SIGLA AND SYMBOLS

Sigla in parentheses refer to works only occasionally quoted; they are listed on the opposite page below the list of editions collated. For full descriptions of the works, see pp. xiv ff.

ALEX	Alexander, 1951	(mF2J)	Anon., –1700
ARD	ARD1 & ARD2	(mF2TCC)	Anon., –1800
ARD1	Case, 1906	(mF4FL33)	Anon., –1723
ARD2	Ridley, 1954	(mF4Q)	Anon., 1685–
(BAYF)	Bayfield, 1920	(mLONG)	Long, –1733?
(BLUM)	Blumhof, 1870	(mPOPE)	Pope, –1723
(BOAS)	Boas, 1935	(mSTV2)	Steevens & Reed, 1791–1802
CAM	CAM1, CAM3a, & CAM3b	(mTBY2, 3, 4)	Thirlby, 1723–33, 1733–47, 1747–53
CAM1	Clark & Wright, 1866		
(CAM2)	Wright, 1892	(mTHEO1, 2, 3)	Theobald, 1723–33, 1729–34, 1729–36
CAM3	CAM3a & CAM3b		
CAM3a, 3b	Wilson, 1950, 1964 (rpt.)	(mTYR)	Tyrwhitt, –1786
CAP	Capell, 1768	(MUN)	Munro, 1957
(CAPN)	Capell, 1779–83 [1774]	(mWARB)	Warburton, 1747–79
(CLN2)	Houghton, 1962	(N&H)	Neilson-Hill, 1942
COL	COL1, COL2, COL3, & COL4	NLSN	Neilson, 1906
COL1, 2, 3, 4	Collier, 1843, 1853, 1858, 1877	OXF1	Craig, [1891]
(COLNE)	Collier, *Notes*, 1853	(PEL2)	Mack, 1969
(DEL)	DEL2 & DEL4	(PEN1)	Harrison, 1937
(DEL2, 4)	Delius, 1856, 1872	POPE	POPE1 & POPE2
DYCE	DYCE1 & DYCE2	POPE1, 2	Pope, 1723, 1728
DYCE1, 2	Dyce, 1857, 1866	RANN	Rann, 1791–
(EV1)	Herford, 1899	RID	RIDa & RIDb
(EV2)	Pink, 1935	RIDa, b	Ridley, 1935, 1954 (rpt.)
EVNS	Evans, 1974	(RLF1)	Rolfe, 1895
Ff	F1, F2, F3, & F4	ROWE	ROWE1, ROWE2, & ROWE3
F1, 2, 3, 4	Folios, 1623, 1632, 1663–4, 1685	ROWE1, 2, 3	Rowe, 1709, 1709, 1714
		SING	SING1 & SING2
(GAR)	Garrick & Capell, 1758	SING1, 2	Singer, 1826, 1856
GLO	Clark & Wright, 1864	SIS	Sisson, 1954
HAL	Halliwell, 1865	(SISNR)	Sisson, 1956
(HALD)	Halliday, 1873	STAU	Staunton, 1859
HAN1, (2), (3)	Hanmer, 1744, 1745, 1771	THEO	THEO1, THEO2, (THEO3), & THEO4
(HAN47)	Hanmer, 1747		
(HTR)	Hunter, 1870	THEO1, 2, (3), 4	Theobald, 1733, 1740, 1752, 1757
HUD	HUD1 & HUD2		
HUD1, 2	Hudson, 1855, 1881	v1773, v1778	Johnson & Steevens, 1773, 1778
(IRV)	Irving & Marshall, 1889		
JOHN1, (2), (3)	Johnson, 1765, 1765, 1768	(v1785)	Johnson, Steevens, & Reed, 1785
KIT1	Kittredge, 1936		
KNT1	Knight, 1841	v1793	Steevens & Reed, 1793
KTLY	Keightley, 1864	v1803	Reed, 1803
MAL	Malone, 1790	v1821	Boswell, 1821
(MAUN)	Maunder, 1839	(v1907)	Furness, 1907
(mCAP2)	Capell, –1751	WARB	Warburton, 1747
(mCOL1)	Collier, –1853	WH	WH1 & WH2
(mF2FL20)	Anon., –1765	WH1, 2	White, 1861, 1883
(mF2FL21)	Anon., 1754–65	(WORD1)	Wordsworth, 1883
		(YAL2)	Phialas, 1955

Symbols used in the textual notes:

∧   punctuation missing or omitted
~   verbal form of the lemma unchanged (while punctuation varies)
-   (between two sigla) all fully collated eds. between and including the
+   (after a siglum) and all succeeding fully collated eds.
(−)   all sigla following the minus sign within parentheses indicate eds. th
    with the Variorum text (i.e., with F1)

A New Variorum Edition of Shakespeare

Founded by Horace Howard Furness (1833–1912),
continued by Horace Howard Furness, Jr. (1865–1930),
and now issued under the sponsorship of
The Modern Language Association of America.

Richard Knowles and Robert Kean Turner,
General Editors

A New Variorum Edition of Shakespeare

ANTONY AND CLEOPATRA

Edited by

MARVIN SPEVACK

Associate Editors

MICHAEL STEPPAT AND
MARGA MUNKELT

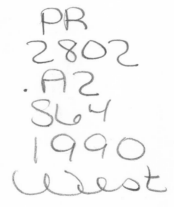
The Modern Language Association of America

Library of Congress Cataloging-in-Publication Data

Shakespeare, William, 1564–1616.
    Antony and Cleopatra / edited by Marvin Spevack; associate editors, Michael Steppat and Marga
Munkelt.
       p.   cm.—(A new variorum edition of Shakepeare)
    Includes bibliographical references.
    ISBN 0-87352-286-9
    1. Antonius, Marcus, 83?–30 B.C.—Drama. 2. Cleopatra, Queen of Egypt, d. 30 B.C.—Drama.
3. Shakespeare, William, 1564–1616. Antony and Cleopatra. I. Spevack, Marvin. II. Title. III. Series: Shakespeare, William, 1564–1616. Works. 1977.
PR2802.A2S64 1990
822.3′3—dc20   89-13691

Permission to use copyrighted material is hereby gratefully acknowledged:

The "Through Line Numbers" as established by Charlton Hinman in *The Norton Facsimile: The First Folio
of Shakespeare* and *Norton Shakespeare* are copyright © 1968 by W. W. Norton & Company, Inc., and
used in this volume with their permission.

Adelman, Janet. *The Common Liar: An Essay on* Antony and Cleopatra. New Haven: Yale University Press,
1973. Copyright © 1973 by Yale University Press. By permission of Yale University Press.

Alvis, John Edward. "Unity of Subject in Shakespeare's Roman Plays." *Publications of the Arkansas Philological Association* 3.3 (1977): 68–75. By permission of University of Central Arkansas Press.

Barroll, J. Leeds. "The Characterization of Octavius." *Shakespeare Studies* 6 (1970): 231–88. By permission
of *Shakespeare Studies*.

Barroll, J. Leeds. "Shakespeare and the Art of Character: A Study of Anthony." *Shakespeare Studies* 5 (1969):
159–235. By permission of *Shakespeare Studies*.

Boas, Guy, ed. *Antony and Cleopatra*. Scholar's Library. London: Macmillan, 1935. By permission of Macmillan Publishers Ltd.

Bowling, Lawrence Edward. "Duality in the Minor Characters in *Antony and Cleopatra*." *College English*
18 (1956–57): 251–55. Copyright 1956 by the National Council of Teachers of English. Reprinted with
permission.

Brower, Reuben A. *Hero and Saint: Shakespeare and the Graeco-Roman Heroic Tradition*. Oxford: Oxford
University Press, 1971. By permission of Oxford University Press.

Cecil, David. "'Antony and Cleopatra.'" *Poets and Story-Tellers*. Pp. 3–24. Glasgow: Constable, 1944, 1949.
By permission of Constable Publishers.

Coates, John. "'The Choice of Hercules' in 'Antony and Cleopatra.'" *Shakespeare Survey* 31 (1978): 45–52.
By permission of Cambridge University Press.

Colie, Rosalie L. *Shakespeare's Living Art*. Copyright © 1974 by Princeton University Press.

Commager, Steele. "Horace, *Carmina* 1.37." *The Phoenix: The Journal of the Classical Association of Canada*
12 (1958): 47–57. By permission of the Classical Association of Canada.

Croce, Benedetto. *Ariosto, Shakespeare and Corneille*. Tr. Douglas Ainslie. New York: Henry Holt and London: George Allen and Unwin, 1920. By permission of Henry Holt and Company.

Dickey, Franklin M. *Not Wisely But Too Well: Shakespeare's Love Tragedies*. San Marino: Huntington Library, 1957. Reprinted with permission of the Henry E. Huntington Library.

Draper, John W. "Shattered Personality in Shakespeare's Antony." *Psychiatric Quarterly* 39 (1965): 448–56.
By permission of Human Sciences Press.

Erskine-Hill, Howard. "Antony and Octavius: The Theme of Temperance in Shakespeare's 'Antony and
Cleopatra.'" *Renaissance and Modern Studies* 14 (1970): 26–47. By permission of the Committee of *Renaissance and Modern Studies*.

Fichter, Andrew. "'Antony and Cleopatra': 'The Time of Universal Peace.'" *Shakespeare Survey* 33 (1980):
99–111. By permission of Cambridge University Press.

Fisch, Harold. "'Antony and Cleopatra': The Limits of Mythology." *Shakespeare Survey* 23 (1970): 59–67.
By permission of Cambridge University Press.

Garber, Marjorie B. *Dream in Shakespeare: From Metaphor to Metamorphosis*. New Haven: Yale University
Press, 1974. Copyright © 1974 by Yale University Press. By permission of Yale University Press.

Goethe, Johann Wolfgang von. *Goethe's Literary Essays: A Selection in English Arranged by J. E. Spingarn*. Copyright © 1921 by the Frederick Ungar Publishing Company. Reprinted by permission of the publisher.

Goldberg, S. L. "The Tragedy of the Imagination: A Reading of *Antony and Cleopatra*." *Critical Review* 4 (1961): 41–64. By permission of the author.

Granville-Barker, Harley. *Prefaces to Shakespeare*. Vol. 1. Copyright 1946, © 1974 renewed by Princeton University Press.

Griffiths, G. S. "Antony and Cleopatra." *Essays and Studies* (Oxford) 31 (1945): 34–67. By permission of the publisher.

Grindon, Rosa Leo. *A Woman's Study of* Antony and Cleopatra. Manchester: Manchester University Press, 1909. By permission of Manchester University Press.

Harris, Duncan C. "'Again for Cydnus': The Dramaturgical Resolution of *Antony and Cleopatra*." *SEL: Studies in English Literature, 1500–1900* 17 (1977): 219–31. By permission of *SEL*.

Heilman, Robert B. "From Mine Own Knowledge: A Theme in the Late Tragedies." *Centennial Review* 8 (1964): 17–38. By permission of *Centennial Review* and the author.

Herford, Charles H. "Shakespeare's Treatment of Love and Marriage." *Edda* 3 (1916): 92–111. By permission of Universitetsforlaget.

Hope, Alec D. "All for Love, or Comedy as Tragedy." *The Cave and the Spring: Essays on Poetry*. Adelaide: Rigby, 1965. By permission of Curtis Brown (Aust) Pty Ltd.

Jones, Emrys. Introduction to *Antony and Cleopatra*. New Penguin Shakespeare. Copyright © 1977 Emrys Jones, 1977. Reproduced by permission of Penguin Books Ltd.

Jones, Emrys. *Scenic Form in Shakespeare*. Oxford: Oxford University Press, 1971. By permission of Oxford University Press.

Knight, G. Wilson. *The Imperial Theme: Further Interpretations of Shakespeare's Tragedies including the Roman Plays*. London: Methuen & Co. 1931. By permission of the publisher.

Krook, Dorothea. "Tragic and Heroic: Shakespeare's *Antony and Cleopatra*." Rpt. from *Scripta Hierosolymitana* (Jerusalem) 19 (1967): 231–61 in *Elements of Tragedy*. New Haven: Yale University Press, 1969. Copyright © 1969 by Yale University Press. By permission of Yale University Press.

Lings, Martin. *Shakespeare in the Light of Sacred Art*. London: Allen and Unwin, 1966. Extract reproduced by kind permission of Unwin Hyman Ltd. Copyright © 1966 by George Allen and Unwin.

Lloyd, Michael. "Cleopatra as Isis." *Shakespeare Survey* 12 (1959): 88–94. By permission of Cambridge University Press.

Long, Michael. *The Unnatural Scene: A Study in Shakespearean Tragedy*. London: Methuen & Co. 1976. By permission of the publisher.

Lyman, Dean B. "Janus in Alexandria: A Discussion of 'Antony and Cleopatra.'" *Sewanee Review* 48 (1940): 86–104.

MacCallum, M. W. *Shakespeare's Roman Plays and Their Background*. London: Macmillan, 1910, 1967. By permission of Macmillan Publishers Ltd.

Mack, Maynard, ed. *Antony and Cleopatra*. Pelican Shakespeare. Baltimore: Penguin, 1960. By permission of the publisher. *

Marsh, D. R. C. *Passion Lends Them Power: A Study of Shakespeare's Love Tragedies*. Manchester: Manchester University Press, 1976. By permission of Manchester University Press.

McAlindon, T. *Shakespeare and Decorum*. London: Macmillan, 1973. By permission of Macmillan Publishers Ltd.

McFarland, Thomas. "Antony and Octavius." *Yale Review* 48 (1958–59): 204–28. By permission of *Yale Review*. Copyright Yale University.

Mills, Laurens J. *The Tragedies of Shakespeare's Antony and Cleopatra*. Bloomington: Indiana University Press, 1964. By permission of Indiana University Press.

Nochimson, Richard. "The End Crowns All: Shakespeare's Deflation of Tragic Possibility in *Antony and Cleopatra*." *English* 26 (1977): 99–132. By permission of The English Association.

Phillips, James Emerson, Jr. *The State in Shakespeare's Greek and Roman Plays*. Copyright © 1940, Columbia University Press, New York. Used by permission.

Rees, Joan. "Shakespeare's Use of Daniel." *Modern Language Review* 55 (1960): 79–82. By permission of the Modern Humanities Research Association.

Rice, Julian C. "The Allegorical Dolabella." *College Language Association Journal* 3 (1970): 402–07. Used by permission of the College Language Association.

Ridley, M. R., ed. *Antony and Cleopatra*. Arden Shakespeare. London: Methuen & Co., 1954. By permission of the publisher.

Riemer, A. P. *A Reading of Shakespeare's* Antony and Cleopatra. Sydney Studies in Literature. Sydney: Sydney University Press, 1968. By permission of the author.

Schanzer, Ernest. "Daniel's Revision of His *Cleopatra*." *Review of English Studies* 8 (1957): 375–81. By permission of Oxford University Press.

Schanzer, Ernest, ed. *Shakespeare's Appian: A Selection from the Tudor Translation of Appian's "Civil Wars."* English Reprints 13. Liverpool: Liverpool University Press, 1956.

Schanzer, Ernest. *The Problem Plays of Shakespeare: A Study of* Julius Caesar, Measure for Measure, Antony and Cleopatra. London: Routledge, 1963. By permission of the publisher.

Schücking, Levin L. *Character Problems in Shakespeare's Plays*. London: Harrap, 1919, tr. 1922. By permission of Harrap Publishing Group Ltd.

Schwartz, Elias. "The Shackling of Accidents: *Antony and Cleopatra*." *College English* 23 (1962): 550–58. Copyright 1962 by the National Council of Teachers of English. Reprinted with permission.

Simmons, J. L. *Shakespeare's Pagan World: The Roman Tragedies*. Charlottesville: University Press of Virginia, 1973. By permission of the University Press of Virginia.

Simpson, Lucie. "Shakespeare's Cleopatra." *Fortnightly Review* 129 (March 1928): 332–42. By permission of The Contemporary Review Company Ltd.

Slater, Ann, ed. *Antony and Cleopatra*. Shakespeare Workshop Edition. London: Ginn, 1971. By permission of Ginn & Company Ltd.

Smith, Gordon Ross. "The Melting of Authority in *Antony and Cleopatra*." *College Literature* 1.1 (1974): 1–18. By permission of *College Literature*.

Smith, J. Oates. "The Alchemy of *Antony and Cleopatra*." *Bucknell Review* 12.1 (1964): 37–50. Reprinted by permission of *Bucknell Review*.

Smith, Marion Bodewell. *Dualities in Shakespeare*. Toronto: University of Toronto Press, 1966. By permission of the publisher.

Spurgeon, Caroline F. E. *Shakespeare's Imagery and What It Tells Us*. Cambridge: Cambridge University Press, 1935. By permission of Cambridge University Press.

Stein, Arnold. "The Image of Antony: Lyric and Tragic Imagination." *Kenyon Review* 21 (1959): 586–606. By permission of the author and the publisher.

Stirling, Brents. *Unity in Shakespearian Tragedy: The Interplay of Theme and Character*. Copyright © 1956, Columbia University Press, New York. Used by permission.

Stoll, Elmer Edgar. "Cleopatra." *Modern Language Review* 23 (1928): 145–63. By permission of the Modern Humanities Research Association.

Strachan, L. R. M. "The Spelling 'Anthony.'" *Notes and Queries* 167 (4 Aug. 1934): 85–86. By permission of Oxford University Press.

Tolmie, L. W. "'Least cause' / 'All cause': Roman Infinite Variety: An Essay on *Antony and Cleopatra*." *Southern Review* (Adelaide) 11 (1978): 113–31. By permission of *Southern Review*.

Traversi, Derek. *An Approach to Shakespeare*. 1938. Garden City: Doubleday, 1968–69. By permission of Doubleday.

Traversi, Derek. *Shakespeare: The Roman Plays*. By permission of the author, Stanford University Press, and The Bodley Head.

Uphaus, Robert W. "Shakespearean Tragedy and the Intimations of Romance." *Centennial Review* 22 (1978): 299–318. By permission of *Centennial Review* and the author.

Waddington, Raymond B. "Antony and Cleopatra: 'What Venus did with Mars.'" *Shakespeare Studies* 2 (1966): 210–27. By permission of *Shakespeare Studies*.

Weitz, Morris. "Literature without Philosophy: 'Antony and Cleopatra.'" *Shakespeare Survey* 28 (1975): 29–36. By permission of Cambridge University Press.

Wilson, John Dover, ed. *Antony and Cleopatra*. New Shakespeare Edition. Cambridge: Cambridge University Press, 1950. By permission of Cambridge University Press.

HELGA SPEVACK

Her Book

CONTENTS

ACKNOWLEDGMENTS

The persons who go into the making of a variorum are of course various and many. First, there are the hundreds who are represented in the edition itself. Second, there are those who helped assemble and analyze the contributions. It is my privilege to thank those happy and not so few who made available their expertise and time.

I am most pleased to mention the work of two who have grown with the edition, the associate editors Michael Steppat, for writing the appendixes on criticism and sources, and Marga Munkelt, for "The Text of *Antony and Cleopatra* on the Stage" and "Performances of *Antony and Cleopatra*," as well as the long notes on "Arme-gaunt Steede" and "ribaudred Nagge." Both were fully engaged in every other part as well. Two assistants, Bradley Rubidge and Sabine U. Bückmann-de Villegas, extended their assignments to include responsibility for "Staging of the Monument Scenes at the Globe" and the index respectively. And for the help from almost a generation of students and staff I wish to single out Birgit Beile, Astrid Beckmann-Swan, Dagmar Bruch, Ingrid Buckmann, Karsten Ehmke, Bernhard Friederici, Monika Guerin, Peter Hellfeuer, Michael Hiltscher, Ingrid Kastrup, Wolf Kristen, Thomas Pago, Elisabeth Pirke, Ellen Quackenbos, Maria Rauschenberger, Lydia Remke, Norbert Schneider, Clemens Sorgenfrey, Gertrud Sparding, Krishnan Venkatesh, M. Carlan Wolf, and Martin Wolny. Loretta Schäfer merits special thanks for her unswerving attention to detail.

Among the scholars who were ready with information and advice are Peter Blayney, J. W. Binns, N. F. Blake, G. Blakemore Evans, Horst-Dietrich Helb, Harold Jenkins, Yoshiko Kawachi, Harry Meserole, Paul Morgan, Paola Pugliatti, S. Schoenbaum, Helga Spevack-Husmann, Gary Taylor, Hans-Jürgen Weckermann, and Stanley Wells. Valuable comment on sections of the edition was made by J. Leeds Barroll, David Bevington, Maurice Charney, Andrew Gurr, T. H. Howard-Hill, Cyrus Hoy, Coppélia Kahn, Carol Thomas Neely, Mark Rose, John Velz, Paul Werstine, and George Walton Williams.

Institutions whose rich resources were courteously put at my disposal include the British Library, the Victoria and Albert Museum, the Bodleian Library, Trinity College (Cambridge) Library, the Cambridge University Library, the Birmingham Shakespeare Library, the Shakespeare Birthplace Trust, the Nuffield Library in

Stratford, the Drama Department of the University of Bristol, the Theatre Collection of the New York Public Library, the Museum of the City of New York, and, last and most, the Folger Shakespeare Library, where I began the project while a Senior Fellow and have returned with profit and pleasure over the years. Fellowships at University College London and Wolfson College Cambridge, a travel grant from the Deutsche Forschungsgemeinschaft, and the continued support of the Minister für Wissenschaft und Forschung des Landes Nordrhein-Westfalen played a significant role.

The general editors, Richard Knowles and Robert Kean Turner, and their associate, Virginia J. Haas, were generous in their engagement and tough in their appraisals. I owe them much. James G. McManaway, when general editor, encouraged me to undertake this task and became to me, as to many Shakespeareans, counselor and friend. We remember Mac for his great learning and infinite kindness.

M.S.

Münster
May 1989

PLAN OF THE WORK

This edition contains four main parts: (1) the text of *Antony and Cleopatra* reprinted from the First Folio edition of 1623, (2) textual notes embodying all significant departures from the F1 text in all important editions of the play, (3) a commentary on the text designed to explicate its language where explication is called for and to summarize the notes that a long succession of editors and commentators has written on it, and (4) an appendix that reproduces or summarizes discussions of certain general aspects of the play and that collects data as well as opinions whose bulk or length precludes their incorporation in the commentary.

The text is a modified diplomatic reprint of the copy of F1 now in the Universitäts- und Stadtbibliothek in Cologne, formerly owned by the Earl of Carysfort and categorized in Class I, Division A, No. VI, in Sidney Lee's *Census*. In cases of doubtful legibility, copies in the Folger Shakespeare Library used by Charlton Hinman (in the Norton facsimile) for more than forty pages in all, as well as other copies for especially difficult readings, have been consulted. Pressvariants found in different copies and facsimiles are recorded in the appendix. The reprint does not reproduce typographical features such as the long s, display and swash letters, and ornaments; abbreviations printed as one letter above another are reproduced as two consecutive letters, the second one superscript. Minor typographical blemishes such as irregular spacing, printing space-types, and wrong-font, damaged, turned, transposed, misprinted, or clearly erroneous or missing letters or punctuation marks have been corrected. If the anomaly is likely to have any bibliographical significance, its correction is recorded in the appendix. Where the error is not clearly typographical, or where the correction is not obvious, the text has been left unaltered and various emendations have been recorded in the textual notes. When emendation of an obvious typographical error has resulted in a change from one word to another, the emendation has been treated as substantive and has been recorded in the textual notes. The F1 lineation of both verse and prose has been preserved, except that turned-over and turned-under lines have been printed continuously; such alteration is recorded in the appendix. In general, the attempt has been made to omit and ignore all insignificant typographical peculiarities but to retain or at least record the alteration of any accidental details of possible textual significance.

Through Line Numbers (TLNs) are printed by fives in the right margin; these numbers are used for all notes and cross-references in the edition. Inclusive Globe act-scene-line numbers as determined by the 1891 edition are supplied in arabic numerals in the headline of each page of text, and Globe act-scene division is indicated by boldface arabic numerals in the right margin. The beginning of each Folio column is marked in the right margin by signature-and-column indicators in parentheses.

The textual notes are based on a collation of the following editions. Each entry below is preceded by the siglum representing that edition in the textual notes. All these editions have been fully collated. When not mentioned, the place of publication is London.

F2	THE SECOND FOLIO. *M*ʳ. *William Shakespeares comedies, histories, and Tragedies. . . . The second Impression.*	1632
F3	THE THIRD FOLIO. *M*ʳ. *William Shakespear's Comedies, Histories, and Tragedies. . . . The third Impression.*	1663–4
F4	THE FOURTH FOLIO. *M*ʳ. *William Shakespear's comedies, histories, and tragedies. . . . The Fourth Edition.*	1685
ROWE1	NICHOLAS ROWE. *Works.* 6 vols. 1709. Vol. 6.	1709
ROWE2	NICHOLAS ROWE. *Works.* 6 vols. 1709. Vol. 6.	1709
ROWE3	NICHOLAS ROWE. *Works.* 8 vols. 1714. Vol. 7.	1714
POPE1	ALEXANDER POPE. *Works.* 6 vols. 1723–5. Vol. 5.	1723
POPE2	ALEXANDER POPE. *Works.* 2nd ed. 8 vols. 1728. Vol. 7.	1728
THEO1	LEWIS THEOBALD. *Works.* 7 vols. 1733. Vol. 6.	1733
THEO2	LEWIS THEOBALD. *Works.* 2nd ed. 8 vols. 1740. Vol. 7.	1740
HAN1	THOMAS HANMER. *Works.* 6 vols. Oxford, 1743–4. Vol. 5.	1744
WARB	WILLIAM WARBURTON. *Works.* 8 vols. 1747. Vol. 7.	1747
THEO4	LEWIS THEOBALD. *Works.* 8 vols. 1757. Vol. 7.	1757
JOHN1	SAMUEL JOHNSON. *Plays.* 8 vols. Printed for J. and R. Tonson, C. Corbet . . . , 1765. Vol. 7.	1765
CAP	EDWARD CAPELL. *Comedies, Histories, & Tragedies.* 10 vols. [1768.] Vol. 8.	1768
v1773	SAMUEL JOHNSON & GEORGE STEEVENS. *Plays.* 10 vols. 1773. Vol. 8.	1773
v1778	SAMUEL JOHNSON & GEORGE STEEVENS. *Plays.* 10 vols. 1778. Vol. 8.	1778
MAL	EDMOND MALONE. *Plays & Poems.* 10 vols. 1790. Vol. 7.	1790
RANN	JOSEPH RANN. *Dramatic Works.* 6 vols. Oxford, 1786–[94]. Vol. 5.	1791–
v1793	GEORGE STEEVENS & ISAAC REED. *Plays.* 15 vols. 1793. Vol. 12.	1793
v1803	ISAAC REED. *Plays.* 21 vols. 1803. Vol. 17.	1803
v1821	JAMES BOSWELL. *Plays & Poems.* 21 vols. 1821. Vol. 12.	1821
SING1	SAMUEL W. SINGER. *Dramatic Works.* 10 vols. Chiswick, 1826. Vol. 8.	1826

KNT1	CHARLES KNIGHT. *Comedies, Histories, Tragedies, & Poems*. Pictorial Ed. 55 parts. [1838–43.] Reissued in 8 vols. Part 36 (vol. 6).	1841
COL1	JOHN PAYNE COLLIER. *Works*. 8 vols. 1842–4. Vol. 8.	1843
COL2	JOHN PAYNE COLLIER. *Plays*.	1853
HUD1	HENRY N. HUDSON. *Works*. 11 vols. Boston & Cambridge, Mass., 1851–6. Vol. 8.	1855
SING2	SAMUEL W. SINGER. *Dramatic Works*. 10 vols. 1856. Vol. 10.	1856
DYCE1	ALEXANDER DYCE. *Works*. 6 vols. 1857. Vol. 6.	1857
COL3	JOHN PAYNE COLLIER. *Comedies, Histories, Tragedies, & Poems*. "The Second Edition." 6 vols. 1858. Vol. 6.	1858
STAU	HOWARD STAUNTON. *Plays*. 50 parts. 1856–60. Reissued in 3 vols. 1858–60. Parts 43–45 (vol. 3).	1859
WH1	RICHARD GRANT WHITE. *Works*. 12 vols. Boston, 1857–66. Vol. 12.	1861
GLO	WILLIAM GEORGE CLARK & WILLIAM ALDIS WRIGHT. *Works*. Globe Ed. Cambridge.	1864
KTLY	THOMAS KEIGHTLEY. *Plays*. 6 vols. 1864. Vol. 5.	1864
HAL	JAMES O. HALLIWELL. *Works*. 16 vols. 1853–65. Vol. 15.	1865
DYCE2	ALEXANDER DYCE. *Works*. 2nd ed. 9 vols. 1864–7. Vol. 7.	1866
CAM1	WILLIAM GEORGE CLARK & WILLIAM ALDIS WRIGHT. *Works*. Cambridge Sh. 9 vols. 1863–6. Vol. 9.	1866
COL4	JOHN PAYNE COLLIER. *Plays & Poems*. 8 vols. 1875–8. Vol. 7.	1877
HUD2	HENRY N. HUDSON. *Works*. Harvard Ed. 20 vols. Boston, 1880–1. Vol. 16.	1881
WH2	RICHARD GRANT WHITE. *Comedies, Histories, Tragedies, & Poems*. Riverside Sh. 3 vols. Boston, 1883. Vol. 3.	1883
OXF1	W. J. CRAIG. *Works*. Oxford Sh.	[1891]
NLSN	WILLIAM ALLAN NEILSON. *Works*. Cambridge Ed. Boston & N. Y.	1906
ARD1	R. H. CASE. *Ant*. Arden Sh.	1906
RIDa	M. R. RIDLEY. *Ant*. New Temple Sh.	1935
KIT1	GEORGE LYMAN KITTREDGE. *Works*. Boston.	1936
CAM3a	JOHN DOVER WILSON. *Ant*. [New] Cambridge Sh.	1950
ALEX	PETER ALEXANDER. *Works*.	1951
RIDb	M. R. RIDLEY. *Ant*. New Temple Sh. (1954 rpt.)	1954
SIS	CHARLES JASPER SISSON. *Works*.	1954
ARD2	M. R. RIDLEY. *Ant*. [New] Arden Sh.	1954
CAM3b	JOHN DOVER WILSON. *Ant*. [New] Cambridge Sh. (1964 rpt.)	1964
EVNS	G. BLAKEMORE EVANS et al. *Works*. Riverside Sh. Boston.	1974

The following editions, books, and manuscripts are occasionally quoted in the textual notes (for unusual readings and corrections), commentary, or appendix:

mF2J	MS notes in copy of F2 sold in 1649 by Sarah Jones, *apud* HALLIWELL (1868).	–1700
mF4Q	MS notes *apud* QUINCY (1854).	1685–
mF4FL33	MS notes in F4, Copy 33, Folger Library.	–1723
mPOPE	ALEXANDER POPE. MS notes in F3, Copy 20, Folger Library.	–1723
mTHEO1	LEWIS THEOBALD. MS notes in F2, Copy 20, Folger Library.	1723–33
mTBY2	STYAN THIRLBY. MS notes in Pope's 1723 ed., Yale Library.	1723–33
mTHEO2	LEWIS THEOBALD. Letters to William Warburton. Vol. 1. Phillipps MS 8565, Folger Library.	1729–34
mTHEO3	LEWIS THEOBALD. Letters to William Warburton. Egerton MS 1956, British Library.	1729–36
mLONG	ROGER LONG. MS notes in copy of F2, Pembroke College Library, Cambridge.	–1733?
mTBY3	STYAN THIRLBY. MS notes in Theobald's 1733 ed., Copy 2, Folger Library.	1733–47
HAN2	THOMAS HANMER. *Works.* 6 vols. 1745. Vol. 5.	1745
HAN47	[THOMAS HANMER.] *Works.* 9 vols. 1747. Vol. 7.	1747
mTBY4	STYAN THIRLBY. MS notes in Warburton's 1747 ed., Copy 2, Folger Library.	1747–53
mWARB	WILLIAM WARBURTON. MS notes in Warburton's 1747 ed., Copy 5, Folger Library.	1747–79
mCAP2	EDWARD CAPELL. MS holograph of Capell's 1768 ed. Trinity College Library, Cambridge.	1751
THEO3	LEWIS THEOBALD. *Works.* 8 vols. 1752. Vol. 7.	1752
mF2FL21	MS notes in F2, Copy 21, Folger Library.	1754–65
GAR	DAVID GARRICK & EDWARD CAPELL. *Ant.*	1758
mF2FL20	MS notes in F2, Copy 20, Folger Library.	–1765
JOHN2	SAMUEL JOHNSON. *Plays.* 8 vols. Printed for J. and R. Tonson, H. Woodfall . . . , 1765. Vol. 7.	1765
JOHN3	SAMUEL JOHNSON. *Plays.* 8 vols. Printed for H. Woodfall, C. Bathurst . . . , 1768. Vol. 7.	1768
HAN3	THOMAS HANMER. *Works.* 6 vols. Oxford, 1770–1. Vol. 5.	1771
CAPN	EDWARD CAPELL. *Notes and Various Readings to Shakespeare.* 3 vols. [1779–83.] Vol. 1, Pt. 1, pub. 1774 but withdrawn.	1779–83
v1785	SAMUEL JOHNSON, GEORGE STEEVENS, & ISAAC REED. *Plays.* 10 vols. 1785. Vol. 8.	1785
mTYR	THOMAS TYRWHITT. MS notes in copy of F2, C.39.i.13, British Library.	–1786

mSTV2	GEORGE STEEVENS & ISAAC REED. MS notes in proof sheets for Boydell ed., Folger Library.	1791–1802
mF2TCC	MS notes in Capell's copy of F2, Trinity College Library, Cambridge.	–1800
MAUN	SAMUEL MAUNDER. *Plays.*	1839
mCOL1	JOHN PAYNE COLLIER. MS notes in the Perkins copy of F2 (1632), Huntington Library.	–1853
COLNE	JOHN PAYNE COLLIER. *Notes and Emendations.* 2nd ed., rev. & enl. 1853. (1st ed. 1852.)	1853
DEL2	NICOLAUS DELIUS. *Werke.* 7 vols. Elberfeld, 1854–[61]. Vol. 2.	1856
BLUM	KARL BLUMHOF. *Ant.* Celle.	1870
HTR	JOHN HUNTER. *Ant.* Longmans Series.	1870
DEL4	NICOLAUS DELIUS. *Werke.* "Dritte, Revidirte Auflage." 2 vols. Elberfeld, 1872. Vol. 2.	1872
HALD	ANDREW HALLIDAY. *Ant.*	1873
WORD1	CHARLES WORDSWORTH. *History Plays.* 3 vols. Edinburgh, 1883. Vol. 1.	1883
IRV	HENRY IRVING & FRANK MARSHALL. *Works.* Henry Irving Sh. 8 vols. N. Y., 1888–90. Vol. 6.	1889
CAM2	WILLIAM ALDIS WRIGHT. *Works.* Cambridge Sh., 2nd ed. 9 vols. 1891–3. Vol. 8.	1892
RLF1	WILLIAM J. ROLFE. *Ant.* Rolfe's English Classics. N. Y.	1895
EV1	C. H. HERFORD. *Works.* Eversley Ed. 10 vols. 1899. Vol. 9.	1899
v1907	HORACE HOWARD FURNESS. *Ant.* New Variorum Ed. Philadelphia.	1907
BAYF	M[ATTHEW] A[LBERT] BAYFIELD. *A Study of Shakespeare's Versification. . . . Including a Revised Text of* Ant. Cambridge.	1920
BOAS	GUY BOAS. *Ant.* Scholar's Library.	1935
EV2	M. A. PINK. *Ant.* New Eversley Sh.	1935
PEN1	G. B. HARRISON. *Ant.* Penguin Sh.	1937
N&H	WILLIAM ALLAN NEILSON & CHARLES J. HILL. *Plays & Poems.* Cambridge, Mass.	1942
YAL2	PETER G. PHIALAS. *Ant.* New Yale Sh. New Haven.	1955
SISNR	CHARLES JASPER SISSON. *New Readings in Shakespeare.* Shakespeare Problems 8. 2 vols. Cambridge.	1956
MUN	JOHN MUNRO. *Works.* London Sh. 6 vols. 1957. Vol. 6.	1957
CLN2	R. E. C. HOUGHTON. *Ant.* New Clarendon Sh. Oxford.	1962
PEL2	MAYNARD MACK. *Ant.* In *Works.* Pelican Sh. rev. Gen. Ed. Alfred Harbage. Baltimore.	1969

The following editions are occasionally quoted in the commentary and the appendix only, and hence are not assigned sigla:

PIERRE ANTOINE DE LA PLACE. *Le Théâtre anglois.* 4 vols.
1746. Vol. 3. 1746
DAVID GARRICK. *Ant.* Promptbook used at Drury Lane, 3 Jan.
1759. 1759
FRANCIS GENTLEMAN. *Plays.* Bell's Ed. 9 vols. [1773–4.] Vol. 6. 1774
FRANCIS GENTLEMAN. *Ant.* 1776
JOH[ANN] JOACH[IM] ESCHENBURG. *Schauspiele.* Neue
verbesserte Auflage. 22 vols. Strassburg, 1778–83. Vol. 6. 1778
PIERRE P. F. LE TOURNEUR. *Shakespeare traduit de l'anglois.* 20
vols. Paris, 1776–83. Vol. 6. 1779
[JOSEPH HOPKINSON.] *Plays & Poems.* 8 vols. Philadelphia,
1795–6. Vol. 1. 1795
[ELIZABETH] INCHBALD. *Ant.* British Th. 1808
[GEORGE COLMAN or JOHN PHILIP KEMBLE.] *Shakspeare's
Tragedy of Antony and Cleopatra; with Alterations, and
with Additions from Dryden; as now Perform'd at the
Theatre-Royal, Covent-Garden.* 1813
JOHN PHILIP KEMBLE. *Ant.* Promptbook used at Covent
Garden, 15 Nov. 1813. 1813
JOHN PHILIP KEMBLE. *Ant.* "Second" stage version, in
autograph. [1813–21?]
F. [P. G.] GUIZOT & A. P[ICHOT]. *Œuvres complètes.* 13 vols.
Paris, 1821. Vol. 3. 1821
JOHANN W. O. BENDA. *Dramatische Werke.* 19 vols. Leipzig,
1825–6. Vol. 9. 1825
JOHANN HEINRICH VOSS, HEINRICH VOSS, & ABRAHAM VOSS.
Schauspiele. 9 vols. Leipzig & Stuttgart, 1818–29. Vol. 7, Pt. 2. 1827
LUDWIG TIECK. *Dramatische Werke.* Tr. A. W. von Schlegel. 9
vols. Berlin, 1825–33. Vol. 5. 1831
WILLIAM CHARLES MACREADY. *Ant.* Handwritten acting
version of 13 July 1833. 1833
G[EORGE] D[ANIEL]. *Ant.* Cumberland's British Th. 355. [1833?]
A. J. VALPY. *Plays & Poems.* 15 vols. 1832–4. Vol. 12. 1833
THOMAS CAMPBELL. *Dramatic Works.* 1838
GULIAN C. VERPLANCK. *Plays.* Illustrated Sh. 138 (?) parts,
1844–7. Reissued in 3 vols. N. Y., 1847. Parts 79–83 (vol. 3). 1846
SAMUEL PHELPS. *Ant.* Promptbook used at Sadler's Wells, 22
Oct. 1849. 1849
[HENRY TYRRELL.] *Complete Works.* 4 vols. London & N. Y.:
Tallis, [1851–3]. Vol. [3]. [1851–3]
ISABELLA GLYN. *Ant.* Copy of text used for readings. [1855?]

FRANÇOIS-VICTOR HUGO. *Œuvres complètes.* 18 vols. Paris,
1859–66. (Deuxième éd. 1865–73.) Vol. 7. (Deuxième éd.
1868.)   1860

CHARLES CALVERT. *Ant.* Text marked perhaps for production at
the Prince's at Manchester (1866) or used for Jean Davenport
Lander's production (1874).   [1866?]

CHARLES CALVERT. *Ant.* Edinburgh.   [1867?]

PAUL HEYSE. *Antonius und Kleopatra.* In *Dramatische Werke.*
Ed. Friedrich Bodenstedt. 38 vols. Leipzig, 1867–71. Vol. 7.
(Zweite Auflage 1873.)   1867

THOMAS HAILES LACY. *Ant.* Lacy's Acting Ed. 75.   [1867?]

CHARLES & MARY COWDEN CLARKE. *Plays.* Cassell's
Illustrated Sh. 270 parts, 1864–9. Reissued in 3 vols.
[1864–8.] Parts 242–50 (vol. 3).   1868

MAX [L.] MOLTKE. *Sämmtliche dramatische Werke.* Deutsche
Volksausgabe. 12 vols. Leipzig, [1867–8]. Vol. 1.   [1868]

EMILE MONTÉGUT. *Œuvres complètes.* 10 vols. Paris, 1867–73.
(Deuxième éd. 1873–8.) Vol. 8. (Deuxième éd. 1878.)   1868

ALEXANDER SCHMIDT. *Antonius und Cleopatra.* In
Dramatische Werke. Tr. A. W. von Schlegel & L. Tieck. Ed.
H. Ulrici. 12 vols. Berlin, 1867–71. Vol. 10.   1870

JEAN DAVENPORT LANDER. *Ant.* Promptbook used at Brooklyn
Th., 2 Sept. 1874, and GEORGE BECKS's memorial
reconstruction of the acted version.   1874

F. J. FURNIVALL. *Works.* Leopold Sh.   1877

WILHELM OECHELHÄUSER. *Dramatische Werke.* 27 vols. Berlin
& Weimar, 1870–8. Vol. 21.   1877

F. DINGELSTEDT et al. *Dramatische Werke.* 9 vols. Leipzig:
Bibliographisches Institut, n.d. Vol. 1.   1878

MAX KOCH. *Dramatische Werke.* 12 vols. Stuttgart, [1882].
Vol. 9.   [1882]

ANON. *Ant.* As Performed for the first time under Mrs. [Lillie]
Langtry's Management.   [1890]

KENNETH DEIGHTON. *Ant.* Deighton's Grey Cover Sh.   1891

A. E. MORGAN & W. SHERARD VINES. *Ant.* Warwick Sh.
London & Glasgow.   [1893–8]

LOUIS CALVERT. *Ant.* Manchester.   [1897?]

CHARLES HANFORD. *Ant.* Promptbook used for a touring
production in America.   [1900?]

KENNETH DEIGHTON. *Ant.* Deighton's Red Cover Sh.   1901

SIDNEY LEE. *Shakespeares Comedies, Histories and Tragedies,
Being a Reproduction in Facsimile . . . with Introduction
and Census of Copies.* Oxford.   1902

ARTHUR H. BULLEN. *Works.* Stratford Town Ed. 10 vols.
Stratford-on-Avon, [1904–7]. Vol. 9.   1906

A conjectural emendation is recorded in the textual notes only if an editor has subsequently printed such a reading in the text. When the editor's emendation differs in minor details of spelling or punctuation from the conjecture as originally proposed, the note records only the editor's version, since this form is usually imitated by subsequent editors. A few unadopted conjectures of special interest are discussed in the commentary notes; all other unadopted conjectures are listed in the appendix. Where dating of MSS is uncertain, all sources overlapping chronologically are given. Conjectures withdrawn in the same book or MS (including those of Thirlby marked by his formulas *np, nm, fnm, nnm, ns*) are marked *and withdrawn*; for withdrawals elsewhere the source is added.

The textual notes record substantive or semisubstantive variants from the Variorum text in the editions collated—i.e., either substitutions, omissions, additions, or reorderings of words or passages, or else such changes of details of spelling, punctuation, typography, spacing, and lineation as significantly affect meaning or meter. Typographical features of the editions collated are retained.

(1) Verbal variants: Lexical variants are recorded when two or more distinct morphemes (i.e., including all affixes and inflections) existed or exist. Parallel forms, sometimes called "by-forms" by the *OED*, are also given (e.g., *crownets/coronets*). Not recorded are unambiguous allographic variations for the same phoneme—variant or modernized spellings like *ore/o'er, then/than*—and purely euphonic phenomena like the final *t* in *whil(e)st* or its omission in *affects*

(= *affectst*). Misprints go unnoticed unless they create words in the English vocabulary or appear to have been taken for legitimate words by being repeated in one or more of the four Shakespeare Folios.

(2) Punctuation: Variant punctuation is recorded only when meaning is affected. Thus the fact that in various editions an independent clause ends with a comma, semicolon, colon, dash, or period is ignored if the variant does not change the meaning of the sentence or speech except in minor degrees of pace or emphasis, whereas a change from comma to semicolon that alters meaning is recorded. Similarly, the notes do not record that an obvious rhetorical question is marked with a period in some texts, but they do record a period that distinguishes between a declarative and an interrogative sentence.

(3) Lining and meter: Variant lining that affects meter—i.e., the relining of verse as prose, of prose as verse, of verse as different verse—is recorded. The formula *On one line* indicates, in cases where it is not clear whether relining is done to render verse or prose, that two lines in F1 adding up to one verse line (pentameter or hexameter) are printed as one line of text. *One verse line* is used when part lines of verse, either within a speech or split between two or more speakers (in v1793 and later editions, with indentation), are relined to make a full verse line. The elision or expansion of syllables for metrical purposes, or the addition of diacritical marks to locate accent, is recorded only if the alteration displaces the accent from one syllable to another or changes the number of metrical feet in a line.

Variants in the accessories are recorded more selectively than those in the text proper:

(1) Added stage directions that describe action clearly implied by the text are ignored, as are directions for insignificant bits of stage business or those intended merely as props to a reader's imagination. Variants that affect only secondary details of a stage direction are also ignored; in some cases the abbreviation *subst.* is used to indicate substantial agreement among editions despite differences of detail. The notes record all differences about who enters or exits, or when, or about stage business that affects the interpretation of a speech or scene.

(2) Only those variant speech prefixes that imply disagreement as to the identity of the speaker are recorded; variants of the form or spelling of the prefix are ignored. Variant scene divisions and numberings are recorded, but not alternative ways of indicating them. Added and variant indications of locale are recorded, but not the different ways of indicating and particularizing the same place.

A variant reading in the textual notes appears in the form printed in the first edition to adopt that reading; insignificant variations in the spelling, punctuation, typography, spacing, and lineation of the reading in later editions are not recorded. Thus a variant given as "I, F3 +" does not imply that all editions from F3 onwards print "I," in precisely that form: later renditions of the reading may be spelled "Ay" or punctuated with a semicolon or period, but as these variations do not affect the meaning they are not recorded. When a variant is only a matter of the punctuation after a word, the word in the lemma is not repeated in the note but is replaced by a swung dash (~), and the absence of punctuation in either lemma or variant is indicated by a caret ($_\wedge$). Thus "him$_\wedge$ onely,] $\sim$, $\sim$ $_\wedge$ COL2, COL3, COL4" indicates that COL2, COL3, and COL4 differ significantly from the Variorum text at this point only in adding a comma after "him" and in removing punctuation after "onely."

Four kinds of formulas are used in the textual notes as space-saving devices to avoid listing a long series of sigla for editions that agree on a reading:

(1) When all editions after a certain one agree with that edition, the agreement is shown by a plus sign after its siglum. Thus ROWE1+ means that all editions collated from Rowe's first edition of 1709 through Evans's edition of 1974 agree with Rowe's text at this point.

(2) The abbreviation *etc.* after a siglum for an edition means that all editions collated that are not otherwise accounted for in the note agree with that edition. Thus "you of] Ff; you of; ROWE1, ROWE2; of you . . . KTLY; you off; ROWE3 *etc.*" means that every edition but the four Folios, Rowe's first and second, and Keightley's agrees with ROWE3.

(3) The agreement of three or more editions in chronological succession is indicated by a hyphen between the sigla of the first and last editions in the series. Thus "POPE1-JOHN1" indicates the agreement of all collated editions from Pope's first edition to Johnson's first.

(4) The agreement of a "family" of related editions — that is, editions by the same editor or bearing the same name — is indicated by the siglum root for that family. Thus THEO indicates the agreement of all editions by Theobald (THEO1, THEO2, etc.) that were collated, CAM the agreement of all "Cambridge" editions collated.

A siglum printed in parentheses and with a minus sign after any of the first three of the above formulas indicates an edition in the succession whose text agrees with F1 rather than with the variant in question. Thus "ROWE1+ (−RID, SIS)" indicates the agreement of all editions from ROWE1 on except for those of Ridley and Sisson, which agree with F1.

To facilitate the interpretation of the formulas — e.g., to enable the reader to see quickly which fully collated editions are included in such a formula as "ROWE1-SIS" — a chronological list of sigla is provided inside the front and back covers of this edition. An alphabetical list of sigla on the facing pages both identifies the editors and gives the date whereby any siglum may be located in the chronological list.

The commentary seeks not only to elucidate the text but also at times to trace the history of the criticism to which the word or passage has been subjected. It includes only a selection from all that has been written about this play, and the responsibility for the selection is the editor's. The critical stance is historical and neutral. The aim is to evaluate and qualify rather than to attack or ignore, for it is the editor's duty to render the outlines of commentary at a particular time or over a period of time and the tone of the discussion and of the individual commentators. Specifically: (1) an attempt has been made to give credit to the first to make a particular comment — i.e., annotation is based on a collation of commentary in editions and works devoted to commentary; (2) if only one comment is recorded, a general consensus may be assumed; (3) if there is no note, it may be assumed that no significant or convincing comment was found. This procedure applies as well, albeit more restrictively, to proverbs, sources, parallels, echoes, and the like. Paraphrase and interpretation of passages or scenes have been kept to a minimum, the latter, along with stage business, being more the matter of the appendix. Very occasionally, the commentary records an especially interesting reading of an edition published later than 1974, the date of the last edition represented in the textual notes.

For certain kinds of information, standard reference works have been used: For (1) names and places: early works like Cooper, as well as Pauly and the *OCD*; (2) grammar: Franz (mainly) and Abbott; (3) proverbs: Dent (with reservations owing to his unclear definition of the proverb) and Tilley; (4) word glosses: early dictionaries and editions (heavily relied on because they reflect Shakespeare's immediate semantic context), as well as Schmidt and the *OED*.

In the network of cross-references, "Compare" points to a contrasting statement, "See" to another instance of the same or a similar phenomenon, "See also" to further support or illustration.

All quotations are enclosed in quotation marks (to set them off from paraphrase or from the present editor's comments) and are reproduced as in the source, except that titles of plays or books are printed in italic and obvious typographical errors are corrected. Omissions within quotations are indicated by suspension points; when such omissions remove the beginning or end of a sentence but still leave a sentence complete in itself, that remaining sentence is silently given an initial capital or a final period. Initial capitals are also supplied for direct discourse. Quotations made by the commentators have been verified, documented, and, where necessary, corrected within square brackets. If no specific edition is mentioned, either the standard or the earliest one is used. The commentators' references to passages in this play by act, scene, and line have been replaced by Through Line Numbers within brackets, and quotations of more than a few words have generally been omitted and replaced by a cross-reference (of Through Line Numbers within brackets) to the appropriate passage in this edition. In references to Shakespeare's other plays, Globe act-scene-line numbers (for *Per.* and *TNK* the Riverside ed. is used) are followed by Through Line Numbers within parentheses or square brackets. Quotations from Shakespeare's Poems or Sonnets are made to conform to the texts of the New Variorum edition, and those from the plays, to the most authoritative folio or quarto text; specifically, the following plays are quoted from the best quarto rather than from F1: *Ado, 1H4, 2H4, Ham., LLL, MND, MV, Oth., Per., R2* (+F1), *Rom., Tit., TNK*, and *Tro*. All biblical quotations are printed in the language of the Authorized Version unless some other version is specified.

The notes printed in the commentary are as a rule identified only by the commentator's last name and the date of the book or article; further information is given only when two works of the same date are drawn upon. Full identification will be found in the bibliography or in the lists of editions printed above. Since arabic numerals are used in preference to roman numerals wherever possible, volume-and-page citations appear in the form 9:14 instead of IX, 14 (except for classical authors, to distinguish book and chapter from volume and page). All statements in the commentary not otherwise assigned and all information within square brackets [   ] are the contribution of the editor. When square brackets appear in the work quoted, they have been changed to pointed brackets < >. In general, the style of quotation and citation used in the commentary is also used in the appendix.

The following list of abbreviations and symbols used in this edition does not include many that are in common use or whose full form should be immediately apparent:

a	(in a signature, superscript) left-hand column
ad.	(in a textual note) added, additionally
ad loc.	*ad locum*, referring to this word, line, passage
Ado	*Much Ado about Nothing*
after	a conjecture based on, and expanding, someone else's reading, comment, or conjecture
ALEX	P. Alexander's ed., 1951
AN&Q	*American Notes and Queries*
Anm.	*Anmerkung*, note
Anon., anon.	Anonymous
Ant.	*Antony and Cleopatra*
ante	above
app.	appendix
apud	according to; *see* conj. apud
AR	*Antioch Review*
Archiv	*Archiv für das Studium der Neueren Sprachen und Literaturen*
ARD	ARD1 and ARD2
ARD1	Arden Sh., ed. R. H. Case, 1906
ARD2	New Arden Sh., ed. M. R. Ridley, 1954
ArQ	*Arizona Quarterly*
ASch	*American Scholar*
AWR	*Anglo-Welsh Review*
AWW	*All's Well that Ends Well*
AYL	*As You Like It*
b	(in a signature, superscript) right-hand column
BAYF	M. A. Bayfield's ed., 1920
Blackwood's	*Blackwood's Edinburgh Magazine*
BLUM	K. Blumhof's ed., 1870
BOAS	G. Boas's ed., 1935
BSUF	*Ball State University Forum*
BuR	*Bucknell Review*
(c)	(in citing press-variants) corrected
c.	*capitulum*, chapter

c(a).	century; circa
CahiersE	*Cahiers Elisabéthains*
CAM	CAM1 and CAM3
CAM1	Cambridge Sh., ed. W. G. Clark & W. A. Wright, 1863–6
CAM2	Cambridge Sh., 2nd ed., ed. W. A. Wright, 1891–3
CAM3	CAM3a and CAM3b
CAM3a	New Cambridge Sh., ed. J. D. Wilson, 1950
CAM3b	New Cambridge Sh., ed. J. D. Wilson, 1964 (rpt.)
Cam. Anc. Hist.	*The Cambridge Ancient History*, ed. S. A. Cook et al., 1952
cap.	*capitulum*, chapter
CAP	E. Capell's ed., [1768]
CAPN	E. Capell's *Notes and Various Readings*, 1779–83 [1774]
CE	*College English*
CEA	*CEA Critic*
CentR	*Centennial Review*
cf.	compare
ch(s).	chorus, chapter(s)
CHum	*Computers and the Humanities*
CL	*Comparative Literature*
CLAJ	*College Language Association Journal*
CLN2	New Clarendon Sh., ed. R. E. C. Houghton, 1962
COL	COL1, COL2, COL3, and COL4
COL1	J. P. Collier's ed., 1842–4
COL2	J. P. Collier's ed., 1853
COL3	J. P. Collier's ed., 1858
COL4	J. P. Collier's ed., 1875–8
col(s).	column(s)
CollL	*College Literature*
COLNE	J. P. Collier's *Notes and Emendations*, 2nd ed., 1853
CompD	*Comparative Drama*
conj.	conjecture; conjunction
conj. apud	conjecture recorded in the ed. whose siglum follows
conj. in	conjecture published in
ContempR	*Contemporary Review*
Cor.	*Coriolanus*
cp.	compare
CQ	*Cambridge Quarterly*
CR	*Critical Review*
CritQ	*Critical Quarterly*
Cym.	*Cymbeline*
DA(I)	*Dissertation Abstracts (International)*
DEL	DEL2 and DEL4
DEL2	N. Delius's ed., 1854–[61]
DEL4	N. Delius's ed., 1872

diss.	dissertation
DNB	*Dictionary of National Biography*
DP	Dramatis Personae
DUJ	*Durham University Journal*
DYCE	DYCE1 and DYCE2
DYCE1	A. Dyce's ed., 1857
DYCE2	A. Dyce's ed., 1864–7
EA	*Etudes Anglaises*
E&S	*Essays and Studies by Members of the English Association*
ed.	edited by, edition, editor
edd., eds.	editions, editors
EdL	*Etudes de Lettres*
EIC	*Essays in Criticism*
EJ	*English Journal*
ELH	*Journal of English Literary History*
ELN	*English Language Notes*
ELR	*English Literary Renaissance*
EM	*English Miscellany*
Enc. Brit.	*The Encyclopaedia Britannica*, 11th ed., 1910–11
Eng. Dial. *Dict.*	*The English Dialect Dictionary*, ed. Joseph Wright, 6 vols., 1898–1905
enl.	enlarged
Ep.	Epilogue
Err.	*The Comedy of Errors*
(errata)	(in a textual note) reading as corrected in the errata of the work
ES	*English Studies*
ESA	*English Studies in Africa*
ESELL	*Essays and Studies in English Language and Literature*
et al.	and others
etc.	*et cetera*, and others, and so forth; (in a textual note) all other fully collated editions
Etymol. Dict.	*An Etymological Dictionary of the English Language*, ed. W. W. Skeat, 1882
EV1	C. H. Herford's Eversley ed., 1899
EV2	M. A. Pink's New Eversley ed., 1935
EVNS	Riverside Sh., textual ed. G. B. Evans, 1974
Expl	*Explicator*
f(f).	and following page(s)
F, F., F1	First Folio (1623)
F2	Second Folio (1632)
F3	Third Folio (1663–4)
F4	Fourth Folio (1685)
facs.	facsimile
Ff	F1, F2, F3, and F4

FHP	*Fort Hare Papers*
fig.	figurative, -ly
fn.	footnote
fo.	folio
Folg.	Folger Library
fol(s).	folio(s), leaf (leaves)
F. Q.	*Faerie Queene*
Fr.	French
GAR	D. Garrick & E. Capell's ed., 1758
Gent. Mag.	*The Gentleman's Magazine*
Ger.	German
GLO	Globe Sh., ed. W. G. Clark & W. A. Wright, 1864
GROVE	*The New Grove Dictionary of Music and Musicians,* ed. S. Sadie, 1980
1H4	*1 Henry IV*
2H4	*2 Henry IV*
H5	*Henry V*
1H6	*1 Henry VI*
2H6	*2 Henry VI*
3H6	*3 Henry VI*
H8	*Henry VIII*
HAL	J. O. Halliwell's ed., 1853–65
HALD	A. Halliday's ed., 1873
Ham.	*Hamlet*
HAN1	T. Hanmer's ed., 1743–4
HAN2	T. Hanmer's ed., 1745
HAN3	T. Hanmer's ed., 1770–1
HAN47	T. Hanmer's ed., 1747
HLQ	*Huntington Library Quarterly*
HTR	J. Hunter's ed., 1870
HUD	HUD1 and HUD2
HUD1	H. N. Hudson's ed., 1851–6
HUD2	H. N. Hudson's ed., 1880–1
HudR	*Hudson Review*
HUSL	*Hebrew University Studies in Literature*
ibid.	*ibidem*, at the same place
IDEM	the same person
i.e.	*id est*, that is
int.	interjection, -ory
IRV	Henry Irving Sh., ed. H. Irving & F. Marshall, 1888–90
It.	Italian
JC	*Julius Caesar*
JEGP	*Journal of English and Germanic Philology*
JJCL	*Jadavpur Journal of Comparative Literature*
Jn.	*King John*

JOHN1	S. Johnson's 1st ed., 1765
JOHN2	S. Johnson's 2nd ed., 1765
JOHN3	S. Johnson's ed., 1768
KIT1	G. L. Kittredge's ed., 1936
KN	*Kwartalnik Neofilologiczny*
KNT1	C. Knight's ed., [1838–43]
KTLY	T. Keightley's ed., 1864
l.	*liber*, book
l(l).	line(s)
L&P	*Literature and Psychology*
LC	*Library Chronicle; A Lover's Complaint*
LHY	*Literary Half-Yearly*
lib.	*liber*, book
lit.	literal, -ly; literature, -ry
LLL	*Love's Labour's Lost*
Lr.	*King Lear*
Luc.	*The Rape of Lucrece*
Mac.	*Macbeth*
MAL	E. Malone's ed., 1790
MAUN	S. Maunder's ed., 1839
mCAP2	E. Capell's MS holograph of his 1768 ed., 1751
McNR	*McNeese Review*
mCOL1	J. P. Collier's MS notes in the Perkins Folio (F2), –1853, Huntington Library
ME	Middle English
mF2FL20	MS notes (–1765) in F2, Copy 20, Folger Library
mF2FL21	MS notes (1754–65) in F2, Copy 21, Folger Library
mF2J	MS notes (–1700) in copy of F2 sold in 1649 by Sarah Jones, *apud* Halliwell (1868)
mF2TCC	MS notes (–1800) in Capell's copy of F2, Trinity College Library, Cambridge
mF4FL33	MS notes (–1723) in F4, Copy 33, Folger Library
mF4Q	MS notes (1685–) *apud* Quincy (1854)
MichA	*Michigan Academician*
MLN	*Modern Language Notes*
mLONG	R. Long's MS notes (–1733?) in copy of F2, Pembroke College Library, Cambridge
MLQ	*Modern Language Quarterly*
MLR	*Modern Language Review*
MLS	*Modern Language Studies*
MM	*Measure for Measure*
MND	*A Midsummer Night's Dream*
MP	*Modern Philology*
mPOPE	A. Pope's MS notes (–1723) in F3, Copy 20, Folger Library
MS(S)	manuscript(s)

mSTV2	G. Steevens's & I. Reed's MS notes in proof sheets for Boydell ed., 1791–1802
mTBY2	S. Thirlby's MS notes in POPE1, 1723–33, Yale University Library
mTBY3	S. Thirlby's MS notes in THEO1, 1733–47, Folger Library
mTBY4	S. Thirlby's MS notes in WARB, 1747–53, Folger Library
mTHEO1	L. Theobald's MS notes (1723–33) in F2, Copy 20, Folger Library
mTHEO2	L. Theobald's letters (1729–34) to William Warburton, Phillipps MS 8565, Folger Library
mTHEO3	L. Theobald's letters (1729–36) to William Warburton, Egerton MS 1956, British Library
mTYR	T. Tyrwhitt's MS notes (–1786) in a copy of F2, C.39.i.13, British Library
MUN	J. Munro's London Sh., 1957
MV	*The Merchant of Venice*
mWARB	W. Warburton's MS notes (1747–79) in WARB, Copy 5, Folger Library
n(n).	note(s)
N&H	W. A. Neilson ed., rev. C. J. Hill, 1942
N&Q	*Notes and Queries*
NCF	*Nineteenth-Century Fiction*
n.d.	no date
NED, N.E.D.	*See* OED
NEQ	*The New England Quarterly*
n. F.	*neue Folge*, new series
NLH	*New Literary History*
NLSN	W. A. Neilson's Cambridge ed., 1906
NM	*Neuphilologische Mitteilungen*
n.p.	no place
NS	new series
NS	*Die Neueren Sprachen*
Obs.	*The Observer* (London)
obs.	obsolete
OCD	*The Oxford Classical Dictionary*, ed. N. G. L. Hammond and H. H. Scullard, 2nd ed., 1970
OE	Old English
OED	*Oxford English Dictionary*, originally published as *A New English Dictionary* and abbreviated *NED*
om.	omitted
ON	Old Norse
op. cit.	*opere citato*, in the work cited
Oth.	*Othello*
OUP	Oxford University Press
OXF1	Oxford Sh., ed. W. J. Craig, [1891]

PAULY	*Paulys Real-Encyclopädie der classischen Altertumswissenschaft,* ed. Georg Wissowa et al., 1894–1978
PEL2	Pelican Sh., ed. M. Mack, 1969
PEN1	Penguin Sh., ed. G. B. Harrison, 1937
Per.	*Pericles*
PhT	*The Phoenix and Turtle*
PLL	*Papers on Language and Literature*
PMLA	*Publications of the Modern Language Association of America*
POPE	POPE1 and POPE2
POPE1	A. Pope's ed., 1723–5
POPE2	A. Pope's ed., 1728
post	below
PP	*The Passionate Pilgrim*
PP.A	S. Thirlby's references in his MSS to the first set of his loose papers, not now known to exist, of early 1729
PQ	*Philological Quarterly*
Pr.	Prologue
pt(s).	part(s)
pub.	public, publication, published
QQ	*Queen's Quarterly*
r	(in a signature or folio, superscript) recto
R2	*Richard II*
R3	*Richard III*
RANN	J. Rann's ed., 1786–[94]
RenP	*Renaissance Papers*
RES	*Review of English Studies*
rev.	revised
RID	RIDa and RIDb
RIDa	M. R. Ridley's New Temple Sh., 1935
RIDb	M. R. Ridley's New Temple Sh., 1954 (rpt.)
RLF1	W. J. Rolfe's ed., 1895
RLMC	*Rivista di Letterature Moderne e Comparate*
RLV	*Revue des Langues Vivantes*
RMS	*Renaissance and Modern Studies*
Rom.	*Romeo and Juliet*
ROWE	ROWE1, ROWE2, and ROWE3
ROWE1	N. Rowe's 1st ed., 1709
ROWE2	N. Rowe's 2nd ed., 1709
ROWE3	N. Rowe's ed., 1714
rpt.	reprint, -ed
RSC	Royal Sh. Company
RUS	*Rice University Studies*
St. James's Chr.	*Saint James's Chronicle*, ed. Henry Baldwin, 1765
SAQ	*South Atlantic Quarterly*

SatR	*Saturday Review*
SB	*Studies in Bibliography*
Sc.	Scene
sc(il).	*scilicet*, understand, supply
SD(s)	stage direction(s)
SEL	*Studies in English Literature, 1500–1900*
SELL	*Studies in English Literature and Language*
ser.	series
Sh(n).	Shakespeare(an) (any spelling)
ShAB	*Shakespeare Association Bulletin*
ShakS	*Shakespeare Studies*
ShN	*Shakespeare Newsletter*
Shr.	*The Taming of the Shrew*
ShS	*Shakespeare Survey*
ShStud	*Shakespeare Studies* (Tokyo)
sig(s).	signature(s)
SING	SING1 and SING2
SING1	S. W. Singer's ed., 1826
SING2	S. W. Singer's ed., 1856
SIS	C. J. Sisson's ed., 1954
SISNR	C. J. Sisson's *New Readings*, 1956
SJ	*Shakespeare-Jahrbuch*
SJH	*Shakespeare-Jahrbuch* (Heidelberg)
SJW	*Shakespeare-Jahrbuch* (Weimar)
SN	*Studia Neophilologica*
SoAB	*South Atlantic Bulletin*
Son.	*The Sonnets*
sp.	spelled
Sp.	Spanish
SP(s)	speech prefix(es)
SP	*Studies in Philology*
SQ	*Shakespeare Quarterly*
SR	*Sewanee Review*
SRAZ	*Studia Romanica et Anglica Zagrabiensia*
st.	stanza
STAU	H. Staunton's ed., 1856–60
STC	*Short-title Catalogue* (by A. W. Pollard & G. R. Redgrave; 2nd ed., rev. & enl. W. A. Jackson, F. S. Ferguson, & K. F. Pantzer, 1976–86)
subst.	substantially
s.v.	*sub voce*, under the word
TEAS	Twayne's English Authors Series
(text)	(in a textual note) the reading so printed in the text of the edition
TGV	*The Two Gentlemen of Verona*

THEO	THEO1, THEO2, THEO3, and THEO4
THEO1	L. Theobald's ed., 1733
THEO2	L. Theobald's ed., 1740
THEO3	L. Theobald's ed., 1752
THEO4	L. Theobald's ed., 1757
Tim.	*Timon of Athens*
Tit.	*Titus Andronicus*
TLN	Through Line Number, numbering
TLS	London *Times Literary Supplement*
Tmp.	*The Tempest*
TN	*Twelfth Night*
TNK	*The Two Noble Kinsmen*
tr.	translated by, translation, translator
Tro.	*Troilus and Cressida*
TSE	*Tulane Studies in English*
TxSE	*Texas Studies in English*
(u)	(in citing press-variants) uncorrected
UCTSE	*University of Cape Town Studies in English*
UDQ	*University of Denver Quarterly*
UDR	*University of Dayton Review*
UTQ	*University of Toronto Quarterly*
v	(in a signature or folio, superscript) verso
v.	verb; verse; *vide*, see
v1773	S. Johnson & G. Steevens's ed., 1773
v1778	S. Johnson & G. Steevens's ed., 1778
v1785	S. Johnson, G. Steevens, & I. Reed's ed., 1785
v1793	G. Steevens & I. Reed's ed., 1793
v1803	I. Reed's ed., 1803
v1821	J. Boswell's ed., 1821
v1907	H. H. Furness's ed., 1907
Var.	Variorum
Ven.	*Venus and Adonis*
VeP	*Vita e Pensiero*
ver.	verse (line)
vi(d).	*vide*, see
viz.	*videlicet*, namely
vol(s).	volume(s)
V. R.	*Various Readings* in E. Capell's *Notes and Various Readings*, 1779–83 [1774]
W&L	*Women and Literature*
WARB	W. Warburton's ed., 1747
WascanaR	*Wascana Review*
w.ch, w:ch	which
WH	WH1 and WH2
WH1	R. G. White's ed., 1857–66

WH2	R. G. White's ed., 1883
withdrawn	conjecture made and withdrawn by the same author in; *and withdrawn*: conjecture made and withdrawn in same place; *withdrawn according to*: (place of withdrawal not located)
Wiv.	*The Merry Wives of Windsor*
WORD1	C. Wordsworth's ed., 1883
WRIGHT MS	MS notes by W. A. Wright in a copy of CAM1, Trinity College Library, Cambridge (1866–92)
WRIGHT SHAKE-SPEARIANA	MS notes by W. A. Wright in Trinity College Library, Cambridge (–1892)
wrongly attrib. to	(thus attributed in CAM1)
WT	*The Winter's Tale*
w.^{t}, w:^{t}	what
w.th, w:th	with
WVUPP	*West Virginia University Philological Papers*
YAL2	New Yale Sh., ed. P. G. Phialas, 1955
y.^{e}, y:^{e}	the
YR	*Yale Review*
y.^{t}, y:^{t}	that

Symbols used in the textual notes:

∧	punctuation missing or omitted
∼	verbal form of the lemma unchanged (while punctuation varies)
-	(between two sigla) all fully collated eds. between and including those indicated by the two sigla
+	(after a siglum) and all succeeding fully collated eds.
(−)	all sigla following the minus sign within parentheses indicate eds. that agree, not with the variant, but with the Variorum text (i.e., with F1)

CHRONOLOGY OF
IMPORTANT EVENTS

44 B.C.   Assassination of Julius Caesar.

43 B.C.   The consuls Hirtius and Pansa killed at Mutina; Triumvirate of Antony, Octavius, and Lepidus.

42 B.C.   Battles of Philippi; suicides of Cassius and Brutus.

41 B.C.   Wars of Fulvia and Lucius Antonius against each other and then together in the Perusine War against Octavius; Cleopatra sails up the Cydnus to Tarsus, where she meets Antony.

40 B.C.   Lucius Antonius surrenders Perusia to Octavius; Fulvia dies in Sicyon; Pact of Brundisium; Antony marries Octavia; Pompey occupies Sardinia and Corsica; the Parthians invade Syria.

39 B.C.   Concordat of Misenum between Antony, Octavius, and Pompey; Antony and Octavia winter in Athens.

38 B.C.   War between Octavius and Pompey; victory of Ventidius over the Parthians and the death of Pacorus at Gindarus.

37 B.C.   Antony gives Octavia leave to mediate between Octavius and him; Pact of Tarentum and probable renewal of the Triumvirate; Antony marries Cleopatra at Antioch.

36 B.C.   Expeditions of Octavius, Lepidus, and Taurus against Pompey; defeat of Pompey by Octavius off Naulochus; Lepidus no longer triumvir.

35 B.C.   Octavia reaches Athens with troops and provisions for Antony, who sends her home; Pompey killed in Asia by Titius, Antony's legate.

34 B.C.   In Alexandria Antony celebrates a triumph over Armenia; the "Donations" of Alexandria.

33 B.C.   Letters of remonstrance between Antony and Octavius; Antony assembles his client kings and takes the oath of allegiance from them.

32 B.C.   Octavia divorced by Antony; Antony's will published by Octavius in Rome; Octavius declares war on Cleopatra.

31 B.C.   Octavius's fleets gather at Brundisium and Tarentum; Octavius crosses

the Adriatic and captures Toryne; battle of Actium.

30 B.C.   Suicide of Antony; Octavius enters Alexandria; suicide of Cleopatra.

Chronology by Acts

Act 1   40 B.C.
Act 2   40–39 B.C.
Act 3   38–30 B.C.
Act 4   30 B.C.
Act 5   30 B.C.

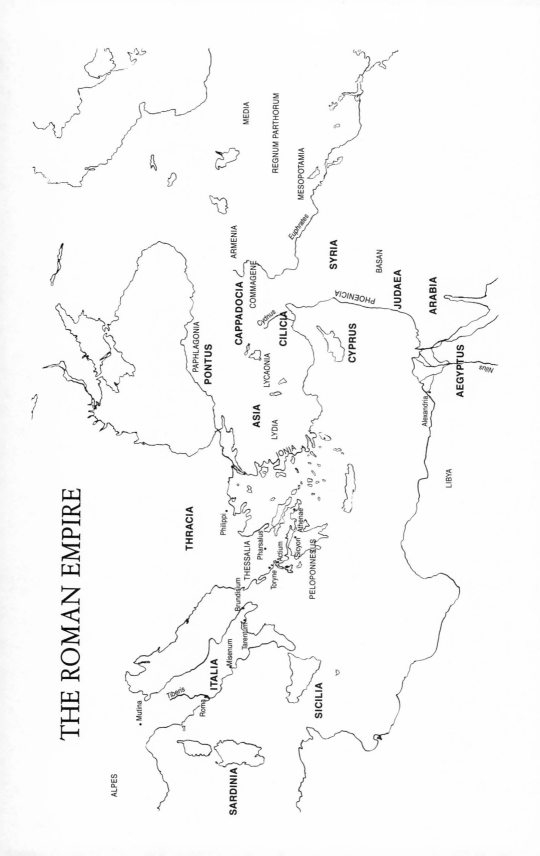

THE ROMAN EMPIRE

ALPES

SARDINIA

SICILIA

ITALIA

Tiberis

Roma

Mutina

Misenum

Tarentum

Brundisium

THRACIA

THESSALIA

Philippi

Pharsalus

Toryne

Actium

Sicyon

Athenae

PELOPONNESUS

IONIA

LYDIA

ASIA

LYCAONIA

PAPHLAGONIA

PONTUS

CAPPADOCIA

COMMAGENE

ARMENIA

CILICIA

Cydnus

SYRIA

PHOENICIA

BASAN

CYPRUS

JUDAEA

ARABIA

AEGYPTUS

Alexandria

Nilus

LIBYA

MEDIA

REGNUM PARTHORUM

MESOPOTAMIA

Euphrates

ANTONY AND CLEOPATRA

[Dramatis Personæ.

Mark Antony.
Octavius Cæsar.
Lepidus.
Sextus Pompeius.   5
Enobarbus,
Ventidius,
Canidius,
Eros,
Scarus,   } *Friends and Followers of* Antony.
Decretas,   10
Demetrius,
Philo,
Mecænas,
Agrippa,   15
Dolabella,
Proculeius,   } *Friends to* Cæsar.
Thidias,
Gallus,
Menas,   20
Menecrates,   } *Friends to* Pompey.
Varrius,
Alexas,
Mardian,   } *Servants to* Cleopatra.
Diomedes,   25
Taurus,
Silius,
Seleucus,
Euphronius,
Lamprius, Rannius, Lucillius,   30
A Soothsayer.
Clown.
Cleopatra, *Queen of* Ægypt.
Octavia, *Sister to* Cæsar, *and Wife to* Antony.
Charmian,   } *Ladies attending on* Cleopatra.   35
Iras,
Ambassadors from Antony *to* Cæsar, *Captains,*
  Soldiers, Messengers, and other Attendants.
The SCENE *lyes in several Parts of the*
  Roman *Empire.*]   40

2

1 **Dramatis Personæ**] Based on ROWE (ed. 1709); there is no list in the Folios. Most editors reproduce Rowe's list with modifications of detail. THEOBALD (ed. 1733) is the first to add Taurus and Silius; HANMER (ed. 1744), the first to add Seleucus; CAPELL (ed. 1768), the first to name Euphronius (STEEVENS [ed. 1793], the first to use Ambassador; WILSON [ed. 1950], the first to use Schoolmaster); COLLIER (1852, p. 470), the first (and only) to assign a name, Elis, to Cleopatra's messenger from Rome (see 1052); RIDLEY (ed. 1935), the first to add the mute Lamprius; and EVANS (ed. 1974), the first to add the nonspeaking Rannius and Lucillius.

2 **Mark Antony**] Marcus Antonius (82–30 B.C.), one of the Second Triumvirate (*Triumviri Reipublicae Constituendae*), with Octavius and Lepidus, a formal magistracy approved by legislative act on 27 Nov. 43 B.C. See PAULY, 1:2595–614 (30); *OCD*.

3 **Octavius Cæsar**] Caius Julius Caesar Octavianus (63 B.C.–A.D. 14), originally Caius Octavius, grandnephew of Julius Caesar and adopted son and heir to three-quarters of his estate, given the title Augustus by the Roman Senate on 17 Jan. 27 B.C. See PAULY, Iulius, 10:275–381 (132); *OCD*, Augustus.

4 **Lepidus**] Marcus Aemilius Lepidus (ca. 90–12 B.C.), triumvir, banished in 36 B.C. to Circeii, deprived by Octavius of his triumviral powers but remained Pontifex Maximus until his death. See PAULY, Aemilius, 1:556–61 (73); *OCD*, Lepidus (3).

5 **Sextus Pompeius**] Sextus Pompeius Magnus (ca. 67–35 B.C.), younger son of Cneius Pompeius Magnus of the First Triumvirate, defeated by Octavius at the sea battle at Naulochus in 36 B.C., then captured on his way to Armenia and executed on order of Antony. See PAULY, 21:2213–50 (33); *OCD*.

6 **Enobarbus**] Cneius Domitius Ahenobarbus (?–31 B.C.), governor of Bithynia (40–34) and consul in 32 B.C. COOPER (1565, *Aeneobarbus*): "A Romayne, so called, because he had a bearde as redde as brasse." See PAULY, Domitius, 5:1328–31 (23); *OCD*.

7 **Ventidius**] Publius Ventidius Bassus (ca. 98 B.C.–? [date of death uncertain, but before Actium]); a coin bearing his likeness was minted in recognition of his victory over the Parthians in 39 B.C. See PAULY, 8A:795–816 (5); *OCD*.

8 **Canidius**] Publius Canidius Crassus (?–30 B.C.), commander of Antony's army at Actium, ordered killed by Octavius in 30 B.C. See PAULY, 3:1475–6 (2); *OCD*.

9 **Eros**] See PAULY, 6:542–3 (8); not in *OCD*.

10 **Scarus**] Possibly Marcus Aemilius Scaurus, half brother of Sextus Pompeius, whom he betrayed to Antony in 35 B.C. Despite CAPELL (1779 [1774], 1:45)—"His name is of the Poet's invention, and himself a person of his creating"—most of those who comment tend to agree with WALKER (1860, 2:323): "*Scarus . . .* is Scaurus." See PAULY, Aemilius, 1:590 (142); not in *OCD*.

11 **Decretas**] Antony's *doryphoros* ("sword bearer"). See PAULY, Derketaios, 5:240; not in *OCD*.

12 **Demetrius**] Not in Plutarch. HONIGMANN (1959, p. 27): "It may be . . . that Antonius' parallel [see *The Comparison of Demetrius with Antonius*, p. 000] influenced Shakespeare." PAULY (4:2803 [52]) mentions a freedman named Demetrius who administered Cyprus for Antony in 39 B.C. and captured and executed Labienus.

13 **Philo**] Not in Plutarch.

14 **Mecænas**] Caius Maecenas (?–8 A.D.), Roman knight, friend and adviser to Octavius, patron of letters. See PAULY, 14:207–29 (6); *OCD*.

15 **Agrippa**] Marcus Vipsanius Agrippa (ca. 64–12 B.C.), consul in 37 B.C., victor over Sextus Pompeius in the naval battle of Naulochus in 36 B.C., and admiral of the Roman fleet at Actium. See PAULY, Vipsanius, 9A:1226–75 (2); *OCD*, Agrippa (3).

16 **Dolabella**] Cornelius Dolabella, probably the son of Publius Cornelius Dolabella (consul with Antony in 44 B.C.). See PAULY, Cornelius, 4:1296–7 (130); mentioned in *OCD*, Dolabella (3). GODSHALK (1977, p. 71): "Caesar's Dolabella is in reality the son of Antony's enemy, but, since North's translation does not distinguish between the father and the son, Shakespeare probably conflates the two."

17 **Proculeius**] Caius Proculeius, wealthy Roman knight, present at the battle of Actium and the capture of Cleopatra. COOPER (1565): "A gentleman of Rome, verye familiar with Augustus." See PAULY, 23:72–4 (2); not in *OCD*.

18 **Thidias**] Freedman sent by Octavius for secret dealings with Cleopatra. See PAULY, Thyrsos, 6A:753 (3); not in *OCD*. Most editions substitute North's spelling *Thyreus* (see p. 000). WILSON's (ed. 1950, p. 125) preference for *Thidias* because *Thyreus* was "so difficult for an actor to speak," like RIDLEY's (ed. 1954) for *Thyreus*, is questionable: a slightly trilled (or flapped) Elizabethan *r* makes *Thyreus* well-nigh indistinguishable from *Thidias*.

19 **Gallus**] Caius Cornelius Gallus (ca. 69–26 B.C.), poet, general under Octavius and prefect of Egypt in 30 B.C. See PAULY, Cornelius, 4:1342–50 (164); *OCD*, Gallus (3).

20 **Menas**] Freedman who captured Sardinia for Sextus Pompeius in 40 B.C. and was appointed governor. He turned it over in 38 B.C. to Octavius, who made him a knight. In 36 B.C. he returned to the service of Pompey and fell in a naval battle off Siscia in 35. See PAULY, 15:774–5 (3) and Menodoros, 15:896–900 (1); *OCD*, Menodorus. See also n. 3108.

21 **Menecrates**] Freedman and naval commander of Sextus Pompeius, sent against Octavius's fleet and the deserter Menas, died in the naval battle off Cumae in 38 B.C. See PAULY, 15:799–800 (15); not in *OCD*.

22 **Varrius**] WALKER (1860, 2:323): "Perhaps L. *Varius* Cotyla, an officer and companion of Antony's. . . . Shakespeare found him in North's Plutarch [see p. 000], and perhaps by a slip of memory took him for a friend of Pompey's. The possibility, however, is . . . slight." See PAULY, Varius, 8A:386–7 (6); not in *OCD*.

23 **Alexas**] Not in PAULY, *OCD*, or Plutarch.

24 **Mardian**] Not in PAULY, *OCD*; in Plutarch (see p. 000).

25 **Diomedes**] Cleopatra's scribe. See PAULY, 5:826 (7); not in *OCD*.

26 **Taurus**] Titus Statilius Taurus, commander of the land army at Actium. See PAULY, Statilius, 3A:2199–203 (34); *OCD*, Statilius.

27 **Silius**] Legate or quaestor of Ventidius. See PAULY, Poppaedius, 22:81 (ll. 36–46); not in *OCD*.

28 **Seleucus**] Slave(?) and procurator of Cleopatra. See PAULY, 2A:1247 (15); not in *OCD*.

29 **Euphronius**] Teacher of the children of Antony and Cleopatra. See PAULY, 6:1220 (2); not in *OCD*.

30 **Lamprius, Rannius, Lucillius**] See n. 77–9.

31 *A Soothsayer*] See n. 77 ("Lamprius").

32 *Clown*] See n. 3492.

33 **Cleopatra**] Cleopatra VII (69–30 B.C.), daughter of Ptolemy XII and last queen of the line of the Ptolemies. COOPER (1565): "The name of diuers great ladies, specially queenes of Aegypte. Of whom one excelling in pleasantnesse and sharpnesse of wit, fyrst allured vnto hir Iulius Cæsar, afterwarde Marcus Antonius, companion in the empyre with Augustus, whom she brought into such dotage, that in folowinge hir appetite, he aspyred vnto the whole empyre: wherfore he was afterward destroyed by Augustus." See PAULY, Kleopatra, 11:750–81 (20); *OCD*, Cleopatra VII.

34 **Octavia**] Octavia minor (ca. 70–11 B.C.), elder sister of Octavius. See PAULY, 17:1859–68 (96); *OCD*.

35 **Charmian**] COOPER (1565): "The handmayde of Cleopatra, that willingly died with hir maistresse." See PAULY, Supp. 3:244 (2); not in *OCD*.

36 **Iras**] PLUTARCH (1579, p. 998): "A woman of *Cleopatraes* bedchamber, that friseled her heare, and dressed her head." See PAULY, Kleopatra, 11:777; not in *OCD*.

THE TRAGEDIE OF
Anthonie, and Cleopatra.

Actus Primus. Scœna Prima.   1.1

Enter Demetrius and Philo.   (vv6ª)

Philo.

Nay, but this dotage of our Generals   4

---

1 *Scœna Prima.*] *Om.* THEO
  SCENE Alexandria *in* Ægypt. ROWE, POPE; *the Palace at* Alexandria *in* Ægypt.
THEO1+ (*subst.*)
  4 Generals] Generall F2-JOHN1

0.1 **Anthonie**] Doubtful derivations of the *th* spelling from Greek (KREBS, 1880, p. 123), Dutch (YONGE *apud* MAYHEW, 1880, p. 264), and German (WOOLRYCH, 1880, p. 453) have been superseded by the explanation of STRACHAN (1934, p. 85): "Some originally Greek words were borrowed from French with *t* instead of *th*, so that the regular Middle English forms were *teatre, apotecarie, catolic, trone, teme.* Learned influence restored the *h* in writing, and then readers might be in doubt about the pronunciation. In the confusion that prevailed the 'learned' spelling with *h* was adopted by mistake in 'Anthony' and 'author'. In some cases the pronunciation *th* was developed in consequence of the new spelling, while in others (such as 'thyme' and 'Thomas' [and British English *Anthony*]) the sound *t* has remained to the present day." For Sh.'s spelling of the name in his other plays, see IDEM, p. 86.

4 **Nay, but**] FRANZ (§404): *Nay* introduces a correction, explanation, also a mild contradiction or rebuttal. See also "Nay then" (1119), "Nay certainly" (1371). Most commentators, however, treat this *Nay* as the stronger *no.*

   of our Generals] MALONE (ed. 1790) is the first to call attention to the double genitive as "the common phraseology of Shakspeare's time." It is still the standard construction; see QUIRK (1972, p. 203). See also 273, 2295.

5

Ore-flowes the measure: those his goodly eyes   5
That o're the Files and Musters of the Warre,
Haue glow'd like plated Mars:
Now bend, now turne
The Office and Deuotion of their view
Vpon a Tawny Front. His Captaines heart,   10
Which in the scuffles of great Fights hath burst
The Buckles on his brest, reneages all temper,

7–8 *One verse line* ROWE1+
7 Mars] Mars' mTBY4 *conj.*, DYCE2, HUD2
10 Captaines] captain UPTON (1748, p. 333) *conj.*, RANN

---

5 **measure**] See nn. 1221, 2191.

5–10 those . . . Front] SCHANZER (1956, *N&Q*, p. 154) compares the Countess of Pembroke's *Antonie* (1595, ll. 1941–2): "In both passages the contrast is drawn between Antony's eyes in the service of Mars and in that of Venus, a contrast sufficiently unusual to make Shakespeare's indebtedness here seem highly probable." For the 1592 *Antonius*, see p. 523.

5 those . . . eyes] FRANZ (§331): At the beginning of the 16th c., the demonstrative collocated with the possessive pronoun is still more frequent than the later construction ("those goodly eyes of his"); in Sh. both forms exist.

6 **Files and Musters**] Only BLUMHOF (ed. 1870) and KITTREDGE (ed. 1941) comment: "Synonymous." See nn. 9, 2404.

7 **Mars**] Only BLUMHOF (ed. 1870) and KITTREDGE (ed. 1941) paraphrase as a genitive; the latter does not add an apostrophe, however. See textual notes and conj., p. 346. For the omission of the apostrophe, see FRANZ §199.

8 **bend, now turne**] WORDSWORTH (ed. 1883) regards *turne* as "*more than 'bend.'*" CASE (ed. 1906): "Editors place a comma after *turn*, but *bend* may be independent, expressing a contrast to the fiery outlook inferred in *glow'd*, and without influence on *the office*, etc."

9 **Office and Deuotion**] DELIUS (ed. 1856): "*Devoted office*," a hendiadys. CASE (ed. 1906) and most commentators disagree. See n. 6.

10 **Tawny**] COTGRAVE (1611, Tanné): "*Also, duskie, swart.*" WHITE (ed. 1883): "Cleopatra was a Greek, the daughter of Ptolemy, and was probably fair, although not with Teutonic fairness." WILSON (ed. 1950, pp. xi f.) reflects the consensus: "Shakespeare had thought of her as an African beauty." See also nn. 14, 1060.

Front] BULLOKAR (1616): "Forehead." See also "Broad-fronted" (556). BLUMHOF (ed. 1870) notes the military sense. WERTIME (1969, p. 17): "A pun reducing the battle-front to the scope of Cleopatra's face and implying, ironically, a similarity between military strife and the domestic strife generated by Cleopatra's 'wrangling' personality."

Captaines] UPTON (1748, p. 333), questionably, "corrects" to *Captain*—"i.e. His warlike heart, such as becomes a captain"—that it may conform to Sh.'s use of (p. 332) "*substantives adjectively*; or, *by way of apposition.*" See also n. 1505.

12 **reneages**] Although all editors agree on the meaning "deny" (ROWE [ed. 1714, 8:Glossary]) or "*renounces*" (POPE [ed. 1723]), there has been inordinate comment on the etymology: HANMER (ed. 1744, 6:Glossary) thinks the word derives from Sp. *rene-*

And is become the Bellowes and the Fan
To coole a Gypsies Lust.

> *Flourish. Enter Anthony, Cleopatra her Ladies, the*   15
> *Traine, with Eunuchs fanning her.*

Looke where they come:
Take but good note, and you shall see in him
(The triple Pillar of the world) transform'd

---

15 *Flourish.*] *Om.* F2-POPE2, HAN1; *ad. within.* DYCE, STAU (*subst.*), HUD2; *after* 20 RID
15–16 *Enter . . . her.*] *After* 20 DYCE, STAU, HUD2, RID
18 in] *Om.* F3-ROWE3

---

gār; BOSWELL (ed. 1821), from Old French *reneyes*; BLUMHOF (ed. 1870), from Latin *renego*. See conj., p. 346.

    temper] MINSHEU (1617): *"Rule or moderate"*; KERSEY (1702): *"Natural disposition"*; DYCHE & PARDON (1740) refer also to "a person of great command over himself." FURNESS (ed. 1907), citing *Oth.* 5.2.233 (3552), senses "a suggestion of the hardening of steel." BLUMHOF (ed. 1870), however, is the first to suggest a pun.

    13 **is become**] See FRANZ §631 for *be* instead of *have* with intransitive verbs in the past and past perfect tenses.

    13–14 **Bellowes . . . coole**] JOHNSON (ed. 1765): "The *bellows* and *fan* being commonly used for contrary purposes, were probably opposed by the authour, who might perhaps have written,— *is become the bellows, and the fan,* To kindle and *to cool a Gypsy's lust."* STEEVENS (ed. 1778) adds, "In Lylly's *Midas,* 1592, the *bellows* is used both to *cool* and to kindle: 'Methinks Venus and Nature stand with *each of them a pair of bellows,* [the] one *cooling* my low birth, the other *kindling* my lofty affections' [5.2.81–3, ed. Warwick Bond, 1902]." And MALONE (*apud* IDEM): "The *bellows,* as well as the *fan, cools* the air by ventilation; and Shakespeare probably considered it in that light only." He compares *Ven.* 51–2 and (in ed. 1790) *F.Q.* 2.9.30. KNOWLES (privately) compares *F.Q.* 2.2.201–5. See conj., p. 347.

    14 **Gypsies**] JOHNSON (ed. 1765): *"Gypsy* is here used, both in the original meaning for an *Egyptian,* and in its accidental sense, for a *bad woman."* BLUMHOF (ed. 1870) mentions Cleopatra's powers of deception and enchantment. IRVING & MARSHALL (ed. 1889) detect "a tone of contemptuous abuse. Compare Romeo and Juliet, [2.4.43–4 (1145–6)]: 'Dido, a dowdy; Cleopatra a *gipsy.*'" See also 2784 ("Gypsie").

    15–16 **Flourish . . . her**] For descriptive, probably authorial, SDs, see also 77–9, 170, et passim, and pp. 375–6.

    17 **Looke where**] FRANZ (§347[b]) suggests that *where* very commonly signifies "there" (or "here") after *look.* See *OED,* Where *adv.* and *conj.* 1b (b).

    18 **but**] For the adverbial use of *but* meaning "only," see FRANZ §434.

    19 **triple Pillar**] Despite many Elizabethan examples of *triple* meaning "threefold," treble" (*OED, adj.* 1), JOHNSON's (ed. 1765) remark (erroneously attributed by STEEVENS [ed. 1773] and others to Warburton)—*"Triple* is here used improperly for *third,* or *one of three"*—misled commentators, causing an extraordinary exchange between BRAE (1851, p. 498) and J. S. W. (1851, p. 27) on the Ovidian precedent for Sh.'s usage. As MALONE (ed. 1790) pointed out, *triple* does mean "third" in *AWW* 2.1.111 (716). BLUMHOF (ed.

Into a Strumpets Foole. Behold and see.   20
   Cleo. If it be Loue indeed, tell me how much.
   Ant. There's beggery in the loue that can be reckon'd.
   Cleo. Ile set a bourne how farre to be belou'd.
   Ant. Then must thou needes finde out new Heauen,
new Earth.   25

---

20 Foole] Stool WARBURTON *conj. apud* THEO1, WARB
24 must thou] thou must COL3

1870) questionably suggests also a pillar of greater or threefold value. The reference, in any event, is to the triumvirate (first defined by BULLOKAR [1616] as "the office of three together"). In the original assignment of geographical spheres of power in 43 B.C. Antony took Cisalpine and Transalpine Gaul, Lepidus Old Gaul and Spain, and Octavius Africa, Sicily, and Sardinia (*Cam. Anc. Hist.* 10:20). In 40 B.C. by the Pact of Brundisium "Antony agreed that Lepidus should be undisturbed in Africa, but the rest of the Empire the two divided between them, Antony taking the East and Octavian the West" (*Cam. Anc. Hist.* 10:44). For Plutarch, see p. 408. STEEVENS (*apud* REED, ed. 1803): "To sustain *the pillars of the earth* is a scriptural phrase," quoting Ps. 75.

   20 **Foole**] WARBURTON *apud* THEOBALD (ed. 1733): "I am much inclin'd to think that *Shakespeare* wrote . . . Stool. Alluding to the common Custom of Strumpets sitting on the Laps of their Lovers. By this Correction the Metaphor is admirably well preserv'd, (for both Stool and Pillar are Things for Support)." Theobald seems to approve the emendation in a letter to Warburton (1731, [fol. 129ʳ]). JOHNSON (ed. 1765) and most others: "This emendation is ingenious, but . . . not necessary." DOUCE (1807, 2:73) cites this instance in discussing the fool in *Tim.*: "Many ancient prints conduce to show that women of this description [Alcibiades's mistresses] were attended by buffoons; and . . . in most brothels such characters were maintained to amuse the guests by their broad jokes and seasonable antics." "Buffoon" or "allowed Fool" is the interpretation of a number of editors, starting with HUDSON (ed. 1881). KITTREDGE (ed. 1941), however: "Dupe. Not here used in the sense of 'buffoon.'" See textual notes and conj., p. 347.

   22 Almost all commentators, starting with THEOBALD (19 Feb. 1729, [fol. 39ʳ]), note the same sentiment in *Rom.* 2.6.32 (1425) and similar expressions in Ovid (*Metamorphoses* 13.824) and Horace (*Ars poetica* 206); STEEVENS (ed. 1778) adds Martial (*Epigrams* 6.34.8), and MALONE (ed. 1790, 10:666) *Ado* 2.1.318 (705–6). WHITING (1968, R62) cites as a proverbial instance: "A right Reckoning comes of a small ragman." Not in TILLEY or DENT.

   23 **bourne**] ROWE (ed. 1714, 8:Glossary, Born): "Limits, Bounds, &c."

   24–5 STEANE (1964, p. 30) compares Jupiter's words to Ganymede, "heaven and earth the bounds of thy delight," in Marlowe's *Dido* 1.1.31 (ed. Tucker Brooke, 1930). SIMMONS (1973, p. 12): "Antony's resounding echo of St. John's Revelation [first noted by SEATON (1946, p. 223)]—'And I sawe a new heauen, & a new earth: for the first heauen, and the first earth were passed away' [21:1]—if it cannot refer to the true transcendent dimension, initiates in the play what Robert Speaight [*Nature in Shakespearian Tragedy*, 1955, p. 129] has called 'Antony's bungling quest of the Absolute.'"

Enter a Messenger.

Mes. Newes (my good Lord) from Rome.
Ant. Grates me, the summe.
Cleo. Nay heare them *Anthony*.
Fuluia perchance is angry: Or who knowes,   30
If the scarse-bearded *Cæsar* haue not sent

---

26 *a Messenger*] *an* Attendant CAP, MAL-OXF1, ARD, CAM3, SIS
27 *Mes.*] *Att.* CAP, MAL-OXF1, ARD, CAM3, SIS
28 Grates me,] Rate me, F2-F4; Rate me ROWE; It grates me. Tell POPE1-THEO4; 'T
grates me:— mTBY4 *conj.*, CAP; ~ ~ ˄ THISELTON (1899, p. 453) *conj.*, ALEX
29 them] it POPE1-JOHN1

---

26 *Messenger*] Most substitute "Attendant"—see textual notes—because of 40. See
also n. 203–7.
28 **the summe**] JOHNSON (ed. 1765) interprets as "Be brief, *sum* thy business in a
few words." THISELTON (1899, *N&Q*, p. 453) paraphrases as "The sum <*i.e.*, news from
Rome> vexes me," explaining that "the function of the comma is to indicate the order
of construction, which has been somewhat dislocated for the sake of emphasis, and also
to mark the distinction between the subject and object of the sentence." He mentions
other instances at 824–5, 1781, 2289. See textual notes and conj., p. 347.
29 **them**] Editors have been at pains to justify Sh.'s use of *news* in both the singular
and plural by quotation from the plays and (MALONE [ed. 1790]) even from Plutarch.
In grammatically unambiguous instances Sh. uses the singular three times more often
than the plural; the instances in which number is not determinable, however, account
for almost 55% of the total. SPENCE (1900, p. 62) makes a finer distinction—"the 'news'
in full, not *it*, the mere 'sum'"—in which he is followed by KITTREDGE (ed. 1941). But
the reference may also be to messengers, according to FURNESS (ed. 1907): Others may
be approaching, or, "by exaggerating the number [see also 40, 60], Cleopatra magnifies
the importance of the news, and veils her jealousy of any control over Antony greater
than her own." See conj., p. 347.
    Anthony] ABBOTT (§469): "Polysyllabic names often receive but one accent at the
end of the line in pronunciation." He cites 38, 435, 548, "&c.," and, for the phenomenon "less frequently in the middle of the line," 640.
30–43 *Fuluia . . . scolds*] NORGAARD (1955, p. 57): "No such incident is to be found
in North, but a strong suggestion for thus staging the embarrassment of Antony when
faced with letters presumably from the wife he had left may have come from the second
stanza of Daniel's *Letter*." See p. 581. REES (1960, p. 82): "*Antony and Cleopatra* opens
with the very scene that Daniel's Octavia imagines . . . but he [Sh.] adds to the effect
by making his Cleopatra taunt Antony with fear of his wife and of Caesar equally."
31 **scarse-bearded *Cæsar***] Comment is confined to Caesar's age—he was 23 at this
time (40 B.C.). In Sh. the beard also indicates manliness; the lack of one, effeminacy.
THEOBALD (6 Jan. 1729, [fol. 8ʳ]), in fact, cites this image to support his emendation
"unhaired sauciness" in *Jn.* 5.2.133 (2387). Compare 686–7 and 938.
    haue] For Sh.'s use of the subjunctive (and indicative) in conditional clauses, see
FRANZ §644.

His powrefull Mandate to you. Do this, or this;
Take in that Kingdome, and Infranchise that:
Perform't, or else we damne thee.
    Ant. How, my Loue?   35
    Cleo. Perchance? Nay, and most like:
You must not stay heere longer, your dismission
Is come from *Cæsar,* therefore heare it *Anthony.*
Where's *Fuluias* Processe? (*Cæsars* I would say) both?
Call in the Messengers: As I am Egypts Queene,   40
Thou blushest *Anthony,* and that blood of thine

---

34 damne] doom mCOL1, COL2
36 Perchance?] ∼ , ROWE1-ARD1 (−CAP)
40 I am] I'm POPE1-JOHN1, DYCE2

---

33 **Take in**] STEEVENS (ed. 1785): "Subdue, conquer." J. D. (1880, p. 304) alone adds "(1) to enclose, and (2) to entrap, to beguile, to deceive and injure by fraud—both derived from the taking of prey in the toils of the hunter." The first sense he applies here, the second in *Cor.* 3.2.59 (2158).

    Infranchise] CAWDREY (1604, enfranchise): "Make free." See also n. 2329 ("enfranched").

34 **damne**] COLLIER (1852, p. 464): "The word 'damn' sounds ill in Cleopatra's mouth . . . and may easily have been misprinted [for] . . . *doom.*" SINGER (1853, p. 288): "*Damn* meant nothing more than *condemn* . . . and would not have offended the ears of his contemporaries. . . . Huloet [*Dictionarie*, 1572] has '*Damne* [or] to condemn.'"

35 **How**] FRANZ (§250): An interjection expressing astonishment, surprise.

36 **like**] FRANZ (§241): Adverbs occur with and without the -*ly* ending, at times, as in *like* or *likely*, with the same base. See 1303 ("sure"), n. 74 ("full").

37 **dismission**] *OED* (3b), quoting this instance: "The written or spoken form of words in which such discharge [from service] is couched." WALKER (1957, p. 97): "The normal English word down to the early nineteenth century." See n. 1009.

38 **Is come**] See n. 13.

39 **Processe**] MINSHEU (1617): "*Our* Common Lawyers *sometime call that the* Processe, *by which a man is called into the Court, and no more.*"

40 **Call . . . Messengers**] See n. 26.

41-3 **Thou . . . scolds**] Following DELIUS (ed. 1872), KITTREDGE (ed. 1941) comments, "By rising to your cheek in a blush of shame, your blood does homage to Cæsar; for such a blush is a confession that what I have said about his authority over you is true. . . . The only other explanation for his blush, Cleopatra says tauntingly, is that he remembers some of Fulvia's reproaches and feels that he deserves them."

Is *Cæsars* homager: else so thy cheeke payes shame,
When shrill-tongu'd *Fuluia* scolds. The Messengers.
   Ant. Let Rome in Tyber melt, and the wide Arch
Of the raing'd Empire fall: Heere is my space,   45
Kingdomes are clay: Our dungie earth alike
Feeds Beast as Man; the Noblenesse of life   (vv6ᵛᵇ)
Is to do thus: when such a mutuall paire,

---

42 else] *Om.* POPE, HAN1, CAP
   cheeke payes] cheeks payes F3; Cheeks pay F4-THEO4
44 in] and ROWE2
45 raing'd] raign'd F3, F4, BLUM (reign'd); rais'd ROWE1-THEO4
48 *Embracing.* POPE1-SING1, COL1+ (−SIS) (*subst.*)

---

42 **else**] WORDSWORTH (ed. 1883): "*Or.*" RIDLEY (ed. 1954, *else so*): "Or else."
43 **The Messengers**] LYONS (1962, p. 271): "May be delivered in one of two ways: as a reiterated, peremptory command to the lingering Attendant; or as an acknowledgment of the entrance of the Messengers and her mocking presentation of them to the reluctant Antony."
44–51 UPTON (1748, p. 89) cites this speech as one example of how Antony, "as Plutarch [see p. 398] informs us, affected the Asiatic manner of speaking, which much resembled his own temper, being ambitious, unequal, and very rodomontade."
44–5 **wide Arch . . . raing'd**] WARBURTON (ed. 1747): "Taken from the *Roman* custom of raising triumphal arches to perpetuate their victories. Extremely noble." JOHNSON (ed. 1765): "A fabrick standing on pillars." CAPELL (1779 [1774], 1:26) and most commentators: "Orderly rang'd; whose parts are now entire and distinct, like a number of well-built edifices." See also n. 2158. STEEVENS (ed. 1773) compares *Cor.* 3.1.206 (1917), "distinctly raunges" (i.e., extends in separate ranks). SEYMOUR (1805, 2:36) and a few others: "The arch (or superb dome, figurative of Roman grandeur,) was wide in proportion to the *range* or excursive scope of the Roman dominion." See textual notes and conj., p. 347.
45 **my space**] Of the few who comment, DEIGHTON (ed. 1891)—"my life in Egypt"— and KITTREDGE (ed. 1941)—"empire enough for me"—agree; WILSON (ed. 1950) specifies, "He flings an arm about her."
46 **alike**] An adverb modifying *feeds.*
48 **thus:**] FURNESS (ed. 1907) objects to POPE's (ed. 1723) insertion of the SD *Embracing*, as it is out of character that the "wrangling" Cleopatra "should tamely submit to be 'embraced.'" KITTREDGE (ed. 1941) adds that "some critics" reject the action as "undignified." SCHANZER (1960, p. 20) believes the *when* clause to be restrictive—*when* meaning "provided"—and the colon to "direct the reader's attention forward." (See n. 722–4.) He adds, "If we are to have an embrace at all, I would prefer it to commence at 'Here is my space' [see n. 45] and to continue throughout the rest of the speech." HAWKES (1973, p. 181): "Antony's embrace of Cleopatra turns out to be paradigmatic. At that moment when their bodies unite on the stage, the word 'thus' and its concomitant gesture stand for, 'embrace', the totality of the Egyptian way of life. . . . [But] to embrace is also to enclose, to restrict."

And such a twaine can doo't, in which I binde
One paine of punishment, the world to weete   50
We stand vp Peerelesse.
   Cleo. Excellent falshood:
Why did he marry *Fuluia*, and not loue her?
Ile seeme the Foole I am not. *Anthony* will be himselfe.
   Ant. But stirr'd by *Cleopatra*.   55

52-4 Excellent . . . not.] *Marked as an aside* JOHN1, v1773, RANN, KTLY
54-5 *Verse lines ending Antony . . . Cleopatra*, POPE1+
54 Ile] I CAP

---

49 **twaine**] CAWDREY (1604): "One for another." Efforts to distinguish *twaine* from *paire* (48) have been unconvincing. For example, SEYMOUR (1805, 2:36): "Two such lovers, with reference to their distinct reciprocal ardours, and to those ardours in union"; DEIGHTON (ed. 1891): "A pair in such complete accord, and a pair so noble in themselves"; DEY (1908, p. 424): "'Such a mutual pair' refers to the love which Antony and Cleopatra bear for each other, their exceptional character as lovers. . . . 'Such a twain' indicates only their high station." See conj., p. 347.

49-50 **in . . . weete**] JONES (ed. 1977): "Antony uses the style of a public proclamation."

49 **in which**] Comment only by DEIGHTON (ed. 1891)—"in which respects"—and KITTREDGE (ed. 1941)—"in this respect (our love)."

50 **One**] BARROLL (1969, *ShakS*, p. 224, n. 17): "F2 emends *One* to *On* and we might concur as we recall [Compositor] B's tendency to carry in his mind more than he can remember." For *one* as a possible spelling and homophone of *on*, see FRANZ §270. See also p. 374.

   weete] MINSHEU (1617): "Knowe." SKEAT (1886, p. 385): "A late spelling of *wit*, verb, to know." VINCENT (1978, p. 44): "The only usage of 'weet' in Shakespeare, and . . . a literary archaism [see *OED*, *v.*[1]], associated with Spenser, and hence, the world of romance."

51 North's Plutarch mentions *Amimetobion*: "As much to say, no life comparable and matcheable." See p. 414.

54 **Ile . . . not**] Those few who comment, beginning with DELIUS (ed. 1856), agree in essence with KITTREDGE's (ed. 1941) paraphrase: "I'll pretend to believe you; though I am not really such a fool as to trust your vows of love."

54-5 **Anthony . . . Cleopatra**] JOHNSON (ed. 1765) glosses *But* as having "the old *Saxon* signification of *without, unless, except. Antony*, says the Queen, *will recollect* [*OED*, *v.*[1] 4: 'recover by an effort'] *his thoughts*, unless *kept*, he replies, *in commotion by* Cleopatra." MASON (1785, p. 280 [= 270]): "By *Antony will be himself*, she means to say, 'that Antony will act like the joint sovereign of the world, and follow his own inclinations, without regard to the mandates of Cæsar, or the anger of Fulvia'. To which he replies, *If but stirr'd by Cleopatra*; that is, if moved to it in the slightest degree by her." Commentators vacillate between these extremes. WILSON (ed. 1950), however, regards *be himselfe* as "two-edged: i.e. (*a*) 'show himself the noble creature he is' . . . (*b*) 'act

Now for the loue of Loue, and her soft houres,
Let's not confound the time with Conference harsh;
There's not a minute of our liues should stretch
Without some pleasure now. What sport to night?
Cleo. Heare the Ambassadors.   60
Ant. Fye wrangling Queene:
Whom euery thing becomes, to chide, to laugh,

---

56 her] his ROWE1-v1778, RANN
59 pleasure now.] pleasure new: mTBY3 *conj.*, WARB, CAM3, SIS; pleasure. Now, JOHN1

---

the fool (cf. l. [20]) he is'. Doting Ant. perceives only (*a*), but immediately exemplifies
(*b*)." The customary glossing of *But* as "only (if)"—see n. 18—fits both views. See AB-
BOTT (§128): "*But* passes naturally from 'except' to 'only', when the negative is omitted."
KITTREDGE (ed. 1941), commenting on *himselfe*: "I.e., a deceiver, as he has always been
(both to Fulvia and to me)." SMITH (1958, p. 371) regards the lines as "thematic. In them
Shakespeare has indicated the whole drama of a man who, in the supreme crisis, failed
to be himself, failed his own integrity." UPTON (1746, p. 261) solves the dilemma by
suggesting that Cleopatra speaks both lines in an aside.
    56 **her**] MALONE (*apud* STEEVENS [1783]): "The *Queen* of love [i.e., Venus]."
    57 **confound**] CAWDREY (1604): "Ouerthrow, destroy, mingle together, or disorder."
MALONE's (*apud* STEEVENS [1780], 1:227) synonym, "consume," SEYMOUR (1805, 2:37)
found "very feeble," yet similar glosses ("waste," "lose") are common later. See also 458,
1142, 1606, and 2291 ("confusion").
    Conference harsh] See Warburton in n. 59.
    58 **stretch**] *OED* (13c): "*Transf.* with reference to time," a nonce use. KITTREDGE (ed.
1941): "Suggests tedium."
    59 **pleasure now**] GÜNTHER (1968, p. 101, n. 30) contrasts Daniel's pejorative use
of *pleasure*—"These momentarie pleasures, fugitive delights" (see p. 542)—with Sh.'s
concept of surrender to the moment, in which lasting fulfillment is sought. *New* is
defended only by WARBURTON (ed. 1747)—"A sentiment much in character of the luxurious and debauched *Antony*. It is the antithesis to *conference harsh*"—and THISELTON
(1899, p. 8), who points out that Plutarch's Cleopatra "still devised sundry new delights
to have Antonius at commandment never leaving him night or day" (see p. 415) and
notes the awkward repetition of *now* from 56, adding, "the letters 'o' and 'e' were exceedingly liable to be confused from the similarity of their manuscript forms." This explanation is accepted only by WILSON (ed. 1950). In Sh. *new* is placed after a noun in only
3 of its 230 occurrences.
    62 **Whom . . . becomes**] Evidently a commonplace. MALONE (ed. 1790) compares
Son. 150.5: "Whence hast thou this beccoming of things il." STEEVENS (*apud* REED,
ed. 1803) adds Marullus (*Epigrammaton* 2.48, ed. Perosa, 1951: "Quicquid dicis seu facis,
omne decet [Whatever you say or do is wholly appropriate]"). BERKOWITZ (privately)
notes the similarity of *cuncta decent* in Ovid's description of Pygmalion's statue (*Metamorphoses* 10.266) and of "Cuncta te apprime decent" in Herodias's address to her daughter
in Grimald's *Archipropheta* 4.2 (ed. Merrill, 1925).

To weepe: who euery passion fully striues
To make it selfe (in Thee) faire, and admir'd.
No Messenger but thine, and all alone, to night   65
Wee'l wander through the streets, and note
The qualities of people. Come my Queene,
Last night you did desire it. Speake not to vs.

                                  Exeunt with the Traine.

   Dem. Is *Cæsar* with *Anthonius* priz'd so slight?   70
   Philo. Sir sometimes when he is not *Anthony,*
He comes too short of that great Property
Which still should go with *Anthony.*

___

63 who] F1; how mTBY2 *conj.,* RIDb, ARD2; whose F2 *etc.*
   fully] fitly mCOL1, COL2
65-6 *Verse lines ending* alone, . . . note ROWE1+
65 Messenger∧] ~ ; MAL, v1793-COL4 (−HUD1, STAU, GLO, CAM1)
73-6 *Four verse lines ending* sorry, . . . liar Fame, . . . hope . . . happy.
POPE1-THEO4; *ending* sorry, . . . who . . . hope . . . happy. mF2FL20, mTYR *conj.,*
and JOHN1+

___

63 **who**] MALONE (*apud* STEEVENS [1783]), regarding F2's emendation, believes the
text corrupt but asserts that "'*whose every* passion' was not . . . the phraseology of Shakspeare's time." STEEVENS (ed. 1793) holds that it "is an undoubted phrase of our author," citing *Tmp.* 2.1.257 (953)—"whose eu'ry cubit"—and *Cym.* 1.6.101 (713): "Whose
euery touch." RIDLEY (ed. 1954) prefers *how* to F1's "clearly impossible" *who* and F2's
"universally accepted" *whose,* for "it is graphically a trifle easier, assuming the transposition of one letter by the compositor rather than the omission of two, and it regularises
somewhat confused syntax, since *in thee* is redundant after *whose.*" *Who* and *how* are
possible spelling variants; see *OED,* How *adv.*
   65 **No . . . thine**] MALONE (*apud* STEEVENS [1783]) defends the Folio punctuation,
paraphrasing as "No common messenger, but thy servant, and without any attendant,
I'll wander." Commenting on the emended punctuation (ed. 1790), he interprets the
line differently: "Talk not to me, says Antony, of messengers; I am now wholly thine,
and you and I unattended will to-night wander through the streets." DELIUS (ed. 1872)
records an interpretation—"No messenger is to come but from you"—that he finds less
convincing but that KITTREDGE (ed. 1941) and WILSON (ed. 1950) follow.
   70 **with**] For *with* denoting an agent (today *by*), see FRANZ §535. ABBOTT (§193)
wavers between "as regards" or "in relation to" and "by."
   71 **Sir**] SCHMIDT (1875): "A general form of address, used to men of any station."
See also nn. 2198, 3100 ("sirs . . . heart"), 3347, 3475 ("Sirra").
   72 **Property**] *OED* (5): "In earlier use sometimes, an essential, special, or distinctive
quality, a peculiarity." See also n. 3301 ("propertied").
   73 **still**] MINSHEU (1617): "*Alwayes, continually.*" See also 400, 1003, et passim.
   Anthony] Only KITTREDGE (ed. 1941) comments: "The name of Antony."

14

Dem. I am full sorry, that hee approues the common
Lyar, who thus speakes of him at Rome; but I will hope   75
of better deeds to morrow. Rest you happy.   *Exeunt*

Enter Enobarbus, Lamprius, a Southsayer, Rannius, Lucilli-   **1.2**
us, Charmian, Iras, Mardian the Eunuch,
and Alexas.

---

74 full] *Om.* POPE1-THEO4
75 Lyar . . . him] liar Fame, Who speaks him thus POPE1-THEO4
77 SCENE II. POPE1+ (−THEO)
  The same. Another Room. CAP+ (*subst.*)
77–9 *Enter* . . .] *Enter* Enobarbus, Charmian, Iras, Alexas, *and a Soothsayer.*
ROWE1-JOHN1; *as* ROWE1, *omitting Enobarbus* CAP-SIS (−NLSN, RID, CAM3)

---

74 **full**] For the absence of the adverbial ending, see FRANZ §241 and n. 36; for the
use of *full* for emphasis, §379. See also 457, 1920.
  approues] CAWDREY (1604): "Alowe, or make good."
74–5 **common Lyar**] CAWDREY (1604, fame): "Report, common talke, credite," from
Latin *fama*. See "vulgar Fame" (2296). Most editions accept POPE's (ed. 1723) qualification of *Lyar* as *Fame* (i.e., rumor)—see textual notes—even if they do not so emend,
attributing it to MALONE (*apud* STEEVENS, ed. 1778). Questionably, DELIUS (ed. 1856):
The lying common man; BLUMHOF (ed. 1870): "*Cæsar.*"
75–6 **hope of**] Sh. uses the prepositional verb *hope of* only half as often as the modern *hope for.* See also FRANZ §513.
76 **Rest you happy**] DELIUS (ed. 1856): Elliptical for "God rest you happy" (a phrase
at parting), where *rest* means "to give rest or repose." See *OED*, Rest *v.*[1] 3b; 7b; 8c. It
is inaccurate to paraphrase *rest you* as "keep you."
  happy] CAWDREY (1604, felicitie): "Happinesse." KITTREDGE (ed. 1941): "Fortunate." For the semantics of *happy*, see COTGRAVE (1611, Felice): "Happie, luckie, blissefull,
prosperous," and *OED, a.* See also 548, 1615, 2553; 856 ("Happily"), 2186 ("happinesse").
77–155 RINEHART (1972, p. 85): "While Plutarch [see p. 417] mentions an Egyptian
soothsayer once, with Antony in Rome, he has nothing to say about reading palms at
court in Egypt. Elizabeth's chief gentlewoman of the Privy Chamber, Blanche Parry, 'loved
to dabble in the dark mysteries of the occult' and had 'made a special study of palmistry'
[Wilson, *Queen Elizabeth's Maids of Honour,* 1922, pp. 7–8], telling the fortunes of
maids of honor on occasion." See also nn. 603, 3407–10.
77–9 *Enter . . . Alexas*] STEEVENS (ed. 1778): None of the characters named in this
SD is mentioned by Plutarch. He adds (*apud* REED, ed. 1803), "*Lamprius, Rannius, Lucilius,* &c. might have been speakers in this scene as it was first written down by Shakspeare, who afterwards thought proper to omit their speeches, though at the same time
he forgot to erase their names as originally announced at their collective entrance"—a
suggestion that most 19th-c. editors accepted as an example of Sh.'s "carelessness." NICHOL-
SON (Wright Shakespeariana, no. 158 [8]) adds a third possibility: "When scenery was

scanty and poor this device [of having nonspeaking characters on stage] was useful in keeping up the vraisemblance, animation, and bye-play of the scene. In the present instance numbers are especially useful in increasing the contagious merriment of the dialogue." CASE (ed. 1906) believes "the scene is mutilated." The most comprehensive view is that of RIDLEY (ed. 1954): "Of the nine characters in F's entry (or eight if we take 'Lamprius' to be the name of the soothsayer) four (or three) have nothing to say throughout the scene, and three of the names occur nowhere else in the play. The usual way . . . of treating this entry has been to excise Lamprius, Rannius, Lucilius and Mardian, to bring in Charmian, Iras, Alexas and the soothsayer together, and defer Enobarbus' entry till after line [90]. . . . It is a good example of what happens when one starts playing fast and loose with Shakespeare's stage-directions, and neglects to keep an eye on the stage. In the first place it makes something near nonsense of Charmian's opening question; if a group of four people enter together it is merely silly for one to ask a second where the fourth member of the quartet is; and Alexas' 'Soothsayer!' is clearly in the nature of a summons. (This no doubt could be met by giving the soothsayer his entry after line [85].) In the second place there is no reason why Enobarbus should not be among the first entrants. No doubt, again, he could enter after line [90], throwing his order over his shoulder as he comes in, but he is then left up in the air, since the others neglect him, and he has no more to say till line [157], which would not matter with a character on already but is dramatically clumsy with a fresh entrant. . . . The characters fall into two groups, one of Enobarbus, a soothsayer, and two (or three) non-speaking figures who, from their names, are presumably Romans; and an Egyptian group, of Cleopatra's waiting women, Mardian and Alexas. (There is just this much to be said for thinking Lamprius to be the soothsayer that this would give the two speaking characters first, followed by the two supers.) Dover Wilson [ed. 1950] saw this, and brings in 'Enobarbus and three other Romans talking with a Soothsayer', and then 'a little after', the Egyptian group. I do not think that this is a possible interpretation of F's entry. A scene-opening in which the entrants are engaged in an inaudible conversation is surely unparalleled in Shakespeare (. . . Shakespeare often covers an entry with *irrelevant* conversation till the characters are well down stage, but he invariably gives the entrants *something* to say). . . . The two groups come in simultaneously, but by different doors. The entry of both is covered by the brisk conversation of one, Enobarbus is there to give his order, and the soothsayer is where we want him, in the non-Egyptian group, so that Alexas can call him over." See p. 376.

77 *Lamprius*] STEEVENS (ed. 1778) mistakenly intimates that this character is Plutarch's grandfather Lamprias, "his author [actually, "one *Philotas* a Physition . . . told him"] for some of the stories he relates of the profuseness and luxury of Antony's entertainments at Alexandria." CANBY (ed. 1921), in noting that only Rannius and Lucillius "take no part in the dialogue," may anticipate RIDLEY (ed. 1954), the first clearly to identify Lamprius as the Soothsayer. See n. 77–9.

Rannius] SINGER (ed. 1826, p. 380): "In the old copy [F1] . . . Ramnus." KITTREDGE (ed. 1941): "Seems to be a misprint for *Ramnus* (i.e., Rhamnus), whom North's Plutarch [see p. 430] mentions as one of Antony's guard in his Parthian campaign." THOMAS (1972, p. 572, n. 23): "If *Rannius* stands for *Rhamnus* . . . then it was he who promised Antony at a time of crisis in the Parthian campaign that if capture seemed imminent he would turn his sword on Antony."

77–8 *Lucillius*] SCHANZER (1960, p. 22) suggests that since in "Shakespeare's preparatory reading [of the Countess of Pembroke's *Antonie*, 1595], the whole of Act III consists of a dialogue between Antonius and Lucilius . . . it is at least possible that . . . Shake-

Char. L. *Alexas,* sweet *Alexas,* most any thing *Alexas,*   80
almost most absolute *Alexas,* where's the Soothsayer
that you prais'd so to'th'Queene? Oh that I knewe this
Husband, which you say, must change his Hornes with
Garlands.
   Alex. Soothsayer.   85
   Sooth. Your will?
   Char. Is this the Man? Is't you sir that know things?

80–4 *Six verse lines ending* sweet Alexas, . . . almost . . . soothsayer . . . queen?
. . . say, . . . garlands! CAP
  80 L.] *Om.* POPE1-THEO4, CAP, v1773; Lord JOHN1, v1778+
      sweet] most sweet mCOL1, COL2, COL3, COL4
  81 almost] nay, almost CAP
  82 so] *Om.* F3-POPE2, HAN1
  83 change] charge mF4FL33, mTHEO1, *and* WARBURTON *conj. apud* THEO1, THEO,
WARB, CAP, MAL, RANN, v1821-ARD2 (−KNT1, STAU, RID)
      his . . . with] for . . . his HAN1
  86 *Sooth.*] *Lam. (throughout scene)* RID
  87 *Prose* POPE2-THEO2, WARB-JOHN1, v1773, OXF1, EVNS; *verse* v1778, v1793-SING2,
STAU-KTLY, NLSN, KIT1-ALEX

---

speare had originally planned a similar role for his Lucillius as Antony's staunchest and
most loyal friend." For the 1592 *Antonius,* see p. 500. In North's Plutarch he is mentioned as "faithfull and frendly" (see p. 445) to Antony.

  80 **most any thing**] KITTREDGE (ed. 1941) is the only modern commentator: "Charmian pretends that she cannot think of an adjective good enough to express her admiration." See conj., p. 347.

  83 **change**] THEOBALD (ed. 1733): "We must restore . . . charge . . . i.e. must be
an honourable Cuckold, must have his Horns hung with Garlands." Most editions agree,
either because *change with* is unidiomatic or because *change* is often misprinted for *charge*
and vice versa. As to the meaning, JOHNSON (ed. 1765) speaks for those who retain *change*:
"To *dress,* or *to dress with changes of* garlands." THISELTON (1899, p. 8) adds, " 'Take
his horns in exchange for garlands'. . . . The 'horns' are symbolic of the cuckold; the
'garlands' of the wedding." The relationship between Mars and Venus may also inform
the image. In the Countess of Pembroke's *Antonius,* Antony laments, "Since then the
Baies so well thy forehead knewe To Venus mirtles yeelded haue their place" (see p. 482);
BULLOKAR (1616) says myrtle was "wont to bee worne of the Romane captaines garland-
wise in triumph, when they had obtained any victory, without slaughter of men: Poets
consecrated this Tree to *Venus.*" STAUNTON (1873, p. 473), defending *chain:* "The allusion is to the sacrificial ox, whose horns were wreathed with flowers." The idea is developed by CASE (ed. 1906) and KITTREDGE (ed. 1941). SCHWALB (1949–50, p. 53) goes
even further: "But the 'sacrifice' . . . is to be Charmian. . . . For this husband . . .
who is he but Death? . . . And it was garlands that North chose for the mortuary account in his Plutarch [see p. 455]." See textual notes and conj., p. 347.

17

Sooth. In Natures infinite booke of Secrecie, a little I
can read.

Alex. Shew him your hand.   90

Enob. Bring in the Banket quickly: Wine enough,
Cleopatra's health to drinke.   (xx1ª)

Char. Good sir, giue me good Fortune.

Sooth. I make not, but foresee.

Char. Pray then, foresee me one.   95

Sooth. You shall be yet farre fairer then you are.

Char. He meanes in flesh.

Iras. No, you shall paint when you are old.

Char. Wrinkles forbid.

Alex. Vex not his prescience, be attentiue.   100

88–90 *Verse lines ending* Secrecy, . . . hand. THEO1+
90 *Enter* ENOBARBUS. CAP-SIS (–NLSN, RID, CAM3)
91–9 *Six verse lines ending* enough, . . . me . . . but foresee. . . . yet . . . flesh.
. . . forbid! HAN1; 91–2 *verse, then as* F1 KNT1, GLO, CAM3, EVNS; 91–2 *prose, then
as* F1 COL3, WH1, HAL; 91–2 *and* 96 *verse,* 93–5 *and* 97–9 *as* F1 STAU, OXF1, NLSN, KIT1,
ALEX
    94 I] Madam, I HAN1
    96 farre] *Om.* v1773
    98 you are] *Om.* HAN1
    100–1 *One verse line* COL4
    100 prescience] patience F3-ROWE3

---

90 If Enobarbus enters here (see textual notes), some modern editions have him first
speak offstage ("within" or "without") or at the door. See n. 77–9.

91 **Banket**] KERSEY (1702, Desert): "*Banquet of sweet-meats.*" MALONE (ed. 1790)
glosses *Banket* in 1334 as "a desert. . . . In [James] Heath's *Chronicle of the Civil Wars*,
1661: '*After dinner*, he was served with a *banquet*' [2nd impression, 1663, p. 662]." See
OED, sb.[1] 3.

97 **in flesh**] *OED* (9b): "In a bodily form." CRAIG (*apud* CASE, ed. 1906): "Plump,
in good condition." Charmian is playfully rejecting the other senses of *fair*: "beautiful"
(DELIUS, ed. 1856) and "fortunate" (WILSON, ed. 1950).

99 **Wrinkles forbid**] DELIUS (ed. 1856): To the allusion to age Charmian replies "Wrinkles forbid" as one would otherwise say "God forbid." BLUMHOF (ed. 1870), questionably: Heaven protect me from wrinkles. DEIGHTON (ed. 1891): "Instead of saying 'Heaven
forbid!' she says, 'may wrinkles not come to make that necessary!'"

100 **his prescience**] DEIGHTON (ed. 1891), translating DELIUS (ed. 1856): "Used jocu-
larly as a title; as we say 'his worship', 'his lordship.'" Agreeing with BLUMHOF (ed. 1870),
WALTER (ed. 1969): "'Prescience' was gained with difficulty and the exercise of natural
magic easily upset. [Compares *Tmp.* 1.2.180 (291), 4.1.158 (1829).]"

Char. Hush.

Sooth. You shall be more belouing, then beloued.

Char. I had rather heate my Liuer with drinking.

Alex. Nay, heare him.

Char. Good now some excellent Fortune: Let mee   105
be married to three Kings in a forenoone, and Widdow
them all: Let me haue a Childe at fifty, to whom *Herode*

---

102 *Verse* v1821, KNT1, STAU, GLO, OXF1, NLSN, KIT1, ALEX
103 with] with much HAN1
105 now‸] ~ , F4+

---

103 JOHNSON (ed. 1765): "To know why the lady is so averse from *heating* her *liver*, it must be remembered, that a heated liver is supposed to make a pimpled face." MASON (1785, p. 280 [= 270]): "The liver was considered as the seat of desire. In answer to the South-sayer, who tells her she shall be very loving, she says, 'She had rather heat her liver, with drinking, if it was to be heated.'" STEEVENS (*apud* REED, ed. 1803) cites *MV* 1.1.81 (90); BLUMHOF (ed. 1870), *Luc.* 47.

105 **Good now**] *OED* (Good *adj.* 6b): "In exclamations containing the name of God or some substituted expression." ABBOTT (§13): "The emphatic nature of this appellative 'good' is illustrated . . . where the noun is omitted." HUDSON (ed. 1881): "An equivalent to *well now*." WORDSWORTH (ed. 1883): "*Dear man!*" KITTREDGE (ed. 1941): "Come now, my good fellow!" See n. 394 ("Good now").

105–8 **Let . . . Homage**] Most commentators are content to repeat and embellish the rather obvious interpretation by STEEVENS (ed. 1793): "This is one of Shakspeare's natural touches. Few circumstances are more flattering to the fair sex, than breeding at an advanced period of life." But BLUMHOF (ed. 1870) detects a reference to Cleopatra's previous marriages, which ended early because of the deaths of her husbands. Others see even more extravagant possibilities. ZIELINSKI (1905, p. 19) asserts that Charmian, who will be fifty in the year of Christ's birth, aspires to be wife of the Magi, Mother of God, and Roman empress. MACCALLUM (1910, pp. 347–8, n. 1): "If fifty years old at the beginning of the Christian era, Charmian could only be ten at the opening of the play: but . . . I think it very likely that Shakespeare intended to rouse some such associations . . . as Professor Zielinski suggests." CUTTS (1966–7, p. 149) holds that the reference is to the mother of John the Baptist and that Charmian's "ambition actually goes further than to be an equal companion to her mistress because her demand that Herod shall do *homage* to her son certainly has more relevance to Christ's power than to John the Baptist's. That Charmian should stop at three kings is mere modesty . . . and yet delightful immodesty . . . in that discerning hearers and readers will thereby catch the world-shattering link with Christ through Elizabeth and John the Baptist."

107–8 *Herode* **of Iewry**] GREY (1754, 2:190): "*Herod* was homager to the *Romans*, for making him King of *Judæa*, and made large presents to *Antony* for befriending him." STEEVENS (ed. 1778) adds, "*Herod* was always one of the personages in the mysteries of our early stage, on which he was constantly represented as a fierce, haughty, blustering tyrant, so that *Herod of Jewry* became a common proverb, expressive of turbulence and rage. [Cites 1625–6 and *Ham.* 3.2.13 (1861).] . . . Charmian wishes for a son who may

of Iewry may do Homage. Finde me to marrie me with
Octauius Cæsar, and companion me with my Mistris.
  Sooth. You shall out-liue the Lady whom you serue.   110
  Char. Oh excellent, I loue long life better then Figs.
  Sooth. You haue seene and proued a fairer former for-
tune, then that which is to approach.

---

108 marrie me] marry CAP-v1778, RANN, CAM3a
110 *Verse* v1793, KNT1, STAU, GLO, OXF1, NLSN, KIT1, ALEX; *prose* v1821
111 *Prose* THEO, JOHN1, v1773, v1778, v1793-v1821, KNT1, STAU, ALEX; *verse* HUD1,
WH1, GLO, OXF1, NLSN, KIT1
112–13 *Verse lines ending* fortune . . . approach. CAP+ (−v1773, HUD1)

---

arrive to such power and dominion that the proudest and fiercest monarchs of the earth
may be brought under his yoke." CANTOR (1976, p. 221, n. 18): "Herod of Jewry is mentioned in the play [at 107–8, 1625, 1627, 1830, 2592], perhaps an attempt to bring Roman events into line with the Biblical chronology." For "Iewry," see n. 2590.
  108 **Finde me**] DELIUS (ed. 1856): I.e., in the lines of the hand. FRANZ (§294): *Me*
is an example of the ethical dative, very frequent in Elizabethan colloquial speech. See
also 144.
  110 SIEGEL (1958, pp. 386–7): One of the many foreshadowings of Cleopatra's death.
Others are at 239–43, 1057, 1099, 2071–3, 2818–21, 3072–4, 3546–7.
  111 **I . . . Figs**] WARBURTON ([2 June 1734, fol. 140ᵛ]): "Spoken ominiously [i.e.,
as an omen]. The Aspicks, by w.ᶜʰ She dy'd, tho' after her Mistress, being brought in
a Basket of Figs." Commentators since HEATH (1765, p. 449) regard this as a "proverbial"
expression, although WHITE (ed. 1861) does "not remember having met with it elsewhere," nor is it to be found in TILLEY or DENT. MCFARLAND (1958–9, p. 206): "The
wonderfully mindless triviality of the line epitomizes the whole aura of the Egyptian
court—epitomizes the trivial present, and in addition prepares for the future sublimities
the play is to unfold."
  Figs] BARTHOLOMAEUS (1582, fol. 291ʳ): "The Figge tree is called *Ficus*, and hath
that name of fruitefulnesse, for it is more fruitful, than other trees, for it beareth fruite
three or foure times in one yeare. . . . And a Figge tree of *Aegypt* is more fructuous
holden. . . . It is said, that figs doe away the shriueling of the skinne of the face, or
wrinckles on the hands of olde men. . . . It is sayd that if the genitals be baulmed
with the iuyce thereof, they be moued to lecherie." BLUMHOF (ed. 1870), anticipating
recent commentators, is aware of a possible phallic allusion. CASE (ed. 1906) "can only
doubtfully suggest possible clues for the choice of figs . . . (1) . . . fruitfulness . . .
(2) the poisoned fig of Spain . . . as a secret means of removing an enemy." LLOYD
(1959, p. 91): "The 'fig leafe signifieth the imbibition and motion of all things: and
besides, it seemeth naturally to resemble the member of generation' ([Plutarch's *Moralia,* tr. Holland, 1603,] p. 1301)." See also nn. 141 ("go"), 979.
  112 **proued**] JOHNSON (1755): "To experience."

Char. Then belike my Children shall haue no names:
Prythee how many Boyes and Wenches must I haue.   115
Sooth. If euery of your wishes had a wombe, & fore-
tell euery wish, a Million.
Char. Out Foole, I forgiue thee for a Witch.
Alex. You thinke none but your sheets are priuie to
your wishes.   120

114–15 *Verse* THEO, WARB, JOHN1, v1773, KTLY; *prose* CAP, v1778, v1793-HUD1, DYCE,
STAU, WH, GLO, OXF1-ALEX, ARD2, EVNS
116–17 *Verse lines ending* Womb, . . . Million. ROWE1+ (−JOHN1, v1773, HUD1)
    foretell] foretold POPE; fertil THEO1-THEO4, CAP, MAL, v1793-COL1,
HUD1-DYCE1, STAU+; fruitful mCOL1, COL2, COL3
118 Out] Out, out HAN1
119–20 *Verse* HAN1

---

114 THEOBALD (ed. 1733) and most commentators: "They shall be illegitimate. [Quotes
TGV 3.1.319–23 (1379–82).]" WARBURTON (ed. 1747) alone: "*I.e.* be of no note, a *Greek*
mode of expression; in which language, διώνυμος signifies both *double-named* and *famous*, because anciently famous men had an agnomen taken from their exploits." JOHN-
SON (ed. 1765): "She here only says, If I have already had the best of my fortune, then
I suppose *I shall never name children*, that is, I am never to be married." MALONE (ed.
1790) compares *Luc.* 522, "namelesse bastardie."
115 **Wenches**] See n. 941.
    must] FRANZ (§607): Occasionally *must* conveys the idea of the future. Thus "must
I haue"="am I to have."
116 **euery**] I.e., every one (when followed by a genitive). See FRANZ §352.
116–17 **& . . . wish**] JOHNSON (ed. 1765) defends the F1 reading: "*If you had as
many wombs as you will have wishes, and* I should *foretel all those wishes, I should
foretel a million of children.* It is an ellipsis very frequent in conversation. . . . *And*
is for *and if.*" MALONE (*apud* STEEVENS, ed. 1785) retorts that "here no personal pronoun has been introduced" and prefers the emendation *fertil* (probably THEOBALD's in
a copy of F2), which most editors since Johnson attribute to Warburton. See textual notes
and conj., p. 347.
118 **Out**] JOHNSON (1755): "An expression of abhorrence or expulsion," here feigned.
    I . . . Witch] STEEVENS (ed. 1793) and most others: "From a common proverbial
reproach to silly ignorant females: —'You'll never be burnt for a witch.'" WILSON (ed.
1950): "I.e. You are no prophet!" See DENT (W585): "I think you are a *Witch*" (though
he calls this phrase questionable as proverb). DELIUS (ed. 1856) and a few recent commentators: Charmian pardons his insult because he is a soothsayer, a wizard; HERFORD
(ed. 1899): "Hence privileged to utter home-truths." In support, BULLOKAR (1616, *Wisard*):
"A Wise man, a Witch, a cunning man." KNOWLES (privately) compares Thomas Heywood, *2 Fair Maid of the West* (*Dramatic Works*, ed. Shepherd, 1874, 2:341): "You are
a witch. . . . A foolish proverbe . . . which . . . is as much as to say, You have hit
the naile on the head."

Char. Nay come, tell *Iras* hers.

Alex. Wee'l know all our Fortunes.

Enob. Mine, and most of our Fortunes to night, shall
be drunke to bed.

Iras. There's a Palme presages Chastity, if nothing els.   125

Char. E'ne as the o're-flowing Nylus presageth Famine.

Iras. Go you wilde Bedfellow, you cannot Soothsay.

Char. Nay, if an oyly Palme bee not a fruitfull Prog-

---

121 come,] come, and HAN1
124 be] be to go ROWE1-JOHN1
125 *Prose* POPE2, THEO1, WARB, JOHN1-v1778, v1793-HUD1, STAU-GLO, OXF1, NLSN,
KIT1-ALEX, EVNS; *verse* THEO2, KTLY; *verse lines ending* chastity, . . . else. HAN1
      There's] There is HAN1
126–7 *Verse* KTLY
126 Nylus] *Nile* HAN1
128 *Prose* v1793-KNT1, HUD1, STAU, GLO, OXF1, NLSN, ALEX; *verse* KIT1

---

122 **know all our Fortunes**] KITTREDGE (ed. 1941) is the only commentator: "Emphatic: '*all* of us.'" For the ambiguity of the construction—either "of us all" or "our
complete"—see FRANZ §324.

123 **most of our Fortunes**] DELIUS (ed. 1856): The fortune of most of us. For the
construction, see n. 122.

125 CAMDEN (1947, p. 7): "If the table line [of the palm] is 'deep, subtle and pale',
at its end, it indicates an honest and chaste person. . . . Perhaps Iras has on her hand
a cross which touches the line of life at its upper corner, for this, as John ab Indagine
writes [*The Book of Palmistry and Physiognomy*, 7th ed., 1683, sig. B6ʳ], 'signifieth a
libidinous and an unshamefac'd woman.'" The same idea is expressed in his *Briefe in-
troductions vnto the art of chiromancy* (1558, sig. B1ᵛ). PHIALAS (ed. 1955): "Because
it [the palm] is dry and cool."

126–7 See n. 382 ("Nylus slime").

128 **Bedfellow**] DELIUS (ed. 1856) alone: Ambiguous, depending on whether Charmian is the bedfellow of Iras or of someone else.

129 **oyly Palme**] DAVIES (1783, 2:339) compares *Oth.* 3.4.36 (2179)—"this hand is
moist my Lady"—and 3.4.42–3 (2185–6)—"heere's a young and swetting diuell here, That
commonly rebels"—in which the sexual implications are clear. MALONE (ed. 1790) compares 3.4.38 (2181)—"This argues fruitfulnesse and liberall heart"—perhaps not recognizing that *liberal* may mean "loose" (see *1H6* 5.4.82 [2722]). Subsequent editors, however,
tend to interpret as a sign of wantonness.

129–30 **fruitfull Prognostication**] I.e., a prognostication of fruitfulness. See n. 2543.

nostication, I cannot scratch mine eare. Prythee tel her   130
but a worky day Fortune.
  Sooth. Your Fortunes are alike.
  Iras. But how, but how, giue me particulars.
  Sooth. I haue said.
  Iras. Am I not an inch of Fortune better then she?   135
  Char. Well, if you were but an inch of fortune better
then I: where would you choose it.
  Iras. Not in my Husbands nose.
  Char. Our worser thoughts Heauens mend.
  Alexas. Come, his Fortune, his Fortune. Oh let him   140
mary a woman that cannot go, sweet *Isis*, I beseech thee,

---

133 *Prose* NLSN, KIT1, ALEX
135 *Verse* JOHN1; *prose* v1793-v1821, KNT1, STAU-GLO, OXF1, NLSN, KIT1, ALEX
139 Heauens] heaven OXF1
    mend] amend KTLY
140-6 *Given to Charmian* mTBY2 *and* THEOBALD (1726, p. 157) *conj.*, POPE2+
140 *Alexas.*] *Om.* mTBY3 (PP.A) *conj. and* POPE2; *Alexas,* — THEOBALD (1726, p. 157) *conj.*, THEO1+

---

130 I . . . eare] Comment, surprisingly, is sparse. DELIUS (ed. 1856) paraphrases, "If I can't see that . . . then I am so dumb that I can't even scratch my ears." WILSON (ed. 1950): "I.e. I shall expect miracles. [Questionably:] An 'itching ear'=one 'eager to hear novelties' (*OED*, ear 3d)"; cites 2 Tim. 4:3–4. TURNER (privately) suggests a pause after *mine*, "whereupon *ear* is substituted for the expected *arse*." But *arse* is not found in any substantive Shn. text.

  mine eare] For *mine* (or *thine*) before words beginning with vowels and *h*, see FRANZ §326. See also 505, 785, et passim.

131 **worky day**] *OED*: "Obs. var. *Workaday*."

134 Following DEIGHTON (ed. 1891), KITTREDGE (ed. 1941): "Spoken with grave emphasis. Compare the use of *dixi* in Latin."

138 Proverbial; see TILLEY (I55): "An *Inch* in a man's nose is much"; excluded by DENT. The bawdy reference is to a more private part, and Charmian responds with mock disapproval.

139 **worser**] For comparatives, see FRANZ §246.

141 **go**] CASE (ed. 1906): "*Go* is constantly employed for walk . . . especially in a varying proverb [not in DENT]: 'Blood (kind, love, bairns, etc.) will creep where it (they) *cannot go*', in print as early as 1481. . . . Does Charmian, then, mean here an old, crippled, or bed-rid woman, whom, on second thoughts, she wills to die and give place to a series of worse in another kind, who will cuckold Alexas as she could not? Another sense of *go* is 'die, depart this life', to which *too* lends some dubious support, as if 'and let her die *too*' were a new and better idea. A third is 'be pregnant' [anticipated by TIESSEN (1879, p. 467)], and go=go with child. . . . Thistleton [sic] — the only commentator, I believe, to offer an explanation — makes 'that cannot go'='that is never satisfied'

23

and let her dye too, and giue him a worse, and let worse
follow worse, till the worst of all follow him laughing to
his graue, fifty-fold a Cuckold. Good *Isis* heare me this
Prayer, though thou denie me a matter of more waight: 145
good *Isis* I beseech thee.

   Iras. Amen, deere Goddesse, heare that prayer of the
people. For, as it is a heart-breaking to see a handsome
man loose-Wiu'd, so it is a deadly sorrow, to beholde a
foule Knaue vncuckolded: Therefore deere *Isis* keep *de-*   150

---

143 worse] worst THEO2, WARB (*corrected to* worse *in* mWARB), THEO4, JOHN1
147–51 *Given to Charmian* F2-POPE1
147 the] thy DANIEL *conj. apud* CAM1, CAM3

[1899, p. 8], without remark or evidence to support his view." E. PARTRIDGE (1947; 1968, p. 115), although admitting "the sense is doubtful": "*Go* must mean one of two things: — Either 'a woman that cannot *go to it*' . . . i.e. cannot effectively copulate . . . or 'one who cannot *come*'. The latter is more likely: . . . *go* is probably elliptic for some such phrase as 'go all the way (with her sexual partner).'" LLOYD (1959, p. 91): "The word 'go' . . . is clearly intended to stress that association of motion with sexual activity [quotes Plutarch's *Moralia*, tr. Holland, 1603, p. 1312]."

   Isis] CASE (ed. 1906) summarizes the main features in commentary beginning with RANN (ed. 1791–): "Originally the Egyptian goddess of the earth and fertility, later of the moon." See PAULY and *OCD*, which characterizes her thus: "In addition to her position as a national deity in Egypt, Isis acquired in the Hellenistic age a new rank as a leading goddess of the Mediterranean world. . . . Isis came more and more to mean all things to all men." *Enc. Brit.* adds, "The goddess absorbed the attributes of all female divinities; she was goddess of the earth and its fruits, of the Nile, of the sea, of the underworld, of love, healing and magic." WALTER (ed. 1969) adds, of "justice." ADELMAN (1973, p. 209, n. 68): "Shakespeare's use of Isis is curious: though there is continued reference to the natural processes associated with her, her name is invoked only . . . to emphasize the exotic strangeness of the Egyptians, and then only in semicomic scenes (cf. 1.2.[65–78 (140–51)]; 1.5.70 [603]; 3.3.[18, 46 (1642, 1678)]) or in Octavian's unflattering portrait of Cleopatra (3.6.17 [1768])."

   143 **follow him**] See n. 3153.

   144 **me**] The ethical dative. See n. 108.

   147 **the**] INGLEBY (1882, pp. 205–6) agrees with Daniel (see textual notes) that *thy* should be preferred, believing the "confusion" of the pronouns "to have arisen from the ear, not the eye." Modern scholarship is not absolutely certain of the homophony: see DOBSON (1957, 2:460).

   149 **loose-Wiu'd**] CAPELL (1779 [1774], Glossary, 1:39) and most others: "Tack'd to a loose Wife." RANN (ed. 1791–): "Unmarried."

   150–1 *decorum*] COOPER (1565): "A seemelinesse in that which becommeth a man." See *OED*, 1, for the customary definition "That which is proper . . . befitting." See also 3220.

   150 **Knaue**] See n. 2839.

corum, and Fortune him accordingly.

Char. Amen.

Alex. Lo now, if it lay in their hands to make mee a
Cuckold, they would make themselues Whores, but
they'ld doo't.   155

Enter Cleopatra.

Enob. Hush, heere comes *Anthony*.

Char. Not he, the Queene.   (xx1^b)

Cleo. Saue you, my Lord.

Enob. No Lady.   160

Cleo. Was he not heere?

Char. No Madam.

Cleo. He was dispos'd to mirth, but on the sodaine
A Romane thought hath strooke him.

---

152 *Char.*] *Iras.* ROWE3, POPE1
156 SCENE III. POPE1-JOHN1 (−THEO)
    Enter Cleopatra.] *After* 158 CAP, v1778-KIT1 (−NLSN); *after* 157 CAM3, ARD2
159–62 *Arranged as verse lines, thus*: 159–61, 162 v1793-KNT1, SING2, DYCE, GLO,
KTLY, HUD2, WH2, NLSN, ARD1, KIT1, SIS+; 159–60, 161–2 ALEX
159 Saue you, my Lord.] Saw you my Lord? F2+
164–5 *One verse line* ROWE1+
164 hath] had F4-POPE2, HAN1

---

153 **Lo now**] In this construction (as in commands) *now* intensifies *Lo*, its temporal
aspect weakened. See *OED*, Now 9.

156 **Enter Cleopatra**] Following FURNESS (ed. 1907), WILSON (1948, p. 392, n. 3)
defends the position of the SD in F1: "Enobarbus would be speaking [157] well in character if jocosely referring to Cleopatra as Antony as soon as he saw her." RIDLEY (ed. 1954)
disagrees "since the actual presence of Cleopatra on the stage would make the remark
[of Enobarbus] nonsensical."

157–69 HARRISON (1948, p. 242): "In his mature plays Shakespeare usually ignored
the restraints of metre in quick conversation."

164 **Romane thought**] This common construction—adjectives with both active and
passive meaning; see ABBOTT §3—is not without ambiguity. CASE (ed. 1906): "Perhaps
a thought such as Roman virtue would inspire, and not merely, as Schmidt [1875] explains it, 'A thought of Rome.'" See conj., p. 347.

    Romane] A variant spelling, along with *Romaine* (1195, 1501, 1581), that appears
only on pages attributed to Compositor E, while Compositor B seems to prefer *Roman*.

    strooke] LLOYD (1960, p. 326), elucidating the influence of Plutarch's theory of
daemons in the *Moralia* (tr. Holland, 1603): "The daemon's communication is as 'a [blow
or] stroke [given unto] the soul' ([1657,] p. 992)."

25

Enobarbus?   165
  Enob. Madam.
  Cleo. Seeke him, and bring him hither: wher's *Alexias?*
  Alex. Heere at your seruice.
My Lord approaches.

                    Enter Anthony, with a Messenger.   170

  Cleo. We will not looke vpon him:
Go with vs.   *Exeunt.*
  Messen. Fuluia thy Wife,
First came into the Field.
  Ant. Against my Brother *Lucius?*   175
  Messen. I: but soone that Warre had end,
And the times state
Made friends of them, ioynting their force 'gainst *Cæsar,*
Whose better issue in the warre from Italy,

━━━

  167 hither:] hither. [*he goes* CAM3
  168–9 *On one line* ROWE1+
  168 Heere] Here, lady, CAP; Here, madam, v1793, v1803, SING1, HUD1
  169 My] see, my HAN1
  170 *After* 172 DYCE, STAU, GLO, CAM1, HUD2, WH2, ARD, RID; *after* 168 SIS; *ad. and Attendants.* ROWE1+ (−RIDb, ARD2)
  171–4 *Verse lines ending* us. . . . field. ROWE1+
  175–8 Ff; *three verse lines ending Lucius?* . . . state . . . *Cæsar,* ROWE1-THEO2, WARB-THEO4; *ending* soon . . . friends . . . *Cæsar,* HAN1, CAP; *ending* Ay: . . . state . . . *Cæsar;* STAU, KTLY; *four verse lines ending Lucius?* . . . Ay. . . . state . . . *Cæsar,* JOHN1 *etc.*
  178 force 'gainst] forces against HAN1, CAP
  179 better] bitter THEO3
      from] of F3-POPE2

───

  165 *Enobarbus*] ABBOTT (§469): "Has but one accent [third syllable], wherever it stands in the verse."
  173–6 For Plutarch, see p. 416. Not in modern histories, like the *Cam. Anc. Hist.*
  176 **end**] A rare construction, possibly for metrical reasons, as in *Son.* 92.6, the only other instance in Sh. of the noun without the indefinite article after *have*. For the omission of the article, see ABBOTT §82. Not commented on elsewhere.
  177–80 *Cam. Anc. Hist.* (10:28–9): "Lucius Antonius, the [younger] brother of the triumvir, who became consul in 41 [see PAULY, Antonius, 1:2585–90 (23); *OCD,* Antonius (6)]," and Fulvia, "persuaded by a steward called Manius that her husband's interests were at stake . . . joined in fierce opposition to Octavian." For Plutarch, see p. 416. He surrendered to Octavius in Perusia, with his troops close to starvation ("*Perusina fames* became a byword"), in February, 40 B.C., and was let off unharmed.

26

Vpon the first encounter draue them.   180
   Ant. Well, what worst.
   Mess. The Nature of bad newes infects the Teller.
   Ant. When it concernes the Foole or Coward: On.
Things that are past, are done, with me. 'Tis thus,
Who tels me true, though in his Tale lye death,   185
I heare him as he flatter'd.
   Mes. Labienus (this is stiffe-newes)

180–1 *Verse lines ending* Well, . . . worse? HAN1, CAP, v1793, v1803, SING; *one verse line* v1821, KNT1, COL1, COL2, DYCE1+

181 worst] worse mTBY2 *conj.*, HAN1, RANN

184 done, with me.] ⁓ . ⁓⁓ , mTBY2 *conj.*, CAM3, SIS

185 his] the ROWE3-v1773 (–CAP)
     lye] lay OXF1

186–96 *Ten verse lines ending* flatter'd. . . . News, . . . *Asia;* . . . conquering . . . *Lydia,* . . . whilst— . . . say. . . . Lord. . . . Tongue, . . . *Rome:* ROWE; *eight verse lines ending* flatter'd. . . . news) . . . *Asia;* . . . shook, . . . *Ionia;* . . . lord! . . . tongue, . . . *Rome.* POPE1-THEO2, WARB-JOHN1, v1773-RANN; *seven verse lines ending Labienus* . . . *Asia,* . . . shook . . . *Ionia;* . . . Lord! . . . tongue, . . . *Rome.* HAN1; *eight verse lines ending Labienus* . . . news) . . . *Asia,* . . . shook, . . . *Ionia;* . . . lord! . . . tongue; . . . *Rome:* CAP; *eight verse lines ending* Labienus . . . force, . . . Euphrätes; (Euphrates his mTYR) . . . Syria . . . Ionia; . . . lord! . . . tongue; . . . Rome: mTYR *conj.*, v1793-KNT1, DYCE, STAU, GLO, CAM1, WH2, NLSN-ALEX, ARD2, EVNS; *nine verse lines ending* Labienus . . . force . . . Euphrätes; . . . Syria . . . whilst— . . . say,— . . . lord! . . . tongue; . . . Rome; COL, HUD, WH1, HAL, OXF1; *eight verse lines ending* Labienus . . . force, . . . Euphrätes; . . . Syria . . . whilst— . . . lord! . . . tongue; . . . Rome: SING2, KTLY; *nine verse lines ending* Labienus— . . . force . . . Euphrates; . . . Syria . . . Ionia, | Whilst— . . . lord! . . . tongue, . . . Rome. SIS; *eight verse lines ending* Labienus— . . . force . . . conquering . . . Lydia . . . say. . . . home. . . . name . . . Rome: YAL2

186 him as] as if POPE1-THEO4

187 (this . . . newes)] *Om.* HAN1

179–80 Commentators do not deal with the complicated syntax. DEIGHTON (ed. 1891): "Whose success in the war drove them at the first encounter out of Italy."

179 **issue**] CAWDREY (1604): "Euent, or successe, or end."

180 **draue**] See FRANZ §170 for the preterit of strong verbs.

186 **as**] I.e., as if. See FRANZ §563a, §582.

187–91 ***Labienus . . . Ionia***] For a description of the Parthian invasion, see *Cam. Anc. Hist.* (10:47–51) and Plutarch, p. 416.

187 **(this is stiffe-newes)**] CAPELL (1779 [1774], 1:27) agrees with HANMER (ed. 1744) that these words should be omitted; they are "a gloss on the other words, put by heedlessness into the manuscript, and creeping thence into print." Commentators agree that *stiff* means—OED, 14c, citing this instance—"Formidable, grave," except JOHNSON (1755, 8), also citing this instance: "Strongly maintained, or asserted with good evidence."

Hath with his Parthian Force
Extended Asia: from Euphrates his conquering
Banner shooke, from Syria to Lydia,   190
And to Ionia, whil'st——
    Ant. Anthony thou would'st say.
    Mes. Oh my Lord.
    Ant. Speake to me home,
Mince not the generall tongue, name   195
Cleopatra as she is call'd in Rome:
Raile thou in *Fuluia's* phrase, and taunt my faults
With such full License, as both Truth and Malice

---

189 Extended] thro' extended HAN1, CAP
    Asia: from Euphrates‸] ~ ‸ ~~ ; v1793-GLO, HAL-SIS (–OXF1, RID); Asia from
Euphrates, and KTLY
189–90 from . . . from] His conqu'ring banner from *Euphrates* shook | And HAN1
190 shooke,] ~ . F2, F3
191 to] *Om.* POPE1-CAP
193 Oh] Oh, no KTLY
197 my] thy F3, F4

---

189 **Extended Asia**] *OED* (Extend 11b) cites this instance as a transferred sense of
a legal term, here meaning "To seize upon, take possession of, by force." JOHNSON (ed.
1765) and all following commentators prefer this sense, of conquering all Asia. CAPELL
(1779 [1774], 1:27): "The extent of Asia, the whole extent of it," misapplying a common
meaning of *extend*—"enlarge"—found in, e.g., CAWDREY (1604).
    Asia] COOPER (1565): "Asia minor . . . nowe called Turkay, and conteyneth in
it . . . Pontus, Bithynia, Phrigia, Caria, Lycia, Lidia, and Lycaonia." See map, p. xxxvii.
    190 **Syria**] COOPER (1565): "A great realme in Asia, whiche hath on the east, the
ryuer of Euphrates: on the weste, the middell sea, and the realme of Aegypte: on the
north, Cilicia and Cappadocia: on the southe, Arabia." See PAULY, 4:1549–1727 (3); *OCD*;
and map, p. xxxvii.
    Lydia] COOPER (1565): "A countrey in Asia, on the east ioygnyng to Phrigia: on
the northe to Mysia: on the south vpon parte of Caria." See PAULY, 13:2122–2202; *OCD*.
    191 **Ionia**] COOPER (1565): "A region in Greece of Asia, wherin were the cities of
Ephesus, Miletus, Priena, and other, and the people therof be called *Iones*, and the tun-
gue *Ionica*, and the sea ioygnyng to it *Mare Ionicum*." See PAULY, 9:1893–4 (4); *OCD*;
and map, p. xxxvii.
    194 **home**] BLUMHOF (ed. 1870): Directly, aptly, openly, plainly. See *OED, adv.* 5.
For the intensive use of the adverb, see FRANZ §381.
    195 **generall tongue**] See n. 164 ("Romane thought").
    generall] See n. 827.
    198 **Malice**] See n. 2363 ("maliciously").

Haue power to vtter. Oh then we bring forth weeds,
When our quicke windes lye still, and our illes told vs   200
Is as our earing: fare thee well awhile.
Mes. At your Noble pleasure.   *Exit Messenger.*

Enter another Messenger.

Ant. From *Scicion* how the newes? Speake there.

---

200 windes] minds mTBY2 *conj.*, HAN1, WARB, MAL, RANN, v1821, SING, HUD1, DYCE1, WH1-ARD2 (–OXF1, SIS)
     illes] ill POPE1-v1773 (–CAP)
201 earing] ear-ring F3; Ear-ring are F4; hearing RANN
202 *Exit Messenger.*] *Om.* ROWE1-POPE2; *after* 206 THEO1-v1773 (–CAP)
203 *Om.* ROWE1+ (–ARD2)
204 how] now mCOL1, COL2; ho, mTBY3 *conj.*, DYCE1-ALEX (–COL3, KTLY)

---

200 **quicke windes**] Whether preferring *winds* or *minds* — the positions are represented respectively by THEOBALD (14 Mar. 1729, [fol. 57ᵛ]) and WARBURTON (ed. 1747) — commentators essentially agree that the active is opposed to the passive, the energetic to the idle. CAPELL (1779 [1774], 1:27) alone: "By '*winds*' are meant — friends." See textual notes and conj., p. 347. KNIGHT (ed. 1841): "The poet knew the old proverb [not identified] of the worth of a bushel of March dust; but 'the winds of March', rough and unpleasant as they are, he knew also produced this good." The dust evidently suppresses weeds.
     200–1 **illes . . . Is**] ABBOTT (§337): "Often . . . a verb preceded by a plural noun (the apparent nominative) has for its real nominative, not the noun, but the noun clause."
     201 **earing**] COLLIER (ed. 1877) alone extends the meaning "ploughing" to "harvest." See also 484 ("eare").
     203–7 The most common treatment — see textual notes — of the occupation and movement of the characters is exemplified by WILSON (ed. 1950), who omits 203, substitutes as speech-prefixes "Attendants" for "Messengers" (205, 207), and adds the SDs "*opens the door and calls*" (205) and "*hurries in*" (207; INCHBALD [ed. 1814] has the line spoken from "*without*"). WELLS (1984, pp. 39–41) assigns 205 and 207 to a second messenger and 206 to Antony: "This permits [207] to be interpreted as a direct response to Antony. . . . It avoids assuming either that [203] is an interpolation or that it means '*Enter two messengers*', and it permits a natural exit of the messenger at TLN 208." See also nn. 26, 205–6.
     204 *Scicion*] COOPER (1565, Sicyon): "A citie in Achaia, not farre from Corynth, called now *Clarentia*." See PAULY, Sikyon, 2A:2528–49 (1); *OCD*, Sicyon; and map, p. xxxvii.
          there] BLUMHOF (ed. 1870), in indirect support of ROWE's (ed. 1709) "*attendants*" (170), considers this a formula of address to followers, not to a particular individual, and cites numerous examples in Sh. See also *OED* (2b): "A brusque mode of address . . . to a person or persons in the place or direction indicated." See 1536, 2105, 2261, 3336, 3596.

1. *Mes.* The man from *Scicion*,   205
Is there such an one?
2. *Mes.* He stayes vpon your will.
Ant. Let him appeare:
These strong Egyptian Fetters I must breake,
Or loose my selfe in dotage.   210

> *Enter another Messenger with a Letter.*

What are you?
3. *Mes.* *Fuluia* thy wife is dead.
Ant. Where dyed she.
Mes. In *Scicion*, her length of sicknesse,   215
With what else more serious,

205–6 *One verse line* ROWE1+
205 1. *Mes.*] *Mes.* ROWE1-JOHN1, v1773; 1. *A.* (*i.e.*, Attendant) CAP, v1778+ (−ARD2)
206 an] a CAP, SING, COL3, KTLY
      Exit first Messenger THEO1-v1773 (−CAP)
207 2. *Mes.*] *Attend.* ROWE1-JOHN1, v1773; 2. *A.* CAP, v1778+ (−ARD2)
210, 212 *One verse line* ROWE1+
211 *with a Letter*] Om. CAP-OXF1, RID
213–18 *Four verse lines ending* she? . . . *Sicyon*, . . . serious . . . me. POPE1-GLO,
HAL+; *three verse lines ending* Sicyon. . . . serious . . . me.— KTLY
213 3. *Mes.*] 2 *Mes.* ROWE1-JOHN1, v1773-RID, CAM3+ (−ARD2); *Mes.* CAP, KIT1
215 *Mes.*] 2 *Mes.* ROWE1-JOHN1, v1773-RID, CAM3-SIS, EVNS; *Third Mess.* ARD2

205–6 R. WATKINS (1950, p. 202): "The contemptuous casual tone of the flunkey
[who 'shouts through the door'] creates for us a vista of crowded ante-chambers and long-
suffering queues outside the stage-door." WALTER (ed. 1969) asks, "Is there perhaps a
quibble 'Sicyon'—'such an one'?" North, incidentally, spells *Sicyone* (p. 416).
    206 **an one**] FRANZ (§270): From the form *such an one*, the elision of the article
before *one* (*th'one*), and wordplay between *one* and the preposition *on* [see *TGV* 2.1.1–2
(398–9)], we may conclude that Sh. knew the pronunciation without the initial *w* (which
is preserved in *alone* and *only*). CERCIGNANI (1981, p. 366) adds that such sequences
"do not . . . rule out the use of variants with *w*, for . . . contemporary usage was . . .
still unsettled."
    210 **loose**] F4's *lose* is justified by the "breake" image in 209.
    212 **What**] FRANZ (§342): Who.
    214 FRANZ (§600): If an interrogative introduces a question that is to be answered,
the construction without *did* predominates.
    215 **her length of sicknesse**] I.e., the length of her sickness. ABBOTT (§423): "Two
nouns connected by 'of' are often regarded as one. Hence sometimes pronominal and
other adjectives are placed before the whole compound noun."
    216 **what else more serious**] Not "something else more serious than the details of
Fulvia's death," but "something else that is very serious." Not commented on elsewhere.

Importeth thee to know, this beares.

   Antho. Forbeare me

There's a great Spirit gone, thus did I desire it:

What our contempts doth often hurle from vs,   220

We wish it ours againe. The present pleasure,   (xx1ᵛᵃ)

By reuolution lowring, does become

The opposite of it selfe: she's good being gon,

The hand could plucke her backe, that shou'd her on.

---

217 Importeth] Importe to F3, F4

218 *Exit second Messenger.* THEO1-KIT1, ALEX, SIS, EVNS; *Messenger and Attendants withdraw* CAM3; *Exeunt Messengers.* ARD2

    me˄] ~ , F4+

219 did I desire] I desir'd POPE, HAN1

220 contempts doth] contempts doe F2-COL3, WH1, KTLY-HUD2, OXF1, KIT1; contempt doth mTBY4 *conj.* (do), STAU, GLO, WH2

220–1 vs . . . The] us. We wish it Hours again, the ROWE1, ROWE2

222 reuolution] repetition mCOL1, COL2, COL3

    lowring] souring mTBY2 *conj.*, mCOL1, COL2, COL3

    does] doth RIDb

224 could] would mTBY4 *conj.*, mCOL1, COL2

---

218 **Forbeare**] BAILEY (1721): "Let alone." See *OED*, 4c. See also 312, 388, et passim.

220–1 **What . . . againe**] THEOBALD (19 Feb. 1729, [fol. 39ʳ]) quotes Horace: "Virtutem præsentem odimus, Sublatam ex oculis quærimus invidi [With envy filled, we hate Virtue while it lives and mourn it only when snatched from sight]" (*Odes* 3.24.31–2). CAPELL (1779 [1774], 1:28) regards this sentence as a "general maxim."

220 **doth**] FRANZ (§156) thinks that this form is less likely a survival of the ME Southern -(*e*)*th* plural than one created on the analogy of the third person singular. BARBER (1976, p. 242): "In the later 16th century, plural -*eth* is rare."

221–3 **The . . . selfe**] FURNESS (ed. 1907, p. 515): A "condensation" of Daniel's *Cleopatra*, ll. 549–52. See p. 549.

221 **present pleasure**] RUSHTON (1872, p. 330) illustrates its consequences in a quotation from Roger Ascham's *Toxophilus*: "Gamninge hath joyned with it, a vayne *presente pleasure*, but there foloweth, losse of name, losse of goodes, and winning of an hundred gowtie, dropsy diseases, as every man can tell [1545, fol. 17ʳ]." See also 462.

222–3 **By . . . it selfe**] WARBURTON (ed. 1747): "The allusion is to the sun . . . which rising in the *east*, and *by revolution lowering*, or setting in the *west*, becomes *the opposite of itself*." HUDSON (ed. 1855): "The image is of a wheel." IRVING & MARSHALL (ed. 1889) add, "Perhaps that of Fortune." See n. 474–8.

223 **she's . . . gon**] WALTER (ed. 1969): "Perhaps a glance at the proverb, 'The dead are well.'" But see DENT (W924, G298.1): "The *worth* of a thing is best known by the want"; "The *good* is not known until lost." See n. 1065.

224 **could**] HEATH (1765, p. 449): "Doth not denote power, but inclination. The sense is, The hand that drove her off would now willingly pluck her back again." See FRANZ §603.

I must from this enchanting Queene breake off,   225
Ten thousand harmes, more then the illes I know
My idlenesse doth hatch.

                    Enter Enobarbus.

How now *Enobarbus*.
        Eno. What's your pleasure, Sir?   230
        Anth. I must with haste from hence.
        Eno. Why then we kill all our Women. We see how
mortall an vnkindnesse is to them, if they suffer our departure death's the word.
        Ant. I must be gone.   235

---

225 enchanting] *Om.* F2-F4; *Ægyptian* ROWE, POPE
227, 229 *One verse line* ROWE1+
228 *After* 229 ROWE1+ (−NLSN, CAM3a, SIS)
229 How now] Ho mTBY3 *conj.,* CAP, HUD, SING2, DYCE, COL3, WH1, HAL; Ho now
COL4, ARD2, CAM3b
230–1 *One verse line* KTLY

---

225 CASE (ed. 1906) compares the Countess of Pembroke's *Antonie* (1595), "Thou breakest . . . spirit [ll. 79–83]." For the 1592 *Antonius,* see p. 482. ADELMAN (1973, p. 179) compares "enchanting Queene" with Marlowe's *Dido* 4.3.31: "Ticing dame [ed. Tucker Brooke, 1930]." See also n. 642.

226–7 Proverbial; see DENT (I13): "*Idleness* is the mother (nurse, root) of all evil (vice, sin)."

227 **idlenesse**] MINSHEU (1617, Idle): "Lazie, & Slouthfull." The few who comment agree with KITTREDGE (ed. 1941): "Folly, dotage." See also nn. 412, 415.

229 RIDLEY (ed. 1954), summarizing one view: "Enobarbus, as seems clearly implied by his first words, enters in answer to a summons. This has led most editors to shift the entry of Enobarbus to half a line later, but retaining 'How now', and led Capell [ed. 1768], and (independently) Dyce [ed. 1857] to read 'Ho, Enobarbus!' [See textual notes.] . . . 'How' is not infrequently printed for 'Ho' (cf. [2946] *post*). . . . The crucial point is Enobarbus' 'What's your pleasure?' which is almost nonsensical as a reply to a question ('How now?'), but natural as the reply to a summons. . . . (I have retained F's 'now', since, though it makes the line hypermetrical, it is not impossible, but Capell and Dyce may well have been right in omitting it, on the grounds that . . . a compositor, taking 'How' to mean 'How' and not 'Ho' might easily insert the natural 'now'.)" The reasons for retaining the F1 reading are pertinent, however, ranging from NICHOLSON's (Wright *Shakespeariana*, no. 158 [8^v]) "'How now' represents the rousing of himself from an idle purposeless reverie . . . and is a kind of self conscious reproach followed by the call — 'Enobarbus'" to the general assumption, reiterated by KITTREDGE (ed. 1941), that the phrase is not a question but "merely an exclamation of summons." OED (How *adv.* 4b): "Ellipt. for 'How is it now?' Often used interjectionally." Compare nn. 350, 2946.

Eno. Vnder a compelling an occasion, let women die.
It were pitty to cast them away for nothing, though betweene them and a great cause, they should be esteemed
nothing. *Cleopatra* catching but the least noyse of this,
dies instantly: I haue seene her dye twenty times vppon   240
farre poorer moment: I do think there is mettle in death,
which commits some louing acte vpon her, she hath such
a celerity in dying.
    Ant. She is cunning past mans thought.
    Eno. Alacke Sir no, her passions are made of nothing   245
but the finest part of pure Loue. We cannot cal her winds
and waters, sighes and teares: They are greater stormes
and Tempests then Almanackes can report. This cannot
be cunning in her; if it be, she makes a showre of Raine
as well as Ioue.   250

---

236 an] *Om.* ROWE1+
243 a celerity] alacrity HAN1
247 They] And yet they ROWE
248 then] that v1821

---

236 **a compelling an occasion**] Although there is little doubt that *an* is a compositorial
slip, the indefinite article may occur after an attributive adjective, as at 3486. FRANZ
(§275) finds only one other instance in Sh. (*AYL* 1.1.2 [5]) and does not list the present one.
    die] See n. 560.
239–43 See n. 110.
239 **nothing**] For "the equivocal meaning," KIRSCHBAUM (1944, p. 170, n. 13) refers
to Hamlet's "Nothing" as a fair thought to lie between maids' legs (3.2.124–8 [1971–4]),
but it is unclear how the bawdy sense applies. COLMAN (1974, pp. 16–18) discusses the
possible allusion to the vulva in *Ham.* and elsewhere but makes no reference to *Ant.*
240 **dye**] See n. 560.
241 **moment**] CAWDREY (1604): "Weight, or importance." *OED* (5), citing this instance: "Cause or motive of action."
243 **dying**] See n. 560.
244 **cunning**] MINSHEU (1617): "Knowledge, Skill, Experience." KERSEY (1702) is the
first dictionary to give "*craftiness*." EAGLESON (1971, p. 11): "In Elizabethan English . . .
the word was moving in the direction of its modern use and was attracting pejorative
overtones." See *OED*, 5. See also 249, 1001, 2144.
246–7 **winds . . . teares**] MALONE (*apud* STEEVENS [1780], 1:228) conjectures an
inversion of word order (see p. 348), then (ed. 1790) says the original "arrangement of
the text was the phraseology of Shakspeare, and probably of his time," and finally (*apud*
STEEVENS, ed. 1793) holds that the "passage . . . may be understood without any inversion." Commentators who follow seem to have missed his retraction.
249 **cunning**] See n. 244.
250 **Ioue**] BLUMHOF (ed. 1870): Jupiter Pluvius, the rain god of the Romans.

Ant. Would I had neuer seene her.

Eno. Oh sir, you had then left vnseene a wonderfull
peece of worke, which not to haue beene blest withall,
would haue discredited your Trauaile.

Ant. Fuluia is dead.   255

Eno. Sir.

Ant. Fuluia is dead.

Eno. Fuluia?

Ant. Dead.

Eno. Why sir, giue the Gods a thankefull Sacrifice: 260
when it pleaseth their Deities to take the wife of a man
from him, it shewes to man the Tailors of the earth: comforting therein, that when olde Robes are worne out,
there are members to make new. If there were no more
Women but *Fuluia*, then had you indeede a cut, and the   265
case to be lamented: This greefe is crown'd with Conso-

---

262 it shewes] they shew HAN1
    to] the RID
    Tailors] tailor POPE, THEO, WARB
263 therein] him therein ROWE, POPE, HAN1, WARB
264 members] numbers HAN1
266 case] case were ROWE1-v1773 (–CAP)

---

253 **withall**] FRANZ (§536): Used for the preposition *with* at the end of a sentence
or relative clause. See also 1814, 3397.

254 **Trauaile**] *Travail* and *travel* were "orig. the same word" (*OED*, Travel *sb.*), the
arbitrary distinction in spelling and accent occurring after Sh. F3's *Travel*, followed by
all subsequent editions, is justified by "left vnseene" (252).

260 **thankefull**] See n. 2543.

262 **Tailors**] ANON. (*apud* STEEVENS, ed. 1773): "*The Gods have . . . provided you
with a new* [woman] *in Cleopatra . . . as the tailors of the earth, when your old garments are worn out, accommodate you with new ones.*" CAPELL (1779 [1774], 1:28):
"Women, the artificers of other women." CASE (ed. 1906): "'The tailors of the earth'
. . . may be merely reproductive man." COLMAN (1974, p. 217) doubts the senses of
female pudendum and penis.

264 **members**] CAPELL (1779 [1774], 1:28): "Of the community." DEIGHTON (ed. 1891):
"Probably with an allusion to the scriptural narrative of Eve being made out of one of
Adam's ribs." COLMAN (1974, p. 203): "Possible quibble, (a) people, (b) male sexual
organs." See textual notes and conj., p. 348.

265 **cut**] THISELTON (1899, p. 9): "Has a double meaning: (1) 'stroke' or 'blow'; (2)
'shape' or 'fashion.'" COLMAN (1974, p. 190): "Vulva (by quibbles)."

266 **case**] BLUMHOF (ed. 1870): State of things as well as body or shape. See also
3104, n. 2873–4. E. PARTRIDGE (1947; 1968, p. 76): "Pudend."

lation, your old Smocke brings foorth a new Petticoate,
and indeed the teares liue in an Onion, that should water
this sorrow.

Ant. The businesse she hath broached in the State,   270
Cannot endure my absence.

Eno. And the businesse you haue broach'd heere cannot be without you, especially that of *Cleopatra's,* which
wholly depends on your abode.

Ant. No more light Answeres: 275
Let our Officers
Haue notice what we purpose. I shall breake
The cause of our Expedience to the Queene,
And get her loue to part. For not alone

---

270 broached] broach'd here ROWE2-POPE2
273 *Cleopatra's*] *Cleopatra* HAN1
275-6 *One verse line* ROWE1+
275 light] like F2-ROWE3
277 purpose] propose F3, F4
279 loue] leave POPE1-JOHN1, v1773, COL2+ (−SING2)

---

267 **your . . . Petticoate**] There is a distinction between a smock—LINTHICUM (1936, p. 189): "A shirt-like garment worn as underwear, and as a sleeping gown by sixteenth-century women"—and a petticoat (IDEM, p. 187): "By the middle of the sixteenth century, used almost exclusively to designate a woman's underskirt, usually tied by points." As both could be ornamental and elaborate, critical attempts to connect the garments with social status are not always convincing. Possibly proverbial; see DENT (B607): "His old *brass* (etc.) will buy (make) you a new pan (etc.)."

268-9 **teares . . . sorrow**] DAVIES (1783, 2:340): "'Fulvia's death will cause no real grief in you; the tears, which you will shed on this occasion, resemble such as are extracted by the application of an onion to the eye'. *If you cannot cry, clap an onion to your eye,* has been . . . an old sarcasm on forced sorrow." Possibly proverbial; see DENT (O67)—"To weep (It may serve) with an *onion*"—and (P391)—"To water one's *plants* (i.e., to weep)."

272 **broach'd**] DELIUS (ed. 1856): With bawdy wordplay. See E. PARTRIDGE (1947; 1968, p. 71): "To broach a woman—as one broaches a cask."

273 **that of *Cleopatra's***] For the genitive, see n. 4.

278 **Expedience**] HANMER (ed. 1744, 6:Glossary): "Expedition," which CAWDREY (1604) defines as "hast, speede," BULLOKAR (1616) as "quicke dispatch, speede, sometime a setting forth vnto warre; a voiage." See conj., p. 348.

279 **loue**] CAPELL (1779 [1774], 1:28-9) finds the emendation *leave* inappropriate to Antony's dignity: "It seems indeed to have been avoided with some study; and '*love*', a less natural expression, substituted for it: the sense . . . is . . . —and get her, whose love is so great for me, to consent to my parting." MALONE (ed. 1790): "The words must

35

The death of *Fuluia*, with more vrgent touches   280
Do strongly speake to vs: but the Letters too
Of many our contriuing Friends in Rome,
Petition vs at home. *Sextus Pompeius*
Haue giuen the dare to *Cæsar,* and commands
The Empire of the Sea. Our slippery people,   285
Whose Loue is neuer link'd to the deseruer,
Till his deserts are past, begin to throw   (xx1^vb^
Pompey the great, and all his Dignities
Vpon his Sonne, who high in Name and Power,

---

281 Do] Doth HAN1, KTLY
284 Haue] Hath F2+

---

mean, I will get her love to permit and endure our separation. But the word *get* connects much more naturally with the word *leave* than with *love.*" He finds (10:666) "the same errour" (of *loves* for *leaves*) in *Tit.* 3.1.292 (1441). DELIUS (ed. 1856), straddling, glosses *love* as "favor." WILSON (ed. 1950) suggests F's *loue* probably derives from MS *leue.* (See IDEM, *The Manuscript of Shakespeare's* Hamlet, 1934, 1:109–10 and n. 5.1.59.) Most commentators emend, assuming that as guest Antony would courteously request royal permission to leave.

280 **more vrgent touches**] Commentators agree with JOHNSON's (ed. 1765) "Things that touch me more sensibly, more pressing motives," but do not specify what is signified (presumably, the civil wars).

282 **many our**] An old genitive construction. See FRANZ §329 for the word order. See also 346.

contriuing] The sense of "to plot" is first recorded in a dictionary in BAILEY (1721), although this meaning is very common in Sh. The present instance seems to be used in the more neutral sense of CAWDREY (1604): "Make." Apparently following WARBURTON's (ed. 1747, 2:417) explanation of *contriue* in *Shr.* 1.2.276 (848), WALKER (1860, 1:163) alone: "*Contriving* here is not *managing* or *plotting,* but *sojourning; conterentes tempus.*" See conj., p. 348.

282-3 **Rome . . . home**] WALKER (1860, 1:163, 2:114): "Pronounce *Rome*, as usual, *Room*; this removes the jingle between *Rome* and *home.*" DOBSON (1957, 2:678–80) and CERCIGNANI (1981, pp. 184–5) call *Rome* a "special" case since variation was common in the pronunciation of *o.*

283 **Petition . . . home**] JOHNSON (ed. 1765): "Wish us at home; call for us to reside at home." Only DELIUS (ed. 1856) seems to disagree: *At home* refers to the "contriving friends," the counseling friends, who from Rome besiege Antony with their petitions. BLUMHOF (ed. 1870), however, sees both possibilities.

284 **Haue**] An apparent misprint. See textual notes.

288 Only DEIGHTON (ed. 1891) mentions as "a hendiadys for 'all the dignities of Pompey.'" KITTREDGE (ed. 1941): "The name and honours."

Higher then both in Blood and Life, stands vp   290
For the maine Souldier. Whose quality going on,
The sides o'th'world may danger. Much is breeding,
Which like the Coursers heire, hath yet but life,
And not a Serpents poyson. Say our pleasure,
To such whose places vnder vs, require   295

---

290 stands] stand ROWE3
293 heire] hare F3, F4; Hair ROWE1+
295 places vnder vs, require] place is under us, requires F2-THEO4, CAP, v1778-ARD1, KIT1-SIS; places under us, requires v1773; places under us require, RID, EVNS; places under us require ARD2

Pompey **the great**] Cneius Pompeius Magnus (106–48 B.C.). See PAULY, Pompeius, 21:2062–2211 (31); *OCD*, Pompeius (4). Only HUDSON (ed. 1881) and KITTREDGE (ed. 1941) say the title ("the Great") is being conferred.

Dignities] CAWDREY (1604): "Worthinesse." See also 3396.

290 **Blood and Life**] The few who comment agree substantially with DEIGHTON (ed. 1891): "Courage and high spirit, vital energy."

290–1 **stands vp . . . Souldier**] DEIGHTON (ed. 1891): "Asserts himself before the world as its greatest soldier." PHIALAS (ed. 1955): "Aspires to be."

291 **quality**] Early glosses include "reputation" (RANN [ed. 1791–]), "role of soldier" (DELIUS [ed. 1856]), and "*party*" (KINNEAR [1883, p. 449]). 20th-c. commentators seem to have settled, substantially, on CASE's (ed. 1906) "nature and condition, including their potentialities," with some substituting "character" or a synonymous term. WILSON (ed. 1950): "Deliberately vague, summing up what has already been said."

going on] RANN (ed. 1791–): "Increasing." Commentators since DELIUS (ed. 1856): "Continuing."

292 **sides**] Most commentators agree with DELIUS (ed. 1856): Frame, structure. KITTREDGE (ed. 1941) alone: "Body." See n. 319.

danger] Although the *OED* gives 1579 as the last recorded occurrence of the verb *endanger*, "to subject (a person) to the absolute control of another," the noun *danger* with the equivalent meaning is to be found in Sh., as in *MV* 4.1.180 (2089).

293 **Coursers heire**] POPE (ed. 1723): "*Alludes to an old idle notion that the hair of a horse dropt into corrupted water, will turn to an animal.*" CAPELL (1779 [1774], 1:29), referring to "a passage in Holinshed" (which THEOBALD [19 Feb. 1729, (fol. 39ʳ)] had specified as the "Description of England, Vol. 1. p. 224"), continues, "The animal produc'd is call'd there indeed—worm; but the vulgar opinion might make a serpent of it: which being hair-like and very minute when it first assum'd life, was not come to its venom" (1587, 224/1/46–54). HALLIWELL (1866, p. 6): The belief "is even now not obsolete."

295 **places . . . require**] See textual notes for interpretations of syntax.

places] See n. 1509, 1515.

Our quicke remoue from hence.
Enob. I shall doo't.

Enter Cleopatra, Charmian, Alexas, and Iras.   **1.3**

Cleo. Where is he?
Char. I did not see him since.   300
Cleo. See where he is,
Whose with him, what he does:
I did not send you. If you finde him sad,
Say I am dauncing: if in Myrth, report
That I am sodaine sicke. Quicke, and returne.   305

296–7 *One verse line* COL, WH1, KTLY, HAL
297 I shall] I'll POPE1-JOHN1
    doo't] do it COL, WH1, HAL, OXF1; do it, sir KTLY
    Exeunt. F2+
298 SCENE IV. POPE1-JOHN1 (–THEO); *SCENE* III. CAP+
    The same. Another Room. CAP, HUD1+ (–COL3, HAL) (*subst.*)
299–300 *One verse line* v1793+ (–HUD)
301–2 *One verse line* ROWE1+
305 Quicke] Quickly F2-ROWE3
    Exit Alexas. CAP, v1778+

---

297 **I shall**] DEIGHTON (ed. 1891): "With the first person, *shall* indicates what is in-evitable, certain, as being fixed by the speaker himself." KITTREDGE (ed. 1941) disagrees: "More submissive than 'I will', for it indicates that the speaker has no volition in the matter." See FRANZ §608, §611. BROOK (1976, p. 113): "In Shakespeare *shall* is used in all three persons to indicate the normal future; *will* generally involves some volition."

300 **did not see**] FRANZ (§599): In negative declarative statements the periphrastic *do* is the less frequent construction.

301–3 **See . . . send you**] DAPHINOFF (1975, pp. 192–3): An illustration of Plutarch's "For she, were it in sport, or in matter of earnest, still devised sundrie new delights to haue Antonius at commaundement, *neuer leauing him night nor day, nor once letting him go out of her sight.*" See p. 415.

303 **I . . . send you**] JOHNSON (ed. 1765) and most others: "You must go as if you came without my order or knowledge." MALONE (ed. 1790) notes a similar construction in *Tro.* 4.2.73 (2333).

303–5 **If . . . sicke**] Possibly proverbial; see DENT (H839): "When the *husband* is sad (merry) the wife will be merry (sad)."

303 **sad**] COCKERAM (1623): "Dolorous, Disconsolate, Pensiue." HANMER (ed. 1744, 6:Glossary) and most others: "Grave, sober, serious." In Act 1 *sad* is always juxtaposed against *merry* or *mirth*. See also 581, 583, et passim.

305 **Quicke**] MALONE (ed. 1790, 1:xxiv): "Either used adverbially [see FRANZ §241], or elliptically for *Be quick.*"

Char. Madam, me thinkes if you did loue him deerly,
You do not hold the method, to enforce
The like from him.
 Cleo. What should I do, I do not?
 Ch. In each thing giue him way, crosse him in nothing.   310
 Cleo. Thou teachest like a foole: the way to lose him.
 Char. Tempt him not so too farre. I wish forbeare,
In time we hate that which we often feare.

     Enter Anthony.

But heere comes *Anthony.*   315
 Cleo. I am sicke, and sullen.
 An. I am sorry to giue breathing to my purpose.
 Cleo. Helpe me away deere *Charmian*, I shall fall,
It cannot be thus long, the sides of Nature
Will not sustaine it.   320
 Ant. Now my deerest Queene.
 Cleo. Pray you stand farther from mee.
 Ant. What's the matter?
 Cleo. I know by that same eye ther's some good news.

---

311 teachest‸ . . . foole:] ~ , . . . ~ , JOHN1, v1773, COL, SING2, KTLY, HAL
312 farre. I wish‸] ~ , ~~ ; BAYF
 I wish] I wish you mF2J *conj.*, KTLY; iwis CAM3, SIS
314 *After* 316 DYCE, STAU, HUD2
322 farther] further v1793-SING1, HUD, DYCE, OXF1

---

306 **me thinkes**] See n. 1673.
312 **Tempt**] COTGRAVE (1611, Tenter): "*To proue, trie.*" DEIGHTON (ed. 1891): "Provoke, defy."
 too farre] ABBOTT (§434) alone hyphenates and considers it a "phrase-compound."
 I wish forbeare] To the meaning of a simple colloquial ellipsis ("wish you to"), as well as to the interpretations implied by emendations and conjectures (see p. 348), may be added JONES (1908, p. 345): "Charmian is about to remonstrate in such terms as 'I wish you would not be so *shrewish*'; but, as that would be too impertinent, suddenly changes her thought to—'forbear.'"
313 Proverbial; see DENT (L556): "He cannot *love* me that is afraid of me."
319 **sides of Nature**] STEEVENS (ed. 1793) is followed substantially by most others in applying the phrase to the human frame; he quotes *TN* 2.4.96–7 (980–1): "There is no womans sides Can bide the beating of so strong a passion." See also n. 292. For the subjective and objective genitive, see FRANZ §322.

What sayes the married woman you may goe?   325
Would she had neuer giuen you leaue to come.
Let her not say 'tis I that keepe you heere,
I haue no power vpon you: Hers you are.
   Ant. The Gods best know.
   Cleo. Oh neuer was there Queene   330
So mightily betrayed: yet at the fitst
I saw the Treasons planted.
   Ant. Cleopatra.
   Cleo. Why should I thinke you can be mine, & true,
(Though you in swearing shake the Throaned Gods)   335
Who haue beene false to *Fuluia*?
Riotous madnesse,
To be entangled with those mouth-made vowes,
Which breake themselues in swearing.
   Ant. Most sweet Queene.   340

---

325 What∧ . . . woman∧ . . . goe?] F1-F3; ∼ ! . . . ∼ ∧ . . . ∼ ? F4, CAM3,
SIS+; ∼ ∧ . . . ∼ ; . . . ∼ ? RID; ∼ ∧ . . . ∼ ? . . . ∼ ; ROWE1 *etc.*
331 fitst] first F2+
335 in] *Om.* F2-F4; with mF4Q *conj. and* ROWE1, ROWE2-JOHN1, v1773
336-7 *One verse line* ROWE1+
338 those] these ROWE2-JOHN1

325-6 ZIELINSKI (1905, p. 18) is the first to compare Ovid's *Heroides*: "'*Sed jubet
ire deus'. Vellem, vetuisset adire!* ['But you are bid to go—by your god!' Ah, would he
had forbidden you to come]" (7.139). BALDWIN (1944, 2:425): "This rhetorical trick of
ire-adire, go and come, would have forced itself on the attention of any learned gram-
marian of the sixteenth century."
   325 See textual notes for interpretation of the grammar.
   332 **Treasons**] WALKER (1860, 1:246) thinks the *s* an interpolation, a kind of corruption, usually affecting nouns, (1:234) "remarkably frequent in the folio." The word is
probably a normal plural, however.
   334-6 **Why . . . Fuluia**] MIOLA (1983, p. 122) finds an echo of Ovid's Dido (*Heroides*
7.81-4) in Cleopatra's "needling questions about Antony's treatment of Fulvia." Also
at 376-8 and 391-4 ("So . . . Egypt").
   335 JONES (ed. 1977): "Cleopatra alludes hyperbolically to the notion that when Jupiter . . . swore an oath, the whole of Olympus shuddered to its foundations."
   336-7 For the question of divided pentameters and short lines within speeches, see
pp. 362-4.
   339 The few who comment agree with DEIGHTON (ed. 1891): "Which break themselves even as they are uttered."
   breake themselues] I.e., are broken. ABBOTT (§296): "The predilection for transitive verbs was perhaps one among other causes why many verbs which are now used intransitively, were used by Shakespeare reflexively."

Cleo. Nay pray you seeke no colour for your going,
But bid farewell, and goe:
When you sued staying,
Then was the time for words: No going then,
Eternity was in our Lippes, and Eyes, 345
Blisse in our browes bent: none our parts so poore,
But was a race of Heauen. They are so still,
Or thou the greatest Souldier of the world,
Art turn'd the greatest Lyar.
Ant. How now Lady? 350
Cleo. I would I had thy inches, thou should'st know (xx2ᵃ)
There were a heart in Egypt.

342-3 *One verse line* ROWE1+
346 browes bent: none] Brows' bent, none THEO2, WARB-COL1, HUD1-GLO, HAL+
(−OXF1); brows, none of HAN1; brows' bent; none of KTLY
347 race] ray HAN1
349 greatest] greater F2-POPE2

341 **colour**] MINSHEU (1617) points out legal implications: "Colour *signifieth in the common Law, a probable plee, but in truth false.*"
346 **Blisse . . . bent**] This much-admired phrase may be an inflection of a familiar topos. See "hire bende browen, þat bringeþ blisse" (l. 26 of "A Wayle Whyt ase Whalles Bon," *The Harley Lyrics*, ed. Brook, 1948; 3rd ed. 1964), also no. 143, l. 10, in *Secular Lyrics of the XIVth and XVth Centuries* (ed. Robbins, 1952, p. 144). The connection between *Blisse* and *Eternity* (345) is apparent in the *OED's* "beatitude of the blessed in heaven" and, of course, in the collocation "eternal bliss." CAPELL (1779 [1774], 1:29) and most commentators: "'*Bent*' is a substantive, and '*brows' bent*'—the fine arch of the eye-brows." BLAKE (1983, p. 60) alone: "It is equally likely that *bent* is a qualifier to the head [of a nominal group] *browes* for bent in the sense 'arched' collocates frequently at this time with *brows* (*cf. OED Bent ppl.a.* 1b) though parallels are lacking in Shakespeare."
   none our parts] See n. 282.
347 **race of Heauen**] WARBURTON (ed. 1747): "*I.e.* had a smack or flavour of heaven." JOHNSON (1755, *Race*, 6), agreeing: "A particular strength or taste of wine"; IDEM (ed. 1765): "The *race* of wine is the taste of the soil." See *OED, sb.²* 10. MALONE (ed. 1790): "Of *heavenly origin.*" Whereas most 18th-c. editors follow Warburton, the others tend to agree with Malone, despite the ambiguity of the homograph. See textual notes and conj., p. 348.
350 **How now**] FRANZ (§250): An expression of astonishment.
352 **were**] ABBOTT (§301): "The subjunctive . . . [is used] in dependent sentences even after 'know.'"
   Egypt] BLUMHOF (ed. 1870): The word may refer to the country or the queen. Most commentators, following WORDSWORTH (ed. 1883), prefer the latter. See n. 394 ("to Egypt").

Ant. Heare me Queene:
The strong necessity of Time, commands
Our Seruices a-while: but my full heart   355
Remaines in vse with you. Our Italy,
Shines o're with ciuill Swords; *Sextus Pompeius*
Makes his approaches to the Port of Rome,
Equality of two Domesticke powers,
Breed scrupulous faction: The hated growne to strength   360
Are newly growne to Loue: The condemn'd *Pompey,*
Rich in his Fathers Honor, creepes apace
Into the hearts of such, as haue not thriued

---

360 Breed] Breeds POPE1-v1803, SING1-SING2, COL3-WH1, KTLY, HAL, COL4, OXF1
363 thriued] thriv'n ROWE1-v1773 (−CAP)

---

353 **Queene**] The vocative *Queene* without modifier is rare. All three instances in Sh.—two are in *Ant.* (see 3244) and one in *Tit.* 2.3.72 (811)—are in decasyllabic lines, hence perhaps the absence of the modifier.

355 **Seruices**] WELLS & TAYLOR (ed. 1986) interpret F1's *Seruicles* as a misprint for *Seruicies,* an obsolete form of *services. OED* provides no 16th- or 17th-c. quotation or even citation for *Seruicies.*

    full heart] The only commentator is DEIGHTON (ed. 1891): "My heart in all its fulness of love."

356 **in vse**] JOHNSON (ed. 1765): "The poet seems to allude to the legal distinction between the *use* and *absolute possession.*" Commentators struggle with the distinction or accept both possibilities, most (since STEEVENS, ed. 1793) quoting *MV* 4.1.383 (2301).

357 **ciuill Swords**] The few who comment agree with DELIUS (ed. 1856): Swords drawn in civil war. See "ciuil bloud," *Rom.* 1.Pr.4 (0.2+6).

358 **Port**] SINGER (ed. 1826): "Gate." HEYSE (ed. 1867) and most others: Ostia; the sense of "gate" conflicts with the historical facts. Both interpretations may be supported by the etymology, which is ambiguous: Latin *porta* means "gate," *portus* means "harbor."

360 **Breed**] A good number of editors emend to *Breeds,* emphasizing that *Equality* is the subject of the sentence. ABBOTT (§412) explains as "Confusion of proximity," but a prepositional phrase with a plural object may be followed by a plural verb—see FRANZ §675.

    scrupulous] CAWDREY (1604): "Full of doubts." HUDSON (ed. 1881): "The radical meaning of the Latin *scrupulosus* is *full of small, sharp* or *pointed stones.* Hence an epithet of *discussion* or *investigation,* and in the sense of *exact* or *precise.* So that the meaning in the text appears to be, that the opposing parties were *rigidly sifting each other's claims.*" See conj., p. 348. SEN GUPTA (1972, p. 38): "May stand for two different but related ideas—the people wavering between two warring factions who are quarrelling about trifles ('scruple'=1/24 of an ounce)." See *OED, sb.*[1] and *sb.*[2].

362 **creepes apace**] The few who gloss interpret *creepes* as "crawls." But the meaning is more likely "to move quietly and stealthily" (*OED,* 2), as suggested by BLUMHOF (ed. 1870), who compares "secretly into the bosome creepe" (*1H4* 1.3.266 [594]). This interpretation avoids an oxymoron, *apace* meaning "swiftly." See also n. 2631.

Vpon the present state, whose Numbers threaten,
And quietnesse growne sicke of rest, would purge   365
By any desperate change: My more particular,
And that which most with you should safe my going,
Is *Fuluias* death.
    Cleo. Though age from folly could not giue me freedom
It does from childishnesse. Can *Fuluia* dye?   370
    Ant. She's dead my Queene.
Looke heere, and at thy Soueraigne leysure read
The Garboyles she awak'd: at the last, best,
See when, and where shee died.

---

367 safe] save F4-POPE1; salve mTBY2 *and* THEOBALD (1726, p. 183) *conj.*, POPE2,
THEO, HAN1, WARB

---

365 **sicke of**] Most commentators, starting with BLUMHOF (ed. 1870), prefer "ill as
a consequence of." A few, starting with DELIUS (ed. 1856), add "tired of."
    purge] Commentators, following DELIUS (ed. 1856), regard the verb as intransi-
tive, meaning "cleanse or heal itself." Only WILSON (ed. 1950) specifies "periodical blood-
letting," although the medical sense can be, as JOHNSON (1755) puts it, "To have frequent stools."
    366 **particular**] See n. 2178.
    367 **safe**] THEOBALD (1726, p. 183) rejects F4's *save* for *salve* because Antony assures
Cleopatra that "as his Wife *Fulvia* is dead . . . She has no Rival." UPTON (1746, p.
305) explains *safe* as "make safe and secure," the definition adopted by the *OED*, which
cites this instance despite MASON's (1785, p. 273) "to *safe* my going, is not English."
MALONE (ed. 1790): "I.e. should render my going not dangerous, not likely to produce
any mischief to you." STEEVENS (ed. 1793) compares *saf't* at 2607. ABBOTT (§290) explains, "Any noun or adjective could be converted into a verb . . . generally in an active
signification."
    370 **Can *Fuluia* dye?**] STEEVENS (ed. 1778): *"Will there ever be an end of your ex-
cuses? As often as you want to leave me, will not some Fulvia, some new pretext be
found for your departure?"* She [Cleopatra] has already said that though age could not
exempt her from some follies, at least it frees her from a childish belief in all he says."
RITSON (1783, p. 147): "Is it possible that Fulvia should dye? I will not believe it." MA-
LONE (ed. 1790): "Though age has not exempted me from folly, I am not so childish,
as to have apprehensions from a rival that is no more. And is Fulvia dead indeed?" JACK-
SON (1819, p. 286) alone: "A high compliment [is] paid to Antony. The artful Queen
would impress on his mind, that one who had a legal claim to his love should have been
more than mortal."
    373 **Garboyles**] CAWDREY (1604): "Hurlie burly." See also 758.
    at . . . best] STEEVENS (ed. 1793) compares "Malcolm's elogium on the thane
of Cawdor: '—nothing in his life Became him, like the leaving it' [*Mac.* 1.4.7–8 (287–8)]."
BOSWELL (ed. 1821): "Her death was the best thing I have known of her, as it checked
her *garboils*." STAUNTON (ed. 1859): "The word *best* . . . is no more than an epithet

Cleo. O most false Loue!	375
Where be the Sacred Violles thou should'st fill
With sorrowfull water? Now I see, I see,
In *Fuluias* death, how mine receiu'd shall be.
	Ant. Quarrell no more, but bee prepar'd to know
The purposes I beare: which are, or cease,	380
As you shall giue th'aduice. By the fire
That quickens Nylus slime, I go from hence
Thy Souldier, Seruant, making Peace or Warre,
As thou affects.

---

377 Now] *Om.* SING1
378 receiu'd shall be] shall be receiv'd ROWE1-v1773
381 th'aduice] th' advices POPE1-v1773
	By] Now, by v1793, v1803
382 slime] Smile ROWE2, ROWE3
383 Souldier, Seruant] soldier-servant DEL2 *conj.*, STAU, COL4

---

of endearment which Antony applies to Cleopatra . . . *my best one.*" Most modern
editors, however, agree with CASE (ed. 1906), who essentially follows DELIUS (ed. 1856):
"Her attention is last directed — possibly also the last part of a letter — [to the] convincing
intelligence of Fulvia's death."

376 **Violles**] WARBURTON (*apud* THEOBALD, ed. 1733): Sh. "plainly hints here at
the *Lacrymatories* in use amongst the *Greeks* and *Romans.*" THEOBALD finds the same
allusion in *TNK* 1.5.3–6. JOHNSON (ed. 1765) elaborates: "Alluding to the lachrymatory
vials, or bottles of tears, which the *Romans* sometimes put into the urn of a friend."
DELIUS (ed. 1856) alone: Perhaps Antony's eyes.

377 **sorrowfull**] See n. 2543.

381–2 **By . . . slime**] FRIPP (1930, pp. 121–2) detects parallels with *Metamorphoses*
1: "Nilus, which overflows its banks and from its fresh slime quickened by the Sun (*re-
cens exarsit sidere limus* [424]) is born the poisonous serpent (*serpens* [439], *veneno* [444]),
Python." He finds them also in 552, 1361, 1363–4, 1387, 3267–8, 3495. THOMSON (1952,
p. 148) suggests *F.Q.* 1.1.21–4 as a source, although "the 'fire' has a better parallel in
a line of Ovid [qtd. above]." LLOYD (1959, p. 94): "There may be some hint of identification with Osiris when Antony protests his love [thus]."

382 **quickens**] See n. 3047.

Nylus slime] COOPER (1565): "And also Nilus was famous for the vertue of the
water thereof, whiche ouerflowynge the countrey of Aegypte, made the grounde woon-
derfull fertyle many yeres after, so that without labourynge, the earth brought foorth
abundaunce of sundry graynes and plantes, delectable and profitable." See 126–7.

383 BLAKE (1983, pp. 61–2): "The qualifier which follows *Seruant* suggests that Antony will serve Cleopatra in the wars he makes and that consequently there is a much
closer connection between the two words *Souldier* and *Seruant*. This could be achieved
by repunctuating . . . as *Thy Souldier Seruant* or even as *Thy Souldier-Seruant*. The

Cleo. Cut my Lace, *Charmian* come,   385
But let it be, I am quickly ill, and well,
So *Anthony* loues.
   Ant. My precious Queene forbeare,
And giue true euidence to his Loue, which stands
An honourable Triall.   390
   Cleo. So *Fuluia* told me.
I prythee turne aside, and weepe for her,
Then bid adiew to me, and say the teares
Belong to Egypt. Good now, play one Scene

---

389 euidence] credence mCOL1, COL2, COL3, WH1, COL4
392 her] me RIDa

---

absence of a comma after *Souldier* would also allow the two halves of the line to balance each other rhythmically." Compares "Lawrell victory" (421), where a hyphen is not normally added by "modern editors," with "Marble constant" (3490) and "Master leauer" (2719), where it is, the question being whether a "head of a nominal group" or a modifier is intended. See textual notes.

384 **thou affects**] CAWDREY (1604, affect): "To desire earnestly." See also n. 538 ("Affections"). The old *-s* for *-st* inflection after *thou* is usually for ease of pronunciation; see FRANZ §152 and n. 502.

385 **Cut my Lace**] DEIGHTON (ed. 1891): "*I.e.* of her stays, so as to allow her to breathe more freely. . . . Of course an anachronism." CASE (ed. 1906): "The first thought, under emotion, real or pretended, of the coarser female character in old plays." Be that as it may, in Sh. the phrase is also used by Queen Elizabeth (*R3* 4.1.34 [2512]) and Paulina (*WT* 3.2.174 [1359]).

386-7 **I . . . loues**] WARBURTON (ed. 1747): "It should be pointed thus, '*I'm quickly ill and well: So* Antony *loves*'. So, i.e. thus fantastically and capriciously." CAPELL (1779 [1774], 1:29): "Such is Antony's love; fluctuating, and subject to sudden turns, like my health." MALONE (*apud* STEEVENS [1783]) suggests, "'My fears quickly render me ill; and I am as quickly well again, when I am convinced that Antony has an affection for me'. So, for *so that*. If this be the true sense of the passage, it ought to be regulated thus: I am quickly ill, — and well again, So Antony loves." He prefers Steevens's interpretation, however. ABBOTT (§363) holds *So* to be almost the equivalent of *since*.

389 **which**] DELIUS (ed. 1856) says that the grammatical reference is either to Antony (equivalent to *who*) or to "*the love of him*." For the interchangeability of *who* and *which*, see FRANZ §335; also 2113, 2896.

394 **to Egypt**] JOHNSON (ed. 1765): "To me, the queen of *Egypt*."

394-400 **Good . . . mends**] HAWKES (1973, p. 185) alone: "The physical gestures which must accompany this interchange suggest themselves."

394 **Good now**] HUDSON (ed. 1881): "*Well now*." CASE (ed. 1906): "''Please you', as in *Hamlet*, I.i.70 [86]." KITTREDGE (ed. 1941): "A vocative noun." See FRANZ §358, n. 105.

Of excellent dissembling, and let it looke   395
Like perfect Honor.
   Ant. You'l heat my blood no more?
   Cleo. You can do better yet: but this is meetly.
   Ant. Now by Sword.
   Cleo. And Target. Still he mends.   400
But this is not the best. Looke prythee *Charmian*,
How this Herculean Roman do's become

---

395 and] *Om.* POPE, HAN1
397 blood‸ no more?] ~ ; ~~ . ROWE1+
399 by] by my F2+

---

398 **meetly**] Suggested meanings range from "*pretty well*" (WORDSWORTH [ed. 1883]) through "reasonably well" (RIDLEY [ed. 1954]) and "well" (IRVING & MARSHALL [ed. 1889]) to "very well" (CASE [ed. 1906]). The first dictionary gloss of the adverb is COLES (1676): "Handsomely, modestly." SKEAT (1914): "Moderately," quoting "Metely good" in Sir Thomas Elyot's *The boke named the Gouernour* (1531, fol. 214ᵛ). The consensus might be "suitably."

399–400 **Sword . . . Target**] MINSHEU (1617) equates *Target* with *Shield* or *Buckler*, specifying "*a* Target *like an halfe-moone*." KERSEY (1702) defines target as "*a kind of great shield*," SKEAT (1914) as "a light round buckler," quoting among others Plutarch's *Life of Julius Caesar*, where, incidentally, Pompey the Great is reported to have pledged his support to Caesar, adding "that he would come with his sword and target both, against them that would withstand him [Caesar] with their swords [tr. North, 1579, p. 769]." Swearing by the sword was, of course, a soldier's most solemn oath. WILSON (ed. 1950), nevertheless: "*And target* . . . makes it a swashbuckler's oath," since (in his note [ed. 1946] to *1H4* 1.3.230 [558]) "sword and buckler were the weapons of the highwayman . . . or serving-man." See also 2685, n. 1223 ("Targes").

400 **Still . . . mends**] DEIGHTON (ed. 1891) paraphrases, "She says banteringly, he is improving, is he not?" For *mend* meaning "to grow better in quality, improve," see *OED*, 10b; for *still* see n. 73.

401–20 **Looke . . . you**] WILLIAMSON (1974, p. 240): "Daniel's Nuntius seems almost to describe Shakespeare's scene, even to verbal echoes." She compares (pp. 239–41) ll. 952–7 and 1559–67 of *Cleopatra* (1599). For the 1594 *Cleopatra*, see pp. 559, 574.

402–3 Most commentators follow the sense of RANN (ed. 1791–): "How these passionate sallies become him." But they detect as well a sense of premeditation, starting with SEYMOUR (1805, 2:41)—"adapts his deportment to the expression of his anger"—and developing in HUDSON (ed. 1881)—"Cleopatra here assumes that Antony is but playing a part; that his passion is put on for effect. . . . 'Look how well he *carries out* the semblance or make-belief of *being chafed* at my words.'"

402 **Herculean**] UPTON (1746, p. 196): "There was a tradition that the Antonies were descended from Hercules, by a son of his called Anteon." IDEM (1748, p. 188, n. 8):

The carriage of his chafe.

  Ant. Ile leaue you Lady.

  Cleo. Courteous Lord, one word: 405
Sir, you and I must part, but that's not it:
Sir, you and I haue lou'd, but there's not it:
That you know well, something it is I would:
Oh, my Obliuion is a very *Anthony*,
And I am all forgotten.   410

  Ant. But that your Royalty

403–5 F1-RANN; *arranged as verse lines, thus*: 403–4, 405 v1793, v1803, SING, KNT1, KTLY; 403, 404–5 v1821 *etc.*
  403 chafe] chief STAU
  407–8 ₐbut . . . well,ₐ] (∼ . . . ∼ ;) THEO1+ (−RID, ARD2)

"Antony was so fond of this imaginary descent that he had a lion struck on his coin, in allusion to the Nemean lion of Hercules." DELIUS (ed. 1856): Sh. was thinking of Plutarch's description of Antony: *"But besides all this, he had a noble presence and showed a countenance of one of a noble house; he had a goodly thick beard, a broad forehead, crooked-nosed, and there appeared such a manly look in his countenance, as is commonly seen in Hercules' pictures, stamped or graven in metal* [see p. 399]." BLUMHOF (ed. 1870) detects in the adjective both the noble ancestry and the blind wrath; WALTER (ed. 1969), "a glance . . . at the popular stage figure who raged in 'Ercles' vein.'"
  403 **carriage**] BLUMHOF (ed. 1870): "Deportment" and "burden."
      chafe] MINSHEU (1617): *"Fret, or fume."* STAUNTON (ed. 1859) alone: "A silly blunder . . . for 'chief', meaning Hercules, the *head* or *principal* of the house of the Antonii."
  404 WILSON (ed. 1950): "I infer 'bows' (S.D.) from the ironical 'Courteous lord' [405]."
  407 **there's**] SCHMIDT (1875, 3) glosses "that['s]."
  409–10 All commentators who follow F1 agree on the identification of "Obliuion" (defined by BULLOKAR [1616] as "Forgetfulnesse") with Antony. They have differing emphases for "all forgotten," mainly expansions of either "apt to forget every thing" (HANMER [ed. 1744]) or *"makes me forget my self"* (WARBURTON [ed. 1747]). DOUCE (1807, 2:86) and more recent commentators straddle the possibilities: "She compares her memory to Antony, and says she is treacherously abandoned and neglected by *both*." ZIELINSKI (1905, pp. 18–19): "Her 'Obliuion' was indeed 'a very Antony', if only a very small one." That is, as her following image (414–16) indicates—and her pointing gesture at "this" (416) emphasizes—Cleopatra is pregnant. MACCALLUM (1910, pp. 655–6), taking this idea seriously, refutes it at length. He paraphrases, "My forgetfulness is as great as Antony's own." Of the conjecture "O my!" STEEVENS (ed. 1793) wonders whether the oath, short for "O my God," "could . . . have been uttered by the Pagan Cleopatra." See conj., p. 348.
  409 **very**] See n. 749.
  411–13 WARBURTON (ed. 1747): *"But that your charms hold me, who am the* greatest *fool on earth in chains, I should have adjudged you to be the* greatest." STEEVENS (ed.

Holds Idlenesse your subiect, I should take you
For Idlenesse it selfe.
    Cleo. 'Tis sweating Labour,
To beare such Idlenesse so neere the heart   415
As *Cleopatra* this. But Sir, forgiue me,
Since my becommings kill me, when they do not   (xx2^b)
Eye well to you. Your Honor calles you hence,
Therefore be deafe to my vnpittied Folly,
And all the Gods go with you. Vpon your Sword   420
Sit Lawrell victory, and smooth successe
Be strew'd before your feete.
    Ant. Let vs go.
Come: Our separation so abides and flies,

---

420 Vpon] On POPE1-JOHN1
421 Lawrell] Lawrell'd F2-v1778, RANN-v1803, SING, COL, HUD, WH, NLSN
422–4 *Verse lines ending* come, . . . flies, POPE1-ARD2, EVNS; *ending* go. . . . flies, YAL2

1778): *"But that your queenship chuses idleness for the subject of your conversation, I should take you for idleness itself. . . . Or* [the view of most commentators] an antithesis may be designed between *royalty* and *subject.—But that I know you to be a queen, and that your royalty holds idleness in subjection to you, exalting you far above its influence, I should suppose you to be the very genius of idleness itself."*

    412 **Idlenesse**] KITTREDGE (ed. 1941) sums up the meaning of most commentators: "'Foolishness' in thought, language, or conduct." See also n. 227.

    415 **Idlenesse**] KITTREDGE (ed. 1941): "Emphatic: 'what you call absurdity or nonsense'. Cleopatra means that Antony has applied this term to her passion of love and grief."

    417 **becommings**] Most commentators, starting with STEEVENS (ed. 1778), define as "graces," "becoming qualities," or the like (*OED*, 1, cites this instance) and compare "Whom euery thing becomes" (62). JOHNSON (1755), however, defines as "Behaviour," also citing this instance.

    418 **Eye**] ABBOTT (§293): = "Appear," a transitive verb "rarely used intransitively."

    421 **Sit**] The optative subjunctive, with *may* understood. See FRANZ §647.

    Lawrell victory] COLLIER (ed. 1843): "In all probability the letter *d* [Lawrell'd] had dropped out in the press." But for the common use of the substantive as adjective, see FRANZ §367 and n. 383.

    successe] COTGRAVE (1611, Evenement): *"An euent . . . end, issue of a matter."* See also 1022, 1731, 3324.

    422 **strew'd**] KITTREDGE (ed. 1941): "Like flowers or laurel branches in the path of a triumphant general." See "Sweepe . . . way" (2041).

    424 **Our separation . . . flies**] CASE (ed. 1906), comparing *Mucedorus* (*Old English Plays*, ed. Hazlitt, 1874, 7:206 [1.1.12–13]) and Donne's "A Valediction: Forbidding Mourning," summarizes the interpretation of most editors: "Their separation is said to *abide*

That thou reciding heere, goes yet with mee;   425
And I hence fleeting, heere remaine with thee.
Away.   *Exeunt.*

        Enter Octauius reading a Letter, Lepidus,   **1.4**
               and their Traine.

Cæs. You may see *Lepidus,* and henceforth know,   430
It is not *Cæsars* Naturall vice, to hate
One great Competitor. From Alexandria
This is the newes: He fishes, drinkes, and wastes
The Lampes of night in reuell: Is not more manlike
Then *Cleopatra*: nor the Queene of *Ptolomy*   435

---

  428 SCENE II. ROWE; SCENE V. POPE, HAN1, WARB, JOHN1; SCENE IV. CAP+
      Rome. ROWE, POPE; SCENE *changes to* Cæsar*'s Palace in* Rome. THEO1+ *(subst.)*
  431 vice] voice F4-POPE2; wise DEL2
  432 One] A HAN1; Our mTBY2 *and* mF2FL21 *conj.,* SING1, COL2+
  434 reuell] revells F2-POPE2, HAN1
      Is] *Om.* POPE, HAN1
      manlike] Manlie ROWE2-v1773 (−CAP)
  435 of] *Om.* v1803, v1821

---

as resulting from Cleopatra's *abode* in Egypt, and to *fly,* as resulting from Antony's fleeting
thence." STEEVENS (ed. 1793) compares Sidney's *Arcadia* (*Poems,* ed. Ringler, 1962, "Other
Poems," [no.] 4, ll. 169–70). A few editors, beginning with DELIUS (ed. 1856), interpret
as "we remain united though separated."

    425 **goes**] See n. 502.

    431 **vice**] KITTREDGE (ed. 1941): "Fault—in a general sense, not limited as in mod-
ern usage." DELIUS's (ed. 1856) emendation *wise,* probably because *vice* in Sh. is normally preceded by derogatory adjectives or juxtaposed to *virtue,* is ingenious but
unnecessary, even if *OED* also records *vice* as obsolete for *wise.*

    432 **One great Competitor**] SEYMOUR (1805, 2:42): "Octavius observes a stately re-
serve, speaking of Anthony. 'One great competitor' appears . . . equivalent to . . .
a certain personage, our partner; but it may only mean, one of the great Triumviri." The
latter idea is followed only by BOSWELL (ed. 1821)—"*One* competitor is *any one* of his
great competitors"—DELIUS (ed. 1856), and BLUMHOF (ed. 1870). MASON (1785, p. 273):
"*Competitor* means . . . *associate,* or *partner.*" See also 3159, n. 1415, textual notes,
and conj., p. 348.

    435 **Queene of *Ptolomy***] WILSON (ed. 1950): "Actually she married her brother Ptolemy
XIII at J. Caes.'s command, and is said to have poisoned him later. Plut[arch, *Life of
Julius Caesar,* tr. North, 1579, p. 786] only says that J. Caes. 'did reconcile her again
unto her brother the King' and that he disappeared in a battle with Caes. shortly after

More Womanly then he. Hardly gaue audience   436
Or vouchsafe to thinke he had Partners. You
Shall finde there a man, who is th'abstracts of all faults,

436–41 *Five verse lines ending* audience, . . . partners. . . . abstract . . . not think
. . . goodness; POPE1-THEO4; *six verse lines ending* he. . . . to think . . . man, . . .
follow. . . . not think, . . . goodness; JOHN1; *five verse lines ending* or . . . there
. . . faults . . . are . . . goodness: CAP, v1778-SING1, COL1-COL3, WH1-ARD2, EVNS;
six verse lines ending he. . . . or . . . there . . . faults . . . are . . . goodness; v1773;
five verse lines ending audience, . . . there . . . faults . . . are . . . goodness: KNT1,
STAU; *five verse lines ending* audience . . . You . . . faults, . . . think . . . goodness:
YAL2

    437 Or] Or did F2-THEO4
       vouchsafe] vouchsaf'd JOHN1+
       thinke] think that POPE1-JOHN1
       he had] h' had POPE
    438 finde there] there find THEO2, WARB-JOHN1
       th'abstracts] th'abstract F2+

[North, p. 787], but mentions neither marriage nor murder." SCHANZER (1960, pp. 335–6),
responding to the questions of where Sh. learned of the marriage and to which brother
Cleopatra was married, suggests the source to be "almost certainly 'The Legend of Cleopatra'
in Chaucer's *Legend of Good Women*": the opening three lines for the fact of the marriage, and Chaucer's reliance on Vincent of Beauvais's *Speculum historiale* for the information about the husband. "But the Ptolemy mentioned by Vincent is Cleopatra's father,
Ptolemy Auletes. It seems probable that Chaucer, misled by the ambiguity of Vincent's
words, took him to be her deceased husband. . . . Editors [are not] justified in explaining Shakespeare's allusions to Ptolemy as referring either to the older or to the younger
of Cleopatra's brothers, for it is unlikely that he knew much more about the matter than
what he found in Chaucer's lines: that Cleopatra was a widow and that her deceased
husband was called Ptolemy." See also 446–7 and n. 660. For the accenting of the name,
see n. 29 ("*Anthony*").

    436 **Hardly**] FRANZ (§440): This adverbial form of *hard* ("in a hard manner") per-
sisted into the 18th c. North (p. 441) uses the word in much the same sense. See also 3196.

    437 **vouchsafe**] Because of the apparent inflectional lapse, editors have either added
did or substituted *vouchsaf'd*. WALKER (1860, 2:61–2): An "error in the folio: arising in
some instances, perhaps, from the juxtaposition of *d* and *e* in the compositor's case; but
far oftener . . . from something in the old method of writing the final *e* or *d*." His
editor, LETTSOM (*apud* IDEM, 2:62, n. 40): "The *e*, with the last upstroke prolonged and
terminated with a loop, might easily be taken for a *d*." Other examples Walker gives
(2:61–8, 3:299) are at 580, 987, 1039, 3156. FURNESS (ed. 1907) rejects Walker's explanation here: "The dental *d* in 'vouchsafed' was lost in the dental *t* of 'to.'" The linguistic
phenomenon is common. See p. 373.

    438 **there**] WORDSWORTH (ed. 1883): "I.e., *in what the letter tells*."

    th'abstracts] The erroneous plural, immediately corrected by F2, may have been
induced by the plural *faults*. For the misprinting of final *s*, see ABBOTT §338.

That all men follow.

Lep. I must not thinke   440
There are, euils enow to darken all his goodnesse:
His faults in him, seeme as the Spots of Heauen,
More fierie by nights Blacknesse; Hereditarie,
Rather then purchaste: what he cannot change,
Then what he chooses.   445

Cæs. You are too indulgent. Let's graunt it is not
Amisse to tumble on the bed of *Ptolomy,*

---

439 That] *Om.* POPE1-THEO4
441 There are] They're POPE1-JOHN1
    enow] enough ROWE1-SING1, HUD, SING2
442–3 Heauen, More fierie] ermine, Or fires HAN1
446–7 *Verse lines ending* amiss . . . Ptolemy; STAU
446 Let's] Let us POPE1-SING1, COL1-HUD1, DYCE1-OXF1, RID, KIT1
    not] *Om.* F2-ROWE3

---

439 **all men follow**] FURNESS (ed. 1907) alone: "'All men' is here the object, not the subject of 'follow.'" He may have been influenced by BLUMHOF (ed. 1870), who points out that "That" may modify "men" or "faults" (438).

441 **enow**] This plural form existed side by side with the more common *enough*. See FRANZ §358.

442–3 **Spots . . . Blacknesse**] JOHNSON (ed. 1765): "The comparison is forced and harsh, stars having been always supposed to beautify the night; nor do I comprehend what there is in the counter-part of this simile, which answers to night's blackness." MALONE (*apud* STEEVENS, ed. 1778): Sh. considers the stars "only with respect to their *prominence and splendour.* It is sufficient for him that their scintillations appear stronger in consequence of darkness." Much the same interpretation had been offered by KYNASTON (*St. James's Chr.*, no. 733 [14–16 Nov. 1765]) in a reply to Johnson and, in a plagiarism of Kynaston, by Q. in the same journal (no. 2281 [26–28 Sept. 1775]). CASE (ed. 1906): "The simile aims only at force of contrast, disregarding correspondence of quality in the things compared, *faults* and *stars*, *goodness* and *blackness.*" DANBY (1952, p. 147): "Here the ambiguities of the play's moral universe get their completest expression: faults shine like stars, the heaven is black, the stars are spots. Ambivalence need go no further." WATERHOUSE (1974, no. 17) sees the "confused image" as "consistent with Lepidus' dullness," although his "cosmic terms" give Antony "that transcendental quality which also surrounds Cleopatra." See conj., p. 348.

444 **purchaste**] JOHNSON (ed. 1765): "Procured by his own fault or endeavour." J. CAMPBELL (1859, pp. 117–18) remarks on "a Roman being made to talk like an English lawyer. . . . Lawyers consider that 'purchase' is opposed to *descent* . . . and that whatever does not come through operation of law by *descent* is *purchased.*" HUDSON (ed. 1881): May "imply the sense of being acquired *wrongfully* or by *evil ways.*"

445 **Then**] I.e., rather than.

446–7 **Let's . . . *Ptolomy***] See n. 435.

51

To giue a Kingdome for a Mirth, to sit
And keepe the turne of Tipling with a Slaue,
To reele the streets at noone, and stand the Buffet   450
With knaues that smels of sweate: Say this becoms him
(As his composure must be rare indeed,
Whom these things cannot blemish) yet must *Anthony*
No way excuse his foyles, when we do beare

---

451 smels] smell F2-SIS (–KTLY, ARD1)
454 foyles] soils MALONE (1783) *conj.*, MAL, v1793-KNT1, DYCE1-RID (–COL3, KTLY, COL4); foibles COL3 *conj.*, BLUM

---

449 **keepe . . . Tipling**] DEIGHTON (ed. 1891): "Go shares in drinking." RIDLEY (ed. 1935, Glossary): "Drink for drink." TOBIN (1979, p. 226, n. 5): "'Tippling' is unique in the canon." He suggests it came from Adlington's tr. of *The Golden Ass of Apuleius*, 1566 (Tudor Translations, ed. Henley, 1893, p. 123), but the word was common. JOHNSON (1755) cites this instance in defining *Tipple*: "To drink luxuriously; to waste life over the cup."

    Slaue] In Sh. a general term of opprobrium not usually to be understood literally.

450 **reele**] The *OED* gives a separate listing (*v.*[1] 9) for this one usage, supplying without explanation the missing "through" or "along." There is perhaps an analogy to a phrase like "walk the streets." In Sh. see *TN* 3.3.25 (1493), *H5* 2.2.122 (751), and ("passe the streets") *JC* 1.1.47 (49). ABBOTT (§198): "Prepositions are frequently omitted after verbs of motion," more specifically, "Motion *in*." See also FRANZ §630a. SCHMIDT (1875, Wing, *v.* 1) says the verb is used "with an accus[ative] of space." See n. 1443.

451 **knaues**] See n. 2839.

    smels] FRANZ (§679) does not find it absolutely necessary to connect the *s* plural with the Northern form, since an analogous development was to be found in the South. The construction is controversial, some believing the form to be the singular. See BARBER (1976, pp. 242–4). The compositor seems to have dropped the *l* (and the *e* before *s* in "becoms") because the line was too crowded. See also 484 and p. 361.

452 **composure**] KERSEY (1702) is the first dictionary to list this word, but the first to define it—"any thing composed" (i.e., composition)—is BAILEY (1721). For the *-ure* suffix see FRANZ §118. See also nn. 698, 1248.

    rare] See n. 3387.

454 **foyles**] Citing *WT* 2.3.170–2 (1102–4), STEEVENS (ed. 1793) conjectures *fails*, but prefers MALONE's (*apud* STEEVENS [1783]) *soils*. MALONE (*apud* IDEM) also suggests *follies*. COLLIER (ed. 1843) retains *foils* as referring to vices "which *foil* or defeat" virtues—see MINSHEU (1617) and *OED* (*sb.*[2] 2: "a repulse")—but admits "that 'foils' for *soils* would be a very easy misprint, the long *s* and the *f* being frequently mistaken." The possible confusion of the letters was previously noted by MALONE (ed. 1790), but there is no pressing need to emend. To Minsheu's (or *OED*'s) definition may be added SCHMIDT's (1874) gloss "blemish" (echoing the verb on 453—see *OED* [*v.*[1] 6]: "To foul, defile, pollute") and, less likely, a further suggestion mentioned in and rejected by RIDLEY (ed. 1954), that they are faults that "set off" virtues. See textual notes and conj., p. 348.

454–5 **we . . . lightnesse**] JOHNSON (ed. 1765): "His trifling levity throws so much

So great waight in his lightnesse. If he fill'd   455
His vacancie with his Voluptuousnesse,
Full surfets, and the drinesse of his bones,
Call on him for't. But to confound such time,
That drummes him from his sport, and speakes as lowd
As his owne State, and ours, 'tis to be chid: 460

---

455 great] great a OXF1
458 Call] Fall mCOL1, COL2, SING2, COL3, KTLY, COL4
460 'tis] They're CROSBY (1877, p. 465; *withdrawn* 1883–4, p. 46) *conj.*, HUD2

---

burden upon us."
   456 **vacancie**] CAWDREY (1604, vacant): "Voyde, or emptie." MINSHEU (1617) adds, "*At leisure, without vse*," which most commentators accept.
   457 **Full**] See n. 74.
   surfets] MINSHEU (1617): "*To eat and drinke more then one can make good concoction* [digestion]." See *OED, sb.* 5.
   drinesse of his bones] BARTHOLOMAEUS (1582, fol. 114^r) mentions dryness as one of the indications of "*Morbus Galicus . . .* the French Poxe." DELIUS (ed. 1856): Drying out of the marrow. WHITAKER (1972, pp. 62–3): "An excess of blood (hot and moist) would produce a dearth of its opposite, black bile (cold and moist), the humor of the melancholy man. Since melancholy functions as 'a bridle to the other two hot humours, *blood* and *choler*, preserving them in the blood, and nourishing the bones' [Burton, *Anatomy of Melancholy*, ed. Dell & Jordan-Smith, 1927, p. 129], the dearth of melancholy would naturally result in 'dryness of bones.'"
   458 **Call . . . for't**] Early commentators follow JOHNSON (ed. 1765): "*Visit him*"; later ones, HUDSON (ed. 1855): "Demand payment of him for it."
   confound] See n. 57.
   459 **drummes**] Commentators agree with DELIUS (ed. 1856) that the reference is to martial drums, except for DEIGHTON (ed. 1891): "Loudly warns."
   460 **his owne State**] KITTREDGE (ed. 1941) summarizes the position of the few who comment: "His own greatness . . . his own position as Triumvir."
   460–3 **'tis . . . iudgement**] JOHNSON (ed. 1765): "For this *Hanmer* [ed. 1744], who thought the *maturity* of a *boy* an inconsistent idea, has put . . . immature . . . but the words *experience* and *judgment* require that we read mature. . . . By *boys mature in knowledge*, are meant, *boys old enough to know their duty*." HEATH (1765, pp. 450–1), apparently independently, makes substantially the same interpretation. DANIEL (1870, p. 80) thinks that Antony "is to be chidden as a boy" and emends "'tis" and "their" to *he's* and *his*, the verbs to the third person singular. CROSBY (1877, p. 464) objects that this emendation "makes no less than five changes of the original text" and proposes (p. 465) "'They're' for ''Tis'—placing the parenthetical clause between dashes. . . . [Thus] it will be seen . . . that 'who' has for its antecedent 'they' of the previous line, viz., persons generally who do so-and-so, and does not in any way refer to 'boys.'" Despite the adoption of this emendation by HUDSON (ed. 1881), CROSBY (1883–4, p. 46) feels that if "As . . . Boyes" is made parenthetical, there is no need, after all, to substitute *They're* for "'tis." See textual notes and conj., p. 348.

As we rate Boyes, who being mature in knowledge,
Pawne their experience to their present pleasure,
And so rebell to iudgement.

Enter a Messenger.

Lep. Heere's more newes.   465
Mes. Thy biddings haue beene done, & euerie houre
Most Noble *Cæsar,* shalt thou haue report
How 'tis abroad. *Pompey* is strong at Sea,
And it appeares, he is belou'd of those
That only haue feard *Cæsar*: to the Ports   470
The discontents repaire, and mens reports
Giue him much wrong'd.
Cæs. I should haue knowne no lesse,
It hath bin taught vs from the primall state
That he which is was wisht, vntill he were: 475

---

461 rate] rare F4
    being mature] immature HAN1, WARB; being immature KTLY
470 Ports] fleets mCOL1, COL2, COL4, CAM3b; coasts WORD1

---

461 **rate**] MINSHEU (1617): *"Rebuke."* RIDLEY (ed. 1954): "J. C. Maxwell makes the
interesting suggestion that [the word] here means 'estimate'—i.e. 'In the same way that
we count as mere boys those men who, being. . . .'" The homograph is recorded in
Minsheu.
    462 **experience**] WORDSWORTH (ed. 1883): *"Future ex."*
    present pleasure] See n. 221.
    470 **Ports**] COLLIER (1852, pp. 466–7) alone would read *"Fleets* for 'ports'; and it seems
likely that the compositor blundered in consequence of the word 'report' being found
two lines above, and 'reports' just below." IDEM (ed. 1878): *"Fleets* . . . can hardly be
wrong." WILSON (ed. 1964) reads *fleets* but glosses *"ports."*
    471 **discontents**] For the nominalization of adjectives, especially of Romance etymol-
ogy, see FRANZ §359.
    472 **Giue**] WORDSWORTH (ed. 1883): *"Represent."*
    474–8 **It . . . lack'd**] The sentiment is common. CAPELL (1779 [1774], 1:30) regards
it as a maxim. See Antony's response to the news of the death of Fulvia (220–4). WALTER
(ed. 1969), regarding 473–81 as "more self-communing than conversation," suggests "Cæsar
may move aside."
    474 **primall state**] WARBURTON (*apud* THEOBALD, ed. 1733) and most others: "The
earliest Histories." WORDSWORTH (ed. 1883) detects a "reference here to the meaning
of Cain's name, 'a man gotten from the Lord', at his mother's wish." RIDLEY's (ed. 1935,
Glossary) "creation" is perhaps anticipated by DEIGHTON's (ed. 1891) "at the beginning
of the world."
    475 **vntill . . . were**] ABBOTT (§302): *"Were* is used . . . remarkably, after 'until',
referring to the past."

54

And the ebb'd man,
Ne're lou'd, till ne're worth loue,
Comes fear'd, by being lack'd. This common bodie,
Like to a Vagabond Flagge vpon the Streame,
Goes too, and backe, lacking the varrying tyde   480

476–7 *One verse line* ROWE1+
477 ne're] not MALONE (1783) *conj.*, RANN, HUD2
478 fear'd] dear'd WARBURTON *conj. apud* THEO1, THEO1-SING1, HUD1-DYCE1, STAU-GLO, HAL+ (−SIS); lov'd mCOL1, COL2, COL3; dear KTLY
     This] The HAN1
479 to] *Om.* RANN, v1803-SING1, HUD1
480 lacking] lashing mPOPE *conj.*, POPE; lackying THEOBALD (1726, p. 183) *conj.*, THEO1+

---

477 **ne're**] MALONE (*apud* STEEVENS [1783]) substitutes *not*, having "no doubt that [this] second *ne'er* was inadvertently repeated at the press." SEYMOUR (1805, 2:44–5) disagrees: It "was not . . . any error of the press . . . but only another instance of that resolute disposition [of Sh.] to jingle and chime with words." See textual notes and conj., p. 349. Emphatic *never* for *not* is common in Sh. See FRANZ §407.

478 **fear'd**] WARBURTON (*apud* THEOBALD, ed. 1733) explains his emendation *dear'd* (i.e., *endear'd*): "It was not Fear, but Love, that made the People flock to Young *Pompey*." BLUMHOF (ed. 1870) is the first to suggest that *fear* might also signify "awe, reverence" (*OED*, *v.* 6). See textual notes and conj., p. 349.

479 **Vagabond**] CAWDREY (1604): "Runnagate, one that will stay no where." WILSON (ed. 1950) suggests "At once shifty and rascally," PHIALAS (ed. 1955) "Shifty."

     Flagge] GERARDE (1597, pp. 45–6) describes the genus *Iris palustris lutes*, the (p. 45) "water Flower de-luce or water flag." It seems more likely, however, that only a rush (THEOBALD, 1726, p. 183) or common reed (which Gerarde, p. 32, describes as having "flaggie" leaves) is intended. See *OED*, *sb.*[1] 1.

480 **lacking**] THEOBALD (1726, pp. 183–4) rejects *lashing*: "How can a Flag, or Rush, floating upon a Stream . . . be said to *lash* the Tide?" He finds "no Sense" in *lacking* but "Correct [is] . . . *lackying* . . . *i.e.* floating backwards and forwards with the Variation of the Tide, like a Page, or *Lackey* at his Master's Heels." STEEVENS (ed. 1778) supports Theobald with quotations from *Homer's Odysses* 5.130–1 and *Iliads* 24.392 (both tr. Chapman, ed. A. Nicoll, 1957). HALLIWELL (1868, p. 13): "Rather a variation of form [of *lackeying*, not recorded in *OED*] than an error. The same orthography occurs in a MS. dated 1615, quoted by [John Sidney] Hawkins, in his edition of [George] Ruggle's *Ignoramus*, 1787, appendix, p. [cxx]." BLUMHOF (ed. 1870) defends *lacking* as meaning "needing." SISSON (1956, 2:263): "The word was certainly caught up in Shakespeare's mind from *lacked* [lack'd] in l. [478]. There is no graphic implausibility. The spelling *lackijng* could well yield *lacking* to the compositor, or, as Miss Husbands suggests privately, *lackying* could well yield *lackyng* (printed *lacking*), a mere minim error." For detail on these orthographic possibilities, see HULME (1962, pp. 318–19). The frequently cited "fat weed" image in *Ham.* 1.5.32–3 (719–20) may be misleading, because there would seem to be no tide on "*Lethe* wharffe," and the weed there, as SEYMOUR (1805, 2:45–6) holds, "was *stagnantly* rotting." See textual notes and conj., p. 349.

To rot it selfe with motion.   (xx2ᵛ

   Mes. Cæsar I bring thee word,
Menacrates and *Menas* famous Pyrates
Makes the Sea serue them, which they eare and wound
With keeles of euery kinde. Many hot inrodes   485
They make in Italy, the Borders Maritime
Lacke blood to thinke on't, and flush youth reuolt,
No Vessell can peepe forth: but 'tis as soone
Taken as seene: for *Pompeyes* name strikes more
Then could his Warre resisted.   490

   Cæsar. Anthony,
Leaue thy lasciuious Vassailes. When thou once

481–2 *One verse line* v1793+
481 *Enter another Messenger.* CAP, RANN, ARD2
484 Makes] Make F4-SIS (–KTLY, NLSN, ARD1)
485 keeles] kneels F3; knells F4
487 flush youth] flesh youth F2; flesh youth to F3-ROWE3; flush'd youth THEO3, THEO4
492 Vassailes] Vassals F4-ROWE3, KNT1; wassails POPE1-SING1, COL1+

---

483 *Menacrates* and *Menas*] LEVIN (1976, p. 54) rejects Knight's idea (*The Sovereign Flower*, 1958, p. 192) "that the pirates Menas and Menecrates are threatening figures because they have minatory names."

484 **Makes**] See n. 451 ("smels").

   eare] See n. 201.

485 **hot**] DEIGHTON (ed. 1891): "Furious." *OED* (7) adds: "Chiefly of conflict or the like."

486 **Borders Maritime**] The few who comment agree with DELIUS (ed. 1856) that perhaps *bord'rers* is meant (see p. 349)—"dwellers on the coast," as DEIGHTON (ed. 1891) puts it. Delius compares *H5* 1.2.142 (289): "Pilfering Borderers." For the position of the adjective after the noun, see FRANZ §685.

487 **Lacke blood**] All agree with JOHNSON (ed. 1765): "Turn pale."

   flush youth] STEEVENS (ed. 1773): "Youth ripened to manhood; *youth* whose blood is at the flow."

489–90 *Pompeyes . . .* **resisted**] The few who comment agree with DELIUS (ed. 1856) that Pompey's name is more powerful than he himself would be if opposed in battle. RIDLEY (ed. 1954): "But if we take 'resisted' as conditional, it means 'His mere name is more effective than his armed forces would be, if only you opposed them.'"

492 **Vassailes**] GREY (1754, 2:193), glossing *wassails*: "Rioters." KNIGHT (ed. 1841): "The modern reading is *wassals*. Now, in three other passages of the original [F1] . . . it is spelt *wassels* [*LLL* 5.2.318 (2243), *Ham.* 1.4.9 (613); or *Wassell* at *2H4* 1.2.179 (419), *Mac.* 1.7.64 (545)] . . . meaning . . . drunken revelry; and that could scarcely be called 'lascivious'. On the contrary, 'leave thy lascivious *vassals*' expresses Cæsar's contempt for Cleopatra and her minions, who were strictly the vassals of Antony . . . his tributaries." HUDSON (ed. 1855), although finding Knight's explanation "plausible," defends *was-*

Was beaten from *Medena*, where thou slew'st
Hirsius, and *Pansa* Consuls, at thy heele
Did Famine follow, whom thou fought'st against,   495
(Though daintily brought vp) with patience more
Then Sauages could suffer. Thou did'st drinke
The stale of Horses, and the gilded Puddle
Which Beasts would cough at. Thy pallat thē did daine
The roughest Berry, on the rudest Hedge.   500
Yea, like the Stagge, when Snow the Pasture sheets,

---

493 Was] Wert F2-v1773; Wast v1778-CAM3 (−NLSN, ARD1)
     Was . . . *Medena*] From *Mutina* wert beaten HAN1
     Medena] *Mutina* ROWE1-THEO4
495 whom] which HAN1

---

sels: "It [*vassals*] strikes quite from the drift and line of all that Cæsar has been saying of Antony. Besides, it spoils the contrast which Cæsar seems to be aiming at here, between Antony as he is now, with his manhood melting away in the lap of voluptuous indulgence, and as he was at the former time referred to." The spellings of editions through ROWE (ed. 1714) are, of course, ambiguous.

493 **Was**] See n. 502.

     Medena] COOPER (1565, *Mutina*): "A citie in Italy . . . *Modona* . . . wheare was the greate battayle betweene Augustus and Brutus." JOHNSON (ed. 1765) is the first to spell *Modena*, CAPELL (1779 [1774], 1:30) the first to refer to the passage and spelling in Plutarch. See p. 407. See PAULY, Mutina, 16:939–46; *OCD*, Mutina; and map, p. xxxvii.

     494 *Hirsius,* and *Pansa*] Consuls in 43 B.C., they fought with Octavius against Antony, who, attempting to take over Cisalpine Gaul, was beleaguering Decimus Brutus in Mutina. *Cam. Anc. Hist.* (10:15): Antony was defeated and "made for [Transalpine] Gaul and Lepidus. . . . A harassing march awaited him over the Alps. . . . Hirtius had fallen in the moment of victory, Pansa was fatally stricken by his wound [suffered somewhat earlier]." See IDEM (10:13–15); PAULY, Hirtius, 8:1956–62 (2), and Vibius, 8A:1953–65 (16); *OCD*, Hirtius, Pansa.

     495 **whom**] DEIGHTON (ed. 1891): "For *who* personifying irrational antecedents, see Abb[ott] §264." Since *Famine* is capitalized, personification may well be intended.

     496 **daintily**] See Plutarch (p. 407): Antony "was brought vp in all finenes and superfluitie." MINSHEU (1617) defines as "*delicate*" and provides a false but interesting etymology: "Ex *Ital*: & *Lat*: *dente, a tooth . . . because daintie meats much please the* teeth *and palate.*" *Dainty,* of course, is derived from Latin *dignitatem* (*dignitas*).

     498 **gilded Puddle**] Sh.'s embellishment of Plutarch's simple "puddle water" (see p. 407) may have distracted commentators somewhat from the repulsiveness of *puddle* itself, "foul, muddy water"—see *OED, sb.* 3, and Puddle water, 6a. All agree the water is covered by "scum," "slime," or "film" but discuss mainly the color: "yellow," "golden," and "iridescent."

     499 **daine**] MINSHEU's (1617, Daigne) "*Vouchsafe, or thinke worthie of*" is extended by *OED* (Deign 2b), citing this instance: "To condescend or vouchsafe to accept. . . . (The opposite of *to disdain.*)"

The barkes of Trees thou brows'd. On the Alpes,
It is reported thou did'st eate strange flesh,
Which some did dye to looke on: And all this
(It wounds thine Honor that I speake it now)   505
Was borne so like a Soldiour, that thy cheeke
So much as lank'd not.
   Lep. 'Tis pitty of him.
   Cæs. Let his shames quickely
Driue him to Rome, 'tis time we twaine   510
Did shew our selues i'th'Field, and to that end
Assemble me immediate counsell, *Pompey*
Thriues in our Idlenesse.
   Lep. To morrow *Cæsar,*
I shall be furnisht to informe you rightly   515

---

502 brows'd] browsedst F2-KIT1 (−NLSN); browsed CAM3, SIS, ARD2
505 thine] thy OXF1
506 borne] bore THEO2, WARB-JOHN1, v1773
     Soldiour] Souldiers F4
507–11 F1-RANN; *four verse lines ending* not. . . . quickly . . . twain . . . end,
KNT1, ALEX; *three verse lines ending* him. . . . time . . . end, KTLY; *four verse lines
ending* him. . . . quickly . . . twain . . . end, v1793 *etc.*
507 as] as I F3, F4
507–8 lank'd . . . 'Tis] lank'd . . . It is HAN1, JOHN1, v1773-v1803, DYCE2, HUD2,
KIT1; lanked . . . 'Tis KTLY, CAM3, SIS
510 'tis time] time is it that POPE1-v1778, RANN
512 me] we F2+ (−v1778, MAL, KNT1, OXF1, CAM3a)
     immediate] immediately F3, F4

---

502 **brows'd**] Most likely a syncopated form of the preterit second person singular
brows'dst, like *look'st* at 1645. See FRANZ §152. WILSON (ed. 1950): "'Browsedst' is too
awkward for the actor." Editors' expansion to *browsed* for metrical purposes is difficult
to ascertain since it is either inconsistent or fixed by publishers' house styles. PARTRIDGE
(1964, p. 119): The many phonetically awkward *-st* endings in 491–507 made it necessary
"to soften *Wast* to *Was* and *browsedst* to *brows'd* in lines [493] and [502]. The phonetic
simplification . . . was common in the past tense, though the licence was economically
used. It is almost certain that this and the *-s* endings [see 384, 425] derive from the
author, and should be retained as legitimate phonetic or grammatical variants of the time."
   507 **lank'd**] MINSHEU (1617): "*Slender, or thinne in bodie.*" OED (*v.* 2) labels this
single instance obsolete.
   508 **pitty of him**] ABBOTT (§174): "*Of* passes easily from meaning 'as regards' to 'concerning', 'about.'"
   510 **to . . . 'tis**] ABBOTT (§484) suggests the possibility of "dissyllabizing" monosyllables "containing diphthongs and long vowels, since they naturally allow the voice to
rest upon them": i.e., "to Ró | me: 'tís." See also 1056 (*dé | ad*), 1071 (*hé | althfull*),

Both what by Sea and Land I can be able
To front this present time.
    Cæs. Til which encounter, it is my busines too. Farwell.
    Lep. Farwell my Lord, what you shal know mean time
Of stirres abroad, I shall beseech you Sir   520
To let me be partaker.
    Cæsar. Doubt not sir, I knew it for my Bond.   *Exeunt*

      Enter Cleopatra, Charmian, Iras, & Mardian.   **1.5**

    Cleo. Charmian.
    Char. Madam.   525
    Cleo. Ha, ha, giue me to drinke *Mandragora.*

---

516 Both what] With what, both KTLY
517–22 *Five verse lines ending* encounter, . . . lord, . . . abroad, . . . partaker.
. . . bond. Farewel. POPE1-JOHN1, v1773; *six verse lines ending* encounter, . . . too.
Farewel. . . . time . . . you sir . . . not sir . . . bond. mTBY4 *conj.*, CAP, v1793-KNT1,
HUD, SING2-STAU, GLO, KTLY, DYCE2, CAM1, WH2 +; *two verse lines ending* encounter,
. . . too. Farewel *then as* F1 v1778-RANN, COL1, COL2, WH1, HAL, COL4
517 front] 'front CAP-SING1, SING2, KTLY
518 Farwell.] *Om.* HAN1
520–1 Sir To] *Om.* POPE1-v1773 (−CAP)
521 partaker] partaker of KTLY
522 Doubt not sir . . . Bond] Doubt not . . . bond. Farewel POPE; Doubt it not,
Sir . . . bond. Farewel THEO1-THEO4; Doubt it not, Sir . . . bond JOHN1, v1773, v1778,
RANN
      knew] know mTBY2 *conj.*, DYCE2, COL4, HUD2, RID, ARD2
523 SCENE III. ROWE; SCENE VI. POPE, HAN1, WARB, JOHN1; *SCENE* V. CAP +
      Alexandria. ROWE1+ (*subst.*)
526–7 *Verse lines ending* Ha, ha!— . . . madam? v1793+ (−STAU)

1700 (*gŏ* | *od*), and 2655 (*mĭ* | *ne*).
    516–17 **be able To front**] RANN (ed. 1791–) regards *able* as used absolutely—i.e., "can
muster" or the like. Only DEIGHTON (ed. 1891) considers it an auxiliary to *front.*
    517 **front**] RANN (ed. 1791–): "Oppose." See *OED, v.*[1] 3; also 752.
    519–20 **shal . . . shall**] For the use of *shall* in both clauses, see FRANZ §608.
    526 **Ha, ha**] KITTREDGE (ed. 1941): "A yawn of ennui." WALTER (ed. 1969) asks whether
it might be a "melodramatic exclamation" as well.
    giue . . . *Mandragora*] DEIGHTON (ed. 1891) alone: "Not 'give me mandragora
to drink', but 'enable me, put it in my power, to drink mandragora', as in *Oth.* ii.3.209
[1329]." For F1's apparent misprint *Mandragoru*, editions from F2 to THEOBALD (ed. 1757)
substituted the Greek and Latin form *Mandragoras*, JOHNSON (ed. 1765) and the rest

Char. Why Madam?
Cleo. That I might sleepe out this great gap of time:
My *Anthony* is away.
    Char. You thinke of him too much.   530
    Cleo. O 'tis Treason.
    Char. Madam, I trust not so.
    Cleo. Thou, Eunuch *Mardian*?
    Mar. What's your Highnesse pleasure?
    Cleo. Not now to heare thee sing. I take no pleasure   535
In ought an Eunuch ha's: Tis well for thee,
That being vnseminar'd, thy freer thoughts
May not flye forth of Egypt. Hast thou Affections?
    Mar. Yes gracious Madam.
    Cleo. Indeed?   540

---

528 time:] ~ , *or* ~ ‸ ROWE1+ (–RID, SIS)
529–32 F1-JOHN1, v1773-RANN; *two verse lines ending* him . . . so. CAP, v1793, v1803,
SING, KTLY; *three verse lines ending* much. . . . treason! . . . so. WH1, HUD2; *two
verse lines ending* much. . . . so. v1821 *etc.*
531 'tis] that is HAN1; *om.* CAP, v1793, v1803
534 What's] What is HAN1
536 an] a OXF1, RIDb
537 vnseminar'd] unseminaried F2-ROWE3

---

the anglicized *Mandragora.* BARTHOLOMAEUS (1582, fol. 304ʳ): "Poets call it *An-
tropomoros*, for the root therof is some deale shapen as a man: the rinde therof medled
wᵗ Wine is giuen to them to drinke yᵗ shall be cut in the body, for they shuld sleepe
and not feele yᵉ sore cutting." PERCY (*apud* STEEVENS, ed. 1778) quotes Gerarde's *Herball* (1597, pp. 281–2) and *The Golden Asse of Apuleius* (tr. Adlington, 1639, p. 187),
RITSON (*apud* STEEVENS, ed. 1793) adds Pliny's *Natural History* (tr. Holland, 1601, 26.11)
and Plutarch's *Moralia* (tr. Holland, 1603, p. 19).

    531 O] ABBOTT (§482) indicates that this emphatic single syllable takes the place
of a whole foot.

    535 **Not . . . sing**] Probably referring to the castrato. According to GROVE, "A male
singer who has been castrated before puberty in order to preserve the soprano or con-
tralto range of his voice."

    537 **vnseminar'd**] COCKERAM (1623, *Sememare*), mistakenly omitting the *un-*: "A
gelded man." DELIUS (ed. 1856): Deprived of semen. See *OED*, Seminary *a.* and *sb.*²

    freer thoughts] SEYMOUR (1805, 2:47): "Amorous imaginations. . . . 'Free', here,
is *liberal.*"

    538 **May**] FRANZ (§604): Retains in Sh. the original meaning of "can." See also 1209–10,
1971, 2088, 2249, 3293, 3362.

    Affections] CAWDREY (1604, affect): "To desire earnestly." MINSHEU (1617): "A
motion or passion of the minde . . . . a disposition." See n. 384; also 543, 1326, *et passim.*

Mar. Not in deed Madam, for I can do nothing
But what in deede is honest to be done:
Yet haue I fierce Affections, and thinke
What Venus did with Mars.
   Cleo. Oh *Charmion*:   545
Where think'st thou he is now? Stands he, or sits he?
Or does he walke? Or is he on his Horse?   (xx2ᵛᵇ)
Oh happy horse to beare the weight of *Anthony*!
Do brauely Horse, for wot'st thou whom thou moou'st,
The demy *Atlas* of this Earth, the Arme   550
And Burganet of men. Hee's speaking now,

541-2 in deed . . . in deede] indeed . . . indeed F2, F3; in deed . . . indeed
F4-THEO4, CAP, SING1+ (−COL, WH1, HAL, OXF1, SIS)
543 haue I] I have KNT1, STAU, RID
546 Stands he] Stands F3, F4
551 men] man F2-v1778, RANN

---

542 **honest**] COTGRAVE (1611, Honneste) offers the full semantic range of this concept: "*Good, vertuous; iust, vpright, sincere; also, gentle, ciuill, courteous; also, worthie,
noble, honorable, of good reputation; also, comelie, seemelie, handsome, well befitting.*"
The dominant meaning is first stated by CLARK & WRIGHT (ed. 1864, Glossary): "Chaste."
See also 3503.

544 **Venus . . . Mars**] I.e., made love. FRIPP (1930, p. 112) gives the corresponding
passage in Ovid's *Metamorphoses* (4.171-89). THOMSON (1952, p. 149) adds, "Related
by Ovid, *Ars Amat.*, II. 561-92." See n. 5–10.

548-9 **beare . . . Do . . . moou'st**] For the obvious sexual quibbles, see COLMAN
(1974, pp. 184, 191) and n. 141 ("go").

548 *Anthony*] See n. 29.

549 **brauely**] See n. 567.

   wot'st] FRANZ (§182): The old preterit (OE *wāt*, "I know") with the normal inflectional ending of the present tense.

550 **demy *Atlas***] FURNESS (ed. 1907, p. 515), noting a "faint fleeting similarity":
"Daniel's Cleopatra calls Anthony 'My Atlas' [1599, l. 15; 'The *Atlas*' in 1594 ed.]." See
p. 534. In the Countess of Pembroke's *Antonius* (see p. 507) Hercules is one of the "Demy-
gods" unable to subdue pleasure.

550-1 **Arme . . . Burganet**] RANN's (ed. 1791-) "The very flower of chivalry" is modified by WILSON (ed. 1950): "The complete soldier; 'arm' standing for the offensive and
'burgonet' . . . for the defensive. To take 'arm' as 'armour' is lit. to rob the image of
all force." COLLIER (ed. 1843) thought it "probably" meant "weapon"; KITTREDGE (ed.
1941), "Armour." But OED (*sb.*²): "The sing. *arm* is late and rarely used." FAIRHOLT
(1846, p. 470): "Burgonet. A helmet made at the close of the fifteenth century, and
so named from the Burgundians, who invented it." IDEM (p. 281): "The helmets took
the form of the head, having frequently flexible overlapping plates of steel that pro-
tected and covered the neck."

Or murmuring, where's my Serpent of old Nyle,
(For so he cals me:) Now I feede my selfe
With most delicious poyson. Thinke on me
That am with Phœbus amorous pinches blacke,　　　　　　555
And wrinkled deepe in time. Broad-fronted *Cæsar,*
When thou was't heere aboue the ground, I was
A morsell for a Monarke: and great *Pompey*

---

554 Thinke] thinks KTLY
556 time.] ~ ? ROWE, CAP, v1778+ (−WH1, KTLY, RID, ARD2)
558 for] of F3-ROWE3

---

552 **Serpent . . . Nyle**] Commentary ranges from the extravagant to the mundane. SEATON (1946, pp. 222–3): Sh. possibly "was ironically conscious that his heroine . . . would by the moralist be likened . . . to the 'great whore that sitteth upon many waters, With whom have committed fornication the kings of the earth' ([Rev.] xvii. 1–2)." ADELMAN (1973, p. 62): "The crocodile is a fitting emblem for emotional deceit. . . . Not the least duplicitous aspect of the crocodile is the ease with which his meanings change." BROUSSARD (1974, p. 25): Sh. "is pointing out not only that she [Cleopatra] may be considered evil, but also that the evil is linked to her 'fertility', her sexual powers." ADLARD (1975, p. 327): "Shakespeare—even if he has not read the identification of Isis with the asp, the Nile serpent, on [fols.] 117 and 119 of Adlington's *Golden Asse* [1566]—is surely remembering Plutarch's account, on page 1316 of the *Moralia* [tr. Holland, 1603], of the Egyptians' reverence for this creature."

553–4 **Now . . . poyson**] Proverbial; see DENT (P456.1): "Love (Lust, A whore) is sweet *poison.*"

555–6 **That . . . time**] WHITE (ed. 1883): "A great misrepresentation. Cleopatra was at this time only twenty-eight years old; and she was not black." "For the thought" CASE (ed. 1906) compares Daniel's *Cleopatra*, ll. 171–3 (ed. Grosart, 1885). For the 1594 *Cleopatra*, see p. 539; see also n. 10 ("Tawny").

556 **Broad-fronted**] I.e., with a broad front or forehead (see n. 10). Suetonius (*The historie of twelve Cæsars*, tr. Holland, 1606, p. 19) describes Caesar as "somewhat full faced." SEWARD (1750, pp. lxvi f.) explains his conjecture "Bald-*fronted*" (see p. 349): "He was *bald*, and boasted that he would cover his Temples with Laurels instead of Hair; and for that purpose, after he was *Dictator*, constantly wore his Laurel-Crown." Although Suetonius (p. 19) mentions Caesar's employing the "triumphant Lawrel guirland" and his combing "his haire that grew but thin, from the crowne toward his forehead" to cover the "deformity of his bald head," Plutarch in his *Life of Julius Cæsar* (tr. North, 1579, p. 765) says that Cicero observed "howe finely he [Caesar] combeth his faire bush of heare, and how smooth it lyeth."

558 **A . . . Monarke**] Udall describes the beautiful Corinthian harlot Lais as "so deere and costly, that she was no morsell for mowyers" (Erasmus, *Apophthegmes*, tr. Nicolas Udall, 1542, fol. 342ʳ), leading HULME (1962, p. 197) to believe the expression a "current idiom" varied by Sh.

great *Pompey*] CASE (ed. 1906) finds the adjective "misleading"; WILSON (ed. 1950): "It seems that despite Plut[arch]'s explicit statement Sh. took father and son for

Would stand and make his eyes grow in my brow,
There would he anchor his Aspect, and dye   560
With looking on his life.

Enter Alexas from Cæsar.

Alex. Soueraigne of Egypt, haile.
Cleo. How much vnlike art thou *Marke Anthony?*
Yet comming from him, that great Med'cine hath   565
With his Tinct gilded thee.
How goes it with my braue *Marke Anthonie?*
Alex. Last thing he did (deere Queene)
He kist the last of many doubled kisses

561, 563 *One verse line* v1793+ (−ALEX)
562 *from Cæsar*] Ff, GLO; *from Antony* mTYR *conj.*, mCOL1, ARD, CAM3, EVNS; *om.*
ROWE1 *etc.*
564 vnlike art thou] art thou like F3, F4; art thou unlike ROWE1-v1773 (−CAP)
566–8 *Verse lines ending* with . . . Queen, HAN1, RID

---

the same man." Still, although Sh. applies the adjective to all the principals, it is clear
that Cneius Pompey, the father, is meant.
  559 **grow in**] Few comment; the last, WILSON (ed. 1950, Glossary), summarizes: "Take
root in, become part of."
  560 **anchor**] The reference may be appropriate to Cneius Pompey, who among other
things had been given an *imperium infinitum* by sea throughout the Mediterranean.
    Aspect] BULLOKAR (1616): "Sight or the beholding of any thing." ABBOTT (§490)
lists *aspect* among "words in which the accent is nearer the end than with us."
    dye] *OED*'s (7) "to languish, pine away with passion" is anticipated by BLUMHOF
(ed. 1870) in commenting on 236 and accentuated by E. PARTRIDGE's (1947; 1968, p.
93) "To experience a sexual orgasm." See also 236, 240, 243 ("dying").
  561 **his life**] DELIUS (ed. 1856): I.e., Cleopatra. A term of endearment in Sh. See
SCHMIDT (1874, 5).
  562 **Cæsar**] Most likely a memorial error (for *Anthony*) induced by *Cæsar* (556).
  565–6 **great Med'cine . . . thee**] JOHNSON (ed. 1765): "Alluding to the philosopher's
stone, which, by its touch, converts base metal into gold. The Alchemists call the matter,
whatever it be, by which they perform transmutation, a *medicine*." RANN (ed. 1791–)
suggests also "physician," perhaps following CAPELL (1779 [1774], 1:30): "The appellation is given to Antony, as being the curer of all her sorrows."
  566 **Tinct**] KITTREDGE (ed. 1941), glossing as "by its alchemical power," compares
"tinct . . . med'cine" in *AWW* 5.3.102 (2814).
  567 **braue**] COTGRAVE (1611) offers the full semantic range: "*Gay, fine, gorgeous, gallant
(in apparrell;) also, proud, stately, loftie; braggard; magnificall, sumptuous.*" The dominant meaning here is summed up by KITTREDGE (ed. 1941): "Splendid, glorious. A general
word of commendation in Elizabethan English — not referring exclusively to valour." See
also 549, 599, et passim.
  569 **kist . . . kisses**] CAPELL (1779 [1774], 1:31), extravagantly: The "growth [of the

63

This Orient Pearle. His speech stickes in my heart.   570
  Cleo. Mine eare must plucke it thence.
  Alex. Good Friend, quoth he:
Say the firme Roman to great Egypt sends
This treasure of an Oyster: at whose foote
To mend the petty present, I will peece   575
Her opulent Throne, with Kingdomes. All the East,
(Say thou) shall call her Mistris. So he nodded,
And soberly did mount an Arme-gaunt Steede,

---

572 Friend] Friends ROWE2-POPE2
575 peece] pace WARBURTON *conj. apud* mTHEO2 (19 Feb. 1729, [fol. 39ᵛ]), HAN1,
WARB
578 an Arme-gaunt] an arm-girt HAN1, COL2, COL3, WH, HUD2; a termagant MASON
(1785, p. 274) *conj.*, v1793, v1803; an arrogant BOADEN *conj. apud* SING1, SING, HUD1,
KTLY; an Arm-gaud BECKET (1815, 2:177) *conj.*, BLUM (an arm-gaud'd); a Rampant
mF2FL21 *conj.*, HALD; a barbèd WORD1

---

pearl] is effected by the accession of coat after coat. . . . The fish it's mother forms
those coats by a repetition of touchings, which [the poet] calls—'kisses.'"
  570 **Orient Pearle**] BULLOKAR (1616): "Glistring Pearles of great price." IDEM (*Orien-*
tall): "Of, or belonging to the East." GREY (1754, 2:195): "Some *historians* [most likely
Pliny, *Natural History* 9.58] observe, that *Cleopatra* was so extravagant, as to drink the
value of a whole province at a draught, dissolving one of the largest and most beautiful
pearls that ever was seen in the *eastern* part of the world, in strong vinegar, and drinking
it off at a draught; a pearl of an immense value, and thought to be worth 250,000 crowns."
CAPELL (1779 [1774], 1:31): "This, it is probable, was Antony's *'petty present'* [575]."
NORMAN (1956, p. 60) finds a possible "immediate inspiration for the gift of the pearl"
in Ben Jonson's *Volpone* 3.7.191–3: "See, here, a rope of pearle; and each, more orient
Then that the braue *Ægyptian* queene carrous'd: Dissolue, and drinke 'hem [ed. Herford & Simpson, 1937, p. 83]."
  574 **at whose foote**] THEOBALD (19 Feb. 1729, [fol. 39ᵛ]): "Has neither Relation to
Cleopatra, nor her Throne, but . . . means no more than that *at the Sequel* of y.ᵗ
Present, he would enlarge her Pow'r w:ᵗʰ additional Kingdoms." IDEM (ed. 1733) compares "At heele of" (861).
  575 **peece**] MINSHEU (1617): "*To* Peece *one thing with another.*" I.e., "piece out,"
"enlarge." DEIGHTON (ed. 1891): "With a play upon *mend.*" See textual notes and conj.,
p. 349.
  576 **opulent**] DEIGHTON (ed. 1891): Either "'already opulent', or 'which shall thereby
be made opulent.'" Like BLUMHOF (ed. 1870), KITTREDGE (ed. 1941) favors the latter,
explaining it as "proleptic."
  578 **Arme-gaunt Steede**] In most cases commentary interprets according to the etymology of the parts of the compound. MINSHEU (1617), defining *arm* and *to arm*, translates Latin *armus* as "*a shoulder, an Arme*" and *armis* as "armes or weapons." BAILEY
(1721) defines the adjective *gaunt* as "lean, one who hath lost his Fat or Flesh." Hence

the *OED*'s (*sb.*[1]) "with gaunt limbs." JOHNSON (ed. 1765) comments that "*arm* is the Teutonick word for *want*, or *poverty*," and SCHMIDT (1874) derives *gaunt* from "Old English . . . '*gaunt*', the German *ganz*, signifying *whole, healthful, lusty*." HULME (1962, p. 296) goes so far as to detect an etymology of *gaunt* based on a dialect "verb *gain* (adopted from ON *gegna* . . . to be meet, fit or suitable) with the by-form *gawne*."

The main questions seem to be whether the steed thus described is a war-horse and whether the epithet is laudatory or pejorative. Those who cannot make sense of it have contributed numerous conjectures, which, although of varying quality, represent a typical chapter in the history of a famous crux.

(1) While JOHNSON's dictionary (1755) neutrally defines the compound as "Slender as the arm," other commentators find reason for the slenderness in the horse's martial activities. WARBURTON (ed. 1747): "His steed worn lean and thin by much service in war." He compares Fairfax's *stall-worn* in *Godfrey of Bulloigne* (1600, 7.27.1), where the word is actually *stalworth*, but is corrected by UPTON (1748, pp. ix–x) and GREY (1754, 2:196). Warburton's definition is modified by CAPELL (1779 [1774], Glossary, 1:3), as "made gaunt (or thin) by long Use of Armour," and by HUNTER (ed. 1870), as referring less to the horse than to "the angular parts of the horse's armour, as resembling the projecting bones of a gaunt or lean animal." NARES (1822; 1876) includes Antony: "*Worn by military service*. This implies the military activity of the master." KITTREDGE (ed. 1941) explains, "*Gaunt* contrasts the warlike steed — all bone and muscle — with what Puck calls 'a fat and bean-fed horse' ([*MND* 2.1.45 (416)])," and SISSON (1956, 2:263), misinterpreting *fat*, adds, "It is the opposite of 'fat and scant of breath' [*Ham.* 5.2.298 (3756)]."

BOSWELL (ed. 1821) stresses the horse's belligerence: "*Gaunt* is certainly *thin*. . . . It may derivatively have acquired the sense of *fierce*, and an *arm-gaunt* steed may signify a steed looking fierce in armour." Literary comparisons quoted by others seem to corroborate this image: STAUNTON (ed. 1859) compares *gaunt eagle* in Ben Jonson's *Catiline* 3.1.200 (ed. Herford & Simpson, 1937, 5:475); GANTILLON (1879, p. 244) quotes the description in Virgil's *Aeneid* 6.881 of a horse so fierce that it can hardly be controlled: "Seu spumantis *equi* foderet calcaribus *armos* [he dug his spurs into the flanks of his foaming horse]"; THISELTON (1899, p. 10) refers to "the description [of the horse] in the 39th chapter of the Book of Job [quotes Job 39:19, 39:21, 39:24, 39:25]," and BULLEN (ed. 1906) to "such a 'hot and fiery steed' as 'roan Barbary' in *Richard II* [5.5.78 (2746)]." ADELMAN (1973, pp. 59–60) believes the steed suggests the traditional image of "the unreined lust of concupiscence" alluded to by Plutarch (see p. 420). "The image . . . might have reminded Shakespeare of the familiar association [with Plato's horse of the mind]."

(2) Some believe the steed to be unconnected with war. MACKAY (1884, p. 19) erroneously detects a "Keltic etymology" of *gaunt* = "bare or scanty": "*Arm-gaunt* would signify a horse without all or any of its martial trappings." NICHOLSON (1883, p. 179) objects that *gaunt* "has never been found in [the sense] of bare or uncovered." Other attempts at describing the horse in nonmartial terms focus on its breed and beauty. SEWARD (1750, p. lxvii), indignant at Warburton's interpretation —"Why must *Anthony* . . . have nothing to ride but an old batter'd lean War-Horse? Beside, lean Horses are seldom remarkable like this for neighing loud and vigorously"— suggests (p. lxviii) that "*Arm-gaunt* . . . signifies *thin-shoulder'd*, which we know to be one of the principal Beauties of a Horse." EDWARDS (1765, p. 131) agrees —"Mr. Warburton . . . seems to have stolen Don Quixote's Rosinante, to mount the demy Atlas of *this* earth"— as does HEATH (1765, p. 452). The feeling that the horse should have a favorable connotation shows in JOHNSON (ed.

1765), who interprets *arm-gaunt* first as "*lean* for *want*, ill fed," but on second thought holds, "As *armgaunt* seems not intended to imply any defect, it perhaps means, a horse so slender that a man might clasp him, and therefore formed for expedition." RITSON (1783, p. 148): "Dr. Johnsons observation that this steed was a post horse is 'impertinent.'" STEEVENS (ed. 1778), referring to *arm-greet* in Chaucer's *Canterbury Tales* ("The Knight's Tale" I [A] 2145, in *The Poetical Works*, ed. Robinson, 1933), notes, "*Armgrete* is *as big as the arm*, and *arm-gaunt* may mean *as slender as the arm*." MALONE (ed. 1790) summarizes: "It is clear, that whatever epithet was used, it was intended as descriptive of a beautiful horse, such (we may presume) as our authour has described in his *Venus and Adonis* [289–300]."

DAVIES (1783, 2:342) stresses the horse's physical qualities and capabilities: "*Arm-gaunt* means *fine-shaped*, or, *thin-shouldered*. . . . *Thin-shouldered horses move the best.*" CHEDWORTH (1805, p. 284) compares Horace's description of his mule in *Satires* 1.6.106. Similarly, CROFT (1810, p. 19): "A courser, in the jockies' phrase, with a light shoulder and tucked-up belly"; HALLIWELL (1868, p. 15): "A finely-formed swift horse"; J. D. (1879, p. 164): "Slender in the fore-thigh or fore-leg . . . equivalent to 'high-bred'"; and ADAMS (1892, p. 283), who refers, among other works, to Fitzherbert's *Husbandry* (1534): "'To haue leane knees' [§76] and 'to be lathe legged' [§78] were two good properties of a horse" (ed. Skeat, 1882).

(3) THEOBALD (19 Feb. 1729, [fol. 39ᵛ]), anticipating many later commentators, admits, "I don't know how to understand this compound Epithet"; INGLEBY (1875, p. 33) groups the adjective with those "'ugly customers' [he classifies them as '*Ullorxals*' after that unintelligible word in *Tim.* 3.4.112 (1247)], with most of whom every conscientious editor has played a losing game"; KELLNER (1925, p. 1) lists *arm-gaunt* under "Unintelligible Passages in Shakespeare," concluding (p. 21): "A number of word-puzzles beginning with *a* are waiting for their solution on palæographic lines"; WILSON (ed. 1950) finds that "'gaunt', even in its common 16th c. sense of 'slender', strikes the wrong note"; and the *OED* concedes, "meaning not certainly known." Believing the expression corrupt, many would emend.

(a) *termagant, rampant, arrogant*: MASON (1785, p. 274), finding *arm-gaunt* "a blunder of the printers," suggests "*Termagant*. . . . So Douglas, in Henry IV. [Part I] is called the *termagant Scot* [5.4.114 (3079)], an epithet that agrees well with the steed's neighing so high," anticipated in a gloss by HOLT WHITE (1783, p. 935), who refers to *Ham.* 3.2.13 (1861) and quotes Bishop Percy: "*Termagant* was a *Saracen deity*, very clamorous and violent in the old moralities [not identified, but a similar reference in *Libius disconius*, l. 1409, in *Bishop Percy's Folio Manuscript*, vol. 2, 1867]." Mason's reading is adopted by STEEVENS (ed. 1793), who groups the conjecture "among the *feliciter audentia* of criticism," and supported by WALKER (1860, 3:297), who thinks *termagant* "was written *tarmagaunt*." LETTSOM (1853, *Blackwood's*, p. 467), first hesitatingly finds that "of all the substitutes proposed, *termagant* is perhaps the best," then clearly decides for *rampaunt* or *ramping* (1853, *N&Q*, p. 378): "At one period to *ramp* and to *prance* seem to have been synonymous. Spenser makes the horses of night 'fiercely *ramp*' [*F.Q.* 1.5.28], and Surrey exhibits a *prancing* lion [l. 7 of "A song written by the earle of Surrey by a lady that refused to daunce with him," *Tottel's Miscellany*, ed. Rollins, 1928; 1965, 1:207]." WHITE (1854, p. 448) finds that *rampaunt*, misprinted *armegaunt*, "sorts well with what *Alexis* says of the high neighing of the horse." Similarly, PERRING (1885, pp. 339–40) thinks "that *arampaunt* was so written as to look like *aramgaunt*," recalling (p. 339) "the 'ramping lion' [*3H6* 5.2.13 (2814)] and 'rampant bear' [*2H6* 5.1.20 (3203)]" but mentioning neither Lettsom nor (presumably) THEOBALD's correction (see textual notes) "a Rampant." Moreover, he finds (p. 340) "such emendations as 'an argent steed', 'a roan gelt steed', 'an ungelt steed' [sources not identified] . . . bearing but a faint resemblance to the word of the Folios." SINGER (ed. 1826), adopting Boaden's (*apud* IDEM) conjecture *arrogant*, argues that it "answers to the Latin *ferox . . . fierce, proud.*" As an illustration he cites an instance of *caballo arrogante* in Lope de Vega's *Arauco domado* (*Obras*, ed. Marcelino Menéndez Pelayo, 1890–1913; rpt. 1969, 27:241). KEIGHTLEY (1867, p. 312): "In Spanish . . . *caballo arrogante* is simply a gallant, spirited horse. See Calderón, *La Niña de Gómez Arias [Obras completas*, ed. Luis Astrana Marín, 3rd ed. 1951, 1:380]." In addition to *arrogant* he thinks *ardent* possible, finding support in "hot and fiery steed" (*R2* 5.2.8 [2375]) and "angry steede" in Spenser (*F.Q.* 1.1.1). While BAILEY (1866, 2:115) is strongly in favor of *arrogant*—"The . . . similarity of the word here suggested to that in the received text is incontrovertible"—KINNEAR (1883, pp. 450–1) finds it "unsuitable to the metre" and prefers *ardent* because of its contrast to *soberly*, adding evidence from *AWW* 2.3.300 (1191), *Tim.* 3.3.33 (1107–8), and *LC* 108 and pointing out that "*'arrogant'* . . . is only applied by Shakespeare to men."

(b) *war-gaunt, Merchant, arm'd gaunt, wing borne*: JACKSON (1819, pp. 287–8) suggests *war-gaunt*: "The *w* is frequently a *scarce sort* with printers; and when the compositor has not any of them in his case, he puts an *m* in place of it. . . . The proof read—*mar-gaunt*, and the reader, judging that the *m* was transposed, marked it to read *arm-gaunt*." MITFORD (1844, p. 467): "The inversion of one letter, *m*, and the transposition of the other *ar*, would change *arm* into *war*." BULLOCH (1865, p. 2): "The word stood originally in the manuscript as *Marchaunt*, the olde mode of spelling *Merchant*." He regards it as a "euphemistic term" for a "*sumpter horse*, or one employed in carrying baggage." SPENCE (1878, p. 244), suggesting *arm'd gaunt*: "Of the one adjective I make two. . . . An error not of sight but of hearing." *Armed-gaunt* appears much earlier as a manuscript correction made between 1632 and 1649 in Sarah Jones's copy of F2. WORDSWORTH (ed. 1883) reads *barbèd* without comment, and BRONSON (1938, p. 644) assumes—finding an analogy in *Ham.* 4.7.22 (3030), where Q2 has "Arm'd," while F1 reads "Winde"—"that the word misread 'arme-gaunt' began with the letters *win*." His conjecture *wing-borne* is the result of the notion that "the image of the flying, or winged, horse was habitual to Shakespeare's thought [refers to *Ven.* 304–6, *1H4* 4.1.104–10 (2335–41), *Tmp.* 4.1.30 (1683), *AWW* 2.3.300 (1191), *Rom.* 3.2.1 (1645), *Cym.* 2.3.23–4 (983–4), *3H6* 2.6.12 (1292)]." In his opinion "the context . . . implies an epithet belonging to the category of *spirited*—an inference supported by other allusions to high-neighing steeds [refers to *H5* 4.Pr.10 (1799) and 4.2.8 (2176–7), *Oth.* 3.3.352 (1994), *Ven.* 307]."

(c) *arm-girt, -gent, -gowned*, etc.: HANMER's (ed. 1744) emendation *arm-girt* is glossed by HUDSON (ed. 1881): "In the days of chivalry, war-horses were sometimes girded with armour as well as the men who rode them." BECKET (1815, 2:177) conjectures, "*Armgent. Gent is fine*, handsomely clad. 'An arm-gent steed' will therefore mean, *a war-steed, gayly caparisoned*. . . . *Arm-gaud* which comes nearer the *letters* in the text . . . will have the same meaning as *arm-gent.*" His line of thought is continued by BLUMHOF's (ed. 1870) *arm-gaud'd*, i.e., "gaudily attired"; JOICEY's (1891, p. 342) *arm-zoned*, glossed as "armour-clad"; and CASE's (ed. 1906) "*arm-gowned*. . . . The spelling might be *gownd* or even *gound*" analogous to an instance of a *gowned beast* in Spenser ("Mother Hubberd's Tale" 749, in *The Minor Poems*, ed. Greenlaw et al., 1947, 2:125). Without attempting to interfere with F1's word, NICHOLSON (1883, pp. 181–2) narrows down the aspect of attire: "Antony mounts, not an ordinary steed, but his war-horse, trained and

Who neigh'd so hye, that what I would haue spoke,
Was beastly dumbe by him.   580

580–5 *Five verse lines ending* sad . . . between . . . not sad . . . disposition! . . .
but note him, HAN1; *two verse lines ending* merry? . . . extremes *then as* F1 v1793+
   580 beastly] beast-like HAN1; boastfully mCOL1, COL2
         dumbe] dumb'd mF4FL33 *and* mTHEO2 (15 Nov. 1729, [fol. 78]) *conj.*, THEO,
HAN1, CAP, v1778+ (−SING, HUD1); done WARB

---

caparisoned for battle . . . arm-gaunted, armour-gloved. [In Wright *Shakespeariana* (no.
158 [9–10]), he also quotes *R2* 2.1.82 (725), where *gaunt as the grave* 'seems certainly
to involve the meaning of sheathed or fitted like a glove.'] In French it would have been
gante en fer, but Shakespeare spelled it gaunt because he so spelled gauntlet. . . . He
wrote gaunt instead of gaunted . . . [as] he in verbs that ended in *d* or *t* elided the
participial *ed* or made them coalesce." On the other hand, Jackson's gloss on *war-gaunt*
as a "highly-spirited steed"—perhaps anticipated by Becket's remote suggestion of *arm-
vaunt*, "for 'boastful, pampered war-horse'"—as well as GOULD's (1884, p. 45) noun *arme-
g'raunt*, which he considers "a mere metaphrasis for a war-horse," and JOICEY's (1892,
p. 470) suggestions *arm-fam'd*, *arm-proud*, and *arm-gemm'd* stress the horse's state of
mind rather than its outward appearance. WELLS & TAYLOR's (ed. 1986) unrecorded *Arme-
iaunct (arm-jaunced)*—i.e., "jolted by armour"—depends on two premises: an unusual
g for *j* before *a* and an added *c*.
   (4) Questionable etymological approaches to the epithet result in contradictory assertions. JOICEY (1891, p. 342): "Was there any adjective formed from the word *armiger*?";
HALL (1892, p. 283): "To the prefix *arm* add Latin *gero*, to bear, to carry, the construction
would be like 'termagant', where the *r* of *vagari* is lost." IDEM (1893, p. 372): "Shakspeare
conjoined *arma* with *gero*, aiming at *armigerent*, but shortened to 'Arm-gaunt' for the
sake of metre." Hall is ridiculed by ADAMS (1892, p. 426): "Maybe the written original
of the printed 'Arme-gaunt' is 'Armenian'"; modified by SAMPSON (1920, p. 272), who
regards *arme-gaunt* as a misprint for *armigerent*, referring to "the horse's trappings, em-
blazoned with the armorial bearings of his master"; and supported by YATES (1938, p.
678), who quotes *armigero* in *Wiv.* 1.1.10, 11 (13, 14), and *armipotent* in *LLL* 5.2.650,
657 (2600, 2606).
   FURNESS (ed. 1907) evaluates this variety of opinions: "In view of the formidable, not
to say appalling combination of equine qualities and armourer's art which has been detected in this adjective, Anthony would have been more than mortal had he not approached his steed with extreme caution, and mounted it 'soberly.'" Like Furness, the
great majority of Shn. commentators have kept their senses. CROSBY, for example, in
a letter to Joseph Parker Norris (2 Feb. 1877, [sheet 163, p. 38]): "'Arm-gaunt' has always
seemed to me right, & conveyed the idea of a large, mettlesome, spirited war-horse, *thin
in flesh*, but full of fire."
   579 **spoke**] For the past participle of this strong verb, see FRANZ §170; for other instances, 834, 839, et passim.
   580 **beastly**] BLUMHOF (ed. 1870) detects a play on "by the beast" and "like a beast."

Cleo. What was he sad, or merry?

Alex. Like to the time o'th'yeare, between ye extremes
Of hot and cold, he was nor sad nor merrie.

Cleo. Oh well diuided disposition: Note him,
Note him good *Charmian*, 'tis the man; but note him.   585
He was not sad, for he would shine on those
That make their lookes by his. He was not merrie,
Which seem'd to tell them, his remembrance lay
In Egypt with his ioy, but betweene both.
Oh heauenly mingle! Bee'st thou sad, or merrie,   590
The violence of either thee becomes,
So do's it no mans else. Met'st thou my Posts?

Alex. I Madam, twenty seuerall Messengers.

---

581 What$_\wedge$] ~ , ROWE1+ (−KTLY, CAM3)
583 nor sad] not sad F3-POPE2, HAN1
584 Note him,] *Om.* POPE1-JOHN1
587 He] *Om.* WH1
592 mans] man F2-ALEX, ARD2

See textual notes and conj., p. 349. For the characteristics of the -*ly* suffix, see FRANZ §123.

dumbe by] See n. 437 for the possibility of a misprint (*e* for *d*) or the dropping of a final *d* between the *b*'s.

581–3 SOELLNER (1958, *SP*, pp. 549–54): Like many of his contemporaries, Sh. seems to have accepted the classical idea that (p. 549) "all human emotions can be reduced to a basic four" (pleasure, pain, desire, and fear), which Renaissance Neoplatonists made (p. 552) "part of a fourfold universe." IDEM (p. 554): "Besides characterizing joy and grief as extremes of passion, Shakespeare here connected the emotions with the four seasons of the year, an association which can easily be accounted for if we assume that he knew about the basic pattern of four emotions and its correspondencies. This seems to be borne out by the continuation of this passage [584–90]."

581 **What**] See nn. 1539, 2786, et passim.

585 **but**] I.e., only. See FRANZ §434.

591 **violence**] MINSHEU (1617): "*Force.*"

592 **So . . . else**] SISSON (1956, 2:264): F1's reading "is to be defended, in the sense 'So does it become no other man's *violence*; no other man's violence of sadness or merriment so becomes him', a more elliptical, but also more subtle and significant expression than the emended version [of F2: *man* for *mans*]."

So] COLLIER (ed. 1843): "*As*," comparing 387. SINGER (ed. 1856): "Probably . . . *So as.*" FURNESS (ed. 1907): "That is, 'So does it *as*. . . .' For other examples of the omission of *as*, see ABBOTT, §281."

Posts] MINSHEU (1617): "*Messenger in hast.*"

593 **seuerall**] See n. 612.

Why do you send so thicke?

　　Cleo. Who's borne that day, when I forget to send　　　　595
to *Anthonie*, shall dye a Begger. Inke and paper *Charmian.* Welcome my good *Alexas.* Did I *Charmian,* e-
uer loue *Cæsar* so?

　　Char. Oh that braue *Cæsar*!

　　Cleo. Be choak'd with such another Emphasis,　　　　600
Say the braue *Anthony.*

　　Char. The valiant *Cæsar.*

　　Cleo. By *Isis*, I will giue thee bloody teeth,
If thou with *Cæsar* Paragon againe:
My man of men.　　　　　　　　　　　　　　　　　605

　　Char. By your most gracious pardon,
I sing but after you.

　　Cleo. My Sallad dayes,

594–9 *Five verse lines ending* day, . . . *Antony,* . . . Paper, *Charmian.* . . . I,
Charmian, . . . *Cæsar*! ROWE1+
597 *Alexas.*] Alexas. [*Exit Alexas.* BLUM
601 Say] Save ROWE3
602 *Char.*] *Cleo.* WARB (*text*; *Char. in errata*)
604 againe:] ∼ ˌ F2+

---

594 **thicke**] JOHNSON (1755, *adv.* 1): "Frequently; fast."
596 **shall . . . Begger**] The few who comment agree with DELIUS (ed. 1856): For
that day shall be unlucky. RIDLEY (ed. 1954) adds, "Perhaps . . . there is nothing more
than a quaint way of expressing the certainty of a daily despatch." He offers no expression or proverb, however.
599 **braue**] See n. 567.
600 **Emphasis**] CAWDREY (1604): "A forcible expressing." *OED* cites Cawdrey under
4 ("stress of voice"), giving its own definition (and this instance) under 2b: "An emphatic
expression." JENKINS (1981, p. 390), glossing *Ham.* 5.1.278 (3450): "The enforcement
of the sense 'by a word of more than ordinary efficacy' (Puttenham, *Art of Eng. Poesy*,
III.17)."
603 **I . . . teeth**] LLOYD (1959, p. 89), questionably, finds this expression an illustration of "the martial element in Cleopatra. . . . This element is wholly devoted to
her fulfilment as a lover." He cites also 1106, 1879. RINEHART (1972, p. 85), suggesting
"similarities" of behavior between Cleopatra and Elizabeth: "Elizabeth once handled
a maid of honor so roughly, 'telt liberall bothe with bloes and yevell words' [qtd. in Wilson, *Queen Elizabeth's Maids of Honour*, 1922, p. 107], that she broke the maid's finger." See also nn. 77–155, 3407–10.
604 **Paragon**] MINSHEU (1617): "*To* Compare, *to equall.*"
608–10 **My . . . then**] WARBURTON (ed. 1747): "Mr. *Theobald* [ed. 1733; earlier,
19 Feb. 1729, (fol. 39ᵛ)] . . . says, Cleopatra *may speak very naturally here with contempt of her judgment at that period: But how truly with regard to the coldness of her*

When I was greene in iudgement, cold in blood,
To say, as I saide then. But come, away, 610
Get me Inke and Paper,
he shall haue euery day a seuerall greeting, or Ile vnpeo- (xx3ᵃ)
ple Egypt.   *Exeunt*

Enter Pompey, Menecrates, and Menas, in **2.1**
warlike manner. 615

Pom. If the great Gods be iust, they shall assist
The deeds of iustest men.

---

609 iudgement,] ~ .—— WARB, JOHN1, v1773-NLSN (–STAU, OXF1)

611–13 F1-THEO2, WARB, THEO4; *two verse lines ending* day . . . *Ægypt.* HAN1, CAP-
v1803, SING, KNT1, HUD1, STAU, KTLY, RID; *three verse lines ending* paper, . . . greeting,
. . . *Ægypt.* mTBY2 *conj.,* JOHN1 *etc.*

612 a seuerall greeting] seuerall greeting F2, F3; several greetings F4-THEO2, WARB,
THEO4

614 ACT II. SCENE I. ROWE1-POPE2, HAN1, WARB, JOHN1+; ACT II. THEO
        SCENE *in* Sicily. ROWE1-JOHN1; Messina. *A Room in* Pompey'*s House.* CAP+
(*subst.*)

614–15 *in* . . . *manner*] *Om.* ROWE1-OXF1 (–GLO, CAM1, WH2)

617–22 *Four verse lines ending* Pompey, . . . deny. . . . decays . . . our selues,
ROWE1+

---

blood may admit some question . . . for that state which the *Greeks* [i.e., Plutarch]
designed by Κόρη, was the very height of blood. But *Shakespear*'s best justification is
restoring his own sense, which is done merely by a different pointing. . . . *Cold in
blood,* is an upbraiding expostulation to her maid. *Those,* says she, *were my sallad days,
when I was green in judgment; but your blood is as cold as my judgment, if you have
the same opinion of things now as I had then.*" BOSWELL (ed. 1821): "Warburton's reading is . . . spirited, but *cold* and *green* seem to be suggested by the metaphor *sallad*
days." Most who comment agree with Warburton that there is a shift of addressee. But
the vagaries of editorial punctuation make the exact intention of some others difficult
to ascertain. See conj., p. 349. What is clear is the allusion to inexperience, following
Plutarch's "For *Cæsar* and *Pompey* knew her when she was but a young thing, & knew
not then what the worlde ment" (p. 412).

612 **a seuerall**] BAILEY (1721): "A Particular." See also 593.

612-13 **vnpeople Egypt**] JOHNSON (ed. 1765) and most others: "By sending out messengers." Only DEIGHTON (ed. 1891) implies that Cleopatra, extravagantly, will let nothing, not the lives of all her people, hinder her.

616 **shall**] STAUNTON (ed. 1859): "Sh. uses *shall* "to denote futurity, whether in the
second and third persons or in the first." See FRANZ §616, §708 (p. 620).

617 **iustest**] For the comparative and superlative, Sh. prefers *-er* and *-est* to *more* and
most. See FRANZ §215.

Mene. Know worthy *Pompey*, that what they do delay, they not deny.
Pom. Whiles we are sutors to their Throne, decayes   620
the thing we sue for.
Mene. We ignorant of our selues,

618–19 *Given to Menas* mCAP2, JOHN1, v1773, v1778, RANN, CAM3, EVNS
618 what] which F2-ROWE3
620 Whiles] While F3-v1773 (−CAP)
       decayes] delay's WARB, CAP
622–5 *Given to Menas* ROWE2-JOHN1, v1773, v1778, RANN, CAM3

618, 622, 635, 638, 662 F1's assignment of all the speeches to Menecrates is countered by JOHNSON's (ed. 1765) assignment of all to Menas: "I know not why *Menecrates*
appears; *Menas* can do all without him." MALONE (ed. 1790) gives 618 and 622 to Menecrates, the rest to Menas, conceding, "It is a matter of little consequence." CAPELL (1779
[1774], 1:31–2): "The characters themselves will point out who the speeches belong to."
He gives 618 to Menas, who "agrees with Pompey, in thinking — that the gods would
befriend them at last," and 622 to Menecrates, a friend "not in favour," whose "opinion
was rather, that Pompey himself should prepare, and attack the triumvirs." (This attribution also accounts for his approval of *delay's* [620] as emended by Warburton.) Both
speeches, he adds, are "in the form of a maxim." BLUMHOF (ed. 1870) agrees with Malone and provides further reasons: the first two speeches reveal a spirit of peace and con-
ciliation, whereas Menas is a war-minded hothead.
    618–19 **what . . . deny**] Proverbial; see DENT (D198.1): "*Delays* are (not) denials."
    do delay] For the periphrastic *do* for the purpose of emphasis, often antithesis,
see FRANZ §595.
    619 **they not**] For the omission of *do* before *not*, see ABBOTT §305.
    620–1 WARBURTON (ed. 1747), followed only by CAPELL (1779 [1774], 1:31–2), pro-
poses *delay's* for *decayes*: "*Menecrates* had said, *The Gods do not deny that which they
delay*. The other turns his words to a different meaning, and replies, *Delay is the very
thing we beg of them*. *i.e.* the delay of our enemies in making preparation against us."
JOHNSON (ed. 1765), followed by all others, defends *decayes*: "The meaning is, *While
we are praying, the thing for which we pray* is losing its value." HEATH (1765, p. 453)
paraphrases: "Is falling into decay and ruin by the ill conduct of my competitors." BECKET
(1815, 2:179) regards the utterance as a question, "[Pompey's] wishing to be informed
if the Heavens were likely to interfere in the regulation of earthly affairs."
    620 **Whiles**] DEIGHTON (ed. 1891): "The genitive case of *while*, time, used adverbi-
ally, as *needs*, *twi-es* (twice), etc." Also, like *whilst*, for euphony. See FRANZ §555.
    622–5 THEOBALD (ed. 1733): An "imitation" of Juvenal's tenth satire, ll. 4–8, 349–51.
CASE (ed. 1906): As much a commonplace in Sh.'s time as now. WILSON (ed. 1950) points
to "Rom. viii. 26 and last offertory Collect of Communion Service in the Book of Common
Prayer." Not clearly identified; possibly "Almighty God, the fountain of all wisdom . . ."
(1559, p. 266).

Begge often our owne harmes, which the wise Powres
Deny vs for our good: so finde we profit
By loosing of our Prayers.   625
   Pom. I shall do well:
The people loue me, and the Sea is mine;
My powers are Cressent, and my Auguring hope
Sayes it will come to'th'full. *Marke Anthony*
In Egypt sits at dinner, and will make   630
No warres without doores. *Cæsar* gets money where
He looses hearts: *Lepidus* flatters both,
Of both is flatter'd: but he neither loues,
Nor either cares for him.
   Mene. *Cæsar* and *Lepidus* are in the field,   635

---

628 powers are] Pow'r's a mTHEO2 (19 Feb. 1729, [fol. 39ᵛ]) *conj.*, THEO1-KNT1, SING2, HUD2

634–6 *Verse lines ending Lepidus . . .* carry. mTBY2 *conj.*, HAN1, CAP, v1793+ (–STAU)

635–6, 638 *Given to Menas* JOHN1, v1773+

---

628 **powers are Cressent**] THEOBALD (19 Feb. 1729, [fol. 39ᵛ]) emends to *power 's a* because "the Poet's Allusion is to the *Moon* [with which all commentators but BECKET (1815, 2:180) agree] . . . as well as for Concord's Sake." UPTON (1746, p. 325): "The relative *it* agrees, and is to be referred to *power* understood in the plural *powers*." SEYMOUR (1805, 2:49): "The relative 'it' . . . has a *general* reference to the *prosperous state of his affairs*." GOULD (1881, p. 10) after proposing *they* for *it* or *power is*: "But there are a great many false concords in Shakspere besides this," an assertion to be found earlier in DYCE (ed. 1857). See textual notes and conj., p. 349.

   Cressent] BULLOKAR (1616): "In Heraldrie it signifieth the newe Moone." MINSHEU (1617): "*Croissant, or halfe Moone in Blazon* . . . [from Latin] crescere, *to increase*." BECKET (1815, 2:180): "There is no sort of allusion to the moon. 'Crescent', is used merely in the sense of *growing, increasing*." DELIUS (ed. 1856) points to both senses, although most commentators accept the moon metaphor.

   629 **to'th'full**] BECKET (1815, 2:180) alone: "The *full number*: the number which may be necessary in my design. . . . 'Full', is a common military term, as a full company, regiment &c."

   631 **without doores**] MINSHEU (1617): Outdoors. See FRANZ §537. WILSON (ed. 1950): "For 'wars' within doors, cf. [757]." DEIGHTON (ed. 1891) alone: "Abroad, out of Egypt."

   631–2 **Cæsar . . . hearts**] Presumably a reference to the imposition of "grim means and . . . special taxes" to pay the troops. "Some of the proscribed," continues SCULLARD (1959; 1976, p. 164), "managed to escape and to join Sextus Pompeius." For Plutarch's references to Octavius's taxation (at different times), see pp. 409, 436.

   633 **neither loues**] DEIGHTON (ed. 1891): "*I.e.* Cæsar or Antony." For the word order, especially in connection with the meter, see FRANZ §683.

   634 **Nor either cares**] The nonperiphrastic form in negative statements was dominant

A mighty strength they carry.
Pom. Where haue you this? 'Tis false.
Mene. From *Siluius,* Sir.
Pom. He dreames: I know they are in Rome together
Looking for *Anthony*: but all the charmes of Loue,   640
Salt *Cleopatra* soften thy wand lip,
Let Witchcraft ioyne with Beauty, Lust with both,

---

637 haue] had CAP
639–40 *Verse lines ending* looking . . . love, HAN1
639 I know] *Om.* HAN1
640 the] *Om.* v1793, v1803
641 wand] F1-ROWE3, COL1; wan mF4Q *conj. and* POPE1, POPE2-MAL (*text*; wan'd *in errata*), RANN; warm mTHEO2 (19 Feb. 1729, [fol. 39ᵛ]) *conj.*, COL2; wanton BECKET (1815, 2:180) *conj.* (want'), KTLY; fond JOHN1 *conj.*, BLUM; wann'd STEEVENS *conj. apud* v1773, IRV, RID; wan'd mTBY3 *conj.*, v1793 *etc.*

---

in Sh. *Care* seems to be one of the verbs that resisted periphrasis. See FRANZ §599.
638 *Siluius*] Not mentioned in Plutarch, PAULY, *OCD,* or *Cam. Anc. Hist.*
640 *Anthony*] See n. 29.
641 *Salt*] MINSHEU (1617): "*Hot in lust as a bitch.*" HUDSON (ed. 1881), the first to comment, compares *Oth.* 2.1.244 (1023). This meaning—"lecherous, salacious" (*OED, a.*[2] b)—is derived from the Latin *saltus* ("leap"; see BULLOKAR [1616, *Saults*]) and is distinct from *salsus,* salt having been considered salubrious and wholesome by Elizabethans. See BARTHOLOMAEUS (1582, fol. 266 [=268]). Confusion is possible, however. WALTER (ed. 1969) "notes that salt was given to animals to awaken lust for breeding," citing Plutarch's *Moralia* (tr. Holland, 1603, p. 728), where one also finds, "As for salt, haply those who have vowed to live a chaste and pure life, doe forbeare it, for that by the heat which it hath . . . it provoketh those who use it, unto lecherie." The meaning "pungent, stinging," used regarding speech, wit, etc. and derived from *salsus* (*OED, a.*[1] 5), might also be applied to Cleopatra. COOPER (1565) cites Quintilian [see *Institutio oratoria* 6.3.13, 18, 30, 89, 101], translating *salsus* as "Mery: pleasant: wittie: sharpe or quicke spoken." The meaning "shrewd, cunning" may also be implied. For the absence of the inflectional ending, see FRANZ §367.
    wand] The ambiguous spelling has been interpreted in two questionable ways: "Allud[ing] to magic" (JACKSON [1819, p. 288], followed only by COLLIER [ed. 1843]), and "*want*' contracted of *wanton*" (BECKET [1815, 2:180]). WILSON (ed. 1950) explains the generally accepted reading *waned*: "I.e. ageing, withered. . . . I conj[ecture] an *e:d* error for 'wan'=dusky (v. O.E.D. 'wan' 1), sp. 'wane.'" See textual notes and conj., p. 349. See n. 665.
642 **Witchcraft**] ADELMAN (1973, pp. 64–5): "The suggestion that Cleopatra was aided by supernatural powers in her conquest of Antony was a familiar part of the tradition. . . . Tasso associates his enchantress Armida with her [*Jerusalem Delivered,* tr. Fairfax, ed. Nelson, 1963, 16.3–7, 20.118]." See also 225, 2781.

Tye vp the Libertine in a field of Feasts,
Keepe his Braine fuming. Epicurean Cookes,
Sharpen with cloylesse sawce his Appetite,   645
That sleepe and feeding may prorogue his Honour,
Euen till a Lethied dulnesse —

Enter Varrius.

How now *Varrius*?
   Var. This is most certaine, that I shall deliuer: 650
Marke Anthony is euery houre in Rome
Expected. Since he went from Egypt, 'tis
A space for farther Trauaile.
   Pom. I could haue giuen lesse matter
A better eare. *Menas*, I did not thinke   655
This amorous Surfetter would haue donn'd his Helme
For such a petty Warre: His Souldiership
Is twice the other twaine: But let vs reare

---

643 Tye . . . field] Lay . . . flood mCOL1, COL2
647 till] to mF4Q *conj. and* HAN1
653 farther] further v1793-SING1, HUD, DYCE, GLO, WH2, OXF1, RIDb

---

643 CASE (ed. 1906) thinks that if there is any specific reference it is "to the large pasture fields . . . in which the severally owned portions were not enclosed." He quotes ELTON (1904, p. 144): "The word 'tyings' meant the right of tethering a horse, hobbled with a 'tye' or chain, so as to graze on the neighbour's herbage." SISSON (1956, 2:264–5) develops the interpretation of DELIUS (ed. 1856) and DEIGHTON (ed. 1891): "Pompey's imagery is that of a soldier, and the *field* is a field of battle or of tournament." He compares 629–31. BLUMHOF (ed. 1870) prefers *field* in the figurative sense of plenty, abundance; RIDLEY (ed. 1935, Glossary) and most others, the more literal "field of rich pasture (*from which the animal would not stray*)."

644 **fuming**] DEIGHTON (ed. 1891): "Muddled with the fumes of wine; cp. *Temp.* [5.1.67 (2023)]." KITTREDGE (ed. 1941): "The fumes of wine were thought to rise from the stomach into the brain and thus to cause drunkenness. Cf. *Macbeth* [1.7.63–7 (544–8)]."

   Epicurean] ABBOTT (§492): "The double accent [-*ean*] seems to have been disliked by the Elizabethans . . . [who] generally did not accent the *e* in such words."

646 **prorogue**] CAWDREY (1604): "Put off . . . deferre."

647 **till**] The northern form of *to*. See ABBOTT §184.

651 **euery**] I.e., each. See FRANZ §352.

652–3 **Since . . . Trauaile**] STEEVENS (ed. 1778), following a series of letters in *St. James's Chr.* (esp. nos. 2409 [15–17 Aug. 1776], 2411 [20–22 Aug. 1776]): "I.e. since he quitted Egypt, a space of time has elapsed in which a longer journey might have been performed than from Egypt to Rome."

656 **donn'd**] See n. 2520 ("daft").

The higher our Opinion, that our stirring
Can from the lap of Egypts Widdow, plucke   660
The neere Lust-wearied *Anthony*.
   Mene. I cannot hope,
Cæsar and *Anthony* shall well greet together;
His Wife that's dead, did trespasses to *Cæsar,*
His Brother wan'd vpon him, although I thinke   665
Not mou'd by *Anthony*.
   Pom. I know not *Menas,*

---

661 neere] near F3-POPE1; ne'er mTBY2 *and* THEOBALD (1726, p. 184) *conj.*, POPE2+
662–6 *Given to Menas* ROWE2+
663 greet] 'gree mF2FL21 *conj.*, RIDb, ARD2
664 that's] who's POPE1-v1773 (−CAP)
665 wan'd] warr'd F2+

---

659 **our Opinion**] I.e., the opinion of us. See FRANZ §322.

660 **Egypts Widdow**] STEEVENS (ed. 1793): "Julius Cæsar had married her to young Ptolemy [actually, the older Ptolemy XIII], who was afterwards drowned." SCHMIDT (1842, p. 318) states that the reference is to Cleopatra's younger brother and consort Ptolemy XIII (actually, XIV), whom she had poisoned. SCHANZER (1960, pp. 335–6), however, finds that neither view can be "justified"; see n. 435.

661 **neere Lust-wearied**] THEOBALD (1726, p. 184) explains his disambiguation of *neere* to *ne'er*: "If *Antony*, tho' *never* tir'd of Luxury, yet mov'd from that Charm upon *Pompey's* Stiring, it was Reason for *Pompey* to pride himself upon being of such Consequence."

662 **hope**] STEEVENS (ed. 1778): I.e., expect. "So, [Chaucer] in *The Reve's Tale*, v. 4027: 'Our manciple I *hope* he wol be ded.'" BOSWELL (ed. 1821): "A blundering expression in the days of Queen Elizabeth." He quotes George Puttenham, *The Arte of English Poesie* (ed. Willcock & Walker, 1936, p. 256): "The Tanner of Tamworth . . . said . . . *I hope I shall be hanged to morrow.* For (*I feare me*)." *OED* (*v.* 4), citing both examples: "To expect or anticipate (without implication of desire)." KITTREDGE (ed. 1941): "The word was often used of disagreeable expectation as well as of that which is pleasant." See also n. 2479.

663 **greet together**] BLUMHOF (ed. 1870): Very likely Sh. intends to present two concepts—greeting and agreeing—in one word. KITTREDGE (ed. 1941): "I.e., 'come to an amicable agreement.'" FURNESS (ed. 1907) finds *greet together* unidiomatic and regards *greet* as "an error of the compositor, who . . . has added to the verb *gree* the *t* of the next word, 'together.'" But *together* is a recognized substitute for the reciprocal pronoun (i.e., each other)—see FRANZ (§312, *Anm.* 2), who refers to examples in SCHMIDT (1875, *Together*, 4) and regards the construction a typical pleonasm (§457). See also 871, 2247, 2495.

664–6 See n. 177–80.

665 **wan'd vpon**] SISSON (1956, 2:265): Possibly "'made defection from'. But the F2 reading . . . is more natural and apt, and is supported by . . . [732–3]." The error—universally corrected to *warr'd*—may be due to a compositorial misreading of *war'd* or

How lesser Enmities may giue way to greater,
Were't not that we stand vp against them all:
'Twer pregnant they should square between themselues,   670
For they haue entertained cause enough
To draw their swords: but how the feare of vs
May Ciment their diuisions, and binde vp
The petty difference, we yet not know:
Bee't as our Gods will haue't; it onely stands   675
Our liues vpon, to vse our strongest hands
Come *Menas*.   *Exeunt.*

Enter Enobarbus and Lepidus.   **2.2** (xx3^b)

Lep. Good *Enobarbus*, 'tis a worthy deed,
And shall become you well, to intreat your Captaine   680
To soft and gentle speech.

---

668 greater,] ⁓ . F4+ (−SING2)
673 diuisions] division COL4
676 hands∧] ⁓ , F2+
678 SCENE II. ROWE1-POPE2, HAN1, WARB, JOHN1+
    Rome. ROWE1-JOHN1, v1773, v1778, RANN; Rome. *A Room in* Lepidus' *House.*
CAP, MAL, v1793+ (*subst.*)

---

perhaps a memorial error induced by *wand* (641).
    668 Possibly proverbial; see DENT (G446): "The greater (One) *grief* (sorrow) drives
out the less (another)."
    670 **pregnant**] COTGRAVE (1611): "Raisons pregnantes. *Plaine, apparent, important,
or pressing reasons.*" From "ready" (BOSWELL [ed. 1821, 21:Glossary]) more recent commentators have shifted to "*Highly probable*" (WORDSWORTH [ed. 1883]).
    should] "Would" (RANN's [ed. 1791–] paraphrase). See FRANZ §616, §708 (pp.
620–1). See also 878.
    square] COTGRAVE (1611, Se quarrer): "*To strout, or square it, looke big on't, carrie
his armes a kemboll braggadochio-like.*" ROWE (ed. 1714, 8:Glossary): "To quarrel, &c."
    671 **entertained**] Those who comment are split between "*Harboured*" (WORDSWORTH
[ed. 1883])—see *OED*, 14c—and "received" (KITTREDGE [ed. 1941])—see *OED*, 14. SEY-
MOUR (1805, 2:50), incorrectly: "'Entertained' is here a participle," modifying *cause*. See
also 1407, nn. 2320 ("entertainment"), 2595.
    673 **Ciment**] ABBOTT (§492) lists among "words in which the accent was nearer the
beginning than with us."
    675–6 **it . . . vpon**] JOHNSON (1755, *Stand* [*upon*], 64): "To concern; to interest."
ABBOTT (§204): "This use of *upon* in 'stand *upon*' is not a mere poetical transposition,
but a remnant of an old idiom imperfectly understood." For the dative, see FRANZ §293.

77

Enob. I shall intreat him
To answer like himselfe: if *Cæsar* moue him,
Let *Anthony* looke ouer *Cæsars* head,
And speake as lowd as Mars. By Iupiter,   685
Were I the wearer of *Anthonio's* Beard,
I would not shaue't to day.
  Lep. 'Tis not a time for priuate stomacking.
  Eno. Euery time serues for the matter that is then
borne in't.   690
  Lep. But small to greater matters must giue way.
  Eno. Not if the small come first.

---

683 moue] mov'd RANN
686 *Anthonio's*] Antonius' mTBY4 *conj.*, v1773-ARD2 (–KTLY, CAM3)
687–94, 696 F1-ROWE2; *three verse lines ending* Day. . . . Stomaching. . . . in't
then as F1 ROWE3; *six verse lines ending* time . . . in't. . . . way. . . . passion; . . .
comes . . . *Cæsar.* POPE1-THEO2, WARB-JOHN1, v1773-RANN; *seven verse lines ending*
a time . . . Every time . . . in't. . . . way. . . . passion; . . . comes . . . *Cæsar.*
HAN1 *etc.*
687 shaue't] shave v1803
690 borne] born F3+

---

683 **like himselfe**] KITTREDGE (ed. 1941): "In a way . . . worthy of his own greatness. . . . Common in this intensive meaning. See H. T. Price, [*RES* 16 (1940), 178–81]."
  684 **looke ouer**] KERSEY (1702, over-look): "*To look scornfully upon.*" WILSON's (ed.
1950) "but suggesting Ant.'s stature also" was anticipated by BLUMHOF (ed. 1870).
Suetonius reports Caesar's "stature but short" (*The historie of twelve Cæsars*, tr. Holland,
1606, p. 74).
  686–7 **Were . . . shaue't**] Modifying WARBURTON's (ed. 1747) "Alluding to the phrase,
I will beard him" (*OED*, 3: "To oppose openly and resolutely"), JOHNSON (ed. 1765):
"I believe he means, *I would meet him undressed, without shew of respect.*" Most commentators agree, despite some slight difference in detail about the dress or beard. CASE
(ed. 1906), followed only by WILSON (ed. 1950) and RIDLEY (ed. 1954), finds the interpretation "too tame" and suggests the literal action: "I would not remove the temptation to pluck or shake it, if he dare." See also nn. 31, 938. MALONE (ed. 1790) notes
that Sh. perhaps had in mind Plutarch's (see p. 408) mentioning that Antony grew a
beard after his defeat at Mutina.
  686 *Anthonio's*] See n. 1056.
  688 **stomacking**] I.e., resentment. COCKERAM (1623, *Stomaked*): "Angered." See nn.
740, 1697.
  689–90, 691 The phrasing seems to suggest proverbs or sententiae, but none has been
put forward. Perhaps, for the first, TILLEY (T314): "There is a *time* for all things (Everything has its time)." And, for the second, IDEM (G437): "The *greater* embraces (includes,
hides) the less."
  690 **borne**] I.e., born. See textual notes.

Lep. Your speech is passion: but pray you stirre
No Embers vp. Heere comes the Noble *Anthony.*

            Enter Anthony and Ventidius.   695

Eno. And yonder *Cæsar.*

       Enter Cæsar, Mecenas, and Agrippa.

Ant. If we compose well heere, to Parthia:
Hearke *Ventidius.*
Cæsar. I do not know *Mecenas,* aske *Agrippa.*   700
Lep. Noble Friends:
That which combin'd vs was most great, and let not
A leaner action rend vs. What's amisse,
May it be gently heard. When we debate
Our triuiall difference loud, we do commit   705
Murther in healing wounds. Then Noble Partners,
The rather for I earnestly beseech,
Touch you the sowrest points with sweetest tearmes,
Nor curstnesse grow to'th'matter.

---

693 you] you, sir, RIDb
697 *After* 699 KTLY, RIDb; *after* 694 SIS; *ad. by another door* CAM3, SIS
699–701 *Verse lines ending* know, . . . friends, CAP, v1778+ (−KNT1, STAU, ALEX)
699 Hearke] Hark thee HAN1; Hark you mTBY3 *conj.*, CAP, v1778-SING1, COL1-SING2,
COL3, WH1, KTLY, COL4; Hark ye DYCE2, HUD2, OXF1
700 know_ᴧ] ~ ; ROWE1-THEO2, WARB-JOHN1

698–700 DELIUS (ed. 1856) believes that Antony and Octavius pretend not to see
each other, each waiting for the other to make the first conciliatory move; WILSON (ed.
1950), that they "check an animated conversation at sight of each other."
    698 **compose**] CAWDREY (1604): "Ioyne together." RANN (ed. 1791–): "Terminate
amicably." STEEVENS (ed. 1793): "Come to a lucky *composition*, agreement." See also
nn. 452, 1248.
    Parthia] COOPER (1565): "A countrey in Asia, whiche hath on the south the redde
sea: on the north, the sea called *Hircanum*: on the east, the people called *Arii*: on the
west, the realme called *Media*." See PAULY, 18B:1968–2029; *OCD*; and map, p. xxxvii.
    707 **The . . . for**] BLUMHOF (ed. 1870): The more so because. ABBOTT (§94) con-
siders *the* the "ablative of the demonstrative and relatives, with comparatives to signify
the measure of excess or defect."
    709 JOHNSON (ed. 1765) and the others: "Let not *ill humour* [i.e., curstnesse, de-
fined even more pejoratively by *OED*, 4] be added to the real *subject* of our difference."
The absence of *neither* as a complement to *nor* usually presupposes a foregoing *not* clause,
as in the somewhat distant 702. See FRANZ §588.
    grow to'th'matter] *OED* (5b): "To arise or come into existence to the benefit or

Ant. 'Tis spoken well: 710
Were we before our Armies, and to fight,
I should do thus.   *Flourish.*
    Cæs. Welcome to Rome.
    Ant. Thanke you.
    Cæs. Sit.   715
    Ant. Sit sir.
    Cæs. Nay then.
    Ant. I learne, you take things ill, which are not so:
Or being, concerne you not.
    Cæs. I must be laught at, if or for nothing, or a little, I   720

---

711 Armies] Armes F2
712 *Flourish.*] *Om.* HAN1, CAP-COL1, HUD, DYCE, STAU, WH1, HAL, OXF1; *Shake hands.*
mCOL1, COL2, SING2, KTLY; *ad. They shake hands.* COL3, COL4, CAM3
713–17 *Arranged as verse lines, thus:* 713–17 KNT1, DYCE, GLO, WH2, NLSN-CAM3,
ARD2, EVNS; 713–14, *then as* F1 COL, WH1, HAL; 713–16, 717 KTLY; *two verse lines divided*
Nay, | Then— v1793-v1821, SING
714 Thanke] I Thank mTBY2 *conj.*, KTLY
719–20 *Verse lines ending* at, . . . I ROWE1+
720 little, I] little, F2-F4

---

injury of." ABBOTT (§364), citing this instance under "subjunctive used optatively or
imperatively": "The juxtaposition of an imperative [*Touch* (708)] sometimes indicates
the imperative use." Mentions also *take* (824).
    712 **do thus**] CAPELL (1779 [1774], 1:32): "Talk the difference over gently." COLLIER
(in PERKINS FOLIO and ed. 1853): "Shake handes" (see textual notes). DELIUS (ed. 1856)
proposes an accompanying gesture of greeting, as do most others.
    Flourish] SHIRLEY (1963, p. 77) suggests that flourishes may also be used for "build-
ing up our excitement before some sort of formal contest."
    715–17 STEEVENS (ed. 1773): "Antony appears to be jealous of a circumstance which
seemed to indicate a consciousness of superiority in his too successful partner in power;
and accordingly resents the invitation of Cæsar to be seated: Cæsar answers, *Nay then—*
i.e. *if you are so ready to resent what I meant an act of civility, there can be no reason
to suppose you have temper enough for the business on which at present we are met.*"
ANON. (*St. James's Chr.*, no. 2404 [3–6 Aug. 1776]): "It is only a Contention of Civility,
between two Persons of equal Dignity, who shall give Place to the other; and Caesar
puts an End to it, by saying nay then; that is, I will not take up the Time by mere useless
Ceremony." G. R. SMITH (1974, p. 2), questionably: "Whichever man sat first, while
the other still stood, presumably had the higher rank. . . . When Antony tells Caesar
to sit first, he slips himself into a subordinate position, and Caesar promptly takes the
superior."
    719 **being**] WORDSWORTH (ed. 1883): "I.e., *So.*" KITTRIDGE (ed. 1941): "If they *are*
ill,—i.e., objectionable."
    720 **or . . . or**] I.e., either . . . or. See FRANZ §586.

Should say my selfe offended, and with you
Chiefely i'th'world. More laught at, that I should
Once name you derogately: when to sound your name
It not concern'd me.
   Ant. My being in Egypt *Cæsar,* what was't to you?   725
   Cæs. No more then my reciding heere at Rome
Might be to you in Egypt: yet if you there
Did practise on my State, your being in Egypt
Might be my question.
   Ant. How intend you, practis'd?   730
   Cæs. You may be pleas'd to catch at mine intent,
By what did heere befall me. Your Wife and Brother
Made warres vpon me, and their contestation

723-5 F1-ROWE3, SING2, KTLY; *three verse lines ending* sound . . . me. . . . you?
POPE1-JOHN1, v1773; *ending* sound . . . Egypt, . . . you? RID, ARD2; *ending* your name
. . . *Cæsar,* . . . you? CAP *etc.*
   726 at] in RIDb
   727 yet] *Om.* POPE, HAN1
   732 me] *Om.* POPE1-v1773 (−CAP)
   733-4 their . . . for you] their contestation Was theam'd for you mTBY2 *and*
WARBURTON *conj. apud* THEO1, THEO1-THEO4, CAP; for contestation Their theme was
you MASON (1785, p. 275) *conj.,* RANN; their contestation For theme was you COL3; your
contestation Was theme for them KTLY; their contestation Was then for you DEIGHTON
(1898, p. 41) *conj.* (thenne), CLN2, CAM3b

722-4 **More . . . me**] SCHANZER (1960, p. 20) compares the colon after *derogately*
with that after *thus* (see n. 48). It too "points forward to a restrictive 'when' clause. Its
function in both cases is to indicate the restrictive nature of the succeeding clause, a
function which in modern punctuation can only be performed by the omission of any
punctuation mark."
   723 **derogately**] CAWDREY (1604, derogate): "To take away, or to diminish." BUL-
LOKAR (1616, *Derogation*): "A taking away from ones honour or estimation."
   725 **being**] SCHMIDT (ed. 1870): Not simply Antony's stay in Egypt but the special
kind of existence and life, as in *TGV* 3.1.57 (1126) and *Tim.* 4.3.246 (1873).
   728 **practise on**] Although the sense of "To practise tricks or artifices upon" (*OED,*
11) was common, the first dictionary so to define is BAILEY (1721): "To endeavour to
bring over, win or draw into ones Hands, to tamper with." STEEVENS (ed. 1778) cites
the Countess of Pembroke's *Antonie:* "Nothing killes me so, As that I so my *Cleopatra*
see Practise with *Cæsar*" (1595, ll. 882–4). For the 1592 *Antonius,* see p. 500.
   729 **be my question**] Commentators follow MALONE (*apud* STEEVENS, ed. 1778): Be
"my theme or subject of conversation." WILSON (ed. 1950) is the exception: "Set me asking."
   733-4 **and . . . you,**] As is apparent from the textual notes and conj. (p. 350), the

Was Theame for you, you were the word of warre.

Ant. You do mistake your busines, my Brother neuer   735
Did vrge me in his Act: I did inquire it,
And haue my Learning from some true reports
That drew their swords with you, did he not rather
Discredit my authority with yours,
And make the warres alike against my stomacke,   740
Hauing alike your cause. Of this, my Letters

---

735 your] the mTBY2 *conj.*, HAN1
736 his] this HAN1
    inquire] require THEO2, WARB, THEO4
737 reports] reporters POPE, HAN1
740 warres] war COL4
741 cause.] ∼ ? F3+

---

crux of the seemingly simple grammatical construction is *for you*, the handling of which causes a change in *Theame* or itself, or both. The subsequent clause suggests that the sense is either "You were the subject of their contestation" or "The contestation was waged in your behalf." Or, as CAPELL (1779 [1774], 1:32) has it, "The fault is in the Poet himself, whose licence of expression is sometimes excessive."

734 **word of warre**] The few who comment regard the phrase as either an intensifying appositive of *Theame* or as meaning "watchword." CANBY (ed. 1921): "You were the excuse for their going to war." See n. 1529.

736 **vrge me**] WARBURTON (ed. 1747): "*I.e.* never did make use of my name." See Pompey's "Not mou'd by *Anthony*" (666) but also Antony's name as a "magicall word of Warre" (1528-9).

737 **reports**] UPTON (1746, p. 320): "*He* [Sh.] *uses the abstract for the concrete.*" Only DELIUS (ed. 1856) disagrees, paraphrasing as "*from the true reports of some.*" The comparison by CASE (ed. 1906) and others with *discontents* (471) is not quite accurate as far as the grammar is concerned. *Discontents* is an example of a nominalized adjective — see n. 471; *reports* may simply be a parallel form to *reporters* — see FRANZ §94. Both are products of conversion, as modern grammatical description would have it.

739 **with**] THISELTON (1899, p. 12): "Along with."

740 **stomacke**] COOPER (1565): "The . . . appetite of one that abhorreth a thing, or deliteth in a thing." See nn. 688, 1697.

741 **Hauing . . . cause**] JOHNSON (ed. 1765): "*Having the same cause as you to be offended with me.*" Still, Johnson asks, "But why, because he was offended with *Antony*, should he make war upon *Cæsar?*" and proposes "Hating *alike* our *cause?*" STEEVENS (ed. 1778) and MALONE (ed. 1790) — and others — disagree with the grammatical reference: "That is, *I* having alike your cause. . . . Dr. Johnson supposed that *having* meant, *he* having." CASE (ed. 1906): "Since I had as much cause to resent them as you." KIT-TREDGE (ed. 1941): "Having as much reason as you had to be displeased with him. *Having* agrees with *me* implied in *my* (i.e., of me) in [740]."

Before did satisfie you. If you'l patch a quarrell,
As matter whole you haue to make it with,
It must not be with this.
  Cæs. You praise your selfe, by laying defects of iudge-   745
ment to me: but you patcht vp your excuses.
  Anth. Not so, not so:
I know you could not lacke, I am certaine on't,

---

742 you'l] you F2-ROWE3; you will mCAP2, CAPN (*errata*)
743 As] No mCOL1, COL2
     you haue] Ff, RANN, KNT1-HUD1, COL3, WH1, COL4, OXF1, RIDb, ARD2, CAM3b,
EVNS; you lack ANON. *conj. apud* CAM1, HUD2; you'd have SIS; you've not ROWE1 *etc.*
     make] take F2-F4
744-7 *Three verse lines ending* self, . . . but . . . not so; POPE1+ (-KNT1)
745-6 defects . . . me] to me defects of judgment CAP, RANN
746 patcht] patch F3-JOHN1
     excuses] excuse WALKER (1860, 1:246) *conj.*, HUD2
748 on't,] of the mTBY4 *conj.* (*and withdrawn*), KTLY (on't——The)

742-3 **If . . . with**] PARTRIDGE (1964, p. 121): "'If you want to patch a quarrel, you will have to make your *patch* out of the *whole* (affair), not out of this isolated instance'. The contrast is almost certainly between the noun *patch* (or 'part'), assumed from the verb, and *whole*. The latter is an adjective in post-position, qualifying *matter*."

742 **patch**] While the verb is not always depreciatory in Sh., Caesar's caustic "patcht vp" (746) exemplifies the *OED* qualification (*v.* 2): "Usually with *up*, and implying a hasty, clumsy, imperfect, or temporary manner."

743 Most commentators accept ROWE's (ed. 1709) insertion of the negative after "haue," their interpretation aptly paraphrased by KITTREDGE (ed. 1941): "As [you must do if you wish to quarrel with me, for] you have no substantial material to make a quarrel out of." Those who defend the F1 reading do so mainly in their interpretation of *As*. Whereas Kittredge regards it as "the elliptical use," WILSON (ed. 1950, Glossary) cites *OED* (3b): "In parenthetical clauses forming an extension of the subject or predicate, the antecedent (*so, as*) formerly present is now omitted, and the relative has acquired somewhat of a concessive force=Though, however"; RIDLEY (ed. 1954) cites *OED* (8d): "In antithetical or parallel clauses, introducing a known circumstance with which a hypothesis is contrasted . . . whereas"; INGLEBY (1877, 1:146), crediting "Professor Sylvester, the world-renowned mathematician," regards it as the *"conjunction of reminder . . .* to introduce a subsidiary statement, qualifying, or even contradicting, what goes before, which the person addressed is required to take for granted [quotes 'Say . . . indeed' (451-2); *AYL* 3.5.37-8 (1810-11), 'though . . . you'; and *MM* 2.4.88-9 (1096-7)]," thus supporting those starting with STEEVENS (ed. 1778) who believe the line alludes "to Antony's acknowledged neglect in aiding Cæsar," a belief also held by those who regard *As* as meaning "since" (like DELIUS [ed. 1856]), "as though" (like THISELTON [1899, p. 12]), "inasmuch as" (like FURNESS [ed. 1907]). Perhaps the simplest and most satisfactory explanation is ABBOTT's (§111), citing this instance: "*As* is used in a transitional manner for 'as regards which' or 'for indeed.'" See textual notes and conj., p. 350.

Very necessity of this thought, that I
Your Partner in the cause 'gainst which he fought,   750
Could not with gracefull eyes attend those Warres
Which fronted mine owne peace. As for my wife,
I would you had her spirit, in such another,
The third oth'world is yours, which with a Snaffle,
You may pace easie, but not such a wife.   755
   Enobar. Would we had all such wiues, that the men
might go to Warres with the women.
   Anth. So much vncurbable, her Garboiles (*Cæsar*)

---

751 gracefull] grateful POPE1-v1773, CAM3b
756-7 *Verse lines ending* might . . . women! COL4
    Marked as an aside BLUM
758 vncurbable] uncurable v1803, SING1, HUD1

---

749 **Very . . . thought**] SCHMIDT (1875, Very): "Generally placed before substantives to indicate that they must be understood in their full and unrestricted sense." See
also 409. Thus HUDSON (ed. 1881) and the few who comment: "This *truly inevitable*
thought." The adjective *very* without a preceding article or pronoun accounts for only
36 of a total of 849 occurrences, 18 alone in the last plays. The 4 occurrences in *Ant.*
are matched only by *WT.* See 1985, 2069, 2881.

   751 **gracefull**] HUDSON (ed. 1881): "*Graceful* for *gracious* or *favourable*; these being
among the many words of common origin that had not become fully differentiated in
the Poet's time." For the suffixes *-ful* and *-ous*, see FRANZ §121, §131, and n. 2543.

   attend] Following STEEVENS's (ed. 1778) paraphrase ("look . . . on"), SCHMIDT
(1874, 4a): "To regard with attention, to take notice of, to witness." See also 3634.

   752 **fronted**] JOHNSON (1755): "To oppose directly." See 517.

   753 MALONE (ed. 1790): "I wish you were married to such another spirited woman."

   spirit, in such] BOSWELL (ed. 1821), commenting on STEEVENS's (ed. 1793) suggestion that *such* be omitted: "Spirit was generally pronounced as a monosyllable." See
conj., p. 350.

   754 **Snaffle**] MINSHEU (1617): "A Bitte *for a horse.*" Since a snaffle lacks a curb, it
is too gentle a restraint for a headstrong horse. See 758.

   755 **pace**] KERSEY's (1702) "*To pace,* or *amble as a horse does*" is explained by DYCHE
& PARDON (1740): "To make a horse move in a particular manner for women to travel
or ride upon easily." Commentators tend to RANN's (ed. 1791-) "Manage."

   756 **had all**] I.e., all of us had. For the construction, see FRANZ §324.

   757 **go . . . women**] BLUMHOF (ed. 1870) first detected an ambiguity: To fight along
with the women (with a reference to Antony's inactivity compared to Fulvia's) and also
to fight against the women (with reference to Antony's subjugation by Cleopatra). In
all other instances of *war with* in Sh. the meaning is clearly "against." The allusion is
of course bawdy. See also n. 631.

   758 **vncurbable**] Commentators agree with DELIUS (ed. 1856) that the reference is
to Fulvia. KITTREDGE (ed. 1941) adds, "Antony pursues the figure he has used in his

Made out of her impatience: which not wanted
Shrodenesse of policie to: I greeuing grant,   760
Did you too much disquiet, for that you must,
But say I could not helpe it.
    Cæsar. I wrote to you, when rioting in Alexandria you
Did pocket vp my Letters: and with taunts
Did gibe my Misiue out of audience.   765
    Ant. Sir, he fell vpon me, ere admitted, then:
Three Kings I had newly feasted, and did want
Of what I was i'th'morning: but next day
I told him of my selfe, which was as much

762–3 *Verse lines ending* to you, . . . you ROWE1+
763 Alexandria ⟨⟩] ~ ; mWARB *conj.*, v1778-NLSN, KIT1, ALEX
765–6 *Verse lines ending* Sir, . . . then CAP, MAL, v1793+
765 gibe] beg F4-ROWE3
766 vpon] on ROWE1-JOHN1, v1773, v1778, RANN
    then:] ~ ⟨⟩ ROWE1-ARD1, RIDa, KIT1, ALEX

---

preceding speech. Even a *curb bit* would not hold Fulvia."
    Garboiles] See n. 373.
    760 **Shrodenesse**] Although SCHMIDT (1875) defines as "cunning," the original sense
and implications ought not be overlooked here. BULLOKAR (1616) defines *Shrew* as "A
kinde of field Mouse, which if he goe ouer a beasts backe, will make him lame in the
chine; and if he bite, the beast swelleth to the heart, and dieth." See also n. 2699.
    policie] CAWDREY (1604): "A wittie shift." MINSHEU (1617) adds, "*A stratageme.*"
See also 1314, n. 3559.
    to] I.e., too.
    761 **Did . . . disquiet**] All commentators beginning with BLUMHOF (ed. 1870) re-
gard *disquiet* as a noun. It could be a verb, however.
    765 **Misiue**] COTGRAVE (1611): "*A letter sent.*" Most commentators, starting with JOHN-
SON (1755), who cites this instance, gloss as "messenger," the sense implicit in THEOBALD
(3 Mar. 1729, [fol. 50ʳ]). WALKER (1957, p. 99): "An example of metonymy, frequently
employed by Shakespeare in talks at high level, and Shakespeare's contemporaries would
consequently have deduced that Caesar was very much on his dignity."
    766 **fell vpon**] RANN (ed. 1791–): "Approached . . . without due ceremony."
    767 **Three Kings**] Not identified, but see SCULLARD (1959; 1976, p. 172): "As a precau-
tionary measure before his Parthian campaign, he reorganized other client-kingdoms,
setting up Amyntas in Galatia, an Archelaus in Cappadocia, and Polemo in an extended
Pontus: all these men, together with Herod, served him well." See also 106, 1826–33.
    767–8 **did . . . was**] Those who comment agree with DELIUS (ed. 1856): Was not
as sober as I had been.
    769 **I . . . selfe**] WARBURTON (ed. 1747) and most others: "*I.e.* told him the condi-
tion I was in, when we had his last audience." DELIUS (ed. 1856) alone: I.e., of my own
volition.

As to haue askt him pardon. Let this Fellow   770
Be nothing of our strife: if we contend
Out of our question wipe him.
　　Cæsar. You haue broken the Article of your oath,
which you shall neuer haue tongue to charge me with.
　　Lep. Soft *Cæsar.*   775
　　Ant. No *Lepidus*, let him speake,
The Honour is Sacred which he talks on now,
Supposing that I lackt it: but on *Cæsar,*
The Article of my oath.
　　Cæsar. To lend me Armes, and aide when I requir'd   780
them, the which you both denied.
　　Anth. Neglected rather:
And then when poysoned houres had bound me vp
From mine owne knowledge, as neerely as I may,
Ile play the penitent to you. But mine honesty,   785
Shall not make poore my greatnesse, nor my power

772–6 Ff; *three verse lines ending* broken . . . never . . . with *then as* F1
ROWE1-THEO2, WARB-JOHN1, v1773-RANN; *four verse lines ending* broken . . . never
. . . No, . . . speak, HAN1, CAP, v1793, SING2, DYCE, GLO, WH2-ARD1, KIT1, ALEX,
SIS; *ending* broken . . . never . . . with. . . . speak; STAU; *ending* broken . . . never
. . . Cæsar. . . . speak; v1803 *etc.*
775 *Cæsar*] Cæsar, soft KTLY
776 No‸] ~ ; ALEX
780–2 *Verse lines ending* them, . . . rather. F4+

---

772 **question**] Whereas early commentators gloss as "Conversation" (BOSWELL [ed.
1821, 21:Glossary]), later ones tend to sharpen to "Subject or cause of quarrel" (WILSON
[ed. 1950, Glossary]).
775 **Soft**] MINSHEU (1617, Softly): "Litle and Litle, [or] Leasurely." *OED* (*adv.* 8):
"Used as an exclamation with imperative force, either to enjoin silence or deprecate haste."
777–8 **The . . . it**] JOHNSON (ed. 1765) and MALONE (*apud* STEEVENS, ed. 1778):
Now modifies *talks on.* MASON (1785, p. 276) and others: "The adverb *now* refers to
is, not to *talks on.*"
778 **Supposing**] Most commentators follow MALONE (*apud* STEEVENS, ed. 1778) in
taking *Supposing* as a participle modifying *he* (Caesar). A few follow JOHNSON's (ed.
1765) adverbial "*even* supposing"—i.e., even if one supposes.
780 **requir'd**] See n. 2123.
781 **the which**] FRANZ (§337): Has the same grammatical function as *which* and serves
for clarity or stress.
784 **mine owne knowledge**] I.e., knowledge of my own self. For the construction, see
FRANZ §322.
785 **honesty**] Most commentators equate *honesty* and *Honour* (777), in the sense
given by COCKERAM (1623, [Pt. 2, sig. D1ʳ]): "*Probity, Integrity.*" Compare 2199, n. 542.

Worke without it. Truth is, that *Fuluia,*
To haue me out of Egypt, made Warres heere,
For which my selfe, the ignorant motiue, do
So farre aske pardon, as befits mine Honour   790
To stoope in such a case.
Lep. 'Tis Noble spoken.
Mece. If it might please you, to enforce no further
The griefes betweene ye: to forget them quite,
Were to remember: that the present neede,   795
Speakes to attone you.
Lep. Worthily spoken *Mecenas.*
Enobar. Or if you borrow one anothers Loue for the
instant, you may when you heare no more words of
Pompey returne it againe: you shall haue time to wrangle   800
in, when you haue nothing else to do.
Anth. Thou art a Souldier, onely speake no more.

---

792 Noble] Nobly F2-v1778, RANN-v1803, SING, COL2, HUD1, COL3, WH1, KTLY, COL4
793, 821 further] farther COL, WH1, HAL
794 ye] you v1773, v1778, RANN
796 Speakes] Speak CAP (*text*; Speaks *in corrigenda*)
797 Worthily] Worthy F2
    spoken] spoke mTBY4 *conj.*, v1793, v1803, COL4
802 Souldier, onely␣] ~ ␣ ~ ;— mTHEO2 (19 Feb. 1729, [fol. 39ᵛ]) *conj.*, THEO1+
(−WARB)

---

787 it] Nearly all commentators follow MALONE's (ed. 1790) "mine honesty"; DELIUS
(ed. 1856), CASE (ed. 1906), and RIDLEY (ed. 1954) also suggest "greatness." BARROLL
(1969, *ShakS*, p. 221, n. 4): "If we take the antecedent of 'it' to be 'honesty', the best
that can be gained is a contradiction. 'Greatness' and 'power' seem, if not synonymous,
at least appositive, with 'greatness' thus the logical antecedent of the pronoun."
    789 **motiue**] CAWDREY (1604): "Cause moouing, or the thing, and reason, that
mooueth to doe any thing."
    792 **Noble**] All commentators, starting with MALONE (*apud* BOSWELL, ed. 1821),
note that "substantives [elsewhere Malone correctly refers to "adjectives . . . used as
adverbs"] were frequently used adjectively by Shakspeare." Only WHITE (ed. 1883) does
"not doubt that here 'noble' is a mere phonetic spelling of *nobly.*" See also n. 2895.
    793 **If . . . you**] CAPELL (1779 [1774], 1:33): "This imperfect and conditional mode
of expressing a wish, may be intended as a mark of submissiveness: in any other light
. . . *Would* were greatly better than '*If.*'"
    794 **griefes**] JOHNSON (1755) and all others: "Grievance."
    796 **attone**] MINSHEU (1617, Attonement): "*Agreement.*" From "at one."

Enob. That trueth should be silent, I had almost forgot.

Anth. You wrong this presence, therefore speake no   805
more.

Enob. Go too then: your Considerate stone.

Cæsar. I do not much dislike the matter, but
The manner of his speech: for't cannot be,
We shall remaine in friendship, our conditions   810 (xx3ᵛ
So diffring in their acts. Yet if I knew,

803–4 *On one line* ROWE1-POPE1, THEO1-HAN1, THEO4, MAL, RANN, COL2, DYCE1,
COL3, HAL-WH2, ARD1, RID, SIS+; *verse* WARB, JOHN1, v1773, v1778, CAM3

805–6 Ff; *on one line* ROWE1-POPE1, HAN1, RANN, DYCE, COL3, HAL, CAM1, HUD2,
WH2, ARD, RID; *verse* POPE2 *etc.*

807 your] you JOHN1 *conj.*, COL2

808–9 matter . . . manner] manner . . . matter WARB, CAP

809 his] this WARB

803–4 GREY (1754, 2:197): "The proverbial sentence, All truth must not be told at
all times . . . *Ray's* [*Collection of English Proverbs*, 1678], p. 211." See also DENT (T594),
citing this instance.

805 **this presence**] Those who comment agree with DEIGHTON (ed. 1891): "This noble
company." CASE (ed. 1906) adds, "As often in Shakespeare." HODGSON (1936, pp. 90–1):
"Very probably it was a not too covert gibe at 'the young Roman boy.'"

807 **Go too**] See n. 1069.

your Considerate stone] STEEVENS (ed. 1773): "*If I must be chidden, hencefor-
ward I will be mute as a marble statue, which seems to think, though it can say nothing.*"
IDEM (ed. 1778) and many others: "*As silent as a stone* . . . might have been once a
common phrase." (See DENT [S879].) IDEM (ed. 1793) quotes Horace's *Epistles* 2.2.83–4,
for the statue image.

Considerate] CAWDREY (1604, consideratly): "Wisely, and with aduise." I.e., ad-
vised, cautious.

808–9 **I . . . speech**] WARBURTON (ed. 1747): "*Shakespear* wrote, *I do not much
dislike the* manner, *but The* matter *of his speech:* —*i.e.* 'tis not his liberty of speech,
but the mischiefs he speaks of, which I dislike. This agrees with what follows, and is
said with much urbanity, and show of friendship." JOHNSON (ed. 1765): "I think the
old reading right. I do not, says *Cæsar*, think the man wrong, but too free of his interpo-
sition; *for't cannot be, we shall remain in friendship: yet if it were possible, I would
endeavour it.* The consideration of the ceremony due from *Cæsar* to the Lieutenant of
Antony, is a criticism of the lowest rate, unworthy of confutation." HEATH (1765, p. 454)
concurs. Only CAPELL (1779 [1774], 1:33) agrees with Warburton.

810 **conditions**] MINSHEU (1617): "*Propertie, nature, disposition, manner, one vseth
or is of.*" Those who gloss follow VALPY (ed. 1833): "Dispositions."

What Hoope should hold vs staunch from edge to edge
Ath'world: I would persue it.
   Agri. Giue me leaue *Cæsar.*
   Cæsar. Speake *Agrippa.*   815
   Agri. Thou hast a Sister by the Mothers side, admir'd
Octauia? Great *Mark Anthony* is now a widdower.
   Cæsar. Say not, say *Agrippa*; if *Cleopater* heard you, your

---

812 should] would POPE1-v1773 (–CAP)
812–13 staunch$_\wedge$ . . . world:] ~ , . . . ~ , ROWE, THEO, WARB, JOHN1, ALEX;
~ , . . . ~ $_\wedge$ POPE, HAN1, CAP-KIT1, SIS
   813–15 *Arranged as verse lines, thus:* 813–14, 815 v1793-CAM3, SIS+; 813, 814–15 ALEX
   816–21 *Lines* 816–17 *three verse lines ending* side, . . . *Antony* . . . Widower., 818–19
prose, 820–1 *two verse lines ending* hear . . . speak. ROWE; *seven verse lines ending*
side, . . . *Antony* . . . *Agrippa*; . . . were . . . rashness. . . . hear . . . speak. POPE;
seven verse lines ending side, . . . *Antony* . . . *Agrippa*; . . . Approof . . . rashness.
. . . hear . . . speak. THEO1-ARD2; *six verse lines ending* side, . . . Antony . . .
Agrippa; . . . [reproof] . . . Caesar; . . . speak. EVNS
   816 the] thy F2-ROWE3
   817 *Octauia?*] ~ ! ROWE1+ (–ARD2)
   818 not, say] not so, ROWE1+

   812–13 **Hoope . . . world**] STEEVENS (ed. 1793) compares "Hoope of Gold, to binde
thy Brothers in," *2H4* 4.4.43 (2417). DEIGHTON (ed. 1891) adds *Ham.* 1.3.63 (528): "Grap-
ple them vnto thy soule with hoopes of steele." WILSON (ed. 1950), fancifully: "The
F. pointing implies that the hoop which binds them together would also encircle the
globe." BERRY (1973, pp. 29–30): "The image here is that of a barrel whose staves must
be tightly fastened with a hoop to prevent leaking. . . . The marriage . . . is not the
only hoop which encloses the two warriors. Caesar's vow to pursue the means of union
with Antony 'from edge to edge o' the world' suggests another, larger hoop — the world
itself, still too small and confining to hold two such titans without becoming the circular
ground for their mortal combat."
   812 **staunch**] MINSHEU (1617, Stanch): "Stoppe, *or* Restraine." Citing this instance,
OED (1b): "Cf. the phrase *to hold water.*"
   816 **Sister . . . side**] DEIGHTON (ed. 1891): "Octavia was the daughter of Caius Octavius by his second wife Atia, as also was the emperor; but Shakespeare here follows
Plutarch who says, 'There was Octavia, the eldest sister of Cæsar, not by one mother,
for she came of Ancharia, and Cæsar himself afterwards of Accia' [see p. 416]." But the
phrase means that the two had the same mother, as CASE (ed. 1906) was the first to
point out. See PAULY, Octavia, 17:1859–68 (96), and *OCD* (2) for Antony's wife-to-be;
PAULY, 17:1859–68 (95), and *OCD* (1) for Octavius's half sister. The article *the* for the
possessive pronoun was common — see "the feet" (1756) and FRANZ §263.
   817 *Octauia?*] RIDLEY (ed. 1954) alone favors F1's question mark rather than an exclamation point or other stop because "Agrippa's is a half-rhetorical question — 'you can't
have forgotten that.'"
   818–19 **your . . . rashnesse**] ABBOTT (§423), explaining "transpositions in Noun-

89

proofe were well deserued of rashnesse.
    Anth. I am not marryed *Cæsar*: let me heere *Agrippa*   820
further speake.
    Agri. To hold you in perpetuall amitie,
To make you Brothers, and to knit your hearts
With an vn-slipping knot, take *Anthony,*
Octauia to his wife: whose beauty claimes   825
No worse a husband then the best of men: whose
Vertue, and whose generall graces, speake
That which none else can vtter. By this marriage,
All little Ielousies which now seeme great,
And all great feares, which now import their dangers,   830
Would then be nothing. Truth's would be tales,
Where now halfe tales be truth's: her loue to both,
Would each to other, and all loues to both

---

819 proofe] Approof THEO, WARB; Reproof HAN1, JOHN1+
    of] for HAN1, COL2
826–7 *Verse lines ending* men: . . . speake F2+
831 would be] would be but POPE1-JOHN1, v1793, v1803, SING2, DYCE2, HUD2, OXF1;
would then be CAP, COL4; would be half RANN
    tales] tales only KTLY

---

clauses containing two nouns connected by 'of' ": "We should say 'the reproof of your
rashness' (unless 'of' here means 'about', 'for')." Since the nouns are normally not so far
apart in this construction — see also FRANZ (§322) — the second suggestion is the more likely.
    819 **proofe**] See textual notes.
    822–5 **To . . . wife**] WILSON (ed. 1950) cites a parallel from the Argument of the
Countess of Pembroke's *Antonie* (1595, ll. 9–11): "Antonius . . . *for knitting a straiter
bonde of amitie betweene them, had taken to wife* Octauia." SCHANZER (1956, p. 153)
finds the work "again echoed" in 1316–18. For the 1592 *Antonius*, see pp. 479–80.
    824 **an vn-slipping knot**] BLUMHOF (ed. 1870) mentions the lover's knot and mar-
riage. ADELMAN (1973, p. 61), more extravagantly: "The Gordian knot is traditionally
associated with marriage; according to legend, he who can loose the Gordian knot will
rule Asia." For the "knot intrinsicate," see n. 3556.
    824–5 **take . . . wife**] See n. 28.
    824 **take**] For the subjunctive, see n. 709.
    827 **generall**] SCHMIDT (1874, 4): "Taken as a whole." See also 195.
    828 **vtter**] Possibly with the secondary meaning "To vanquish, conquer, or overcome."
See *OED, v.*[2].
    830 **import**] Although MINSHEU (1617) refers to "Implie," commentators beginning
with HUDSON (ed. 1881) prefer his more literal "*bring in.*"
    831 **tales**] MINSHEU (1617): "*To tell* Tales, *or blase abroad rumors or reports.*" COCK-
ERAM (1623) equates *tale* with *lie* in defining *Comment.* Generally in Sh., however, the
word seems to signify a narrative, something told or reported.

Draw after her. Pardon what I haue spoke,
For 'tis a studied not a present thought,   835
By duty ruminated.
    Anth. Will *Cæsar* speake?
    Cæsar. Not till he heares how *Anthony* is toucht,
With what is spoke already.
    Anth. What power is in *Agrippa*,   840
If I would say *Agrippa*, be it so,
To make this good?
    Cæsar. The power of *Cæsar,*
And his power, vnto *Octauia.*
    Anth. May I neuer   845
(To this good purpose, that so fairely shewes)
Dreame of impediment: let me haue thy hand
Further this act of Grace: and from this houre,
The heart of Brothers gouerne in our Loues,

---

836 By] My COL2
839–40 *One verse line* v1793+
839 spoke] spoken F3-ROWE3
    already] *Om.* HAN1
842–5 *Verse lines ending* and . . . never THEO1-COL3, WH1+; *ending* Cæsar, . . .
never STAU
844 vnto] to POPE2
847 hand‸] ~ ; THEO1-SIS (–RIDb)
849 heart] hearts mCOL1, COL2

834–5 **Pardon . . . thought**] There has been no comment on why Agrippa should
ask pardon for a meditated rather than spontaneous suggestion. He is most likely being
extremely courteous and tactful.
    835 **present**] COTGRAVE (1611): *"Readie; in sight, in view; at hand, hard by."* See
n. 863 ("presently").
    836 **ruminated**] CAWDREY (1604): "To chewe ouer againe, to studie earnestlie vppon."
    844 **his**] DEIGHTON (ed. 1891): Caesar's. RANN (ed. 1791–) alone: *"Agrippa's."*
    845–7 **May . . . impediment**] WILSON (ed. 1950), noting CASE's (ed. 1906) citation
of *Son.* 116.1–2: "Both prob. derive from the Marriage Service in the Book of Common
Prayer" (i.e., "if either of you do know any impediment why ye may not be lawfully
joined together"). See also n. 2450.
    847–8 **hand Further**] RIDLEY (ed. 1954): "A good example of a tinkering with F's
punctuation [see textual notes for the punctuation after *hand*] which destroys the intended sense. Antony means 'I hope your hand-clasp will ratify this act of grace'. For
this use of 'have' cf. *Othello,* v.ii.87 [3348]."
    849 **heart . . . gouerne**] Not the subject *heart* but the proximity of *Brothers* to *gouerne*
determines the number of the verb. See FRANZ §675 and, for "confusion of proximity,"
ABBOTT §412. See also 3158–60 for a similar collocation.

91

And sway our great Designes.   850
    Cæsar. There's my hand:
A Sister I bequeath you, whom no Brother
Did euer loue so deerely. Let her liue
To ioyne our kingdomes, and our hearts, and neuer
Flie off our Loues againe.   855
    Lepi. Happily, Amen.
    Ant. I did not think to draw my Sword 'gainst *Pompey*,
For he hath laid strange courtesies, and great
Of late vpon me. I must thanke him onely,
Least my remembrance, suffer ill report: 860
At heele of that, defie him.
    Lepi. Time cals vpon's,
Of vs must *Pompey* presently be sought,

---

858 laid] *Om.* F3, F4
859 him‸ onely,] ～ , ～ ‸ COL2, COL3, COL4
862 vpon's] on's HAN1

---

850 **Designes**] CAWDREY (1604, deseigne): "An appoynting how any thing shall be done." See also 3160.

855 **Flie off**] KITTREDGE (ed. 1941), following DEIGHTON (ed. 1891): "An idiom for sudden alienation. [Compares *Lr.* 2.4.91 (1364).]" Understood is the *Let* of 853, continuing the optative subjunctive construction.

856 **Happily**] The only commentator is DEIGHTON (ed. 1891): "This is a happy conclusion." See n. 76.

858 **strange**] COTGRAVE (1611, Estrange): "*Vnusuall.*" DELIUS's (ed. 1856) "conspicuous" or "striking" is typical of the semantic shift in modern glosses.

859 **thanke him onely**] JOHNSON (ed. 1765) and most others: "Must barely return him thanks." DAVIES (1783, 2:347), defending Antony's generosity: "'Let me first', says Antony, 'return the obligation I owe Pompey in such a manner as becomes me.'" Refinements are offered by DELIUS (ed. 1856): "Must therefore say thanks"; and DEIGHTON (ed. 1891): "Must give him thanks, though I cannot do more than that."

861 **At heele of**] Commentators follow JOHNSON's (ed. 1765) "and then," some adding DELIUS's (ed. 1856) "immediately after." FRANZ (§268): *At* is very possibly equivalent to the ME *atte* (contraction of *at the*) or even the rendition of a careless pronunciation that results in the absorption of *the* into *at*. ABBOTT (§89) cites "At heele" as an example of *the* "frequently omitted before a noun already defined by another noun, especially in prepositional phrases." See also 1018–19, 2777, 3326, and n. 574.

defie] JOHNSON (ed. 1765) and most others: "I will defy." Only DELIUS (ed. 1856), without explanation, holds that what is understood is "I may" or "let us." For the apparent absence of the pronominal subject, see FRANZ §306.

863 **Of**] I.e., by. For *of* before personal pronouns, see FRANZ §519.

presently] COTGRAVE (1611, Presentement): "*Quickly, anon, at an instant, at hand, readily, speedily, suddenly.*" FRANZ (§412) holds that the sense of "shortly, soon" and

Or else he seekes out vs.
    Anth. Where lies he?   865
    Cæsar. About the Mount-Mesena.
    Anth. What is his strength by land?
    Cæsar. Great, and encreasing:
But by Sea he is an absolute Master.
    Anth. So is the Fame,   870
Would we had spoke together. Hast we for it,
Yet ere we put our selues in Armes, dispatch we
The businesse we haue talkt of.

864–5 *One verse line* v1793 +

865 Where] And where HAN1, v1793, v1803
    he] he, Cæsar CAP; he now KTLY

866–70 F1-POPE2, KNT1; *four verse lines ending Misenum. . . . Land? . . . Sea
. . . fame.* THEO, WARB, JOHN1, v1773-RANN, STAU, GLO, WH2, NLSN, KIT1, ALEX, EVNS;
three verse lines ending strength? . . . sea . . . fame. mTBY2 *conj. (and withdrawn),*
HAN1 *etc.*

866 Mount-Mesena] *Mount-Misenum* ROWE1-THEO4, CAP-ALEX (– ARD1); Mount
Misenus JOHN1

867 What is] What's HAN1, CAP, v1793-RID (– KNT1, STAU, GLO, WH2, NLSN)
    by land] *Given to Caesar* mTBY2 *conj. (and withdrawn),* HAN1, KTLY, ARD2

870 Fame] Frame F3-ROWE3

---

that of "immediately, at once" are both found in Sh. It is often difficult to make a distinction, however. See 1700, 1733, 1747, n. 835.

866 **Mesena**] COOPER (1565, *Misenum*): "A promontorie by *Cumæ.*" *OCD*: "The northern headland of the Bay of Naples." See PAULY, Misenum, 15:2043–8, and map, p. xxxvii.

867 **by land**] RIDLEY (ed. 1954) finds HANMER's (ed. 1744) assignment to Caesar
"almost as certain as such things can be. . . . Antony was not likely to narrow the scope
of his question to the enemy's land forces." See textual notes, however.

870 **Fame**] See n. 74–5.

871 **Would we**] WILSON (ed. 1950) holds that *we* refers to Caesar and Antony: "Ant.
means: if only *you and I* had taken counsel together (instead of quarrelling) this disaster
(Pomp.'s mastery of the sea) would never have happened." Only RIDLEY (ed. 1954) and
EVANS (ed. 1974) agree. The rest seem to assume that *we* refers to Antony and Pompey.
BARROLL (1969, *ShakS*, p. 222, n. 8): "Possibly, the term is intentionally ambiguous,"
although it is not clear why Antony would wish to be equivocal here.

    spoke] SCHMIDT (ed. 1870) interprets as "fought," citing 1205 and *Cor.* 1.4.4 (488).
KITTREDGE (ed. 1941) prefers the "more probable sense": "Antony wishes the preliminary conference with Pompey were over." NEILSON & HILL (ed. 1942): "I.e., to thank him."

    together] See n. 663.

    Hast . . . it] Only DEIGHTON (ed. 1891) comments: "Let us hasten our prepara-
tions for the encounter: *it*, used indefinitely."

872 **dispatch we**] FRANZ (§649): The old subjunctive used imperatively.

Cæsar. With most gladnesse,
And do inuite you to my Sisters view,   875
Whether straight Ile lead you.   (xx4

Anth. Let vs *Lepidus* not lacke your companie.

Lep. Noble *Anthony*, not sickenesse should detaine
me.

                                        Flourish. Exit omnes.   880

            Manet Enobarbus, Agrippa, Mecenas.

Mec. Welcome from Ægypt Sir.

Eno. Halfe the heart of *Cæsar*, worthy *Mecenas*. My
honourable Friend *Agrippa*.

Agri. Good *Enobarbus*.   885

Mece. We haue cause to be glad, that matters are so
well disgested: you staid well by't in Egypt.

Enob. I Sir, we did sleepe day out of countenaunce:
and made the night light with drinking.

876–9 *Three verse lines ending Lepidus, . . . Antony, . . .* me. mTBY2 *conj.*, HAN1,
CAP, v1778+
878 Noble] Nobld F2
880 *Flourish.*] *Om.* F2-POPE2, HAN1, JOHN1, CAP
881 SCENE III. POPE, HAN1, WARB, JOHN1
887 disgested] digested F2-SIS (–ARD1, KIT1)

---

874 **most**] For *most* "frequently used as the . . . superlative of the adjective 'great,'"
see ABBOTT §17.

875 **And do**] For the omission of the subject *I* when "there can be no doubt what
is the nominative," see ABBOTT §399. Here perhaps omitted for metrical reasons.

    my Sisters view] WHITE (ed. 1883): "View of my sister." See FRANZ §322.

876 **Whether**] See 2077, n. 1504.

878 **should**] See n. 670.

883 **Halfe the heart**] DEIGHTON (ed. 1891): "*I.e.* who are very dear to Cæsar; the
translation of a Latin poetical phrase used by Horace of Vergil, *Odes* [1.3.8], '*animæ
dimidium meæ.*'" KITTREDGE (ed. 1941): "Mæcenas and Agrippa were equally favoured
by Octavius."

887 **disgested**] CAWDREY (1604, digest): "Bring into order, to deuide, & distribute
things into their right place." A punning reference to food, suggested by BLUMHOF (ed.
1870) and THISELTON (1899, p. 13), is unlikely.

    staid well by't] Evidently a conversational idiom. The sparse comment, beginning
with BLUMHOF (ed. 1870), includes only slight variations of "have stood your ground"
(SCHMIDT, 1875, *v.* 1a) and "[kept] things going" (ONIONS, 1911).

888–9 **we . . . drinking**] DEIGHTON (ed. 1891), following BLUMHOF (ed. 1870): The
allusion is to the sun, "with a pun upon *out of countenance* in the sense of a person
put to shame by being stared hard at, and of the daylight put to shame by being of
no use to them; and a second pun upon *light* in the sense of *merry* and of *bright*."

Mece. Eight Wilde-Boares rosted whole at a break-   890
fast: and but twelue persons there. Is this true?
   Eno. This was but as a Flye by an Eagle: we had much
more monstrous matter of Feast, which worthily deserued noting.
   Mecenas. She's a most triumphant Lady, if report be   895
square to her.
   Enob. When she first met *Marke Anthony,* she purst
vp his heart vpon the Riuer of Sidnis.
   Agri. There she appear'd indeed: or my reporter de-
uis'd well for her.   900

---

892 as] *Om.* ROWE2-POPE2
893 Feast] feasts KNT1
899–901 *Verse lines ending* reporter . . . you, sir: CAP-v1778, RANN

890–2 **Eight . . . Eagle**] BARROLL (1958, *JEGP,* p. 711): "Shakespeare alters [Plutarch's
(see p. 414) emphasis on 'waste and careless expense'] to suggest that Antony ate great
amounts of food."
   890–1 **breakfast**] In Plutarch (see p. 414), supper.
   892 **This . . . Eagle**] Proverbial; see DENT (E1): "The *eagle* does not catch flies."
The application is questionable.
   by] Commentators starting with SCHMIDT (ed. 1870) gloss as "compared with."
FURNESS (ed. 1907) alone shifts the emphasis somewhat: "So far from eight boars having
been considered an inordinate repast, it was no more than a fly would be considered
a hearty breakfast by an eagle."
   895 **triumphant**] SCHMIDT (1875): "Glorious, of supreme magnificence and beauty."
KITTREDGE (ed. 1941) adds, "From *triumph* in the sense of 'a splendid show' (like a
Roman *triumph* or procession)." See n. 2666.
   895–6 **be square to**] STEEVENS (ed. 1778): "*Quadrates* with . . . or suits with." RANN
(ed. 1791–): Be "just" to. See also n. 970–1.
   897–8 MASON (1785, pp. 276–7): "Enobarbus is made to say, that Cleopatra gained
Anthony's heart on the river Cydnus; but it appears from the conclusion of his own description that Anthony had never seen her there; that whilst she was on the river, Anthony
was sitting alone enthroned in the market-place, whistling to the air, all the people having left him to gaze upon her, and that when she landed, he sent to her to invite her
to supper [quotes 'The Citty . . . Nature' (926–31)]." CLARKE (ed. [1868]): "The expression, 'upon the river of Cydnus', is here used to signify 'the district on the shores
of the river Cydnus'. . . . The idiom 'upon the Seine', or 'upon the Thames' [see *OED,*
Upon *prep.* 3a] is employed to express the adjacent shores of those rivers, the country
in their neighbourhood."
   899 **appear'd indeed**] DELIUS (ed. 1856): *Appear'd* is emphatic and is emphasized
by *indeed.* KITTREDGE (ed. 1941): "Made a truly magnificent appearance." See conj.,
p. 350.
   899–900 **deuis'd**] MINSHEU (1617): "Invent."

Eno. I will tell you,
The Barge she sat in, like a burnisht Throne
Burnt on the water: the Poope was beaten Gold,
Purple the Sailes: and so perfumed that
The Windes were Loue-sicke.   905
With them the Owers were Siluer,
Which to the tune of Flutes kept stroke, and made
The water which they beate, to follow faster;
As amorous of their strokes. For her owne person,

---

901 you] you, sir mTBY3 *conj.*, CAP
905-6 *One verse line* POPE1+
    Loue-sicke. With them ∧] ~ ∧ ~~ ; POPE1+ (–KNT1)
909 their] her F3, F4

902–31 Following the suggestion of ELLIS-FERMOR (1927, pp. 19–21) HARRISON (1956, pp. 58–9): "Shakespeare had not forgotten this play [Marlowe's *Dido*] and . . . Marlowe himself remembered Plutarch. [Compares Dido's promise to mend Aeneas's sails, 3.1.112–14 (ed. Tucker Brooke, 1930), as well as 3.1.115–18 and 4.4.48–9, with 906–9 ('the . . . strokes'), 913–17 ('On . . . did'), and 922–3 ('The . . . hands').]" For Plutarch, see p. 413. BARROLL (1958, *TxSE*, p. 76): Possibly a reminder of "The 'great whoore' who also 'sytteth vpon many waters', and 'with whome haue committed fornication the kynges of the earth' . . . the subject of Dekker's play, *The Whore of Babylon* (1607)." MORRIS (1968–9, p. 277) compares Cleopatra's and Queen Elizabeth's barges and also their personal appearance, using descriptions by foreign travelers to Elizabethan England. FRIEDMAN (1969, p. 482) compares Drayton's description of Isabella's voyage to France to meet her lover (*Mortimeriados*, ll. 988–1006 [*Works*, ed. Hebel, vol. 1, 1931] and *The Barons Warres* 3.369–90 [*Works*, ed. Hebel, vol. 2, 1932]). ERSKINE-HILL (1970, pp. 27–8) compares the description of Acrasia's *"Bowre of blis"* (mentioned by Barroll) in *F.Q.*, citing 2.12.81, 72, 61, 59, and 2.5.27–8. WHITAKER (1972, p. 157) compares "one of the rituals of worship" of the cult of Isis in *The Golden Asse of Apuleius* (tr. Adlington, 1566, fols. 120 f.).

902–3 **The Barge . . . water**] STEEVENS (*apud* REED, ed. 1803): "The same idea occurs in Chapman's translation of the tenth Book of the *Odyssey*: '—In a *throne* she plac'd My welcome person. Of a curious frame 'Twas, and so bright, I *sat as in a flame*' [ed. Nicoll, 1957, ll. 418–20]." CASE (ed. 1906): "Compare Fairfax's Tasso, *Godfrey of Bulloigne* (1600), XVI.iv., of a representation of the battle of Actium: —'The waters *burnt* about their vessels good, Such flames the gold therein enchased threw' [ll. 5–6], etc."

903 **beaten Gold**] DEIGHTON (ed. 1891): "Plates of hammered gold."

906–9 **Owers . . . strokes**] SPEAIGHT (1977, p. 309) surmises: "Giulio Landi's *Life of Cleopatra* (1551) gave the dramatist . . . the silver oars that ferried the 'barge she sat in' and 'when they struck the water . . . gave out a musical sound, various and sweeter than flutes or other such instruments' [*La vita di Cleopatra*, p. 21]."

907 **Flutes**] STERNFELD (1963, pp. 222–3) finds Sh.'s reduction of "the band [of all the instruments mentioned by Plutarch] to a single family of instruments, the amorous

It beggerd all discription, she did lye   910
In her Pauillion, cloth of Gold, of Tissue,
O're-picturing that Venus, where we see

---

911 cloth . . . Tissue] cloth of gold and tissue mCOL1, COL2, COL3, KTLY; cloth-of-
gold of tissue DYCE1, STAU, GLO, HAL-KIT1 (−ARD1)

---

flute . . . [an example of] musical economy in Shakespeare's treatment of Plutarch."
He notes a similar instance in 2467–2501.

911 **cloth . . . Tissue**] CASE (ed. 1906) summarizes the discussion: "One of the two
current explanations, *viz.*, 'cloth of gold in tissue or texture', may, I think, be dismissed;
for . . . '*of tissue*' added to the otherwise sufficient '*cloth of gold*' must denote something, in view of the independent existence of *tissue* and *cloth of tissue*; whether the
intermixture of coloured silks, or else quality, depending on the number of threads in
the warp." As illustrations he quotes from Skelton's *Bouge of Court* (n.d., 9.2–3) and
MINSHEU's (1617) definitions: "Tissu, *of the French* Tissu, *i*.[*e*.] *wouen cloth of* Tissu,
with vs cloth of silke and siluer, or of siluer and gold wouen together [and] Tissue, *made
of three threeds of diuers colours of* Tissue." Case repeats Craig's quotation from Pliny's
Natural History 8.48 (tr. Holland, 1634, p. 228: "To weaue cloth of tissue with twisted
threeds both in woofe and warp, and the same in sundry colours was the inuention of
Alexandria") and continues: "The other explanation current is Staunton's [ed. 1859] '*cloth
of gold* on a ground *of tissue*', which suggests no objection save that the reversal of the
positions of *gold* and *tissue* is possible, indeed probable, judging by the frequency of
examples. [Quotes from Hall's *Union of the Two Noble and Illustrate Famelies of Lancas-
tre & Yorke* (1548), "Henry VIII," fols. lxv and lxxviii, and from Sylvester's *Du Bartas*,
"The third Day of the first Week" (1620; ed. Snyder, 1979, p. 204, l. 1133) and "The
Magnificence" (ibid., p. 664, l. 22).] The Collier MS. [Perkins Folio] correction, '*cloth
of gold, and tissue*', was therefore needless, though the phrase apparently occurs. See
Nichols, *Progresses of James I.* (1828), ii. 550." See p. 413 for Plutarch's phrase. Case
is, however, incomplete. For one thing, the first of the "current explanations" is unidentified. The explanation of DELIUS (ed. 1856)—*gold of tissue* is a unit—is not considered,
nor is the modification of STAUNTON (ed. 1859) by HUDSON (ed. 1881): "We should
say 'cloth-of-gold *on* tissue'; but *of* and *on* were often used indiscriminately." In short,
most recent commentators follow Staunton, pithily compressed by ONIONS (1911, tissue): "Stuff made of gold thread and silk woven together." See LINTHICUM (1936, pp.
114–15, "*Cloth of Gold and Silver*," and pp. 117–18, "TISSUE").

912–13 **O're-picturing . . . Nature**] For the semantics of *O're-picturing*, meaning
here "out-picturing" or "surpassing in depicting," and *out-worke*, see FRANZ §144, §145.
The same concept is noted by THEOBALD (ed. 1733) in *Cym.* 2.4.82–5 (1246–9), by SINGER
(ed. 1856, 10:483) in *Cym.* 5.5.163–5, "for Feature . . . Nature" (3442–4), and by BON-
JOUR (1962, pp. 76–7) in *Ven.* 289–92. See also n. 3317–20.

912 **Venus**] Some believe Sh. alludes to a specific picture, THEOBALD (ed. 1733), for
example, to "*Venus* done by *Apelles* . . . call'd . . . Venus *rising out of the Sea*," and
WARBURTON (ed. 1747) to "the *Venus* of *Protogenes* mentioned by *Pliny*, l.35.c.10." The
latter is corrected by CASE (ed. 1906): "As Pliny records no Venus by Protogenes we must
surely substitute that of Apelles (Pliny, *Nat. Hist.* lib. XXXV. 36 <x>)." Other pictures

The fancie out-worke Nature. On each side her,
Stood pretty Dimpled Boyes, like smiling Cupids,
With diuers coulour'd Fannes whose winde did seeme,   915
To gloue the delicate cheekes which they did coole,
And what they vndid did.
    Agrip. Oh rare for *Anthony.*
    Eno. Her Gentlewoman, like the Nereides,
So many Mer-maides tended her i'th'eyes,   920

---

914 pretty Dimpled] pretty-dimpled DEL4 *conj.*, OXF1
915 diuers coulour'd] divers-colour'd F3+ (–SIS)
916 gloue] glove F2-F4; glow ROWE1-JOHN1, v1773+; glow CAP (*text*; *rejected reading misprinted as* love, *corrected to* glove *in corrigenda*)
919 Her] Here WARB (*text*; Her *in errata*)
    Gentlewoman] Gentlewomen F2+
    Nereides] *Nereids* POPE1-THEO2, WARB-v1773, DYCE1 (*text*; Nereides *in corrigenda*), WH1, HUD2; *Nereids*, *or* HAN1
920 i'th'eyes] i'the guise MASON (1785, p. 278) *conj.*, SING2

---

that may have stimulated Sh.'s imagination are mentioned by BLUMHOF (ed. 1870) and SHAW-SMITH (1973, p. 93).
    913 **fancie**] CAWDREY (1604, fantacie [the expanded form of *fancy*]): "Imagination." See also 3318, 3319.
    each side her] See n. 3008.
    914 **like**] KITTREDGE (ed. 1941): "In the guise of—not merely, resembling. So in l. [919]."
    916 **gloue**] Only ANDREWS (ed. 1989) seems to defend this reading, which can make sense of a sort.
    delicate] CAWDREY (1604): "Daintie, giuen to pleasure." See also 1458.
    917 **what . . . did**] Neither the conjecture of JOHNSON (ed. 1765), to make the line "be read less harshly," nor that of STAUNTON (ed. 1859), to indicate "a new glow from the warmth of their own tints," has been adopted. See conj., p. 350.
    918 **rare**] See n. 3387.
    919 **Nereides**] COOPER (1565): "Fayries of the sea." See PAULY, 17:1–23; *OCD*, Nereus.
    920 **Mer-maides**] COLERIDGE (1836, 2:145) does not believe "that Shakspeare wrote . . . 'mermaids'. He never . . . would have so weakened by useless anticipation the fine image immediately following. The epithet 'seeming' [922] becomes so extremely improper after the whole number had been positively called 'so many mermaids.'" BARROLL (1958, *TxSE*, p. 76, n. 32): "The definition of 'Nereid' as 'mermaid' is not from Plutarch [pointed out by HALLIWELL (ed. 1865)]. It is North's translation [see p. 413] of Amyot's 'les fées des eaux' and thus a Renaissance and especially an English concept." Barroll also (pp. 65–6) identifies Circe, siren, and mermaid as having a similar mythological allusiveness: "A symbol of temptation to incontinence and most often to lechery."
    920–1 **tended . . . adornings**] Most commentators agree with JOHNSON (ed. 1765) on 920—"Discovered her will by her eyes"—or with MALONE (ed. 1790): "They performed their duty in the sight of their mistress." A refinement is added by H. INGLEBY (1891,

And made their bends adornings. At the Helme,   921
A seeming Mer-maide steeres: The Silken Tackle,
Swell with the touches of those Flower-soft hands,

---

921 adornings] adorings HAN1, WARB, JOHN1; adornings WH1 (*text*; adoring *in errata*)
922 Tackle] Tackles F2-JOHN1, v1773, v1778, RANN
923 Swell] Smell mCOL1, COL2, HUD1, COL3, COL4

---

p. 182): "The place assigned to the Cupids is *at the side* [913–14], and to the personal attendants *in front*, of their mistress." The same commentators tend to accept, or elaborate on, WARBURTON's (ed. 1747) explanation of 921: "Her maids bowed with so good an air, that it added new graces to them." Many commentators, starting with DELIUS (ed. 1856), regard the *bends* not only as adornments of the gentlewomen but to Cleopatra and the whole tableau. Specific details are discussed by HEATH (1765, p. 455): "*Bend*, is . . . an arch, and the *bends of the eyes* are the eye-brows. . . . These seeming nereids were employed in adjusting Cleopatra's eye-brows, as often as they happened to be discomposed by the fanning of the boys, or any other accident." MALONE (*apud* STEEVENS, ed. 1778) first regards the *bends* as referring to Cleopatra's eyes, but then changes his mind (ed. 1790); THISELTON (1899, p. 13) continues this interpretation, however, and CROSBY (2 Feb. 1877, [sheet 163, p. 36]) holds that they refer as well to the attendants' eyes, comparing Antony's eyes that "bend" (8). Taking a cue from Plutarch's "Her gentlewomen . . . tended the tackles and ropes of the barge" (see p. 413), JACKSON (1819, pp. 292–3) inaugurates a tangle of nautical explanations, sometimes advanced without reference to the context: "The *bends* are the chief support of a ship's sides [see Manwayring, 1644], and form a kind of belt or zone of heavy plank." The rigging, he continues, is connected to the chain plates "by ropes which run through the *eyes*, or, as they are more commonly called, the *dead eyes*." C. F. B. (1857, pp. 286–7) says *eyes* are "Bows of a vessel"; INGLEBY (1875, p. 119), "Hawseholes"; MARSHALL (1902, p. 342), "The common name for a loop of cord or rope." ABSENS (1902, p. 342) detects a pun on *bends* as "bows or curtsies . . . and 'bends', the latter nautically from the verb 'to bind'. The sailor's 'bends' are tied knots." PRENTER (1902, p. 223) supports this interpretation by quoting Manwayring (1644, *To Bend*). CASE (ed. 1906, p. 207) adds, "Any ornamental band, tie, or sash, fillet or chaplet." He believes (p. 211) that "the least unsatisfactory explanation remains that of Warburton and Steevens"; the latter (ed. 1793) was so exasperated by this "very powerful instance of the uncertainty of verbal criticism" that he facetiously proposed reading, "omitting only a single letter,—'made their *ends* adornings.'"

923 **Swell**] COLLIER (1852, p. 470): "The printer . . . mistook *m* for *w*: the poet is alluding to the perfume derived by the silken cordage from the flower-soft hands through which it passed." He conjectures *smell*. WHITE (1854, p. 450) rejects Collier—"Cordage will swell with handling"—as does DYCE (1859, p. 204), who doubts that the hands could impart "*a perfume to the tackle, and so strong a perfume, too, that it reached even the adjacent wharfs*" and asks (ed. 1857): "To say nothing else of the alteration, is 'Smell *with*' the phraseology of Shakespeare's time?" KEIGHTLEY (1867, p. 314) thinks that Collier is "probably right" but that "'Swell' (*sc.* with pride, *i.e.* are elate) no doubt makes good sense." BLUMHOF (ed. 1870) and most others believe because of "Swell" that the tackle includes sails as well as ropes. THISELTON (1899, p. 13), fancifully: "The yielding softness of their hands gives rise to the illusion that the silken tackle swells."

That yarely frame the office. From the Barge
A strange inuisible perfume hits the sense   925
Of the adiacent Wharfes. The Citty cast
Her people out vpon her: and *Anthony*
Enthron'd i'th'Market-place, did sit alone,
Whisling to'th'ayre: which but for vacancie,
Had gone to gaze on *Cleopater* too,   930
And made a gap in Nature.
    Agri. Rare Egiptian.
    Eno. Vpon her landing, *Anthony* sent to her,
Inuited her to Supper: she replyed,
It should be better, he became her guest: 935
Which she entreated, our Courteous *Anthony*,
Whom nere the word of no woman hard speake,
Being barber'd ten times o're, goes to the Feast;
And for his ordinary, paies his heart,
For what his eyes eate onely.   940

---

931 made] make ROWE2, ROWE3
936 our] *Om.* POPE, HAN1

---

924 **yarely**] COLES (1676) has two lemmas: *yare* (of Suffolk origin), meaning "nimble,
smart," and *yare* (*old word*), meaning "ready." Most commentators merge the two. *OED*
(Yare *adv.* 1c) adds, "Esp. in nautical use." See also 2309, 3534, n. 1905.
    frame] MINSHEU (1617): "*Forme*." KERSEY (1702): "*Fashion, build, devise* or *forge*."
Thus RANN (ed. 1791–): "Perform." See also 3174.
    927 **Her**] I.e., the city's. See FRANZ §209 for the Romance feminine gender's appear-
ing also in Sh. as feminine.
    928 **Enthron'd**] HALLIWELL (ed. 1865) provides a drawing of a Roman coin to show
"public inthronization as practised by the Emperors of Rome."
    929–31 **but . . . Nature**] WARBURTON (ed. 1747): "Alluding to an axiom in the
peripatetic philosophy then in vogue, that *Nature abhors a vacuum*." See DENT (N42).
TIESSEN (1879, p. 470) is alone and unconvincing in rejecting the customary interpretation by proposing for *vacancie* "lacking vision."
    929 **vacancie**] See n. 456.
    932 **Rare**] See n. 3387.
    935 **should**] ABBOTT (§326): "Was used in a subordinate sentence after a simple past
tense. . . . We should now say 'might.'" See 2086.
    937 **hard**] I.e., heard. See CERCIGNANI (1981, p. 66).
    938 **barber'd**] WILSON (ed. 1950): "Prof. J. A. K. Thomson suggests to me that Ant.
wore a beard, contrary to the fashion of Roman nobles or the Egyptian Ptolemies, in
imitation of his ancestor Hercules. . . . On Sh.'s stage, it contrasted him with 'the scarce-
bearded Caesar' ([31])." See also nn. 31, 686–7, and, for Plutarch, p. 399.
    939 **ordinary**] KERSEY (1702): "*An eating-house*, or *set meal*." BAILEY (1721): "A
Victualling-house, where Persons may eat at so much per Meal." Thus JOHNSON (1755),
citing this instance: "Regular price of a meal."

Agri. Royall Wench:

She made great *Cæsar* lay his Sword to bed, (xx4ᵇ)

He ploughed her, and she cropt.

    Eno. I saw her once

Hop forty Paces through the publicke streete, 945

And hauing lost her breath, she spoke, and panted,

That she did make defect, perfection,

And breathlesse powre breath forth.

    Mece. Now *Anthony*, must leaue her vtterly.

948–50 *Verse lines ending Antony* . . . not. mTBY2 *conj.*, HAN1, CAP, KTLY, EVNS

948 breathlesse powre breath] F1; breathlesse power breath F2, ROWE; breathless power breathe F3, F4, POPE1-THEO2, WARB-JOHN1, v1773; breathless, power breathe HAN1 *etc.*

---

940 STEEVENS (*apud* REED, ed. 1803): "Thus Martial: 'Inspexit molles pueros, *oculisque comedit*' [Inspected and devoured with his eyes dainty boys]" (*Epigrams* 9.59.3).

    eate] The few who gloss agree with KITTREDGE (ed. 1941): "Ate." *Eat(e)* is the only spelling of both the present and past (and, with *eaten*, past perfect) tenses in Sh.

    941 **Wench**] MINSHEU (1617): "Maide & Girle." THEOBALD (31 Mar. 1730, [fol. 118ᵛ]): "*Wench & Lass* [(3570) and *girl* (2672)] . . . were not used in that low & vulgar Acceptation as they are at this Time of Day." But KERSEY (1702, Wench): "*A young girl; light housewife*, or *strumpet*." EAGLESON (1971, p. 11): "The modification [Royall] . . . together with the general context of praise for Cleopatra . . . indicates that *wench* is not being used in a derogatory sense." *Wench* in Sh. is neutral, positive or negative overtones dependent on the preceding adjective. See also 115.

    942–3 For the sexual overtones, see E. PARTRIDGE (1947; 1968, *plough*, p. 163, and *sword*, p. 196). WALTER (ed. 1969), fancifully: "Perhaps an echo of *Isaiah*, ii.4, 'beat their swords into ploughshares.'"

    943 **cropt**] RANN (ed. 1791–): "Yielded a noble harvest." For Plutarch, see p. 434. CASE (ed. 1906) refers also to Plutarch's *Julius Caesar* (tr. North, 1579, p. 787) and, for "the word in a similar connection," to Marston's *2 Antonio and Mellida* [*Antonio's Revenge*] (1602, 1.1.26).

    948 **breathlesse powre breath**] The orthographical ambiguity of *powre* and *breath*, as well as the grammatical alternatives, are summarized by BLAKE (1983, p. 59): *Breathlesse* could modify *powre*, which could be the object of *breath* with the sense "and breathes out breathless charm," or it could modify *she* (947) so that the sense becomes "'And she breathless breathes forth charm'. If *breathlesse* is taken as a qualifier to *she* . . . the meaning would be 'And breathless she pours forth breath'. . . . If, however, *breath* is taken as a nominal group rather than as a verb, it would mean that *powre* is better understood as the verb 'pour' rather than the functionally shifted verb 'power'. When *powre* is understood as a noun . . . it has to be understood in an otherwise unattested sense of 'charm.'" CAPELL'S (1779 [1774], 1:33–4) gloss represents the view of the great majority of commentators: "'*Power*' is — power of charming; this . . . Cleopatra breath'd forth even by being breathless; making . . . defects perfections, by the grace that went along with her panting." See textual notes and conj., p. 351.

Eno. Neuer he will not: 950
Age cannot wither her, nor custome stale
Her infinite variety: other women cloy
The appetites they feede, but she makes hungry,
Where most she satisfies. For vildest things
Become themselues in her, that the holy Priests   955

---

950 Neuer‸] ∼ , F3+ (−SIS)
951 stale] steale F2-ROWE3
952-3 *Verse lines ending* women . . . hungry, v1793, v1803, SING1
954 vildest] wildest BLUM

---

950 **Neuer he will not**] DYCE (ed. 1857): "This does not read like a passage where
the author meant to use the double negative." RIDLEY (ed. 1954): "'He will not' is something of an anticlimax after the emphatic 'never', and I suspect that F's unpunctuated
reading . . . with double negative, is right; or perhaps even more probably that 'Never'
and 'he will not' were alternatives, neither of which was clearly marked for omission."
But if F1's reading is a "double negative," it is the only one in Sh. with "never . . . not."

951-2 **Age . . . variety**] STEEVENS (ed. 1793): "Cleopatra, as appears from the
tetradrachms [Greek coins] of Antony, was no Venus; and indeed the majority of ladies
who most successfully enslaved the hearts of princes, are known to have been less remarkable for personal than mental attractions. The reign of insipid beauty is seldom lasting;
but permanent must be the rule of a woman who can diversify the sameness of life by
an inexhausted variety of accomplishments." ADLARD (1975, p. 327) notes the identification of Isis with the asp in Plutarch's *Moralia* (tr. Holland, 1603, p. 1316: "The *Aspis*
also they compare to the planet of the Sunne, because he doth never age and wax old"),
"which may remind the reader of Enobarbus' famous tribute. . . . The 'varietie' of Isis
is shown in her 'habiliments' ['of different tinctures and colours'], according to the *Moralia*, page 1318." See also n. 1768.

951 **custome stale**] Possibly proverbial; see DENT (C930): "As stale as *custom*." Although CERCIGNANI (1981, p. 158) dismisses as "unquestionably unreliable" suggestions
by Kökeritz of a *stale-steal* homonymic pun (though not here), the fact is that these
words are spelling variants of each other, and F2-ROWE's (ed. 1714) spelling *steal*, though
not proposed by anyone, does make sense of a sort.

952 **infinite variety**] Commentators have found only remote parallels. PHIALAS (ed.
1955): "The phrase occurs in Florio's Montaigne [1603; Tudor Translations, ed. Henley,
1892, 1:150], in a passage contrasting the weaknesses of present 'indiscreet writers' with
the excellence of Plutarch." WALTER (1969, p. 137) suggests that a description of Isis in
Plutarch's essay "Isis and Osiris" (*Moralia*, tr. Holland, 1603, p. 1309: "An infinite number of names, for that she receiveth all formes and shapes") may have influenced Sh.
Also "it may be that the phrase was occasionally used to describe the works of the creator
as, for example, by Helkiah Crooke, *Microcosmographia* [1615], p. 651."

952-4 **other . . . satisfies**] MALONE (*apud* STEEVENS, ed. 1778) compares *Per.*
5.1.113–14, and IDEM (ed. 1790) adds *Ven.* 19–20. DICKEY (1957, p. 186, n. 6) gives numerous examples of the Elizabethan association of lust and gluttony.

954 **vildest**] See n. 2851 ("vilde").

955 **Become themselues**] I.e., are becoming. FRANZ (§628): The Elizabethan reflex-

Blesse her, when she is Riggish.

    Mece. If Beauty, Wisedome, Modesty, can settle
The heart of *Anthony*: *Octauia* is
A blessed Lottery to him.

    Agrip. Let vs go. Good *Enobarbus*, make your selfe   960
my guest, whilst you abide heere.

    Eno. Humbly Sir I thanke you.   *Exeunt*

    Enter Anthony, Cæsar, Octauia betweene them.   **2.3**

    Anth. The world, and my great office, will
Sometimes deuide me from your bosome.   965

    Octa. All which time, before the Gods my knee shall
bowe my prayers to them for you.

959–62 *Three verse lines ending* go. . . . Guest, . . . you. ROWE1+
959 blessed Lottery] blest allott'ry WARBURTON *conj. apud* THEO1, THEO1-THEO4, CAP
962 *Exeunt*] *Om.* ROWE2, ROWE3
963 *SCENE* III. CAP+
    The same. A Room in Cæsar's *House.* CAP, MAL, v1793+ *(subst.)*
    Enter . . .] *Ad. Attendants behind, and* Soothsayer. CAP-KNT1
964–8 *Four verse lines ending* sometimes . . . time, . . . Prayers . . . *Octavia,*
ROWE1+
967 my] in mF4Q *conj. and* ROWE1, ROWE2-v1778, RANN, CAM3b; with mCOL1, COL2

---

ive is often replaced in modern English by the intransitive form of the verb. MALONE
(*apud* STEEVENS [1783]) compares *Son.* 150.5; SEYMOUR (1805, 2:54), *Ant.* 62.

    956 **Riggish**] MINSHEU (1617, Rigge): "*Impudent wanton girle.*" BAILEY (1721): "[Of
ridendo, L(atin). Laughing.] A wanton ramping [i.e., romping] Girl." It may be that
commentators interpret the word somewhat too severely, as in *OED*'s "licentious," given
Bailey's whimsical etymology and DYCHE & PARDON's (1740) definition of *To rig about*:
"To jump, skip, or play the wanton, to ramp, to be frisky, &c."

    957 **Modesty**] See nn. 1115–16, 3034. MUIR (1957, p. 210) points out Daniel's use
of *modestie* to describe Octavia's "entertainment" (conversation, social behavior). See
p. 580.

    959 **Lottery**] CAWDREY (1604): "Casting of lots." Or, as the *OED* (*sb.* 3) puts it, cit-
ing this instance: "Something which comes to a person by lot or fortune." THEOBALD
(ed. 1733) calls this word a "very indifferent Compliment in *Mecænas* to call *Octavia*
a *Lottery*, as if She might turn up *blank*, as well as prove a *Prize* to *Antony*," a remark
that led to WARBURTON's conjectures (see textual notes), CAPELL's (1779 [1774], Glossary, 1:2, Allottery) gloss "Allotment," RANN's (ed. 1791–) "A glorious prize," and BECKET's
(1815, 2:184) conjecture *votary*: "The woman who thus is *destined* to him."

    967 **bowe**] *OED* (*v.*[1] 7b), citing this instance: "To express by bowing."

Anth. Goodnight Sir. My *Octauia*
Read not my blemishes in the worlds report:
I haue not kept my square, but that to come   970
Shall all be done byth'Rule: good night deere Lady:
Good night Sir.
   Cæsar. Goodnight.   *Exit.*

               Enter Soothsaier.

Anth. Now sirrah: you do wish your selfe in Egypt?   975

---

972 *Given to Octavia* F2-v1778, RANN-v1803, SING, KNT1, HUD, COL3, STAU, DYCE2, COL4, OXF1, KIT1+
   973 *Exit*] *Exeunt* Cæsar *and* Octavia ROWE1+
   974 SCENE IV. POPE, HAN1, WARB, JOHN1
      Enter Soothsaier.] *Om.* CAP-KNT1
      Soothsaier] *Lamprius* (*throughout scene*) RID
   975–83 *Lines* 975–82 *prose,* 983 *verse* ROWE, THEO, WARB; *prose* POPE (*continuing prose through* 989); 975–82 *prose,* 983 *two verse lines ending Cæsar's. . . .* side. mTBY2 *conj.,* HAN1, JOHN1, COL, HUD1, WH1, HAL, CAM; *eight verse lines ending Egypt? . . . you . . . it in . . . yet . . . me, . . . mine?* | *Soo.* Cæsar's. . . . side: CAP-SING1, SING2, DYCE1, OXF1, RID, ARD2; 975–80 *prose,* 981–3 *four verse lines ending* me, . . . mine? | *Sooth.* Cæsar's. . . . side: KNT1, STAU, DYCE2, HUD2; *nine verse lines ending* Egypt? . . . you | Thither! . . . it in . . . yet . . . me, . . . mine? | *Sooth.* Cæsar's. . . . side: GLO, WH2, NLSN, ARD1; *seven verse lines ending* Egypt? . . . you . . . it in . . . yet . . . whose . . . *Sooth.* Cæsar's ⌃ . . . . side: KTLY; 975 *verse,* 976–7 *prose,* 978–83 *six verse lines ending* reason! . . . tongue. . . . me, . . . mine? | *Sooth.* Cæsar's. . . . side! KIT1, SIS; 975 *and* 978 *verse,* 976–7 *and* 979–80 *prose,* 981–3 *four verse lines ending* me, . . . mine? | *Sooth.* Cæsar's. . . . side. ALEX; 975 *and* 978–82 *verse,* 976–7 *prose,* 983 *two verse lines ending* Caesar's. . . . side. EVNS
   975 you do] do you F3-THEO4

---

968 **Goodnight Sir**] GRAY (1917–18, p. 44, n. 1) alone: "The folios and all modern editors . . . give the . . . words to Antony, while many editors have followed the Second Folio in giving the *second* 'Good night, sir' [972] to Octavia on the ground that Antony has already said 'good night' to Caesar. But, as Malone says [*apud* STEEVENS (1780), 1:230], Caesar immediately answers this [972], and for Antony to say 'Good night, sir' *twice* to Caesar is, as Ritson remarks [1792, p. 85], absurd. It is equally absurd for him to turn and say 'Good night, sir' to Caesar before answering Octavia, and for Shakespeare to leave her with no 'good night' to Antony." No edition gives this line to Octavia, however; see textual notes.
   970–1 **kept my square . . . byth'Rule**] COLLIER (ed. 1843): "The last part of the sentence explains the first." Summarizing the dominant view, first explicated by DELIUS (ed. 1856), CASE (ed. 1906): "Kept within due bounds." RIDLEY (ed. 1935, Glossary): "Stayed true (*met. from carpentry*)." IDEM (ed. 1954): "'Kept to the straight line'. The metaphor is from a carpenter's set square, by which a line can be ruled not only straight

Sooth. Would I had neuer come from thence, nor you
thither.
Ant. If you can, your reason?
Sooth. I see it in my motion: haue it not in my tongue,
But yet hie you to Egypt againe.   980

---

976 nor] or HAN1
977 thither] Hither MASON (1785, p. 279) *conj.*, RANN, HUD2, CAM3b; Come thither
KTLY
979 motion] notion mTHEO2 (19 Feb. 1729, [fol. 39ᵛ]) *conj.*, THEO, HAN1, KTLY,
HUD2
980 to Egypt againe] again to *Egypt* CAP-SING1 (–MAL)

---

but in the right relation to another." BARROLL (1958, *JEGP*, p. 719), citing George Wither's *Collection of Emblemes* [1635, 3.35]: "The square is law." HANKINS (1978, p. 71):
"In a comment upon Aristotle's *Nicomachean Ethics*, Donatus Acciaiolus states that the
virtuous and happy man is 'squared' (*quadratus*). Right angles and straight (*recta*) lines
become symbols of up*right*ness and *rectitude* [*Commentarium in ethica ad Nicomachum*,
tr. Argyropylos, 1565, pp. 53–4]." See also n. 895–6.
  975 sirrah] See n. 3475.
  977 thither] MASON (1785, p. 279): "Both the sense and grammar require that we
should read *hither.*" FURNESS (ed. 1907): "The Soothsayer means, 'would I had never
left Egypt nor you gone thither'. It is merely a confusion of two constructions. He says
afterward, 'But yet hie you *again* to Egypt' [980], which seems to refer to this 'thither.'"
GRAY (1917–18, p. 44, n. 2): "'Either', or perhaps the double negative 'neither', should
. . . be substituted. The line with 'thither' or with 'hither' implies some sort of contrast
in the coming of Antony and the Soothsayer, which, of course, is not the case." See p. 351.
  979 motion] THEOBALD (19 Feb. 1729, [fol. 39ᵛ]) conjectures *notion*, comparing
Ham. 1.2.185 (374) and 1.2.250 (450), and states (ed. 1733): "What *Motion*? I can trace
no Sense in this Word here, unless the Author were alluding to that *Agitation* of the
Divinity, which Diviners pretend to when the Fit of Foretelling is upon them; but then,
I think verily, he would have wrote, *Emotion*. . . . The Soothsayer should say, he saw
a Reason in his *Thought* or *Opinion*, tho' he gave that Thought or Opinion no Utterance. . . . And *Notion* is a Word which our Author frequently chuses, to express the
mental Faculties." This emendation seems to anticipate WARBURTON's ([2 June 1734,
fol. 141ʳ]) explanation: "Motion not dependant on Sense. Shakespeare alluded to that
famous peripatetick principle. Nihil sit in *Intelectu* quod priùs non fuerit in *Sensu* [Nothing
can exist in the mind that has not previously existed in the senses]." Later commentators
are imprecise in defining the "motion"; glosses range from "a cool deliberate observation
of certain indications in nature" (HEATH [1765, p. 455]) to "a something *moving* within"
(CAPELL [1779 (1774), 1:34]) to astrological observation (BLUMHOF [ed. 1870]) to "mind"
(IRVING & MARSHALL [ed. 1889]) to "feel" (WILSON [ed. 1950]). See *OED*, *sb.* 4, 7,
9. LLOYD (1959, p. 91) thinks Sh. is echoing a concept of motion peculiar to the cult
of Isis, which he found in Holland's tr. of Plutarch's *Moralia*, 1603. See also nn. 111, 141.
  980 hie] MINSHEU (1617): "*Make speede.*"
  againe] I.e., back. See FRANZ §433.

Antho. Say to me, whose Fortunes shall rise higher
Cæsars or mine?
Sooth. Cæsars. Therefore (oh *Anthony*) stay not by his side.
Thy Dæmon that thy spirit which keepes thee, is
Noble, Couragious, high vnmatchable,   985
Where *Cæsars* is not. But neere him, thy Angell
Becomes a feare: as being o're-powr'd, therefore

---

981 Fortunes] Fortune F4-THEO4, COL2
984 that] that's F2-THEO4, CAP, v1778-SING1, COL2-COL3, GLO, DYCE2, COL4, WH2, OXF1
985 high‸] ～, F3-ALEX, ARD2
987-8 *Verse lines ending* overpower'd; . . . you. HAN1
987 feare: . . . o're-powr'd,] ～, . . . ～; POPE2+ (–CAM3, ARD2)
    a feare] afeard mTBY2 *conj.*, mCOL1, COL2, SING2, COL3, KTLY, RID, ARD2
    therefore] and therefore F2-THEO4, CAP

981–1007 For Plutarch, see p. 417.
984 **Dæmon**] WARBURTON (*apud* THEOBALD, ed. 1733): "*Shakespeare* calls That *Dæmon* in one Line, which he calls *Angel* in another [986]: and This, I conceive, not accidentally, but knowingly. It is to be observ'd, that the antient *Greek* Authors always used the Word *Dæmon* in the Sense of *God, Demi-god*, or *celestial Being*; and that it had not the Signification of *Devil, malignant* or *infernal Being*, 'till after the Time of Christianity. Since that Period, it has been used for Both; but by the Christian Writers most commonly in the latter sense." Sh.'s practice is otherwise. Following earlier and partial attempts by RANN (ed. 1791–), BLUMHOF (ed. 1870), and BULLOCH (1878, p. 255), KITTREDGE (ed. 1941) gives a definitive statement: "The same as *angel*. . . . *Dæmon* and *angel* are synonymous with *genius* in the sense of 'guardian spirit', as is shown by a passage in *Macbeth* [first quoted by Rann] which mentions this very incident in Antony's life (iii, 1, 55–57 [1045–7])." He also quotes from Chapman's *Cæsar and Pompey* 4.3 (ed. Shepherd, 1873, 3:169), as well as from *Cæsar's Revenge*, ll. 1311 ff. (ed. Boas, 1911), and Lodge's *The Wounds of Civil War*, ll. 2514 ff. (ed. Wilson, 1910). See n. 986.
    that thy spirit] MALONE (ed. 1790): *That's* (see textual notes) "is supported by . . . Plutarch [see p. 418]." ROLFE (ed. 1895), defending F1, compares 1743 and 2916. For the demonstrative pronoun *that* with a relative clause following, see FRANZ §313.
    keepes] MINSHEU (1617): "*Defend.*" See also 1580.
985 **high vnmatchable**] BLAKE (1983, p. 67), in discussing hyphenation of nominal groups, sees "*high* as a separate modifier, though *high-unmatchable* would seem a reasonable interpretation. [Compares 'hye battel'd' (2185) and 'trebble-sinewed, hearted, breath'd' (2362).]" For other possibilities, see textual notes and conj., p. 351.
986 **Angell**] CAWDREY (1604, genius): "The angell that waits on man, be it a good or euill angell."
987 **a feare**] WARBURTON (ed. 1747): "A fearful thing." Although JOHNSON (ed. 1765) found "the common reading . . . more poetical" and STEEVENS (ed. 1773) recognized "a personage [not identified] in some of the old moralities," the few advocates of the

Make space enough betweene you.

   Anth. Speake this no more.

   Sooth. To none but thee no more but: when to thee,   990
If thou dost play with him at any game,
Thou art sure to loose: And of that Naturall lucke,
He beats thee 'gainst the oddes. Thy Luster thickens,
When he shines by: I say againe, thy spirit
Is all affraid to gouerne thee neere him: 995
But he alway 'tis Noble.

   Anth. Get thee gone:
Say to *Ventigius* I would speake with him.   *Exit.*
He shall to Parthia, be it Art or hap,
He hath spoken true. The very Dice obey him,   1000
And in our sports my better cunning faints,
Vnder his chance, if we draw lots he speeds,

---

988 Make] make thou HAN1
     enough] *Om.* WH2, NLSN
990 but:] ～ ∧ F2+
992 And] he's HAN1
996 alway 'tis] alway is F2-ROWE3; away, 'tis POPE1-CAM1, COL4+; all 'way, 't is BLUM
998 *Exit.*] *Exit* Sooth. ROWE1+; *after* Parthia *in* 999 HUD2, CAM3
1000 spoken] spoke POPE1-v1773 (–CAP)

---

emendation *afear'd* produce many reasons: consistency with Plutarch's (see p. 418) "Thy Demon is *afraid* of his" and parallelism to 994–5 (COLLIER [1852, p. 470]); an instance of "final *d* and *e* being . . . confounded with one another" (WALKER [1860, 3:299]); doubt as to whether "*a fear* is used as the denomination of a particular species of beings, whether real or imaginary" (HEATH [1765, p. 456]); "a Fear [being] a source of terror, not an object of it" (KEIGHTLEY [1867, p. 314]); and "*a fear*" being not "characteristic of the soothsayer. . . . In lines [995, 996] he makes precisely the same distinction between *afraid* and *noble*" (RIDLEY [ed. 1954]). ABBOTT (§24) explains it simply as an adverb with the prefix *a*—"*i.e. 'a-fear'* [fearful]." See also n. 437.

   992 of] WORDSWORTH (ed. 1883): "*In consequence of.*" See FRANZ §517.
     lucke] See also 3537.
   995 **gouerne**] MINSHEU (1617): "*Guide . . . protect.*"
   998 *Ventigius*] MAXWELL (1951, p. 337): "Editors have noted it as an oddity but have failed to comment that the *gi* is phonetic: <dʒ>. In *Timon of Athens* no fewer than four spellings occur: *Ventidius, Ventiddius, Ventigius* and *Ventidgius.*" See also 1007, 1008, and pp. 374, 376.
   999 hap] MINSHEU (1617): "Accident, Aduenture, Chaunce." See also "haply" (2209, 2445).
   1001 **cunning**] See n. 244.
   1002 **speeds**] IRVING & MARSHALL (ed. 1889): "Is fortunate." DEIGHTON (ed. 1891): "Is successful; the radical meaning of the substantive *speed* is *success.*"

His Cocks do winne the Battaile, still of mine,
When it is all to naught: and his Quailes euer
Beate mine (in hoopt) at odd's. I will to Egypte: 1005
And though I make this marriage for my peace,   (xx4ᵛ
I'th'East my pleasure lies. Oh come *Ventigius.*

Enter Ventigius.

You must to Parthia, your Commissions ready:
Follow me, and reciue't.   *Exeunt* 1010

_____

Enter Lepidus, Mecenas and Agrippa.   **2.4**

Lepidus. Trouble your selues no further: pray you
hasten your Generals after.

_____

1005 (in hoopt) at] in-coop'd at HAN1; in whoop'd-at SEWARD (1750, p. lxv) *and* mTBY4
(hoop'd-at) *conj.*, CAP
  1011 *SCENE* IV. CAP+
    The same. A Street. CAP, v1778+ *(subst.)*
  1012–15 *Prose (cont. through* 1023) F2-F4; *two verse lines ending* hasten . . . after
then prose ROWE, POPE; *three verse lines ending* hasten . . . Antony . . . follow. mTBY2
conj., THEO1+
  1012 your selues] your selfe F2-ROWE3
    further] farther F2-RANN, COL, WH1, HAL

_____

1003 **of**] See n. 1781.
1004 **all to naught**] RANN (ed. 1791–): "When, at the onset, I have every prospect
of success." WORDSWORTH (ed. 1883): *"The odds in my favour are as all to nothing."*
  Quailes] HANMER (ed. 1744): "Lucian [*Anacharsis* 37] *relates that at* Athens *Quail-
fighting was exhibited at shews: and many other ancient Authors mention it as a sport
much in use."* Quail combats are described by DOUCE (1807, 2:87).
  1005 **(in hoopt)**] Although THEOBALD (19 Feb. 1729, [fol. 39ᵛ]) uncharacteristically
cannot comment ("This is a Term I dont know what to make of, thro my Ignorance in
Quaii-fighting") and HANMER (ed. 1744) offers no explanation for his emendation (*in-
coop'd*), other commentators are ready to correct and explain. SEWARD (1750, p. lxv):
Bettors "on my Side *shout* and *whoop* for Victory." JOHNSON (ed. 1765), however, and
most others: *"Inhoop'd is inclosed, confined,* that they may fight." FARMER (*in* STEEVENS,
ed. 1773, 10:Qq2): "John Davies begins one of his epigrams . . . : 'He sets cocke *on*
the hoope', *in*, you would say; 'For cocking *in hoopes* is now all the play' [*Works*, ed.
Grosart, 1878, "Vpon English Prouerbes", 2:(no.) 287]."

Agr. Sir, *Marke Anthony*, will e'ne but kisse *Octauia*,
and weele follow.   1015
Lepi. Till I shall see you in your Souldiers dresse,
Which will become you both: Farewell.
Mece. We shall: as I conceiue the iourney, be at
Mount before you *Lepidus.*
Lepi. Your way is shorter, my purposes do draw me   1020
much about, you'le win two dayes vpon me.

───────────────────────────────

1016 Souldiers] F1, F2, POPE2; Souldier's F3-POPE1, HAN1, CAP, MAL, v1793-SIS, EVNS;
Soldiers' THEO1 *etc.*
1017–23 *Seven verse lines ending* Farewel. . . . be . . . *Lepidus.* . . . shorter, . . .
about, . . . success. | *Lep.* Farewel. ROWE; *six verse lines ending* shall, . . . th' mount
. . . shorter, . . . about, . . . success. | *Lep.* Farewel. POPE1-COL2, SING2-GLO, HAL+;
five verse lines ending shall, . . . Mount . . . shorter; . . . about: . . . me *then as*
F1 HUD1; *five verse lines ending* shall, . . . Mount Misenum . . . shorter; . . . about.
. . . Farewell. KTLY
1018 at] at the F2-v1773, RANN, KNT1, DYCE, GLO, CAM1, HUD2+ (−RID)
1019 Mount] Mount Misenum KTLY
1020 way] stay v1778, RANN

─────────────────

   at odd's] SEWARD (1750, p. lxv): "When the Odds are on my Side." See "'gainst
the oddes" (993).
   1007, 1008 *Ventigius*] See n. 998.
   1009 **Commissions**] MINSHEU (1617): "*Delegation, a Mandate.*" See "dismission" (37)
and *OED, sb.*[1] 1 ("Instruction") or 2 ("Authority").
   1011–23 LEE (ed. 1907, p. xxviii) complains Sh.'s use of Plutarch is aimless, and he
offers this scene as an example of "the digressive tendency of the middle currents of the
piece." Begrudgingly, TRAVERSI (1963, p. 119) acknowledges that the short scene "recalls
the continued pressure of public events"; JONES (1971, p. 245), finding it "otherwise
otiose," that it "is included simply in order to recall . . . the journeying involved . . .
and to insist once more on the space-time dimension."
   1012 **Trouble . . . further**] KITTREDGE (ed. 1941): "Lepidus dismisses them courteously."
   1013 DELIUS (ed. 1856): Make your generals hasten after. BLUMHOF (ed. 1870) prefers
"Hasten after your generals" since it is inappropriate for Caesar's "subordinates" to have
such power. DEIGHTON (ed. 1891) agrees, citing ABBOTT §203 on the transposition of
prepositions. BLAKE (1983, p. 112), however: "*After* is a postponed preposition," or "an
adverb . . . to express manner."
   1014 **e'ne**] Only DEIGHTON (ed. 1891) comments: "Emphasizing *but.*"
   1018–19 **at Mount**] See n. 866 for the identification of the place. CHEDWORTH (1805,
p. 287) alone: "Heron (in his *Letters of Literature* [1785, letter 38, p. 301]) says, *at mount*
means ready to mount our horses." MALONE (ed. 1790): "Our authour probably wrote—*a'*
the mount." FURNESS (ed. 1907): "Is it not more likely that there is an absorption of
the in the final *t* of 'at'?" See n. 861, textual notes, and conj., p. 351.
   1021 **much about**] KITTREDGE (ed. 1941): "By a very roundabout way."

Both. Sir good successe.
Lepi. Farewell.   *Exeunt.*

Enter Cleopater, Charmian, Iras, and Alexas.   **2.5**

Cleo. Giue me some Musicke: Musicke, moody foode   1025
of vs that trade in Loue.
Omnes. The Musicke, hoa.

Enter Mardian the Eunuch.

Cleo. Let it alone, let's to Billards: come *Charmian.*
Char. My arme is sore, best play with *Mardian.*   1030

1022 Sir] *Om.* HAN1
1024 SCENE III. ROWE; SCENE V. POPE, HAN1, WARB, JOHN1+
    Alexandria. ROWE1+ (*subst.*)
1025-7, 1029 *Three verse lines ending* food . . . hoa! . . . *Charmian.* ROWE1-THEO2,
WARB-JOHN1, v1773-RANN, COL1-HUD1, DYCE1, COL3, WH1+; *four verse lines ending* food
. . . hoa! . . . come, | *Charmian.* HAN1, CAP; *four verse lines ending* food . . . ho!
. . . billiards: . . . Charmian. v1793-KNT1, SING2, STAU
1029 let's] let us HAN1, CAP-KNT1, STAU

1022 **successe**] See n. 421.
1025 **moody**] JOHNSON (ed. 1765): "The *mood*, is the *mind*, or *mental disposition*.
. . . Perhaps here is a poor jest intended between *mood* the *mind* and *moods* of musick." STEEVENS (ed. 1778): "*Melancholy*." (His assertion that "Cotgrave [1611] explains
moody, by the French words, *morne* and *triste*" is incorrect; the two French words are
defined by *melancholy* among others.) SEYMOUR (1805, 2:56) rejects Steevens as "not
accurate" and proposes "fitful, suiting any particular gust or strain of passion." The first
dictionaries with the lemma *moody* are KERSEY (1702)—"*Humoursome*"—and BAILEY
(1730)—"Sullen, &c."
1026 **trade in**] Expanding FURNESS (ed. 1907), KITTREDGE (ed. 1941): "Deal with;
have to do with. In Elizabethan usage the word does not suggest *mercenary* dealing.
Cf. *Hamlet* iii, 2, 346 [2204]."
1027 **Omnes.**] WILSON (ed. 1950): "'All' is the usual prefix in 'good' Sh. texts." See
p. 368.
    hoa] Only this variant spelling of *ho* occurs in *Ant.* OED (Ho *int.*[1] 2): "An excla-
mation to attract attention," in *Ant.* most often with commands. See also 1446, 1493,
2262, 2801, 2808, 2982, 2983, 3580. Compare n. 2946.
1029 **Billards**] MALONE (ed. 1790): "This game was not known in ancient times."
VERPLANCK (ed. 1846): Sh. "employed the familiar English word for the game most like
that he supposed might have been played in old times." ADEE (1883, p. 131): Sh. "cribbed
the idea from . . . Chapman's *Blind Beggar of Alexandria* [1598] . . . that billiards

Cleopa. As well a woman with an Eunuch plaide, as
with a woman. Come you'le play with me Sir?
Mardi. As well as I can Madam.
Cleo. And when good will is shewed,
Though't come to short   1035
The Actor may pleade pardon. Ile none now,
Giue me mine Angle, weele to'th'Riuer there
My Musicke playing farre off. I will betray
Tawny fine fishes, my bended hooke shall pierce
Their slimy iawes: and as I draw them vp,   1040
Ile thinke them euery one an *Anthony*,

1031–2 *Verse lines ending* play'd, . . . Sir? ROWE1+
1031 an] a OXF1
1034–5 *One verse line* ROWE1+
1037–8 Riuer ͜ . . . off.] ~ , . . . ~ , F4+ (−RID, ARD2)
1039 Tawny fine] Tawny-fine F3, F4; Tawny-fin ROWE, POPE, HAN1; Tawny-finn'd
mTBY2 *conj.*, THEO1, THEO2, WARB+
        fishes] fish POPE1-v1773 (−CAP)

---

was an *Egyptian* game, and a favorite pastime of *women*." He quotes, "Send for some
Ladies to goe play with you, At chesse, at Billiardes, and at other game" (Sc. 4.12–13,
ed. Holaday, 1970, p. 29), although Chapman probably was anachronistic too. Recent
commentators concentrate on the obvious bawdy aspects of the game, its implements
and language. See, for example, E. PARTRIDGE (1947; 1968, p. 66). For the acceptability
of the F1 spelling, see CERCIGNANI (1981, p. 284).

1034–6 And . . . pardon] Although a number of commentators, beginning with
DELIUS (ed. 1856), regard the actor as the doer or agent (or as player in the game of
billiards), Sh.'s usage strongly suggests the theatrical sense (in all but 4 of the 24 instances). TIESSEN (1879, p. 470), however, is unconvincing in citing 1032 as evidence therefor. More convincing is the repetition of a "similar sentiment," cited first by STEEVENS
(ed. 1793), in *MND* 5.1.82–3 (1879–80): Theseus will hear the play of the handicrafts-
men, "For neuer any thing Can be amisse, when simplenesse and duty tender it." But
the bawdy implications of the passage are, of course, powerful.

1037 Angle] *OED* (*sb.*[1] 1), citing this instance: "A fishing-hook; often, in later use,
extended to the line or tackle . . . and the rod."

1038–42 I . . . caught] ADELMAN (1973, p. 60): "Everyone knew that pleasure was
a baited hook. The image was so familiar that Spenser could describe the false Una as
'vnder blake stole hyding her bayted hooke' (*FQ* 1.1.49): the image is not grotesque only
because its familiarity enables us to recognize it at once as a moral rather than a literal
description. Garnier explicates the association." She quotes Pembroke's *Antonie* (1595,
ll. 1176–9), a comparison made earlier by GÜNTHER (1968, p. 102, n. 31). For the 1592
Antonius, see p. 506.

1039 fine] See n. 437.
        bended] For weak verbs ending either in *-ed* or in *-t*, see FRANZ §160.

And say, ah ha; y'are caught.

   Char. 'Twas merry when you wager'd on your Angling, when your diuer did hang a salt fish on his hooke
which he with feruencie drew vp.   1045

   Cleo. That time? Oh times:
I laught him out of patience: and that night
I laught him into patience, and next morne,
Ere the ninth houre, I drunke him to his bed:
Then put my Tires and Mantles on him, whilst   1050
I wore his Sword Phillippan. Oh from Italie,

1042–6 *Four verse lines ending* merry when . . . diver . . . he . . . times!—
POPE1+
1049 drunke] drank v1773, v1778, RANN
1051 Phillippan] Philippian COL, WH1, KTLY

1043–5 For Plutarch, see p. 415. Similar stories involving other persons are given by
GREY (1754, 2:198–9), from M. C. Baronne D'Aulnoy, *Memoirs of the Court of England
in 1675* (1707, pp. 489–90; tr. Mrs. Arthur, ed. G. D. Gilbert, 1913, pp. 314–15), and
DOUCE (1807, 2:87–90), from [Thomas] *Nashes Lenten Stuffe* (1599, p. 60).

1044 **salt fish**] Plutarch refers to "a fishe . . . which they had taken before." See p. 415.

1046 **That time**] DELIUS (ed. 1856) and others: Not an exclamation but indicating
when "I laught. . . ." WILSON (ed. 1950) points to the colon after "Oh times" as "marking a parenthesis." For the colon, a compositorial characteristic, see pp. 368–9.

1049 **ninth houre**] WORDSWORTH (ed. 1883) alone: "By the Roman reckoning of time,
3 P.M." DEIGHTON (ed. 1891) and the rest: "Before nine o'clock in the morning. . . .
Shakespeare is here reckoning according to English time." WILSON (ed. 1950) compares
JC 2.4.23 (1172), in which the same early hour is mentioned in connection with Caesar's
appearance at the Capitol.

   I . . . bed] BLAKE (1983, p. 54): "*Drunke* means 'made him so drunk that he
had to take to his bed' and this sense is not recorded elsewhere." See *OED* (Drunk *v.*
2)—"To saturate or fill with drink . . . to make drunken"—which gives the year 1388
as the last instance, and *OED* (Drink *v.*[1] 9)—"To provide with drink"—which gives 1883
as the first instance.

1050–1 **Then . . . Phillippan**] WARBURTON (ed. 1747): "The speaker is supposed
to do this in imitation of *Omphale*, in her treatment of *Hercules* the great ancestor of
Antony." WILSON (ed. 1950): "Did Sh. get this direct from Ovid's *Fasti* [2.317–26]?"
WARNER (1957, pp. 139–40) suggests Plutarch's *Comparison of Demetrius with Antonius*
(see p. 458) as a possible source; SCHANZER (1960, p. 21, n. 2), the Countess of Pembroke's *Antonius* (see p. 507). LLOYD (1959, p. 93): "Cleopatra likewise [as the moon
(female) contains an element of Osiris (male)] has taken to herself an element of Antony's virility symbolized in the sword. [Cites also 2851.]" WADDINGTON (1966, p. 214)
adds the "mythic prototype" of Mars and Venus, among others.

1050 **Tires**] Most commentators follow MINSHEU (1617, Attire)—"In English commeth from the Latine word *Tiãra*, which is an ornament of the heads of the Persian Kings,

Enter a Messenger.

Ramme thou thy fruitefull tidings in mine eares,
That long time haue bin barren.
Mes. Madam, Madam.   1055
Cleo. Anthonyo's dead,
If thou say so Villaine, thou kil'st thy Mistris:

1052 *Enter*] *Enter* ELIS mCOL1, COL2
1053 Ramme] Rain HAN1, CAP, RANN, SING, KTLY, CAM3b
    fruitefull] faithful THEO2, WARB, THEO4
1055–6 Madam. | *Cleo. Anthonyo's*] madam, | Antony— | *Cleo.* O, is BAYF
1056–9 *Four verse lines ending* dead? . . . mistress: . . . free, . . . here POPE1-
JOHN1, v1773-HUD1, COL3, WH1, HAL, COL4; *three verse lines ending* so, . . . free, . . .
here CAP; *three verse lines ending* villain, . . . free, . . . here SING2, DYCE, STAU, GLO,
KTLY, CAM1, HUD2+
1056 *Anthonyo's*] Anthony's F2-HUD1, SING2-WH1, HAL, DYCE2, COL4, HUD2, OXF1,
KIT1, ALEX, SIS; Antonius DEL2, GLO, CAM1, WH2, ARD, RID; Oh, Antony is KTLY
1057 so] so, thou ANON. *conj. apud* CAM1, HUD2
    kil'st] killest KTLY
    Mistris] *Trisyllabic* mTBY2 *conj.*, KTLY

Priests, and Women"—rather than KERSEY (1702): "Attire, or *dress*." The customary reference in Sh. is to a headdress (despite Minsheu's incorrect etymology).
   Mantles] MINSHEU (1617): "*Pendula, a long hanging cloake.*"
   1051 **Sword Phillippan**] THEOBALD (ed. 1733): "We are not to suppose, nor is there
any Warrant from History, that *Antony* had any particular Sword so call'd. The dignify-
ing Weapons, in this Sort, is a Custom of much more recent Date." CAPELL (1779 [1774],
1:34): "The sword that was worn at Philippi."
   1053 **Ramme**] The supporters of the F1 reading apparently follow the reasoning of
MALONE (ed. 1790): "The term employed . . . is much in the style of the speaker; and
is supported incontestably by a passage in *Julius Cæsar* [quotes 'I . . . ears,' 5.3.73–5
(2558–60)]." Those supporting Hanmer's (ed. 1744) emendation evidently follow STEEVENS
(ed. 1773): "*Rain* agrees better with . . . *fruitful* and *barren*." Agreeing, CAPELL (1779
[1774], 1:34) thinks, "In . . . '*Ramme*', there is a grievous and striking indelicacy that
could not come from Cleopatra." Perhaps less convincingly, JACKSON (1819, p. 294) believes *Rain* was misread as *Ram*, "the dot being omitted over the *i*." HUDSON (ed. 1855):
"The word is spelt *ramme* in the original, so that it could hardly be a misprint for *rain*."
   1056 **Anthonyo's**] DELIUS (ed. 1856) emends, giving no other reason than that F1's
spelling is frequently used for *Antonius*, as at 686 and *JC* 1.2.3 (91). WILSON (ed. 1950):
"The [F1] spelling suggests intimacy, natural to the context." RIDLEY (ed. 1954), emending, finds Wilson's remark "over-subtle." One important reason is that only this spelling
requires a stress on the second syllable; *Antony* is never stressed so. See n. 29 and p. 376.
   dead] See n. 510.
   1057 See n. 110.
   Villaine] COTGRAVE (1611): "*Slaue, bondman, seruile tenant. . . . Hence also,*

But well and free, if thou so yeild him.
There is Gold, and heere
My blewest vaines to kisse: a hand that Kings   1060
Haue lipt, and trembled kissing.
  Mes. First Madam, he is well.
  Cleo. Why there's more Gold.
But sirrah marke, we vse
To say, the dead are well: bring it to that,   1065
The Gold I giue thee, will I melt and powr
Downe thy ill vttering throate.
  Mes. Good Madam heare me.
  Cleo. Well, go too I will: (xx4ᵛ)

1058 thou so] so thou JOHN1, v1773, v1778, RANN
    him.] ～, POPE2+
1061–4 Ff;   *arranged as verse lines, thus:* 1061, 1062, 1063–4 ROWE1-RANN, HUD1,
HAL; 1061–2, 1063–4 v1793, v1803, SING, KNT1, STAU, KTLY; 1061, 1062–3, 1064 v1821 *etc.*
1065 it] me F2-ROWE3
1066 thee] *Om.* F4
1068–9 *One verse line* v1793+

---

a churle, carle, boore, clowne; *and*, *a miser, micher, pinch-pennie, pennyfather*; *and*,
a knaue, rascall, varlet, filthie fellow; *any base-humored, ill-borne, and worse-bred hinde*,
cullion, or clusterfist." Modern glosses, although not so picturesque, reflect the same
range. See also 1105, 2611, 3386.

    Mistris] ABBOTT (§477): "R, and liquids in dissyllables, are frequently pronounced
as though an extra vowel were introduced between them and the preceding consonant.
. . . 'Frús | t(*e*)ráte.'" See also 3111.

    1058 **But . . . free**] RANN (ed. 1791–) alone: "Say but he is well; and thou gain'st
thy freedom." All others agree that the reference in both instances is to Antony, KIT-
TREDGE (ed. 1941) adding, "Explained by l. [1078]."

    1060 **blewest vaines**] Blue veins would seem to presuppose a fair complexion. See
10 and 555, as well as *Luc.* 407, 440, 1454.

    1064 **sirrah**] See n. 3475.

    1064–5 **vse To**] For the present tense of *use* plus the prepositional infinitive with the
meaning "in the habit of" or "accustomed to," see FRANZ §620, *Anm.* 2. See also 1937.

    1065 **dead are well**] Proverbial; see DENT (H347): "He is well since he is in *heaven*."

    1066–7 CASE (ed. 1906): "Perhaps suggested by the treatment of Crassus' body by
Orodes," related in n. 1497. BALDWIN (1944, 2:576) suggests Florus, *Epitome of Roman
History* 1.46—following THEOBALD (1909, p. 165)—and not Dio Cassius as the source
for this "particular story," although no one else seems to trace the idea to Dio.

    1069 **go too**] FRANZ (§454): A now-obsolete but earlier often-used expression of an-
ger, impatient displeasure, and the like, on the one hand, and of soothing encourage-
ment, on the other. Commentators beginning with DEIGHTON (ed. 1891) prefer the second

But there's no goodnesse in thy face if *Anthony*   1070
Be free and healthfull; so tart a fauour
To trumpet such good tidings. If not well,
Thou shouldst come like a Furie crown'd with Snakes,
Not like a formall man.
    Mes. Wilt please you heare me?   1075
    Cleo. I haue a mind to strike thee ere thou speak'st:
Yet if thou say *Anthony* liues, 'tis well,
Or friends with *Cæsar,* or not Captiue to him,
Ile set thee in a shower of Gold, and haile
Rich Pearles vpon thee.   1080
    Mes. Madam, he's well.
    Cleo. Well said.

1070 face ∧] ~ . ROWE1-ALEX (−KNT1, HUD1, RID)
1071 so] Why so ROWE1-CAP, RANN-SING1, COL2, COL3, DYCE2, COL4, HUD2, KIT1, ALEX
        fauour] favour suits not KTLY
1077 'tis] is mF4FL33 *and* mTBY2 *conj.*, CAP, v1778-KNT1, HUD1-DYCE1, GLO+ (−HAL, NLSN, EVNS)
1078 Captiue] Captaine F2-ROWE3
1079 set] see F3-POPE2
1080–2 *One verse line* v1793+

---

possibility here. See 807, 1623. *To* and *too* were not consistently differentiated in spelling until about the first half of the 17th c. See *OED*, Go (to) 91b.
    1070 **goodnesse**] THISELTON (1899, p. 13) alone: "Worth. Modern editors, taking this word in the wrong sense have altered the punctuation," by inserting a period after *face.* See textual notes.
    1071 **healthfull**] See n. 510.
    fauour] MINSHEU (1617): "*Countenance.*"
    1073 **Furie . . . Snakes**] FRIPP (1930, p. 101) cites Ovid's "crinibus angues [(combing black) snakes from their hair]" (*Metamorphoses* 4.454). THOMSON (1952, p. 149): "See *Aeneid*, VII. 328, 329 . . . Seneca often."
    1074 **formall**] Comment is diverse and not unambiguous, but three main interpretations emerge. Two are almost equally represented, both derived from the early lexicographers CAWDREY (1604) and BULLOKAR (1616). One is first proposed by MALONE (*apud* STEEVENS, ed. 1778): "*In form,* i.e. *shape*"; the other by WARBURTON (ed. 1747)— "Ordinary"—and JOHNSON (ed. 1765): "Rather decent, regular." The third interpretation, less frequent, is to be found in EDWARDS (1765, p. 234): "In his senses."
    1077 **'tis**] TYRWHITT (1766, p. 11) justifies his emendation *is* only by paraphrasing with it. SISSON (1956, 2:267), agreeing, at least adds: "'*Tis well* is awkward here and in the air."
    1078 **Or . . . or**] See n. 720.
    Captiue] DELIUS (ed. 1856) is alone in suggesting that this word, like *free* (1071),

115

Mes. And Friends with *Cæsar.*
Cleo. Th'art an honest man.
Mes. *Cæsar,* and he, are greater Friends then euer.   1085
Cleo. Make thee a Fortune from me.
Mes. But yet Madam.
    Cleo. I do not like but yet, it does alay
The good precedence, fie vpon but yet,
But yet is as a Iaylor to bring foorth   1090
Some monstrous Malefactor. Prythee Friend,
Powre out the packe of matter to mine eare,
The good and bad together: he's friends with *Cæsar,*
In state of health thou saist, and thou saist, free.
    Mes. Free Madam, no: I made no such report,   1095
He's bound vnto *Octauia.*
    Cleo. For what good turne?
Mes. For the best turne i'th'bed.
Cleo. I am pale *Charmian.*
Mes. Madam, he's married to *Octauia.*   1100
Cleo. The most infectious Pestilence vpon thee.
                                  Strikes him downe.

Mes. Good Madam patience.
Cleo. What say you?   *Strikes him.*
Hence horrible Villaine, or Ile spurne thine eyes   1105

1086 Make] Marke F2-ROWE3, CAP
1089 precedence] precedent mTBY3 *conj. and* HAN1
1092 the] thy mTBY2 *conj.*, HAN1, CAP, RANN
1093 friends] friend v1803, SING1
1095 I made . . . report] I made . . . sport F3-ROWE3; I have made . . . sport POPE
1103–5 *Verse lines ending* Hence, . . . eyes mTYR *conj. and* CAP, v1778-HUD1,
SING2+; *ending* you?— . . . eyes DEL2
1103 patience] have but patience HAN1

---

is not to be taken in its literal sense: rather, it refers to Antony's independence of will.
    1084 **honest**] KITTREDGE (ed. 1941): "Honourable, worthy." See 1195, 2425, 2916.
    1089 **precedence**] CAWDREY (1604, precedent): "Going before." COCKERAM (1623,
Precedency): "A going before." For the differences of suffixation, see FRANZ §113, §114.
    1092 **packe**] RIDLEY (ed. 1954): "Cleopatra thinks of the messenger with his news
as like a pedler with his pack, and elaborates the image later, in lines [1157–9]."
    1097–8 Proverbial; see DENT (T616): "One good *turn* asks (requires, deserves) another."
    1099 See n. 110.
    1101–9 WALTER (ed. 1969): "Cleopatra's curses are suggestive of venereal disease and
its treatment . . . and the whipping of prostitutes."
    1105 **Villaine**] See n. 1057.

Like balls before me: Ile vnhaire thy head,

She hales him vp and downe.

Thou shalt be whipt with Wyer, and stew'd in brine,
Smarting in lingring pickle.
   Mes. Gratious Madam,   1110
I that do bring the newes, made not the match.
   Cleo. Say 'tis not so, a Prouince I will giue thee,
And make thy Fortunes proud: the blow thou had'st
Shall make thy peace, for mouing me to rage,
And I will boot thee with what guift beside   1115
Thy modestie can begge.
   Mes. He's married Madam.
   Cleo. Rogue, thou hast liu'd too long.   *Draw a knife.*
   Mes. Nay then Ile runne:
What meane you Madam, I haue made no fault.   *Exit.* 1120

1106 before] from v1773
1115 beside] beside. BLUM; besides HUD2
1118-19 *One verse line* v1793+ (−KNT1, STAU)

1105-7 **Ile . . . *downe*] See n. 603.
1105-6 **Ile . . . me**] Only BLUMHOF compares the football image in *Err.* 2.1.83 (359).
1105 **spurne**] MINSHEU (1617): "*Kicke.*" See also n. 1741-2.
1107 ***vp and downe***] SCHMIDT (1874, Down, 2a): "To and fro."
1108 **whipt . . . Wyer**] CASE (ed. 1906): "So in Nash, *The Unfortunate Traveller* (1594; ed. Gosse, 1892), p. 195: 'Then did they scourge hys backe parts so blistered and basted, with burning whips of red hot *wire*'; Sylvester's Du Bartas, *The Decay* [1620; ed. Snyder (1979, p. 744, l. 386): 'With wyerie Rods thou shalt to death be whipt']."
1109 **lingring pickle**] MINSHEU (1617, Pickle): "*Brine.*" DELIUS (ed. 1856) interprets *lingring* as referring to the duration of the "smarting." CASE (ed. 1906): "*Either* long-continuing pickle, *or* pickle whose effects will be so."
1115-16 **I . . . begge**] DEIGHTON (ed. 1891): "I will in addition present you with whatever gift you may in moderation ask." KITTREDGE (ed. 1941): "Cleopatra means that any gift that he can beg, however great, will seem moderate to her." WILSON (ed. 1950): "I.e. however immoderate thy demand." SCHMIDT (1875) defines *modesty* as "freedom from arrogance or obtrusive impudence," following MINSHEU (1617): "*To* Abashe." IDEM (Abash): "*Make ashamed.*" See also 957, n. 3034.
1115 **boot**] MINSHEU's (1617) "*Helpe, succour, aid and aduantage*" is followed by most commentators. A few, starting with IRVING & MARSHALL (ed. 1889), blend in "give . . . to boot"—i.e., "over and above." See *OED, v.*[1] 1 and 2. See also "Make boote" (2400).
   beside] FRANZ (§469): The Elizabethans made no distinction between *beside* and *besides.*
1118 ***Draw a knife***] See pp. 375-6.
1119 **Nay then**] See n. 4.

117

Char. Good Madam keepe your selfe within your selfe,
The man is innocent.

Cleo. Some Innocents scape not the thunderbolt:
Melt Egypt into Nyle: and kindly creatures
Turne all to Serpents. Call the slaue againe,   1125
Though I am mad, I will not byte him: Call?

Char. He is afeard to come.

Cleo. I will not hurt him,
These hands do lacke Nobility, that they strike
A meaner then my selfe: since I my selfe   1130
Haue giuen my selfe the cause. Come hither Sir.

Enter the Messenger againe.

Though it be honest, it is neuer good

1124 kindly] kindled F2-ROWE3
1127 afeard] afraid POPE1-JOHN1, v1773
1128 *Exit Charmian.* DYCE, STAU, GLO, CAM1, HUD2-RIDa, CAM3, SIS
1132 *Enter*] *Re-enter* ELIS COL2; *Re-enter* CHARMIAN *and* DYCE, STAU, GLO, CAM1, HUD2-RIDa, CAM3, SIS

1121 **keepe . . . within your selfe**] STEEVENS (ed. 1793): "I.e. contain yourself, restrain your passion within bounds." WILSON (ed. 1950): "The opposite of 'beside yourself.'"

1123 Commentators strain for interpretations of the simple fact that cataclysms afflict all. DOUCE (1807, 2:89): "This alludes to a superstitious notion among the ancients, that they who were stricken with lightning were honoured by Jupiter and therefore to be accounted holy." CASE (ed. 1906): *Innocents* is "perhaps a play on the sense fools, naturals, occurring *e.g.* in *King Lear*, III.vi.8 [2005]." RICE (1968, p. 320): "Cleopatra's line contributes to the skeptical texture of the play through the inevitable Renaissance association of references to the thunderbolt's inaccuracy with pagan skepticism."

1124 **Melt . . . Nyle**] Editors since STEEVENS (ed. 1778) compare 44. THISELTON (1899, p. 13) adds, "The affinity of nature between Anthony and Cleopatra is suggested by their similar imprecations when the continuance of their connection is threatened."

kindly] Either "Natural" (BOSWELL [ed. 1821, 21:Glossary]) or "Of gentle nature" (DEIGHTON [ed. 1891]) or both (EVANS [ed. 1974]). The F2-ROWE (ed. 1714) *kindled* is defined by KERSEY (1702) as "*Bring forth young, as a hare does.*" See also *AYL* 3.2.359 (1528).

1125 **all**] Most likely the intensive adverb meaning "completely," "entirely." See FRANZ §371.

1129–31 **These . . . cause**] GREY (1754, 2:199): "Alluding to the laws of *chivalry*, which forbid a superior to engage with an inferior." DELIUS (ed. 1856) paraphrases: Cleopatra herself deserves the blows, being herself to blame. Most follow DEIGHTON (ed. 1891) in explaining the "cause" as being her infatuation for Antony; some follow FURNESS (ed. 1907), her "ever allow[ing] Anthony to leave her." In addition MALONE (*apud* STEEVENS [1783]), without evidence: "Perhaps here was intended an indirect cen-

To bring bad newes: giue to a gratious Message
An host of tongues, but let ill tydings tell   1135   (xx5ᵃ)
Themselues, when they be felt.
    Mes. I haue done my duty.
    Cleo. Is he married?
I cannot hate thee worser then I do,
If thou againe say yes.   1140
    Mes. He's married Madam.
    Cleo. The Gods confound thee,
Dost thou hold there still?
    Mes. Should I lye Madame?
    Cleo. Oh, I would thou didst: 1145
So halfe my Egypt were submerg'd and made
A Cesterne for scal'd Snakes. Go get thee hence,
Had'st thou *Narcissus* in thy face to me,
Thou would'st appeere most vgly: He is married?
    Mes. I craue your Highnesse pardon.   1150
    Cleo. He is married?
    Mes. Take no offence, that I would not offend you,
To punnish me for what you make me do
Seemes much vnequall, he's married to *Octauia.*

1135 An] A OXF1
     ill] it F2
1136–8 *Arranged as verse lines, thus:* 1136–7, 1138 v1793, v1803, SING, KNT1, DYCE,
STAU, GLO, KTLY, CAM1, HUD2+; 1136, 1137–8 COL, WH1, HAL
1137 haue] have but CAP
1140 thou] you ROWE2-JOHN1
1142–3 *One verse line* ROWE1+
1145 I] *Om.* F3-POPE2
1149, 1151 married?] ～ . POPE, KTLY
1152 that] for POPE, HAN1

---

sure of Queen Elizabeth, for her unprincely and unfeminine treatment of the amiable
Earl of Essex."
    1139 **worser**] See n. 139.
    1142 **confound**] See n. 57.
    1143 **hold there**] WORDSWORTH (ed. 1883) and the others: *"Persist in saying that."*
    1146 **So**] BLUMHOF (ed. 1870): Even if. See FRANZ §565 and conj., p. 352.
    1147 **scal'd Snakes**] GREY (1754, 2:201) and others take as "the *crocodile*, with which
the *Nile* abounded," but, of course, all snakes are scaly.
    1147–9 **Go . . . vgly**] STEEVENS (ed. 1793) compares *Jn.* 3.1.36–7 (957–8).
    1152 **that**] ABBOTT (§284): "Since *that* represents different cases of the relative, it
may mean 'in *that*', 'for *that*', 'because' ('quod')."
    1154 **vnequall**] DELIUS (ed. 1856) and the others: "Unjust."

Cleo. Oh that his fault should make a knaue of thee,   1155
That art not what th'art sure of. Get thee hence,
The Marchandize which thou hast brought from Rome
Are all too deere for me:
Lye they vpon thy hand, and be vndone by em.

1155 that‸ his fault‸] ∼ , ∼∼ , WH1
1156 That] Thou JOHN3
     art not] say'st but HAN1, WARB, CAP; art but WH; art in HUD2
     art not what . . . of.] ∼∼ !— ∼ ? . . . of't? DAVIES (1783, 2:349) *conj.*,
v1793, v1803, HUD1, SING2, COL3, KTLY; ∼∼ !— ∼ ? . . . ∼ — SING1, COL1,
COL2, COL4
1157 Marchandize which] Merchandises which F4-ROWE3; merchandises POPE1-JOHN1
1158–60 *Verse lines ending* hand, . . . patience. mTBY2 *conj.*, CAP+ (−ARD2)
1159 *Exit Mes.* ROWE1+

1155–6 **Oh . . . of**] Most commentators who do not emend seem to accept the paraphrase of MALONE (ed. 1790): "Strange, that his fault should make thee appear a knave, who art not that information of which thou bringest such certain assurance." JOHNSON (ed. 1765) fancies "the line consists only of abrupt starts" and interprets, "*That . . . thee that art* — but what *shall I say thou art* not? — Thou art then sure of this *marriage*." TOLLET (*apud* STEEVENS, ed. 1778) is followed by DELIUS (ed. 1856) and BLUMHOF (ed. 1870): "Thou art not an honest man, of which thou art thyself assured, but thou art in my opinion a knave by thy master's fault alone." RANN (ed. 1791–), followed by WILSON (ed. 1950) and PHIALAS (ed. 1955): "O, that a fault of his should make thee appear the knave thou art not, but which, I perceive by thy tale, thou art confident he is." WHITE (ed. 1861), emending *art not* (1156) to *art but*, paraphrases: "O that, <i.e., Antony's marriage,> which is his fault, should make a knave of thee, that art but what thy tidings are." JOICEY (1891, p. 342): "Is not Cleopatra about to say 'that art not married'? . . . The meaning would be, 'O that Antony's knavish fault of getting married should cause thee — thee that art not married — to be treated as a knave.'" NICHOLSON (1892, p. 182) rejects Joicey by saying that Cleopatra "cannot . . . have known whether he was [married] or was not" and proposes that Sh. "meant that Cleopatra — looking to what she had just done — would assume that such a knave was sure to be whipped or carted." Of the emendations that may require explanation, MALONE (*apud* STEEVENS [1783]), proposing *sore* for *sure*: "Alas, is it not strange, that the fault of Antony should make thee appear to me a knave, thee, that art innocent, and art not the cause of that ill news, in consequence of which thou art yet *sore* with my blows!" And MASON (1785, p. 280), following DAVIES (1783, 2:348–9), paraphrases the last clause: "What? are you sure of what you tell me, that he is married to Octavia?" See textual notes and conj., p. 352.

     1155 **knaue**] See n. 2839.
     1157–9 See n. 1092. STULL (1956, p. 77) is alone in thinking that the messenger carries a small casket and in regarding Cleopatra's utterance as an example of her magnanimity. She rejects the "merchandise" — "Antony's gifts" — presents them to the messenger, and thus enunciates the "primary idea . . . one familiar enough in Shakespeare: wealth is a curse."

Char. Good your Highnesse patience.   1160
Cleo. In praysing *Anthony*, I haue disprais'd *Cæsar.*
Char. Many times Madam.
Cleo. I am paid for't now: lead me from hence,
I faint, oh *Iras, Charmian*: 'tis no matter.
Go to the Fellow, good *Alexas* bid him   1165
Report the feature of *Octauia*: her yeares,
Her inclination, let him not leaue out
The colour of her haire. Bring me word quickly,
Let him for euer go, let him not *Charmian*,

1161 praysing] praying F2
1162-4 *Three verse lines ending* now. . . . hence, . . . matter: — CAP, v1793-CAM3,
SIS, EVNS; *ending* madam. . . . faint, . . . matter. ARD2
1163 for't] for it POPE1-JOHN1, v1773-RANN
1168 *Exit* Alexas. CAP, v1778+
1169 go,] ~ ?— COL2, COL3
     him not] him — no, TYRWHITT (1766, p. 11) *conj.*, RANN

1160 **Good your Highnesse**] ABBOTT (§13): "*The possessive Adjectives*, when unem-
phatic, are sometimes transposed, being really combined with nouns." See also 1810,
2285, 2990.
1165-8 **bid . . . haire**] GREY (1754, 2:201): "This is a manifest allusion to the questions put by Queen *Elisabeth* to Sir *James Melvil*, concerning his mistress the Queen
of *Scots.* [Quotes *The Memoires of Sir James Melvil*, 1683, pp. 50-1.]" Emphatically rejected by FURNESS (ed. 1907).
1166 **feature**] BULLOKAR (1616): "Hansomnesse, comelinesse, beautie." KERSEY (1702):
"*Lineament of the face.*" BECKET (1815, 2:186): "*Feature*, with the earlier writers, is not
at all times *lineament of the visage.* It frequently signifies *make* or *shape* in general —
faiture — (form) old French. [Quotes *F.Q.* 3.9.33.]"
1167 **inclination**] COTGRAVE (1611): "*A humor, disposition, or affection, vnto.*" See
OED, 6d, which cites this instance.
1167-8 **let . . . haire**] HENLEY (*apud* STEEVENS, ed. 1785): "As from thence [her
hair color] she might be able to judge for herself, of her rival's propensity to those pleasures, upon which her passion for Antony was founded." AMNER (*apud* STEEVENS, ed.
1793): "I can in no wise divine what coloured hair is to be regarded as most indicative
of venereal motions: — perhaps indeed the κόμαι χρύσειαι; and yet, without experience,
certainty may still be wanting to mine appetite for knowledge. *Cuncta prius tentanda*,
saith that waggish poet Ovidius Naso [I have already tried all other means]" (*Metamorphoses* 1.190).
1169 **Let him . . . him**] JOHNSON (ed. 1765): "She is now talking in broken sentences, not of the Messenger, but *Antony.*" Because commentators agree and make no
distinction between the two *hims*, the assumption is that Antony is meant and that *Let*
means "allow." THISELTON (1899, p. 14) is the notable and unconvincing exception: "*I.e.*
hinder him not. On hearing Cleopatra apparently express a wish to have no more of

Though he be painted one way like a Gorgon,   1170
The other wayes a Mars. Bid you *Alexas*
Bring me word, how tall she is: pitty me *Charmian*,
But do not speake to me. Lead me to my Chamber.

Exeunt.

Flourish. Enter Pompey, at one doore with Drum and Trum-   **2.6**
pet: at another Cæsar, Lepidus, Anthony, Enobarbus, Me-   1176
cenas, Agrippa, Menas with Souldiers Marching.

1171 other wayes] F1-F3; other way he's mTHEO1 *conj.* (other he's), THEO2-THEO4,
v1773-SING2, COL3, KTLY, HAL, COL4; other way's F4 *etc.*
    a] *Om.* RANN, COL3
    to Mardian. CAP, v1778+
1172-3 Bring me . . . do not speake] Bring . . . speak not POPE1-v1773 (–CAP)
1175 SCENE IV. ROWE; SCENE VI. POPE, HAN1, WARB, JOHN1+
    The Coast of Italy, *near* Misenum. ROWE1+ *(subst.)*
    Flourish.] *Om.* F2-JOHN1, v1773-KNT1, HUD1, SING2, KTLY
1177 *Agrippa,*] *Om.* v1773-OXF1, ARD1, SIS
    Menas] *After Pompey in* 1175 ROWE1+ (–ARD2)

---

the Messenger, Charmian, we must understand, makes a movement as if she would tell
Alexas, who has already started in quest of the Messenger, not to bring the latter back
with him. Cleopatra noticing this corrects herself and bids Charmian not to interfere.
The first 'him' in this line refers to the Messenger: the second to Alexas." As dubious
evidence he compares Gorgon (1170) with 1073, "which shows that the Messenger is here
referred to."
    1170-1 **Though . . . Mars**] STAUNTON (ed. 1859): "An allusion to the 'double' pic-
tures in vogue formerly, of which Burton says,—'Like those double or turning pictures;
stand before which you see a fair maid, on the one side an ape, on the other an owl'
[*Anatomy of Melancholy*, ed. Jackson, 1932, p. 115]." HILL (1984, p. 230) detects an
echo of the "description of Hector in the Iliad, 'The eyes of Gorgon burnt in him and
warre's vermilion God' (Chapman's translation [8.304, ed. Nicoll, 1957])."
    1170 **Gorgon**] COOPER (1565, Gorgones): "Monstruous women, whiche were van-
quished by Perseus." WIGGINTON (1980, p. 367): Cleopatra's Gorgon, representing rage,
"derives primarily from Sir Thomas Elyot's translation of, and commentary on, a passage
from Ovid's *Art of Love* [3.501-4], and secondarily from Christopher Marlowe's echo [*1
Tamburlaine* 4.1.18-19, ed. Bowers, 1973] of a line from Spenser's *Faery Queene* [1.1.37]."
    1171 **wayes**] The F1 spelling, as well as F4's *way's*, is ambiguous. It has been inter-
preted as a contracted form of *way he is* by most, as *way as* by some. See KÖKERITZ (1953,
p. 271). In many instances *way's* is given without explanation.
    1177 *Menas*] RIDLEY (ed. 1954) explains why he deviates from the practice of all edi-

Pom. Your Hostages I haue, so haue you mine:
And we shall talke before we fight.
   Cæsar. Most meete that first we come to words,   1180
And therefore haue we
Our written purposes before vs sent,
Which if thou hast considered, let vs know,
If'twill tye vp thy discontented Sword,
And carry backe to Cicelie much tall youth,   1185
That else must perish heere.
   Pom. To you all three,
The Senators alone of this great world,
Chiefe Factors for the Gods. I do not know,
Wherefore my Father should reuengers want,   1190
Hauing a Sonne and Friends, since *Iulius Cæsar,*
Who at Phillippi the good *Brutus* ghosted,
There saw you labouring for him. What was't

1179–81 *Verse lines ending* meet . . . have we ROWE1+
1181 we] *Om.* STAU (*text;* we *in corrigenda*)
1186 must] much F2
1193 him] me F3-ROWE3

---

tions (see textual notes) since ROWE (ed. 1714): "The S.D. is interpretable as it stands. There enter first, by their respective doors, Pompey, the triumvirs, Enobarbus and Maecenas; they are followed by Agrippa (who does not talk at all) and Menas (who does not talk till all but he and Enobarbus have left), each as leader of a group of soldiers, and they stand in the background." WILSON (ed. 1950): "F. places 'Menas' last, which groups him with Caes.'s party. Perh. Sh. added the name to the list after writing a prose epilogue to the scene [presumably 1280–1332]."

1185 **Cicelie**] COOPER (1565, *Sicilia*): "A noble yle first called *Trinacria*, afterwarde *Sicania*, and at the laste *Sicilia*." See PAULY, Sicilia, 2:2461–2522 (1); *OCD*, Sicily; and map, p. xxxvii.

     tall] HANMER (ed. 1744, 6:Glossary): "Eminent, notable, considerable." JOHNSON (1755) and most others: "Sturdy; lusty."

1187–9 **To . . . Gods.**] DELIUS (ed. 1856) finds the sentence elliptical, requiring something like "I speak." See n. 1189 ("Gods. I"). WILSON (ed. 1950): "Sarcastic."

1188 **Senators**] CANTOR (1976, p. 220, n. 11), questionably: "The word 'senators' appears only once in the play . . . and even then is misapplied," possibly reflecting Pompey's irony.

1189 **Factors**] CAWDREY (1604): "One that doth busines for another."

     Gods. I] RIDLEY (ed. 1954): "The heavy punctuation of F is surely right. Pompey starts with a formal address, and then states his case; and *To you I do not know* is almost impossibly awkward." See n. 1187–9.

1192 **ghosted**] JOHNSON (1755), citing this instance: "To haunt with apparitions of departed men."

That mou'd pale *Cassius* to conspire? And what
Made all-honor'd, honest, Romaine *Brutus*,   1195
With the arm'd rest, Courtiers of beautious freedome,
To drench the Capitoll, but that they would
Haue one man but a man, and that his it
Hath made me rigge my Nauie. At whose burthen,
The anger'd Ocean fomes, with which I meant   1200
To scourge th'ingratitude, that despightfull Rome   (xx5
Cast on my Noble Father.
    Cæsar. Take your time.

1194–5 *Verse lines ending* And . . . Brutus, v1778-RANN
1195 all-honor'd] the all-honor'd F2-ROWE1, HAN1, CAP, v1793-SING1, COL2-ARD2
(–HAL, SIS); thee all-honour'd ROWE2-THEO2, WARB-JOHN1, v1773
        honest, Romaine ₐ] ~ ₐ ~ ₐ F2-THEO4, v1773, SING1, HUD1, KTLY; ~ ₐ ~ ,
mWARB *conj.*, JOHN1, DYCE, STAU, GLO, CAM1, COL4-ALEX, ARD2
    1196 Courtiers] courters mTHEO2 (19 Feb. 1729, [fol. 39ᵛ]; *withdrawn according to*
v1907) *conj.*, HAN1
    1198 one man but] but one man POPE
        his] is F2+

1194 **pale**] DEIGHTON (ed. 1891): "Symptomatic of his envious nature."
1195–7 **Made . . . To drench**] See n. 2894.
1195 **all-honor'd . . . *Brutus***] BLAKE (1983, p. 63): "Romaine" may modify "*Brutus*" or "*Brutus*" may be in apposition to "Romaine." "Both structures . . . are quite acceptable . . . and it is not clear why some modern editors wish to break away from the Folio here since its reading might be thought preferable rhythmically." See textual notes.
    honest] See n. 1084.
1196 **Courtiers . . . freedome**] See Spenser, "Mother Hubberds Tale" 717–18 (*The Minor Poems*, ed. Greenlaw et al., 1947, 2:124): "Yet the braue Courtier, in whose beauteous thought Regard of honour harbours more than ought."
    beautious] For the suffix, added to words of French or Latin origin, see FRANZ §131.
1198 **Haue . . . a man**] BLUMHOF (ed. 1870) compares *JC* 1.2.152–7 (251–6); KITTREDGE (ed. 1941), *JC* "And this Man, Is now become a God . . . him" (1.2.115–18 [213–16]).
1200 **meant**] JACKSON (1819, p. 295) proposes *mean* (see p. 352) because Pompey "displays a fixed determination," the F1 reading making him "speak like one already conquered." But this interpretation ignores the fact that *meant*, occurring at the same time as "Hath made me rigge" (1199), continues into the present. For the tense, see FRANZ §635.
1201 **despightfull**] COTGRAVE (1611, Despiteux): "*Testie, fumish . . . stomackfull, exceeding angrie, or moodie.*"
1203 **Take your time**] RANN (ed. 1791–): "Begin when you please." DELIUS (ed. 1856) and others, substantially: Don't rush.

124

Ant. Thou can'st not feare vs *Pompey* with thy sailes.
Weele speake with thee at Sea. At land thou know'st   1205
How much we do o're-count thee.
    Pom. At Land indeed
Thou dost orecount me of my Fatherrs house:
But since the Cuckoo buildes not for himselfe,
Remaine in't as thou maist.   1210
    Lepi. Be pleas'd to tell vs,
(For this is from the present how you take)
The offers we haue sent you.
    Cæsar. There's the point.
    Ant. Which do not be entreated too,   1215
But waigh what it is worth imbrac'd.
    Cæsar. And what may follow to try a larger Fortune.
    Pom. You haue made me offer
Of Cicelie, Sardinia: and I must
Rid all the Sea of Pirats. Then, to send   1220

1212 present_∧ . . . take)] ~) . . . ~ _∧ mTHEO2 (19 Feb. 1729, [fol. 40]) *conj.*,
THEO1+
        how you take] now you talke F2-POPE2
1213 offers] offer HAN1, DYCE2, HUD2
1215–18 *Three verse lines ending* weigh . . . follow . . . offer ROWE1+

1204 **feare**] For verbs used in the causative, see FRANZ §630.
1205 **speake**] See n. 871 ("spoke").
1208 **orecount**] CAPELL (1779 [1774], 1:35): "A perversion of [o're-count] in . . .
[1206]; for where Antony meant—over-number, this speaker means—over-reach." MA-
LONE (ed. 1790) says it seems to be used in both senses.
1209–10 JOHNSON (ed. 1765): "Since like the cuckow, that seizes the nests of other
birds, you have invaded a house which you could not build, keep it while you can."
STEEVENS (ed. 1778) quotes Pliny, *Natural History* 10.9 (tr. Holland, 1601, p. 273) on
this habit of "cuckows." For *may* in the sense of "can," see n. 538.
1212 **from**] ABBOTT (§158): "Frequently . . . in the sense of 'apart from', 'away from',
without a verb of motion."
    how you take] Rejecting F2-POPE (ed. 1728), THEOBALD (19 Feb. 1729, [fols.
39ᵛ f.]) defends F1, modifying its punctuation (see textual notes): "What, was Pompey
to tell them the [offers] that They had sent to him? Lepi[dus, most assuredly, does not
talk so] absurdly." Incidentally, F2 may read *now* because in some copies of F1 the *h*
in *how* is broken and resembles an *n*.
1216 **it**] Although the antecedent appears to be *offers* (1213)—see "offer" (1218)—*it*
is probably influenced by the intervening singular noun *point* (1214). For this type of
concord, see FRANZ §676.
1219, 1231 **Cicelie**] See n. 1185.

Measures of Wheate to Rome: this greed vpon,
To part with vnhackt edges, and beare backe
Our Targes vndinted.
　　Omnes. That's our offer.
　　Pom. Know then I came before you heere,   1225
A man prepar'd
To take this offer. But *Marke Anthony,*
Put me to some impatience: though I loose
The praise of it by telling. You must know
When *Cæsar* and your Brother were at blowes,   1230
Your Mother came to Cicelie, and did finde
Her welcome Friendly.
　　Ant. I haue heard it *Pompey,*
And am well studied for a liberall thanks,
Which I do owe you.   1235
　　Pom. Let me haue your hand:
I did not thinke Sir, to haue met you heere.
　　Ant. The beds i'th'East are soft, and thanks to you,
That cal'd me timelier then my purpose hither:

───

1223–7 *Three verse lines ending* offer. . . . Man . . . *Antony,* ROWE; *ending* then
. . . prepar'd . . . *Antony* POPE1+
　　1223 Our] *Om.* mTBY4 *conj.,* mCOL1, COL2
　　　　Targes] targets F4-ROWE3, OXF1; targe POPE1-v1773, v1793, v1803, SING1, HUD1,
COL4
　　1224 *Omnes.*] *CÆS. ANT. LEP.* CAP, MAL, v1793+ (–KIT1, ALEX)
　　1228 Put] Puts HAN1
　　1229 telling.] ~ , mTHEO2 (19 Feb. 1729, [fol. 40]) *conj.,* THEO1+ (–HAN1, SING2,
RID)
　　1230 Brother] brothers v1793-SING1, HUD1

───

　　1221 **Measures**] COTGRAVE (1611, Mesure): *"Containing about a bushell and a halfe."*
See also 5, n. 2191.
　　1223 **Targes**] I.e., targets. See n. 399–400.
　　　　vndinted] MINSHEU (1617, Dint): "Dent." JOHNSON (1755), citing this instance:
"Not impressed by a blow."
　　1228–9 **though . . . telling**] Proverbial; see DENT (M476): "A *man's* praise in his
own mouth does stink."
　　1234 **well studied**] MINSHEU (1617, Studious): *"Adicted vnto, desirous or greedie of,
painefull, earnest carefull."* Commentators take their pick. RANN (ed. 1791–): Have "long
wished." SEYMOUR (1805, 2:59): Have "long meditated on." WORDSWORTH (ed. 1883):
"Prepared by thought." IRVING & MARSHALL (ed. 1889): "Well disposed or inclined to."
CASE (ed. 1906): "Well equipped."
　　1239 **timelier**] JOHNSON (1755, *Timely*), citing this instance: "Early; soon."

For I haue gained by't.   1240
   Cæsar. Since I saw you last, ther's a change vpon you.
   Pom. Well, I know not,
What counts harsh Fortune cast's vpon my face,
But in my bosome shall she neuer come,
To make my heart her vassaile.   1245
   Lep. Well met heere.
   Pom. I hope so *Lepidus*, thus we are agreed:
I craue our composion may be written
And seal'd betweene vs.
   Cæsar. That's the next to do.   1250
   Pom. Weele feast each other, ere we part, and lett's
Draw lots who shall begin.
   Ant. That will I *Pompey.*
   Pompey. No *Anthony* take the lot: but first or last,
your fine Egyptian cookerie shall haue the fame, I haue   1255

1240–2 *Verse lines ending* last, . . . not, ROWE1+
1240 I haue] I've POPE1-JOHN1
    by't] by it POPE1-JOHN1, v1773-KNT1, COL, SING2, KTLY, HAL
1241 ther's] There is ROWE1-ARD2 (−SING2, CAM3, SIS)
1242 Well,] ∼ ∧ POPE, HAN1
1243–4 harsh . . . shall she] hard . . . she shall F3-v1773 (−CAP)
1245 her] a F2-POPE2, HAN1
1248 composion] composition F2+
1252–7 *Five verse lines ending* begin. . . . lot: . . . Cookery . . . *Cæsar* . . . much.
ROWE1-JOHN1, v1773, KTLY; *ending Pompey.* . . . first, . . . cookery . . . *Cæsar* . . .
much. CAP, v1778-HUD1, SING2-COL3, WH1, GLO, HAL, DYCE2, COL4-WH2, NLSN, ARD1,
EVNS; *ending* Pompey. . . . lot; . . . cookery . . . *Cæsar* . . . much. DEL2, CAM1,
OXF1, RID-SIS; 1252–3 *one verse line, then prose* STAU; *five verse lines ending* Pompey.
. . . last, . . . shall have . . . *Cæsar* . . . much. ARD2
1253 will I] I will THEO2, WARB-JOHN1, v1773
1254 No] No, noble CAP

1243 **counts . . . cast's**] WARBURTON (ed. 1747) and the rest: "Metaphor from mak-ing marks or lines in casting accounts in arithmetick." See also n. 1557 ("cast").
1246 **met**] SCHMIDT (1875, 5): "Joined with an adverb, as a kind of salutation."
1247 Only RIDLEY (ed. 1954) comments: "I think F's punctuation makes Pompey more deliberately courteous to the unimportant member of the triumvirate. *Thus* then = 'if you also are content.'"
1248 **composion**] Although *composition* is doubtless correct, the F1 reading is well formed, a possible word formation from *compose* + *ion.* See "composure" (n. 452) and "compose" (n. 698).

heard that *Iulius Cæsar,* grew fat with feasting there.
    Anth. You haue heard much.
    Pom. I haue faire meaning Sir.
    Ant. And faire words to them.
    Pom. Then so much haue I heard,   1260
And I haue heard *Appolodorus* carried——
    Eno. No more that: he did so.
    Pom. What I pray you?
    Eno. A certaine Queene to *Cæsar* in a Matris.
    Pom. I know thee now, how far'st thou Souldier?   1265
    Eno. Well, and well am like to do, for I perceiue
Foure Feasts are toward.   (xx5ᵛ)
    Pom. Let me shake thy hand,
I neuer hated thee: I haue seene thee fight,
When I haue enuied thy behauiour.   1270
    Enob. Sir, I neuer lou'd you much, but I ha'prais'd ye,

1258–9 *One verse line* v1793+
1258 meaning] meanings mTBY2 *conj.*, v1773, MAL+ (−RID)
1259 them] it HAN1
1260–3 *Three verse lines ending* have heard, . . . carry'd—— . . . you? CAP
1262, 1264 *Marked as an aside* CAM3
1262 more] more of F3+
1265–6 *Verse lines ending* Well; . . . perceive, THEO1+ (−HAN1)
1270–1 *Verse lines ending* Sir, . . . ye, POPE1+
1271 ye] you CAP-SING2, COL3, WH1, KTLY, COL4

1256 *Iulius Cæsar,*] SIMPSON (1911, p. 27), illustrating the emphasizing comma: "The comma . . . points the innuendo with a significant pause. The real reference is of course to Antony himself. Here . . . we have a punctuation expressly intended to guide the actor; it is equivalent to a stage direction." But this ignores the tendency to punctuate at midline.

1258 **meaning**] HEATH (1765, p. 457): "The following reply, *And fair words to them,* makes it evident we should read, *meanings.*" MALONE (ed. 1790), supporting Heath: "The transcriber's ear being probably deceived, in consequence of the next word [Sir] beginning with the final letter of this." But it is doubtful that there was a transcriber. See p. 373.

1261–4 *Appolodorus . . .* **Matris**] An account of this event is given in Plutarch's *Julius Caesar* (tr. North, 1579, p. 786). HUDSON (ed. 1881) adds, "The incident is dramatized with much spirit, in Fletcher's *False One* [1.2 and 2.3]" (*Works,* ed. Waller, 1906, 3:314–15, 325–30).

1267 **toward**] JOHNSON (1755): "Near; at hand; in a state of preparation."

1271 **ha' . . . ye**] WILSON (ed. 1950): "Short forms prob. due to the limitation of the F. column." *Ha* is found only once again, at 2673, another full line. *Ye* occurs in lines that are not full — 794, 1309, and 3295 — but only three times in all. Enobarbus uses both words only here.

When you haue well deseru'd ten times as much,
As I haue said you did.
  Pom. Inioy thy plainnesse,
It nothing ill becomes thee: 1275
Aboord my Gally, I inuite you all.
Will you leade Lords?
  All. Shew's the way, sir.
  Pom. Come.   *Exeunt. Manet Enob. & Menas*
  Men. Thy Father *Pompey* would ne're haue made this   1280
Treaty. You, and I haue knowne sir.
  Enob. At Sea, I thinke.
  Men. We haue Sir.
  Enob. You haue done well by water.
  Men. And you by Land.   1285
  Enob. I will praise any man that will praise me, thogh
it cannot be denied what I haue done by Land.
  Men. Nor what I haue done by water.
  Enob. Yes some-thing you can deny for your owne
safety: you haue bin a great Theefe by Sea.   1290
  Men. And you by Land.
  Enob. There I deny my Land seruice: but giue mee

1277–9 *Arranged as verse lines, thus*: 1277–9 v1793-COL2, SING2-CAM3, SIS+; 1277, 1278–9 ALEX

1278 *All.*] CÆS. ANT. LEP. CAP, MAL, v1793+ (−KIT1, ALEX)
    Shew's] Shew us mTBY3 *conj. and* HAN1, CAP-KIT1

1280–3 *Lines* 1280–1 *as verse lines ending* treaty. . . . Sir *then prose* POPE2-THEO2, WARB-JOHN1, v1773, v1778, RANN, ALEX; *two verse lines ending* treaty.— . . . have, sir. KTLY; 1280–1 *two verse lines ending* made . . . sir *then prose* COL4

1280–1 Thy . . . Treaty.] *Marked as an aside* JOHN1+ (−OXF1)

1280 this] *Om.* F3-ROWE3

1284–5 *One verse line* KTLY

1290 great] good F2-ROWE3

1274 **Inioy**] KERSEY (1702, enjoy): *"To have the use,* or *profit of."*

1281 **knowne**] STEEVENS (ed. 1793): "I.e. been acquainted. So, in *Cymbeline*: 'Sir, we have *known together* at Orleans' [1.4.36–7 (349)]." ABBOTT (§382): Elliptical for "one another."

1286 **I . . . me**] GREY (1754, 2:203): "Da mihi mutuum testimonium. *Cic.* Orat. pro *Flacco* [4.10]. To which answer our *English proverbs. Ka me,* and I'll *ka thee.* [Or] *Claw me,* and I'll *claw* [you]. *Commend* me, and I'll *commend* [you]. *Ray's* [*Collection of English Proverbs,* 1678], p. 163." See TILLEY (K1); not in DENT.

1292 **Land seruice**] JONES (ed. 1977): "Military (as opposed to naval) service," and may also be associated with the "idea of thieving." Compares *2H4* 1.2.154 (402).

129

your hand *Menas*, if our eyes had authority, heere they
might take two Theeues kissing.

Men. All mens faces are true, whatsomere their hands   1295
are.

Enob. But there is neuer a fayre Woman, ha's a true
Face.

Men. No slander, they steale hearts.

Enob. We came hither to fight with you.   1300

Men. For my part, I am sorry it is turn'd to a Drinking. *Pompey* doth this day laugh away his Fortune.

Enob. If he do, sure he cannot weep't backe againe.

Men. Y'haue said Sir, we look'd not for *Marke Anthony* heere, pray you, is he married to *Cleopatra*?   1305

Enob. *Cæsars* Sister is call'd *Octauia*.

Men. True Sir, she was the wife of *Caius Marcellus*.

1293 our] your F4-ROWE3, v1773
1294 take] have F3-ROWE3
1295 whatsomere] whatsoere F2-WH1, KTLY-HUD2, OXF1, RID
1297–8 *Verse* WARB

1293 **authority**] Following DELIUS (ed. 1856), SCHMIDT (1874): "Legal and official
power."

1294 **two Theeues kissing**] RANN (ed. 1791–): "Thievish hands." WORDSWORTH (ed.
1883) takes *kissing* literally, for his gloss of *true* (1295)—"*Honest*"—indicates that "This
is said as they kiss each other." CASE (ed. 1906): "*I.e.* fraternising, in a general sense,
if the speakers are the 'two thieves', as lines [1290, 1291] indicate [so interpreted by DELIUS
(ed. 1856)]; but line [1295–6] points rather to their hands, which the word *kissing* would
suit very well. [Compares *Rom.* 1.5.101–2 (677–8) and Kyd, *The First Part of Ieronimo*
2.1.52–8 (ed. Boas, 1901).]"

1295 **true**] All commentators, beginning with BLUMHOF (ed. 1870), gloss as "honest."
WILSON (ed. 1950, Glossary) adds "natural, not 'made up.'"

1297–8 Proverbial; see TILLEY (F3): "Fair *Face* foul heart." Excluded by DENT. CASE
(ed. 1906): *True* means "unsophisticated as well as honest. Mr. [W. J.] Craig suggests
that in [1295], *true* means (as well as 'honest') 'true indices of character, of their thoughts.'"
(In CROSBY [2 Feb. 1877, (sheet 163, p. 40)], the "*true* index of the mind.")

1299 **No slander**] SEYMOUR (1805, 2:61): "Speak no slander." DELIUS (ed. 1856) and
most others: It is no slander.

1302–3 *Pompey . . . againe*] CASE (ed. 1906): "Proverbial, perhaps, but I fail to
trace it." So has everyone else.

1303 **sure**] See n. 36.

1304 **Y'haue said**] DELIUS (ed. 1856): You're right. HUDSON (ed. 1881): "A common
phrase of assent; and equivalent to our 'just so.'"

1307 *Caius Marcellus*] See PAULY, Claudius, 3:2734–6 (216); *OCD*, Marcellus (5).

Enob. But she is now the wife of *Marcus Anthonius.*
Men. Pray'ye sir.
Enob. 'Tis true.   1310
Men. Then is *Cæsar* and he, for euer knit together.
Enob. If I were bound to Diuine of this vnity, I wold
not Prophesie so.
Men. I thinke the policy of that purpose, made more
in the Marriage, then the loue of the parties.   1315
Enob. I thinke so too. But you shall finde the band
that seemes to tye their friendship together, will bee the
very strangler of their Amity: *Octauia* is of a holy, cold,
and still conuersation.
Men. Who would not haue his wife so?   1320
Eno. Not he that himselfe is not so: which is *Marke*
Anthony: he will to his Egyptian dish againe: then shall

1308 she is now] now she is F3-v1778, RANN
1309 ye] you CAP-KNT1, COL, HUD1, WH1
1311 together.] ～ ? COL3
1317 their] the THEO4
1318 strangler] stranger F2-F4; estranger ROWE

1309 **Pray'ye]** *OED* (8a): "*I pray you (thee)*: used parenthetically to add instance or deference to a question or request." Paraphrases range from "Pray, do you mean it?" (IRVING & MARSHALL [ed. 1889]) to "Pray repeat that, for I didn't quite catch it" (KIT-TREDGE [ed. 1941]); the latter (following DEIGHTON [ed. 1891]) calls it "A phrase of sur-prised incredulity" and compares "the colloquial 'You don't say so!'" The pronoun *ye*, here in the infrequent accusative usage, "seems"—ABBOTT (§236)—"to be generally used in questions, entreaties, and rhetorical appeals." See n. 1271.

1311 COLLIER (ed. 1858): "Menas must intend to ask the question, whether it [the knitting] be so: if not, he contradicts himself in his next speech [1314–15]." This interpre-tation is rejected by DEY (1909, p. 465): "While Enobarbus agrees as to the motive of policy in the marriage, he begins his further remarks with the adversative 'But' [1316], showing that he is opposing Menas." COLLIER (ed. 1877) abandons the question mark. For inversion of subject and verb, especially after adverbs like *then*, see FRANZ §682; for the frequent use of *is* with a plural subject, see FRANZ §672.

1312 **wold]** An occasional spelling of *would*, here possibly because of a crowded (or full) line.

1314 **policy]** See n. 760.

1316–18 **But . . . Amity]** See n. 822–5.

1319 **still conuersation]** See "still Conclusion" (3033).

　　conuersation] CAWDREY (1604, conuerse): "Companie with." BULLOKAR (1616): "To vse ones company, to liue with." BAILEY (1721) and most others specify as "behavior." RUSHTON (1870, pp. 33–4) adds, "In this sense it is used in some of the ancient statutes. [Quotes 26 *Henry VIII*, cap. 14, in *Statutes of the Realm*, ed. Luders, 1810–28, 3:509–10.]"

the sighes of *Octauia* blow the fire vp in *Cæsar,* and (as I
said before) that which is the strength of their Amity,
shall proue the immediate Author of their variance. *An-*   1325
thony will vse his affection where it is. Hee married but
his occasion heere.
   Men. And thus it may be. Come Sir, will you aboord?
I haue a health for you.
   Enob. I shall take it sir: we haue vs'd our Throats in   1330
Egypt.
   Men. Come, let's away.   *Exeunt.*

            Musicke playes.   **2.7** (xx5
    Enter two or three Seruants with a Banket.

1 Heere they'l be man: some o'th'their Plants are ill   1335
rooted already, the least winde i'th'world wil blow them
downe.
2 *Lepidus* is high Conlord.

1333 SCENE V. ROWE; SCENE VII. POPE, HAN1, WARB, JOHN1+
    Pompey's *Galley.* ROWE1+ (*subst.*)
1335 o'th'their] o' their F2+
1338 high Conlord] high coloured F2+

1326 **vse . . . is**] DELIUS (ed. 1856) and the other commentators: Gratify his love
where it is to be found—i.e., in Egypt.
    affection] See n. 538.
1327 **occasion**] COTGRAVE (1611): "*Opportunitie.*"
1329 **haue a health**] WORDSWORTH (ed. 1883): "*Toast,* in drinking."
1330 **take**] DEIGHTON (ed. 1891): "Accept; drink the toast."
    vs'd] CASE (ed. 1906): "Whether we take this as=made use of *or* accustomed, the
inference of practised pledging is the same."
1333–1493 Speculating on a court performance of *Ant.,* DAVIES (1985, pp. 141–9)
suggests that shipboard feasts given by James I and the visiting Danish king Christian
in August 1606 may be (p. 141) "a real-life contributory source" for 2.7.
    1333 *Musicke playes*] WALTER (ed. 1969) suggests "A broken consort, that is a mixed
orchestra of wind and string instruments," citing STERNFELD (1963, p. 206).
    1334 *two or three Seruants*] An instance of what—according to GREG (1955, p. 135)—
"may be called permissive or petitory directions." See also 2984 and pp. 375–6.
    Banket] See n. 91.
    1335 **Plants**] JOHNSON (ed. 1765): "Besides its common meaning . . . here used
for the *foot,* from the *Latin* [*planta*]."
    1338 **Conlord**] GOULD (1884, pp. 45–6) alone defends the F1 reading: "He was one

1 They haue made him drinke Almes drinke.

2 As they pinch one another by the disposition, hee   1340
cries out, no more; reconciles them to his entreatie, and
himselfe to'th'drinke.

1 But it raises the greater warre betweene him & his
discretion.

2 Why this it is to haue a name in great mens Fel-   1345
lowship: I had as liue haue a Reede that will doe me no

---

of the triumviri or conlords, and this is the subject of conversation." For this possible
word formation, unlikely here, see FRANZ §81.

1339 **Almes drinke**] Most commentators follow WARBURTON (ed. 1747): "A phrase,
amongst good-fellows, to signify that liquor of another's share which his companion drinks
to ease him. But it satirically alludes to *Cæsar* and *Antony's* admitting him into the
triumvirate, in order to take off from themselves the load of envy." COLLIER (ed. 1858):
"Wine that did not properly belong to his share, but which each had contributed, in
order to intoxicate Lepidus." BLUMHOF (ed. 1870) offers the second most frequent interpretation: leftovers of food and drink meant for servants and the poor. The meaning
here is that they have treated him like a mere beggar. THISELTON (1899, p. 14): "This
expression may contain all or any of four ideas: (1) drink had for the asking; (2) drink
that is not paid for or 'answered' (compare [1451]) by the others present also drinking;
(3) drink whose quantity is increased by the others present foregoing their share; and
(4) . . . 'the remains of liquor reserved for alms-people' [*OED*, Alms 4b]. . . . The
last signification by no means implies inferiority, but merely that the wine was not used
on the occasion for which it was provided, and would apply to liquor drunk by Lepidus
after the others had left off." KITTREDGE (ed. 1941): "It was each man's duty to drain
his cup whenever any one had drunk to him. To relieve a man of this duty by drinking
in his place was to *drink alms-drink*, i.e., charitably to relieve a weaker brother of his
obligation. Thus Iago promises Cassio, who has a weak head for wine: 'I'll drink *for* you'
(*Othello*, ii, 3, 39 [1148–9]). In the present passage the meaning is that the others have
(as a practical joke) tricked Lepidus into drinking more than his share by pledging him
frequently. Pompey continues the joke (see ll. [1366, 1379, 1431])." PHIALAS (ed. 1955):
"Toast drunk for one too infirm to answer a pledge." The expression does not seem to
occur elsewhere, one reason for the dubiety of HULME's (1958, p. 385) explanation: "The
servant is merely changing the known idiom 'drunk as a beggar', getting his laugh by
delaying recognition of a current phrase."

1340 **pinch . . . disposition**] Most commentators follow WARBURTON (ed. 1747):
"*Touching one in a sore place.*" COLLIER (ed. 1858): "Refer[s] to the sign they give each
other regarding 'the disposition' of Lepidus to drink." WORDSWORTH (ed. 1883): They
"*straiten . . . by the arrangement, disposal of the drink*" in order that Lepidus may
have to drink more. DEIGHTON (ed. 1891): "They ply each other hard with the mischievous desire of seeing one another under the table . . . [although] we have no reason
for thinking that they were quarrelsome in their cups." IDEM (ed. 1901): "Cp. 'disposed',
used absolutely as=inclined to merriment, *L.L.L.* [2.1.249 (754)]." See conj., p. 352.

1345 **name**] WORDSWORTH (ed. 1883): "I.e., *without the reality*." KITTREDGE (ed.
1941): "Emphatic: 'the mere *name* of being a partner with great men.'"

1346 **liue**] A spelling variant of *lief*.

seruice, as a Partizan I could not heaue.

1 To be call'd into a huge Sphere, and not to be seene
to moue in't, are the holes where eyes should bee, which
pittifully disaster the cheekes.   1350

A Sennet sounded.
Enter *Cæsar, Anthony, Pompey, Lepidus, Agrippa, Mecenas,*
Enobarbus, Menes, with other Captaines.

Ant. Thus do they Sir: they take the flow o'th'Nyle
By certaine scales i'th'Pyramid: they know   1355

1352 *Agrippa, Mecenas,*] *Om.* CAP
1354 *to* Cæs. CAP, MAL, v1793+ (−OXF1)
    do they] they do v1773
1355 scales] scale F2-THEO4

1347 **as . . . heaue**] WILSON (ed. 1950): "I.e. as fill a role I cannot play."

Partizan] *OED* (*sb.*[2] 1): "Military weapon used . . . by footmen . . . consisting of a long-handled spear, the blade having one or more lateral cutting projections, variously shaped."

1348–50 JOHNSON (ed. 1765): "This speech seems to be mutilated . . . but perhaps the sense was . . . *To be called into a huge sphere, and not to be seen to move in it,* is a very ignominious state; great offices *are the holes where eyes should be, which,* if eyes be wanting, *pitifully disaster the cheeks.*" Most others agree in the main with the interpretation, although MASON (1785, p. 280) finds the "thought miserably expressed," not mutilated, and MALONE (ed. 1790): "I do not believe a single word has been omitted." ADELMAN (1973, p. 118): "The servant's shift from the cosmic and outsized to the human and minute in mid-metaphor ['the effect is comic'] is wholly appropriate: for poor Lepidus is in a sense a mere mortal caught in a world filled with hyperbolical figures."

1350 BLUMHOF (ed. 1870) is the first to connect *disaster* with an astrological context. NICHOLSON (Wright Shakespeariana, no. 158 [11[r]]), comparing "Disasters in the sunne" in *Ham.* 1.1.118 (124+11): "Not merely as meaning 'disfigure or do damage to' but [*disastre, dis-star*] as 'blotch or take the lustres or lights out of the cheeks." CASE (ed. 1906): "An adjective *disastered* (compare 'ill-starred') occurs thrice in the Countess of Pembroke's *Antonie* (1595), *e.g.* in Act II.: 'us *disastered* men' [515], 'this *disastered* woe' [665]." For the 1592 *Antonius,* see pp. 492, 495.

cheekes] WALTER (ed. 1969) identifies as both "human face" and "slope of the heavens," as in *Tmp.* 1.2.4 (85), *Cor.* 5.3.151 (3508), and *Son.* 132.6.

1351 *Sennet*] NARES (1822; 1876): "Set of notes on the trumpet, or [Elizabethan] cornet, different from a flourish," in its "greater length" (STERNFELD [1963, p. 197]). For a discussion of the etymology, which may hint at a "signal" rather than a "sounding," see NAYLOR (1896, p. 172). SHIRLEY (1963, p. 73): "In the later plays, Shakespeare usually reserved the sennets for occasions of greater pageantry."

1354–60 SCHANZER (1956, p. 154) suggests that "the words of the Chorus in Act

By'th'height, the lownesse, or the meane: If dearth
Or Foizon follow. The higher Nilus swels,
The more it promises: as it ebbes, the Seedsman
Vpon the slime and Ooze scatters his graine,
And shortly comes to Haruest.   1360
    Lep. Y'haue strange Serpents there?

1358 promises:] ∼ ∧ F2-F4
1360 And] And't ANON. *conj. apud* CAM2, CAM3
1361-2 *One verse line* COL, WH1, KTLY, HAL
1361 there?] ∼ . ROWE1-SIS (−NLSN, RID, CAM3)

II of *Antonius* [ll. 768 ff.; see p. 497] . . . contributed, together with a passage [as
first pointed out by GREY (1754, 2:204)] in Holland's Pliny (Bk. 5, ch. 9 [1601, p. 98]),
and [as first mentioned by MALONE (*apud* STEEVENS, ed. 1793)] possibly one in [John]
Pory's translation [1600] of [John] Leo's *History [and Description] of Africa* (Dd6v [ed.
R. Brown, 1896, 3:879–81]), to the formulation. . . . There is no mention of the slime
in either Pliny or Leo. [Earlier than Schanzer, ANDERS (1904, p. 37) had found the influence of Pliny and Leo "uncertain"; Ovid (*Metamorphoses* 1.416–37), however, mentions the slime.] And both of them state that if the water rises beyond a certain mark
it threatens famine. Only from *Antonius* could Shakespeare have derived the notion that
'the higher . . . promises.'" ADELMAN (1973, pp. 220–1, n. 27): "The overflow of the
Nile determines the size of the crop, but the use of the pyramids as a scale is not mentioned by Conti, Cartari, Spenser, Whitney, or any of the other mythographers, emblem
writers, Egyptologists, or poets with whom I am familiar. . . . The natural history of
the Nile . . . is a celebration of temperance: only the mean is fertile. But temperance
is totally foreign to Shakespeare's Nile. Shakespeare may have suppressed the implicit
warning about the disastrous effects of excessive overflow because it was untrue to the
scheme of his play, where the only fertility comes through excess." DELIUS (ed. 1856):
Although editors often add *To Caesar*, Antony could just as well be addressing Lepidus.
    1355 **scales**] RANN (ed. 1791–) apparently with knowledge of the passage in Leo (see
n. 1354–60): "Digits or cubits, marked on a marble pillar, called the Niloscope, or
Nilometer."
    Pyramid] COOPER (1565, Pyramis): "A great thinge of stone or other mattier broade
and fowersquare beneath, vpwardes small and sharpe: a steeple." There is doubt as to
whether an obelisk is meant. BLOUNT (1656, Obelisk) gives a cross-reference from *Pyramid*:
"The difference between an *Obeliske* and a *Pyramid* was this, the *Obelisk* was all of one
entire stone or peece, and therefore of no such height as the *Pyramids*, which were of
divers stones; and again the *Obelisk* is four square, whereas the *Pyramis* may be of other
figure." See also 3270, n. 1371–2.
    1357 **Foizon**] COTGRAVE (1611, Foison): "*Store, plentie, abundance, great fullnesse.*"
COLLIER (ed. 1877) suggests an interesting but incorrect etymology: "Possibly, from the
Fr. *fois*, because it is *timely, seasonable.*"
    1361–4 ANDERS (1904, pp. 235–6) cites "De Jode's Atlas (Speculum Orbis Terrae,
Antwerp, 1593, see 'Africa') . . . which throws light on Lepidus's remarks regarding the

Anth. I *Lepidus.*

Lep. Your Serpent of Egypt, is bred now of your mud
by the operation of your Sun: so is your Crocodile.

Ant. They are so.   1365

Pom. Sit, and some Wine: A health to *Lepidus.*

Lep. I am not so well as I should be:
But Ile ne're out.

Enob. Not till you haue slept: I feare me you'l bee in
till then.   1370

1364 of your] of the F2-ROWE2, CAP
1366 Sit, and] Sir, and F3, F4; Sirrah, mF4Q *conj. and* ROWE1, ROWE2-THEO4
1367–8 F1-THEO2, WARB-JOHN1, v1773; *on one line* HAN1, MAL, RANN, SING2-COL3,
HAL-WH2, ARD, RID, SIS; *prose* CAP *etc.*
1367 well] *Om.* THEO2, WARB, THEO4
1369–70 *Marked as an aside* CAP, STAU, KTLY

---

abiogenetic origin of serpents and crocodiles." Mentioning 381–2, he continues, "The
belief in equivocal generation [i.e., without parents] seems to have been general in
Shakespeare's days. [Quotes Bacon's *Natural History*, ed. Ellis & Spedding, 1859, 2:557,
638, and *Oth.* 4.1.256–7 (2640–1).]" WILSON (ed. 1950) compares 381–2, his note on
Ham. 2.2.181–2 (1218–19), and Ovid's *Metamorphoses* 1.495–522 (tr. Golding, 1567; ed.
Rouse, 1904), for spontaneous generation. HANKINS (1978, p. 162): "The reference to
the Nile suggests Ovid's *Metamorphoses* [see Wilson] as the probable immediate source,
though the idea had become a commonplace. . . . Consult C. W. Lemmi's 'Monster-
Spawning Nile-Mud in Spenser' [*MLN* 41 (1926), 234–8], where there is mention of similar
passages by Strabo, Herodotus, Aelian, Diodorus Siculus, and Albertus Magnus."

1361 **strange Serpents**] WILSON (ed. 1950): "Sh. gives tipsy Lep. plenty of sibilants
to slur." See n. 552.

1363–4 **Your . . . your Sun**] BLUMHOF (ed. 1870): The repetition of *your* is a sign
of a tipsy conviviality. CASE (ed. 1906) quotes ABBOTT on this "common colloquialism"
(§221)—"Though in this instance the *your* may seem literally justified, the repetition
of it indicates a colloquial vulgarity which suits the character of Lepidus"—and adds,
"It certainly sets off his temporary condition." KITTREDGE (ed. 1941): "The repetition
of *your* gives Lepidus's remarks an indescribably comic air of a drunken attempt to speak
in an offhand manner, as if thoroughly familiar with the subject." But ABRAHAM (1982–3,
p. 103) disagrees: Since *serpent, mud* (of the Nile), *operation of your sun*, and *crocodile*
are alchemical terms, and the "alchemists almost always referred to the metals, materials,
forces, arcane substances and vessels used in their work as 'Our,'" *your* is appropriate
to Lepidus, "an outsider to the 'mysteries' of Egypt."

1367 FURNESS (ed. 1907): "Lepidus takes the 'health' literally and replies that he is
not very well."

1368 DELIUS (ed. 1856): I.e., of the round of drinking. THISELTON (1899, p. 15) regards
the utterance as "support" for the servant's "gaug[ing]" the vanity of Lepidus' character"
at 1348–50.

Lep. Nay certainly, I haue heard the *Ptolomies* Pyramisis are very goodly things: without contradiction I
haue heard that.

Menas. Pompey, a word.

Pomp. Say in mine eare, what is't.   1375

Men. Forsake thy seate I do beseech thee Captaine,
And heare me speake a word.

Pom. Forbeare me till anon.   *Whispers in's Eare.*
This Wine for *Lepidus.*

Lep. What manner o'thing is your Crocodile?   1380

Ant. It is shap'd sir like it selfe, and it is as broad as it
hath bredth; It is iust so high as it is, and mooues with it
owne organs. It liues by that which nourisheth it, and
the Elements once out of it, it Transmigrates.

1371 *Ptolomies*] *Ptolemie's* F3-JOHN1; *Ptolemies'* CAP+ (−RID)
1371-2 Pyramisis] Pyramids mCOL1, COL2
1372 I] *Om.* F2
1374-8 *Marked as asides* ROWE1+ (−OXF1) (*subst.*)
1374-5 *One verse line* v1793+ (−OXF1, SIS)
1376 seate] feate F2
1377-9 *Verse lines ending* word. . . . *Lepidus.* CAP-RANN; *ending* anon.— . . .
Lepidus. v1793+
1378 Forbeare] For F3-ROWE3
1382-6 with it . . . it] with it's . . . it's F3-COL3, WH1, HAL-HUD2 (−CAM1)

1369 **in**] DELIUS (ed. 1856): Enobarbus plays on the opposite of *out, in*: "Enveloped
in something." IRVING & MARSHALL (ed. 1889): "In liquor."
1371 **Nay certainly**] See n. 4.
1371-2 **Pyramisis**] MALONE (*apud* STEEVENS [1780], 1:230): "*Pyramis* for *pyramid*
was in common use. . . . From this word Shakspeare formed the English plural, *pyramises*,
which perhaps he preferred, as better suited to the pronunciation of a man nearly intoxicated. In other places he has introduced the Latin plural *pyramides*. . . . So, in this
play [3270]." See also n. 1355 ("Pyramid").
1372 **goodly**] KITTREDGE (ed. 1941): "Handsome. A ridiculously inadequate adjective to apply to the pyramids." But Sh. also uses it to describe size, as in structures, buildings, cities. *OED* (*a.* 2): "Notable or considerable in respect of size, quantity, or number."
1378 **anon**] MINSHEU (1617): "By and by." IDEM (By *and* by): "Presently." See n. 863
("presently") and FRANZ §412 for the development.
1382-3 **it owne**] For the older genitive, see FRANZ §320. DEIGHTON (ed. 1891), finding *it* used (according to ABBOTT, §228) in Sh. "especially when a child is mentioned,"
surmises, "Here probably marking Antony's contempt for the half-drunken Lepidus."
However, there may be no more room for an *s* in 1382; there is an *it* directly above in
1381; and *it* occurs 11 times in the speech.
1384 **Elements . . . Transmigrates**] DELIUS (ed. 1856) is the first to compare trans-

Lep. What colour is it of?   1385
Ant. Of it owne colour too.
Lep. 'Tis a strange Serpent.
Ant. 'Tis so, and the teares of it are wet.
Cæs. Will this description satisfie him?
Ant. With the Health that *Pompey* giues him, else he   1390
is a very Epicure.
Pomp. Go hang sir, hang: tell me of that? Away:
Do as I bid you. Where's this Cup I call'd for?
Men. If for the sake of Merit thou wilt heare mee,

1389–91 *Marked as asides* CAP, STAU
1390 Health] healths HAN1
1391 *Menas whispers again* CAM3, EVNS
1392–9 *Marked as asides*: 1392–9 Go . . . say? (*except* 1393 Where's . . . for?)
JOHN1-WH2, NLSN, ARD1, KIT1+; 1396–9 I . . . say? OXF1; 1394–9 If . . . say? RID
    1393 this] the F2-JOHN1, v1773, v1778, RANN
    1394–6 *Lines* 1394–5 *as* F1, 1396 *prose* JOHN1, v1773; *two verse lines ending* me, . . .
matter? v1793+ (−SIS)

---

migration of souls in *AYL* 3.2.186–8 (1373–4). KITTREDGE (ed. 1941): "Antony probably
means merely 'it passes from life to death.'" WILSON (ed. 1950): "A quasi-'philosophical'
flourish to a series of profound truths. Sh. can hardly have known that in Egypt the
crocodile was worshipped and transmigration believed in."
    Elements] BULLOKAR (1616): "The first matter of visible substance, from whence
all things take their beginning: wherof there be foure, namely fire, ayre, water, and earth."
    1388 **teares . . . wet**] HALLIWELL (ed. 1865) quotes *Topsell's Historie of Serpents*,
1608: "The common prouerbe also, *Crocodili lachrimæ*, the crocodiles teares, iustifieth
the treacherous nature of this beast, for there are not many bruite beasts that can weepe,
but such is the nature of the Crocodile, that to get a man within his danger, he will
sob, sigh & weepe, as though he were in extremitie, but suddenly he destroyeth him.
Others say, that the crocodile weepeth after he hath deuoured a man. How-soeuer it
be, it noteth the wretched nature of hypocriticall harts [sig. N2ʳ]." CASE (ed. 1906) quotes
BARTHOLOMAEUS (1582, fol. 359ʳ) for the same information. Both take Antony's amusing substitution of the obvious for the profound too seriously. Although its form is hardly
that of a proverb, DENT (C831) includes it.
    1390–1 DAVIES (1783, 2:349) and most others: "Antony's answer is ironical: 'Lepidus,
with the help of wine, will take up with this solution of his question: but, when he
is sober, his judgement is so strong, that he is a perfect epicure in the art of doubting.'"
    1391 **Epicure**] RANN (ed. 1791–) and the others: "Nice indeed." RIDLEY (ed. 1935):
"Fastidious gourmet." WILSON (ed. 1950) alone: "Atheist. Cf. *Caes.* 5.1. [77–9 (2416–18)]
and Latimer, *Seven Sermons* ([1549], ed. Arber [1869], p. 54): 'beleue (as yᵉ Epecurs
do) that after this life ther is neither hel nor heauen.'"
    1394 TIESSEN (1879, p. 471) rejects RANN's (ed. 1791–) and DELIUS's (ed. 1856) ex-

Rise from thy stoole.   1395   (xx6ᵃ)
   Pom. I thinke th'art mad: the matter?
   Men. I haue euer held my cap off to thy Fortunes.
   Pom. Thou hast seru'd me with much faith: what's
else to say? Be iolly Lords.
   Anth. These Quicke-sands *Lepidus,*   1400
Keepe off, them for you sinke.
   Men. Wilt thou be Lord of all the world?
   Pom. What saist thou?
   Men. Wilt thou be Lord of the whole world?
That's twice.   1405
   Pom. How should that be?
   Men. But entertaine it, and though thou thinke me
poore, I am the man will giue thee all the world.

1395 thy] the F4-POPE2
1398–1400 *Verse lines ending* say? . . . *Lepidus,* HAN1, CAP+
1399 Be] By ROWE3
1401 off, them ₐ] ~ ₐ ~ , F2+
     for] 'fore mTHEO2 (19 Feb. 1729, [fol. 40]) *conj.*, THEO, WARB, JOHN1, v1773, COL4; or mTBY3 *conj.*, DYCE2, HUD2
1402–26 *Marked as asides* JOHN1+ (*subst.*)
1404–5 Ff; *on one line* ROWE1-POPE1, HAN1, MAL, DYCE, HAL, CAM1, HUD2, WH2, ARD1; *verse* POPE2 *etc.*
1406–9 F1-F3; *four verse lines ending* be? . . . poor, . . . world. . . . well? F4-ROWE3; *three verse lines ending* and . . . man . . . well? mTBY3 *conj. and* HAN1, v1793-SING1, KTLY; *ending* it, . . . man . . . well? POPE1 *etc.*
1406 should] shall ROWE1-JOHN1, v1773-RANN
1407 though thou] though you POPE2-THEO2, WARB-JOHN1, v1773, v1778, RANN; Although thou mTBY3 *conj.* (you) *and* HAN1, v1793-SING1, HUD1, SING2, KTLY
1408 thee] me JOHN2

---

planatior that Menas wants to be heard because of the service he has done, suggesting instead he wants to be heard because what he has to say merits hearing. Most commentators follow Rann and Delius.
   1397 **cap off**] THEOBALD (28 Mar. 1730, [fol. 116ʳ]) compares *Oth.* 1.1.10 (14), *Off-capt*: "I.e. stood Cap in hand solliciting him." CASE (ed. 1906): "From the etiquette of service at a time when head-coverings were more constantly worn than now, [rather] than from occasional acts of deference or courtesy, such as . . . in *Othello.*"
   1400–1 Commentators since RANN (ed. 1791–)—"You are half seas over"—point to the progressive drunkenness of Lepidus or (WILSON [ed. 1950]) the triumvirs. CASE (ed. 1906): "Perhaps Lepidus collapses here."
   1407 **entertaine**] See n. 671.

Pom. Hast thou drunke well.

Men. No *Pompey*, I haue kept me from the cup,   1410
Thou art if thou dar'st be, the earthly Ioue:
What ere the Ocean pales, or skie inclippes,
Is thine, if thou wilt ha't.

Pom. Shew me which way?

Men. These three World-sharers, these Competitors   1415
Are in thy vessell. Let me cut the Cable,
And when we are put off, fall to their throates:
All there is thine.

Pom. Ah, this thou shouldst haue done,
And not haue spoke on't. In me 'tis villanie,   1420
In thee, 't had bin good seruice: thou must know,
'Tis not my profit that does lead mine Honour:
Mine Honour it, Repent that ere thy tongue,
Hath so betraide thine acte. Being done vnknowne,
I should haue found it afterwards well done,   1425
But must condemne it now: desist, and drinke.

Men. For this, Ile neuer follow

1409 Hast thou] Thou hast CAP, RANN

1411 Thou art] That F3, F4

1418 there] then mF4FL33 *conj.*, POPE1-v1778, RANN, COL2, COL3, KTLY, DYCE2, COL4, HUD2, CAM3

   is] is is FURNESS (v1907) *conj.*, BAYF

1420 spoke on't] spoken on't F3-JOHN1; spoke of it mCAP2 *and* GREY (1754, 2:204) *conj.* (spoken of it), CAP-v1778, RANN

1423 it] is F2-ROWE3

1427–30 *Marked as an aside* CAP, MAL, v1793+

1427–8 *Verse lines ending* this . . . more; POPE1-COL3, WH1+; *one verse line* STAU

1409 CAPELL (1779 [1774], 1:36): "A sarcastical affirmation of Pompey's; and no interrogation . . . [involving] a transposition of '*hast*' and '*thou*.'" As a question, of course, the line is equally ironical.

1412 **pales**] MINSHEU (1617): "*Hedge in with pales.*"

   inclippes] THEOBALD (1726, p. 32): "*Embracing.*" See 3629, n. 2656.

1415 **Competitors**] CAWDREY (1604): "Hee that sueth for the same thing, or office, that another doth." But "partners" is more likely. See 3159, n. 432.

1418 **there**] See textual notes and conj., p. 352.

1423 **ere**] ever.

1428 **paul'd**] MINSHEU (1617, Appale): "*Dismay.*" KERSEY (1702, pall): "*Die, or grow flat, as wine and other liquors do.*" WARBURTON (ed. 1747): "*I.e.* dead." EDWARDS (1765, p. 206): "*Decayed.*" Most commentators follow Kersey as elaborated by HEATH (1765, p. 457) and JOHNSON (ed. 1765), the latter saying, "*Vapid*, past its time of excellence;

Thy paul'd Fortunes more,
Who seekes and will not take, when once 'tis offer'd,
Shall neuer finde it more.   1430
   Pom. This health to *Lepidus.*
   Ant. Beare him ashore,
Ile pledge it for him *Pompey.*
   Eno. Heere's to thee *Menas.*
   Men. Enobarbus, welcome.   1435
   Pom. Fill till the cup be hid.
   Eno. There's a strong Fellow *Menas.*
   Men. Why?
   Eno. A beares the third part of the world man: seest
not?   1440
   Men. The third part, then he is drunk: would it were
all, that it might go on wheeles.

1430-5 *Arranged as verse lines, thus*: 1430-1, 1432-3, 1434-5 POPE1-JOHN1, v1773-COL2, SING2+; 1430, 1431-2, *then as* F1 HUD1

1436 LEPIDUS *born off.* CAP

1437–40 *Lines* 1437-8 *as* F1, 1439-40 *on one line* ROWE1-POPE1, HAN1, DYCE, STAU, GLO, CAM1, WH2, ARD1-ARD2; *verse lines ending* bears . . . not? CAP, v1778-v1821, SING, COL, WH1, KTLY, HAL; 1437-8 *as* F1, 1439-40 *verse* HUD2

1437 *Pointing to* Lepidus. ROWE1-JOHN1; *Pointing to the attendant who carries off Lepidus.* v1773+

        strong] strang F2; strange F3-ROWE3

1439 seest] seest thou KTLY

1441-3 *Three verse lines ending* all, . . . wheels! . . . reels. mTBY2 *conj.*, THEO1-SING1, COL1-GLO, HAL+; *two verse lines ending* all, . . . reels. KTLY

1441 he] *Om.* ROWE1-v1773, MAL-KNT1, COL2+ (−KTLY, HAL, COL4, RID)

---

palled wine, is wine that has lost its original spriteliness." See *OED, v*[1] 3.

1429–30 STEEVENS (ed. 1793): "From the ancient proverbial rhyme: 'He who will not, when he may, When he will, he shall have nay.'" DENT (N54) regards the passage as "sententious" rather than proverbial, but see WHITING (W275) and TAYLOR (1963, p. 159). SEYMOUR (1805, 2:61) compares *JC* 4.3.218-21 (2217-20).

1439 A] FRANZ (§226): A form of *he* characteristic of the south of England and employed in Sh. by both educated and uneducated speakers. See also 1492, 2103.

1441 he] Most editions omit, although not explicitly for the reason, now discredited (see p. 373), given by MALONE (ed. 1790): "The transcriber's ear deceived him." FURNESS (ed. 1907), however: "Had there been an interrogation mark after 'The third part', or even a dash, would anyone have suggested a change?"

1442 go on wheels] MALONE (ed. 1790): "'The World goes [correctly: runs] upon wheels', is the title of a pamphlet written by [John] Taylor the Water-poet [*Workes*, 1630 (Pt. 2), pp. 232-44]." SINGER (ed. 1826): "'The third part of the world is drunk (meaning Lepidus, one of the *triumvirs*), would it were all so, that it might go on wheels, i.e.

Eno. Drinke thou: encrease the Reeles.

Men. Come.

Pom. This is not yet an Alexandrian Feast.   1445

Ant. It ripen's towards it: strike the Vessells hoa.

Heere's to *Cæsar.*

Cæsar. I could well forbear't, it's monstrous labour

when I wash my braine, and it grow fouler.

1445 yet] *Om.* THEO2, WARB-JOHN1
1446 towards] toward v1785, HUD2
1447–50 *Three verse lines ending* forbear it, . . . brain, . . . time. POPE1+
1449 and] An SING2
      grow] growes F2+ (−SING2, KTLY, ARD, EVNS)

---

turn round or change'. To which Enobarbus replies, 'Drink thou . . .', i.e. increase its giddy course." COLLIER (ed. 1843) calls the expression "proverbial." KINNEAR (1883, p. 456), glossing as "go easily," compares *TGV* 3.1.317 (1377) and explains, "Menas wishes Antony and Cæsar drunk as well as Lepidus, that he might carry out his own plans easily." KITTREDGE (ed. 1941): "Would that the whole world were drunk, that the saying 'The world runs on wheels' might be fulfilled." WILSON (ed. 1950): "Quibbling on 'wheel' = to reel (O.E.D. [*v.* 1c]) as Enob.'s retort shows." The two proverbs implied would seem to be "He that is giddy thinks the *world* turns round" (DENT, W870) and "(To drink until) the *world* goes round" (DENT, W885.1). See also n. 1470–1.

1443 **Reeles**] Most commentators accept the meaning "A whirl or whirling movement" (*OED*, *sb.*[2] 1); a few add "Revels," for which *OED* (1b) cites this instance. See n. 450 and conj., p. 353.

1446 **strike the Vessells**] JOHNSON (ed. 1765): "Try whether the casks sound as empty." STEEVENS (ed. 1773): "*A mark of our unanimity in drinking,* as we now say, *chink glasses.*" HOLT WHITE (1787, p. 479): "*Vessels* probably mean *kettle-drums* [see also p. 353], which were beaten when the health of a person of eminence was drunk." BOSWELL (ed. 1821) compares Fletcher's *Monsieur Thomas*, "*strike a fresh piece of wine*" (5.12.42, ed. Bowers, 1979) to show that *strike* means "tap." THISELTON (1899, p. 16): "*I.e.* 'let down the cups by drinking off the wine'. The metaphor is the nautical one of striking a sail or topmast." CASE (ed. 1906): "'Fill the vessels (*i.e.* the cups) full'. . . . . A 'strike' was 'an instrument with a straight edge for levelling (striking off) a measure of grain' (Skeat, *Etymol. Dict.* § v.). . . . The adverb *strike* = full to the top. Again, the sense 'fill' might conceivably be reached from that of 'to lade a fluid from one vessel into another'. . . . This is clearly the sense in Harrison's directions for brewing (Holinshed's Chronicle, 1587, *Description of England*, book ii. chap. vi. p. 170)." Most commentators agree with Boswell.

    hoa] See n. 1027.

1448–9 **it's . . . fouler**] KNOWLES (privately): "A clear allusion to the labor of the Augean stables."

1449 **and it grow**] CASE (ed. 1906): "*And* = if." RIDLEY (ed. 1954): "*And* is more probably the ordinary copula, and *grow* a subjunctive, caused by the feeling that *when* is in effect a conditional, not temporal, conjunction." See ABBOTT (§102): "The hypothe-

Ant. Be a Child o'th'time.   1450
Cæsar. Possesse it, Ile make answer: but I had rather
fast from all, foure dayes, then drinke so much in one.
Enob. Ha my braue Emperour, shall we daunce now
the Egyptian Backenals, and celebrate our drinke?
Pom. Let's ha't good Souldier.   1455

1451–6 *Lines* 1451-2, 1455-6 *verse,* 1453-4 *prose* THEO2, WARB, THEO4; 1451-6 *verse*
CAP; *five verse lines ending* fast . . . one. . . . now . . . drink? . . . hands, HAN1,
MAL; *seven verse lines ending* it, . . . fast . . . one. . . . Emperor, . . . Bacchanals,
. . . Soldier. . . . hands; JOHN1, v1773, v1778, RANN; *six verse lines ending* fast . . .
one. . . . emperor! . . . Bacchanals, . . . soldier. . . . hands; v1793-SING1, COL1-
SING2, COL3, WH1, KTLY, HAL, COL4; *six verse lines ending* answer: . . . days, . . .
emperor! . . . Bacchanals, . . . soldier. . . . hands; mTBY2 *conj.,* KNT1, DYCE, STAU,
GLO, CAM1, HUD2-ARD1, KIT1+; *seven verse lines ending* answer: . . . days, . . . emperor,
. . . Bacchanals, . . . drink? . . . soldier. . . . hands, RID
   1451 Possesse] Profess mCOL1, COL2, COL3
         Ile] I will JOHN1, v1773, v1778, RANN
         make] *Om.* HAN1
   1453 *to* Ant. CAP, v1778+

---

sis, the *if,* is expressed not by the *and,* but by the subjunctive . . . . *And* merely means
with the addition of, plus."
   1450 DELIUS (ed. 1856) and others: Comply with the time. DEIGHTON (ed. 1891)
seems to imply a proverb: "Do at Rome as the Romans do." See TILLEY (R165); not in DENT.
   1451 **Possesse it**] THEOBALD'S (19 Feb. 1729, [fol. 40ʳ]) "I am a Stranger to this
Phrase" has not deterred extensive comment. RANN (ed. 1791–): "Take it off." VALPY
(ed. 1833): "Understand." COLLIER (1852, p. 471): "*Profess it* . . . that is, profess to
be a child of the time; but Cæsar follows it up by stating his dislike of drinking to excess.
In . . . 'King Lear' [1.1.76 (79)] we have had the converse of this misprint—*professes*
for 'possesses.'" LETTSOM (1853, *Blackwood's,* p. 467) gives the dominant view: "*Be master of it."* STAUNTON (ed. 1859) gives the second most favored view: "It was the practice,
when one good fellow drank to another, for the latter to 'do him right' by imbibing
a quantity of wine equal to that quaffed by the health giver. Antony proposes a health
to Cæsar, but Cæsar endeavors to excuse himself, whereupon Antony urges him by saying, 'Be a child o' the time', *i.e. do as others do; indulge for once.* Cæsar then consents
to pledge the health, and says '*possess* it' or *propose* it,—I'll do it justice." BLUMHOF
(ed. 1870) detects an ambiguity, *it* referring both to the cup Antony has handed Octavius and to the time. COLLIER (ed. 1877): "*Pass* it, viz., the cup." THISELTON (1899,
p. 16): "Have your wish." DEIGHTON (1907, p. 86), proposing "Possess *us*": "*I.e.* tell us
what you mean by 'Be a child o' the time'; as in *Twelfth Night,* ii. 3, 149 [832], and
elsewhere." See textual notes and conj., p. 353.
   make answer] KITTREDGE (ed. 1941) sums up comment since RANN (ed. 1791–):
"Drink in response to your toast."
   1453 **Emperour**] COOPER (1565, Imperator): "A chiefe capitain in warres." Applied
throughout to Antony (except 3338).

Ant. Come, let's all take hands,
Till that the conquering Wine hath steep't our sense,
In soft and delicate Lethe.
  Eno. All take hands:
Make battery to our eares with the loud Musicke,   1460
The while, Ile place you, then the Boy shall sing.   (xx6ᵛ
The holding euery man shall beate as loud,
As his strong sides can volly.

Musicke Playes. Enobarbus places them hand in hand.

The Song.   1465
Come thou Monarch of the Vine,

1462 beate] bear THEO1-HAN1, THEO4-KIT1, CAM3+ (–SIS); bear 't PEN1
1463 can] the ROWE2, ROWE3

1458 **delicate**] See n. 916.
1461 **Ile place you**] See 1464.
1462 **holding**] Although many commentators gloss as "burden" or "refrain"—
STERNFELD (1963, p. 82) uses both to define *holding*—there is some confusion, since
OED (*vbl. sb.* 5) defines *holding* as "The burden of a song" but defines *burden* (9) as
"The bass, 'undersong', or accompaniment" and (10) as "The refrain or chorus of a song;
a set of words recurring at the end of each verse." RIDLEY (ed. 1954): "But the meaning
here must be rather 'refrain', since if Enobarbus' directions were followed the boy's song
would be drowned by an 'undersong.'"
1462–3 **euery . . . volly**] THEOBALD (ed. 1733) reads *bear* for "beate" because the
singers could not beat the holding with their sides. The majority of editions, which also
emend, interpret similarly; COLLIER (ed. 1843) adds, "No misprint is perhaps more common than to substitute *t* for *r.*" The others follow JOHNSON (*apud* STEEVENS, ed. 1773):
"Every man shall accompany the chorus by drumming on his sides, in token of concur-
rence and applause." THISELTON (1899, p. 16): "'Beate' of the Folio is evidently right
after 'battery' in [1460]." And SISSON (1956, 2:267) agrees substantially with Johnson—
"One can also *beat* the rhythm and emphasize it by singing it loudly"—and (*pace* Collier) adds, "A misreading of *beare* as *beate* is not at all self-evident graphically."
1463 **volly**] KERSEY (1702): "*A great shout.*"
1464 *Musicke Playes*] The extent of Sh.'s indebtedness to Plutarch "for the musical
portions of the drinking party" is discussed by LONG (1964, pp. 29–33), whose main
point is that (p. 29) "for Antony, his association with music, other than military signals,
has sinister connotations. . . . [p. 33] The musical details . . . [show] that, for Antony,
Bacchus is his evil genius."
1465 **The Song**] NOBLE (1923, p. 127): "A Bacchanalian equivalent of *Veni Creator*
[*Spiritus*]." STERNFELD (1963, pp. 86–7) agrees: "The transmutation of a hymn addressed
to the holy spirit into a poem supplicating Bacchus was only one instance of the many
wandering melodies (contrafacta) that were characteristic of the interplay between sacred
and secular Renaissance poetry." SENG (1965, p. 5) finds that Noble "offers no evidence
at all for his assertion that it is [a parody]" and that, although Sternfeld "adduces other

> *Plumpie Bacchus, with pinke eyne:*
> *In thy Fattes our Cares be drown'd,*
> *With thy Grapes our haires be Crown'd.*
> *Cup vs till the world go round,*   1470
> *Cup vs till the world go round.*

Cæsar. What would you more?
Pompey goodnight. Good Brother

1472–3 *One verse line* ROWE1-ARD2, EVNS; *two verse lines ending* good night. . . . brother, PEL2

---

trochaic songs of the time of Shakespeare beginning with the word 'Come' . . . there is, in fact, no evidence that even these are related in more than a coincidental way to the great Whit Sunday hymn. . . . If, however, we want to argue that Shakespeare's song is a parody of a church hymn, we can find a much more likely model. [Quotes (p. 6) 'Veni sancte spiritus.']" LLOYD (1959, p. 93): A "climax" of the identification of Antony, "who exhorts them to a Bacchic dance with the praise of wine, and presides over these 'Egyptian Bacchanals,'" with Bacchus, an identification Lloyd finds in Plutarch (see pp. 411, 449). Sternfeld (1963, p. 87): "Although no contemporary melody survives . . . there is no lack of music to fit Shakespeare's stanza. [Names four lyrics (pp. 86–7) with "contemporary musical settings."]"

1467 **Plumpie**] For the development of the ending *-ie*, see FRANZ §759.

pinke eyne] MINSHEU (1617) gives two verbs under *Pinke*: "*wake in slumbering* . . . *to* Winke" and "*cut full of small holes* . . . *to* Iagge." Citing this instance, JOHNSON (1755, *Pink*, 2): "A small eye." STEEVENS (ed. 1778) alone but for VALPY (ed. 1833): "*Red eyes*: eyes inflamed with drinking, are very well appropriated to Bacchus. So, in *Julius Cæsar*: '—such *ferret* and such fiery eyes' [1.2.186 (288)]. . . . Again, in a song sung by a drunken Clown in *Marius and Sylla*, 1594: 'Thou makest some to stumble, and many mo to fumble, And me have *pinky eyne*, most brave and jolly wine!' [Thomas Lodge, *The Wounds of Civil War*, ll. 1769 f. (ed. Wilson, 1910)]. IDEM (*apud* REED, ed. 1803): "From the following passage in P. Holland's translation of the 11th Book of Pliny's *Natural History* [1601], it appears that *pink*-eyed signified the smallness of eyes: '—also them that were *pinke-eyed* and had verie small eies, they termed *ocellæ*' [p. 335]." Voluminous citations are to be found in CASE (ed. 1906). KITTREDGE (ed. 1941), like most commentators, combines the two possibilities in Minsheu: "Little; here, 'half shut, blinking.'" See *OED*, Pink-eyed *a.*[1]. Also, DELIUS (ed. 1856) identifies *eyne* as the old *-n* plural (see FRANZ §189b), which Sh. uses here as elsewhere mainly for the rhyme; instances are listed in SCHMIDT (1874).

1468 **Fattes**] HUDSON (ed. 1881): "Old form of *vats*." CERCIGNANI (1981, p. 325): "Southern and SW Midland initial *v* for Anglian *f.*"

1470–1 Proverbial; see DENT (W885.1): "(To drink until) the *world* goes round."

1472–86 **What . . . fall not**] For the figurative implications of these lines as analogues to the successive defeats of Lepidus, Pompey, and Antony, see ALDUS (1955, pp. 409–14) and his exchange with MILLS (1956, pp. 133–4).

1473 **Good Brother**] G. A. SMITH (1974, p. 284): "When 'good-brother' appears as

Let me request you of our grauer businesse
Frownes at this leuitie. Gentle Lords let's part,   1475
You see we haue burnt our cheekes. Strong *Enobarbe*
Is weaker then the Wine, and mine owne tongue
Spleet's what it speakes: the wilde disguise hath almost
Antickt vs all. What needs more words? goodnight.
Good *Anthony* your hand.   1480
    Pom. Ile try you on the shore.

1474 you of] Ff; you of; ROWE1, ROWE2; of you . . . KTLY; you off; ROWE3 *etc.*
1476 cheekes] cheeke F2-THEO1, HAN1
    Enobarbe] *Enobarbus* POPE1-v1773 (–CAP)
1477 Wine] wind F3-THEO4
1478 Spleet's] Splits F4-ARD2
    speakes: the] F1(c); speakest: he F1(u)
1480–1 *One verse line* v1793+

---

a hyphenated word in Elizabethan English, it means brother-in-law. [Quotes *OED* and *Lr.* 4.2.44 (2303+13).] Similarly, but with perhaps less probability [because of the omission of the hyphen], Octavius Caesar . . . requests his brother-in-law to leave." BLUMHOF (ed. 1870) also refers to this passage in glossing *Brothers* at 1539 as meaning "brothers-in-law," following DELIUS (ed. 1856).

    1474 **of**] THISELTON (1899, p. 16) alone: "For the sake of." WORDSWORTH (ed. 1883), reading *off*: "*To come away.*" *OED* (Request 3c) agrees, citing this "elliptical" instance.

    1476 **burnt our cheekes**] DELIUS (ed. 1856): Our cheeks are glowing from the wine as if they had been burnt.

    1478 **Spleet's**] CERCIGNANI (1981, p. 140): "An adoption from MLG *splete*[*n*] obscurely related to *split* (MDu *splitten*)."

    1478–9 **wilde disguise . . . Antickt**] Taken by most—following JOHNSON's (1755) definition (4) of the verb *disguise* as "To deform by liquor"—as a euphemism for excessive drinking, which has made them all appear like antics or buffoons. WORDSWORTH (ed. 1883): "*Disorder by drink.*" CASE (ed. 1906) gives illustrations of this sense from the *OED* (Disguise *sb.* 7), which quotes this passage. Taken by some, like KITTREDGE (ed. 1941), as referring to masquelike singing and dancing: "This wild guising (playacting in the dance) has almost turned us all into fantastic mummers." And, most recently, taken by a few—starting with WILSON (ed. 1950)—in both senses. STERNFELD (1963, p. 82) is the most positive: "The term 'antick'd' divulges the fact that several magic forces, beside song, are exercising their enchantment on the three rulers of the world. The entire banquet scene is in the nature of a masque with its attendant antics—a Bacchanalian dance with clasped hands, to the accompaniment of instrumental music; the boy's singing and, finally, the triumvirs joining in the 'holding.'"

    1480 WILSON (ed. 1950): "Evidently Ant.'s legs seem steadier than his own."

    1481 Following DELIUS (ed. 1856), CASE (ed. 1906) and most others: "This may mean 'I'll test your hospitality ashore', with time of so doing undefined; but more probably Pompey . . . wants to continue the debauch, offers to vie drinking powers on shore

146

Anth. And shall Sir, giues your hand.
Pom. Oh *Anthony*, you haue my Father house.
But what, we are Friends?
Come downe into the Boate.   1485
Eno. Take heed you fall not *Menas*: Ile not on shore,

1482–90 *Three verse lines ending* Hand. . . . House. . . . Boat *then as* F1 ROWE,
POPE, THEO, WARB; *seven verse lines ending* hand. . . . house. . . . boat. . . . shore:
. . . what! . . . farewel . . . out! HAN1; 1482-5 *three verse lines ending* hand. . . .
house. . . . boat., 1486-8 *prose, then as* F1 JOHN1; *seven verse lines ending Antony*,
. . . friends: . . . not.—— . . . cabin.—— . . . hear, . . . fellows: . . . out. CAP;
eight verse lines ending hand. . . . house, . . . boat. . . . Menas: . . . cabin.——
These . . . what! . . . farewell . . . out. v1773; *eight verse lines ending* hand. . . .
house, . . . boat. . . . not.—— . . . cabin.—— . . . what!—— . . . farewel . . . out.
v1778-RANN; *seven verse lines ending* Antony, . . . friends: . . . not.—— . . . cabin.——
. . . what!—— . . . farewell . . . out. v1793-SING1, COL1-COL3, WH1+; *eight verse
lines ending* hand. . . . house,—— . . . boat. . . . shore. . . . cabin.—— . . .
what!—— . . . farewell . . . out! KNT1, STAU
    1483 haue] hate mPOPE *and* mLONG *conj.*, POPE
        Father house] Fathers house F2+ (-KNT1)
    1484 Friends?] ~ ; THEO1-SIS
    1486 fall not] fall not.—— [*Exeunt* POM. CÆS. ANT. *and Attendants*. CAP, MAL,
v1793+
        Menas] *As speech prefix* ROWE, JOHN1
    1486–90 Ile . . . out.] *Given to Menas* ROWE1-JOHN1; 1486 *given to Enobarbus*,
1487–90 *to Menas* mTBY2 *conj.*, CAP-CAM1, COL4+; 1486 *given to Enobarbus*, 1487 No
. . . Cabin *to Menas*, 1487–90 these . . . out *to Enobarbus* BLUM

---

then." BLUMHOF (ed. 1870), alone, regards this line simply as an offer of help in getting
ashore, a view supported by THISELTON (1899, p. 16): "'To keep a ship at try' meant
to keep it close to the wind, and Pompey simply means that he himself will navigate
or conduct Cæsar safely on to the shore."
    1482 **And**] ABBOTT (§97): "Introducing a statement in *exact* conformity with a previ-
ous statement, comes almost to mean 'exactly'. . . . *I.e.* 'You say well, *and* you shall',
or 'So you shall', 'that you shall', emphatically."
        giues your hand] WHITAKER (1972, p. 132): Antony "staggers, and calls to Pompey."
    1483-4 KITTREDGE (ed. 1941): "Pompey is slightly maudlin. His mind reverts to his
pet grievance [1207–10]—Antony's seizure of the mansion of Pompey the Great; but he
adds, sentimentally—'What of *that*? We're friends!'" For Plutarch, see pp. 403, 409, and
417.
    1483 **my Father house**] Probably the genitive *s* was mistakenly omitted from *Father*
(compare 1208), but the older genitive construction is still found in Sh. See FRANZ §201,
§202.
    1486-7 **Take . . . Cabin**] CAPELL (1779 [1774], 1:36) gives the now generally ac-
cepted explanation: "Speaking to some of them, (Pompey, probably) whom he sees stag-

No to my Cabin: these Drummes,
These Trumpets, Flutes: what
Let Neptune heare, we bid aloud farewell
To these great Fellowes. Sound and be hang'd, sound out.   1490

                          Sound a Flourish with Drummes.

    Enob. Hoo saies a there's my Cap.
    Men. Hoa, Noble Captaine, come.   *Exeunt.*

    Enter Ventidius as it were in triumph, the dead body of Paco-   **3.1**
               rus borne before him.   1495

    Ven. Now darting Parthya art thou stroke, and now

1488 Flutes] *Om.* HAN1
1489 heare] F1(c); heere a F1(u)
    aloud] a loud ROWE3+ (−CAP)
1492-3 *Lines divided* captain! | Come. v1793, v1803, SING, KTLY; *one verse line* v1821,
COL, WH1, HAL
    1494 ACT III. SCENE I. ROWE1-POPE2, HAN1, WARB, JOHN1+; ACT III. THEO
        SCENE *A Camp.* ROWE, POPE; SCENE, *a Camp in a Part of* Syria. THEO1+
(*subst.*)
    1494-5 *Enter . . .*] *Ad.* Silius THEO1+ (−JOHN1) (*subst.*)

---

ger: After which, the boat puts off with it's company [see textual notes]; and Enobarbus,
who has not yet had his dose, turns [and speaks] to Menas [who replies]." RIDLEY (ed.
1954) conjectures "that the MS. had *Menas* twice . . . and that we should read *Eno.*
Take . . . fall not, Menas. *Men.* I'll . . . cabin." He believes Enobarbus should address
his equal rather than the triumvirs and Pompey, that "'Menas' is a rather awkwardly formal opening to 'I'll not on shore,'" and that Enobarbus would not "force his continued
company on Menas." No one agrees.
    1487-8 KEIGHTLEY (ed. 1864) suspects words missing at the end of 1488, GOULD
(1884, p. 63) at the end of both lines. ELZE (1886, p. 274) suggests adding *ho* after "what"
(1488) because of Enobarbus's reply on 1492. See p. 353.
    1490 **be hang'd**] DEIGHTON (ed. 1891): "Curse you for being so long about it."
    1492 **Hoo**] FRANZ (§249): An exclamation of triumphant joy. See nn. 1555, 1557,
1561-2.
        saies a] RIDLEY (ed. 1935) alone: "Perhaps an auditory error for '*sessa*' [*OED*: "An
exclamation of uncertain meaning"]?" TURNER (privately): "Enobarbus, drunkenly ex-
uberant, refers to himself in the third person." For *a* as "he," see n. 1439.
    1493 **Hoa**] See n. 1027.
    1494-1537 X. Z. (1851, p. 139): This scene "appears to be totally unconnected with
what goes before and what follows." C. B. (1851, p. 190): The scene serves "two objects —

Pleas'd Fortune does of *Marcus Crassus* death
Make me reuenger. Beare the Kings Sonnes body,
Before our Army, thy *Pacorus Orades*,
Paies this for *Marcus Crassus*.   1500

1499 Army] host POPE1-JOHN1

---

one to gain time, the other for the sake of naturalness," comparing *Mac.* 1.6.1–10 (434–44)
and 4.3.146–59 (1978–91). BRADLEY (1909, p. 291) also finds the scene "totally useless
to the plot and purely satiric in its purport . . . to show how Ventidius fears to pursue
his Parthian conquests because it is not safe . . . to outdo his master. . . . We know
too well what must happen in a world so splendid, so false, and so petty." RIEMER (1968,
p. 47): "The episode *is* justified (if we keep in mind the complex design of the play)
and its effect is a telling one. This is the world of history remote from the rivalry of
great men: it is the process of armies moving across the face of the earth, fighting battles,
exacting revenge. . . . The great men, despite their sway and mastery, despite the fact
that history can be understood by concentrating on their actions and personalities, are
nevertheless subject to events and activities not entirely in their control." WILLIAMSON
(1971, p. 188): "The scene reveals another perspective on . . . leader-follower relationships. . . . Ventidius' decision forms an echo of the situation we have just witnessed
on Pompey's barge, when Menas suggests to his leader that they assassinate the triumvirs.
. . . Leaders and followers, we conclude from the conjunction of these scenes, may hold
the chivalric values of honor, loyalty, glory, but often their relationships are corrupted
by the simple fact of power in a constantly changing world." For Sh.'s possible debt to
Dio, see IDEM (1971, pp. 180–90). For Plutarch, see p. 418.

1494 *triumph*] CAWDREY (1604): "Great ioy outwardly shewed." See n. 895.

1496 **darting . . . stroke**] JOHNSON (*apud* STEEVENS, ed. 1773): "*Struck* alludes to
darting. Thou whose darts have so often struck others, art struck now thyself." DEIGHTON
(ed. 1891): "A reference . . . to the Parthian method of fighting, their horsemen pour-
ing in a shower of darts as they swarmed round the enemy, and then, as they fled to
avoid close combat, turning in their saddles and discharging flights of arrows." See also
2905. For the form *stroke*, see FRANZ §170. For the events in Plutarch, see p. 418.

1497 *Marcus Crassus* **death**] COOPER (1565): "Finally, beynge steered with couetous-
nesse and enuy, at the greate honours that Cæsar and Pompei had obteyned, he procured
warre against the Parthians, by whom both he and his sonne with .30000. Romaynes
were slayne, many also were taken, whiche as Plutarche wryteth, hapned by his negligence, beynge more industriouse aboute the gatherynge of money, then in gouerninge
his army." CASE (ed. 1906): "Crassus (who formed the first triumvirate with Pompey and
Cæsar) was defeated B.C. 53, in the plains of Mesopotamia, by Surenas, the general of
Orodes, King of Parthia and father of Pacorus; and was treacherously killed during a
conference proposed by the victor. Orodes poured melted gold into the dead man's mouth,
bidding him take his fill of what he had so coveted in life." See PAULY, Licinius, 13:295–331
(68), and Pakoros, 18:2437–8 (1); *OCD*, Crassus (4) and Orodes II.

Crassus] For the genitive in words ending in *s*, see FRANZ §199.

1499 **thy**] I.e., Orodes, King of Parthia.

1500 **this**] DEIGHTON (ed. 1891): "*Sc.* the penalty of death."

149

Romaine. Noble *Ventidius,*
Whil'st yet with Parthian blood thy Sword is warme,
The Fugitiue Parthians follow. Spurre through Media,
Mesapotamia, and the shelters, whether
The routed flie. So thy grand Captaine *Anthony*   1505
Shall set thee on triumphant Chariots, and
Put Garlands on thy head.
   Ven. Oh *Sillius, Sillius,*
I haue done enough. A lower place note well
May make too great an act. For learne this *Sillius,*   1510
Better to leaue vndone, then by our deed

1501–7, 1525–7, 1533 *Given to Silius* THEO1+
1503 Spurre] Spurne F2–ROWE3
1506 Chariots] chariot WALKER (1860, 1:253) *conj.,* COL4, HUD2
1507–12 *Five verse lines ending* done . . . make . . . better . . . acquire . . .
away. HAN1; *ending* O Silius, Silius, . . . well, . . . Silius; . . . acquire . . . away.
v1793, v1803, COL, WH1, HAL
   1508 Oh *Sillius, Sillius*] *Silius* HAN1
   1511 to] *Om.* v1793, v1803
      deed] deeds COL1, COL2, COL3, WH1

1503 **Parthians follow**] DELIUS (ed. 1856): *Parthians* is the object of the imperative *follow.*
   follow] See n. 3153.
   Media] See n. 1832.
1504 **Mesapotamia**] COOPER (1565): "A countrey in the orient, liynge betweene the twoo noble ryuers Tigris and Euphrates, and hath on the southe Babylon, and on the northe, the great mountayne called *Caucasus.*" See PAULY, 15:1105–63; *OCD*; and map, p. xxxvii.
   whether] For the interchangeability of pronunciation of *whether* and *whither,* see FRANZ §26. CERCIGNANI (1981, p. 51) adds, "The common variation between *i* and *e* in words of this type makes orthographic practice rather indecisive." See 876, 2077.
1505 **grand Captaine**] Very likely, from CASE's (ed. 1906) examples, a military title of highest rank. MINSHEU (1617) defines *"a cheife Captaine ouer an Army"* as *"a* Generall," following COTGRAVE (1611, Capitaine), who applies the phrase to the "Colonel general de l'Infanterie Françoise." See also n. 10 ("Captaines").
1506 **triumphant**] See nn. 895, 2666.
1508–12 THEOBALD (ed. 1733): *"Plutarch* [see p. 418] particularly takes notice, that *Ventidius* was careful to act only on Lieutenantry; and cautious of aiming at any Glory in his own Name and Person. But the Sentiments, he throws in here, seem directly copied from *Quintus Curtius,* in *Antipater's* Behaviour with Regard to *Alexander.* [Quotes 6.1.18–19.]"
1508 *Sillius*] Not in Plutarch. See DP.
1509, 1515 **place**] COTGRAVE (1611): *"Office, Function, Dignitie, Charge."* See also 295.

Acquire too high a Fame, when him we serues away.
Cæsar and *Anthony*, haue euer wonne
More in their officer, then person. *Sossius*
One of my place in Syria, his Lieutenant,   1515
For quicke accumulation of renowne,
Which he atchiu'd by'th'minute, lost his fauour.
Who does i'th'Warres more then his Captaine can,
Becomes his Captaines Captaine: and Ambition
(The Souldiers vertue) rather makes choise of losse   1520
Then gaine, which darkens him.
I could do more to do *Anthonius* good,
But 'twould offend him. And in his offence,
Should my performance perish.   (xx6ᵛᵃ)
  Rom. Thou hast *Ventidius* that, without the which a   1525

1512 him] he POPE1-v1778, RANN
1513–14 *Cæsar* . . . person.] *Given to Silius* UPTON (1748, p. 276) *conj.*, RANN
1517 he] *Om.* F3, F4
1521–7 *Seven verse lines ending* him. . . . good, . . . offence, . . . perish. . . .
which . . . distinction: . . . *Antony.* ROWE1-THEO2, WARB-JOHN1, v1773; *six verse lines
ending* more . . . him; . . . perish. . . . which . . . distinction: . . . *Antony.* HAN1;
six verse lines ending him. . . . good, . . . offence . . . that, . . . sword, . . . *Antony?*
CAP, v1778-RANN, v1821+; *six verse lines ending* him. . . . good, . . . offence . . .
Ventidius, . . . sword, . . . Antony? v1793, v1803
1525 the] *Om.* CAPN *conj.*, v1793, v1803

1514 **then**] FURNESS (ed. 1907) alone: "It is possible that in the final *n* . . . there
is an absorption of *in*."
  Sossius] Appointed governor of Syria and Cilicia by Antony in 38 B.C. See PAULY,
Sosius, 3:1176–80 (2); *OCD*, Sosius (1).
  1517 **by'th'minute**] RANN (ed. 1791–): "Every minute," to which BLUMHOF (ed. 1870)
adds "quickly"; WORDSWORTH (ed. 1883), "*incessantly*."
  lost his fauour] DELIUS (ed. 1856): Not in Plutarch; *his* signifies Antony's.
  1519–20 **Ambition . . . vertue**] CASE (ed. 1906) compares *Oth.* 3.3.349–50 (1992–3);
KNOWLES (privately) compares *AYL* 4.1.13 (1928–9): "The Souldiers [melancholy], which
is ambitious." WILSON (ed. 1950): *Ambition*, "like 'place' [1509, 1515], stands for the
man, here a general."
  1521 **him**] BLUMHOF (ed. 1870) and others: "The captain"; CASE (ed. 1906) and RIDLEY
(ed. 1954): "The soldier." KITTREDGE (ed. 1941) adds, "Emphatic: himself."
  1523 **his offence**] WORDSWORTH (ed. 1883): "*His being offended*." DEIGHTON (ed.
1891) and others: "[My] offending him." For the subjective and objective genitive, see
FRANZ §322.
  1525–6 **that . . . distinction**] WARBURTON (*apud* THEOBALD, ed. 1733) and others:
"Thou hast That, *Ventidius*, which, if Thou hadst not, there is scarce any Distinction
betwixt a Soldier and his Sword: they are equally cutting and senseless. But what Thing

151

Souldier and his Sword graunts scarce distinction: thou
wilt write to *Anthony.*
     Ven. Ile humbly signifie what in his name,
That magicall word of Warre we haue effected,
How with his Banners, and his well paid ranks,   1530
The nere-yet beaten Horse of Parthia,
We haue iaded out o'th'Field.
     Rom. Where is he now?
     Ven. He purposeth to Athens, whither with what hast
The waight we must conuay with's, will permit: 1535
We shall appeare before him. On there, passe along.

                                        Exeunt.

         Enter Agrippa at one doore, Enobarbus at another.   **3.2**

===

     1526 graunts] grant HAN1, WARB, JOHN1, v1773; Gains mCOL1, COL2, COL3, KTLY,
COL4
     1527 *Anthony.*] ~ ? THEO1+ (−HAN1)
     1531 The] That ROWE2-POPE2
     1534 whither] *Om.* POPE1-JOHN1; where mTBY3 *conj.*, CAP
     1536 On there,] *Om.* POPE, HAN1
     1538 SCENE II. ROWE1+ (−THEO)
          Rome. ROWE1-JOHN1, v1773; Rome. *An Anti-room in* Cæsar's *House.* CAP,
v1778+ (*subst.*)

---

is That here meant? Why, Wisdom, or a Knowledge of the World. . . . 'Tis Wisdom
makes the Man; without That, the Soldier and his Sword are equally two senseless Pieces
of Matter." COLLIER (1853, p. 493): "The corrector of the folio, 1632, writes *gains* for
'grants' in his margin: . . . The soldier and his sword scarcely gain distinction where
judgment and prudence are deficient." DEIGHTON (ed. 1891) detects "a confusion of
thought between 'Thou hast that [intelligence] the absence of which scarce grants distinction between a soldier and his sword' and 'Thou hast that without which a soldier
and his sword have scarcely any distinction.'" Unclear too is the subject of *graunts*: either
the singular noun nearest it (see FRANZ §677) or the coordinated subject *a Souldier and
his Sword*, in which case the final *s* could be in the plural (see FRANZ §679). Furthermore, if the subject is *that* (without the which), *graunts* might have to be in the passive;
if not, a preposition is omitted before *Souldier*—e.g., *to* or *between*. Finally, *distinction*
in the sense of "honor" (KITTREDGE [ed. 1941]) is not the customary usage in Sh., nor
is it so glossed by others. *OED* gives no examples before the 18th c. See CAWDREY (1604):
"A difference, or seperation."
     1529 **word of Warre**] WARBURTON (ed. 1747): "What the *Romans* meant by their
Auspicium Ducis: in which they were so remarkably superstitious." See n. 734.

Agri. What are the Brothers parted?
Eno. They haue dispatcht with *Pompey,* he is gone,   1540
The other three are Sealing. *Octauia* weepes
To part from Rome: *Cæsar* is sad, and *Lepidus*
Since *Pompey's* feast, as *Menas* saies, is troubled
With the Greene-Sicknesse.
Agri. 'Tis a Noble *Lepidus.*   1545
Eno. A very fine one: oh, how he loues *Cæsar.*
Agri. Nay but how deerely he adores *Mark Anthony.*
Eno. Cæsar? why he's the Iupiter of men.
Ant. What's *Anthony,* the God of Iupiter?
Eno. Spake you of *Cæsar?* How, the non-pareill?   1550
Agri. Oh *Anthony,* oh thou Arabian Bird!

1539 are] F1(c); art F1(u)
1549 *Ant.*] *Agr.* ROWE1+
    Anthony, . . . Iupiter?] ~ ? . . . ~ . JOHN1+
1550 Spake] Speak F3-v1773 (–CAP)
    How] Oh F2-THEO4, CAP; Ho MAL *conj.,* STAU; Hoo KIT1
1551 Oh . . . thou] Of . . . the mF4Q, mTBY2 *conj., and* HAN1; Of . . . thou
DYCE2, COL4, HUD2

1532 **iaded**] RANN (ed. 1791–): "Driven out like jades."
1535 **waight**] BLUMHOF (ed. 1870): "Baggage." WALTER (ed. 1969): "I.e. booty, captives, and Pacorus."
1536 **passe along**] Continuing the procession that began at 1494–5. See n. 1973–4.
1539 **What**] SCHMIDT (1875, 1e): "A word of exclamation, expressing surprise [as here],
or exultation, or impatience." See also n. 2786. For interjections with this function, see
FRANZ §250.
    Brothers] See n. 1473.
    parted] KITTREDGE (ed. 1941): "Departed."
1544 **Greene-Sicknesse**] WORDSWORTH (ed. 1883): "Characterised by a pale, lurid
complexion." HERFORD (ed. 1899) adds, "And incident to maidens in love. Lepidus, it
is insinuated, is languishing for love of Cæsar and Antony." If, as BLUMHOF (ed. 1870)
and most others suggest, the reference is to the aftereffects of Lepidus's heavy drinking,
of which greenness and pallor are characteristic, then KITTREDGE's (ed. 1941) citing of
Mac. 1.7.35–8 (512–15) is most appropriate.
1545 **'Tis**] KITTREDGE (ed. 1941): "*It,* when thus used of *persons,* is sometimes affectionate, sometimes contemptuous"; the latter adjective is used by DEIGHTON (ed. 1891).
1546 **fine**] HUDSON (ed. 1855): "Alluding, perhaps, ironically, to the signification
of the word *lepidus.*" WILSON (ed. 1950): "App[arently] a jest upon 'lepidus'=fine, delicate." But COOPER (1565): "Neate: pleasant . . . mery."
1551 **oh**] RITSON (1792, p. 87): "*Ho* [see textual notes] . . . is nothing more than
an accidental transposition of *oh.*" But compare n. 1027 ("hoa").
    Arabian Bird] BARTHOLOMAEUS (1582, fol. 212ᵛ): "There [Arabia] breedeth a Birde

Eno. Would you praise *Cæsar,* say *Cæsar* go no further.
Agr. Indeed he plied them both with excellent praises.
Eno. But he loues *Cæsar* best, yet he loues *Anthony*:
Hoo, Hearts, Tongues, Figure,   1555
Scribes, Bards, Poets, cannot
Thinke speake, cast, write, sing, number: hoo,

1552 further] farther CAP, COL, WH1, HAL
1555–6 *One verse line* ROWE1+
1555 Figure] figures HAN1, CAP, v1778+
1557–60 *Three verse lines ending Antony. . . . wonder. . . . loves.* HAN1; *ending
love . . . Cæsar, . . . loves.* mTBY2 *conj.*, CAP-v1778, RANN-KNT1, HUD1
      1557 Thinke] Ever think KTLY
            number:] *Om.* HAN1

---

that is called *Phœnix*." WALTER (ed. 1969) adds, "with gorgeous plumage, famed for
its chastity and fabled to be the only one of its kind. Perhaps a satirical glance at Antony's Egyptian dress and his unchastity."
      1555–7 JOHNSON (ed. 1765): "Not only the tautology of *bards* and *poets*, but the
want of a correspondent action for the *Poet*, whose business in the next line is only to
number, makes me suspect some fault in this passage, which I know not how to mend."
STEEVENS (ed. 1778): "This puerile arrangement of words was much studied in the age
of Shakespeare, even by the first writers. So in *An excellent Sonnet of a Nymph*, by Sir
P. Sidney; printed in *England's Helicon*, 1614." MALONE (*apud* STEEVENS, ed. 1793)
adds, "Again, in Daniel's 11th Sonnet, 1594 [quotes ll. 13–14, sig. B6ʳ]." LEE (*apud* HER-
FORD, ed. 1899): "A parody of the so-called 'reporting sonnet,'" the title of a poem [no.
162] in *A Poetical Rhapsody* (1602, ed. Rollins, 1931, 1:223). See also "Knife . . . operation" (3030–1).
      1555 Hoo] CASE (ed. 1906): "Characteristic of the speaker and also appropriate to
the semi-hysterical adulation of Lepidus which he mimics." See nn. 1492, 1561–2.
      1555–7 Hearts . . . Thinke] SLATER (ed. 1971): "The heart was not the seat of emo-
tions . . . but of thoughts." BARTHOLOMAEUS (1582, fol. 54ᵛ): "Therin is all businesse
and cause of wit and of knowing." Compare n. 103.
      1555 Figure] JOHNSON (1755, 8), citing this passage: "A character denoting a num-
ber." Commentators agree, CANBY (ed. 1921) adding, "*mathematical figures of the horoscope* (?)," which is sense 9 in Johnson ("The horoscope; the diagram of the aspects of
the astrological houses"). Possibly "*a . . . flourish of Rhetoricke*" (COTGRAVE [1611]),
sense 11 in Johnson.
      1557 cast] MINSHEU (1617): "*To* Count." JOHNSON (1755, 21), citing this passage:
"To compute; to reckon; to calculate." Commentators agree. See also n. 1243.
      number] STEEVENS (ed. 1773): "Verses are often called *numbers*, and to *number*,
a verb (in this sense) of Shakespeare's coining, is *to make verses*."
      hoo] KITTREDGE (ed. 1941): "The metre [of 1557–8] is perfect. *Hoo!* is prolonged
so as to make three syllables ('hoo — oo — oo'), in ludicrous and splendid parody of Lepidus's whoop of admiration." See nn. 1492, 1561–2.

His loue to *Anthony*. But as for *Cæsar,*
Kneele downe, kneele downe, and wonder.
  Agri. Both he loues.   1560
  Eno. They are his Shards, and he their Beetle, so:
This is to horse: Adieu, Noble *Agrippa.*
  Agri. Good Fortune worthy Souldier, and farewell.

      Enter Cæsar, Anthony, Lepidus, and Octauia.

1558 *Cæsar*] *Cæsar*, kneel CAP-v1778, RANN
1559 Kneele downe] kneel HAN1
1562 Noble] most noble KTLY
    Agrippa.] *Agrippa.* [*Trumpets.* ROWE1-JOHN1, v1773-RANN; *SD after* Beetle *in*
1561 CAP, DYCE, GLO, CAM1, HUD2-SIS; *SD after* so *in* 1561 v1793-SING2, COL3-WH1,
KTLY, HAL, COL4, ARD2, EVNS
    Trumpets. ROWE1+ (*subst.*)
1564 *Enter*] *Enter above* BLUM

1561 **Shards . . . Beetle**] CAPELL (1779 [1774], Glossary, 1:61): "The husky and glaz'd
Shells or outer Wings of the Beetle." IDEM (1:37): "By those shards, the poor beetle Lepidus was enabl'd to soar as he had done; and, if they were taken from him, would be
in that beetle's condition,—fall to the ground." BECKET (1815, 2:187), alone and unconvincingly: As shards "serve as shelter" to the "blind" beetle, so Lepidus, "*blind* to the
designs of Cæsar and Antony . . . *covers* himself from censure . . . by allowing his
colleague to be the prominent character on every occasion." WALTER (1969, pp. 137–8):
"The *O.E.D.* [*sb.*[2]] maintains that 'shards' means patches of dung, and that the rendering wing-cases or wings is based on a misunderstanding of 'shard-borne' in *Macbeth*,
III.ii.42 [1200]. . . . Enobarbus's words are clearly intended to epitomize with a final,
impressively scornful image the ridicule with which he and Agrippa have mimicked Lepidus's fulsome two-way flatteries of Caesar and Antony." IDEM (ed. 1969): "In Plutarch
["Isis and Osiris," *Moralia* (tr. Holland, 1603, pp. 1291, 1316)] the beetle is described
as rolling a ball of dung backwards and forwards just as the sun appears to travel west
by day and east by night. The image is a brilliant caricature of Lepidus scurrying to and
fro with his fulsome praise between Antony east and Cæsar west."
    1561–2 **Beetle, so: This**] DELIUS (ed. 1856): ROWE's (ed. 1709) insertion of the SD
Trumpets makes *so* refer to the trumpets (*This*) summoning him to horse. BLUMHOF (ed.
1870) suggests that *so* refers to a mocking hand gesture underlining what has just been
said. WALTER (ed. 1969): "Enobarbus may give a lively representation of a beetle running to and fro. On the other hand 'so' may be Enobarbus' repetition of the trumpet
call [compares 'Hoo' (1555, 1557) and 1492, 'where "Hoo" echoes the "flourish"']."
    1562–3 RIDLEY's (ed. 1954) "Two more unmistakable exit lines it would be hard to
find" may have been anticipated by BLUMHOF (ed. 1870): The speakers, ready to depart,
remain to overhear the dealings of their superiors and later comment confidentially on
them. For the interrupted withdrawal (in this instance a modification of the standard
double entry), see URKOWITZ (1978, pp. 203–10).

Antho. No further Sir.   1565
Cæsar. You take from me a great part of my selfe:
Vse me well in't. Sister, proue such a wife
As my thoughts make thee, and as my farthest Band
Shall passe on thy approofe: most Noble *Anthony*,
Let not the peece of Vertue which is set   .   1570
Betwixt vs, as the Cyment of our loue
To keepe it builded, be the Ramme to batter
The Fortresse of it: for better might we
Haue lou'd without this meane, if on both parts

1565 *to* Cæsar. CAP
       further] farther F2-THEO4, CAP, COL, WH1, HAL
1568 as] *Om.* POPE1-THEO4
       farthest] furthest JOHN1, v1773, v1778, RANN-SING1, DYCE, OXF1
1573 Fortresse] Fortune F2-POPE2
       it] it down KTLY
       for] for much HAN1; for far mTBY3 *conj.*, CAP, DYCE2, HUD2

1565 **No further Sir**] KITTREDGE (ed. 1941): "Antony politely protests against Cæsar's taking the trouble to escort him farther."

1568-9 **as . . . approofe**] JOHNSON (ed. 1765): "As I will venture the greatest pledge of security on the trial of thy conduct." Johnson's implied legal context is made explicit by WILSON (ed. 1950): "Commercial language."

1569 **passe on**] JOHNSON (1755, *Pass*, 19): "To determine finally; to judge capitally."

approofe] Commentators, following Johnson's paraphrase in the main, define as "prove by testing." DEIGHTON (ed. 1891) and others cite *AWW* 2.5.3 [1272]—"of very valiant *approof*', *i.e.* of approved valour"—or, as CASE (ed. 1906) has it, "the proved possession of a quality."

1570 **peece**] Most commentators agree with STEEVENS's (ed. 1793) citation of *Tmp.* 1.2.56 (148), "Thy Mother was a peece of vertue." Some suggest further semantic possibilities. DEIGHTON (ed. 1891): "Here *piece* is used both of a constituent part of a building [quotes 'All . . . is,' *H8* 5.5.26-7 (3395-6)], and of something of supreme excellence"; CASE (ed. 1906): "*Piece* often=masterpiece, as here (most probably) and in [3319] *post*, but is also used merely for 'creature' and like words." FURNESS (ed. 1907): "'Piece' may mean a 'specimen, or example, and be applied to an abstract thing' [citing *OED*, 8b]; and it may also mean a woman [citing *OED*, 9b] which is, I think, the better meaning here." WILSON (ed. 1950): "Also poss. a quibble on 'piece' (vb.)=join, unite."

1572 **builded**] For the endings *-ed* and *-t* in weak verbs terminating in *n*, *l*, *r*, and *d*, see FRANZ §160.

1574 **meane**] WORDSWORTH (ed. 1883): "*Medium*." HERFORD (ed. 1899) adds "mediator." KITTREDGE (ed. 1941): "Means (of cementing our love)." See also 2616. IRVING & MARSHALL (ed. 1889): "*Mean* is often used by Shakespeare in the singular, though oftener in the plural." In fact Sh. favored the substantive *means* over *mean* by almost seven to one. See FRANZ §194.

This be not cherisht.   1575
   Ant. Make me not offended, in your distrust.
   Cæsar. I haue said.
   Ant. You shall not finde,
Though you be therein curious, the lest cause
For what you seeme to feare, so the Gods keepe you,   1580
And make the hearts of Romaines serue your ends:
We will heere part.
   Cæsar. Farewell my deerest Sister, fare thee well,
The Elements be kind to thee, and make
Thy spirits all of comfort: fare thee well.   1585
   Octa. My Noble Brother.
   Anth. The Aprill's in her eyes, it is Loues spring,
And these the showers to bring it on: be cheerfull.
   Octa. Sir, looke well to my Husbands house: and——   (xx6ᵛᵇ)
   Cæsar. What *Octauia?*   1590

1575–8 *Verse lines ending* offended . . . find, ROWE1+
1579 therein] certain ROWE2-POPE2
1589–91 *Verse lines ending* What, . . . ear. HAN1, CAP, v1793-KNT1, SING2, DYCE,
STAU, GLO, KTLY, CAM1, HUD2-ARD1, KIT1+ (–SIS); *ending* What, | Octavia? . . . ear. RID

1577 WORDSWORTH (ed. 1883): "*I will add no more*: Lat. '*dixi*.'"
1579 **curious**] CAWDREY (1604, curiositie): "Picked diligence, greater carefulnes, then
is seemely or necessarie."
1580 **keepe**] See n. 984 ("keepes").
1584–5 **The . . . comfort**] JOHNSON (ed. 1765): "*May the different* elements *of the
body, or principles of life, maintain such proportion and harmony as may keep you cheerful*." STEEVENS (ed. 1773): "*May the four elements, of which this world is composed,
unite their influences to make thee chearful*." IDEM (ed. 1778): "There is, however, a
thought which seems to favour Dr. Johnson's explanation . . . [quotes 'My . . . heart,'
TNK 1.3.8–11, 61–3, and 'Does . . . say,' *TN* 2.3.9–11 (708–10)]. These parting words
of Cæsar to his sister, may indeed mean no more than the common compliment which
the occasion of her voyage very naturally required. He wishes *that serene weather and
prosperous winds may keep her spirits free from every apprehension that might disturb
or alarm them*." Despite MASON's (*apud* IDEM, ed. 1793) proposing the elements of earth
and water and MALONE's (*apud* IDEM) of air and water, most commentators tend to agree
with HOLT WHITE (1783, p. 935): "Surely this expression means no more than, *I wish
you a good voyage*."
1585 **all**] For the intensive meaning "wholly," "completely," see FRANZ §371.
1587–8 **The . . . on**] Proverbial; see DENT (S411): "April *showers* bring May flowers."
Expanding on BLUMHOF (ed. 1870), WALTER (ed. 1969): "In Roman myth showery April
was sacred to Venus, whose wet shining eyes were expressive of love."

 Octa. Ile tell you in your eare.

 Ant. Her tongue will not obey her heart, nor can

Her heart informe her tongue.

The Swannes downe feather

That stands vpon the Swell at the full of Tide: 1595

And neither way inclines.

 Eno. Will *Cæsar* weepe?

 Agr. He ha's a cloud in's face.

1592–6 *To Lepidus.* BLUM
1593–4 *One verse line* ROWE1+
1593 informe] obey OXF1
1595 That] Thus WALKER (1860, 3:301) *conj.*, COL4, HUD2
  the full of] full of F2-v1778, RANN-SING1, STAU, GLO, DYCE2-NLSN, RID, KIT1,
CAM3; the full COL3; full of th' N&H
1596–8 *Arranged as verse lines, thus*: 1596, 1597–8 v1793-COL2, SING2-COL3,
WH1-HUD2, OXF1, ARD, KIT1, CAM3, SIS; 1596–8 RID; 1596–7, 1598 EVNS

1591 FURNESS (ed. 1907) facetiously: "Voss [ed. 1827] is the sole commentator who
overhears what Octavia whispers. He says that she begs her brother not to be too exacting
when dealing with Anthony, or else to remain constant to her, should Anthony's former
fascination for Cleopatra re-awaken. But see [1609–10]."

1592–6 CASE (ed. 1906): "It is not clear whether Octavia's heart is the swan's down-
feather [proposed by CAPELL (1779 [1774], 1:37)], swayed neither way on the full tide
of emotion at parting with her brother to accompany her husband, or whether it is merely
the *inaction* of heart and tongue [proposed by DELIUS (ed. 1856)], on the same occasion,
which is elliptically compared to that of the feather." KITTREDGE (ed. 1941): "Antony
means that Octavia's tongue cannot express her conflicting emotions, and that her heart
is too full to allow her tongue utterance. Her state of feeling is so delicately balanced
between sorrow at parting with her brother and desire to accompany her husband that
it is like a 'swan's down-feather' on the water when the tide is at the pause between flood
and ebb. [Compares "'tis . . . backe,' *2H4* 2.3.62–6 (1022–6).]" LEE (1971, p. 33): "Octavia's soft, defenceless quality and inevitable destruction are suggested by the image
of the feather, and her uselessness as a force to bind the ever-moving tide is clear. . . .
We come back again to the vacillation and perpetual change which characterises the play."

1595 **full of Tide**] DELIUS (ed. 1856): The height of the flood, when the forces of
ebb and flow are equal and the water motionless.

1598–9 **He . . . Horse**] STEEVENS (ed. 1778): "A horse is said to have *a cloud in
his face*, when he has a black or dark-coloured spot in his forehead between his eyes.
This gives him a sour look, and being supposed to indicate an ill-temper, is of course
regarded as a great blemish." STEEVENS (*apud* REED, ed. 1803): "The same phrase occurs
in Burton's *Anatomy of Melancholy*, edit. 1632, 524: 'Every lover admires his mistress,
though she be very deformed of her selfe — thin leane, chitty face, have *clouds in her
face*, be crooked', etc." RIDLEY (ed. 1954): "According to . . . [Richard] Sadler, *De
Procreandis*, etc., *equis*, 1587: *Equus nebula (ut vulgo dicitur) in facie, cujus vultus tris-
tis est et malancholicus, jure vituperatur* [A horse with a cloud (as it is commonly called)

Eno. He were the worse for that were he a Horse, so is
he being a man.   1600
    Agri. Why *Enobarbus*:
When *Anthony* found *Iulius Cæsar* dead,
He cried almost to roaring: And he wept,
When at Phillippi he found *Brutus* slaine.
    Eno. That year indeed, he was trobled with a rheume,   1605
What willingly he did confound, he wail'd,
Beleeu't till I weepe too.
    Cæsar. No sweet *Octauia*,
You shall heare from me still: the time shall not
Out-go my thinking on you.   1610
    Ant. Come Sir, come,
Ile wrastle with you in my strength of loue,
Looke heere I haue you, thus I let you go,

1599–1601 *Verse lines ending* horse; . . . *Enobarbus?* POPE1+
1607–8 *One verse line* v1793+ (–ALEX)
1607 weepe] wept mTHEO2 (19 Feb. 1729, [fol. 40]) *conj.*, THEO, WARB, JOHN1,
SING2-ARD2 (–COL3, KTLY, ALEX)
1610 my] her ROWE2, ROWE3

---

in his face, whose mien is sad and melancholy, is justly found fault with (sig. B2ʳ)]. Such
a horse . . . is Arcite's unlucky steed in *The Two Noble Kinsmen*, V.iv.[50–1]." KNOWLES
(privately): "The meaning elaborated here is a quibbling one. The primary one is that
Caesar's features promise tears as a cloud promises rain. See 'weeping clowdes' (*2H4* 1.3.61
[562]), 'the . . . clouds, contend in teares' (*2H6* 3.2.384 [2101]). For clouds=gloom,
Tim. 3.4.42 (1171), et passim."
    1605 **rheume**] CAWDREY (1604): "Catarre, a distilling of humors from the head."
    1606 **confound**] See n. 57.
    1607 **Beleeu't . . . weepe**] THEOBALD (ed. 1733): "*Enobarbus* would say, '. . . be-
lieve me, [Antony] bewail'd all the Mischiefs he did, till I my self wept too'. This appears
to me very sarcastical. *Antony's* Tears, he would infer, were dissembled: but *Enobarbus*
wept in real Compassion of the Havock and Slaughters committed on his Countrymen."
STEEVENS (ed. 1773) and most commentators: "*Believe it*, (says Enobarbus) *that Antony
did so*, i.e. *that he wept over such an event, till you see me weeping on the same occasion, when I shall be obliged to you for putting such a construction on my tears, which,
in reality, (like his) will be tears of joy*." CAPELL (1779 [1774], 1:37) adds, "Which he
[Enobarbus] thought [he would] never [weep]." Only MASON (1797, p. 52) believes Antony was sincere.
    1609–10 FURNESS (ed. 1907): "Is it not here revealed what Octavia told in Caesar's
ear?" See n. 1591.
    1610 **Out-go**] MINSHEU (1617): "Goe beyond." For the prefix *out-*, see n. 912–13.
    1613–14 For conj., see p. 353.

And giue you to the Gods.
　Cæsar. Adieu, be happy.   1615
　Lep. Let all the number of the Starres giue light
To thy faire way.
　Cæsar. Farewell, farewell.   *Kisses Octauia.*
　Ant. Farewell.   *Trumpets sound. Exeunt.*

　　　Enter Cleopatra, Charmian, Iras, and Alexas.   **3.3**

　Cleo. Where is the Fellow?   1621
　Alex. Halfe afeard to come.
　Cleo. Go too, go too: Come hither Sir.

　　　　　Enter the Messenger as before.

　Alex. Good Maiestie: *Herod* of Iury dare not looke   1625
vpon you, but when you are well pleas'd.
　Cleo. That *Herods* head, Ile haue: but how? When

1617–19 *One verse line* v1793+ (−ALEX)
1618 *Kisses Octauia.*] *Om.* v1773
1620 SCENE III. ROWE1+ (−THEO)
　　Alexandria. ROWE1+ (*subst.*)
1622 afeard] afraid POPE1-JOHN1, v1773
1623–9 *Five verse lines ending* majesty, . . . upon you, . . . head . . . gone, . . .
near. POPE1+
1624 *Enter*] *Enter* ELIS mCOL1, COL2

1615 **happy**] See n. 76.
1617 **faire**] DEIGHTON (ed. 1891): "Used proleptically; which will thus be rendered fair."
1618 TURNER (privately) suggests the first "farewell" is addressed to Octavia, the second to Antony.
1620–83 GREY (1754, 2:201–2) quotes *The Memoires of Sir James Melvil* (1683, pp. 50–1) for the similarity of the questions asked by Queen Elizabeth about her rival Mary Queen of Scots. See also n. 1165–8. RITSON (*apud* STEEVENS, ed. 1793) remarks, however, that the conversation occurred in 1564, the year of Sh.'s birth, and was not printed until 1683, but grants, "Such enquiries, no doubt, are perfectly natural to rival females, whether queens or cinder-wenches."
1623 **Go too**] See n. 1069.
1624 COLLIER (ed. 1858) identifies him as the same messenger; WILSON (ed. 1950) takes him to be in the same state, "dishevelled as . . . in 2.5."
1625–6 See n. 107–8.
1625 **Iury**] See n. 2590.

Anthony is gone, through whom I might commaund it:
Come thou neere.
    Mes. Most gratious Maiestie.   1630
    Cleo. Did'st thou behold *Octauia*?
    Mes. I dread Queene.
    Cleo. Where?
    Mes. Madam in Rome, I lookt her in the face: and
saw her led betweene her Brother, and *Marke Anthony.*   1635
    Cleo. Is she as tall as me?
    Mes. She is not Madam.
    Cleo. Didst heare her speake?
Is she shrill tongu'd or low?
    Mes. Madam, I heard her speake, she is low voic'd.   1640
    Cleo. That's not so good: he cannot like her long.

1630–7 *Lines* 1630-3 *as* F1, 1634-7 *four verse lines ending* face: . . . Brother, and
. . . me? . . . Madam. ROWE, POPE, HAN1; *five verse lines ending* behold, . . . *Rome*,
Madam. . . . led . . . *Antony.* . . . Madam. THEO, WARB, JOHN1-COL3, WH1, KTLY-
HUD2, OXF1, ARD, RID, CAM3; 1630-3 *as* F1, 1634-7 *four verse lines ending* Rome; . . .
led . . . Antony. . . . madam. STAU, GLO, WH2, NLSN, KIT1; *five verse lines ending*
Octavia? . . . Rome; . . . led . . . Antony. . . . madam. BAYF, EVNS; *six verse lines
ending* Majesty! . . . Queen. . . . Rome . . . led . . . Antony. . . . madam. ALEX;
1630-1 *line divided* behold | Octavia?, 1632-7 *four verse lines ending* Rome, . . . led
. . . Antony. . . . madam. SIS
1634 Madam in Rome] In *Rome*, Madam THEO, WARB, JOHN1
1638–9 *One verse line* ROWE1+

1627–8 WILSON (ed. 1950) cites Plutarch's account (see p. 420) of Antony's beheading of Antigonus; PHIALAS (ed. 1955), also of his beheading of Cicero (see p. 409). DICKEY
(1957, p. 189): In a characteristic burst of rage, spoken "quite gratuitously."
    1639 **shrill tongu'd**] THISELTON (1899, p. 17): "Cleopatra is evidently wishing to com-
pare Octavia with shrill-tongued Fulvia [43]."
    1641 MALONE (*apud* STEEVENS [1783]): "Cleopatra perhaps does not mean—'That
is not so good a piece of intelligence as your last'; but, '*That*, i.e. a low voice, is not so
good as a shrill tongue'. That she did not herself esteem a low voice . . . as a merit
in a lady, appears from what she adds [at 1643.]—If the words be understood in the
sense first mentioned, the latter part of the line will be found inconsistent with the foregoing." IDEM (ed. 1790): "Perhaps, however, the authour intended no connexion between
the two members of this line; and that Cleopatra, after a pause, should exclaim—He
cannot like her, whatever her merits be, for any length of time. My first interpretation
I believe to be the true one." Most commentators agree. But IRVING & MARSHALL (ed.
1889): "Cleopatra means that a low voice is so good a thing in itself that it is 'not so
good' for *her*, as it denotes a charm in Octavia"—to which THISELTON (1899, p. 17) adds,
"But in her anxiety . . . she immediately clutches at another possible meaning of the
word 'low.'"

 Char. Like her? Oh *Isis*: 'tis impossible.
 Cleo. I thinke so *Charmian*: dull of tongue, & dwarfish,
What Maiestie is in her gate, remember
If ere thou look'st on Maiestie.   1645
 Mes. She creepes: her motion, & her station are as one:
She shewes a body, rather then a life,
A Statue, then a Breather.
 Cleo. Is this certaine?
 Mes. Or I haue no obseruance.   1650
 Cha. Three in Egypt cannot make better note.
 Cleo. He's very knowing, I do perceiu't,
There's nothing in her yet.
The Fellow ha's good iudgement.   (yy1ᵃ)
 Char. Excellent.   1655

1645–6 *Verse lines ending* creeps; . . . one: ROWE1+
1645 look'st] look'dst POPE1-SIS (−v1773)
1649–50 *Line* 1649 *given to Messenger,* 1650 *to Cleopatra* F3, F4
1650–3 *Three verse lines ending Ægypt* . . . knowing, . . . yet. THEO1+
1651 Three . . . cannot] Not three . . . can POPE

1643 TURNER (privately): "The compositor did not set a comma after 'dwarfish,' as the proofsheet in HINMAN (1963, 1:234) in the uncorrected state reveals. In the corrected state, a comma appears flush right on 1645, however, although its insertion is not marked on the proofsheet. This may indicate — barring a second round of correction — that during proof correction the compositor himself decided to add it, but somehow got it on the wrong line, 1645." DAWSON (privately) suggests that the comma may have been a mistaken replacement for a quad pulled during printing.

 1646 **station**] COCKERAM (1623): "A standing." STEEVENS (ed. 1778) and most others: "*The act of standing.* So in *Hamlet*: 'A *station* like the herald Mercury' [3.4.58 (2442)]." SEYMOUR (1805, 2:64) disagrees with this "literal and primitive sense. . . . It means attitude, position; and might as well be the act of sitting." Thus, following BLUMHOF (ed. 1870), some commentators refer to the manner of standing — e.g., WILSON (ed. 1950): "She holds her body stiff."

 1647 **shewes**] I.e., appears. For transitive verbs used intransitively, see FRANZ §629.

 1648 **Statue**] MINSHEU's (1617) definition — "*standing image*" — is to be compared with that of *station* (1646).

 1650 **obseruance**] BULLOKAR (1616): "Diligent heede, or attendance." Most commentators, however, follow HANMER (ed. 1744): "*Is here used for* Observation."

 1651 GREY (1754, 2:205): "Alluding to the old catches, which were in three parts"; RANN (ed. 1791–): "Three of the best performers in *Ægypt* cannot make sweeter musick." WILSON (ed. 1950): "Charm.'s support (?ironical) suggests previous collusion, v. [p. 182, n. SD: "The Messenger has also learnt wisdom, perhaps in private from Charmian"] and cf. l. [1671]."

Cleo. Guesse at her yeares, I prythee.

Mess. Madam, she was a widdow.

Cleo. Widdow? *Charmian*, hearke.

Mes. And I do thinke she's thirtie.

Cle. Bear'st thou her face in mind? is't long or round?   1660

Mess. Round, euen to faultinesse.

Cleo. For the most part too, they are foolish that are
so. Her haire what colour?

Mess. Browne Madam: and her forehead
As low as she would wish it.   1665

1656–8 *Verse lines ending* madam? . . . hark. CAP, v1793+

1657 Madam,] Her years, madam? CAP

1659–66 *Six verse lines ending* thirty. . . . or, round? . . . faultiness. . . . so. . . . forehead. . . . thee. F3-ROWE3, CAM, ARD, RID, ALEX, SIS; *six verse lines ending* thirty. . . . or round? . . . too, . . . colour? . . . forehead . . . thee. POPE1-JOHN1, v1773-RANN; *five verse lines ending* face . . . faultiness. . . . so.— . . . forehead . . . thee. CAP; *six verse lines ending* thirty. . . . or round? . . . too, . . . colour? . . . low . . . thee. v1793, v1803; *seven verse lines ending* thirty. . . . or round? . . . faultiness. . . . so.— . . . colour? . . . forehead . . . thee. v1821-DYCE2, COL4-NLSN, KIT1, EVNS

1660 is't] it's THEO2, WARB-JOHN1

1664 and her forehead] *Given to Cleopatra* NARES (*s.v.* FOREHEAD, HIGH) *conj.*, SING2

1665 As] is as v1793, v1803
   she] you mF4FL33 *conj.*, mCOL1, COL2, COL4

1659 **she's thirtie**] ADLER (1895, p. 295, n. 1) uses this line as evidence that Cleopatra was younger than 30, that to Sh. she was the 28 history makes her when she first met Antony. But RIDLEY (ed. 1954): "Cleopatra passes on without comment. She was herself thirty-eight."

1661–3 **Round . . . so**] STEEVENS (ed. 1793): "This is from the old writers on Physiognomy. So, in [Thomas] Hill's *Pleasant History* &c. 1613. 'The head [. . .] *very round*, to be forgetful and *foolish*'. Again, 'the head *long* [. . .] to be prudent and wary'.—'a *low forehead* to be sad'. &c. &c. [fol.] 218 [wrongly paged 118]." CASE (ed. 1906) adds examples from fols. 86, 26, and 220 (wrongly paged 120).

1664 **Browne**] Blond hair was preferred. For the ideal of feminine beauty, see BREWER (1955, pp. 257–69).

1665 RANN (ed. 1791–): "Somewhat lower—*as you could wish it.*" MALONE (ed. 1790): "Low foreheads were in Shakspeare's age thought a blemish. [Quotes *Tmp.* 4.1.250 (1923).] . . . *You* and *She* are not likely to have been confounded; otherwise we might suppose that our authour wrote—'As low as *you* would wish it.'" STEEVENS (ed. 1793): "The phrase employed by the Messenger, is still a cant one. I once overheard a chambermaid say of her rival,—'that her legs were as thick *as she could wish them.*'" WILSON (ed. 1950): "Sarcastic; really 'as Cleo.' etc."

Cleo. There's Gold for thee,
Thou must not take my former sharpenesse ill,
I will employ thee backe againe: I finde thee
Most fit for businesse. Go, make thee ready,
Our Letters are prepar'd.   1670
  Char. A proper man.
  Cleo. Indeed he is so: I repent me much
That so I harried him. Why me think's by him,
This Creature's no such thing.
  Char. Nothing Madam.   1675
  Cleo. The man hath seene some Maiesty, and should
know.
  Char. Hath he seene Maiestie? *Isis* else defend: and

1666 There's] There is v1793-SING1
1669 ready,] ready, while CAP
1670 *Exit Mes.* HAN1, CAP, MAL, v1793+
1673 so I] I so THEO3, v1773, v1778, RANN, SING1, HUD1
    Why] *Om.* POPE, HAN1
1674–5 *One verse line* v1793+ (−v1821, COL, WH1, HAL)
1675 Nothing] O nothing POPE1-CAP, v1793, v1803; No, nothing KTLY
1676–7 F1-ROWE3; *on one line* POPE1, HAN1, MAL, DYCE, COL3, HAL, COL4-WH2, ARD, RID; *verse* POPE2 *etc.*
1678–82 *Five verse lines ending* defend! . . . long. . . . *Charmian*: . . . me . . . enough. ROWE1+

1668 **backe againe**] DEIGHTON (ed. 1891): "To carry back letters." For *againe* emphasizing *backe*, see FRANZ §433. See also *Lr.* 4.2.91 (2339): "I met him backe againe."
    1671 **proper**] COTGRAVE (1611, Propre): "*Handsome, seemelie, comelie, well accommodated, vnto the purpose.*"
    1672 **repent me**] For the reflexive pronoun in the dative case, see FRANZ §307.
    1673 **me think's**] For impersonal verbs with no expressed subject but a pronoun in the dative, see FRANZ §627. An intrusive apostrophe before *s* is not uncommon.
      by him] SEYMOUR (1805, 2:64): "*I.e.* by his description."
    1674 **Creature's**] Sh.'s usage is not pejorative. See MINSHEU (1617): "*Omne quod viuit & sentit* [All that lives and feels]."
      no such thing] DELIUS (ed. 1856) continues, "To worry about." WHITE (ed. 1861) and others paraphrase: "I.e., nothing very remarkable—a colloquial phrase."
      thing] SEYMOUR (1805, 2:64): "'Thing' often occurs, when either an object of superlative dignity or remarkable insignificance is to be expressed; thus Coriolanus, blazing in the splendour of his victory, is accosted, 'Thou noble thing!' [*Cor.* 4.5.122 (2774)] and thus, in the extremity of contempt, is Hostess Quickly saluted, 'Thou thing!' [*1H4* 3.3.131 (2123); in Qq 'you thing,' in F1 'you nothing']."
    1675 **Nothing**] I.e., not at all. For the adverbial use, see FRANZ §405. ELZE (1886, p. 274): "Pope's and Keightley's conjectures [see textual notes] are unnecessary" if there is a syllable pause before *Nothing*.
    1678 **else defend**] WORDSWORTH (ed. 1883): "*Forbid it should be otherwise.*"

seruing you so long.

Cleopa. I haue one thing more to aske him yet good   1680
Charmian: but 'tis no matter, thou shalt bring him to me
where I will write; all may be well enough.

Char. I warrant you Madam.   *Exeunt.*

Enter Anthony and Octauia.   **3.4**

Ant. Nay, nay *Octauia*, not onely that,   1685
That were excusable, that and thousands more
Of semblable import, but he hath wag'd
New Warres 'gainst *Pompey*. Made his will, and read it,
To publicke eare, spoke scantly of me,

1684 SCENE IV. ROWE1+ (−THEO)
         Athens. ROWE1-JOHN1; Athens. *A Room in* Antony's *House*. CAP+ (*subst.*)
1685–6 *Verse lines ending* only that,— that . . . more MAL
1687–90 *Four verse lines ending* wag'd . . . it . . . eàr: . . . not CAP-GLO, HAL+;
three verse lines ending wars . . . ear; . . . not KTLY
1689 scantly] scantily THEO1-v1778, RANN

1680–1 I . . . matter] WILLIAMS (privately) sees this as Sh.'s "planting" a reference
in this scene to which he may return if he discovers he needs another little scene in Egypt
(like 1.5, 2.5, 3.3).
    1682 I will write] Apparently contradicts "Our Letters are prepar'd" (1670).
    1685–94 PARTRIDGE (1964, pp. 117–18): "The passage is patently corrupt at three points,
possibly four. A full-stop is by no means impossible after *Pompey*; but the next two words
are curious, since Plutarch [see p. 436] avers that Octavius took Antony's will (not his
own) and read it publicly, to which the latter naturally objected. The emendation *ta'en*
[for *Made his*—see p. 353] has been suggested. The line-arrangement has gone awry from
eare in the next line, apparently implying a marginal insertion difficult for the compositor to read. *Them* should be read for *then* at [1692], and *took't* for *look't* in the next
line." See textual notes.
    1687 semblable] BULLOKAR (1616): "Like."
    1688–9 Made . . . eare] KELLNER (1925, p. 124) defends his emendation *maim'd*
(see p. 436): "The corresponding passage in North's Plutarch shows that Cæsar denounced
Antony's will by which he gave away large territories to Cleopatra's sons." RIDLEY (ed.
1954), without supporting detail: "It is unlike Shakespeare to desert North on so specific
a point, and I think there is certainly corruption. The vagaries of F's punctuation, as
well as other awkwardnesses, suggest an unusually difficult passage in MS." But THISEL-
TON (1899, p. 17): "The commas after 'it' [and] 'of me' . . . mark the close of the coordinate sentences and indicate the impetuosity of Antony's utterance."
    1689 scantly] MINSHEU (1617, Scarcely): "*Scantly, hardly.*" The usage is often neutral

When perforce he could not   1690
But pay me tearmes of Honour: cold and sickly
He vented then most narrow measure: lent me,
When the best hint was giuen him: he not look't,
Or did it from his teeth.
  Octaui. Oh my good Lord,   1695
Beleeue not all, or if you must beleeue,

1690 When] And when at any time HAN1
1691-2 Honour: . . . then˄ . . . measure:] ~ , . . . ~ ; . . . ~ ˄ ROWE1+
1692 then] them ROWE1+
1692-3 me, . . . him:] ~ ; . . . ~ , ROWE1-SING1, COL1+
1693 not look't] had look't F2-F4; o'er-look'd ROWE, POPE; not took't mTBY2 *conj.*,
THEO1-SING1, COL1, HUD1-DYCE1, WH1+; but look'd mCOL1, COL2; not took'd STAU

---

in Sh.'s time, but some modern editors stress the pejorative here, as, for example,
DEIGHTON (ed. 1891)—"grudgingly"—and FURNESS (ed. 1907), "slightingly."

1691 **cold and sickly**] All commentators refer to the manner of Octavius. Suetonius,
however, describes his weak constitution: "Most commonly he was sickish and had a faint-
nesse upon him. . . . His body beeing so shaken and crasie, hee could not well endure
either colde or heat. In winter time clad he went against the colde with foure coates,
together with a good thicke gowne, and his Wastcoate or Peticoate bodie of woollen:
well lapped also about the thighes and legges" (*The historie of twelve Cæsars*, tr. Holland, 1606, p. 75).

1693 **not look't**] COLLIER (ed. 1843) defends *took't* ("Had *look't* been merely meant
for *looked*, it would probably not have had an apostrophe" [which is incorrect]), then
(IDEM [1852, p. 472]) prefers *but look'd* ("There appears no sufficient ground for doing
more than amend the frequent error of 'not' for *but*"), and finally (IDEM [ed. 1858])
echoes KNIGHT (ed. 1841) in restoring F1 ("Cæsar would not look to avoid taking the
least hint, or if he did look, and took the hint, his praise was superficial and insincere").

1694 **from his teeth**] RANN (ed. 1791–): "Reluctantly." STEEVENS (ed. 1793): "Whether
this means, as we now say, *in spite of his teeth*, or that he spoke through his teeth, so
as to be purposely indistinct, I am unable to determine." IDEM (*apud* REED, ed. 1803)
adds examples, two of which—from Thomas Fuller's *The historie of the holy warre* 4.17
(1639, p. 197) and *Homer's Iliads* 15.99 (tr. Chapman, ed. A. Nicoll, 1957)—are used
by SINGER (ed. 1826) to illustrate the meaning stated by CHEDWORTH (1805, p. 289):
"Not heartily . . . does not come from the heart." Agreeing, PYE (1807, p. 267) quotes
Dryden's *The Wild Gallant*: "I am confident she is only angry from the teeth outwards
[4.1.197–8, *Works*, ed. Hooker, Swedenborg, et al., vol. 8, 1962]." CASE (ed. 1906): "Compare '*Frae the teeth* forward <Not from the heart>' ([Andrew] Henderson's *Scottish
Proverbs*, ed. 1876, p. 110)." Possibly proverbial; see DENT (T423): "From the *teeth*
outwards."

Stomacke not all. A more vnhappie Lady,
If this deuision chance, ne're stood betweene
Praying for both parts:
The good Gods wil mocke me presently,   1700
When I shall pray: Oh blesse my Lord, and Husband,
Vndo that prayer, by crying out as loud,
Oh blesse my Brother. Husband winne, winne Brother,
Prayes, and distroyes the prayer, no midway
'Twixt these extreames at all.   1705
    Ant. Gentle *Octauia*,
Let your best loue draw to that point which seeks
Best to preserue it: if I loose mine Honour,

1699–1701 *Verse lines ending* me, . . . Husband, ROWE1-THEO4, CAP, v1773, RANN;
ending presently . . . *husband!* v1778, MAL, v1821, SING, KTLY
    1700 The] And the v1793, v1803; Sure, the DYCE2, HUD2
        presently] *Om.* ROWE1-THEO4, CAP-v1778, RANN
    1701 pray] praying ROWE
        Lord, and] *Om.* CAP, v1773, RANN
        Husband,] *husband!* presently CAP (*text*; husband! CAPN [*errata*]), v1773;
husband! and presently mTBY4 *conj.*, RANN
    1702 Vndo] And undo KTLY

    1697 **Stomacke**] WALKER (1957, pp. 98–9): "Figuratively for 'resent'. . . . [The word]
was never used for physical digestion until the nineteenth century. . . . The transferred
sense was not only pre-Shakespearian but also the primary meaning in English." See nn.
688, 740.
    1697–1705 **A . . . all**] STEEVENS (ed. 1793): "The situation and sentiments of Oc-
tavia resemble those of Lady Blanch in *King John*. [Cites 3.1.326–36 (1259–69).]" FRYE
(1970, p. 190): "A near perfect example of the ways in which the mature Shakespeare
used a basic iambic pentameter pattern, but varied it, so as to provide a union of poetic
power and of colloquial speech. . . . Exclamations and assertions, heavy and unexpected
pauses, the irregular, often violent beat of the rhythm, sudden starts and stops, are combined with passages of perfect regularity to convey an appropriate sense of conflict and
confusion, as the speech of Octavia reflects her inner turmoil in utterly credible verse."
For Plutarch, see p. 419.
    1700 **good**] See n. 510.
        presently] See nn. 835, 863.
    1702 **Vndo**] DELIUS (ed. 1856): *I* or *I shall* completes the verb.
    1704 **Prayes, and distroyes**] DELIUS (ed. 1856): The subject of these verbs is "Hus-
band winne, winne Brother" (1703).
        prayer] DELIUS (ed. 1856): The one who prays, Octavia. BLUMHOF (ed. 1870) alone:
The prayer, not the one who prays.
    1707 **to that point**] WORDSWORTH (ed. 1883): "I.e., *of the compass*; here, *that side*."
DEIGHTON (ed. 1891): "Viz. to what is honourable."

I loose my selfe: better I were not yours
Then your so branchlesse. But as you requested,   1710
Your selfe shall go between's, the meane time Lady,
Ile raise the preparation of a Warre
Shall staine your Brother, make your soonest hast,
So your desires are yours.
    Oct. Thanks to my Lord,   1715
The Ioue of power make me most weake, most weake,
You reconciler: Warres 'twixt you twaine would be,

1710 your] yours F2+
1713 staine] strain THEO, HAN1, CAP; 'stain RANN; stay WARBURTON *conj. apud*
mTHEO3 (28 July 1733, [fol. 39ᵛ]), mCOL1, COL2, HUD1, COL3, DYCE2, COL4
        soonest] sooner v1773
1716 most weake, most] although most HAN1
1717 You] Your F2+

1710 **branchlesse**] Earlier commentators gloss as "bare" (WORDSWORTH [ed. 1883]),
more recent ones as "maimed" (RIDLEY [ed. 1935]).
    1713 **staine**] THEOBALD (28 July 1733, [Egerton MS 1956, fol. 39ᵛ]): "You [i.e., War-
burton] very justly observe, that it was a very odd way of satisfying his Wife, to tell her
he should raise a preparation for War y.ᵗ should stain, i.e. cast an Odium on her Brother.
You therefore advise, Shall *staie* your Brother, i.e. keep him back from invading Me. I
read, Shall *strain* your Brother. i.e. put him to all his Shifts, lay him under such Con-
straints, that he shall not be able to injure Me." JOHNSON (ed. 1765): "*Stain* may be
allowed to remain unaltered, meaning no more than *shame* or *disgrace*." MASON (1785,
p. 281) agrees with Theobald but supposes "that *strain* means rather to *restrain* than
to *constrain*." MALONE (ed. 1790): "I believe a line betwixt these two [1712–13] has been
lost, the purport of which probably was, *unless I am compell'd in my own defence, I
will do no act that* shall stain, &c. After Antony has told Octavia that she shall be a
mediatrix between him and his adversary, it is surely strange to add that he will do an
act that shall disgrace her brother." RANN (ed. 1791–) prefers *'stain*: "Sustain, in defence
of him." SINGER (ed. 1826): "To *stain* is . . . used . . . for to *eclipse, extinguish*, throw
into the shade, *to put out*; from the old French *esteindre*." INGLEBY (1875, p. 96): "Compromise." FURNESS (ed. 1907): "Be it as offensive as it will, it still remains the word of
the text. Anthony's bearing towards Octavia is not deferential—hardly gentle." See textual notes and conj., p. 354.
    1714 DELIUS (ed. 1856): In that I permit you to act as intermediary, you have got
what you desired. BLUMHOF (ed. 1870): Everything else you may desire (i.e., travel arrangements) is up to you. RIDLEY (ed. 1954): "'So you have what you want'. But it could
equally well mean 'Granted that is what *you* want, and not something that your brother
has instigated you to want.'"
    1717 **You reconciler**] MALONE (ed. 1790): "Manifest error of the press." See textual
notes and p. 374.

As if the world should cleaue, and that slaine men
Should soader vp the Rift.
   Anth. When it appeeres to you where this begins,   1720 (yy1[b])
Turne your displeasure that way, for our faults
Can neuer be so equall, that your loue
Can equally moue with them. Prouide your going,
Choose your owne company, and command what cost
Your heart he's mind too.   *Exeunt.* 1725

         Enter Enobarbus, and Eros.   **3.5**

   Eno. How now Friend *Eros*?
   Eros. Ther's strange Newes come Sir.
   Eno. What man?

1718 should] would RLF1; shall YAL2
1725 he's] has F2+
1726 *SCENE* V. CAP+
    The same. Another Room in the same. CAP, v1778+ (*subst.*)
1727–37 *Three verse lines ending* Sir. . . . man? . . . *Pompey then as* F1 THEO1,
THEO2, v1773, v1778, RANN; *eleven verse lines ending* Sir. . . . made war . . . success?
. . . i' th' wars . . . rivalty: . . . glory of them; . . . letters . . . *Pompey.* . . . him,
. . . inlarge . . . confine. HAN1; 1727–31 *as* F1 *then seven verse lines* Cæsar, . . . wars
| 'Gainst . . . rivalty; | Would . . . glory: And | Not . . . letters | He had formerly
wrote (*or* He had Wrote formerly CAPN) to *Pompey:* seizes him | On his appeal; so . . .
up, | 'Till . . . confine. mCAP2, CAPN; *ten verse lines ending* man? . . . upon . . .
Cæsar, . . . Pompey, . . . let him . . . and not . . . had . . . appeal, . . . Death
. . . confine. KTLY

1717–19 **Warres . . . Rift**] WARBURTON (ed. 1747): "The thought is wonderfully
sublime. It is taken from *Curtius*'s leaping into the gulf in the Forum, in order to close
the gap [see PAULY, 4:1864–5 (7, 9); *OCD*]. As that was closed by one *Roman*, so it is
insinuated that if the whole world were to cleave, *Romans* only could *solder* up the chasm.
The expression is exact. For as metal is soldered by metal more pure and noble, so the
globe was to be soldered up by men, who are only a more refined earth." JOHNSON
(ed. 1765): "The sense is, that war between *Caesar* and *Antony* would engage the world
between them, and that the slaughter would be great in so extensive a commotion."
   1718 **that**] KITTREDGE (ed. 1941): "As if. *That* is often used to continue or repeat
a preceding particle or relative adverb (*if, when, though,* etc.)." See FRANZ §546.
   1721–3 **for . . . them**] CASE (ed. 1906), expanding DELIUS (ed. 1856): "*I.e.* for our
faults cannot possibly be so equally balanced as not to decrease your love for one or the
other in a greater degree." WILSON (ed. 1950): "Spoken resentfully, it seems, these words
are his own condemnation, and he knows it."

Ero. Cæsar & *Lepidus* haue made warres vpon *Pompey.*   1730
Eno. This is old, what is the successe?
Eros. Cæsar hauing made vse of him in the warres
'gainst *Pompey*: presently denied him riuality, would not
let him partake in the glory of the action, and not resting
here, accuses him of Letters he had formerly wrote to   1735
Pompey. Vpon his owne appeale seizes him, so the poore
third is vp, till death enlarge his Confine.
Eno. Then would thou hadst a paire of chaps no more,

1730 warres] Warre F2-JOHN1
    vpon] On HAN1
1733 riuality] rivalty ROWE2-THEO4, CAP
1734 in] of F3-POPE2, HAN1
    the action, and] action, and F2; them; HAN1
1735-6 Letters . . . wrote . . . appeale] letters Which . . . written . . . appeal
he HAN1
1736 owne] *Om.* CAP
1738-40 *Three verse lines ending* more: . . . hast, . . . *Antony?* mTBY2 *conj.*, HAN1,
CAP+
1738 would thou hadst] World! thou hast HAN1, CAP, MAL-COL1, COL2-KIT1,
CAM3-ARD2, EVNS; would thou hast PEN1; world, thou hadst mCOL1, MUN

1731 successe] See n. 421.
1733 presently] See nn. 835, 863.
    riuality] CAWDREY (1604, riuall): "One suing, and striuing for the same thing."
1735 had . . . wrote] For the use of the preterit form for the past participle, see
FRANZ §167.
1736 appeale] MINSHEU (1617): "*Commonly vsed in the Common Law for a priuate
accusation.*"
    seizes] CAWDREY (1604), possibly: "To forfaite to the prince." A legal term, now
technically written *seise.* See *OED*, 1.
1737 vp] RANN (ed. 1791–): "Shut up." RIDLEY (ed. 1954), agreeing, compares Richard
Brome, *The Antipodes* 4.12 (1640; ed. Haaker, 1966, 4.13.45–9) and Beaumont and
Fletcher, *The Island Princess* 5.1 (1620–1; *Works*, ed. Waller, 1910, 8:158). FURNESS (ed.
1907): "*Finished, done,* as in the current phrase, 'the game is up.'"
    enlarge] CAWDREY (1604): "Set at libertie."
    Confine] For the productive verb-to-noun conversion, see FRANZ §149.
1738-40 would . . . the other] MALONE (ed. 1790): "*World* and *would* were easily
confounded." THISELTON (1899, p. 18): "One form of 'r' in manuscript was very liable
to be taken for 'u.'" MALONE (ed. 1790): "The omission in the last line, which Dr. Johnson [ed. 1765] has supplied, is one of those errors that happen . . . when the same
words are repeated near to each other in the same sentence. . . . The compositor's eye
. . . glancing on the second *the,* after the first had been composed, the words now
recovered were omitted."

and throw betweene them all the food thou hast, they'le
grinde the other. Where's *Anthony?*   1740
 Eros. He's walking in the garden thus, and spurnes
The rush that lies before him. Cries Foole *Lepidus,*
And threats the throate of that his Officer,
That murdred *Pompey.*
 Eno. Our great Nauies rig'd.   1745
 Eros. For Italy and *Cæsar,* more *Domitius,*
My Lord desires you presently: my Newes
I might haue told heareafter.
 Eno. 'Twillbe naught, but let it be: bring me to *Anthony.*
 Eros. Come Sir.   *Exeunt.* 1750

1740 the] each HANMER *conj. apud* mTBY2, HAN1, RANN, COL, HUD1; the one the
JOHN1 *conj.,* CAP, MAL, v1793-KNT1, SING2, DYCE1, STAU-DYCE2, HUD2+
 Where's] Where is HAN1, CAP-v1778, COL, HUD1, WH1, KTLY, HAL
1748–50 *Three verse lines ending* naught, . . . *Antony.* . . . Sir. mTBY2 *conj.,* HAN1,
CAP-GLO, HAL+; *two verse lines ending* naught; . . . sir. KTLY

1738 **no more**] MALONE (ed. 1790): "Has the same meaning as . . . *and* no more.
Thou hast now a *pair* of chaps, and *only* a pair."
 1741 **thus**] Those who comment agree that Eros imitates Antony's manner of walking; BLUMHOF (ed. 1870) says that it shows his indignation; FURNESS (ed. 1907), his
impatience. WALTER (ed. 1969) alone: "Perhaps with his arms folded, the customary sign
of grief and frustration."
 1741–2 **spurnes The rush**] RIDLEY (ed. 1935): "Is it possible that this is not so appropriate to Antony in the garden [as all believe] as to Eros' illustrative action, kicking
the rushes on the floor of the apartment?" Most commentators, however, starting with
BLUMHOF (ed. 1870), regard the phrase as figurative, with *rush* signifying "trifle," and
compare *Ham.* 4.5.6 (2751).
 1743–4 **Officer . . . Pompey**] For the account of the deed by Antony's lieutenant
Titius, CASE (ed. 1906) cites Goulart's *Life of Octavius.* See p. 466. MACCALLUM (1910,
pp. 648–9) adds Appian (see p. 475), where the question of Antony's responsibility is
left open. GREY (1754, 2:205) paraphrases from Livy's *Romanæ historiæ* 112 (see tr. Holland, 1600, p. 1258), refers to Plutarch's *Life of Julius Caesar,* and (p. 206) quotes from
William Alexander's *Tragedy of Julius Cæsar* 2.2 (3rd ed., 1616, sig. 58ʳ).
 1746 **more**] JOHNSON (ed. 1765): "I have something *more* to tell you."
 1747 **presently**] See nn. 835, 863.
 1749 **'Twillbe naught**] Commentators are divided among "awkward" (RANN [ed.
1791-]), "of no value" (DELIUS [ed. 1856]), and "*bad*" (HUDSON [ed. 1881]). See also
3093, n. 1977. CAPELL (1779 [1774], 1:38) alone: "Has no relation to Eros' last words,
but means—the event will be naught; and is spoke with a look of much thoughtfulness,
and after a silence of some length." THISELTON (1899, p. 18): An example of "Enobarbus'
prescience," citing also 950, 1861, and 1977.

Enter Agrippa, Mecenas, and Cæsar.   **3.6**

Cæs. Contemning Rome he ha's done all this, & more
In Alexandria: heere's the manner of't:
I'th'Market-place on a Tribunall siluer'd,
Cleopatra and himselfe in Chaires of Gold   1755
Were publikely enthron'd: at the feet, sat
Cæsarion whom they call my Fathers Sonne,
And all the vnlawfull issue, that their Lust
Since then hath made betweene them. Vnto her,

1751 SCENE V. ROWE1-JOHN1 (–THEO); *SCENE* VI. CAP+
    Rome. ROWE1+ (*subst.*)
1752 this, & more‸] ~ , ~~ ; STAU, KTLY
1753 manner] matter F3-POPE2, HAN1, RID
1756 the] their mTBY2 *conj.*, mCOL1, COL2
1757 *Cæsarion*] *Cæsario* ROWE1-JOHN1 (–HAN1)
    Fathers] father F2

1751 **Enter . . . Cæsar**] Regarding the order of entrance, RIDLEY (ed. 1954) conjectures "that there may at some stage have been a brief interchange between Agrippa and Maecenas, covering the entrance and also giving Cæsar a point of departure for his statement, which at present begins somewhat in mid-air."

1752–91 WILSON (ed. 1950): "A good illustration of versified Plut[arch]." See p. 434.

1753 **heere's . . . of't**] CAPELL (1779 [1774], 1:38): Octavius "puts into their hands the dispatch he receiv'd it by." DEIGHTON (ed. 1891): "I will give you a specimen of his behaviour."

1754–6 **I'th'Market-place . . . enthron'd**] See, for irony, 928–9.

1754 **Tribunall**] HUDSON (ed. 1881): "In the Latin sense of *platform* or *stage.*"

1756 **the**] For the definite article for the possessive pronoun, see FRANZ §263.

1757 FURNESS (ed. 1907) discusses the testamentary adoption of Octavius by Julius Caesar; according to Plutarch (*Life of Brutus*, tr. North, 1579, p. 1065), he was the son of Julius Caesar's niece. VINCENT (1978, p. 193): "Shakespeare ironically alludes to this fact when he has Octavius irritably mention the son of Cleopatra and Julius Caesar . . . apparently not noticing that he also 'calls' himself the son of Julius Caesar."

Cæsarion] Ptolemy XV Caesar, the eldest son of Cleopatra, born in 47 B.C., and killeᴅ on Octavius's command in 30 B.C. See PAULY, Ptolemaios, 23:1760–1 (37); *OCD*, Caesarion.

1759–61 **Vnto . . . Queene**] MORRISON (1974, p. 118): "Authors seem to enjoy making a sort of litany . . . of the territories bestowed by Antony on Cleopatra (Jodelle [*Cléopâtre captive*, ed. L. B. Ellis, 1946, p. 69], [Act] I, 195–6; Garnier [*Marc Antoine*, ed. Pinvert, 1923], [Act] IV, p. 218 [for the 1592 *Antonius*, see p. 512]; Brandon [*Octavia*, ed. McKerrow, 1909], [Act] III, 1397–1412])." See also n. 1825–33. On the transcendental significance

He gaue the stablishment of Egypt, made her   1760
Of lower Syria, Cyprus, Lydia, absolute Queene.
  Mece. This in the publike eye?
  Cæsar. I'th'common shew place, where they exercise,
His Sonnes hither proclaimed the King of Kings,
Great Media, Parthia, and Armenia   1765
He gaue to *Alexander.* To *Ptolomy* he assign'd,
Syria, Silicia, and Phœnetia: she

1761–2 *Verse lines ending Lydia,* . . . *Eye?* ROWE3+
1761 Lydia] *Libya* mTBY2 *conj.,* JOHN1
1762 in] is F2-F4
1764 hither] were there ROWE1-THEO4; he there mF2FL21 *conj.,* JOHN1+
    King] Kings ROWE1+
1766 he] *Om.* HAN1
1767 Silicia] Sicilia F3, F4

---

of these and the following lines (1752–70), KNIGHT (1931, p. 248): "Antony and Cleopatra are here symbolically enthroned in love's regality."

1760 **stablishment**] MINSHEU (1617, Establishment): "*Assurance of* dower *made to the* wife *by the* husband *or his* friends, *before or at* mariage." Modern commentators prefer "permanent inheritance" (IRVING & MARSHALL [ed. 1889]) or "government, rule" (KITTREDGE [ed. 1941]). For Plutarch, see p. 420.

1761 **Cyprus**] COOPER (1565): "An yle in the sea called Carpathium, against the countrey called Syria: on the northe it hath Cilicia: on the south and the east, Aegipt." See PAULY, Kypros, 12:59–117 (1); *OCD*; and map, p. xxxvii.

Lydia] See n. 190. JOHNSON (ed. 1765): "For *Lydia* Mr. *Upton* [1746, p. 244, and earlier, Thirlby; see textual notes], from [the Greek of] *Plutarch,* has restored *Lybia.*" FARMER (1767, pp. 10–11) traces the "origin of the mistake" to Amyot and North. See p. 434. But MASON (1785, pp. 281–2): "*Lydia* was evidently what he [Sh.] intended to write; for . . . he gives the Kingdom of Lybia to [Bocchus]." See n. 1826 ("Lybia").

1763 **they exercise**] DEIGHTON (ed. 1891): "The athletic exercises take place."

1764 **hither**] RIDLEY (ed. 1954), expanding on WILSON (ed. 1950): "Very probably a compositor's handling of an MS. *hether* (cf. the frequent printing of *whether* for *whither*) so crowded that the space had disappeared; if so, Johnson's emendation is nearer the original than at first glance looks likely." But see p. 373.

1765 **Armenia**] COOPER (1565): "The name of two regions: *Maior,* and *Minor. Armenia maior,* hath on the north Colchis, Iberia, and Albania: on the weast, parte of Cappadocia: on the east, parte of the Hircane sea: on the southe, Mesopotamia, and the mountaine Taurus. *Armenia minor,* hath on the northe and weast part Cappadocia: on the east the noble riuer Euphrates, and *Armenia maior:* on the south parte, the mountaine Taurus." See PAULY, 2:1181–6; *OCD*; and map, p. xxxvii.

1767 **Silicia**] COOPER (1565, *Cilicia*): "A countrey in Asia, partely inclosed with the highest part of the mountaine Taurus." See PAULY, Kilikia, 11:385–9; *OCD*, Cilicia; and map, p. xxxvii.

Phœnetia] COOPER (1565, *Phœnicia*): "A region in Syria, next to Judea." See PAULY,

In th'abiliments of the Goddesse *Isis*
That day appeer'd, and oft before gaue audience,
As 'tis reported so.   1770
    Mece. Let Rome be thus inform'd.
    Agri. Who queazie with his insolence already,
Will their good thoughts call from him.
    Cæsar. The people knowes it,
And haue now receiu'd his accusations.   1775
    Agri. Who does he accuse?
    Cæsar. Cæsar, and that hauing in Cicilie
Sextus Pompeius spoil'd, we had not rated him
His part o'th'Isle. Then does he say, he lent me
Some shipping vnrestor'd. Lastly, he frets   1780
That *Lepidus* of the Triumpherate, should be depos'd,

1770–3 *Three verse lines ending* thus . . . insolence . . . him. HAN1, CAP,
v1778-SING1, COL1-COL3, WH1-CAM1, COL4-SIS, EVNS; *ending* inform'd. . . . already,
. . . him. KNT1, STAU, ARD2; *ending* thus . . . already, . . . him. DEL4
1770 reported˄] ~ , F2+ (−v1821, HAL)
1772–3 *Given to Mecænas* HAN1
1774–6 *Verse lines ending* receiv'd . . . accuse? POPE1+
1774 knowes] know F3-OXF1, KIT1, CAM3
1776 Who] Whom F2-SING2, COL3, WH1, KTLY, COL4, OXF1
1777 and] for HAN1

Phoinikia, 20:350–80; *OCD*; and map, p. xxxvii.
    1768 **th'abiliments**] ADLARD (1975, p. 325): Plutarch (see p. 434) "has Cleopatra in
'the apparell of the Goddesse Isis'. It is to Holland's version of the *Moralia* [1603, p.
1318] that we must look for the word 'habiliments.'" See n. 951–2.
    1770 **so**] DELIUS (ed. 1856): Referring to "In th'abiliments."
    1772 **queazie**] KERSEY (1702): "*Apt to vomit.*" Commentators prefer the transferred
sense found in VALPY (ed. 1833): "Disgusted."
    insolence] CAWDREY (1604, insolent): "Proude, disdainefull." BULLOKAR (1616)
adds "also strange and vnwonted." HUDSON (ed. 1881): "*Outlandishness*, aping of foreign manners; like the Latin *insolentia.*"
    1774–5 **people knowes . . . haue now**] CASE (ed. 1906): "*Have now*, etc., appears
to show that *people* is not a singular collective here." *Knowes* could be the plural form,
because *people* in Sh. otherwise always takes the plural.
    1778 **spoil'd**] MINSHEU (1617): "Waste, Destroy."
    rated] VALPY (ed. 1833): "Assigned." CASE (ed. 1906): "Apportioned by estimate,
a rare extension of the usual meaning 'computed', 'valued.'" See also n. 2100.
    1779 **does**] For the periphrastic *do*, here most likely for metrical reasons, see FRANZ
§597.
    1781 **of**] For the use of both *of* and *from* with verbs of freeing, discharging, deliver-

And being that, we detaine all his Reuenue.
Agri. Sir, this should be answer'd.
Cæsar. 'Tis done already, and the Messenger gone:
I haue told him *Lepidus* was growne too cruell,   1785
That he his high Authority abus'd,   (yy1ᵛᵃ)
And did deserue his change: for what I haue conquer'd,
I grant him part: but then in his Armenia,
And other of his conquer'd Kingdoms, I demand the like.
Mec. Hee'l neuer yeeld to that.   1790
Cæs. Nor must not then be yeelded to in this.

        Enter Octauia with her Traine.

Octa. Haile *Cæsar,* and my L. haile most deere *Cæsar.*
Cæsar. That euer I should call thee Cast-away.
Octa. You haue not call'd me so, nor haue you cause.   1795

1781–3 *Three verse lines ending* Triumvirate . . . detain . . . answered. ROWE1+
1782 being‸ that,] ~ , ~ ‸ ROWE3+ (−v1821, COL1, COL3, WH1, HAL, COL4, SIS)
1784 the] his F2-v1773 (−CAP); a mCOL1, COL2
1785 haue] *Om.* ROWE2-v1773 (−CAP)
1786 he] *Om.* F2-F4
1787 change:] chance‸ F2-F4; chance. ROWE
1789–90 *Verse lines ending* I . . . that. ROWE1+
1791 not] he POPE1-THEO4
1792 *with her Traine*] *Om.* CAP-KNT1
1793 L.] Lord F3-ARD1, KIT1-SIS, EVNS; lords BROOKS *conj. apud* ARD2, RIDb, ARD2

---

ing, cleansing, and the like, see FRANZ §509 and 1003, 2675. FURNESS (ed. 1907), however: "It may be observed from the punctuation of the Ff . . . that the compositor did
not recognize this idiom, but supposed the sense to be, as it is quite possible it may
be, '. . . Lepidus, he of the Triumvirate. . . .'"
    Triumpherate] FRANZ (§688) considers this a Shn. blending of *triumvirate* and
triumph. WILSON (ed. 1950, p. 124) considers it an excellent example of a Shn. spelling.
Yet Sh. was not given to serious coinages of this kind, and *OED* calls the spelling erroneous. See p. 375.
    1782 **Reuenue**] CAWDREY (1604, reuenewe): "Rents comming in."
    1787 **for**] I.e., as for, as regards. See also 3278. For this restrictive use, see FRANZ §483.
    1788 **Armenia**] See n. 1765.
    1793 **my L.**] DEIGHTON (ed. 1891) and almost all others: "Cæsar, ruler of Rome . . .
[and] the head of her family." Only BROOKS (*apud* RIDLEY, ed. 1954): "L. stands for
the plural. . . . Octavia thus greets both Maecenas and Agrippa—as she naturally
would—instead of only one of them."
    1794 **Cast-away**] In Sh., the three occurrences of the singular (also *Tit.* 5.3.75 [2579]
and *Luc.* 744) appear to be used, as WILSON (ed. 1950) points out, "for a 'ruined' woman."

Cæs. Why haue you stoln vpon vs thus? you come not
Like *Cæsars* Sister. The wife of *Anthony*
Should haue an Army for an Vsher, and
The neighes of Horse to tell of her approach,
Long ere she did appeare. The trees by'th'way   1800
Should haue borne men, and expectation fainted,
Longing for what it had not. Nay, the dust
Should haue ascended to the Roofe of Heauen,
Rais'd by your populous Troopes: But you are come
A Market-maid to Rome, and haue preuented   1805
The ostentation of our loue; which left vnshewne,
Is often left vnlou'd: we should haue met you

1796 haue you] hast thou F2-THEO4, CAP
     vs] me F2-POPE2, HAN1
     come] came F2-ROWE3
1799 Horse] horse' HUD2
1806 ostentation] ostent mTHEO2 (19 Feb. 1729, [fol. 40]) *conj.*, THEO, HAN1, CAP,
v1793, v1803
     1807 left] held mCOLL1, COL2, WH1; felt SINGER (1853, p. 293) *conj.*, HUD2

1798 **Vsher**] MINSHEU (1617): "*Is properly* one that keepes or opens a doore for entrance . . . *also vsed for* those that goe before the person of a Prince or great personage."
1804 **Troopes**] See n. 2886.
1804–7 **But . . . vnlou'd**] RICE (1968, p. 137): "In Caesar appearance merges with
substance. . . . Caesar neither recognizes nor feels any difference between the ostentation of love and love itself. For him, the act, the show, is the full reality." But for other
views, compare n. 1806–7.
     1805 **preuented**] COTGRAVE (1611, Prevenir): "*Anticipate . . . forestall.*"
     1806 **ostentation**] BULLOKAR (1616): "A proud setting forth to shew." THEOBALD (19
Feb. 1729, [fol. 40ʳ]): "We have an unharmonious Alexandrine here, & without any
Necessity. I read . . . *ostent.*"
     1806–7 **which . . . vnlou'd**] SEYMOUR (1805, 2:66–7): "'Which' must refer either
to 'love' or 'ostent'; if to love, what can be meant by 'love left unlov'd'? (perhaps *unvalued*). If to 'ostent', besides the tautology of ostent or ostentation left unshewn, what
is intended by its being also left unloved? (perhaps, as in the other case, *unvalued*)."
COLLIER (1852, p. 473) emends the second *left* to *held*: "Where the ostentation was omitted, it was often held, or considered, that love did not exist." LEO (1853, p. 320), pointing to the frequent use of the active for the passive voice, paraphrases as "seems unloving."
SINGER (1853, p. 293) emends *left* to *felt*, transposition being "a common accident at
press," and paraphrases: "When love is not manifested by acts, the neglect is *often felt*
as if we were unloved." LETTSOM (1853, p. 467) rejects *held* and *felt*, for they "should
require to read . . . '*unloving*', and this the measure will not permit. . . . The meaning . . . is often left *unreturned*." BLUMHOF (ed. 1870) regards the display as also a
means of evoking the love of the Roman people. DEIGHTON (ed. 1891): "It, (*sc.* love)

By Sea, and Land, supplying euery Stage
With an augmented greeting.
   Octa. Good my Lord,   1810
To come thus was I not constrain'd, but did it
On my free-will. My Lord *Marke Anthony,*
Hearing that you prepar'd for Warre, acquainted
My greeued eare withall: whereon I begg'd
His pardon for returne.   1815
   Cæs. Which soone he granted,
Being an abstract 'tweene his Lust, and him.
   Octa. Do not say so, my Lord.
   Cæs. I haue eyes vpon him,
And his affaires come to me on the wind: wher is he now?   1820

1811 was I] I was RIDb
     it] *Om.* WH2, NLSN
1812 On] Of mCOL1, COL2
1814 greeued] greeving F2-v1773
1817 abstract] Obstruct mTHEO1 *and* WARBURTON *conj. apud* THEO1, THEO1-SING1,
COL1-GLO, HAL-RID, ALEX, SIS; obstruction KTLY
1820–1 *Verse lines ending* Wind: . . . *Athens.* ROWE1+
1820 is he] say you, he is CAP

---

when denied the opportunity of showing itself, oftentimes ceases to be felt." RIDLEY
(ed. 1954): Possibly "*left*=written off as."
   1807 **should**] KITTREDGE (ed. 1941), expanding BLUMHOF (ed. 1870): "This does not
imply *duty*, but what would actually have occurred if Octavia had not come so privately."
See FRANZ §612.
   1808 **Stage**] KERSEY (1702): "*Station in a journey.*"
   1810 See n. 1160.
   1814 **withall**] See n. 253.
   1815 **pardon**] DELIUS (ed. 1856): Permission. DEIGHTON (ed. 1891) adds, "Excusing
myself for wishing to leave him."
   1817 **abstract**] CAWDREY (1604): "Drawne away from another." STEEVENS (ed. 1793):
"One of the meanings of *abstracted* is—*separated, disjoined*; and therefore our poet,
with his usual license, might have used it for *a disjunctive*." DOUCE (1807, 2:93–4) concludes: "The sense is obviously, 'Octavia drew away or *abstracted* Cleopatra from Antony.'" Some commentators, beginning with DELIUS (ed. 1856), believe the reference
is to "pardon for returne" (1815). Thus SCHMIDT (1874): "The shortest way for him and
his desires"; and THISELTON (1899, p. 18): "'Removal of an obstacle', or perhaps 'a thing
that completes connection.'" But most commentators follow THEOBALD (ed. 1733), proposing *obstruct*: "His wife being an Obstruction, a Bar, to the Prosecution of his wanton
Pleasures with *Cleopatra.*"
   1820 **on the wind**] SCHMIDT (1875), glossing this instance: "From every side."
DEIGHTON (ed. 1891): "By every wind, *i.e.* by every vessel."

177

Octa. My Lord, in Athens.

Cæsar. No my most wronged Sister, *Cleopatra*
Hath nodded him to her. He hath giuen his Empire
Vp to a Whore, who now are leuying
The Kings o'th'earth for Warre. He hath assembled,   1825
Bochus the King of Lybia, *Archilaus*
Of Cappadocia, *Philadelphos* King
Of Paphlagonia: the Thracian King *Adullas*,

1821 in] he is in HAN1
1822 wronged] wrong'd OXF1
1824 who now are] who now is mTBY3 (and he — is) *conj. and* mCAP2, CAPN (*errata*),
RANN; they now are mTBY3 *conj.* (and they are), mCOL1, COL2, KTLY
1825 He] She mCAP2, CAPN (*errata*), RANN
    assembled] dissembled F3, F4

1824 **who**] MALONE (ed. 1790): "Which two persons." For the apparent lack of concord, see FRANZ §§671–8.
1825 **The Kings o'th'earth**] SEATON (1946, p. 223): "The phrase comes like a refrain
in *Revelation*; on Cæsar's lips (its only use in the play), it sounds an exaggeration. . . .
The superfluous kings of Asia Minor are thus given an unmerited magnificence."
1825–33 For Plutarch's catalog, see p. 438. The first to point out Sh.'s confusion as
to the names is UPTON (1746, pp. 238–40). See also textual notes and n. 1759–61. WIL-
LIAMS (privately): "The manifest pleasure Caesar takes in rattling off his catalogue speaks
clearly his lack of interest in his sister's welfare; the catalogue has a keen dramatic purpose."
1826 *Bochus*] See PAULY, Bocchus, 3:578–9 (2); *OCD*.
    Lybia] COOPER (1565): "Was amonge the Greekes, the generall name of all Af-
frica: Not withstandynge it is of the Romaines taken onely for that parte of Afffrica, whiche
is from Aegypte to the west Oceean." See PAULY, Libye, 13:149–202 (2); *OCD*, Libya;
and map, p. xxxvii.
    Archilaus] In response to the charms of his mother, Glaphyra, Antony made him
king in 41 B.C., although he had rivals until 36 B.C. See PAULY, Archelaos, 2:451–2 (15);
not in *OCD*.
1827 **Cappadocia**] COOPER (1565): "A countrey in Asia, hauynge on the south Cilicia,
and the mountaine Taurus: On the easte, Armeny, and dyuers other nations: On the
north, the sea Euxinum: On the weast, Galatia: and is diuided from Armeny the more
with the famous ryuer Euphrates. In this countrey are bredde plentie of excellent good
horses." See PAULY, Kappadokia, 10:1910–17; *OCD*, Cappadocia; and map, p. xxxvii.
    Philadelphos] The nickname of the tetrarch of western Galatia, Deiotarus. See
PAULY, Deiotarus, 4:2404 (4); *OCD*.
1828 **Paphlagonia**] COOPER (1565): "A countrey in the lesse Asia, ioygning to Galatia, where dwelled the people called *Veneti*, of whom came the Venecians." See PAULY,
18:2486–550 (2); *OCD*; and map, p. xxxvii.
    Thracian] COOPER (1565, *Thrace*): "A region in Europe. On the northe it is bounded
with the lower Mysia, on the easte with the higher: on the south with the sea *Aegeum*:

King *Mauchus* of Arabia, King of Pont,
Herod of Iewry, *Mithridates* King   1830
Of Comageat, *Polemen* and *Amintas,*
The Kings of Mede, and Licoania,

1829 *Mauchus*] *Malichus* ROWE1-POPE2; *Malchus* THEO1-KIT1 (−ARD1); Manchus
mTBY3 *conj.*, CAM3+ (−SIS)
    King of] the King of KTLY
1829–32 Pont . . . Mede] *Medes* . . . *Pont* HEATH (1765, p. 459) *conj.* (Mede), CAP
1831 Comageat] *Comagene* ROWE1-GLO, HAL-ARD2; Comagenè KTLY; Comagena EVNS
1832–4 F1-RANN; *verse lines ending* with a . . . wretched, v1793-v1821, SING, HUD,
DYCE, KIT1, ALEX; *ending* Lycaonia, . . . wretched, KNT1 *etc.*
1832 The . . . Licoania] Of Lycaonia; and the king of Mede UPTON (1746, p. 240)
conj., RANN
    Kings] King F2-JOHN1 (−HAN1)
    Licoania] Lycaonia F2+

---

on the weast with *Bosphorus Thracius,* and *Propontis.* Therein is the citie of Constan-
tinople, sometyme called *Byzantium.*" See PAULY, Thrake, 6A:443; *OCD,* Thrace; and
map, p. xxxvii.
    Adullas] Mentioned by Plutarch (p. 438) but not in PAULY or *OCD.* The figure
may be Sadalas.
    1829 *Mauchus*] See PAULY, Malchos, 14:857 (3); *OCD,* Malchus (2). WILSON (ed. 1950),
finding F1's reading "an obvious misp[rint]," follows Amyot and North and reads *Manchus,* although admitting, "Plut[arch]'s name is Μάλχος."
    Arabia] COOPER (1565): "In hebrue *Saba,* is a countrey in Asia [Minor]." See PAULY,
2:344–62; *OCD*; and map, p. xxxvii.
    King of Pont] COOPER (1565, *Pontus*): "A great countrey ioygninge to the same
sea, which conteineth these realmes, Colchis, Cappadocia, Armenia, and diuers other
countreis." See PAULY, Pontos, Supp. 15:396–442 (2); *OCD,* Pontus; and map, p. xxxvii.
KEIGHTLEY (1867, p. 316): Probably "a proper name has been lost."
    1830 **Iewry**] See n. 2590.
    Mithridates] COOPER (1565): "A puissaunt kyng of Pontus in Asia, of great strengthe
both of bodie and mynde, and of singular memory." See PAULY, 15:2213–14 (30); *OCD,*
Commagene.
    1831 **Comageat**] COOPER (1565, *Comagene*): "A parte of Syria." See PAULY, Kom-
magene, Supp. 4:978–90; *OCD*; and map, p. xxxvii.
    Polemen] King of Pont from 38 to 8 B.C. See PAULY, Polemon, 21:1281–5 (2); *OCD,*
Polemon (1).
    Amintas] COOPER (1565, *Amynthas*): "Was the .xv. kyng of Macedonie." See PAULY,
Amyntas, 1:2007–8 (21); *OCD,* Amyntas (2).
    1832 **Mede**] COOPER (1565, *Media*): "A countrey in Asia, hauyng on the north, the
sea called *Hircanum*: on the west, Armenie the more, and Assyria: on the south, Persia:
on the east *Hircania,* and *Parthia.*" See PAULY, Media Provincia, Supp. 6:289–91; *OCD*;
and map, p. xxxvii.
    Licoania] COOPER (1565, *Lycaonia*): "A countrey in Asia. After some writers, it

With a more larger List of Scepters.

   Octa. Aye me most wretched,

That haue my heart parted betwixt two Friends,   1835

That does afflict each other.

   Cæs. Welcom hither: your Letters did with-holde our breaking forth

Till we perceiu'd both how you were wrong led,

And we in negligent danger: cheere your heart,

Be you not troubled with the time, which driues   1840

O're your content, these strong necessities,

But let determin'd things to destinie

1833 more] *Om.* HAN1, CAP

1834 Aye] Ah HAN1, CAP, MAL-KNT1, COL, HUD, SING2, KTLY, HAL

1836–7 *Verse lines ending* hither, . . . forth F4+

1836 does] doe F2-NLSN, KIT1, CAM3

1838 perceiu'd . . . wrong led] perceived . . . wrong'd mTBY3 *conj.*, CAP, STAU, DYCE2, HUD2, KIT1; perceiv'd . . . wronged mF2FL21 *conj.*, v1773, COL2, SING2, COL4; perceived . . . wronged mTBY2 *conj.*, RANN, COL3, KTLY; perceived . . . be-wronged DEIGHTON (1898, p. 41) *conj.*, BOAS, EV2

---

is a parte of Arcadia." See PAULY, Lykaonia, 13:2253–65 (2); *OCD*, Lycaonia; and map, p. xxxvii.

1833 **more larger**] For the double comparative, see FRANZ §217a.

1834 **Aye me**] *OED* (*int.* 2): "Alas! Ah me!—an ejaculation of regret, sorrow, pity."

1836 **does**] For the rather free choice of the predicate verb in a relative clause, see FRANZ §§678–9.

   afflict] KITTREDGE (ed. 1941): "Clash with, attack."

1837 **with-holde**] MINSHEU (1617): "*To* Detaine." See also n. 2904.

   our breaking forth] DEIGHTON (ed. 1891): "My giving vent to my anger by an attack upon him."

1838 **wrong led**] RIDLEY (ed. 1954): "Capell's emendation [see textual notes] assumes a compositor's error not so easy to account for . . . since . . . it involves the supposed insertion . . . of a space and two letters. . . . On the other hand it is impossible to be happy with F's reading. Not only does it produce a very awkward rhythm, but it makes it almost impossible to put the stress on *you* which is demanded by the contrast with *we* in the next line." Most editors disagree.

1839 **negligent danger**] Most commentators agree with CAPELL (1779 [1774], 1:39): "*I.e.* in danger from negligence." But CASE (ed. 1906): "Danger which we were neglecting." For the construction, see n. 2381.

1840 **time**] DEIGHTON (ed. 1891): "The circumstances of the time." WILSON (ed. 1950, Glossary): "Present state of affairs."

1840–1 **which . . . necessities**] Only DEIGHTON (ed. 1891) comments on the metaphor: "Of a tempest driving clouds across the serene face of the heaven."

1842–3 **But . . . way**] Proverbial; see DENT (G453): "Never *grieve* for that you cannot help."

1842 **determin'd . . . destinie**] DEIGHTON (ed. 1891): "But let things that are fated

Hold vnbewayl'd their way. Welcome to Rome,
Nothing more deere to me: You are abus'd
Beyond the marke of thought: and the high Gods   1845
To do you Iustice, makes his Ministers
Of vs, and those that loue you. Best of comfort,
And euer welcom to vs.   *Agrip.* Welcome Lady.
   Mec. Welcome deere Madam,
Each heart in Rome does loue and pitty you,   1850
Onely th'adulterous *Anthony,* most large

1845 Gods] God COL3 *conj.*, KTLY
1846 makes his] make his F2-POPE2, COL1, COL2, CAM3; make their mF4Q *and*
mTHEO2 (19 Feb. 1729, [fol. 40]) *conj.*, THEO1-JOHN1, v1773, v1778, RANN, KNT1,
HUD1-DYCE1, WH1, HAL, OXF1, RID, ALEX; make them CAP, MAL, v1793-SING1, COL3,
STAU, GLO, DYCE2-WH2, NLSN, KIT1
1847 Best] Be ROWE1-v1778, RANN
1848 *Agrip. . . . Lady.*] *Separate line* F4+

---

go on their way to destiny without your mourning them. It is possible, however, that
the construction may be 'things determined to destiny', *i.e.* on which destiny has resolved."
RIDLEY (ed. 1954) rejects the latter as "awkward in syntax and redundant in sense."
   1844 **Nothing . . . me**] DELIUS (ed. 1856) and others regard as an ellipsis: "*Nothing is more dear to me than you.*" Only BLUMHOF (ed. 1870) implies a vocative, comparing "Best of comfort" (1847).
   1845 **marke**] For the metaphor from archery, mentioned by commentators since
DEIGHTON (ed. 1891), see MINSHEU (1617): "*White, or pricke to shoote at.*" Also interesting is IDEM (1617, Marque): "The limits or borders, whereof comes our *English
Marches.*" See *OED, sb.*[1] 1.
   1846 **makes his**] CASE (ed. 1906) summarizes the essentials of the discussion of concord and reference: "*Makes* (plural) is probably correct . . . and its identity with the
singular form may be responsible for *his* of the folios; but if the reading had been *its*
instead of *his,* there would have been no doubt that Collier ([ed.] 1843), who retained
his, did right in referring it to justice instead of to *the high gods.* In [ed.] 1858, he meekly
accepted Singer's [ed. 1856] rebuke and objection that justice is not personified here,
and that if it were, *his* would still be inapplicable (presumably, as not feminine), apparently not reflecting that if *his*=its, as often, both objections are invalid."
   Ministers] See n. 2179.
   1847 **Best of comfort**] MALONE (*apud* STEEVENS [1783]) and most commentators:
"*Thou best of comforters!* [See] *the Tempest* [5.1.58 (2014)]." IDEM (ed. 1790) alone:
"Cæsar however may mean, that what he has just mentioned is the best kind of comfort
that Octavia can receive." STEEVENS (ed. 1793) and others: "*May the best of comfort
be yours!*" ROWE's (ed. 1709) emendation *Be* makes the easier emendation *Be'st* tempting, although Octavia is addressed with the familiar *you.*
   1851 **large**] BOSWELL (ed. 1821, 21:Glossary): "Not kept within bounds." CLARK &
WRIGHT (ed. 1864, Glossary): "Licentious, free. [Cites *Ado* 4.1.53 (1709).]" DEIGHTON

In his abhominations, turnes you off,   (yy1^{vb})
And giues his potent Regiment to a Trull
That noyses it against vs.
   Octa. Is it so sir?   1855
   Cæs. Most certaine: Sister welcome: pray you
Be euer knowne to patience. My deer'st Sister.   *Exeunt*

     Enter Cleopatra, and Enobarbus.   **3.7**

   Cleo. I will be euen with thee, doubt it not.

1854 noyses] Noses ROWE1-THEO4
1856 Most . . . you] It is most . . . you POPE1-JOHN1, v1773; Most . . . you, now
mCAP2, CAP
1858 SCENE VI. ROWE1-JOHN1 (–THEO); *SCENE* VII. CAP+
    Actium. ROWE1-JOHN1, CAM3, SIS; *Near* Actium. Antony's *Camp.* CAP-KIT1,
ALEX, ARD2, EVNS (*subst.*)

(ed. 1891) adds, "There may also be a play upon the word in the sense of *spacious, ex-*
travagant."
   1852 **turnes . . . off**] JOHNSON (1755, 37): "To dismiss contemptuously."
   1853 **Regiment**] CAWDREY (1604): "Gouernment, guidance, rule, or dominion." Following BAILEY (1730), JOHNSON (1755), citing this instance: "A body of soldiers under
one colonel."
     Trull] JOHNSON (ed. 1765): "It may be observed, that *trull* was not, in our authour's
time, a term of mere infamy, but a word of slight contempt, as *wench* is now." Despite
STEEVENS's (ed. 1778) illustrations in support of Johnson, many modern commentators
agree with RITSON (1783, p. 149), who was "certain, that *trull* . . . signified a *strum-*
pet," and MASON (1785, p. 282): "It was evidently the intention of Mecenas to call Cleopatra
by the grossest name he could think of. . . . La Pucelle is called, 'the Dauphin's courtesan, concubine, and trull' [*1H6* 2.2.28 (799), 3.2.45 (1477)]." MINSHEU (1617, Pusle):
"*Trull, or stinking wench.*" HALLIWELL (1868, p. 20) quotes Reginald Scot's *The discoverie*
of witchcraft (1584, pp. 521–2): "*Guteli* or *Trulli* are spirits (they saie) in the likeness
of women, shewing great kindnesse to all men: & hereof it is that we call light women,
truls."
   1854 **noyses it**] FURNESS (ed. 1907) alone: Rowe's *noses* (see textual notes) imparts
"a novel and coquettish charm."
   1857 **Be . . . patience**] CASE (ed. 1906): "Compare this circumlocution for 'patient'
with the scriptural 'acquainted with grief'" (Isa. 53:3).
   1859 **euen**] MINSHEU (1617): "*Plaine.*" BLUMHOF (ed. 1870): Settle accounts (*OED,*
a. 10b). KNOWLES (privately): "Have revenge" (*OED, a.* 10c), as in *Oth.* 2.1.308 (1082).

Eno. But why, why, why?   1860
Cleo. Thou hast forespoke my being in these warres,
And say'st it it not fit.
Eno. Well: is it, is it.
Cleo. If not, denounc'd against vs, why should not
we be there in person.   1865
Enob. Well, I could reply: if wee should serue with
Horse and Mares together, the Horse were meerly lost:
the Mares would beare a Soldiour and his Horse.
Cleo. What is't you say?
Enob. Your presence needs must puzle *Anthony,*   1870

1862–3 *One verse line* v1793+ (−WH1)
1862 it it] it is F2+
1864–9 *Five verse lines ending* we . . . reply; . . . together, . . . bear . . . say?
mTBY2 *conj.,* HAN1, CAP+
1864 If . . . vs,] Is't not denounc'd against us? ROWE1-JOHN1, v1773, v1778, RANN,
SING1, HUD1, KIT1-SIS; Is't not denounc'd 'gainst us? CAP, HUD2; If not, denounce't against
us, MAL, WH1; Is't not? Denounce against us, TYRWHITT (1766, p. 9) *conj.,* v1793, v1803;
If they're denounc'd against us, WORD1; If now denounced against us, DEIGHTON (1898,
p. 42) *conj.,* BOAS, EV2
1866 Well,] ~ ∧ HAN1
1867 Horse . . . Horse] horse' . . . horse' HUD2
      lost] lust ROWE
1870 presence] present F2

1860 KITTREDGE (ed. 1941): "Note the characteristic masculine impatience of
Enobarbus at what he regards as pure feminine unreason."
1861 **forespoke**] JOHNSON (1755), citing this instance: "To forbid." But IDEM (ed.
1765) and others modify to "*speak against.*"
1864 **If . . . vs**] The standpoints in the extensive discussion of these words may be
deduced from the textual notes. Omitting punctuation after *not* (or *now*) refers to denun-
ciations of Cleopatra or to war's (wars') being declared — see CAWDREY (1604, denounce):
"Declare, or giue warning of, or proclaime," and MINSHEU (1617): "*Proclaime warre.*"
Those with punctuation after *not* refer to *not fit* in 1862. HUDSON (ed. 1855) points
out that Plutarch mentions (see p. 438) that Rome declared war against Cleopatra; his
comment has been noted by only a few commentators and has not always been accepted
as supporting evidence.
1866–8 RIEHLE (1964, p. 84), classifying the speech as an "overheard" aside: Cleopatra's
response indicates that she has heard but not quite made out Enobarbus's words.
1867 **meerly**] MINSHEU (1617, Meere): "*Onely of it selfe,* not mixt." JOHNSON (1755):
"Simply; only." See also 1915, 2201, 2226. BLUMHOF (ed. 1870) suggests a pun on "mare-ly."
1868 For the same pun, see 548.
1870 **puzle**] KERSEY (1702): "*Confound.*" KITTREDGE (ed. 1941): "Paralyze. A very
strong word."

Take from his heart, take from his Braine, from's time,
What should not then be spar'd. He is already
Traduc'd for Leuity, and 'tis said in Rome,
That *Photinus* an Eunuch, and your Maides
Mannage this warre.   1875
    Cleo. Sinke Rome, and their tongues rot
That speake against vs. A Charge we beare i'th'Warre,
And as the president of my Kingdome will
Appeare there for a man. Speake not against it,
I will not stay behinde.   1880

Enter Anthony and Camidias.

    Eno. Nay I haue done, here comes the Emperor.
    Ant. Is it not strange *Camidius*,
That from Tarrentum, and Brandusium,

1871 from's] take from's F3-ROWE3
1872 then] thence WALKER (1860, 3:303) *conj.*, HUD2
1874 *Photinus*ᴧ an Eunuch,] ∼ , ∼∼ ᴧ DEL2 *conj.*, CAM1
    an] a SING, KTLY, OXF1
1876 their] there WARB
1878 will] will I POPE1-THEO4, KTLY
1880, 1882–3 *Verse lines ending* done: . . . *Canidius*, HAN1, CAP, v1793+
1881 *Camidias*] Canidius (*throughout*) ROWE1+

1874 **Photinus an Eunuch**] DELIUS (ed. 1856): In Plutarch (p. 438) *an Eunuch* is not
in apposition to *Photinus* but is a coordinate subject; the eunuch is Mardian. Evidently
an error in Plutarch, since the historical Photinus had been put to death by Julius Caesar.
BLUMHOF (ed. 1870): Plutarch used the Greek spelling *Pothinus*, which became *Photinus* in Amyot and then North. See PAULY, Potheinos, 22:1176 (1, 2); not in *OCD*.
    1876 **Sinke . . . rot**] For the optative subjunctive, see FRANZ §637.
    1877–9 **A . . . man**] For Plutarch, see p. 435. LLOYD (1959, p. 89), questionably:
"Bellona is the servant of Venus. That Roman contrast between love and war is in Cleopatra
a synthesis." MORRIS (1968–9, pp. 276–7) finds "this character in no way like Plutarch's
Cleopatra," but compares Queen Elizabeth "in the Armada year [addressing] her troops
at Tilbury." ADELMAN (1973, pp. 92–3): "Cleopatra on her way to do battle would have
been dressed literally as a man, in armor. At this moment, Cleopatra may enact the role
of her divine prototype [Venus Victrix] on stage."
    1877 **Charge**] WORDSWORTH (ed. 1883): "Share of the expense." KITTREDGE (ed.
1941): "A certain responsibility." See also n. 2528.
    1878 **president**] BULLOKAR (1616): "A chiefe Iudge or ruler." See also *OED*, *sb*. 1b,
and Precedent, *sb*. 1.
    1879 **for a man**] See n. 603.
    1884 **Tarrentum**] COOPER (1565): "A noble citie in Calabria." See PAULY, 4A:2302–13
(1); *OCD*; and map, p. xxxvii.

He could so quickly cut the Ionian Sea,   1885
And take in Troine. You haue heard on't (Sweet?)
   Cleo. Celerity is neuer more admir'd,
Then by the negligent.
   Ant. A good rebuke,
Which might haue well becom'd the best of men   1890
To taunt at slacknesse. *Camidius,* wee
Will fight with him by Sea.
   Cleo. By Sea, what else?
   Cam. Why will my Lord, do so?
   Ant. For that he dares vs too't.   1895
   Enob. So hath my Lord, dar'd him to single fight.

1886 Troine] Toryne F2+
1890 becom'd] become THEO2, WARB-JOHN1, COL, WH1, KTLY, RID
    men_∧] ~ . BLUM
1891 at] a ROWE2, ROWE3
    slacknesse.] slackness. Come, HAN1; slackness.— My CAP
1894–5 *One verse line* v1793+
1895 that] *Om.* v1793, v1803
    too't] *Om.* HAN1

   Brandusium] COOPER (1565, *Brundusium*): "A citie in the realme of Naples." See
PAULY, Brundisium, 3:902–6; *OCD*; and map, p. xxxvii.
   1886 **take in**] See n. 33.
   Troine] Sh. does not seem to have taken advantage of the wordplay in Plutarch
(see p. 439): "This word Toryne . . . signifieth a citie of Albania, and also, a ladell
[the shape of the city] to scoome the pot with: as if she ment, Cæsar sat by the fire side
scomming of the pot." See PAULY, Toryne, 6A:1809; not in *OCD*. See map, p. xxxvii.
   1887–8 The form suggests a proverb or axiom.
   1890 **becom'd**] For weak forms derived from strong verbs, especially in southern English dialects, see FRANZ §161.
   1891 **To . . . slacknesse**] BLUMHOF (ed. 1870) alone regards this as an independent
phrase, an exclamation of astonishment. HUDSON's (ed. 1881) grammatical description—a
"gerundial use of the infinitive"—is possibly less accurate than FRANZ's (§658) the nominative with the infinitive.
   slacknesse] WALKER's (1854, p. 20) suggestion, obtaining an extra syllable by
pronouncing "slackeness," is rejected by FURNESS (ed. 1907): "The pause necessitated
by the change of address supplies the rhythm." ABBOTT (§477), like Walker, conceives
of the pronunciation of *slacknesse* as trisyllabic. See textual notes and p. 354.
   1893 **what else**] SCHMIDT (1874, Else), citing this instance: "Of course." G. R. SMITH
(1974, p. 17, n. 16) alone: "Her . . . words cannot be her agreeing with Antony, partly
because no one has yet disputed Antony on the matter and partly because 'What else'
is in a class with 'Now what?' and 'What next?'—brief idiomatic forms connoting skepticism and irritation when used as expletives after the repetition of someone else's assertion."

Cam. I, and to wage this Battell at Pharsalia,
Where *Cæsar* fought with *Pompey.* But these offers
Which serue not for his vantage, he shakes off,
And so should you.   1900
    Enob. Your Shippes are not well mann'd,
Your Marriners are Militers, Reapers, people
Ingrost by swift Impresse. In *Cæsars* Fleete,
Are those, that often haue 'gainst *Pompey* fought,
Their shippes are yare, yours heauy: no disgrace   1905
Shall fall you for refusing him at Sea,
Being prepar'd for Land.
    Ant. By Sea, by Sea.
    Eno. Most worthy Sir, you therein throw away
The absolute Soldiership you haue by Land,   1910
Distract your Armie, which doth most consist

1897   this] his F3-ROWE3, OXF1
1899   serue] serues F3, F4
1902   are Militers] muleteers and HAN1
          Militers] Muliters F2+
1904   'gainst] against WARB
1906   Shall] Can CAP
1909   worthy‸] ~ , DYCE2, HUD2

1897 **Pharsalia**] COOPER (1565, *Pharsalos*): "A citie in Thessalie, nighe to the whiche was the great and sharpe battaile betweene Cæsar and Pompeius, where Pompeius was vanquished, and fledde. It is also called of Lucanus *Pharsalia.*" See PAULY, Pharsalos, Supp. 12:1038–84; *OCD*; and map, p. xxxvii.

1902 **Militers**] MALONE (ed. 1790): "The [F2] correction . . . is confirmed by the old translation of Plutarch: '—for lacke of watermen his captains did presse by force all sortes of men out of Græce . . . as travellers, *muliters*, reapers, harvestmen', &c. [See p. 439.] *Muliter* was the old spelling of *muleteer.*" WILSON (ed. 1950): "Minim error" for *Muleters*.

1903 **Ingrost**] BULLOKAR (1616, Ingrosse): "To buy vp all for himselfe." RANN (ed. 1791–): "Levied, collected."

Impresse] KERSEY (1702, *imprest*): "*Compell Soldiers to enter into the publick service.*" OED credits Sh. with being the first to convert the verb into the noun (*sb.* 2).

1905 **yare**] BAILEY (1721): "[Among *Sailors*] nimble, ready, quick, expeditious." See n. 924 and Plutarch's "yarage" (p. 439).

1906 **fall**] JOHNSON (1755, 24): "To happen; to befall."

you] The dative.

1910 **absolute Soldiership**] Like BLUMHOF (ed. 1870), KITTREDGE (ed. 1941) and others: "Perfect generalship; skill in land tactics." DEIGHTON (ed. 1891): "Unchallenged supremacy."

1911 **Distract**] CAWDREY (1604, distracted): "Drawne into diuerse parts." CASE (ed.

Of Warre-markt-footmen, leaue vnexecuted
Your owne renowned knowledge, quite forgoe
The way which promises assurance, and
Giue vp your selfe meerly to chance and hazard,   1915
From firme Securitie.
   Ant. Ile fight at Sea.
   Cleo. I haue sixty Sailes, *Cæsar* none better.   (yy2ᵃ)
   Ant. Our ouer-plus of shipping will we burne,
And with the rest full mann'd, from th'head of Action   1920
Beate th'approaching *Cæsar.* But if we faile,
We then can doo't at Land.   *Enter a Messenger.*
Thy Businesse?
   Mes. The Newes is true, my Lord, he is descried,

1912 leaue] leaving RID
1918 I] Why, I HAN1
   sixty] full sixty SEYMOUR (1805, 2:68) *conj.*, HUD2
   better] better hath KTLY
1919 Our] Come: | Our CAP
1920 th'head] th' heart F2-ROWE3
   Action] Actium F2+
1921 But] *Om.* HAN1
1922–3 *One verse line* CAP, v1778+

1906): "*Distract* had the senses 'confuse', as now, and 'disjoin', 'divide'. See [*distractions*, 1951, and *distract*] in *A Lover's Complaint*, 231. Schmidt [1874] assigns the latter here." Most commentators agree.

   1912 **Warre-markt-footmen**] Although Compositor B was fond of hyphens—there are 84 in *Ant.*—this construction is morphologically unusual, as is "Honour'd-gashes" (2659).

   1914 **assurance**] COTGRAVE (1611, Asseurement): "*Protection, safegard, or safeconduct.*"

   1915 **meerly**] See n. 1867.

   chance and hazard] Commentators make no distinction; apparently rhetorical repetition. Hendiadys is not proposed.

   1919 **ouer-plus**] CAWDREY (1604): "More then needeth."

   1920 **full**] See n. 74.

   th'head] COLES (1676, *Head-land*): "A point of Land lying farther out (at Sea) than the rest."

   Action] COOPER (1565, *Actium*): "A towne in Epyre, and an elbowe of lande liynge into the sea." See PAULY, Aktion, 1:1214–15; *OCD*; and map, p. xxxvii. WILSON (facs. 1929, Introd.) cites as evidence of Sh.'s nonchalant spelling habits: "What did it matter how he spelt a name in the prompt-book so long as it sounded all right on the stage? Thus he spells . . . 'Actium' 'Actiom', which not unnaturally appears as 'Action' in the Folio." There is no evidence that Sh. wrote *Actiom*; even if he did, there is no reason why there should be still another change to *Action*, natural or not. The *-ion* ending is the Greek form. See p. 374.

187

Cæsar ha's taken Toryne.   1925
   Ant. Can he be there in person? 'Tis impossible
Strange, that his power should be. *Camidius,*
Our nineteene Legions thou shalt hold by Land,
And our twelue thousand Horse. Wee'l to our Ship,
Away my *Thetis.*   1930

Enter a Soldiour.

How now worthy Souldier?
   Soul. Oh Noble Emperor, do not fight by Sea,
Trust not to rotten plankes: Do you misdoubt
This Sword, and these my Wounds; let th'Egyptians   1935
And the Phœnicians go a ducking: wee
Haue vs'd to conquer standing on the earth,
And fighting foot to foot.
   Ant. Well, well, away.   *exit Ant. Cleo. & Enob.*

1926 there‸ in person?] ∼ ? ∼∼ ‸ CAM3b
    impossible‸] ∼ . POPE1+ (−SIS, EVNS)
1927 be] be so F2-JOHN1 (−HAN1)
1930, 1932 *One verse line* CAP, v1778+

1925 **Toryne**] See n. 1886 ("Troine").
1926 **impossible**] SISSON (1956, 2:268) defends F1's lack of punctuation: "Antony has already allowed for the possibility of *Octavius* arriving, in this scene. What seems 'impossible' is that his whole *army*, and not only an advance-guard, should have arrived." Although *impossible* may be the adverb without an ending (see FRANZ §241) and although Sh. does use adjective-adjective ("impossible Strange") compounds (see FRANZ §242), both constructions seem unconvincing here. See textual notes.
1930 *Thetis*] STEEVENS (ed. 1778): "Antony addresses Cleopatra by the name of this sea-nymph, because she had just promised him assistance in his naval expedition." See PAULY, 6A:206–41; *OCD*. WILSON (ed. 1950): "She was often confused as here with her grandmother Tethys, greatest of sea deities, wife of Oceanus, mother of the Nile and other rivers." LLOYD (1959, p. 92): "In that case Antony was intended to give Cleopatra one of the names of Isis, for 'they say, that *Osiris* is the Ocean, and *Isis, Tethys* . . . the nourse that suckleth and feedeth the whole world' ([Plutarch, *Moralia*, tr. Holland, 1603] p. 1301)." See PAULY, Tethys, 5A:1065–9 (1); *OCD*.
1933–9 For Plutarch, see p. 441.
1934 **misdoubt**] MINSHEU (1617): "Mistrust."
1936 **a ducking**] MINSHEU (1617, *to* Ducke): "*Diue vnder water as* Duckes *doe.*" WORDSWORTH (ed. 1883): "Take to the water, like ducks." CASE (ed. 1906): "As a result of 'rotten planks' perhaps."
1937 **vs'd**] See n. 1064–5.
1939 **Well, well**] BARROLL (1969, *ShakS*, p. 227, n. 30), citing *MM* 1.2.58–62 (151–4):

Soul. By *Hercules* I thinke I am i'th'right.   1940
Cam. Souldier thou art: but his whole action growes
Not in the power on't: so our Leaders leade,
And we are Womens men.
Soul. You keepe by Land the Legions and the Horse
whole, do you not?   1945
Ven. Marcus Octauius, Marcus Iusteus,

1940 right] light F2
1941 his] the F2-ROWE3; this CAP
1942 Leaders leade] leader's led mTBY2 (leader's lead) *and* mLONG *conj.*, THEO1+
1943–5 *Verse lines ending* Land . . . not? ROWE1+
1946–9 *Given to Canidius* POPE1+

"Notwithstanding what you say, I have my own thoughts." Possibly proverbial; see DENT
(W269): "*Well, well* is a word of malice."

1941–2 **action . . . on't**] JOHNSON (ed. 1765): "That is, his whole conduct becomes
ungoverned by the right, or by reason." Anticipated by CAPELL (1779 [1774], 1:39) is
MALONE (ed. 1790): "His whole conduct in the war is not founded upon that which
is his greatest strength, (namely his *land force*,) but on the caprice of a woman, who
wishes that he should fight by sea. . . . [*On't*] refers to *action*." Most commentators
follow Malone, expanding (after SEYMOUR, 1805, 2:69) the scope to Antony's "general
conduct."

1942 **on't**] For *on* used after *win* and *grow* to indicate a gradual advantage, see FRANZ
§487 and 1021.

so] NICHOLSON (Wright Shakespeariana, no. 158 [11ᵛ]) believes "that '*so*' should
have a comma after it (if not,—) and that a depreciating jerk of the head and a look
in the direction of Cleopatra, or a pointing with the finger explained his meaning to
the audience."

leade] See textual notes and n. 2077.

1943 **Womens men**] Most commentators agree with DELIUS (ed. 1856): Servants of
women. TURNER (privately) suggests "sissies, milksops," citing *OED* (Woman 8): "A lady's
man, a gallant."

1945 **whole**] WILSON (ed. 1950, Glossary) collects the possibilities: "(*a*) undivided,
(*b*) healthy, (hence here of an army) unimpaired." See also 1948, 1964, 2659.

1946 *Ven.*] For the SP, commentators have offered explanations based on the incorrect idea that the text derives from a promptbook. See p. 376. COLLIER (ed. 1858): "Perhaps for *Vennard*, an actor in the part of Canidius." WALKER (1860, 2:185) holds that
the abbreviation stands for Ventidius and should be changed to Canidius. WILSON (ed.
1950): "Suggests doubling." TURNER (privately): "Could *Ven.* be a false start on the name
of one who is for sea, mistaken for a SP? Ventidius perhaps? See doubtful SP at 2015."

Marcus Octauius] One of Antony's commanders at Actium. See PAULY, 17:1825
(34); not in *OCD*.

Marcus Iusteus] Another of Antony's commanders at Actium. See PAULY, M. In-
steius, 9:1562 (3); not in *OCD*. Sh.'s spelling follows North's tr. See p. 441.

Publicola, and *Celius*, are for Sea:
But we keepe whole by Land. This speede of *Cæsars*
Carries beyond beleefe.
   Soul. While he was yet in Rome.   1950
His power went out in such distractions,
As beguilde all Spies.
   Cam. Who's his Lieutenant, heare you?
   Soul. They say, one *Towrus*.
   Cam. Well, I know the man.   1955

Enter a Messenger.

   Mes. The Emperor cals *Camidius*.
   Cam. With Newes the times with Labour,
And throwes forth each minute, some.   *exeunt*

1949–50 *One verse line* v1793+
1950 he was] *Om.* HAN1
     Rome.] ∼ ∧ F2+
1951–3 *Verse lines ending as* . . . you? POPE1-SING1, COL1-COL3, WH1+; *ending*
distractions . . . you? KNT1, STAU
   1955 Well,] ∼ ∧ ROWE3+ (−JOHN1, KNT1, HUD1)
1957–9 *Three verse lines ending Canidius.* . . . forth . . . some. ROWE1-GLO, HAL+;
two verse lines ending Time's . . . some. KTLY
   1957 cals] calls for HAN1, v1793, v1803
   1958 with] in mF4Q *conj. and* ROWE1, ROWE2-JOHN1, CAPN (*errata*), v1773, RANN,
ARD2, CAM3b
   1959 throwes] throes THEO, v1773, v1793+ (−COL, WH1, KTLY, ARD2)

   1947 **Publicola**] Consul in 36 B.C. and commander of a wing of the fleet at Actium.
See PAULY, L. Gellius Poplicola, 7:1003–5 (18); not in *OCD*.
   Celius] PAULY, Q. Caelius, 3:1256 (14) remarks that the name of this commander,
mentioned in Plutarch (see p. 441), seems to be a perversion of L. *Gellius* Poplicola;
not in *OCD*.
   1949 **Carries**] STEEVENS (ed. 1793): "Perhaps . . . from archery [quotes *2H4* 3.2.52–3
(1580–1)]." *OED* (9): "A bow, a gun, or the like is said to *carry* an arrow, a ball, or other
missile to a specified distance or in a specified way." Commentators are split between
"*passes*" (SINGER, ed. 1826) and "sweeps him forward" (WILSON, ed. 1950).
   1950–3 WILSON (ed. 1950): "Nothing of this in Plut[arch]."
   1951 **distractions**] JOHNSON (ed. 1765): "Detachments; separate bodies." See n. 1911.
DELIUS (ed. 1856) is the first to mention the tactical advantages of such ruses.
   1954 **Towrus**] See DP.
   1958 **with**] Citing the *OED*'s "efforts of childbirth," figuratively (Labour *sb.* 6b),
WALKER (1957, p. 96) argues that the repeated *with* is "contrary to Elizabethan idiom"
rather than a compositor's error, as WILSON (ed. 1950) and RIDLEY (ed. 1954) thought.

Enter Cæsar with his Army, marching.   **3.8**

Cæs. *Towrus?*   1961
Tow. My Lord.
Cæs. Strike not by Land,
Keepe whole, prouoke not Battaile
Till we haue done at Sea. Do not exceede   1965
The Prescript of this Scroule: Our fortune lyes
Vpon this iumpe.   *exit.*

Enter Anthony, and Enobarbus.   **3.9**

1960 *SCENE* VIII. CAP+
   The same. Plain between both Camps. CAP+ (*subst.*)
   1961–7 Ff; *three verse lines ending Torus? . . . Lord. . . .* Battel *then as* F1 ROWE1-
RANN, DYCE, WH, GLO, CAM1, HUD2, OXF1+; *four verse lines ending* whole: . . . sea.
. . . scroll: . . . jump. v1793 *etc.*
   1968 SCENE IX. DYCE, STAU, GLO, CAM1, HUD2, WH2, NLSN+
   Another part of the plain. DYCE, STAU, GLO, CAM1, HUD2, WH2, NLSN+ (*subst.*)

   1959 **throwes**] The great majority agree with STEEVENS (ed. 1793), reading *throes*:
"I.e. emits as in parturition. So, in *The Tempest*: '—proclaim [. . .] a birth [. . .] Which
throes [F1: throwes] thee much to yield' [2.1.229–31 (918–20)]." HUDSON (ed. 1855):
"In Shakespeare *throe* and *throw* are always spelt alike; so that it is not quite certain
which word was intended here." Thus RIDLEY (ed. 1954) and some recent commentators: "Theobald's emendation (or rather re-spelling . . .) has been almost universally
accepted [see textual notes], but it is less convincing on examination than at first sight.
. . . Here [as opposed to the *Tmp.* passage] the object is the thing born [not the person
in labor], and the image is that of a *series* of births, with no question of difficulty, as
of an animal producing a litter." Noting the lack of direct support in the *OED* for the
majority opinion, KNOWLES (privately) suggests *OED* (Throw $v.^{1}$ 6) in the sense of creating or fashioning by turning, with *Labour* (1958) referring not to birth but to work.
   1967 **iumpe**] JOHNSON (1755), citing this instance: "A lucky chance." CAPELL (1779
[1774], Glossary, 1:36): "Minute or critical Minute." CASE (ed. 1906)—supporting Johnson, who is followed by most commentators—notes the *OED* citation [not verified] of
Pliny, *Natural History* 2.219 (tr. Holland, 1601), for a contemporary usage. STEEVENS
(*apud* REED, ed. 1803) first noted the obvious comparison with *Mac.* 1.7.7 (481).

Ant. Set we our Squadrons on yond side o'th'Hill,
In eye of *Cæsars* battaile, from which place   1970
We may the number of the Ships behold,
And so proceed accordingly.   *exit.*

Camidius Marcheth with his Land Army one way ouer the   **3.10**
stage, and Towrus the Lieutenant of Cæsar the other way:
After their going in, is heard the noise of a Sea-fight.   1975
Alarum. Enter Enobarbus and Scarus.

Eno. Naught, naught, al naught, I can behold no longer:

1970 In] In the v1773
1973 SCENE VII. POPE, HAN1, WARB, JOHN1; SCENE X. DYCE, STAU, GLO, CAM1,
HUD2, WH2, NLSN+
    Another part of the plain. DYCE, STAU, GLO, CAM1, HUD2, WH2, NLSN+ (*subst.*)
1976 *and Scarus*] *Om.* ROWE3+

1969–72 WILSON (ed. 1950): "Thus Sh. gives Enob. a look-out whence to see the
battle." See also 2755.
    1970 **battaile**] MINSHEU (1617): "*Arraie.* G[allicum]. Ordre de bataille, Armée en
bon arroy." Plutarch (see p. 425) mentions Antony's making "his army march in a square
battell." See n. 2065 ("squares").
    1971 **may**] See n. 538.
    1973–4 *Marcheth . . . ouer the stage*] NICOLL (1959, p. 48): This formula applies
"to a stately procession, or to the walking across of one or more persons, passers-by, who
do not speak but are observed and commented upon by others." It may entail (IDEM,
p. 53) "a movement from yard to platform to yard again" or more likely (KING [1971,
p. 18]) "enter at one door and exit the other." WILSON (ed. 1950) adds, "It also conveniently marks the passage of time."
    1975 *going in*] I.e., into the tiring-house. Stage terminology for what is from the
audience's point of view "going out." See GREG (1955, pp. 122–4).
    noise] Citing HODGES (1968, p. 82), JONES (ed. 1977): "It probably involved gun-
fire from the cannon just outside the [Globe] theatre."
    1976 *Alarum . . . Scarus*] RIDLEY (ed. 1954): "F, though it has '*Enter Scarrus*' at
line [1981], also brings him in along with Enobarbus at the opening of the scene. This
is probably an example of the not uncommon 'anticipatory' S.D. (cf. [3574] and [3588])."
But for the copy for *Ant.*, see pp. 375–6.
    Alarum] FLORIO (1598, Al'arma): "*To armes or weapons. Also a march so called,
sounded vpon the drum or trumpet.*"
    1977 **Naught**] MINSHEU (1617): "*Ill* . . . Bad." Some commentators, beginning with
SCHMIDT (1875), modify to "lost, ruined." See also 3093, n. 1749.

Thantoniad, the Egyptian Admirall,
With all their sixty flye, and turne the Rudder:
To see't, mine eyes are blasted.   1980   (yy2[b])

Enter Scarrus.

Scar. Gods, & Goddesses, all the whol synod of them!
Eno. What's thy passion.
Scar. The greater Cantle of the world, is lost
With very ignorance, we haue kist away   1985
Kingdomes, and Prouinces.
Eno. How appeares the Fight?
Scar. On our side, like the Token'd Pestilence,
Where death is sure. Yon ribaudred Nagge of Egypt,

1978 *Thantoniad*] Th' *Antonias* POPE1-JOHN1
1979 flye . . . turne] flies . . . turns HAN1
1980, 1982-3 *Verse lines ending* Goddesses, . . . passion? THEO1+ (−HAN1)
1984 lost∧] ~ . RIDb
1985 away] way v1821
1988 like] *Om.* v1821
1989 Yon] You F2; Your F3-THEO4 (−HAN1)
    ribaudred] ribauld ROWE1-v1778, RANN, COL2, HUD, COL3, COL4; ribald-rid STEEVENS *conj. apud* v1778, MAL, v1793-v1821, KNT1, COL1, KIT1, CAM3; ribauded BLUM
    Nagge] hag mTBY3 *conj.* (*and withdrawn*), TYRWHITT (1766, p. 9) *conj.*, SING, COL2, COL3, COL4

1978 *Thantoniad*] POPE (ed. 1723): "*Th'* Antonias . . . (*which* Plutarch *says was the name of* Cleopatra's *ship.*)." See p. 438. SKEAT (1880, p. 312, n. to p. 207, l. 17): "The nominative case is rather *Antonias*; but we speak in the same way of the *Iliad*. Such words in English most often follow the accusative form of the noun; and occasionally, the genitive."
    Admirall] Plutarch (p. 438): "The Admirall galley"—i.e., the admiral's ship.
1980 **blasted**] MINSHEU (1617): "*Seared, or singed as trees or fruits.*" See also 2280.
1985 **very**] See n. 749.
    ignorance] DEIGHTON (ed. 1891): "Sheer folly." WILSON (ed. 1950, Glossary): "Stupidity (cf. *Lear*, 4.5.9 [2394])."
1988 **Token'd**] MINSHEU (1617, *a* Token): "*Note, or marke.*" JOHNSON (ed. 1765): "Spotted." STEEVENS (ed. 1778): "The death of those visited by the plague was certain when particular eruptions appeared on the skin; and these were called *God's tokens*. [Cites 'Lords tokens,' *LLL* 5.2.423 (2356).]" DELIUS (ed. 1856) cites "death tokens" (*Tro.* 2.3.187 [1384]). WALTER (ed. 1969): "They [spots] were known as God's tokens because of their resemblance to the halfpenny or farthing tokens issued by tradesmen, and the belief that the plague was God's punishment—the wages of sin."
1989 **Yon ribaudred Nagge**] This expression has launched numerous conjectures and interpretations, but also perplexity and speculation. COLLIER (1852, p. 473): "The line

is overloaded by a syllable." Most eds. who agree emend to *ribald, ribauld,* or *ribaud* to regularize the meter. Others attempt more elaborate improvements. STEEVENS (ed. 1778) offers: "*Yon* ribald-rid *nag of Egypt.* . . . It appears . . . from [John] Barrett's *Alvearie,* 1580 [also in the 1573 ed.], that the word was sometimes written *ribaudrous.*" HALL's *ribaldish (apud* HUDSON, ed. 1881) is similar. JACKSON (1819, p. 300) sees *ribaudred* as a corruption of the "French adjective—*rebours* . . . or low French—*reboured* . . . sounded as a dissyllable [in contrast to F1's trisyllabic form], which leaves the verse perfect." GOULD (1884, p. 64) suggests *ribanded,* and THISELTON (1899, *N&Q,* p. 361) "'riband-red', signifying 'red with ribands.'" PERRING (1907, p. 301) finds that *-red* "has got detached from its first syllable, which has been tacked on to *ribald.* . . . Briefly, in *red-nagge* I distinctly see *renegade, ren-gade.*" CAIRNCROSS (1975, p. 173), regarding *-red* as a "printer's pie," thinks that "the appropriate place for the pied letters would seem to be with 'Yon', to give 'Yonder.'" In contrast, RAY (1976, p. 21) prefers "to separate 'ribaud' and 'red' by adequate space," citing examples of Compositor B's spacing errors in F1.

Though the *OED* (12:114) lists F1's *ribaudred* under "Spurious Words," a number of commentators leave it unchanged and try to explain form and meaning. BECKET (1787, p. 131): "*Ribaude,* in the French language, is a *whore,* a *strumpet.*" SINGER (1851, p. 274): "Although we have not the participle *ribaudred,* which may be peculiar to the poet . . . *ribaudrie* and *ribauldrie* . . . indicates its sound and derivation from the French." BLUMHOF (ed. 1870) thinks that *ribaudred* is actually *ribauded,* i.e., the participle of a verb "To (ribauld) ribaud," which derives from both the French *ribaud* and the Italian *ribaldo.* FURNESS (ed. 1907) expands on Singer: "Ribauldried . . . is the very word, phonetically spelled, in our present 'ribaudred.'" SISSON (1956, 2:269): "*Ribaudred—ribaudered—ribaldered,* i.e. rotted by ribaldry and licence." EAGLESON (1971, p. 6): "Today, we tend to interpret past participles in a passive sense. . . . We need [here, however,] some such sense as 'full of ribaldry'. . . . The formative element [*-ed*] that takes a noun through a verb into a past participial modifier has a different denotation in Elizabethan English from Present-Day English."

The overwhelming majority of commentators—whether they suggest emendation or not—apply the epithet to Cleopatra. Its meaning concerns mainly her (and in rare cases Antony's) extravagance if not immorality. CAPELL (1779 [1774], 1:39), representing almost all editors before him: "*Ribald nag* . . . brazen hackney . . . calling her so in his anger, by reason of her forwardness and her prostitutions." JACKSON (1819, p. 300): "Cleopatra has appeared *obstinate,* to an excess, even in the manner of conducting the war. . . . To this *obstinacy* Scarus alludes." FRANCISCUS (1851, p. 465) suggests a praise of Cleopatra, "a queen celebrated for her beauty, her cunning, her debauchery, nay, even adultery." THISELTON (1899, *N&Q,* p. 362), comparing "Carnation Ribbon" in *LLL* 3.1.146 (911): "Cleopatra is a nag adorned with red ribbons rather than a war-horse." IDEM (1899, p. 19), conjecturing *riband-red*: "Cleopatra's red ribands . . . suggest the figure of the red plague to Scarrus." SCHANZER (1960, p. 22), comparing Enobarbus's speech at 1866–8: "The allusion here . . . exemplifies Enobarbus's dictum: just as it refers to a particular nag, Cleopatra, so it refers to a particular ribald (i.e. licentious) horse, Antony, whose utter loss has been brought about by her insistence that in this battle they 'should serve with horse and mares together.'" MIOLA (1983, p. 139) sees the same connection and finds that "behind this [Enobarbus's] fanciful figure and the 'ribaudred nag' lies Vergil's *Georgics* [3.209–17]" and also (n. 27) "Plutarch's mention of Plato's metaphor for concupiscence, the 'horse of the minde'" (which ADELMAN—see n. 578—associates with "Arme-gaunt Steede").

Only a few think the epithet refers to Cleopatra's numerous lovers or to Antony alone. POPE (ed. 1723) glosses *"a luxurious squanderer"*; STEEVENS (ed. 1778), more precisely, "a lewd fellow," quoting *Arden of Feversham* 1.1.37–8 (1592; *The Shakespeare Apocrypha*, ed. C. F. Tucker Brooke, 1908). He applies the epithet to Cleopatra's men and glosses *ribald-rid nag* as "Yon strumpet who is common to every wanton fellow." MALONE (ed. 1790) narrows *ribald* down to Antony only: "Scarus . . . means the lewd Antony in particular, not *'every* lewd fellow.'"

Some commentators discuss whether *nag* or *hag* (or *rag*; see p. 354) is the appropriate term for Cleopatra. Arguments for or against *nag* reflect conceptions of horses manifold and contradictory as regards nature, build, and age. Preceded by TYRWHITT (1766, p. 9), BECKET (1787, p. 131) suggests *"Ribaudred hag,* i.e. a woman who has been the property of several men; as was the case with Cleopatra"; he is backed by JACKSON (1819, p. 301): "Certainly, neither the age, sex, beauty, nor majestic stature of Cleopatra can warrant the term—*nag."* COLLIER (1852, p. 474): *"Ribald hag* is most appropriate to Cleopatra on account of her profligacy, as well as her witchcraft. . . . Besides, how was leprosy [1990] to afflict a *nag?"* LEO (1853, p. 325) ridicules Collier's argument: Of course Scarus does not apply *leprosy* to the *nag* itself but to the person who is likened to that nag, i.e., Cleopatra. HUDSON (ed. 1855): "The Poet meant to use the term *nag,* in reference to her speedy flight from the battle, carrying Antony off, as it were, on her back." He compares 1993–4. WHITE (ed. 1861): "So *Leontes* in his jealous fit exclaims, 'Then say my wife's a *hobby-horse'* [*WT* 1.2.276 (368)]." KEIGHTLEY (1867, p. 317): "'Nag', like *hackney*, etc., was used of unchaste women." DELAMAINE (1916, p. 8), however, seeing a connection between Cleopatra's tanned complexion and the *nag,* conjectures *brinded* (i.e., brindled) *nag.* HENN (1972, p. 123) compares "Dürer's picture of 'Death Riding': . . . the misery and dejection of the beast. Behind or before it [*ribaudred nag*] there is the horse-jade pun for a light woman, whose leprosy will, like Cresseid's, be the result of her promiscuity." Sickness is also stressed by RAY (1976, p. 23): "Calling Cleopatra a 'ribaud red Nagge' equates her with a plague spot. . . . She not only is seen in animalistic terms ('Nagge'), but she is depicted also in terms of a disease."

Most of the glosses on *ribald* or *ribaudred* overlap with definitions of *ribald, ribaudry,* or *ribaudrous* in such early dictionaries as HULOET (1552 and 1572), BARET (1573), COTGRAVE (1611), RIDER (1612), and COCKERAM (1623). The common idea is rudeness in appearance, words, or action. Accordingly, the meaning is almost always negative and associated with Cleopatra's (or Antony's) lewdness; only a few other characteristics—such as Cleopatra's obstinacy, beauty, vanity, and "feminine adornments"—are touched on. See also textual notes and conj., p. 354.

1989–93 **Nagge . . . Cow**] LLOYD (1959, p. 92), somewhat extravagantly: "If Actium shows us the values of Isis claiming an Antony they will destroy and remake, this hint is followed up and the process shown in little by replacing the Roman image of the horse with that of the cow, symbol of Isis." For further identification of Isis with the cow according to Plutarch's *Moralia* (tr. Holland, 1603) and *The Golden Asse of Apuleius* (tr. Adlington, 1566), see WHITAKER (1972, pp. 156–8). For a "series of equations: Cleopatra=a cow in June=Io=Isis=Cleopatra" derived from allusions in Rabelais, Virgil, Ovid, and Cooper's *Thesaurus,* see HUNTER (1969, pp. 236–9).

(Whom Leprosie o're-take) i'th'midst o'th'fight,   1990
When vantage like a payre of Twinnes appear'd
Both as the same, or rather ours the elder;
(The Breeze vpon her) like a Cow in Inne,
Hoists Sailes, and flyes.
   Eno. That I beheld: 1995
Mine eyes did sicken at the sight, and could not
Indure a further view.
   Scar. She once being looft,

1990 o're-take) i'th'] o're) i'th' F2-F4; o'er, i'th' very ROWE
1991 vantage] vantages KTLY
1992 as] of F2-ROWE3
1993 Inne] Iune F2+
1994–6 *Verse lines ending* eyes . . . not CAP, v1793, v1803; *ending* beheld: . . . not v1821, SING, COL, HUD, STAU, WH1, KTLY, HAL, OXF1, ALEX, EVNS
1994 Hoists] Hoist ROWE2
1995 beheld] beheld myself KTLY
1996 sight] sight of it CAP; sight on't v1793, v1803
1997 further] farther COL4

1990 **Leprosie**] JOHNSON (ed. 1765): "An epidemical distemper of the *Ægyptians.*"
STEEVENS (ed. 1778): "*Leprosy* was one of the various names by which the *Lues venerea* was distinguished. [Quotes Robert Greene's *A disputation betweene a hee conny-catcher, and a shee conny-catcher,* 1592; ed. Grosart, 1881–6, 10:232.]"
   o're-take] SCHMIDT (1875) notes the application of *take,* meaning "to seize, to attack," to diseases. Compare n. 3324.
   1992 **elder**] WILSON (ed. 1950): "And so the heir of victory."
   1993–4 **(The . . . flyes**] BARTHOLOMAEUS (1582, fol. 383ᵛ): "When she [the fat Cowe] is stong with a great flie, then she reeseth vp hir taile in a wonderfull wise, & stertleth [rushes], as she wer mad, about fields and plaines."
   1993 HUDSON (ed. 1855): "In this line, *her* refers to *cow,* not to *ribald nag*; the logical order being thus: 'Like a cow in June, the brize upon her.'"
   Breeze] MINSHEU (1617, Brie): "*Brieze, Horsefly, or Gadfly.*" JOHNSON (ed. 1765): "The *brieze* is the *gad fly,* which in summer stings the cows, and drives them violently about." CASE (ed. 1906) cites Ben Jonson's *The New Inne*: "Runns like a Heyfar, bitten with the Brieze" (5.3.4, ed. Herford & Simpson, 1938). BLUMHOF (ed. 1870) and others: A pun on *wind* and *gadfly.* THOMAS (1974, p. 24) cites a parallel metaphor in William Stevenson's *Gammer gurtons Nedle* (1575, sig. A3ʳ), in which "the cow's *tail* is her *sail,*" although "Bees" incite the cow.
   1998 **looft**] There is uncertainty as to whether *looft* (Modern English *luffed*) means simply, as in COLES (1676, *Loof-up*), "Keep the Ship close to the wind" — usually for the purpose of changing direction — or whether it already means the new direction has been taken and the ship is "aloof," or, as defined by MINSHEU (1617), "farre off." The ten-

The Noble ruine of her Magicke, *Anthony,*
Claps on his Sea-wing, and (like a doting Mallard)   2000
Leauing the Fight in heighth, flyes after her:
I neuer saw an Action of such shame;
Experience, Man-hood, Honor, ne're before,
Did violate so it selfe.
    Enob. Alacke, alacke.   2005

Enter Camidius.

    Cam. Our Fortune on the Sea is out of breath,
And sinkes most lamentably. Had our Generall
Bin what he knew himselfe, it had gone well:
Oh his ha's giuen example for our flight,   2010

2000 and] *Om.* POPE1-JOHN1
2010 his] hee F2+

---

dency is toward the latter, especially since STEEVENS (ed. 1778) points out that "this expression is in the old translation of Plutarch ['he was driuen also to loofe of'; see p. 442]." IDEM (*apud* REED, ed. 1803) adds, "It also occurs frequently in [Richard] Hackluyt's *Voyages.* See Vol. III. 589 [*Principal Navigations,* 1589; rpt. 1598–1600]." COLLIER (ed. 1843): "We may doubt if it be not put for *aloof'd,* and the meaning would then be, 'She having once borne away, or made off.'"

    2000 **Sea-wing**] *OED* (1), citing this instance: "*Poet. nonce-use.* Means of 'flight' by sea." JONES (ed. 1977): "Sails." CROFT (1810, p. 19), alone and questionably: "Two rows of long flat pieces of wood, which are suspended in the air when the vessel sails, and which they let down in concert when they are becalmed or have the wind against them."

    Mallard] VALPY (ed. 1833): "Drake." PHIALAS (ed. 1955): "Eager to follow his mate." HARTING (1864, p. 237): Such wildfowl, "as soon as they become aware of the approach of the enemy, ignominiously take to flight. [Quotes 'theres . . . wilde ducke,' *1H4* 2.2.107–8 (835–6).]"

    2009 **Bin . . . himselfe**] CASE (ed. 1906): "Literally, Been what he knew himself to be — another way of saying, acted in character, displayed the courage and skill he consciously possessed — or . . . *formerly* is implied in *knew,* as Delius [ed. 1856] seems to think, and the sense consequently, *either* Been the man he once knew in his own person, *or* Been the man he was once conscious of being." Delius compares Plutarch, p. 443; but Case, p. 444.

    2010 **his**] MAXWELL (1951, p. 337): "All editors accept F2's *he* for *his,* and this was undoubtedly Shakespeare's final intention. Thiselton's [1899, p. 20] view that *his* meant 'his general', i.e. Cleopatra, is absurd. It is possible that *his* was simply an anticipation of *ha's,* but surely it is more likely that Shakespeare originally wrote l. [2010] as complete in itself, with *his* meaning 'his flight'. He may then have decided that this was too compressed, or even changed course without a deliberate decision, and gone on to add the next half line without going back to change *his* to *he.*"

Most grossely by his owne.
    Enob. I, are you thereabouts? Why then goodnight
indeede.
    Cam. Toward Peloponnesus are they fled.
    Scar. 'Tis easie toot,   2015
And there I will attend what further comes.
    Camid. To *Cæsar* will I render
My Legions and my Horse, six Kings alreadie
Shew me the way of yeelding.
    Eno. Ile yet follow   2020

    2011–17 *As* F1 *but for* 2012-13 *on one line* ROWE, POPE1; *six verse lines ending* own.
. . . good-night | Indeed. . . . fled. . . . attend . . . render HAN1, CAP, v1778-SING1,
COL, SING2, WH1, HAL, RID; *four verse lines ending* own. . . . good night | Indeed.
. . . fled *then as* F1 v1773; *two verse lines ending* own. . . . indeed *then as* F1 KNT1,
HUD1; *five verse lines ending* thereabouts? . . . indeed. . . . fled. . . . attend . . .
render DYCE, STAU, GLO, CAM1, HUD2-NLSN, KIT1-SIS, EVNS; *three verse lines ending*
thereabouts? . . . indeed. . . . to't *then as* F1 KTLY; *five verse lines ending* own! . . .
good-night . . . fled. . . . attend . . . render ARD
    2012–13 *Marked as an aside* CAP, MAL, v1793-KNT1, HUD, SING2, KTLY
    2014 Toward] Towards WARB, JOHN1, v1773-SING2, COL3-WH1, KTLY, HAL, COL4, OXF1
    2016 I will] will I THEO3, v1778, RANN
        further] farther COL, HAL
    2016, 2019 *Exit marked by* CAP

    2012 **I . . . thereabouts**] DELIUS (ed. 1856) and the others (substantially): Is that
what you're up to, is that (i.e., flight) your idea?
    2014 **Peloponnesus**] COOPER (1565): "A countrey in Greece. . . . On the northe,
it hath the gulphe of Corinthe, Isthmos, and the sea of Crete: on the weste and south,
the sea Adriatike: on the east, the sea of Crete: so that it is almoste cleane enuironned
with the sea. In it were the famous kyngdomes of *Mycenæ*, of *Argos*, *Lacedæmon*, *Arcadia*, *Sicyonia*, &c." See PAULY, 19:380–91; *OCD*; and map, p. xxxvii.
    2015–16 RIDLEY (ed. 1954): "A very odd remark from Scarus. It looks as though it
must mean 'It's easy enough to get there, and I'll make my way there and watch events'.
But that is certainly not what Scarus does, and the last thing one would expect him to
do. See IV.vii [2621–46], viii [2647–93], x [2736–46] and xii [2752–2808] *post*. I wonder
whether all that really belongs to Scarus is a scornful aside, "Tis easy to't', and the rest
belongs to Canidius, to whose present frame of mind it is perfectly appropriate." But
the transition to 2017 would be awkward. KNOWLES (privately) conjectures that 2015
and 2016 could be transposed.
    2016 **attend**] COTGRAVE (1611, Attendre): "*Wait, stay, tarrie* [for]."
    2017–18 **To . . . Horse**] This expression may recall the formula of capitulation found
in Caesar's *Gallic Wars*: "Se suaque omnia Caesari dediderunt [Themselves and all their
belongings they rendered up to Caesar]."
    2018 **six Kings**] For Plutarch, see p. 440.

The wounded chance of *Anthony*, though my reason
Sits in the winde against me.

Enter Anthony with Attendants.   **3.11**

Ant. Hearke, the Land bids me tread no more vpon't,
It is asham'd to beare me. Friends, come hither,   2025
I am so lated in the world, that I
Haue lost my way for euer. I haue a shippe,
Laden with Gold, take that, diuide it: flye,
And make your peace with *Cæsar.*
Omnes. Fly? Not wee.   2030
Ant. I haue fled my selfe, and haue instructed cowards
To runne, and shew their shoulders. Friends be gone,
I haue my selfe resolu'd vpon a course,
Which has no neede of you. Be gone,
My Treasure's in the Harbour. Take it: Oh,   2035
I follow'd that I blush to looke vpon,
My very haires do mutiny: for the white
Reproue the browne for rashnesse, and they them

2023 SCENE VIII. POPE, HAN1; *SCENE* IX. CAP-SING2, COL3, WH1, KTLY, HAL, COL4,
OXF1; SCENE XI. DYCE, STAU, GLO, CAM1, HUD2, WH2, NLSN +
    Alexandria. *A Room in the Palace.* CAP + (*subst.*)
    with] *with* Eros *and other* POPE1-JOHN1, v1773, v1778, RANN
2034 gone] gone, be gone CAP; gone, I pray you KTLY

2021 **wounded chance**] JOHNSON (ed. 1765), although retaining the F1 reading: Perhaps "*The wounded* chase *of* Antony,—The allusion is to a deer wounded and chased,
whom all other deer avoid. *I will*, says *Enobarbus, follow Antony*, though *chased* and
wounded." See n. 2022. MALONE (ed. 1790): "A phrase nearly of the same import as
the broken fortunes of Antony. The old reading is indisputably the true one. [Quotes
3403-4.]" COTGRAVE (1611, Fortune): "*Hap, chaunce, luck, lot, hazard, aduenture.*"
2022 **Sits . . . winde**] CAPELL (1779 [1774], 1:39) and most others: "Taken from
field-sports. . . . Scents coming down the wind, or from game that sits or lyes in the
wind, are always the strongest." WILLIAMSON (1968, p. 424): "The image here involves
one of Fortune's most familiar attributes, her winds."
2026 **lated**] JOHNSON (ed. 1765): "Alluding to a benighted traveller."
2031 **my selfe**] FURNESS (ed. 1907): "Does this mean, 'I myself have fled', or 'I have
fled *from* myself'?" Although commentators have not answered the question, the former
seems more likely.
2032 **shoulders**] JOHNSON (1755): "The upper part of the back."
2036 **that**] I.e., that which. For constructions in which *that* is at the same time a demonstrative and a relative pronoun, see FRANZ §348.

199

For feare, and doting. Friends be gone, you shall
Haue Letters from me to some Friends, that will   2040
Sweepe your way for you. Pray you looke not sad,
Nor make replyes of loathnesse, take the hint
Which my dispaire proclaimes. Let them be left
Which leaues it selfe, to the Sea-side straight way;
I will possesse you of that ship and Treasure.   2045
Leaue me, I pray a little: pray you now,   (yy2ᵛᵃ
Nay do so: for indeede I haue lost command,
Therefore I pray you, Ile see you by and by.   *Sits downe*

          Enter Cleopatra led by Charmian and Eros.

Eros. Nay gentle Madam, to him, comfort him.   2050
Iras. Do most deere Queene.
Char. Do, why, what else?
Cleo. Let me sit downe: Oh *Iuno*.

2043 them] that CAP+
2044 leaues it selfe] leave themselves ROWE1-JOHN1
     the] *Om.* F2-F4
          Sea-side straight way;] sea-side. Straight-way ∧ JOHN1, v1773; sea-side straight
away; CAP
     2048 *Sits downe*] *Ad. Exeunt* Attendants CAP; *om.* v1773-RANN
     2049 *Eros*] *Iras* POPE1-JOHN1, v1773; *Iras, and Eros* CAP, v1778+ (*subst.*)
     2051–9 *Four verse lines ending* me . . . no. . . . *Char.* Madam! . . . Sir, Sir, my
Lord! HAN1; *five verse lines ending* me . . . Juno!— . . . fye! . . . Empress! . . .
sir . . . KTLY
     2052 *Char.*] *Cleo.* HAN1

     2041 **Sweepe . . . way**] See n. 422.
     2044 **leaues it selfe**] DEIGHTON (ed. 1891): "Abandons itself."
     2045 **possesse you of**] DEIGHTON (ed. 1891): "Put you in possession of." For this causa-
tive use, see FRANZ §630c and *OED* (8), which cites this instance.
     2047 **for . . . command**] JOHNSON (ed. 1765): "I am not master of my own emo-
tions." STEEVENS (ed. 1778): "I *intreat* you to leave me, because I have lost all power
to *command* your absence."
     2048 **by and by**] See n. 1378.
     2049 *Enter . . . Eros*] RIDLEY (ed. 1954): "There has been a general tendency of
editors not only to complete F's S.D. by the necessary addition of Iras, but also to change
it, by having Cleopatra led in by Charmian and Iras, with Eros following. This, I think,
misses the point. Not only is he the first to speak, so that his entry behind the other
three is awkward, but he has, one imagines, been instrumental in persuading Cleopatra
to come to comfort his master, and it is therefore appropriate that he should conduct her."
     2053 Although no comment has been found, it seems that Cleopatra is so much in
despair that she must sit, perhaps next to Antony.

Ant. No, no, no, no, no.
Eros. See you heere, Sir?   2055
Ant. Oh fie, fie, fie.
Char. Madam.
Iras. Madam, oh good Empresse.
Eros. Sir, sir.
Ant. Yes my Lord, yes; he at Philippi kept   2060
His sword e'ne like a dancer, while I strooke

2058 oh] *Om.* CAP
2059 sir] Sir, my Lord HAN1
2060 my Lord] *Om.* HAN1

2054 DELIUS (ed. 1856): Antony rejects Eros's attempts to bring him closer to Cleopatra. BLUMHOF (ed. 1870) regards the repeated *no* as referring not to the attempts at reconciliation (these come later) but to Antony's self-torturing brooding over his shameful flight, as also at 2056.

2057–8 The lines suggest a swoon. See the similar words by the same characters at 3084–5.

2060–5 CAPELL (1779 [1774], 1:39–40): "Bury'd in thought and sightless, without knowledge of what is said to him or where he is, he just hears a voice; replies to it, as it had come from some courtier or other great person, and relapses immediately into the same train of thinking that engag'd him before; nor is he wak'd out of it, 'till Eros (either raising his voice, or shaking him) says—'*Sir, the queen.*'" BLUMHOF (ed. 1870): The following words are not spoken to an imaginary third person but, along with the previous speeches, are part of a bitter dialogue with himself. Most commentators lean more toward Blumhof than toward Capell. SCHANZER (1956, p. 153) finds the description of Octavius in the Countess of Pembroke's *Antonie* (1595, ll. 1060–1: "A man, a woman both in might and minde, In *Mars his* schole who neuer lesson learn'd")—noted by MACCALLUM (1910, p. 57)—"somewhat closer" to Antony's words than WILSON's (ed. 1950) comparison of ll. 1088–1101: "A man who neuer saw enlaced pikes With bristled points against his stomake bent, Who feares the field, and hides him cowardly Dead at the very noise the souldiors make." For the 1592 *Antonius*, see pp. 504, 505.

2060 my Lord] STAUNTON (ed. 1859): "This kind of rejoinder, sometimes in play, sometimes in petulance, is not unfrequent in our old dramas." IDEM (1:413), in a note on *MV* 2.9.85 (1199), compares *R2* 5.5.67 (2734–5) and *1H4* 2.4.314–15 (1240–1). HUDSON (ed. 1881): "He is referring to Cæsar." KITTREDGE (ed. 1941), following FURNESS (ed. 1907), maintains that Antony "inattentively replies to Eros." KNOWLES (privately): "He is my Lord."

2061 His . . . dancer] JOHNSON (ed. 1765): "In the *Morisco*, and perhaps anciently in the *Pyrrhick* dance, the dancers held swords in their hands with the points upward." TOLLET (*apud* STEEVENS, ed. 1778): "The Goths in one of their dances held swords in their hands with the points upwards, sheathed and unsheathed." RITSON (1783, p. 149): "In these dances the sword-points are generally over the shoulders of the performers. Antony means that Cæsar stood inactive with his sword on his shoulder." But STEEVENS

The leane and wrinkled *Cassius*, and 'twas I
That the mad *Brutus* ended: he alone
Dealt on Lieutenantry, and no practise had
In the braue squares of Warre: yet now: no matter.   2065
    Cleo. Ah stand by.
    Eros. The Queene my Lord, the Queene.
    Iras. Go to him, Madam, speake to him,

2063 mad] sad mTBY3 *conj. and* HAN1
2066–70 *Three verse lines ending* the queen. . . . unquality'd . . . O! CAP; *four verse lines ending* by. . . . madam, . . . shame. . . . Oh! KTLY
2066 Ah] Ah me CAP

(ed. 1778) and most commentators: "Cæsar never offered to draw his sword, but kept it in the scabbard, like one who dances with a sword on, which was formerly the custom in England." He compares *Tit.* 2.1.38–9 (593–4). MALONE (*apud* IDEM [1783]) cites *AWW* "I . . . with" (2.1.30–3 [630–3]). See also n. 2186–7.

2063 **mad**] UPTON (1746, p. 297), objecting to Hanmer's (ed. 1744) emendation *sad*: "How agreeable is it to the character of the wild, undisciplin'd Antony, to call even Brutus *Mad*, the sober Brutus, the philosopher and patriot? Such as Antony look on all virtue and patriotism, as enthusiasm and madness." Starting with DELIUS (ed. 1856), most commentators do not mention Antony's character but do point out his appraisal of Brutus as, in one way or another, "an unbalanced enthusiast" (KITTREDGE [ed. 1941]). Developing a "hint" from WILSON (ed. 1950), WALTER (ed. 1969): "Perhaps Shakespeare momentarily confused Brutus with his ancestor Lucius Junius Brutus who feigned witlessness to save his life."

    ended] Normally, with *sword*, "killed" in Sh.—see *1H4* 5.3.9 (2900)—but here "defeated" since Brutus committed suicide.

2063–4 **he . . . Lieutenantry**] JOHNSON (ed. 1765): Means either "that *Cæsar* only acted as lieutenant at *Philippi*, or that he made his attempts only on lieutenants, and left the Generals to *Antony*." STEEVENS (ed. 1773): "Means only,—*fought by proxy*, made war by his lieutenants." Almost all commentators agree. MASON (1785, p. 283) adds, "Shakespeare represents Augustus in the next act, as giving his orders to Agrippa, and remaining unengaged himself [quotes 2577 and 2586]." MALONE (ed. 1790) cites Plutarch (p. 419). See also 1513–14 ("*Cæsar* . . . person").

2064 **Dealt**] In Sh. normally neutral in connotation.

    on] SCHMIDT (1875): "Denoting the ground or occasion of any thing done." FRANZ (§492): "*On the strength of . . . by*."

2065 **braue**] See n. 567. KITTREDGE (ed. 1941) emphasizes that "valiant" is not meant.

    squares] JOHNSON (1755, 6): "Squadron; troops formed square." *OED* (9), also citing this instance and following BAILEY (1730): "A body of troops drawn up in a square formation, either with solid ranks or leaving an open space in the centre." See also n. 1970.

2066 DEIGHTON (ed. 1891): "Help me; pretending that she is about to faint."

2069 **vnqualitied**] MALONE (ed. 1790): "*Unsoldiered.*" Subsequent commentary tends to define it in terms of personal condition, starting with RANN (ed. 1791–)—"rendered

Hee's vnqualitied with very shame.
    Cleo. Well then, sustaine me: Oh.   2070
    Eros. Most Noble Sir arise, the Queene approaches,
Her head's declin'd, and death will cease her, but
Your comfort makes the rescue.
    Ant. I haue offended Reputation,
A most vnnoble sweruing.   2075
    Eros. Sir, the Queene.
    Ant. Oh whether hast thou lead me Egypt, see
How I conuey my shame, out of thine eyes,
By looking backe what I haue left behinde
Stroy'd in dishonor.   2080
    Cleo. Oh my Lord, my Lord,

2069 Hee's] Hee is F2-ARD2
     vnqualitied] unqualified HUD2
2072 cease] seize F2+ (−HUD1)
2073–6 *Verse lines ending* offended . . . Queen. KTLY
2073 makes] make SEYMOUR (1805, 2:71) *conj.* (only, now can make), HUD
2075 A] By mCOL1, COL2
2079 backe] back, on ROWE1-KNT1, HUD1, KTLY, COL4

---

incapable of exertion, depressed, dejected"—and continuing to EVANS (ed. 1974): "Without his natural powers, not himself." F1's spelling *vnqualited* is conceivable but most likely incorrect, since the structure is *un* + *qual* + *iti* + *ed* and the two items are not normally homophonic. The *OED* credits Sh. with the first use.

    very] See n. 749.

    2071–3 See n. 110.

    2072 **cease**] HUDSON (ed. 1855) alone among editors does not disambiguate to *seize*, preferring *cease*, which "was not unfrequently thus used as a transitive verb, in the sense of to *end*, or *put an end to*." He quotes *Tim.* "be . . . deniall" (2.1.16–17 [633–4]), *Cym.* "I . . . life" (5.5.253–6 [3543–6]), and *2H6* "Now . . . cease" (5.2.43–5 [3265–7]).

    but] JOHNSON (ed. 1765) and most commentators: "*But* has here . . . the force of *except*, or *unless*." MALONE (ed. 1790): "*But* has here its ordinary signification. If it had been used for *unless*, Shakspeare would, I conceive, have written, according to his usual practices, *make* [see FRANZ §644]." FURNESS (ed. 1907), preferring *but* in the sense of "if . . . not"—already in CROSBY (14 Sept. 1880, [sheet 1, pp. 1–2])—cites FRANZ §566. For *but* as conjunction, preposition, and adverb, see FRANZ §287a.

    2077 **whether**] See 876 and n. 1504.

    lead] I.e., led (most likely a homophone). See CERCIGNANI (1981, p. 77). See also 1942.

    2078–80 JOHNSON (ed. 1765): "How, by looking another way, I withdraw my ignominy from your sight." STAUNTON (ed. 1859) and others: "How I *pass by sleight* my shame out of thy sight, in looking another way."

    2079 **looking**] I.e., looking at. For the absence of a preposition after the verb, see FRANZ §630.

Forgiue my fearfull sayles, I little thought
You would haue followed.
    Ant. Egypt, thou knew'st too well,
My heart was to thy Rudder tyed by'th'strings,   2085
And thou should'st stowe me after. O're my spirit
The full supremacie thou knew'st, and that
Thy becke, might from the bidding of the Gods
Command mee.
    Cleo. Oh my pardon.   2090
    Ant. Now I must
To the young man send humble Treaties, dodge
And palter in the shifts of lownes, who
With halfe the bulke o'th'world plaid as I pleas'd,
Making, and marring Fortunes. You did know   2095
How much you were my Conqueror, and that

2085 strings] string ROWE2-JOHN1
2086 stowe] towe mLONG *conj. and* ROWE1+
2087 The] Thy mTBY2 *and* mLONG *conj.*, THEO2+ (−COL1, WH1)
2089–91 *One verse line* v1793+
2093 shifts] shift ROWE2-THEO4

2082 **fearfull**] See n. 2543.
2085–6 **My . . . after**] For the image WILSON (ed. 1950) compares Plutarch (see p. 443) and, as was first noted by STEEVENS (ed. 1778), the Countess of Pembroke's *Antonie* (1595, ll. 439–40). SCHANZER (1956, p. 153): "Plutarch is closer." For the 1592 *Antonius*, see p. 490.
2085 **by'th'strings**] COTGRAVE (1611, Precordiaux): "*The heart-strings, or filme of the heart.*" OED (Heart-strings 1): "In old notions of Anatomy, the tendons or nerves supposed to brace and sustain the heart."
2086 **should'st stowe**] See p. 373.
2088 **becke**] FRIPP (1930, p. 100) detects a reference to Jove's "'nod' or 'beck.'" See also "nodded" (1823).
    might] See n. 538.
    from] For the sense "away from," see n. 1212.
2092 **Treaties**] JOHNSON (1755), citing this instance: "For entreaty: supplication; petition; solicitation."
2093 **palter**] KERSEY (1702): "*Prevaricate, or deal indirectly.*" OED (3), citing this instance: "Equivocate . . . deal crookedly or evasively."
    shifts] MINSHEU (1617): "*Subtil dealing.*"
    of lownes] Adapting RANN's (ed. 1791–) "condescend to," RIDLEY (ed. 1935): "Humility." But DEIGHTON (ed. 1891) and most others: "As those employ whose fortune is at the lowest ebb."
2095 **Making, and marring**] CASE (ed. 1906): "Nothing is commoner than the collocation of *make* and *mar*, and 'To make *or* mar' is a proverbial phrase. [See DENT (M48).] Yet, in conjunction with 'play'd' (line [2094]), there seems to be an allusion here to a

My Sword, made weake by my affection, would
Obey it on all cause.
    Cleo. Pardon, pardon.
    Ant. Fall not a teare I say, one of them rates   2100
All that is wonne and lost: Giue me a kisse,
Euen this repayes me.
We sent our Schoolemaster, is a come backe?
Loue I am full of Lead: some Wine
Within there, and our Viands: Fortune knowes,   2105
We scorne her most, when most she offers blowes.   *Exeunt*

Enter Cæsar, Agrippa, and Dollabello, with others.   **3.12**

2098 cause] causes CAP, HUD2

2099 Pardon] O, pardon THEO1-JOHN1, v1793-SING1, HUD1, KTLY

2102-5 *Three verse lines ending* schoolmaster, . . . lead; . . . knows, HAN1, CAP, v1778-KIT1, CAM3a, ALEX-ARD2, EVNS; *four verse lines ending* me. . . . back? . . . lead. . . . knows CAM3b

2102 me] *Om.* F2-ROWE3

2105 Within] *Om.* HAN1, CAP, v1778, RANN

2107 SCENE VII. ROWE; SCENE VIII. POPE (*see* 2023), WARB, JOHN1; SCENE IX. HAN1; *SCENE* X. CAP-SING2, COL3, WH1, KTLY, HAL, COL4, OXF1; SCENE XII. DYCE, STAU, GLO, CAM1, HUD2, WH2, NLSN+
        Cæsar's Camp. ROWE1-JOHN1; A Camp in Egypt. Cæsar's Tent. CAP+ (subst.)
        Agrippa] Agrippa, Thidias ROWE1-JOHN1, NLSN, KIT1+ (subst.); THYREUS CAP-OXF1, ARD1, RID

---

game of some kind. [William Lowes] Rushton, *Shakespeare Illustrated by the Lex Scripta* (1870), p. 57, cites [*2 and 3 Philip and Mary*, Ch. 9]: '. . . places for bowling, tennis, dicing, white and black, *making and marring*, and other unlawful games prohibited by the laws and statutes of this realm' [*Statutes of the Realm*, ed. Luders, 1810–28, 4:285]."

2097 **affection**] See n. 538.

2100 **Fall**] DELIUS (ed. 1856) and others paraphrase as "let fall," regarding the verb as transitive. FRANZ (§630c), however, regards the usage as causative, with *tear* as subject.
        rates] RANN (ed. 1791-): "Is equivalent to." See n. 1778.

2102 **Euen**] SCHMIDT (1874, 5): "Like the adj. *very*, sometimes=mere, alone." For this emphatic use, see FRANZ §438.

2103 **Schoolemaster**] See DP (Euphronius) and for Plutarch, p. 447.
        a] I.e., he. See n. 1439.

2104 **Loue . . . Lead**] Proverbial; see DENT (L134): "As heavy as *lead*."

2105 **Within there**] DELIUS (ed. 1856): A call to the servants inside the palace.

2105-6 **Fortune . . . blowes**] The form suggests an axiom.

2107 COLLIER (ed. 1843): "The . . . stage-direction includes the name of Agrippa,

Cæs. Let him appeare that's come from *Anthony.*
Know you him.
    Dolla. Cæsar, 'tis his Schoolemaster,   2110   (yy2^vb)
An argument that he is pluckt, when hither
He sends so poore a Pinnion of his Wing,
Which had superfluous Kings for Messengers,
Not many Moones gone by.

Enter Ambassador from Anthony.   2115

    Cæsar. Approach, and speake.
    Amb. Such as I am, I come from *Anthony*:
I was of late as petty to his ends,
As is the Morne-dew on the Mertle leafe
To his grand Sea.   2120
    Cæs. Bee't so, declare thine office.
    Amb. Lord of his Fortunes he salutes thee, and
Requires to liue in Egypt, which not granted

2108 from] for F2-F4

2115 *Ambassador*] EUPHRONIUS (*throughout*) CAP, v1803-KIT1, ALEX (*subst.*)

2120 his] the mF4Q, mTBY3 *conj.*, *and* HAN1, JOHN1, WH1, HUD2; this mTHEO2 (21 Feb. 1729, [fol. 40]; *withdrawn* 18 Nov. 1731, [fol. 86]), mTYR *conj.*, KTLY

---

but he does not appear [in the scene]." RIDLEY (ed. 1954): "Shakespeare not infrequently includes a non-speaker, either (perhaps) because he at first intended him to speak and then forgot or changed his mind, or (as more probably here) because it was natural for the character to be there."

2113 **Which**] See n. 389.

2118 **to**] I.e., compared to. See FRANZ §529.

2119–20 THEOBALD (19 Feb. 1729, [fol. 40^r]): "The Sea that might skirt one Side of Cæsar's Camp." IDEM (18 Nov. 1731, [fol. 86^r]): "That great *Flood* & *Confluence* of Allies & Depen[dants that follow'd] Anthony." STEEVENS (ed. 1778): "The sea from which the dew-drop is exhaled. Shakespeare might have considered the sea as the source of dews as well as rain [an idea found earlier in CAPELL (1779 [1774], 1:40)]." RIDLEY (ed. 1935): "The grand sea, which is what Antony is in comparison with me." WALTER (ed. 1969) cites *Rom.* 2.2.133–4 (934–5) and *TN* 1.1.9–11 (13–15) "for the association of the sea with the greatness of love."

2119 **Mertle**] WALTER (ed. 1969) alone: "The emblem of love sacred to Venus."

2120 **his**] STEEVENS (ed. 1778): "*His* is used instead of *its.*" WORDSWORTH (1864, pp. 16–18) agrees, holding that "'it' . . . was indebted for its declension to the pronouns masculine and feminine of the same person, and instead of *its,* *his* and *hers* were used with reference to a thing spoken of." See also n. 3163 ("his") and FRANZ §320.

2123 **Requires**] MINSHEU (1617, Request): "*Require.*" HUDSON (ed. 1881): "To *require* and to *request* were formerly synonymous." See also 780, 2141, 2232.

He Lessons his Requests, and to thee sues
To let him breath betweene the Heauens and Earth   2125
A priuate man in Athens: this for him.
Next, *Cleopatra* does confesse thy Greatnesse,
Submits her to thy might, and of thee craues
The Circle of the *Ptolomies* for her heyres,
Now hazarded to thy Grace.   2130
  Cæs. For *Anthony*,
I haue no eares to his request. The Queene,
Of Audience, nor Desire shall faile, so shee
From Egypt driue her all-disgraced Friend,
Or take his life there. This if shee performe,   2135
She shall not sue vnheard. So to them both.
  Amb. Fortune pursue thee.
  Cæs. Bring him through the Bands:
To try thy Eloquence, now 'tis time, dispatch,

2124 Lessons] Lessens F2-ALEX, ARD2
2138 *Exit Ambassador.* ROWE1+

2124 **Lessons**] Although almost all editions emend to *lessens*, none explains why. Only DEY (1908, p. 424) argues that "'Requests' . . . denotes a product which Antony, in obedience to Caesar's pleasure, properly 'lessens.'" THISELTON (1899, p. 20), followed by only a few, disagrees: "'Lessons' is undoubtedly Shakespeare's word here in the sense of 'schools' or 'disciplines'. . . . The ambassador is . . . a schoolmaster."

2126 **A . . . Athens**] BARROLL (1969, *ShakS*, p. 230, n. 45): Appian contains "suggestive parallelisms in the section [*Auncient Historie*, 1578, p. 311] glossed '*Antony* priuate'. The hero 'tarried the winter' with Cleopatra in Egypt after he first met her, living 'lyke a priuate man in an other mans kingdome. . . . And leauing all cares of a Captaine, he put on a *Greekes* robe, and such a garment, as the *Athenienses* and *Egiptians* Priestes do vse. And he resorted onely to temples, scooles, and assemblies of Philosophers, keping company with the Grecians that obeyed *Cleopatra*.'"

2128 **her**] For the simple pronoun used reflexively, see FRANZ §307.

2129 **Circle**] JOHNSON (ed. 1765): "The diadem; the ensign of royalty."

2130 **hazarded to**] RANN (ed. 1791–): "Subject to . . . dependant on." DELIUS (ed. 1856): By chance subject to. BLUMHOF (ed. 1870): Subject uncertainly to. SCHMIDT (1874), glossing this instance: "Staked and lost . . . as at gaming." KITTREDGE (ed. 1941): "Lost, but for the chance [of]." WALTER (ed. 1969) alone: "Derived from tennis where a player won a point by driving the ball into his opponent's 'hazard', a hole or gallery in the wall. The original stake was usually a couronne (crown)."

2133 **Audience**] For the occasional absence of the negative (*neither*) before this first correlative, see FRANZ §587b.

  so] Provided that, if (FRANZ §565).

2134 **all-disgraced**] For *all* as intensifier meaning "completely," see FRANZ §371.

2138 **Bands**] CAWDREY (1604, band): "Company of men."

From *Anthony* winne *Cleopatra*, promise   2140
And in our Name, what she requires, adde more
From thine inuention, offers. Women are not
In their best Fortunes strong; but want will periure
The ne're touch'd Vestall. Try thy cunning *Thidias*,
Make thine owne Edict for thy paines, which we   2145
Will answer as a Law.
   Thid. *Cæsar,* I go.
   Cæsar. Obserue how *Anthony* becomes his flaw,
And what thou think'st his very action speakes
In euery power that mooues.   2150
   Thid. *Cæsar,* I shall.   *exeunt.*

2140 promise] *Om.* ROWE2, ROWE3; promise; THEO, WARB
2141 Name, what] Name, when F2-THEO2, WARB-JOHN1; name; when HAN1
    adde] and WALKER (1860, 1:253) *conj.*, WORD1, CAM3a
2142 From . . . offers] As thine invention offers HAN1, CAM3b; Offers from thine
invention mF2FL21 *conj.*, KTLY, HUD2; From thine invention, offer WHALEY *conj. apud*
mTBY2, WORD1, CAM3a
2144 *Thidias*] *Thyreus* (*throughout*) THEO1-KIT1, ALEX
2145 Edict] edicts RID

2141 **requires**] See n. 2123.
2141–2 **adde . . . offers**] DEIGHTON (ed. 1891): "The position of *offers* seems to
be intentionally emphatic." See textual notes and conj., p. 355.
2144 **ne're touch'd Vestall**] UPTON (1748, p. 305): Sh. "makes Latin words English,
and uses them according to their original idiom and latitude. . . . [p. 307] So Horace
calls Pallas, I. Ode. 7. *Intacta* [l. 5]."
    cunning] See n. 244.
    Thidias] See DP and p. 374.
2145–6 Like BLUMHOF (ed. 1870), DEIGHTON (ed. 1891) and most others: "Fix your
own reward, if you succeed, and I will consider its payment as binding upon me as a
law. Edicts at Rome were rules promulgated by magistrates upon entry into office; and
when the practice became common of magistrates adopting the edicts of their predecessors, these edicts practically had the force of ordinary laws." Only WALTER (ed. 1969)
disagrees: "Cæsar is giving Thidias a free hand to make offers, 'edict' is not a statement
of costs or valuation."
2148 **becomes his flaw**] JOHNSON (ed. 1765) and most others: "Conforms himself
to this breach of his fortune." Colloquially, WILSON (ed. 1950): "Carries off his little
lapse, i.e. his flight."
2150 **power**] DELIUS (ed. 1856) and others: (Bodily) organ. Since DEIGHTON (ed.
1891), most commentators expand to "bodily and mental faculties."
2151 **I shall**] ABBOTT (§315): "'I *shall*' has a trace of its old meaning, 'I ought': or
perhaps there is a mixture of 'I am bound to' and 'I am sure to'. Hence it is often used
in the replies of inferiors to superiors." See also 2580, 3189.

Enter Cleopatra, Enobarbus, Charmian, & Iras.   **3.13**

Cleo. What shall we do, *Enobarbus?*
Eno. Thinke, and dye.
Cleo. Is *Anthony,* or we in fault for this?   2155
Eno. Anthony onely, that would make his will
Lord of his Reason. What though you fled,
From that great face of Warre, whose seuerall ranges
Frighted each other? Why should he follow?
The itch of his Affection should not then   2160
Haue nickt his Captain-ship, at such a point,

2152 SCENE VIII. ROWE; SCENE IX. POPE, WARB, JOHN1; SCENE X. HAN1; *SCENE* XI. CAP-SING2, COL3, WH1, KTLY, HAL, COL4, OXF1; SCENE XIII. DYCE, STAU, GLO, CAM1, HUD2, WH2, NLSN +

    Alexandria. ROWE1+ *(subst.)*
2154 Thinke] Drink HAN1, WARB, CAP
2157 though] although POPE1-THEO4, v1793, v1803, KNT1
2159 follow] follow you POPE1-THEO4, CAP, KTLY, HUD2

2154 HANMER (ed. 1744), reading *Drink,* cites Plutarch (see p. 447): *"That after their defeat at* Actium *they* [Antony and Cleopatra] *instituted a society of friends who enter'd into engagement to die with them, not abating in the mean time any part of that luxury, excess, and riot, in which they had lived before."* UPTON (1748, p. 236, n. 2), agreeing, compares 123–4. JOHNSON (ed. 1765), "not being convinced that it [emendation] is necessary": *"Think, and die*; that is, *Reflect on your folly, and leave the world,* is a natural answer." TYRWHITT (1766, p. 10): "A very proper answer from a Moralist or a Divine; but *Enobarbus,* I doubt, was neither the one nor the other. . . . The true reading is,— *Wink* and die," a phrase he finds in Beaumont and Fletcher's *The Sea-Voyage* 1.1 (*Works,* ed. Waller, 1910, 9:3). STEEVENS (ed. 1778) cites *JC*—"All that he can do Is to himselfe; take thought, and dye for *Cæsar"* (2.1.186–7 [820–1])—and Holinshed (1587, 3:50 [/2/35–6]): *"—taking thought* for the losse of his houses and money, he pined away and died." TYRWHITT (*apud* IDEM), changing his mind: *"Die of thought,* or *melancholy.* In this sense is *thought* used below [2615–17]."
    2156 will] DELIUS (ed. 1856): Desire, lust. KITTREDGE (ed. 1941): "A regular mild synonym."
    2158 ranges] COTGRAVE (1611, Rang): *"A ranke, row, list, file."* See also n. 44–5.
    2160 itch] BAILEY's (1866, 2:348) conjecture *edge* is interesting, given its frequent collocations in Sh. with cutting instruments like swords and knives.
    Affection] See n. 538. DELIUS (ed. 1856) sets it against *Captain-ship* (2161), as *will* (2156) is set against *Reason* (2157).
    2161 nickt] STEEVENS (ed. 1793): "I.e., set the mark of folly on it. [Quotes 'and . . . foole,' *Err.* 5.1.174–5 (1647–8).]" VALPY (ed. 1833): "Defeated." STAUNTON (ed. 1859):

When halfe to halfe the world oppos'd, he being
The meered question? 'Twas a shame no lesse
Then was his losse, to course your flying Flagges,
And leaue his Nauy gazing.   2165
   Cleo. Prythee peace.

        Enter the Ambassador, with Anthony.

Ant. Is that his answer?   *Amb.* I my Lord.

2163 meered] meer ROWE; mooted JOHN1 *conj.*, COL2
     'Twas] Tis F2-ROWE3
2167 *Enter*] *Enter, above,* BLUM
2168–73 *Six verse lines ending* Lord. . . . courtesie, . . . so. . . . know't. . . .
Head, . . . brim, ROWE1-THEO2, WARB-JOHN1, v1773, v1778, RANN; *five verse lines
ending* Queen . . . yield . . . know't. . . . head, . . . brim HAN1, CAP, v1793, v1803;
five verse lines ending lord. . . . she . . . know it.— . . . head, . . . brim MAL,
v1821, SING1, COL1+; *five verse lines ending* lord. . . . yield . . . know it.— . . .
head, . . . brim KNT1
2168 that] this F2-ROWE3, MAL, v1793-SING1, HUD1

"*Emasculated.*" WHITE (ed. 1861), proposing with "hardly a doubt," *prick'd*: "His 'captainship' meaning not his military skill, but himself." HUDSON (ed. 1881), elaborating
on Steevens's explanation: "*Disgrace* or *discredit*; a sense that probably grew from the
hair of Fools being cut in nicks or notches as a badge of their vocation." CASE (ed. 1906):
"A *nick* [is] a winning throw in the game of hazard—*to nick* came to mean to cheat,
or merely *to get the better of.* So, in many passages [quotes, among others, *The Tragedy
of Sir John Van Olden Barnavelt* 5.2 (*A Collection of Old English Plays*, ed. A. H. Bullen,
1882–5, 2:303) and George Chapman's *Two Wise Men* 6.4 (1619, p. 82)]. . . . The *Eng.
Dial. Dict.* [ed. Wright, 1898–1905] has many examples. . . . The *Century Dict.* [ed.
Whitney, 1889–91] explains cut short, abridged, because 'a false bottom in a beer can,
by which customers were cheated, the *nick* below and the froth above filling up part
of the measure', was called a *nick*; and for the verb quotes a reference of Halliwell's to
The Life of Robin Goodfellow, 1628 [*The Mad Pranks and Merry Jests of* . . . , ed. Collier, 1841, Pt. 2, p. 29]." DUHRING (*apud* FURNESS, ed. 1907), "An acknowledged authority
on *Cutaneous Diseases*": "Not the itch, or scabies, but, without question, the common
'ringworm of the scalp' . . . which causes the destruction of the hair, giving to the area
invaded a nicked or cropped appearance." CHARNEY (1961, p. 131): "'Nick'd' implies
that Antony's 'captainship' is conceived as the blade of a sword, which Cleopatra has
damaged and made useless." OED (*v.*[2] 2), citing this instance: "To cut into or through;
to cut short."
   2163 **meered**] MINSHEU (1617): "*Marke-stone in the field.*" HANMER (ed. 1744,
6:Glossary): "Relating to a boundary: *meer* being a boundary or mark of division." MA-
LONE (*apud* STEEVENS [1783]) and most commentators: "May be a word of our author's
own formation, from *mere.* He being the *sole*, the entire subject of dispute." A few com-

Ant. The Queene shall then haue courtesie,
So she will yeeld vs vp.   2170
    Am. He sayes so.
    Antho. Let her know't. To the Boy *Cæsar* send this
grizled head, and he will fill thy wishes to the brimme,
With Principalities.
    Cleo. That head my Lord?   2175
    Ant. To him againe, tell him he weares the Rose   (yy3ᵃ)
Of youth vpon him: from which, the world should note
Something particular: His Coine, Ships, Legions,
May be a Cowards, whose Ministers would preuaile
Vnder the seruice of a Childe, as soone   2180
As i'th'Command of *Cæsar.* I dare him therefore
To lay his gay Comparisons a-part,

2171 He] My Lord, he HAN1, CAP
2175 That] Thy THEO2, WARB, THEO4
2179 Ministers] ministries mWARB *conj.*, CAP, RANN
2182 Comparisons] caparisons mPOPE *conj.*, POPE, HAN1, SING2, WH1, KTLY, HUD2

---

mentators, starting with DELIUS (ed. 1856), propose both possibilities. See textual notes
and conj., p. 355.

2164 **course**] MINSHEU (1617), inaccurately: "The action of running, as a *shippe* at
sea." KERSEY (1702): *"Chase wild beasts."*

2170 **So**] See n. 2133.

2173 **grizled head**] WILSON (ed. 1950) compares the "gray hayres" in the Countess
of Pembroke's *Antonie* (1595, l. 1058). For the 1592 *Antonius*, see p. 504.

2176 **Rose**] SCHMIDT (1875): "Symbol of youth and beauty." DEIGHTON (ed. 1891):
"Flower and glory."

2177 **should**] Only DEIGHTON (ed. 1891): "May well."

2178 **particular**] COTGRAVE (1611, Particulier): *"Ones owne; also, distinct . . . speciall."*
See 366, 2717.

2179 **Ministers**] COTGRAVE (1611, Ministre): *"Seruant; Officer; Deputie; Assistant;
Instrument."* See 1846, 3133, 3204.

2180 **Vnder**] I.e., in.

2182 **gay Comparisons**] WARBURTON (ed. 1747): *"Shakespear* coined the word *comparisons* analogically from the *Italian*, which says, *vestito positivamente*, to signify one
cloathed simply and modestly, in opposition to the *comparative* and *superlative*. [This
false etymology is vehemently rejected by HEATH (1765, p. 460).] But, as usual, he has
made it serve to quibble to—*decline* [2183], another term of Grammar." JOHNSON (ed.
1765): "I require of *Cæsar* not to depend on that superiority which the *comparison* of
our different fortunes may exhibit to him." MALONE (*apud* STEEVENS, ed. 1778): "I suspect Shakespeare wrote, his gay *caparisons*. Let him divest himself of the splendid trappings of power. . . . *Caparison* is frequently used by our author and his contemporaries,
for *an ornamental dress*. [Quotes 'though . . . man,' *AYL* 3.2.205 (1390–1) and *WT*

211

Antony and Cleopatra

And answer me declin'd, Sword against Sword,
Our selues alone: Ile write it: Follow me.
    Eno. Yes like enough: hye battel'd *Cæsar* will   2185
Vnstate his happinesse, and be Stag'd to'th'shew
Against a Sworder. I see mens Iudgements are
A parcell of their Fortunes, and things outward
Do draw the inward quality after them
To suffer all alike, that he should dreame,   2190

2183 me⌃ declin'd,] ∼, ∼⌃ SING2
2184 *Exit* Antony. ROWE1-JOHN1, v1773; *Exeunt* ANTONY, *and* EUPHRONIUS. CAP, v1778+ (*subst.*)
2185–93 *Marked as an aside* CAP, DYCE1+ (−COL3, WH1, HAL, COL4)
2189 Do] To SING1
      quality] qualities mCOL1, COL2

4.3.27 (1694–5).]" MASON (1785, p. 283) mediates: "The word *gay* seems rather to favour Malone's conjecture [see textual notes], that we should read *caparisons*; on the other hand, the following passage . . . appears to favour the present reading [quotes 'that . . . emptinesse' (2190–2)]." WILLIAMS (1962, no. 79), comparing *Ven.* 285–6: Sh. almost "invariably uses 'gay' to modify nouns of clothing . . . or to suggest brave finery that may be worn."

    2183 **declin'd**] JOHNSON (ed. 1765): "In this decline of my age or power." CAPELL (1779 [1774], 1:41): "These advantages [accruing to Caesar from comparisons], he dares Cæsar to lay aside or *decline*." MALONE (*apud* STEEVENS, ed. 1778), agreeing, quotes *Tim.* 1.1.88 (110). SINGER (ed. 1856): "*Declined* must mean inclined, *sloped*, as swords are sloped one against another at the commencement of a combat. The word is technical, and we have it elsewhere twice. [Quotes *Ham.* 2.2.499–500 (1518–19) and *Tro.* 4.5.188–9 (2756–7).]" See textual notes and conj., p. 356.

    2185 **hye battel'd**] RANN (ed. 1791–): "In his plenitude of power." DELIUS (ed. 1856): With great armies. See also n. 985.

    2186 **Vnstate his happinesse**] RANN (ed. 1791–): "Descend from his dignity." CASE (ed. 1906): "*I.e.* strip it of state and dignity." KITTREDGE (ed. 1941): "Strip himself of the splendid advantages which fortune has given him." See n. 76.

    2186–7 **Stag'd . . . Sworder**] DAVIES (1783, 2:352): "Fight with him, like a gladiator upon a stage, for the diversion of the populace." DEIGHTON (ed. 1891) compares *2H6* 4.1.135–6 (2303–4)—"A Romane Sworder, and Bandetto slaue Murder'd sweet *Tully*"— an instance that reveals the pejorative connotations of the word. KITTREDGE (ed. 1941): "Prize fights with swords were common London shows in Elizabethan times and later. [William] Lambarde (*A Perambulation of Kent*, 1596, p. 233) speaks of persons who visit 'Parisgardein, the Bell Sauage, or Theatre, to beholde Beare baiting, Enterludes, or Fence play.'" For the *-er* suffix, see also n. 2304.

    2188 **parcell**] COTGRAVE's (1611) "*peece*" is given a proper focus by *OED* (1b): "Emphasizing comprehension in the whole, rather than partitive character." See also n. 3393.

    2190 **suffer**] STAUNTON (ed. 1859) alone: "The verb is apparently used here in an active sense, meaning to *punish* or *afflict*." Most commentators prefer meanings like "to

Knowing all measures, the full *Cæsar* will
Answer his emptinesse; *Cæsar* thou hast subdu'de
His iudgement too.

Enter a Seruant.

Ser. A Messenger from *Cæsar.*   2195
Cleo. What no more Ceremony? See my Women,
Against the blowne Rose may they stop their nose,
That kneel'd vnto the Buds. Admit him sir.
Eno. Mine honesty, and I, beginne to square,
The Loyalty well held to Fooles, does make   2200
Our Faith meere folly: yet he that can endure
To follow with Allegeance a falne Lord,
Does conquer him that did his Master conquer,
And earnes a place i'th'Story.

2191 measures] miseries mCOL1 (*withdrawn* COLNE, 1852, p. 512), COL2
2193, 2195 *One verse line* v1793+ (−ALEX)
2197 nose] noses WALKER (1860, 3:305) *conj.*, HUD2
2198 Buds] bud mTBY4 *conj.*, COL2
    Exit Attendant. CAP, DYCE1, STAU, GLO, DYCE2+
2199–2204 *Marked as an aside* HAN1, CAP, v1778+
2200 The] Tho' mTBY3 (PP.A, *withdrawn*) *and* mTHEO2 (19 Feb. 1729, [fol. 40ᵛ])
conj., THEO, HAN1, WARB (*errata*; The *in text*)
    held ᴧ to Fooles,] ∼ , ∼∼ ᴧ mTHEO2 (19 Feb. 1729, [fol. 40ᵛ]) *conj.*, THEO,
HAN1, WARB
2204, 2206–8 *Arranged as verse lines, thus:* 2204 *and* 2206, 2207 *and* 2208
v1793-SING1, COL1-COL3, WH1-COL4, WH2-CAM3, SIS+; 2204 *and* 2206, 2207, 2208 KNT1,
STAU, HUD2; 2204, 2206–7, 2208 ALEX
2204 earnes] earn RID

---

be affected" (WORDSWORTH [ed. 1883]) or "decline" (KITTREDGE [ed. 1941]).
    that] DEIGHTON (ed. 1891) and others, substantially: "To think that."
    2191 **Knowing all measures**] COLLIER (1852, pp. 474–5, 512) cautiously proposes *miseries* for the "hastily misread" *measures*: "Enobarbus refers to the miserable plight and prospects of Antony at the time." LETTSOM (1853, p. 467): "*Full* [2191] and *emptiness* [2192] prove . . . that 'measure' is the right word." His interpretation of the phrase — "experienced every measure of fortune" — is followed by most commentators. RIDLEY (ed. 1954): "Being so good a judge of men's 'capacities.'" See also 5, n. 1221.
    2197 **blowne**] See nn. 2615, 3269, and 3618.
    2198 **sir**] FURNESS (ed. 1907): "An instance of the use of 'sir' in addressing persons of humble rank." See also nn. 71, 2228.
    2199 **honesty**] See n. 785.
    square] See n. 670.
    2201 **meere**] See n. 1867.
    2204 **Story**] MINSHEU (1617): "Historie." See nn. 2359, 3630–3.

Enter Thidias.   2205

Cleo. *Cæsars* will.

Thid. Heare it apart.

Cleo. None but Friends: say boldly.

Thid. So haply are they Friends to *Anthony*.

Enob. He needs as many (Sir) as *Cæsar* ha's,   2210

Or needs not vs. If *Cæsar* please, our Master

Will leape to be his Friend: For vs you know,

Whose he is, we are, and that is *Cæsars*.

Thid. So. Thus then thou most renown'd, *Cæsar* intreats,

Not to consider in what case thou stand'st   2215

2208 None] None here HAN1; Here's none mTBY4 *conj.*, KTLY
    say] say on CAP
2210–13 *Given to Cleopatra* MAL *conj.*, RANN
2211 vs. . . . please,] — ‸ . . . — . WARB
2212 For vs] For as F2-THEO4; Or, as CAP (*text*; for us mCAP2, CAPN [*errata*])
2213–14 *Verse lines ending* So. . . . intreats POPE1+
2214 intreats] entreats thee KTLY

2208 **None but Friends**] DEIGHTON's (ed. 1891) paraphrase, "*i.e.* are present here," repeats HANMER's (ed. 1744) emendation. See textual notes.

2209 **haply**] See n. 999.

2210–13 MALONE (ed. 1790): "I suspect that the . . . speech belongs to Cleopatra, not to Enobarbus. . . . The whole dialogue naturally proceeds between Cleopatra and Thyreus [Thidias], till Enobarbus thinks it necessary to attend to his own interest, and says what he speaks when he goes out. The plural number, (*us*) . . . suits Cleopatra." STEEVENS (ed. 1793): "Enobarbus, who is the buffoon of the play, has already presumed [see 798–801] to interfere between the jarring Triumvirs, and might therefore have been equally flippant on the occasion before us." See textual notes.

2212–13 **For . . . *Cæsars***] HEATH (1765, p. 461): "For, as you know very well, though we are indeed our master's friends, yet both he and we are at present pretty much at Cæsar's discretion." CAPELL (1779 [1774], 1:41) and others: "'*For us*', (*i.e.* As for us,)." See textual notes.

2214–16 **Cæsar . . . Cæsars**] WARBURTON (ed. 1747), for the majority who adopt F2's *Cæsar* at 2216: "I.e. Cæsar *intreats, that at the same time you consider your desperate fortunes, you would consider he is* Cæsar: That is, generous and forgiving, able and willing to restore them." MALONE (ed. 1790): "It has been just said, that whatever *Antony* is, all his followers are; 'that is, *Cæsar's*'. Thyreus [Thidias] now informs Cleopatra that Cæsar entreats her not to consider *herself* in a state of subjection, further than as she is connected with Antony, who is *Cæsar's*: intimating to her, (according to the instructions he had received from Cæsar, to detach Cleopatra from Antony, see [2138–46],) that she might make separate and advantageous terms for herself." KITTREDGE (ed. 1941): "[Thidias] speaks with such equivocation that he actually promises nothing whatever."

Further then he is *Cæsars.*
  Cleo. Go on, right Royall.
  Thid. He knowes that you embrace not *Anthony*
As you did loue, but as you feared him.
  Cleo. Oh.   2220
  Thid. The scarre's vpon your Honor, therefore he
Does pitty, as constrained blemishes,
Not as deserued.
  Cleo. He is a God,

2216 Further] Farther COL, WH1, KTLY
    Cæsars] *Cæsar* F2-v1778, v1793+ (−v1821, COL1)
2218 embrace] embrac'd mTBY2 *conj.*, CAPN (*errata*), RANN, HUD2, CAM3, ARD2
2219–20 *One verse line* v1793+ (−NLSN)
2220 *Marked as an aside* ROWE1-JOHN1, v1773
2221 scarre's] scarres F2+
2223–8 *Three verse lines ending* deserued. . . . right. . . . meerly *then as* F1 ROWE;
four verse lines ending knows . . . yielded, . . . that, . . . leaky POPE1+
2223–4 deserued. . . . He is] deservèd (*trisyllabic*). . . . He's WALKER (1860, 3:305)
conj., DYCE2, HUD2

2217 **right Royall**] WILSON (ed. 1950): "I.e. a truly royal message! She purrs." See
n. 2425.
2219 **As**] DELIUS (ed. 1856): "*As if.*" For the conjunction with the subjunctive, see
FRANZ §644, *Anm.* 3.
2220 FURNESS (ed. 1907): "If we believe that she [Cleopatra] is here playing false
to Anthony, this 'Oh' must be a shudder. If she is true to Anthony . . . and is merely,
with consummate skill, drawing on the Ambassador in order to probe to the bottom
Cæsar's plans so that she can protect Anthony and herself, then this 'Oh' is shocked surprise. . . . With whatever tone it was uttered, the Ambassador was quick to interpret
it not otherwise than as a confirmation of his insinuation." KITTREDGE (ed. 1941): Conveys "not only eager acceptance of Cæsar's theory of her union with Antony, but also
gratified surprise that Cæsar should have shown so sympathetic an understanding of the
case. All this she expresses in plain terms in her next speech [2224–6]." RIDLEY (ed.
1954): "Cleopatra, in North [see p. 453], during the scene in which she deludes Cæsar,
says the same ['as . . . him' (2219)] of herself. This may help to clarify the way in which
Cleopatra's *O!* should be delivered." Ridley does not "clarify" further. MILLS (1960, p.
151, n. 15): "The Folio 'Oh' followed by a period may suggest only a distressful moan;
Thyreus goes on speaking as if he heard nothing. Maybe modern editors imply too much
by inserting an exclamation point." WALTER (ed. 1969) epitomizes the commentary: "Is
this—surprise, incredulity, irony, coyness, amusement?"
2224 FURNESS (ed. 1907): "Which is the better emphasis: 'He's a *God*', implying
astonishment, and that the knowledge of Cæsar's divinity has just dawned on the speaker;
or 'He *is* a God', implying that Cæsar's divinity is well-known, and that in this reluctant
assent lies a fresh and convincing proof of it?" DEY (1909, p. 465): "We do know that

And knowes what is most right. Mine Honour   2225
Was not yeelded, but conquer'd meerely.
   Eno. To be sure of that, I will aske *Anthony.*
Sir, sir, thou art so leakie
That we must leaue thee to thy sinking, for
Thy deerest quit thee.   *Exit Enob.* 2230
   Thid. Shall I say to *Cæsar,*
What you require of him: for he partly begges
To be desir'd to giue. It much would please him,
That of his Fortunes you should make a staffe
To leane vpon. But it would warme his spirits   2235
To heare from me you had left *Anthony,*
And put your selfe vnder his shrowd, the vniuersal Landlord.
   Cleo. What's your name?

2227–30 *Marked as an aside* HAN1, CAP, v1778+
2228 sir,] *Om.* POPE1-THEO4
2229 to] *Om.* F2-F4
2232 for] *Om.* POPE1-THEO4
2234 should] would ROWE3-JOHN1, v1773, v1778, RANN
2235–8 *Four verse lines ending* spirits, . . . *Antony,* . . . shrowd, the great, . . .
name? HAN1, CAP, v1778+; *five verse lines ending* upon. . . . me . . . yourself . . .
landlord. . . . name! JOHN1, v1773
2237 the] the great, The HAN1, CAP; who is the mCOL1, COL2, COL3, KTLY, COL4,
HUD2

Cleopatra is now being favoured with what are accepted as evidences of Cæsar's godlike
knowledge, but we do not know from the text that the evidence in question is in confirmation of any such previous estimate of his sagacity. In the absence of an antecedent
reference, the new idea, I think, indicates that 'god' is the emphatic word, rather than,
as suggested by Furness, 'He *is* a god.'" WALTER (ed. 1969): "Is this pretended humility,
irony, or gratification that Cæsar is sympathetic?"
   2225 **right**] MINSHEU (1617): "Iust." Following WILSON (ed. 1950), RIDLEY (ed. 1954):
"True."
   2226 **meerely**] See n. 1867.
   2228 **Sir, sir**] RANN (ed. 1791–): "Apostrophising the absent *Antony,* and reflecting
on his fallen state."
   2232 **require**] See n. 2123.
   2235 **warme his spirits**] DELIUS (ed. 1856): An intensification of "please him" (2233)
indicated by the introductory *But.*
   2237 **shrowd**] JOHNSON (1755), citing this instance: "Shelter." WILSON (ed. 1950)
fancifully: "The language of feudalism. . . . Sh. himself worked 'under the shroud' of
the Lord Chamberlain."
   2238 WILSON (ed. 1950): "An invitation to personal relations, which he follows up
at ll. [2249–50]."

Thid. My name is *Thidias.*

Cleo. Most kinde Messenger, 2240
Say to great *Cæsar* this in disputation,
I kisse his conqu'ring hand: Tell him, I am prompt (yy3[b])
To lay my Crowne at's feete, and there to kneele.
Tell him, from his all-obeying breath, I heare
The doome of Egypt. 2245
Thid. 'Tis your Noblest course:

2241 this in disputation,] this; in Deputation WARBURTON *conj. apud* THEO1,
THEO1-v1773, RANN, SING2, DYCE1, WH1-KTLY, DYCE2-NLSN, KIT1, ALEX, SIS, CAM3b;
this, in disputation v1778, MAL, v1793-v1821, KNT1, COL1, STAU, HAL; that in deputation
mCOL1, COL2, HUD1, COL3; this in deputation, mTHEO1 *conj.*, ARD, RID, EVNS
2244-5 *Verse lines ending* breath, . . . *Ægypt.* ROWE1-THEO4
2244 Tell him] Tell him that ROWE1-JOHN1; Till mTYR *conj.*, CLN2

2241 **this in disputation**] THEOBALD (ed. 1733), asserting Warburton's agreement as
to the punctuation: "The Poet certainly wrote . . . *this*; *in* Deputation . . . i.e. by
Proxy; I *depute* you to pay him that Duty in my Name. . . . [Quotes 'Lent . . . powre,'
MM 1.1.20-2 (22-4); 'And . . . drawn,' *1H4* 4.1.32-3 (2256-7), 4.3.86-7 (2555-6); 'Sometime . . . on,' *Tro.* 1.3.151-2 (611-12).]" STEEVENS (ed. 1778), however: "*I kiss his hand
in disputation*—may mean, I own he has the better in the controversy.—I confess my
inability to *dispute or contend* with him. To *dispute* may have no immediate reference
to words or language by which controversies are agitated. [Cites 'Dispute . . . man,'
Mac. 4.3.220 (2069) and *TN* 4.3.9 (2123).]—If Dr. Warburton's change [to 'this';] be
adopted, we should read—'*by* deputation.'" MALONE (ed. 1790), defending Warburton,
quotes *Jn.* 1.1.2-4 (6-9) and *1H4* 4.3.86-7 (2555-6), adding, "Supposing *disputation*
to mean . . . struggle for power, or the contention of adversaries, to say that one kisses
the hand of another *in contention*, is surely a strange phrase: but to *kiss by proxy*, and
to *marry by proxy*, was the language of Shakspeare's time, and is the language of this
day. I have, however, found no example of *in deputation* being used in the sense required here." THISELTON (1899, p. 20): "The presence of the long non-final 's' [in 'disputation'] is against the substitution of 'deputation.'" CASE (ed. 1906): "In deputed authority,
as my representative." As to F1's reading, "*dis-* [results from] the attractive proximity of
this and *kiss.*" See also textual notes and conj., p. 356.

2244 **Tell**] MUIR (1961, p. 142): "Both rhythm and sense would be improved if we
changed the full-stop to a comma in the previous line, and emended 'Tell him' to 'Till'.
. . . The scribe or the compositor misread 'Till' as 'Tell' under the influence of 'Tell
him' two lines above." See textual notes.

all-obeying] JOHNSON (ed. 1765) alone: "*Doom* [i.e., judgment upon; see also
3130] is declared rather by an *all-commanding*, than an *all-obeying breath*. I suppose
we ought to read,—*all* obeyed breath." But RANN (ed. 1791-): "The active participle
may, perhaps, as elsewhere, be used passively [i.e., which all obey]." See FRANZ §664
and ABBOTT §372.

2245 **Egypt**] WORDSWORTH (ed. 1883) and others: "*Queen of Egypt.*" Only DEIGHTON

Wisedome and Fortune combatting together,
If that the former dare but what it can,
No chance may shake it. Giue me grace to lay
My dutie on your hand.   2250
   Cleo. Your *Cæsars* Father oft,
(When he hath mus'd of taking kingdomes in)
Bestow'd his lips on that vnworthy place,
As it rain'd kisses.

                Enter Anthony and Enobarbus.   2255

   Ant. Fauours? By Ioue that thunders. What art thou Fellow?
   Thid. One that but performes
The bidding of the fullest man, and worthiest
To haue command obey'd.
   Eno. You will be whipt.   2260

2250–2 *Verse lines ending* father . . . in, v1793, v1803, SING, KNT1, HUD1, KTLY;
ending oft, . . . in, v1821, COL1, COL2, DYCE1-GLO, HAL+
  2251 oft] *Om.* HAN1
  2254, 2256–7 *Verse lines ending* thunders. . . . performs F4+
  2254 rain'd] reign'd ROWE3
  2255 SCENE X. POPE, WARB, JOHN1; SCENE XI. HAN1
  2260 *Marked as an aside* CAP, DYCE, GLO, CAM1, HUD2+; *Aside to* THYR. STAU

(ed. 1891) of those who comment at all seems to imply the country Egypt.
  2247 **together**] See n. 663.
  2249 **may**] See n. 538.
    Giue me grace] JOHNSON (ed. 1765): "Grant me the favour."
  2251 ***Cæsars* Father**] See n. 1757.
  2252 **taking . . . in**] See 1886, n. 33.
  2254 **As**] I.e., as if. See n. 2219.
  2256–2332 VINCENT (1978, p. 195): "Antony's overbearingly personal revenge on
Thidias does seem to have a kind of poetic justice. . . . The attempt to torture Antony
with the loss of his lover has the effect of raising him to Herculean proportions in his
wrath. . . . Antony becomes at once a more ironic and a more heroic figure in this scene."
   2256 **Fauours?**] FURNESS (ed. 1907) asks "why the astonished interrogation of the
Folio should be deserted, as it is, by all editors since Capell [except a few recent ones
like RIDLEY (eds. 1935, 1954) and EVANS (ed. 1974)]."
    Fellow] SCHMIDT (1874): "An appellation of familiarity," usually from one of higher
station to one of lower and often with a negative adjective or context, as here. But compare 2507, 2515.
    2258 **fullest**] MALONE (ed. 1790): "The most complete, and perfect. So, in *Othello*
[1.1.66 (72)]." BLUMHOF (ed. 1870): Refers not to personal qualities but to power; compares "full *Cæsar*" (2191).

Ant. Approch there: ah you Kite. Now Gods & diuels
Authority melts from me of late. When I cried hoa,
Like Boyes vnto a musse, Kings would start forth,
And cry, your will. Haue you no eares?
I am *Anthony* yet. Take hence this Iack, and whip him.   2265

Enter a Seruant.

Eno. 'Tis better playing with a Lions whelpe,
Then with an old one dying.
Ant. Moone and Starres,
Whip him: wer't twenty of the greatest Tributaries   2270
That do acknowledge *Cæsar,* should I finde them

2261 ah] Ay v1793-COL1, HUD1, DYCE, COL3, WH1, HAL, COL4, OXF1

2262–5 *Four verse lines ending* I . . . would . . . ears? . . . him. HAN1; *ending*
ho! . . . forth, . . . am . . . him. mTYR *conj. and* CAP, v1773+ (−KNT1, STAU, CAM,
ARD, RID, SIS)

2262 me‸ of late.] ~ . Of ~ ‸ mTBY4 *conj.,* JOHN1, v1773+ (−RID, SIS)

2266 *a Seruant*] *Servants* THEO1+ (−NLSN) (*subst.*)

2267–8 *Marked as an aside* CAP, DYCE, STAU, GLO, CAM1+ (−ALEX)

2270 wer't] were F3-POPE2

2261 **Approch there**] WORDSWORTH (ed. 1883): "To attendants."

ah you Kite] BLUMHOF (ed. 1870): Directed to Cleopatra. CASE (ed. 1906): "On
the other hand, Thyreus might be so addressed." WILSON (ed. 1950): "'You' (cf. 'thou',
l. [2256]) and 'kite' (=whore; cf. *Hen. V,* 2.1.[80 (576)]) show that this is hissed at Cleo."

2262 **hoa**] See n. 1027.

2263 **musse**] FLORIO (1598, Fare alla grappa piu): "*To play at musse . . . to skamble*
for." OED (Muss *sb.*[1]): "A game in which small objects are thrown down to be scrambled
for."

2265 **I . . . yet.**] BULMAN (1985, p. 202) detects an echo of Seneca's *Medea* 166,
"Medea superest [Medea is left]" (ed. Miller, 1917 [Loeb]).

Iack] MALONE (ed. 1790, 2:214, n. 5): "A term of contempt. [Quotes *1H4* 3.3.99
(2089) and 'Rascall . . . tearmes,' *Shr.* 2.1.158–9 (1025–6).] See in *Minsheu's Dict.* 1617,
'A *Jack* sauce, or saucie *Jack.*'" DELIUS (ed. 1856) adds: For upstarts. See also 2278. JONES
(ed. 1977) alone adds "substitute," citing *OED, sb.*[1]. For an extended discussion of the
term, see BARROLL (1969, *ShakS,* p. 231, n. 48).

2266 ***Enter a Seruant***] BARROLL (1969, *ShakS,* p. 230, n. 46): "It is plausible that
[Compositor] B could very easily have forgotten the final *s* of a hypothetical *Servants,*
but is it as plausible that in the process he would also add the indefinite article? . . .
The issue at hand is the waning influence of Anthony over his attendants. . . . The
tardy entrance of only one servant would reinforce the point." See textual notes and n. 2984.

2267–8 Proverbial; see DENT (L321.1): "It is dangerous to play with *lions.*"

So sawcy with the hand of she heere, what's her name
Since she was *Cleopatra?* Whip him Fellowes,
Till like a Boy you see him crindge his face,
And whine aloud for mercy. Take him hence.   2275
    Thid. Marke Anthony.
    Ant. Tugge him away: being whipt
Bring him againe, the Iacke of *Cæsars* shall
Beare vs an arrant to him.   *Exeunt with Thidius.*
You were halfe blasted ere I knew you: Ha?   2280
Haue I my pillow left vnprest in Rome,
Forborne the getting of a lawfull Race,
And by a Iem of women, to be abus'd
By one that lookes on Feeders?

2272 she] her HAN1
2278 the] this POPE1-SING1, HUD1+ (−COL3, WH1, HAL, RID, ALEX, EVNS)
    Cæsars] Cæsar COL2
2279 *Exeunt*] *Exeunt Attendants* CAP, v1778-OXF1, ARD1+; *Exit Servant* NLSN

2272 **she**] THEOBALD (1726, p. 40): "Grammar requires that it should be . . . *her*
here." WHITE (ed. 1883): "Not English." KITTREDGE (ed. 1941): "Often used as a noun
and therefore uninflected." For the use of the personal pronoun in the nominative case
instead of the accusative, see FRANZ §287g, §287h. SEYMOUR (1805, 2:74) would avoid
the problem by repunctuating: "'With the hand of—She here. (It is she here whom I
mean,) What's her name?' &c."
2273 **Since . . . *Cleopatra*]** MASON (1785, p. 284) and most commentators: "Since
she ceased to be Cleopatra." DELIUS (ed. 1856): The sentence is unfinished; it should
close with: I should have them whipped like this one. ABBOTT (§132): "'*Since* (though
she is not now worthy of the name) she once *was* (emphatical) Cleopatra'. Else 'What
is her new name since she ceased to be Cleopatra?' If *since*, in the sense of 'ago', could
be used absolutely for 'once' [not in Sh.], a third interpretation would be possible: 'What's
her name? *Once* she was Cleopatra.'"
2274 **crindge**] JOHNSON (1755), citing this instance, is the first to define: "To draw
together; to contract."
2278 **Iacke**] See n. 2265.
2279 **vs**] I.e., for us. For the dative, see FRANZ §307.
    arrant] I.e., errand. MINSHEU (1617, Arrand): "Message."
2280 **blasted**] See n. 1980.
    Ha] WILSON (ed. 1950): "Goes with ll. [2281] ff."
2282 SINGER (ed. 1856): "In point of fact Antony did have issue by Octavia." For
Plutarch, see p. 419.
2283 **abus'd**] COTGRAVE (1611): "*Misuse . . . also to deceiue, disappoint, gull, cou-*
sine, beguile." Most commentators prefer the latter meanings. Plutarch (see p. 412) mentions Antony's being "easely abused by the praises they gaue him."
2284 **one . . . Feeders**] JOHNSON (ed. 1765): "One that waits at the table while

220

Cleo. Good my Lord.   2285
Ant. You haue beene a boggeler euer,
But when we in our viciousnesse grow hard
(Oh misery on't) the wise Gods seele our eyes
In our owne filth, drop our cleare iudgements, make vs

2287 But] And WH2, NLSN
    grow] grew F2-ROWE3
2288 seele] seale F3-THEO4, WH1
2288–9 eyes˄ . . . filth,] ∼ : . . . ∼ ˄ mTBY3 *conj.*, WARB, v1778+ (−KNT1)
2289 drop] dark LETTSOM *conj. apud* WALKER (1860, 3:305), HUD2; drown mTBY2
conj., WORD1

---

others are eating." STEEVENS (ed. 1778), quoting Ben Jonson's *Epicoene* 3.5.33–5 (ed. Herford & Simpson, 1937): "*One who looks on feeders,* is one who throws away her regard on *servants,* such as Antony would represent Thyreus to be." DELIUS (ed. 1856): Parasite. Modern eds. tend toward the derogatory usage, although CASE (ed. 1906) with numerous citations: "The weight of evidence is wholly against [the] explanation, *parasites.*"
    2285 See n. 1160.
    2286–97 **You . . . out**] BERKELEY (1964, pp. 139–40): "In Plutarch, Antony never addresses an angry word to Cleopatra; but in Shakespeare he twice gives her the rough side of his tongue [2286–97, 2788–97]."
    2286 **boggeler**] SKINNER (1671, Boggle): Hesitate, stagger. BAILEY (1721): "To be uncertain what to do, to waver, to scruple." Although JOHNSON (1755, *Boggle,* 3) and *OED* (Boggle *v.* 3), agreeing, cite this instance, commentators starting with RANN (ed. 1791-)—"a dastard, a dissembler"—stress duplicity, shiftiness. MACCALLUM (1910, p. 442, n. 1): "I take it as certain that with Thyreus she is for the moment at least 'a boggler', and then she has already sent her private message to Caesar."
    2287–91 KITTREDGE (ed. 1941): "The old Greek doctrine of infatuation or *atē* (ἄτη). When a man imagines himself superior to humanity, the gods let him go on in his mad folly until he accomplishes his own ruin. The same idea underlies Shakespeare's treatment of Cæsar's character in *Julius Cæsar* (ii, 2 [983 ff.]; iii, 1 [1200 ff.]). He veritably 'struts to his confusion'. Cf. *Psalm* ii, 4: 'He that sitteth in the heavens shall laugh; the Lord shall have them in derision'; *Proverbs,* xvi, 18: 'Pride goeth before destruction, and an haughty spirit before a fall.'" WILSON (ed. 1950), after quoting Kittredge: "A more prob. source is Isa. vi. 10, John xii. 40, which suggest 'grow hard' and 'seel our eyes.'" Proverbial; see DENT (G257): "When *God* will punish he will first take away the understanding."
    2288 **seele**] MINSHEU (1617): "*Sow vp the eye-lids.*" COLLIER (ed. 1843): "To 'seel' [i.e., close up] the eyes of a hawk was a term in falconry [as an aid in training]. . . . It was perhaps only another form of *seal,* and it is sometimes doubtful which form should be preserved." See also n. 3373.
    2289 **In . . . iudgements**] DEIGHTON (ed. 1891) alone: "Another metaphor from hawking, in which the hawk after long confinement was subjected to a course of scouring diet; the technical term for which was to *enseam.*"

Adore our errors, laugh at's while we strut   2290
To our confusion.
   Cleo. Oh, is't come to this?
   Ant. I found you as a Morsell, cold vpon
Dead *Cæsars* Trencher: Nay, you were a Fragment
Of *Gneius Pompeyes*, besides what hotter houres   2295
Vnregistred in vulgar Fame, you haue
Luxuriously pickt out. For I am sure,
Though you can guesse what Temperance should be,
You know not what it is.
   Cleo. Wherefore is this?   2300
   Ant. To let a Fellow that will take rewards,
And say, God quit you, be familiar with
My play-fellow, your hand; this Kingly Seale,
And plighter of high hearts. O that I were
Vpon the hill of Basan, to out-roare   2305
The horned Heard, for I haue sauage cause,

2292 is't] is it v1773-KNT1, COL, WH1, KTLY, HAL
2295 *Pompeyes*] *Pompey* HAN1
2303 this] that mCOL1, COL2

2291 **confusion**] See n. 57.
2294 **Fragment**] In addition to the food metaphor, see *OED* (2c): "Applied to a person as a term of contempt."
2295 **Of . . . Pompeyes**] For the genitive, see n. 4.
2296 **vulgar**] CAWDREY (1604): "Common, much vsed." For *Fame*, see n. 74–5.
2297 **Luxuriously**] CAWDREY (1604): "Riotous, and excessiue in pleasure, and wontonnesse."
    pickt] WALTER (ed. 1969): "Can also mean to eat fastidiously, and here perhaps . . . continue the 'morsel'—'trencher'—'fragment' image."
2301 **Fellow**] See n. 2256.
2302 **God quit you**] DELIUS (ed. 1856): Said by servants on receiving a sought-after gratuity. DEIGHTON (ed. 1891): "The common thanks of beggars." For *quit*, see n. 2331.
2303 **this Kingly Seale**] Because of *this*, COLLIER (ed. 1858) suggests that Antony may take Cleopatra's hand.
2304 **plighter**] Although the *-er* suffix is the most common in Sh., this may be one of the instances that point to pejorative connotations. See n. 2186–7.
    high] SCHMIDT (1874, 5): "Proud, lofty."
2304–6 **O . . . Heard**] GREY (1754, 2:208) refers to Ps. 58:15 ("The hill of God is *as* the hill of Bashan; an high hill *as* the hill of Bashan") and compares Ps. 22:12 ("Many bulls have compassed me: strong *bulls* of Bashan have beset me round").
2305 **Basan**] COOPER (1565): "A countrey beyonde the ryuer of Iordan in Iudea." See PAULY, Batanaia, 3:115–17 (1), and map, p. xxxvii; not in *OCD*.
2306 **horned Heard**] JOHNSON (ed. 1765): "It is not without pity and indignation

And to proclaime it ciuilly, were like
A halter'd necke, which do's the Hangman thanke,
For being yare about him. Is he whipt?

Enter a Seruant with Thidias.   2310

Ser. Soundly, my Lord.
Ant. Cried he? and begg'd a Pardon?
Ser. He did aske fauour.
Ant. If that thy Father liue, let him repent
Thou was't not made his daughter, and be thou sorrie   2315
To follow *Cæsar* in his Triumph, since
Thou hast bin whipt. For following him, henceforth
The white hand of a Lady Feauer thee,
Shake thou to looke on't. Get thee backe to *Cæsar,*
Tell him thy entertainment: looke thou say   2320
He makes me angry with him. For he seemes
Proud and disdainfull, harping on what I am,
Not what he knew I was. He makes me angry,

2309 Is he whipt?] *Separate line* COL, HAL
2310 *a Seruant*] *Attendants* CAP-SIS (−NLSN, KIT1, ALEX)
2312 a] a' THEO1+ (−HAN1, NLSN, RIDa)
2317 whipt. . . . him,] ~ , . . . ~ . ROWE1+
2319 Shake . . . Get] Shake to looke on't. Get F2-F4; Shake to look on't. Go get ROWE1-THEO4; Shake thee to look on't.──Get MAL; Shake but to looke on't. Get mCOL1, COL2
2321 makes] make ROWE2, ROWE3

---

that the reader of this great Poet meets so often with this low jest [on cuckold's horns], which is too much a favourite to be left out of either mirth or fury."

sauage cause] SCHMIDT (1875, Savage, adj. 2): "Cause to act like a wild beast."

2308 BLUMHOF (ed. 1870): In England it was customary for the hangman to ask forgiveness of the man he was about to hang. Compares "the . . . pardon," *AYL* 3.5.3–6 (1773–6), and *MM* 4.2.53–4 (1903–5).

2309 yare] See nn. 924, 1905.

2312 a] The article or the pronoun. See textual notes and n. 1439. Modern editions usually add an apostrophe to mark the pronoun.

2315 **Thou . . . daughter**] WORDSWORTH (ed. 1883): "*Because being a man, thou hast taken too great a liberty.*"

2319–31 **Get . . . me**] For Plutarch's version, see p. 448.

2320 **entertainment**] DYCHE & PARDON (1740): "The usage or reception a person meets with, either from his friends or enemies." See also nn. 671, 2595.

looke] *OED* (3b): "To take care, make sure, see (*that* or *how* something is done; also with omission of *that*)."

And at this time most easie 'tis to doo't:
When my good Starres, that were my former guides   2325
Haue empty left their Orbes, and shot their Fires
Into th'Abisme of hell. If he mislike,
My speech, and what is done, tell him he has
Hiparchus, my enfranched Bondman, whom
He may at pleasure whip, or hang, or torture,   2330
As he shall like to quit me. Vrge it thou:
Hence with thy stripes, be gone.   *Exit Thid.*
     Cleo. Haue you done yet?
     Ant. Alacke our Terrene Moone is now Eclipst,

2326 shot] shut F3, F4
2327 th'] their OXF1
2329 enfranched] enfranchis'd THEO1-SING2, COL3, WH1, KTLY, COL4, OXF1
2333-6 *Three verse lines ending* moon . . . alone . . . time. CAP, v1778+

2324 **doo't:**] RIDLEY (ed. 1954): "Most edd. print a comma. F is right, I think, marking the pause before he amplifies *this time*."

2325-7 **When . . . hell**] WILSON (ed. 1950): "Spoken to himself rather than to Thidias and marking the ebb of his wrath."

2329 *Hiparchus*] CASE (ed. 1906): "Antony is not abandoning an innocent man thus, but a revolter." For Plutarch, see pp. 444, 448; PAULY, Hipparchos, 8:1664–5 (9); not in *OCD*.

enfranched] See n. 33 ("Infranchise"). The more common *enfranchised* is not used attributively in Sh.

2331 **like**] SCHMIDT (1874, *adj.* 4): "Likely. . . . [The] personal use, with an inf. following." KNOWLES (privately), noting the following comma since ROWE (ed. 1714) and the lack of comment, suggests there is a consensus for considering *like* a verb.

quit me] JOHNSON (ed. 1765): "To repay me this insult; to *requite* me." Compare n. 2302.

2334 **Terrene Moone**] Most commentators agree substantially with CAPELL (1779 [1774], 1:42): "The moon in the heavens . . . might be call'd—'*terrene*', as being the earth's attendant, or satellite: But the speaker means it of Cleopatra, who was call'd—the new Isis . . . the moon." However, there are other, not entirely convincing, views. HOTSON (1949, p. 10): "*Terrene* is a short form of *Mediterranean*, favourite with the geographer Ortelius and the dramatist Marlowe: 'not far from Alexandria, Whereas the Terrene and the Red Sea meet' [*2 Tamburlaine* 5.3.131–2, ed. Bowers, 1973]. The mighty battle-crescent of their Mediterranean fleet has suffered eclipse, giving infallible omen of Antony's fall." WILLIAMSON (1968, p. 425): "Antony seems here to be using an image associated with 'fortune-following love', which 'eclipses soon As does the moon that falls into the shade Of mother earth' [Guillaume de Lorris and Jean de Meun, *The Romance of the Rose*, ll. 4799–4801, tr. Robbins, 1962, p. 104]." BARROLL (1969, *ShakS*, p. 229, n. 43): "Based in its simplest sense on the equation of the moon with Cynthia and chastity, for the hero's argument has to do with his version of a manner in which Cleopatra has somehow sexually defiled herself." TOBIN (1979, p. 227): "It seems more likely (given the themes

And it portends alone the fall of *Anthony*.   2335
  Cleo. I must stay his time?
  Ant. To flatter *Cæsar*, would you mingle eyes
With one that tyes his points.
  Cleo. Not know me yet?
  Ant. Cold-hearted toward me?   2340
  Cleo. Ah (Deere) if I be so,
From my cold heart let Heauen ingender haile,
And poyson it in the sourse, and the first stone
Drop in my necke: as it determines so

2336 *to her Women.* CAP; *marked as an aside* KTLY
2340 me?] ~ ! THEO, WARB, JOHN1, v1773, HUD
2341 Ah (Deere)] *Om.* HAN1

---

of the immediate context and the uniqueness of the adjective recalled from [Apuleius's] *The Golden Asse* [tr. Adlington, 1566, Tudor Translations, ed. Henley, 1893, pp. 99, 128, 236]) that the 'terrene moon' is Antony himself. His eclipse logically precedes his fall; first loss of power, then loss of position."

2336 **stay his time**] DEIGHTON (ed. 1891): "Wait till his passion subsides." BLUMHOF (ed. 1870): Spoken aside, half-aloud.

2338 **one . . . points**] DAVIES (1783, 2:353): "The office of a menial servant. . . . Metaphorically . . . a low and servile office." MALONE (ed. 1790): "*Points* were laces with metal tags, with which the old trunk-hose were fastened [to the doublet]." LINTHICUM (1936, p. 282, n. 3): "A row of points were fastened to the waistline of the hose, and a corresponding row of eyelets made at the waistline of the doublet. After the gentleman had donned these garments, his 'boy' drew the points of the hose through the eyelets on the doublet, and tied the two ends of each point in a bow-knot. This process was called trussing."

2340–2 HENINGER (1960, p. 56) "illuminates" by means of BARTHOLOMAEUS's (1582, fol. 162ᵛ) theory of the generation of hail: "Her heart would compare to a cold cloud, and the great heat of her love for Antony (suffused throughout her body) would act to compress her heart into hail. [She] turns Antony's accusation into a statement of her fervent devotion to him."

2340 RIDLEY (ed. 1954), supporting Theobald (ed. 1733): "Antony, not yet relenting, is bitterly answering Cleopatra's question: 'Yes, only too well I know your cold heart.'"

2341–50 **if . . . prey**] WALTER (ed. 1969) sees an allusion to the plagues in Exod. 8:21–4 ("Flies"), 9:18–29 ("haile"), and especially 12:12, 29–30 ("Cæsarian," Cleopatra's firstborn).

2343 **the sourse**] DEIGHTON (ed. 1891): "*Sc.* my heart."

2344 **in**] DEIGHTON (ed. 1891): "On."

as] BLUMHOF (ed. 1870) suggests both "when" and "in the way in which." For Sh.'s use of *as . . . so*, see FRANZ §578.

determines] CAWDREY (1604): "Resolue, conclude." MASON (1785, p. 284): "Dissolves." Commentators interpret the verb both literally, as does Mason—i.e., the hail

Dissolue my life, the next Cæsarian smile,   2345
Till by degrees the memory of my wombe,
Together with my braue Egyptians all,
By the discandering of this pelleted storme,
Lye grauelesse, till the Flies and Gnats of Nyle
Haue buried them for prey.   2350
      Ant. I am satisfied:

2345 Cæsarian] *Cæsario* ROWE1-THEO2, WARB-JOHN1
      smile] smite ROWE1+
2348 discandering] discattering ROWE1-POPE2; discandying mTBY2 *and* mTHEO2 (19
Feb. 1729, [fol. 40ᵛ]) *conj.*, THEO1+ (−KNT1)

---

dissolves—or figuratively, as does MALONE (ed. 1790): "Comes to its end, or dissolution.
The word is so used in legal conveyances, but I believe no *poet* but Shakspeare has employed it in this sense." COLLIER (ed. 1843): "But for the verse, we might, perhaps, more
properly and intelligibly read, 'as it *dissolves*, so *determine* (or *end*) my life'. 'Determine'
and 'dissolve' may, however, be taken as convertible terms."
      2345 **next Cæsarian**] DEY (1909, p. 85): "I believe the line should be punctuated
thus: 'The next [i.e., the next stone], Cæsarion smite!'" WALTER (1969, p. 138), noting
"Biblical overtones," relates the smiting of the Egyptian firstborn (Exod. 12:12) to
Cleopatra's "next," or firstborn. For *Cæsarian*, see n. 1757.
      2346 **memory . . . wombe**] CAPELL (1779 [1774], 1:42): "The memorials of my womb,
the things by which it will be remember'd . . . her children."
      2348 **discandering**] Most commentators favor THIRLBY's and THEOBALD's emenda-
tion *discandying*, meaning—THEOBALD (19 Feb. 1729, [fol. 40ᵛ])—"melting, dissolving."
IDEM (ed. 1733): "The congealing of the Water into Hail he [Sh.] metaphorically calls
candying." Quotes 2776–9; "Twentie . . . mollest," *Tmp.* 2.1.278–80 (977–9); "Will . . .
surfet," *Tim.* 4.3.225–7 (1846–8); *Ham.* 3.2.65 (1911); and *1H4* 1.3.251–2 (578–9). KNIGHT
(ed. 1841) is in the minority: Misinterpreting *discandying* as "melting into sweetness,"
he proposes "To *squander* [as in *MV* 1.3.22 (346)] is to scatter. . . . To *dis-scander*, we
believe then, is to *dis-squander.*" HUDSON (ed. 1855), in fact, suggests adopting
disquandering, though he does not do so. MACKAY (1884, p. 34) offers a fantastic explanation: "Formed from the Keltic *dith* (*di*), to crowd or press together, and *sqannradh*,
dispersion, a panic flight, a rout; corrupted by the London compositors into *discander*,
and allowed to pass unquestioned by the correctors of the press." See n. 2778.
      pelleted] See FRANZ §662 for adjectives, with the sense of "having," formed by
the addition of the inflectional suffix *-ed*. ABBOTT (§374) suggests *-ed* "loosely employed for *-ful, -ing*, or some other affix expressing connection." For *-ed* in Sh., see SMITHERS
(1970, pp. 27–37).
      2349–50 **till . . . prey**] DEIGHTON (ed. 1891) and others: "Till they have found a
grave in the stomachs of the flies and gnats of the Nile [i.e., have been devoured]." TURNER
(privately) suggests, "The flies and gnats cover—bury—the decomposing bodies."
      2351 WILSON (ed. 1950): "Ant.'s 'satisfaction' with this highly extravagant protesta-
tion [2341–50] is one more proof of his infatuation." But WALTER (ed. 1969): "Antony
apparently recovers his balance impressed by the weight of Cleopatra's curse." DELIUS

Cæsar sets downe in Alexandria, where
I will oppose his Fate. Our force by Land,
Hath Nobly held, our seuer'd Nauie too
Haue knit againe, and Fleete, threatning most Sea-like.   2355
Where hast thou bin my heart? Dost thou heare Lady?
If from the Field I shall returne once more
To kisse these Lips, I will appeare in Blood,
I, and my Sword, will earne our Chronicle,

2352 sets] sits JOHN1, v1773+ (–SIS, CAM3b, EVNS)
    in] 'fore HAN1
2354 our] and F2-ROWE3
2355 and] a mF2J *conj.* (and is a), COL2
    Fleete] Float ROWE1-v1773 (–CAP)
2357 shall] should POPE2-THEO2, WARB-JOHN1, v1773, v1778, RANN
2359 our] my F2-v1778 (–CAP)

(ed. 1856), however, holds that the reference is to what follows and not to what precedes. This view is supported by SORGENFREY (privately), who finds this instance an example of the "frequent use of the colon"—i.e., between unlinked coordinate clauses—here to "indicate that the succeeding clause is an explication or fulfilment of the preceding one."

2352 **sets downe**] BLUMHOF (ed. 1870) prefers the F1 reading, holding that it means "encamps," and compares *Cor.* 1.3.110 (462) and 5.3.2 (3348). See *OED,* Set *v.* 143a (*b*). But *sits down* also means "To encamp *before* a town, etc., in order to besiege it"; see *OED,* Sit *v.* 21c (*b*), which cites *Cor.* 4.7.28–9 (3119–20).

2353 **I . . . Fate**] FURNESS (ed. 1907): "A revelation of the conviction forced on Anthony both by the Soothsayer [983–8], and by his own experience, that it was Cæsar's 'fate' to be Anthony's superior." KITTREDGE (ed. 1941), agreeing, compares *Mac.* 3.1.71–2 (1061–2).

2355 **Fleete**] CAPELL (1779 [1774], 1:42), defending F1's reading: "'*Fleet*' . . . implies —a moving with nimbleness, a skimming lightly on water . . . and is therefore fitter than—*float* . . . which carries with it an idea of inaction and stillness." TYRWHITT (*apud* STEEVENS, ed. 1778): "*Fleet* is the old word for *float.*" See *OED,* Fleet *v.*[1]. Practically all commentators gloss as "float."

   Sea-like] SCHMIDT (1875): "Likely to keep the sea." DEIGHTON (ed. 1891) and others: "Sea-worthy."

2356 **heart**] DELIUS (ed. 1856): Antony is referring to his courage. Only BLUMHOF (ed. 1870) and FURNESS (ed. 1907) hold that the reference is to Cleopatra—"Lady."

2358 **in Blood**] In addition to "bloody," DEIGHTON (ed. 1891) and most commentators: "With an allusion to the phrase as used of a stag when in full vigour [compares *1H6* 4.2.48–50 (1999–2001) and *Cor.* 4.5.224–5 (2869–70)]."

2359 MALONE (*apud* STEEVENS [1780], 1:231): Alluding to "the swords belonging to the heroes of ancient romances, which are chronicled, and dignified with names."

   our] I.e., of us. For the subjective and objective genitive, see FRANZ §322.

   Chronicle] See n. 2204.

227

There's hope in't yet.   2360
    Cleo. That's my braue Lord.
    Ant. I will be trebble-sinewed, hearted, breath'd,
And fight maliciously: for when mine houres
Were nice and lucky, men did ransome liues
Of me for iests: But now, Ile set my teeth,   2365
And send to darkenesse all that stop me. Come,
Let's haue one other gawdy night: Call to me

2360–1 *One verse line* v1793-SING2, COL3-HAL, COL4, HUD2, OXF1, ALEX, EVNS
2360 There's hope in't] There is hope in it HAN1, CAP, v1778-SING1
2363 mine] my THEO2, WARB-JOHN1

2362 See n. 985.
    breath'd] HUDSON (ed. 1881): "*Exercised.* Repeatedly so. [Compares 'breathing time,' *Ham.* 5.2.181 (3639).]" CASE (ed. 1906): "But here a treble strength of breath goes with the like of heart and sinews."
    2363 **maliciously**] CAWDREY (1604, malitious): "Hating, or enuying." COTGRAVE (1611, Malicieusement): "*With an ill meaning, with a bad intent.*" See also "Malice" (198).
    2363–5 **when . . . me**] STEEVENS (*apud* REED, ed. 1803) compares *Homer's Iliads* 21.100–2: "Till his death, I did grace to Troy, and many lives did rate At price of ransome: but none now of all the brood of Troy (Who ever Jove throwes to my hands) shall any breath enjoy" (tr. Chapman, ed. A. Nicoll, 1957).
    2363 **houres**] WALTER (ed. 1969) alone: "May be an astrological image."
    2364 **nice**] The entire semantic spectrum is represented. CAWDREY (1604): "Slow, laysie." MINSHEU (1617): "Daintie, Coy . . . *effeminate.*" WARBURTON (ed. 1747): "Delicate, courtly, flowing in peace." JOHNSON (ed. 1765): "*Just fit for my purpose, agreeable to my wish.*" STEEVENS (ed. 1778): "*Trifling.* So in [*Rom.* 5.2.18 (2837)]." DAVIES (1783, 2:353): "Pleasure, gaiety, and happiness." RANN (ed. 1791–): "Glided smoothly on." DOUCE (1807, 2:94): "In a sense bordering on that of *amorous* or *wanton.*" SINGER (ed. 1826) adds, "Equivalent to *soft, tender, wanton,* or *luxurious.*" DELIUS (ed. 1856): Without care, careless. BLUMHOF (ed. 1870): Weak, unimportant. CANBY (ed. 1921): "*Fastidious, particular.*"
    2365 **Of**] I.e., from.
    for iests] WALTER (ed. 1969) compares 448: "To giue a Kingdome for a Mirth."
    2366 **stop**] MINSHEU (1617): "*Hinder.*"
    2367 **one other**] I.e., one more. This expression, unique in Sh., seems to have given way to *another* before Sh.'s time. For possible confusion of *one* and *on* (*an*), see n. 50.
    gawdy] BLOUNT (1656): "Grand days. In the Inns of Court there are four of these in the yeer, that is, one in every Term, viz. *Ascension day* in Easter Term, *Midsummer day* in Trinity Term, *All Saints day* in *Michaelmas* Term, and *Candlemas day* in Hillary Term. . . . The Etymology of the word may be taken from Judge *Gawdy*, who (as some affirm) was the first instituter of those days, or rather from *gaudium*, because (to say

All my sad Captaines, fill our Bowles once more:
Let's mocke the midnight Bell.
   Cleo. It is my Birth-day,   2370
I had thought t'haue held it poore. But since my Lord
Is *Anthony* againe, I will be *Cleopatra.*
   Ant. We will yet do well.
   Cleo. Call all his Noble Captaines to my Lord.   (yy3^{vb})
   Ant. Do so, wee'l speake to them,   2375
And to night Ile force
The Wine peepe through their scarres.
Come on (my Queene)
There's sap in't yet. The next time I do fight
Ile make death loue me: for I will contend   2380
Euen with his pestilent Sythe.   *Exeunt.*
   Eno. Now hee'l out-stare the Lightning, to be furious
Is to be frighted out of feare, and in that moode

2368 Bowles$_\wedge$ once more:] ~ ; ~~ $_\wedge$ ROWE1-SING1, COL1-HUD1, DYCE1-WH1, HAL-
HUD2 (−CAM1)
2371-2 *Verse lines ending* is . . . *Cleopatra.* HAN1
2375-8 *Arranged as verse lines, thus*: 2375-6, 2377-8 ROWE1+
2381 *Exeunt*] *Exeunt* ANT. CLE. Cha. Ira. *and Att.* CAP, v1778+ (*subst.*)
2383 be . . . and] frighted out of fear: CAP (*text*; be *restored in corrigenda*)

---

truth) they are days of *joy*, as bringing good cheer to the hungry Students. In Colledges
they are most commonly called *gawdy*, in Inns of Court *Grand days*, and in some places
they are called *Coller-days.*"
   2373 **will**] FURNESS (ed. 1907) detects "simple futurity" and refers to FRANZ §462
(now §616). KITTREDGE (ed. 1941): "Expresses determination."
   2380-1 STEEVENS (ed. 1785): "This idea seems to have been caught from the 12th
book [st. 60] of [John] Harrington's translation of the *Orlando Furioso*: 'Death goeth
about the field rejoicing mickle, To see a sword that so surpast his sickle' [1591, p. 93]."
   2380 DEIGHTON (ed. 1891) and most commentators: "*I.e.* as to which of us shall reap
the greater slaughter." WORDSWORTH (ed. 1883) in the minority: "*As if armed with.*"
   2381 **pestilent Sythe**] SCHMIDT (1875, Pestilent): "The scythe of pestilence, the deaths
occasioned by pestilence." For adjectives, "especially those ending in *ful*, *less*, *ble*, and
ive [and *ant*, *ent*, which] have both an active and a passive meaning," see ABBOTT §3
and FRANZ §121.
   2382-3 **to . . . feare**] SEYMOUR (1805, 2:74): "Fear, pressed to extremity, turns to fury."
   2382 **furious**] MINSHEU (1617, Furye): "*Rage, madnesse, outragiousnesse, frenzie.*"
   2383 **frighted**] ABBOTT (§472): "Ed following d or t . . . when written [is] often
not pronounced."
      out of] DELIUS (ed. 1856): Beyond.

The Doue will pecke the Estridge; and I see still
A diminution in our Captaines braine,   2385
Restores his heart; when valour prayes in reason,
It eates the Sword it fights with: I will seeke
Some way to leaue him.   *Exeunt.*

2384 and] *Om.* HAN1, HUD2, KIT1
2386 prayes in] preys on COTGRAVE (1655, p. 282) *conj.*, ROWE1+
2387 Sword] Swords ROWE2-POPE1
2388 *Exeunt.*] *Exit.* ROWE1-THEO4, CAP, v1778+

2384 **Estridge**] Which bird—the ostrich or the estridge—Sh. meant has troubled commentators. The first to gloss as "the ostrich" was RANN (ed. 1791–), perhaps following early dictionaries starting with COCKERAM (1623, Of Birds, [Pt. 3], sig. G8ʳ): "A huge bird which will swallow downe a peece of Iron halfe as bigge as a horseshooe, his feathers serue for Plumes for Nobles, and he runnes as fast as a horse"—a description taken substantially from Pliny's *Natural History* 10.1. The major dictionaries list only *ostrich*, although KERSEY (1702) refers to "Ostrich *or* estridge" and JOHNSON (1755) lists "*Estrich* . . . <commonly written *ostrich.*>" Evidently, the 18th c. had little doubt about which bird, indigenous to Africa or Ethiopia, was meant. DOUCE (1807, 1:436–7), however: "It has been quite overlooked that *estridge* signifies a *goshawk*. . . . It would be absurd to talk of a dove pecking an ostrich; the allusion is to the practice of flying falcons at pigeons. Thus Golding in his translation of *Ovid's metamorphoses* [1567, Bk. 2], fo. 9: 'With flittering feather[s] sielie *doves* so from the *gosshawk* flie'. The manor of Radeclyve in Nottinghamshire was held by the service of 'mewing a goshawk'; in the original charter, 'mutandi unum *estricum*'. In the romance of *Guy earl of Warwick* we have, '*Estrich falcons*, of great mounde [i.e., power]' [l. 176, ed. Zupitza, 1883, p. 12]. Falconers are often called *ostregers* and *ostringers* in the old books of falconry, and elsewhere. *Estridge* for *ostrich* or *ostridge* is a corrupt spelling that crept into the language at the commencement of Queen Elizabeth's reign, and it appears that after that period the two words were very often confounded together, and used one for the other." Since Douce, commentators have been split. They use the same passage in Sh. to prove both the opposing views: *1H4* 4.1.98 (2329), for example, is first used by Douce (1:435) for "estridge" and first used by IRVING & MARSHALL (ed. 1889) for "ostrich." Even Douce's (1:436) citing of *3H6* 1.4.41 (501), in which "*doves* do peck the *faulcon's* piercing talons," is cited by KITTREDGE (ed. 1941) for his gloss "ostrich." (WILSON [ed. 1950], glossing "ostrich" as "appropriate to Egypt," repeats this note in ed. 1964, but his glossary gives "goshawk.") Obviously, there is a linguistic complication, as sensed by 17th- and 18th-c. lexicographers and by the *OED*. For further discussion and illustration, see FURNESS (ed. 1907), WILSON (ed. 1950), and RIDLEY (ed. 1954).

2386 **heart**] See n. 10 ("Captaines").

2386–7 **when . . . with**] Possibly sententious; HALLIWELL (1868, p. 29): "This passage is . . . given in [John] Cotgrave's English Treasury [of Wit and Language], 1655 . . . [p. 282]."

2386 **prayes in**] WHITE's (ed. 1861) defense of F1—"'in' having the sense of upon"—is unlikely: *in* for *on* is usually found in reference to location, position, or time. See FRANZ §502.

  Enter Cæsar, Agrippa, & Mecenas with his Army, **4.1**
     Cæsar reading a Letter.   2390

Cæs. He calles me Boy, and chides as he had power
To beate me out of Egypt. My Messenger
He hath whipt with Rods, dares me to personal Combat.
Cæsar to *Anthony*: let the old Ruffian know,
I haue many other wayes to dye: meane time   2395
Laugh at his Challenge.

2389 ACT IV. SCENE I. ROWE, POPE, HAN1, WARB, JOHN1+; ACT IV. THEO
  SCENE Cæsar's *Camp.* ROWE1+ (*subst.*)
2395 I haue] He hath mTBY3 *conj.* (He has) *and* HAN1, JOHN1, CAP
2396–7 *One verse line* v1793+
2396 Laugh . . . Challenge] Laugh at this Challenge F2-POPE2; I at this challenge
laugh HAN1; I laugh at his challenge mTBY3 *and* UPTON (1746, p. 240) *conj.*, CAP (*text*;
his fond challenge *in* mCAP2 *and corrigenda*), RANN

2391–6 STAPFER (1880, p. 411), finding Caesar colorless: "When Antony . . .
challenged Octavius to single combat, it was not necessary for him [Octavius] to be a
wise man, to shrug his shoulders at a challenge so obviously absurd,—not to be a hero
was quite sufficient." DEIGHTON (ed. 1891): "Said with scorn at the idea of one like
himself deigning to fight with one like Antony."
  2391 He . . . Boy] JONES (ed. 1977) notes a similar insult in Suetonius (*The historie
of twelve Cæsars*, tr. Holland, 1606, p. 42). See also n. 2770.
   as] I.e., as if.
  2394 RIDLEY (ed. 1954) alone: "F's punctuation very probably right. *Cæsar to Antony* is then the opening of his reply (as though he was dictating a letter). . . . For
to . . . meaning 'versus', cf. [*1H6* 1.3.47 (414)], 'Blue coats to tawny coats.'"
   Ruffian] MINSHEU (1617, Ruffin): "*Swashbuckler* . . . Swaggerer."
  2395 I . . . dye] UPTON (1746, pp. 240–1) defends *He hath* for "I haue" by reference to Plutarch: "After this Antony sent a challenge to Caesar to fight him hand to
hand, and received for answer, *That* HE <viz., Antony> *might find several other ways
to end* HIS LIFE [see p. 449]." FARMER (*apud* STEEVENS, ed. 1773) elaborates: "Most indisputably this is the sense of Plutarch, and given so in the modern translations; but
Shakespeare was misled by the ambiguity of the old one [North]." WILSON (ed. 1950):
"North correctly translates Amyot." BLUMHOF (ed. 1870) and others find that the words
reflect not Caesar's scorn but rather his calm and prudence. DEIGHTON (ed. 1891), speaking
for still others: "If I wish to die there are plenty of ways of doing so without demeaning
myself to single combat with him."
  2396 **Laugh**] FURNESS (ed. 1907): "'Laugh' is . . . in the imperative . . . 'Let's
laugh.'" For the addition of *I*, as subject, see textual notes.

Mece. Cæsar must thinke,
When one so great begins to rage, hee's hunted
Euen to falling. Giue him no breath, but now
Make boote of his distraction: Neuer anger   2400
Made good guard for it selfe.
    Cæs. Let our best heads know,
That to morrow, the last of many Battailes
We meane to fight. Within our Files there are,
Of those that seru'd *Marke Anthony* but late,   2405
Enough to fetch him in. See it done,
And Feast the Army, we haue store to doo't,
And they haue earn'd the waste. Poore *Anthony.*   *Exeunt*

2397 must] we must WALKER (1860, 2:262) *conj.*, HUD2
      thinke,] ~ . MAL
2401–3 *Verse lines ending* heads . . . battels mTBY2 *and* mTHEO2 (21 Feb. 1729,
[fol. 41]) *conj.*, THEO1+
2403 many] *Om.* ROWE2-POPE2
2406 it] it be POPE1-CAP, v1793, v1803, KTLY, HUD2

2397 RIDLEY (ed. 1954): "Apart from the halting rhythm, this is an oddly third-personal
way for Maecenas to address Cæsar. . . . Should we perhaps read *Cæsar, we must think?*"
Previously suggested by WALKER (1860, 2:262). See textual notes.
2398–9 **When . . . falling**] BLUMHOF (ed. 1870) detects references to Ajax and the
boar of Thessaly (see 2810–12) or to Hercules (see 2802–6). WILSON (ed. 1950): "The
image of the embossed [see n. 2812] stag at bay."
2400 **Make boote**] See n. 1115 ("boot").
2400–1 **Neuer . . . selfe**] TILLEY (N307): "*Nothing* is well said or done in a passion
(in anger)." Excluded by DENT.
2402 **best heads**] DEIGHTON (ed. 1891): "Ablest generals." Implied in SCHMIDT's (1874)
"Pars pro toto; *head*=the whole person."
2404 **Files**] FORTESCUE (1916, 1:114, n. 1): "The file was . . . the unit . . . in which
the strength of an army was expressed. Men took their places in the *files*, not in the
ranks of an army." See also n. 6.
2406 **fetch him in**] BOSWELL (ed. 1821, 21:Glossary): "Apprehend, or subdue." BLUM-
HOF (ed. 1870): The phrase implies the hunting image (of closing in on), perhaps also
Caesar's desire that Antony be taken alive.
2408 **waste**] MINSHEU (1617): "*Consume.*" Commentators straddle two possibilities:
"Total consumption . . . without restraint" (SCHMIDT [1875]) and, mainly, "*Expense
. . . cost*" (HUDSON [ed. 1881]).
    Poore *Anthony*] KITTREDGE (ed. 1941): "An expression rather of pity and regret
than of scorn."

Enter Anthony, Cleopatra, Enobarbus, Charmian,   **4.2**
           Iras, Alexas, with others.   2410

Ant. He will not fight with me, *Domitian*?
Eno. No?
Ant. Why should he not?
Eno. He thinks, being twenty times of better fortune,
He is twenty men to one.   2415
Ant. To morrow Soldier,
By Sea and Land Ile fight: or I will liue,
Or bathe my dying Honor in the blood
Shall make it liue againe. Woo't thou fight well.
Eno. Ile strike, and cry, Take all.   2420
Ant. Well said, come on:
Call forth my Houshold Seruants, lets to night

                              Enter 3 or 4 Seruitors.

2409 SCENE II. ROWE1+ (–THEO)
     Alexandria. ROWE1+ (*subst.*)
2410 *Alexas,*] *Om.* CAP
2411 *Domitian*] *Domitius* ROWE1+
     Domitian?] ∼ . F3-NLSN (–HAN1, KNT1, COL2, HUD1, KTLY)
2412 No?] ∼ . THEO1+ (–NLSN)

2412 **No?**] CAPELL (1779 [1774], 1:42) justifies the substitution of a period for the
question mark: "This sullen affirmative negation expresses admirably the state of the
speaker's mind."
    2417 **or**] I.e., either; see FRANZ §586.
    2418 CASE (ed. 1906): "Perhaps an allusion to baths of blood as a remedy." WILSON
(ed. 1950) in support cites *OED*, blood-bath (Blood *sb.* 19).
        in the blood] BLUMHOF (ed. 1870): "In my blood" or "in the blood of my enemies."
    2419 **Woo't**] FRANZ (§176): A sporadically occurring form for *wilt*, in which the *l*
is not sounded. The apostrophe may indicate the missing *l*. KITTREDGE (ed. 1941): "This
form was employed only in very familiar language; hence its use implied either intimacy
. . . or contempt."
    2420 JOHNSON (ed. 1765): "Let the survivor take all. No composition, victory or death."
COLLIER (ed. 1858): "From the gaming table, meaning, let all depend upon this hazard,
and let the successful competitor 'take all.'" DENT (A192.1): "He that wins shall take *all*."
        strike] WILSON (ed. 1950): "Deliberately ambiguous: (a) fight desperately . . .
[and improbably] (b) strike sail and surrender."
    2421–2 **come . . . Seruants**] Only BLUMHOF (ed. 1870) explicitly suggests that an
attendant is addressed.
    2423 *Seruitors*] WILSON (ed. 1950, Glossary): "Attendant[s] (theatr. term)." Not sup-
ported by *OED*.

Be bounteous at our Meale. Giue me thy hand,
Thou hast bin rightly honest, so hast thou,   2425
Thou, and thou, and thou: you haue seru'd me well,
And Kings haue beene your fellowes.
    Cleo. What meanes this?
    Eno. 'Tis one of those odde tricks which sorow shoots
Out of the minde.   2430
    Ant. And thou art honest too:
I wish I could be made so many men,
And all of you clapt vp together, in
An *Anthony*: that I might do you seruice,
So good as you haue done.   2435
    Omnes. The Gods forbid.   (yy4ᵃ)
    Ant. Well, my good Fellowes, wait on me to night:
Scant not my Cups, and make as much of me
As when mine Empire was your Fellow too,
And suffer'd my command.   2440
    Cleo. What does he meane?
    Eno. To make his Followers weepe.
    Ant. Tend me to night;
May be, it is the period of your duty,

  2426 Thou] And thou ROWE1-v1778, RANN-SING1, DYCE2, HUD2, KIT1
      haue] have all KTLY
  2429 tricks] freaks HAN1; traits WARB
  2430-1 *One verse line* v1793+ (−ALEX)
  2435 done] done me WALKER (1860, 2:254) *conj.*, HUD2

    2424-7 **Giue . . . fellowes**] MURRY (1936, p. 362): "There is the double touch, which makes Antony Antony—the simple humanity of his handshake with his servants and the reminder that kings have done him the like office. . . . If kings were his servants, so his servants are now made kings. It is . . . the Last Supper of Antony."
    2425 **rightly**] SCHMIDT (1875): "Truly, really." See also FRANZ §389 and n. 2217.
    honest] See nn. 785, 1084.
    2427 **haue . . . fellowes**] DEIGHTON (ed. 1891): "Have shared your duties as servants."
    2429 **odde tricks**] Rejecting previous emendations—see textual notes—JOHNSON (ed. 1765): "*Trick* is here used in the sense in which it is uttered every day by every mouth elegant and vulgar." See also n. 3290. RANN (ed. 1791–) and most others: "An irregular sally, or transport of grief." SCHMIDT (1875, 6): "Out of passion or caprice." See "odde" (3509).
    2433 **clapt vp**] SCHMIDT (1874): "Shut up."
    2437-66 For Plutarch, see p. 449.
    2440 **suffer'd**] MINSHEU (1617): "Tollerate."
    2444 **period**] CAWDREY (1604): "The end of a perfect [i.e., full] sentence." Thus KERSEY (1702) and all commentators: "*Close*, or *conclusion*."

Haply you shall not see me more, or if,   2445
A mangled shadow. Perchance to morrow,
You'l serue another Master. I looke on you,
As one that takes his leaue. Mine honest Friends,
I turne you not away, but like a Master
Married to your good seruice, stay till death: 2450
Tend me to night two houres, I aske no more,
And the Gods yeeld you for't.
     Eno. What meane you (Sir)
To giue them this discomfort? Looke they weepe,
And I an Asse, am Onyon-ey'd; for shame,   2455
Transforme vs not to women.
     Ant. Ho, ho, ho:

2446 A] You do, a KTLY
     Perchance] It may chance POPE1-JOHN1
2452 yeeld] shield JOHNSON *conj. apud* CAM1 (*erroneous*), JOHN1
2454 they] you F2-ROWE3

2445 **Haply**] See n. 999.

2446 **Perchance**] CAPELL (1779 [1774], 1:43) rejects emendation (see textual notes) because "verses wanting . . . their full measure . . . have, upon some occasions, a singular beauty; [this one] being a kind of painting of the disturb'd mind of the person it comes from." For the common addition of a syllable before or after the caesura, see SIPE (1968, p. 33).

2449–50 RIDLEY (ed. 1954), following KITTREDGE (ed. 1941): "'You have served me well and I will remain your master till I die', but I think that the *like* is slightly awkward, and that the natural sense (though it cannot be extracted from the text) would be 'I ask you to stay with me till I die' (which, the whole context implies, will be soon). It is perhaps worth considering a 'transposed pointing' so that the passage will read: —I . . . stay till death, Tend me. . . . Then, taking *but*=except, the lines will mean 'I am not turning you away except as any master would warn loyal servants of his approaching death: stay with me till death comes.'"

2450 DEIGHTON (ed. 1891) alone detects "an allusion to the words of the Marriage Service, 'I *M.* take thee *N.* . . . till death us do part.'" See also n. 845–7.

2452 **yeeld**] FRANZ (§707): Elliptical for "yield reward."

2454 **they weepe**] CANTOR (1976, p. 221, n. 21): "Antony's ability to summon up tears and call on men's pity is already evident in [*JC* 3.2.173 (1706), 197–8 (1730–1)]. See also [Plutarch, pp. 408, 426]."

2455 **I . . . Onyon-ey'd**] JOHNSON (ed. 1765): "I have my eyes as full of tears as if they had been fretted by onions." CASE (ed. 1906): "Enobarbus' mocking reference to his own probably real emotion is quite in character . . . but just possibly it indicates some impatience of feeling in an intending 'master-leaver.'" Proverbial; see DENT (O67): "To weep (It may serve) with an *onion*."

2457 **Ho, ho, ho**] HOLT WHITE (*apud* STEEVENS, ed. 1793): "I.e. *stop*, or *desist* [*OED, int.*²]. Antony desires his followers to cease weeping." BOSWELL (ed. 1821): "These words

Now the Witch take me, if I meant it thus.
Grace grow where those drops fall (my hearty Friends)
You take me in too dolorous a sense,   2460
For I spake to you for your comfort, did desire you
To burne this night with Torches: Know (my hearts)
I hope well of to morrow, and will leade you,
Where rather Ile expect victorious life,
Then death, and Honor. Let's to Supper, come,   2465
And drowne consideration.   *Exeunt.*

Enter a Company of Soldiours.   **4.3**

1. *Sol.* Brother, goodnight: to morrow is the day.

2459 grow] grows mTBY4 *conj. and* THEO3
2461 For] *Om.* POPE1-v1773, v1793, v1803, SING1
    spake] speake POPE
2467 SCENE III. HAN1, JOHN1+
    SCENE, *a Court of Guard before the Palace.* THEO1+ (*subst.*)

---

may have been intended to express an hysterical laugh, in the same way as Cleopatra
exclaims—'*Ha! ha!* Give me to drink mandragora' [526]." CASE (ed. 1906): "After his
brief indulgence in sentiment and pathos, Antony laughs it off."

2458 **Witch . . . me**] WARBURTON (ed. 1747): "*I.e.* blast, bewitch" me. KITTREDGE
(ed. 1941) adds, "To *take* often means to 'infect,' 'enchant,' 'bewitch'. [Quotes *Ham.* 1.1.163
(162), 'No fairy takes, nor witch hath power to charm.']" See *OED*, Take 7.

2459 **Grace grow**] STEEVENS (ed. 1778) compares *R2*: "*Here did she drop a tear*; here,
in this place, I'll set a bank of rue, sour *herb of grace*" (3.4.104–5 [1916–17]). BAR-
THOLOMAEUS (1582, fol. 317ᵛ): "Rew is called *Ruta*, and is a medicinable hearbe . . .
Ruta Hortensis, and *Ruta Silvestris*, hearbe grace." See *OED*, Herb-grace. DELIUS (ed.
1856) seems the first to mention the possibility as well of grace in the customary sense
of "virtue, goodness."

2462 **burne**] DELIUS (ed. 1856): Destroy—i.e., by making bright. He quotes *Wiv.*
2.1.54 (599), "Wee . . . day-light."

2465 **death, and Honor**] UPTON (1746, p. 308): "*He* [Sh.] *sometimes expresses one
thing by two substantives*; which the rhetoricians call "Εν διὰ δυοῖν [i.e., hendiadys]
. . . honourable death." FURNESS (ed. 1907): Possibly "I'll expect a victorious life rather
than death, and I'll expect honour."

2466 **consideration**] SCHMIDT (1874): "Meditation, reflection."

2467, 2474, 2477 Although only two soldiers have lines, editors, following BLUMHOF
(ed. 1870), agree that two detachments, each with one speaker, meet at 2467 and are
joined by a third detachment with a speaker at 2474. RIDLEY (ed. 1954): "They go on

2. *Sol.* It will determine one way: Fare you well.
Heard you of nothing strange about the streets.   2470
   1 Nothing: what newes?
   2 Belike 'tis but a Rumour, good night to you.
   1 Well sir, good night.
They meete other Soldiers.

   2 Souldiers, haue carefull Watch.   2475
   1 And you: Goodnight, goodnight.
They place themselues in euery corner of the Stage.

   2 Heere we: and if to morrow

2471–3, 2475–6 *Three verse lines ending* rumour: . . . Soldiers, . . . good night.
v1793, v1803, SING, KNT1, STAU, KTLY; 2471 *as* F1, 2472 *prose, then as* F1 v1821, HUD1;
2471–2 *and* 2476 *as* F1, 2473 *and* 2475 *one verse line* DEL4, ARD, KIT1
   2472 to] *Om.* ROWE3
   2475 2] *Third Sold.* ARD2
      to first party SIS
   2476 1] 3. *S.* CAP, MAL, v1793-CAM3, EVNS
   2477 *They* . . . *Stage*] *the two first go to their Posts* CAP, MAL, v1793-OXF1 (−GLO, CAM1, WH2)
   2478–81, 2483–90 *Seven verse lines ending* to-morrow . . . hope . . . army, . . .
List, list! . . . earth. . . . say. . . . mean? mTBY2 *conj.*, CAP, DYCE, GLO, CAM1, HUD2+;
seven verse lines ending to-morrow . . . hope . . . army, . . . List, list! | 2. *SOLD.*
Hark! . . . well, . . . mean? v1793, v1803, SING, KNT1, STAU, KTLY; *four verse lines
ending* to-morrow . . . hope . . . army, . . . purpose *then as* F1 v1821, COL, WH1,
HAL; *prose* HUD1
   2478 2] 4. *S.* CAP, MAL, v1793-CAM3
      we:] we: [*going to theirs*] CAP, MAL, v1793-OXF1 (−GLO, CAM1, WH2)

---

their way to their posts . . . which are, by the space-destroying conventions of the Elizabethan stage, improbably close together. . . . Thus they are in a position not only to hear
the music, which in fact they could have done, but to interchange comments on it, which
in fact they could not." As an Elizabethan company consisted of 100–200 men (CRUICK-
SHANK, 1946; 1966, p. 54), the SD at 2467 must mean the more general sense of "party."
   2469 **It**] DELIUS (ed. 1856): The next day. BLUMHOF (ed. 1870): Or the present situation.
     determine] CAWDREY (1604): "Resolue, conclude." See also n. 2550.
   2477 DELIUS (1873, p. 200), citing this instance: The movements of armies and soldiers are documented with precision as orientation for the actors. For symbolic interpretations of the symmetry, see n. 2482–2501. The reference to "corners" argues against the
idea that the Globe stage was round. GREG (1955, p. 398): The SD reveals no promptbook connection; it is "not of a kind that would be convenient in actual performance."
See pp. 375–6.
   2478 **Heere we**] DEIGHTON (ed. 1891): "*I.e.* will keep watch."

Our Nauie thriue, I haue an absolute hope
Our Landmen will stand vp.   2480
 1 'Tis a braue Army, and full of purpose.
                Musicke of the Hoboyes is vnder the Stage.
 2 Peace, what noise?
 1 List list.

2480 Landmen] landsmen KTLY
2481 1] 3. *S.* CAP, MAL, v1793-ALEX
2483 2] 4. *S.* CAP, MAL, v1793-CAM3 (–NLSN, KIT1)
2484, 2490, 2493 1] 3 *Sold.* ALEX

2479 **hope**] COTGRAVE (1611, Esperance): *"Trust, confidence."* See also n. 662.
2481 **braue**] See n. 567.
2482–2501 CHARNEY (1957, pp. 158–9): "The dissolution theme is acted out on a mythological plane. . . . This scene is in the symbolic tradition of the medieval pageant wagon, where the stage itself represented the world, with heaven above and hell below. As a matter of structure, the departure of Hercules occurs at almost the same time as the desertion of Enobarbus; in some sense Enobarbus has been Antony's Hercules, and IV.iii gives his desertion a mythological compulsion." For other discussions of the nature of the scene, see BARROLL (1958, *TxSE*, pp. 72–3), TRAVERSI (1963, p. 159), STROUP (1964, p. 293), and SHAW (1974, pp. 227–32). STERNFELD (1963, pp. 223–4): "Supernatural strains presage that the gods are about to forsake Antony. . . . Plutarch's noise [p. 449] is not specified, however, it is performed by sundry sorts of instruments, which suggest a broken consort [i.e., concerted music]. Shakespeare . . . reduces the instruments used to a single family, oboes under the stage," perhaps because (p. 217) "the squealing of oboes was held to be an ill omen." See nn. 907, 2482. LONG (1964, p. 33): Sh. "replaced the singing, dancing, and music of the [i.e., Plutarch's] supernatural bacchantes with the more austere, yet still mysterious, music of hautboys; he replaced the citizens of Alexandria with sentries in a military setting; and he replaced the genius Bacchus with the genius Hercules. . . . Plutarch suggested the use of music to mark the departure of Antony's genius."
2482 *Musicke . . . Stage*] Crediting Thomas Warton (*History of English Poetry* [ed. Hazlitt, 1871, 3:291]), STEEVENS (ed. 1793) suggests that Sh. may have been influenced "by some of the machineries in Masques." He also mentions that Holinshed (*Description of England*, 1587, 3:1297/2/5–8) describes a "spectacle presented before Queen Elizabeth," in which music came "secretlie and strangelie *out of the earth*." COWLING (1913, p. 55): "Consorts of hautboys were the music prescribed by etiquette for banquets" and were also used (NAYLOR [1896, p. 169]) in masques and processions.
 Hoboyes] COWLING [1913, p. 54): "Conical wooden tubes with six holes in front for the fingers and a thumb-hole behind. . . . Their popular names were 'shawms' and 'waits.'"
2483 **noise**] DELIUS (ed. 1856): Music.

2 Hearke.   2485
1 Musicke i'th'Ayre.
3 Vnder the earth.
4 It signes well, do's it not?
3 No.
1 Peace I say: What should this meane?   2490
2 'Tis the God *Hercules*, whom *Anthony* loued,
Now leaues him.
1 Walke, let's see if other Watchmen
Do heare what we do?
2 How now Maisters?   *Speak together.* 2495

2485 *advancing from their Posts.* CAP
2486 1] 4 *Sold.* SING2, KTLY; 3 *Sold.* ALEX
2487 3] 4 *Sold.* ALEX
2488 4] *Om.* F2-JOHN1; 5 *Sold.* ALEX
       signes] singes F3; sings F4-POPE2
2489 3] 2 *Sold.* ROWE1-JOHN1; 4 *Sold.* ALEX
2491-7 *Four verse lines ending* lov'd, . . . watchmen . . . *Sol.* How now? (2496)
. . . strange? CAP, v1793, v1803, SING, KNT1, DYCE, STAU, GLO, KTLY, HUD2+ (−RID);
2491-5 *prose,* 2496-7 *two verse lines ending SOLD.* How now? . . . strange? v1821;
2491-5 *as* F1, 2496-7 *two verse lines ending Omnes.* How now! . . . strange? COL, WH1,
HAL; *two verse lines ending* lov'd, . . . watchmen *then as* F1 HUD1
2491 whom *Anthony* loued] who loved *Antony* ROWE1-JOHN1; who *Anthony* loved
mCOL1, COL2, HUD2
2494 *going. Enter other Soldiers, meeting them.* CAP; *They advance to another post.*
MAL, v1793-ARD1 (−CAM1)
2495 2] 1. F4; 1.2.3.4. CAP
       Speak together.] *Om.* HAN1, CAP, HUD1, OXF1

2488 **signes**] MINSHEU (1617): "Token." IDEM (Token): "*Signe of some great good or euill chance to come.*"
2491 *Hercules*] THEOBALD (21 Feb. 1729, [fol. 41ʳ]) conjectures *Bacchus*, following Plutarch (see n. 2482-2501), but later (acc. to CLARK & WRIGHT [ed. 1866]) changes his mind. UPTON (1746, p. 196): "But Bacchus was his [Antony's] tutelary God." CAPELL (1779 [1774], 1:43): "Bacchus, the god his author [Plutarch] intended, could not stand in his [Sh.'s] verse along with these words ['whom Antony loued']: . . . 'tis observable, he speaks only of '*musick*'; and has omitted the other signs mention'd [by Plutarch], which determine them to have proceeded from Bacchus." PHIALAS (ed. 1955): "Shakespeare substituted Hercules, the more appropriately to forecast Antony's defeat on the morrow." For Antony and Hercules, see n. 402.
2495 **Maisters**] OED (Master 20): "Used vocatively as a term of respect or politeness." IDEM (b): "Sirs, gentlemen." Also 2498.
       together] See n. 663.

239

Omnes. How now? how now? do you heare this?

1 I, is't not strange?

3 Do you heare Masters? Do you heare?

1 Follow the noyse so farre as we haue quarter.
Let's see how it will giue off.   2500   (yy4ᵇ)

Omnes. Content: 'Tis strange.   *Exeunt.*

Enter Anthony and Cleopatra, with others.   **4.4**

Ant. *Eros*, mine Armour *Eros*.

Cleo. Sleepe a little.

Ant. No my Chucke. *Eros*, come mine Armor *Eros*.   2505

Enter Eros.

Come good Fellow, put thine Iron on,

2497 I,] *Om.* F3-JOHN1

2499–2501 *Verse lines ending* quarter; . . . strange. v1793-COL2, SING2+ (–CAM1, RID, KIT1, ALEX); *prose* HUD1

2500 *Music.* COL4

2502 SCENE III. POPE, WARB; SCENE IV. HAN1, JOHN1+

  Cleopatra's *Palace.* POPE1+ (*subst.*)

  Cleopatra,] *Ad.* Charmion JOHN1, v1773-SING2, COL3, WH1-HAL, CAM, WH2-RID, ARD2, EVNS (*subst.*); *ad.* CHARMIAN, Iras CAP, DYCE, STAU, COL4, HUD2, KIT1, ALEX, SIS

2505 *Line divided* armour, | *Eros.* THEO1, THEO2, WARB

2507 good] my good ROWE1-CAP, v1793, v1803, KTLY, DYCE2, HUD2

  thine] mine mTBY2 *conj.*, HAN1, COL2-ALEX (–WH1, HAL, RID, CAM3)

2496 Despite the SP, the questions suggest that they were distributed rather than spoken in unison. See also 2501.

2498 **heare . . . heare**] ABBOTT (§480): "Monosyllables ending in r or re, preceded by a long vowel or diphthong, are frequently pronounced as dissyllables."

2499 **so . . . quarter**] RANN (ed. 1791–): "To the extent of our station."

2500 **giue off**] JOHNSON (1755, *Give, v. n.* 6): "Cease."

2502 **Enter . . . others**] RIDLEY (ed. 1954): "F's omission of Charmian may be just an oversight, but it may suggest that Charmian's few words and Cleopatra's two words of rejoinder [2547–8] were [added by Sh. as] an afterthought." Charmian is normally mentioned in SDs; see p. 376.

2505 **Chucke**] JOHNSON (1755): "A word of endearment, corrupted from chicken or chick."

2507 **thine**] MALONE (ed. 1790), comparing *H5* 4.8.41 (2756): "*Thine iron* is the iron which thou hast in thy hands, i.e. Antony's armour." HUDSON (ed. 1855): "The occurrence of *mine* in the two preceding lines shows that it should be mine here." SINGER

If Fortune be not ours to day, it is
Because we braue her. Come.
   Cleo. Nay, Ile helpe too, *Anthony.*   2510
What's this for? Ah let be, let be, thou art
The Armourer of my heart: False, false: This, this,
Sooth-law Ile helpe: Thus it must bee.
   Ant. Well, well, we shall thriue now.
Seest thou my good Fellow. Go, put on thy defences.   2515
   Eros. Briefely Sir.
   Cleo. Is not this buckled well?
   Ant. Rarely, rarely:
He that vnbuckles this, till we do please
To daft for our Repose, shall heare a storme.   2520

2509–11 *Verse lines ending* too. . . . art HAN1, JOHN1+
2510 *Anthony.*] *Om.* mTBY2 *conj.*, HAN1, JOHN1+
2511–12 *Given to Antony*: What's . . . this, this. mTBY2 *conj.*, HAN1, JOHN1-v1778;
Ah . . . this, this. mTBY2 *conj.*, MAL+
2513–16 *Three verse lines ending* well, . . . fellow? . . . Sir. HAN1, CAP, v1778+
2513 Thus . . . bee.] *Given to Antony* mCOL1, COL2, HUD1, COL3
2516 *Eros.*] *Eno.* F4-v1773 (–HAN1, CAP)
2518 Rarely] Oh! rarely HAN1, CAP, KTLY
2520 heare] bear mTBY4 *conj.*, COL2, SING2, COL3, COL4

(ed. 1856), questioning Malone, compares "thy defences" of 2515. RIDLEY (ed. 1954):
"Antony is, I think, being slightly humorous: 'Come on, Eros, put your whole ironmonger's
shop on me.'" SISSON (1956, 2:270), agreeing with Malone: "The word *iron* for *armour*
invites the familiar touch of *thine.*"
   2509 **braue**] MINSHEU (1617): "*Affront, or abuse to ones face, to swagger with.*"
   2510–13 COATES (1978, p. 50): "Cleopatra . . . arms Antony, recalling the many
Renaissance paintings of Venus arming Mars, love aiding courage." Opinions of which
piece is being put on, and how, are abundant but inconclusive.
   2510–12 ***Anthony* . . . this**] WILSON (ed. 1950): "A speech [with *Anthony* as SP]
added in the margin and wrongly inserted by the compositor." RIDLEY (ed. 1954): "'Sooth-
law Ile helpe' [2513] was also part of the addition, with the appropriate speech-heading
for Cleopatra. . . . Her speech originally stood simply: *Cleo.* Nay, Ile helpe too, what's
this for? Thus it must bee." Both views are purely speculative. See textual notes.
   2511–12 **thou . . . heart**] DEIGHTON (ed. 1891): "Your work is to steel my heart
with courage, not to arm my body with iron."
   2513 **Sooth-law**] I.e., sooth (truly) law. *OED* (Law *int.*): "An exclamation . . . in
early use chiefly asseverative."
   2518 **Rarely**] See n. 3387.
   2520 **daft**] I.e., daff't. MINSHEU (1617, Doffe): "*Doe of, as* Doff your cap, *i.*[*e.*,] *put
off your cap.*" JOHNSON (1755) mistakenly conceives of the verb as *to daft,* "contracted
from *do aft*; that is, to *throw back,* to *throw off.*" CERCIGNANI (1981, p. 113): "In certain

Thou fumblest *Eros*, and my Queenes a Squire
More tight at this, then thou: Dispatch. O Loue,
That thou couldst see my Warres to day, and knew'st
The Royall Occupation, thou should'st see
A Workeman in't.　　　　　　　　　　　　　　　　　　　　2525

Enter an Armed Soldier.

Good morrow to thee, welcome,
Thou look'st like him that knowes a warlike Charge:
To businesse that we loue, we rise betime,
And go too't with delight.　　　　　　　　　　　　　　　　2530
　　Soul. A thousand Sir, early though't be, haue on their
Riueted trim, and at the Port expect you.　　　　　　　*Showt.*
　　　　　　　　　　　　　　　　　　　Trumpets Flourish.

2522 then thou] *Om.* F2-ROWE3
2530-2 *Three verse lines ending* Sir, . . . trim, . . . you. ROWE1-ARD1, KIT1+; *ending*
delight. . . . on . . . you. RID
2532 *Showt*] *Ad. within* CAP, DYCE, STAU, HUD2, ALEX
2533 *After* 2536 COL4

forms of Middle English speech, the tendency to lower and unround the reflex of OE
ŏ . . . operated so fully that ME ŏ was eventually identified with ME ă, as can be seen
from such phonological variants as . . . *daff* beside original . . . *doff*. The development . . . was apparently a feature not only of the Western and South-Western but
also of the Eastern dialects, with which Cockney English is closely allied."
　　　heare a storme] COLLIER (1852, p. 476): "An enemy . . . was not likely to 'hear
a storm' of words, but 'to *bear* a storm' of blows." HUDSON (ed. 1855) and most others:
"The change [by Collier] is plausible, but not necessary." See textual notes. THISELTON
(1899, p. 22) in support of Collier compares "battery . . . heart" (2872) and "burst
. . . brest" (11–12).
　　2522 **tight**] MALONE (ed. 1790): "Expert . . . adroit." SINGER (ed. 1826) compares
Wiv. 1.3.88 (370); HUDSON (ed. 1855), Fletcher's *Fair Maid of the Inn* 2.1 (*Works*, ed.
Waller, 1910, 9:167).
　　2524 **Royall Occupation**] WORDSWORTH (ed. 1883): "*Trade of kings.*" DELIUS (ed.
1856) compares "*Othello's* occupation's gone" (*Oth.* 3.3.357 [2000]).
　　2528 **Charge**] MINSHEU (1617): "*Command.*" SCHMIDT (1874, 7) and most others:
"Military post or command." WILSON (ed. 1950) alone: "Message." Compare nn. 1877,
2748 ("charg'd").
　　2529 **betime**] COTGRAVE (1611, De bonne heure): "*In good time . . . early, betimes.*"
See 2539. Plutarch speaks of the "breake of day" (p. 449). See n. 2698. DEIGHTON (ed.
1891): "The form *betimes* is more common." See FRANZ §237.
　　2532 **trim**] JOHNSON (1755): "Dress; geer; ornaments." MALONE (*apud* STEEVENS
[1780], 1:231) compares *H5* 4.Pr.12–13 (1801–2).
　　　　Port] RANN (ed. 1791–): "The gates." Compare n. 358. TURNER (privately): "More
likely a sallyport."

Enter Captaines, and Souldiers.

Alex. The Morne is faire: Good morrow Generall.	2535
All. Good morrow Generall.	
Ant. 'Tis well blowne Lads.	
This Morning, like the spirit of a youth	
That meanes to be of note, begins betimes.	
So, so: Come giue me that, this way, well-sed.	2540
Fare thee well Dame, what ere becomes of me,	
This is a Soldiers kisse: rebukeable,	
And worthy shamefull checke it were, to stand	
On more Mechanicke Complement, Ile leaue thee.	
Now like a man of Steele, you that will fight,	2545

2535 *Alex.*] *Cap*[*tain*]. ROWE1+
2537 Lads] Lad F2-POPE2
2540 this way, well-sed] what ere becomes of me F2-ROWE3; this way; well set BLUM
2541 becomes] become F2
2543 checke] cheek THEO2, THEO4, WARB (*text*; check *in errata*)
2544 more] mere v1785
2544-5 thee. . . . Steele,] ~ , . . . ~ . ROWE1+

2535 *Alex.*] CAPELL (1779 [1774], 1:44) suggests that the parts of Alexas and a Captain were doubled. But there is no evidence for this view. Since there is no captain of such a name in the source, *Alex.* might be Alexas or Alexander Cooke, the actor. Both possibilities are remote, however: the first because "*Alexas* did reuolt" (2590), the second because of the nature of the copy (see p. 364).

2537 **blowne**] Commentators are split between "bright" (RANN [ed. 1791–]) or "*blossoming*" (HUDSON [ed. 1881]) — both referring to "Morning" (2538) — and the trumpets sounding the flourish at 2533 (DELIUS [ed. 1856]).

2539 **betimes**] See n. 2529. DEIGHTON (ed. 1891): "The final *-s* being due to the habit of adding *-s* or *-es* to form adverbs, as in *whiles, besides*, etc."

2540 KITTREDGE (ed. 1941): "Addressed to Cleopatra, who is still busy adjusting Antony's armour."

well-sed] DELIUS (ed. 1856) and most commentators: Bravo, good, well done. See *AYL* 2.6.14 (964). BLUMHOF (ed. 1870) emends to *well set*, referring to the armor, which is now in place, and noting that F1 always prints *said* when this word is meant.

2542 **rebukeable**] *OED*: "Now *rare*" but "Freq. in 16th c."

2543 **shamefull**] I.e., causing shame. For the active and passive sense in adjectives ending in *-ful*, see FRANZ §121. See also 129–30, 260, 377, 751, 2082, 2705.

2544 **Mechanicke Complement**] DELIUS (ed. 1856), followed by most commentators: A ceremonious farewell such as might be appropriate to common people, artisans. Citing this line, *OED* (Mechanic 3): "Vulgar, low, base." BLUMHOF's (ed. 1870) emphasis on a purely formal, time-wasting farewell, like CASE's (ed. 1906) preference for "the early use of *mechanic* for unspontaneous, and so ceremonious or conventional," is not sup-

Follow me close, Ile bring you too't: Adieu.　　　　　*Exeunt.*
　Char. Please you retyre to your Chamber?
　Cleo. Lead me:
He goes forth gallantly: That he and *Cæsar* might
Determine this great Warre in single fight;　　　　　　　2550
Then *Anthony*; but now. Well on.　　　　　*Exeunt*

　　　　　Trumpets sound. Enter Anthony, and Eros.　　　**4.5**

Eros. The Gods make this a happy day to *Anthony.*
Ant. Would thou, & those thy scars had once preuaild
To make me fight at Land.　　　　　　　　　　　　　2555

2546 *Exeunt*] *Ad.* EROS, ANTONY, Officers, *and* Soldiers CAP, v1778+
2547 you] you to ROWE3-THEO2, WARB-THEO4, v1773
　　　retyre] retire you SEYMOUR (1805, 2:75) *conj.*, HUD2
2552 SCENE IV. POPE, WARB; SCENE V. HAN1, JOHN1+
　　　SCENE *changes to a Camp.* THEO1-JOHN1, v1773; *Under the Walls of* Alexandria.
Antony's *Camp.* CAP, MAL, v1793-KIT1, ALEX, ARD2, EVNS; *Near Alexandria.* v1778, RANN,
CAM3, SIS (*subst.*)
　　　Eros] *Ad. a Soldier meeting them* mTBY2 *and* mTHEO2 (21 Feb. 1729, [fol. 41])
conj., THEO1+ (*subst.*)
2553 *Eros.*] *Sold.* mTBY2 *and* mTHEO2 (21 Feb. 1729, [fol. 41]) *conj.*, THEO1+

---

ported by the Shn. semantics, which is not always negative — certainly not in the cheerful
bravado of this speech — and never "mechanical" in the modern sense. See 3451.
　2549 **That**] The optative subjunctive, here elliptical. See FRANZ §637.
　2550 **Determine**] ALLEN (1900, p. 55): "'Determination' is once used [by Sh.] in
its legal sense, as signifying the end. . . . 'Determine' is also twice used in a like sense.
[Quotes 'So . . . determination,' *Son.* 13.5–6; *Cor.* 5.3.120 (3475); and this line.]" See
n. 2469.
　2553, 2556, 2561 *Eros.*] THEOBALD (21 Feb. 1729, [fol. 41ʳ]): "The 3 first Speeches,
here given to Eros, should belong to that *Soldier* [whom Antony met at 1931]. [Please]
to observe, a Soldier twice speaks in this Scene, tho None is mark'd to enter. Besides
E[ros had] but just before quitted the Stage w:ᵗʰ Antony, & could not well know the
News of Enoba[rbus's] Desertion." CAPELL (1779 [1774], 1:44), also reassigning the speeches:
"Their style is . . . most unsuitable to the dependant condition of Eros, the gentleness
of his manners, and his extream love of his master." RIDLEY (ed. 1954): "One might
suppose that Shakespeare had intended to operate with only Antony and Eros, but found
that later he wanted another speaker, and hurriedly inserted a soldier."
　2553 **happy**] See n. 76.

Eros. Had'st thou done so,
The Kings that haue reuolted, and the Soldier
That has this morning left thee, would haue still
Followed thy heeles.
    Ant. Whose gone this morning?　　　　　　　　　　2560
    Eros. Who? one euer neere thee, call for *Enobarbus,*
He shall not heare thee, or from *Cæsars* Campe,　　　　　(yy4^{va})
Say I am none of thine.
    Ant. What sayest thou?
    Sold. Sir he is with *Cæsar.*　　　　　　　　　　　2565
    Eros. Sir, his Chests and Treasure he has not with him.
    Ant. Is he gone?
    Sol. Most certaine.
    Ant. Go *Eros*, send his Treasure after, do it,
Detaine no iot I charge thee: write to him,　　　　　　　　2570
(I will subscribe) gentle adieu's, and greetings;
Say, that I wish he neuer finde more cause
To change a Master. Oh my Fortunes haue
Corrupted honest men. Dispatch *Enobarbus.*　　　　*Exit*

2556–9, 2561–3 *Given to Soldier* mTBY2 *and* mTHEO2 (21 Feb. 1729, [fol. 41]) *conj.,*
CAP, MAL, v1793+

2559–61 *Verse lines ending* Who? . . . *Enobarbus,* POPE1+

2563–8 *Three verse lines ending Sold.* Sir, . . . treasure . . . certain. THEO1-COL2,
SING2-ARD2, EVNS; 2563–4 *one verse line,* 2565–8 *prose* HUD1; *three verse lines ending*
thine.' . . . Caesar. . . . him *then as* F1 YAL2

2570 iot] jot of it CAP

2571 (I will subscribe)] ˌ ~ ~ ~ ˌ POPE1-THEO4

2574 Dispatch *Enobarbus*] Dispatch *Eros* F2-ROWE3, WH1; dispatch my *Eros*
POPE1-JOHN1; Dispatch.——O *Enobarbus* CAP; Dispatch. Enobarbus v1773-MAL,
v1821-STAU, GLO+; Eros! dispatch RITSON (1792, pp. 5, 25) *conj. and* RANN, v1793, v1803

2568 ELZE (1886, p. 276) conjectures, "The words . . . belong to Eros. . . . Antony, unwilling to believe him [the Soldier], appeals to the higher authority of Eros."

2569–74 See n. 2600–4. HUDSON (ed. 1881): "Plutarch [see p. 440] represents this
as having occurred before the battle of Actium."

2570 **iot**] MINSHEU (1617): "A thing of no value."

2571 **subscribe**] CAWDREY (1604): "Write vnder, or to agree with another in any matter." Most prefer the former—i.e., sign.

2574 **Dispatch *Enobarbus***] See textual notes and conj., p. 356. RITSON (1792, pp.
3–5): "'Anthony . . . desires . . . *Eros* to dispatch, and then pronounces the name
Enobarbus. . . . [F2] supposed that Enobarbus must have been an error of the press,
and therefore reads; "Dispatch, *Eros*."' Such is Mr. Malones account [ed. 1790, 1:xxvi;
Malone does not, however, mention that the line's meter] . . . would be defeated by
the word *Enobarbus*. . . . The manuscript, it is probable, had, in this place, only an

Flourish. Enter Agrippa, Cæsar, with Enobarbus,   **4.6**
and Dollabella.   2576

Cæs. Go forth *Agrippa*, and begin the fight:
Our will is *Anthony* be tooke aliue:
Make it so knowne.
   Agrip. Cæsar, I shall.   2580
   Cæsar. The time of vniuersall peace is neere:
Proue this a prosp'rous day, the three nook'd world

2575 SCENE III. ROWE; SCENE V. POPE, WARB; SCENE VI. HAN1, JOHN1+
   Cæsar's *Camp.* ROWE1-JOHN1, v1773, v1778, RANN, EVNS; *Before* Alexandria.
Cæsar's *Camp.* CAP, MAL, v1793-KIT1, ALEX, ARD2 (*subst.*); *The same.* CAM3, SIS (*subst.*)
   Flourish.] *Om.* F2-JOHN1, v1773, v1778, RANN
2579–80 *One verse line* KNT1, STAU, KTLY, ALEX, EVNS
2580 *Exit* AGRIPPA. CAP, v1778+
2582 a] is a RIDb

E. of which the original printer improperly made *Enobarbus.* . . . The editor of [F2] . . . has therefor rightly corrected the word, but, at the same time, has neglected to observe the transposition which had been made by his predecessor. . . . Take the line, therefor, as Shakspeare gave it. . . . —*Eros! dispatch.*" Ritson was unaware that "polysyllabic names often receive but one accent at the end of a line" (ABBOTT §469). HUDSON (ed. 1881), summarizing various attitudes: "*Dispatch* is addressed to Eros, for hastening the work just committed to him; and . . . *Enobarbus!* is an exclamation of grief and surprise, or wonder, at the desertion of his friend."

   2575–6 *Enter . . . Dollabella*] RIDLEY (ed. 1954): "The placing of Agrippa first may be due to mere carelessness, but does it perhaps indicate that Agrippa is to enter by a different door (on his return from seeing that the troops are ready for action, or the like)?"

   2577 See n. 2063–4.

   2578 **tooke**] For strong verbs in Sh., see FRANZ §170.

   2580 See n. 2151.

   2581 WILSON (ed. 1950): "This, which reflects the coming of Christ ([see] the interpolation in [Goulart, *Life of Octavius Caesar*, tr. North, 1612, p. 1179]), also voices the aspiration of many in England about 1606–7, especially of James I," probably referring to the marginal gloss "At the birth of Christ war ceaseth." WALTER (ed. 1969): "Also perhaps a recollection of Virgil's 'messianic' Eclogue IV."

   2582 **Proue this**] If this prove. Cited by FRANZ (§644, *Anm.* 4c) as an instance of the inversion of subject to indicate a conditional sentence, widespread in Sh.

      three nook'd world] KERSEY (1702, Nook): "*Corner.*" THEOBALD (ed. 1733): "*Europe, Asia,* and *Africk* making . . . three Angles of the Globe . . . the *American* Parts not being then discover'd." MALONE (ed. 1790) cites *Jn.* 5.7.116 (2727), "three corners of the world," and John Lyly's *Euphues and his England* (1580; ed. Warwick Bond, 1902, p. 32). BLUMHOF (ed. 1870): The three parts of the earth divided among the triumvirate.

Shall beare the Oliue freely.

Enter a Messenger.

Mes. *Anthony* is come into the Field.   2585
Cæs. Go charge *Agrippa*,
Plant those that haue reuolted in the Vant,

2583, 2585-6 *Verse lines ending Antony . . . Agrippa* CAP, v1778+
2585 *Anthony*] *Mark Antony* POPE1-JOHN1

HERFORD (ed. 1899): "The Roman world . . . conceived as the triangle formed by its
three seats of sovereignty." CASE (ed. 1906): "The Roman world fell naturally into such
a division of East and West provinces and Africa. See also *Julius Cæsar*, IV. i. 14 [1868].
A trine aspect of the world was familiar to contemporary poets . . . [Thomas Heywood,
The Brazen Age]: 'Il'e make her Empresse ore the *triple* world' [*Dramatic Works*, ed.
Shepherd, 1874, 3:242]; *Locrine*, III. iv. [35–]36: 'Stout Hercules . . . That tam'd the
monsters of the *three-fold* world'; *ibid.* V. iv. 5[–6]: 'The great foundation of the *triple*
world, Trembleth' [both in *The Shakespeare Apocrypha*, ed. Tucker Brooke, 1908], etc.
In such cases the phrase was probably caught from the *triplex mundus* of Ovid, *Metam*[*or-
phoses* 12.]40, involving sky, land and sea. [Sylvester's] Du Bartas . . . speaks of the
earth as divided 'in *three* vnequall Portions' by the sea and its arms [1620; ed. Snyder,
1979, p. 174, l. 90], and again [ed. Snyder, 1979, p. 443, ll. 46, 47], of 'this spacious
Orb' as parted by the Creator 'Into *three* Parts', east, south and west, 'Twixt *Sem*, and
Cham, and *Japheth*.'" Still more possibilities are discussed by FURNESS (ed. 1907). Of
special interest is the answer to the question in HUDSON (ed. 1855): "How the world
came to be thus spoken of as having *three corners* only?" BLAKISTON's (1964, p. 868)
explanation, developed by ANDERSON (1979, p. 106), apparently unaware of Blakiston:
Gloss as "three-sectored world. Elizabethans would have thus construed the phrase for
two reasons: (1) One meaning of *nook*, now obsolete, was 'sector of a circle'; a pie was
cut into 'nooks'. (2) A geometrical symbol for the Old World . . . was that used in the
so-called T-in-O maps: a 'T' circumscribed by an 'O', with the top half (nook) of the
circle representing Asia, and the lower left-hand and right-hand quadrants (nooks)
representing, respectively, Europe and Africa." See also 1984 and conj., p. 357.

2583 **beare . . . freely**] WARBURTON (ed. 1747) and most commentators prefer "produce": "*I.e.* shall spring up every where spontaneously and without culture." MASON
(1785, pp. 284–5) and a few others: "To *bear* does not mean to *produce*, but to *carry*;
and the meaning is, that the world shall then enjoy the blessings of peace, of which
olive branches were the emblem."

freely] COTGRAVE (1611, Liberalement): "*Freely, bountifully.*" See also 3227.
2586 See n. 2063–4.
2587–9 This tactic is not described by Frontinus in his manual on strategy, although
there are similar ones. He does mention (*Stratagems* 3.16) Hannibal, in a campaign against
Scipio in Africa, placing auxiliaries in front of the Carthaginians so that the former might
be unable to run away. Frontinus makes no moral judgments on the stratagems he describes.
2587 **Vant**] COTGRAVE (1611, Avant-garde): "*The Forward, or vauntgard, of an armie.*" In *vanguard* the *t* is elided.

247

That *Anthony* may seeme to spend his Fury
Vpon himselfe.   *Exeunt.*
    Enob. Alexas did reuolt, and went to *Iewry* on   2590
Affaires of *Anthony*, there did disswade
Great *Herod* to incline himselfe to *Cæsar*,
And leaue his Master *Anthony*. For this paines,
Cæsar hath hang'd him: *Camindius* and the rest
That fell away, haue entertainment, but   2595
No honourable trust: I haue done ill,
Of which I do accuse my selfe so sorely,
That I will ioy no mote.

              Enter a Soldier of Cæsars.

    Sol. Enobarbus, Anthony   2600
Hath after thee sent all thy Treasure, with

2589 *Exeunt*] *Ad.* CÆSAR, *and Train* CAP, v1778+
2590–1 *Verse lines ending* Jewry, . . . did persuade v1793, v1803, SING, KNT1, COL3, KTLY, CAM1, RID
2590 did] doth ROWE3, POPE
     and] he CAP, KTLY
2591 *Anthony*] Antony's KTLY
     did] did he RANN
     disswade] perswade ROWE1-KNT1, COL2-STAU, GLO-ARD1
2593 this] his mTBY2 *conj.*, HAN1
2598, 2600 *One verse line* v1793+ (−ALEX)
2598 mote] more F2+

2588 **spend**] See n. 3121.
2590–4 *Alexas . . . him*] For Plutarch's version, see pp. 446, 447. Alexas was the friend of Antony. See PAULY, Alexas von Laodikeia, Supp. 1:56 (1a); not in *OCD*.
2590–1 *Alexas . . . Anthony*] CAPELL (1779 [1774], 1:44): "The revolt of Alexas was not nor could not be prior to his going to Herod."
2590 *Iewry*] IRVING & MARSHALL (ed. 1889): "Judea." See also 108, 1625 ("Iury"), 1830.
2591 **disswade**] CAWDREY (1604): "To perswade to the contrarie." Those who emend do so on the basis of Plutarch's use of *perswaded* (p. 447).
2593 **this paines**] FRANZ (§194): In Sh. *pains*, in the abstract sense, can be both singular and plural.
2595 **entertainment**] COTGRAVE (1611, Entretien): "*Maintenance, meanes, nourishment.*" Agreeing, BOSWELL (ed. 1821, 21:Glossary) and all others: "Admission of a soldier into pay." See also nn. 671, 2320.
2600–4 GREY (1754, 2:210) points out a parallel in Plutarch's *Julius Cæsar* (tr. North, 1579, p. 780): Caesar showed "the same generosity towards *Labienus*, who had been his particular friend, and lieutenant, and fought by him very vigorously in the *Gallic wars*;

His Bounty ouer-plus. The Messenger
Came on my guard, and at thy Tent is now
Vnloading of his Mules.
    Eno. I giue it you.   2605
    Sol. Mocke not *Enobarbus,*
I tell you true: Best you saf't the bringer
Out of the hoast, I must attend mine Office,
Or would haue done't my selfe. Your Emperor
Continues still a Ioue.   *Exit* 2610
    Enob. I am alone the Villaine of the earth,
And feele I am so most. Oh *Anthony,*
Thou Mine of Bounty, how would'st thou haue payed
My better seruice, when my turpitude
Thou dost so Crowne with Gold. This blowes my hart,   2615

2604–7 *Three verse lines ending* mules. . . . Enobarbus. . . . bringer v1793, v1803, SING, KNT1, STAU; *ending* you. . . . Enobarbus. . . . bringer COL1-HUD1, DYCE1, COL3, WH1, GLO, HAL+; *ending* you. . . . not, . . . bringer KTLY

2606 Mocke] Mock me THEO1-THEO4, v1793, v1803; I mock CAP

2607 Best you saf't] Best you see safe ROWE3, POPE, HAN1, WARB, CAP; best, you see safe't THEO; Best that you saf'd v1793, v1803, HUD2; 't were best you safed RID *conj.*, CAM3b

2615 blowes] bows ROWE1-THEO4, CAP

2615–16 hart, . . . not:] ~ ; . . . ~ , ROWE1+

---

yet when he deserted, and went over to *Pompey*, *Cæsar* sent all his money and equipage after him."

2602 **ouer-plus**] See n. 1919.

2603 **on my guard**] Most commentators prefer "While I was on guard" (KITTREDGE [ed. 1941]); some, "*Where I was on duty*" (WORDSWORTH [ed. 1883]). HUDSON (ed. 1881) alone: "*Under* my guard."

2607 **saf't**] See n. 367.

2608 **hoast**] MINSHEU (1617): "*Of Souldiers, or Armie.*" See also 2687.

2611 **alone**] REED (*apud* STEEVENS, ed. 1793): "*Pre-eminently* the *first*, the *greatest.* . . . To stand alone, is still used in that sense." See ABBOTT §18.

    alone the] ABBOTT (§92) says *the* is "used to denote notoriety, &c."; FRANZ (§259) refers to the emphatic use of the article.

    Villaine] See n. 1057.

2612 **most**] MASON (1785, p. 285): "More than any one else thinks it."

2615 **blowes**] JOHNSON (ed. 1765): "Swells." Most commentators agree (see *OED*, *v.*[1] 22); MALONE (*apud* STEEVENS, ed. 1778) cites 3617–18 (compare nn. 3269, 3618). But MASON (1785, p. 285), although the *OED* (*v.*[1] 4) gives only an intransitive use of this sense: "When a man is out of breath . . . we say he is *blown*"; WHITE (ed. 1883) glosses as "smites"; and FURNESS (ed. 1907) suggests "breaking" (see *OED*, *v.*[1] 24).

If swift thought breake it not: a swifter meane
Shall out-strike thought, but thought will doo't. I feele
I fight against thee: No I will go seeke
Some Ditch, wherein to dye: the foul'st best fits
My latter part of life.   *Exit.* 2620

Alarum, Drummes and Trumpets.   **4.7**
Enter Agrippa.

Agrip. Retire, we haue engag'd our selues too farre:

2616 swifter] swifted F2-ROWE3
2617 doo't. I feele˄] ~ , ~~ . ROWE1+
2619 wherein to] where to F2-F4; where I may ROWE1-v1773 (–CAP)
2621 SCENE IV. ROWE; SCENE VI. POPE, WARB; SCENE VII. HAN1, JOHN1+
   Before the Walls of Alexandria. ROWE1+ (*subst.*)
   Drummes and Trumpets] Om. CAP
2622 *Ad. and his Forces* CAP, v1778+

2616 **If . . . not**] WALTER (ed. 1969): "Sudden intense grief rushed the melancholy
humour to the heart so that the heart was choked. [Compares *Ven.* 990 and 'heart . . .
corroborate,' *H5* 2.1.130 (621–2).]"
   swift thought] Proverbial; see DENT (T240): "As swift as *thought.*"
   thought] MALONE (ed. 1790): "*Melancholy.* [Compares 2154.]" Most agree, except COLLIER (ed. 1858): "Reflection on his own turpitude"; HUDSON (ed. 1881): "Grief";
FURNESS (ed. 1907): "Very blackest despair."
   meane] See n. 1574.
   2616–17 **swifter . . . out-strike thought**] The first to suggest suicide is BLUMHOF
(ed. 1870).
   2617 **out-strike**] DELIUS (ed. 1856): Strike better than. KITTREDGE (ed. 1941) adds
"sooner . . . than."
   2620 **My . . . life**] I.e., the latter part of my life. For this type of genitive, see FRANZ
§322.
      latter] SCHMIDT (1874): "Last," as a rule in Sh., along with *latest.* See FRANZ §219.
   2621 *Alarum*] See n. 1976. The use of both drums and trumpets in connection with
an alarum—the only such instance in F1—would seem to indicate a special effect. But
WELLS & TAYLOR (1987, p. 552), regarding both as normal, find the SD "repetitive"
unless referring to "musicians who appear on stage."
   2623 **Retire**] WELLS & TAYLOR (1987, p. 552): "Could well be an instruction to sound
a retreat." SHIRLEY (1963, p. 58): "Generally, the retreat is sounded in combination with
alarums."

Cæsar himselfe ha's worke, and our oppression
Exceeds what we expected.   *Exit.* 2625

Alarums.   (yy4^vb)
Enter Anthony, and Scarrus wounded.

Scar. O my braue Emperor, this is fought indeed,
Had we done so at first, we had drouen them home
With clowts about their heads.   *Far off.* 2630
Ant. Thou bleed'st apace.
Scar. I had a wound heere that was like a T,
But now 'tis made an H.

2624 and] *Om.* HAN1
        oppression] opposition mTBY2 *and* WARBURTON *conj. apud* mTHEO2 (21 Feb.
1729, [fol. 41]), HAN1, KTLY
2625 *Exit.*] *Om.* ROWE3; *Retreat. Exeunt.* CAP, v1778+
2627 *and*] *and Forces; with* CAP
2629 drouen] driven CAP-WH1, HAL, DYCE2, COL4, HUD2
2630 heads] head F2-ROWE3
        Far off.] *Om.* ROWE3-JOHN1, v1773-COL1, HUD1-DYCE2, COL4-NLSN, ALEX;
Retreat afar off. (after 2633) CAP, COL2, CAM, ARD1-KIT1, SIS+ *(subst.)*

2624 **our**] I.e., of or on us. For the subjective and objective genitive, see FRANZ §322.
        oppression] COTGRAVE (1611): "*Ouercharging, ouerlaying . . . a grieuous bur-
then.*" BULLOKAR (1616, *Pressure*): "An oppression."
2626 *Alarums*] See n. 1976.
2628 **braue**] See n. 567.
2629 **drouen**] JOHNSON (1755) includes this old participle as a headword and cites
this instance, but under *drive* he does not mention it among the principal parts. WHITE
(ed. 1883) is surely wrong in saying "not Elizabethan 'grammar'; mere heedlessness."
For strong verbs in Sh., see FRANZ §170.
2630 **clowts**] MINSHEU (1617): "*Ragge*"—i.e., bandages (DELIUS [ed. 1856]).
        Far off] See textual notes.
2631 **apace**] MINSHEU (1617): "*A swift pace.*" See also 2874, 3579, n. 362.
2632-3 **T . . . H**] DELIUS (ed. 1856) and most commentators: The *T* must be understood as lying on its side, made into an *H* by one or two new slashes. STAUNTON
(1873, p. 535): "A pun upon the letter H and the word *ache.*" He compares *Ado* 3.4.56
(1553), as does JOHNSON (ed. 1765, 3:229, n. 8). For the pronunciation, see CERCIGNANI
(1981, p. 324). CASE (ed. 1906): "There would be more confidence about it [i.e., the
pun] if we could find any particular reason for selecting T just before." RIDLEY (ed. 1954)
answers with Delius's explanation, "if we are thinking of printed capitals. And see Dover
Wilson's [ed. 1950] note *ad loc.* giving Maunde Thompson's comment on the minuscule
letters in 'secretary' hand [in Pollard, *Shakespeare's Hand*, 1923, p. 91, n. 1: 'But substitute for the capitals T and H the old English cursive minuscules *t* (a straight-cut letter)
and *h* (a sinuous letter like a mangled wound), and the meaning is clear']."

Ant. They do retyre.

Scar. Wee'l beat 'em into Bench-holes, I haue yet   2635
Roome for six scotches more.

Enter Eros.

Eros. They are beaten Sir, and our aduantage serues
For a faire victory.

Scar. Let vs score their backes,   2640
And snatch 'em vp, as we take Hares behinde,
'Tis sport to maul a Runner.

Ant. I will reward thee
Once for thy sprightly comfort, and ten-fold
For thy good valour. Come thee on.   2645

Scar. Ile halt after.   *Exeunt*

Alarum. Enter Anthony againe in a March.   **4.8**
Scarrus, with others.

2642 'Tis] 'Tis a F3, F4
2645-6 *One verse line* v1793+ (−ALEX)
2645 thee] *Om.* HAN1
2647 *SCENE* VIII. CAP+
      Gates of Alexandria. CAP, v1778+ (*subst.*)
      Alarum.] *Om.* CAP

   2635 **Bench-holes**] RANN (ed. 1791–): "Augre-holes." MALONE (*apud* BOSWELL, ed. 1821): "The hole in a bench, ad levandum alvum," i.e., a privy seat. CASE (ed. 1906) cites Thomas Dekker, *Northward Ho* (1607), Act 5 (ed. Shepherd, 1873, 3:78), and John Fletcher, *Women Pleased* 4.3 (Beaumont and Fletcher Folio, 1679, p. 201).
   2636 **scotches**] HANMER (ed. 1744, 6:Glossary): "To hack, to bruise, to crush." But JOHNSON (1755), citing this instance, and most others: "A slight cut; a shallow incision."
   2638-9 **our . . . victory**] CAPELL (1779 [1774], 1:45): "Circumstances favour'd them [Antony's forces], and they had now an opportunity of obtaining '*a fair victory.*'" DELIUS (ed. 1856): The advantage we have gained is as good as a complete, declared victory.
   2641 **snatch 'em vp**] DEIGHTON (ed. 1891): "Catch them by the neck, as dogs snap up ('pinch', in the old technical language) hares."
   2642 **maul**] BAILEY (1721): "To bang or beat soundly." See *OED, v.* 2. Possibly connected with a game called *pall-mall* in which a wooden ball was driven with a mallet.
      Runner] WORDSWORTH (ed. 1883): "*One who runs away.*"
   2645 **thee**] FRANZ (§283): The form of reflexive verbs in the imperative (like *retire thee*) may have helped cause *thee* to follow other verbs that otherwise would take *thou*. See also ABBOTT §212.

Ant. We haue beate him to his Campe: Runne one
Before, & let the Queen know of our guests: to morrow   2650
Before the Sun shall see's, wee'l spill the blood
That ha's to day escap'd. I thanke you all,
For doughty handed are you, and haue fought
Not as you seru'd the Cause, but as't had beene
Each mans like mine: you haue shewne all *Hectors.*   2655
Enter the Citty, clip your Wiues, your Friends,
Tell them your feats, whil'st they with ioyfull teares
Wash the congealement from your wounds, and kisse
The Honour'd-gashes whole.

                    Enter Cleopatra.   2660

Giue me thy hand,

2649–50 *Verse lines ending* before, . . . to morrow ROWE1+
2650 guests] Gests mTHEO1 (*withdrawn* mTHEO2, 21 Feb. 1729, [fol. 41]) *and*
WARBURTON *conj. apud* mTHEO2 (21 Feb. 1729, [fol. 41]), THEO1-THEO4, CAP, COL2+
2654 the] my HAN1
2655 shewne all] shewn your selves all POPE1-THEO4, KTLY; all shewn you CAP
    Hectors.] Hectors. Go, WALKER (1860, 3:307) *conj.*, HUD2
2659, 2661 *One verse line* ROWE1-RID (−NLSN)
2660 *attended.* CAP, MAL, v1793+ (−ARD2)
2661 *To* Scarus. ROWE1+ (−COL1, COL2, COL3, WH1, HAL)

2647 *Alarum*] See n. 1976.
2650 **guests**] THEOBALD (21 Feb. 1729, [fol. 41[r]]): "Tho' tis [*gests*] a word very familiar w:[th] *Spenser*, we no where [else find] it in our Poet: He always chuses, *feats.* I
think we should read . . . *her* [guests−] i.e. Anthony, & his Commanders [quotes
2686-7]." But most editors disagree. LEO (1853, p. 321) even uses 2686-8 to support
gests, since there was not enough room in Antony's "Pallace" for guests. THISELTON's
(1899, p. 22) argument—"'gests' was pronounced 'guests'"—is surely wrong, however:
see DOBSON (1957, 1:124). FURNESS (ed. 1907) cites *feats* (2657) in support of *gests*.
2654 **seru'd**] DELIUS (ed. 1856): Were only servants to.
2654-5 **as't . . . mine**] Commentators give positive shadings. DELIUS (ed. 1856):
As if it were each man's own cause not mine. KITTREDGE (ed. 1941): "As truly as it was
mine." WILSON (ed. 1950): "As if the cause had been yours as much as mine."
2655 **mine**] See n. 510.
    shewne] See n. 1647.
    all] See n. 1585.
2656 **clip**] MINSHEU (1617, Clippe): "*Colle or Cull, as one clippeth or Colleth about
the necke.*" IDEM (Coll): "Embrace." See 3629, n. 1412 ("inclippes").
2659 **Honour'd-gashes**] See n. 1912.
    whole] See n. 1945.

To this great Faiery, Ile commend thy acts,
Make her thankes blesse thee. Oh thou day o'th'world,
Chaine mine arm'd necke, leape thou, Attyre and all
Through proofe of Harnesse to my heart, and there   2665
Ride on the pants triumphing.
 Cleo. Lord of Lords.
Oh infinite Vertue, comm'st thou smiling from
The worlds great snare vncaught.

2665 heart] part F2–F4

2662 **Faiery**] MINSHEU (1617, Hagge) offers synonyms: "Witch, Sorceresse, Enchauntresse, Fairie." HANMER (ed. 1744): "Inchantress [a sense] . . . *which it often carries in the old Romances.*" UPTON (1748, p. 327): "Sometimes . . . mischievous bugs [hobgoblins] and furies, at other times *fair* and benign beings of a superior race." CAPELL (1779 [1774], 1:45): "Something more than humanity, and of a middle nature between that and the gods." BECKET (1815, 2:193), whimsically: "*Faire*, in old language, is happiness, *good fortune*, and I think that Shakspeare has here used 'fairy', written, perhaps, *faerie*, in the sense of one who occasions, *who brings good fortune.*" ADELMAN (1973, p. 65): "By no means unambiguous: dealings with the fairy queen were apt to be dangerous. . . . Much of the attraction of faerie was that it seemed to occupy a terrain outside the usual moral categories. Fairies were spirits who were neither devils nor angels, yet were clearly nonhuman."

2664 **Chaine . . . necke**] WARBURTON (ed. 1747): "Alluding to . . . men of worship wearing gold chains about the neck." EDWARDS (1765, p. 201) and all others: "Entwine me, armed as I am, in thy embraces."

 Attyre and all] Of the four who comment, three agree with DELIUS (ed. 1856): All that you have on. SLATER (ed. 1971) alone: "Armed as I am."

2665 **proofe of Harnesse**] STEEVENS (ed. 1778): "I.e. armour of proof." MINSHEU (1617, Harnesse): "*For the breast* . . . Breast-plate."

2666 WARBURTON (ed. 1747): "Alluding to an admiral ship on the billows after a storm." EDWARDS (1765, p. 202) objects, "I thought victories gained, not storms escaped, had been the matter of triumphs; and I suppose, other ships dance on the billows, just after the same manner as the Admiral's does." DELIUS (ed. 1856) compares a ride in a triumphant chariot, to which CASE (ed. 1906) offers a passage from Fletcher's *The False One* 4.2 (Beaumont and Fletcher Folio, 1679, p. 329), which he thinks "imitates" Sh. See also nn. 895, 1494.

2667–9 MCFARLAND (1958–9, p. 223): "The absolute thematic center of the play. . . . In hypostasis stand the pride of Cleopatra, the power of Antony, the exhilaration of the lovers, the discomfiture of the Machiavellian world."

2668 **infinite Vertue**] DELIUS (ed. 1856): All manly virtues in unlimited number. IRVING & MARSHALL (ed. 1889) and most others: "The Latin *virtus*, valour."

2669 **worlds great snare**] STEEVENS (*apud* REED, ed. 1803): "I.e. the war. So, in the 116th *Psalm*: 'The *snares of death* compassed me round about' [l. 3]." BLUMHOF (ed. 1870) adds further biblical references: Ps. 119, 110, and 140:4. MILLS (1960, p. 153, n. 18): "War, 'all the snares the world can set' [RIDLEY, ed. 1954], or Caesar?"

Ant. Mine Nightingale,　　　　　　　　　　　　　　　　2670
We haue beate them to their Beds.
What Gyrle, though gray
Do somthing mingle with our yonger brown, yet ha we
A Braine that nourishes our Nerues, and can
Get gole for gole of youth. Behold this man,　　　　　2675
Commend vnto his Lippes thy sauouring hand,
Kisse it my Warriour: He hath fought to day,
As if a God in hate of Mankinde, had
Destroyed in such a shape.
　　Cleo. Ile giue thee Friend　　　　　　　　　　　　　2680
An Armour all of Gold: it was a Kings.

2670 Mine] My F2+ (−ALEX, EVNS)
2671–2 *One verse line* ROWE1+
2673–5 *Three verse lines ending* brown, . . . nerves, . . . man, JOHN1, v1773, KNT1, SING2, KTLY
2673 yonger] *Om.* HAN1, CAP, v1793, v1803
2676 sauouring] favouring mTBY2 *and* THEOBALD (1726, p. 184) *conj.*, THEO1+

2670 **Mine Nightingale**] See p. 373.
　　Nightingale] DEIGHTON (ed. 1891) and others: "A compliment to the fascination of her voice." For Plutarch, see p. 413.
2672 **Gyrle**] See n. 941.
2673 **somthing**] More common in Sh. than *somewhat*, though meaning much the same. See FRANZ §398. See also 3504.
　　yonger] STEEVENS (ed. 1793) omits as hypermetrical and superfluous to meaning. The full line of type may account for the absence of *u* (as it may for *ha*).
2674 **Braine . . . Nerues**] BARTHOLOMAEUS (1582, fols. 36ᵛ–37ʳ): "The braine is . . . the beginning and principall of the sinewes [i.e., nerves] of all the bodie. . . . [It] is a member moouing and ruling all the lower members of the bodie, and giueth to all these limmes feeling and mouing."
2675 **Get . . . of youth**] Commentators make subtle distinctions. RANN (ed. 1791–): "Dispute the prize with youth." DELIUS (ed. 1856): Win one prize after another from youths. DEIGHTON (ed. 1891): "Win as many goals as younger men." For *of*, see also n. 1781.
　　gole for gole] JOHNSON (ed. 1765) and KITTREDGE (ed. 1941) believe *goal* derives from tilting at barriers, Johnson glossing "to *win a goal*" as "to be superiour in a contest of activity." WILSON (ed. 1950) points out that the *OED* does not support the association with barriers; he suggests that Sh. possibly "had football in mind." DELIUS (ed. 1856) conceives of *goal* as the end of a race. See *OED* (2c): "Used for 'contest, race.'"
2676 **Commend**] MINSHEU (1617): "Commit."
　　sauouring] THEOBALD (1726, p. 184), emending to *favouring*: "*Antony* did not want his Captain to grow in Love with his Mistress, on Account of the Flavour and Lusciousness of her Hand; but only to have a Reward of Honour."
2680–1 For Plutarch's version, see p. 449.

Ant. He has deseru'd it, were it Carbunkled
Like holy Phœbus Carre. Giue me thy hand,
Through Alexandria make a iolly March,
Beare our hackt Targets, like the men that owe them.   2685
Had our great Pallace the capacity
To Campe this hoast, we all would sup together,
And drinke Carowses to the next dayes Fate
Which promises Royall perill, Trumpetters   (yy5ᵃ
With brazen dinne blast you the Cities eare,   2690
Make mingle with our ratling Tabourines,

2682 has] hath COL3
2683 holy] glowing mCOL1, COL2
2687 all would] would all THEO2, WARB-JOHN1, v1773, v1778, RANN
2691 with] with it KTLY

2682–3 **Carbunkled . . . Carre**] For the luminous qualities of carbuncle, a fiery precious stone, see BARTHOLOMAEUS (1582, fol. 257ᵛ). DELIUS (ed. 1856) compares *Cym.*
5.5.189–90, "had it beene a Carbuncle Of Phœbus Wheele" (3470–1); CASE (ed. 1906),
Ovid's *Metamorphoses* 2.107–10: "Along the yoke [of the Sun's chariot] chrysolites and
jewels . . . gave back their bright glow to the reflected rays of Phoebus" (trans. Miller,
1960 [Loeb]). *OED* (Car *sb.*¹ 1b): "Since 16th c. chiefly poetic, with associations of dignity, solemnity, or splendour." TAYLOR (1985, pp. 54–5) traces carbuncle to Golding's
mistranslation of Ovid's word for "bronze" (*pyropo*), which "by an association of ideas,
he [Sh.] had transferred from the walls of Phoebus' palace [*Metamorphoses* 2.1–2] to
the more suitable setting of his chariot wheels."
    2684 **iolly**] MINSHEU (1617): "Braue . . . Gallant." Commentators prefer "gay, lively."
    2685 WARBURTON (ed. 1747): "*I.e.* hackt as much as the men are, to whom they
belong." JOHNSON (ed. 1765): "*Bear our hack'd targets* with spirit and exaltation, such
as becomes the brave warriors *that own them.*" ABBOTT (§419a), citing this line: "Even
when the adjective cannot immediately precede the noun, yet the adjective comes first,
and the adverb afterwards. . . . So probably [this line]"—i.e., hack'd-like-the-men-that-
own-them targets.
    Targets] See n. 399–400.
    2686–7 See n. 2650.
    2687 **hoast**] See n. 2608.
    2688 **Carowses**] MINSHEU (1617): "*In drinking* . . . of two Germane words, viz. gar
. . . altogether, & ausz, *i.*[*e.*,] out." JOHNSON (1755): "A hearty dose of liquour." See
also 2768.
    2689 **Royall perill**] DEIGHTON (ed. 1891): "Right glorious hazard." WILSON (ed. 1950)
compares 2524 ("Royall Occupation").
    2691 **Tabourines**] COTGRAVE (1611): "*A Drumme; and a little Drumme; also, the
Drumme, or Drummer belonging to a Companie of footmen.*" CASE (ed. 1906): "The
tabourine appears to have been 'the full-sized military drum, corresponding to the modern side-drum', while the tabor was a little drum devoted to peaceful amusements. See
Naylor, *Shakespeare and Music*, 1896, pp. 161, 162."

That heauen and earth may strike their sounds together,
Applauding our approach.   *Exeunt.*

Enter a Centerie, and his Company, Enobarbus followes.   **4.9**

Cent. If we be not releeu'd within this houre,   2695
We must returne to'th'Court of Guard: the night
Is shiny, and they say, we shall embattaile
By'th'second houre i'th'Morne.
1. *Watch.* This last day was a shrew'd one too's.

2692 may] make CAM3a
2693 approach] reproach F3, F4
       Flourish. CAP, COL4
2694 SCENE V. ROWE; SCENE VII. POPE, WARB; SCENE VIII. HAN1, JOHN1; *SCENE
IX.* CAP+
       Cæsar's Camp. ROWE1-KIT1, ALEX, ARD2, EVNS (*subst.*); *The same.* CAM3, SIS
(*subst.*)
       Centerie] *Century* F3-POPE2 (*and* CAM3, ALEX: Centurion); *Centry* THEO1-JOHN1,
v1773, NLSN, KIT1, ARD2, EVNS; Sentinels *or Centinel* CAP, v1778-OXF1, ARD1, RID, SIS
(*subst.*)
       Enobarbus followes] *After* 2699 DYCE, STAU, GLO, CAM1-RID (−NLSN)
2695, 2707, 2722, 2725, 2730 *Cent.*] 3. *S.* CAP
2697 we] she JOHN2
2698–2702 *Three verse lines ending* was . . . night! . . . him. HAN1, CAP, MAL,
v1793-SING1, COL1-COL3, WH1-COL4, WH2+; *ending* day . . . night,— . . . him. STAU;
four verse lines ending was . . . to's. . . . this! . . . him. WALKER (1860, 3:307) *conj.*,
HUD2

2694 *Centerie*] Commentators are divided between *Centerie*—i.e., a centurion or captain of a hundred men—and *sentry*, or sentinel. The speech prefixes following are also
affected; see textual notes. RIDLEY (ed. 1954): "Enobarbus' entry . . . is awkward, partly
because . . . an abrupt entry after the watchmen are more or less in position ought
to be the occasion for a challenge."
2695 **releeu'd**] See n. 3248.
2696 **Court of Guard**] STEEVENS (ed. 1778): "I.e. the guard-room, the place where
the guard musters."
2697 **embattaile**] COLES (1676, *Embattel'd*): "Set in battel aray."
2698 Presumably 2 a.m. Sh. observes the Elizabethan custom of counting the hours
from midnight on. See also n. 2529.
2699 **shrew'd**] MINSHEU (1617): "*Ill.*" Most commentators agree, adding synonyms
like "cursed," "evil," "severe." KNOWLES (privately): "Injurious" (*OED*, 4). See n. 760.

Enob. Oh beare me witnesse night.   2700
2 What man is this?
1 Stand close, and list him.
Enob. Be witnesse to me (O thou blessed Moone)
When men reuolted shall vpon Record
Beare hatefull memory: poore *Enobarbus* did   2705
Before thy face repent.
    Cent. Enobarbus?
2 Peace: Hearke further.
    Enob. Oh Soueraigne Mistris of true Melancholly,
The poysonous dampe of night dispunge vpon me,   2710
That Life, a very Rebell to my will,

2701–2, 2707–8, 2721–6 *Marked as asides* CAP
2702 list] listen to HAN1; list to v1793, v1803, KTLY
    they go aside CAM3
2703 to me] *Om.* RIDb
2706–8 *Verse lines ending* Peace; . . . further. HAN1, v1793+ (−HUD)
2708 further] farther COL, WH1, HAL
2710 dispunge] disperge HAN1
2711 *Lying down.* COL2; *SD after* 2715 COL3; *SD after* 2720 COL4

2700–20 JORGENSEN (1951, p. 391): "Readers of [Sir Lewis Lewkenor's] *The Estate [of English Fugitives under the King of Spaine* (1595)] would have seen no inappropriate strain in Enobarbus' terminal agonies. In Lewkenor it is not the exception but the rule that prominent deserters should die with passionate melancholy and distraction. . . . Nor would this audience [i.e., of *Ant.*] have been likely to ask whether Enobarbus had ever displayed sufficient delicacy to die of remorse." Plutarch (p. 440) makes the connection between Enobarbus's repentance for "open treason" and his dying "immediatly after." He also mentions that Enobarbus was "sicke of an agewe."

    2702 **close**] BULLOKAR (1616, *Clandestine*): "Priuy, close, secret." For the uninflected adverb, see FRANZ §241.

    list him] Listen to him. For the dative construction, see FRANZ §630a.

    2704 **men reuolted**] For the transposition of the adjective, here perhaps for metrical reasons, see FRANZ §685.

    Record] MINSHEU (1617): "*Call to minde.*" I.e., remembrance. See also 2941, 3344.

    2705 **hatefull**] I.e., exciting hate. For the active and passive meanings of the suffix *-ful*, see FRANZ §121.

    2709 CAPELL (1779 [1774], 1:45): "To which of the fabulous deities is this prayer of Enobarbus address'd? It cannot be Night; for she is desir'd to '*despunge*', or pour down upon him, '*the poisonous damp of night*': it must therefore be Hecate, the Night's companion." HUDSON (ed. 1881) and most others prefer "Moon."

    Melancholly] CAWDREY (1604): "Black choler, a humor of solitarines, or sadnes."

    2710 **dispunge**] WARBURTON (ed. 1747): Sh.'s "own invention, from the squeezing out a spunge upon any one."

May hang no longer on me. Throw my heart
Against the flint and hardnesse of my fault,
Which being dried with greefe, will breake to powder,
And finish all foule thoughts. Oh *Anthony*,   2715
Nobler then my reuolt is Infamous,
Forgiue me in thine owne particular,
But let the world ranke me in Register
A Master leauer, and a fugitiue:
Oh *Anthony*! Oh *Anthony*!   2720

2720–30, 2732–5 *Lines* 2720–30, 2732 *as* F1, *then verse lines ending* he is . . . on,
. . . yet. HAN1; 2720–5 *as* F1, *then verse lines ending* Awake, sir, . . . hand . . . him.
. . . sleepers: . . . he is . . . then; . . . yet. CAP; 2720–30, 2732 *as* F1, *then verse
lines ending* he is . . . then; . . . yet. v1778, RANN; 2720–9 *as* F1, *then verse lines
ending* drums . . . him . . . hour . . . out. . . . yet. MAL; *eleven verse lines ending*
speak . . . speaks . . . sleeps. . . . his . . . him. . . . sir? . . . drums . . . him
. . . hour . . . then, . . . yet. v1793-v1821, SING, DYCE, GLO, KTLY, WH2, NLSN, KIT1;
2720–9 *prose, then verse lines ending* drums . . . him . . . hour . . . then; . . . yet.
KNT1, STAU (2727 *erroneously indented*); *twelve verse lines ending* Antony! O Antony!
. . . to him. . . . speaks . . . sleeps. . . . his . . . him. . . . sir? . . . drums . . .
him . . . hour . . . then; . . . yet. COL, WH1, HAL, OXF1; *twelve verse lines ending*
Antony! O Antony! . . . to him. . . . speaks . . . sleeps. . . . his . . . him. . . .
sir? . . . drums . . . him . . . hour . . . out. . . . yet. HUD; *eleven verse lines ending*
to him. . . . speaks . . . sleeps. . . . his . . . him. . . . sir? . . . drums . . . him
. . . hour . . . out. . . . yet. CAM1, ARD, RID, EVNS; *six verse lines ending* to him.
. . . speaks . . . sleeps. . . . his . . . him. . . . sir *then as* F1 CAM3; *thirteen verse
lines ending* Antony! O Antony! . . . to him. . . . speaks . . . sleeps. . . . his . . .
him. . . . us. . . . sir? . . . drums . . . him . . . hour . . . then; . . . yet. ALEX;
eleven verse lines ending to him. . . . speaks . . . sleeps. . . . his . . . him. . . .
sir? . . . drums . . . him . . . hour . . . then. . . . yet. SIS

2720 *Dies.* ROWE1+

2712–14 **Throw . . . powder**] JOHNSON (ed. 1765): "The pathetick of *Shakespeare*
too often ends in the ridiculous. It is painful to find the gloomy dignity of this noble
scene destroyed by the intrusion of a conceit so far-fetched and unaffecting." MALONE
(ed. 1790): "Shakspeare in most of his conceits is kept in countenance by his contemporaries. Thus Daniel, in his 18th Sonnet, 1594, somewhat indeed less harshly, says, 'Still
must I whet my young desires abated, Vpon the Flint of such a heart rebelling' [ll. 9–10]."
KITTREDGE (ed. 1941): "'Destroyed' is too strong a word. Substitute 'impaired', and Johnson's criticism must be accepted." WILSON (ed. 1950), however: Probably "not 'far-fetched'
to Jacobeans, for whom l. [2714] was at least sound psychology."

2712–15 **heart . . . thoughts**] See n. 1555–7.

2713 **flint and hardnesse**] For hendiadys, see n. 9.

2714 **dried with greefe**] KITTREDGE (ed. 1941): "Every sigh was supposed to take away
a drop of blood from the heart." WILSON (ed. 1950) compares *Rom.* 3.5.59 (2092): "Drie
sorrow drinkes our bloud." BABB (1951, p. 103): "Immoderate sorrow deprives the body

1 Let's speake to him.

Cent. Let's heare him, for the things he speakes

May concerne *Cæsar.*

2 Let's do so, but he sleepes.

Cent. Swoonds rather, for so bad a Prayer as his   2725

Was neuer yet for sleepe.

1 Go we to him.

2 Awake sir, awake, speake to vs.

1 Heare you sir?

Cent. The hand of death hath raught him.   2730

Drummes afarre off.

2722 him] him further CAP
2726 for] 'fore mTBY2 *conj.*, mCOL1, COL2, SING2, COL3, KTLY, COL4
      sleepe] sleeping v1793, v1803
2728 sir, awake] awake, sir v1793-SING1
2730 hath] has POPE2-v1773 (−HAN1, CAP)
      raught] caught F4-POPE2, HAN1

---

of the natural heat and moisture which reside in the vital spirit of the blood. . . . The constriction of the grief-stricken heart prevents generation and distribution of spirit. Through loss of spirit, the blood degenerates into cold, dry melancholy. Grief, furthermore, stimulates the spleen to emit melancholy, which chills and dries the vital spirit and the heart. Grief means loss of blood and increase of melancholy. Since cold and dryness, the qualities of melancholy, are inimical to life, the grief-stricken person becomes thin and ill. He may die. Immoderate sorrow is a disease."

2717 **in . . . particular**] CASE (ed. 1906): "As far as you yourself are concerned." See n. 2178.

2718 **Register**] BULLOKAR (1616): "Writings of record kept for memory." See n. 2704 ("Record").

2719 **Master leauer**] KITTREDGE (ed. 1941): "A runaway servant. Enobarbus is willing to be ranked with fugitive slaves and masterless vagabonds. According as it is uttered, this word will mean either 'one who abandons his master' or 'a master-workman in the trade of desertion.'" See n. 383.

2726 **for sleepe**] DOUCE (1807, 2:95), on STEEVENS's (ed. 1793) emendation to *sleeping*: "The *harmony* is certainly improved, as the accent is to be laid on *to* in the ensuing line [2727]." COLLIER (1852, p. 477) conjectures *'fore* (before). Starting with WORDSWORTH (ed. 1883)—*"Fit for"*—most commentators, however, retain F1, stressing the incompatibility of sleep and bad conscience.

2730 **raught**] STEEVENS (ed. 1778): "The ancient preterite of the verb to *reach.*" For weak forms of what were originally strong verbs, see FRANZ §161.

2732 **demurely**] MINSHEU (1617, Demure): "Sober, mannerly, or modest"; KERSEY (1702): *"Seemingly grave* or *bashfull."* Most commentators amalgamate to "solemnly, gravely." Quoting this line, *OED* (b): "In a subdued manner." But NICHOLS (1865, p.

Hearke the Drummes demurely wake the sleepers:
Let vs beare him to'th'Court of Guard: he is of note:
Our houre is fully out.
2 Come on then, he may recouer yet.   *exeunt* 2735

Enter Anthony and Scarrus, with their Army.   **4.10**

Ant. Their preparation is to day by Sea,

2732 Hearke] Hearke how F2-v1778, RANN
        demurely wake] din early wakes HAN1; Do early wake mCOL1, COL2, COL3, COL4;
Do merrily wake DYCE1 *conj.*, KTLY
    2735 then] *Om.* HAN1
        exeunt] Ad. *with the Body.* CAP, v1778+
    2736 SCENE VI. ROWE; SCENE VIII. POPE, WARB; SCENE IX. HAN1, JOHN1; *SCENE
X.* CAP+
        Between the two Camps. ROWE1-JOHN1, v1773-KIT1, ALEX, ARD2, EVNS (*subst.*);
Hills without the City. CAP; *The same.* CAM3, SIS (*subst.*)
    2737 by] for CAP, RANN

---

264), mistakenly deriving from Latin *de more*, "according to custom": "The customary
drums." NICHOLSON (1871, p. 41) adds "another and [doubtful] second meaning": "The
drum-reveillé of the non-Latin races was not a lively, merry, or clamorous din, but a measured and somewhat solemn beat." Still more doubtful are his etymologies (Wright
Shakespeariana, no. 158, [12ʳ]): "In Italian law êssere in môra is to be due the term being expired. In this sense de-murely might mean unduly untimely. Or it might have
been capriciously and euphuistically derived from mora delay and mean undelayingly."
THISELTON (1899, p. 22): "The opposite of 'forward' . . . descriptive of the gradual increase in the volume of the sound of the drums." CASE (ed. 1906): "Perhaps the soldier
inconsistently treats the mellowed sound, that reaches him at a distance, as if it were
similarly heard by those in camp." HUNTER (ed. 1870) alone: "Cause the sleepers to wake
demurely." See also textual notes and conj., p. 357, and also n. 3034.
    2737–46 SISSON (1956, 2:270-1) speculates: "Most [eds.] suggest a missing line or
phrase after *the haven* [2744]. . . . The compositor had a complicated piece of copy
here, with six regular lines revised by two marginal additions, *order for sea . . . the
haven* for Scarus at l. [2738] (the words are surely a part of Scarus' report), and *where
their . . . discover* for Antony at l. [2742]. The compositor read both consecutively and
inserted all into Antony's speech." He refers to the scene's source in Plutarch (see p. 449).
"Scarus, be it noted, is Antony's co-general and is reporting on his fleet, the practical
man of war. Antony is on the heights of optimism." For Sisson's lineation and the views
of others, see textual notes and conj., p. 357.
    2737 by] CAPELL (1779 [1774], 1:45): "Instead of '*for.*'" The "printers [of F1] let their
eye slip upon '*by*' in the next line. . . . That '*for*' is the true word, is evinc'd . . .
by Scarus' reply." But only RANN (ed. 1791-) agrees.

We please them not by Land.
  Scar. For both, my Lord.
  Ant. I would they'ld fight i'th'Fire, or i'th'Ayre,   2740
Wee'ld fight there too. But this it is, our Foote
Vpon the hilles adioyning to the Citty
Shall stay with vs. Order for Sea is giuen,
They haue put forth the Hauen:
Where their appointment we may best discouer,   2745
And looke on their endeuour.   *exeunt*

           Enter Cæsar, and his Army.   **4.11**

2738–9 *One verse line* v1793+ (−SIS)
2739 Lord.] lord. Order for sea is given, | They have put forth the haven. SIS (*transposed from 2743–4*)
2742 hilles] hill SING1
2743 Shall . . . vs.] *Before* And *in* 2746, *omitting period* SIS
2744 They] And they KTLY
    Hauen:] Haven: Further on, ROWE1-THEO4, RANN-v1803, HAL; haven: Hie we on, CAP; haven: Let's seek a spot, MAL, v1821, SING1; haven: ——forward, now, DYCE; haven.——Ascend we then WH1; haven. We'll take our stand KTLY; haven: mount we, then, HUD2; haven. Go we up WH2, NLSN, KIT1; haven: ——let us on, NICHOLSON *conj. apud* CAM1, IRV
2747 SCENE XI. DYCE, STAU, GLO, CAM1, HUD2, WH2, NLSN+
    Another part of the same. DYCE, STAU, GLO, CAM1, HUD2, WH2, NLSN+ (*subst.*)

2741 **Foote**] IRVING & MARSHALL (ed. 1889): "Infantry."
2743–4 **Order . . . Hauen**] KNIGHT (ed. 1841) appears to be alone in believing that the "sentence . . . is parenthetical." The editors who add to 2744—see textual notes and conj., p. 357—"corrupt the text," for they "allow nothing for the rapidity of utterance, and the modulation with which such parenthetical passages are given upon the stage."
2745 **Where**] DELIUS (ed. 1856) finds *Where* refers to the whole sentence "They . . . Hauen"; CASE (ed. 1906), comparing 1969–70, to "hills" (2742). KITTREDGE (ed. 1941): "Plutarch [p. 449] shows that *where* . . . must refer to the hills, not to the haven."
    their] Most commentators interpret as a reference to the enemy's ships. A minority led by DELIUS (ed. 1856): Antony is referring to his own ships. WHITE (ed. 1861), citing Plutarch's account: "And *there* he stoode to behold his gallies which departed from the haven."
    appointment] WARBURTON (ed. 1747) and most others: "*Numbers.*" But JOHNSON (1755), citing this instance: "Equipment; furniture." KITTREDGE (ed. 1941): "Appearance and array of their ships." BARROLL (1969, *ShakS*, p. 226, n. 22), citing *OED* (5), where this line is quoted: "Resolution, purpose."
    discouer] COTGRAVE (1611, Descouvrir) specifies: "*To descrie, discerne, perceiue*

Cæs. But being charg'd, we will be still by Land,
Which as I tak't we shall, for his best force
Is forth to Man his Gallies. To the Vales,   2750
And hold our best aduantage.   *exeunt.*   (yy5ᵇ)

Alarum afarre off, as at a Sea-fight.   **4.12**
Enter Anthony, and Scarrus.

Ant. Yet they are not ioyn'd:
Where yon'd Pine does stand, I shall discouer all.   2755

2748–9 But . . . shall] Not . . . shall not HAN1
2752 SCENE XII. DYCE, STAU, GLO, CAM1, HUD2, WH2, NLSN+
    Another part of the same. DYCE, STAU, GLO, HUD2, WH2, NLSN-RID, SIS+ (*subst.*);
Hills adjoining to Alexandria. CAM1, KIT1-ALEX
    Alarum . . . Sea-fight.] *After* 2763 CAP, v1778-ARD1, KIT1, ALEX; *after* 2756
GRANVILLE-BARKER (1930; 1946, 1:397, n. 21) *conj.*, RIDa, CAM3, SIS, EVNS
    2754–7 *Three verse lines ending* stand, . . . word . . . built CAP, v1778+ (−SING2)
    2755 yon'd Pine does stand] yond Pine stands ROWE1-JOHN1; yonder pine does stand
CAP-SING1 (−MAL)

---

a farre off." See also 2755.
    2748 **But being**] WARBURTON (ed. 1747): "*Unless we be.*" More precisely, for *but*
in the sense of "if not," see FRANZ §566b.
    charg'd] BAILEY (1721): "[An *Enemy*] to attack, encounter, or fall upon him." Com-
pare nn. 1877, 2528.
    2749 **Which . . . shall**] WARBURTON (ed. 1747): "Which quiet I suppose we shall
keep."
    2750 **To the Vales**] WILSON (ed. 1950): "Sh. sends him in a direction different from
Ant., who has gone up to the hills."
    2751 DEIGHTON (ed. 1891): "Let us post ourselves to the best advantage."
    2752 *Alarum . . . Sea-fight*] The position of the SD has caused problems: see tex-
tual notes. WILSON (ed. 1950): The SD was placed "(wrongly, as 'Yet they are not joined'
in l. [2754] shows), prob[ably] because it was written somewhat indefinitely in the margin." RIDLEY (ed. 1954): The position "well illustrates the troubles that are sometimes
created by the post-Elizabethan division into scenes. . . . The S.D. does not belong
to either 'scene', but occupies the empty-stage interval between *exeunt* and *Enter.*" WALTER
(ed. 1969) finds no problem at all: "The alarum is only the prelude to a sea-fight, as
Antony correctly notes [2754], not the fight itself." See also n. 1976.
    2754 **Yet . . . not**] For *yet* in the sense of "till now," at times preceding the negative
particle, see FRANZ §423.
    2755 See n. 1969–72.
    discouer] See n. 2745.

Ile bring thee word straight, how 'tis like to go.   *exit.*

    Scar. Swallowes haue built
In *Cleopatra's* Sailes their nests. The Auguries
Say, they know not, they cannot tell, looke grimly,
And dare not speake their knowledge. *Anthony,*   2760
Is valiant, and deiected, and by starts
His fretted Fortunes giue him hope and feare
Of what he has, and has not.

                    Enter Anthony.

    Ant. All is lost: 2765
This fowle Egyptian hath betrayed me:
My Fleete hath yeelded to the Foe, and yonder
They cast their Caps vp, and Carowse together
Like Friends long lost. Triple-turn'd Whore, 'tis thou

2756 thee] the F3
2758 Auguries] augurs POPE1-JOHN1, v1773; augurers mTBY3 *conj.*, CAP, v1778-v1821,
KNT1, COL2-GLO, HAL-ALEX, ARD2; augures SING1
2763, 2765-6 *Arranged as verse lines, thus*: 2763, 2765-6 THEO, WARB, JOHN1, v1773,
HUD2; 2763 *and* 2765, 2766 v1793-COL4, WH2+ (−ALEX)
2763 *Exit.* ROWE1-JOHN1, v1773, v1778, RANN
2764 SCENE VII. ROWE; SCENE IX. POPE, WARB; SCENE X. HAN1, JOHN1
    Alexandria. ROWE1-JOHN1 (*subst.*)

2757-8 **Swallowes . . . nests**] For Plutarch's version of this "maruelous ill signe,"
see p. 438. WILSON (ed. 1950): "In Plut[arch] the omen precedes Actium."
    2758 **In . . . Sailes**] Plutarch says "vnder the poop."
       Auguries] RIDLEY (ed. 1954): Possibly "*augures,* a Latin plural [of *augur*]." SINGER
(ed. 1826) had this reading and explanation but subsequently changed to *augurers* (ed.
1856). The ambiguity of the spelling notwithstanding, commentators gloss as "augurs"
or "soothsayers." See also MUIR (*Mac.*, ed. 1951, n. 3.4.123) on *Augures* (3.4.124 [1406]).
    2762-3 The few who comment follow DEIGHTON (ed. 1891): "His fortunes of min-
gled good and evil alternately elate him with the hope of retaining what he has and
depress him with the fear of disaster befalling him; in *fretted* the figure is that of lines
interlacing or crossing each other, as in [*JC* 2.1.104 (735)]; *fret* being a term in heraldry
meaning a bearing composed of bars crossed and interlaced, though Shakespeare may
have also had in his mind the idea of 'to fret' in the sense of to vex, harass, literally
to eat into, to corrode." Both definitions appear in MINSHEU (1617).
    2764 ***Enter Anthony***] LEVIN (1976, p. 175): "Antony, coming down from his vantage-
point after the battle or hoisted up to Cleopatra's Monument in death, acts out the movement of his destiny."
    2768 **Carowse**] See n. 2688.
    2769 **Triple-turn'd Whore**] JOHNSON (ed. 1765): "She was first for *Antony,* then was

Hast sold me to this Nouice, and my heart   2770
Makes onely Warres on thee. Bid them all flye:
For when I am reueng'd vpon my Charme,
I haue done all. Bid them all flye, be gone.
Oh Sunne, thy vprise shall I see no more,
Fortune, and *Anthony* part heere, euen heere   2775

2772, 2781 Charme] charmer KTLY
2773 all flye] fly v1773
       Exit SCARUS. CAP, MAL, v1793+

---

supposed by him to have *turned* to *Cæsar*, when he found his messenger kissing her hand, then she *turned* again to *Antony*, and now has *turned* to *Cæsar*. [Suggests *triple-tongued*.] *Double-tongued* is a common term of reproach, which rage might improve to *triple-tongued*." TOLLET (*apud* STEEVENS, ed. 1778): "She was first for Julius Cæsar, then for Pompey the great, and afterwards for Antony." MASON (1785, p. 286): "She first belonged to Julius Cesar, then to Anthony, and now as he supposes, has turned to Augustus. It is not likely, as Tollet surmises, that in recollecting her turnings, Anthony should not have had that in his contemplation which gave him most offence." Developing his objection (*apud* STEEVENS [1780]) to Johnson, MALONE (ed. 1790): "According to this [Mason's] account of the matter, her connexion with Cneius Pompey is omitted, though the poet certainly was apprized of it, as appears [in 2293–5]. 2. There is no ground for supposing that Antony meant to insinuate that Cleopatra had granted any personal favour to Augustus, though he was persuaded that she had '*sold* him to the novice'. Mr. Tollet supposed that Cleopatra had been mistress to Pompey *the Great*; but her lover was his eldest son, Cneius Pompey." STEEVENS (ed. 1793), agreeing with Mason: "The sober recollection of a critick should not be expected from a hero who has this moment lost the one half of the world." STAUNTON (ed. 1859): "From Julius Cæsar to Cneius Pompey, from Pompey to Antony, and, as he suspects now, from him to Octavius Cæsar." Later commentators are more or less equally divided among the alternatives. See also n. 902–31 and conj., p. 357.

2770 **Nouice**] I.e., Octavius. See the "Boy *Cæsar*" (2172), "Boy" (2391), the "young Roman Boy" (2807).

2771 **onely . . . thee**] DEIGHTON (ed. 1891): "Upon thee alone." For the transposition of adverbs, see ABBOTT §420.

2772–3 **For . . . done all**] BERKELEY (1964, p. 140): "In Plutarch, Antony's characterization is completely free from a desire to gain revenge upon Cleopatra for betrayal to Octavius. Shakespeare, however, thrice sounds this distinctive note [quotes 'For . . . done all' (2772–3), 'The Witch . . . for't' (2806–8), and 'she . . . death' (2855–6)]." Expanding THOMSON (1952, p. 149), WAITH (1962, pp. 118–19) notes the similar motivation in Seneca's *Hercules Oetaeus* 1449–55.

2772 **Charme**] Although most commentators regard this as a rhetorical example of the abstract for the concrete—i.e., charmer (see 2781)—WILSON (ed. 1950) remarks, "She has ceased to be a woman and become a foul piece of black magic."

265

Do we shake hands? All come to this? The hearts   2776

2776–8 **hearts . . . dis-Candie**] The commentators have produced a gallery of gorgeous inventions. First, WARBURTON (*apud* THEOBALD, ed. 1733): "*Pannelling at Heels* must mean here, *following*: but where was the Word ever found in such a Sense? . . . *Shakespeare* must certainly have wrote; *That* pantler'd *me at Heels*; i.e. run after Me like Footmen, or *Pantlers* . . . the Servants who have the Care of the Bread; but is used by our Poet for a menial Servant in general, as well as in its native Acceptation." To which GREY (1755, p. 27) correctly responds: Sh. "never used the Word in that Sense." Second, RURICOLA (1747, p. 179): "'Tis very usual in our language to form verbs of substantives. . . . Thus if we say of one, who follows another at some distance, that he *dogs* him; why may it not be said . . . of a fawning flatterer, that he *spannels* one at the heels?" And TOLLET (*apud* STEEVENS, ed. 1778): "*Spaniel* was often formerly written *spannel*. Hence there is only the omission of the first letter." PYE (1807, pp. 268–9) agrees but qualifies: "To spaniel, here, is to follow fawningly, as a spaniel does his master." NARES (1822; 1876, *discandy*): "*Hearts . . . spaniel'd . . .* heels, *melting their sweets* upon Cæsar, forms a masterpiece of incongruity." WILSON (ed. 1950): "For the assoc. in Sh.'s mind of fawning dogs with melting sweets, and flatterers, due to the unclean practice of feeding dogs at meals under the table, [see] Spurgeon, *Sh.'s Imagery*, 1935, pp. 195–9, and cf. *Caes.* 3.1.42–3 [1249–50]; *Ham.* 3.2.[65–7 (1911–13)]; *1 Hen. IV*, 1.3.251[–2 (578–9)]. [The cluster was] noticed by Whiter, 1794 (p. 138), who was 'unable to discover' the cause [ed. Over, 1967, pp. 123–7, n. 1]." Third, UPTON (1746, pp. 203–4) compares *Tim.* 4.3.224, "page thy heeles" (1845), and reads "*pag'd* me at the heels." IDEM (1748, p. 200, n. 3), however: Sh.'s "words ought not to be changed. . . . The allusion here, licentious as it is, is to the pannel of a wainscot." He cites "ioyne Wainscot" (*AYL* 3.3.88 [1592–3]) to show "that by *the hearts that pannell'd me at heels*, he means *the hearts that* JOIN'D *me, united themselves to me, &c.*" Fourth, MACKAY's (1884, p. 33) questionable etymology: "The Keltic word *pannel* or *bannal*, means a band, a troop, a company, an assemblage of men; whence the modern English to *empanel* (or collect) a jury. The obvious meaning is 'The hearts (men) that followed in troops, or crowds, at my heels have forsaken me to bestow their attentions upon Cæsar.'" Fifth, THISELTON's (1899, p. 23) puzzling explanation: "A panel is defined by Schmidt [1875] as 'a piece of board inserted into the groove of a thicker surrounding frame'. Though it thus becomes a part of the structure, it is distinguished by its surface being on a lower level than that of the frame. And in this way Anthony's followers may be said to have 'pannelled' him 'at heeles.'" Sixth, HULME (1962, p. 108): "In the one verb 'pannelled' Shakespeare combines two meanings: the noun 'panel' (a form of earlier 'parnel') has the sense 'prostitute'; a second noun 'panele' has the meaning 'sugar'. And I would not deny—what Hanmer [ed. 1744] recognised—that it may be part of the function of Shakespeare's 'pannelled', through the shape and sound of the word, to bring to mind also, in this context, the 'spaniel' image." And EAGLESON (1971, p. 4): Sh. "has caught up the twin ideas of unfaithfulness and flattery, or if you like, sugar-coated treachery." Seventh, JACKSON (1819, p. 309), advocating *pan-kneel'd*: "The *knee* is merely a joint; the *knee-pan*, the convex bone that protects the joint. Thus, the slight bending of the knee is not the desired figure; it is the bending the knee in its *knee-pan* to the ground, and following on heel and toe, at Antony's heels, until the suit was granted." Eighth, MEREDITH (1974, p. 124), in the most extensive commentary of all: "It retains the idea . . . of dogs, in this case panting

266

That pannelled me at heeles, to whom I gaue
Their wishes, do dis-Candie, melt their sweets
On blossoming *Cæsar*: And this Pine is barkt,
That ouer-top'd them all. Betray'd I am.   2780
Oh this false Soule of Egypt! this graue Charme,
Whose eye beck'd forth my Wars, & cal'd them home:

2777 pannelled] pantler'd WARBURTON *conj. apud* THEO1, THEO, WARB; spaniel'd
HAN1, JOHN1+ (−v1773)

2780–1 am. Oh] am‸ On F4

2781 Soule] soil CAP; spell mTBY3 *conj.*, mCOL1, COL2, SING2, COL3, COL4; snake
WALKER (1860, 3:309) *conj.*, WORD1

       graue] gay mPOPE *conj.*, POPE1-THEO4; great mCOL1, COL2, COL3, COL4; grand
SING2; brave WORD1

2782 eye] eyes OXF1

---

behind Antony; the word *pantle*d with its belittling suffix perfectly conveying the scorn-
in-grief that he feels for his followers. . . . Subsidiary meanings . . . [link] this word
and the other parts of the passage. The connection between *hearts* and *panting* is . . .
common. . . . Not only is *pantled* appropriate to *hearts* but it combines both the meanings of *pant*, 'quick, short breathing' and 'throbbing', both of which fit in here; the one
leading to the idea of dogs panting breathlessly at his heels, the other to the ironical
one of hearts throbbing devotedly for him. . . . [Meredith (pp. 122–4) also describes]
two ways in which *pantled* might have become the Folio *pannelled*, both involving a
scribal or compositorial misreading." See also p. 357 for further conjectures. The overwhelming majority accepts Hanmer's emendation—see textual notes—on the basis of
the association of dogs, melting sweets, and flatterers elsewhere in Sh.

    2777 **at heeles**] See n. 861.

    2778 **dis-Candie**] Cited by HURD (1757; 1811, 1:77–8)—along with "dislimes" (2836)—
as an example of Sh.'s "artful management . . . by which you may be able to give a
new air and cast to old [words]" in adding *dis*- to "known words . . . [to] express the
contrary ideas." First appearance credited to Sh. by the *OED*. See n. 2348.

    2779–80 **Pine . . . all**] WILSON (ed. 1950): "The pine is always lofty to [Sh.]." Com-
pares *MV* 4.1.75 (1981), *R2* 3.2.42 (1398), *2H6* 2.3.45 (1101), *Cym.* 4.2.175 (2469).

    2779 **barkt**] MINSHEU (1617): "*Pill* [i.e., peel] *trees*." WILSON (ed. 1950): "I suspect
it was a comb. of 'pine' . . . and 'spanielled' which [suggested] it [to] Sh."

    2781 **graue**] CAWDREY (1604) offers synonyms: "Waightie, sober, sage, discrete." JOHN-
SON (ed. 1765), rejecting *gay*: "*Sublime . . . majestick.*" Most commentators tend toward
CAPELL's (1779 [1774], 1:46) "that leads to death or the grave," which STEEVENS (ed.
1778), glossing as "*deadly*, or *destructive*," says is "employed in the sense of the Latin
word *gravis*." Others range from "heavy" (DELIUS [ed. 1856]) or "oppressive" (IRVING
& MARSHALL [ed. 1889]) to "potent" (THISELTON [1899, p. 23]) or "commanding" (CASE
[ed. 1906]). For the numerous conjectures, see textual notes and p. 357.

        Charme] Most commentators favor the agent—e.g., "enchantress" (RANN [ed.
1791–]). See 2772. The others compare 2788.

    2782 **beck'd**] See n. 2088.

Whose Bosome was my Crownet, my chiefe end,
Like a right Gypsie, hath at fast and loose
Beguil'd me, to the very heart of losse.   2785
What *Eros, Eros?*

Enter Cleopatra.

Ah, thou Spell! Auaunt.
   Cleo. Why is my Lord enrag'd against his Loue?
   Ant. Vanish, or I shall giue thee thy deseruing,   2790
And blemish *Cæsars* Triumph. Let him take thee,
And hoist thee vp to the shouting Plebeians,

2792 to] unto KTLY

2783 **Crownet**] JOHNSON (1755), citing this instance: "Chief end; last purpose; probably from *finis coronat opus* [The end justifies the means]."
   2784 **right**] See n. 2425.
   Gypsie] See n. 14.
   fast and loose] HAWKINS (*apud* STEEVENS, ed. 1778): "A term to signify a cheating game. . . . A leathern belt is made up into a number of intricate folds, and placed edgewise upon a table. One of the folds is made to resemble the middle of the girdle, so that whoever should thrust a skewer into it would think he held it fast to the table; whereas, when he has so done, the person with whom he plays may take hold of both ends and draw it away. This trick . . . perhaps was practised by the Gypsies in the time of Shakespeare." STEEVENS (ed. 1778): "Sir John Hawkins's supposition is confirm'd by the following Epigram in an ancient collection called [*Rubbe*] *and a great Cast*, by Tho[mas] Freeman, 1614 [quotes Pt. 2, *Rvnne, And a great Cast*, Epigram 95]."
   2785 **heart of losse**] Expanding on WARBURTON (ed. 1747), CAPELL (1779 [1774], 1:46): "The most perfect and absolute loss, *i.e.* ruin; and is taken from trees, whose heart or centre is commonly perfecter than their extreams."
   2786 MILLS (1964, p. 46) alone and improbably: "He calls for Eros, but Cleopatra appears, having mistakenly thought, perhaps, that Antony was summoning her by calling on the deity of love, Eros."
   What] DEIGHTON (ed. 1891): "An exclamation of impatience in summoning an attendant." See also n. 1539.
   2788–97 See n. 2286–97.
   2788 **Auaunt**] MINSHEU (1617): "*A terme of disdaine* . . . Fie on thee, Away, Get thee from before mee, *or*, Out of my sight." See FRANZ §252. See also "Vanish" (2790) and n. 3494.
   2791 **Triumph**] KITTREDGE (ed. 1941): "Triumphal procession."
   2792 **hoist . . . vp**] Captives were not exhibited in cages or the like (as they are in Marlowe's *1 Tamburlaine* 4.2 [ed. Bowers, 1973]), but effigies were displayed. Plutarch notes (p. 456): "In his [Caesar's] triumphe he caried *Cleopatraes* image." See 3264 and n. 3562.

Follow his Chariot, like the greatest spot
Of all thy Sex. Most Monster-like be shewne
For poor'st Diminitiues, for Dolts, and let   2795
Patient *Octauia*, plough thy visage vp
With her prepared nailes.   *exit Cleopatra.*

2794 Most . . . shewne] Monster-like be the shew HAN1
2795 for Dolts] for doits mTBY2 *and* WARBURTON *conj. apud* mTHEO2 (21 Feb. 1729, [fol. 41]), WARB, CAP, v1773, MAL, v1821, SING1, COL1-NLSN, KIT1, ALEX; to dolts TYRWHITT *conj. apud* v1778, v1778, v1793, v1803
2797–8 *One verse line* ROWE1+

2793 **Follow his Chariot**] In reality, captives preceded the chariot. See PAULY, Triumphus, 7:503 (1). See 2911–13 ("whil'st . . . ensued"), n. 2913.
2795 **Diminitiues, for Dolts**] THEOBALD (21 Feb. 1729, [fol. 41ʳ]): "She shall be made a Sight for the most *contemptible* Part of the *Rabble*. [Compares 'Shall . . . Rome' (3264–6) and 'Mechanicke . . . view' (3451–3) as well as *Tro.* 5.1.37–9, 'Ah . . . nature' (2900–1).]" IDEM (ed. 1733), although retaining *Dolts*, explains Warburton's *doits*: "Both Dr. *Thirlby* [in a letter (7 May 1729, [fol. 67ʳ]) and in his MS notes in a copy of POPE (ed. 1723)] and Mr. *Warburton* have suspected, that *Shakespeare* wrote—*for* Doits: i.e. for that small Piece of Money, so call'd. I should not be stagger'd at the Transgression against Chronology in this Point." Quotes *Cor.* 1.5.7 (577). CAPELL (1779 [1774], 1:46): "Had '*dolts*' been the word, the Poet would have said—*to* dolts,—*to* poor'st diminutives; as he has, two lines higher [2792], '*to the shouting plebeians*'; which very words led him to '*for*' and to '*doits*', to avoid a co-incidence of thoughts and expression in lines so near one another." TYRWHITT (*apud* STEEVENS, ed. 1778), proposing *to dolts*: "This aggravates the contempt of her supposed situation; to be shewn, *as monsters are*, not only *for the smallest pieces of money*, but *to the most stupid and vulgar spectators*." SISSON (1956, 2:271) finds "no difficulty" in F1, interpreting as "in place of (*for*) dwarfs and idiots." See textual notes and conj., p. 357. Thirlby's emendation is doubtful: Sh. otherwise uses *doit* only in the singular and never following the preposition *for*, and he does not elsewhere employ *shown for.*
2797 **prepared nailes**] WARBURTON (ed. 1747) and most commentators: "*I.e.* with nails which she suffered to grow for this purpose." SEYMOUR (1805, 2:77) and some others: "*Cut* or *sharpened* for the purpose." DELIUS (ed. 1856) and a few others: Held in readiness, made ready. ROBERTS (1983, p. 111) detects a reference to the "belief that to draw blood on a witch [to whom Cleopatra is often likened], especially from her face, was a way of removing her *maleficium.*"
exit Cleopatra] SMITH (1967, p. 9): "Shakespeare's observance of the law [of Reentry (p. 7): 'Shakespeare avoided having a character enter the stage at the beginning of an act or scene after having been on-stage at the end of the preceding act or scene'] is evidenced. . . . Cleopatra leaves the stage at [2797], just ten lines before the end of the scene. She reenters at the beginning of IV. xiii [2809], having in the meantime traveled from a hill outside Alexandria to a room inside her palace. Antony makes the same journey ten lines later. He leaves the hillside just ten lines after Cleopatra [2808]

'Tis well th'art gone,
If it be well to liue. But better 'twere
Thou fell'st into my furie, for one death   2800
Might haue preuented many. *Eros*, hoa?
The shirt of *Nessus* is vpon me, teach me
Alcides, thou mine Ancestor, thy rage.
Let me lodge *Licas* on the hornes o'th'Moone,
And with those hands that graspt the heauiest Club,   2805

2800 into] under mCOL1, COL2, COL3, COL4

2803–4 rage. Let me] rage, Led thee mTHEO2 (21 Feb. 1729, [fol. 41ᵛ]) *conj.* (Let
thee), HAN1, WARB

2804 lodge˄ *Licas*˄] ~ , ~ , v1773

---

and reaches the palace just ten lines after her [2823], having made the trip during the
course of IV. xiii [2809–22], which is just ten lines long."

2799–2801 **better . . . many**] BLUMHOF (ed. 1870) finds that Antony may mean
many deaths that you will cause, or many that in my anger I will cause, or many deaths
that you will undergo. DEIGHTON (ed. 1891): "Better for you to die by my fury than
to suffer death many times, as you will in the terrors to which your cowardice will be
exposed." FURNESS (ed. 1907): "Her death (in time past) *'might have prevented* many'
(others, of soldiers slain in battle). In this case, 'better 'twere thou fell'st' is equivalent
to 'better 'twere thou shouldst have fallen',—the sequence of tenses will hardly permit
'fell'st' to be the perfect indicative. Can it be that in Anthony's present conviction of
Cleopatra's treachery there rise in his memory past occasions when he mistrusted her,
notably her reception of Cæsar's messenger? and he now sees that it would have been
better had she fallen under his fury then? and by one death 'might have prevented many'?"

2801, 2808 **hoa**] See n. 1027.

2802 **shirt of *Nessus***] COOPER (1565, *Nessus*): "A Centaure, whiche rauished Deianira
Hercules wyfe: who beynge wounded to death, gaue to Deianyra a poyson, wherwith
Hercules shyrte beynge washed, and put on him, his body did rotte with most horrible
peynes, which he not susteinynge, did enter into a great fyre, and let himselfe be burned."

2803 ADELMAN (1973, p. 135): "Hercules is the type of gigantic excess, a figure whose
native region is the impossible and whose native speech is hyperbole. . . . Antony's
hyperboles are Hercules' literal actions."

Alcides] For Hercules as ancestor of Antony, see PAULY, Alkaios, 1:1498 (2); *OCD*,
Heracles.

2804 *Licas*] COOPER (1565, *Lica*): "The name of one of Hercules companions." WAR-
BURTON (ed. 1747): "From *Seneca*'s *Hercules* [*Oetaeus* 817–18], who says *Lichas* being
lanched into the air, sprinkled the clouds with his blood." CAPELL (1779 [1774], 1:46):
"Lichas was not lodg'd by Hercules quite upon '*the horns of the moon*', but was thrown
from the top of mount Oeta into the sea: Antony's exaggeration in this place, and the
puffiness of what he speaks next, should be consider'd as specimens of that Asiatick tumour
of diction, which the Poet (using Plutarch's authority [see p. 398]) has made a part of
his character." STEEVENS (ed. 1793) cites Ovid's *Metamorphoses* 9.211–38 (tr. Golding,
1575, fol. 119ᵛ). See PAULY, 13:210–11 (1); not in *OCD*.

Subdue my worthiest selfe: The Witch shall die,   2806
To the young Roman Boy she hath sold me, and I fall
Vnder this plot: She dyes for't. *Eros* hoa?   *exit.*

Enter Cleopatra, Charmian, Iras, Mardian.   **4.13**

Cleo. Helpe me my women: Oh hee's more mad   2810
Then *Telamon* for his Shield, the Boare of Thessaly

2806 my] thy mTHEO2 (21 Feb. 1729, [fol. 41ᵛ]) *conj.*, HAN1, WARB
2807 young] *Om.* HAN1, CAP, v1793, v1803, HUD2
2808 this] his F3-THEO2, WARB-JOHN1, v1773; her mTBY2 *conj.*, HAN1
2809 *SCENE* XI. CAP-SING2, COL3, WH1, KTLY, HAL, COL4, OXF1; SCENE XIII. DYCE,
STAU, GLO, CAM1, HUD2, WH2, NLSN+
     Alexandria. *A Room in the Palace.* CAP, v1778+ (*subst.*)
2810 women] woman F2-F4
     hee's] he is F2-KIT1, ALEX

2806 **my worthiest selfe**] THEOBALD (21 Feb. 1729, [fol. 41ᵛ]) proposes *thy* because
Antony would not call "himself here *his worthiest Self*" and because (IDEM [ed. 1733])
worthiest is properly "apply'd to *Hercules*, whom *Antony* was fond to esteem his Ancestor." HEATH (1765, p. 464): Calling himself *worthiest* "proceeds wholly from a transport
of the fancy, which represents him to himself for that moment as the very Hercules in
person." JOHNSON (ed. 1765): "The meaning is, Let me do something in my rage, becoming the successor of *Hercules*." STAUNTON (ed. 1859) alone conjectures *worthless elf*,
since "it [is] more probable [that] he is thinking of Cleopatra." IRVING & MARSHALL
(ed. 1889): "Myself most deserving of the fate I suffer." FURNESS (ed. 1907): "That part
of his nature which is noblest and best,—this had been in subjection to Cleopatra; he
now prays for strength to control it, 'subdue' it, and make it again subservient to his will."
   2806–8 **The . . . for't**] See n. 2772–3.
   2807 **young . . . Boy**] STEEVENS (ed. 1793) omits for the same reason given at n.
2673. See textual notes. HUDSON (ed. 1881): "Probably the Poet wrote *boy* as a substitute for *young*, and then both words got printed together. 'Roman *boy*' conveys a sneer
which '*young* Roman' does not."
   2808 *exit*] See n. 2797.
   2809 *Enter Cleopatra*] See n. 2797.
   2811 *Telamon* **. . . Shield**] COOPER (1565, *Aiax*): "(The sone of Thelamon by He-
sione, daughter of Laomedon kyng of Troy) was the strongest man of all the Greekes
nexte to Achilles: but after Achilles was slayne, Aiax contending with Ulisses for Achilles
armour, and Ulisses by force of eloquence, obteyninge sentence on his parte, became
madde. And in his fury slewe many beastes, supposing them to be Ulisses and his company." STEEVENS (ed. 1778): "*Ajax Telamon* for the armour of *Achilles*, the most valu-

Was neuer so imbost.

    Char. To'th'Monument, there locke your selfe,

And send him word you are dead:

The Soule and Body riue not more in parting,   2815   (yy5ᵛ)

Then greatnesse going off.

    Cleo. To'th'Monument:

Mardian, go tell him I haue slaine my selfe:

Say, that the last I spoke was *Anthony*,

And word it (prythee) pitteously. Hence *Mardian*,   2820

And bring me how he takes my death to'th'Monument.

                                      Exeunt.

    2812–14 *Verse lines ending* monument, . . . dead: POPE1+

    2815 in] at v1773, v1778, RANN

    2820–1 *Three verse lines ending* Hence, . . . death.—— . . . monument. v1793-
SING1, COL1-SING2, COL3, WH1, KTLY, HAL, COL4, OXF1; *ending* Mardian, . . . death.——
. . . monument. KNT1, STAU

    2821 death‸] ~ . POPE1+ (–HAN1, SIS, ARD2)

---

able part of which was the shield." See PAULY, Aias, 1:930–6 (3); *OCD*, Aias (1).

    Boare of Thessaly] COOPER (1565, *Meleager*): "Or *Meleagrus*, The sonne of Oeneus,
kyng of Calydon." He killed a giant boar sent by Diana to ravage the land. CASE (ed.
1906) cites Ovid's *Metamorphoses* 8.284 (tr. Golding, 1567, fol. 100ᵛ). See PAULY,
Meleagros, 15:446–78 (1); *OCD*, Meleager (1).

    2812 **imbost**] HANMER (*apud* STEEVENS, ed. 1773): "When a deer is hard run and
foams at the mouth, he is said to be *imbost*." *N&Q* was flooded with suggestions in
1868 and again in 1873, when there were more than a dozen. FURNIVALL (1873, p. 507),
e.g., cites the etymological alternatives found in COTGRAVE (1611), preferring the sense
of "foamed with rage," the meaning now generally accepted. And he rejects such explanations as *aux abois* (F. J. V. [1873, p. 210]), which gave rise to "at bay," and "hunted
to extremity . . . to exhaustion" (ADDIS [1868, p. 454]). Possibly the word is connected
with the shield, which was presumably "embossed." The battle of Actium was depicted
on the shield of Virgil's Aeneas (8.675–713) and Mars appears "embossed in steel" (*caela-
tus ferro*, l. 701).

    2813 **Monument**] CAWDREY (1604): "A remembrance of some notable act, as Tombs."

    2815–16 MALONE (ed. 1790) compares *H8* 2.3.15–16 (1218–19): "'Tis a sufferance,
panging [suffering, painful] As soule and bodies seuering."

    2815 **riue**] MINSHEU (1617): "Rent [rend], & Teare."

    2818–21 **go . . . death**] See n. 110.

    2821 **death**] SISSON (1956, 2:271) rejects the emendation of POPE (ed. 1723)—see
textual notes—"for which violent change in punctuation and sense I see no need"—and
its defense by RIDLEY (ed. 1954)—"Pope's emendation does undoubtedly provide a more
emphatic exit": "The Folio text has clear sense, 'Bring (the news) to me to the monument
how he takes my death.'"

    2823 **Enter Anthony**] See n. 2797.

    2824–47 FERGUSSON (1978, p. 21): "Analogous to the Sophoclean choral ode [*An-*

Enter Anthony, and Eros.   **4.14**

Ant. Eros, thou yet behold'st me?
Eros. I Noble Lord.   2825
Ant. Sometime we see a clowd that's Dragonish,
A vapour sometime, like a Beare, or Lyon,
A toward Cittadell, a pendant Rocke,

2823 SCENE VIII. ROWE; SCENE X. POPE, WARB; SCENE XI. HAN1, JOHN1; *SCENE*
XII. CAP-SING2, COL3, WH1, KTLY, HAL, COL4, OXF1; SCENE XIV. DYCE, STAU, GLO, CAM1,
HUD2, WH2, NLSN+
    Cleopatra's *Palace.* ROWE, CAP, v1778+ (*subst.*)
2826 Sometime] Sometimes OXF1
2828 toward] tower'd ROWE1+

---

tigone, tr. Fitts & Fitzgerald, 1947, pp. 462–3]. . . . Antony is its *persona*, and his action is to see through the cloudy shapes before him to himself, as he really is. When
he sees *that*, he too cannot hold his visible shape; the lyric ends, and he sees Cleopatra
as the cause of his non-entity. As he speaks we remember his wavering course throughout
the play, and the shifting actions of his antagonists, who tried to keep up with him.
His vision, or daydream, illuminates both his action and that of the play."
    2825–37 RANSOM (1947, pp. 190–1) illustrates Sh.'s poetic "way of compounding la-
tinical elements with his native English" (p. 191)—as in "blew Promontorie" and "blacke
Vespers Pageants."
    2826–31 Various sources or parallels are offered. RAWLINSON (*apud* STEEVENS, ed.
1773) quotes Aristophanes, *Nubes* 345 ([346–7]; *The Clouds*, tr. Theobald, 1715, p. 20).
STEEVENS (ed. 1778) adds Pliny's *Natural History* 2.3.7, and Chapman's *Monsieur D'Olive*
2.2.91 ff. (1606; ed. Holaday, 1970, p. 424). MALONE (ed. 1790) compares Chapman's
Bussy d'Ambois 3.1.23–5 (1607; ed. Parrott, 1910) or "[Pierre Le Loyer's] *A Treatise of
Spectres [or straunge Sights]*, &c. quarto, 1605 . . . : 'The *cloudes* sometimes will seem
to be monsters, *lions*, bulls, and wolves; *painted* and figured: albeit in truth the same
be nothing but a *moyst humour mounted in the ayre*, and drawne up from the earth,
not having any figure or colour, but such as the *ayre* is able to give unto it' [fol. 59ᵛ]."
More recently, CASE (ed. 1906) quotes parallels from Sylvester's *Du Bartas*, "The Im-
posture" (ed. Snyder, 1979, p. 342, ll. 151–6), and Fairfax's translation of Tasso's *Godfrey
of Bulloigne* (1600), 16.69. And HANKINS (1953, p. 230, n. 3) adds Lucretius, *De rerum
natura* 4.129–42. "To illustrate the susceptibility of the human mind to illusion," RICE
(1968, pp. 123–4) adds Daniel's *Cleopatra*, ll. 33–40 (ed. Grosart, 1885)—for the 1594
Cleopatra, see p. 535—and *Ham.* 3.2.393–9 (2247–53). MACCALLUM (1910, pp. 303–4)
believes there is a connection between *Bussy* and *Ant.*, "and if there is Shakespeare must
have been the debtor; but as *Bussy d'Ambois* was acted before 1600, this loan is without
much value" in closely dating *Ant.*
    2828 **toward**] THISELTON (1899, p. 24): "Probably a misprint for 'tower'd'"—an *e: a*

A forked Mountaine, or blew Promontorie
With Trees vpon't, that nodde vnto the world,   2830
And mocke our eyes with Ayre.
Thou hast seene these Signes,
They are blacke Vespers Pageants.
   Eros. I my Lord.
   Ant. That which is now a Horse, euen with a thoght   2835
The Racke dislimes, and makes it indistinct

2830 world] wind CAP (*text*; world mCAP2, CAPN [*errata*])
2831–2 *One verse line* ROWE1+
2836 it] *Om.* F4

---

misreading. But see p. 374. BARROLL (1969, *ShakS*, p. 233, n. 63): Sh. frequently associates *tower* with *clouds* (as do many writers).

   2831 **mocke**] MINSHEU (1617): "*Deceiue.*"

   2833 **Vespers**] WALTER (ed. 1969): "It has been suggested that F reading 'Vespers'
is plural and was used here with a glance at its association with the eve of the Passion
of Our Lord." See *OED*, 5b.

   Pageants] Commentators in the main stress staged spectacles—WARTON (*apud*
STEEVENS, 1780, 1:231) mentions "the frequency and the nature of these shows in Shakspeare's age"—or natural beauty, like RANN (ed. 1791–): "A part of that unsubstantial
pageantry, which an evening's sky exhibits." WHITER (1794; ed. Over, 1967, pp. 164–6)
believes that since *Racke* (2836) is associated with masques, *Pageants* here, as in *Tmp.*
4.1.155 (1826), must mean "masque." In support he cites Jonson's *Hymenæi* 212–29 (ed.
Herford & Simpson, 1941). SINGER (ed. 1826) attributes to Boswell the following from
a sermon by Bishop Hall: "I feare some of you are like the *pageants* of your great solemnities, wherein there is a show of a solid body, whether of a lion, or elephant, or unicorne;
but if they be curiously look'd into, there is nothing but cloth, and sticks, and ayre"
(from "The Righteous Mammon" [1618] in *Works*, 1634, p. 666). BLUMHOF (ed. 1870)
compares the natural beauty with life's evening, with its increasing shadows. CASE (ed.
1906) "explains the allusion" with a quotation from Whetstone's *2 Promos and Cassan-
dra* 1.5: "*Phallax.* With what strange showes doo they their *Pageaunt* grace? *Bedell.* They
have *Hercules* of monsters conqueryng, Huge great *Giants* in a forest fighting With *Lyons,
Beares, Wolues, Apes, Foxes,* and *Grayes, Baiards, Brockes,* &c. [*Six old Plays,* ed. John
Nichols, 1779, 1:65]." KITTREDGE (ed. 1941) makes reference to Robert Withington, *English Pageantry,* 1918–20. See also n. 3292–3320.

   2835 **euen . . . thoght**] DEIGHTON (ed. 1891): "With the swiftness of thought."
See n. 2616 and *JC* 5.3.19 (2499). For the intensive *even,* see FRANZ §438. The spelling
thoght is doubtless due to the full line, as at 3407.

   2836 **Racke**] UPTON (1748, pp. 209–10): "I once red, *wracking clouds* . . . tossing
them like waves of the sea." He refers to "mist, clouds driven by the wind" in Gavin
Douglas's translation (1553) of Virgil (*Poetical Works,* ed. Small, 1874, 4:320). Also in
JOHNSON (1755, 5). For an extensive discussion of the meaning, see FURNESS (ed. 1892)
on *Tmp.* 4.1.156 (1827).

As water is in water.

   Eros. It does my Lord.

   Ant. My good Knaue *Eros*, now thy Captaine is

Euen such a body: Heere I am *Anthony*,   2840

Yet cannot hold this visible shape (my Knaue)

I made these warres for Egypt, and the Queene,

Whose heart I thought I had, for she had mine:

Which whil'st it was mine, had annext vntoo't

A Million moe, (now lost:) shee *Eros* has   2845

Packt Cards with *Cæsars*, and false plaid my Glory

2845 moe] more ROWE1-OXF1 (−KTLY, CAM1)
2846 *Cæsars*] *Cæsar* ROWE1-KNT1, HUD1+ (−HAL, EVNS)

---

   dislimes] MINSHEU (1617, Limne): "*Paint with colours.*" JOHNSON (1755), citing this instance: "To unpaint; to strike out of a picture." See n. 2778. JONES's (ed. 1977) "wordplay involving the idea of a *body* [2840] being 'dislimbed' [first conjectured by KEIGHTLEY (1867, p. 320)] — torn limb from limb — on a rack" is questionable because, among other things, it is not recorded by the *OED* before 1662. Puzzling is WELLS & TAYLOR's (ed. 1986) *distaines* (*distains*), adopted because it "makes equally good sense" and is used elsewhere in Sh. Though ROWE (ed. 1709) was the first to add the *n*, the spelling *limn* was current in Sh.'s time.

   2839 Knaue] MINSHEU (1617): "*A man seruant.*" SINGER (ed. 1826) adds, "But it had already begun to have no favourable signification when [John] Baret published his Alvearie [or Triple Dictionarie], in 1573 [defining it as 'a lying beggerly or saucy fellow']." Still, HUDSON (ed. 1881) and most commentators in this instance: "*Knave* was often used as a playful or familiar term of endearment." Of the six instances in *Ant.* the two spoken to Eros (the other at 2841) seem positive, three are so qualified as to appear negative (150, 451, 1155), and one is neutral (3203).

   2840 Heere] KITTREDGE (ed. 1941): "Here and now; at this moment."

   2844 it] DEIGHTON (ed. 1891): I.e., Antony's heart.

   2845 moe] FRANZ (§221): As distinct from *more*, used generally with count nouns in the plural.

   2846 Packt Cards] KERSEY's (1702) simple definition, "*Put 'em together,*" is orchestrated by JOHNSON (1755), citing this instance: "To sort the cards so as that the game shall be iniquitously secured. It is applied to any iniquitous procurement of collusion." MAHOOD (1957, p. 21): The "card-playing image" is produced by the "play upon the further meanings of *Knave* [2841], *Queen* [2842] and *heart* [2843] . . . and . . . *triumph* [2847]."

   Cæsars] COLLIER (ed. 1843): "Cæsar's cards." WHITE (ed. 1861), perhaps following WALKER (1860, 1:233) on "final *s* frequently interpolated and frequently omitted in the first folio," supports *Cæsar*: "We have had the same error before in this play [*Figure* for *Figures*, 1555]."

   2846–7 false . . . triumph] WARBURTON (ed. 1747) detects a pun, "which either signifies *Octavius's* conquests, or what we now call, contractedly, the *trump* at cards, then

Vnto an Enemies triumph.
Nay, weepe not gentle *Eros*, there is left vs
Our selues to end our selues.

                Enter Mardian.   2850

Oh thy vilde Lady, she has rob'd me of my Sword.
    Mar. No *Anthony*,
My Mistris lou'd thee, and her Fortunes mingled
With thine intirely.
    Ant. Hence sawcy Eunuch peace, she hath betraid me,   2855
And shall dye the death.
    Mar. Death of one person, can be paide but once,
And that she ha's discharg'd. What thou would'st do

2849, 2851–2 *Verse lines ending* Lady! . . . *Antony*, ROWE1+
2851 thy] the F4-POPE2
2854–6 *Verse lines ending* peace, . . . death. HAN1, CAP+
2856 And] And she ROWE1-JOHN1 (–HAN1)
2858 ha's] hath CAP-v1778, RANN

---

called the *triumph.*" The legitimacy of the pun, a matter of controversy for a century after Warburton, is no longer doubted (*OED*, Triumph *sb.* 8a). WALTER (ed. 1969) sums up the implications: "By such card-sharping betrayed my glory so that it became my enemy's triumph (or, so that my glory was trumped by my enemy)."

2851 CAPELL (1779 [1774], 1:47): "Words that should not be taken metaphorically . . . but literally; for that he had no sword of his own, appears by what he says to Eros in [2916–17]. . . . Cleopatra's action proceeded from tenderness: she saw the rage he was in; and, fearing the effects of it, withdrew, (or caus'd to be withdrawn) the instrument of his harm." Most others, starting with BLUMHOF (ed. 1870), take the expression metaphorically. See nn. 1051, 2944–5.

    vilde] Apart from *vildest* (954), the only instance in the play of this frequent form. FRANZ (§60) is of the (minority) opinion that it derives from the participle *aviled* (of the obsolete verb *avile*). CERCIGNANI (1981, p. 318), agreeing with *OED*, holds that it is the "very common" form in Sh. of an excrescent final *d* after *l*, others, such as *rascald* and *scrich-ould*, being only "occasional." Compare n. 3568.

2855–6 **she . . . death**] See n. 2772–3.

2856 **dye the death**] For the use of the article in connection with *death*, a pronouncement meaning something like "be put to death," see FRANZ §262 and *OED*, *v.*[1] 2c, which cites JOHNSON's (ed. 1765, 1:311, n. 8) comment on *MM* 2.4.165 (1179): "This seems to be a solemn phrase for death inflicted by law. [Compares *MND* 1.1.65 (74).]" CASE (ed. 1906) compares *Cym.* 4.2.96 (2374) as well.

2857–8 **Death . . . discharg'd**] WALTER (ed. 1969) alone: "A quibble on 'debt' and 'death.'"

2857 Proverbial; see DENT (M219): "A *man* can die but once."

    of] Only KITTREDGE (ed. 1941) comments: "By."

Is done vnto thy hand: the last she spake
Was *Anthony*, most Noble *Anthony*:   2860
Then in the midd'st a tearing grone did breake
The name of *Anthony*: it was diuided
Betweene her heart, and lips: she rendred life
Thy name so buried in her.
    Ant. Dead then?   2865
    Mar. Dead.
    Ant. Vnarme *Eros*, the long dayes taske is done,
And we must sleepe: That thou depart'st hence safe
Does pay thy labour richly: Go.   *exit Mardian.*
Off, plucke off,   2870
The seuen-fold shield of *Aiax* cannot keepe

2863 rendred] tendred F2-F4
2864–6 *One verse line* v1793+
2864 Thy] The v1778, RANN
2867 Vnarme *Eros*] Unarm me, *Eros* ROWE1-CAP, COL2, KTLY, DYCE2, COL4, HUD2, KIT1; Eros, unarm RITSON *conj. apud* CAM1, v1793, v1803
2868 *To* Mardian. HAN1, JOHN1+ (−ALEX) (*subst.*)
2869–70 *One verse line* ROWE1-POPE2, HAN1, CAP, v1778+
2870 Off,] Oh, F2-POPE2; *om.* HAN1, CAP

2859 **vnto thy hand**] DELIUS (ed. 1856) and others: Is already done for you. WILSON (ed. 1950, Glossary) alone: "In readiness."
    2861–5 WILSON (ed. 1950): "Mard. a little overplays the pathos Cleo. ordered."
    2861 **breake**] SCHMIDT (1874, 5), citing this instance: "To interrupt . . . (cut it in two)."
    2862–3 **it . . . lips**] DEIGHTON (ed. 1891): "Only half of it was pronounced by her lips, the other half getting no further than her heart."
    2863 **rendred**] See n. 2017–18.
    2864 **so**] DELIUS (ed. 1856): As it were.
    2867 **Vnarme *Eros***] See textual notes. STEEVENS (ed. 1793) regards F1's reading as "in defiance of metre" and emends to "Eros, unarm." COLLIER (ed. 1858): "[F2] puts it 'Unarm *me*, Eros', which we cannot believe to be right, because the measure is thus unnecessarily disturbed." RIDLEY (ed. 1954): Rowe's (ed. 1709) "emendation is, of course, graphically easy, and the intrusive *me*, though I think it produces a rhythm less suiting to the context, is metrically quite defensible (it is more awkward if we are pronouncing the name as Ērŏs rather than Ĕrōs)." For Plutarch's "vnarmed him selfe," see p. 450.
    2871 **seuen-fold shield of *Aiax***] The shield is described in *Homer's Iliads* (7.193, tr. Chapman), which WILSON (ed. 1950) considers Sh.'s source: "The right side brasse, and seven Oxehides within it quilted hard [ed. A. Nicoll, 1957]." As BLUMHOF (ed. 1870) notes, it is also mentioned in Ovid's *Metamorphoses* 13.1–2.
    2871–2 **keepe . . . heart**] BOSWELL (ed. 1821) and most 19th-c. commentators: "The battery [i.e., heartbeats] *proceeding from* my heart, which is strong enough to break

The battery from my heart. Oh cleaue my sides.
Heart, once be stronger then thy Continent,
Cracke thy fraile Case. Apace *Eros*, apace;
No more a Soldier: bruised peeces go,   2875
You haue bin Nobly borne. From me awhile.   *exit Eros*
I will o're-take thee *Cleopatra*, and
Weepe for my pardon. So it must be, for now
All length is Torture: since the Torch is out,

2872 The] This mTBY3 *conj.*, RANN, CAM3b
     cleaue~] ~ , THEO1+ (−v1773, SING1)
2876 *exit Eros*] *After* borne DEL2
2879 the] thy HAN1

---

through the seven-fold shield of Ajax." DELIUS (ed. 1856) and 20th-c. commentators:
Any blow [i.e., tidings] that threatens the heart and against which armor or shield cannot
protect.
    2872–4 **cleaue . . . Case**] FURNESS (ed. 1907) alone: "The period in the Folio after
'sides' . . . makes Anthony adjure his sides to cleave, *scil.* themselves. This intransitive
or reflexive use of 'cleave' is rare; see Murray (*N.E.D.*) where comparatively few examples
of it are given. Replace the period with a comma, and 'cleave' then becomes the imperative of a transitive verb with 'sides' as an object, and 'Heart' as the subject: 'Oh, Heart,
cleave my sides!' Then, in a manner thoroughly Shakespearian, the idea is repeated, but
in a different form: 'for once be stronger than thy continent, crack thy frail case.'"
    2873–4 **Heart . . . Case**] SINGER (ed. 1856): "Perhaps pathologically accurate, a bro-
ken heart being, when it does occur, a rupture of the wall or cell that contains the heart,
not of the heart itself." CASE (ed. 1906): "For this frequent appeal, compare *King Lear*,
II. iv. 200: 'O sides, you are too tougʰ' [1488]; and from [Thomas] Heywood, one of
several passages ([*Dramatic Works*, ed. Shepherd, 1874] ii, 299), *Faire Maid of the West*,
[Act] iii." RIDLEY (ed. 1954) adds, "Antony is not asking his heart to break (as in *Lear*,
V. iii. [312 (3285)]) but to have for once the strength to break out into freedom from
the confining body." WILSON (ed. 1950), however: "In death the heart cracks (cf. *Ham.*
5.2.[370 (3848)]; *Lear*, 5.3.196–9 [3159–62], 216–17 [3168+12 f.]; *K. John*, 5.7.52 [2662]);
but Ant.'s heart must be kept for Cleo. (cf. ll. [2883–7]) so that for 'once' the 'case' (body)
must 'crack' first to release it." See also 3104 ("case"), n. 266.
    2873 **thy Continent**] STEEVENS (ed. 1778): "I.e. the thing that contains thee." For
the genitive construction, see FRANZ §322.
    2874 **apace**] See n. 2631.
    2876 **From me awhile**] DELIUS (ed. 1856), practically alone, says this is directed not
to Eros but to Cleopatra, as the passage in Plutarch (see p. 450) confirms. Eros goes out
by himself to carry off the armor. WILSON (ed. 1950) agrees: "Even Eros must not hear
his words to Cleo.'s spirit, whispered, I think, like a prayer, on his knees."
    2879 Despite FURNESS's (ed. 1907) doubts of the connection, VINCENT asserts (1978,
p. 266): "Antony's torture and his torch are joined by wordplay."
    length] CHEDWORTH (1805, p. 293): "Protraction of life." HUDSON (ed. 1855) alone:

Lye downe and stray no farther. Now all labour   2880
Marres what it does: yea, very force entangles   (yy5^{vb})
It selfe with strength: Seale then, and all is done.
Eros? I come my Queene. *Eros*? Stay for me,
Where Soules do couch on Flowers, wee'l hand in hand,
And with our sprightly Port make the Ghostes gaze: 2885
Dido, and her *Æneas* shall want Troopes,

2880 stray] stay ROWE3
        farther] further ROWE2-JOHN1, v1773, v1778, RANN, v1793-SING1, HUD, DYCE,
OXF1
2882 Seale] sleep HAN1
2883 Stay] Say F2-F4
2886 *Æneas*] *Sichæus* WARBURTON *conj. apud* mTHEO2 ([18 Nov. 1731, fol. 85^{v}]),
HAN1, WARB

"All length of *journey* or *travel*; as is shown by the following part of the sentence."
    Torch is out] COATES (1978, p. 50): "A well-known Renaissance emblem of the
soul being freed from the body [cites Henry Green, *Shakespeare and the Emblem Writers*,
1870, pp. 455–6]." See also 3100.
    2880–1 **Now . . . does**] BATTENHOUSE (1969, p. 164), too ingeniously: "Note how
Shakespeare puns on the irony of this situation, by having the Mars-like Antony [pun
on *Marres*]."
    2881 **very**] See n. 749.
    2882 **Seale**] THEOBALD (ed. 1733): "*Antony* . . . thinks, stabbing himself will *seal*
That [Cleopatra's] Pardon." WARBURTON (ed. 1747) and most commentators: "Metaphor taken from civil contracts, where, when all is agreed on, the *sealing* compleats the
contract; so he had determined to die, and nothing remain'd but to give the stroke."
JOHNSON (ed. 1765) and only a few others: "The reading is,—seel. . . . To *seel hawks*,
is to close their eyes. The meaning will be . . . Close thine eyes *for ever, and be quiet*."
    2884 **Where . . . Flowers**] DELIUS (ed. 1856): The reference is to the Elysian Fields.
MACCALLUM (1910, p. 58): The detail may have been suggested by the Countess of Pembroke's *Antonius* (see p. 523), but "there is a great difference in the tone of the context."
    hand in hand] See ADELMAN (1973, p. 199, n. 35), listing and discussing the sig-
nificance of repeated episodes of hand play: "Antony's vision [of himself and Cleopatra
in Elysium] subsumes both handshaking and hand kissing. Finally, they can trust only
their own hands and each other's."
    2885 **sprightly**] DELIUS (ed. 1856) is the first to suggest the double sense of "gay,
lively," and "spectral, spiritlike." RANN (ed. 1791–) alone: "Majestic."
    Port] COTGRAVE (1611): "*The carriage, behauior, or demeanour*."
    2886–7 **Dido . . . ours**] KITTREDGE (ed. 1941) summarizes the main trend initiated
by DELIUS (ed. 1856): "All the resort shall be to us; we alone shall be the pair of lovers
that the ghosts will throng to behold."
    2886 **Æneas**] While most commentators compare Virgil (6.467–76), ZIELINSKI (1905,
pp. 17–18) prefers Ovid's Dido. Forgetting the unhappy meeting with Dido in the under-

279

And all the haunt be ours. Come *Eros, Eros.*

Enter Eros.

Eros. What would my Lord?

Ant. Since *Cleopatra* dyed,   2890
I haue liu'd in such dishonour, that the Gods
Detest my basenesse. I, that with my Sword,
Quarter'd the World, and o're greene Neptunes backe
With Ships, made Cities; condemne my selfe, to lacke
The Courage of a Woman, lesse Noble minde   2895
Then she which by her death, our *Cæsar* telles

2891 haue liu'd] live HAN1
2895 minde] minded ROWE1-v1773, COL2, KTLY, DYCE2, COL4, HUD2
2896 our] her OXF1

---

world (*Aeneid* 6.469), MACCALLUM (1910, p. 411, n. 1): "Perhaps he [Sh.] remembered only that Æneas . . . between his two authorised marriages with ladies of the 'superior' races, intercalated the love-adventure . . . with an African queen."

Troopes] COTGRAVE (1611, Troupe) offers synonyms: "*Crue, rout, rable, throng, or multitude of people, &c.*" See also 1804.

2887 **haunt**] WILSON (ed. 1950): "Used quibblingly like 'sprightly' in l. [2885]." See *OED, sb.* 2b ("company"), 3 ("resort"); the first instance of "ghost" (*OED*, 5) is 1878. SCHANZER (1956, p. 154) compares "haunt'st" in the Countess of Pembroke's *Antonie* (1595, l. 1973) as evidence for the relationship of the two works. For the 1592 *Antonius*, see p. 523.

2893 **Quarter'd**] MINSHEU (1617): "*Dismember.*" EVERETT (ed. 1964) adds "covered with troops."

2893–4 **o're . . . Cities**] DEIGHTON (ed. 1891): "*I.e.* his vessels being so capacious as to carry in each of them the population of a city." FURNESS (ed. 1907), however, compares *H5* 3.Pr.14–16, "behold A Citie on th'inconstant Billowes dauncing: For so appeares this Fleet Maiesticall" (1058–60).

2894 **condemne . . . to lacke**] For Sh.'s use of the prepositional infinitive, especially in connection with meter, see FRANZ §651 and 1195–7, 2990–1.

2895 **lesse Noble minde**] MALONE (*apud* STEEVENS [1783]): "Antony is made to say . . . that he is *destitute* of [lacks] a less noble mind than Cleopatra. But he means to assert the very contrary;—that he *has* a less noble mind than she. I . . . read . . . noble-*minded*." STEEVENS (ed. 1793), advocating *nobly* for *noble*: "To *mind*, in this instance, may be a verb, signifying to *incline*, or *be disposed*. So, in Spenser's *State of Ireland* [ll. 821–2, *Spenser's Prose Works*, ed. Gottfried, 1949, p. 71]." SINGER (ed. 1826), agreeing: "The termination *bly* is often written *ble* by old writers, and is frequently to be found so in Shakespeare. [Quotes *3H6* 4.1.106 (2136) and 4.1.140 (2174).]" See also n. 792. BLUMHOF (ed. 1870): Either in apposition to the subject *I* [2892] or an expansion of "condemne my selfe" [2894]—i.e., to be less noble-minded or of less noble mind. Most commentators accept the latter.

I am Conqueror of my selfe. Thou art sworne *Eros*,
That when the exigent should come, which now
Is come indeed: When I should see behinde me
Th'ineuitable prosecution of disgrace and horror,   2900
That on my command, thou then would'st kill me.
Doo't, the time is come: Thou strik'st not me,
'Tis *Cæsar* thou defeat'st. Put colour in thy Cheeke.
    Eros. The Gods with-hold me,
Shall I do that which all the Parthian Darts,   2905
(Though Enemy) lost ayme, and could not.
    Ant. Eros,
Would'st thou be window'd in great Rome, and see

2898 should] is v1773
2900–4 *Five verse lines ending* disgrace . . . then . . . come: . . . defeat'st. . . .
me, ROWE1-JOHN1, KNT1; *ending* of . . . command, . . . come: . . . defeat'st. . . .
me! mTYR *conj. and* CAP, v1773-SING1, COL1-GLO, HAL+; *ending* prosecution . . .
command, . . . come.— . . . defeatest. . . . me! KTLY
2902 Doo't] Do it, for POPE1-JOHN1
2903 'Tis] 'Till F4-ROWE3
    thy] my F2-POPE2
2906 Enemy] enemies KTLY

2896 **which**] See n. 389.
2898 **exigent**] COTGRAVE (1611): "*Necessitie, extremitie.*" MINSHEU (1617) mentions
a legal writ so called because it "requireth [an] appearance *or foorthcomming to answer
the Law.*"
2899–2900 **When . . . horror**] DEIGHTON (ed. 1891): "The figure is that of hounds
running down their prey [quotes *H5* 1.Pr.6–8, *'and . . . employment'* (7–9)]; though
there the hounds are represented as waiting to be sent in pursuit." But as at 2898, legal
terminology is also apparent.
2900 FURNESS (ed. 1907): "This line, with its eight feet catalectic . . . is certainly
a notable violation of the laws of blank verse. . . . Anthony's . . . emotion must have
been almost uncontrollable before he could bring himself to utter 'disgrace' and 'horror'.
. . . I would . . . put 'disgrace and horror' in a separate line." See textual notes.
    prosecution] CAWDREY (1604, prosequute): "Follow after, or finish."
2903 **defeat'st**] BULLOKAR (1616): "To deceiue, or beguile: to take craftilie from one."
DEIGHTON (ed. 1891) and most commentators: "Foil, disappoint." See also 3185.
2904 **with-hold**] COTGRAVE (1611, Retenir): "*Withhold; stay . . . restraine.*" See also
n. 1837.
2905 **Parthian Darts**] See n. 1496.
2906 **lost ayme**] I.e., missed the target.
2908 **window'd**] JOHNSON (1755), citing this instance: "To place at a window." Most
commentators agree. DAVIES (1783, 2:357): "Gazed at from *windows.*"

Thy Master thus with pleacht Armes, bending downe
His corrigible necke, his face subdu'de   2910
To penetratiue shame; whil'st the wheel'd seate
Of Fortunate *Cæsar* drawne before him, branded
His Basenesse that ensued.
   Eros. I would not see't.
   Ant. Come then: for with a wound I must be cur'd.   2915
Draw that thy honest Sword, which thou hast worne
Most vsefull for thy Country.
   Eros. Oh sir, pardon me.
   Ant. When I did make thee free, swor'st y^u not then
To do this when I bad thee? Do it at once,   2920
Or thy precedent Seruices are all
But accidents vnpurpos'd. Draw, and come.

2909 Thy] The F4
2917–18 *One verse line* v1793+ (–COL4)
2919 I did] did I CAM3a

2909 **pleacht Armes**] COTGRAVE (1611, Plesser): "*Fould, or plait young branches one within another.*" DAVIES (1783, 2:357): "Arms tied behind him." FURNESS (ed. 1907) refers to the frontispiece of Burton's *Anatomy of Melancholy*, where "Inamorato" is represented with arms folded, "as a sign of sadness." See also *TGV* 2.1.19–20 (414–15): "Wreath . . . Armes like a Male-content."

2910 **corrigible**] CAWDREY (1604): "Easily corrected." RANN (ed. 1791–): "Submissive, yielding to correction."

2910–11 **subdu'de To**] I.e., subject to. KITTREDGE (ed. 1941) alone: "To *subdue* to another means to 'bring it into full agreement' therewith. [Quotes *Son.* 111.6–7 and 'let . . . paine,' *Oth.* 3.4.146–8 (2303–5).]"

2911 **penetratiue**] For the suffix *-ive*, which implies a constant or lasting tendency and is not necessarily identical with the gloss "penetrating," see FRANZ §130.

2912 **Fortunate**] See also 3029, 3234.

2913 SINGER (ed. 1856): "This is a little inaccurate; the captives came before the victor in the order of a Roman triumph." But see 2793 and, for Plutarch, p. 431. For the passive genitive, i.e., the baseness of him, see FRANZ §322.

2916–17 See n. 2851.

2916 **honest**] See nn. 785, 1084.

2917 **vsefull**] See n. 74.

2919–22 CASE (ed. 1906) compares "the inferior scene between Cassius and Pindarus in *J.C.* V.iii.[36–50 (2517–32)]."

2919 **make . . . free**] A slave made free became a Roman citizen, although not necessarily of the rank of the *civis Romanus*. He owed his patron obedience (*obsequium*) and reverence (*reverentia*). See PAULY, Libertini, 8:104–10; *OCD*, Freedmen.

2922 **accidents vnpurpos'd**] RANN (ed. 1791–) and most others: "Will appear to have been the effects of accident, not intentional." BLUMHOF (ed. 1870) alone: *Vnpurpos'd*

Eros. Turne from me then that Noble countenance,
Wherein the worship of the whole world lyes.
   Ant. Loe thee.   2925
   Eros. My sword is drawne.
   Ant. Then let it do at once
The thing why thou hast drawne it.
   Eros. My deere Master,
My Captaine, and my Emperor. Let me say   2930
Before I strike this bloody stroke, Farwell.
   Ant. 'Tis said man, and farewell.
   Eros. Farewell great Chiefe. Shall I strike now?
   Ant. Now *Eros.*   *Killes himselfe.*
   Eros. Why there then: 2935
Thus I do escape the sorrow of *Anthonies* death.
   Ant. Thrice-Nobler then my selfe,
Thou teachest me: Oh valiant *Eros*, what
I should, and thou could'st not, my Queene and *Eros*
Haue by their braue instruction got vpon me   2940
A Noblenesse in Record. But I will bee
A Bride-groome in my death, and run intoo't
As to a Louers bed. Come then, and *Eros*,

2927 at once] *Om.* HAN1
2934 *SD after* 2935 *or* 2936 ROWE1+
2935–7 *Verse lines ending* sorrow . . . self! POPE1+
2936 I do] do I THEO2, WARB-JOHN1, v1773, v1778, RANN, v1803-SING1, COL, WH1,
HAL, OXF1, ALEX
2939 thou] *Om.* F3, F4

---

means "without content or worth."
   2925 DEIGHTON (ed. 1891): "As though the word were a verb [i.e., look], not an interjection." See *OED,* Lo *int.* b. For *thee,* see n. 2645.
   2934 *Killes himselfe.*] The SD may very well have been aligned with 2936 in the MS since the action refers to the stabbing, not the dying, of Eros. Because there is no room on 2936 and the col. is tight, the compositor seems to have placed it mistakenly on 2934 instead of 2935.
   2940 **got vpon me**] DELIUS (ed. 1856): Won or gained from or over. For *upon* in connection with power or superiority, see FRANZ §499. In the minority are IRVING & MARSHALL (ed. 1889): "gained before me"; following TIESSEN (1879, pp. 473–4), THISELTON (1899, p. 24): "here in the procreative sense"; and RIDLEY (ed. 1935): "Put before me . . . the emphasis lying on what they have done for Antony, not what glory they have won for themselves."
   2941 **Record**] See n. 2704.

Thy Master dies thy Scholler; to do thus
I learnt of thee. How, not dead? Not dead?   2945
The Guard, how? Oh dispatch me.

Enter a Guard.   (yy6ᵃ)

1. *Guard.* What's the noise?
Ant. I haue done my worke ill Friends:
Oh make an end of what I haue begun.   2950
2 The Starre is falne.

2944 *Falling on his Sword.* ROWE1+ (*subst.*)
2945 not] not yet POPE1-CAP, v1793, v1803, HUD2
2946, 2948–57 *Three verse lines ending* noise? . . . end . . . fall'n *then as* F1 HAN1,
CAP-RANN; *five verse lines ending* noise? . . . end . . . fallen. . . . woe! . . . Not
I *then as* F1 v1793-SIS, EVNS; *six verse lines ending* noise? . . . end . . . fall'n. . . .
woe! . . . Not I. . . . one. ARD2; *five verse lines ending* me! . . . friends. . . . begun.
. . . period. . . . dead *then as* F1 YAL2; *six verse lines ending* noise? . . . end . . .
fall'n. . . . woe! . . . dead. . . . one. PEL2
2946 how] ho mTHEO2 (21 Feb. 1729, [fol. 41ᵛ]) *conj.*, THEO, WARB, JOHN1, v1773,
RANN-SING1, HUD1+ (−COL3)
2947 SCENE XI. POPE; SCENE XII. HAN1, JOHN1; SCENE IX. WARB
     Enter a Guard.] *Enter* Decretas *and Guard.* ROWE1+ (POPE1-SIS: Dercetas
throughout; CAP, ARD2: Guard, *and* DERCETAS. [*subst.*])
2949 worke∧ ill∧] ~, ~ ∧ F3-ROWE1, v1773; ~ ∧ ~ , ROWE2-CAP, v1778+

2944–5 CAPELL (1779 [1774], 1:47) believes that Antony uses Eros's sword. See n.
2851, and also p. 753.
2944 **Scholler**] COTGRAVE (1611, Escolier): "*A Scholler, Learner; Pupill, Student.*"
WALTER (ed. 1969): "An intensifying paradox with a quibble on 'master.'"
2946 **how?**] The regular spelling for *ho* is *hoa*. Compare n. 1027. Of 57 instances
in *Ant.*, this one and that at 204 are the only ambiguous spellings—see textual notes.
COLLIER (ed. 1858): "'How?' in Antony's mouth is equivalent to 'What shall I do?'"
WILSON (ed. 1950): "Poss[ibly] . . . should be printed 'Ho!' to represent a groan," the
question mark, as customarily, standing for an exclamation mark.
2947 *Enter a Guard*] RIDLEY (ed. 1954): "We clearly have to get Decretas on at some
point, and the usual method has been to give 'Enter Decretas (or Dercetas or Dercetus)
and Guard' but that rather suggests that he is in command of the guard, which he pretty
clearly is not. We can bring him in after the guard's exit at line [2957], but that makes
his first speech abrupt—he needs a short while in which to take in the situation. I suggest therefore that he comes in behind the guard (like Enobarbus in [2694]), and watches
and listens."
2951–2 SEATON (1946, pp. 219–20) compares the "apocalyptic suggestion of the splendid phrases" with Rev. 10:6, 8:13, 9:6. SCHANZER (1963, p. 137): Presumably "the day-
star, the sun, which measures time, and to which Antony has been repeatedly compared
in the course of the play." See also n. 3560.

1 And time is at his Period.
All. Alas, and woe.
Ant. Let him that loues me, strike me dead.
1 Not I.　　　　　　　　　　　　　　　2955
2 Nor I.
3 Nor any one.　　　　　　　　　*exeunt*
Dercetus. Thy death and fortunes bid thy folowers fly.
This sword but shewne to *Cæsar* with this tydings,
Shall enter me with him.　　　　　　　　　2960

Enter Diomedes.

Dio. Where's *Anthony*?
Decre. There *Diomed* there.
Diom. Liues he: wilt thou not answer man?
Ant. Art thou there *Diomed*?　　　　　　2965
Draw thy sword, and giue mee,
Suffising strokes for death.
Diom. Most absolute Lord:
My Mistris *Cleopatra* sent me to thee.

2956 Nor] Not F4-POPE2, HAN1
2957 *exeunt*] *Ad.* Guard CAP, MAL, v1793+
2958 *Dercetus.*] *Decre.* F2-ROWE3, ARD2, EVNS (*at* 2963 F1 *reads Decre.*, 3114 *and* 3117 *Decretas*, 3117, 3125, 3132 *Dec.*; POPE1-SIS: Dercetas *or Der. throughout*)
2959 this] these HAN1
2962–4 *Verse lines ending* he? . . . man? v1793, v1803, SING, KNT1, HUD, DYCE, STAU, GLO, KTLY, CAM1, WH2+; 2962–3 *as* F1, *then verse lines ending* he? . . . man? v1821, COL, WH1, HAL
2963 *hiding Antony's sword in his cloak* CAM3
2964 man] *Om.* HAN1
　　　Exit DERCETAS, *with the Sword.* CAP, v1778+ (*subst.*)
2965–6 *One verse line* ROWE1+

2952 **Period**] See n. 2444.
2958 **Dercetus**] An uncorrected misreading of *Decretas*, which occurs six times in full or abbreviated.
2959 **this tydings**] Like *news*, *tydings*—always spelled with a final *s* in Sh.—is found with both singular and plural modifiers; in the main, it is plural. See n. 29 ("them").
2960 **enter**] Following DELIUS (ed. 1856), SCHMIDT (1874, 2d): "To introduce favourably, to recommend." See *OED* (17b)—"To admit into a society, etc."—which quotes this instance.
2968 **absolute**] CAWDREY (1604): "Perfect, or vpright." *OED* (8) gives 1612 as first instance of the meaning "despotic."

Ant. When did shee send thee?   2970
Diom. Now my Lord.
Anth. Where is she?
Diom. Lockt in her Monument: she had a Prophesying feare
Of what hath come to passe: for when she saw
(Which neuer shall be found) you did suspect   2975
She had dispos'd with *Cæsar,* and that your rage
Would not be purg'd, she sent you word she was dead:
But fearing since how it might worke, hath sent
Me to proclaime the truth, and I am come
I dread, too late.   2980
   Ant. Too late good *Diomed:* call my Guard I prythee.
   Dio. What hoa: the Emperors Guard,
The Guard, what hoa? Come, your Lord calles.

          Enter 4. or 5. of the Guard of Anthony.

   Ant. Beare me good Friends where *Cleopatra* bides,   2985
'Tis the last seruice that I shall command you.
   1 Woe, woe are we sir, you may not liue to weare
All your true Followers out.
   All. Most heauy day.

2970-2 *One verse line* v1793+
2970 thee] *Om.* POPE2
2973 *Verse lines ending* monument. . . . fear HAN1
     had] had, alas! HAN1
2976 dispos'd] compos'd mCOL1, COL2
2977 you] *Om.* POPE1-v1773 (-CAP)
2982-3 *Verse lines ending* guard, what hoa! . . . calls. POPE1+
2987 Woe,] *Om.* POPE1-THEO4, CAP, v1793, v1803

2975 **found**] DELIUS (ed. 1856): Found true.
2976 **dispos'd**] JOHNSON (1755, *v. n.*), citing this instance: "To bargain; to make terms."
See also 3418.
2982, 2983 **hoa**] See n. 1027.
2984 **4. or 5. of the Guard**] For the indefinite number, compare *Tit.* 1.1.69 (88),
"*and others, as many as can be,*" and n. 1334. See p. 376.
2987 **we**] ABBOTT (§230): "In the earliest writers 'woe!' is found joined with the dative inflection of the pronoun. . . . As early as Chaucer, and probably earlier, the sense
of the inflection was weakened, and 'woe' was used as a predicate: 'I am woe', 'we are
woe', &c."
   you] WORDSWORTH (ed. 1883): "*That you.*"
2987-8 **weare . . . out**] BLUMHOF (ed. 1870) and most others: To live longer than.
Following DEIGHTON (ed. 1891), WILSON (ed. 1950): "I.e. in your service."

Ant. Nay good my Fellowes, do not please sharp fate   2990
To grace it with your sorrowes. Bid that welcome
Which comes to punish vs, and we punish it
Seeming to beare it lightly. Take me vp,
I haue led you oft, carry me now good Friends,
And haue my thankes for all.   *Exit bearing Anthony*   2995

     Enter Cleopatra, and her Maides aloft, with   **4.15**
         Charmian & Iras.

Cleo. Oh *Charmian*, I will neuer go from hence.
Char. Be comforted deere Madam.
Cleo. No, I will not: 3000
All strange and terrible euents are welcome,
But comforts we dispise; our size of sorrow
Proportion'd to our cause, must be as great
As that which makes it.

         Enter Diomed.   3005

How now? is he dead?
Diom. His death's vpon him, but not dead.

2996 ACT V. SCENE I. ROWE; SCENE XII. POPE, WARB; SCENE XIII. HAN1, JOHN1-SING2, COL3, WH1, KTLY, HAL, COL4, OXF1; SCENE XV. DYCE, STAU, GLO, CAM1, HUD2, WH2, NLSN+
     SCENE *A magnificent Monument.* ROWE1+ (*subst.*)
     3004, 3006 *One verse line* CAP, v1778+
     3005 *Ad. below* COL1+ (−SING2, KTLY)
     3007–9, 3011 *Three verse lines ending* out . . . him hither. . . . sun, HAN1; *ending* out . . . monument,——But see, . . . O sun, sun, CAP; *ending* dead. . . . monument, . . . sun, v1793, v1803, SING, DYCE, STAU, GLO, KTLY, CAM1, HUD2+ (−ALEX)
     3007 but] but he is mTBY2 *conj.*, KTLY

     2990 **good my Fellowes**] See n. 1160.
     2990–1 **please . . . To grace**] See n. 2894.
     2991–3 **Bid . . . lightly**] WILSON (ed. 1950): "The Stoic philosophy; cf. the reception by Brutus of the news of Portia's death in *Caes.* 4.3.[144–97 (2131–93)]." WALTER (ed. 1969): "Perhaps a variation of the proverb, 'He that endures is not overcome, he who suffers overcomes.'" See TILLEY (E136); excluded by DENT.
     2996–3050 For the textual and staging problems, see pp. 778–81.
     3002 **our . . . sorrow**] I.e., size of our sorrow. For this genitive construction, see FRANZ §324.

Looke out o'th other side your Monument,
His Guard haue brought him thither.

                    Enter Anthony, and the Guard.   3010

Cleo. Oh Sunne,   (yy6

Burne the great Sphere thou mou'st in, darkling stand
The varrying shore o'th'world. O *Antony, Antony, Antony,*

3008 your Monument] *Om.* HAN1
3009 thither] hither F2-POPE2, HAN1, CAP, KTLY, COL4
3011 Oh] O thou POPE1-JOHN1, v1793, v1803, SING1
3012 Burne] Turn from WARBURTON *conj. apud* mTHEO2 ([2 June 1734, fol. 140ᵛ]),
HAN1, WARB

       great] *Om.* HAN1

       stand] stand on KTLY

3013–16 *Line* 3013 *divided* O Antony! | *Antony, Antony then as* F1 JOHN1, v1773,
v1778, RANN; *three verse lines ending* O Antony, . . . *Iras*; . . . Peace: CAP, v1793,
v1803; *ending* O Antony! . . . Iras, help; . . . Peace: MAL, KNT1, HUD1-DYCE1, STAU,
GLO-CAM1, HUD2 +; *ending* Antony, Antony, Antony, . . . friends . . . Peace: v1821,
SING1, COL, WH1

3013 The] Thou COL2

       shore] star STAUNTON (1873, p. 535) *conj.*, HUD2, OXF1

       O *Antony, Antony, Antony*] O *Antony* POPE1-THEO4

3008 **side your Monument**] For the replacement of an expected preposition (here *of*)
by a prepositional phrase, see FRANZ §542d.

3009 **thither**] Questioning DYCE's (ed. 1857) "The original word agrees well enough
with [3008]," FURNESS (ed. 1907) recommends *hither* as *thither*: "Refers to *that* place,
away from the speaker, on the other side of the monument." See textual notes.

3011–13 **Sunne . . . o'th'world**] WARBURTON ([2 June 1734, fol. 140ᵛ]) proposes
Turn from for *Burn*: "I.e. forsake & fly off from it, & then the Earth would be dark."
IDEM (ed. 1747): "*The varying shore o' th' world! i.e.* of the *Earth*, where light and darkness make an incessant *variation*. But then, if the Sun should set on fire the whole Sphere,
in which he was supposed to move, how could the Earth *stand darkling*? On the contrary
it would be in perpetual light." JOHNSON (ed. 1765) and most others: "She desires the
Sun to *burn* his own *orb*, the vehicle of light, and then the earth will be dark." HEATH
(1765, p. 465): "The sun was [thought to be] a planet, and was whirled round the earth
by the motion of a solid sphere, in which it was fixed. If the sun therefore was to set
fire to this sphere, so as to consume it, the consequence would be, that itself, for want
of support, must drop through, and wander in endless space; and in that case the earth
would be involved in endless night." Expanding on DEIGHTON (ed. 1891) and THISEL-
TON (1899, p. 24), FURNESS (ed. 1907): "It was more than the mere shores that Cleopatra
wished might stand darkling; it was the whole world, of which the shores were the limit.
And the image of the whole world, the *orbis terrarum*, which, possibly, Shakespeare had
here in mind, was the same as that, which, with its irregular outline, its deeply indented,
its 'varying' shore, he had already called the '*three-nook'd* world.'" JONES (ed. 1977) alone:

Helpe *Charmian*, helpe *Iras* helpe: helpe Friends
Below, let's draw him hither.   3015
   Ant. Peace,
Not *Cæsars* Valour hath o'rethrowne *Anthony*,
But *Anthonie's* hath Triumpht on it selfe.
   Cleo. So it should be,
That none but *Anthony* should conquer *Anthony*,   3020
But woe 'tis so.
   Ant. I am dying Egypt, dying; onely
I heere importune death a-while, vntill

3014 Helpe . . . helpe:] *Charmian*, help; help, *Iras*; CAP, v1793, v1803; Help,
Charmian, help; Iras, help; v1773-RANN
   3015 let's] there, let us HAN1
   3018 *Anthonie's* . . . it selfe] *Anthonie* . . . it selfe F2-F4; *Antony* . . . himself
ROWE1-THEO4
   3019-21 *Verse lines ending* but *Antony* . . . so. ROWE1+
   3022 onely] only yet POPE1-CAP, HUD2

"The word *shore* may . . . be a term of contempt, meaning 'sewer'. . . . Cleopatra
would then mean that the world without Antony is nothing but a ceaselessly flowing
sewer [cites other expressions in the play for contempt of the world, like 3073-4]."
   3012 **darkling**] I.e., in the dark. For the retention of the old adverbial suffix, see FRANZ
§243.
   stand] WORDSWORTH (ed. 1883): "Optative [may it stand]." For this use of the
subjunctive, see FRANZ §638. WALTER (ed. 1969) alone: "Perhaps a glance at 'standing'
water between ebb and flow."
   3013 **shore**] STAUNTON (1873, p. 535): "An *erratum* for *star* . . . Egypt's queen,
in her wretchedness, calls, like Othello, for 'a huge *eclipse of sun and moon*' [*Oth.*
5.2.99-100 (3362-3)]." HUDSON (ed. 1881), also reading *star*: "The *changing* Moon; which
would stand *darkling* . . . if the Sun should break loose and run away." But CASE (ed.
1906): "If 'darkling stand', etc. is a consequence, Cleopatra would make it apply to the
orb that held herself and Antony rather than to the moon." WALKER (1957, p. 105):
"Any reader of Latin poets would have recognised what [it] meant [*luminis orae* (shores
of light) = (poet.) the world], though he might, with reason, have suspected that the
plural 'shores' was more in accordance with poetic idiom." See also n. 3011-13.
   3014-15 WILSON (ed. 1950): "Indubitable interpolation, since if she proposes this
now, ll. [3022-8, 'I . . . taken'] become unnecessary. . . . Omit the words and Ant.'s
'Peace!' is seen to be the answer to her passion in ll. [3011-13]." RIDLEY (ed. 1954) rejects
this suggestion in a long technical note, and SISSON (1956, 2:272) in a pithy one: "But
this is a laying of plans, a preparation, interrupted by Antony who, apparently dead,
now speaks."
   3016-20 For the same idea, CASE (ed. 1906) compares Ovid's *Metamorphoses* 13.390
(tr. Golding, 1567, fol. 163ᵛ), and *JC* 5.5.56-7 (2705-6).
   3023 **heere**] WALTER (ed. 1969): "Below, outside the monument." TURNER (privately):
"At this point."

Of many thousand kisses, the poore last
I lay vpon thy lippes.   3025
   Cleo. I dare not Deere,
Deere my Lord pardon: I dare not,
Least I be taken: not th'Imperious shew
Of the full-Fortun'd *Cæsar,* euer shall
Be brooch'd with me, if Knife, Drugges, Serpents haue   3030
Edge, sting, or operation. I am safe:

3025–7 *Verse lines ending Cleo.* I dare not, . . . dare not;) THEO1-v1778 (–JOHN1);
ending dear, . . . not, v1793-GLO, HAL+; *ending* lips. . . . not, KTLY
   3025 lippes.] lips.——Come down mTHEO2 (21 Feb. 1729, [fol. 41ᵛ]) *conj.,*
THEO1-THEO4, CAP
   3026 not‸] ～ . v1773
   3027 pardon:] your pardon, that mTHEO2 (21 Feb. 1729, [fol. 41ᵛ]) *conj.,*
THEO1-THEO4, CAP; pardon, pardon me— HUD2
       not] not descend MALONE (1783) *conj.,* RANN; not come down mTBY2 *conj.,*
WORD1; not open ANON. *conj. apud* CAM1 (not ope the gates), CAM3
   3029 full-Fortun'd] dull-fortun'd F4
   3030 Knife] knives mTBY4 *conj.,* CAP
   3031 sting, or operation.] operation, or sting, HAN1
       operation.] ～ , F2-SIS (–RID, CAM3)

3026–30 **I . . . me**] WILSON (ed. 1950): "Not stated in Plut[arch]. But cf. *Antonie,*
1595 (the Argument): '. . . the tombe. Which she not daring to open least she should
bee made a prisoner to the Romaines, and carried in Caesar's triumph.'" For the 1592
Antonius, see p. 480.
   3027 For his emendation (see textual notes) THEOBALD (21 Feb. 1729, [fol. 41ᵛ])
claims improvement in sense and meter as well as "a Sort of warrant from Plutarch [see
p. 450]." RIDLEY (ed. 1954), commenting on emendations: "There is a compression,
or ellipse, in Cleopatra's words as they stand: it is not that she dare not take his last
kiss—though that is what she says—but that even for that she dare not come down."
Also rejecting MALONE (*apud* STEEVENS [1783]) and WILSON (ed. 1950), SISSON (1956,
2:272): "Cleopatra is not reporting the situation to Antony, who is dying. She is speaking her own thoughts. She cannot leave the monument and go to him. He must be
lifted to her."
   3028 **Imperious**] CAWDREY's (1604) definition—"desiring to rule, full of commaunding,
stately"—shows that the modern distinction between *imperious* and *imperial* was not
yet observed. The modern equivalent here would be *imperial,* which Cawdrey defines
as "belonging to the crowne." A very productive suffix, -*ous* is to be found with words
of French or Latin origin. See FRANZ §131.
   3029 **full-Fortun'd**] See also 2912, 3234.
   3030 **brooch'd**] CAWDREY (1604, brooch): "Iewell." Citing this instance, JOHNSON
(1755): "To adorn with jewels." Sh. is credited with the conversion of the noun to a verb
by the *OED* (which erroneously locates it in *Tro.*). KITTREDGE (ed. 1941) compares 2790–7
for Cleopatra as "chief ornament of Cæsar's triumphal procession."

Your Wife *Octauia*, with her modest eyes,
And still Conclusion, shall acquire no Honour
Demuring vpon me: but come, come *Anthony*,
Helpe me my women, we must draw thee vp:　　　　3035
Assist good Friends.
　　Ant. Oh quicke, or I am gone.
　　Cleo. Heere's sport indeede:
How heauy weighes my Lord?

3033 Conclusion] condition mTBY4 *conj.*, mCOL1, COL2, COL3
　　no] *Om.* F3, F4
3034 Demuring] Demurring FURNESS (v1907) *conj.*, CAM3
3038-9 *One verse line* ROWE1+
3038 sport] port JACKSON *conj.* (his port), COL2, COL3, COL4

3032 **modest**] See n. 3034.
3033 **still Conclusion**] Commentators offer a range of interpretations. WARBURTON (ed. 1747) and a few others: "*I.e.* sedately collected in herself, which even the sight of me could not stir up into passion." JOHNSON (ed. 1765) and some others: "Sedate determination." LETTSOM (1853, *Blackwood's*, p. 468) and most others: "*Drawing her quiet inferences.*" Following NARES (1822; 1876), VERPLANCK (ed. 1846) and a few: "Quiet censure." See "still conuersation" (1319).
3034 **Demuring vpon me**] CAWDREY (1604, modest): "Sober, demure." IDEM (demurre): "To stay, to linger, or vse delaies." Commentary, often unaware of or even contaminating the two forms, ranges from "Taking a cool, but scornful survey of me" (RANN [ed. 1791-]), to "*with affected modesty*" (WORDSWORTH [ed. 1883]), to "with . . . quiet disdain" (DEIGHTON [ed. 1891]), to "with an air of innocence" or possibly with "leisurely consideration" (CASE [ed. 1906]), to "looking doubtfully askance upon me" (FURNESS [ed. 1907]), to "with pondering eyes" (WILSON [ed. 1950, Glossary]), to "putting in a demurrer" (TURNER, privately; *OED, v.* 5). See also 3263-4, n. 2732. The adjective-to-verb conversion is credited to Sh. by the *OED*, which also regards it as a *hapax legomenon*. See textual notes, 957, and n. 1115-16. See pp. 377-8.
3037 **or**] Possibly also "before."
3038 Commentators are troubled. JOHNSON (ed. 1765): "*Here's* trifling, *you* do not work *in earnest.*" MALONE (ed. 1790): "Perhaps rather, here's a curious game, the last we shall ever play with Antony! Or perhaps she is thinking of fishing with a line, a diversion of which we have been already told she was fond [1037-42]." STEEVENS (ed. 1793): "Cleopatra, perhaps, by this affected levity . . . only wishes to inspire Antony with cheerfulness, and encourage those who are engaged in the melancholy task of drawing him up into the monument." Other characterizations of Cleopatra's mood range along the scale from "bitter irony" (DELIUS [ed. 1856]) to "grim humour" (CASE [ed. 1906]). See textual notes and conj., p. 358.
　　sport] JACKSON (1818, pp. 10-11) conjectures *port*, meaning "haven, harbor." COLLIER (1852, p. 479) uses the same spelling "as a substantive to indicate weight. . . . The French use *port* for burden."

Our strength is all gone into heauinesse,   3040
That makes the waight. Had I great *Iuno*'s power,
The strong wing'd Mercury should fetch thee vp,
And set thee by Ioues side. Yet come a little,
Wishers were euer Fooles. Oh come, come, come,
        They heaue Anthony aloft to Cleopatra.   3045
And welcome, welcome. Dye when thou hast liu'd,
Quicken with kissing: had my lippes that power,
Thus would I weare them out.
   All. A heauy sight.
   Ant. I am dying Egypt, dying.   3050
Giue me some Wine, and let me speake a little.
   Cleo. No, let me speake, and let me rayle so hye,
That the false Huswife Fortune, breake her Wheele,
Prouok'd by my offence.
   Ant. One word (sweet Queene)   3055
Of *Cæsar* seeke your Honour, with your safety. Oh.
   Cleo. They do not go together.

3045 *After* 3036 CAP
3046 when] where POPE1-KNT1, COL2-KIT1, ALEX
3049 A] Oh ROWE1-JOHN1; Ah ANON. *conj. apud* CAM1, CAM3
3056 Oh.] *Om.* HAN1; you—— WARB

3040 **heauinesse**] MALONE (ed. 1790): "Used equivocally for *sorrow* and *weight*."
3041 **That**] KITTREDGE (ed. 1941): "Emphatic."
3041-3 **Had . . . side**] ARDINGER (1976, p. 93): "After thunderbolts destroyed his funeral pyre, Hercules was transported to Olympus, where he was welcomed by Jupiter and the other gods and adopted by Juno through the ceremony of rebirth."
3044 **Wishers . . . Fooles**] Proverbial; see TILLEY (W539): "*Wishers* and woulders are never good householders." Excluded by DENT. Following WORDSWORTH (ed. 1883), KITTREDGE (ed. 1941): "Alluding to her impossible wish that she had 'great Juno's power.'"
3046 **Dye . . . liu'd**] Defending F1, COLLIER (ed. 1843): "In consequence of being quickened, or restored, by my kissing thee"; THISELTON (1899, p. 24): "This simply means 'live ere thou diest.'"
3047 **Quicken**] MINSHEU (1617): "*Put life into,*" i.e., come alive or revive. See also 382. ADELMAN (1973, p. 179) compares Marlowe's *Dido* 4.4.123 (ed. Tucker Brooke, 1930), which "may have suggested the dimension of immortality."
3053 **false Huswife Fortune**] JOHNSON (1755): "A bad manager; a sorry woman. It is common to use *housewife* in a good, and *huswife* or *hussy* in a bad sense." Dictionaries before Johnson record only the former. The latter sense is not recorded in the *OED* for Sh.'s time, except "with qualification (*light*, etc.), or contextual." See *sb.* 3. Proverbial; see DENT (F603.1): "*Fortune* is a strumpet (whore, huswife)."
3056-7 **seeke . . . together**] Proverbial; see DENT (D35): "The more *danger* the more honor."

Ant. Gentle heare me,
None about *Cæsar* trust, but *Proculeius.*
Cleo. My Resolution, and my hands, Ile trust,   3060
None about *Cæsar.*
Ant. The miserable change now at my end,
Lament nor sorrow at: but please your thoughts
In feeding them with those my former Fortunes
Wherein I liued. The greatest Prince o'th'world,   3065
The Noblest: and do now not basely dye,
Not Cowardly put off my Helmet to
My Countreyman. A Roman, by a Roman

3064 those my former] these my v1773
3065 liued.] F1-POPE2; ∼ ᴧ THEO, WARB, JOHN1, v1773, COL2, SING2, KTLY, DYCE2, COL4, HUD2, ARD1, KIT1, ALEX; ∼ ; *or* ∼ , *or* ∼ : HAN1 *etc.*
3066 Noblest . . . not] Noblest: and doe not F3, F4; noblest once; and do now not ROWE1, ROWE2; noblest once; and now not ROWE3-POPE2, HAN1; noblest once; and do not now THEO, WARB
3067 Not] Nor ROWE1-JOHN1, v1773, v1778, RANN-KNT1, COL2-SING2, COL3, DYCE2, HUD2

    Cowardly ᴧ] ∼ , F4, ROWE; ∼ ; v1773, v1778, RANN-v1821, SING
    Helmet ᴧ] ∼ ; CAP

3059 BERKELEY (1950, p. 535): "Does Antony deliberately try to betray Cleopatra for what he has at times regarded as her treachery, or does he recommend Proculeius in ignorance of the man's attachment to Caesar? The question, I think, cannot be definitely answered. . . . The fact that Shakespeare borrows this ambiguous touch from Plutarch [see p. 451] should not obviate comment." Most commentators, however, tend to agree with MACCALLUM (1910, p. 450) that Antony "has no thought of himself but only of her."
3062-6 **The . . . Noblest**] For Plutarch, see p. 451.
3062 **miserable**] NEWBOLT (1925, p. 22): North added to Plutarch "that one word 'miserable' [see p. 451] which makes the profound pathos of the line."
3065 **Wherein**] *OED* (3): "In which (matter, fact, action, condition, etc.); in respect of which."
3065-8 **liued . . . Countreyman**] WILSON (ed. 1950), inserting ellipsis points after *liued, Noblest,* and *Countreyman:* "He [Antony] finds speech more and more difficult." RIDLEY (ed. 1954) believes F1's full stops after *liued* and *Countreyman* indicate that "Antony is, literally, at the last gasp, and his utterance is broken, with heavy pauses."
3067-8 **Not . . . Countreyman**] CAPELL (1779 [1774], 1:48) defends his pointing (see textual notes), which "is strongly confirm'd by the words of the translated Plutarch [see p. 451], out of whom this whole speech is taken almost verbatim." CASE (ed. 1906): "Rowe [ed. 1709] placed a comma after *cowardly* with F4, thus connecting it with *die,* and changed *not* to *nor.* This is defensible; but surely those who, with Pope [ed. 1723], read *Nor cowardly put off* . . . weaken the connection of the negative with *cowardly;* to which alone it applies and not to *put off.*"
3068-9 **A . . . vanquish'd**] BROWER (1971, p. 124) compares Ovid's description of

Valiantly vanquish'd. Now my Spirit is going,
I can no more.   3070
  Cleo. Noblest of men, woo't dye?
Hast thou no care of me, shall I abide
In this dull world, which in thy absence is
No better then a Stye? Oh see my women:
The Crowne o'th'earth doth melt. My Lord?   3075
Oh wither'd is the Garland of the Warre,
The Souldiers pole is falne: young Boyes and Gyrles   (yy6ᵛᵃ
Are leuell now with men: The oddes is gone,
And there is nothing left remarkeable
Beneath the visiting Moone.   3080

3070 Antony *Dies.* ROWE1-JOHN1, v1773-SING2, COL3, WH1, KTLY, HAL; *SD after* 3074
CAP, DYCE, STAU, GLO, CAM1, HUD2-SIS, EVNS; *after* 3075 COL4; *after* melt *in* 3075 ARD2
  3075 Lord] lord! my lord mTBY4 *conj.*, DYCE2, HUD2
  3077 Souldiers] soldier's POPE1-ALEX, ARD2, EVNS; soldiers' SIS
  3080-4 *Arranged as verse lines, thus*: 3080-1, 3082-4 v1793+ (–HUD, ALEX)

Ajax's death, "Ne quisquam Aiacem possit superare nisi Ajax [lest anyone conquer Ajax
save Ajax]" (*Metamorphoses* 13.390).
  3070 **can**] For *can* as finite verb, see FRANZ §603.
  3071 **woo't**] See n. 2419.
  3072-4 **shall . . . Stye**] See n. 110.
  3076 **Garland**] See "Lawrell victory" (421).
  3077 **Souldiers pole**] JOHNSON (ed. 1765): "He at whom the soldiers pointed, as at
a pageant held high for observation." RANN (ed. 1791-): "Standard," now generally accepted. SCHMIDT (1875) and a few others: "The pole-star . . . loadstar." DEIGHTON
(ed. 1891): "The word *garland* in the previous line [3076] evidently suggested the word
pole, Shakespeare thinking of the village festivities in which a pole, the central point
of the sports, is decked with garlands of flowers. There may also be the idea [already
suggested by SEYMOUR (1805, 2:79)] of a conspicuous mark round which the soldier might
rally, as in *Cor.* v.3.72-5 ['that thou . . . thee!' (3425-8)]." WHITAKER's (1965, p. 295)
assertion—"an all too appropriate though indecent double meaning of the kind Shakespeare uses elsewhere to deflate the emotion of a potentially tragic situation"—is rejected by COLMAN (1974, pp. 14-15) as thematically and theatrically inappropriate.
  3078 **oddes**] FURNESS (ed. 1907) and most others: Distinguishing or distinctive "difference[s]." Where grammatically unambiguous, it is singular in Sh. See FRANZ §194.
  3079 **remarkeable**] CAWDREY (1604): "Able or worthy to be marked [i.e., noted] againe."
STAUNTON (ed. 1859): Applied to "something profoundly striking and uncommon."
  3081-8 **Oh . . . Woman**] RIDLEY (ed. 1954): "Rowe's S.D. [*She faints* (3080)] is clearly
justified, since otherwise there is no point of reference for Iras's first speech [3082], and
so is Wilson's, as the occasion for Charmian's *Peace, peace, Iras!* [3087] (if that should
be hers). I think that Charmian's *O quietness* [3081] is addressed to Iras, and her *Lady!*
[3083] to Cleopatra, like her own and Iras's subsequent exclamations. . . . Cleopatra's

Char. Oh quietnesse, Lady.
Iras. She's dead too, our Soueraigne.
Char. Lady.
Iras. Madam.
Char. Oh Madam, Madam, Madam.   3085
Iras. Royall Egypt: Empresse.
Char. Peace, peace, *Iras.*
Cleo. No more but in a Woman, and commanded

3085–7 *Verse lines divided Egypt!* | Emperess *then as* F1 CAP, v1793-COL2, SING2-DYCE2, COL4, WH2-ARD1, KIT1, ARD2, EVNS; *verse lines ending* Egypt, . . . Iras! RID; *ending* Empress! . . . Iras! SIS

3085 Oh Madam] Oh HAN1

3087 *Char.*] *Cleo.* HAN1

     Iras] *Isis* WARB

3088 in a] a meer ROWE1-THEO4; e'en a mTBY4 *conj.,* CAP+

No more but e'en a woman [3088] is a correction of Iras's *Empress!* [3086], and if so Charmian's *Peace, peace, Iras!* must be given as a rapid aside. But it is very tempting to attribute the words to Cleopatra herself, comparing her *Peace, peace!* at [3561] *post,* where also the words check an excited address."

3081–5 SCHANZER (1956, p. 154): "In feeling, situation, and wording" the lines have "much in common" with the Countess of Pembroke's *Antonie,* 1595, ll. 1879–84 ("Her face . . . up"). For the 1592 *Antonius,* see p. 521.

3081 **Oh quietnesse**] WILSON (ed. 1950): "Suggests the loud passion Sh. expected of the boy Cleo."

3087 *Iras*] JOHNSON (ed. 1765), objecting to WARBURTON's (ed. 1747) idea that Cleopatra is addressed by the name of the goddess Isis: Charmian "sees the Queen recovering, and thinks speech troublesome."

3088 **No . . . Woman**] JOHNSON (ed. 1765), interpreting F1's *in* as *e'en,* glosses it with the reading adopted by ROWE (ed. 1709), *meer.* CAPELL (1779 [1774], 1:48) charges "the whole set of them . . . [with] putting the gloss for the text." MASON (1785, p. 288): Cleopatra "naturally replies to Iras who had addressed herself to her, and not to Charmian, who only interposed to prevent Iras from continuing to speak; strike out the speech of Charmian which is said aside to Iras, and the sense will be evident." RANN (ed. 1791–), adding a dash after *more:* "I am now convinced that I am a mere woman." NICHOLS (1861–2, 1:7): "A continuation of the soliloquy which was interrupted by her fainting [3071–80]; the train of thought remained, though its utterance had been suspended, and, as she recovered, she resumed the thread—*'There* [. . .] *moon'* . . . *'No more but in a woman'.* Nothing more remarkable in me now than is to be found in any woman." Finally, KNOWLES (privately): "Possibly a response to 3081, as interpreted by WILSON (ed. 1950) above, and to 3086, Cleopatra not fainting but perhaps just sobbing, and continuing here to justify an even louder outcry. She does not lament like an Empress, but like a milkmaid (3089), when she ought to be assailing the gods."

3088–90 **a Woman . . . chares**] To show that Sh. "came uncannily close to contem-

By such poore passion, as the Maid that Milkes,
And doe's the meanest chares. It were for me,   3090
To throw my Scepter at the iniurious Gods,
To tell them that this World did equall theyrs,
Till they had stolne our Iewell. All's but naught:
Patience is sottish, and impatience does
Become a Dogge that's mad: Then is it sinne,   3095
To rush into the secret house of death,
Ere death dare come to vs. How do you Women?
What, what good cheere? Why how now *Charmian?*
My Noble Gyrles? Ah Women, women! Looke
Our Lampe is spent, it's out. Good sirs, take heart,   3100

3089 passion] passions mTBY4 *conj.*, v1773
3100 *to the guard below.* MAL, v1793-SING2, COL3, KTLY, COL4

---

porary examples of queenly behavior," MUIR (1969, pp. 199–200) quotes from "a speech to Parliament in 1576, [in which] Elizabeth replied to a petition that she should take a husband—'If I were a milk-maid, with a pail on my arm, whereby my private person might be little set by, I would not forsake that poor and single state to match with the greatest monarch' [see J. E. Neale, *Elizabeth I and her Parliaments 1559–1581*, 1953, p. 366]."

3089 **poore passion**] WALTER (1969, pp. 138–9): "May not mean pitiful grief for a dead lover, it may refer to *hysterica passio*, or the Mother, a condition common to women according to Elizabethan medical views. . . . It was caused . . . by any strong passion . . . and it began and ended suddenly, and its symptoms were 'swounding, the very image of death', palpitation, and a feeling of choking, together with seizures of various kinds. . . . Her [Cleopatra's] words may therefore express resentment that she is humbled and degraded by a condition that ranks her with a milkmaid. . . . 'Poore' is then parallel to 'meanest' [3090]."

3090 **It . . . me**] JOHNSON (ed. 1765): "*Were I what I once was.*"

were] HUDSON (ed. 1881) and most others: "Were *right*," i.e., fitting.

3091 **iniurious**] CAWDREY (1604): "Wrongfull, or hurtfull." For the suffix, see n. 3028.

3093 **naught**] See nn. 1749, 1977.

3094 **sottish**] CAWDREY (1604, sotte): "Foole, dunse."

3094–5 **impatience . . . mad**] BLUMHOF (ed. 1870) detects an old proverb, though without a contemporary citation. WALTER (ed. 1969): "An echo of the proverb 'Patience perforce is a medicine for a mad dog.'" TILLEY's (P112) first instance is dated 1659. Perhaps also DENT's (M2.1): "As mad as a *mad dog*."

does Become] See n. 402–3.

3100 **Our . . . out**] See n. 2879 ("Torch is out").

sirs . . . heart] DYCE (ed. 1857): "To the words . . . is usually added a stage-direction '[*To the Guard below*]': but by '*sirs*' does not Cleopatra mean Charmian and

Wee'l bury him: And then, what's braue, what's Noble,
Let's doo't after the high Roman fashion,
And make death proud to take vs. Come, away,
This case of that huge Spirit now is cold.
Ah Women, Women! Come, we haue no Friend   3105
But Resolution, and the breefest end.

Exeunt, bearing of Anthonies body.

Enter Cæsar, Agrippa, Dollabella, Menas, with   **5.1**
his Counsell of Warre.

Cæsar. Go to him *Dollabella*, bid him yeeld,   3110

3101 what's Noble] what Noble F2, F3
3108 SCENE VII. ROWE (*for* II; *see* 2996); ACT V. SCENE I. POPE, HAN1, WARB,
JOHN1+; ACT V. THEO

  Cæsar's *Camp.* ROWE1+ (*subst.*)

  Menas,] *Om.* mTBY2 *and* mTHEO2 (21 Feb. 1729, [fol. 41ᵛ]) *conj.*, THEO1+
(*subst.*)

3108–9 *with . . . Warre*] *Om.* ROWE, POPE

Iras?" He finds women addressed as "sirs" in Beaumont and Fletcher, *The Coxcomb*
4.3.47–8 (ed. Bowers, 1966) and *A King and No King* 2.1.236–9 (ed. Bowers, 1970).
See also n. 3475 ("Sirra"). The infrequent plural is not sociologically identical with the
singular form; it is often used for servants of both sexes.

  3104 case] See nn. 266, 2873–4.

  3107 *of*] I.e., off. F1 is unusual; the only other instance following *bearing* (*3H6* 2.5.78
[1216]) is an entrance. But the exit here justifies *off*, the reading of practically all editors
since ROWE (ed. 1709).

  3108 *Menas*] THEOBALD (ed. 1733): "*Menas* and *Menecrates* . . . were the two famous Pirates link'd with *Sextus Pompeius* . . . [not] to *Octavius*'s Party. . . . In the
two places in the Scene, where this Character [Menas] is made to speak, they [Ff.] have
mark'd in the Margin MEC. so that, as Dr. *Thirlby* [see textual notes] sagaciously conjec-
tur'd, we must cashier *Menas*, and substitute *Mecænas* in his Room." See also DP.

  3110 **Go** . . . *Dollabella*] WILSON (ed. 1950): "Here dispatched to Ant., Dolabella
is still 'on' at ll. [3143] ff. in F., while at l. [3190] Caes. proposes to send him with Proc.
to Cleo., is surprised (as we are) not to find him present, and then recollects that he
has been employed otherwise. Yet Dol. does 'second Proculeius' after all in [3276]. Something odd here." See nn. 3113, 3438–45.

Being so frustrate, tell him,
He mockes the pawses that he makes.
Dol. Cæsar, I shall.

   Enter Decretas with the sword of Anthony.

   Cæs. Wherefore is that? And what art thou that dar'st   3115
Appeare thus to vs?
   Dec. I am call'd *Decretas,*
Marke Anthony I seru'd, who best was worthie
Best to be seru'd: whil'st he stood vp, and spoke
He was my Master, and I wore my life   3120
To spend vpon his haters. If thou please
To take me to thee, as I was to him,
Ile be to *Cæsar*: if y^u pleasest not, I yeild thee vp my life.

3111–13 *Two verse lines ending* mocks . . . shall. HAN1, CAP, v1778-KNT1, HUD1-KTLY, DYCE2, CAM1, HUD2+; *three verse lines ending* mocks . . . makes. . . . shall. COL2, HAL, COL4

3111 frustrate] frustrated CAP, v1778

3112 He mockes] he but mocks HAN1; he mocks us by MALONE (1783) *conj.*, MAL-COL1, HUD, SING2, KTLY, COL4; that he mocks STEEVENS (v1793) *conj.*, COL2; that he mocks us By COL3

3113 *Exit* Dolabella. mTHEO2 (21 Feb. 1729, [fol. 41^v]) *conj.*, THEO1+

3123–4 *Verse lines ending* not, . . . sayest? F4+

3111 **frustrate**] CAWDREY (1604): "Make voyde [i.e., defeat], deceiue." Commentators split about evenly: either a syllable or word is missing (see textual notes) or this word is pronounced trisyllabically (DELIUS [ed. 1856]). For this form of the participial adjective, see FRANZ §132. See also n. 1057 ("Mistris").

3112 **mockes . . . makes**] STEEVENS (ed. 1778): "I.e. he plays wantonly with the intervals of time which he should improve to his own preservation. Or . . . being thus defeated in all his efforts, and left without resource, tell him that these affected pauses and delays of his in yielding himself up to me, are mere idle mockery. . . . *He makes a mockery of us by these pauses*; i.e. he trifles with us." See textual notes.

3113 THEOBALD (21 Feb. 1729, [fol. 41^v]): "Mark here; *Exit Dolabella.* 'Tis reasonable to imagine, he should presently go upon Cæsar's Commands; [so the] Speeches plac'd to him [at 3143–5, 3147–9], must be transferr'd to *Agrippa*, or He does [not] speak at all: Besides y.^{t} He should be gone, appears from [3190], where Cæsar asks [for him, but recollects he had sent him on business]." See n. 3110.

3116 **thus**] STEEVENS (ed. 1793): "I.e. with a drawn and bloody sword in thy hand."

3120 **wore**] COTGRAVE (1611, Vser): "*To weare, occupie, imploy . . . consume, spend.*"

3121 **spend**] COTGRAVE (1611, Despendre): "*Expend . . . bestow, imploy, lay out vpon.*" See also 2588, 3554.

Cæsar. What is't thou say'st?
Dec. I say (Oh *Cæsar*) *Anthony* is dead.   3125
Cæsar. The breaking of so great a thing, should make
A greater cracke. The round World
Should haue shooke Lyons into ciuill streets,
And Cittizens to their dennes. The death of *Anthony*
Is not a single doome, in the name lay   3130
A moity of the world.
      Dec. He is dead *Cæsar,*
Not by a publike minister of Iustice,
Nor by a hyred Knife, but that selfe-hand
Which writ his Honor in the Acts it did,   3135
Hath with the Courage which the heart did lend it,

3127–9 *Three verse lines ending* shook . . . Citizens . . . *Antony* THEO, WARB,
JOHN1, RANN, KTLY, COL4; *ending* shook . . . streets, . . . Antony MAL, v1793-SING1,
COL1, COL2, WH1, HAL
    3127 cracke] crack in nature HAN1, CAP
        round] round-uproarèd HUD2; wounded WH2
        World] world, so bereft, WORD1
    3129 to] Into THEO, WARB, JOHN1, RANN, KTLY
    3130 the] that POPE1-v1773, CAM3b

3126 **breaking**] WALTER (ed. 1969): "(*a*) death, (*b*) breaking of news."
    3127 **cracke**] KITTREDGE (ed. 1941): "When used of sound, *crack* was a far more emphatic and dignified word than at present, as may be seen in the old phrase 'the crack of doom', of which, indeed, line [3130] suggests that Shakespeare was thinking." WILSON (ed. 1950) detects a quibble on *breaking* (3126) as meaning also "disclose."
        The . . . World] For attempts to complete the line, see textual notes and conj., p. 358. CASE (ed. 1906): "As the sense is plain, may not the short line have been intentional? a pause here would be natural and impressive."
        round] Unsupported is WELLS & TAYLOR's (ed. 1986) *reaued* (modern spelling *rived*), which "seems more likely to have given rise to 'round' than 'riued,'" although the well-known "parallel" in *JC* 437–8 ("I . . . Winds Haue riu'd the knottie Oakes"), a "passage which also offers lions in the streets," and the metrical deficiency are mentioned. *OED* first records *rived* in 1631; *reaved* as adj. is not recorded.
    3128 **haue shooke**] For the forms of strong verbs in Sh., see FRANZ §170.
        ciuill streets] IRVING & MARSHALL (ed. 1889): "City streets." But KITTREDGE (ed. 1941): "*Civil* implies *civilization* or *well regulated society* as opposed to *wildness* and *savagery.*"
    3129 **their dennes**] The dens of the lions.
    3130 **doome**] See n. 2244 ("all-obeying").
    3131 **moity**] CAWDREY (1604): "Halfe."
    3133 **minister**] See n. 2179.
    3134 **selfe-hand**] For *self* as pronominal adjective meaning "same," see ABBOTT §20.

Splitted the heart. This is his Sword,
I robb'd his wound of it: behold it stain'd
With his most Noble blood.

    Cæs. Looke you sad Friends,   3140
The Gods rebuke me, but it is Tydings   (yy6^{v}
To wash the eyes of Kings.

    Dol. And strange it is,
That Nature must compell vs to lament
Our most persisted deeds.   3145

    Mec. His taints and Honours, wag'd equal with him.

    Dola. A Rarer spirit neuer
Did steere humanity: but you Gods will giue vs

3137 Splitted the heart] Splitted the heart it self HAN1, CAP; Split that self noble
heart mCOL1, COL2, COL3

3138 behold it] behold is ROWE2

3140 you$_\wedge$sad$_\wedge$] ~ , ~ $_\wedge$ ~ F3-POPE2; ~ $_\wedge$ ~ , THEOBALD (1726, p. 152) *conj.*, THEO1+

3141 The] May the v1773

       is Tydings] is a Tydings F2–F4, CAP, v1778, RANN-v1803, DYCE2, COL4, HUD2,
ARD2; is a Tiding ROWE1-THEO4; tidings is KTLY

3143-5 *Given to Agrippa* mTHEO2 (21 Feb. 1729, [fol. 41^{v}]) *conj.*, THEO1-COL4,
WH2+; *given to Caesar* DANIEL (1870, p. 83) *conj.*, HUD2

3144 That] The ROWE2, ROWE3

3145-7 *Verse lines ending* honours . . . never POPE1+

3146, 3150-1 *Given to Menas* F3-POPE2

3146 wag'd equal with] way equall with F2; may equall with F3, F4; weigh'd equal
in ROWE1-THEO4; Waged equal in JOHN1; Weigh'd equal with CAP, COL2, COL3, COL4

3147-9 *Given to Agrippa* mTHEO2 (21 Feb. 1729, [fol. 41^{v}]) *conj.*, THEO1+

3137 **Splitted**] IRVING & MARSHALL (ed. 1889): "The form of the participle in the
four instances in which Shakespeare uses it; the [simple] past tense does not occur in
his works." FRANZ (§159), however, mentions two instances of *split* as participle.

    3140 **you sad**] THEOBALD (1726, p. 152): "Why . . . *sad friends*? . . . *Octavius*
enjoins his Friends to be concern'd at the News." Adds comma after *sad*. See textual notes.

    3141 **The . . . me**] JOHNSON (ed. 1765): "*May the Gods rebuke me.*"

    but] For *but* meaning "if not," especially after oaths, protestations, and the like,
see FRANZ §566.

    it is Tydings] RIDLEY (ed. 1954): "F's rhythm is . . . awkward [and] a too
grammatically-minded compositor might . . . have dropped the *a* in the interest of
supposed correctness." He follows F2; see textual notes. See also n. 2959 on the number
of *Tydings.*

    3146 **with**] ABBOTT (§193): "In."

    3147 **Rarer**] See n. 3387.

    3148-9 **Gods . . . men**] Proverbial; see DENT (M116): "Every *man* has (No man is
without) his faults."

Some faults to make vs men. *Cæsar* is touch'd.
  Mec. When such a spacious Mirror's set before him,   3150
He needes must see him selfe.
  Cæsar. Oh *Anthony,*
I haue followed thee to this, but we do launch
Diseases in our Bodies. I must perforce
Haue shewne to thee such a declining day,   3155
Or looke on thine: we could not stall together,
In the whole world. But yet let me lament
With teares as Soueraigne as the blood of hearts,
That thou my Brother, my Competitor,
In top of all designe; my Mate in Empire,   3160
Friend and Companion in the front of Warre,
The Arme of mine owne Body, and the Heart

3149 make] mark CAP
3149-51 *Cæsar . . . him selfe.*] *Marked as an aside* KTLY
3153 I haue] Have I mCOL1, COL2
3156 looke] look'd mF4Q *conj. and* HAN1, WH1, DYCE2, COL4, HUD2, RID

3148 **will**] Used for a habitual action — e.g., are wont to; see FRANZ §620.

3149 *Cæsar* **is touch'd**] For Plutarch, see p. 451.

3151 WORDSWORTH (ed. 1883): *"What may be his own fate."*

3153 **followed**] MINSHEU (1617): *"Pursue."* RANN (ed. 1791-): "Driven." See also 143, 1503.

3153-4 **launch . . . Bodies**] HULOET (1552, Launce) and practically all commentators: "Launche open a soore." MALONE (*apud* STEEVENS, ed. 1778) alone: "When we *launch* on the sea of life, the principles of decay are interwoven with our constitution." See conj., p. 358.

3156 **looke**] See n. 437.

3158 WALTER (ed. 1969): "As blood distilled by the heart that rules the body, so precious are the tears shed by me the ruler of Rome."

Soueraigne] THISELTON (1899, p. 25): "In Coriolanus I.i.[140 (143)] the heart is called 'the Court', *i.e.* the residence of the Sovereign." CASE (ed. 1906), "The thought being, perhaps, of a sovereign remedy," compares 2418 (see n.), where he quotes Ben Jonson's *Discoveries,* "Morbi," ll. 1058-62 (ed. Herford & Simpson, 8:596), and *Gesta Romanorum* no. 230 (ed. Oesterley, 1872-1963, p. 633).

3158-60 **hearts . . . Brother . . . designe**] For a similar collocation, see 849-50.

3159-63 BLUMHOF (ed. 1870) suggests that Sh. characterizes Caesar's emotional involvement by having him not complete the thought begun at 3159. That is, there is no verb for this clause.

3159 **Brother**] See n. 1473. The reference may be to "fellow ruler" or to "brother-in-law."

Competitor] See n. 432.

3160 **In top of**] DELIUS (ed. 1856): In the height of.

designe] See n. 850.

Where mine his thoughts did kindle; that our Starres
Vnreconciliable, should diuide our equalnesse to this.
Heare me good Friends,   3165
But I will tell you at some meeter Season,
The businesse of this man lookes out of him,
Wee'l heare him what he sayes.

Enter an Ægyptian.

Whence are you?   3170
    Ægyp. A poore Egyptian yet, the Queen my mistris
Confin'd in all, she has her Monument

3163 his] its POPE1-THEO4
3164-5 *Verse lines ending* should have divided . . . friends, POPE1+
3164 Vnreconciliable] Unreconcilable F3-THEO2, WARB-JOHN1, SING, COL, HUD1, WH1, HAL
        diuide] have divided POPE1-JOHN1 (–HAN1)
3168, 3170 *One verse line* ROWE1+
3170 Whence are you] Now whence are you HAN1; Whence are you, sir CAP, HUD2
3171 Egyptian∧ yet,] ∼ , ∼ ∧ mTYR *conj.*, CAM3-SIS
        yet] *Om.* mTBY3 *conj.*, CAP
3172 all, she has∧ her Monument∧] ∼ ∧ ∼∼ , ∼∼ , ROWE1+

3163 **mine**] I.e., my heart.
    his] RANN (ed. 1791–): "*Its.*" See n. 2120.
    Starres] DEIGHTON (ed. 1891): "Destinies."
3164 **Vnreconciliable**] Sh. also uses *irreconcil'd* (*H5* 4.1.160 [2000]) and *unreconcil'd* (*Oth.* 5.2.27 [3269]). For such pairs (the Ger. *un-* and the Latin *in-*), see FRANZ §79. For the suffix, see n. 3509.
    diuide . . . this] JOHNSON (ed. 1765): "That is, *should have made us,* in our equality of fortune, disagree *to* a pitch like this, that one of us must die."
3167 **lookes out of**] SCHMIDT (1874, 2): "To show itself [in]." For the reflexive use, as with the verbs *feel, taste, smell,* etc., see FRANZ §628a.
3168 **him**] For this "redundant object," see ABBOTT §414. FRANZ (§304): It follows verbs of knowing, perceiving, and thinking.
3170 **Whence**] DEIGHTON (ed. 1891): "Of what country?"
3171 **A . . . yet,**] JOHNSON (ed. 1765): "If this punctuation be right, the man means to say, that he is *yet an* Ægyptian; that is, *yet a servant of the Queen of* Ægypt; though soon to become a subject of *Rome.*" HUNTER (ed. 1870): "Cleopatra [is] the 'poor Egyptian'. . . . The line should be written thus: 'A poor Egyptian, yet . . . '; where *yet* means *but not less.*" DEY (1909, p. 465): "This 'Egyptian' . . . would [not] speak of Cleopatra as a 'poor Egyptian' . . . to say nothing of the rather saucy '*but not less* the queen, my mistress', the significance attached to 'yet.'" CASE (ed. 1906): "From what is yet Egypt, till your intents pronounce its fate."
    yet] STAUNTON (ed. 1859) alone: "*Now.*"

Of thy intents, desires, instruction,
That she preparedly may frame her selfe
To'th'way shee's forc'd too.   3175
   Cæsar. Bid her haue good heart,
She soone shall know of vs, by some of ours,
How honourable, and how kindely Wee
Determine for her. For *Cæsar* cannot leaue to be vngentle.
   Ægypt. So the Gods preserue thee.   *Exit.* 3180

3173 desires,] ∼ ‸ ROWE2+
3178 honourable] honourably POPE1-v1778, RANN, WH2; honourable WH1 (*text*; honourably *in errata*)
3179–80 *Verse lines ending* cannot live . . . thee. POPE1-JOHN1, v1773+; *ending* cannot . . . thee! CAP
3179 Determine . . . vngentle] Determin'd have . . . gentle CAP
      leaue] live mF4FL33 *conj. and* ROWE3, POPE1-JOHN1, v1773-SING2, COL3-HAL, CAM1-CAM3, SIS+; learn mTYR *conj.*, DYCE, ALEX
3180 So] *Om.* ROWE2, ROWE3; May POPE1-THEO4

3172 See textual notes for pointing.
3173 **desires,**] WILSON (ed. 1950): "Emphasizing comma (v. Simpson [1911], §7)."
3174 **frame**] See n. 924.
3176–9 PHILLIPS (1940, p. 200), very questionably: "Elyot [*The Boke Named the Gouernour*, 1531; ed. Watson, 1907, pp. 142–7] had cited the case of Augustus as an example of lack of vindictiveness in a ruler; Shakespeare's Octavius no less demonstrates the same compassion in victory."
3177 **some of ours**] DEIGHTON (ed. 1891): "Some messenger of ours." Later commentators generalize with KITTREDGE (ed. 1941): Some of "our men; our officers."
3178 **honourable . . . kindely**] In a series of adverbs it is not uncommon for only one to have the characteristic adverbial ending. See FRANZ §244a. ABBOTT (§397): "In [its] old pronunciation [honourable] would approximate to 'honourably.'" Less satisfactory explanations are given by MALONE (ed. 1790)—"Our authour often uses adjectives adverbially"—and SINGER (ed. 1826)—"The laxity of old orthography."
3179 **Determine**] See nn. 2469, 2550.
      leaue . . . vngentle] RIDLEY (ed. 1954): The emendation *Live* "has been almost universally accepted. It is fairly easy graphically (especially if we accept Dover Wilson's [ed. 1950] suggestion of a MS. *leue* [not found in Sh. meaning "live" or "leave"], a spelling which would account for F's *love* for *leaue* in [279]) and even easier auditorily; and it makes quite adequate sense. None the less [he prefers] *leave* . . . with the sense 'stop being gentle' or even more nearly 'stop being himself so as to become ungentle.'" See textual notes and conj., p. 359.
      vngentle] COTGRAVE (1611, Discourtois): "*Vngentle, vnciuile, rude, harsh, without humanitie.*" See also 3267.
3180 **So**] SCHMIDT (1875, 2): "Introducing an optative sentence ['May the Gods . . . '], after or before asseverations."

Cæs. Come hither *Proculeius.* Go and say
We purpose her no shame: giue her what comforts
The quality of her passion shall require;
Least in her greatnesse, by some mortall stroke
She do defeate vs. For her life in Rome,   3185
Would be eternall in our Triumph: Go,
And with your speediest bring vs what she sayes,
And how you finde of her.
    Pro. Cæsar I shall.   *Exit Proculeius.*
    Cæs. Gallus, go you along: where's *Dolabella,* to se-   3190
cond *Proculeius?*
    All. Dolabella.
    Cæs. Let him alone: for I remember now
How hee's imployd: he shall in time be ready.
Go with me to my Tent, where you shall see   3195
How hardly I was drawne into this Warre,

3183 quality] equality KTLY
3186 eternall in] eternaling mTBY2 *conj.*, HAN1, WARB, CAP
3188–9 *One verse line* v1793+ (–STAU)
3188 of] *Om.* mTBY3 *conj.*, WARB
3190–2 *Two verse lines ending* where's *Dolabella,* . . . *Dolabella!* POPE1-CAM3, SIS+;
three verse lines ending Where's Dolabella, . . . Proculeius? | *All.* Dolabella! ALEX
3190 go you] you go SING1, HUD1
3191 *Exit* Gallus. THEO1+
3192 *All.*] *Agr. Mec.* MAL, v1793-KNT1, HUD, SING2, DYCE, STAU, KTLY, OXF1

3181–6 **Go . . . Triumph**] For Plutarch, see p. 451.
3183 **quality**] MINSHEU (1617): "*State, or condition.*"
3185 **defeate**] See n. 2903.
3185–6 **For . . . Triumph**] Summing up most commentators' views since JOHNSON
(ed. 1765), KITTREDGE (ed. 1941): "To exhibit her as a living captive would make my
triumphal procession eternally memorable." CASE (ed. 1906): *Eternal* may have "become
merely intensive" and may mean "her presence . . . would contribute in the highest
degree to my triumph"; his illustration—"eternall villaine" in *Oth.* 4.2.130 (2839)—is
not convincing.
3187 **speediest**] For the nominalization of adjectives, even of comparatives and su-
perlatives, see FRANZ §362b.
3188 **of**] FRANZ (§517): "*With regard to, about, concerning.*"
3189 See n. 2151.
3193–4 **Let . . . imployd**] PERRET (1966, p. 70) interprets Caesar's "forgetting" as
revealing his "callousness," BARROLL (1970, p. 271) as a "depiction of hypocrisy."
3194 **in time**] SCHMIDT (1875): "One day or other; by degrees," in the course of things
(1); "at the right moment" (3), not citing this passage.
3195–9 For Plutarch, see p. 451.
3196 **hardly**] See n. 436.

How calme and gentle I proceeded still
In all my Writings. Go with me, and see
What I can shew in this.   *Exeunt.*

Enter Cleopatra, Charmian, Iras, and Mardian.   **5.2**

Cleo. My desolation does begin to make   3201
A better life: Tis paltry to be *Cæsar*:
Not being Fortune, hee's but Fortunes knaue,
A minister of her will: and it is great
To do that thing that ends all other deeds,   3205   (zz1ᵃ)
Which shackles accedents, and bolts vp change;
Which sleepes, and neuer pallates more the dung,

3200 SCENE VIII. ROWE (*for* III; *see* 2996); SCENE II. POPE1+ (−THEO)
The Monument. ROWE1+ (*subst.*)
Enter . . .] *Ad. above* THEO1-JOHN1, OXF1, SIS
and Mardian] *Ad. and* Seleucus ROWE1-JOHN1; *om.* CAP-OXF1, ARD, RIDa, SIS;
and Seleucus RIDb
3206 change;] change; | Lulls wearied nature to a sound repose WARB
3207 sleepes, . . . pallates] makes us sleep, nor palate HAN1
dung] dugg mTBY2 *and* WARBURTON *conj. apud* THEO1, THEO1, HAN1, WARB,
COL2, DYCE1-STAU, GLO, HAL-COL4, WH2, OXF1, ALEX

3198 **In . . . Writings**] DEIGHTON (ed. 1891) implies that the phrase (like 3196)
modifies *see* in 3195.
3200 *Mardian*] KITTREDGE (ed. 1941): "Most editors omit his name [see textual notes];
but obviously he had come to the monument, as Cleopatra had bidden him, and had
told her how Antony had taken his report of her suicide." RIDLEY (ed. 1954): Mardian
"must be omitted. (a) He says nothing throughout the scene; not a strong argument,
in view of Agrippa in III.[xii (2107–51)]. (b) North [see p. 455] stresses the absence of
everyone but the two waiting-women; a trifle stronger, but not at all decisive. (c) There
is no place [for] 'Exit Mardian', so that if he is to be there we must imagine him as a
silent spectator throughout. But . . . at the moment of Cleopatra's farewell (l. [3543]),
[or] after Cæsar's entry (l. [3597]) . . . he would naturally be questioned. I fancy that
Shakespeare intended to include him in the dialogue, but then found that the scene
was better without him, and forgot to delete his entry."
3201-2 **My . . . life**] Some commentators, starting with RANN (ed. 1791–), lean toward
a life that "grows less irksome"; others, starting with DELIUS (ed. 1856), toward death
or the preparation for it: "A better life" is death, which is regarded as imminent.
3203 **hee's . . . knaue**] Proverbial; see DENT (F617.1): "He is (To be) *Fortune's fool.*"
knaue] JOHNSON (ed. 1765): "*Servant.*" See also n. 2839.
3204 **minister**] See n. 2179.
3207-8 Warburton and Johnson state the basic positions; the rest of the commentary

The beggers Nurse, and *Cæsars.*

Enter Proculeius.

Pro. Cæsar sends greeting to the Queene of Egypt,   3210
And bids thee study on what faire demands
Thou mean'st to haue him grant thee.
Cleo. What's thy name?
Pro. My name is *Proculeius.*

3208 The] O' th' HAN1
3209 *Ad. and* Gallus HAN1, CAP-OXF1, ARD1, RIDa, KIT1, ALEX, SIS; *ad. with Soldiers* CAP-ARD1, RIDa, KIT1, ALEX, SIS; *As he speaks with* CLEOPATRA *through the bars,* GALLUS *and soldiers enter, unseen by those within, mount to the top with ladders, and go down into the monument* CAM3
3212 CLEOPATRA, CHARMIAN, *and* IRAS *exeunt above, and re-enter below behind the bars of the gates.* SIS

---

is largely details supporting one or the other. WARBURTON (*apud* THEOBALD, ed. 1733): "While in life like slumbering Children, we *palate* and *tamper for the* Dug; but in the sleep of Death, we hone no more after transitory Enjoyments. Death rocks us all into a fast and unbroken sleep; and is equally a Nurse to the Beggar, in this respect, as it is to *Cæsar.*" IDEM (ed. 1747) supplies a line after 3206 (see textual notes) to strengthen the argument. JOHNSON (ed. 1765) counters, "The difficulty of the passage, if any difficulty there be, arises only from this, that the act of suicide, and the state which is the effect of suicide, are confounded. Voluntary death . . . produces a state . . . which has no longer need of the gross and terrene sustenance, in the use of which *Cæsar* and the beggar are on a level. The speech is abrupt, but perturbation in such a state is surely natural." The same point about the "trash and dung of this earth" is made by HEATH (1765, p. 466), both deriving from SEWARD (1750, 4:140), who had observed that "*both the Beggar and* Caesar are fed and nursed by *the Dung of the Earth*" and cited "dungie earth" (46). MALONE (*apud* STEEVENS, ed. 1785): "The word *dug* was not . . . coarse or inelegant." DEIGHTON (ed. 1891): "There seems a considerable difference between speaking of the earth as fertilized by manure into furnishing food, and a human being feeding on dung." CASE (ed. 1906): "The attraction of an inoffensive for an unpleasant idea . . . has caused so many editors to read '*dug*' for '*dung.*'" SISSON (1956, 2:275): "Between *dung* and *dug* there is only the presence or absence of a nunnation mark over the *u*, and there is no easier misreading. It is, moreover, not the *dung*, but 'the dungy *earth*' that feeds man and beast in Antony's words. *Dug* is a woman's image, as *dung* is not. [Yet] all canons of textual criticism are in favour of the Folio *dung*, which gives good and relevant sense. The more probable spellings of *dug* and *dung*, *dugge* and *dunge*, are less likely to be confused. Finally, *dung* is the *durior lectio* here." For an explanation of the principle of choosing a *durior lectio*, see Slater in n. 3305. See also textual notes and conj., p. 359.

3207 **pallates**] The *OED* credits Sh. with the first usage of the transitive verb.

3208 Whether this refers to *dung* (*dug*) or *thing* (3205), meaning "death," a question posed by BLUMHOF (ed. 1870), is the subject of an exchange, generating more heat than light, in *TLS* from 14 Oct. 1926 to 13 Jan. 1927. Most commentators favor the former.

Cleo. Anthony   3215
Did tell me of you, bad me trust you, but
I do not greatly care to be deceiu'd
That haue no vse for trusting. If your Master
Would haue a Queene his begger, you must tell him,
That Maiesty to keepe *decorum*, must   3220
No lesse begge then a Kingdome: If he please
To giue me conquer'd Egypt for my Sonne,
He giues me so much of mine owne, as I
Will kneele to him with thankes.
    Pro. Be of good cheere: 3225
Y'are falne into a Princely hand, feare nothing,
Make your full reference freely to my Lord,
Who is so full of Grace, that it flowes ouer
On all that neede. Let me report to him
Your sweet dependancie, and you shall finde   3230
A Conqueror that will pray in ayde for kindnesse,

3221 Kingdome: If he please∧] ~ ; ~~~ . JOHN1
3224 kneele] kneel for HAN1
      thankes] thanks for mTBY3 *conj.* (*withdrawn* mTBY4), GAR (p. 100) *conj.*, KTLY
3227 reference] reverence WORD1
3228 so] *Om.* F3, F4

3217 **care to be deceiu'd**] DELIUS (ed. 1856) and others: Care whether or not I am deceived.
3218 **haue . . . for**] I.e., am not in the habit of, am not accustomed to. See also n. 1064–5.
3218–21 **If . . . Kingdome**] NORMAN (1958, p. 13, n. 7) suggests as source "Daniel's lines [63–74 (ed. Grosart, 1885, 3:34–5)], with their picture of a queen who feels it beneath her to stoop to pick up others' charity." For the 1594 *Cleopatra*, see p. 536.
3220 *decorum*] See n. 150–1.
3223 **as**] For *as* after *so* and *such*, in the sense of "that," see FRANZ §572, and conj., p. 359.
3227 **Make . . . reference**] Commentators split evenly between the sense of "*refer the whole matter*" (CANBY, ed. 1921) and, beginning with DEIGHTON (ed. 1891), that of "appeal." KNOWLES (privately): "Submit yourself."
    freely] See n. 2583.
3231 **pray in ayde**] HANMER (ed. 1744): "*A Law-term used for a petition made in a Court of Justice for the calling in of help from another that hath an interest in the cause in question.*" The lemma ("Praie *in aide*") exists in MINSHEU (1617), but without an exact definition. See *OED*, Pray 6.

Where he for grace is kneel'd too.

Cleo. Pray you tell him,
I am his Fortunes Vassall, and I send him
The Greatnesse he has got. I hourely learne   3235
A Doctrine of Obedience, and would gladly
Looke him i'th'Face.

Pro. This Ile report (deere Lady)
Haue comfort, for I know your plight is pittied
Of him that caus'd it.   3240

Pro. You see how easily she may be surpriz'd:

3234 send him] bend to HAN1
3240 it.] it. Fare you well.——Hark, Gallus! CAP
    Here Gallus, *and Guard, ascend the Monument by a Ladder, and enter at a*
back-Window. THEO, WARB, RIDb, SIS, ARD2; *SD after* 3241 HAN1, JOHN1, v1773, v1778
(*subst.*); *Here* PROCULEIUS (*then as* THEO, *but after* 3241) MAL-COL1, COL2-OXF1, NLSN
(*after* 3240), ARD1-KIT1, ALEX (*subst.*); *The soldiers approach Cleopatra from behind.*
mCOL1 (Enter Guards *after* 3241), PEN1, EVNS (*subst.*)
    3241–2 *Given to Charmian* F2-ROWE3; 3241 *given to Charmian*, 3242 *to Proculeius*
POPE; 3241 *given to Gallus*, 3242 *to Proculeius* mTBY2 *and* mTHEO2 (21 Feb. 1729, [fol.
42]) *conj.*, THEO1-THEO4; 3241–2 *given to Gallus* MAL-ARD2 (–NLSN)
    Marked as an aside: 3241 JOHN1, v1773, v1778; 3241–2 *aside to Gallus* CAP; 3241
aside to Proc. HAN3 (*giving line to Gallus, who enters monument after* 3241)
    3241 she] he YAL2

3234 **Fortunes**] See also 2912, 3029.
    3234–5 **I send . . . got**] WARBURTON (ed. 1747) alone: "*I.e.* I have nothing to send
him, alluding to the presents sent by vassals to their lords." JOHNSON (ed. 1765) and
almost all other commentators: "I allow him to be my conqueror; I own his superiority
with complete submission." MASON (1785, p. 289): "She means her crown which he has
won; and I suppose that when she pronounces these words, she delivers to Proculeius
either her crown, or some other ensign of royalty."
    3240 **Of**] I.e., by. For this archaic use of *of* in connection with concepts of pity, com-
passion, etc., see FRANZ §494, *Anm.* 1.
    3241–4 TURNER (privately): "3243 and 3244 sound like warnings; 3244 is flat as a
statement of fact. I suspect that Cleopatra is not actually taken until 3246 and that 3241–2
are a false start that should be cancelled."
    3241 Alluding to F2's SP, THEOBALD (21 Feb. 1729, [fol. 42ʳ]): "Here Charmian . . .
is made to countenance & give Directions for her [Cleopatra's] being made prisoner:
tho Charmian immediately after says [3244]. . . . Gallus, who climbs up to the hinder
Windows of the Monument, speaks it to the Guard y.ᵗ attend him." IDEM (ed. 1733)
adds, "This Blunder is for want of knowing, or observing, the historical Fact. . . . I
have reform'd the Passage therefore . . . from the Authority of *Plutarch* [see p. 451]."
JOHNSON (ed. 1765): "To him [Proculeius] it certainly belongs, though perhaps misplaced. I would put it [as aside after 3232]. Then while *Cleopatra* makes a formal answer,

Guard her till *Cæsar* come.

Iras. Royall Queene.

Char. Oh *Cleopatra*, thou art taken Queene.

Cleo. Quicke, quicke, good hands.   3245

Pro. Hold worthy Lady, hold:

Doe not your selfe such wrong, who are in this

Releeu'd, but not betraid.

Cleo. What of death too that rids our dogs of languish?

3242-3 *One verse line* KTLY

3242 *Exit* PROCULEIUS. Gallus *maintains Converse with* Cleopatra. *Re-enter, into the Monument, from behind*, PROCULEIUS, *and Soldiers, hastily.* CAP; *Exit.* v1778; *Exit* Gallus. MAL-ARD2 (−NLSN)

3243 Royall] O Royal THEO1-CAP, KTLY

3245-6 *One verse line* v1793+ (−HUD1)

3245 *Drawing a Dagger.* THEO1+ (*subst.*); Proculeius *rushes in* THEO, WARB, JOHN1, v1773, v1778 (*subst.*)

3248-50 *Three verse lines ending* too, . . . *Cleopatra,* . . . by CAP, MAL, v1793+; *four verse lines ending* betray'd. . . . languish? | *Pro.* Cleopatra, . . . by v1773, v1778, RANN

3248 Releeu'd] Bereav'd PECK (1740, p. 254) *conj.* (*for* betraid *on same line*), WARB

Gallus, upon the hint given, seizes her." MALONE (ed. 1790): "It is clear from . . . Plutarch . . . that it belongs to Gallus; who, after Proculeius hath, according to his suggestion, ascended the monument, goes out to inform Cæsar that Cleopatra is taken." THISELTON (1899, p. 26): "To follow Plutarch the simplest way would be, perhaps, to regard this line as the commencement of a new scene, the interval being taken up with the movements of Proculeius, but the fact that Gallus, whose presence talking with Cleopatra is essential to Plutarch's account, does not enter till later shows that Shakespeare did not intend to follow his authority slavishly. It therefore seems preferable to suppose that the ladder was fixed by the soldiers during Proculeius' previous conversation with Cleopatra, and that he, instead of going to Cæsar as he pretended, climbed up the ladder with the soldiers and almost immediately appeared behind Cleopatra and her companions who were still standing at the gate. This view will account for the two speeches in succession being attributed to Proculeius by the Folio." BARROLL (1969, *ShakS*, p. 215): "The effect [Gallus as speaker] is to remove from Proculeius a relatively contemptuous comment about the queen. Hence, a contrast: the sympathetic Proculeius opposed to the unsympathetic Gallus." For the repeated SP and the staging of Cleopatra's capture, see pp. 788-9.

3248 **Releeu'd**] DAVIES (1783, 2:360) stresses the military aspect: "Alludes to a town besieged . . . freed from the besiegers." See 2695.

3249 **What . . . too**] CAPELL (1779 [1774], 1:50): "What, am I rob'd of death too, as well as of my kingdom? and [the words] have no relation to those that Proculeius had just spoke, which perhaps were not heard by her." Everyone else, however, feels that Cleopatra is indeed responding to 3248.

languish] CAWDREY (1604): "Pining, consuming, wearing away with griefe or sicknes."

Pro. Cleopatra, do not abuse my Masters bounty, by   3250
Th'vndoing of your selfe: Let the World see
His Noblenesse well acted, which your death
Will neuer let come forth.
  Cleo. Where art thou Death?
Come hither come; Come, come, and take a Queene   3255
Worth many Babes and Beggers.
  Pro. Oh temperance Lady.
  Cleo. Sir, I will eate no meate, Ile not drinke sir,
If idle talke will once be necessary
Ile not sleepe neither. This mortall house Ile ruine,   3260

3250 *Cleopatra*,] *Om.* POPE1-JOHN1
    my] our v1773, v1778
3255 Come, come] Come F3, F4; Oh! Come ROWE1-JOHN1
    a] the ROWE
3256-7 *One verse line* v1793+
3259 *As a parenthesis* SING, ARD, RID, CAM3, SIS
    talke] time WARB
    necessary] accessary HAN1, COL2, COL3, STAU, COL4
3260 sleepe] speak CAP

3250 **abuse**] See n. 2283.
3259-60 **If . . . neither**] JOHNSON (ed. 1765), rejecting the HANMER (ed. 1744) and WARBURTON (ed. 1747) emendations: "An easy explanation . . . is, *I will not eat,* and *if it will be necessary now for once* to waste a moment in *idle talk* of my purpose, *I will not sleep neither*." HEATH (1765, p. 466) concurs. CAPELL (1779 [1774], 1:50): "'*Necessary*' in this line, means—necessary to life; and '*idle talk*',—conversation and talk among friends: and this being so, '*sleep*' . . . must be a mistake . . . for—'*speak*': After declaring first against '*meat*', and then against '*drink*', she crowns the whole by threat'ning him with,—the greatest possible female atchievement,—a renouncing of *speech*." STEEVENS (ed. 1778): "*Once* may mean *sometimes*. . . . If *idle talking* be sometimes necessary to the prolongation of life, why I will not *sleep* for fear of *talking idly in my sleep*. The sense designed, however, may be—If it be necessary to talk of performing impossibilities, why, I'll not sleep neither." MALONE (ed. 1790): "A line has been lost after the word *necessary*, in which Cleopatra threatened to observe an obstinate silence. The line probably began with the words *I'll*, and the compositor's eye glancing on the same words in the line beneath, all that intervened was lost. . . . The words *I'll not sleep neither*, contain a new and distinct menace. I once thought that Shakespeare might have written— I'll not *speak* neither; but in [3419], Cæsar comforting Cleopatra, says, 'feed, and *sleep*'; which shews that *sleep* in the passage before us is the true reading." SINGER (ed. 1826), agreeing with Johnson, feels the statement is "evidently parenthetical." CASE (ed. 1906), also regarding the line as parenthetical, expands: "Most editors point, *sir; If . . . necessary, I'll . . . neither*: F has no stop save comma after *sir* and full stop after *neither*. Hitherto (and she reverts to this course in her interview with Cæsar) Cleopatra has si-

Do *Cæsar* what he can. Know sir, that I
Will not waite pinnion'd at your Masters Court,
Nor once be chastic'd with the sober eye
Of dull *Octauia*. Shall they hoyst me vp,
And shew me to the showting Varlotarie   3265
Of censuring Rome? Rather a ditch in Egypt.
Be gentle graue vnto me, rather on Nylus mudde
Lay me starke-nak'd, and let the water-Flies
Blow me into abhorring; rather make

3263 Nor once] Not once to F3-ROWE3; Not once POPE
3266–7 Egypt. Be gentle‸ graue‸] ∼ , ∼∼ ‸ ∼ ‸ F2, POPE1+; ∼ . ∼∼ , ∼ ,
F3, F4; ∼ . But ∼ , ∼ , ROWE
3267 vnto] to HAN1, v1793-SING1, COL, HUD1, WH1, HAL
3268 starke-nak'd . . . the] stark naked, and let HUD2

---

lently nursed her purpose and deceived her conquerors. Now, shaken out of her self-
possession, she reveals it in threats, idle talk, as she calls them by contrast with her settled and previously dissembled purpose. 'Words', says Daniel's Cleopatra, 'are for them
that can complaine and liue' (*Works*, [ed.] Grosart [1885], iii. 73, *Cleopatra*, [Act] IV.
line 1154). The line will then mean: 'If for once I must weakly deal in words': and it
seems more naturally to follow the first threats than to be confined to that of not sleeping. . . . [Compares Thomas Heywood's *A Woman Kilde with Kindnesse*, 1607 (*Dramatic Works*, ed. Shepherd, 1874, 2:151).]" For the 1594 *Cleopatra*, see p. 564.
    3260–7 **This . . . me**] NORMAN (1958, pp. 12–13) compares her abhorrence of cap-
tivity and Octavia's view (noted by CASE [ed. 1906, p. x] in Daniel's *Cleopatra*, ll. 63–74
[ed. Grosart, 1885, 3:34–5]). For the 1594 *Cleopatra*, see p. 536.
    3262 **waite**] CAWDREY (1604, attendance): "Watching, staying for, or wayting vpon."
KITTREDGE (ed. 1941) adds, "As a slave."
    3263–4 **Nor . . . Octauia**] See n. 3034.
    3264 **hoyst me vp**] See n. 2792.
    3265 **Varlotarie**] COTGRAVE (1611, Valet): "*A groome, yeoman, or household seruant
of the meaner sort: In old time it was a more honorable title.* . . . [It] *grew into disesteeme, and is, at the length, become opposite vnto that of* Gentilhomme [see *gentle*
(3267)]." *Varlet* is a variant of *valet*; *Varloterie*, "Varlets collectively; a number or crowd
of attendants or menials" (*OED*, Varletry).
    3266 **censuring**] BULLOKAR (1616): "A iudgement: an opinion." Most commentators
prefer a neutral connotation, which seems more common in Sh., although it is often
difficult to decide; some also give the sense of "critical."
    3267 **gentle**] See n. 3179.
    3268 **starke-nak'd**] DYCE (ed. 1857): "Here '*nak'd*' is . . . a monosyllable."
    3269 **Blow**] JOHNSON (1755, *v. a.*, 11), citing this instance: "To infect with the eggs
of flies." See also nn. 2615, 3618.
    abhorring] UPTON (1746, p. 310): Sh. uses the "active participle passively . . .
i.e. into being abhorred." See ABBOTT §372.

My Countries high pyramides my Gibbet,   3270
And hang me vp in Chaines.   (zz1ᵇ)
  Pro. You do extend
These thoughts of horror further then you shall
Finde cause in *Cæsar.*

Enter Dolabella.   3275

  Dol. Proculeius,
What thou hast done, thy Master *Cæsar* knowes,
And he hath sent for thee: for the Queene,
Ile take her to my Guard.
  Pro. So *Dolabella,*   3280
It shall content me best: Be gentle to her,
To *Cæsar* I will speake, what you shall please,
If you'l imploy me to him.   *Exit Proculeius*

3270 high pyramides] high Pyramids F3, F4, v1773, STAU (*text*; high pyramides *in corrigenda*); highest *Pyramid* HAN1
  3273 further] farther CAP, COL, WH1, HAL
  3274, 3276 *One verse line* v1793+ (−ALEX)
  3274 cause] cause for it CAP
  3275 SCENE III. WARB, JOHN1
  3277 thy] my F4-POPE2, HAN1
  3278 sent] sent me DYCE1 *conj.*, KTLY, DYCE2, KIT1
    for the] as for the F2-v1778, RANN-v1803, HUD2, OXF1
  3282 *To* Cleopatra. HAN1, JOHN1+ (*subst.*)
  3283 *Exit Proculeius*] *After* 3284 POPE1-THEO2, HAN1 (*Exeunt* Proculeius *and* Gallus.), WARB+

3270 STEEVENS (ed. 1773): "The poet seems either to have designed we should read the word *country* as a trissyllable, or *pyramides*, Lat. instead of *pyramids*. The verse will otherwise be defective." IDEM (ed. 1778)—and others—prefers the quadrisyllabic *pyramides* (accented on the second syllable), quoting among others Marlowe's *Dr. Faustus* 823–4 and *1 Tamburlaine* 4.2.103 (both ed. Bowers, 1973). See n. 1371–2 and CERCIGNANI (1981, p. 43).

  3271 BLUMHOF (ed. 1870) compares *3H6* "if I digg'd vp thy fore-fathers Graues, And hung their rotten Coffins vp in Chaynes" (1.3.27–8 [429–30]). KNOWLES (privately) cites Marlowe's *2 Tamburlaine* 5.1.108, "Hang him up in chaines upon the citie walles" (ed. Bowers, 1973), and 5.1.147 SD.

  3275 *Enter Dolabella*] CASE (ed. 1906): "In North [see p. 452] it is Epaphroditus who is sent at this stage." WILSON (ed. 1950): "Cf. Plut[arch]'s [see p. 454] different use of Dol."

  3278 **for the**] See n. 1787.
  3279 **Guard**] WORDSWORTH (ed. 1883): "*Guardianship.*"

312

Cleo. Say, I would dye.

Dol. Most Noble Empresse, you haue heard of me.   3285

Cleo. I cannot tell.

Dol. Assuredly you know me.

Cleo. No matter sir, what I haue heard or knowne:
You laugh when Boyes or Women tell their Dreames,
Is't not your tricke?   3290

Dol. I vnderstand not, Madam.

Cleo. I dreampt there was an Emperor *Anthony.*
Oh such another sleepe, that I might see
But such another man.

Dol. If it might please ye.   3295

Cleo. His face was as the Heau'ns, and therein stucke
A Sunne and Moone, which kept their course, & lighted

3295 ye] you CAP, v1778-KNT1, COL, HUD1, SING2, KTLY, HAL
3296 Heau'ns] heaven's DEL2 *conj.*, BLUM

3283 **imploy**] FRANZ (§531): The phrasal verb *employ to*, meaning "to send with a message or commission to," developed under the influence of the similar sounding verb *to envoy* and the substantive *envoy*. See *OED*, Employ *v.* 3b.

3286 WILSON (ed. 1950): "Cleo.'s indifference to this 'young gentleman' (Plut[arch; see p. 454]) who cannot conceal his admiration, as compared with her attitude towards Thidias in 3.13. [2152 ff.] is significant of the change in her."

3290 **tricke**] JOHNSON (1755, 6): "A practice; a manner; a habit." See n. 2429.

3292–3320 WHITER (1794; ed. Over, 1967, pp. 161–3): "An imitation of the *sphere* of the Heavens with the attributes and ornaments belonging to it, the sweetness of its music and the noise of its thunder, the Sun, the Moon, and the Earth, colossal figures — armorial bearings — a magnificent procession of monarchs and their attendants — floating islands — and a prodigal distribution of wealth and honors, are the known and familiar materials, which formed the motley compound of the Masque, the Pageant, or the Procession. The reader will, perhaps, be gratified in discovering that all these ideas accompany the imagery of the *dolphin*, and are introduced by the Poet as the *visionary* objects of a delightful *dream*." See also nn. 2833, 3306–8.

3293 **might**] See n. 538.

3295, 3299, 3311 STIRLING (1956, pp. 179–80), alone and questionably: "Dolabella . . . is apparently assigned the function of reducing her [Cleopatra's] illusion in a single, well-turned line. . . . Note Dolabella's interruptions which seem to imply that a public airing of nobility in these terms approaches travesty and destroys a dignity which should be maintained by reticence." See n. 3299.

3296–8 WILSON (ed. 1950) compares Cleopatra's words spoken over the body of Antonius in the Countess of Pembroke's *Antonie* (1595, l. 1941), "Thy eies, two Sunnes." For the 1592 *Antonius*, see p. 523.

The little o'th'earth.
Dol. Most Soueraigne Creature.
Cleo. His legges bestrid the Ocean, his rear'd arme   3300
Crested the world: His voyce was propertied
As all the tuned Spheres, and that to Friends:
But when he meant to quaile, and shake the Orbe,

3298 o'th'] O o'th' THEO, WARB, JOHN1, CAP; orb o'th' HAN1; O the v1773+
3302 and] when mTHEO2 (21 Feb. 1729, [fol. 42]) *conj.*, THEO1-v1773 (–HAN1)

3298 **o'th'earth**] THEOBALD (ed. 1733): "There is but a Syllable wanting, and that . . . was but of a single Letter; which the first Editors not understanding, learnedly threw it out as a Redundance. I restore, *The little O o'th' Earth*, i.e. the little Orb or Circle." COLLIER (ed. 1843), reading "O, the earth": "This is substantially Theobald's amendment. . . . There seems no necessity to add to the text." BLUMHOF (ed. 1870), wildly, detects a possible wordplay on the exclamation of pain *O* or on the sense of little importance, as in the figure *O*. See textual notes.

3299 BLUMHOF (ed. 1870), alone and unconvincingly, regards this utterance as an acknowledgment of the picture of Antony Cleopatra has been drawing and also regards as unnecessary the dash inserted by editors since ROWE (ed. 1709)—except SINGER (ed. 1856) and KEIGHTLEY (ed. 1864)—to indicate an interruption. Compare n. 3295.

3300–10 MOSELEY (1986, p. 121) draws attention to "two emblems in George Wither's *A Collection of Emblemes* (London, 1635), numbers I.xxxi and III.xxix, which have a remarkable similarity to this imagined picture."

3300 **His . . . Ocean**] MALONE (ed. 1790) quotes *JC*: "Why man, he doth bestride the narrow world Like a Colossus" (1.2.135–6 [234–5]). See PAULY, Chares, 3:2130–1 (15); not in *OCD*. JACKSON (1819, p. 313) alone: "Alludes to his naval forces: though seas divided his territories, yet he united them."

3301 **Crested the world**] PERCY (*apud* MALONE, ed. 1790): "Alluding to some of the old crests in heraldry, where a raised arm on a wreath was mounted on the helmet." See conj., p. 359.

3301–2 **His . . . Spheres**] DEIGHTON (ed. 1891): "His voice was endowed with all the music of the tuneful spheres. The harmony of the spheres was a doctrine of Pythagoras, according to whom the heavenly bodies in their motion could not but occasion a certain sound or note, the notes of them altogether forming a regular musical scale or harmony."

3301 **propertied**] An unusual conversion of noun to adjective. Cited as first instance in *OED*. See n. 72.

3302 **and that**] FURNESS (ed. 1907), rejecting the conjectures of Staunton and Elze (see p. 359): "'That' is perfectly correct. Its antecedent is 'voice'. 'That' (or *such*) was his voice when addressing his friends." For *and* introducing emphatic additions, see FRANZ §590.

3303 **quaile**] Some early commentators tend to follow HANMER's (ed. 1744, 6:Glossary) "*to droop, to languish*." Most, however, favor the more active "*quell*" (MINSHEU, 1617), "overpower" (BLUMHOF, ed. 1870), "overawe" (SCHMIDT, 1875). For the causative use ("make quail"), see FRANZ §630c.

He was as ratling Thunder. For his Bounty,
There was no winter in't. An *Anthony* it was,   3305

3304 as] a HUD2
3305 *Anthony* it was] Autumn 'twas mTHEO2 (8 Apr. 1729, [fol. 63]) *conj.*,
THEO1-HUD1, SING2-ALEX, ARD2; Autumn it was mTBY2 *and* mF2FL21 *conj.*, DEL2, SIS,
EVNS

3304–6 **For . . . reaping**] ERSKINE-HILL (1970, p. 42) finds a source to be Plutarch's
Life of Alcibiades (tr. North, 1603, p. 197): "For where *Euripides* saith, that of all the
faire times of the yeare, the Autumne or latter season is the fairest: that commonly falleth
not out true. And yet it proued true in *Alcibiades*, though in few other: for he was passing faire euen to his latter time, and of good temperature of body." IDEM (p. 38): "This
is the final Magnificence of Antony . . . a *noble* intemperance."
    3305 **An *Anthony* it was**] The main arguments for emending to *Autumn*: THEOBALD
(ed. 1733): "How could an *Antony* grow the more by reaping? [F's reading] might easily
arise from the great Similitude of the two Words in the old way of spelling, *Antonie*
and *Automne*." COLLIER (ed. 1843): "The error, doubtless, arose from autumn having
been written with a capital letter." RIDLEY (ed. 1954): The spelling of F's copy "was regularly *Anthony* (very occasionally *Anthonie*). And easy though the *Automne-Antonie* confusion would be, to misread *Automne* as a word containing (probably) *y*, and (almost
certainly) distinctive long-tailed *h*, would be much less natural. Further, if . . . the copy
. . . indicated proper names for italicization, the absence of such indication for the
hypothetical *Automne* ought to have made the compositor suspicious. However, as Dr.
[H. F.] Brooks points out, F's reading at [2345], where the compositor apparently took
Cæsarion as an adjective, suggests that the copy was at least not consistent in such indication. . . . I have little doubt that *Automne* is what Shakespeare wrote."
    The main arguments for retaining *Antony*: CORSON (1873, pp. 144–5): "If 'An An-
thony it was' is not right, 'an autumn 'twas' is certainly wrong. It is too tame for the
intensely impassioned speech in which it occurs, or rather into which it has been introduced by the editors. Again, if 'autumn' could, by metonymy, be wrenched to mean
the crops of autumn, it could hardly be said that an autumn *grows* the more by reaping.
. . . [In] 'An Anthony it was' . . . 'it' stands, of course, for 'Bounty.'" THISELTON (1899,
p. 27): "Nothing seems to be gained by substituting 'autumn' for 'Anthony', since the
idea so arrived at is already contained by implication in the preceding sentence. 'An Anthony' is required (1) in order that all his great qualities may be included in the statement of inexhaustibility, and (2) in order to mark the contrast between Cleopatra's dream
of him and the worldly reality, Anthony from the point of view of mortality having now
been reaped once for all. The emendation greatly reduces the pathos, and is due to that
cast of mind—admirable enough in its way—that must have everything directly expressed,
and will leave no scope for the suggestion, which is the soul of poetry." FURNESS (ed.
1907): "Reaping in the autumn is done when the grain is ripe, and grain thus reaped
never grows again. . . . 'Anthony' [implies] inexhaustible perfection in face, in form,
in voice, in bounty, which for Cleopatra so far lay in that single name that once, in order
to express the height and depth and boundlessness of her self-absorption she exclaimed,
'Oh, my oblivion is a very Anthony!' [409]." SPENCER (1942, p. 165, n. 4): "If it [the

315

That grew the more by reaping: His delights   3306
Were Dolphin-like, they shew'd his backe aboue

3307 his] their HAN1; the KTLY

---

line] is properly spoken, it is quite clear that Shakespeare meant Cleopatra's thought
to come suddenly back to Antony, so that by a particularly intense reversion, he appears
to her more than ever a microcosm of bounty. If we see a sexual reference, which is by
no means unlikely, all difficulties of meaning disappear." SLATER (ed. 1971): "In F Antony is spelt with an 'h' throughout [169 times] (with one exception, where two lines
are crammed into one, and it is the obvious abbreviation to make, the name appearing
three times in one line [3013]). 'There is no doubt that "Anthony" was Shakespeare's
spelling' (Greg: *The Shakespeare First Folio* [1955] p. 289, fn. 2). The graphic ease of
the emendation is therefore unacceptable. Furthermore, a compositor rarely invents an
obscure word, rather than an obvious one to replace something illegible in the MS. The
notorious compositorial instinct is: 'When in doubt, simplify'. Since unanimous editorial
insistence on 'autumn' shows this to be the word commonly expected from the context,
the compositor might well have read the obvious 'autumn' for an illegible 'Antonie', but
he would never have extracted the masterly and unexpected 'Anthony' from an illegible
'autumn'. On grounds of style the contrast with *winter* and the link with *reaping* in the
next line are attractive, but pedestrian, whereas for Cleopatra to call Antony's bounty
'an Anthony' is wholly in accord with her style [quotes 't'imagine . . . peece' (3318 f.),
409, and 1041]. All things are absorbed into the giant figure of her lover, as this whole
speech shows. This attitude is central to the play. . . . 'Anthony' is Cleopatra's all-
embracing superlative: the greatest name she can give his generosity is his own: *An Anthony it was*." Other details are worth mentioning, though in themselves they do not
necessarily preclude compositorial error. *Autumn* is never written with an *o* in Sh., and
in six of eight instances with *mne(s)*. *Autumn* is never used with an indefinite article
in Sh. With only two exceptions (one of which is due to line justification) it is written
with an *mn* in all quartos and F1: in this spelling there are too many strokes in *mn* for
it to be mistaken for *ni*. Furthermore, it is often overlooked that *it was* is of metrical
necessity emended to *'twas*. But in all the possible substantive eds. of Sh. only one verse
line ends in *'twas* (*Tit.* 5.1.95 [2211]), which the following quartos and F1 place at the
beginning of the next line and read *And 'twas*; thirteen verse lines in Sh. end in *it was*.
Finally, Corson (1873, pp. 144–5), SPEDDING (1874, pp. 303–4), CROSBY (*apud* HUD-
SON, ed. 1881), and others fruitlessly discuss whether Antony's bounty may derive from
Greek ἄνθος or whether Sh. knew Greek at all. For although the etymology of *Antony*
is incorrect, it was evidently popular in his day and later. See CAMDEN (1605, p. 43):
"*Anthonie*, [Greek]: as *Antheros*, flourishing, from the greeke *Anthos* a floure. . . .
There are yet some that drawe it from *Anton* a companion of *Hercules*."
    3306 **by reaping**] RANN (ed. 1791–): "Produced successive crops." All commentators
agree except KNOWLES (privately), who suggests "by conquest—harvesting what others
have sown."
    3306-8 **His . . . in**] DELIUS (ed. 1856) and most commentators: Antony was not
submerged in his pleasures but knew how to keep himself always above them. Variations
are offered by BLUMHOF (ed. 1870): His joys were of a lively nature and showed him

The Element they liu'd in: In his Liuery
Walk'd Crownes and Crownets: Realms & Islands were
As plates dropt from his pocket.   3310
   Dol. Cleopatra.
   Cleo. Thinke you there was, or might be such a man
As this I dreampt of?
   Dol. Gentle Madam, no.
   Cleo. You Lye vp to the hearing of the Gods: 3315
But if there be, nor euer were one such
It's past the size of dreaming: Nature wants stuffe

3309 Crownes] crown HUD2
    Crownets] coronets POPE1-JOHN1; crownlets OXF1
    were] *Om.* F2-POPE2
3310–11 *One verse line* v1793+ (−HUD1)
3316 nor] or F3-CAM3, SIS, ARD2

---

as master within the element; WORDSWORTH (ed. 1883): "*His pleasures were not secret or selfish.* [Cites Plutarch; see p. 426.]"; and EVANS (ed. 1974): "In his pleasures he rose above the common as a dolphin rises out of its element, the sea." The lines have elicited a considerable number of ingenious, at times questionable, interpretations, two of which may serve as characteristic. FURNESS (ed. 1907) quotes WHITER (1794; ed. Over, 1967, p. 160): "The *back of the dolphin* is deeply associated in the mind of Shakspeare with the splendid scenery of the pageant or the procession. Would the reader believe that the following idea . . . is to be referred to this source? [Quotes this passage.]" PROSER (1965, p. 226, n. 46): "Motion suggests sexual 'motion' as well as other kinds of creative motion. . . . Within Cleopatra's hyperbole lives a sexual innuendo one can be sure is meant to amuse and delight us." FRIPP (1930, p. 126) compares Ovid's *Metamorphoses* 2.265–6. ADELMAN (1973, p. 72): Sh. "may have deliberately recalled Vulcan's shield" as described in Virgil's *Aeneid* 8.671–7. E. JONES (1977, p. 12) mentions the "Delphino lascivior" of Erasmus (*Opera*, 1703, 2:12) and "wonders whether Shakespeare recalled it . . . and whether for him it coloured the meaning of the simile." See also n. 3292–3320.

   3308 **Element**] See nn. 1384, 3540–1.

   3310 **plates**] MINSHEU (1617, *Vocabularium Hispanicolatinvm*, Pláta): "*Silver, money.*" STEEVENS (ed. 1778) illustrates by quoting Marlowe's *Jew of Malta* 2.3.97–8, 102, and 107 (ed. Bowers, 1973). See also 3366.

   3316 **nor**] THISELTON (1899, p. 27): " 'Nor' of the Folio has been unwarrantably changed to 'or', owing to its being overlooked that this line is in direct contrast with the preceding, and that 'nor' implies an ellipsis of 'neither' or 'not'. Cleopatra would ask, 'But assuming for the moment you are right, how came I to dream of such a one?' " CASE (ed. 1906): "This [explanation of Thiselton] is ingenious, but Shakespeare's ellipses of *neither* are always unmistakable and cause no ambiguity." The main point, however, is that *nor* in Sh. is not used alone except as part of an ellipsis, as in the explanation of JONES (ed. 1977): "If there neither [understood] is nor ever was such a man."

   3317–20 **Nature . . . quite**] BLUMHOF (ed. 1870) notes the same hyperbole in Enobar-

317

To vie strange formes with fancie, yet t'imagine
An *Anthony* were Natures peece, 'gainst Fancie,
Condemning shadowes quite.   3320
    Dol. Heare me, good Madam:
Your losse is as your selfe, great; and you beare it
As answering to the waight, would I might neuer
Ore-take pursu'de successe: But I do feele
By the rebound of yours, a greefe that suites   3325

3318 t'imagine] to form HAN1
3319 were] with F3, F4
      peece] Prize WARBURTON *conj. apud* THEO1, THEO1-THEO4
      Fancie] Fancy's KTLY
3323–4 waight, . . . successe:] ~ : . . . ~ , ROWE1+
3325 suites] shoots POPE1-JOHN1, v1773-KNT1, KTLY, WH2; smites mF2FL21 *conj.*,
CAP, COL1-GLO, HAL-HUD2, OXF1+

---

bus's description of Cleopatra, "where we see The fancie out-worke Nature" (912–13).
    3318 **vie**] MINSHEU (1617): "*As at Cardes,* [from] Lat: Vieo, i.[e.,] vincio, *to binde,*
because players at cards are bound *to see the* Vie, *or they lose it.*" CASE (ed. 1906) expands, "'To vie' in gaming was to stake or counter-stake, originally (see Skeat, *Etymol.
Dict.* [1882]) 'to draw on or invite a game' [subst.] by staking a sum, *vie* and *invite* being
different forms of one original."
    3318, 3319 **fancie**] See n. 913.
    3318–20 **yet . . . quite**] WARBURTON (*apud* THEOBALD, ed. 1733): "'*Nature* in
general has not Materials sufficient to furnish out real Forms, for ev'ry Model that the
boundless Power of the *Imagination* can sketch out. < This is the Meaning of the Words,
Nature wants Matter to vye strange Forms with Fancy.> . . . Yet it must be own'd, that
when *Nature* presents an *Antony* to us, she then gets the better of *Fancy*, and makes
even the *Imagination* appear poor and narrow; or . . . *condemns shadows quite'*. The
Word *Prize*, which I have restored, [figures] a Contention between *Nature* and *Imagination* about the larger Extent of their Powers; and Nature gaining the Prize by producing
Antony." JOHNSON (ed. 1765) and most others: "The word *piece*, is a term appropriated
to works of art. Here Nature and Fancy produce each their *piece*, and the *piece* done
by Nature had the preference. *Antony* was in reality *past the size of dreaming*; he was
more by *Nature* than *Fancy* could present in sleep." See textual notes.
    3323 **As . . . waight**] DEIGHTON (ed. 1891): "In a manner corresponding to its bur-
den." KITTREDGE (ed. 1941) adds, "I.e., heavily, grievously."
    3324 **Ore-take**] MINSHEU (1617, Ouer-take): "*Attaine.*" Compare n. 1990.
    successe] See n. 421.
    But] See n. 3141.
    3325 **rebound**] To the customary meaning JOHNSON (1755), citing this instance, adds
"resilition" (in BLOUNT [1656] the lemma is "Resilience"). WALTER (ed. 1969), unconvincingly, flattens it to "repetition, iteration."
    suites] Reading *smites*, CAPELL (1779 [1774], 1:50): "*Shoots* is hardly less uncouth

My very heart at roote.
Cleo. I thanke you sir:
Know you what *Cæsar* meanes to do with me?
Dol. I am loath to tell you what, I would you knew.
Cleo. Nay pray you sir.   3330
Dol. Though he be Honourable.
Cleo. Hee'l leade me then in Triumph.
Dol. Madam he will, I know't.   *Flourish.*

Enter Proculeius, Cæsar, Gallus, Mecenas,
and others of his Traine.   3335

All. Make way there *Cæsar.*

3329 what,] ~ ‿ ROWE3+ (−ARD2)
3330–1 *One verse line* v1793+ (−HUD1)
3332–3, 3336–9 *Two verse lines ending* will, . . . know't *then as* F1 HAN1, KNT1,
SING2; *four verse lines ending* will; . . . queen . . . Arise, . . . kneel:— v1793, v1803,
SING1; *three verse lines ending* know it. . . . Egypt? . . . kneel. KTLY; *two verse lines
ending* triumph? . . . Caesar *then as* F1 DEL4
3332 then] *Om.* THEO2, WARB-CAP
3333 *Flourish.*] *Om.* F2-SING2, COL3, WH1, KTLY, HAL, OXF1
3334–5 *After* 3336 POPE1-ARD2 (−NLSN); *ad. and* SELEUCUS CAP, MAL, v1793+
(−CAM3, RIDb, ARD2)
3334 SCENE III. POPE, HAN1; SCENE IV. WARB, JOHN1
     Proculeius . . . Mecenas] Cæsar, Gallus, Mecænas, Proculeius ROWE1-SIS (*subst.*)
3336 *All*] *within* CAP, MAL, v1793-ARD2 (−NLSN) (*subst.*)

---

than the word it is chang'd for [*suites*]." MALONE (ed. 1790) reads *shoots* and mentions
the possible pun: "The error arose from the two words . . . being pronounced alike."
(See CERCIGNANI [1981, p. 347].) THISELTON (1899, p. 27) points out the similarity to
the *shoot* metaphors in *Cor.* 5.1.44 (3200) and *Per.* 4.4.26. CASE (ed. 1906) objects that
shoots "does not agree with 'at root', as *smites* does"—to which RIDLEY (ed. 1954) adds,
"and also produces an impossible assonance," an assertion found in COLLIER (ed. 1843).
     3326 **at roote**] For the omission of the article in adverbial phrases, see n. 861.
     roote] *OED* (*sb.*[1] 10b): "The bottom."
     3333–6 **Flourish . . . there Cæsar**] RIDLEY (ed. 1954): "'Make way' must surely pre-
cede Cæsar's entry. And . . . what is Proculeius doing apparently leading the procession? The usual modern method of dealing with it has been to have a 'shout within'
along with the flourish, and to demote Proculeius to a humbler place. . . . But it is
not wholly satisfying. . . . First, on the Elizabethan stage the 'Make way' would need
to precede Cæsar's appearance at the entrance door by very little, if at all. He still has
to make his way some distance down stage, and a certain amount of noise and bustle

Cæs. Which is the Queene of Egypt.   (zz1

Dol. It is the Emperor Madam.   *Cleo. kneeles.*

Cæsar. Arise, you shall not kneele:

I pray you rise, rise Egypt.   3340

Cleo. Sir, the Gods will haue it thus,

My Master and my Lord I must obey.

Cæsar. Take to you no hard thoughts,

The Record of what iniuries you did vs,

Though written in our flesh, we shall remember   3345

As things but done by chance.

Cleo. Sole Sir o'th'World,

I cannot proiect mine owne cause so well

To make it cleare, but do confesse I haue

Bene laden with like frailties, which before   3350

3338 *Cleo. kneeles.*] *Om.* CAP
3340–3 *Three verse lines ending* Gods . . . lord . . . thoughts: POPE1+
3342 must] much F2-F4
3348 proiect] parget HAN1; procter WARB

---

would not be amiss. Second, the guard have presumably, from the time of Cleopatra's capture, been lining the back of the stage, guarding the exits, and it is they who have to make way. Is it possible that Proculeius does in fact enter first, perhaps with a few soldiers, as a kind of advance party, and that the 'Make way' comes from the guard, clearing the doors under his instructions, and not from 'voices off'?" BERKELEY (1964, p. 140), agreeing, adds, "Retaining the F1 stage-direction obviously enhances the role of Proculeius as Caesar's agent and directs our querying attention to the advice given by the dying Antony to Cleopatra."

3337 WILSON (ed. 1950): "What a question! Caesar's opening shot in the duel of wits." But this assertion, developed from GRINDON (1909, p. 63) and GRANVILLE-BARKER (1930; 1946, 1:401), ignores the physical condition of Cleopatra described by Plutarch [see p. 453] and the effort to rouse Cleopatra that is apparent in 3338. See also 3435, 3575.

3344 **Record**] See n. 2704.

3345 **written . . . flesh**] DEIGHTON (ed. 1891): "Felt so acutely." WALTER (ed. 1969): "I.e. in warfare."

3347 **Sir**] COTGRAVE (1611): "*Maister; A title of honor which, without addition, is giuen onely to the King; but with addition, vnto Marchants, or Tradesmen . . . and vnto Knights . . . and vnto some few owners of Fiefs, or Seigniories.*"

3348 **proiect**] COTGRAVE (1611, Projecter): "*To draw, purtray, describe, delineate, proportion, a thing before it be done.*" HANMER (ed. 1744) emends to *parget*, defining (6:Glossary) as "to daub or plaister over." WARBURTON (ed. 1747) emends to *procter*: "The technical term, to plead by an advocate." HEATH (1765, p. 466): "To *project* is properly a term of perspective, signifying to represent an object truly." JOHNSON (ed. 1765) and most others: "To *project a cause*, is to *represent* a cause; to *project* it *well*, is to *plan* or *contrive* a scheme of defence."

3349 **cleare**] MINSHEU (1617): "Plaine, apparent, manifest, pure, transparent, bright." DYCHE & PARDON (1740) and all commentators: "Free from blame, innocent."

Haue often sham'd our Sex.

　　Cæsar. *Cleopatra* know,

We will extenuate rather then inforce:

If you apply your selfe to our intents,

Which towards you are most gentle, you shall finde　　　　3355

A benefit in this change: but if you seeke

To lay on me a Cruelty, by taking

Anthonies course, you shall bereaue your selfe

Of my good purposes, and put your children

To that destruction which Ile guard them from,　　　　3360

If thereon you relye. Ile take my leaue.

　　Cleo. And may through all the world: tis yours, & we

Your Scutcheons, and your signes of Conquest shall

Hang in what place you please. Here my good Lord.

　　Cæsar. You shall aduise me in all for *Cleopatra.*　　　　3365

　　Cleo. This is the breefe: of Money, Plate, & Iewels

3355 towards] toward HUD2
3362–4 And . . . please.] *Marked as an aside* BLUM
3364 Here] Hear COL4
3365 in all for] of all ROWE3-POPE2
3366 breefe: of] ～ ∧ ～ POPE1-SIS

　　3354 **apply your selfe**] COTGRAVE (1611, s'Appliquer à): *"Follow the humor of."* KIT-
TREDGE (ed. 1941): "To *apply* means literally to '*fit* (one object) to the *folds* or outlines
(of another)'. [See MINSHEU (1617): 'To fold, or plait, or applie or bend vnto.'] Hence
to *apply one's self* denotes complete submission of the will."

　　3361 **thereon**] SCHMIDT (1875, Rely): Refers to "my good purposes."

　　3362–4 **And . . . please**] BLUMHOF (ed. 1870): An aside, since it contradicts the
subservience in Cleopatra's preceding and following speeches.

　　3362 **may**] I.e., can. See n. 538.

　　3363 **signes**] Only WALTER (ed. 1969) specifies as "banners, ensigns."

　　3364 **Hang**] BLUMHOF (ed. 1870): I.e., as mementoes of conquest.

　　Here] COLLIER (ed. 1877) alone: "Always misprinted [for *Hear*], as if offering Cæsar
an inventory; but Cæsar's answer shows that he was ready to listen to her in all things."
KNOWLES (privately), disagreeing: "Sudden change of direction suggests that *Here* indicates that Cleopatra produces and thrusts on Caesar her 'brief.'"

　　3365 **in all for**] THEOBALD (21 Feb. 1729, [fol. 42ʳ]), defending the F1 reading:
"What a mean Rascal do our modern Editors [reading *of all*; see textual notes] make
of Cæsar, who is afraid least Cleopatra should not give him in her whole Inventory!"
IDEM (ed. 1733) continues, "*Cæsar* takes pains to comfort her; and tells her, that she
herself shall direct him in ev'ry Thing for her own Relief and Satisfaction [as support
refers to 'Therefore . . . counsell' (3416–19)]." *For* can mean "as regards"; see FRANZ §483.

　　3366 **Plate**] See n. 3310.

321

I am possest of, 'tis exactly valewed,
Not petty things admitted. Where's *Seleucus*?
  Seleu. Heere Madam.
  Cleo. This is my Treasurer, let him speake (my Lord)   3370
Vpon his perill, that I haue reseru'd
To my selfe nothing. Speake the truth *Seleucus*.
  Seleu. Madam, I had rather seele my lippes,
Then to my perill speake that which is not.
  Cleo. What haue I kept backe.   3375
  Sel. Enough to purchase what you haue made known.
  Cæsar. Nay blush not *Cleopatra*, I approue
Your Wisedome in the deede.
  Cleo. See *Cæsar*: Oh behold,

3368 admitted] omitted mTHEO1 *and* mTBY2 *conj.*, THEO1-THEO4, CAP
    Where's] Whereas F3, F4
    Enter SELEUCUS. ARD2
3373–5 *Two verse lines ending* peril . . . back? HAN1; *three verse lines ending* Madam,
. . . peril, . . . back? CAP, v1778+
3373 Madam,] *Om.* HAN1
    seele] seale F3-THEO4, CAP, KNT1-SIS (–SING2, KTLY, KIT1)
3378–9 *One verse line* v1793+
3379 See *Cæsar*: Oh] *Cæsar!* HAN1

3367–8 'tis . . . admitted] THEOBALD (ed. 1733), emending to *omitted*: "For this Declaration lays open her Falshood; and makes her angry, when her Treasurer detects her in a direct Lye." JOHNSON (ed. 1765) and most others: "She is angry afterwards, that she is accused of having reserved more than petty things." KITTREDGE (ed. 1941): "Being allowed me as necessities and therefore omitted from the list. But *admitted* may be a mere misprint for *omitted*, as Theobald thought." See also "I haue reseru'd . . . nothing" (3371–2).

3368–3406 Where's . . . *Seleucus*] See n. 3383–7. MUIR (1969, pp. 202–5) compares the "theatrical violence" of Cleopatra's behavior in Jodelle's *Cléopâtre captive*, Act 3 (ed. Gohin, 1925, pp. 75–7), and Daniel's *Cleopatra*, ll. 681–94 (ed. Grosart, 1885), citing (n. 17) Rees (1952, pp. 1–10) "for an account of Daniel's debt to Jodelle." For the 1594 *Cleopatra*, see p. 552; for the episode in Plutarch, see p. 454.

3368–70 Where's . . . Treasurer] RIDLEY (ed. 1954): "Capell [ed. 1768], followed by most editors since [see textual notes], brought on Seleucus in Cæsar's train at [3334–5]. But what is he doing there? And if he had already gone over to Cæsar why does Cleopatra here explain who he is?" Doubtless so that the audience knows.

3371 Vpon his perill] *OED* (Peril *sb.* 3b): His "taking the risk or responsibility of the consequences."

3373 seele my lippes] JOHNSON (ed. 1765): "Sew up my mouth." COLLIER (ed. 1843): Commentators understand "*seeling* the eyes of a hawk; but the common expression of *sealing* the lips requires no such explanation." WILSON (ed. 1950): "'Seel' . . . is only used of the eyes." See also n. 2288.

How pompe is followed: Mine will now be yours,   3380
And should we shift estates, yours would be mine.
The ingratitude of this *Seleucus*, does
Euen make me wilde. Oh Slaue, of no more trust
Then loue that's hyr'd? What goest thou backe, y^u shalt
Go backe I warrant thee: but Ile catch thine eyes   3385
Though they had wings. Slaue, Soule-lesse, Villain, Dog.
O rarely base!
  Cæsar. Good Queene, let vs intreat you.
  Cleo. O *Cæsar,* what a wounding shame is this,
That thou vouchsafing heere to visit me,   3390

3386 Soule-lesse,] ∼ ‸ POPE1+

3380 **Mine**] RANN (ed. 1791–): "My followers."

3383-7 **Oh . . . base**] FURNESS (ed. 1907) translates STAHR (1864, p. 270): "This little comedy, pre-arranged and agreed upon, between her and her faithful treasurer is a masterstroke of the bold lady, which completely attains the purpose for which it was designed." Furness agrees that no excuses are needed for "simulated rage." WILSON (ed. 1950) notes the "put-up job between Cleo. and Sel." as starting at 3368. Those who may not believe in the collusion do not comment except for VERPLANCK (1877, p. 321), who finds no evidence in Plutarch's account (see p. 454) for a prearrangement. There of course need be none.

3384-6 **What . . . wings**] DEIGHTON (ed. 1891): "What (said as she advances to strike him), do you retreat before me? you will be ready enough, I warrant, to desert me; *Go back* being used in the literal and the figurative sense." CASE (ed. 1906): "Said as Seleucus recoils before Cleopatra's threatening looks. I very much question the existence of any figurative meaning in *Go back*, line [3385], such as 'succumb', 'get the worst' (Schmidt [1874]). . . . The whole equals this: So you go back, do you? yes, you shall do that, yet find no escape from the look that dismays you."

3386 **Soule-lesse, Villain**] RIDLEY (ed. 1954), omitting the comma: "The crescendo of invective [rises] from a creature despicable but still human, through something barely human, to something not human at all." See n. 1057.

3387 **rarely**] MINSHEU (1617): "Singular." See also 2518, "rare" (452, 918, 932), "Rarer" (3147).

3389-3400 **O . . . mediation**] NORMAN (1958, p. 15) compares Daniel's *Cleopatra*, ll. 684-94 (ed. Grosart, 1885), holding "that while Shakespeare versified North's translation independently of Daniel, he has modified it in petty but telling ways suggested by Daniel. He prefers, for example, the rhythm of Daniel's sentence order in 'what a wounding shame is this'; he adapts the word *toys* to his own use; he borrows the verb *mediate* and perhaps echoes Daniel's word *Lord* (line 686) with *lordliness* (line [3391]); and he follows Daniel in mentioning Caesar's wife before his sister." For the 1594 *Cleopatra*, see p. 552; for Plutarch's version, see p. 454.

3390-4 **That . . . Enuy**] BLUMHOF (ed. 1870): The break in the grammatical construction—the absence of a finite verb for *thou*—reflects Cleopatra's agitated state

Doing the Honour of thy Lordlinesse
To one so meeke, that mine owne Seruant should
Parcell the summe of my disgraces, by
Addition of his Enuy. Say (good *Cæsar*)
That I some Lady trifles haue reseru'd,   3395
Immoment toyes, things of such Dignitie
As we greet moderne Friends withall, and say
Some Nobler token I haue kept apart
For *Liuia* and *Octauia*, to induce
Their mediation, must I be vnfolded   3400

3392 meeke] weak mTHEO1 *and* THIRLBY *conj. apud* mTBY4, THEO1-THEO4; mean
mTBY3 *conj. and* mCAP2, GAR, CAP, RANN
3393 disgraces] disgrace OXF1
3395 haue] had v1778, RANN
3400 mediation] meditation F3, F4

---

of mind. But the construction may be absolute; see FRANZ §660.
   3392 **meeke**] Despite the general acceptance of *meeke*, THEOBALD (ed. 1733): "Surely,
Cleopatra must be bantering *Cæsar*, to call herself *meek*. . . . I correct [to *weak*] i.e.
so shrunk in Fortune and Power: vanquish'd, and spoil'd of her Kingdom. Besides, she
might allude to her bodily Decay." CAPELL (1779 [1774], 1:50–1): "'*Meek*' is corrupt.
. . . *Weak* is ambiguous, and therefore improper; and '*mean*', a word as near it in characters, bids fairer to be the true one, from it's opposition to '*lordliness*' in the same sentence." The parallel passage in Plutarch (see p. 454: "poore wretche, and caitife creature,
brought into this pitiefull & miserable estate") is inconclusive.
   3393 **Parcell**] COTGRAVE (1611, Parcelé): "*Peecemealed; cut, or made, into parcels.*"
JOHNSON (1755), citing this instance: "To make up into a mass"; IDEM (*apud* STEEVENS,
ed. 1773): "In vulgar language, *to bundle up.*" DAVIES (1783, 2:360) and most others
settle for "adding another item to." See also n. 2188.
   3394 **Enuy**] BULLOKAR (1616, *Malignitie*): "Spitefulnesse . . . malice."
   3396 **Immoment**] CAWDREY (1604, moment): "Weight, or importance." JOHNSON
(1755): "Trifling; of no importance or value." The *OED* credits Sh. with the first and
only usage in English.
   Dignitie] See n. 288.
   3397 **moderne**] CAWDREY (1604): "Of our time." So dictionaries until JOHNSON (1755):
"In *Shakespeare*, vulgar; mean; common." Most commentators, avoiding negative connotations, prefer HANMER's (ed. 1744, 6:Glossary) "Common, ordinary."
   withall] See n. 253.
   3398 **Nobler token**] MACCALLUM (1910, p. 435): "If we imagine she was keeping back
her regalia for this last display [her death], we can understand why Shakespeare inserted
the 'nobler token' in addition to the unconsidered trifles which she was quite ready to
own she had reserved, and of which indeed in Shakespeare though not in Plutarch she
had already made express mention as uninventoried." IDEM (p. 435, n. 1): "It is a rather
striking coincidence that Jodelle, too, heightens Plutarch's account of the treasures she

With one that I haue bred: The Gods! it smites me
Beneath the fall I haue. Prythee go hence,
Or I shall shew the Cynders of my spirits   (zz1^{vb})
Through th'Ashes of my chance: Wer't thou a man,
Thou would'st haue mercy on me.   3405
    Cæsar. Forbeare *Seleucus.*
    Cleo. Be it known, that we the greatest are mis-thoght

3401 With] By ROWE3-JOHN1, v1773; Of CAP
      The] Ye mTBY4 *conj.*, mCOL1, COL2-SING2, COL3, KTLY, COL4
3402 *To* Seleucus. JOHN1+ (*subst.*)
3403 spirits] spirit mTBY2 *conj.*, mCOL1, KTLY, COL4, HUD2
3404 my chance] mischance HAN1, COL2, COL3, COL4; my glance INGLEBY (1875,
p. 158) *conj.*, HUD2
3405–6 *One verse line* v1793+
3406 *Exit* SELEUCUS. CAP+

---

has retained, and includes among them the crown jewels and royal robes. [Quotes *Cléopâtre
captive*, Act 3 (ed. Gohin, 1925, pp. 75, 77).]"
    3399 *Liuia*] Livia Drusilla, divorced by Nero, married Octavius in 39 B.C. See PAULY,
13:900–24 (37); *OCD*.
    3400 **vnfolded**] COTGRAVE (1611, Desplié): "*Displayed . . . vnfoulded; manifested,
made plaine, layed open.*"
    3401 **With**] For *with* in the sense of *by* in connection with a person used or serving
as a means, see FRANZ §535.
    The Gods] COLLIER (1852, p. 482): "As *the* was often formerly written *ye*, the article
was mistaken for it in this instance." DELIUS (ed. 1856) and DYCE (ed. 1857), however,
find instances of the exclamation with *the*, so spelled, in *Cor.* 2.3.60 (1444), 4.1.37 (2477),
Tro. 4.2.88 (2346), *Cym.* 1.1.123 (145), *Lr.* 2.4.171 (1452), and *Ant.* 3465.
    3403–4 **Or . . . my chance**] See textual notes and conj., p. 360.
    3404 **Wer't . . . man**] HEYSE (ed. 1867) and only a few others hold that Cleopatra
implies that Seleucus is a eunuch.
    3407–10 RINEHART (1972, p. 85) compares Cleopatra and Queen Elizabeth in their
awareness "of their public characters as queens," quoting (n. 5) from "Elizabeth's reply
to a deputation from Parliament, 12 November 1586, urging her to carry out the death
sentence on Mary, Queen of Scots: 'For we Princes are set as it were upon stages, in the
sight and view of all the world. The least spot is soon spied in our garments, a blemish
quickly noted in our doings. It behoveth us therefore to be careful that our proceedings
be just and honourable' [Chamberlin, *Sayings of Queen Elizabeth*, 1923, p. 242, quoting (subst.) Camden, *History of Elizabeth*, 1688, p. 364]." See also nn. 77–155, 603.
    3407 **mis-thoght**] Following BAILEY (1730), JOHNSON (1755, *Misthink*), citing this
instance: "To think ill; to think wrong." Most commentators, beginning with SCHMIDT
(1875), prefer the latter, i.e., "misjudge." A few, beginning with CLARK & WRIGHT (ed.
1864, Glossary), prefer the former. Slightly more, beginning with KITTREDGE (ed. 1941),
follow Johnson in giving both meanings. The spelling *thoght* is doubtless due to the
full line, as 2835.

For things that others do: and when we fall,
We answer others merits, in our name
Are therefore to be pittied.   3410
  Cæsar. Cleopatra,
Not what you haue reseru'd, nor what acknowledg'd
Put we i'th'Roll of Conquest: still bee't yours,
Bestow it at your pleasure, and beleeue
Cæsars no Merchant, to make prize with you   3415
Of things that Merchants sold. Therefore be cheer'd,
Make not your thoughts your prisons: No deere Queen,
For we intend so to dispose you, as
Your selfe shall giue vs counsell: Feede, and sleepe:
Our care and pitty is so much vpon you,   3420
That we remaine your Friend, and so adieu.
  Cleo. My Master, and my Lord.
  Cæsar. Not so: Adieu.   *Flourish.*
                                    Exeunt Cæsar, and his Traine.

3409 answer . . . name] answer others merits, in our Names ROWE, POPE, THEO;
pander others merits with our names, HAN1; answer. Others' merits, in our names
WARBURTON *conj. apud* LOUNSBURY (1906, p. 360), WARB; answer others' merits in our
names; HEATH (1765, p. 467) *conj.*, JOHN1, v1773, v1778, RANN; answer others' merits
in our name, mTYR *conj.*, MAL, v1793+
  3410 Are] And HAN2, COL2
  3413 we] me ROWE, POPE
  3415 prize] price ANON. *conj. apud* CAM1, RID, CAM3, SIS
  3417 prisons] poison HAN1; prison HAN2, KTLY, HUD2
  3423 *Flourish.*] *Om.* F2-KNT1, HUD1, SING2, KTLY
  3424 *Cæsar*] *Ad.* DOLABELLA CAP

  3409 JOHNSON (ed. 1765) and the majority of commentators: We *"answer in our
own names for the merits* [i.e., faults] *of others."* DELIUS (ed. 1856) and a somewhat
smaller group: We answer faults committed by others in our name. KNOWLES (privately):
"[Those] in our name [i.e., we the greatest] are therefore to be pitied." See textual notes
and conj., p. 360.
    merits] JOHNSON (ed. 1765): "In this place taken in an ill sense, for actions *merit-
ing* censure."
  3415 **make prize**] Earlier commentators, beginning with STAUNTON (ed. 1859,
3:Glossary), gloss as *"rate"* or—WORDSWORTH (ed. 1883)—as *"estimation"*; a somewhat
larger number of more recent ones follow KITTREDGE's (ed. 1941) "haggle."
  3417 **Make . . . prisons**] JOHNSON (ed. 1765) and the others: *"Be not a prisoner
in imagination, when in reality you are free."*
  3418 **dispose**] See n. 2976.
  3423 **Not so**] BLUMHOF (ed. 1870): This comment refers either to Cleopatra's attempt
to show submissiveness, which Caesar gallantly prevents, or to his rejection of the titles

Cleo. He words me Gyrles, he words me,   3425
That I should not be Noble to my selfe.
But hearke thee *Charmian.*
Iras. Finish good Lady, the bright day is done,
And we are for the darke.
Cleo. Hye thee againe,   3430
I haue spoke already, and it is prouided,
Go put it to the haste.
Char. Madam, I will.

                        Enter Dolabella.

Dol. Where's the Queene?   3435
Char. Behold sir.

3425–7 *Verse lines ending* not . . . *Charmian.* HAN1, CAP+
3425 SCENE V. POPE, WARB, JOHN1; SCENE IV. HAN1
3431 spoke] spoken COL, HUD1, WH1
3433 *Exit* Charm. THEO1-JOHN1, v1773; *exit after* 3436 CAP, v1778+
3435–7 *One verse line* v1793+ (−HUD1)
3435 Where's] Where is POPE1-KIT1 (−HUD1)
3436 *Char.*] Iras. mF4Q *conj.* (*erroneously at* 3576) *and* HAN1

(3422) with which he has been addressed.

3425 **words**] WALKER (1957, p. 99) cites this as an example of "words that he [Sh.] coined and his strategic use of figurative language for dramatic ends. . . . The Oxford Dictionary describes this use of 'word' as obsolete and rare, glossing as = 'to ply or urge with words' [*v.* 3a] and citing only this instance. Onions [1911], following Schmidt, more plausibly glosses as 'to flatter with words'. This may be a Latinism (*dare verba* = to flatter, deceive) [already noted by WORDSWORTH (ed. 1883) and cited by KITTREDGE (ed. 1941) as *verba facere*] and . . . 'words' in *Cymbeline*, I.iv.[16–17 (330–1)] . . . possibly means 'flatters' too, though the Oxford Dictionary cites it as a nonce use, meaning 'to represent as in words', and Onions glosses as 'to speak of.'"

3430 **Hye . . . againe**] See n. 980.

3431 THEOBALD (ed. 1733): "She has spoke for the Asp, and it is provided, tho' she says not a Word of it in direct Terms." CAPELL (1779 [1774], 1:51): "Her further directions about it, are convey'd in a whisper [3427]."

3432 **the haste**] For the use of the definite article for purposes of emphasis, see FRANZ §259.

3434 *Enter Dolabella*] WILSON (ed. 1950): "He goes out with Caes., overhears his plans, and returns to tell them."

3435 See n. 3337.

3436 See textual notes at 3433 for added SD. RIDLEY (ed. 1954): "Another example of Elizabethan exit, not easy to indicate, as the discrepancy between Theobald [ed. 1733] and Capell [ed. 1768] interestingly shows. Charmian begins to move off on *Madam, I will,* and meets Dolabella on her way to the door."

Cleo. Dolabella.

Dol. Madam, as thereto sworne, by your command
(Which my loue makes Religion to obey)
I tell you this: *Cæsar* through Syria   3440
Intends his iourney, and within three dayes,
You with your Children will he send before,
Make your best vse of this. I haue perform'd
Your pleasure, and my promise.

Cleo. Dolabella, I shall remaine your debter.   3445

Dol. I your Seruant:
Adieu good Queene, I must attend on *Cæsar.*   *Exit*
Cleo. Farewell, and thankes.
Now *Iras*, what think'st thou?
Thou, an Egyptian Puppet shall be shewne   3450
In Rome aswell as I: Mechanicke Slaues
With greazie Aprons, Rules, and Hammers shall
Vplift vs to the view. In their thicke breathes,
Ranke of grosse dyet, shall we be enclowded,

3444–6 *Verse lines ending Dolabella*, . . . servant. POPE1+
3448–9 *One verse line* ROWE1+ (−CAP)
3450 shall] shalt F2-v1821, KNT1-COL2, SING2-WH2, RID-CAM3

3438–45 WILSON (ed. 1950): "Based on Plut[arch; see p. 454]. . . . But not led
up to in the play, unless a scene with Dolabella has been cut." See n. 3110. NORMAN
(1958, p. 16) compares *Cleopatra* (ll. 1090–7, ed. Grosart, 1885): "The paraphrase of
Daniel's 'I must die his debter' and Dolabella's allusion to his 'love' alone hint that Shakespeare had Daniel's scene in mind." For the 1594 *Cleopatra*, see p. 562.

3445 GRANVILLE-BARKER (1930; 1946, 1:402): Cleopatra "makes his name sound beautiful in his ears (it is a name that can be lingered on), perhaps gives him her hand to
kiss . . . and he goes."

3449 thou] WILSON (ed. 1950): "Emphatic. She knows Charmian's mind."

3450 Puppet] JOHNSON (1755), citing this instance (but mistakenly as occurring in
Cym.): "A word of contempt." See also *OED* (3c): "A living personator in dramatic action." Most commentators follow DELIUS (ed. 1856) in stressing the allusion to Elizabethan acting figures on moving pageants or drawn platforms.

3451–3 Mechanicke . . . view] See nn. 2795, 3264.

3451 Mechanicke] See n. 2544.

   Slaues] See n. 449.

3453 Vplift . . . view] BLUMHOF (ed. 1870) compares 2792 and 3264–5.

3454 Ranke] COTGRAVE (1611, Ranci): "*Mustie, fustie . . . tainted, stale, putrified
. . . stinking, vnsauorie, ill-smelling.*"

   of] I.e., from. For the interchangeability, see FRANZ §509.

3455 drinke] JOHNSON (1755): "To suck up; to absorb."

And forc'd to drinke their vapour.   3455
  Iras. The Gods forbid.
  Cleo. Nay, 'tis most certaine *Iras*: sawcie Lictors
Will catch at vs like Strumpets, and scald Rimers
Ballads vs out a Tune. The quicke Comedians
Extemporally will stage vs, and present   3460
Our Alexandrian Reuels: *Anthony*
Shall be brought drunken forth, and I shall see
Some squeaking *Cleopatra* Boy my greatnesse
I'th'posture of a Whore.
  Iras. O the good Gods!   3465

3458 scald] stall'd HAN1
3459 Ballads vs] Ballad us F2-ARD2; Ballad 's EVNS
3461 Alexandrian] Alexandria F2-F4
3463 squeaking *Cleopatra* Boy] speaking-*Cleopatra*-Boy F2, F3; speaking *Cleopatra*-Boy F4; speaking *Cleopatra* Boy ROWE
3465–6 *Om.* RANN

3457 **Lictors**] COOPER (1565): "Sergeants or like ministers to execute corporall punishment. . . . They caried in their handes a bundel of roddes bounde with an axe, therewith to doe execution at the chiefe officers commaundement." FURNESS (ed. 1907): "Lear (IV, vi, 166 [2605]) attributes to the 'beadle' that which, I think, Cleopatra attributes, in imagination, to the saucy lictors." WILSON (ed. 1950): "Sh. thinks of beadles, who officially dealt with 'strumpets.'" See PAULY, 13:507–18; *OCD*, Lictores.

3458 **catch**] MINSHEU (1617): "*Snatch.*"

  scald] KERSEY (1702, *Scall*): "*Scurf on the head.*" BAILEY (1730): "[*Q. d.* a scaly Head] a scurfy, scabbed Head." Here, a general term of opprobrium: "Mean . . . contemptible" (*OED, a.*[1] and *sb.*[5] 2).

3459 **Ballads . . . Tune**] STERNFELD (1963, p. 239): "The model for Cleopatra's phrase again derives from Horace [*Satires* 2.1.46] . . . 'insignis [. . .] cantabitur.'" The *OED* credits Sh. with the first use of the transitive verb.

  Ballads] FURNESS (ed. 1907) refers to ABBOTT §338 for "this superfluous *s.*" Abbott's section heading, however, is "S final misprinted," where he implies that a comma was sometimes misread as the letter. Citing this instance, he qualifies: "Sometimes (even without the possibility of mistake for a comma) the -*s* is inserted." For the possibility of -*s* as the plural inflectional form, see FRANZ §155.

  a] Commentators interpret not as the indefinite article but as the worn-down form of the preposition *of*.

  quicke] MINSHEU (1617): "*Liuelie.*" JOHNSON (ed. 1765) and most others stress "gay inventive."

3463 **squeaking *Cleopatra* Boy**] All commentators agree that the phrase refers to the boy actors. There is, however, some uncertainty about the word class of *Boy*. Most take it as a verb, as does the *OED*, citing this instance. See textual notes and conj., p. 360.

Cleo. Nay that's certaine.

Iras. Ile neuer see't? for I am sure mine Nailes

Are stronger then mine eyes.

Cleo. Why that's the way to foole their preparation,   (zz2ᵃ)

And to conquer their most absurd intents.   3470

Enter Charmian.

Now *Charmian.*

Shew me my Women like a Queene: Go fetch

My best Attyres. I am againe for *Cidnus,*

To meete *Marke Anthony.* Sirra *Iras,* go   3475

3466 that's] this is GAR, CAPN
3467 I] *Om.* ROWE3
        mine] my F2+ (−ALEX, EVNS)
3468-70, 3472 *Three verse lines ending* way . . . conquer . . . *Charmian.* ROWE1+
3470 to] *Om.* F2-F4
        absurd] assur'd mTHEO2 (21 Feb. 1729, [fol. 42]) *conj.,* THEO, HAN1, CAP, COL2,
HUD, COL4
3471 *After* 3472 ROWE1-SING2, COL3, KTLY, HAL, COL4

3467 **mine Nailes**] See p. 373.

3470 **absurd**] THEOBALD (21 Feb. 1729, [fol. 42ʳ]), although finding F1 "plausible,"
emends to *assur'd*: "*I.e.* the purposes yᵗ they are most determin'd to put in Practise;
make themselves most sure of accomplishing." UPTON (1746, p. 296) points out that
absurd, following the Latin sense, means "harsh, grating," but early dictionaries give only
the customary meaning—e.g., CAWDREY (1604): "Foolish, irksome." JOHNSON (ed. 1765):
"The design certainly appeared *absurd* enough to *Cleopatra,* both as she thought it unreasonable in itself, and as she knew it would fail." See conj., p. 360.

3473-5 **Shew . . . Anthony**] FURNESS (ed. 1907, p. 515) finds a "faint fleeting similarity" with Daniel's *Cleopatra,* ll. 1473-84 (ed. Grosart, 1885). For the 1594 *Cleopatra,*
see p. 572. SEATON (1946, p. 223) compares Rev. 21:2: "Prepared as a bride trimmed
[see also n. 3609] for her husband."

3474 *Cidnus*] See n. 897-8. F1's *Cidrus* is regarded by WILSON (ed. 1950, p. 126)
as a minim error "involving *a, r, u, n.*"

3475 **Sirra Iras**] DYCE (ed. 1866): Eds. "wrongly put a comma between these words."
BLUMHOF (ed. 1870), defending the comma, holds that *Sirra* is probably a general exclamation, like "go someone," then, specifically, Iras. It is difficult, however, to determine
the intent in early eds. whose punctuation is unsystematic.

Sirra] MINSHEU (1617): "*A contemptuous word, ironically compounded of* Sir, *and*
a, ha, *as much to say,* ah sir, *or* sir boye, *&c.*" Minsheu's (and *OED*'s) etymology may
be open to doubt—although none better has been proposed—and the term is a relatively neutral address to persons of the lowest social rank (as well as the term they use
to address one another). See also 975, 1064. Of interest here is its application to a woman
and to one who is not of a low social rank. The only such instance in Sh., it must be

(Now Noble *Charmian*, wee'l dispatch indeede,)
And when thou hast done this chare, Ile giue thee leaue
To play till Doomesday: bring our Crowne, and all.
A noise within.
Wherefore's this noise?   3480

Enter a Guardsman.

  Gards. Heere is a rurall Fellow,
That will not be deny'de your Highnesse presence,
He brings you Figges.
  Cleo. Let him come in.   *Exit Guardsman.* 3485
What poore an Instrument
May do a Noble deede: he brings me liberty:
My Resolution's plac'd, and I haue nothing
Of woman in me: Now from head to foote
I am Marble constant: now the fleeting Moone   3490

3479 *Exit* IRAS. CAP, MAL, v1793-ALEX, SIS, EVNS (*subst.*); *Exeunt Charmian and Iras.*
RIDb, ARD2
3480 Wherefore's] Wherefore F3-v1773 (−CAP)
3485–6 *One verse line* ROWE1+ (−HUD1)
3486 What poore an] How poore an F2-v1773, v1793, v1803, SING, COL2, HUD1; What
a poor v1778, RANN, KTLY

---

interpreted affectively. Less convincing are STEEVENS (ed. 1793): "From hence it appears
that *Sirrah*, an appellation generally addressed to males, was equally applicable to females"; and ORGER (1890, p. 102) alone: *Sirra* "cannot . . . be spoken to Iras, on account of her sex, and her mistress's affection"; he conjectures *Swift*.
  3482 **rurall**] CAWDREY (1604): "Clownish, vplandish, or churlish, and vnmannerly."
MINSHEU (1617, Uplandish): "Rusticke *or* Clowne, *because the* people *that dwell among*
Mountaines, *are seuered from the* Ciuilitie *of* Cities." See also n. 3492.
  3486 **What . . . an**] MALONE (*apud* BOSWELL, ed. 1821), rejecting STEEVENS's (ed.
1793) rejection of *What* as "nonsensical": "We have many inversions equally harsh in
these plays." For Sh.'s use of transposed articles and this particular instance, see ABBOTT
§422; for the letter "A . . . pleonastically used," IDEM §85, which adds that "'what'
is used for 'how.'" FRANZ (§275) refers to the positioning of the indefinite article after
the attributive adjective. See n. 236.
  3488 **plac'd**] COTGRAVE (1611, Placé): "*Seated, lodged, settled, fixed, planted.*"
  3490 **Marble constant**] See n. 383.
  3490–1 **now . . . mine**] WARBURTON (ed. 1747): "Alluding to the *Egyptian* devotion
paid to the moon [as] *Isis.*" STEEVENS (ed. 1773): "Cleopatra having said, *I have nothing
of woman in me*, added, by way of amplification, that she had not *even the changes of
disposition peculiar to the sex, and which sometimes happen as often as those of the moon.*"
  3490 **fleeting**] KERSEY (1702, flit): "*Remove from one place to another.*" IDEM (Flit-

331

No Planet is of mine.

     Enter Guardsman, and Clowne.

 Guards. This is the man.
 Cleo. Auoid, and leaue him.   *Exit Guardsman.*
Hast thou the pretty worme of Nylus there,   3495
That killes and paines not?
 Clow. Truly I haue him: but I would not be the par-
tie that should desire you to touch him, for his byting is
immortall: those that doe dye of it, doe seldome or neuer recouer.   3500
 Cleo. Remember'st thou any that haue dyed on't?
 Clow. Very many, men and women too. I heard of
one of them no longer then yesterday, a very honest woman, but something giuen to lye, as a woman should not
do, but in the way of honesty, how she dyed of the by-   3505
ting of it, what paine she felt: Truely, she makes a verie

3491, 3493–4 *Arranged as verse lines, thus:* 3491 *and* 3493, 3494 v1793-CAM3, SIS+;
3491, 3493–4 ALEX
 3498 that] *Om.* POPE2-v1773 (–HAN1, CAP)

---

ting): *"Uncertain."* See *OED*, Fleeting *ppl. a.* 2 and Flitting *ppl. a.* 2.
 3492–3530 For Plutarch's account of the meeting, see p. 455.
 3492 *Clowne*] MINSHEU (1617): *"Clumperton, or Peasant."* See also n. 3482.
 3494 **Auoid**] FRANZ (§252): *"Be gone."* See n. 2788.
 3495 **pretty**] *OED* (4b): "Frequently applied in a coaxing or soothing way, esp. to children." Plutarch uses the adjective in describing the "two litle pretie bytings in her arme,
scant to be discerned" (p. 456), which SKEAT (1880, p. 228) inaccurately glosses as "minute."
 worme] JOHNSON (ed. 1765): *"Worm* is the Teutonick word for *serpent."* Although
early dictionaries define as "insect" (KERSEY, 1702) or "creeping Insect" (BAILEY, 1721),
Sh. and his contemporaries often prefer this more archaic but poetic form. See also 3507,
3509, et passim. JONES (ed. 1977): "In this scene . . . *worm* has three applications:
(1) Snake, asp [3495]; (2) the male sexual organ [3507]; (3) earth-worm [3522]."
 3499 **immortall**] The few who comment generally agree with DELIUS (ed. 1856) that
this is a rustic blunder for "mortal." But ANON. (1790, *Gent. Mag.*, p. 126): "He means,
that though by the bite of the asp the mortal scene is closed, yet by it we become immortal; so, figuratively, he says his biting is immortal."
 3503 **honest**] See n. 542.
 3504 **something**] See n. 2673.
 3504–5 **giuen . . . honesty**] WILSON (ed. 1950): "Prob. a double quibble intended."
IDEM (Glossary): "(*a*) truthfulness, (*b*) chastity." *Lye*, of course, means "tell falsehoods"
as well as "have sexual intercourse."

good report o'th'worme: but he that wil beleeue all that
they say, shall neuer be saued by halfe that they do: but
this is most falliable, the Worme's an odde Worme.

Cleo. Get thee hence, farewell.   3510

Clow. I wish you all ioy of the Worme.

Cleo. Farewell.

Clow. You must thinke this (looke you,) that the
Worme will do his kinde.

Cleo. I, I, farewell.   3515

Clow. Looke you, the Worme is not to bee trusted,
but in the keeping of wise people: for indeede, there is
no goodnesse in the Worme.

Cleo. Take thou no care, it shall be heeded.

Clow. Very good: giue it nothing I pray you, for it   3520
is not worth the feeding.

Cleo. Will it eate me?

Clow. You must not think I am so simple, but I know
the diuell himselfe will not eate a woman: I know, that
a woman is a dish for the Gods, if the diuell dresse her   3525

3507–8 all . . . halfe] half . . . all WARBURTON *conj. apud* THEO1, THEO1, HAN1,
WARB

3509 odde] adder mCOL1, COL2

3516–18, 3520–1, 3523–8, 3530 *Given to Cleopatra* F2

3519 thou] *Om.* F2-POPE2, HAN1

3507–8 **but . . . do**] WARBURTON (*apud* THEOBALD, ed. 1733): "This must be read
the contrary way, and *all* and *half* change places with one another." Following HEATH
(1765, p. 468), STEEVENS (ed. 1773) and most others: "Probably Shakespeare designed
that confusion which the critick would disentangle." WILSON (ed. 1950): "He seems to
have been listening to sermons on Salvation by Faith, not Works." FISCH (1970, p. 64):
"The man who believed what the woman said of the serpent (worm) but could not be
saved by what she had done is of course Adam; just as Cleopatra is Eve."

3509 **falliable**] A blunder for "infallible." See n. 3499. The spelling *ia* may be an
error, a dialectlike form (especially after *ll*), or a form derived by analogy with forms
like *amiable, malleable,* and, perhaps of importance here, *unreconciliable* (see 3164).
For suffixes in general, see FRANZ §93; for *-able,* see IDEM §124.

   odde] See n. 2429.

3514 **do his kinde**] JOHNSON (ed. 1765): "Act according to his nature."

3524 **the . . . woman**] No source has been found for the Clown's comment.

3525 **dresse**] BLUMHOF (ed. 1870) detects a play on the culinary sense of preparing
and on adorning. Those who follow prefer the first sense, with WILSON (ed. 1950) adding "for cooking (in hell)."

not. But truly, these same whorson diuels doe the Gods
great harme in their women: for in euery tenne that they
make, the diuels marre fiue.

    Cleo. Well, get thee gone, farewell.

    Clow. Yes forsooth: I wish you ioy o'th'worm.   *Exit* 3530

    Cleo. Giue me my Robe, put on my Crowne, I haue
Immortall longings in me. Now no more
The iuyce of Egypts Grape shall moyst this lip.
Yare, yare, good *Iras*; quicke: Me thinkes I heare
Anthony call: I see him rowse himselfe   3535 (zz2ᵇ
To praise my Noble Act. I heare him mock
The lucke of *Cæsar*, which the Gods giue men
To excuse their after wrath. Husband, I come:
Now to that name, my Courage proue my Title.
I am Fire, and Ayre; my other Elements   3540

3528 fiue] nine mCOL1, COL2
3531 SCENE VI. POPE, WARB, JOHN1; SCENE V. HAN1
    Re-enter IRAS CAP, MAL, v1793-ALEX, SIS, EVNS (*subst.*); *Re-enter Charmian and Iras* RIDb, ARD2
3533 this] his F3-ROWE3
3535 call] calls ROWE2

3526 **whorson**] JOHNSON (1755): "A bastard. It is generally used in a ludicrous dislike."

3527 **their**] DELIUS (ed. 1856): A possessive referring to the women of the gods. FURNESS (ed. 1907): "'Their' is here used ethically": i.e., as a colloquialism. Compare n. 1363–4.

3530 **forsooth**] MINSHEU (1617): "Truely." BAILEY's (1721) "Interjection of Contempt or Derision" is not followed here by most others, who prefer SCHMIDT's (1874) "used by low persons as a phrase of honest asseveration."

3531–3 For Plutarch, see p. 455.

3531–2 **I . . . me**] CRANE (1951, p. 180): Cleopatra "is capable of picking up his [Clown's] line [quotes 'but . . . immortall' (3497–9)], and making of it her own exquisite [line]."

3534 **Yare**] See nn. 924, 1905. OBERTELLO (1955, p. 697) alone: Iras is slow in attiring Cleopatra, for she has paused already to put her hand in the basket and has been bitten. See n. 3544.

    Me thinkes] See n. 1673.

3537 **lucke of Cæsar**] See also 992.

3537–8 **Gods . . . wrath**] KITTREDGE (ed. 1941) best summarizes those who (beginning with DELIUS [ed. 1856]) explain: "That a man's constant and (as it were) unbridled good fortune makes the gods envious and leads to his sudden downfall is an ancient idea. It persists in a modified form in the feeling that too much good luck is dangerous."

3538 **Husband, I come**] See n. 3473–5.

3540–1 **I . . . life**] DEIGHTON (ed. 1891): "I leave to be eaten by worms." CASE (ed.

I giue to baser life. So, haue you done?
Come then, and take the last warmth of my Lippes.
Farewell kinde *Charmian*, *Iras*, long farewell.
Haue I the Aspicke in my lippes? Dost fall?

3541 to] no F3, F4
3543 Iras *falls and dies.* CAP, MAL, v1793+ (*subst.*)

1906): "'Fire and air' are that part of Cleopatra which she supposes to escape through death to immortal life: her other elements she leaves with the *baser* conditions she is quitting, baser whether compared with the new life or with death, by which that is to be nobly attained." COOK (1947, no. 9) notes that of the "Aristotelian elements here mentioned, air and fire have the special property of rising, earth and water of falling. Air and fire are metaphorical for the soul which will rise to Antony . . . earth and water, for the body which will be interred in the ground ('baser life')." LLOYD (1960, p. 327) quotes Plutarch's *Moralia* (tr. Holland, 1603; 1657, p. 1079): "There is a transformation as well of bodies as soules: and like as we may observe, that of earth is ingendred water, of water aire, and of aire fire, whiles the nature of the substance still mounteth on high: even so the better soules are changed, first from men to Heroes or Demi-gods, and afterwards from them to Daemons, and of Daemons some few after long time, being well refined and purified by vertue, came to participate the divination of the gods." FARNHAM (1950, p. 171) compares Daniel's "Base life" (see p. 575). HANKINS (1978, p. 41): Cleopatra "echoes" Cicero's idea "that the human soul is made entirely of air and fire, lacking any traces of earth and water." See also nn. 1384, 3308.

3543 *Charmian, Iras*] CASE (ed. 1906): "So the folio; with the result in sound of slow, unbroken movement befitting farewells, and in sense, of uniting both women in the long adieu. The usual separative pointing, *Charmian*; *Iras*, gains nothing but a paltry contrast of the halves of the line."

long farewell] Despite CASE's (ed. 1906) paraphrase as "long adieu," and the absence of further comment, the sense is more likely "for a long time."

3544 STEEVENS (ed. 1773): "Iras must be supposed to have applied an asp to her arm while her mistress was settling her dress, or I know not why she should fall so soon." CAPELL (1779 [1774], 1:53–4) commenting on 3568: "Iras, either in setting down the basket, or in leaning over it to take her farewel, gets a bite from an asp; and being it's first bite, when it's poison was most vigorous, she dies almost instantly." ANON. (1790, *Gent. Mag.*, p. 127) offers another singular variation: "I apprehend a mistake in the stage-direction,—that it should be, *Applying the asp to Iras*, in order to see the effect of the poison, and the pain she had to encounter in death." MALONE (ed. 1790): "Are my lips poison'd by the aspick, that my kiss has destroyed thee?" DELIUS (ed. 1856), rejecting Steevens, feels that Iras dies of grief. CASE (ed. 1906), agreeing, compares the "improbability" of Enobarbus's death. FURNESS (ed. 1907) names the cause of death a "broken heart." He is followed by KITTREDGE (ed. 1941), but rejected by WILSON (ed. 1950): "If so, Sh. would surely have given her an 'aside' to make that clear. Cf. Enob.'s death in 4.9 [2694 ff.] and [IDEM on 3552] . . . *This* i.e. the death of Iras. Implying surely a self-sought death."

Aspicke] MINSHEU (1617): "*Aspe*, is but a little, but a most venomous serpent,

If thou, and Nature can so gently part,   3545
The stroke of death is as a Louers pinch,
Which hurts, and is desir'd. Dost thou lye still?
If thus thou vanishest, thou tell'st the world,
It is not worth leaue-taking.
    Char. Dissolue thicke clowd, & Raine, that I may say   3550
The Gods themselues do weepe.
    Cleo. This proues me base:
If she first meete the Curled *Anthony,*
Hee'l make demand of her, and spend that kisse
Which is my heauen to haue. Come thou mortal wretch,   3555
With thy sharpe teeth this knot intrinsicate,

3548 vanishest] vanquishest ROWE2, ROWE3
3549 Iras *dies.* POPE1-JOHN1, v1773, v1778, RANN
3553 first meete] proves F2-F4; approves ROWE
     Curled] cursed F4
3555 thou] *Om.* POPE1-CAP, v1793, v1803

---

whose venome is deadly, mortall, and vncurable, except you cut off the member poisoned. . . . Also more of the nature of the Aspicke in *Plyn*[y]: *lib*: 8: *cap*: 28 [23 in tr. Holland, 1601]." MALONE (ed. 1790): "Poison" (from the aspic). PEARCE (1953, no. 17), referring to Pliny, *Natural History* 8.33, is very much alone (despite the allusions to the aspic) in identifying the creature as the basilisk: "It is the sight of Death in Cleopatra's face, the basilisk glance and touch, which kills Iras."

3546-7 See n. 110.

3552 **This**] KITTREDGE (ed. 1941): "The fact that Iras died first."

3553-4 **If . . . kisse**] JOHNSON (ed. 1765): "He will enquire of her concerning me, and kiss her for giving him intelligence." RIDLEY (ed. 1954): "Shakespeare's Cleopatra knew her Antony better than Johnson did." WALTER (ed. 1969) specifies: "He will embrace her and waste on her his kiss."

3554 **spend**] See n. 3121.

3555 **wretch**] SCHMIDT (1875): "Used as a word of tenderness (mixed with pity)." He lists only two other instances in Sh.: *Rom.* 1.3.44 (392) and *Oth.* 3.3.90 (1691). For the application to "animals, birds, or insects," see *OED, sb.* 2d.

3556 **knot intrinsicate**] WARBURTON (ed. 1747): "The expression is fine; it signifies a hidden, secret [*intrinsecus*] knot, as that which ties soul and body together." Later critics disagree. EDWARDS (1765, pp. 184-5): Sh. "uses *intrinsecate* for *intricate, intangled,* or *tied in hard knots*: [quotes *Lr.* 2.2.80-1 (1147-8), first cited by THEOBALD (30 Dec. 1729, [fol. 113ʳ])]. Had it signified *hidden, secret,* it could no more have been *bitten in twain,* than *untied,* before it was *found out.*" Nevertheless — and although the F1 reading in *Lr.* is *intrinse* — morphologically *intrinsecate* cannot be derived from *intrico,* "to wrap"; it must derive from *intrinsecus,* "within, inner." HALLIWELL (1868, p. 41) quotes two instances of *intrinsecate* (meaning "make familiar") "as a verb in [Edward] Blount's [translation of Lorenzo Ducci's] Ars Aulica, or the Courtier's Arte, 1607, p. 206." Still, it is

Of life at once vntye: Poore venomous Foole,
Be angry, and dispatch. Oh could'st thou speake,
That I might heare thee call great *Cæsar* Asse, vnpolicied.
   Char. Oh Easterne Starre.   3560
   Cleo. Peace, peace:
Dost thou not see my Baby at my breast,

3559–61 *Verse lines ending* ass, . . . peace! POPE1+

---

tempting to regard this construction not simply as a contamination but, following the suggestion of DELIUS (ed. 1856), as an artistic word formation combining both bases, an "intricate inner" knot. KITTREDGE (ed. 1941): "This word implies not only (1) that vitality is so closely involved in our bodily frames that death (except by violence) is not a simple matter, but also (2) that life itself is a complicated affair." For the stylistic impact of this word (and other apparent inkhornisms), see SCHÄFER (1973, pp. 64–6). WILSON (ed. 1950): "The 'knot' is not Life itself, which was immortal, but what ties Life to the 'baser life' or elements of the body. [Compares 3540–1 and Sherrington, *Endeavour of Jean Fernel*, 1946, pp. 89–91, 94–5.]" WALTER (ed. 1969): "Perhaps . . . the 'heart strings' [cites *Lr.* as above and 'the . . . cracke,' 5.3.216–17 (3168+12 f.), *Jn.* 5.7.52–6 (2662–6)]." See also n. 824.

3557 **Poore . . . Foole**] STEEVENS (1780, 1:261), commenting on *Lr.* 5.3.305 (3277), cites this phrase, which "was an expression of tenderness." Cites also *Rom.* 1.3.48 (395) and *3H6* 2.5.36 (1170).

3558 **dispatch**] Only WILSON (ed. 1950, Glossary): "Hasten (with quibble on [finish with])."

3559 **Asse**] WILSON (ed. 1950) detects a "poss[ible] . . . quibble on 'ace', the lowest throw at dice." KOZIKOWSKI (1977, p. 8) overingeniously detects a "barbed allusion, found in Plutarch [see p. 441], to the very sign of Caesar's victory at Actium. . . . Cleopatra's asp becomes the sign of her triumph over Caesar, just as the ass had been the symbol of Caesar's victory over Antony."

vnpolicied] STEEVENS (ed. 1778): "*Without more policy* than to leave the means of death within my reach, and thereby deprive his triumph of its noblest decoration." More recent commentary ranges from "without policy" to "senseless, stupid" (IRVING & MARSHALL [ed. 1889]), "unskilled" (PHIALAS [ed. 1955]), or "with plans gone awry" (WILSON [ed. 1950]), "outdone in craftiness" (EVANS [ed. 1974]). FURNESS (ed. 1907) prefers F1's comma: "A pause after the word . . . seems . . . to impart an emphasis, with concentrated bitterness, to 'unpolicied.'" WILSON (ed. 1950) agrees, and he presents another possible but unlikely meaning, apparently thinking of "unpoliced": "Wild, or turned out to grass; cf. *Caes.* 4.1.26 [1881], and 'wild ass' in Old Testament." WALTER (ed. 1969): "Perhaps a glance at the proverb, 'A king unlearned is a crowned ass.'" See TILLEY (K69). See also n. 760.

3560 *OED* (Morning star): "The planet Venus when visible in the east before sunrise." BLUMHOF (ed. 1870) compares "Bright Starre of *Venus*," *1H6* 1.2.144 [351]. See also n. 2951–2.

3562 BUCKNILL (1860, p. 221): "It is curious that Shakespeare makes Cleopatra ap-

That suckes the Nurse asleepe.
  Char. O breake! O breake!
  Cleo. As sweet as Balme, as soft as Ayre, as gentle.   3565
O *Anthony*! Nay I will take thee too.

---

ply the aspic both to the breast and to the arm, since we find a discussion in old [James]
Primrose's *Popular Errors*, on this point. . . . In his chapter [7] on the mountebank's
antidote, he says [tr. Robert Wittie, 1651, pp. 29–30]: '. . . *Petrus Victorius* blames the
painters, that paint *Cleopatra* applying the aspe to her paps, seeing it is manifest out
of *Plutarch*, in the *Life of Antonius* [as noted by THEOBALD, n. 3566], and out of *Plinie*
likewise [not identified], that she applyed it to her arme. [Johannes] *Zonaras* relates that
there appeared no signe of death upon her, save two blew spots on her arme [*Epitome
historiarum* 10.31 (ed. Dindorf, 1868–75, 2:433)]. *Cæsar* also in her statute [statue] which
he carryed in triumph, applyed the aspe to her arme: For in the armes there are great
veines and arteries, which doe quickly and in a straight way convey the venome to the
heart, whereas in the paps the vessels are slender, which, by sundry circumvolutions onely,
do lead to the heart.'" "Her arme" is mentioned in Daniel's *Cleopatra* as well; see p.
574. For the figure of the nurse, CASE (ed. 1906) compares George Peele's *Edward I* (*Works*,
ed. Bullen, 1888, 1:187) and Thomas Nashe's *Christ's Tears* (*Works*, ed. Grosart, 1883–4,
4:211–12). RIBNER's (1952, pp. 244–6) regarding Peele as a source here is convincingly
rebutted by REEVES (1952, pp. 441–2) and NORGAARD (1952, pp. 442–3), the latter also
providing interesting material on the "literary history of Cleopatra's suicide." LLOYD (1959,
p. 93) compares Apuleius's Isis, "the originall and motherly nource of all fruitfull things
in earth" (*The Golden Asse*, tr. Adlington, 1566; Chiltern Library, 1946, p. 221)—TOBIN
(1979, p. 227) suggests Apuleius's pregnant Psyche as well (Tudor Translations, ed. Henley, 1893, p. 129)—and Plutarch's "the nourse that suckleth and feedeth the whole world"
(*Moralia*, tr. Holland, 1603, p. 1301). ADELMAN (1973, p. 64): "When Shakespeare transferred the serpent's bite from Cleopatra's arm to her breast, he may have tapped the
force of an ancient image for Terra, the generative mother earth, who was frequently
portrayed nourishing serpents. That this figure was transformed during the Middle Ages
into an emblem for Luxuria is characteristic of the double nature of woman, as nourisher
and devourer." See also n. 3495 ("worme").
  3563 **asleepe**] See n. 3614.
  3564 WORDSWORTH (ed. 1883): "I.e., *my heart.*"
  3566 THEOBALD (29 Dec. 1729, [fol. 111ᵛ]): "Thinking her Death slow . . . She
takes up another [asp], & claps it to her Arm. For Confirmation [quotes 3617–19]." IDEM
(ed. 1733) continues: "*Dion Cassius*, in the 51st Book [Ch. 14] of his *Roman* History
is express as to small Punctures of the Asp being discover'd only on her Arm. . . . And
Plutarch says . . . that she had two Marks imprinted by the Sting of the Asp: and that
Cæsar carried a Statue of her in Triumph, with an Asp fix'd to her Arm [see p. 456].
However, the Application of the Aspick to her Breast is not the Invention of our Poet.
Virgil, who says nothing of the Locality of her Wounds, plainly intimates that she ap-
plied two of these venomous Creatures. [Quotes *Aeneid* 8.697, and cites numerous others.]"
Although only one asp is mentioned at 3495 ff., COCKERAM (1623, *Aspe*, [Pt. 3], sig.
K3ʳ) adds: "A venemous Serpent, that alwaies goe two and two together, and if one of
them be slaine, the other will pursue him eagerly that slue him, and if a man chance

What should I stay——   *Dyes.*
    Char. In this wilde World? So fare thee well:
Now boast thee Death, in thy possession lyes
A Lasse vnparalell'd. Downie Windowes cloze,   3570
And golden Phœbus, neuer be beheld
Of eyes againe so Royall: your Crownes away,

3567 What] Why mTBY2 *conj.* (*and withdrawn*), mCOL1, COL2
3568 In . . . World?] *Given to Cleopatra* mTBY4 *conj. and* HAN47
    wilde] vile mTBY2 *and* mF2FL21 *conj.*, CAP, SING2, DYCE1, STAU, GLO-CAM1,
HUD2, WH2, NLSN+ (−KIT1, CAM3); wide MAUN, OXF1
3572 away] awry ROWE3+

---

to be bitten by this Serpent, it is present death if he cut not off the member so bitten:
they are of a blacke earthly colour and sometime yellow. [From Pliny; see n. 3544
("Aspicke").] *Cleopatra*, by applying these Serpents to her body, wilfully slue her selfe."
    take] OBERTELLO (1955, p. 699), rejecting the second asp theory, alone glosses
as "join."
    3567 BROWN (1966, pp. 40–1): "There must be some compulsive movement at this
point, for her crown is jerked 'awry.'" See n. 3572. LAMB (1980, p. 39): "Even today,
one bit of business from [Dryden's] *All for Love* survives in Shakespearean production:
Cleopatra still dies in the hierarchical ['hieratic' in 1976 diss.] seated pose of Egyptian
funerary sculpture instead of on her Jacobean daybed [see n. 3626]." But BOWERS (1983,
p. 289): Cleopatra calls to mind the "realistic marble effigies [which] were the vogue
in early seventeenth-century England."
    What] Means "why" in questions in which the speaker anticipates a negative re-
sponse. See FRANZ §342.
    3568 wilde] STEEVENS (ed. 1778): "This world which by the death of Antony is be-
come a *desert* to her. A *wild* is a desert. Our author, however, might have written *vild*
. . . for worthless." The latter explanation follows CAPELL (1779 [1774], 1:53). Compare
n. 2851 ("vilde").
    So] OBERTELLO (1955, p. 698) alone: Charmian puts her wrist down for the asp
to bite.
    3570 Lasse] See n. 941.
    Downie . . . cloze] RITSON (*apud* STEEVENS, ed. 1793): "Charmian . . . must
be conceived to close Cleopatra's eyes; one of the first ceremonies performed toward a
dead body."
    3572 Of] ABBOTT (§170): "*Of* meaning 'from' is placed before an agent (*from* whom
the action is regarded as proceeding) where we use 'by.'"
    away] STEEVENS (ed. 1778) supports *awry* (see textual notes) with a quotation from
Daniel's *Cleopatra*: "And sencelesse, in her sinking downe she wryes The Diademe which
on her head she wore" (1599, sig. K2ᵛ). For the 1594 *Cleopatra*, see p. 576. Agreeing
are MALONE (ed. 1790), who cites Plutarch (see p. 455), and WILSON (ed. 1950), who
detects "an *a:r* error." See also n. 3567. FURNESS (ed. 1907) likes NICHOLS's (1861–2,
2:3–4) explanation of *away*: "As she dies, her head naturally falls backward on the couch,
the position of the face becomes horizontal, and the crown, compressed between the

Ile mend it, and then play—

      Enter the Guard rustling in, and Dolabella.

1. *Guard.* Where's the Queene?   3575
Char. Speake softly, wake her not.
1 *Cæsar* hath sent
Char. Too slow a Messenger.
Oh come apace, dispatch, I partly feele thee.
1 Approach hoa,   3580
All's not well: *Cæsar's* beguild.
2 There's *Dolabella* sent from *Cæsar*: call him.
1 What worke is heere *Charmian?*

3573, 3575-6 *Arranged as verse lines, thus*: 3573, 3575-6 v1793-GLO, HAL+; 3573
and 3575, 3576 KTLY
    3574 *and Dolabella*] *Om.* ROWE1+
    3577-8 *One verse line* v1793+ (−HUD1)
    3577 sent‸] ~ . F2-F4, THEO1; ~ — ROWE1-POPE2, THEO2+
    3579 come‸] ~ . *or* ~ ; JOHN1, v1773-SING2, COL3, WH1, KTLY, HAL, COL4
    3580-1 *One verse line* THEO1+
    3583-4 *One verse line* ROWE1+
    3583 heere‸ *Charmian?*] ~ ?— ~ , CAP-SIS (−RID)

---

back of the head and the couch, necessarily springs *away* from the forehead." BLUMHOF
(ed. 1870) also defends *away* because it may be applied to both the literal and the
metaphoric senses of *crown* and also because Sh. employs tag rhymes (*away-play*) at the
end of certain actions or scenes.
    3573 **play—**] RANN (ed. 1791-): "My part in this tragedy." STEEVENS (ed. 1793)
adds, "Or she may mean, that having performed her last office for her mistress, she will
accept the permission given her in [3478], to '*play* till doomsday.'" DELIUS (ed. 1856):
"Dally" since she no longer has employment. FURNESS (ed. 1907), not accepting Steevens's
"universally adopted" explanation: "But the fact that the sentence is broken off renders
possible a different conclusion [not given, however]." He objects to the substitution of
a full stop for the dash (see textual notes). COLLIER (ed. 1843) had explained the long
dash as indicating Charmian's being "interrupted by the sudden arrival of the Guard."
For the play-actor image WILSON (ed. 1950) compares Daniel's *Cleopatra*: "Come . . .
vndergoe" (1607, fol. 34ʳ).
    3574 *rustling*] BAILEY (1721): "To make a Noise as Armour or new Garments do."
Commentators stress swift movement (rush) as well.
    3575 See n. 3337.
    3579 **apace**] See n. 2631.
    3580 **hoa**] See n. 1027.
    3582 **There's**] Commentators are silent on whether *there* is an introductory adverb
or, more likely, the beginning of an existential sentence ("Dolabella has been sent").
See FRANZ §348.

Is this well done?

Char. It is well done, and fitting for a Princesse   3585
Descended of so many Royall Kings.
Ah Souldier.   *Charmian dyes.*

Enter Dolabella.

Dol. How goes it heere?
2. *Guard.* All dead.   3590
Dol. Cæsar, thy thoughts
Touch their effects in this: Thy selfe art comming
To see perform'd the dreaded Act which thou
So sought'st to hinder.

Enter Cæsar and all his Traine, marching.   3595

All. A way there, a way for *Cæsar.*
Dol. Oh sir, you are too sure an Augurer: (zz2^{va})
That you did feare, is done.
Cæsar. Brauest at the last,
She leuell'd at our purposes, and being Royall   3600

3585 It is] Is't ROWE2
3587 Souldier] Soldiers ROWE1-JOHN1
      dyes] and Iras Die ROWE
3589–91 *One verse line* v1793+
3594, 3596 *One verse line* v1793, v1803, SING, KNT1, HUD1, STAU, KTLY, RID, ALEX
3596 *All] within* CAP, v1778-ARD2 (–NLSN) (*subst.*)
      A way . . . a way] Make way . . . make way F3-THEO2, WARB-JOHN1; Make
way . . . way HAN1; A way . . . way CAP, v1793, v1803; A way . . . make way v1773
3599 the] *Om.* POPE1-JOHN1
3600 purposes] purpose POPE1-JOHN1, KTLY

3584 SINGER (ed. 1856): "This refers to a deception. Charmian . . . went out to
manage the introduction of the Clown with the asps." But FURNESS (ed. 1907) finds
"that the question is exactly copied from North's *Plutarch* [see p. 455], where the Guard
could not have known of Charmian's agency in the matter. Charmian's reply, moreover,
shows that it refers to the dead queen."
3592 **Touch . . . effects]** RANN's (ed. 1791–) "Are justified" is more directly phrased
by WORDSWORTH (ed. 1883) and all who follow: "*Are realised.*"
3598 **That]** That which. *That* "contains" the relative pronoun; see FRANZ §348f.
3599 **at the last]** SCHMIDT (1874, 2), glossing this instance: "At the close." Interchangeable with "at last"; see FRANZ §268.
3600-1 **She . . . way]** HUNTER (1845, 2:290–1) quite alone: "Cleopatra, brave in
her death, is represented under the image of a hawk [to which] Shakespeare transfers
the attribute of a *hart-royal*, which had the privilege of roaming at large unmolested,

Tooke her owne way: the manner of their deaths,
I do not see them bleede.
  Dol. Who was last with them?
  1. *Guard.* A simple Countryman, that broght hir Figs:
This was his Basket.   3605
  Cæsar. Poyson'd then.
  1. *Guard.* Oh *Cæsar*:
This *Charmian* liu'd but now, she stood and spake:
I found her trimming vp the Diadem;
On her dead Mistris tremblingly she stood,   3610
And on the sodaine dropt.
  Cæsar. Oh Noble weakenesse:
If they had swallow'd poyson, 'twould appeare
By externall swelling: but she lookes like sleepe,
As she would catch another *Anthony*   3615
In her strong toyle of Grace.
  Dol. Heere on her brest,   (zz2ᵛ
There is a vent of Bloud, and something blowne,

3601 their] her F4
3605–7 *One verse line* v1793+
3605 his] the v1773
3609–10 Diadem; . . . Mistris∧] ~ , . . . ~ , F3+ (−ROWE2)

and taking its own way to its lair. Thus Cleopatra being 'royal' had 'taken her own way'
in self-destruction."
   3600 **leuell'd**] DYCHE & PARDON (1740): "To aim." See *OED, Level v.*[1] 7. But, more
likely, JOHNSON (1755): "To conjecture . . . guess." See *OED,* 7b.
   3604 **hir**] *OED:* "Obs. ME. form of *Her.*"
   3609 For Plutarch, see p. 455.
      trimming vp] MINSHEU (1617): "*Make* [a thing] *seeme fairer.*"
   3612 **Noble weakenesse**] KNOWLES (privately): "The deathly weakness which reveals
their noble courage in committing suicide."
   3614 **she . . . sleepe**] THEOBALD (ed. 1733) cites classical sources on the "stupifying
Quality" of the asp's bite to show that Sh. "in this Description . . . is precisely just
to History."
   3615 **As**] As if. See FRANZ §582.
   3616 **toyle**] COTGRAVE (1611, Toiles): "*A Hay* [net] *to inclose, or intangle, wild beasts
in.*"
      Grace] COTGRAVE (1611) and those few who comment at all: "Beautie, seemelinesse,
comelinesse, handsomenesse." BETHELL (1944, p. 131) almost alone: "Perhaps . . . the
word 'grace' may have a tinge of theological significance."
   3618 **vent**] JOHNSON (1755, 4) and most commentators: "Emission."
      blowne] JOHNSON (ed. 1765) and most others: "*Puffed* or *swoln.*" DELIUS (ed.

The like is on her Arme.

    1. *Guard.* This is an Aspickes traile,   3620
And these Figge-leaues haue slime vpon them, such
As th'Aspicke leaues vpon the Caues of Nyle.

    Cæsar. Most probable
That so she dyed: for her Physitian tels mee
She hath pursu'de Conclusions infinite   3625
Of easie wayes to dye. Take vp her bed,
And beare her Women from the Monument,
She shall be buried by her *Anthony.*

3619–23 *Four verse lines ending* arm. . . . . fig-leaves . . . leaves . . . probable,
JOHN1, v1773-GLO, HAL+; *ending* trail, . . . as . . . Nile. . . . probable, KTLY
    3620 is] *Om.* F2-F4
    3625 hath] has THEO2, WARB-JOHN1, v1773

1856) considers *something* not an adverb but a noun. But RIDLEY (ed. 1954), rejecting
Johnson: The Guard's *This* refers "to whatever Dolabella has discovered on breast and
arm. I think therefore that *blown* must refer to something like the track of a snail." At
3614 he gives CASE's (ed. 1906) note on the absence of swelling in Sylvester's *Du Bartas*,
"The Lawe" (ed. Snyder, 1979, p. 548, ll. 99–104). JONES (ed. 1977): "Deposited." Compare nn. 2615, 3269.

    3622 **Caues**] HUDSON (ed. 1881): "Alexandria was supplied with water brought from
the Nile in underground canals; which may be the caves meant." Most commentators
are less specific, like KITTREDGE (ed. 1941): "Hollows in the banks of the river." The
suggestion *canes* or reeds—see p. 360—had tempted editors like Hudson and, especially,
RIDLEY (ed. 1954), who believes that if caves were meant the text would have read *upon
the walls of the caves* or *in the caves,* "whereas the parallel between the *canes* and the
fig-leaves is appropriate. The misreading of *n* as *u* is easy."

    3624 **Physitian**] WORDSWORTH (ed. 1883): "Named Olympus: see . . . Plut[arch]
p. [453]."

    3625 **Conclusions**] MALONE (*apud* STEEVENS [1780], 1:232) and most others: "Ex-
periments. [Compares 'is't . . . Conclusions,' *Cym.* 1.5.16–18 (508–10); Thomas Middleton and William Rowley, *The Spanish Gipsie* (1653, sig. C3^r); and John Davies's
Epigram 180 (*The Scourge of Folly* [1611], p. 85).]" STEEVENS (ed. 1793) compares "like
. . . conclusions," *Ham.* 3.4.194–5 (2570–1). CASE (ed. 1906) adds *Luc.* 1160 and quotes
Richard Brathwait's *His Odes: or, Philomel's teares* (in *Natures embassie,* 1621 [1623]):
"*These,* conclusions try on man, *Surgeon* and *Physician*" (Ode 7, st. 6). See *OED,* 8,
which cites this instance. For Plutarch, see p. 447.

    infinite] COTGRAVE (1611, Infini): "*Endlesse; innumerable.*" The few who com-
ment, beginning with MALONE (*apud* STEEVENS [1780], 1:232), prefer the latter. For
the position of the adjective, see FRANZ §685.

    3626–7 **Take . . . Monument**] WILSON (ed. 1950): "Proves that the deaths take place
on the outer stage." For the staging, see pp. 777–93.

    3626 **bed**] Plutarch (p. 453): "A litle low bed in poore estate." See n. 3567.

No Graue vpon the earth shall clip in it
A payre so famous: high euents as these   3630
Strike those that make them: and their Story is
No lesse in pitty, then his Glory which
Brought them to be lamented. Our Army shall
In solemne shew, attend this Funerall,
And then to Rome. Come *Dolabella*, see   3635
High Order, in this great Solemnity.   *Exeunt omnes*

FINIS.

3631 Strike] Strikes RIDb

3629-30 **No . . . famous**] BURCKHARDT (1968, p. 26): Octavius "is doing more than comparing two disparate things. By saying 'clip' he makes of the grave a nuptial bed and beyond that of the bed one of the partners to the nuptials. As the bridegroom clips the bride, so the grave will embrace the now finally united and inseparable pair." FELPE-RIN (1977, p. 110): "Here the Romans' historical and rhetorical model of epic glory ('A pair so *famous*') has apparently been reconciled with the lovers' model of saving passion ('No grave shall *clip* . . . '), since the spokesman of the former has adopted the vocabulary of the latter."

3629 **clip in**] See nn. 1412, 2656.

3630-3 **high . . . lamented**] CAPELL (1779 [1774], 1:54): "The very causers of events like the present, cannot help being touch'd by them: and the pitifulness of them will set them as high in fame, as conquest will the person that wrought them." STEEVENS (ed. 1793): "The narrative of such events demands not less compassion for the sufferers, than glory on the part of him who brought on their sufferings." CASE (ed. 1906): "Apparently elliptical for: and the tale of these events is as pitiful as the renown of him who caused their lamentable nature is glorious. But in an uncritical perusal, the mind—and perhaps rightly after all—may refer *their* in *their story* to A pair so *famous*, and understand: and there is as much to pity in their story as glory for him who made them objects of pity." MACCALLUM (1910, p. 389): "So the last word is a testimonial to himself. These are eulogies of the understanding, not of the heart." See also 2204.

3631 **Strike**] BAILEY (1730): "Affect or make an Impression on the Mind."

3634 **attend**] See n. 751.

3635-6 **Come . . . Solemnity**] LEVIN (1976, p. 43): "All drama oscillates between order and disorder. . . . More broadly, actions may be scaled to a moral order, incidents be framed within a world-order. Every drama must terminate, in effect, with the kind of resolution that Augustus Caesar formulates in [this] tag-line."

344

APPENDIX

Emendations of Accidentals in F1

The following list records emendations made in the Variorum text of obvious typographical irregularities that have no substantive importance. Such palpable defects
in F1 as the misalignment of types or irregular spacing not creating a true word
(e.g., 604 Parago nagaine) have been corrected silently. In each note the lemma is
the reading of the Variorum text as emended, and the first siglum is that of the
edition from which the emendation is drawn. This is followed by the rejected F1
reading.

22 reckon'd.] F3; ～ ∧ F1, F2 (*full line in* F1)
201 awhile] F2; awhlle F1
268 and] F2; aud F1
355 Seruices] F2 (Services); Seruicles F1
494 *Pansa*] F2; *Pausa* F1
526 *Mandragora*] F2 (*Mandragoras*); *Mandragoru* F1
568 Queene] F2; Qu ene F1
583 sad ∧] F3; ～ ∧ F1 (a fleck, probably not a comma, in some copies); ～ , F2
716 *Ant.*] F2; ～ , F1
912 Venus] F2; Venns F1
918 *Agrip.*] F2; ～ · F1 (*turned period*)
921 Helme,] F3 (Helm,); ～ . F1, F2
957 *Mece.*] F2; ～ ∧ F1
967 prayers] F2; ptayers F1
983 *Sooth.*] F4; *Soot* . F1; *Soot.* F2, F3
       side.] F3; ～ ∧ F1, F2 (*full line*)
1090 But] F2; Bur F1
1216 imbrac'd.] F2; ～ ∧ F1
1237 heere.] F3; ～ , F1, F2
1243 Fortune] F2; Fotune F1
1249 vs.] F3; ～ , F1, F2
1343 greater] F2; greatet F1
1380 What] F2; Whar F1
1387 *Lep.*] F2; ～ · F1 (*turned period*)
1444 *Men.*] F2; ～ ∧ F1
1492 *Enob.*] F2; *Enor.* F1
1499 Army,] F2; ～ , F1 (?)
1509 A lower] F2; Alower F1
1574 on both] F2; onboth F1

345

1593 tongue] F2; tougue F1
1605 year indeed] F2; yearindeed F1
1643 dwarfish,] ~ , F1 (c) (*comma flush right, line* 1645); ~ ∧ F1 (u). *See CN* 1643.
1750 Sir.] F2; ~ , F1
1789 like.] F4; ~ ∧ F1–F3 (*full line*)
1797 Sister.] F3 (~ ;); ~ , F1, F2
1837 our breaking forth] our | (breaking forth (*turnover*) F1
1926 *Ant.*] F2; ~ , F1
2069 vnqualitied] THEO1 (unqualitied); vnqualited F1-POPE2
2100 *Ant.*] F2; ~ ∧ F1
2237 Landlord.] Land- | lord. (*turnunder*) F1
2256 thou Fellow?] thou | (Fellow? (*turnunder*) F1
2556 Had'st] F2 (Hadst); Had''st F1
2590 *Iewry*] F2; *Iewrij* F1 (possibly an *ij* ligature with a damaged second point; cf. *Tit.* 696.)
2597 sorely] F2; forely F1
2623 *Agrip.*] F2; ~ ∧ F1
2694 *Enter*] F2; *Euter* F1
2747 *Cæsar*] F2; *Cæsvr* [turned *a*]
2756 'tis] F2 (tis); 'ris F1
2836 The] F3; the F1, F2
2919 *Ant.*] F2; ~ , F1
2958 fly.] F3; ~ ∧ F1, F2 (*full line*)
2972 *Anth.*] F2 (*Ant.*); ~ · F1 (*turned period*)
2973 Prophesying feare] Prophesying | (feare (*turnover*) F1
3013 [last] *Antony,*] F3; ~ ∧ F1, F2 (*full line*)
3179 vngentle.] ROWE1; ~ ∧ Ff (*full line*)
3219 Queene] F2; Queece F1
3230 dependancie] F2 (dependancy); dependacie F1
3249 languish?] F2; ~ ∧ F1 (*full line*)
3342 obey.] F4; ~ , F1–F3
3363 Your] F3; your F1, F2
3376 known.] F3; ~ ∧ F1, F2 (*full line*)
3430 thee] (*first e weakly inked in Cologne copy*)
3474 *Cidnus*] ROWE1; *Cidrus* Ff
3636 Solemnity] F2; Solmemnity F1

Conjectural Emendations

The following is a list of the first occurrences of conjectural emendations of the text unadopted by any editor. They are taken from editions, commentaries, notes, and, selectively, manuscript sources. Explanations in quotation marks are from these sources as well.

7 like] like a mF2J
   Mars] stars GOULD (1884, p. 63)
12 reneages] reneyes [renounces] BOSWELL (v1821); rejects WRAY *in* WRIGHT SHAKE-SPEARIANA

14 coole] kindle and to cool JOHN1; heat and cool STAUNTON (1873, p. 473)

20 Foole] tool GREY (1754, 2:190)

28 Grates me] *Continued to Messenger* M. H. (1790, p. 307)

29 them] them all, I pr'ythee, SEYMOUR (1805, 2:35)

32 Mandate . . . Do] mandate, Do you SEYMOUR (1805, 2:35)

36–7 *Verse lines* Perchance? . . . not now | Stay longer here; for your dismission SEYMOUR (1805, 2:35)

38 Is . . . therefore] From Cæsar comes; so SEYMOUR (1805, 2:35)

39 both?] *Om.* SEYMOUR (1805, 2:35)

42 so] *Om.* SEYMOUR (1805, 2:36)

45 *Embracing* SCHANZER (1960, p. 20)

the raing'd] the rank'd ["high, of great importance . . . French *rang*, anglicised"] BECKET (1815, 2:172)

space] span GOULD (1884, p. 63)

48 thus:] ∼ ∧ SCHANZER (1960, p. 20)

49 a] a constant *or* a faithful STAUNTON (1873, p. 473)

50 weete] eat SIGURDSON (1986, p. 52)

52 Excellent] O excelling SEYMOUR (1805, 2:36)

53 Why∧] ∼ , ARD2

54–5 *Continued to Cleopatra as an aside* I'll . . . Cleopatra. UPTON (1746, p. 261)

55 But] buts ["but's, for *but is*"] ANON. MS *apud* HALLIWELL (1868, p. 8)

70 slight] light GREY (1754, 2:190)

77–9 *Enter . . .*] *Entrance of Enobarbus after* 99 KÖNIG (1875, p. 381); *entrance of Lamprius, Rannius, and Lucillius after* 90 KITTREDGE (ed. 1941)

77 *Rannius*] Ramnus ["i.e., Rhamnus"] KITTREDGE (ed. 1941)

80–1 any thing . . . absolute] absolute . . . anything ELZE (1886, p. 268)

83–4 change . . . Garlands] change his horns for garlands SEYMOUR (1805, 2:37); chain his horns with garlands JACKSON (1819, p. 285); hange his Horns with Garlands WILLIAMS (1862, p. 89); change his garlands with horns SCHMIDT (ed. 1870)

87 know] know all LLOYD (1891, p. 82)

91–2 *After* 99 KÖNIG (1875, p. 381)

97 flesh] face GOULD (1884, p. 63)

101 *Given to Enobarbus or spoken to Enobarbus* KÖNIG (1875, p. 381)

103 *Given to Enobarbus* KÖNIG (1875, p. 381)

106 in a forenoone] one after one KELLNER (1925, §194)

108 me to] me(a)n(s) to KELLNER (1925, §180)

114–15 *Three verse lines ending* children . . . boys . . . have? ARD1

116–17 & foretell] I might foretell for mF2J; And fourfold THEOBALD *apud* L. H. (*in* mTHEO2, 16 Dec. 1732, [fol. 154ʳ])

125–8 *Four verse lines ending* chastity, . . . Nilus . . . bedfellow, . . . soothsay. WALKER (1860, 1:18)

139 *Given to Alexas* COBDEN-SANDERSON (1912, p. 206)

worser] worse ANON. *in* mF2TCC

140–6 *Given to Iras* mLONG

164 Romane] Roaming GREY (1754, 2:191)

176 I] Ay, my lord SEYMOUR (1805, 2:38)

178 ioynting] joyning mCOL1

180 Vpon] on FLEAY (1881, 2:87)

181 what] what's the mF2J

197 phrase] praise GOULD (1884, p. 63)

199 then] *Om.* SEYMOUR (1805, 2:38)

200 windes] wints ["furrows"] COL1

219 thus . . . it] I it desir'd *or* I this desir'd SEYMOUR (1805, 2:39)

220 from vs,] from 's, gone WALKER (1860, 3:294)

236 a] so NICHOLSON *apud* CAM1; as ANON. *apud* CAM1

    let] let not ANON. MS *apud* HALLIWELL (1868, p. 9)

246–7 winds . . . teares] sighs and tears, winds and waters MALONE (1780; *withdrawn* MAL)

262–3 man . . . therein] men . . . them JOHN1

264 members] menders ORGER (1890, p. 96)

268 liue] lie WALKER (1860, 2:210)

273 be] be done ANON. *apud* CAM1

278 Expedience] expedition mF2J

281 Do] Do's HEATH (1765, p. 450)

282 contriuing] continuing GOULD (1884, p. 44)

295–6 *Verse lines ending* us, . . . hence. MASON (1785, p. 282 [= 272])

295 whose] who've MASON (1785, p. 282 [= 272])

296 Our] Their JOHN1

298 Scene 2 mCOL1

    and Iras] *Om.* ANON. *apud* CAM1

299 he] he now STEEVENS (v1793); he, Charmian ANON. *apud* CAM1

312 I wish] the wish *or* your wish NICHOLSON *apud* CAM1; I wis ANON. *apud* CAM1; shrewish DEY (1908, p. 165)

314 *Anthony*] *Ad.* with Alexas ANON. *apud* CAM1

332 Treasons] treason WALKER (1860, 1:246)

    planted] planned mWARB

335 in] by mF2J

347 a] a'th' [o'th'] CAM3

    race] trace HTR; grace KELLNER (1925, §220)

360 scrupulous] emulous GOULD (1887, p. 72)

364 state, whose] state. War's STAUNTON (1873, p. 473)

365 rest] rust SEYMOUR (1805, 2:40)

367 safe] 'safe [vouchsafe] BECKET (1815, 2:174); 'scuse KELLNER (1925, §55)

381 th'aduice] them aidance ANON. *apud* CAM1

386 well] well again MALONE (1783)

389 euidence] audience CAMPBELL *apud* CAM2

409 Oh, my] Oh me! EDWARDS MS *apud* v1778; O my! HENLEY *apud* v1785

    Obliuion is] oblivion!—'Tis JOHN1

410 forgotten] forgeting mTHEO2 (19 Feb. 1729, [fol. 39ʳ]; *withdrawn according to* CAM1); forgone JOHN1; forlotten ["i.e. forlorn, deserted"] BECKET (1815, 2:174)

416 *Cleopatra*] Cleopatra doth mF2J

428 Scene 3 mCOL1

432 One] ane ["i.e. any"] BECKET (1815, 2:175)

436–8 *Three verse lines* More . . . he; he scarce gave audience, | Or vouchsaf'd think he had partners: you shall find | In him, a man the abstract of all faults SEYMOUR (1805, 2:42)

437 to thinke] think STEEVENS (v1793); that CAM3

442 Spots] stars mF4Q

443 Blacknesse] black SEYMOUR (1805, 2:42)

445 chooses] chooses. Cæsar, think it so SEYMOUR (1805, 2:42)

452 As] And JOHN1

454 foyles] follies MALONE (1783); fails STEEVENS (v1793); sports KELLNER (1925, §96, §114)

460 'tis] he's DANIEL (1870, p. 80)

462–3 Pawne their . . . their . . . rebell] Pawns his . . . his . . . rebels DANIEL (1870, p. 80)

475 That he] He BECKET (1815, 2:176)

477 Ne're . . . loue,] worth love, (ne'er lov'd till near) BECKET (1815, 2:176)

478 fear'd] 'feer'd [*"affeer'd, i.e.*, estimated"] CROSBY (1883–4, p. 47; *attrib. to* INGLEBY)

479 Like to] E'en like SEYMOUR (1805, 2:45)

     Flagge] Ragge mCOL1 (*originally, according to* CAM2)

480 backe] fro KEIGHTLEY (1867, p. 312)

     lacking the varrying] backing the varying mF4FL33; the lashing varying ["(with)
the lashing, varying"] BECKET (1815, 2:177); tacking the varying GOULD (1881, p. 10);
taking the varying KNOWLES (1986, privately)

481 it selfe] *Om.* STEEVENS (v1793)

482 *Cæsar* . . . thee] I bring SEYMOUR (1805, 2:45)

484 eare] tear mF2J

486 Borders] bord'rers DEL2

487 flush] fresh ANON. MS *apud* HALLIWELL (1868, p. 15)

496 with] bore with WRAY *in* WRIGHT SHAKESPEARIANA

499 did] did not ANON. *in* mF2TCC

507–10 *Two verse lines ending* shames . . . twain FLEAY (1881, 2:87)

508 'Tis] Ay, 'tis ANON. *apud* CAM1

510 Rome] Rome disgrac'd MALONE (1783); Rome: Lepidus ANON. *apud* CAM1

     time] time indeed STEEVENS (v1793)

516 Both] With ANON. *apud* CAM1

     be able] assemble ANON. *apud* CAM1; leavie ["levy"] KELLNER (1925, §60, §192)

518 Farwell] Farewell good Lepidus SEYMOUR (1805, 2:46)

523 Sc 4 mCOL1

538 Hast thou] Hast' SEYMOUR (1805, 2:47)

553–4 Now . . . poyson] *As Antony's words* SEWARD (1750, p. lxvi)

553 Now] How mTYR

554 poyson. . . . me ∧] ⌢ ? . . . ⌢ ? mTYR

556 Broad-fronted] Bald-fronted SEWARD (1750, p. lxvii)

558 *Pompey*] Pompey's son ANON. MS *apud* v1907

563 Soueraigne of Egypt,] Egypt, all SEYMOUR (1805, 2:47)

573 firme] first WALKER (1860, 3:295)

575 peece] space GREY (1754, 2:195)

578 an Arme-gaunt] an armed-gaunt mF2J; an arm-gent *or* an arm-vaunt BECKET (1815,
2:177); a war-gaunt JACKSON (1819, p. 287); a ramping LETTSOM (1853, p. 378); a merchant
BULLOCH (1865, p. 2); an ardent *or* an angry KEIGHTLEY (1867, p. 312); an arme-g'raunt
(*omitting* Steede) GOULD (1884, p. 45); on a rampant PERRING (1885, p. 339); an arm-zoned
JOICEY (1891, p. 342); an arm-gowned ARD1; an armigerent SAMPSON (1920, p. 272); a
wing-borne BRONSON (1938, p. 644)

579 Who . . . hye] He neigh'd so high BECKET (1815, 2:178)

580 beastly dumbe] basely dump ["dumpish"] BECKET (1815, 2:178); beastly drown'd
COLNE (1852, p. 512, *and withdrawn*), BAILEY (1866, 2:117)

608 Sallad] ballad BECKET (1815, 2:178)

614 *Menecrates*] *Om.* JOHN1

628 powers are Cressent] power is Crescent BECKET (1815, 2:180); power's a-crescent
ANON. *apud* CAM1

629 it] they GOULD (1881, p. 10)

641 Salt . . . soften . . . wand] Soft . . . salt . . . wanton INGLEBY (1891, p. 3, *and
withdrawn*)

     wand] tand ["tann'd"] KEIGHTLEY (1867, p. 313)

642 ioyne] ioynd ARD2

643 field] fold WILLIAMS (1862, p. 89); file CAM3

646 Honour] hour MAL

647 Lethied] Lethe ANON. *apud* CAM1

653–5 *Two verse lines* A . . . given | Less matter better ear.—I did not think— STEEVENS (v1793)

653 space . . . farther] race . . . farthest GOULD (1884, p. 45)

654 lesse] less weighty GOULD (1884, p. 45)

662 hope] hold DANIEL (1870, p. 80)

670 square] Quare ["*contracted of* quarrel"] BECKET (1815, 2:181)

678 ACT II. SCENE I. JOHN1

703 leaner] meaner mF4Q; lesser GOULD (1884, p. 45)

704 heard] mov'd *or* urg'd GOULD (1884, p. 45)

723 derogately] derogate SEYMOUR (1805, 2:50)

730 practis'd] practise ANON. *apud* CAM1

734 Was . . . were] Had theme from you, you were *or* You were theme for, you were JOHN1; Was theam'd from you, you were MALONE *apud* v1778; For you: yes you, the theme BECKET (1815, 2:181); Was ta'en for your's,—you were JACKSON (1819, p. 290); Was you for theme, you were MITFORD (1844, p. 467); Had you for theme, you were STAU; Was tak'n from you, you were LEO (1885, p. 118); Was known for yours, you were ORSON (1891, p. 6)

    of warre] o' th'war *or om.* JOHN1

735 your] their ANON. *apud* CAM1

741 Hauing alike your] Hating alike our JOHN1

743 you haue] you n'have STAU; you've nought ANON. *apud* CAM1; you halve ANON. *apud* CAM1; you'll have SISNR

747 Not so] No SEYMOUR (1805, 2:50)

753 spirit,] ⁓ ; MALONE (1783)

    in] e'en MALONE (1783; *withdrawn* MAL)

    such] *Om.* STEEVENS (v1793)

769 told] told it SCHMIDT (ed. 1870); called KELLNER (1925, §155)

775 Soft] Nay, softly SEYMOUR (1805, 2:51)

776 *Lepidus*] Lepidus, I pr'ythee SEYMOUR (1805, 2:51)

793 If] Would CAPN

807 your Considerate stone] your confederates love HEATH (1765, p. 454); you considerate ones JOHN1; your consideratest one BLACKSTONE *apud* v1785; now I'm your considerate stone SEYMOUR (1805, 2:52); your confederate's tone BECKET (1815, 2:182); you're considerate as stone JACKSON (1819, p. 291); your considerate tone NICHOLS (1861–2, 1:10; *withdrawn* 1862, p. 11); your confederates atone LLOYD *apud* CAM1 (Addenda); your considerate stone am I KEIGHTLEY (1867, p. 313); your confederate is gone LEO (1869, p. 191); your confederate atone BROWNE *in* WRIGHT SHAKESPEARIANA; you (*or* you're *or* you are a) considerate stone ELZE (1886, p. 273); you're considerate stone ELZE (1889, p. 285); *spoken aside* NICHOLSON *in* WRIGHT SHAKESPEARIANA

815 *Agrippa*] Agrippa, speak ANON. *apud* CAM2

818 not, say] it not, mCOL1

830 import] impart mCOL1

831 tales] as tales STEEVENS (v1793); mere tales NICHOLSON *apud* CAM1

832 both,] each. ARD2

836–40 *Three verse lines ending* speak? . . . what . . . Agrippa. ELZE (1886, p. 273)

858 laid] done mF4FL33

859 vpon] unto mF4FL33

864–70 *Four verse lines ending* About . . . land? . . . is . . . Fame, mTYR

899 indeed] indeed triumphantly *or* indeed in triumph CAM3

903 Burnt] flam'd *or* blaz'd SEYMOUR (1805, 2:52)

908 faster] after GOULD (1884, p. 63)

917 vndid did] did, undid JOHN1; undy'd, dy'd STAU

920 Mer-maides] seamaids CARTWRIGHT (1862, p. 169)

920–1 tended . . . adornings] tended her by th' eyes, And made their Bends adorings JOHN1; *as* F1 *but for* ends adornings STEEVENS (v1793); tended her: and made Their tends, i' the eyes, adorings BECKET (1815, 2:184); *as* F1 *but for* the bends adornings JACKSON (1819, p. 293); tended her i' the bends, And made their eyes adorings STAU; *as* F1 *but for* the bends' adornings INGLEBY (1875, p. 119); *as* F1 *but for* I'th' dais *and* bands adornings *or* ribands adornings GOULD (1884, p. 63); bended to the oars *then as* F1 SMITH (1890, pp. 402–3); tended in her eyes *or* tended her wi' their eyes *then as* F1, *or* tend her in her eyes And make their bends adornings JOICEY (1891, pp. 62, 263); 'tended her i' the eyes, And marked their bends, adoring LLOYD (1891, p. 4); 'tended on her eyes And marked their bends, adoring *or* tended her wi' their eyes And made their bends adornings C.C.B. (1891, p. 63); 'tended her wi' th' eyes *then as* F1 PRIDEAUX (1891, p. 203)

922–3 Tackle, Swell] tackles Swerve *or* tackle Swerves NICHOLSON *apud* CAM1

923 Swell] move GOULD (1884, p. 63); serv'd KINNEAR (1883, p. 451)

924 frame] serve GOULD (1884, p. 63)

the office] their office KEIGHTLEY (1867, p. 314)

925 inuisible] invincible BECKET (1815, 2:184); invasible *or* invasive ["permeative"] GOULD (1884, p. 45); inticible ["seductive"] KELLNER (1925, §171)

937 Whom . . . woman] Whom never the word—no woman CAPN (V. R.); Whom woman ne'er the word of 'No' ELZE (1886, p. 273)

939 for] at SEYMOUR (1805, 2:54)

948 breathlesse powre breath] breathless, pour breath DANIEL *apud* CAM1 (Addenda)

950 Neuer . . . not] Never; he will not. Be assured of it SEYMOUR (1805, 2:54); Never *or* he will not ARD2

958–9 *Octauia* . . . him] he is aye blessed: | Octavia votary to him BECKET (1815, 2:184)

966–7 knee . . . prayers] prayers . . . knee COL3

968 Goodnight Sir.] *Continued to Octavia* GRAY (1917–18, p. 44)

976 from] *Om.* SEYMOUR (1805, 2:55)

976–7 you thither.] you. Thither! *or* you Thither again[!] ARD2

977 thither] either *or* neither GRAY (1917–18, p. 44)

978–9 If . . . in] *One verse line, thus:* If you can, sir, . . . in SEYMOUR (1805, 2:55)

983 Therefore (oh *Anthony*)] so, Antony, SEYMOUR (1805, 2:56)

984 thy] shy BULLOCH (1878, p. 255)

spirit] sprite SEYMOUR (1805, 2:56)

985 high vnmatchable] high-unmatchable ANON. *apud* CAM2

987 a feare] afear WALKER (1860, 2:68; 3:299)

therefore] *Om.* SEYMOUR (1805, 2:56)

989 Speake] Of SEYMOUR (1805, 2:56)

993 thickens] sickens GOULD (1884, p. 45)

1006 And] For CAPN (V. R.)

1018–19 at Mount] *at mount* ["ready to mount"] CHEDWORTH (1805, p. 287)

1018 at] at' ANON. *apud* CAM2

1024 Scene 4 mCOL1

1039 bended] bent ANON. *apud* CAM1

1046 time? Oh] time of mTHEO2 (19 Feb. 1729, [fol. 39ᵛ])

1053 Ramme] Cram BECKET (1815, 2:185)

1057 say] [do?] say (*reading* 1056–7 *as one line,* Antony's . . . villain,) WALKER (1854, p. 48)

1058–61 *Three verse lines ending* There . . . kisse: . . . kissing. mTYR

1062 Madam] *Om.* SEYMOUR (1805, 2:57)

1065 it to] to me mCOL1

1067 throate] throat. Therefore look to't SEYMOUR (1805, 2:57)

1071 so] needs so MALONE (1783); hast too NICHOLSON *apud* CAM1

1084 Th'art] *Om.* SEYMOUR (1805, 2:57)
1086 Gives again. NICHOLSON *apud* CAM1
1088 alay] alloy GOULD (1884, p. 63)
1099 pale] faint GOULD (1884, p. 63)
1108 stew'd] stood GOULD (1884, p. 63)
1122–3 *Verse lines ending* innocents . . . thunderbolt. WALKER (1860, 3:300)
1146 So] Tho' SEYMOUR (1805, 2:58)
1152 that] *Om.* GOULD (1884, p. 63)
1154 he's . . . *Octauia.*] *Given to Cleopatra as a question* ORGER (1890, p. 97)
1156 art . . . of] art—not what?—Thou'rt sure on't JOHN1; art not what thou'rt sore of MALONE (1783); That art not!—What? thou art assured of SEYMOUR (1805, 2:59); thwart not what thou art sure of BECKET (1815, 2:185); wot not what thou 'rt sure of JERVIS (1860, p. 25); art's not what thou'rt sure of BULLOCH (1878, p. 256); sharest in what thou'rt sure of HUD2; art not what thou utter'st KINNEAR (1883, p. 454); art not—what thou art sure of JOICEY (1891, p. 342); art no whit th' author of 't DEIGHTON (1898, p. 41); act not what thou 'rt sure of ARD1
1158–64 *Six verse lines ending* upon . . . highness . . . have . . . I . . . hence, . . . matter. ANON. *apud* ARD2
1163–6 *Verse lines ending* faint; . . . Go . . . report . . . years, WALKER (1860, 3:300)
1169 him not *Charmian,*] him go, Charmian GOULD (1884, p. 63)
1175 Scene 5 mCOL1
1200 meant] mean JACKSON (1819, p. 295)
1205 Weele speake] weere weake GOULD (1884, p. 63)
1212 present] purpose DANIEL (1870, p. 81)
1216 imbrac'd] embracing WRAY *in* WRIGHT SHAKESPEARIANA
1223 vndinted] unindented mLONG
1243 counts] change GOULD (1884, p. 45)
Fortune cast's] fortune's cast ["*has cast*"] ARD2
1253 That . . . *Pompey*] I, Pompey, will SEYMOUR (1805, 2:60)
1254 take] take we STEEVENS (v1793); let's take SEYMOUR (1805, 2:60)
1260 heard] heard. Mark Antony ELZE (1886, p. 274)
1262 *Eno.* No . . . so] LEPIDUS. No more of that. ENO. He did so ["aside to Pompey."] ORGER (1890, p. 98)
more] rumour KELLNER (1925, §206)
1275–7 *Two verse lines* It . . . galley | I do . . . lords? SEYMOUR (1805, 2:60)
1275 thee] thee, Enobarbus ELZE (1886, p. 274)
1324 Amity] unity ELZE (1886, p. 274)
1333 Scene 6 mCOL1
1335 man] mad ANON. *in* mF2TCC; anon LLOYD (1891, p. 82)
1335–6 ill rooted] un-rooted GOULD (1884, p. 45)
1339 drinke Almes] drink, always KELLNER (1925, §118)
1340–1 by the disposition, hee . . . to his] he . . . to his disposition by the DEIGHTON (1907, p. 303)
1340 by the disposition] by the disputation ["*in the controversy*"] STAU; by the doing reason KINNEAR (1883, p. 454); at the imposition CROSBY (1883–4, p. 122, *and withdrawn*)
1371–2 Pyramisis] Pyramides RANN
1377 a word] *Om.* STEEVENS (v1793)
1392 tell me of that?] *To Antony and Caesar* NICHOLSON *apud* CAM1
1399–1407 *Five verse lines* Be . . . Lepidus | Keep . . . lord | Of all the world | What . . . whole world | That's . . . entertain't. NICHOLSON *in* WRIGHT SHAKESPEARIANA
1401 for] for fear ANON. *apud* CAM1
1407 entertaine] enter into ANON. *apud* CAM1
1418 there] theirs STEEVENS *apud* v1778

1436 cup] lip GOULD (1884, p. 63)

1443 encrease the Reeles] and grease the wheels STEEVENS (v1793); increase the revels DOUCE (1807, 2:91); increase the rules ["signifying revel"] ARD1 (*and withdrawn*)

1446 Vessells] kettles ["kettle-drums"] CROSBY (1883–4, p. 123)

1451–2 Possesse it, . . . make answer: . . . fast] *One verse line, thus*: Possess, . . . answer, . . . fast MITFORD (1844, p. 468)

1451 Possesse it] Possess MITFORD (1844, p. 468); propose it STAU; Proface it NICHOLSON *apud* CAM1; pass it GOULD (1884, p. 46); Pledge it KINNEAR (1883, p. 456); Pass it, pass it CROSBY (1883–4, p. 123); Possess us DEIGHTON (1907, p. 86)

1456 hands] hands, and beat the ground STEEVENS (v1793)

1462 holding] burden WRAY *in* WRIGHT SHAKESPEARIANA
    beate] peat ["repeat"] BECKET (1815, 2:186); bleat DANIEL *apud* CAM1

1467–71 eyne: . . . Cup] eyne; | *Thine it is to cheer the soul,* | *Made, by thy enlarging bowl,* | *Free from wisdom's fond controul,* | Bur. *Free from* &c. | 2. | *Monarch, come; and with thee bring* | *Tipsy dance, and revelling:* | [1468–70 *as in* F1] Bur. *Cup* CAPN (*wrongly attrib. by Capell to* GAR)

1481 on the shore] ashore *or* on shore WALKER (1860, 3:300)

1487–8 *Some words missing at end of each line* GOULD (1884, p. 63)

1487 these Drummes, These] Where now are these drums, these STAUNTON (1873, p. 534); Speak, drums! speak, DEIGHTON (1907, p. 86)

1488 Flutes: what] these flutes! what ho! ELZE (1886, p. 274)

1492 saies a] sessa RID

1511–12 *Three verse lines ending* undone, . . . fame, . . . away. WALKER (1860, 3:300)

1520–1 *Verse lines* The . . . a choice | Of loss, than of that gain which darkens him. SEYMOUR (1805, 2:62)

1525 Thou . . . that] Thou'st that, Ventidius ELZE (1889, p. 288)
    Ventidius] *Om.* ELZE (1886, p. 274)

1526 graunts] Wants NICHOLSON *apud* CAM1

1534–6 *Four verse lines ending* purposeth . . . weight . . . shall . . . along. WALKER (1860, 3:300–1)

1538 Act 3 Scene 1 mCOL1

1552 go] *Om.* STEEVENS (v1793)

1555–7 Hoo . . . hoo] Oh . . . oh NICHOLSON *apud* CAM2

1557 number] thunder BULLOCH (1878, p. 257)

1558 to *Anthony*] Unto Antonius SEYMOUR (1805, 2:62)

1582–3 *One verse line, omitting* fare thee well, SEYMOUR (1805, 2:63)

1582 heere part] part here SEYMOUR (1805, 2:63)

1592–6 *Spoken aside* FURNESS (v1907)

1598 a] indeed, a watry SEYMOUR (1805, 2:63)

1613–14 thus: . . . Gods.] *Given to Cæsar and addressed to Octavia* ARD2

1620 Scene 2 mCOL1

1636 me] I SEYMOUR (1805, 2:63)

1665 As low as] Lower than CAPN
    she would] you could RANN; ye would ANON. *apud* CAM2

1669 Go,] Go, and SEYMOUR (1805, 2:64)

1676–7 *Continued to Charmian* ANON. *apud* CAM1

1678 Hath . . . Maiestie?] *Continued to Cleopatra* ANON. *apud* CAM1

1684 Scene 3 mCOL1

1688 Made his] ta'en my CAMPBELL *in* WRIGHT MS; maim'd my KELLNER (1925, §180)

1689 eare] ear to win the multitude SEYMOUR (1805, 2:65)

1700 good] *Om.* WALKER (1860, 3:301)

1701 Husband,] husband! and then SEYMOUR (1805, 2:65)

1712–13 *Intervening line lost* MAL

1712 the . . . a] no preparation of LETTSOM *apud* WALKER (1860, 3:301)
1713 Shall staine] Shall stun JACKSON (1819, p. 298); T' assail LETTSOM *apud* WALKER (1860, 3:301); Shall slack ANON. *apud* CAM1; Shall stem JOICEY (1891, p. 343)
  Brother] brother's BAILEY (1866, 2:117)
1716 weake, most weake] weak, most strong SEYMOUR (1805, 2:66)
1720 begins] began KELLNER (1925, §92)
1723 equally] equal, SEYMOUR (1805, 2:66)
1731 This . . . what is] Pho! this . . . What's CAPN
1737 is] is pent GOULD (1884, p. 46)
1738 chaps no more] chaps! Go now GOULD (1884, p. 46)
1739 they'le] or they'll GOULD (1884, p. 46)
1740 the] one th' HEATH (1765, p. 458)
1746 more *Domitius*] Now, Enobarbus GOULD (1884, p. 63)
1751 Scene 4 mCOL1
1764 the] *Om.* ANON. *apud* CAM1
1787 his change] disgrace *or* discharge ANON. *apud* CAM1
1806 ostentation] ostention ["*ostension*"] WALKER (1860, 3:302)
1807 vnlou'd] unvalued SEYMOUR (1805, 2:66); unpriz'd STAU; uncared for *or* unknown BAILEY (1866, 2:119)
1817 abstract] abstract: ["for *separated from*; an estranged person"] BECKET (1815, 2:188); obstacle CARTWRIGHT (1866, p. 38)
  'tweene] 'tweyn'd ["intwine"] BECKET (1815, 2:188)
1820-2 *Three verse lines* And . . . wind. | Where . . . *Cæsar.* No, | No, . . . Cleopatra WALKER (1860, 2:145)
1820 he] he, 'pray you, STEEVENS (v1793)
1834 Aye] *Om.* SEYMOUR (1805, 2:67)
1838 wrong led] wrangled ARD2
1847 Best] Rest JACKSON (1819, p. 298)
1854-7 *Four verse lines* That . . . us. | *Octa.* Is . . . welcome! | Pray . . . patience:— | My dearest sister! WALKER (1860, 3:303); *three verse lines* That . . . sir? | *Cæs.* Most . . . be | ever acknown . . . sister! ANON. *apud* CAM1
1854 noyses] poises GOULD (1884, p. 46)
1858 Scene 5 mCOL1
1860-1 *One verse line* Why? . . . Thou'st . . . wars. (*reading* Why *for* But why, why, why) SEYMOUR (1805, 2:67)
1870 Your] You mCOL1 (*and withdrawn*)
1891 slacknesse] slacknesses BULLOCH (1878, p. 258)
  Camidius, wee] we, Canidius SEYMOUR (1805, 2:68)
1918 *Cæsar*] Cæsar himself STEEVENS (v1793)
1921 Beate] meet GOULD (1884, p. 46)
1923 Businesse] business, briefly SEYMOUR (1805, 2:68)
1925 ha's taken] hath march'd a power and ta'en SEYMOUR (1805, 2:69)
1958-9 *Verse lines* Can. I come to him with news; methinks the time's | In labour . . . some. SEYMOUR (1805, 2:69)
1960 Scene 6 mCOL1
1967 iumpe] junct' ["contracted of juncture"] BECKET (1815, 2:189)
1989 Yon ribaudred Nagge] Yon ribald rag ANON. *apud* CAM1; Yon ribald ren'gade PERRING (1907, p. 301); You brinded nag DELAMAINE (1916, p. 8); Yonder ribaud Nagge CAIRNCROSS (1975, p. 173)
  ribaudred] reboured JACKSON (1819, p. 300); ribanded GOULD (1884, p. 64); ribaldish HALL *apud* HUD2; riband-red THISELTON (1899, p. 19) *and* EV1; ribaud red RAY (1976, p. 22)
1992 as] ag'd STAU

1994 Sailes] sail GAR (p. 100); tail STAUNTON (1873, p. 534)
    flyes] flies, Enobarbus ELZE (1886, p. 274)
2011 owne] own. And let him bide it SEYMOUR (1805, 2:70)
2013 indeede] indeed, Canidius ELZE (1886, p. 275)
2015 'Tis easie toot] 'Tis easy way KEIGHTLEY (1867, p. 317); *spoken aside* ARD2
2016 *Given to Canidius* ARD2
2020 Ile yet] Yet I'll SEYMOUR (1805, 2:70)
2021-2 *Verse lines ending* although . . . direct against me. SEYMOUR (1805, 2:70)
2021 chance] chase JOHN1
2023 A seaport town in Peloponnesus. CAMPBELL *apud* CAM2
2034 Be gone] be gone, I say STEEVENS (v1793); begone, I pray KEIGHTLEY (1867,
p. 317)
2039 Friends] Fellows WALKER (1860, 1:288)
2043 Let them] Let him mF2J; lest that JACKSON (1819, p. 302); Let then BLUM
2044 Which . . . selfe] who leaves himself mF2J
2052 *Om.* SEYMOUR (1805, 2:70)
2054 No, no, no, no, no] No, no, no SEYMOUR (1805, 2:70)
2056 fie, fie, fie] fy! fy SEYMOUR (1805, 2:70)
2058 Madam] Nay, madam SEYMOUR (1805, 2:70)
2059 Sir, sir] Sir SEYMOUR (1805, 2:70)
2063 mad] Lad mTHEO1 (*withdrawn* mTHEO2, 19 Feb. 1729, [fol. 40^r]); mild mTHEO2
(19 Feb. 1729, [fol. 40^r]); man GAR (p. 100; *withdrawn* CAPN)
2064 Lieutenantry] lieutenancy mF2J
2068 him] him, beseech you SEYMOUR (1805, 2:71)
2070-3 *Four verse lines ending* Sir, . . . see, her head's . . . quickly seize her; but . . .
only, now can make the rescue SEYMOUR (1805, 2:71)
2074 Reputation] reputation by GOULD (1887, p. 72)
2080 Stroy'd] Strew'd *or* Strow'd GAR (p. 100)
2119 Morne-dew] morning-dew KEIGHTLEY (1867, p. 317)
2133 Of . . . faile] Nor . . . lack SEYMOUR (1805, 2:71)
2139 now 'tis] now's the CAPN (V. R.)
2141 And . . . requires,] What she requires; and in our name WH1
2142 From] Frame KINNEAR (1883, p. 457)
2143 periure] pervert KELLNER (1925, §79)
2152 Act IIII Sc 1 mCOL1 (*withdrawn* COLNE, 1852, p. 474)
    A seaport town in Peloponnesus. CAMPBELL *apud* CAM2
2153 do] *Om.* STEEVENS (v1793)
2154 Thinke] Wink TYRWHITT (1766, p. 10; *withdrawn apud* v1778); Swink BECKET
(1815, 2:192)
2157 though] an though WALKER (1860, 2:157)
    you] you, timorous, STAUNTON (1873, p. 534)
2158 ranges] rages STAU
2159 Why] wherefore SEYMOUR (1805, 2:72)
    follow] ha' follow'd ANON. *apud* CAM1
2160 itch] edge BAILEY (1866, 2:348)
2161 nickt] prick'd WH1
2162 he being] begins ORGER (1890, p. 99)
2163 meered] meeted [measured] mWARB; meetest BECKET (1815, 2:192); admired MIT-
FORD (1844, p. 468); me in *or* me o' the NICHOLS (1861-2, 1:12); empery BULLOCH (1865,
p. 2); vexed GOULD (1881, p. 10); merest ["entire, veriest"] KINNEAR (1883, p. 457); mortal
ORGER (1890, p. 99); moved ARD1; verie KELLNER (1925, §117)
2172 Let] We'll let JACKSON (1819, p. 303)
    know't] know it then STEEVENS (v1793)

2177 from which] whence SEYMOUR (1805, 2:72)
2183 declin'd, . . . against Sword] sword against sword declin'd WH1; declined sword 'gainst sword RID
2186 Vnstate] stake GOULD (1884, p. 64)
2191 the] that the COLNE (1852, p. 475)
2197 their] the KINNEAR (1883, p. 458)
    nose] sense STAUNTON (1873, p. 534)
2199 square] sparre PECK (1740, p. 224)
2208 None] None hear JACKSON (1819, p. 303); No one WALKER (1860, 3:305)
2213 that is] that, if JACKSON (1819, p. 304)
2217–19 right . . . him.] *Given to Thyreus* DANIEL *apud* CAM1 (Addenda)
2237 your selfe] yourself instead *or* your self and realm ANON. *apud* CAM1
    shrowd] stewardship BULLOCH (1865, p. 2); shield GOULD (1884, p. 64)
2241 *Cæsar* this] Cæsar,— BECKET (1815, 2:192)
    in disputation] by deputation STEEVENS *apud* v1778; in disreputation BECKET (1815, 2:192); in disposition ["*in inclination*"] STAU
2244 all-obeying] all obeyed JOHN1; all-swaying ANON. *apud* CAM1
2262 me . . . cried] me; cried I but SEYMOUR (1805, 2:73)
2286 You haue] Indeed we know you've SEYMOUR (1805, 2:74)
2289 drop] dull GOULD (1881, p. 10)
2344–5 determines so Dissolue] dissolves, so determine *or* dissolves, so end COL1
2348 discandering] disquandering HUD1 (*after* KNT1)
    pelleted] polluted STAUNTON (1873, p. 534)
2354 our] and our mF2J
2355 Fleete] steere GOULD (1884, p. 64)
2359 I] ay BECKET (1815, 2:193)
2371–2 *Three verse lines ending* poor: . . . again, . . . Cleopatra. WALKER (1860, 3:306)
2372–3 *Verse lines* Is . . . again, again I will | Be . . . well. BLAIR *apud* CAM2
2372 againe] *Om.* STEEVENS (v1793)
    I will be] I'm SEYMOUR (1805, 2:74)
2381–3 *Three verse lines* Even . . . outstare | The . . . is to be | Affrighted . . . mood, WALKER (1860, 3:306)
2382 out-stare] outflare DANIEL *apud* CAM1 (Addenda)
2389 Scene 2 mCOL1 (*withdrawn* COLNE, 1852, p. 474)
2395–7 *Two verse lines* He hath many . . . die than so. | Meantime, I laugh . . . must know. MAGINN (1839, p. 265)
2397 must] needs must RITSON *apud* v1793; must needs STAUNTON (1873, p. 535)
2400 Neuer anger] Anger never SEYMOUR (1805, 2:74)
2409 Scene 3 mCOL1
2419 Woo't] Wo'n't mSTV2
2426 Thou] Thou too ANON. *apud* CAM1
2446 Perchance] nay, perchance, STEEVENS (v1793)
2467 Scene 4 mCOL1
2491 *Hercules*] Bacchus mTHEO2 (21 Feb. 1729, [fol. 41^r]; *withdrawn according to* CAM1)
2500 giue] go CAPN (V. R.)
2502 Scene 5 mCOL1 (*withdrawn* COLNE, 1852, pp. 475–6)
2528 knowes] loves KELLNER (1925, §103)
2547 Chamber] chamber, madam ELZE (1886, p. 276)
2549 That . . . might] Might he and Cæsar SEYMOUR (1805, 2:75)
2552 Scene 6 mCOL1
2568 *Given to Eros* ELZE (1886, p. 276)
2574 Dispatch] Dispatch! To JOHN1; Domitius ANON. *apud* CAM1
2575 Scene 7 mCOL1

2579 knowne] known, Agrippa ELZE (1886, p. 276)

2582 three nook'd] three-nuk'd ["*Nuke* is the *head*"] BECKET (1815, 2:190); threaten'd GOULD (1884, p. 46)

2585 *Anthony*] Sir, Mark Antony ELZE (1886, p. 276)

2589–91 *Verse lines ending* revolt, . . . Antony, . . . persuade FLEAY (1881, 2:87)

2607 saf't] save mF4FL33; saw safe CAPN (V. R.)

2616 meane] dream mF2J

2617 out-strike] outstrip GOULD (1884, p. 46)

2621 Scene 8 mCOL1

2624 our] the GOULD (1884, p. 46)

2635 Bench-holes] bung-holes GOULD (1884, p. 46)

2647 Scene 9 mCOL1

2650 our] her mTHEO2 (21 Feb. 1729, [fol. 41^r])

2655 haue] all have NICHOLSON *apud* CAM2

       Hectors] as Hectors ANON. *apud* CAM1

2663 thou day] thou ray JACKSON (1819, p. 307); wonder GOULD (1884, p. 46)

2673 yet ha we] *Separate line* FLEAY (1881, 2:88)

2691 Make mingle] Make't tingle DANIEL (1870, p. 82)

2691–2 *Intervening line lost* ELZE (1886, p. 276)

2694 Scene 10 mCOL1

2722 Let's] Nay, let us ELZE (1886, p. 276)

2732 demurely wake the] wake the demurely BECKET (1815, 2:193)

       demurely] clam'rously SING2; do mournfully CARTWRIGHT (1866, p. 38); Do matinly NICHOLSON *apud* CAM1 (*withdrawn* 1871, p. 41); Do rudely KINNEAR (1883, p. 458); Do yarely ELZE (1886, p. 276)

2736 Scene 11 mCOL1

2741 this] thus COL3

2744 Hauen:] haven: let us go mTYR; haven: Let's further, JACKSON (1819, p. 307); haven: forward then, STAU; haven. To the hills! ANON. *apud* CAM1; haven: Haste we, then, HTR; haven let us up NICHOLSON *in* WRIGHT SHAKESPEARIANA

2745 Where] Here *or* There ANON. *apud* CAM1

       discouer] discern ANON. *apud* CAM1

2769 Triple-turn'd] triple-tongued JOHN1 (*and withdrawn*); Triple-train'd JACKSON (1819, p. 308)

2777 pannelled me at] pag'd me at the UPTON (1746, p. 204; *withdrawn* 1748, p. 200)

       pannelled] pan-kneel'd JACKSON (1819, p. 309); pantled ["diminutive of . . . *pant*"] MEREDITH (1974, p. 122)

2778 sweets] suits MACKAY (1884, p. 34)

2779 barkt] lopp'd *or* hack'd mTHEO2 (21 Feb. 1729, [fol. 41^r]; *withdrawn according to* CAM1)

2781 Soule] fowl BULLOCH (1865, p. 2)

       this graue] haggard BULLOCH (1865, p. 2)

       graue Charme] grave-charm FRIPP (1938, 2:680)

2795 For . . . for] 'Fore . . . 'fore MAL

2796 Patient] Passion'd mTHEO2 (21 Feb. 1729, [fol. 41^v]; *withdrawn according to* CAM1)

2804 Let me] Help'd thee THEO1

2806 worthiest selfe] worthless elf ["witch or fairy"] STAU

2807–8 *Three verse lines* To . . . and | I . . . for it. | Eros, ho! MALONE (1783)

2809 Scene 12 mCOL1

2836 dislimes] dislimbs KEIGHTLEY (1867, p. 320)

2847 Vnto] into PYE (1807, p. 269)

2872 sides.] ⁓ , FURNESS (v1907)

2879 length] life STEEVENS (v1793)

357

2882 Seale] seel JOHN1

2893 backe] breast *or* plain ANON. *apud* CAM1

2895 Noble] nobly STEEVENS (v1793)

2922 come] home ANON. *apud* CAM1

2925 thee] there WH1

2946 how] now BARRY *apud* COL1

2958 *Enter Decretas.* ARD2 *(and withdrawn)*

2959–60 *Spoken aside* FURNESS (v1907)

2973 Prophesying] *Om.* GAR (p. 100); prophet's STEEVENS (v1793)

3009, 3011–12 *Two verse lines ending* burn . . . stand MALONE (1783)

3014–22 *Seven verse lines ending* below! . . . valour . . . Antony's . . . itself. . . . but Antony . . . Antony; . . . only WALKER (1860, 3:310)

3014–15 *Om.* CAM3

3022, 3050 I] O, I SEYMOUR (1805, 2:78–9)

3022 dying;] dying, dying; STEEVENS (v1793); *om.* WALKER (1860, 3:310)

3027 *Some words missing at end of line* WALKER (1860, 3:307)

not] not come ELZE (1886, p. 277); not ope the door NICHOLSON *apud* CAM2

3030 brooch'd] brook'd WRAY *in* WRIGHT SHAKESPEARIANA

3033 Conclusion] countenance GOULD (1884, p. 46); complexion KINNEAR (1883, p. 459)

3038 Heere's sport] Here's su'port ["support"] BECKET (1815, 2:196); He's spent BAILEY (1866, 2:120)

3050 dying.] dying; pry'thee SEYMOUR (1805, 2:79)

3066 and] and I mF4FL33

3067 put off] but doff STAU

Helmet] helm but ANON. *apud* CAM1

3071 woo't] wo'n't mSTV2

3075 o'th'earth] of all the earth ANON. *apud* CAM1

melt] melt away SEYMOUR (1805, 2:79)

Lord] lov'd, lov'd lord ANON. *apud* CAM1

3086–7 *Verse lines ending* Empress, my royal mistress! . . . Iras. SEYMOUR (1805, 2:79)

3087 Peace, peace, *Iras*] Iras, peace SEYMOUR (1805, 2:79)

3108 Scene 2. mCOL1

3111 frustrate] prostrate JACKSON (1819, p. 311)

tell him] *Om.* RITSON (1792, p. 88)

3126 thing] thing, Dercetas *(reading* The . . . Dercetas *as one verse line)* SPRENGER (1891, p. 9)

3127 cracke . . . World] crack: The ruin'd world STEEVENS *apud* v1778; crack than this: The ruin'd world STEEVENS (v1793); crack: The round world convulsive SING1; crack, and the rebounding world *or* crack: and the surrounding world BULLOCH (1865, p. 2, *and withdrawn*); crack: the round world in rending NICHOLSON *apud* CAM1; crack in the round world DANIEL *apud* CAM1; crack: the ruinated world CAMPBELL *in* WRIGHT MS; crack: the drowned world SPRENGER (1891, p. 8)

3128 *Line lost after* shooke JOHN1

shooke Lyons] shook, Thrown raging lions MALONE *apud* v1778; shook; Thrown hungry lions MAL; shook, Lions been hurtled MALONE *apud* v1793

3137 the heart] the heart. Cæsar *or* that very heart ELZE (1886, p. 277)

3144 must compell] most compels STAUNTON (1873, p. 535)

3145 persisted] perfited DANIEL *apud* CAM1

3146 wag'd] wagged ANON. *in Gent. Mag.* (1790, p. 126); way'd GOULD (1884, p. 64)

3148 steere] sterre ["star," brighten] BECKET (1815, 2:196); weare GOULD (1884, p. 64)

3153 launch] blaunch: ["Blanchir, to lose vigor"] BECKET (1815, 2:197)

3156 thine] mine GOULD (1884, p. 46)

3170 Whence] Whence, and who STEEVENS (v1793)

    you] you? What WALKER (1860, 3:311)

3171 *Two verse lines* A . . . yet the minister | Of royal purposes. The . . . mistress ANON. *apud* CAM1

    yet,] yet by me mTYR

3179 leaue] beare GOULD (1884, p. 46)

3188 her] her; go SEYMOUR (1805, 2:80)

3200 Scene 3 mCOL1

3202 better] bitter GOULD (1884, p. 46)

3206 accedents] accident ANON. *apud* CAM1

    change] chance WARBURTON *apud* mTHEO2 (21 Feb. 1729, [fol. 42^r]; *withdrawn according to* CAM1)

3207 pallates] quillets BECKET (1815, 2:198)

    dung] tongue BECKET (1815, 2:198); tong ["tongue"] NICHOLSON (1865, p. 395); wrong CARTWRIGHT (1866, p. 38); doom BAILEY (1866, 2:123)

3208 Nurse, and] nurse alike, and mighty SEYMOUR (1805, 2:80); curse and BAILEY (1866, 2:123)

3223 as] and MASON *apud* v1803; that SEYMOUR (1805, 2:80)

3231 pray in ayde] prove mayde GOULD (1884, p. 46)

3234 send] lend ANON. *apud* CAM1

3241 *After* 3232 JOHN1

3248 Releeu'd . . . betraid] Betray'd not, but relev'd ["Relevé . . . raised up"] BECKET (1815, 2:199)

3249 languish] anguish mF4FL33

3257 Oh] *Om.* SEYMOUR (1805, 2:81)

3258 *After* 3259 BECKET (1815, 2:200)

    Ile] I will ANON. *apud* CAM2

3259 *After* 3257 (*continued to Proculeius*) JOICEY (1891, p. 343); *om.* ANON. *apud* ARD2

    necessary] necessary, | I'll not so much as syllable a word; MALONE *apud* v1793; necessary, | I will not speak; if sleep be necessary, RITSON *apud* v1793

3269 into] unto GRIMES *apud* CAM1

3298 little] little world mF2J

3301 Crested] clefted JACKSON (1819, p. 313)

3301–2 propertied . . . that] that of all The tuned spheres, and property'd BECKET (1815, 2:200)

3302 and that] addrest ANON. *apud* CAM1; and sweet STAUNTON (1873, p. 535); and soft *or* and sweet ELZE (1886, p. 277)

    Friends] foes JACKSON (1819, p. 314)

3305 An *Anthony*] an entity BULLOCH (1878, p. 263); A bounty GOULD (1887, p. 72)

3306–7 His delights Were . . . they shew'd] in his delights, He, . . . display'd SEYMOUR (1805, 2:82)

3307 backe] backs BAILEY (1866, 2:125)

3308 they] he SEYMOUR (1805, 2:82)

3319 were] was GAR (p. 100)

3326 at] at' FURNESS (v1907)

3348 project] prolate ["Latin . . . shew, set forth"] BECKET (1815, 2:201); perfect ORGER (1890, p. 101)

3350 which] as SEYMOUR (1805, 2:82)

3358 *Anthonies*] Antonius' ANON. *apud* CAM1

3365 to Seleucus mWARB

    all for] all, fair GOULD (1884, p. 47)

3368 Not] No DANIEL *apud* CAM1

3404 chance] Cheeks WARBURTON *apud* THEO1 (*withdrawn according to* CAM1); change WALKER (1860, 3:312)

3407 the] at JOHN1

3409 We answer] And answer HEATH (1765, p. 468); We, answering BULLOCH (1878, p. 264)

3416 sold] hold ANON. *apud* CAM1

3417 prisons] poisons GOULD (1884, p. 47)

3425 words . . . words] mocks . . . mocks GOULD (1884, p. 47)

3430 againe] amaine mTHEO1 *and* mTHEO2 (21 Feb. 1729, [fol. 42^r]; *withdrawn according to* CAM1), mWARB

3431 *Given to Charmian* mTHEO1 *and* mTHEO2 (21 Feb. 1729, [fol. 42^r])

3456 The Gods] Ye GOULD (1884, p. 47)

3458 catch at] chastise ORGER (1890, p. 101)

3463 Boy] buoy BECKET (1815, 2:201); bow SPRENGER (1891, p. 9); bog LEO (1892, p. 223)

3466 *Cleo.* Nay that's certaine.] *Om. or CLE.* Nay, this is certain; CAPN
   certaine] certain. Be you well assur'd on't SEYMOUR (1805, 2:82)

3469 foole] foile mCOL1 (*withdrawn* COLNE, 1852, p. 483)

3470 absurd] absolute ANON. *apud* CAM1; abhorr'd KINNEAR (1883, p. 462); obscene CAM3

3475 Sirra] Swift, ORGER (1890, p. 102)

3541 life] earth mTHEO2 (21 Feb. 1729, [fol. 42^r]; *withdrawn according to* CAM1)

3543 Applying the asp to Iras ANON. *in Gent. Mag.* (1790, p. 127)

3553 first] first should mCOL1 (*and withdrawn*)

3555 Which . . . wretch] *Verse lines* Which . . . have. | Come | Thou mortal wretch ABBOTT (1870, §512)

3556 intrinsicate] intricate WRAY *in* WRIGHT SHAKESPEARIANA

3564 O breake! O breake] A snake! a snake GOULD (1884, p. 47)

3566 To Charmian. ANON. *apud* CAM1

3566–7 Nay . . . stay—] *Given to Charmian* mLONG

3567–8 *Two verse lines* What! shall . . . world, alone? | No, I will follow strait—O, fare thee well! SEYMOUR (1805, 2:83); *two verse lines* What . . . world? | So . . . well. NICHOLSON *apud* CAM2

3568 wilde] viled NICHOLSON *apud* CAM1

3570 Lasse] loss SPRENGER (1891, p. 10)

3596 A . . . a] Way there, WALKER (1860, 1:89)

3609–10 Diadem; On] ~ ∧ Of mTYR

3614–15 *Verse lines* By some . . . looks | Like . . . *Antony* GAR (p. 100)

3614 externall] Extern WALKER (1860, 3:312)

3622 leaues] voids BAILEY (1866, 2:126)
   Caues] canes BARRY *apud* COL1; eaves ANON. *apud* CAM1; course PERRING (1885, p. 345)

3632 then his] his, than BADHAM *apud* CAM2

The Text

The First Folio Text of Antony and Cleopatra *(1623)*

Ant. occupies 29 double-column pages of F1: sig. vv6^v (p. 340), quire xx (mistakenly x; pp. 341–52), quire yy (yy2, yy3 mistakenly y2, y3; pp. 353–64), and sigs.

$zz1$–$zz2^v$ (pp. 365–8). Type-recurrence and box-rule evidence lead H INMAN (1963, 2:303, 307, 311, 315–16, 517) to conclude that the order of printing was normal for F1—that is, from the innermost sheet of each quire to the outermost, as follows:

vv– –	– –	– –	– –	1^v:6	1:6^v
$xx3^v$:4	3:4^v	2^v:5	2:5^v	1^v:6	1:6^v
$yy3^v$:4	3:4^v	2^v:5	2:5^v	1^v:6	1:6^v
$zz3^v$:4	3:4^v	2^v:5	2:5^v	1^v:6	1:6^v

Forme $vv1$:6^v, containing the first type page of *Ant.*, was followed by a one-page piece of job printing, a Heralds' Visitation Summons dated 5 Aug. 1623; thereafter, work on *Ant.* resumed with the setting of forme $xx3^v$:4. "Headline evidence," Hinman remarks (2:307), "in some measure confirms [the sequence advocated for quire xx], for a roman instead of an italic 'n' appears in the '*Anthony*' of the recto-page headline in $xx3^v$:4 and $xx3$:4^v but not elsewhere. Evidently the roman 'n' represents the original setting, correction having been effected before $xx2^v$:5 went to press." He also demonstrates (2:303–16) that the type pages were composed in the following sequence:

vv –	–	–	–	–	–	–	–	–	–	–	6^v
$xx3^v$	4	4^v	3	2^v	5	2	5^v	1^v	6	6^v	1
$yy3^v$	4	4^v	3	2^v	5	2	5^v	6	1^v	1	6^v
zz –	–	–	–	2^v	–	–	2	1^v	–	–	1

The text is undivided, although it is headed "*Actus Primus. Scœna Prima.*," as are the other half-dozen undivided plays in F1. Sig. $zz2^v$ has only 40 lines of text, 20 in each column, the rest of the page being filled out with a "FINIS.," horizontal rules, and the "satyr" tailpiece (Hinman, 1:21 et passim).

The Composition of F1

Until recently it was believed that the F1 text of *Ant.* was the work of Compositor B because of the spelling of certain high-frequency words: W ILLOUGHBY (1932), A. W ALKER (1953), M CKENZIE (1959), H INMAN (1963), K ABLE (1968), and R EID (1976), among others, call attention to B's preference for *do* (rather than *doe*), *go* (vs. *goe*), *heere* (vs. *here*), *yong* (vs. *young*), and so on; to final *y* rather than *ie*, to medial *i* rather than *y*; and to a single terminal consonant in the third person singular (e.g., *cals* for *calls* at 553, 862, 1957). Other features brought forward as supporting evidence include B's centering of SDs involving entries, his placing of exits full out to the right-hand margin of the column, and his use of italics for quotations and letters. Hinman, cautious as to the absolute value of orthographical evidence, also emphasizes "physical evidence," primarily typecase identifications, in the determination of compositorial responsibility. Because he found that in *Ant.* only the case he designated "y" was employed, and because the only other workman suggested by the evidence, Compositor E, (1957, p. 20) "was not regarded as competent to deal with manuscript copy," Hinman is certain B set all of *Ant.*

This view has been challenged by HOWARD-HILL (1977), who finds E setting from MS in plays preceding *Ant.* in F1—one type page in *Tim.* and ten in *Oth.* (assuming that *Oth.* derives from MS). In *Ant.* Howard-Hill attributes xx3^v–5, 6–6^v, and yy1 to Compositor E. As proof he cites (p. 35) E's use of elisions with *xth'* (e.g., "oth'world" [754] as opposed to *o'thworld* or *o th'world*); of verbal auxiliaries with a final *e* (*they'le, weele, you'le* in contrast to B's *they'l, wee'l, you'l*); (pp. 35–6) of shorter forms of pronouns ending in *-e* (*he's, she's* in contrast to B's *hee's, shee's*); and of distinctive SPs (pp. 37–8): "B favours *'Ant., Caes./Caesar., Eno./Enob.',* whereas E uses *'Ant./Anth., Caesar., Eno.'*" In addition, in *Oth.* B preferred *-oo-* in *doo't, too't*, etc.; in *Ant.* (p. 37) "only -oo- spellings occur, all in B's pages." Howard-Hill's (1976) distinguishing of E on the basis of a strong preference for nonspaced medial commas is especially convincing evidence, for this mechanical trait could not be influenced by the printer's MS copy. His overall position is conveniently summarized in HOWARD-HILL (1980). A detailed comparison of B and E as to sophistications and errors involving transpositions, literal changes, substitutions, omissions, interpolations, semisubstantives, and SDs—mainly in *Tit., Rom.,* and *Tro.*—appears in WERSTINE (1983), a supplement to his earlier study (1978) of these practices by B in *1H4* and the comedies.

A troublesome consequence of the reassignment to E of work formerly attributed to B is that, according to Hinman's analysis, they must be supposed to have set from the same typecase, case y. Thus B would have set vv6^v, stepped aside (or busied himself elsewhere) while E set xx3^v through 4^v, returned for 3 and 2^v, stepped aside again while E set 5, and so on. Such a pattern is not impossible, but it is unique in the Folio, for elsewhere when two compositors collaborated on material for the same quire they seem to have worked simultaneously at two typecases. Aware of this problem earlier (1977, p. 19), HOWARD-HILL (1980, p. 176) asserts that "rather than the single case y hereabouts which Hinman records, there were *two* typecases. No other hypothesis will resolve the conflict between the case evidence and the unassailable witness of the spacing and spellings." And this hypothesis may prove correct. In a paper as yet unpublished, Paul Werstine reinterprets Hinman's type-recurrence evidence to show that B and E set from two typecases, not one, in their collaboration on *Oth.*, and he privately expresses the opinion, based on preliminary work, that a similar revision of the evidence pertaining to *Ant.* may show that two typecases were employed there as well.

Some Features of the Printed Text

Lineation

Mislining, considered by GREG (1942; 1954, p. 147) "rather frequent" in *Ant.*, is not a simple term because it presupposes a "clear and consistent distinction between verse and prose" that McKERROW (1939, p. 44) finds absent from dramatic writing, where "little regard, even in what is clearly verse, seems to have been paid to the formation of complete lines" (i.e., lines with five regular feet). Be that as it may, the origin of mislining is explained from apparently different directions. According to Greg (p. 147), mislineation of verse in *Ant.* "seems mainly due to the author running on half-lines to economize space." McKerrow (pp. 47–9), however, concentrating on the breaking of lines in F1 and the later Folios, especially on the breaking of one long line into two at the beginning of speeches, finds (p. 49) "sufficient evidence that this peculiarity of the Folio is not based on the copy from which it was printed, and we may safely assume that it is due to the compositor alone, who may for some reason have disliked the appearance of a turnover in the first line of a speech." An analysis of such split pentameters in *Ant.* reveals that most seem compositorial. MS leaves seem generally to have been wide enough to accommodate on one line a SP and a full pentameter. In F1, however, because they occupy space in the narrow column of type, SPs may have caused the pentameter immediately following to be run over to a new line. The resulting split pentameters at the opening of speeches in *Ant.* appear (in the order of typesetting) at 1034–5, 1063–4 (xx4^v), 1142–3 (xx5), 1274–5 (xx5^v), 301–2 (xx1^v), 1400–1, 1427–8, 1432–3, 1472–3 (xx6), 1638–9 (xx6^v), 176–7, 187–8, 194–5, 215–16 (xx1), 2375–6 (yy3^v), 1963–4 (yy2), 3038–9 (yy6), 3448–9 (zz1^v). Other instances, where there is room on one line for the pentameter, seem to result from the compositor's miscalculation—275–6 (xx1^v)—or perhaps from his dislike of giving a short SD a line to itself, as at 171–2 (xx1).

Another group of split pentameters attributable to physical restrictions on the compositor consists of those within a speech (and so not affected by a SP or SD) that are simply too long for the narrow F1 column, as at 7–8 (vv6^v), where the line is crowded by the ornamental "N" occupying 4–8; 905–6 (xx4); 1555–6 and 1593–4 (xx6^v); 2377–8 (yy3^v); 2671–2 (yy4^v); 2831–2 (yy5^v).

A further group is regularly split because an entrance SD intrudes, as at 14–17 (vv6^v), 210–12 (xx1), 647–9 (xx3), 1922–3, 1930–2 (yy2), 2525–7 (yy4), 2659–61 (yy4^v), 2786–8, 2797–8 (yy5), 2869–70 (yy5^v), 3004–6 (yy6), 3168–70 (yy6^v), 3470–2 (zz2). In all instances the second short line involves a shift by the speaker of focus or theme (most often a direct response to the action or person in the SD); in all instances but 212 and 3006 the second short line is followed either by a normal pentameter line or, being the conclusion of a speech, by a pentameter opening the next speech. The two short lines thus almost invariably must be taken as one pentameter. This type of intrusive SD is found solely on pages set by Compositor B. Only on xx4^v does the situation present itself to E, and there at 1007–8, 1051–2, and 1131–2 he sets the entrance SD after the entering person has been addressed.

Another group consists of pentameters split, although there is room for both parts on the same line, probably to meet the requirements of casting off. Once xx2^v had been composed, the pentameter on xx2 now comprising 476–7 was divided to waste space. For the same reason, 336–7 and 342–3 were divided on xx1^v and 168–9, 173–4, and 205–6 on xx1. A tight page no doubt resulted in the turnover at 1837 (yy1^v) and perhaps the squeezing of Agrippa's speech on to the same line (1848) as the conclusion of Caesar's, although several opportunities for the same maneuver occur in col. b.

Eds. have also relined single short lines within verse speeches, often normatively but more often with individual and erratic differences. These single lines are integrated into a larger context or expanded, as may be seen in the textual notes involving 566, 611, 1158, 1181, 1484, 1521, 1653, 1690, 1699, 2102, 2228, 2744, 2849 (with a centered SD on 2850), 3111, 3127, 3137, and 3165. Yet Sh. did write short lines within speeches, as the instances in *Ant.*—e.g., 2279 and 2847—that have withstood both compositorial and editorial manipulation prove.

In his survey of nineteen Folio texts WERSTINE (1984) has shown that (p. 111) "distinctive kinds of mislineation in these plays are associated with individual compositors" and that instances in *Ant.* of two verse lines set as one, for example, are (p. 96) "distributed fairly evenly" between B and E. Thus, the irregularities cannot always be due to the physical requirements of typesetting or the compositor's idiosyncrasies. Some, like 1487–8, set by Compositor E, seem to be caused by a tangle in the MS; Werstine observes (p. 101) that the amount of irregular verse in B's part of *Ant.* shows that he also "reproduced irregularities in his copy when he found them," and he found them because Sh. put them there. Seeking principles to govern the lineation of Sh.'s verse, BOWERS (1980) refers to *Ant.* as (p. 81) "the metrically most irregular of Shakespeare's plays," an opinion doubtless shared by its eds., who on numerous occasions cannot agree on whether lines have been mislined and if so how they are to be relined. At 186–96, one among countless examples, two eds. propose 10 lines, two 9 lines, five 8 lines, and one 7 lines. At 975–83 there is a notable disagreement on the number of lines and a bewildering mixture of verse and prose within them. The textual notes at 2720–30 and 2732–5 testify to a medley of interpretations so variegated as to exceed the possible causes of variation: the incapacity of the compositor, the disposition of the eds., and perhaps even the intention of the author. Since each strives for "regularity" according to his own fashion and ability, the reconstruction of an original text can be only partial, the attribution of responsibility at best tentative. Assertions that F1's lineation is "swarming with vital clues to pauses and emphasis" (BERTRAM, 1981, p. 55) or reveals the "rhetorical pattern of the verse" (SLATER, ed. 1971, p. 41) are too impressionistic or heedless of compositorial practice to be tenable.

Speech-Prefixes

The SPs in *Ant.* have been regularly abbreviated, in the main. Their use in compositor identification is discussed below. The most telling are the 200 instances of *Cleo.*, as opposed to 1 instance of *Cle.* (1660) and 2 of *Cleopa.* (1031, 1680) adopted by Compositor E in full lines of type; 61 instances of *Char.*, with 1 *Ch.* in a full line (310; B) and 1 *Cha.* (1651; E) possibly caused by a shortage of *r*'s; 26 of *Eros.*, with 1 *Ero.* in a full line (1730). The relatively minor characters are also completely regularized (*Alex.*, *Clow.*, *Dem.*, *Iras.*, *Philo.*, *Pro.*, *Scar.*, *Sooth.*) or have but one or at most two deviations not occurring in full lines (*Agri., Amb., Cam., Dec., Diom., Dol., Lep., Mar., Mece., Men., Mes., Octa., Pom.*). Each of these variants is most often restricted to a single page of F1: Compositor B varies *Am., Camid., Decre., Dio., Dolla., Menas., Mene.,* and *Messen.*; Compositor E *Agr., Lepi., Mardi., Oct., Octaui.*; and both compositors *Agrip., Mec.,* and *Mess.*

Enobarbus, Cæsar, and *Anthony* are somewhat more complicated. A survey of the pages in order of typesetting helps clarify the situation.

Comp.	Sig.	F1 Page	Prefixes (f = full lines; s = short lines)
B	vv6^v	340	*Enob.* (1s)
E	xx3^v	346	*Enobar.* (2f) *Enob.* (1f) *Enob.* (1s)
E	4	347	*Eno.* (1f) *Enob.* (1f) *Eno.* (1f) *Enob.* (1f) *Eno.* (6s)
E	4^v	348	
B	3	345	*Enob.* (1s) *Eno.* (3s)
B	2^v	344	
E	5	349	*Eno.* (3s)
B	2	343	
B	5^v	350	*Enob.* (1f) *Enob.* (2s) *Enob.* (4f) *Enob.* (3s)
			Enob. (1f) *Enob.* (1s) *Enob.* (2f) *Eno.* (1f) *Enob.* (1f)
B	1^v	342	*Eno.* (1s) *Eno.* (4f) *Eno.* (2s) *Eno.* (2f) *Enob.* (1s)
E	6	351	*Eno.* (2s) *Eno.* (1f) *Eno.* (1s) *Enob.* (1f) *Eno.* (1s)
			Eno. (1f) *Enor.* (1s)
E	6^v	352	*Eno.* (4s) *Eno.* (1f) *Eno.* (3s) *Eno.* (2f)
B	1	341	*Enob.* (1f) *Enob.* (3s)
B	yy3^v	358	*Eno.* (1f) *Eno.* (1s) *Eno.* (1f) *Eno.* (1s) *Eno.* (1f)
B	4	359	*Eno.* (2s)
B	4^v	360	*Enob.* (1s) *Eno.* (1s) *Enob.* (1s)
B	3	357	*Eno.* (2s) *Enob.* (1s) *Eno.* (3s)
B	2^v	356	*Eno.* (2s)
B	5	361	*Enob.* (3s)
B	2	355	*Eno.* (1f) *Eno.* (3s) *Enob.* (1s) *Enob.* (1f) *Eno.* (1s)
B	5^v	362	
B	6	363	
B	1^v	354	*Eno.* (2s) *Enob.* (1f) *Enob.* (1s) *Eno.* (1s) *Enob.* (2s)
			Eno. (1s)
E	1	353	*Eno.* (3s) *Eno.* (1f) *Eno.* (1s) *Eno.* (1f)

An analysis of the instances found in short lines reveals that Compositor E, after some variation between *Enob.* and *Eno.*, preferred *Eno.* B vacillated between *Enob.* (22 times) and *Eno.* (26 times). His choice may have been affected partly by a desire for uniformity on the page, as is apparent in his use of *Enob.* in close alternation with the equally wide *Men.* in col. a of xx5^v (p. 350) and, on the next page he set, of *Eno.* with *Ant.* in col. a of xx1^v (p. 342). On the whole, there is regularity, for with the exception of yy1^v (p. 354) only seven anomalies occur, no more than one to a page: five instances of *Enob.* by B at 297, 682, 2005, 2012, and 2210; one of *Enor.* by E at 1492; one of *Eno.* by B at 2605. An explanation is of course difficult, but the irregularities have in common their appearance just before or after a SD. Whatever the exact reason for minor variations (type shortage might be one), the general pattern is clear. Even the irregularity of yy1^v (p. 354) does not greatly disturb the overall picture.

The 59 instances of *Cæsar.* and 37 of *Cæs.* are likewise regular in distribution.

Comp.	Sig.	F1 Page	Prefixes (f = full lines; s = short lines)
B	vv6^v	340	
E	xx3^v	346	*Cæs.* (1f) *Cæsar.* (3f) *Cæsar.* (2s) *Cæsar.* (1f) *Cæsar.* (6s)
E	4	347	*Cæsar.* (1s)
E	4^v	348	
B	3	345	*Cæsar.* (1s) *Cæs.* (3s) *Cæs.* (1f) *Cæs.* (2s)
B	2^v	344	*Cæsar.* (1s) *Cæs.* (1s) *Cæs.* (1f) *Cæsar.* (1f)
E	5	349	*Cæsar.* (3s) *Cæsar.* (2f) *Cæsar.* (1s)
B	2	343	*Cæs.* (3s)
B	5^v	350	*Cæs.* (1s)
B	1^v	342	
E	6	351	*Cæsar.* (2f) *Cæsar.* (1s)
E	6^v	352	*Cæsar.* (7s)
B	1	341	
B	yy3^v	358	*Cæs.* (2s)
B	4	359	
B	4^v	360	*Cæs.* (1s) *Cæsar.* (1s) *Cæs.* (1s)
B	3	357	
B	2^v	356	*Cæs.* (1s) *Cæsar.* (1s) *Cæs.* (3s) *Cæsar.* (1s)
B	5	361	*Cæs.* (1s)
B	2	355	*Cæs.* (2s)
B	5^v	362	
B	6	363	
B	1^v	354	*Cæs.* (1s) *Cæsar.* (1s) *Cæs.* (1f) *Cæs.* (2s) *Cæsar.* (1s) *Cæs.* (1f) *Cæs.* (1s)
E	1	353	*Cæs.* (1f) *Cæsar.* (1f) *Cæsar.* (3s)
B	6^v	364	*Cæsar.* (1s) *Cæs.* (1f) *Cæsar.* (1s) *Cæsar.* (1f) *Cæs.* (1s) *Cæsar.* (2s) *Cæs.* (1s) *Cæs.* (1f) *Cæs.* (1s)
		[Three pages of *Cym.*]	
B	zz2^v	368	*Cæsar.* (4s)
		[Two pages of *Cym.*]	
B	2	367	
B	1^v	366	*Cæs.* (1s) *Cæsar.* (9s)

Compositor E consistently prefers *Cæsar.*; he uses it for all 24 short lines. Whereas in *JC* B employed *Cæs.* 39 times and *Cæsar.* but once (as the prefix to the first speech after the scene-opening SD at 985), he here vacillates throughout in short lines between *Cæsar.* (24 times) and *Cæs.* (29 times), finishing strongly with 13 uses of *Cæs.* on the last pages (zz2^v, 1^v). Some instances of *Cæsar.* may be due to their following a SD, at xx3 (p. 345), yy2^v (p. 356), yy1^v (p. 354), yy6^v (p. 364) (although the last two are not the only ones on the page). Five instances occur when the SP follows a line of text in which the name *Cæsar* appears, at 2580–1, 2147–8, 1793–4, 3123–4, 3125–6. If these instances are taken into account, as well as those that might be attributed to the fear of type shortages arising from the name's use in both text and SPs, the irregularities, considered page by page, are fairly infrequent.

As for the abbreviation for *Anthony*, Compositor B's 127 usages of *Ant.* in short lines (as against 3 of *Anth.* and 1 each of *An.* and *Antho.*) affirm his consistency. E's 20 uses help establish the dominance if not regularity of the SP. E, however, also uses *Anth.* in an equal number of short lines. Yet 15 occur in the first two pages he set (xx3^v and 4), after which he adopted the more economical form with fair regularity.

Comp.	Sig.	F1 Page	Prefixes (f = full lines; s = short lines)
B	vv6^v	340	*Ant.* (2f) *Ant.* (5s)
E	xx3^v	346	*Anth.* (2s) *Ant.* (2s) *Anth.* (2s) *Anth.* (2f) *Anth.* (3s) *Ant.* (1f) *Anth.* (3s)
E	4	347	*Anth.* (3s) *Anth.* (1f) *Ant.* (1s) *Antho.* (1f) *Anth.* (2s)
E	4^v	348	
B	3	345	*Ant.* (7s) *Ant.* (1f)
B	2^v	344	
E	5	349	*Ant.* (1f) *Ant.* (4s) *Anth.* (1s) *Ant.* (1s)
B	2	343	*Ant.* (9s)
B	5^v	350	*Ant.* (1f) *Anth.* (1s) *Ant.* (1s) *Ant.* (1f) *Ant.* (2s) *Ant.* (1f)
B	1^v	342	*Anth.* (1s) *Ant.* (8s) *An.* (1s) *Ant.* (6s)
E	6	351	*Anth.* (1s) *Ant.* (4s) *Anth.* (1s)
E	6^v	352	*Ant.* (1s) *Antho.* (1s) *Ant.* (2s) *Anth.* (1s) *Ant.* (3s)
B	1	341	*Ant.* (2s) *Ant.* (1f) *Ant.* (5s) *Antho.* (1s)
B	yy3^v	358	*Ant.* (14s)
B	4	359	*Ant.* (1f) *Ant.* (3s) *Ant.* (1f) *Ant.* (3s) *Ant.* (1f) *Ant.* (1s)
B	4^v	360	*Ant.* (6s) *Ant.* (1f) *Ant.* (2s)
B	3	357	*Ant.* (1s) *Ant.* (2f) *Ant.* (5s)
B	2^v	356	*Ant.* (10s) *Antho.* (1f)
B	5	361	*Ant.* (5s)
B	2	355	*Ant.* (4s) *Ant.* (2f)
B	5^v	362	*Ant.* (2s) *Ant.* (1f) *Ant.* (1s) *Ant.* (1f) *Ant.* (4s) *Ant.* (2f) *Ant.* (5s)
B	6	363	*Ant.* (4s) *Anth.* (1s) *Ant.* (3f) *Ant.* (7s)
B	1^v	354	*Ant.* (5s)
E	1	353	*Ant.* (2s) *Anth.* (1s)

Eds. emend a number of SPs—for example, the possible confusion of *Mene.* for *Menas.* at 618, 635, 638, 662. As the textual notes show, however, not all eds. accept that *Mene.* means *Menas.* Indisputable errors are F1's *Ant.* (corrected by ROWE [ed. 1709] to *Agr.*) at 1549, *Ven.* (corrected by POPE [ed. 1723] to *Can.*) at 1946, and *Alex.* (corrected by Rowe to *Cap.*) at 2535, because Antony, Ventidius, and Alexas are not on stage at the required time. Another oversight was corrected by

THEOBALD (ed. 1733) when he added an entrance for a Soldier at 2552 and changed *Eros.* to *Sold.* at 2553, 2556, and 2561. Still another is the attribution of two speeches to Dolabella at 3143 and 3147. Theobald was the first to introduce an exit for him at 3113 and to substitute Agrippa as speaker of the lines. F1's *Alexas.* at 140 is a compositorial confusion of the name, written in the Italian hand, for the SP. (ROLFE's [ed. 1895] assertion that the normal SP is *Alex.* is not convincing, since numerous SPs give names in full: *Cæsar, Eros, Iras, Dercetus, Lepidus, Mecenas, Menas, Pompey.*) Most eds. follow Theobald (see textual notes) in regarding Alexas as spoken of, since his fortune is to be laughed out, and continue the speech to Charmian. Editorial substitution of North's Canidius for F1's *Camidius* or *Camidias* or *Camindius* (with *Cam.* or once [at 2017] *Camid.* as SPs) does not correct a series of misreadings but alters an authorial form.

Of some significance is the repeated *Pro.* at 3241. Assigned by eds. to various speakers (see textual notes), the repeated SPs are regarded by HINMAN (1963, 2:508) as indicating a missing SD dealing with Cleopatra's capture, an omission due to the "decidedly 'tight' page" and resulting (2:509) "in almost every modern edition [in an] unnecessary emendation, '*Gal.*' (for *Gallus*) having been substituted for the Folio's second '*Pro.*' (for *Proculeius*)." Another is the apparent confusion concerning the numbering of the messengers at 203–17: see textual notes and commentary. Still another is the unusual SP *Omnes.*, which occurs six times in *Ant.*—in the order of typesetting, on xx4^v at 1027 (E); xx5, 1224 (E); yy4, 2436, 2496, 2501 (B); and yy2, 2030 (B)—and only four times in all other substantive eds. of Sh.: twice in *Cor.* (823 [Compositor A], 3065 [B]) and twice in *Per.* Q1 (1.4.97, 2.4.40). According to WELLS & TAYLOR (1987, pp. 556–7, 593–4), *Cor.* shows strong signs of having been printed from scribal copy, and *Per.* Q1 is a reported text. The customary SP in Sh., *All.*, occurs very often in 23 substantive eds., including eight times in *Ant.*, all set by Compositor B: 1278, 2536, 2953, 2989, 3049, 3192, 3336, and 3596. Since both SPs have significance for copy, however, it is probable that the first instance of *Omnes.* at 1027 (xx4^v), set by Compositor E, was the copy's form. The other instances, set by B, are typical of his vacillating between what may be copy and the more economical *All.* The possibility that B used *All.* because of a shortage of type is remote since so few O's are required, especially as the SPs for *Octavius* are always *Cæsar.* and *Cæs.* and for *Octavia.* are only thirteen in all. Besides, there is no evidence elsewhere in F1 of a shortage of O's in case y.

Colons and Semicolons

If Hand D's punctuation of the *Sir Thomas More* fragment is Sh.'s, the pointing of F1 *Ant.* cannot be his. Instead of Hand D's extremely light pointing, that of *Ant.* is relatively heavy, as evidenced by its 563 colons, which appear in roughly the same proportion in pages set by Compositors B and E (who uses 165). The same is true of semicolons: there are 48 on 20 pages set by B, 6 on 4 pages set by E. Attempts to explain these marks on the basis of structural punctuation, the most favored theory, or even less convincingly on that of rhetorical or dramatic considerations—for a convenient summary of opinion see SPEVACK (1985, 2:346–9)—are of little consequence as far as the copy is concerned, since either way the great number of colons—about half as many as full stops—is enough to indicate that the punctuation is not Shn.

Other Accidental Details

Most accidental irregularities appear to be compositorial, as is apparent in the list of emended accidentals (pp. 345–6) and press-variants (pp. 370–1) and in certain commentary notes, such as 1643. In addition, the short verse line at 611, followed by the catchword "Hee" at xx2^v (Compositor B), is completed at 612–13 (xx3, also B) in prose beginning with "he," perhaps because xx2^v was set after xx3, with Compositor B employing his favored -*ee* spelling for this pronoun when it does not appear in a full line. B's vacillation may account for a similar discrepancy between the CW "Hee" at yy4 (p. 359) and the text word "He" at 2562 (yy4^v, p. 360), although the two type pages were set sequentially. A blunder may account for B's incorrect CW *"Dol."* at zz2, which was set just before the first SP, *"Cæs."* (3337), of zz1^v. Other compositorial features are the 24 ampersands used in full lines or occasionally for the centering or accommodating of SDs set flush right, as at 523, 1279, 1939, 2152, 2389, 2997, all set by B. Likewise, the four thorn logotypes (582, 2919, 3123, 3384) are found in full or nearly full lines. The same is true of the tildes—e.g., at 499; at 3230, however, what may be a missing tilde in "dependacie" is more likely a simple error (note the *n* before the *d*), for there is ample space in the line. A blank line after 1563 suggests a SD may have been overlooked, but since the same situation is correctly handled at 1537 and 1619, it is more likely that the SD never existed. Considering Compositor B's fondness for long dashes to indicate broken-off speeches, the absence of one at 3577 (after two appear at 3567 and 3573) must be an oversight. The absence of end punctuation at 218 may be connected with a missing SD to provide for the exit of the Messenger and to enable Antony to deliver 219–27 solus. Finally, HINMAN (1963, 2:312) attributes the use of lowercase *e* for the *E* of exit directions in quire yy—four times in yy2, once in yy2^v, six times in yy5, twice in yy5^v, and once in yy6—to Compositor B's concern over having enough *E*'s to set "a play in which *Eros* and (especially) *Enobarbus* have important parts and in which directions beginning with '*Enter*' are more than ordinarily abundant."

Press-Variants in F1

The following table of press-correction variants—the uncorrected state preceding the corrected one—given by HINMAN (1963, 1:316–18) is based on his collations of approximately fifty copies of F1 at the Folger Library, of the Barton copy in the Boston Public Library, and of the Lee (1902) and Kökeritz-Prouty (Yale, 1954) facsimiles of the Chatsworth and the Elizabethan Club copies. Also collated in this ed. is the copy formerly owned by the Earl of Carysfort, now in the University of

Cologne; unless otherwise mentioned, it agrees with the corrected copies. Discussion of certain variants is also found on pp. 376–7, in the list of emended accidentals (pp. 345–6), and in the commentary. The characteristics of Compositor E, who set all the press-variant pages, are discussed on p. 362.

Sig. xx3ᵛ (p. 346)
   a18 (761)
      youm uſt,] 16 copies (e.g., Folg. 8 and 38)
      You muſtt,] all others; also Lee and Yale
   a19 (762)
      it?
      it.
   a47 (790)
      as b efits
      as befits

Sig. xx4ᵛ (p. 348)
   a59 (1061)
      l pt] 5 copies (Folg. 1, 21, 43, 47, and 67)
      [Because the "p" is more than type-high, the "t" after it is partly obscured and perhaps an "i" before it is totally obscured.]
      lipt] all others; also Lee and Yale

Sig. xx6 (p. 351)
   a33 (1427)
      Mǝn.] 6 copies (Folg. 1, 9, 10, 12, 54, and 73)
      Men.] all others; also Lee and Yale
   b20 (1478)
      ſpeakest: he
      ſpeakes: the
   b31 (1489)
      heere a, (mistakenly "heare a," in Hinman)
      heare,
   b32 (1490)
      theſe great
      theſe great
   b35 (1493)
      Hoa Noble . . . *Exenut.*
      Hoa, Noble . . . *Exeunt.*
   b38 (1495)
      beȷore
      before
   b44 (1501)
      Ventidus
      Ventidius
   b55 (1512)
      to high
      too high

b60 (1517)
by.th'
by'th'

Sig. xx6ᵛ (p. 352)

a13 (1536)
their ,] 4 copies (Folg. 8, 26, 29, and 50, plus a fragment of the proof sheet)
there,] all others; also Lee and Yale

a16 (1539)
art
are

a55 (1577)
Cæſar,
Cæſar.

a59 (1581)
ſpeure
ſerue

a63 (1585)
farethee
fare thee

b1 (1589)
[Foreign matter, inked, over "Husbands house."]
[This foreign matter not in evidence.]

b7 (1595)
the of full tide
the full of Tide

b11 (1599)
that, . . . Horſe
that . . . Horſe,

b17 (1605)
yeare indeed . . . troubled . . . rume
[Because the letters "bl" are more than type-high, the "u" and "e" beside them are partly obscured.]
yearindeed . . . trobled . . . rheume

b25 (1613)
I, let ʎou
I let you

b39 (1626)
plaes'd
pleas'd

b53 (1640)
ſpeake . . . voic'c.
ſpeake, . . . voic'd.

That all the press-variant pages were set by Compositor E may be due to an accident of survival, but it is more likely that his work, known to be poor, was closely supervised. And since the uncorrected states have so few errors, the variants listed here are likely survivors of at least one previous round of correction—in other words, the variants are not from raw proof but from revises.

The extant proof sheet for xx6ᵛ (p. 352), set by Compositor E and reproduced by HINMAN (facs. 1968, p. 922), is also important for what it reveals about proof-reading. The proof corrector made some 19 corrections, "mostly of pure compositor's blunders" (SIMPSON, 1935, p. 82) and probably without reference to copy, in order to "ensure a comprehensible text" whose spellings were "most likely" in "accord with what he imagined the standard usage of the time" (H[oward-]HILL, 1963, p. 15). Thus among the spelling corrections called for are "there" for "their" (1536) and "rheume" for "rume" (1605). Interesting too are the corrections that may not have been necessary (the "S" in "Should" at 1524, the final "d" in "builded" at 1572, both poorly inked, are not typesetting errors, though the corrector could not see the "S", and the "d" looked broken), that were not carried out ("onboth" at 1574), that were incorrectly executed (the spelling changes made to accommodate "rheume" at 1605 did not prevent the running together of "yearindeed"), and that were not marked by the corrector (e.g., the erroneous SP at 1549, the missing SD after 1563 and end punctuation at 1643). Simpson finds that the corrections "indicate the normal standard of a professional corrector" (p. 82); WILLOUGHBY (1932, p. 64) characterizes the work as "moderately careful but not meticulous." BLAYNEY (1982, 1:238) uses the page to illustrate that corrections could be marked in the wrong order: "Had the compositor taken the corrections in order the line [1605] would have read: *Eno.* That yearhee indeed, he was trobled with a ume,".

The Copy for F1

Since F1 (1623) offers the first and only text of *Ant.*, the textual situation should be simple or at least notably simpler than that of plays with both quarto and folio versions. To a certain extent it is simpler, yet although the existence of only one text limits the evidence, it has not restricted the speculations and conclusions, for uncertainty remains about the printer's copy as well as about the accuracy of the printed text in some details. Many eds. up to FURNESS (ed. 1907, pp. vi–vii)—most notably HUDSON (ed. 1855, 8:441) and WHITE (ed. 1861, 12:5)—agree substantially, if not verbatim, with the first to comment explicitly, KNIGHT (ed. 1841, 6:277): "The text is, upon the whole, remarkably accurate; although the metrical arrangement is, in a few instances, obviously defective. The positive errors are very few. Some obscure passages present themselves; but, with one or two exceptions, they are not such as to render conjectural emendation desirable." Yet in his second ed. Hudson (ed. 1881, 16:3)—no doubt influenced by DELIUS (ed. 1856), whose opinion he seems to translate literally—changes his mind strikingly: "I must add that the original text of this play is not very well printed, even for that time or that volume, and has a number of corruptions [presumably the punctuation and lineation mentioned by Delius (2:1)] that are exceedingly trying to an editor." Twentieth-c. eds. often take a benevolent position, like KITTREDGE's (ed.

1941, p. vii) almost casual "Misprints are plentiful, but they are usually easy to correct" or EVERETT's (ed. 1964, p. 187) "As a text, it is relatively good: it contains many slips but few real difficulties." WILSON (facs. 1929, Introd., [p. 1]) even makes a virtue of the vice of irregularity: "The very roughness of the text . . . is a guarantee of its authenticity."

It is precisely this paradox—a "good" text, one generally representing Sh.'s intention, but marked or marred by certain aberrations and corruptions—that enables scholars to make inferences about the copy, for the "minor" difficulties— spelling, punctuation, even lineation—are thrown into relief by the otherwise "good" text. So too the coincidence of opposites on another level, as in HUDSON's (ed. 1881, 16:4) explanation of the underlying situation: "The style of the play is so superlatively idiomatic, and abounds in such splendid audacities of diction and imagery, that it might well be very puzzling to any transcriber or printer or proof-reader, unless the author's hand-writing were much plainer than it appears to have been."

The evidence provided by the text of F1 has led to two speculations about the copy that reflect the eminently Elizabethan concern with the interaction of speaking and writing in the evolution of modern English orthography. The first theory is evident in commentary notes by THEOBALD (ed. 1733) and supported in one way or another by MALONE (ed. 1790) and STEEVENS (ed. 1793), reaching a climax of sorts in FURNESS (ed. 1907, p. viii), who attributes many orthographic peculiarities to aural misapprehensions, notably the "practice of reading the copy aloud to the compositor." Not only has the notion that printshops followed this practice been rejected (see McKERROW [1927, pp. 239 ff.] and ALBRIGHT [1927, pp. 325 ff.]), but Furness's (pp. viii–ix) "errors of the ear" evaporate under scrutiny. "Mine Nightingale" (2670) for "My Nightingale" and "mine Nailes" (3467) for "my Nailes," for example, may not be very common, but they are not necessarily errors and are most unlikely examples of mishearing, for they create longer units, whereas the euphony underlying such mishearings normally leads to shorter ones through elision, telescoping, and other means of assimilation. "Thantoniad" (1978) for "The Antoniad" and "places" (295) for "place is" ("place's") are ordinary elisions. In "vouchsafe to" (437) for "vouchsafed to" there is less a particular compositor's hearing error than assimilation, if not a simple compositorial blunder, as "should'st stowe" (2086) for "should'st towe" most certainly is (WILSON [ed. 1950, p. 125] calls these "seeming dittographs"). Still less is "vouchsafe to" a compositorial confusion resulting, as WALKER (1860, 2:61–2) asserts, from the "old method of writing" final *e*/*d*. "Whose" (302) for "Who's" is a common Elizabethan spelling (the opening words of *Ham.* Q2 are "Whose there?"); "neere" (Lust-wearied) at 661 is ortho-graphically interchangeable with the homophone "ne'er," which Furness suggests is "correct" (although both readings have their supporters). Finally, "hither" (1764) and "he there" are unconvincing aural alternatives because of the difference in stress; a compositorial blunder seems a more reasonable explanation, especially as the line contains a second error ("King" for "Kings").

The few examples cited by Furness that fulfill the formal requirements for mishearing are also not convincing. Although both readings, as the textual notes attest, have their advocates, "greet together" (663) for "gree together," "your proofe" (818–19) for "your reproof," "wayes a Mars" (1171) for "way he's a Mars," "your so branchlesse" (1710) for "yours so branchless," and "Vnarme *Eros*" (2867) for "Unarm me Eros" are possibly sophistications, misreadings, or eye-skip errors, and "your so branchlesse" (1710) for "yours so branchless" and "You reconciler" (1717) for "Your reconciler," both corrected by F2, could result from misreading or haplography. Instead of a mishearing, "toward Cittadell" (2828) for "tower'd Citadel" may just as likely be a compositorial misreading of the minuscule *e* for *a* in *toward*, or even a spelling variant (the *OED* gives *towerde* as a form of *toward*).

More recently, the study of orthographic features has enabled investigators to identify not only compositors but also, some think, distinctive characteristics of the author. The collaborative effort of POLLARD et al. (*Sh.'s Hand*, 1923), a seminal work of the New Bibliography, attempted to establish the connection between spellings in the *Sir Thomas More* fragment held to be in Sh.'s hand and parallels in the quartos. Certain spellings, deemed "abnormal," were declared to be Sh.'s. And although the evidence was at first limited to "good" (albeit badly printed) quartos, it was extended, on the strength of only a few spellings, to the entire corpus, to multiple-text as well as to Folio-only plays. The staunchest advocate of Sh.'s own MS of *Ant.* as the copy for F1 is WILSON (ed. 1950, pp. 124 ff.), who, applying the methodology of the investigation reported in *The Manuscript of Shakespeare's 'Hamlet'* (1934) and expanding somewhat the view he had proposed in the introduction to his facsimile of the F1 text of *Ant.* (1929), finds three interrelated groups of words directly associated with Sh.: forms attributable to odd spelling, to odd penmanship, and to a combination of both spelling and penmanship.

As SPEVACK (1987, pp. 94–7) points out, Wilson's evidence is not always convincing. His first group includes common variants—e.g., *one* for *on* (50), *to* for *too* (1035) and vice versa (3175), and *reciding* for *residing* (425, 726)—that were randomly employed, although the principle of convergence applies to a certain extent because some of the same forms are found in *STM* as well as in texts thought to have been printed from Sh.'s MS. Presuming that Sh. worked "with North under his eye," Wilson thinks (p. 124) he was "restrained by no habits of 'correctness' or consistency so long as the names sounded all right on the stage." Indeed, some of Sh.'s names are simply phonetic equivalents rather than errors (*Towrus* for *Taurus* [1954], *Ventigius* for *Ventidius* [998, 1007, 1008]) or are readily attributable to misreading (*Medena* for *Modena* [493] and *Brandusium* for *Brundusium* [1884], as Wilson remarks, but equally *Action* for *Actium* [1920]; all are words that occur only once). Others may have originated with Sh.: *Scicion* for *Sicyon* (204, 205, 215), which may be compared with *scilens* in *STM* and *2H4* Q (1745 et passim), *Sceneca* in *Ham.* Q2 (1448), and *Scicinius* for *Sicinius* in *Cor.* (1122, 1241, 1530, 1699); *Camidius* for *Canidius* (1881 [as *Camidias*], 1883, 1891, 1927, 1957, 1973, 2006, and 2594 [as *Camindius*, perhaps thought by Compositor B to be a different character]); and *Thidias* for *Thyreus* (2144, 2205, 2239, 2310, and 2332 [as *Thid.*]). They differ from the orthodox forms because Sh. clearly did not have North's version under his eye, nor was he obliged to reproduce exactly all the names in his source. Also in this group, besides the proper names that may be Sh.'s, are two forms that likely are his: *triumpherate* for *triumvirate* (1781) and *in* for *e'en* (3088). The former, more likely a phonetic spelling than "erroneous . . . by confusion with *triumph*" (*OED*), is documented only in Sh., here and as *triumpherie* in *LLL* Q1 (1385). The latter, also a likely "phonetic spelling" (KÖKERITZ, 1953, p. 204), "agrees with the form *ivn* recorded by both [John] Hart . . . and [Alexander] Gil" (CERCIGNANI, 1981, p. 152) and is found, as Wilson points out, in *AWW* (1419), *Err.* (496), *MV* Q1 (1833), and *Rom.* Q2 (2747).

Wilson's second and third groups are similar in effect to his first. He blames Sh.'s penmanship for several types of minim error: confusion of *m*, *n*, *u*, *v*, *i*, *w*; of *a*, *r*, *u*, *n*; of *e*, *o*; of *e*, *d*; and of *l*, *t*. No doubt the author's careless handwriting was responsible for misreadings, but since many secretary hands were susceptible to misunderstanding in the same categories, it is impossible by such misreadings to identify the writer specifically. The same objection holds for "the few misprints involving both spelling and handwriting," and methodological weaknesses apparent here are also present in the earlier sections. Wilson argues, for example, that "*Anthony*" (3305) is an error for *autumn*, as Theobald first suggested, and that the error was caused by a misreading of that word spelled *autome* and taken for *antonie*. The problems are, first, that although nearly all eds. accept Theobald's emendation, a few do not, and some critics as well as these eds. argue that *Anthony* should be retained (see n. 3305). Second, if *autumn* is right, inventing "autome" to explain it is fanciful when the spelling in *MND* Q1 (487) is "Autumne" and that of *MV* Q1 (408) is "Autume." The mistake—if it is one—could have resulted from Antony's being the subject of the speech and from the surrounding instances of the pronoun *his*. In sum, many of the Shn. characteristics Wilson finds in *Ant.* will not stand scrutiny. The few that will are insufficient to prove that "the copy for F . . . was Shakespeare's own manuscript," but they may indicate that traces of Sh.'s linguistic preferences were present in whatever MS did immediately underlie F1.

Attempts to use SDs to explain the nature of the copy for *Ant.* have been convincing in showing what it was not. At first, however, critics did not agree on the quality of the SDs. Evidently finding them suited to production, POLLARD (1920, pp. 67–8) offered the unsupported opinion that F1 was based on prompt copy. CHAMBERS (1930, 1:477) observed that the SDs "are not markedly full, but there are occasional notes for action or for the grouping and attitude of personages." GREG (1942; 1954, pp. 147–8), on the other hand, thinks "the directions are unusually full and afford beautiful examples of what the author writes. . . . Even when we find notes that might be the prompter's, I . . . ascribe them to the author. . . . I can see only a very carefully written copy, elaborately prepared by the author for the stage with directions respecting the manner of production. There is no sign of its having been used as a prompt-book, and the directions are not of a kind that would be convenient in actual performance. In fact it is a producer's [i.e., director's] copy not a prompter's." What the author writes, he continues, are SDs specifying the characters' function or nature as well as their names (*Lamprius*, *a Southsayer* [assuming Lamprius is the Soothsayer's name] . . . *Mardian the Eunuch* [77–8]), the effect wanted without explanation of how it is to be obtained (*in warlike manner* [614–15], *They heaue Anthony aloft to Cleopatra* [3045], and *Enter the Guard rustling in* [3574]), grouping (*Octauia betweene them* [963]), business (*Enobarbus places them hand in hand* [1464]), and an indefinite number of characters (*Enter 4. or 5. of the Guard* [2984]).

GREG later (1955, pp. 398–402) retreats somewhat. He quotes Chambers, then comments drily (p. 398), "A few directions are detailed, but on the whole their elaboration may have been over-stressed," citing his own opinion of 1942. Yet he reiterates his assessment of the F1 MS as "a producer's copy, not a prompter's," and in his survey of the "most noteworthy" SDs he finds oversights and irregularities that presumably would have been unwelcome in a promptbook: for example, the omission of some needed characters (Silius at 1494–5, Taurus at 1960, Thidias at 2107, Proculeius and Gallus at 3108–9, Seleucus at 3334–5) and of exits (at 297, 1563, 2138, and 2184) and the inclusion of ghost characters (at 77–8). The lack of directions for Cleopatra's capture (p. 401) alone "suffice[s] to show that we are not dealing with prompt-copy."

A comparison of Compositor E's share with B's may provide stronger clues as to the copy. According to Joseph Moxon's *Mechanick Exercises on the Whole Art of Printing* (1683–4), a compositor copyedited as he typeset and in doing so tended to regularize variations in the copy (see, for example, the discussion of F1's speech prefixes, pp. 364–8). It seems safe to assume, however, that the compositor, as he proceeded to work out a system of normalization for a particular text, more often followed the irregularities of his copy early in his stint than later. It is probably also true that an experienced workman would be less likely to follow copy than an inexperienced, for the neophyte would not as fully know what kinds of normalization were either available or desirable.

On these suppositions, Compositor E's pages should be especially revealing of MS characteristics. Found in them are the 16 SDs of an authorial nature already mentioned (pp. 375–6), the SPs *Omnes.* (1027, 1224), and the unique *Both.* (1022). The unusual spellings *Cleopater* and *Ventigius* probably also come from copy. *Cleopater* appears only on pages set by E consecutively: xx3^V (818), xx4 (930), xx4^V (1024); *Cleopatra* appears later on his xx6^v (1620) and yy1 (1755). While E and the proofreader evidently thought *Cleopater* was an (if not *the*) acceptable form, *Cleopatra* is the only form found on B's pages: the 38 instances, plus 3 of *Cleopatra's*, suggest that B standardized any variant of the more common spelling he may have found. *Ventigius* also appears only on pages set by E consecutively: xx4 (998) and xx4^v (1007, 1008); *Ventidius* appears on a page set by B (xx3 at 695, 699) and two set by E (xx6 at 1494, 1501, and xx6^v at 1525). Since, unlike *Cleopatra*, the name is rare—although it was not the business of the compositor to inquire—it is likely that E set what he found in his copy. The unorthodox spelling *Anthonyo's* (1056) on E's xx4^v is somewhat different: the meter calls for a stress on the second syllable. The same is true of B's *Anthonio's* (686). Still, it is tempting to regard both as Shn. spellings

rather than either mistakes for the more common *Anthonius*, which many eds. substitute (see textual notes), or examples of E's preference for medial *y* and B's for *i*.

Apparently the MS did not always clearly distinguish verse from prose. On
xx3^v (744–875), E's first page, Enobarbus is a prose speaker, but the others—
mainly Caesar and Antony—speak verse. Caesar's first speech (745–6), however, is
lined as prose. His second (763–5) is verse, but his third (773–4), fourth (781–2),
and one other (818–19) are prose-lined. Otherwise his speeches are lined as verse.
Antony fares better: he speaks verse to 820–1, where, perhaps under the influence
of Caesar's immediately preceding prose, he too shifts to prose, though he returns
to verse immediately thereafter. The incorrect lineation was probably inspired by
the MS rather than by a desire to save space: verse lineation of all the prose-lined
speeches would have required but three more type lines, and three white lines appear
on xx4 (above 880 and above and below 963), the forme-mate of xx3^v. It could be
that the incorrectly lined speeches were cast-off as verse but mistaken by the compositor.

Another type of evidence, assumed literary irregularities indicating revision or
intent to revise, has also been adduced, although not recently. JENKIN's (1945)
theory that Sh. wrote two versions of the early part of 4.15 (see pp. 779–80) struck
WILSON (ed. 1950, pp. 128–30) as evidence for traces not of Sh.'s but (p. 128)
"of the prompter's hand," which had (p. 130) "casually jotted down in the margin
. . . a couple of notes with a view to making a cut in the prompt-book later." (P.
129): "Clearly Cleopatra's speech [3011–15] once ended 'O *Antony, Antony, Antony*',
since the two lines that follow not only interpose most awkwardly between her
passion and Antony's proud rebuke, but render quite unnecessary [3022–8] (Antony's request for the door to be opened and her refusal) and anticipate [3034–6,
the last words of which], intended to express a sudden inspiration on Cleopatra's
part, repeat her previous command in similar words." Moreover, 3050 repeats 3022.
"If one omits all that lies between [3016 and 3036], the context runs straight
on. . . . We are here confronted with notes for a proposed cut of some seventeen
lines, and should explain the repetition in [3022 and 3050] as due to a consciousness
on the part of the abridger that by omitting [3022–5] in particular he had left
Antony's dying condition insufficiently emphasized, so that he tried to make all
well by transferring a scrap of it to [3050]."

Although he prints the lines supposed to have been excised, RIDLEY (ed. 1954)
admits the possibility of revision by explaining the supposed anomalies differently,
both Sh. and a "cutter" being involved. Rejecting the prompter's complicity, GREG
(1955, p. 403) more enthusiastically accepts the notion of revision. The most likely
explanation of the phenomena observed by Wilson is "that when Shakespeare got
to [3034], 'Demuring vpon me', he became dissatisfied with what he had written
—as well he might, with its contradiction, its obscure allusion to opening the door,
and its irrelevant elaboration of 'th'Imperious shew' [3028] that tends to dissipate
the tension—cancelled all after ['o'th'world' (3013)] and continued with ['but come,'
(3034)], and later at [3050] retrieved Antony's 'I am dying Egypt, dying.'" "The

undoubted source of F [was therefore] in foul papers," he concludes. Since this idea does not sit comfortably with the "very carefully written copy" of GREG (1942; 1954, p. 148), one can see why in 1955 he emphasized the irregularities of the text.

The case for revision rests, however, on the conviction that the two repetitions—"help Friends Below, let's draw him hither" (3014–15) and "we must draw thee vp: Assist good Friends" (3035–6) and "I am dying Egypt, dying" (3022, 3050)—are unnecessary and are therefore literary faults not intended to be part of the finished play. Its refutation lies in disproving that they are faults, the argument of GALLOWAY (1958, pp. 330–5). (P. 334): "To cut [the first] 'repetition' is to suggest that Cleopatra has a practical efficiency which she does not actually possess and to iron out the so-called 'contradictions and confusions' is to iron out the character of Cleopatra at one of the great moments of the play." As for the second, Antony is "reminding Cleopatra that he has not long to live—a fact which, outwardly, she has seemed to be in danger of forgetting." Since recent eds. have implicitly or explicitly accepted Galloway's opinion, the idea that the play contains one patch of revision has disappeared.

To summarize, F1 has none of the strictly professional SDs that characterize promptbooks and none of the formal appurtenances, such as act-and-scene division with a *finis* after each act, that may reveal the hand of a professional scribe. All responsible critics agree that despite some obvious irregularities the text is generally clean and in all major respects—the dialogue, its assignment to speakers, and its government by SDs—complete and superficially correct. Beneath the surface, however, lies error or confusion enough to require modern eds. to emend 200 or so substantives. Some of these alterations are trifling, and by comparison with those required in a text evidently set from a truly foul MS, such as *AWW*, the number is not great. Yet even after allowance is made for the vagaries of the compositors there are errors enough to suggest that the MS was not always easy to read. Authorial traits are present in orthographical details and SDs. All these characteristics underlie the recent consensus that the MS was in whole or in part a Shn. fair copy, the opinion of BEVINGTON (ed. 1988, p. 140): "It is a good text, set evidently from Shakespeare's own draft in a more finished state than most of his foul or working papers, though not yet prepared to be a promptbook." Yet, as mentioned earlier, the SP *Omnes* and the system of punctuation are uncharacteristic of Sh., and, as WELLS & TAYLOR (1987, p. 549) point out, the exclamation *oh* is predominantly spelled *oh* in *Ant.* rather than *o*, as it is almost invariably spelled in texts thought to derive directly from Shn. MSS. The comparison is striking. For example, in *MND* Q1, *MV* Q1, and *Ham.* Q2, all typeset from foul papers, *o* outnumbers *oh* 60 to 3, 33 to 0, and 103 to 5. In *Ant.*, however, the reverse occurs: *oh* outnumbers *o* 83 to 13. All the *o*'s were set by Compositor B, and 6 of them fall on zz2–1^v, pages set one after the other, the first *o* generating the others.

The conclusion therefore seems inescapable that F1 was typeset from what WELLS & TAYLOR (1987, p. 549) call "some sort of transcript of foul papers." The copy may have been in a few respects rather rough, but it represented, as far as one can tell, a full text with reasonably uniform and complete SDs and SPs. Possibly it was prepared for use by the company rather than for printer's copy or for a private patron. If so, it might be the kind of transcript intermediate between foul papers and the promptbook hypothecated by A. WALKER (1953, pp. 109–13) and BOWERS (privately in GREG [1955, pp. 467–8] and 1955; 1966, pp. 3–32).

The Date of Composition

On 20 May 1608 Edward Blount entered two plays in the Stationers' Register: "Entred for his copie vnder thande of Sr Geo. Buck knight & m^r warden Seton a booke called. The booke of Pericles Prynce of Tyre . . . Entred also for his copie by the lyke Aucthoritie. A booke Called. Anthony. & Cleopatra" (GREG, 1939, 1:24). The latter work, however, has neither been found to have been published nor positively identified as Sh.'s play. The title, in fact, was reregistered by Blount and Isaac Jaggard on 8 Nov. 1623 as one of sixteen plays "not formerly entred to other men" (Greg, 1939, 1:33).

Why Blount, a respectable publisher, should register the "booke" and not publish it remains a subject of speculation. COLLIER's (ed. 1843, 8:3) theory that Blount was unable to obtain a copy is questionable because an entry would presuppose that he had a copy, as required for the license (issued by Buc) and the warrant (granted by Seton), and that he was acting with the approval of Sh.'s company. It is of course conceivable that the copy was returned to the company or to Sh., but no existing evidence supports that possibility.

Since it is generally accepted that after 1600 the company tended to keep its new plays out of print, POLLARD (1909, p. 78) explains the first registration as having "been of the nature of 'blocking' entries rather than inspired with any intention of early publication": that is, Sh.'s company attempted, as WILSON (ed. 1950, p. vii) explains, "to protect themselves against an anticipated piracy by employing a friendly publisher . . . to register his copyright in the plays." There is no solid evidence to support this hypothesis—on the contrary, that the practice was common is very much open to doubt, as KNOWLES (1977, pp. 353–64) demonstrates in his discussion of the "staying entry" of 4 Aug. 1600—and considerably less for the supposition (often mentioned in connection with the suspicious publication of *Per.* in 1609) that the closing of the London theaters from 28 July 1608 to Dec. 1609, owing to the plague, may have increased, as HOENIGER (1963, p. xxv) suggests, the "temptation of piracy . . . for the unemployed minor dramatist, actor, or bookkeeper of theatrical companies." That Blount moved his shop in 1608 from Over against the Great North Door of St. Paul's to The Black Bear, St. Paul's Churchyard, may at most account for a possible delay in publication: after issuing only one work (*STC* 1201) in 1608, Blount produced his customary annual average of four or five titles in 1609. Furthermore, these explanations do not respond to GREG's (1940, [p. 1]) suggestion that the deleted "R" (which indicated receipt) under the fee of six pence "probably" means the entry was canceled, a situation that

would apply to *Ant.* as well since its entry fee of six pence also has a deleted "R."
Why (and when) Blount's 1608 entry was canceled (if it was)—Greg (1939, 1:7 et
passim) lists only seven other instances, all by different stationers, in the entire
period 1557–1689—is, however, a mystery. *Per.* might be easier to explain. Henry
Gosson's two eds. in 1609, although unregistered, might have superseded Blount's:
Gosson does not seem to have been prosecuted, nor was an authorized version
forthcoming, as in the case of Q2 of *Ham. Ant.* is more difficult because no separate
printed version seems to have followed the entry. Perhaps *Ant.* was unpopular—
another argument against a blocking entry or, for that matter, against entry
altogether—and publication was deemed ill-advised. Perhaps the copy was lost or
otherwise unavailable. But as they rest on the purest speculation, such conjectures
are idle.

CHAMBERS (1930, 1:477), perhaps following HALLIWELL (ed. 1865, 15:195),
somewhat cavalierly attributes the second registration to Blount's appearing "to have
forgotten it [the first]"; BULLOUGH (1964, 5:215) laconically adds, "or ignored"
it. True, fifteen years had passed, and the new copyright was now granted to two
owners, Blount and Jaggard. But if Greg is correct about the cancellation of the
first entry, then a more potent reason for the second entry is evident.

Despite the uncertainty about the exact circumstances of the two entries, the
overwhelming consensus is that the work registered in 1608 was indeed Sh.'s—
TURNER notes (privately) the improbability that Blount, who published plays on
classical subjects, would have acquired two non-Shn. works with titles identical to
those of plays by Sh.—and that 1608 is the terminus ad quem; in further support
of the latter view, almost all commentators accept MALONE's (ed. 1790, 1:372)
assertion that an allusion to Sh.'s play may be made in Ben Jonson's *Epicoene or The
Silent Woman* (1609), 4.4.16–18 (ed. Herford & Simpson, 1937): "*Mor[ose].* Nay I
would sit out a play, that were nothing but fights at sea, drum, trumpet, and
target!" (The acceptance of this one allusion is surprising since any number of
romances or adventure plays of the time—Thomas Heywood and William Rowley's
Fortune by Land and Sea has been mentioned—may be expected to contain the same
ingredients.)

Only KNIGHT (ed. 1841) and VERPLANCK (ed. 1846) disagree. The former
(6:148) holds it "more than probable" that the play "entered in 1608 was not
Shakspere's tragedy," being the only play of Sh.'s to contradict the 1623 registration
of "many of the said copies as are not . . . entered to other men," and states
"unhesitatingly"—but without details—"that there is no *internal* evidence whatever
for the dates of any of the three Roman plays," which he regards as an organic cycle.
The latter, as often, agrees with Knight that the cycle was written in Sh.'s last
years, finding resemblances to *Tmp.* in the (p. 6) "larger number than usual of lines
hypermetrical by redundant syllables," as well as strong verbal similarities—he
compares only "blacke Vespers Pageants" (2833) with Prospero's "insubstantiall
Pageant" (4.1.155 [1826])—and even contrasts (Miranda and Cleopatra) "so marked"
as to be "not merely accidental."

Considering that the play was registered in May 1608, COLLIER (ed. 1843,

8:3) infers it was written "late in 1607." This view dominates in the 19th c., dubiously supported by impressionistic psychologizing, as exemplified by HUDSON (ed. 1855, 8:442), who groups *Ant.* with *Mac.* and *Lr.*: "It will hardly be questioned . . . that at the time of writing these stupendous dramas the Poet's mind was equal to any achievement lying within the compass of human thought. Nor can we taste in this play any peculiarities of style, as distinguished from the proper tokens of dramatic power, that should needs infer more ripeness of the author's mind, than in case of the other dramas reckoned to the same period [1605–10]." WHITE (ed. 1883, 3:787) is equally and typically vague in simply mentioning that "internal evidence [i.e., style] shows that it must have been produced soon after the great tragedies [i.e., *Ham.*, *Oth.*, *Lr.*], and just before its author fell into the daring indifference of his latest style; quite surely between 1605 and 1608; and probably about 1607." Somewhat more convincing is the stylistic "kinship," especially with *Mac.* (1605–6), stressed by IRVING & MARSHALL (ed. 1889, 6:113), who note (but do not specify) "various interesting links connecting the characters of Macbeth and Antony," and by HERFORD (ed. 1899, 9:259), who detects but does not analyze *Ant.*'s conceptual affinity with *Mac.* and the "symptoms" in its versification of [Sh.'s] latest manner . . . in particular," the weak ending, of which he finds twenty-eight instances.

The 20th c. has not produced more conclusive evidence. That the terminus a quo cannot be exactly pinpointed has not deterred commentators. Thus the discussion of the connection between Sh.'s play and Samuel Daniel's *Cleopatra* of 1607—see pp. 528–30—given new impetus by CASE (ed. 1906), effected a small modification favored by many 20th-c. commentators, who tend to recognize Daniel's debt to Shakespeare. As Case says (pp. xi–xii), "Though this evidence is by no means overwhelming . . . just so much probability follows that we should finally exclude 1608 . . . and admit 1606 to competition with 1607." As further external evidence, he thinks (p. xii) "some resemblances which occur in other plays are perhaps worth mentioning": the anonymous *No-body and Some-body* (undated, but registered in 1606, probably in a rev. version; ed. R. Simpson, *The School of Shakspere*, 1878, vol. 1), in which ll. 34–39 ("There's *Elydure* Your elder brother next unto the King; He plies his booke; when shall you see him trace Lascivious *Archigallo* through the streets, And fight with common hacksters hand to hand To wrest from them their goods and dignities?") are compared with 449–51 of *Ant.*; Barnabe Barnes's *The Divils Charter* (a revised version registered 16 Oct. 1607 but played before the king, according to the title page, on 2 Feb.; ed. McKerrow, 1904), of which ll. 2546–69—containing references to aspics ("*Cleopatraes* birds") applied to the breasts of the young princes, "competitors, With *Cleopatra* . . . in death and fate," who are wafted to the "*Elisian* fields"—are compared with 3542–66 of *Ant.*; George Chapman's *Bussy D'Ambois* (published in 1607–8 as acted by the Paul's children; ed. Holaday, 1987), of which 3.1.21–4 ("and like empty clouds In which our faulty apprehensions fordge The formes of Dragons, Lions, Elephants, When they hold no proportion") are compared with 2826–31 and 2841 of *Ant.* (as first noted by MALONE [ed. 1790]). Chapman's *Monsieur D'Olive* (published in 1606, following performances at Blackfriars, according to the title page; ed. Holaday, 1970), of which 2.2.91–6 ("Our great men Like to a Masse of clowds that now seeme like An Elephant, and straight wayes like an Oxe And then a Mouse, or like those changeable creatures That liue in the Burdello, now in Satten Tomorrow next in Stammell") are compared with 2826–31 of *Ant.* (first noted by STEEVENS [ed. 1778]), is mentioned again by PHIALAS (ed. 1955, pp. 158–9). With the possible exception of those in Barnes's play, which seem to merit attention—although WELLS & TAYLOR (1987, p. 129) feel that "Barnes's treatment resembles . . . more closely" a similar episode (sig. I2^r) in George Peele's *Edward I* (1593, rpt. 1599) than it does Sh.'s description—either the resemblances are fairly remote or, as CHAMBERS (1930, 1:478) points out, "The ideas [of *No-body* and *Bussy*] are . . . of still older standing." MACCALLUM's (1910, p. 301) "evidence that in the preceding years Shakespeare was occupied with and impressed by [North's tr. of Plutarch's] *Life of Antony*" rests (pp. 301–2) on a single reference to Timon (see p. 445) and two others that may have found their way into *Mac.*: the first (p. 302) "describing the scarcity of food among the Roman army in Parthia," which (see p. 428) "made them out of their witts," in "Root, That takes the Reason Prisoner" (1.3.84–5 [186–7]), and the second, "an unmistakable reminiscence of the soothsayer's warning to Antony" (983–8 and p. 418) in "My *Genius* is rebuk'd, as it is said *Mark Anthonies* was by *Cæsar*" (3.1.56–7 [1046–7]).

In addition to works by other authors, commentators have tried to find connections between *Ant.* and contemporary events and persons. MASSEY's (1866; 1872, p. 482) questionable thesis that the model for Cleopatra was Lady Rich is matched by CARTWRIGHT's dubious one (1859, p. 22) that it was the Dark Lady of *Son.*—more specifically, according to HARRIS (1909, p. 304), Mary Fitton. And WALTER (ed. 1969, pp. 5, 305–6) speculates that the play's (p. 5) "appearance at this time [1606] . . . may have been inspired by the well-known love-affair of Charles Blount, Lord Mountjoy, and Penelope Rich": both couples were (p. 306) "approaching middle age"; both "had children born out of wedlock"; both men were highly regarded generals; both women had "links with Venus"—(p. 305) "Penelope [having] played the part of Venus in Daniel's masque *The Vision of the Twelve Goddesses* presented at Hampton Court in January, 1604." Speculations concerning psychological aspects of Sh. himself, fuzzy contributions of 19th-c. commentators to the dating of *Ant.*, are also not infrequent in the 20th c. Thus HUDSON's (ed. 1855, 8:442) reference to Sh.'s having been in "his forty-fourth year" when he wrote *Ant.* may have led to MACCALLUM's (1910, pp. 314–15) direct comparison of Sh. and Antony: "Shakespeare would imagine Antony at the outset [of the play] as between forty-two and forty-six, practically on the same *niveau* of life as himself. . . . They had reached the same stadium in their career, had the same general outlook on the future, had their great triumphs behind them." Even CHAMBERS (1930, 1:86) mirrors this approach to dating, blending the personal and stylistic: "Shakespeare's spirit must have been nearly submerged in *Lear* [1605–6], and although the wave passed, and he rose to his height of poetic expression in *Antony and Cleopatra*, I think that he went under in the unfinished *Timon of Athens* [1607–8]." And the equally blurry application of dramatic conception and weltanschauung finds typical expression in MacCallum (p. 308), who places *Ant.* "shortly after [*Mac.*, 1605–6] and shortly before [*Cor.*, 1607–8], near the end of 1607": "As in *Macbeth* we accept without demur the penalty exacted for the offence. As in *Coriolanus* we welcome the magnanimity that the offenders recover or achieve at the close. If there is [in *Ant.*] less of acquiescence in vindicated justice than in the first, if there is less of elation at the triumph of the nobler self than in the second, there is yet something of both."

The application to dating of versification, meter, and diction, though as unconvincing as it was in the 19th c., has not ceased in the 20th. INGRAM's (1874, p. 450) table of light and weak endings, evidence that can at best group plays in "periods" of Sh.'s "poetic life" but not fix the precise position of the individual plays, is summarized by MACCALLUM (1910, p. 305) for *Ant.*: "Thus the sudden outcrop of light and weak endings [unstressed final monosyllables] . . . the preponderance of the light [mainly pronouns and auxiliaries] over the weak [prepositions and conjunctions] in that play, the increase in the total percentage of such endings and especially in the relative percentage of weak endings in the dramas that for various reasons are believed to be later, all confirm its position after *Macbeth* and before *Coriolanus*." (CHAMBERS's [1930, 2:401] count of seventy-one light endings in *Ant.* and only sixty in *Cor.* casts some doubt on this assertion.) GRAY's (1931, p. 148) average of the percentage of double (feminine) endings, run-on lines, and speeches ending within the line also places *Ant.* (49.1 percent) between *Mac.* (46.7) and *Cor.* (51.1) without indicating specific dates. Similarly, the various metrical tests collected and compared by WENTERSDORF (1951, pp. 182–8)—of extra syllables, "overflows" (run-on lines), pauses in unsplit lines, and split lines—reveal a "regular increase in metrical freedom" if the historical plays are not taken fully into account. Other stylistic criteria—unspecified references to the "concise, bold and difficult" diction (MacCallum, p. 305) or the increase in the percentage of split lines (REINHOLD, 1942, pp. 87–9)—likewise almost inherently too sparse or imprecise, are nevertheless employed to justify the generally accepted date of composition, 1606–7, although they too can apply only to speculations about the approximate order of the plays or the period in which they may have been written. The quirky BAYFIELD (1920, p. 399) alone considers *Ant.* Sh.'s last play, because it contains more "resolutions"—metrical feet (p. 3) "containing more than two syllables"—than does any other; the frequency of such "resolutions" ranges from 31 percent in *3H6* to 73 percent in *Ant.*

LAW's (1936, pp. 50–1) "tabulation" of the dates proposed by seven authorities between 1923 and 1935 offers no noteworthy deviations. Nor does MCMANAWAY (1950), reviewing (p. 22) "significant contributions which scholars have made in the two succeeding decades" since Chambers's 1930 summary of results of previous investigations: (p. 30) "There has been no attempt to alter the dates [1606–7] accepted by Chambers." BARROLL's (1965, pp. 115–62) detailed investigation of the intricate performance and printing history of the Daniel and Barnes plays, as well as the effect of the plague, indicates a possible first playing of *Ant.* as early as

the spring of 1605. But since this possibility is heavily based on admitted speculations about *Ant.* as a source for Daniel's and Barnes's plays, and since it calls into
question the traditional order of all the tragedies after *Ham.*, it may be best for the
present to leave the last word with McManaway—for the only evidence for the
dating of *Ant.* that might merit the designation "hard" is the initial registration.

Sources, Influences, and Analogues

Major Sources and Influences

PLUTARCH

LANGBAINE (1691, p. 455), followed by GILDON (1699, p. 126, and 1710, p. 416),
identifies *Ant.*'s classical sources: "The Ground of this Play is founded on History:
see *Plutarch*'s Life of *Anthony; Appian, Dion Cassius, Diodorus, Florus,* &c." Whereas
many consider Sh. an unlettered natural genius, ROWE (ed. 1709, 1:xxx–i) praises
his biographical accuracy and historical propriety (though not the play's multiplicity
of action) in showing Antony "exactly as . . . describ'd by [*xxxi*] *Plutarch*," and
UPTON (1746; 1748) infers from such evidence as the way Sh. (p. 90) "very artfully,
and learnedly" makes use of Plutarch's Antony's (p. 89) "Asiatic manner of speaking"
that Sh. knew Plutarch in the Greek. Hence Upton restores "Libya" at 1761 (see
n.), a passage used by FARMER (1767, pp. 10–11), in refuting Upton, as evidence
that Sh. was familiar only with North. Sh.'s use of North is stressed first by JOHNSON
(ed. 1765; 1968, 7:83) and in more detail by CAPELL (ed. 1768, 1:50), who praises
Sh. for having, "with much judgment, introduc'd no small number of speeches into
these [Roman] plays, in the very words of that translator," but making these speeches
indistinguishable from those he invented.

    Nineteenth-c. scholars more extensively specify parallels and differences be-
tween Sh. and Plutarch. SKOTTOWE (1824, 2:233) emphasizes Sh.'s "originality"
in characterization and finds that, although his representation of Antony's "voluptuousness" under the "witchery of Cleopatra" accords with Plutarch, Sh. ennobles
Antony: "The most repulsive feature in his character, cruelty, the dramatist has
entirely suppressed, whilst he has taken frequent opportunities to enlarge upon, and
give instances of, his courage, constancy, nobility, and generosity." (For Cleopatra,
see below.) Others who see Sh.'s Antony as ennobled include CAMPBELL (ed. 1838,
p. lxi), TRENCH (1872; 1874, pp. 70–1), MORGAN & VINES (ed. 1893–8, pp.
xxiii–v), ADLER (1895, pp. 287–92), HERFORD (ed. 1899, 9:265), MacCALLUM
(1910, pp. 336–7), CREIZENACH (1916, 5:441–2), HILLEBRAND (ed. 1926, pp.
xxvii–ix), ELLEHAUGE (1930–1, p. 203), OAKESHOTT (1954, pp. 119–23), MUNRO
(ed. 1957, 6:1211), SCHIRMER (in SCHÜCKING, ed. 1962, p. 186), RIEMER (1968,
p. 18), INGLEDEW (ed. 1971, pp. xxxv–vi), and G. R. SMITH (1974, p. 16). CASE
(ed. 1906, p. xvi): "It is said that Shakespeare softened or suppressed Antony's worst
traits as he found them in North; but his instanced cruelties and oppressions precede
as much of the story as is retold in the play [noted also by TRENCH, 1872; 1874,

p. 71], and a dramatist must have gone out of his way to reveal in him anything beyond what we gather from his treacherous and cold-blooded treatment of Octavia. It is even questionable whether his good qualities are not more conspicuous in Shakespeare than in Plutarch only because of the diminished size of the canvas; but the former certainly gives them full dramatic effect."

Among others who point to differences between Sh.'s Antony and Plutarch's, MORGAN & VINES (ed. 1893–8, p. xxiv) note that Sh. mitigates Plutarch's reports of Antony's debauchery by putting them in Octavius's mouth in 1.4, and ADLER (1895, pp. 287–92) finds that whereas Plutarch's lack of understanding of Antony leads to inconsistent characterization, with cruelty, dishonesty, courage, and generosity juxtaposed, Sh. shows him as motivated by love (similarly MACCALLUM, 1910, p. 341) to rouse sympathy for him. MacCallum affirms also (pp. 336–7) that the positive traits Plutarch gives Antony (see Adler) are brought to the forefront by Sh. HILLEBRAND (ed. 1926, p. xxix): "Plutarch makes clear that with all his faults Antony was much beloved, and this is even more true of Shakespeare's Antony. Yet unlike Plutarch's Antony, Shakespeare's never gave cause for men to hate him." PHIALAS (ed. 1955, p. 168) points out that "whereas Plutarch's Antony in the end bows before the moral principles he has violated, Shakespeare's reaffirms his adherence to the values he has espoused." WILSON (1957, pp. 165, 168) sees Cleopatra's spell on Sh.'s Antony as continuous: "It is not simply in the interest of dramatic condensation that Shakespeare passes briefly over Plutarch's account of Antony's stay in Rome and Athens after he married Octavia, of how she bore him three children and, during this time, reconciled a difference between Antony and Octavius which had nothing to do with Cleopatra. In fact, Antony's second (and fatal) infatuation for Cleopatra occurred after an interval of some years, during which time, as far as we may judge from Plutarch's story, Antony had given up all serious thought of returning to her. In the historical account, only when his affairs necessitated his going into Asia and thus leaving Octavia, did the impulse strike him to send for Cleopatra to join him in Syria. Shakespeare suggests that the spell Cleopatra cast upon Antony was never broken and thus avoids raising questions about his activities and motives that Plutarch never answers. For Shakespeare, Antony is even simpler than Plutarch represents him. From the beginning, Cleopatra has laid enchantment on him, and we see him rouse for a moment to shore the ruins of his empire against the ominously encroaching Octavius, only to revert to his 'Egyptian dish' [1322] when all is quiet. . . . [*168*] Plutarch saw clearly enough Antony's infatuation for Cleopatra. He hardly suspected—what Shakespeare was so clearly to show us in his tragic hero—that the simplicity and impetuosity of Antony's love for Cleopatra went together with a rash and impetuous sense of honour that impaired his tactical judgment when he had need of his greatest skill." NORMAN (1956, pp. 60–1) briefly notes that while Octavius in 1.4 judges Antony by Plutarch's Roman standards (as observed by Morgan & Vines, ed. 1893–8), essentially of manliness, Sh. gives full effect throughout the play to Cleopatra's judgment of Antony as the best of men. BERKELEY (1964, pp. 138–42) tries inconclusively to show that Sh.'s Antony, unlike Plutarch's, is obsessed by enigmatic love-hate toward Cleopatra, evidenced by purposely false advice on Proculeius (3059). EVANS (1979, pp. 265–8) argues similarly. Earlier versions of Berkeley's interpretation (1950, pp. 534–5; 1955–6, pp. 96–9) do not compare Sh. with Plutarch. Berkeley's view is rejected by HOOK (1955–6, pp. 365–6) and GRILL (1960, p. 191). SIMMONS (1973, *Shakespeare's Pagan World*, pp. 124–5) believes Sh. regards Antony's vices as interwoven with his virtues, Plutarch having been unable to see their paradoxical relationship (contrast FARNHAM, 1950, pp. 139, 146, who is more illuminating on the subtlety of Plutarch's view). ALVIS (1978, p. 186) claims that, contrary to Plutarch, Sh.'s Antony acts nobly in choosing a life of love, and DILLON (1979, pp. 334–5) observes that Sh. rejects the physical isolation of Plutarch's Antony after Actium in favor of "solitude of mind," or inability to commit oneself to others. ZANCO (ed. 1931, pp. xxi–v) and HONDA (1958, pp. 1–15) discuss Sh.'s effective shaping of Plutarch's Antony into a complex dramatic figure.

Scholars who note parallels between Sh.'s concept of Antony and Plutarch's include ELLEHAUGE (1930–1, p. 203), who thinks, rather superficially, that Sh. copies Antony's military energy, generosity, boastfulness, and dotage from Plutarch, and, more persuasively, FARNHAM (1950, p. 146), who regards both figures as paradoxes: "Plutarch presents Antony as having exhibited a baffling conglomeration of good and bad qualities all through his career, and in his analysis of him he obviously takes care to show that the good qualities at times even made one with the bad. . . . In the comparison of Demetrius and Antony [see p. 459] . . . Plutarch grants that Antony is to be given credit for bringing himself to the point of ending his life in time to keep his enemy from having power over his person, but he says that the manner of his death was cowardly, pitiful, and ignoble. Doubtless Plutarch is thinking of the fact that Antony did not steel himself to end his life until he thought that Cleopatra had ended hers, and of the fact that he used his sword so clumsily when he did turn it against himself that he died a lingering death." This paradoxical character Sh. (p. 139) "was willing to accept with minor changes." RIEMER (1968, p. 20), believing "there is a distinct empathy between the humanism of *Antony and Cleopatra* and the detached, classical humanity of the *Lives*," also refers to the *Comparison of Demetrius with Antonius*, where (p. 19) "Antony is not a schematic figure of didactic literature, he is a disturbingly complex human being, and the biographer's attitude is one of wonder and admiration for his subject. But this admiration is tempered by a wise and essentially civilized awareness of his faults. . . . This Antony is not a moral *exemplum* whose faults and vices are presented in a coherent didactic pattern; he is unique, individual, and the uniqueness we find in Plutarch's narrative reappears in Shakespeare's treatment of the material." SIMMONS (1973, *Shakespeare's Pagan World*, p. 125), however, rather sweepingly objects that Plutarch's judgment of Antony is consistently severe. DRAPER (1965, *Psychiatric Quarterly*, pp. 450–3) stresses Sh.-Plutarch parallels when he argues that the writers' psychological insight allows them to depict Antony's progress from soldier to sybarite.

LLOYD (1959, *ShS*, pp. 93–4) notes that Sh. adapts suggestions from Plutarch's *Lives* as well as from *Moralia* in likening Antony to Bacchus and Hercules; the latter analogy is discussed also by DAPHINOFF (1975, pp. 189–90). On Herculean analogies see also p. 609. Some see an Antony-Hercules and Cleopatra-Omphale parallel, implied at 1050–1, as suggested to Sh. by Plutarch's *Comparison*, especially WARNER (1957, p. 139), BARROLL (1958, *TxSE*, pp. 70–1), SCHANZER (1960, "Three Notes on *Ant.*," p. 21, and 1963, p. 158), KERMODE (1961; 1971, p. 98, n. 20), WADDINGTON (1966, pp. 211–12), ADELMAN (1973, p. 209, n. 69), and MACK (1973, p. 96). Among others who comment on Sh.'s use of the *Comparison*, MACCALLUM (1910, p. 341) and BROWER (1971, pp. 349–50) observe that Plutarch's account of Antony's fall denigrates him far more than Sh.'s. MacCallum (p. 452) also points out that Cleopatra's claim to be Antony's wife (3538) finds support in the *Comparison*. For Farnham (1950) and Riemer (1968), see quotations above. HONIGMANN (1959, p. 27) thinks Plutarch's implied contempt in the *Comparison* for Antony's feasting and lovemaking before battle is turned by Sh. in Antony's favor in 4.4, especially 2510–13; SCHANZER (1963, p. 140), agreeing, believes Plutarch's passage also suggested 455–63 (similarly SIMMONS, 1973, *Shakespeare's Pagan World*, p. 125).

Sh.'s reworking of Plutarch's Cleopatra has received similarly diverse comment. SKOTTOWE (1824, 2:240), launching a debate on Cleopatra's queenliness, complains that Sh. "has not been successful in conveying an idea of the elegance of Cleopatra's mind," since he gives her none of the accomplished "manners, thoughts, nor language" she has in Plutarch. CORSON (1889, pp. 270–1) agrees that Sh.'s Cleopatra is less queenly than Plutarch's but thinks Sh.'s moral purpose is to distance her from the audience's sympathy. SCHÜCKING (1919, tr. 1922, p. 121), rather like Skottowe, believes that Plutarch's Cleopatra has considerable cultural refinement while Sh.'s is a great though vulgar courtesan in the play's first half. In answering, CRAIG (1948, pp. 272–3) holds that Sh.'s Cleopatra is no less gracious than Plutarch's, to whose character description Sh. added little, BULLOUGH (1964, 5:250–1) that Sh.'s queen, no less consistently than Plutarch's, is a royal seductress throughout.

Among those who stress Sh.'s modifications of Plutarch's Cleopatra, ADLER (1895, pp. 294–301) and ROTHSCHILD (1976, p. 419) point out that Sh. tries more than Plutarch to understand her complexity; others go further, finding Sh.'s Cleopatra nobler than Plutarch's: especially HERFORD (ed. 1899, 9:265: Sh. effaces the hoyden in her), KELLER (ed. 1912, 5:193: Sh.'s Cleopatra is more royal than Plutarch's), TRAUB (1938, pp. 21–3: heroic stature), PHIALAS (ed. 1955, p. 168: tragic stature), INGLEDEW (ed. 1971, p. xl: more sympathetic than Plutarch's), SIMMONS (1973, *Shakespeare's Pagan World*, pp. 126–7: Plutarch's Cleopatra is motivated by political ambition; Sh. tries to understand her love), and FITZ (1977, pp. 310–13: Sh. mitigates Plutarch's harsh views of her).

FARNHAM (1950, pp. 146–8): "Plutarch presents Cleopatra . . . as having shown a character basically composed of bad qualities until some time after the Battle of Actium. Beauty she certainly had when she cast a spell over Antony, and charm even more certainly, but the moral Plutarch is not the man to [*147*] lose his head over beauty and charm. . . .

"Did Cleopatra really rise to a true love for Antony when she drew toward the end of her life? Plutarch leaves it to the reader to answer that question, though he encourages him to answer that she did. . . . [*148*] Shakespeare departs from Plutarch by making Cleopatra thoroughly paradoxical . . . both before and after Actium. He is more kind than Plutarch to the earlier Cleopatra and less kind to the later. But he makes her rise to grandeur in death even more surely than Plutarch does." SPENCER's (1958, p. 375) and DAPHINOFF's (1975, pp. 184, 187–8) views are similar.

In Plutarch, she commits suicide, ADLER (1895, pp. 285, 300) maintains, for fear of humiliation and captivity, in Sh. for love of Antony. In contrast, MORGAN & VINES (ed. 1893–8, pp. xxvii–ix) and ELLEHAUGE (1930–1, pp. 203–8) claim that Sh. departs from Plutarch in making fear of Octavius's triumph her main motive. CASE (ed. 1906, pp. xvii–xix) more perceptively believes Sh. departs from Plutarch by suggesting mixed motives: "His Queen of Egypt is a figure of coarser fibre than that which moves in the prose narrative, even allowing for the strong lights of dialogue. . . . [*xviii*] Shakespeare intentionally represented Cleopatra less favourably than Plutarch in dealing with the motive of her death. . . .

"In Plutarch, there is no direct mention of . . . Cleopatra's dread of being made part of Cæsar's triumph in Rome. . . . In a moving speech at Antony's tomb, she lays stress on her preservation by Cæsar [*xix*] only that he may triumph over Antony: there is no word of her own fear of ignominy. . . .

"Shakespeare's omissions throw into strong relief his development of the mere hint of a second motive for self-destruction, but it is not absolutely certain that he meant us to infer that this second motive was the only efficient one, and that Cleopatra would gladly have survived. He inserts in the final scene with Antony [3060] and after his death [3094 ff.] expressions on the part of Cleopatra of determination to die, which rest as much or more on the desire not to outlive Antony as on the unwillingness to endure ignominy. He gives us no right to judge this determination weakened."

FARNHAM (1950, pp. 145, 147, 196–200) observes that in Plutarch, who dwells on her grief for Antony, she decides to die on learning she is to be taken to Rome, whereas Sh. shows love and fear alternately swaying her during Act 5. GREEN (1979, pp. 114–19) finds Plutarch's account of Cleopatra's motives inconsistent and concludes, as does Case, that Sh. gives her mixed reasons but, following BULLOUGH (1964, 5:247), that after Antony's death her resolve to die is constant.

A few put weight on various parallels with Plutarch's Cleopatra, such as MACCALLUM (1910, pp. 413–38, in particular pp. 416–18: though Sh. unlike Plutarch makes Cleopatra beautiful, he agrees with Plutarch in making beauty the least part of her attraction), HILLEBRAND (ed. 1926, p. xxxii: Plutarch and Sh. believe in Cleopatra's single-hearted devotion to Antony), SCHIRMER (in SCHÜCKING, ed. 1962, pp. 189–90: Sh., using Plutarch's description, makes her beautiful and seductive), and GRANT (1972, pp. 242–3: Sh. and Plutarch agree in dwelling at length on her death, not just Antony's).

As for Enobarbus, most scholars point out that he is an independent creation of Sh.'s from a few bare anecdotes in Plutarch (e.g., ADLER, 1895, pp. 303–4). MACCALLUM (1910, p. 351) neatly if speculatively sums up Plutarch's Enobarbus:

"He is capable; he is honest and bold in recommending the right course; when Antony wilfully follows the wrong one, he forsakes him; but, touched perhaps by his magnanimity, dies, it may be, in remorse" (on Sh.'s Enobarbus see pp. 704–5). NORMAN (1956, p. 60) notes that Sh. confuses Plutarch's Domitius, the soldier who deserts Antony, with Domitius Aenobarbus, who survives Antony. And SPENCER (1964; 1968, p. 16) observes that "although Aenobarbus is an insignificant person in Plutarch," Sh. "had absorbed a great deal of the miscellaneous information he found about Antony into building up the character and dramatic function of Enobarbus. . . . He created Enobarbus in *Antony and Cleopatra* for the purpose (at least partly) of giving a standard of equanimity, shrewdness, normal affection, and common sense." DAWSON (1987, pp. 216–17) discusses Sh.'s alteration of the historical character's name.

Among the few who compare Sh.'s Octavius with Plutarch's, MORGAN & VINES (ed. 1893–8, pp. xxv–vii) consider Sh.'s more coldly Machiavellian than Plutarch's, whereas to ADLER (1895, pp. 301–2) Sh.'s prudential statesman is essentially Plutarch's. MACCALLUM (1910, pp. 385–6), however, notes that Sh. in 3.7 alters Plutarch, who has Octavius take the lead in daredevilry, by having him coolly propose a sea battle that will disadvantage Antony; ALTMANN (1969, p. 185) remarks that Sh. in 5.2 replaces the cupidity of Plutarch's Octavius with a quest for glory as he seeks to outwit Cleopatra. INGLEDEW (ed. 1971, p. xliv) claims that Sh.'s Octavius, unlike Plutarch's, is a purely public figure with no private dimension (similarly EMERSON, 1890, pp. 519–21, without comparing Plutarch). And SLATER (ed. 1971, p. 36) observes that "Plutarch's Caesar is full of extraordinarily petty motives, which Shakespeare omits." SIMARD (1986, pp. 69–74) compares Sh.'s Octavia with Plutarch's.

Scholars disagree over Sh.'s interpretation of Plutarch's material. Among those who stress Sh.'s modification of Plutarch, VATKE (1868, pp. 322–3, 338) notes a priority of personal over historical and political matters in the play, at least after 3.6, as against Plutarch's consistently political interest. MACCALLUM (1910, p. 339) agrees, in the main. WILCOX (1936, pp. 531–2) finds Sh. not so concerned with moral precepts as Plutarch is; GOURLAY (1969, pp. 223–41) sees Sh. as dissenting from Plutarch's Roman morality; and KOPPENFELS (1972; 1978, pp. 578–80) thinks Sh. stresses the love affair but avoids Plutarch's moralism. According to GRIFFIN (1966, pp. 257–8), Sh. enlists sympathy for the lovers from the beginning, Plutarch only toward the end. ROTHSCHILD (1976, p. 417) sees Plutarch as a moralizer, Sh. as an observer: "The 'Roman' consciousness to which Philo and Demetrius give voice is the same consciousness that Shakespeare found in his Plutarch. There it colors the entire presentation of Antony's involvement with Cleopatra. . . . For Plutarch as well as for Philo and Demetrius, she is but a fatal temptation to ruinous luxury. . . . Shakespeare conceived of his historical source as a limited presentation of the truth of the life it took for its subject." A similar view is that of SLATER (ed. 1971, p. 37).

Others point to interpretive similarities. Thus HUGO (ed. 1860; 1868, 7:12) notes Sh.'s and Plutarch's concern with the impotency of human will against higher forces directing events, MÉZIÈRES (1860; 1886, pp. 452, 458) their interest in the influence of passion on the human spirit.

HERFORD (ed. 1899, 9:261–2) believes Sh. follows Plutarch's tragic and moralistic concept in general: Plutarch portrayed "the tragic collapse of Roman nerve and stamina in the arms of the Greek enchantress on the throne of Egypt. The subject . . . resembled a kind of political 'Choice of Hercules', where Antony, unlike his fabled ancestor, preferred Pleasure to Virtue. Plutarch, however, throws the full burden of the tragic issue upon Cleopatra. . . .

"This Plutarchian conception Shakespeare entirely adopted, together with almost all the detail in which it is worked out. It fell in with the disposition [262] apparent in the dramas of the preceding years,—in *Lear, Troilus and Cressida, Macbeth*,—to connect tragic ruin with the intervention of a woman." Sh. and Plutarch also share a sense of fate (p. 268): "The conflict is drawn, too, with touches of the mystic fatalism which, through the medium of Plutarch, seems to have coloured Shakespeare's conception of the great catastrophes of the ancient world. Portents foreshadow Antony's fall as they had done Cæsar's; unearthly music is heard on the eve of the last battle: [quotes 2491–2]. A soothsayer warns him to avoid Cæsar, for 'near him thy angel becomes a fear as being o'erpower'd' [986–7]; and Shakespeare applied the phrase to Macbeth's subduing fear of Banquo. But Shakespeare has provided a new and significant augurer of his own [i.e., Enobarbus]."

For BROOKE (1909, 2:xiv), both show the "infinite pity" of Antony's ruin. MACCALLUM (1910, pp. 333–9), noting that Sh.'s changes in Plutarch's characterizations add vividness without altering fundamentals, finds that Sh.'s (p. 335) "most far-reaching modifications concern in the main the manner in which the persons appeal to our sympathies," mainly by omissions from Plutarch. The effect is (p. 339) "to concentrate the attention on the purely personal relations of the lovers." As to political events, Sh. (p. 333) "could give the history of the time, not as it was but as Plutarch represented it, and as Plutarch's representation explained itself to an Elizabethan. It is hardly to his discredit if he underestimates Cleopatra's political astuteness, and has no guess of the political projects that recent criticism has ascribed to Antony, for of these things his author has little to say." HILLEBRAND (ed. 1926, p. xi) sees Sh. as attracted by Plutarch's being "before all else a moral philosopher, for whom history was an object lesson in wisdom and folly, right and wrong, vice and virtue. If one man was successful, he looked for the virtues to which this success was to be accounted; if another failed, he laid it not to fate but to vices within the man's character. . . . That he [Sh.] approved of Plutarch's theories of human action is shown by the fact that his judgment on the heroes of his Roman plays is the same as the historian's. But he would not have delighted in the moralist if the moralist had not spoken so authoritatively to the man and the dramatist in him. . . . The liveliness of his [Plutarch's] action, the sureness with which he divides his story and projects the important scenes, the vividness of his characterization and the illuminating quality of his dialogue,—these are graces that appealed to Shakespeare's dramatic sense." THOMSON (1952, pp. 216–21) traces close Sh.-Plutarch similarities in characterization and political background, with a difference chiefly in Sh.'s choric Enobarbus. And KERMODE (1961; 1971, pp. 98–9, n. 20) observes that Sh. takes over from Plutarch the conflict of heroic virtue and sensuality, with mythic allusions: Antony appears as Hercules (see also p. 609) and Cleopatra as Venus, yet she comes not to play with Bacchus as in Plutarch but to betray Hercules.

Scholars note that various thematic or moral interpretations in Plutarch are given added significance by Sh. Thus SATIN (1966, p. 574) finds Sh. expansive on idealism in love: "The love of Antony and Cleopatra 'needs find out new heaven, new earth' [24–5] . . . and in time it becomes apparent that each finds the perfect universe in the other's love and that their deaths destroy that universe, which may well symbolize the passing of the Renaissance—certainly the cold scientism of Octavius suggests the manner of a later age. Their kind of love is the culmination of a Renaissance tradition that began with Dante's idealism of Beatrice and developed by stages into the mutual idealization of lovers in Spenser's The Faerie Queene (Britomart and Artegall, Arthur and Gloriana). Shakespeare could have found the concept in Spenser, or Tasso or Ariosto among other sources, but he at least finds reinforcement of it in Plutarch's Amimetobion." BROWER (1971, pp. 348–50) believes Sh. expands suggestions in Plutarch to give dramatic life to the history of a noble mind defeated by itself.

ADELMAN (1973, pp. 173–5), who perceives that Plutarch suggested to Sh. the validity both of measured reason and of imaginative transcendence, judiciously comments, "For the most part, Plutarch's tone in North's translation of the *Life* is that of a judicious and morally upright Roman: though he is aware of Cleopatra's charms, he is far more aware of the enormous damage that she did to Antony's public and private career. Antony and Cleopatra are merely erring human beings in his account, though they err magnificently. But interspersed within his rational and moral history of the lovers are a few phrases which imply a paradoxical or a mythic view of the lovers [e.g., p. 399]. Though Plutarch frequently uses these phrases ironically, they nonetheless suggest a language beyond the moral and rational language of Rome.

"Plutarch acknowledges the complexity of his subject in terms which are occasionally contrary to strict Roman logic. He hints at the possibility that Antony's defects are his perfections. . . .

[*174*] "The possibility of a perspective distinct from the merely human is implied in Plutarch's frequent associations of the lovers with gods; though Plutarch never seems to take these associations seriously, they might have jostled Shakespeare's [*175*] imagination."

JONES (ed. 1977, p. 32) agrees with critics such as ROTHSCHILD (1976, p. 417; see p. 389) that "in most traditional accounts, Antony was stigmatized as a great man ruined by sexual passion [as shown by DICKEY, 1957, pp. 146–55]. This is clearly what Plutarch thought." Jones points out (pp. 16–17), "Plutarch had a special interest in the private moments of the famous personages who were his subjects. . . . [*17*] Plutarch is as much interested in behaviour, a man's habits and way of living, as in the great events of his life. . . . Some of this detail shows a curiosity about human behaviour for its own sake, while sometimes he conveys a strong sense of its perplexing paradoxicality. . . . Confronted by such splendidly generous folly [as Antony's], moral judgement seems for a moment disarmed and confused." The play also is (p. 33) "ambiguous" on the value of the love relationship. ALVIS (1978, p. 186) believes Sh. expands Plutarch's *Amimetobion* and *Synapothanumenon* in portraying a passion that combines "erotic exaltation with a yearning for death."

Concerning structure, WHITE (ed. 1883, 3:787) finds *Ant.* "little more than a very bald dialoguing" of Plutarch. ADLER (1895, pp. 264–86), however, examines Sh.'s scene sequence in detail to show the extent of his independence from the Plutarchan narrative. LEE (ed. 1907, 36:xxv–vii), frowning on Sh.'s haphazard selections from Plutarch, believes his omissions leave (p. xxvii) "many jagged edges," as in Ventidius's sudden innuendo on Antony's jealousy in 3.1: intelligible in Plutarch, it conflicts with Antony's generally "chivalric tenour" in Sh. Lee sees Sh. making "hurried and fragmentary allusion to Plutarchan episode [e.g., the Parthian wars] with which he deals either very perfunctorily or not at all." MACCALLUM (1910, pp. 332–9) sees Sh. as closely following Plutarch's structure but is surprised (p. 334) "to find how persistently he rearranges and regroups the minor details, and how by this means he gives them a new significance. The portions of the play where he has made the narrative more compact are also, roughly speaking, those in which he has taken most liberties in dislocating the sequence." The fruit of this recasting is "not merely greater conciseness but an original interpretation," mainly—as Vatke (1868) finds—a focus on the lovers' personal relations. SATIN (1966, p. 573) notes that Sh.'s recasting of incidents serves his concept of dramatic time and space: he "typically cuts through intervals of tangential importance, such as Antonius's campaign against the Parthians and the year's delay of the Roman-Egyptian war after the Battle of Actium, but he still weights this play with a sense of the slow passage of time. He manages this in part by a spread out canvas . . . in part by a piling up of small incidents almost all from Plutarch. . . . By unfurling the four corners of the world and by sowing small incidents densely among them Shakespeare makes space as vast as time in this play, converting his source material into a massive structure." ALTMANN (1969, p. 8), however, argues that Sh. narrows the scene: "Comparison with Plutarch shows that had Shakespeare wanted to encompass more of the world, he might easily have used his material to do so. Plutarch's narrative involves many places and much movement of the characters from place to place. But in the play, only four places are represented, and dramatically there are only two. Misenum, where the triumvirs meet with Pompey [2.6], and Athens, where Antony takes Octavia after their marriage [3.4], are essentially not-Alexandria, and therefore Rome. Shakespeare's characters, in comparison, do not move about their world very much. Although Plutarch's lovers often met outside of Alexandria . . . Shakespeare's lovers do not. Except for the few scenes in Actium, we always see them together in Alexandria. In fact, all roads seem to lead to Alexandria." JONES (ed. 1977, p. 19) perceives that Sh.'s focusing attention on Antony, onstage or off, "can be seen as responding to a Plutarchan emphasis": Sh. finds a "dramatic equivalent" for Plutarch's "small-scale" progression in a narrative held together by anecdotes concerning Antony. Hence the play's (p. 20) "peculiar drifting movement," since Sh.'s and Plutarch's "concern is more with ethics, even manners, than with the growth of passion." *Ant.* falls into two "movements," with a break at 3.6 (previously noted by JONES, 1971, p. 230; suggested first by GRANVILLE-BARKER, 1930; 1946, 1:379–80). Jones continues (p. 24), "In the first movement, Antony leaves Cleopatra for Rome, marries Octavia, but then abandons her for Cleopatra. This prompts the war between Antony and Caesar, which, together with its aftermath in the deaths of the lovers, occupies the second movement. Both movements open with Antony and Cleopatra together, and both of them end with Caesar. He has the last word in both sequences—an arrangement which can be interpreted as having an expressive value. It is a way of dramatizing the actual historical outcome—for since Caesar survived Antony and Cleopatra, he can be said historically to have had the last word." Both phases (p. 25) "correspond to two massive blocks of Plutarch's *Life*, where they are separated by the long account of Antony's Parthian campaign for which Shakespeare had no use." PELLING (1988, p. 38) takes issue with Jones's description of Plutarch's structure. GREEN (1979, pp. 12–18) surveys commentary on *Ant.*'s structure and discusses in detail (pp. 19–129) Sh.'s transformation of Plutarch into the same two blocks of dramatic action. Surveys of Sh.-Plutarch parallels and comments on Sh.'s selections include those by VOLLMER (1887, pp. 215–19: parallels, adding Appian, Dio, and other historians), ADLER (1895, pp. 264–86 et passim), MACCALLUM (1910, pp. 300–453), MUNRO (ed. 1957, 6:1211–12), WALTER (ed. 1969, pp. 299–301), LEE (1971, pp. 58–60), and SLATER (ed. 1971, pp. 31–7).

On language, scholars have pointed out Sh.'s debt to North's skillful prose (e.g., WYNDHAM, 1895, 1:xciv–vi; BULLOUGH, 1964, 5:251–2), especially to North's idiomatic informality and manly dignity (HILLEBRAND, ed. 1926, pp. xii–xiii), his opulence (MURRY, 1929; 1931, pp. 82–9), his as well as Plutarch's mythological allusions and use of hyperbole (MCALINDON, 1973, pp. 187–9). RALEIGH (1907, pp. 71–2) thinks Sh. even falls short of North in 4.3 and 5.2, while NEWBOLT (1925, pp. 22–3) remarks on Sh.'s creative power in translating North into 4.15 and 5.2. Some discuss the extent of Sh.'s poetic "improvements" on North (e.g., ADLER, 1895, pp. 305–17) and his freedom in revision (e.g., MACCALLUM, 1910, pp. 318–25). GÜNTHER (1968, pp. 103–4) notes the cosmic scope of Sh.'s language, unlike North's smaller compass. Scholars who comment on Sh.'s humorous tone include LEE (ed. 1907, 36:xxix), who thinks Sh.'s humor has no model in Plutarch, while JONES (ed. 1977, p. 20) believes the comic passages in *Ant.* reflect Plutarch's approach to biography as "comedy of manners" (a phrase borrowed from RUSSELL, 1973, p. 102). Scholars who compare Enobarbus's "barge" speech (901–31) with Plutarch include MURRY (1929; 1931, pp. 11–12), EDWARDS (1933, pp. 109–13), HIGHET (1949, pp. 212–14), THOMSON (1952, pp. 234–6), PHIALAS (ed. 1955, pp. 168–70), MACK (ed. 1960, pp. 16–18), ALTMANN (1969, pp. 60–102: extended discussion of characterization of Cleopatra and Enobarbus), INGLEDEW (ed. 1971, pp. xxxi–iv), ADAMS (1973, pp. 79–81), and FISKIN (1975, pp. 97–8). For various other influences on the speech, see nn. 902–31, 902–3, 906–9, and p. 608.

Comments on Sh.'s techniques in transforming Plutarch into drama include, after KOCH's (ed. 1882, 9:244–5) praise, especially STAMM (1959; 1967, pp. 74–84: Sh.'s use of techniques such as dramatic exposition or impulses for action given in speeches, as against Plutarch's narrative; 1965, pp. 91–4: Sh.'s ability to express abstract ideas as dramatic event) and INGLEDEW (ed. 1971, pp. xxvi–xxxv: Sh.'s adaptation of Plutarch to dramatic situation and characterization), as well as the comprehensive accounts by ADLER (1895, pp. 263–317), MACCALLUM (1910, pp. 300–453), THOMAS (1956, passim), ALTMANN (1969, passim), and GREEN (1979, pp. 19–129).

MUIR (1957, pp. 201–5, slightly rev. in 1977, pp. 220–3), apart from citing verbal parallels especially in 491–507 and 901–31, finds allusions in *Ant.* to Plutarch's mythic references and (in 1957 only) sees both authors as agreeing on Seleucus's secret collusion with Cleopatra in 5.2. LLOYD (1960, pp. 324–7) examines Sh.'s reflecting Plutarch's notion that daemons move men to action; SCHANZER (1960, "Three Notes on *Ant.*," p. 21) the development of proper names in the play from hints in Plutarch; WILLIAMSON (1970, pp. 244–5) the added emphasis given in *Ant.* to Plutarch's reports of loyalty, deception, and betrayal; and FISKIN (1975, pp. 93–8) fortune, Roman virtue, and cosmic dimension in the *Life* and *Ant.* Scholars who compare single scenes or passages with Plutarch include NORMAN (1956, pp. 59–61: on 1.4, 1.5, and 4.10), THOMAS (1958, pp. 153–7: on 4.15; 1972, pp. 566, 568, 572: opening scenes), LONG (1964, pp. 28–34: on 2.7 and 4.3), STIRLING (1964, pp. 299–311: on the Seleucus episode in 5.2), and KIMURA (1981–2, pp. 91–107: on ll. 59, 1785, 2370, 2769).

Other *Lives* are cited for particular aspects and episodes: that of Julius Caesar by GREY (1754, 2:205, 210; see nn. 1743–4, 2600–4), SKEAT (1914; see n. 399–400), and DRAPER (1933, p. 234: for the augurer and further details of local color), that of Cato (Tudor Translations, ed. W. E. Henley, 1896, 5:178) by BARROLL (1969, p. 234, n. 67: for the description of Cato's suicide, which serves as an "ideal" for Antony's). Comparisons of Plutarch's description of Isis in *Moralia* with references or allusions to her in the play are offered by LLOYD (1959, *ShS*, pp. 91–4; see nn. 111, 141, 979, 3562, and the [p. 92] "transfiguration of Isis" recalled at 3560), WALTER (1969, pp. 137–8; see n. 952), FISCH (1970, p. 61), WHITAKER (1972, pp. 156–8), COLIE (1974, p. 195), and ADLARD (1975, pp. 325–8; see nn. 552, 951–2, 1768, and, overingeniously, P. Holland's tr. of 1603, p. 1304, for 129). LLOYD (1960, pp. 326–7) sees Sh. as drawing on Plutarch's theory of daemons, explained not only in the *Lives* but also in *Moralia*—see n. 164 and, rather remotely, p. 992 of Holland's tr. (1603, ed. of 1657) as a source for the imagery at 2084–6, Holland's p. 994 for 2325–7—and he suggests (1962, pp. 548–54) that Sh.'s imagery of fortune recalls Plutarch's statements on fortune and chance in *Moralia*. See also n. 641. The account summarizing the fable of Mars and Venus in *De Homero*, an essay attributed by Xylander to Plutarch, with its emphasis

on harmony born from the gods' union, is cited—along with *Moralia*—by WAD-
DINGTON (1966, p. 221) to illuminate Sh.'s interpretation of the lovers; see also
p. 610.

The Life of Marcus Antonius and *The Comparison of Demetrius with Antonius* (1579)

"PLUTARK*s Lyves*" was entered on the Stationers' Register to Thomas Vautrollier
and J. Wighte on 6 Apr. 1579 (ARBER, 2:159). A folio was published with the
following title page: "THE LIVES | OF THE NOBLE GRE- | CIANS AND RO-
MANES, COMPARED | *together by that graue learned Philosopher and Historiogra-* |
pher, Plutarke of Chæronea: | Translated out of Greeke into French by IAMES AMYOT,
Abbot of Bellozane, | Bishop of Auxerre, one of the Kings priuy counsel, and great
Amner | of Fraunce, and out of French into Englishe, by | *Thomas North.* | [device]
| Imprinted at London by Thomas Vautroullier dvvelling | in the Blacke Friers by
Ludgate. | 1579." Before the writing of *Ant.*, two further editions of the work
appeared, in 1595 (*STC* 20067) and 1603 (*STC* 20068). LAW (1942–3, pp. 197–
203) discusses evidence, particularly spelling, for the ed. Sh. used, concluding—
as does BROOKE (1909, 1:xxii)—that 1579 is the most likely.

The text below is a modified diplomatic reprint of 1579. The folio's marginal
section divisions are not reproduced. Typographical ornaments have been removed.
The prose is relined, and the beginning of each page in 1579 indicated by bracketed
italic numbers. Ornamental initials have been replaced by regular capitals, and the
capitals that conventionally follow display letters reduced. Long *s* is printed *s*, and
other archaic types are represented by modern equivalents. Obvious typographical
errors have been silently corrected.

The text is based on the copy in the Huntington Library (*STC* 20065). Variants
in the University of Illinois Library's copy of the 1595 and the British Library's
copy of the 1603 edition are recorded in notes. The full text of North's version of
The Life of Antonius has been edited by SKEAT (1875; 1880), LEO (1878), WYNDHAM
(1895), ROUSE (1898), CARR (1906), BROOKE (1909), TURNER (1963), and SPEN-
CER (1964; 1968), as well as in editions of North's Plutarch by the Sh. Head Press
in 1928 and the Nonesuch Press in 1929.

Passages corresponding with *Ant.* are preceded by bracketed TLNs. The following parallels have been found (numbers without parentheses are *Ant.* TLNs;
numbers in parentheses are Plutarch page numbers in this edition):

The Life 19 (408), 42–3 (403), 44–51 (398), 51 (414, 447), 57–68 (416), 59
(415), 66–7 (415), 77 (414, 417, 430), 77–8 (444), 79 (447), 84 (455), 163–4
(415), 173–4 (416), 173–80 (416), 173–91 (414), 187–91 (416), 209–10 (416),
213–15 (416), 225–7 (416), 283–5 (417), 299–322 (433), 301–3 (415), 402
(399, 420, 438), 432–4 (414), 433 (415), 436 (441), 448–51 (399), 450–1 (415),
458–61 (414), 468 (417), 483–90 (417), 492–4 (407), 495–504 (407), 495–6
(407), 554 (421), 556–61 (412), 578–80 (420), 608–9 (412), 631–2 (409, 436),

643–7 (416), 686 (399, 408), 688 (416), 693–4 (416), 701–9 (416), 753–62 (416), 754–5 (403), 787–8 (416), 787–91 (416), 792–7 (416), 816–17 (416), 820 (416), 822–34 (417), 852–3 (416), 858–9 (417), 866 (417, 417), 883–4 (419), 890–1 (414), 898–928 (413), 933–8 (413), 936 (412), 938 (399), 942–3 (412, 434), 957 (417), 981–1005 (417), 984 (418), 1043–5 (415), 1207–10 (403, 409, 417), 1218–21 (417), 1229–32 (417), 1251–2 (417), 1276 (417), 1307 (416), 1314–15 (417), 1402–26 (417), 1466–7 (411, 413, 438, 449), 1483 (403, 409, 417), 1496–1500 (418), 1501–5 (418), 1508–12 (418), 1513–17 (419), 1531 (419), 1534 (419), 1566–9 (418), 1583–9 (418), 1627–8 (409, 420), 1685–94 (419), 1687–8 (420, 434), 1688–9 (436), 1697–1705 (419), 1710–11 (419), 1730 (420, 434), 1745–6 (419), 1752–67 (434), 1759–61 (420), 1767–70 (434), 1775–89 (434), 1792–1857 (419), 1810–16 (419), 1825–33 (438), 1834–6 (419), 1844–5 (433), 1850–2 (434), 1861 (435), 1864 (438), 1872–5 (438), 1874 (438), 1877–9 (435), 1883–6 (439), 1884 (439), 1891–3 (439), 1896–8 (439), 1897–1900 (440), 1901–5 (439), 1903–7 (440), 1908–10 (439), 1909–16 (440), 1917 (439), 1919–20 (441), 1919–21 (439), 1924–6 (439), 1927–30 (435), 1928–9 (438, 444), 1933–9 (441), 1944–8 (444), 1944–5 (441), 1946–7 (441), 1948 (441), 1953–4 (441), 1961–7 (441), 1970 (425), 1978–9 (442), 1978 (438), 1988–94 (442), 1998–2011 (443), 1998 (442), 2000 (441), 2009 (443, 444), 2014 (442), 2017–19 (444, 446), 2018–19 (440), 2025–45 (443), 2047 (442), 2048 (443), 2049–59 (443), 2063–4 (419), 2067–9 (443), 2085–6 (443), 2103 (447), 2110–14 (447), 2122–30 (447), 2131–6 (448), 2144 (448), 2181–4 (439), 2218–26 (453), 2251–65 (448), 2282 (419), 2283–4 (412), 2293–5 (412), 2319–31 (448), 2328–9 (444), 2353–5 (443), 2370–2 (448), 2393–5 (449), 2416–19 (449), 2422–7 (449), 2437–40 (449), 2443–51 (449), 2453–65 (449), 2454 (408, 426), 2482–2501 (449), 2491 (438), 2529 (449), 2562–74 (440), 2590–4 (447), 2591–3 (446), 2594–5 (444), 2600–4 (440), 2628–50 (449), 2664–6 (449), 2675–81 (449), 2703–20 (440), 2741–6 (449), 2754–6 (449), 2757–60 (438), 2766 (449), 2767–9 (449), 2780 (449), 2803 (399, 420, 438), 2804–6 (398), 2813–18 (450), 2842–7 (449), 2867 (450), 2876–7 (450), 2883 (450), 2889–96 (450), 2897–2902 (450), 2911–13 (431), 2919–22 (450), 2923–36 (450), 2937–9 (450), 2944–57 (450), 2958–60 (451), 2961 (450), 2985–95 (450), 3014–15 (450), 3026–8 (450), 3035–6 (450), 3038–45 (450), 3045 (450), 3049 (450), 3051 (450), 3056 (451), 3059 (451), 3062–9 (451), 3117–39 (451), 3140–65 (451), 3181–6 (451), 3190 (451), 3195–9, (451), 3200 (455), 3215–16 (451), 3217–18 (451), 3218–27 (451), 3241 (451), 3244 (451), 3245 (451), 3246–53 (452), 3258–61 (453), 3275 (452), 3275 ff. (454), 3308–10 (399, 420, 426), 3308 (440), 3336–8 (453), 3339–42 (453), 3356–61 (453), 3357 (452), 3359–61 (452), 3366–3405 (454), 3411–21 (454), 3435–42 (454), 3450–64 (451), 3472–5 (455), 3474 (455), 3482–3530 (455), 3482–4 (455), 3495 (456), 3495–6 (447), 3531 (455), 3538 (450), 3544 (455), 3557–8 (455), 3559 (441), 3561–3 (447), 3566 (456), 3567–3601 (455), 3572–3 (455), 3583–7 (455), 3603–5 (455), 3608–11 (455), 3613–14 (455), 3614 (447), 3617–19 (456), 3620–2 (455, 455), 3623–4 (456), 3624–6 (453), 3625–6 (447), 3626

(453), 3626–33 (456); *The Comparison* 455–63 (457), 1050–1 (458), 2510–13 (458), 3538 (458).

THE LIFE OF   [970]

Marcus Antonius.

ANTONIVS grandfather was that famous Orator whome *Marius* slue, bicause he tooke *Syllaes* parte. His father was an other *Antonius* surnamed *Cretan, who was not so famous, nor bare any great sway in the common wealth: howbeit otherwise he was an honest man, and of a very good nature, and specially very liberall in giuing, as appeareth by an acte he did. He was not very wealthie, and therefore his wife would not let him vse his liberalitie and francke nature. One day a friend of his comming to him to praye him to helpe him to some money, hauing great neede: *Antonius* by chaunce had no money to giue him, but he commaunded one of his men to bringe him some water in a siluer basen, & after he had brought it him, he washed his beard as though he ment to haue shauen it, and then found an arrant for his man to send him out, and gaue his friend the siluer basen, and bad him get him money with that. Shortly after, there was a great sturre in the house among the seruaunts, seeking out[1] this siluer basen. Insomuch as *Antonius* seeing his wife maruelously offended for it, & that she would examine all her seruaunts, one after another about it, to know what was become of it: at length he confessed he had giuen it away, & prayed her to be contented. His wife was *Iulia*, of the noble house and familie of *Iulius Cæsar*: who for her vertue & chastitie, was to be compared with the noblest Lady of her time. *M. Antonius* was brought vp vnder her, being married after her first husbands death, vnto *Cornelius Lentulus*, whom *Cicero* put to death with *Cethegus*, and others, for that he was of *Catilines* conspiracie against the common wealth. And this seemeth to be the originall cause and beginning of the cruell and mortall hate *Antonius* bare vnto *Cicero*. For *Antonius* selfe sayth, that he would neuer giue him the body of his father in law to bury him, before his mother went first to intreat *Ciceroes* wife: the which vndoubtedly was a flat lye. For *Cicero* denied buriall to none of them, whom he executed by law. Now *Antonius* being a fayer younge man, and in the pryme of his youth: he fell acquainted with *Curio*, whose friendship and acquaintance (as it is reported) was a plague vnto him. For he was a dissolute man, giuen ouer to all lust and insolencie, who to haue *Antonius* the better at his commaundement, trayned him on into great follies, and vaine expences [971] vpon women, in rioting & banketing. So that in short time, he brought *Antonius* into a maruelous great det, & too great for one of his yeres, to wete: of two hundred & fifty talents, for all which summe *Curio* was his suertie. His father hearing of it, did put his sonne from him, and forbad him his house. Then he fell in with *Clodius*, one of the desperatest and most wicked Tribunes at that time in ROME. Him he followed for a time in his desperate attempts, who bred great sturre and mischiefe in ROME: but at length he forsooke him, being weary of his rashnes and folly, or els for that he was affraid of them that were bent against *Clodius*. Therevppon

(marginal notes)
Antonius parentage.
*Bicause that by his death he ended the warre which he vnfortunately made against those of Creta. The liberalitie of Antonius father.

Iulia the mother of M. Antonius.

Antonius corrupted by Curio.

---

[1] out] out of 1603

397

he left ITALY, and went into GRÆCE, and there bestowed the most parte of his tyme, sometime in warres, and otherwhile in the studie of eloquence. [TLN 44–51, 2804–6] He vsed a manner of phrase in his speeche, called Asiatik, which caried the best grace and estimation at that time, and was much like to his manners and life: for it was full of ostentation, foolishe brauerie, and vaine ambition. After he had remayned there some tyme, *Gabinius* Proconsul going into SYRIA, perswaded him to goe with him. *Antonius* tolde him he would not goe as a priuate man: Wherefore *Gabinius* gaue him charge of his horsemen, and so tooke him with him. So, first of all he sent him against *Aristobulus*, who had made the IEVVES to rebell, & was the first man him selfe that got vp to the wall of a castell of his, and so draue *Aristobulus* out of all his holds: and with those few men he had with him, he ouercame al the IEVVES in set battel, which were many against one, and put all of them almost to the sword, and furthermore, tooke *Aristobulus* him selfe prisoner with his sonne. Afterwards *Ptolomy* king of ÆGYPT, that had bene driuen out of his contry, went vnto *Gabinius* to intreate him to goe with his armie with him into ÆGYPT, to put him againe into his kingdom: and promised him if he would goe with him, tenne thowsand talents. The most part of the Captaines thought it not best to goe thither, & *Gabinius* him selfe made it daintie to enter into this warre: although the couetousnes of these tenne thowsand talents stucke sorely with him. But *Antonius* that sought but for oportunitie and good occasion to attempt great enterprises, and that desired also to gratifie *Ptolomyes* request: he went about to perswade *Gabinius* to goe this voyage. Now they were more affrayd of the way they should goe, to come to the citie of PELVSIVM, then they feared any daunger of the warre besides: bicause they were to passe through deepe sandes & desert places, where was no freshe water to be had all the marisses thorough, which are called the marisses Serbonides, which the ÆGYPTIANS call the exhalations or fume, by the which the Gyant *Typhon* breathed. But in truth it appeareth to be the ouerflowing of the red sea, which breaketh out vnder the ground in that place, where it is deuided in the narrowest place from the sea on this side. So *Antonius* was sent before into ÆGYPT with his horsemen, who did not onely winne that passage, but also tooke the citie of PELVSIVM, (which is a great citie) with all the souldiers in it: and thereby he cleared the way, and made it safe for all the rest of the armie, and the hope of the victorie also certaine for his Captaine. Nowe did the enemies them selues feele the frutes of *Antonius* curtesie, and the desire he had to winne honor. For when *Ptolomy* (after he had entred into the citie of PELVSIVM) for the malice he bare vnto the citie, would haue put all the ÆGYPTIANS in it to the sword: *Antonius* withstoode him, & by no meanes would suffer him to doe it. And in all other great battells and skirmishes which they fought, and were[3] many in number, *Antonius* did many noble actes of a valliant and wise Captaine: but specially in one battell, where he compassed in the enemies behind, giuing them the victorie that fought against them[4], whereby he afterwards had such honorable reward, as his val-

Antonius vsed in his pleading the Asiatik phrase.

Antonius had charge of horsemen, vnder Gabinius Proconsul going into Syria. Antonius acts against[2] Aristobulus. Antonius tooke Aristobulus prisoner.

Antonius acts in AEgypt vnder Gabinius.

---

[2] *against*] *gainst* 1603
[3] and were] being 1603
[4] against them] in front 1603

liantnes deserued. So was his great curtesie also much commended of all, the
which he shewed vnto *Archelaus*. For hauing bene his very friend, he made warre
with him against his will while he liued: but after his death he sought for his
bodye, and gaue it honorable buriall. For these respects he wanne him selfe
great fame of them of ALEXANDRIA, and he was also thought a worthy man of
all the souldiers in the ROMANES campe. But besides all this, he had a noble
presence, and shewed a countenaunce of one of a noble house: [TLN 686, 938]
he had a goodly thicke beard, a broad forehead, crooke⁵ nosed, and there
appeared such a manly looke in his countenaunce, as is commonly seene in
Hercules pictures, stamped or grauen in mettell. Now it had bene a speeche of
old time, [TLN 402, 2803] that the familie of the *Antonij* were discended from
one *Anton*, the sonne of *Hercules*, whereof the familie tooke name. This opinion
did *Antonius* seeke to confirme in [972] all his doings: not onely resembling
him in the likenes of his bodye, as we haue sayd before, but also in the wearing
of his garments. For when he would openly shewe him selfe abroad before many
people, he would alwayes weare his cassocke gyrt downe lowe vpon his hippes,
with a great sword hanging by his side, and vpon that, some ill fauored cloke.
Furthermore, things that seeme intollerable in other men, as to boast commonly,
to ieast with one or other, [TLN 448–51] to drinke like a good fellow with
euery body, to sit with the souldiers when they dine, and to eate and drinke
with them souldierlike: it is incredible what wonderfull loue it wanne him
amongest them. And furthermore, being giuen to loue: that made him the
more desired, and by that meanes he brought many to loue him. For he would
further euery mans loue, and also would not be angry that men should merily
tell him of those he loued. But besides all this, that which most procured his
rising and aduauncement, [TLN 3308–10] was his liberalitie, who gaue all to
the souldiers, and kept nothing for him selfe: and when he was growen to great
credit, then was his authoritie and power also very great, the which notwithstanding him selfe did ouerthrowe, by a thowsand other faults he had. In this
place I will shewe you one example onely of his wonderful liberalitie. He
commaunded one day his coferer that kept his money, to giue a friend of his
25. Myriades: which the ROMANES call in their tongue, Decies. His coferer
marueling at it, and being angry withall in his minde, brought him all this
money in a heape together, to shewe him what a maruelous masse of money it
was. *Antonius* seeing it as he went by, asked what it was: his⁶ coferer aunswered
him, it was the money he willed him to giue vnto his friend. Then *Antonius*
perceiuing the spight of his man, I thought, sayd he, that Decies had bene a
greater summe of money then it is, for this is but a trifle: and therefore he
gaue his friend as much more another tyme, but that was afterwardes. Nowe
the ROMANES mainteyning two factions at ROME at that tyme, one against the
other, of the which, they that tooke part with the Senate, did ioyne with *Pompey*
being then in ROME: and the contrary side taking part with the people, sent
for *Cæsar* to ayde them, who made warres in GAVLE. Then *Curio Antonius* friend,
that had chaunged his garments, and at that tyme tooke parte with *Cæsar*,

Antonius curtesie vnto Archelaus being dead.

Antonius shape & presence. The house of the Antonij discended from Hercules.

Antonius liberalitie.

---

⁵ crooke] crooked 1603
⁶ his] the 1603

whose enemie he had bene before: he wanne *Antonius*, and so handled the matter, partly through the great credit and swaye he bare amongest the people, by reason of his eloquent tongue: and partly also by his exceeding expence of money he made which *Cæsar* gaue him: that *Antonius* was chosen Tribune, and afterwards made Augure. But this was a great helpe and furtheraunce to *Cæsars* practises. For so soone as *Antonius* became Tribune he did oppose him selfe against those thinges which the Consul *Marcellus* preferred: (who ordeyned that certaine legions which had bene already leauied and billed, should be giuen vnto *Cneus Pompey*, with further commission and authoritie to leauye others vnto them) and set downe an order, that the souldiers which were already leauied and assembled, should be sent into SYRIA, for a newe supplie vnto *Marcus Bibulus*, who made warre at that tyme against the PARTHIANS. And furthermore,[7] prohibition that *Pompey* should leauy no more men, and also that the souldiers should not obey him. Secondly, where *Pompeys* friends and followers would not suffer *Cæsars* letters to be receiued, and openly red in the Senate: *Antonius* hauing power and warrant by his person, through the holines of his tribuneship, did read them openly, and made diuers men chaunge their mindes: for it appeared to them that *Cæsar* by his letters required no vnreasonable matters. At length, when they preferred two matters of consideracion vnto the Senate, whether they thought good that *Pompey*, or *Cæsar*, should leaue their armie: there were few of the Senators that thought it meete *Pompey* should leaue his armie, but they all in manner commaunded *Cæsar* to doe it. Then *Antonius* rising vp, asked whether they thought it good that *Pompey* and *Cæsar* both, should leaue their armies. Thereunto[8] all the Senators ioyntly together gaue their whole consent, and with a great crye commending *Antonius*, they prayed him to referre it to the iudgement of the Senate. But the Consuls would not allowe of that. Therefore *Cæsars* friendes preferred other reasonable demaunds and requests againe, but *Cato* spake against them: and *Lentulus*, one of the Consuls draue *Antonius* by force out of the Senate, who at his going out made greuous curses against him. After that, he tooke a slaues gowne, and speedily fled to *Cæsar*, with *Quintus Cassius*, in a hyered coch. When they came to *Cæsar*, they cryed out with open mouth, that all went hand [973] ouer head at ROME: for the Tribunes of the people might not speake their mindes, and were driuen away in great daunger of their liues, as many as stoode with lawe and iustice. Hereuppon *Cæsar* incontinently went into ITALY with his army, which made *Cicero* say in his Philippides: that as *Hellen* was cause of the warre of TROY, so was *Antonius* the author of the ciuill warres, which in deede was a starke lye. For *Cæsar* was not so fickle headed, nor so easily caried away with anger, that he would so sodainly haue gone and made warre with his[9] contry, vpon the sight onely of *Antonius* and *Cassius*, being fled vnto[10] him in miserable apparell, and in a hyered coche: had he not long before determined it with him selfe. But sith in deed *Cæsar* looked of long time but for some culler, this came as he wished, and gaue him iust occasion of warre. But to say truely, nothing els

Antonius Tribune of the people, and Augure.

Antonius acts for Cæsar.

Antonius flyeth from Rome vnto Cæsar.

Cicero reproued for lying.

---

[7] furthermore,] further, gaue a 1603
[8] Thereunto] Thereupon 1603
[9] his] the 1603
[10] vnto] to 1603

moued him to make warre with all the world as he did, but one selfe cause, which first procured *Alexander* and *Cyrus* also before him: to wit, an insatiable desire to raigne, with a senseles couetousnes to be the best man in the world, the which he could not come vnto, before he had first put downe *Pompey*, and vtterly ouerthrowen him. Now, after that *Cæsar* had gotten ROME at his commaundement, & had driuen *Pompey* out of ITALY, he purposed first to goe into SPAYNE, against the legions *Pompey* had there: and in the meane time to make prouision for shippes and marine preparacion, to follow *Pompey*. In his absence, he left *Lepidus* that was Prætor, gouernor of ROME: and *Antonius* that was Tribune, he gaue him charge of all the souldiers, and of ITALY. Then was *Antonius* straight maruelously commended and beloued of the souldiers, bicause he commonly exercised him self among them, and would oftentimes eate and drinke with them, and also be liberall vnto them, according to his abilitie. But then in contrary manner, he purchased diuers other mens euill willes, bicause that through negligence he would not doe them iustice that were iniuried[11], & delt very churlishly with them that had any sute vnto him: and besides all this, he had an ill name to intise mens wiues. To conclude, *Cæsars* friends that gouerned vnder him, were cause why they hated *Cæsars* gouernment (which in deede in respect of him selfe was no lesse then a tyrannie) by reason of the great insolencies & outragious parts that were committed: amongst whom *Antonius*, that was of greatest power, and that also committed greatest faultes, deserued most blame. But *Cæsar* notwithstanding, when he returned from the warres of SPAYNE, made no reckoning of the complaints that were put vp against him: but contrarily, bicause he found him a hardy man, & a valliant Captaine, he employed him in his chiefest affayres, and was no whit deceiued in his opinion of him. So he passed ouer the IONIAN sea vnto BRVNDVSIVM, being but slenderly accompanied: & sent vnto *Antonius*, & *Gabinius*, that they should imbarke their men as soone as they could, and passe them ouer into MACEDON. *Gabinius* was affrayd to take the sea, bicause it was very roughe, and in the winter time: & therefore fetched a great compasse about by land. But *Antonius* fearing some daunger might come vnto *Cæsar*, bicause he was compassed in with a great number of enemies: first of all he draue away *Libo*, who roade at ancker with a great armie, before the hauen of BRVNDVSIVM. For he manned out such a number of pynnasies, barks, and other small boates about euery one of his gallies, that he draue him thence. After that, he imbarked into shippes twenty thowsand footemen, and eyght hundred horsemen, and with this armie he hoysed sayle. When the enemies sawe him, they made out to followe him: but the sea rose so highe, that the billowes put backe their gallies that they could not come neare him, and so he scaped that daunger. But withall he fell vppon the rockes with his whole fleete, where the sea wrought very highe: so that he was out of all hope to saue him selfe. Yet by good fortune, sodainely the winde turned Southwest, and blewe from the gulffe, driuing the waues of the riuer into the mayne sea. Thus *Antonius* loosing from the lande, and sayling with safetie at his pleasure, soone after he sawe all the coastes full of shippe-wracks. For the force and boysterousnes of the winde, did cast away the gallies

---

[11] iniuried] iniured 1603

that followed him: of the which, many of them were broken and splitted, and diuers also cast away, and *Antonius* tooke a great number of them prisoners, with a great summe of money also. Besides all these, he tooke the citie of Lyssvs, and brought *Cæsar* a great supplie of men, and made him coragious, comming at a pynche with so great a power to him. Now there were diuers hotte skyrmishes and encownters, in the which *Antonius* fought so valliantly, that he caried the prayse from them all: but specially at two seuerall tymes, [974] when *Cæsars* men turned their backes, and fled for life. For he stepped before them, and compelled them to returne againe to fight: so that the victorie fell on *Cæsars* side. For this cause he had the seconde place in the campe amonge the souldiers, and they spake of no other man vnto *Cæsar*, but of him: who shewed playnely what opinion he had of him, when at the last battell of Pharsalia (which in deede was the last tryall of all, to giue the Conqueror the whole Empire of the worlde) he him selfe did leade the right wing of his armie, and gaue *Antonius* the leading of the left wing, as the valliantest man, and skilfullest souldier of all those he had about him. After *Cæsar* had wonne the victorie, and that he was created Dictator, he followed *Pompey* steppe by steppe: howbeit before, he named *Antonius* generall of the horsemen, and sent him to Rome. The generall of the horsemen is the second office of dignitie, when the Dictator is in the citie: but when he is abroad, he is the chiefest man, and almost the onely man that remayneth, and all the other officers and Magistrates are put downe, after there is a Dictator chosen. Notwithstanding, *Dolabella* being at that tyme Tribune, and a younge man desirous of chaunge and innouation: he preferred a law which the Romanes call Nouas tabulas (as much to saye, as a cutting of and cancelling of all obligacions and specialties, & were called the[13] newe tables, bicause they were driuen then to make bookes of daily receit and expense) and perswaded *Antonius* his friend (who also gaped for a good occasion to please and gratifie the common people) to aide him to passe this lawe. But *Trebellius* & *Asinius* disswaded from it al they could possible. So by good hap it chaunced that *Antonius* mistrusted *Dolabella* for keeping of his wife, and tooke suche a conceite of it, that he thrust his wife out of his house being his Cosin Germane, & the daughter of *C. Antonius*, who was Consul with *Cicero*: & ioyning with *Asinius*, he resisted *Dolabella*, & fought with him. *Dolabella* had gotten the market place where the people doe assemble in counsel, & had filled it ful of armed men, intending to haue this law of the newe tables to passe by force. *Antonius* by cōmaundement of the Senate, who had giuen him authoritie to leauy men,[14] to vse force against *Dolabella*: he went against him, & fought so valliantly, that men were slaine on both sides. But by this meanes, he got the il will of the cōmon people, & on the other side, the noble men (as *Cicero* saith) did not only mislike him, but also hate him for his naughty life: for they did abhor his banckets & dronkē feasts he made at vnseasonable times, & his extreme wastful expences vpon vaine light huswiues, & then in the day time he would sleepe or walke out his dronkennes, thinking to weare away the

Antonius manhood in warres.[12]

Antonius led the left wing of Cæsars battell at Pharsalia where Pompey lost the field.

The dignitie of the general of the horsemen.

Dissention be twixt Antonius and Dolabella.

---

[12] *warres*] *warre* 1595, 1603
[13] the] *Om.* 1603
[14] men,] men & 1603

fume of the aboundaunce of wine which he had taken ouer night. In his house
they did nothing but feast, daunce, & maske: and him selfe passed away the
time in hearing of foolish playes, or in marrying these plaiers, tomblers, ieasters,
& such sort of people. As for profe hereof it is reported, that at *Hippias* mariage,
one of his ieasters, he drank wine so lustely all night, that the next morning
when he came to pleade before the people assembled in counsel, who had sent
for him: he being quesie stomaked with his surfet he had takē, was compelled
to lay¹⁵ all before them, & one of his friends held him his gowne in stead of
a basen. He had another pleasaunt player called *Sergius*, that was one of the
chiefest men about him, & a woman also called *Cytheride*, of the same profession,
whom he loued derely: he caried her vp & downe in a litter vnto all the townes
he went, & had as many men waiting apon her litter, she being but a player,
as were attending vpon his owne mother. It greued honest men also very much,
to see that when he went into the contry, he caried with him a great number
of cubbords ful of siluer & gold plate, openly in the face of the world, as it
had ben the pompe or shewe of some triumphe: & that eftsoones in the middest
of his iorney he would set vp his hales and tents hard by some greene groue or
pleasaunt riuer, and there his Cookes should prepare him a sumptuous dinner.
And furthermore, Lyons were harnesed in trases to drawe his carts: and besides
also, in honest mens houses in the cities where he came, he would haue common
harlots, curtisans, & these tumbling gillots lodged. Now it greued men much,
to see that *Cæsar* should be out of ITALY following of his enemies, to end this
great warre, with such great perill and daunger: and that others in the meane
time abusing his name and authoritie, should commit such insolent and outragious parts vnto their Citizens. This me thinkes was the cause that made the
conspiracie against *Cæsar* increase more and more, and layed the reynes of the
brydle vppon the souldiers neckes, whereby they durst boldlier¹⁶ commit many
[975] extorsions, cruelties and robberies. And therefore *Cæsar* after his returne
pardoned *Dolabella*, & being created Consul the third time, he tooke not *An-*
tonius, but chose *Lepidus*, his colleague and fellow Consul. [TLN 1207–10,
1483] Afterwards when *Pompeys* house was put to open sale, *Antonius* bought
it: but when they asked him money for it, he made it very straung, and was
offended with them, and writeth him selfe that he would not goe with *Cæsar*
into the warres of AFRICK, bicause he was not well recompenced for the seruice
he had done him before. Yet *Cæsar* did somewhat bridle his madnes and
insolencie, not suffering him to passe his faulte¹⁷ so lightly away, making as
though he sawe them not. And therefore he left his dissolute manner of life,
and married *Fuluia* that was *Clodius* widowe, a woman not so basely minded
to spend her time in spinning and housewiuery, [TLN 42–3] and was not
contented to master her husband at home, but would also rule him in his office
abroad, [TLN 754–5] and commaund¹⁸ him, that commaunded legions and
great armies: so that *Cleopatra* was to giue *Fuluia* thankes for that she had
taught *Antonius* this obedience to women, that learned so well to be at their

Antonius abominable life.

Antonius laid vp his stomack before the whole assembly.

Antonius insolency.

Cæsar, & Lepidus, Consuls.
Antonius byeth Pompeys house.

Antonius married Fuluia, Clodius widow. Fuluia ruled Antonius, at home, and abroad.

¹⁵ lay] ley vp 1603
¹⁶ boldlier] more boldly 1603
¹⁷ faulte] faults 1603
¹⁸ commaund] commaunded 1603

commaundement. Nowe, bicause *Fuluia* was somewhat sower, and crooked of condition, *Antonius* deuised to make her pleasaunter, & somewhat better disposed: and therefore he would playe her many prety youthfull partes to make her mery. As he did once, when *Cæsar* returned the last time of all Conqueror out of SPAYNE, euery man went out to meete him: and so did *Antonius* with the rest. But on the sodeine there ranne a rumor through ITALY, that *Cæsar* was dead, and that his enemies came againe with a great armie. Thereuppon he returned with speede to ROME, and tooke one of his mens gownes, and so apparelled came home to his house in a darke night, saying that he had brought *Fuluia* letters from *Antonius*. So he was let in, and brought to her muffled as he was, for being knowen: but she taking the matter heauily, asked him if *Antonius* were well. *Antonius* gaue her the letters, and sayd neuer a word. So when she had opened the letters, and beganne to read them: *Antonius* ramped of her necke, and kissed her. We haue told you this tale for examples sake onely, and so could we also tell you of many such like as these. Nowe when *Cæsar* was returned from his last warre in SPAYNE, all the chiefest nobilitie of the citie road many dayes iorney from ROME to meete him, where *Cæsar* made maruelous much of *Antonius*, aboue all the men that came vnto him. For he always tooke him into his coche with him, through out all ITALY: and behind him, *Brutus Albinus*, and *Octauius*, the sonne of his Nece, who afterwards was called *Cæsar*, and became Emperor of ROME long time after. So *Cæsar* being afterwards chosen Consul the fift time, he immediatly chose *Antonius* his colleague and companion: and desired by deposing him selfe of his Consulship, to make *Dolabella* Consul in his roome, and had already moued it to the Senate. But *Antonius* did stowtly withstand it, and openly reuiled *Dolabella* in the Senate: and *Dolabella* also spared him as litle. Thereuppon *Cæsar* being ashamed of the matter, he let it alone. Another time also when *Cæsar* attempted againe to substitute *Dolabella* Consul in his place, *Antonius* cryed out, that the signes of the birdes were against it: so that at length *Cæsar* was compelled to giue him place, and to let *Dolabella* alone, who was maruelously offended with him. Now in truth, *Cæsar* made no great reckoning of either of them both. For it is reported that *Cæsar* aunswered one that did accuse *Antonius* and *Dolabella* vnto him for some matter of conspiracie: tushe said he, they be not those fat fellowes and fine comed men that I feare, but I mistrust rather these pale and leane men, meaning by *Brutus* and *Cassius*, who afterwards conspired his death, and slue him. *Antonius* vnwares afterwards, gaue *Cæsars* enemies iust occasion and culler to doe as they did: as you shall heare. The ROMANES by chaunce celebrated the feast called Lupercalia, & *Cæsar* being apparelled in his triumphing robe, was set in the Tribune where they vse to make their orations to the people, and from thence did behold the sport of the runners. The manner of this running was this. On that day there are many young men of noble house, and those specially that be chiefe Officers for that yeare: who running naked vp & downe the citie annointed with the oyle of olyue, for pleasure do strike them they meete in their way, with white leather thongs they haue in their hands. *Antonius* being one amonge the rest that was to ronne, leauing the auncient ceremonies & old customes of that solemnitie: he ranne to the Tribune where *Cæsar* was set, and caried a laurell crowne in his hand, hauing a royall band or diademe wreathed about it, which in old time was the auncient marke

Cæsar, & Antonius, Consuls.

Antonius vnwittingly gaue Cæsars enemies occasion to conspire against him.

and token of a king. When he [976] was come to *Cæsar*, he made his fellow ronners with him lift him vp, & so he did put this laurell crowne vpon his head, signifying thereby that he had deserued to be king. But *Cæsar* making as though he refused it, turned away his heade. The people were so reioyced at it, that they all clapped their hands for ioy. *Antonius* againe did put it on his head: *Cæsar* againe refused it, and thus they were striuing of and on a great while together. As oft as *Antonius* did put this laurell crowne vnto him, a fewe of his followers reioyced at it: & as oft also as *Cæsar* refused it, all the people together clapped their hands. And this was a wonderfull thing, that they suffered all things subiects should doe by commaundement of their kings: & yet they could not abide the name of a king, detesting it as the vtter destructiõ of their liberty. *Cæsar* in a rage rose out of his seate, and plucking downe the choller of his gowne from his necke, he shewed it naked, bidding any man strike of his head that would. This laurel crowne was afterwards put vpõ the head of one of *Cæsars* statues or images, the which one of the Tribunes pluckt of. The people liked his doing therein so well, that they wayted on him home to his house, with great clapping of hands. Howbeit *Cæsar* did turne thē out of their offices for it. This was a good incoragemēt for *Brutus* & *Cassius* to conspire his death, who fel into a cõsort with their trustiest friends, to execute their en-terprise: but yet stood doubtful whether they should make *Antonius* priuy to it or not. Al the rest liked of it, sauing *Trebonius* only. He told them, that when they rode to meete *Cæsar* at his returne out of SPAYNE, *Antonius* & he alwaies keping company, & lying together by the way, he felt his mind a farre of: but *Antonius* finding his meaning, would harken no more vnto it, & yet notwith-standing neuer made *Cæsar* acquainted with this talke, but had faithfully kept it to him self. After that they cõsulted whether they should kil *Antonius* with *Cæsar*. But *Brutus* would in no wise consent to it, saying: that ventring on such an enterprise as that, for the maintenãce of law & iustice, it ought to be clere from all villanie. Yet they fearing *Antonius* power, & the authoritie of his office, appointed certain of the cõspiracy, that when *Cæsar* were gone into the Senate, and while others should execute their enterprise, they should keepe *Antonius* in a talke out of the Senate house. Euen as they had deuised these matters, so were they executed: and *Cæsar* was slaine in the middest of the Senate. *Antonius* being put in a feare withall, cast a slaues gowne vpon him, and hid him selfe. But afterwards when it was told him that the murtherers slue no man els, and that they went onely into the Capitoll: he sent his sonne vnto them for a pledge, & bad them boldly come downe vpon his word. The selfe same day he did bid *Cassius* to supper, and *Lepidus* also bad *Brutus*. The next morning the Senate was assembled, & *Antonius* him selfe preferred a lawe that all things past should be forgotten, and that they should appoint prouinces, vnto *Cassius* and *Brutus*: the which the Senate confirmed, and further ordeyned, that they should cancell none of *Cæsars* lawes. Thus went *Antonius* out of the Senate more praysed, and better esteemed, then euer man was: bicause it seemed to euery man that he had cut of all occasion of ciuill warres, and that he had shewed him selfe a maruelous wise gouernor of the common wealth, for the appeasing of these matters of so great waight & importance. But nowe, the opinion he conceiued of him selfe after he had a litle felt the good will of the people towards him, hoping thereby to make him selfe the chiefest man if he might ouercome *Brutus*:

Antonius Lupercian putteth the diademe vpon Cæsars head.

Brutus & Cassius conspire Cæsars death.

Consultation about the murther of Antonius with Cæsar.

did easily make him alter his first mind. And therefore when *Cæsars* body was brought to the place where it should be buried, he made a funeral oration in cõmendacion of *Cæsar*, according to the auncient custom of praising noble men at their funerals. When he saw that the people were very glad and desirous also to heare *Cæsar* spoken of, & his praises vttered: he mingled his oration with lamentable wordes, and by amplifying of matters did greatly moue their harts and affections vnto pitie & compassion. In fine to conclude his oration, he vnfolded before the whole assembly the bloudy garments of the dead, thrust through in many places with their swords, & called the malefactors, cruell & cursed murtherers. With these words he put the people into such a fury, that they presently toke *Cæsars* body, & burnt it in the market place, with such tables & fourmes as they could get together. Then whē the fire was kindled, they toke firebrands, & ran to the murtherers houses to set thē afire, & to make thē come out to fight. *Brutus* therfore & his accomplices, for safety of their persons were driuē to fly the city. Then came all *Cæsars* friends vnto *Antonius*, & specially his wife *Calpurnia* putting her trust in him, she brought the moste part of her money into [977] his house, which amounted to the summe of foure thowsand talents, & furthermore brought him al *Cæsars* bokes & writings, in the which were his memorials of al that he had done & ordeyned. *Antonius* did daily mingle with them such as he thought good, and by that meanes he created newe officers, made newe Senators, called home some that were banished, and deliuered those that were prisoners: and then he sayde that all those thinges were so appoynted and ordeyned by *Cæsar*. Therefore the ROMANES mocking them that were so moued, they called them CHARONITES: bicause that when they were ouercome, they had no other helpe but to saye, that thus they were found in *Cæsars* memorialls, who had sayled in *Charons* boate, and was departed. Thus *Antonius* ruled absolutely also in all other matters, bicause he was Consul, and *Caius* one of his brethren Prætor, and *Lucius* the other, Tribune. Now thinges remayning in this state at ROME, *Octauius Cæsar* the younger came to ROME, who was the sonne of *Iulius Cæsars* Nece, as you haue heard before, and was left his lawefull heire by will, remayning at the tyme of the death of his great Vncle that was slayne, in the citie of APOLLONIA. This young man at his first arriuall went to salute *Antonius*, as one of his late dead father *Cæsars* friendes, who by his last will and testament had made him his heire: and withall, he was presently in hande with him for money and other thinges which were left of trust in his handes, bicause *Cæsar* had by will bequeathed vnto the people of ROME, three score and fifteene siluer Drachmas to be giuen to euery man, the which he as heire stoode charged withall. *Antonius* at the first made no reckoning of him, bicause he was very younge: and sayde he lacked witte, and good friendes to aduise him, if he looked to take such a charge in hande, as to vndertake to be *Cæsars* heire. But when *Antonius* saw that he could not shake him of with those wordes, and that he was still in hande with him for his fathers goods, but specially for the ready money: then he spake and did what he could against him. And first of all, it was he that did keepe him from being Tribune of the people: and also when *Octauius Cæsar* beganne to meddle with the dedicating of the chayer of gold, which was prepared by the Senate to honor *Cæsar* with: he threatned to send him to prison, and moreouer desisted not to

Antonius maketh vprore among the people, for the murther of Cæsar.

Calpurnia, Cæsars wife.

Charonites, why so called.

M. Antonius Consul.
Caius Antonius Prætor.
Lucius Antonius Tribune, all three brethren.

Variance betwixt Antonius and Octauius Cæsar, heire vnto Iulius Cæsar.

put the people in an vprore. This young *Cæsar* seeing his doings, went vnto *Cicero* and others, which were *Antonius* enemies, and by them crept into fauor with the Senate: and he him self sought the peoples good will euery manner of way, gathering together the olde souldiers of the late deceased *Cæsar*, which were dispersed in diuers cities and colonyes. *Antonius* being affrayd of it, talked with *Octauius* in the capitoll, and became his friend. But the very same night *Antonius* had a straunge dreame, who thought that lightning fell vpon him, & burnt his right hand. Shortly after word was brought him, that *Cæsar* lay in waite to kil him. *Cæsar* cleered him selfe vnto him, and told him there was no such matter: but he could not make *Antonius* beleue the contrary. Whereuppon they became further enemies then euer they were: insomuch that both of them made friends of either side to gather together all the old souldiers through ITALY, that were dispersed in diuers townes: & made them large promises, & sought also to winne the legions of[19] their side, which were already in armes. *Cicero* on the other side being at that time the chiefest man of authoritie & estimation in the citie, he stirred vp al mē against *Antonius*: so that in the end he made the Senate pronoūce him an enemy to his contry, & appointed young *Cæsar* Sergeaunts to cary axes before him, & such other signes as were incident to the dignitie of a Consul or Prætor: [TLN 492–4] & moreouer sent *Hircius* and *Pansa*, then Consuls, to driue *Antonius* out of ITALY. These two Consuls together with *Cæsar*, who also had an armye, went against *Antonius* that beseeged the citie of MODENA, and there ouerthrew him in battell: but both the Consuls were slaine there. *Antonius* flying vpon this ouerthrowe, fell into great miserie all atonce: [TLN 495–6] but the chiefest want of all other, & that pinched him most, was famine. Howbeit he was of such a strong nature, that by pacience he would ouercome any aduersitie, and the heauier fortune lay vpon him, the more constant shewed he him selfe. Euery man that feleth want or aduersitie, knoweth by vertue and discretion what he should doe: but when in deede they are ouerlayed with extremitie, and be sore oppressed, few haue the harts to follow that which they praise and commend, and much lesse to auoid that they reproue and mislike. But rather to the contrary, they yeld to their accustomed easie life: and through faynt hart, & lacke of corage, doe chaunge their first mind and purpose. And therefore it was a wonderfull [978] example to the souldiers, [TLN 495–504] to see *Antonius* that was brought vp in all finenes and superfluitie, so easily to drinke puddle water, and to eate wild frutes and rootes: and moreouer it is reported, that euen as they passed the Alpes, they did eate the barcks of trees, and such beasts, as neuer man tasted of their flesh before. Now their intent was to ioyne with the legions that were[20] on the other side of the Mountaines, vnder *Lepidus* charge: whō *Antonius* tooke to be his friend, bicause he had holpen him to many things at *Cæsars* hand, through his meanes. When he was come to the place where *Lepidus* was, he camped hard by him: and when he saw that no man came to him to put him in any hope, he determined to venter him selfe, and to goe vnto *Lepidus*. Since the ouerthrow

Octauius Cæsar ioyned in friendship with Cicero.

Antonius and Octauius became friends. Antonius dreame.

Antonius iudged an enemy by the Senate.

Hircius and Pansa Consuls.

Antonius ouerthrowen in battell by the citie of Modena.

Antonius pacient in aduersitie.

Antonius hardnes in aduersitie, notwithstanding his fine bringing vp.

---

[19] of] on 1595, 1603
[20] were] was 1595

he had at MODENA, [TLN 686] he suffred his beard to grow at length and neuer clypt it, that it was maruelous long, and the heare of his heade also without koming: and besides all this, he went in a mourning gowne, and after this sort came hard to the trenches of *Lepidus* campe. Then he beganne to speake vnto the souldiers, [TLN 2454] and many of them their hartes yerned for pitie to see him so poorely arrayed, and some also through his wordes beganne to pitie him: insomuch that *Lepidus* beganne to be affrayd, and therefore commaunded all the trompetts to sownd together to stoppe the souldiers eares, that they should not harken to *Antonius*. This notwithstanding, the souldiers tooke the more pitie of him, & spake secretly with him by *Clodius* & *Lælius* meanes, whom they sent vnto him disguised in womens apparel, & gaue him counsel that he should not be affraid to enter into their campe, for there were a great number of souldiers that would receiue him, and kill *Lepidus*, if he would say the word. *Antonius* would not suffer them to hurt him, but the next morning he went with his army to wade a ford, at a litle riuer that ranne betweene them: and him selfe was the foremost man that tooke the riuer to get ouer, seeing a number of *Lepidus* campe that gaue him their handes, plucked vp the stakes, and layed flat the bancke of their trenche to let him in to their campe. When he was come into their campe, and that he had all the army at his commaundement: he vsed *Lepidus* very curteously, imbraced him, and called him father: and though in deede *Antonius* did all, and ruled the whole army, yet he alway gaue *Lepidus* the name and honor of the Captaine. *Munatius Plancus*, lying also in campe hard by with an armye: vnderstanding the report of *Antonius* curtesie, he also came and ioined with him. Thus *Antonius* being a foote againe, and growen of great power, repassed ouer the Alpes, leading into ITALY with him seuenteene legions, and tenne thowsand horsemen, besides six legions he left in garrison amonge the GAVLES, vnder the charge of one *Varius*, a companion of his that would drinke lustely with him, and therefore in mockery was surnamed *Cotylon*: to wit, a bibber. So *Octauius Cæsar* would not leane to *Cicero*, when he saw that his whole trauail and endeuor was onely to restore the common wealth to her former libertie. Therefore he sent certaine of his friends to *Antonius*, to make them friends againe: and thereuppon all three met together, (to wete, *Cæsar, Antonius*, & *Lepidus*) in an Iland enuyroned round about with a litle riuer, & there remayned three dayes together. Now as touching all other matters, they were easily agreed, [TLN 19] & did deuide all the Empire of ROME betwene them, as if it had bene their owne inheritance. But yet they could hardly agree whom they would put to death: for euery one of them would kill their enemies, and saue their kinsmen and friends. Yet at length, giuing place to their gredy desire to be reuenged of their enemies, they spurned all reuerence of bloud, and holines of friendship at their feete. For *Cæsar* left *Cicero* to *Antonius* will, *Antonius* also forsooke *Lucius Cæsar*, who was his Vncle by his mother: and both of them together suffred *Lepidus* to kill his owne brother *Paulus*. Yet some writers affirme, that *Cæsar* & *Antonius* requested *Paulus* might be slain, & that *Lepidus* was contēted with it. In my opinion there was neuer a more horrible, vnnatural, & crueller chaunge then this was. For thus chaunging murther for murther, they did aswel kill those whom they did forsake & leaue vnto others, as those also which others left vnto them to kil: but so much more was their wickednes & cruelty great vnto their friends, for that they put them to death

Antonius wan all Lepidus army from him.

Varius, surnamed Cotylon.

The conspiracie and meeting of Cæsar, Antonius, & Lepidus.

The proscription of the Triumviri.

408

being innocents, & hauing no cause to hate them. After this plat[21] was agreed
vpon betwene thē: the souldiers that were thereabouts, would haue this friendship & league betwixt them cōfirmed by mariage, & that *Cæsar* should mary
Claudia, the daughter of *Fuluia*, & *Antonius* wife. This mariage also being
agreed vpon, they condēned three hūdred of the chiefest citizens of ROME, to
be put to death by proscriptiō. [TLN 1627–8] And *Antonius* also cōmaū-
[979]ded thē to whō he had geuen cōmission to kil *Cicero*, that they should
strik of his head & right hand, with the which he had written the inuectiue
Orations (called Philippides) against *Antonius*. So whē the murtherers brought   *Antonius cruelty vnto Cicero.*
him *Ciceroes* head & hand cut of, he beheld them a long time with great ioy,
& laughed hartily, & that oftentimes for the great ioy he felt. Then when he
had taken his pleasure of the sight of them, he caused them to be set vp in an
open place, ouer the pulpit for Orations (where when he was aliue, he had often
spoken to the people) as if he had done the dead man hurt, and not bleamished
his owne fortune, shewing him selfe (to his great shame and infamie) a cruell
man, and vnworthie the office and authoritie he bare. His vncle *Lucius Cæsar*
also, as they sought for him to kill him, and followed him hard, fledde vnto
his sister. The murtherers comming thither, forcing to breake into her chamber,
she stoode at her chamber dore with her armes abroade, crying out still: you   *Lucius Cæsars*
shall not kill *Lucius Cæsar*, before you first kill me, that bare your Captaine in   *life saued, by*
my wombe. By this meanes she saued her brothers life. Now the gouernment   *his sister.*
of these Triumuiri grewe odious and hatefull to the ROMANES, for diuers
respects: but they most blamed *Antonius*, bicause he being elder then *Cæsar*,   *Antonius riot in*
and of more power and force then *Lepidus*, gaue him selfe againe to his former   *his Triumuirate.*
riot and excesse, when he left to deale in the affaires of the common wealth.
But setting aside the ill name he had for his insolencie, [TLN 1207–10, 1483]
he was yet much more hated in respect of the house he dwelt in, the which
was the house of *Pompey* the great: a man as famous for his temperaunce,   *The praise of*
modestie, and ciuill life, as for his three triumphes. For it grieued them to see   *Pompey the*
the gates commonly shut against the Captaines, Magistrates of the citie, and   *great.*
also Ambassadors of straunge nations, which were sometimes thrust from the
gate with violence: and that the house within was full of tomblers, anticke
dauncers, iuglers, players, ieasters, and dronkards, quaffing and goseling, and
that on them he spent[22] and bestowed the most parte of his money he got by
all kind of possible extorcions, briberie and policie. For they did not onely sell
by the crier, the goods of those whom they had outlawed, and appointed to
murther, slaunderously deceiued the poore widowes and young orphanes, [TLN
631–2] & also raised all kind of imposts, subsidies, and taxes: but vnderstanding
also that the holy vestall Nunnes had certaine goods & money put in their
custodie to keepe, both of mens in the citie, and those also that were abroade:
they went thither, and tooke them away by force. *Octauius Cæsar* perceiuing
that no money woulde serue *Antonius* turne, he prayed that they might deuide
the money betwene them, and so did they also deuide the armie, for them both
to goe into MACEDON to make warre against *Brutus* and *Cassius*: and in the

---

[21] plat] plot 1595, 1603
[22] he spent] *Om.* 1603

meane time they left the gouernment of the citie of ROME vnto *Lepidus*. When
they had passed ouer the seas, and that they beganne to make warre, they being
both camped by their enemies, to wit, *Antonius* against *Cassius*, and *Cæsar*
against *Brutus: Cæsar* did no great matter, but *Antonius* had alway the vpper
hand, and did all. For at the first battell *Cæsar* was ouerthrowen by *Brutus*,
and lost his campe, and verie hardly saued him selfe by flying from them that
followed him. Howebeit he writeth him selfe in his Commentaries, that he fled
before the charge was geuen, bicause of a dreame one of his frends had. *Antonius*
on the other side ouerthrewe *Cassius* in battell, though some write that he was
not there him selfe at the battell, but that he came after the ouerthrowe, whilest
his men had the enemies in chase. So *Cassius* at his earnest request was slaine
by a faithfull seruaunt of his owne called *Pindarus*, whom he had infranchised:
bicause he knewe not in time that *Brutus* had ouercomen[23] *Cæsar*. Shortly after
they fought an other battell againe, in the which *Brutus* was ouerthrowen, who
afterwardes also slue him selfe. Thus *Antonius* had the chiefest glorie of all this
victorie, specially bicause *Cæsar* was sicke at that time. *Antonius* hauing found
Brutus body after this battel, blaming him muche for the murther of his brother
Caius, whom he had put to death in MACEDON for reuenge of *Ciceroes* cruell
death, and yet laying the fault more in *Hortensius* then in him: he made *Hortensius*
to be slaine on his brothers tumbe. Furthermore, he cast his coate armor (which
was wonderfull rich and sumptuous) vpon *Brutus* bodie, and gaue commaundement to one of his slaues infranchised, to defray the charge of his buriall. But
afterwards, *Antonius* hearing that his infranchised bondman had not burnt his
coate armor with his bodie, bicause it was verie riche, and worth a great summe
of money, and that he had also kept backe much of the ready money appointed
for his funerall & tombe: he also put him to death. [980] After that *Cæsar* was
conueied to ROME, and it was thought he would not liue long, nor scape[24] the
sickenes he had. *Antonius* on thother side went towardes the East prouinces and
regions, to leauie money: and first of all he went into GRÆCE, and caried an
infinite number of souldiers with him. Now, bicause euerie souldier was promised fiue thowsande siluer Drachmas, he was driuen of necessitie to impose
extreame tallages and taxacions. At his first comming into GRÆCE, he was not
hard nor bitter vnto the GRÆCIANS, but gaue him selfe onely to heare wise men
dispute, to see playes, and also to note the ceremonies & sacrifices of GRÆCE,
ministring iustice to euerie man, and it pleased him maruelously to heare them
call him *Philellen*, (as much to say, a louer of the GRÆCIANS) and specially the
ATHENIANS, to whom he did many great pleasures. Wherefore the MEGARIANS,
to excede the ATHENIANS, thinking to shew *Antonius* a goodly sight: they
prayed him to come & see their Senate house, & counsell hall. *Antonius* went
thither to see it: so when he had seene it at his pleasure, they asked him, my
Lord, how like you our hall? Me thinkes (quot he) it is litle, old, and ready to
fall downe. Furthermore, he tooke measure of the temple of *Apollo Pythias*, and
promised the Senate to finish it. But when he was once come into ASIA, hauing
left *Lucius Censorinus* Gouernor in GRÆCE, and that he had felt the riches and

The valliantnes of Antonius against Brutus.

The death of Cassius.

Brutus slue him selfe.

Antonius gaue honorable buriall vnto Brutus.

Antonius great curtesie in Græce.

---

[23] ouercomen] ouercome 1595, 1603
[24] scape] escape 1595, 1603

pleasures of the East partes, and that Princes, great Lordes and Kinges, came to waite at his gate for his comming out, and that Queenes and Princesses to excell one an other, gaue him verie riche presentes, and came to see him, curiously setting forth them selues, and vsing all art that might be to shewe their beawtie, to win his fauor the more: (*Cæsar* in the meane space turmoyling his wits and bodie in ciuill warres at home, *Antonius* liuing merily & quietly abroad) he easely fell againe to his old licētious life. For straight one *Anaxenor* a player of the citherne, *Xoutus* a player of the flutes[25], *Metrodorus* a tombler, and such a rabble of minstrells & fit ministers for the pleasures of ASIA, (who in finenes & flattery passed all the other plagues he brought with him out of ITALIE) all these flocked in his court, & bare the whole sway: & after that, all went awry. For euery one gaue them selues to riot and excesse, when they saw he delighted in it: and all ASIA was like to the citie *Sophocles* speaketh of in one of his tragedies:

The plagues of Italie, in riot.

> VVas full of svveete perfumes, and pleasant songs,
> VVith vvoefull vveping mingled thereamongs.

For in the citie of EPHESVS, women attyred as they goe in the feastes and sacrifice of *Bacchus*, came out to meete him with such solemnities & ceremonies, as are then vsed: with men and children disguised like Fawnes and Satyres. Moreouer, the citie was full of Iuey, & darts wreathed about with Iuey, psalterions, flutes and howboyes, [TLN 1466–7] and in their songes they called him *Bacchus*, father of mirth, curteous, and gentle: and so was he vnto some, but to the most parte of men, cruell, and extreame. For he robbed noble men and gentle men of their goods, to geue it vnto vile flatterers: who oftentimes begged mens goods liuing, as though they had bene dead, and would enter their houses by force. As he gaue a citizens house of MAGNESIA vnto a cooke, bicause (as it is reported) he dressed him a fine supper. In the ende he doubled the taxacion, and imposed a seconde vpon ASIA. But then *Hybræas* the Orator sent from the estates of ASIA, to tell him the state of their contrie, boldly sayd vnto him: if thou wilt haue power to lay two tributes in one yere vpon vs, thou shouldest also haue power to geue vs two sommers, two autumnes, and two haruests. This was gallantly and pleasauntly spoken vnto *Antonius* by the Orator, and it pleased him well to heare it: but afterwardes amplifying his speache, he spake more boldly, and to better purpose. ASIA hath payed the two hundred thowsand talents. If all this money be not come to thy cofers, then aske accompt of them that leauied it: but if thou haue receiued it, and nothing be left of it, then are we vtterly vndone. *Hybræas* words nettled *Antonius* roundly. For he vnderstoode not many[26] of the thefts and robberies his officers committed by his authoritie, in his treasure and affaires: not so muche bicause he was carelesse, as for that he ouersimply trusted his men in all things. For he was a plaine man, without suttletie, and therefore ouerlate founde out the fowle faultes they committed against him: but when he heard of them, he was muche offended,

Antonius crueltie in Asia.

Hybræas wordes vnto Antonius, touching their great payments of money vnto him.

Antonius simplicity.

---

[25] flutes] flute 1603
[26] many] *Om.* 1603

and would plainly confesse it vnto them whome his officers had done iniurie vnto, by countenaunce of his authoritie. He had a noble minde, as well to punish offendors, as to reward well doers: and yet [*981*] he did exceede more in geuing, then in punishing. Now for his outragious manner of railing he commonly vsed, mocking and flouting of euerie man: that was remedied by it selfe. For a man might as boldly exchaunge a mocke with him, & he was as well cõtented to be mocked, as to mock others. But yet it oftentimes marred all. For he thought that those which told him so plainly, & truly in mirth: would neuer flatter him in good earnest, in any matter of weight. [TLN 2283–4] But thus he was easely abused by the praises they gaue him, not finding howe these flatterers mingled their flatterie, vnder this familiar and plaine manner of speach vnto him, as a fine deuise to make difference of meates with sharpe and tart sauce, & also to kepe him by this franke ieasting & bourding with him at the table, that their common flatterie should not be troublesome vnto him, as men do easely mislike to haue too muche of one thing: and that they handled him finely thereby, when they would geue him place in any matter of waight, and follow his counsell, that it might not appeare to him they did it so muche to please him, but bicause they were ignoraunt, and vnderstoode not so muche as he did. *Antonius* being thus inclined, the last and extreamest mischiefe of all other (to wit, the loue of *Cleopatra*) lighted on him, who did waken and stirre vp many vices yet hidden in him, and were neuer seene to any: and if any sparke of goodnesse or hope of rising were left him, *Cleopatra* quenched it straight, and made it worse then before. The manner how he fell in loue with her was this. *Antonius* going to make warre with the PARTHIANS, sent to commaunde *Cleopatra* to appeare personally before him, when he came into CILICIA, to aunswere vnto suche accusacions as were layed against her, being this: that she had aided *Cassius* and *Brutus* in their warre against him. The messenger sent vnto *Cleopatra* to make this summons vnto her, was called *Dellius*: who when he had throughly considered her beawtie, the excellent grace and sweetenesse of her tongue, he nothing mistrusted that *Antonius* would doe any hurte to so noble a Ladie, but rather assured him selfe, that within few dayes she should be in great fauor with him. Thereupon he did her great honor, and perswaded her to come into CILICIA, as honorably furnished as she could possible, and bad her not to be affrayed at all of *Antonius*, for he was [TLN 936] a more curteous Lord, then any that she had euer seene. *Cleopatra* on thother side beleuing *Dellius* wordes, and gessing by [TLN 556–61, 942–3, 2293–5] the former accesse and credit she had with *Iulius Cæsar*, and *Cneus Pompey* (the sonne of *Pompey* the great) only for her beawtie: she began to haue good hope that she might more easely win *Antonius*. [TLN 608–9] For *Cæsar* and *Pompey* knew her when she was but a young thing, & knew not then what the worlde ment: but nowe she went to *Antonius* at the age when a womans beawtie is at the prime, and she also of best iudgement. So, she furnished her selfe with a world of gifts, store of gold and siluer, and of riches and other sumptuous ornaments, as is credible enough she might bring from so great a house, and from so wealthie and rich a realme as ÆGYPT was. But yet she caried nothing with her wherein she trusted more then in her selfe, and in the charmes and inchauntment of her passing beawtie and grace. Therefore when she was sent vnto by diuers letters, both from *Antonius* him selfe, and also from his

Antonius maners.

Antonius loue to Cleopatra whom he sent for into Cilicia.

frendes, she made so light of it, and mocked *Antonius* so much, that she disdained to set forward otherwise, [TLN 898–928] but to take her barge in the riuer of Cydnus, the poope whereof was of gold, the sailes of purple, and the owers of siluer, which kept stroke in rowing after the sounde of the musicke of flutes, howboyes, citherns, violls, and such other instruments as they played vpon in the barge. And now for the person of her selfe: she was layed vnder a pauillion of cloth of gold of tissue, apparelled and attired like the goddesse *Venus*, commonly drawen in picture: and hard by her, on either hand of her, pretie faire boyes apparelled as painters doe set forth god *Cupide*, with litle fannes in their hands, with the which they fanned wind vpon her. Her Ladies and gentle-women also, the fairest of them were apparelled like the nymphes *Nereides* (which are the mermaides of the waters) and like the *Graces*, some stearing the helme, others tending the tackle and ropes of the barge, out of the which there came a wonderfull passing sweete sauor of perfumes, that perfumed the wharfes side, pestered with innumerable multitudes of people. Some of them followed the barge all alongest the riuers[27] side: others also ranne out of the citie to see her comming in. So that in thend, there ranne such multitudes of people one after an other to see her, that *Antonius* was left post alone in the market place, in his Imperiall seate to geue audience: and there went a rumor in the peoples mouthes, that the goddesse *Venus* [982] was come to play [TLN 1466–7] with the god *Bacchus*, for the generall good of all ASIA. [TLN 933–8] When *Cleopatra* landed, *Antonius* sent to inuite her to supper to him. But she sent him word againe, he should doe better rather to come and suppe with her. *Antonius* therefore to shew him selfe curteous vnto her at her arriuall, was contented to obey her, & went to supper to her: where he found such passing sumptuous fare, that no tongue can expresse it. But amongest all other thinges, he most wondered at the infinite number of lightes and torches hanged on the toppe of the house, geuing light in euerie place, so artificially set and ordered by deuises, some round, some square: that it was the rarest thing to behold that eye could discerne, or that euer books could mencion. The next night, *Antonius* feasting her, contended to passe her in magnificence and finenes: but she ouercame him in both. So that he him selfe began to skorne the grosse seruice of his house, in respect of *Cleopatraes* sumptuousnes and finenesse. And when *Cleopatra* found *Antonius* ieasts and slents to be but grosse, and souldier like, in plaine manner: she gaue it him finely, and without feare taunted him throughly. Now her beawtie (as it is reported) was not so passing, as vnmatchable of other women, nor yet suche, as vpon present viewe did enamor men with her: but so sweete was her companie and conuersacion, that a man could not possiblie but be taken. And besides her beawtie, the good grace she had to talke and discourse, her curteous nature that tempered her words & dedes, was a spurre that pricked to the quick. Furthermore, besides all these, her voyce and words were maruelous pleasant: for her tongue was an instrument of musicke to diuers sports and pastimes, the which she easely turned to any language that pleased her. She spake vnto few barbarous people by interpreter, but made them aunswere her selfe, or at the least the most parte of them: as the ÆTHIOPIANS, the ARABIANS,

The wonderfull sumptuousnes of Cleopatra, Queene of AEgypt, going vnto Antonius. Cydnus fl.

The sumptuous preparations of the suppers of Cleopatra and Antonius.

Cleopatraes beawtie.

---

[27] riuers] riuer 1603

the TROGLODYTES, the HEBRVES, the SYRIANS, the MEDES, and the PARTHI-
ANS, and to many others also, whose languages she had learned. Whereas diuers
of her progenitors, the kings of ÆGYPT, could scarce learne the ÆGYPTIAN
tongue only, and many of them forgot to speake the MACEDONIAN [TLN
173–91]. Nowe, *Antonius* was so rauished with the loue of *Cleopatra*, that
though his wife *Fuluia* had great warres, and much a doe with *Cæsar* for his
affaires, and that the armie of the PARTHIANS, (the which the kings Lieutenauntes had geuen to the onely leading of *Labienus*) was now assembled in
MESOPOTAMIA readie to inuade SYRIA: yet, as though all this had nothing
touched him, [TLN 432–4, 458–61] he yeelded him selfe to goe with *Cleopatra*
into ALEXANDRIA, where he spent and lost in childish sports, (as a man might
say) and idle pastimes, the most pretious thing a man can spende, as *Antiphon*
sayth: and that is, time. [TLN 51] For they made an order betwene them,
which they called Amimetobion (as much to say, no life comparable and matcheable with it) one feasting ech other by turnes, and in cost, exceeding all measure
and reason. And for proofe hereof, I haue heard my grandfather [TLN 77]
Lampryas report, that one *Philotas* a Phisition, borne in the citie of AMPHISSA,
told him that he was at that present time in ALEXANDRIA, and studied Phisicke:
and that hauing acquaintance with one of *Antonius* cookes, he tooke him with
him to *Antonius* house, (being a young man desirous to see things) to shew him
the wonderfull sumptuous charge and preparation of one only supper. When
he was in the kitchin, and saw a world of diuersities of meates, and amongst
others, [TLN 890–1] eight wilde boares rosted whole: he began to wonder at
it, and sayd, sure you haue a great number of ghests to supper. The cooke fell
a laughing, and answered him, no (quot he) not many ghestes, nor aboue twelue
in all: but yet all that is boyled or roasted must be serued in whole, or else it
would be marred straight. For *Antonius* peraduenture will suppe presently, or
it may be a pretie while hence, or likely enough he will deferre it longer, for
that he hath dronke well to day, or else hath had some other great matters in
hand: and therefore we doe not dresse one supper only, but many suppers,
bicause we are vncerteine of the houre he will suppe in. *Philotas* the Phisition
tolde my grandfather this tale, and sayd moreouer, that it was his chaunce
shortly after to serue the eldest sonne of the sayd *Antonius*, whome he had by
his wife *Fuluia*: and that he sate commonly at his table with his other frendes,
when he did not dine nor suppe with his father. It chaunced one day there
came a Phisition that was so full of words, that he made euery man wearie of
him at the bord: but *Philotas* to stoppe his mouth, put out a[29] suttle proposition
to him. It is good in some sorte to let a man drinke colde water that hath an
agew:[30] euery man that hath an agew hath it in some sorte, ergo it is good for
a[31] [983] man that hath an agew to drinke cold water. The Phisition was so
grauelled and amated withall, that he had not a word more to say. Young
Antonius burst out in[32] such a laughing at him, and was so glad of it, that he

*An order set vp
by Antonius &
Cleopatra.*

*The excessiue
expences of*[28]
*Antonius and
Cleopatra in
AEgypt.*

*Eight wilde
boares rosted
whole.*

*Philotas a
Phisition, borne
in Amphissa,
reporter of this
feast.
Philotas,
Phisition to the
younger
Antonius.
Philotas subtil
proposition.*

---

[28] *The . . . of*] *Om.* 1603
[29] a] this 1603
[30] agew:] ague: But 1603
[31] a] euery 1603
[32] in] into 1603

sayd vnto him: *Philotas*, take all that, I geue it thee: shewing him his cubbord full of plate, with great pots of gold and siluer. *Philotas* thanked him, and told him he thought himselfe greatly boūd to him for this liberality, but he would neuer haue thought that he had had power to haue geuen so many things, and of so great value. But muche more he maruelled, when shortly after one of young *Antonius* men brought him home all the pots in a basket, bidding him set his marke and stampe vpon them, and to locke them vp. *Philotas* returned the bringer of them, fearing to be reproued if he tooke them. Then the yoūg gentleman *Antonius* sayd vnto him: alas poore man, why doest thou make it nise to take them? Knowest thou not that it is the sonne of *Antonius* that geues them thee, and is able to do it? If thou wilt not beleue me, take rather the readie money they come to: bicause my father peraduenture may aske for some of the plate, for the antike & excellent workemanship of them. This I haue heard my grandfather tell oftentimes. But now againe to *Cleopatra*. *Plato* wryteth that there are foure kinds of flatterie: but *Cleopatra* deuided it into many kinds. [TLN 59, 301–3] For she, were it in sport, or in matter[33] of earnest, still deuised sundrie new delights to haue *Antonius* at commaundement, neuer leauing him night nor day, nor once letting him go out of her sight. For she would play at dyce with him, drinke with him, and hunt commonly with him, and also be with him when he went to any exercise or actiuity of body. [TLN 66–7] And somtime also, when he would goe vp and downe the citie disguised like a slaue in the night, & would peere into poore mens windowes & their shops, [TLN 450–1] and scold & brawle with them within the house: *Cleopatra* would be also in a chamber maides array, & amble vp & downe the streets with him, so that oftentimes *Antonius* bare away both mockes & blowes. Now, though most men misliked this maner, yet the ALEXANDRIANS were commonly glad of this iolity, & liked it well, saying verie gallantly, and wisely: [TLN 163–4] that *Antonius* shewed them a commicall face, to wit, a merie countenaunce: and the ROMANES a tragicall face, to say, a grimme looke. But to reckon vp all the foolishe sportes they made, reuelling in this sorte: it were too fond a parte of me, and therefore I will only tell you one among the rest. [TLN 433, 1043–5] On a time he went to angle for fish, and when he could take none, he was as angrie as could be, bicause *Cleopatra* stoode by. Wherefore he secretly commaunded the fisher men, that when he cast in his line, they should straight diue vnder the water, and put a fishe on his hooke which they had taken before: and so snatched vp his angling rodde, and brought vp fish twise or thrise. *Cleopatra* found it straight, yet she seemed not to see it, but wondred at his excellent fishing: but when she was alone by her selfe among her owne people, she told them howe it was, and bad them the next morning to be on the water to see the fishing. A number of people came to the hauen, and got into the fisher boates to see this fishing. *Antonius* then threw in his line and *Cleopatra* straight commaunded one of her men to diue vnder water before *Antonius* men, and to put some old salte fish vpon his baite, like vnto those that are brought out of the contrie of PONT. When he had hong the fish on his hooke, *Antonius* thinking he had taken a fishe in deede, snatched vp his line presently. Then

Plato writeth of foure kinds of flatterie. Cleopatra Queene of all flatterers.

Antonius fishing in AEgypt.

[33] matter] matters 1595, 1603

415

they all fell a laughing. *Cleopatra* laughing also, said vnto him: leaue vs (my Lord) ÆGYPTIANS (which dwell in the contry of PHARVS and CANOBVS) your angling rodde: this is not thy profession: thou must hunt after conquering of realmes and contries. [TLN 57–68] Nowe *Antonius* delighting in these fond and childish pastimes, verie ill newes were brought him from two places. [TLN 173–80] The first from ROME, that his brother *Lucius*, and *Fuluia* his wife, fell out first betwene them selues, and afterwards fell to open warre with *Cæsar*, & had brought all to nought, that they were both driuen to flie out of ITALIE. The seconde newes, as bad as the first: [TLN 187–91] that *Labienus* conquered all ASIA with the armie of the PARTHIANS, from the riuer of Euphrates, and from SYRIA, vnto the contries of LYDIA and IONIA. [TLN 209–10, 225–7, 643–7] Then began *Antonius* with much a doe, a litle to rouse him selfe as if he had bene wakened out of a deepe sleepe, and as a man may say, comming out of a great dronkennes. So, first of all he bent him selfe against the PAR-THIANS, and went as farre as the contrie of PHOENICIA: but there he receiued lamentable letters from his wife *Fuluia*. Whereuppon he straight returned towards ITALIE, with two hundred saile: and as he went, tooke vp his frendes by the way that fled out of ITALIE, to come to him. By them he was in-[984]formed, [TLN 173–4, 787–8] that his wife *Fuluia* was the only cause of this warre: who being of a peeuish, crooked, and troublesome nature, had purposely raised this vprore in ITALIE, in hope thereby to withdraw him from *Cleopatra*. But by good fortune, [TLN 213–15] his wife *Fuluia* going to meete with *Antonius*, sickened by the way, and dyed in the citie of SICYONE: and therefore *Octauius Cæsar*, and he were the easelier made frendes together. For when *Antonius* landed in ITALIE, and that men saw *Cæsar* asked nothing of him, [TLN 753–62, 787–91] and that *Antonius* on the other side layed all the fault & burden on his wife *Fuluia*: [TLN 688, 693–4, 701–9, 792–7] the frendes of both parties would not suffer them to vnrippe any olde matters, and to proue or defend who had the wrong or right, and who was the first procurer of this warre, fearing to make matters worse betwene them: but they made them frendes together, and deuided the Empire of ROME betwene them, making the sea Ionium the bounds of their diuision. For they gaue all the prouinces Eastward, vnto *Antonius*: and the contries Westward, vnto *Cæsar*: and left AFRICKE vnto *Lepidus*: and made a law, that they three one after an other should make their frendes Consuls, when they would not be them selues. This seemed to be a sound counsell, but yet it was to be confirmed with [TLN 816–17, 852–3, 1307] a straighter bonde, which fortune offered thus. There was *Octauia* the eldest sister of *Cæsar*, not by one mother, for she came of *Ancharia*, & *Cæsar* him self afterwards of *Accia*. It is reported, that he dearly loued his sister *Octauia*, for in deede she was a noble Ladie, and left the widow of her first husband *Caius Marcellus*, who dyed not long before: and it seemed also that *Antonius* had bene widower euer since the death of his wife *Fuluia*. [TLN 820] For he denied not that he kept *Cleopatra*, but so did he not[34] confesse that he had her as his wife: & so with reason he did defend the loue he bare vnto this ÆGYPTIAN *Cleopatra*. Thereupon euerie man did set

The warres of Lucius Antonius and Fuluia, against Octauius Cæsar.

The death of Fuluia Antonius wife.

All the Empire of Rome deuided betwene the Triumuiri.

Octauia, the halfe sister of Octauius Cæsar, & daughter of Ancharia which was not Cæsars mother.

---

[34] but . . . not] neither did he 1603

forward this mariage, hoping thereby that [TLN 957] this Ladie *Octauia*, hauing an excellent grace, wisedom, & honestie, ioyned vnto so rare a beawtie, that when she were with *Antonius* (he louing her as so worthy a Ladie deserueth) she should be [TLN 822–34, 1314–15] a good meane to keepe good loue & amitie betwext her brother and him. So when *Cæsar* & he had made the matche betwene them, they both went to ROME about this mariage, although it was against the law, that a widow should be maried within tenne monethes after her husbandes death. Howbeit the Senate dispensed with the law, and so the mariage proceeded accordingly. [TLN 283–5, 468, 483–90] *Sextus Pompeius* at that time kept in SICILIA, and so made many an inrode into ITALIE with a great number of pynnasies and other pirates shippes, of the which were Captaines two notable pirats, *Menas*, and *Menecrates*, who so scoored all the sea thereabouts, that none durst peepe out with a sayle. [TLN 858–9, 1229–32] Furthermore, *Sextus Pompeius* had delt verie frendly with *Antonius*, for he had curteously receiued his mother, when she fled out of ITALIE with *Fuluia*: and therefore they thought good to make peace with him. [TLN 866] So they met all three together by the mount of Misena, vpon a hill that runneth farre into the sea: *Pompey* hauing his shippes ryding hard by at ancker, and *Antonius* and *Cæsar* their armies vpon the shoare side, directly ouer against him. [TLN 1218–21] Now, after they had agreed that *Sextus Pompeius* should haue SICILE and SARDINIA, with this condicion, that he should ridde the sea of all theeues and pirats, and make it safe for passengers, and withall that he should send a certaine of wheate to ROME: [TLN 1251–2] one of them did feast an other, and drew cuts who should beginne. It was *Pompeius* chaunce to inuite them first. Whereupon *Antonius* asked him: & where shall we suppe? [TLN 1207–10, 1276, 1483] There, said *Pompey*, and shewed him his admirall galley which had six bankes of owers: that (sayd he) is my fathers house they haue left me. He spake it to taunt *Antonius*, bicause he had his fathers house, that was *Pompey* the great. So he cast ankers enowe into the sea, to make his galley fast, and then built a bridge of wodde to conuey them to his galley, from the heade of [TLN 866] mount Misena: and there he welcomed them, and made them great cheere. Now in the middest of the feast, when they fell to be merie with *Antonius* loue vnto *Cleopatra*: [TLN 1402–26] *Menas* the pirate came to *Pompey*, and whispering in his eare, said vnto him: shall I cut the gables of the ankers, and make thee Lord not only of SICILE and SARDINIA, but of the whole Empire of ROME besides? *Pompey* hauing pawsed a while vpon it, at length aunswered him: thou shouldest haue done it, and neuer haue told it me, but now we must content vs with that we haue. As for my selfe, I was neuer taught to breake my faith, nor to be counted a traitor. The other two also did likewise feast him in their campe, and then he returned into SICILE. *Antonius* after this agreement made, sent *Ventidius* before into ASIA to stay the PARTHIANS, and to keepe them they should come [985] no further: and he him selfe in the meane time, to gratefie *Cæsar*, was contented to be chosen *Iulius Cæsars* priest and sacrificer, & so they ioyntly together dispatched all great matters, concerning the state of the Empire. [TLN 981–1005] But in all other maner of sportes and exercises, wherein they passed the time away the one with the other: *Antonius* was euer inferior vnto *Cæsar*, and alway lost, which grieued him much. [TLN 77] With *Antonius* there was a soothsayer or astronomer of ÆGYPT, that coulde cast a figure, and

A law at Rome for marying of widowes.
Antonius maried Octauia, Octauius Cæsars halfe sister.

Antonius and Octauius Cæsar, doe make peace with Sextus Pompeius.

Sextus Pompeius taunt to Antonius.

Sextus Pompeius being offered wonderfull great fortune: for his honestie and faithes sake, refused it.

iudge of mens natiuities, to tell them what should happen to them. He, either to please *Cleopatra*, or else for that he founde it so by his art, told *Antonius* plainly, that his fortune (which of it selfe was excellent good, and very great) was altogether bleamished, and obscured by *Cæsars* fortune: and therefore he counselled him vtterly to leaue his company, and to get him as farre from him as he could. For thy *Demon* said he, ([TLN 984] that is to say, the good angell and spirit that kepeth thee) is affraied of his: and being coragious & high when he is alone, becometh fearefull and timerous when he commeth neere vnto the other. Howsoeuer it was, the euents ensuing proued the ÆGYPTIANS words true. For, it is said, that as often as they two drew cuts for pastime, who should haue any thing, or whether they plaied at dice, *Antonius* alway lost. Oftentimes when they were disposed to see cockefight, or quailes that were taught to fight one with an other: *Cæsars* cockes or quailes did euer ouercome. The which spighted *Antonius* in his mind, although he made no outward shew of it: and therefore he beleued the ÆGYPTIAN the better. [TLN 1566–9, 1583–9] In fine, he recommended the affaires of his house vnto *Cæsar*, & went out of ITALIE with *Octauia* his wife, whom he caried into GRÆCE, after he had had a daughter by her. So *Antonius* lying all the winter at ATHENS, newes came vnto him of the victories of *Ventidius*, who had ouercome the PARTHIANS in battel, in the which also were slaine, *Labienus*, and *Pharnabates*, the chiefest Captaine king *Orodes* had. For these good newes he feasted all ATHENS, and kept open house for all the GRÆCIANS, and many games of price were plaied at ATHENS, of the which he him selfe would be iudge. Wherfore leauing his gard, his axes, and tokens of his Empire at his house, he came into the show place (or listes) where these games were played, in a long gowne and slippers after the GRÆCIAN facion, and they caried tippestaues before him, as marshalls men do cary before the Iudges to make place: and he himselfe in person was a stickler to part the young men, when they had fought enough. After that, preparing to go to the warres, he made him a garland of the holy Oliue, and caried a vessell with him of the water of the fountaine Clepsydra, bicause of an Oracle he had receiued that so commaunded him. [TLN 1496–1500] In the meane time, *Ventidius* once againe ouercame *Pacorus*, (*Orodes* sonne king of PARTHIA) in a battell fought in the contrie of CYRRESTICA, he being come againe with a great armie to inuade SYRIA: at which battell was slaine a great number of the PARTHIANS, & among them *Pacorus*, the kings owne sonne slaine[35]. This noble exployt as famous as euer any was, was a full reuenge to the ROMANES, of the shame and losse they had receiued before by the death of *Marcus Crassus*: [TLN 1501–5] and he made the PARTHIANS flie, and glad to kepe them selues within the confines and territories of MESOPOTAMIA, and MEDIA, after they had thrise together bene ouercome in seuerall battells. [TLN 1508–12] Howbeit *Ventidius* durst not vndertake to follow them any further, fearing least he should haue gotten *Antonius* displeasure by it. Notwithstanding, he led his armie against them that had rebelled, and conquered them againe: amongest whome he besieged *Antiochus*, king of COMMAGENA, who offered him to giue a thowsand talentes to be pardoned his rebellion, and promised euer after to be at *Antonius* com-

Antonius told by a Soothsayer, that his fortune was inferior vnto Octauius Cæsar.

Antonius vnfortunate in sport and earnest, against Octauius Cæsar.

Orodes king of Parthia.

Ventidius notable victorie of the Parthians. The death of Pacorus, the king of Parthiaes sonne.

---

[35] slaine] *Om.* 1603

maundement. But *Ventidius* made him aunswere, that he should send vnto *Antonius*, who was not farre of, and would not suffer *Ventidius* to make any peace with *Antiochus*, to the end that yet this litle exployt should passe in his name, and that they should not thinke he did any thing but by his Lieutenaunt *Ventidius*. The siege grew verie long, bicause they that were in the towne, seeing they coulde not be receiued vpon no reasonable composition: determined valliantly to defende them selues to the last man. Thus *Antonius* did nothing, and yet receiued great shame, repenting him much that he tooke not their first offer. And yet at[36] last he was glad to make truce with *Antiochus*, and to take three hundred talentes for composition. [TLN 1534] Thus after he had set order for the state & affaires of SYRIA, he returned againe to ATHENS: and hauing giuen *Ventidius* suche honors as he deserued, he sent him to ROME, to triumphe for the PARTHIANS. [TLN 1531] *Ventidius* was the only man that euer triumphed of the PARTHIANS vn-[986]till this present day, a meane man borne, and of no noble house nor[37] family: who only came to that he attained vnto, through *Antonius* frendshippe, the which deliuered him happie occasion to achieue to great matters. [TLN 1513–17] And yet to say truely, he did so well quit him selfe in all his enterprises, that he confirmed that which was spoken of *Antonius* and *Cæsar*: to wit, [TLN 2063–4] that they were alway more fortunate when they made warre by their Lieutenants, then by them selues. For *Sossius*, one of *Antonius* Lieutenauntes in SYRIA, did notable good seruice: and *Canidius*, whom he had also left his Lieutenaunt in the borders of ARMENIA, did conquer it all. So did he also ouercome the kinges of the IBERIANS and ALBANIANS, and went on with his conquests vnto mount Caucasus. By these conquests, the fame of *Antonius* power increased more and more, and grew dreadfull vnto all the barbarous nations. [TLN 1685–94] But *Antonius* notwithstanding, grewe to be maruelously offended with *Cæsar*, vpon certaine reportes that had bene brought vnto him: [TLN 1745–6] and so tooke sea to go towards ITALIE with three hundred saile. And bicause those of BRVNDVSIVM would not receiue his armie into their hauen, he went further vnto TARENTVM. [TLN 1710–11, 1810–16] There his wife *Octauia* that came out of GRÆCE with him, besought him to send her vnto her brother: the which he did. [TLN 2282] *Octauia* at that time was great with child, and moreouer had a second daughter by him, and yet she put her selfe in iorney, [TLN 883–4, 1792–1857] and met with her brother *Octauius Cæsar* by the way, who brought his two chiefe frendes, *Mæcenas* and *Agrippa* with him. [TLN 1697–1705, 1834–6] She tooke them aside, and with all the instance she could possible, intreated them they would not suffer her that was the happiest woman of the world, to become nowe the most wretched and vnfortunatest creature of all other. For now, said she, euerie mans eyes doe gaze on me, that am the sister of one of the Emperours and wife of the other. And if the worst councell take place, (which the goddes forbidde) and that they growe to warres: for your selues, it is vncertaine to which of them two the goddes haue assigned the victorie, or ouerthrowe. But for me, on which side soeuer victorie fall, my state can be but most miserable still. These words

Ventidius the only man of the Romanes, that triumphed for the Parthians.

Canidius conquests.

Newe displeasures betwext Antonius and Octauius Cæsar.

The wordes of Octauia vnto Mæcenas and Agrippa.

---

[36] at] at the 1603
[37] nor] or 1603

of *Octauia* so softned *Cæsars* harte, that he went quickely vnto TARENTVM. But
it was a noble sight for them that were present, to see so great an armie by
lande not to sturre, and so many shippes aflote in the roade, quietly and safe:
and furthermore, the meeting and kindenesse of frendes, louinglie imbracing
one an other. First, *Antonius* feasted *Cæsar*, which he graunted vnto for his
sisters sake. Afterwardes they agreed together, that *Cæsar* should geue *Antonius*
two legions to go against the PARTHIANS: and that *Antonius* should let *Cæsar*
haue a[38] hundred gallies armed with brasen spurres at the prooes. Besides all
this, *Octauia* obteyned of her husbande, twentie brigantines for her brother:
and of her brother for her husbande, a thowsande armed men. After they had
taken leaue of eache other, [TLN 1687-8, 1730] *Cæsar* went immediatly to
make warre with *Sextus Pompeius*, to gette SICILIA into his handes. *Antonius* also
leauing his wife *Octauia* and litle children begotten of her, with *Cæsar*, and his
other children which he had by *Fuluia*: he went directlie into ASIA. Then
beganne this pestilent plague and mischiefe of *Cleopatraes* loue (which had slept
a longe tyme, and seemed to haue bene vtterlie forgotten, and that *Antonius*
had geuen place to better counsell) againe to kindle, and to be in force, so
soone as *Antonius* came neere vnto SYRIA. [TLN 578-80] And in the ende, the
horse of the minde as *Plato* termeth it, that is so hard of rayne (I meane the
vnreyned lust of concupiscence) did put out of *Antonius* heade, all honest and
commendable thoughtes: for he sent *Fonteius Capito* to bring *Cleopatra* into
SYRIA. [TLN 1759-61] Vnto whome, to welcome her, he gaue no trifling
things: but vnto that she had already, he added the prouinces of PHOENICIA,
those of the nethermost SYRIA, the Ile of CYPRVS, and a great parte of CILICIA,
and that contry of IVRIE where the true balme is, and that parte of ARABIA
where the NABATHEIANS doe dwell, which stretcheth out towarde the Ocean.
These great giftes much misliked the ROMANES. But now, though [TLN
3308-10] *Antonius* did easely geue away great seigniories, realmes, & mighty
nations vnto some priuate men, and that also he tooke from other kings their
lawfull realmes: ([TLN 1627-8] as from *Antigonus* king of the IEWES, whom
he openly beheaded, where neuer king before had suffred like death) yet all
this did not so much offend the ROMANES, as the vnmeasurable honors which
he did vnto *Cleopatra*. But yet he did much more aggrauate their malice & il
wil towards him, bicause that *Cleopatra* hauing brought him two twinnes, a
sonne and a daughter, he named his sonne *Alexander*, & his daughter *Cleopatra*,
and gaue them to their surnames, the [987] Sunne to the one, & the moone
to the other. This notwithstanding, he that could finely cloke his shamefull
deedes with fine words, said that the greatnes & magnificence of the Empire
of ROME appeared most, not where the ROMANES tooke, but where they gaue
much: & nobility was multiplied amongest men, by the posterity of kings,
when they left of their seede in diuers places: and that by this meanes [TLN
402, 2803] his first auncester was begotten of *Hercules*, who had not left the
hope and continuance of his line and posterity, in the wombe of one only
woman, fearing *Solons* lawes, or regarding the ordinaunces of men touching the

*Octauia pacifieth
the quarrell
betwixt
Antonius, and
her brother
Octauius Cæsar.*

*Plato calleth
cõcupiscence: the
horse of the
minde.*

*Antonius sent
for Cleopatra
into Syria.*

*Antonius gaue
great prouinces
vnto Cleopatra.*

*Antigonus king
of Iurie, the first
king beheaded by
Antonius.
Antonius
twinnes by
Cleopatra, &
their names.*

---

[38] a] an 1603

procreacion of children: but that he gaue it vnto nature, and established the
fundacion of many noble races and families in diuers places. Nowe when *Phraortes*
had slaine his father *Orodes*, and possessed the Kingdom: many gentlemen of
PARTHIA forsooke him, and fled from him. Amongst them was *Monæses*, a noble
man, and of great authority among his contry men, who came vnto *Antonius*,
that receiued him, & compared his fortune vnto *Themistocles*, and his owne riches
& magnificence, vnto the kings of PERSIA. For he gaue *Monæses* three cities,
LARISSA, ARETHVSA, & HIERAPOLIS, which was called before BOMBYCE. Howbeit the king of PARTHIA shortly after called him home againe, vpon his faith
& word. *Antonius* was glad to let him go, hoping thereby to steale vpon *Phraortes*
vnprouided. For he sent vnto him, & told him that they would remaine good
frends, & haue peace together, so he would but only redeliuer the standerds &
ensignes of the ROMANES, which the PARTHIANS had wonne in the battell
where *Marcus Crassus* was slaine, & the men also that remained yet prisoners
of this ouerthrow. In the meane time he sent *Cleopatra* backe into ÆGYPT, &
tooke his way towards ARABIA & ARMENIA, & there tooke a general muster of
all his army he had together, & of the kings his côfederats that were come by
his cômaundement to aide him, being a maruelous number: of the which, the
chiefest was *Artauasdes*, king of ARMENIA, who did furnish him with six thowsande horsemen, and seuen thowsand footemen. There were also of the ROMANES
about three score thowsand footmen, & of horsemen (SPANIARDS & GAVLES
reckoned for ROMANES) to the number of ten thousand, & of other nations
thirty thowsand men, reckoning together the horsemen and light armed footemen. This so great & puisant army which made the INDIANS quake for feare,
dwelling about the contry of the BACTRIANS, and all ASIA also to tremble:
serued him to no purpose, & all for the loue he bare to *Cleopatra*. For the earnest
great desire he had to lye all winter with her, made him begin his[40] warre out
of due time, and for hast, to put all in hazard, being so rauished & enchaunted
with the [TLN 554] sweete poyson of her loue, that he had no other thought
but of her, & how he might quickly returne againe: more then how he might
ouercome his enemies. For first of all, where he should haue wintered in AR-
MENIA to refresh his men, wearied with the long iorney they had made, hauing
comen[41] eight thowsand furlongs, and then at the beginning of the spring to
go and inuade MEDIA, before the PARTHIANS should stirre out of their houses
& garrisons: he could tary no lenger[42], but led them forthwith vnto the prouince
of ATROPATENE, leauing ARMENIA on the left hand, & forraged al the contry.
Furthermore, making all the hast he coulde, he left behinde him engines of
battery which were caried with him in three hûdred carts, (among the which
also there was a ramme foure score foote long) being things most necessary for
him, and the which he could not get againe for money if they were once lost
or marred. For the hie prouinces of ASIA haue no trees growing of such height
and length, neither strong nor straight enough to make such like engines of

Phraortes slue
his father Orodes
king of
Persia[39].

Antonius great
& puisant army.

Antonius dronke
with the loue of
Cleopatra.

[39] *Persia*] *Parthia* 1603
[40] his] this 1603
[41] comen] come 1595, 1603
[42] lenger] longer 1595, 1603

battery. This notwithstanding, he left them all behind him, as a hinderance
to bring his matters & intent speedily to passe: and left a certaine number of
men to keepe them, and gaue them in charge vnto one *Tatianus*. Then he went
to besiege the citie of PHRAATA, being the chiefest and greatest citie the king
of MEDIA had, where his wife and children were. Then he straight founde[43]
his owne fault, and the want of his artillerie he left behinde him, by the worke
he had in hande: for he was fayne for lacke of a breache (where his men might
come to the sworde with their enemies that defended the walle) to force a mount
of earth hard to the walles of the citie, the which by litle and litle with greate
labour, rose to some height. In the meane time king *Phraortes* came downe with
a great armie: who vnderstanding that *Antonius* had left his engines of batterie
behind him, he sent a great number of horsemen before, which enuironed
Tatianus with all his cariage, and slue him, and ten thowsand men he had with
him. After this, [988] the barbarous people tooke these engines of battery and
burnt them, and got many prisoners, amongst whom they tooke also king
Polemon. This discomfiture maruelously troubled all *Antonius* army, to receiue
so great an ouerthrow (beyond their expectacion) at the beginning of their
iorney: insomuche that *Artabazus*, king of the ARMENIANS, dispairing of the
good successe of the ROMANES: departed with his men, notwithstanding that
he was him selfe the first procurer of this warre and iorney. On the other side,
the PARTHIANS came coragiously vnto *Antonius* campe, who lay at the siege of
their chiefest citie, and cruelly reuiled and threatned him. *Antonius* therefore
fearing that if he lay still and did nothing, his mens harts would faile them:
he tooke ten legions, with three cohorts or ensignes of the Prætors, (which are
companies appointed for the gard of the Generall) and all his horsemen, and
caried them out to forrage, hoping therby he should easely allure the PARTHIANS
to fight a battell. But when he had marched about a dayes iorney from his
campe, he saw the PARTHIANS wheeling round about him to geue him the
onset, & to skirmish with him, when he would thinke to march his way.
Therefore he set out his signall of battell, & yet caused his tents and fardells
to be trussed vp, as though he ment not to fight, but only to lead his men
back againe. Then he marched before the army of the barbarous people, the
which was marshall like a cressant or halfe moone: and commaunded his
horsemen, that as soone as they thought the legions were nere enough vnto
their enemies to set vpon the voward, that then they should set spurres to their
horses, & begin the charge. The PARTHIANS standing in battell ray, beholding
the countenaunce of the ROMANES as they marched: they appeared to be souldiers
in deede, to see them marche in so good array as was possible. For in their
march, they kept the[44] rankes a like[45] space one from an other, not straggling
out of order, and shaking their pikes, speaking neuer a word. But so soone as
the allarom was giuen, the horsemen sodainly turned head vpon the PARTHIANS,
and with great cries gaue charge on them: who at the first receiued their charge
coragiously, for they were ioined nerer thē within an arrowes shoote. But when

Antonius
besiegeth the city
of Phraata in
Media.

The Parthiās
tooke Antonius
engines of
battery.

Battell betwext
the Parthians &
Antonius.

The Romanes
good order in
their march.

---

[43] founde] found out 1603
[44] the] their 1603
[45] like] litle 1595, 1603

the legions also came to ioine with them, showting out alowde, & ratling of
their armors: the PARTHIANS horses and them selues were so affrayed and amazed
withall, that they all turned taile and fled, before the ROMANES could come
to the sword with them. Then *Antonius* followed thē hard in chase, being in
great good hope by this conflict to haue brought to end all, or the most part
of this warre. But after that his footemen had chased them fiftie furlonges of,
and the horsemen also thrise as farre: they found in all but thirty prisoners
taken, and about foure score men only slaine. But this[46] did much discorage
them, when they cōsidered with them selues, that obtaining the victory, they
had slaine so few of their enemies: and where[47] they were ouercome, they lost
as[48] many of their men, as they had done at the ouerthrow when the cariage
was taken. The next morning, *Antonius* army trussed vp their cariage, and
marched backe towards their campe: and by the way in their returne they met
at the first a fewe of the PARTHIANS: then going further, they met a few moe.
So at length when they all came together, they reuiled them, & troubled them
on euery side, as freshly & coragiously, as if they had not bene ouerthrowen:
so that the ROMANES very hardly got to their campe with safety. The MEDES
on the other side, that were besieged in their chiefe city of PHRAATA, made a
saly out vpon them that kept the mount, which they had forced and cast against
the wall of the city, and draue them for feare, from the mount they kept.
Antonius was so offended withall, that he executed the Decimation. For he
deuided his men by ten legions, and then of them he put the tenth legion to
death, on whom the lot fell: and to the other nine, he caused them to haue
barley giuen them in stead of wheate. Thus this warre fell out troublesome
vnto both parties, and the ende thereof muche more fearefull. For *Antonius*
could looke for no other of his side, but famine: bicause he could forrage no
more, nor fetche in any vittells, without great losse of his men. *Phraortes* on the
other side, he knew well enough that he could bring the PARTHIANS to any thing
els, but to lye in campe abroad in the winter. Therefore he was affrayed, that
if the ROMANES continued their siege all winter long, & made warre with him
still: that his mē would forsake him, & specially bicause the time of the yere
went away apace, & the ayer waxed clowdy, & cold, in the equinoctiall autumne.
Therupon he called to mind this deuise. He gaue the chiefest of his gentlemē
of the PARTHIANS charge, that when they met the ROMANES out of their campe,
going to forrage, or to water [989] their horse, or for some other prouision:
that they should not distresse them too muche, but should suffer them to carie
somewhat away, and greatly commend their valliantnes and hardines, for the
which their king did esteeme them the more, and not without cause. After
these first baytes and allurements, they beganne by litle and litle to come neerer
vnto them, and to talke with them a horsebacke, greatly blaming *Antonius*
selfewill that did not geue their king *Phraortes* occasion to make a good peace,
who desired nothing more, then to saue the liues of so goodly a companie of
valliant men: but that he was too fondly bent to abide two of the greatest and

Decimacion a marshall punishment.

The craft of the Parthians against the Romanes.

[46] But this] which 1603
[47] where] when 1603
[48] as] so 1603

most dreadfull enemies he could haue, to wit: winter, and famine, the which they should hardly away withall, though the PARTHIANS did the best they could to aide & accompany them. These words being oftentimes brought to *Antonius*, they made him a litle pliant, for the good hope he had of his returne: but yet he woulde not sende vnto the king of PARTHIA, before they had first asked these barbarous people that spake so curteously vnto his men, whether they spake it of them selues, or that they were their maisters words. When they told them the king him selfe sayd so, and did perswade them further not to feare or mistrust them: then *Antonius* sent some of his frends vnto the king, to make demaund for the deliuery of the ensignes and prisoners he had of the ROMANES, since the ouerthrow of *Crassus*: to the ende it should not appeare, that if he asked nothing, they shoulde thinke he were glad that he might only scape with safety out of the daunger he was in. The king of PARTHIA answered him: that for the ensignes & prisoners he demaunded, he should not breake his head about it: notwithstãding, that if he would presently depart without delay, he might depart in peaceable maner, and without daunger. Wherefore *Antonius* after he had giuen his men some time to trusse vp their cariage, he raised his campe, & tooke his way to depart. But though he had an excellent tongue at will, and very gallant to enterteine his souldiers and men of warre, and that he could passingly well do it, as well, or better then any Captaine in his time: yet being ashamed for respects, he would not speake vnto them at his remouing, but willed *Domitius AEnobarbus* to do it. Many of them tooke this in very ill parte, & thought that he did it in disdaine of them: but the most part of them presently vnderstoode the truth of it, and were also ashamed. Therefore they thought it their dueties to carie the like respect vnto their Captaine, that their Captaine did vnto them: and so they became the more obedient vnto him. So *Antonius* was minded to returne the same way he came, being a plaine barren contry without wodde. But there came a souldier to him, borne in the contry of the MARDIANS, who by oft frequenting the PARTHIANS of long time, knew their facions very wel, and had also shewed him selfe very true & faithfull to the ROMANES, in the battell where *Antonius* engines of battery and cariage were taken away. This man came vnto *Antonius*, to counsell him to beware how he went that way, and to make his army a pray, being heauily armed, vnto so great a number of horsemen, all archers in the open field, where they should haue nothing to let them to compasse him round about: and that this was *Phraortes* fetch to offer him so frendly cõdicions & curteous words to make him raise his siege, that he might afterwards meete him as he would, in the plaines: howbeit, that he would guide him, if he thought good, an other way on the right hand, through woddes & mountaines, a farre neerer way, and where he should finde great plenty of all things needefull for his army. *Antonius* hearing what he said, called his counsel together, to consult vpon it. For after he had made peace with the PARTHIANS, he was loth to geue them cause to thinke he mistrusted them: and on thother side also he would gladly shorten his way, and passe by places wel inhabited, where he might be prouided of al things necessary: therfore he asked the MARDIAN what pledge he would put in, to performe that he promised. The MARDIAN gaue himself to be bound hand and foote, till he had brought his army into the contry of ARMENIA. So he guided the army thus bound, two dayes together, without any trouble or sight of

Antonius returneth from the iorney of the Parthiãs.

enemy. But the third day, *Antonius* thinking the PARTHIANS would no more follow him, & trusting therin, suffred the souldiers to march in disorder as euery mā listed. The MARDIAN perceiuing that the dammes of a riuer were newly broken vp, which they should haue passed ouer, & that the riuer had ouerflowen the bankes and drowned all the way they shoulde haue gone: he gessed straight that the PARTHIANS had done it, and had thus broken it open, to stay the ROMANES for getting too farre before them. Therupon he bad *Antonius* looke to him selfe, and told him [990] that his enemies were not farre from thence. *Antonius* hauing set his men in order, as he was placing of his archers & sling men to resist the enemies, & to driue them backe: they discried the PARTHIANS that wheeled round about the army to compasse them in on euery side, & to breake their rankes, & their light armed men gaue charge apon them. So after they had hurt many of the ROMANES with their arrowes, and that they them selues were also hurt by them with their dartes and plummets of leade: they retyred a litle, and then came againe and gaue charge. Vntill that the horsemen of the GAVLES turned their horses, & fiercely gallopped towards them, that they dispersed them so, as al that day they gathered no more together. Therby *Antonius* knew what to do, and did not only strengthen the rereward of his army, but both the flanks also, with darters[49] and sling men, [TLN 1970] and made his army march in a square battell: commaunding the horsemen, that when the enemies should come to assaile them, they shoulde driue them backe, but not follow them too farre. Thus the PARTHIANS foure daies after, seeing they did no more hurte to the ROMANES, then they also receiued of them: they were not so hotte vpon them as they were commaunded, but excusing them selues by the winter that troubled them, they determined to returne backe againe. The fift day, *Flauius Gallus*, a valliant man of his handes, that had charge in the armie: came vnto *Antonius* to pray him to let him haue some moe of his light armed men then were alreadie in the rereward, and some of the horsemen that were in the voward, hoping thereby to doe some notable exploite. *Antonius* graunting them vnto him, when the enemies came according to their maner to set vpon the taile of the army, and to skirmish with them: *Flauius* coragiously made them retire, but not as they were wont to doe before, to retire and ioyne presently with their army, for he ouerrashly thrust in among them to fight it out at the sword. The Capteines that had the leading of the rereward, seeing *Flauius* stray too farre from the army: they sent vnto him to will him to retire, but he would not harken to it. And it is reported also, that *Titius* himselfe the Treasorer, tooke the ensignes, & did what he could to make the ensigne bearers returne backe, reuiling *Flauius Gallus*, bicause that through his folly and desperatnes he caused many honest and valliant men to be both hurt & slaine to no purpose. *Gallus* also fel out with him, and commaunded his men to stay. Wherefore *Titius* returned againe into the army, and *Gallus* stil ouerthrowing and driuing the enemies backe whom he met in the voward, he was not ware that he was compassed in. Then seeing him selfe enuironned of all sides, he sent vnto the army, that they should come and aide him: but there the Captaines that led the legions (among the which *Canidius*, a man of great

The Parthiās doe set vpon Antonius in his returne.

The bold act of Flauius Gallus.

Canidius fault, Antonius Captaine.

---

[49] darters] darts 1595, 1603

estimacion about *Antonius* made one) committed many faults. For where they should haue made head with the whole army vpon the PARTHIANS, they sent him aide by small cōpanies: and when they were slaine, they sent him others also. So that by their beastlinesse and lacke of consideracion, they had like to haue made all the armie flie, if *Antonius* him selfe had not come frō the front of the battell with the third legion, the which came through the middest of them that fled, vntill they came to front of [50] the enemies, & that they stayed them from chasing any further. Howbeit at this last conflict there were slaine no lesse thē three thowsand men, and fiue thowsande besides brought sore hurt into the campe, and amongest them also *Flauius Gallus*, whose body was shot through in foure places, whereof he died. [TLN 2454] *Antonius* went to the tents to visite & comfort the sicke & wounded, and for pities sake he could not refraine from weeping: and they also shewing him the best countenaunce they coulde, tooke him by the hand, and prayed him to go and be dressed, and not to trouble him selfe for them, most reuerently calling him their Emperour & Captaine: & that for them selues, they were whole & safe, so that he had his health. For in deede to say truly, there was not at that time any Emperour or Captaine that had so great & puisant an army as his together, both for lusty youths, & corage of the souldiers, as also for their pacience to away with so great paines & trouble. Furthermore, the obedience & reuerēce they shewed vnto their captaine, with a maruelous earnest loue & good wil, was so great: & all were indifferētly (as wel great as smal, the noble men, as meane men, the Captaines and[51] souldiers) so earnestly bent to esteeme *Antonius* good will & fauor, aboue their owne life & safety: that in this point of marshall discipline, the auncient ROMANES could not haue don any more. But diuers things were cause therof, as we haue told you before: *Antonius* nobility & ancient house, his eloquence, his plaine nature, [TLN 3308–10] his liberality & ma-[*991*]gnificence, & his familiarity to sport & to be mery in company: but specially the care he tooke at that time to help, visite, & lament those that were sicke & woūded, seing euery man to haue that which was meete for him: that was of such force & effect, as it made them that were sicke & wounded to loue him better, & were more desirous to do him seruice, then those that were whole & soūd. This victory so encoraged the enemies, (who otherwise were weary to follow *Antonius* any further) that all night longe they kept the fieldes, and houered about the ROMANES campe, thinking that they would presently flie, & then that they should take the spoile of their campe. So the next morning by breake of daye, there were gathered together a farre greater nūber of the PARTHIANS, then they were before. For the rumor was, that there were not much fewer then forty thowsand horse, bicause their king sent thither euen the very gard about his person, as vnto a most certaine and assured victorie, that they might be partners of the spoyle and booty they hoped to haue had: for as touching the king him selfe, he was neuer in any conflict or battell. Then *Antonius* desirous to speake to his souldiers, called for a blacke gowne, to appeare the more pitifull to them: but his friends did disswade him from it. Therefore he put on his coate armor,

Flauius Gallus slaine.
Antonius care of them that were wounded.

The loue and reuerence of the souldiers vnto Antonius.

The rare and singular gifts of Antonius.

The king of Parthia neuer came to fight in the field.

---

[50] of] *Om.* 1603
[51] and] as 1603

and being so apparelled, made an oration to his armie: in the which he highly commended them that had ouercome and driuen backe their enemies, and greatly rebuked them that had cowardly turned their backes. So that those which had ouercome, prayed him to be of good chere: the other also to cleere them selues, willingly offred to take the lotts[52] of *Decimation* if he thought good, or otherwise, to receiue what kind of punishment it should please him to laye vpon them, so that he would forget any more to mislike, or to be offended with them. *Antonius* seeing that, did lift vp his hands to heauen, and made his prayer to the goddes, that if in exchaunge of his former victories, they would nowe sende him some bitter aduersitie: then that all might light on him selfe alone, and that they would giue the victorie to the rest of his armie. The next morning, they gaue better order on euery side of the armie, and so marched forward: so that when the PARTHIANS thought to returne againe to assaile them, they came farre short of the reckoning. For where they thought to come not to fight, but to spoyle and make hauock of all: when they came neare them, they were sore hurt with their slings and darts, and such other iauelings as the ROMANES darted at them, & the PARTHIANS found them as rough and desperat in fight, as if they had bene fresh men they had delt withall. Whereuppon their harts beganne againe to fayle them. But yet when the ROMANES came to goe downe any steepe hills or mountaines, then they would set on them with their arrowes, bicause the ROMANES could goe downe but fayer and softly. But then againe, the souldiers of the legion that caried great shields, returned backe, and inclosed them that were naked or light armed, in the middest amongest them, and did kneele of one knee on the ground, and so set downe their shields before them: and they of the second ranck also couered them of the first rancke, and the third also couered the second, and so from ranck to rancke all were couered. Insomuch that this manner of couering and sheading them selues with shields, was deuised after the facion of laying tiles vpon houses, and to sight, was like the degrees of a Theater, and is a most stronge defence and bulwarke against all arrowes and shot that falleth vpon it. When the PARTHIANS saw this countenaunce of the ROMANE souldiers of the legion, which kneeled on the ground in that sorte vpon one knee, supposing that they had bene wearied with trauell: they layed downe their bowes, & tooke their speares & launces, and came to fight with them man for man. Then the ROMANES sodainely rose vpon their feete, and with the darts that they threwe from them, they slue the formost, and put the rest to flight, and so did they the next dayes that followed. But by meanes of these daungers and lets, *Antonius* armie could winne no way in a day, by reason whereof they suffred great famine: for they could haue but litle corne, and yet were they driuen daily to fight for it, and besides that, they had no instruments to grynd it, to make bread of it. For the most part of them had bene left behind, bicause the beasts that caried them were either dead, or els imployed to cary them that were sore and wounded. For the famine was so extreame great, that the eight parte of a bushell of wheate was sold for fifty Drachmas, and they sold barley bread by the waight of siluer. In the ende, they were compelled to liue of erbes and rootes, but they found few of them

Antonius charitable prayer to the gods for his army.

The Romanes testudo, and couering against shot.

Great famine in Antonius army.

---

[52] lotts] lot 1603

that men doe commonly eate of, and were inforced to tast of them that were
neuer eaten be-[992]fore: among the which there was one that killed them, and
made them out of their witts. For he that had once eaten of it, his memorye
was gone from him, and he[53] knewe no manner of thing, but onely busied him
selfe in digging and hurling of stones from one place to another, as though it
had bene a matter of great waight, and to be done with all possible speede.
All the campe ouer, men were busily stouping to the ground, digging and
carying of stones from one place to another: but at the last, they cast vp a great
deale of choller, and dyed sodainly, bicause they lacked wine, which was the
onely soueraine remedy to cure that disease. It is reported that *Antonius* seeing
such a number of his men dye dayly, and that the PARTHIANS left them not,
nether would suffer them to be at rest: he oftentymes cryed out sighing, and
sayd: O, tenne thowsand. He had the valliantnes of tenne thowsand GRÆCIANS
in such admiration, whome *Xenophon* brought away after the ouerthrow of
CYRVS[54]: bicause they had comen[55] a farder iorney from BABYLON, and had
also fought against much moe enemies many tymes told, then them selues, and
yet came home with safetie. The PARTHIANS therfore seeing that they could
not breake the good order of the armie of the ROMANES, and contrarily that
they them selues were oftentymes put to flight, and welfauoredly beaten: they
fell againe to their olde craftie suttelties. For when they found any of the
ROMANES scattered from the armie to goe forrage, to seeke some corne, or other
vittells: they would come to them as if they had bene their friends, and shewed
them their bowes vnbent, saying, that them selues also did returne home to
their contry as they did, and that they would follow them no further, howbeit
that they should yet haue certaine MEDES that would follow them a dayes iorney
or two, to keepe them that they should doe no hurt to the villages from the
high wayes: and so holding them with this talke, they gently tooke their leaue
of them, and bad them farewell, so that the ROMANES began againe to thinke
them selues safe. *Antonius* also vnderstanding this, being very glad of it, determined to take his way through the plaine contry, bicause also they should
find no water in the mountaines, as it was reported vnto him. So as he was
determined to take this[56] course, there came into his hoast one *Mithridates*, a
gentleman from the enemies campe, who was Cosen vnto *Monæzes*[57] that fled
vnto *Antonius*, and vnto whome he had giuen three cities. When he came to
Antonius campe, he praied them to bring him one that could speake the PAR-
THIAN, or SYRIAN tongue. So one *Alexander* ANTIOCHIAN, a famillier of *Antonius*,
was brought vnto him. Then the gentleman told him what he was, and sayde,
that *Monæzes*[58] had sent him to *Antonius*, to requite the honor and curtesie he
had shewed vnto him. After he had vsed this ceremonious speeche, he asked
Alexander if he sawe those highe Mountaines a farre of, which he poynted vnto

A deadly erbe incurable without wine.

The valliantnes of tenne thowsand Græcians, whome Xenophon brought away after the ouer throw of Cyrus.

The Parthians very suttell and craftie people.

Mithridates a Parthian, bewrayeth vnto Antonius the conspiracie of his own contry men against him.

---

53 he] *Om.* 1603
54 CYRVS] CYPRVS 1595
55 comen] come 1595, 1603
56 this] his 1603
57 *Monæzes*] *Monæxes* 1603
58 *Monæzes*] *Monexes* 1603

him⁵⁹ with his finger. *Alexander* aunswered he did. The PARTHIANS (sayd he)
doe lye in ambushe at the foote of those Mountaines, vnder the which lyeth a
goodly playne champion contry: and they thinke that you beeing deceiued with
their craftie suttill wordes, will leaue the way of the Mountaines, and turne
into the plaine. For the other way, it is very hard and painefull, and you shall
abide great thirst, the which you are well acquainted withall: but if *Antonius*
take the lower way, let him assure him selfe to runne the same fortune that
Marcus Crassus did. So *Mithridates* hauing sayd, he departed. *Antonius* was
maruelously troubled in his mind when he heard thus much, & therfore called
for his friends, to heare what they would say to it. The MARDIAN also that was
their guide, being asked his opinion, aunswered: that he thought as much as
the gentleman *Mithridates* had sayd. For, sayd he, admit that there were no
ambushe of enemies in the valley, yet is it a long crooked way, and ill to hit:
where taking the Mountaine waye, though it be stonye and painefull, yet there
is no other daunger, but a whole dayes trauelling without any water. So *Antonius*
chaūging his first mind and determination, remoued that night, and tooke the
Mountaine way, commaunding euery man to prouide him selfe of water. But
the most part of them lacking vessells to cary water in, some were driuen to
fill their salletts and murrians with water, and others also filled goates skinnes
to cary water in. Nowe they marching forwarde, worde was brought vnto the
PARTHIANS that they were remoued: whereuppon, contrary to their manner,
they presently followed them the selfe same night, so that by breake of day
they ouertooke the rereward of the ROMANES, who were so lame and wearied
with going, and lacke of sleepe, that they were euen done. For, beyond expectacion, they had gone that night, two hundred [993] and forty furlong⁶⁰,
and further, to see their enemies so sodainly at their backs, that made them
vtterly dispaire: but moste of all, the fighting with them increased their thirst,
bicause they were forced to fight as they marched, to driue their enemies backe,
yet creeping on still. The voward of the armie by chaunce met with a riuer *A salt riuer.*
that was very cleere, and colde water, but it was salt and venemous to drinke:
for straight it did gnawe the gutts of those that had dronke it, and made them
maruelous drye, and put them into a terrible ache and pricking. And notwithstanding that the MARDIAN had told them of it before, yet they would not
be ruled, but violently thrust them backe that would haue kept them from
drinking, and so dranke. But *Antonius* going vp and downe amongst them,
prayed them to take a litle pacience for a while, for hard by there was another
riuer that the water was excellent good to drinke, & that from thenceforth the
way was so stony and ill for horsemen, that the enemies could followe them
no further. So he caused the retreate to be sownded to call them backe that
fought, and commaunded the tents to be set vppe, that the souldiers might
yet haue shadow to refreshe them with. So when the tents were set vp, and the
PARTHIANS also retyred according to their manner: the gentleman *Mithridates*
before named, returned againe as before, and *Alexander* in like manner againe

⁵⁹ him] *Om.* 1603
⁶⁰ furlong] furlongs 1603

brought vnto him for Interpreter. Then *Mithridates* aduised him, that after the armie had reposed a litle, the ROMANES should remoue forthwith, and with all possible speede get to the riuer: bicause the PARTHIANS would goe no further, but yet were cruelly bent to follow them thither. *Alexander* caried the report thereof vnto *Antonius*, who gaue him a great deale of gold plate to bestowe vpon *Mithridates*. *Mithridates* tooke as much of him as he could well cary away in his gowne, and so departed with speede. So *Antonius* raysed his campe being yet day light, and caused all his army to marche, & the PARTHIANS neuer troubled any of them by the way: but amongest them selues it was as ill and dreadfull a night as euer they had. For there were Villens of their owne company, who cut their fellowes throates for the money they had, and besides that, robbed the sumpters and cariage of such money as they caried: and at length, they set vpon *Antonius* slaues that draue his owne sumpters and cariage, they brake goodly tables & riche plate in peeces, and deuided it among them selues. Thereuppon all the campe was straight in tumult and vprore: For the residue of them were affraid it had bene the PARTHIANS that had giuen them this alarom, and had put all the armie out of order. Insomuch that *Antonius* called for one [TLN 77] *Rhamnus*, one of his slaues infranchised that was of his gard, and made him giue him his faith that he would thrust his sword through him when he would bid him, and cut of his head: bicause he might not be taken aliue of his enemies, nor knowen when he were dead. This grieued his friends to the hart, that they burst out a weeping for sorrow. The MARDIAN also did comfort him, and assured him that the riuer he sought for was hard by, and that he did gesse it by a sweete moyst wind that breathed vpon them, and by the ayer which they found fresher then they were wont, and also, for that they fetched their wind more at libertie: and moreouer, bicause that since they did set forward, he thought they were neare their iorneys ende, not lacking much of day. On the other side also, *Antonius* was informed, that this great tumult and trouble came not through the enemies, but through the vile couetousnes and villany of certaine of his souldiers. Therefore *Antonius* to set his armie againe in order, and to pacifie this vprore, sownded the trompet that euery man should lodge. Now day began to breake, and the army to fall againe into good order, and all the hurly burly to cease, when the PARTHIANS drewe neare, and that their arrowes lighted among them of the rereward of his army. Thereuppon the signall of battell was giuen to the light armed men, and the legioners did couer them selues as they had done before with their shields, with the which they receiued & defended the force of the PARTHIANS arrowes, who neuer durst any more come to hand[61] strokes with them: and thus they that were in the voward, went downe by litle and litle, till at length they spyed the riuer. There *Antonius* placed his armed men vpon the sands to receiue and driue backe the enemies, and first of all, got ouer his men that were sicke and hurt, and afterwards all the rest. And those also that were left to resist the enemies, had leysure enough to dr:nke safely, and at their pleasure. For when the PARTHIANS saw the riuer, they vnbent their bowes, and bad the ROMANES passe ouer without any feare, and greatly commended their valliantnes. When they had all passed ouer the

Antonius great liberalitie vnto Mithridates, for the care he had of his saftie.

The tumult of Antonius soldiers through couetousnes.

Antonius desperat minde.

---

[61] hand] handy 1595, 1603

[994] riuer at their ease, they tooke a litle breath, and so marched forward
againe, not greatly trusting the PARTHIANS. The sixt daye after this last battell, *Araxes fl.*
they came to the riuer of Araxes, which deuideth the contry of ARMENIA from
MEDIA: the which appeared vnto them very daungerous to passe, for the depth
and swiftnes of the streame. And furthermore, there ranne a rumor through
the campe, that the PARTHIANS lay in ambushe thereabouts, and that they
would come & set vpon them whilest they were troubled in passing ouer the
riuer. But now, after they were all comen[62] safely ouer without any daunger,
and that they had gotten to the other side, into the prouince of ARMENIA: then
they worshipped that land, as if it had bene the first land they had seene after
a long and daungerous voyage by sea, being now arriued in a safe and happy
hauen: and the teares ranne downe their cheekes, and euery man imbraced eache
other for the great ioy they had. But nowe, keeping the fields in this frutefull
contry so plentifull of all things, after so great a famine and want of all thinges:
they so crammed them selues with such plenty of vittells, that many of them
were cast into flyxes and dropsies. There *Antonius* mustring his whole army,
found that he had lost twenty thowsand footemen, and foure thowsand horsemen, which had not all bene slayne by their enemies: for the most part of them
dyed of sicknes, making seuen and twenty dayes iorney, comming from the
citie of PHRAATA into ARMENIA, and hauing ouercome the PARTHIANS in *18 seuerall*
battels fought
with the
Parthians.
eighteene seuerall battells. But these victories were not throughly performed
nor accomplished, bicause they followed no long chase: and thereby it easily
appeared, that *Artabazus* king of ARMENIA, had reserued *Antonius* to end[63] this *The trechery of*
Artabazus king
of Armenia,
warre. For if the sixteene thowsand horsemen which he brought with him out *vnto Antonius.*
of MEDIA, had bene at these battells, considering that they were armed and
apparelled much after the PARTHIANS manner, and acquainted also with their
fight: When the ROMANES had put them to flight that fought a battell with
them, & that these ARMENIANS had followed the chase of them that fled, they
had not gathered them selues againe in force, neither durst they also haue
returned to fight with them so often, after they had bene so many times
ouerthrowen. Therefore, all those that were of any credit and countenaunce in
the army, did perswade and egge *Antonius* to be reuenged of this ARMENIAN
king. But *Antonius* wisely dissembling his anger, he told him not of his trechery,
nor gaue him the worse[64] countenaunce, nor did him lesse honor then he did
before: bicause he knew his armie was weake, & lacked things necessary. Howbeit *Antonius*
triumphed of
Artabazus king
afterwards he returned againe into ARMENIA with a great army, and so with *of Armenia, in*
fayer wordes, and sweete promises of Messengers, he allured *Artabazus* to *AEgypt.*
come vnto[65] him: whome he then kept prisoner, [TLN 2911–13] and led in
triumphe in the citie of ALEXANDRIA. This greatly offended the ROMANES,
and made them much to mislike it: when they saw that for *Cleopatraes* sake
he depriued his contry of her due honor and glory, onely to gratifie the ÆGYP-
TIANS. But this was a prety while after. Howbeit then, the great haste he made

---

[62] comen] come 1595, 1603
[63] reserued . . . to end] kept . . . from ending 1603
[64] worse] worst 1595
[65] vnto] to 1603

to returne vnto *Cleopatra*, caused him to put his men to so great paines, forcing them to lye in the field all winter long when it snew vnreasonably, that by the way he lost eight thowsand of his men, and so came downe to the seaside with a small companye, to[66] a certaine place called BLANCBOVRG, which standeth betwixt the cities of BERYTVS and SIDON, and there taried for *Cleopatra*. And bicause she taried longer then he would haue had her, he pined away for loue and sorrow. So that he was at such a straight, that he wist not what to doe, and therefore to weare it out, he gaue him selfe to quaffing and feasting. But he was so drowned with the loue of her, that he could not abide to sit at the table till the feast were[67] ended: but many times while others bankette, he ranne to the sea side to see if she were comming. At length she came, and brought with her a worlde of apparell and money to giue vnto the souldiers. But some saye notwithstanding, that she brought apparell, but no money, and that she tooke of *Antonius* money, and caused it to be giuen amonge[68] the souldiers in her owne name, as if she had giuen it them. In the meane time it chaunced, that the king of the MEDES, and *Phraortes* king of the PARTHIANS, fell at great warres together, the which began (as it is reported) for the spoyles of the ROMANES: and grew to be so hot betwene them, that the king of MEDES was no lesse affrayd, then also in daunger to lose his whole Realme. Thereuppon he sent vnto *Antonius* to pray him to come and make warre with the PARTHIANS, promising him that he would ayde him to his vttermost power. This put *Antonius* againe in good comfort, conside-[995]ring that vnlooked for, the onely thing he lacked, (which made him he could not ouercome the PARTHIANS, meaning that he had not brought horsemen, and men with darts and slings enough) was offred him in that sort: that he did him more pleasure to accept it, then it was pleasure to the other to offer it. Hereuppon, after he had spoken with the king of MEDES at the riuer of Araxes, he prepared him selfe once more to goe through ARMENIA, and to make more cruell warre with the PARTHIANS, then he had done before. Now whilest *Antonius* was busie in this preparation, *Octauia* his wife, whome he had left at ROME, would needes take sea to come vnto him. Her brother *Octauius Cæsar* was willing vnto it, not for his respect at all (as most authors doe report) as for that he might haue an honest culler to make warre with *Antonius* if he did misuse her, and not esteeme of her as she ought to be. But when she was come to ATHENS, she receiued letters from *Antonius*, willing her to stay there vntill his comming, & did aduertise her of his iorney and determination. The which though it grieued her much, and that she knewe it was but an excuse: yet by her letters to him of aunswer, she asked him whether he would haue those thinges sent vnto him which she had brought him, being great store of apparell for souldiers, a great number of horse, summe[69] of money, and gifts, to bestow on his friendes

Antonius pined away looking for Cleopatra.

Cleopatra came to Blächourg vnto Antonius.

VVarres betwixt the Parthians and Medes.

Octauia, Antonius wife, came to Athens to meete with him.

---

[66] to] vnto 1603
[67] were] was 1603
[68] amonge] amongst 1595, 1603
[69] summe] summes 1603

and Captaines he had about him: and besides all those, she had two thowsand souldiers chosen men, all well armed, like vnto the Prætors bands. When *Niger*, one of *Antonius* friends whome he had sent vnto ATHENS, had brought these newes from his wife *Octauia*, and withall did greatly prayse her, as she was worthy, and well deserued: *Cleopatra* knowing that *Octauia* would haue *Antonius* from her, and fearing also that if with her vertue and honest behauior, (besides the great power of her brother *Cæsar*) she did adde thereunto her modest kind loue to please her husband, that she would then be too stronge for her, and in the end winne him away: she suttelly seemed to languish for the loue of *Antonius*, pyning her body for lacke of meate. [TLN 299–322] Furthermore, she euery way so framed her countenaunce, that when *Antonius* came to see her, she cast her eyes vpon him, like a woman rauished for ioy. Straight againe when he went from her, she fell a weeping and blubbering, looked[70] rufully of the matter, and still found the meanes that *Antonius* should oftentymes finde her weeping: and then when he came sodainely vppon her, she made as though she dryed her eyes, and turned her face away, as if she were vnwilling that he should see her weepe. All these tricks she vsed, *Antonius* being in readines to goe into SYRIA, to speake with the king of MEDES. Then the flatterers that furthered *Cleopatraes* mind, blamed *Antonius*, and tolde him that he was a hard natured man, and that he had small loue in him, that would see a poore Ladye in such torment for his sake, whose life depended onely vpon him alone. For, *Octauia*, sayd they, that was maryed vnto him as it were of necessitie, bicause her brother *Cæsars* affayres so required it: hath the honor to be called *Antonius* lawefull spowse and wife: and *Cleopatra*, being borne a Queene of so many thowsands of men, is onely named *Antonius* Leman, and yet that she disdayned not so to be called, if it might please him she might enioy his company, and liue with him: but if he once leaue her, that then it is vnpossible she should liue. To be short, by these their flatteries and enticements, they so wrought *Antonius* effeminate mind, that fearing least she would make her selfe away: he returned againe vnto ALEXANDRIA, and referred the king of MEDES to the next yeare following, although he receyued newes that the PARTHIANS at that tyme were at ciuill warres amonge them selues. This notwithstanding, he went afterwardes and made peace with him. For he maried his Daughter which was very younge, vnto one of the sonnes that *Cleopatra* had by him: and then returned, beeing fully bent to make warre with *Cæsar*. [TLN 1844–5] When *Octauia* was returned to ROME from ATHENS, *Cæsar* commaunded her to goe out of *Antonius* house, and to dwell by her selfe, bicause he had abused her. *Octauia* aunswered him againe, that she would not forsake her husbands house, and that if he had no other occasion to make warre with him, she prayed him then to take no thought for her: for sayd she, it were too shamefull a thinge, that two so famous Captaines should bringe in ciuill warres among the ROMANES, the one for the loue of a womã, & the other for the ielousy betwixt one an other. Now as she spake the worde, so did she also performe the deede. For she kept still in *Antonius* house, as if he had bene there, and very honestly and honorably kept his children, not

The flickering enticements of Cleopatra, vnto Antonius.

The occasion of ciuil warres betwixt Antonius and Cæsar.

The loue of Octauia to Antonius her husband, and her wise and womanly behauior.

[70] looked] looking 1603

433

those onely she had by him, but the other which her husband had by *Fuluia*.
Further-[996]more, when *Antonius* sent any of his men to ROME, to sue for any
office in the cōmon wealth: she receiued him[71] very curteously, and so vsed her
selfe vnto her brother, that she obtained the thing[72] she requested. Howbeit
thereby, thinking no hurt, she did *Antonius* great hurt. [TLN 1850–2] For her
honest loue and regard to her husband, made euery man hate him, when they
sawe he did so vnkindly vse so noble a Lady: but yet the greatest cause of their
malice vnto him, [TLN 1752–67] was for the diuision of lands he made amongst
his children in the citie of ALEXANDRIA. And to confesse a troth, it was too
arrogant and insolent a part, and done (as a man would say) in derision and
contempt of the ROMANES. For he assembled all the people in the show place,
where younge men doe exercise them selues, and there vpon a high tribunall
siluered, he set two chayres of gold, the one for him selfe, and the other for
Cleopatra, and lower chaires for his children: then he openly published before
the assembly, that first of all he did establish *Cleopatra* Queene of ÆGYPT, of
CYPRVS, of LYDIA, and of the lower SYRIA, and at that time also, *Cæsarion* king
of the same Realmes. [TLN 942–3] This *Cæsarion* was supposed to be the sonne
of *Iulius Cæsar*, who had left *Cleopatra* great with child. Secondly he called the
sonnes he had by her, the kings of kings, and gaue *Alexander* for his portion,
ARMENIA, MEDIA, and PARTHIA, when he had conquered the contry: and vnto
Ptolomy for his portion, PHENICIA, SYRIA, and CILICIA. And therewithall he
brought out *Alexander* in a long gowne after the facion of the MEDES, with a
high copped tanke[73] hat on his head, narrow in the toppe, as the kings of the
MEDES and ARMENIANS doe vse to weare them: and *Ptolomy* apparelled in a
cloke after the MACEDONIAN manner, with slippers on his feete, and a broad
hat, with a royall band or diademe. Such was the apparell and old attyre of the
auncient kinges and successors of *Alexander* the great. So after his sonnes had
done their humble duties, and kissed their father and mother: presently a
company of ARMENIAN souldiers set there of purpose, compassed the one about,
and a like company of the[74] MACEDONIANS the other. [TLN 1767–70] Now
for *Cleopatra*, she did not onely weare at that time (but at all other times els
when she came abroad) the apparell of the goddesse *Isis*, and so gaue audience
vnto all her subiects, as a new *Isis*. *Octauius Cæsar* reporting all these thinges
vnto the Senate, and oftentimes accusing him to the whole people and assembly
in ROME: he thereby stirred vp all the ROMANES against him. [TLN 1687–8,
1730, 1775–89] *Antonius* on thother side sent to ROME likewise to accuse him,
and the chiefest poyntes of his accusations he charged him with, were these.
First, that hauing spoyled *Sextus Pompeius* in SICILE, he did not giue him his
parte of the Ile. Secondly, that he did deteyne in his hands the shippes he lent
him to make that warre. Thirdly, that hauing put *Lepidus* their companion and
triumuirate out of his part of the Empire, and hauing depriued him of all
honors: he retayned for him selfe the lands and reuenues thereof, which had

Antonius arrogantly deuideth diuers prouinces vnto his children by Cleopatra. Cæsarion, the supposed sōne of Cæsar, by Cleopatra.

Alexander & Ptolomy, Antonius sonnes by Cleopatra.

Accusations betwixt Octauius Cæsar, & Antonius.

---

[71] him] thē 1603
[72] thing] things 1603
[73] copped tanke] coppe-tanke 1603
[74] of the] of 1603

bene assigned vnto him for his part. And last of all, that he had in manner deuided all ITALY amongest his owne souldiers, and had left no part of it for his souldiers. *Octauius Cæsar* aunswered him againe: that for *Lepidus*, he had in deede deposed him, and taken his part of the Empire from him, bicause he did ouercruelly vse his authoritie. And secondly, for the conquests he had made by force of armes, he was contented *Antonius* should haue his part of them, so that he would likewise let him haue his part of ARMENIA. And thirdly, that for his souldiers, they should seeke for nothing in ITALY, bicause they possessed MEDIA and PARTHIA, the which prouinces they had added to the Empire of ROME, valliantly fighting with their Emperor and Captaine. [TLN 1927–30] *Antonius* hearing these newes, being yet in ARMENIA, commaunded *Canidius* to goe presently to the sea side with his sixteene legions he had: and he him selfe with *Cleopatra*, went vnto the citie of EPHESVS, & there gathered together his gallies and shippes out of all parts, which came to the number of eight hundred, reckoning the great shippes of burden: and of those, *Cleopatra* furnished him with two hundred, and twenty thowsand talents besides, and prouision of vittells also to mainteyne al the whole army in this warre. [TLN 1861] So *Antonius*, through the perswasions of *Domitius*, commaunded *Cleopatra* to returne againe into ÆGYPT, and there to vnderstand the successe of this warre. But *Cleopatra*, fearing least *Antonius* should againe be made friends with *Octauius Cæsar*, by the meanes of his wife *Octauia*: she so plyed *Canidius* with money, and filled his purse, that he became her spokes man vnto *Antonius*, and told him [TLN 1877–9] there was no reason to send her from this warre, who defraied so great a charge: neither that it was for his profit, bicause that[75] thereby the ÆGYPTIANS [997] would then be vtterly discoraged, which were the chiefest strength of the army by sea: considering that he could see no king of all the kings their confederats, that *Cleopatra* was inferior vnto, either for wisedom or iudgement, seeing that longe before she had wisely gouerned so great a realme as ÆGYPT, & besides that she had bene so long acquainted with him, by whom she had learned to manedge great affayres. These fayer perswasions wan him: for it was predestined that the gouernment of all the world should fall into *Octauius Cæsars* handes. Thus, all their forces being ioyned together, they hoysed sayle towards the Ile of SAMOS, and there gaue them selues to feasts and sollace. For as all the kings, Princes, & communalties, peoples[76] and cities from SYRIA, vnto the marishes Mæotides, and from the ARMENIANS to the ILLYRIANS, were sent vnto, to send and bringe all munition and warlike preparation they could: euen so all players, minstrells, tumblers, fooles, and ieasters, were commaunded to assemble in the Ile of SAMOS. So that, where in manner all the world in euery place was full of lamentations, sighes and teares: onely in this Ile of SAMOS there was nothing for many dayes space, but singing and pyping, and all the Theater full of these common players, minstrells, and singing men. Besides all this, euery citie sent an oxe thither to sacrifice, and kings did striue one with another who should make the noblest feasts, & giue the richest gifts. So that euery man sayd, what can they doe more for ioy of victorie, if they winne the

Antonius came with eight hundred saile against Octauius Cæsar.

Antonius carieth Cleopatra with him to the warres, against Octauius Cæsar: & kept great feasting at the Ile of Samos together.

---

[75] that] *Om.* 1603
[76] peoples] people 1603

battell? When they make already such sumptuous feasts at the beginning of
the warre? When this was done, he gaue the whole rabble of these minstrells,
& such kind of people, the citie of PRIENE to keepe them withal, during this
warre. Then he went vnto the citie of ATHENS, and there gaue him selfe againe
to see playes and pastimes, and to keepe the Theaters. *Cleopatra* on the other
side, being ielous of the honors which *Octauia* had receiued in this citie, where
in deede she was maruelously honored and beloued of the ATHENIANS: to winne
the peoples good will also at ATHENS, she gaue them great gifts: and they
likewise gaue her many great honors, and appointed certain Ambassadors to
cary the decree to her house, amõg the which *Antonius* was one, who as a Citizen
of ATHENS reported the matter vnto her, & made an oration in the behalfe of
the citie. Afterwards he sent to ROME to put his wife *Octauia* out of his house,
who (as it is reported) went out of his house with all *Antonius* children, sauing
the eldest of them he had by *Fuluia*, who was with her[77] father, bewailing &
lamenting her cursed hap that had brought her to this, that she was accompted
one of the chiefest causes of this ciuill warre. The ROMANES did pitie her, but
much more *Antonius*, & those specially that had seene *Cleopatra*: who nether
excelled *Octauia* in beawtie, nor yet in young yeares. *Octauius Cæsar* vnderstanding the sodain & wonderful great preparation of *Antonius*, he was not a litle
astonied at it, (fearing he should be driuen to fight that sommer) bicause he
wanted many things, [TLN 631–2] & the great and grieuous exactions of
money did sorely[78] oppresse the people. For all manner of men els, were driuen
to pay the fourth part of their goods and reuenue: but the Libertines, (to wete,
those whose fathers or other predecessors had some time bene bond men) they[79]
were sessed to pay the eight part of all their goods at one payment. Hereuppon,
there rose[80] a wonderfull exclamation and great vprore all ITALY ouer: so that
among the greatest faults that euer *Antonius* committed, they blamed him most,
for that he delayed to giue *Cæsar* battell. For he gaue *Cæsar* leysure to make
his preparacions, and also to appease the complaints of the people. When such
a great summe of money was demaunded of them, they grudged at it, and
grewe to mutinie vpon it: but when they had once paied it, they remembred
it no more. Furthermore, *Titius* and *Plancus* (two of *Antonius* chiefest friends
and that had bene both of them Consuls) for the great iniuries *Cleopatra* did
them, bicause they hindered all they could, that she should not come to this
warre: they went and yelded them selues vnto *Cæsar*, [TLN 1688–9] and tolde
him where the testament was that *Antonius* had made, knowing perfitly what
was in it. The will was in the custodie of the Vestall Nunnes: of whom *Cæsar*
demaunded for[81] it. They aunswered him, that they would not giue it him;
but if he would goe and take it, they would not hinder him. Thereuppon *Cæsar*
went thither, & hauing red it first to him self, he noted certaine places worthy
of reproch: so assembling all the Senate, he red it before them all. Whereuppon

*Antonius put his
wife Octauia out
of his house at
Rome.*

*Octauius Cæsar
exacteth grieuous
payments of the
Romanes.*

*Titius and
Plancus reuolt
from Antonius,
and doe yeld to
Cæsar.*

---

[77] her] his 1595, 1603
[78] sorely] sore 1603
[79] they] *Om.* 1603
[80] rose] arose 1603
[81] for] *Om.* 1603

diuers were maruelously offended, and thought it a straunge matter that he being aliue, should be punished for that he had appoynted by his will to be done after his death. *Cæsar* chiefly tooke hold of this that he [998] ordeyned touching his buriall: for he willed that his bodie, though he dyed at ROME, should be brought in funerall pompe through the middest of the market place, and that it should be sent into ALEXANDRIA vnto *Cleopatra*. Furthermore, among diuers other faultes wherewith *Antonius* was to be charged, for *Cleopatraes* sake: *Caluisius*, one of *Cæsars* friends reproued him, bicause he had franckly giuen *Cleopatra* all the libraries of the royall citie of PERGAMVM, in the which she had aboue two hundred thowsand seueral bookes. Againe also, that being on a time set at the table, he sodainly rose from the borde, and trode vpon *Cleopatraes* foote, which was a signe giuen betwene them, that they were agreed of. That he had also suffred the EPHESIANS in his presence to call *Cleopatra*, their soueraine Ladye. That diuers times sitting in his tribunall and chayer of state, giuing audience to all kings and Princes: he had receiued loue letters from *Cleopatra*, written in tables of onyx or christall, and that he had red them, sitting in his imperial seate. That one day when *Furnius*, a man of great accompt, and the eloquentest man of all the ROMANES, pleaded a matter before him: *Cleopatra* by chaunce cōming through the market place in her litter where *Furnius* was a pleading: *Antonius* straight rose out of his seate, and left his audience to followe her litter. This notwithstanding, it was thought *Caluisius* deuised the most part of all these accusations of his owne head. Neuertheles they that loued *Antonius*, were intercessors to the people for him, and amongest them they sent one *Geminius* vnto *Antonius*, to pray him he would take heede, that through his negligence his Empire were not taken from him, and that he should be counted an enemie to the people of ROME. This *Geminius* being arriued in GRÆCE, made *Cleopatra* ielous straight of his cōming: bicause she surmised that he came not but to speake for *Octauia*. Therefore she spared not to tawnt him all supper tyme, and moreouer to spyte him the more, she made him be[82] set lowest of all at the borde, the which he tooke paciently, expecting occasion to speake with *Antonius*. Now *Antonius* commaunding him at the table to tell him what wind brought him thither: he aunswered him[83], that it was no table talke, and that he would tell him to morrow morning fasting: but dronke or fasting, howsoeuer it were, he was sure of one thing, that all would not go well on his side, vnles *Cleopatra* were sent backe into ÆGYPT. *Antonius* tooke these wordes in very ill part. *Cleopatra* on the other side aunswered him, thou doest well *Geminius*, sayd she, to tell the truth before thou be compelled by torments: but within fewe dayes after, *Geminius* stale away, and fled to ROME. The flatterers also to please *Cleopatra*, did make her driue many other of *Antonius* faithfull seruaunts and friends from him, who could not abide the iniuries done vnto them: amonge the which these two were chiefe, *Marcus Syllanus*, and *Dellius* the Historiographer: who wrote that he fled, bicause her Phisitian *Glaucus* tolde him, that *Cleopatra* had set some secretly to kill him. Furthermore he had *Cleopatraes* displeasure, bicause he sayde one night at supper, that they made

A famous librarie in the citie of Pergamum.

Furnius, an eloquent Orator among the Romanes.

Geminius sent from Rome to Antonius, to bid him take heede to him selfe.

Many of Antonius friends doe forsake him.

---

[82] be] to be 1595, 1603
[83] him] *Om.* 1603

them drinke sower wine, where *Sarmentus* at ROME drancke good wine of
FALERNA. This *Sarmentus* was a pleasaunt younge boye, such as the Lordes of
ROME are wont to haue about them to make them pastyme, which they call
their ioyes, and he was *Octauius Cæsars* boye. Nowe, after[84] *Cæsar* had made
sufficient preparation, [TLN 1864] he proclaymed open warre against *Cleopatra*,
and made the people to abolishe the power and Empire of *Antonius*, bicause he
had before giuen it vppe vnto a woman. [TLN 1872–5] And *Cæsar* sayde
furthermore, that *Antonius* was not Maister of him selfe, but that *Cleopatra* had
brought him beside him selfe, by her charmes and amorous poysons: and that
they that should make warre with them, should be *Mardian* [TLN 1874] the
Euenuke, *Photinus*, and *Iras*, a woman of *Cleopatraes* bedchamber, that friseled
her heare, and dressed her head, and *Charmion*, the which were those that ruled
all the affaires of *Antonius* Empire. Before this warre, as it is reported, many
signes & wonders fel out. First of all, the citie of PISAVRVM which was made
a colony to ROME, and replenished with people by *Antonius*, standing vpon the
shore side of the sea Adriatick, was by a terrible earthquake sonck into the
ground. One of the images of stone which was set vp in the honor of *Antonius*,
in the citie of ALBA, did sweate many dayes together: and though some wyped
it away, yet it left not sweating still. In the citie of PATRAS, whilest *Antonius*
was there, the temple of *Hercules* was burnt with lightning. And at the citie of
ATHENS also, in a place where the warre of the gyants against the goddes is
set out in imagerie: the statue of *Bacchus* with a terrible winde was thrown
downe in the Theater. [999] [TLN 402, 2491, 2803] It was sayd that *Antonius*
came of the race of *Hercules*, as you haue heard before, [TLN 1466–7] and in
the manner of his life he followed *Bacchus*: and therefore he was called the new
Bacchus. Furthermore, the same blustering storme of wind, ouerthrew the great
mōstrous images at ATHENS, that were made in the honor of *Eumenes* and
Attalus, the which men had named and intituled, the *Antonians*, and yet they
did hurt none of the other images which were many besides. [TLN 1978] The
Admirall galley of *Cleopatra*, was called Antoniade, in the which there chaunced
a maruelous ill signe. [TLN 2757–60] Swallowes had bred vnder the poope of
her shippe, & there came others after them that draue away the first, & plucked
downe their neasts. Now when all things were ready, and that they drew neare
to fight: it was found that *Antonius* had no lesse then fiue hundred good ships
of warre, among the[85] which there were many gallies that had eight & ten
bancks of owers, the which were sumptuously furnished, not so meete for fight,
as for triumphe: [TLN 1928–9] a[86] hundred thowsand footemen, & twelue
thowsand horsemen, [TLN 1825–33] & had with him to ayde him these kinges
and subiects following. *Bocchus* king of LYBIA, *Tarcondemus* king of high CILICIA,
Archelaus king of CAPPADOCIA, *Philadelphus* king of PAPHLAGONIA, *Mithridates*
king of COMAGENA, and *Adallas* king of THRACIA. All the[87] which were there
euery man in person. The residue that were absent sent their armies, as *Polemō*

Antonius Empire taken from him.

Signes and wonders before the ciuill warres betwixt Antonius and Oct. Cæsar. Pesaro, a citie in Italy, sonck into the groūd by an earthquake.

An ill signe, foreshewed by swallowes breding in Cleopatraes shippe. Antonius power against Oct. Cæsar.

Antonius had eyght kings, & their power to ayde him.

[84] after] after that 1603
[85] the] *Om.* 1603
[86] a] an 1603
[87] the] *Om.* 1595, 1603

king of PONT, *Manchus* king of ARABIA, *Herodes* king of IVRY: & furthermore, *Amyntas* king of LYCAONIA, & of the GALATIANS: and besides all these, he had all the ayde the king of MEDES sent vnto him. Now for *Cæsar*, he had two hundred and fifty shippes of [88] warre, foure score thowsand[89] footemen, & well neare as many horsemen as his enemy *Antonius*. *Antonius* for his part, had all vnder his dominiō from ARMENIA, & the riuer of Euphrates, vnto the sea IONIVM & ILLYRICVM. *Octauius Cæsar* had also for his part, all that which was in our HEMISPHÆRE, or halfe part of the world, from ILLYRIA, vnto the Occean sea vpon the west: then all from the Occean, vnto Mare Siculū: & from AFRICK, all that which is against ITALY, as GAVLE, & SPAYNE. Furthermore, all from the prouince of CYRENIA, vnto[90] ÆTHIOPIA, was subiect vnto *Antonius*. [TLN 1891–3, 1908–10, 1917] Now *Antonius* was made so subiect to a womans will, that though he was a great deale the stronger by land, yet for *Cleopatraes* sake, he would needes haue this battell tryed by sea: [TLN 1901–5] though he sawe before his eyes, that for lacke of water men, his Captaines did presse[91] by force all sortes of men out of GRÆCE that they could take vp in the field, as trauellers, muletters, reapers, haruest men, and younge boyes, and yet could they not sufficiently furnishe his gallies: so that the most part of them were empty, and could scant rowe, bicause they lacked water men enowe. But on the contrary side, *Cæsars* shippes were not built for pompe, highe, and great, onely for a fight and brauery, but they were light of yarage, armed and furnished with water men as many as they needed, and had them all in readines, [TLN 1884] in the hauens of TARENTVM, and BRVNDVSIVM. So *Octauius Cæsar* sent vnto *Antonius*, to will him to delay no more time, but to come on with his army into ITALY: and that for his owne part he would giue him safe harber, to lande without any trouble, and that he would withdraw his armie from the sea, as farre as one horse could runne, vntil he had put his army a shore, & had lodged his men. [TLN 1896–8, 2181–4] *Antonius* on the other side brauely sent him word againe, and chalenged the combate of him man to[92] man, though he were the elder: and that if he refused him so, he would then fight a battell with him in the fields of PHARSALIA, as *Iulius Cæsar*, and *Pompey* had done before. Now whilest *Antonius* rode at anker, lying idely in harber at the head of ACTIVM, in the place where the citie of NICOPOLIS standeth at this present: [TLN 1883–6, 1924–6] *Cæsar* had quickly passed the sea Ionium, and taken a place called TORYNE, before *Antonius* vnderstoode that he had taken shippe. Then began his men to be affraid, bicause his army by land was left behind. But *Cleopatra* making light of it: and what daunger, I pray you, said she, if *Cæsar* keepe at *TORYNE? The next morning by breake of day, his enemies comming with full force of owers in battell against him, *Antonius* was affraid that if they came to ioyne, they would take and cary away his shippes that had no men of warre in them. [TLN 1919–21] So he armed all his water men, and

The army & power of Octauius Cæsar against Antonius.

Antonius dominions. Octauius Cæsars dominiōs.

Antonius too much ruled by Cleopatra.

Antonius rode at anker at the head of Actiū: where the citie of Nicopolis stādeth.

**The grace of this tawnt can not properly be expressed in any other tongue,*

439

set them in order of battell vpon the forecastell of their shippes, and then lift vp all his rancks of owers towards [TLN 3308] the element, as well of[93] the one side, as the other[94], with the prooes against the enemies, at the entry and mouth of the gulfe, which beginneth at the point of ACTIVM, and so kept them in order of battell, as if they had bene armed and furnished with water men and souldiers. Thus *Octauius Cæsar* beeing finely deceyued by this stratageame, re-[*1000*]tyred presently, and therewithall *Antonius* very wisely and sodainely did cut him of from fresh water. For, vnderstanding that the places where *Octauius Cæsar* landed, had very litle store of water, and yet very bad: he shut them in with stronge ditches and trenches he cast, to keepe them from salying[95] out at their pleasure, and so to goe seeke water further of. [TLN 2562–74, 2600–4] Furthermore, he delt very friendely and curteously with *Domitius*, and against *Cleopatraes* mynde. For, he being sicke of an agewe when he went and tooke a litle boate to goe to[96] *Cæsars* campe, *Antonius* was very sory for it, but yet he sent after him all his caryage, trayne, and men: [TLN 2703–20] and the same *Domitius*, as though he gaue him to vnderstand that he repented his open treason, he[97] died immediatly after. [TLN 2018–19] There were certen kings also that forsooke him, and turned on *Cæsars* side: as *Amyntas*, and *Deiotarus*. Furthermore, his fleete and nauy that was vnfortunate in all thinges, and vnready for seruice, compelled him to chaunge his minde, and to hazard battell by land. [TLN 1897–1900] And *Canidius* also, who had charge of his army by land, when time came to follow *Antonius* determination: he turned him cleane contrary, and counselled him to send *Cleopatra* backe againe, and him selfe to retyre into MACEDON, to fight there on the maine land. And furthermore told him, that *Dicomes* king of the GETES, promised him to ayde him with a great power: and that it should be no shame nor dishonor to him to let *Cæsar* haue the sea, ([TLN 1903–7] bicause him selfe & his men both had bene well practised & exercised in battels by sea, in the warre of SICILIA against *Sextus Pompeius*) [TLN 1909–16] but rather that he should doe against all reason, he hauing so great skill and experience of battells by land as he had, if he should not employ the force and valliantnes of so many lusty armed footemen as he had ready, but would weaken his army by deuiding them into shippes. But now, notwithstanding all these good perswasions, *Cleopatra* forced him to put all to the hazard of battel by sea: considering with her selfe how she might flie, & prouide for her safetie, not to helpe him to winne the victory, but to flie more easily after the battel lost. Betwixt *Antonius* campe & his fleete of shippes, there was a great hie point of firme lande that ranne a good waye into the sea, the which *Antonius* often vsed[98] for a walke, without mistrust of feare or daunger. One of *Cæsars* men perceiued it, & told his Maister that he would laugh &[99] they could take vp *Antonius* in the middest of his walke.

bicause of the equiuocation of this word Toryne, which signifieth a citie of Albania, and also, a ladell to scoome the pot with: as if she ment, Cæsar sat by the fire side scomming of the pot.

Domitius forsaketh Antonius, & goeth vnto Octauius Cæsar. Amyntas, and Deiotarus, do both reuolt from Antonius and goe vnto Cæsar.

Antonius in daunger of taking at Actium.

93 of] on 1603
94 the other] on the other 1603
95 salying] sailing 1603
96 to] vnto 1595, 1603
97 he] *Om.* 1603
98 often vsed] vsed often 1603
99 &] if 1595, 1603

Thereuppon *Cæsar* sent some of his men to lye in ambush for him, & they missed not much of taking of[100] him: for they tooke him that came before him, bicause they discouered to soone, & so *Antonius* scaped verie [TLN 436] hardly. [TLN 1919–20] So when *Antonius* had determined to fight by sea, he set all the other shippes a fire, but three score shippes of ÆGYPT, & reserued onely but the best & greatest gallies, from three bancks, vnto tenne bancks of owers. Into them he put two & twenty thowsand fighting men, with two thowsand darters & slingers. [TLN 1933–9] Now, as he was setting his men in order of battel, there was a Captaine, &[101] a valliant man, that had serued *Antonius* in many battels & conflicts, & had all his body hacked & cut: who as *Antonius* passed by him, cryed out vnto him, & sayd: O, noble Emperor, how commeth it to passe that you trust to these vile brittle shippes? what, doe you mistrust these woundes of myne, and this sword? let the ÆGYPTIANS & PHÆNICIANS fight by sea, and set vs on the maine land, where we vse to conquer, or to be slayne on our feete. *Antonius* passed by him, and sayd neuer a word, but only beckoned to him with his hand & head, as though he willed him to be of good corage, although in deede he had no great corage him selfe. For when the Masters of the gallies & Pilots would haue let their sailes alone, [TLN 2000] he made them clap them on, saying to culler the matter withall, that not one of his enemies should scape. All that day, & the three dayes following, the sea rose so high, & was so boysterous, that the battel was put of. The fift day the storme ceased, & the sea calmed againe, & thē they rowed with force of owers in battaile one against the other: [TLN 1946–7] *Antonius* leading the right wing with *Publicola*, & *Cælius* the left, & *Marcus Octauius*, & *Marcus Iusteius* the middest. *Octauius Cæsar* on thother side, had placed *Agrippa* in the left winge of his armye, and had kept the right winge for him selfe. [TLN 1944–5, 1948] For the armies by lande, *Canidius* was generall of *Antonius* side, [TLN 1953–4, 1961–7] and *Taurus* of *Cæsars* side: who kept their men in battell raye the one before the other, vppon the sea side, without stirring one agaynst the other. Further, touching both the Chieftaynes: *Antonius* being in a swift pinnase, was caried vp and downe by force of owers through his army, & spake to his people to encorage them to fight valliantly, as if they were on maine land, bicause of the steadines & heauines of their ships: & commaunded the Pilots & masters of the [1001] gallies, that they should not sturre, none otherwise then if they were at anker, and so to receiue the first charge of their enemies, and that they should not goe out of the straight of the gulfe. *Cæsar* betymes in the morning going out of his tent, to see his ships thorough out: met a man by chaunce that draue an asse before him. *Cæsar* asked the man what his name was. The poore man told him, his[103] name was *Eutychus*, to say, fortunate: and his asses name Nicon, to say, Conquerer. Therefore *Cæsar* after he had wonne the battell, setting out the market place with the spurres of the gallies he had taken, for a signe of his victorie: he caused also the man and his [TLN 3559] asse to be

Antonius regardeth not the good counsell of his souldier[102].

Battail by sea at Actium, betwixt Antonius and Cæsar.

A lucky signe vnto Octauius Cæsar.

Eutychus Nicon, fortunate Conqueror.

---

[100] of] *Om.* 1603
[101] &] *Om.* 1603
[102] *souldier*] *souldiers* 1603
[103] his] that his 1603

set vp in brasse. When he had visited the order of his armie thorough out, he tooke a litle pinnase, and went to the right wing, and wondered when he sawe his enemies lye stil in the straight, & sturred not. For, decerning them a farre of, men would haue thought they had bene shippes riding at anker, and a good while he was so perswaded: So he kept his gallies eight furlong[104] from his enemies. About noone there rose[105] a litle gale of winde from the sea, and then *Antonius* men waxing angry with tarying so long, and trusting to the greatnes and height of their shipps, as if they had bene inuincible: they began to march forward with their left wing. *Cæsar* seeing that, was a glad man, and began a litle to giue backe from the right wing, to allure them to come further out of the straight & gulfe: to thend that he might with his light shippes well manned with water men, turne and enuirone the gallies of the enemies, the which were heauy of yarage, both for their biggenes, as also for lacke of watermen to row them. When the skirmish began, and that they came to ioyne, there was no great hurt at the first meeting, neither did the shippes vehemently hit one against the other, as they doe commonly in fight by sea. For on the one side, *Antonius* shippes for their heauines, could not haue the strength and swiftnes to make their blowes of any force: and *Cæsars* shippes on thother side tooke great heede, not to rushe & shocke with the forecastells of *Antonius* shippes, whose proues were armed with great brasen spurres. Furthermore they durst not flancke them, bicause their points were easily broken, which way soeuer they came to set vpon his shippes, that were made of great mayne square peeces of tymber, bounde together with great iron pinnes: so that the battel was much like to[106] a battel by land, or to speake more properly, to the assault of a citie. For there were alwaies three or foure of *Cæsars* shippes about one of *Antonius* shippes, and the souldiers fought with their pykes, halberds, and darts, and threw pots and darts with fire. *Antonius* ships on the other side bestowed among them, with their crosbowes and engines of battery, great store of shot from their highe towers of wodde, that were apon their shippes. Now *Publicola* seing *Agrippa* put forth his left wing of *Cæsars* army, to compasse in *Antonius* shippes that fought: [TLN 1998] he was driuen also to loofe of to haue more roome, & going[107] a litle at one side, to put those further of that were affraid, and in the middest of the battel. For they were sore distressed by *Aruntius*[108]. [TLN 1978–9, 1988–94] Howbeit the battell was yet of euen hand, and the victorie doubtfull, being indifferent to both: when sodainely they saw the three score shippes of *Cleopatra* busie[109] about their yard masts, and hoysing saile to flie. So they fled through the middest of them that were in fight, for they had bene placed behind the great shippes, & did maruelously disorder the other shippes. [TLN 2014] For the enemies them selues wondred much to see them saile in that sort, with ful saile towards PELOPONNESVS. [TLN 2047] There *Antonius*

Cleopatra flyeth.

---

[104] furlong] furlongs 1603
[105] rose] arose 1603
[106] to] vnto 1603
[107] going] to go 1603
[108] *Aruntius*] *Antonius* 1603
[109] busie] busily 1603

shewed plainely, that he had not onely lost the corage and hart of an Emperor, but also of a valliant man, [TLN 2009] & that he was not his owne man: (prouing that true which an old man spake in myrth, that the soule of a louer liued in another body, and not in his owne) he was so caried away with the vaine loue of this woman, [TLN 2085–6] as if he had bene glued vnto her, & that she could not haue remoued without mouing of him also. [TLN 1998–2011] For when he saw *Cleopatraes* shippe vnder saile, he forgot, forsooke, & betrayed them that fought for him, & imbarked vpon a galley with fiue bankes of owers, to follow her that had[110] already begon to ouerthrow him, & would in the end be his vtter destruction. When she knew this[111] galley a farre of, she lift vp a signe in the poope of her shippe, and so *Antonius* comming to it, was pluckt vp where *Cleopatra* was, howbeit he saw her not at his first comming, nor she him, [TLN 2048] but went and sate down alone in the prowe of his shippe, and said neuer a word, clapping his head betwene both his hands. In the meane time came certaine light brigantynes of *Cæsars* that followed him hard. So *Antonius* straight turned the prowe of his shippe, and presently put the rest to flight, sauing one *Eurycles*[112] LACEDÆMONIAN, that follow-[*1002*]ed him neare, and prest vpon him with great corage, shaking a dart in his hand ouer the prow, as though he would haue throwen it vnto *Antonius*. *Antonius* seing him, came to the forecastell of his ship, & asked him what he was that durst follow *Antonius* so neare? I am, aunswered he, *Eurycles* the sonne of *Lachares*, who through *Cæsars* good fortune seketh to reuenge the death of my father. This *Lachares* was condemned of fellonie, and beheaded by *Antonius*. But yet *Eurycles* durst not venter on[113] *Antonius* shippe, but set vpon the other Admirall galley (for there were two) and fell with[114] him with such a blowe of his brasen spurre, that was so heauy and bigge, that he turned her round, and tooke her, with another that was loden with very rich stuffe and cariage. After *Eurycles* had left *Antonius*, he returned againe to his place, and sate downe, speaking neuer a word as he did before: and so liued three dayes alone, without speaking to any man. [TLN 2049–59, 2067–9] But when he arriued at the head of Tænarus, there *Cleopatraes* women first brought *Antonius* and *Cleopatra* to speake together, and afterwards, to suppe and lye together. Then beganne there agayne a great number of Marchaunts shippes to gather about them, and some of their friends that had escaped from this ouerthrow: who brought newes, [TLN 2353–5] that his army by sea was ouerthrowen, but that they thought the army by land was yet whole. Thē *Antonius* sent vnto *Canidius*, to returne with his army into ASIA, by MACEDON. Now for him self, he determined to crosse ouer into AFRICK, [TLN 2025–45] & toke one of his carects or hulks loden with gold and siluer, and other rich cariage, and gaue it vnto his friends: commaunding them to depart, and to[115] seeke to saue them selues. They

The soule of a louer liueth in another body.

Antonius flyeth after Cleopatra.

Antonius lycenceth his

---

[110] had] was 1595
[111] this] his 1603
[112] *Eurycles*] *Eurycles* a 1603
[113] on] vpon 1603
[114] with] vpon 1603
[115] to] *Om.* 1603

aunswered him weeping, that they would nether doe it, nor yet forsake him. Then *Antonius* very curteously and louingly did comfort them, and prayed them to depart: and wrote vnto *Theophilus* gouernor of CORINTHE, that he would see them safe, and helpe to hide them in some secret place, vntil they had made their way and peace with *Cæsar*. This *Theophilus* was the father of [TLN 2328–9] *Hipparchus*, who was had in great estimation about *Antonius*. He was the first of all his infranchised bondmen that reuolted from him, and yelded vnto *Cæsar*, and afterwardes went and dwelt at CORINTHE. And thus it stoode with *Antonius*. Now for his armie by sea, that fought before the head or foreland of ACTIVM: they helde out a longe tyme, and nothing troubled them more then a great boysterous wind that rose full in the prooes of their shippes, and yet with much a doe, his nauy was at length ouerthrowen, fiue howers within night. There were not slaine aboue fiue thowsand men: but yet there were three hundred shippes taken, as *Octauius Cæsar* writeth him selfe in his commentaries. Many plainely sawe *Antonius* flie, and yet could[116] hardly beleeue it, [TLN 1928–9] that he that had nyneteene legions whole by lande, and twelue thowsand horsemen vpon the sea side, would so haue forsaken them, and haue fled so cowardly: [TLN 2009] as if he had not oftentimes proued both the one and the other fortune, & that he had not bene throughly acquainted with the diuers chaunges and fortunes of battells. And yet his souldiers still wished for him, and euer hoped that he would come by some meanes or other vnto them. [TLN 1944–8] Furthermore, they shewed them selues so valliant and faithfull vnto him, that after they certainly knewe he was fled, they kept them selues whole together seuen daies. [TLN 2017–19, 2594–5] In the ende *Canidius, Antonius* Lieuetenant, flying by night, and forsaking his campe: when they saw them selues thus destitute of their heads and leaders, they yelded themselues vnto the stronger. This done, *Cæsar* sailed towards ATHENS, and there made peace with the GRÆCIANS, and deuided the rest of the corne that was taken vp for *Antonius* army, vnto the townes and cities of GRÆCE, the which had bene brought to extreme misery & pouerty, cleane without money, slaues, horse, & other beastes of cariage. So that my grandfather *Nicarchus* tolde, that all the Citizens of our citie of CHÆRONEA, (not one excepted) were driuen them selues to cary a certaine measure of corne on their shoulders to the sea side, that lieth directly ouer against the Ile of ANTICYRA, & yet were they driuen thether with whippes. They caried it thus but once: for, the second tyme that they were charged againe to make the like cariage, all the corne being ready to be caried, newes came that *Antonius* had lost the battel, & so scaped our poore city. For *Antonius* souldiers & deputies fled immediatly, & the citizens deuided the corne amongst them. *Antonius* being arriued in LIBYA, he sent *Cleopatra* before into ÆGYPT from the citie of PARÆTONIVM: & he him selfe remained very solitary, hauing onely two of his friends with him, with whom he wandred vp & down, both of them orators, the one *Aristocrates* a GRÆCIAN, [TLN 77–8] & the other *Lu-*[1003]*cilius* a ROMANE. Of whom we haue written in an other place, that at the battell where *Brutus* was ouerthrowen, by the citie of PHILIPPES, he came & willingly put him self into the hands of those that followed *Brutus*, saying

friends to depart, and giueth them a shippe loden with gold and siluer.

Antonius nauy ouerthrowen by Cæsar.

Antonius legions doe yeld them selues vnto Octauius Cæsar.

Lucilius spoke of in Brutus life.

---

[116] could] could very 1595, 1603

that it was he: bicause *Brutus* in the meane time might haue liberty to saue him selfe. And afterwards bicause *Antonius* saued his life, he still remained with him and was very faithfull and frendly vnto him till his death. But when *Antonius* heard, that he whom he had trusted with the gouernment of LIBYA, and vnto whom he had geuen the charge of his armie there, had yelded vnto *Cæsar*: he was so madde withall, that he would haue slaine him selfe for anger, had not his frendes about him withstoode him, and kept him from it. So he went vnto ALEXANDRIA, and there found *Cleopatra* about a wonderfull enterprise, and of great attempt. Betwixt the redde sea, and the sea betwene the landes that poynt vpon the coast of ÆGYPT, there is a litle peece of land that deuideth both the seas, and separateth AFRICKE from ASIA: the which straight is so narrow at the end where the two seas are narrowest, that it is not aboue three hundred furlonges ouer. *Cleopatra* went about to lift her shippes out of the one sea, and to hale them ouer the straight into the other sea: that when her shippes were come into this[117] goulfe of ARABIA, she might then carie all her gold & siluer away, and so with a great companie of men goe and dwell in some place about the Ocean sea farre from the sea Mediterranium, to scape the daunger and bondage of this warre. But now, bicause the ARABIANS dwelling about the citie of PETRA, did burne the first shippes that were brought alande[118], and that *Antonius* thought that his armie by lande, which he left at ACTIVM was yet whole: she left of her enterprise, and determined to keepe all the portes and passages of her realme. *Antonius*, he forsooke the citie and companie of his frendes, and built him a house in the sea, by the Ile of PHAROS, vpon certaine forced mountes which he caused to be cast into the sea, and dwelt there, as a man that banished him selfe from all mens companie: saying that he would lead *Timons* life, bicause he had the like wrong offered him, that was affore[119] offered vnto *Timon*: and that for the vnthankefulnes of those he had done good vnto, and whom he tooke to be his frendes, he was angry with all men, and would trust no man. This *Timon* was a citizen of ATHENS, that liued about the warre of PELOPONNESVS, as appeareth by *Plato*, and *Aristophanes* commedies: in the which they mocked him, calling him a vyper, & malicious man vnto mankind, to shunne all other mens companies, but the companie of young *Alcibiades*, a bolde and insolent youth, whom he woulde greatly feast, and make much of, and kissed him very gladly. *Apemantus* wondering at it, asked him the cause what he ment to make so muche of that young man alone, and to hate all others: *Timon* aunswered him, I do it sayd he, bicause I know that one day he shall do great mischiefe vnto the ATHENIANS. This *Timon* sometimes would haue *Apemantus* in his companie, bicause he was much like to[120] his nature & condicions; and also followed him in maner of life. On a time when they solemnly celebrated the feasts called Choæ at ATHENS, (to wit, the feasts of the dead, where they make sprincklings and sacrifices for the dead) and that they two then feasted together by them selues, *Apemantus* said vnto the other:

The fidelitie of Lucilius vnto Antonius.

The wonderful attempt of Cleopatra.

Antonius followeth the life and example of Timō Misanthropus the Athenian.

Plato, & Aristophanes testimony of Timon Misanthropus, what he was.

---

[117] this] the 1595, 1603
[118] alande] to land 1595, 1603
[119] affore] before 1595, 1603
[120] to] of 1595, 1603

O, here is a trimme banket *Timon. Timon* aunswered againe, yea said he, so
thou wert not here. It is reported of him also, that this *Timon* on a time (the
people being assembled in the market place about dispatch of some affaires)
got vp into the pulpit for Orations, where the Orators commonly vse to speake
vnto the people: & silence being made, euerie man listning to heare what he
would say, bicause it was a wonder to see him in that place: at length he began
to speake in this maner. My Lordes of ATHENS, I haue a litle yard in[121] my
house where there groweth a figge tree, on the which many citizens haue hãged
them selues: & bicause I meane to make some building vpon[122] the place, I
thought good to let you all vnderstand it, that before the figge tree be cut
downe, if any of you be desperate, you may there in time goe hang your selues.
He dyed in the citie of HALES, and was buried vpon the sea side. Nowe it
chaunced so, that the sea getting in, it compassed his tombe rounde about,
that no man coulde come to it: and vpon the same was wrytten this epitaphe.

The epitaphe of
Timon
Misanthropus.

> *Heere lyes a vvretched corse, of vvretched soule bereft,*
> *Seeke not my name: a plague consume you vvicked vvretches left.*

It is reported, that *Timon* him selfe when he liued made this epitaphe: for
that which is [*1004*] commonly rehearsed was not his, but made by the Poet
Callimachus.

> *Heere lye I Timon vvho aliue all liuing men did hate,*
> *Passe by, and curse thy fill: but passe, and stay not here thy gate.*

Many other things could we tell you of this *Timon*, but this litle shall
suffice at this present. But now to returne to *Antonius* againe. *Canidius* him
selfe came to bring him newes, that he had lost all his armie by land at ACTIVM.
[TLN 2017–19, 2591–3] On thother side he was aduertised also, that *Herodes*
king of IVRIE, who had also certeine legions and bandes with him, was reuolted
vnto *Cæsar*, and all the other kings in like maner: so that, sauing those that
were about him, he had none left him. All this notwithstanding did nothing
trouble him, and it seemed that he was contented to forgoe all his hope, and
so to be ridde of all his care and troubles. Thereupon he left his solitarie house
he had built in[123] the sea which he called Timoneon, and *Cleopatra* receiued
him into her royall pallace. He was no sooner comen[124] thither, but he straight
set all the city of[125] rioting and banketing againe, and him selfe, to liberalitie
and giftes. He caused the sonne of *Iulius Cæsar* and *Cleopatra*, to be enrolled
(according to the maner of the ROMANES) amongst the number of young men:
& gaue *Antyllus*, his eldest sonne he had by *Fuluia*, the mans gowne, the which
was a plaine gowne, without gard or imbroderie of purple. For these things,

Antonius rioting
in Alexandria
after his great
losse &
ouerthrow.
Toga virilis.
Antillus, the
eldest sonne of
Antonius by his
wife Fuluia.

---

[121] in] at 1603
[122] vpon] on 1595, 1603
[123] in] by 1595, 1603
[124] comen] com 1595, 1603
[125] of] on 1595, 1603

there was kept great feasting, banketing, and dauncing in ALEXANDRIA many dayes together. In deede they did breake their first order they had set downe, [TLN 51] which they called Amimetobion, (as much to say, no life comparable) & did set vp an other which they called Synapothanumenon (signifying the order and agreement of those that will dye together) the which in exceeding sumptuousnes and cost was not inferior to the first. For their frendes made them selues to be inrolled in this order of those that would dye together, and so made great feastes one to an other: for euerie man when it came to his turne, feasted their whole companie and fraternitie. [TLN 3625–6] *Cleopatra* in the meane time was verie carefull in gathering all sorts of poysons together to destroy men. Now to make proofe of those poysons which made men dye with least paine, she tried it vpon condemned men in prison. For when she saw the poysons that were sodaine and vehement, and brought speedy death with grieuous torments: & in contrary maner, that suche as were more milde and gentle, had not that quicke speede and force to make one dye sodainly: she afterwardes went about to proue the stinging of snakes and adders, and made some to be applied vnto men in her sight, some in one sorte, and[126] some in an other. So when she had dayly made diuers and sundrie proofes, she found none of all them[127] she had proued so fit, [TLN 3495–6, 3561–3, 3614] as the biting of an Aspicke, the which only causeth[128] a heauines of the head, without swounding or complaining, and bringeth a great desire also to sleepe, with a litle swet in the face, and so by litle and litle taketh away the sences and vitall powers, no liuing creature perceiuing that the pacientes feele any paine. For they are so sorie when any bodie waketh[129] them, and taketh them vp: as those that being taken out of a sound sleepe, are very heauy and desirous to sleepe. [TLN 2122–30] This notwithstanding, they sent Ambassadors vnto *Octauius Cæsar* in ASIA, *Cleopatra* requesting the realme of ÆGYPT for her[130] children, and *Antonius* praying that he might be suffered to liue at ATHENS like a priuate man, if *Cæsar* would not let him remaine in ÆGYPT. [TLN 2103, 2110–14] And bicause they had no other men of estimacion about them, for that some were fledde, and those that remained, they did not greatly trust them: they were inforced to sende *Euphronius* the schoolemaister of their children. [TLN 79, 2590–4] For *Alexas* LAODICIAN, who was brought into *Antonius* house and fauor by meanes of *Timagenes*, and afterwards was in greater credit with him, then any other GRECIAN: (for that he had alway[131] bene one of *Cleopatraes* ministers to win *Antonius*, and to ouerthrow all his good determinations to vse his wife *Octauia* well) him *Antonius* had sent vnto *Herodes* king of IVRIE, hoping still to keepe him his frend, that he should not reuolt from him. But he remained there, and betrayed *Antonius*. For where he should haue kept *Herodes* from reuolting from him, he perswaded him to turne to *Cæsar*: & trusting king

An order erected by Antonius, and Cleopatra, called Synapothanumenon, reuoking the former called Amimetobion.

Cleopatra verie busie in prouing the force of poyson.

The property of the biting of an Aspick.

Antonius and Cleopatra send Ambassadors vnto Octauius Cæsar.

---

[126] and] *Om.* 1603
[127] all them] them all 1595, 1603
[128] only causeth] causeth only 1603
[129] waketh] awaketh 1595, 1603
[130] her] their 1595, 1603
[131] alway] euer 1603

Herodes, he presumed to come in *Cæsars* presence. Howbeit *Herodes* did him no pleasure: for he was presently taken prisoner, and sent in chaines to his owne contrie, & there by *Cæsars* commaundement put to death. Thus was *Alexas* in *Antonius* life time put to death, for betraying of him. [TLN 2131–6] Furthermore, *Cæsar* would not graunt vnto *Antonius* requests: but for *Cleopatra*, he made her aunswere, that he woulde deny her nothing reasonable, so that she would either put *Antonius* [1005] to death, or driue him out of her contrie. [TLN 2144] Therewithall he sent *Thyreus* one of his men vnto her, a verie wise and discreete man, who bringing letters of credit from a young Lorde vnto a noble Ladie, and that besides greatly liked her beawtie, might easely by his eloquence haue perswaded her. He was longer in talke with her then any man else was, [TLN 2251–65] and the Queene her selfe also did him great honor: insomuch as he made *Antonius* gealous of him. Whereupon *Antonius* caused him to be taken and well fauoredly whipped, [TLN 2319–31] and so sent him vnto *Cæsar*: and bad him tell him that he made him angrie with him, bicause he shewed him selfe prowde and disdainfull towards him, and now specially when he was easie to be angered, by reason of his present miserie. To be short, if this mislike thee said he, thou hast *Hipparchus* one of my infranchised bondmen with thee: hang him if thou wilt, or whippe him at thy pleasure, that we may crie quittaunce. From thenceforth, *Cleopatra* to cleere her selfe of the suspicion he had of her, she[132] made more of him then euer she did. [TLN 2370–2] For first of all, where she did solemnise the day of her birth very meanely and sparingly, fit for her present misfortune: she now in contrary maner did keepe it with such solemnitie, that she exceeded all measure of sumptuousnes and magnificence: so that the ghests that were bidden to the feasts, and came poore, went away rich. Nowe things passing thus, *Agrippa* by diuers letters sent one after an other vnto *Cæsar*, prayed him to returne to ROME, bicause the affaires there did of necessity require his person and presence. Thereupon he did deferre the warre till the next yeare following: but when winter was done, he returned againe through SYRIA by the coast of AFRICKE, to make warres against *Antonius*, and his other Captaines. When the citie of PELVSIVM was taken, there ran a rumor in the citie, that *Seleucus*, by *Cleopatraes* consent, had surrendered the same. But to cleere her selfe that she did not, *Cleopatra* brought *Seleucus* wife and children vnto *Antonius*, to be reuenged of them at his pleasure. Furthermore, *Cleopatra* had long before made many sumptuous tombes and monumentes, as well for excellencie of workemanshippe, as for height and greatnes of building, ioyning hard to the temple of *Isis*. Thither she caused to be brought all the treasure & pretious things she had of the auncient kings her predecessors: as gold, siluer, emerods, pearles, ebbanie, iuorie, and sinnamon, and besides all that, a maruelous number of torches, faggots, and flaxe. So *Octauius Cæsar* being affrayed to loose suche a treasure and masse of riches[133], and that this woman for spight would set it a fire, and burne it euery whit: he alwayes sent some one or other vnto her from him, to put her in good comfort, whilest he in the meane time drewe neere the citie with his armie. So *Cæsar* came, and pitched

Alexas treason iustly punished.

Pelusium was yeelded vp to Octauius Cæsar.

Cleopatraes monuments set vp by the temple of Isis.

---

[132] she] *Om.* 1603
[133] riches] richesse 1595

his campe hard by the city, in the place where they runne and manage their horses. [TLN 2628–50, 2664–6] *Antonius* made a saly vpon him, and fought verie valliantly, so that he draue *Cæsars* horsemen backe, fighting with his men euen into their campe. Then he came againe to the pallace, greatly boasting of this victorie, and sweetely kissed *Cleopatra*, armed as he was, when he came from the fight, [TLN 2675–81] recommending one of his men of armes vnto her, that had valliantly fought in this skirmish. *Cleopatra* to reward his manlines, gaue him an armor and head peece of cleane gold: howbeit the man at armes when he had receiued this rich gift, stale away by night, and went to *Cæsar.* [TLN 2393–5] *Antonius* sent againe to chalenge *Cæsar*, to fight with him hande to hande. *Cæsar* aunswered him, that he had many other wayes to dye then so. [TLN 2416–19] Then *Antonius* seeing there was no way more honorable for him to dye, then fighting valliantly: he determined to sette vp his rest, both by sea and lande. [TLN 2422–7, 2437–40, 2443–51] So being at supper, (as it is reported) he commaunded his officers and household seruauntes that waited on him at his bord, that they should fill his cuppes full, and make as muche of him as they could: for said he, you know not whether you shall doe so much for me to morrow or not, or whether you shall serue an other maister: and it may be you shall see me no more, but a dead bodie. [TLN 2453–65] This notwithstanding, perceiuing that his frends and men fell a weeping to heare him say so: to salue that he had spoken, he added this more vnto it, that he would not leade them to battell, where he thought not rather safely to returne with victorie, then valliantly to dye with honor. [TLN 2482–2501] Furthermore, the selfe same night within[134] litle of midnight, when all the citie was quiet, full of feare, and sorrowe, thinking what would be the issue and ende of this warre: it is said that sodainly they heard a maruelous sweete harmonie of sundrie sortes of instrumentes of musicke, with the crie of a multitude of people, as they had bene dauncing, [TLN 1466–7] and had song as they vse in *Bacchus* feastes, with mouinges and turninges after the [1006] maner of the Satyres: & it seemed that this daunce went through the city vnto the gate that opened to the enemies, & that all the troupe that made this noise they heard, went out of the city at that gate. Now, such as in reason sought the depth of the interpretacion of this wōder, thought that it was the god vnto whom *Antonius* bare singular deuotion to counterfeate and resemble him, that did forsake them. [TLN 2529, 2741–6, 2754–6] The next morning by breake of day, he went to set those few footemen he had in order vpon the hills adioyning vnto the citie: and there he stoode to behold his gallies which departed from the hauen, and rowed against the gallies of his enemies, and so stoode still, looking what exployte his souldiers in them would do. But when by force of rowing they were come neere vnto them, [TLN 2767–9] they first saluted *Cæsars* men: and then *Cæsars* men resaluted them also, and of two armies made but one, and then did all together row toward the citie. When *Antonius* sawe that his men did forsake him, and yeelded vnto *Cæsar*, and that his footemen were broken and ouerthrowen: he then fled into the citie, [TLN 2766, 2780, 2842–7] crying out that *Cleopatra* had betrayed him vnto them, with whom he had made warre

Straunge noises heard, and nothing seene.

Antonius nauie doe yeeld them selues vnto Cæsar.

Antonius ouerthrowen by Octauius Cæsar.

---

[134] within] within a 1603

for her sake. [TLN 2813–18] Then she being affraied of his fury, fled into the tombe which she had caused to be made, and there locked the dores vnto her, and shut all the springes of the lockes with great boltes, and in the meane time sent vnto *Antonius* to tell him that she was dead. *Antonius* beleuing it, said vnto him selfe: what doest thou looke for further, *Antonius*, sith spitefull fortune hath taken from thee the only ioy thou haddest, for whom thou yet reseruedst thy life? when he had sayd these words, he went into a chamber [TLN 2867] & vnarmed him selfe, and being naked said thus: [TLN 2876–7, 2883, 2889–96] O *Cleopatra*, it grieueth me not that I haue lost thy companie, for I will not be long from thee: but I am sory, that hauing bene so great a Captaine and Emperour, I am in deede condemned to be iudged of lesse corage and noble minde, then a woman. [TLN 2897–2902, 2919–22] Now he had a man of his called *Eros*, whom he loued and trusted much, and whom he had long before caused to sweare vnto him, that he should kill him when he did commaunde him: and then he willed him to keepe his promise. [TLN 2923–36] His man drawing his sworde, lift it vp as though he had ment to haue striken his maister: but turning his head at one side, he thrust his sword into him selfe, and fell downe dead at his maisters foote. [TLN 2937–9] Then said *Antonius*, O noble *Eros*, I thanke thee for this, and it is valliantly done of thee, to shew me what I should doe to my selfe, which thou couldest not doe for me. [TLN 2944–57] Therewithall he tooke his sword, and thrust it into his bellie, and so fell downe vpon a litle bed. The wounde he had killed him not presently, for the blood stinted a litle when he was layed: and when he came somwhat to him selfe againe, he praied them that were about him to dispatch him. But they all fled out of the chamber, and left him crying out & tormenting him selfe: [TLN 2961] vntill at last there came a secretarie vnto him called *Diomedes*, who was commaunded to bring him into the tombe or monument where *Cleopatra* was. [TLN 2985–95] When he heard that she was aliue, he verie earnestlie prayed his men to carie his bodie thither, and so he was caried in his mens armes into the entry of the monument. [TLN 3014–15, 3026–8, 3035–6, 3045] Notwithstãding, *Cleopatra* would not open the gates, but came to the high windowes, and cast out certaine chaines and ropes, in the which *Antonius* was trussed: and *Cleopatra* her owne selfe, with two women only, which she had suffered to come with her into these monumentes, trised *Antonius* vp. [TLN 3049] They that were present to behold it, said they neuer saw so pitiefull a sight. For, they plucked vp poore *Antonius* all bloody as he was, and drawing on with pangs of death, who holding vp his hands to *Cleopatra*, raised vp him selfe as well as he could. [TLN 3038–45] It was a hard thing for these women to do, to lift him vp: but *Cleopatra* stowping downe with her head, putting to all her strength to her vttermost power, did lift him vp with much a doe, and neuer let goe her hold, with the helpe of the women beneath that bad her be of good corage, and were as sorie to see her labor so, as she her selfe. So when she had gotten him in after that sorte, and layed him on a bed: she rent her garments vpon him, clapping her brest, and scratching her face & stomake. Then she dried vp his blood that had berayed his face, and called him her Lord, [TLN 3538] her husband, and Emperour, forgetting her owne miserie and calamity, for the pitie and compassion she tooke of him. [TLN 3051] *Antonius* made her ceasse her lamenting, and called for wine, either bicause he was a

Cleopatra flieth into her tombe or monument.

Eros Antonius seruant, slue him selfe.

Antonius did thrust his sword into him selfe, but died not presently.

Antonius caried vnto Cleopatraes tombe.

A lamentable sight to see Antonius and Cleopatra.

thirst, or else for that he thought thereby to hasten his death. When he had dronke, [TLN 3056] he earnestly prayed her, and perswaded her, that she would seeke to saue her life, if she could possible, without reproache and dishonor: [TLN 3059, 3215–16] and that chiefly she should trust *Proculeius* aboue any man else about *Cæsar*. [TLN 3062–9] And as [*1007*] for him selfe, that she should not lament nor sorowe for the miserable chaunge of his fortune at the end of his dayes: but rather that she should thinke him the more fortunate, for the former triumphes & honors he had receiued, considering that while he liued he was the noblest and greatest Prince of the world, & that now he was ouercome, not cowardly, but valiantly, a ROMANE by an other ROMANE. As *Antonius* gaue the last gaspe, *Proculeius* came that was sent from *Cæsar*. [TLN 2958–60, 3117–39] For after *Antonius* had thrust his sworde in him selfe, as they caried him into the tombes and monuments of *Cleopatra*, one of his gard called *Dercetæus*, tooke his sword with the which he had striken him selfe, and hidde it: then he secretly stale away, and brought *Octauius Cæsar* the first newes of his death, & shewed him his sword that was bloodied. [TLN 3140–65] *Cæsar* hearing these newes, straight withdrewe him selfe into a secret place of his tent, and there burst out with teares, lamenting his hard and miserable fortune, that had bene his frende and brother in law, his equall in the Empire, and companion with him in sundry great exploytes and battells. Then he called for all his frendes, [TLN 3195–9] and shewed them the letters *Antonius* had written to him, and his aunsweres also sent him againe, during their quarrell and strife: & how fiercely and prowdly the other answered him, to all iust and reasonable matters he wrote vnto him. [TLN 3181–6] After this, he sent *Proculeius*, and commaunded him to doe what he could possible to get *Cleopatra* aliue, fearing least otherwise all the treasure would be lost: and furthermore, he thought that if he could take *Cleopatra*, and bring her aliue to ROME, [TLN 3450–64] she would maruelously beawtifie and sette out his triumphe. [TLN 3217–18] But *Cleopatra* would neuer put her selfe into *Proculeius* handes, although they spake together. For *Proculeius* came to the gates that were very[135] thicke & strong, and surely barred, but yet there were some cranewes through the which her voyce might be heard, and so they without vnderstoode, [TLN 3218–27] that *Cleopatra* demaunded the kingdome of ÆGYPT for her sonnes: and that *Proculeius* aunswered her, that she should be of good cheere, and not be affrayed to referre all vnto *Cæsar*. After he had viewed the place verie well, he came and reported her aunswere vnto *Cæsar*. [TLN 3190] Who immediatly sent *Gallus* to speake once againe with her, and bad him purposely hold her with talke, [TLN 3241] whilest *Proculeius* did set vp a ladder against that high windowe, by the which *Antonius* was trised vp, and came downe into the monument with two of his men hard by the gate, where *Cleopatra* stoode to heare what *Gallus* sayd vnto her. [TLN 3244] One of her women which was shut[136] in her monumēts with her, saw *Proculeius* by chaunce as he came downe, and shreeked out: O, poore *Cleopatra*, thou art taken. Then when she sawe *Proculeius* behind her as she came from the gate, [TLN 3245] she thought to haue stabbed her selfe in with a

---

[135] very] *Om.* 1603
[136] shut] shut vp 1603

short dagger she ware[137] of purpose by her side. [TLN 3246–53] But *Proculeius* *Cleopatra taken.*
came sodainly vpon her, and taking her by both the hands, said vnto her.
Cleopatra, first thou shalt doe thy selfe great wrong, and secondly vnto *Cæsar*:
to depriue him of the occasion and oportunitie, openly to shew his bountie and
mercie, and to geue his enemies cause to accuse the most curteous and noble
Prince that euer was, and to appeache him, [TLN 3357] as though he were a
cruell and mercielesse man, that were not to be trusted. So euen as he spake
the word, he tooke her dagger from her, and shooke her clothes for feare of
any poyson hidden about her. [TLN 3275] Afterwardes *Cæsar* sent one of his
infranchised men called *Epaphroditus*, whom he straightly charged to looke well
vnto her, and to beware in any case that she made not her selfe away: and for
the rest, to vse her with all the curtesie possible. And for him selfe, he in the *Cæsar tooke the*
meane time entred the citie of ALEXANDRIA, and as he went, talked with the *citie of*
Philosopher *Arrius*, and helde him by the hande, to the end that his contrie *Alexandria.*
men should reuerence him the more, bicause they saw *Cæsar* so highly esteeme *Cæsar greatly*
and honor him. Then he went into the show place of exercises, and so vp to *honored Arrius*
his chaire of state which was prepared for him of a great height: and there *the Philosopher.*
according to his commaundement, all the people of ALEXANDRIA were assem-
bled, who quaking for feare, fell downe on their knees before him, and craued
mercie. *Cæsar* bad them all stande vp, and told them openly that he forgaue
the people, and pardoned the felonies and offences they had committed against
him in this warre. First, for the founders sake of the same citie, which was
Alexander the great: secondly, for the beawtie of the citie, which he muche
esteemed and wondred at: thirdly, for the loue he bare vnto his verie frend
Arrius. Thus did *Cæsar* honor *Arrius*, who craued pardon for him selfe and many
others, & specially for *Philostratus*, the eloquentest man of all the sophisters and *Philostratus, the*
Orators of his time, for present and sodaine speech: howbeit he falsly [1008] *eloquentest*
named him selfe an Academicke Philosopher. Therefore, *Cæsar* that hated his *Orator in his*
nature & condicions, would not heare his sute. Thereupon he let his gray beard *time, for present*
grow long, and followed *Arrius* steppe by steppe in a long mourning gowne, *speech vpon a*
still bussing in his eares this Greeke verse: *sodaine.*

> *A vvise man if that he be vvise in deede,*
> *May by a vvise man haue the better speede.*

    Cæsar vnderstanding this, not for the desire he had to deliuer *Philostratus*
of his feare, as to ridde *Arrius* of malice & enuy that might haue fallen out
against him: he pardoned him. Now touching *Antonius* sonnes, *Antyllus*, his *Antyllus,*
eldest sonne by *Fuluia* was slaine, bicause his schoolemaister *Theodorus* did betray *Antonius eldest*
him vnto the souldiers, who strake of his head. And the villaine tooke a pretious *sonne by Fuluia,*
stone of great value from his necke, the which he did sowe in his girdell, and *slaine.*
afterwards denied that he had it: but it was founde about him, and so *Cæsar*
trussed him vp for it. [TLN 3359–61] For *Cleopatraes* children, they were verie
honorablie kept, with their gouernors and traine that waited on them. But for
Cæsarion, who was sayd to be *Iulius Cæsars* sonne: his mother *Cleopatra* had sent

---

[137] ware] wore 1603

him vnto the INDIANS through ÆTHIOPIA, with a great summe of money. But one of his gouernors also called *Rhodon*, euen such an other as *Theodorus*, perswaded him to returne into his contrie, & told him that *Cæsar* sent for him to geue him his mothers kingdom. So, as *Cæsar* was determining with him selfe what he should doe, *Arrius* sayd vnto him.

    Too Many Cæsars is not good.

Alluding vnto a certaine verse of *Homer* that sayth:

    Too Many Lords doth not vvell.

The saying of Arrius the Philosopher.

    Therefore *Cæsar* did put *Cæsarion* to death, after the death of his mother *Cleopatra*. Many Princes, great kings and Captaines did craue *Antonius* body of *Octauius Cæsar*, to giue him honorable burial: but *Cæsar* would neuer take it from *Cleopatra*, who did sumptuously and royally burie him with her owne handes, whom *Cæsar* suffred to take as much as she would to bestow vpon his funeralls. [TLN 3258–61] Now was she altogether ouercome with sorow & passion of minde, for she had knocked her brest so pitifully, that she had martired it, and in diuers places had raised vlsers and inflamacions, so that she fell into a feuer withal: whereof she was very glad, hoping thereby to haue good colour to absteine from meate, and that so she might haue dyed easely without any trouble. [TLN 3624–6] She had a Phisition called *Olympus*, whom she made priuie of her intent, to thend he shoulde helpe her[138] to ridde her out of her life: as *Olympus* wryteth him selfe, who wrote a booke of all these thinges. But *Cæsar* mistrusted the matter, by many coniectures he had, [TLN 3356–61] and therefore did put her in feare, & threatned her to put her children to shameful death. With these threats, *Cleopatra* for feare yelded straight, as she would haue yelded vnto strokes: and afterwards suffred her selfe to be cured and dieted as they listed. [TLN 3336–8] Shortly after, *Cæsar* came him selfe in person to see her, and to comfort her. *Cleopatra* being layed vpon [TLN 3626] a litle low bed in poore estate, when she sawe *Cæsar* come into her chamber, she[139] sodainly rose vp, naked in her smocke, and fell downe at his feete maruelously disfigured: both for that she had plucked her heare from her head, as also for that she had martired all her face with her nailes, and besides, her voyce was small and trembling, her eyes sonke into her heade with continuall blubbering and moreouer, they might see the most parte of her stomake torne in sunder. To be short, her bodie was not much better then her minde: yet her good grace and comelynes, and the force of her beawtie was not altogether defaced. But notwithstanding this ougly and pitiefull state of hers, yet she showed her selfe within, by her outward lookes and countenance. [TLN 2218–26, 3339–42] When *Cæsar* had made her lye downe againe, and sate by her beddes side: *Cleopatra* began to cleere and excuse her selfe for that she had done, laying all to the feare she had of *Antonius*. *Cæsar*, in contrarie maner, reproued

Cæsariō Cleopatraes sonne, put to death.

Cleopatra burieth Antonius.

Olympus Cleopatraes Phisition.

Cæsar came to see Cleopatra.

Cleopatra, a martired creature, through her owne passion and fury.

---

[138] her] *Om.* 1603
[139] she] *Om.* 1603

her in euery poynt. Then she sodainly altered her speache, and prayed him to pardon her, as though she were affrayed to dye, & desirous to liue. [TLN 3366–3405] At length, she gaue him a breefe and memoriall of all the readie money & treasure she had. But by chaunce there stoode *Seleucus* by, one of her Treasorers, who to seeme a good seruant, came straight to *Cæsar* to disproue *Cleopatra*, that she had not set in al, but kept many things back of purpose. *Cleopatra* was in such a rage with him, that she flew vpon him, and tooke him by the heare of the head, and boxed him wellfauoredly. *Cæsar* fell a laughing, and parted the fray. Alas, said she, O *Cæsar*: is not this a great shame and reproche, that thou hauing vouchesaued to take the peines [*1009*] to come vnto me, and hast[140] done me this honor, poore wretche, and caitife creature, brought into this pitiefull & miserable estate[141]: and that mine owne seruaunts should come now to accuse me, though it may be I haue reserued some iuells & trifles meete for women, but not for me (poore soule) to set out my selfe withall, but meaning to geue some pretie presents & gifts vnto *Octauia* and *Liuia*, that they making meanes & intercession for me to thee, thou mightest yet extend thy fauor and mercie vpon me? *Cæsar* was glad to heare her say so, perswading him selfe thereby that she had yet a desire to saue her life. [TLN 3411–21] So he made her answere, that he did not only geue her that to dispose of at her pleasure, which she had kept backe, but further promised to vse her more honorably and bountifully then she would thinke for: and so he tooke his leaue of her, supposing he had deceiued her, but in deede he was deceiued him selfe. [TLN 3275ff., 3435–42] There was a young gentleman *Cornelius Dolabella*, that was one of *Cæsars* very great familiars, & besides did beare no euil[142] will vnto *Cleopatra*. He sent her word secretly as she had requested him, that *Cæsar* determined to take his iorney through SVRIA, & that within three dayes he would sende her away before with her children. When this was tolde *Cleopatra*, she requested *Cæsar* that it would please him to suffer her to offer the last oblations of the dead, vnto the soule of *Antonius*. This being graunted her, she was caried to the place where his tombe was, & there falling downe on her knees, imbracing the tombe with her women, the teares running downe her cheekes, she began to speake in this sorte: O my deare Lord *Antonius*, not[143] long sithence I buried thee here, being a free woman: and now I offer vnto thee the funerall sprinklinges and oblations, being a captiue and prisoner, and yet I am forbidden and kept from tearing & murdering this captiue body of mine with blowes, which they carefully gard and keepe, onely to triumphe of thee: looke therefore henceforth for no other honors, offeringes, nor sacrifices from me, for these are the last which *Cleopatra* can geue thee, sith nowe they carie her away. Whilest we liued together, nothing could seuer our companies: but now at our death, I feare me they will make vs chaunge our contries. For as thou being a ROMANE, hast bene buried in ÆGYPT: euen so wretched creature I, an ÆGYPTIAN, shall be buried in ITALIE, which shall be all the good that I haue receiued by thy contrie. If therefore the gods where thou art now haue

Seleucus, one of Cleopatraes Treasorers. Cleopatra bet her treasorer before Octauius Cæsar.

Cleopatraes wordes vnto Cæsar.

Cleopatra finely deceiueth Octauius Cæsar, as though she desired to liue.

Cleopatraes lamentation ouer Antonius tombe.

---

[140] hast] *Om.* 1603
[141] estate] state 1603
[142] euil] ill 1603
[143] not] it is not 1603

any power and authoritie, sith our gods here haue forsaken vs: suffer not thy
true frend and louer to be caried away aliue, that in me, they triumphe of thee:
but receiue me with thee, and let me be buried in one selfe tombe with thee.
For though my griefes and miseries be infinite, yet none hath grieued me more,
nor that I could lesse beare withall: then this small time, which I haue bene
driuē to liue alone without thee. Then hauing ended these dolefull plaints, and
crowned the tombe with [TLN 84] garlands and sundry nosegayes, and maruelous louingly imbraced the same: [TLN 3472–5] she commaunded they
should prepare her bath, and when she had bathed and washed her selfe, she
fell to her meate, and was sumptuously serued. Nowe whilest she was at dinner,
[TLN 3482–3530] there came a contrieman, and brought her a basket. The
souldiers that warded at the gates, asked him straight what he had in his basket.
He opened the basket, and tooke out the leaues that couered the figges, and
shewed them that they were figges he brought. They all of them maruelled to
see so goodly figges. The contrieman laughed to heare them, and bad them
take some if they would. They beleued he told them truely, and so bad him
carie them in. After *Cleopatra* had dined, she sent a certaine table written and
sealed vnto *Cæsar*, [TLN 3200] and commaunded them all to go out of the
tombes where she was, but the two women, then she shut the dores to her.
Cæsar when he receiued this table, and began to read her lamentation and
petition, requesting him that he would let her be buried with *Antonius*, [TLN
3567–3601] founde straight what she ment, and thought to haue gone thither
him selfe: howbeit he sent one before in all hast that might be, to see what it
was. Her death was very sodaine. For those whom *Cæsar* sent vnto her ran
thither in all hast possible, & found the souldiers standing at the gate, mis-
trusting nothing, nor vnderstanding of her death. But when they had opened
the dores, they founde *Cleopatra* starke dead, layed vpon a bed of gold, [TLN
3474, 3531] attired and araied in her royall robes, [TLN 3544] and one of her
two women, which was called *Iras*, dead at her feete: [TLN 3572–3, 3608–
11] and her other woman called *Charmion* halfe dead, and trembling, trimming
the Diademe which *Cleopatra* ware vpon her head. [TLN 3583–7] One of the
souldiers seeing her, angrily sayd vnto her: is that well done *Charmion*? Verie
well sayd she againe, and meete for a Princes discended from the race of so
many noble kings. She sayd no [1010] more, but fell downe dead hard by the
bed. [TLN 3482–4, 3603–5, 3620–2] Some report that this Aspicke was
brought vnto her in the basket with figs, & that she had cōmaunded them to
hide it vnder the figge leaues, that when she shoulde thinke to take out the
figges, the Aspicke shoulde bite her before she should see her: howbeit, that
when she would haue taken away the leaues for the figges, she perceiued it,
and said, art thou here then? And so, her arme being naked, she put it to the
Aspicke to be bitten. Other say againe, she kept it in a boxe, and that she did
pricke and thrust it with a spindell of golde, [TLN 3557–8] so that the Aspicke
being angerd withall, lept out with great furie, and bitte her in the arme.
Howbeit fewe can tell the troth. For they report also, that she had hidden
poyson in a hollow raser which she caried in the heare of her head: [TLN
3613–14] and yet was there no marke seene of her bodie, or any signe discerned
that she was poysoned, neither also did they finde this serpent in her tombe.
But it was reported onely, [TLN 3620–2] that there were seene certeine fresh

The death of
Cleopatra.

Cleopatraes two
waiting women
dead with her.

Cleopatra killed
with the biting
of an Aspicke.

steppes or trackes where it had gone, on the tombe side toward the sea, and specially by the dores side[144]. [TLN 3566, 3617–19, 3623–4] Some say also, that they found two litle [TLN 3495] pretie bytings in her arme, scant to be discerned: the which it seemeth *Cæsar* him selfe gaue credit vnto, bicause in his triumphe he caried *Cleopatraes* image, with an Aspicke byting of her arme. And thus goeth the report of her death. [TLN 3626–33] Now *Cæsar*, though he was maruelous sorie for the death of *Cleopatra*, yet he wondred at her noble minde and corage, and therefore commaunded she should be nobly buried, and layed by *Antonius*: and willed also that her two women shoulde haue honorable buriall. *Cleopatra* dyed being eight and thirtie yeare[145] olde, after she had raigned two and twenty yeres, and gouerned aboue foureteene of them with *Antonius*. And for *Antonius*, some say that he liued three and fiftie yeares: and others say, six and fiftie. All his statues, images, and mettalls, were plucked downe and ouerthrowen, sauing those of *Cleopatra* which stoode still in their places, by meanes of *Archibius* one of her frendes, who gaue *Cæsar* a thowsande talentes that they should not be handled, as those of *Antonius* were. *Antonius* left seuen children by three wiues, of the which, *Cæsar* did put *Antyllus*, the eldest sonne he had by *Fuluia*, to death. *Octauia* his wife tooke all the rest, and brought them vp with hers, and maried *Cleopatra, Antonius* daughter, vnto king *Iuba*, a maruelous curteous & goodly Prince. And *Antonius*, the sonne of *Fuluia* came to be so great, that next vnto *Agrippa*, who was in greatest estimacion about *Cæsar*, and next vnto the children of *Liuia*, which were the second in estimacion: he had the third place. Furthermore, *Octauia* hauing had two daughters by her first husband *Marcellus*, and a sonne also called *Marcellus: Cæsar* maried his daughter vnto that *Marcellus*, and so did adopt him for his sonne. And *Octauia* also maried one of her daughters vnto *Agrippa*. But when *Marcellus* was deade, after he had bene maried a while, *Octauia* perceiuing that her brother *Cæsar* was very busie to choose some one among his frends, whom he trusted best to make his sonne in law: she perswaded him, that *Agrippa* should mary his daughter, (*Marcellus* widow) and leaue her owne daughter. *Cæsar* first was contented withall, and then *Agrippa*: and so she afterwards tooke away her daughter and maried her vnto *Antonius*, and *Agrippa* maried *Iulia, Cæsars* daughter. Now there remained two daughters more of *Octauia* and *Antonius*. *Domitius AEnobarbus* maried the one: and the other, which was *Antonia*, so fayer and vertuous a young Ladie, was maried vnto *Drusus* the sonne of *Liuia*, and sonne in law of *Cæsar*. Of this mariage, came *Germanicus* and *Clodius*: of the which, *Clodius* afterwards came to be Emperour. And of the sonnes of *Germanicus*, the one whose name was *Caius*, came also to be Emperour: who, after he had licentiously raigned a time, was slaine, with his wife and daughter. *Agrippina* also, hauing a sonne by her first husbande *AEnobarbus* called *Lucius Domitius*: was afterwardes maried vnto *Clodius*, who adopted her sonne, and called him *Nero Germanicus*. This *Nero* was Emperour in our time, and slue his owne mother, and[146] had almost destroyed the Empire of ROME, through his madnes and wicked life, being the fift Emperour of ROME after *Antonius*.

The image of Cleopatra, caried in triumphe at Rome, with an Aspicke biting of her arme.

The age of Cleopatra and Antonius.

Of Antonius issue came Emperors.

---

[144] dores side] doore side 1595; dooreside 1603
[145] yeare] yeares 1603
[146] and] *Om.* 1595

THE COMPARISON OF
Demetrius with Antonius.

Now, sithence it falleth out, that *Demetrius* and *Antonius* were one of them much like to the other, hauing fortune a like diuers and variable vnto them: let vs therefore come to consider their power and authoritie, and how they came to be so great. First of all, it is certaine that *Demetrius* power and greatnes fell vnto him by inheritance from his father *Antigonus*: who became the greatest and mightiest Prince of all the successors of *Alexander*, and had won the most parte of ASIA, before *Demetrius* came of full age. *Antonius* in contrary maner, borne of an honest man, who otherwise was no man of warre, and had not left him any meane to arise to such greatnes: durst take vpon him to contend for the Empire with *Cæsar*, that had no right vnto it by inheritaunce, but yet made him selfe successor of the power, the which the other by great paine and trauell had obteyned, and by his owne industrie became so great, without the helpe of any other: that the Empire of the whole worlde being deuided into two partes, he had the one halfe, and tooke that of the greatest countenaunce and power. *Antonius* being absent, oftentimes ouercame the PARTHIANS in battell by his Lieutenaunts, and chased away the barbarous people dwelling about mount Caucasus, vnto the sea Hyrcanium: insomuche as the thing they most reproue him for, did most witnes his greatnes. For, *Demetrius* father made him gladly marrie *Phila, Antipaters* daughter, although she was too old for him: bicause she was of a nobler house then him selfe. *Antonius* on thother side was blamed for marying of *Cleopatra*, a Queene that for power and nobilitie of blood, excelled all other kings in her time, but *Arsaces*: and moreouer made him selfe so great, that others thought him worthie of greater things, then he him selfe required. Now for the desire that moued the one and the other to conquer realmes: the desire of *Demetrius* was vnblameable & iust, desiring to raigne ouer people, which had bene gouerned at all times, & desired to be gouerned by kings. But *Antonius* desire was altogether wicked & tyrannicall: who sought to keepe the people of ROME in bondage and subiection, but lately before rid of *Cæsars* raigne and gouernment. For the greatest and most famous exployte *Antonius* euer did in warres (to wit, the warre in the which he ouerthrew *Cassius* and *Brutus*) was begon to no other ende, but to depriue his contriemen of their libertie and freedom. *Demetrius* in contrarie maner, before fortune had ouerthrowen him, neuer left to set GRÆCE at libertie, and to driue the garrisons away, which kept the cities in bondage: and not like *Antonius*, that bosted he had slaine them that had set ROME at libertie. The chiefest thing they commended in *Antonius*, was his liberalitie and bountie: in the which *Demetrius* excelled him so farre, that he gaue more to his enemies, then *Antonius* did to his frends: although he was maruelously well thought of, for the honorable and sumptuous funerall he gaue vnto *Brutus* bodie. Howbeit *Demetrius* caused all [1012] his enemies be buried that were slaine in battel, and returned vnto *Ptolomy* all the prisoners he had taken, with great giftes and presentes he gaue them. They were both in their prosperitie, verie riotouslie and licentiouslie geuen: [TLN 455–63] but yet no man can euer say, that *Demetrius* did at any time let slippe any oportunitie or occasion to followe great matters, but onelie gaue him selfe in deede to pleasure, when he had nothing else to doe. And

457

further, to say truely, he tooke pleasure of *Lamia*, as a man woulde haue a delight to heare one tell tales, when he hath nothing else to doe, or is desirous to sleepe: [TLN 2510–13] but in deede when he was to make any preparation for warre, he had not then Iuey at his darts end, nor had his helmet perfumed, nor came not out of Ladies closets, picked and princt to go to battell: but he let all dauncing and sporting alone, and became as the Poet *Euripides* saith,

> *The souldier of Mars, cruell, and bloodie.*

But to conclude, he neuer had ouerthrowe or misfortune through negligence, nor by delaying time to followe his owne pleasure: as we see in painted tables, [TLN 1050–1] where *Omphale* secretlie stealeth away *Hercules* clubbe, and tooke his Lyons skinne from him. Euen so *Cleopatra* oftentimes vnarmed *Antonius*, and intised him to her, making him lose matters of great importaunce, and verie needefull iorneys, to come and be dandled with her, about the riuers of Canobus, and Taphosiris. In the ende, as *Paris* fledde from the battell, and went to hide him selfe in *Helens* armes: euen so did he in *Cleopatraes* armes, or to speake more properlie, *Paris* hidde him selfe in *Helens* closet, but *Antonius* to followe *Cleopatra*, fledde and lost the victorie. Furthermore, *Demetrius* had many wiues that he had maried, and all at one time: the which was not dissalowable or not forbidden by the kinges of MACEDON, but had bene vsed from *Philippe* and *Alexanders* time, as also king *Lysimachus* and *Ptolomy* had, and did honor all them that he maried. [TLN 3538] But *Antonius* first of all maried two wiues together, the which neuer ROMANE durst doe before, but him selfe. Secondly, he put away his first ROMANE wife, which he had lawfully maried: for the loue of a straunge woman, he fondly fell in fancy withall, and contrarie to the lawes and ordinaunces of ROME. And therefore *Demetrius* mariages neuer hurt him, for any wrong he had done to his wiues: but *Antonius* contrarily was vndone by his wiues. Of all the lasciuious partes *Antonius* played, none were so abhominable, as this onely fact of *Demetrius*. For the historiographers write, that they would not suffer dogges to come into the castell of ATHENS, bicause of all beastes he is too busie with bitcherie: and *Demetrius*, in *Mineruaes* temple it selfe lay with Curtisans, and there defiled many citizens wiues. And besides all this, the horrible vice of crueltie, which a man would thinke were least mingled with these wanton delightes, is ioyned with *Demetrius* concupiscence: who suffered, (or more properly compelled) the goodliest young boy of ATHENS, to dye a most pitiefull death, to saue him selfe from violence, being taken. And to conclude, *Antonius* by his incontinencie, did no hurte but to him selfe: and *Demetrius* did hurte vnto all others. *Demetrius* neuer hurte any of his frendes: and *Antonius* suffered his Vncle by his mothers side to be slaine, that he might haue his will of *Cicero* to kill him: a thing so damnable, wicked, and cruell of it selfe, that he hardlie deserued to haue bene pardoned, though he had killed *Cicero*, to haue saued his Vncles life. Nowe where they falsefied and brake their othes, the one making *Artabazus* prisoner, and the other killing of *Alexander:* *Antonius* out of doubt had best cause, and iustest colour. For *Artabazus* had betrayed him, and forsaken him in MEDIA. But *Demetrius* (as diuers doe reporte) deuised a false matter to accuse *Alexander*, to cloke the murther he had committed: and some thinke he did accuse him, to whom he him selfe had done

Canobus, and Taphosiris fl.

Demetrius & Antonius wiues.

Antonius the first Romane that euer maried two wiues together.

Demetrius lasciuiousnes.

Dogges not suffred in Athens castle, bicause of bitcherie.

The loue and impietie: the faith & falsehoode of Demetrius and Antonius.

iniurie vnto: and was not reuenged of him, that woulde doe him iniurie. Furthermore, *Demetrius* him selfe did many noble feates in warre, as we haue recited of him before: and contrarilie *Antonius*, when he was not there in person, wanne many famous and great victories by his Lieutenauntes: and they were both ouerthrowen being personallie in battell, but yet not both after one sorte. For the one was forsaken of his men being MACEDONIANS, and the other contrarily forsooke his that were ROMANES: for he fled, & left them that ventred their liues for his honor. So that the fault the one did was, that he made them his enemies that fought for him: and the fault in the other, that he so beastlie left them that loued him best, and were most faithfull to him. And for their deathes, a man can not praise the one nor [1013] the other, but yet *Demetrius* death the more reproachefull. For he suffered him selfe to be taken prisoner, and when he was sent away to be kept in a straunge place, he had the hart to liue yet three yeare longer, to serue his mouth and bellie, as brute beastes doe. *Antonius* on the other side slue him selfe, (to confesse a troth) cowardly, and miserably, to his great paine and griefe: and yet was it before his bodie came into his enemies hands.

Margin note: Demetrius & Antonius acts in warres.

GOULART

That Sh. drew on Simon Goulart's *Life of Octavius Cæsar Augustus* for his Octavius seems unlikely to MACCALLUM (1910, p. 649), who calls the *Life* a "dull performance" merely hinting at ideas better stated by Appian. BULLOUGH (1964, 5:247), however, who calls the *Life* a "probable source" for *Ant.*, is the first to note that Sh. may have found confirmation in Goulart for Octavius's "aloof efficiency" in Plutarch. Far more graphically than Plutarch, Goulart portrays a man who allows no private interests to stand in the way of his public efficiency. ERSKINE-HILL (1983, p. 156; similarly 1970, p. 43) points to Goulart's stress on "Augustus as a bringer of order, whether in civil customs and laws, or in the military and political state of the Empire. He is endowed with some dim intimations of the birth of Christ, but his cunning and politic side is also given due weight. . . . [Goulart] helped Shakespeare to the complex picture he gives of the Caesar just about to become the Emperor Augustus," since the traits Goulart gives to Octavius form an important part of Sh.'s concept of the character. The excerpt given here covers Octavius's life to the death of Antony, omitting a section on the proscriptions. Goulart's account helps explain some aspects of Sh.'s description of the historical situation, especially Fulvia's wars and Pompey's death, but mainly Octavius's character. See also nn. 1743–4 and 2581.

The Life of Octavius Cæsar Augustus (1602)

North's translation of Simon Goulart's *Life of Octavius Caesar* appeared in a folio collection in 1602 with the following title page: "THE LIVES | OF EPAMINON-DAS, | OF PHILIP OF MACEDON, OF | DIONYSIVS THE ELDER, AND OF OCTAVIVS | CÆSAR AVGVSTVS: COLLECTED | out of good Authors. | Also the liues of nine excellent Chieftaines of warre, taken | out of Latine from EMYLIVS

459

PROBVS, by S.G.S. | *By whom also are added the liues of* Plutarch *and of* Seneca: | Gathered together, disposed, and enriched | as the others. | And now translated into English by Sir THOMAS | NORTH Knight. | [device] | Imprinted at London by Richard Field | 1602." The typographical conventions used in the modified diplomatic reprint below are the same as for North's Plutarch.

The text is based on the copy in the Huntington Library (*STC* 20071). The work is also included in the edition of Plutarch by SKEAT (1875; 1880, pp. 230–77).

Parallels with *Ant.* 787–8 and 1743–4 occur on pp. 464 and 466.

THE LIFE OF [*51*]

Octauius Cæsar Augustus.

Thy youth Augustus, and thy tongues good gift,
Thy valour, wisedome, and thy worthy feats,
Thy countries loue, thy lawes and statutes, lift
Thy throne aboue all other princely seates.

Accia, the daughter of *Accius Balbus* and of *Iulia* the sister of *Iulius Cæsar*, was maried vnto the father of this man, whose life we write of now, and who was descended of the auncient race of the *Octauians*, issued out of the countrey of the VOLSCES, and knowne at ROME from the time of *Tarquinius*, and of *Seruius Tullus*. Their sonne *Octauius* was borne in the yeare of the Consulship of *Cicero* and of *Caius Antonius*, at that time when as the conspiracy of *Catiline* was discouered, and suppressed. He was called *Thurinus*: but afterwards, according to the tenor of his vnckles testament, who made him his heire, he was called *Caius Iulius Cæsar*, and lastly *Augustus*, by the aduice of *Munatius Plancus*, and by the decree of the Senate. He was but foure yeares old when his father died, and at twelue yeares he made the funerall oration for his grandmother *Iulia*: foure yeares after that, he became a gowneman, though he were but yong: yet his vnckle gaue him a present at his returne out of AFRICK, such as the souldiers are accustomed to haue of their Captaines. Shortly after he followed his vnckle into SPAINE, whither he was gone against the children of *Pompey*, and passed through many great dangers to ouertake him. This warre being ended, because *Cæsar* vndertooke other longer iourneys, *Octauius* was sent into the city of APPOLONIA: and there plied his booke very diligently. And it chanced him, without hauing any mind to it, that being gone to see *Theogenes* a learned Astronomer, he cast his natiuity, and suddenly he leapt being amazed, and honoured him. The which made *Octauius* conceiue great hope of himselfe, and in memorie of this good hap, he caused certaine peeces of money to be coined, and he himselfe told the opinion of *Theogenes*. Being returned from APPOLONIA to ROME, after his vnckle was slaine by *Cassius, Brutus*, and their allies, he declared himselfe to be his heire, though his mother and *Marcius Philippus* were of another mind. And hauing put himselfe forward, he gouerned [52] the commonwealth of ROME, first with *Antonius* and *Lepidus*: afterwards with *Antonius* the space of twelue yeares: and lastly himselfe alone, the space of foure and forty yeares. But before we speake of his gouernement of common affaires in time of peace and warre, let vs say somewhat (after *Swetonius*) of his family and his maners. He married being yet very young the daughter of *Publius Seruilius Isauricus*: but hauing made peace with *Antonius* after the warre of MVTINE, and at the request of their armies who were desirous to see them friends, he maried with *Clodia*, the daughter of *Publius Clodius* and of *Fuluia* then wife of *Antonius*. But before he knew her, he sent her to her mother, with whom he was somewhat discontented, and because of the warre also of PEROVSE. Immediatly he maried *Scribonia*, and kept not her long because she was too troublesome: yet he had a daughter by her called *Iulia*. But forsaking her, he tooke another which he loued vnto the end: and that was *Liuia Drusilla* the wife of *Tiberius Nero*, whom he caried with him great with child as she was, and had no children by her but one, and yet she went not out her time, and it had no life. His daughter *Iulia* was maried vnto *Marcellus*, the sonne of his sister *Octauia*: and after his death vnto *Marcus Agrippa*, by whom she had three sonnes, *Caius, Lucius*, and *Agrippa*: and two daughters, *Iulia*, and *Agrippine*. After the death of *Marcus Agrippa*, he chose for his sonne in law *Tiberius* the sonne of *Tiberius Nero* and of *Liuia Drusilla*, at that time a knight of ROME, and compelled him to forsake his wife *Vipsamia*, of whom he had a sonne called *Drusus*. But as he was fortunate in managing the affaires of the common wealth, so was he vnfortunate in his race: for his daughter and his neece *Iulia* committed so foule faults in ROME, that he was constrained to banish them. *Agrippine* was maried vnto *Germanicus*, the sonne of his sisters daughter. *Caius* and *Lucius* died in lesse then a yeare and a halfe one after the other: whereupon he adopted his nephew *Agrippa*, and his sonne in law *Tiberius*. But because *Agrippa* was of a churlish nature and vnhonest, he did disinherite him, and confined him to SVRRENTVM. His neece *Iulia* had a child after she was banished, but he would not know it, nor suffer it should be brought vp. He was very modest and continent in all the parts of his life, sauing that he was somewhat giuen to women and play: for the rest, he liked not great pallaces, but was contented with meane lodgings: and if there were any ornament, it was in porches and parkes. His houshold-stuffe and apparell was nothing sumptuous nor costly. It pleased him well to make feasts, he very carefully made choise of his guests, and oftentimes he sate downe at the table a long time after euery body, and would rise before others, which remained after he was vp. In his ordinarie diet he banished superfluity of meates: he delighted to be merry and pleasant among his friends, or to bring in pleasant players of comedies to passe the time away. And he did not tie himselfe to any certaine howres to eate his meate, but when his stomacke serued him he tooke something. So that somtimes he supped not at al, and then when euery man was gone, he made them bring him meate, neither dainty nor delicate. Also he drunke very litle wine, he slept in the day, and by times in the night, talking with some, or reading: so that oftentimes he slept not till the breake of day, and for that he tooke no rest in the night, he might chaunce to sleepe in his litter as they caried him in the streetes in the day time vp and downe ROME. He was a goodly Prince, and that kept himselfe in good state from the beginning of his life to the latter end: not curious to set himselfe out, as litle caring to be shauen, as to weare long haire: and in stead of a looking-glasse, reading in his booke, or writing, euen whilest the Barber was trimming of him. Whether he spake or held his peace, he had so comely a face, that many of his enemies bent to do him hurt, their hearts would not serue them so soone as euer they looked on him. He had very cleare and liuely eyes, but with time he was subiect to many diseases and infirmities, the which he remedied with great care. As for his exercises, he left armes and horses immediatly after the ciuill warres: for he was neuer any great souldier. He would play at tennis, at the ballone, he would go abroad in his coach to walke and stirre himselfe. Sometimes he would go a fishing, or play at the bones, or at nuts with yong children of the MOORES & SYRIANS that had some prety maner and behauiour with them, and alwayes spake words to moue laughter. He was learned in the liberall sciences, very eloquent, and desirous to learne: insomuch that during the warre of MVTINE, in the middest of all his infinite affaires, he did reade, he wrote, and made orations amongst his familiars. He neuer spake vnto the Senate nor people, nor to his souldiers, but he had first written and premeditated that he would say vnto them, although he had speech at commaundement, to propound or aunswer to any thing in the field. And because he would [53] not deceiue his memory, or lose time in superfluous speech: he determined euer to write all that he would say: and he was the first inuenter of it. If he had to conferre with any man, or with his wife in any matters of importance: he would put that downe in his writing tables, because he would speake neither more nor lesse. And he tooke pleasure to pronounce his words with a sweete voyce and good grace, hauing continually about him for this purpose a fine man to frame his voice. But one day hauing a paine in his mouth, he made his oration to the people by an Herauld. He made many bookes and verses of diuerse sorts: but all is dead with time. His speech was as the rest of his life, eloquent, well couched together, and sententious. He delighted to reade good authors, but he gathered nothing other then the sentences teaching good maners: and hauing written them out word by word, he gaue out a copy of them to his familiars: and sent them about to the gouernours of prouinces, and to the magistrates of ROME and of other cities. He was somewhat, and too much giuen vnto deuinations: he was maruellously afraid of thunder and lightning: he had a great confidence in dreames, and in such like vanities. But peraduenture we are too curious searching out his priuate life: yet that may sometime discouer great personages more then their publicke actions, in the which they are more carefull to frame their countenances, and do counterfeit most.

Now, as we haue lightly runne ouer his priuate life before spoken of: so shall the memorable deeds done by his authorite be briefly represented: being vnpossible to comprehend in a few lines so many notable things, vnlesse a man would make a great booke of them. This is to be noted in him, that so young a man hauing so small beginnings, comming out of a meane house in comparison of others, hath excelled all other young and old men in wisedome and greatnesse of courage: should rise so high, that before he had bene Prætor the Senate gaue him the name of *Augustus*, created him maister of the horse, when as yet he neuer had charge of a company of men at armes: proclaimed him Emperour and soueraigne captaine, afore he had bene placed in any publike office by authority of the Senate. Furthermore, for the first time he was chosen Consull when he was but twentie yeares old: and he was thirteene times Consull, and twentie times called Soueraigne captaine. Afterwards, when he was not yet foure and thirtie yeares old, the Senate and people of ROME gaue him this goodly name of father of his country, because he had maintained and preserued the commonwealth. It is a wonderfull thing that he could wind himself out of so many great affaires and warres, that he could within foure and twentie yeares of age, restore againe into so good estate the commonwealth of ROME, turmoiled and troubled with so many proscriptions and ciuill warres as it was. And that afterwards so long as he commaunded alone, he did so firmely establish this Monarchie, that notwithstanding the infinite troubles receiued vnder other Emperours, yet it stood vpright and in so great prosperitie for so many hundred yeares. After the death of *Iulius Cæsar*, this man being but bare eighteene yeares old, came to ROME, where he was welcomed and immediatly did contest with *Antonius*, hated of *Cicero* and of many others: from whence the aduancement of this young *Cæsar* came, and the declaration of the warre against *Antonius*, iudged an enemy of the commonwealth, and ouercome by the Consuls *Hirtius* and *Pansa*. *Cæsar* who was their associate, was called Soueraigne captaine, though he had not yet fought: both the Consuls being dead of their hurts. But the Senate after this ouerthrow, beginning to change their mind, he perceiuing that they were slow to graunt him the Consulship, resolued to possesse it by force of armes, and began to acquaint himselfe with *Antonius* and *Lepidus* which were ioyned together: he made that the souldiers promised by oath the one to the other, that they would fight against none of *Cæsars* troupes, & sent 400 men to ROME to aske for him, in the name of all the army, the office of Cōsull. They hauing deliuered their charge vnto the Senate, *Cornelius* the Centiner chiefe of this

legation or ambassade, perceiuing they wold giue him no present answer, casting vp his
cassocke, & shewing the Senate the pommell of his sword, sayd vnto them: This shall do it,
if you will not do it. So they being returned without obtaining their demand, *Cæsar* made
Antonius and *Lepidus* come into ITALY, & he for his part hauing passed the riuer of Rubicon,
marched with 8 legions right to ROME. This put all ROME in such a feare, as they sent to
Cæsar to present him the Consulship: and twise so much in gift, as they had promised the
legions. Now whilest the Ambassadors were on their way, the Senators beginning again to
take hart to them, encouraged by the arriuall of the legions of AFRICK, they determined to
try all meanes before they wold betray the liberty of their coútry, being minded to cal backe
that which they had sent to *Cæsar*, & so disposed them-[54]selues to make warre. *Cæsar*
being offended with this inconstancie, sent certaine horsemen before to assure the people that
he would make no tumult at all: he drew his legions neare, and made himselfe Lord of ROME
without one stroke striken: and contrariwise, the people and Senate receiued him with shew
of great ioy. Then, in the assembly of all the people he was chosen Consull, iust at the full
accomplishment of twenty yeares of his age. So he demaunded in the field that they should
proceed criminally against those that had killed his father *Cæsar*. *Q. Pedius* his fellow Consull
published the decree. So were *Brutus* and *Cassius*, and all their friends condemned, with
interdiction of water and fire. But for as much as *Augustus* had too small meanes to set vpon
Brutus and *Cassius*, he reconciled *Antonius* and *Lepidus* with the Senate, and made alliance
with them, followed with great armies. They ioyned, and were in consultation of their affaires
the space of three dayes together, neare vnto BOLONIA, or vnto MVTINE, and as if the
ROMAINE Empire had bene their owne inheritance, they deuided it betweene them three.
So that *Cæsar* had the high and base LYBIA, with SICILIA, and SARDINIA. SPAINE and GAVLE
NARBONNESE fell vnto *Lepidus*: and the rest of GAVLE was for *Antonius*. They did decree also
that they should be called *Trium-viri*, appointed for the reestablishment of the commonwealth,
with soueraigne authority for fiue yeares, to dispose and giue the estates and offices to whom
they thought good, without asking aduice of the Senate nor people. So they established
Lepidus Consull for the yeare following, in the place of *Decimus Brutus* that was killed: and
they gaue him the gard of ROME and ITALIE, so long as they two that remained made their
preparations to go against *Brutus* and *Cassius*. Besides the presents they should make vnto
the souldiers after the victory, they promised to giue them leaue to ease themselues, &
eighteene rich townes in ITALIE for them to dwell in. Then they began to set vp a rolle of
all the citizens of ROME appointed by them to be slaine. And they decreed to euery free man
that should bring the *Trium-viri* a head of the proscripts, the sum of two thousand fiue
hundred crownes, and halfe so much vnto the slaues with enfranchisement: and the like
summe also to whosoeuer could discouer any man that had hidden or fauoured the proscripts.
Antonius and *Lepidus* were thought to be the chiefe authors of this horrible tragedie: and
Cæsar seemed willing to none but to the murtherers of his father, and did a long time oppose
himselfe against the other two: but at the length he gaue ouer, and they made wonderfull
changes, abandoning their owne parents and friends the one to the other, to be reuenged of
their enemies. But when the sword was once drawne, he was no lesse cruell then the other
two. *Cicero* was not forgotten, as we may see in his life: and it would be very hard to describe
the wickednesse of that time, the which like a furious streame caried away so many citizens
of ROME. . . .

[57] Now during the cruelties of this *Triumuirate*, *Brutus* and his followers made themselues strong in MACEDON, and did diuers exploits of warre: and were afterwards ouercome
in the fields PHILIPPIANS, as hath bene said in the life of *Brutus*, which we need not rehearse
againe, the principall being comprehended there. After this victorie, *Antonius* went into the

East to dispose of his affaires in ASIA, and to leauie money there to pay his souldiers, hauing promised to euery one of them fiue hundred crownes. *Cæsar* returned into ITALIE to refresh himselfe, to assigne Colonies to his souldiers, to pacifie the troubles *Lepidus* had procured, and to set a pike betwixt him and *Pompey* at a need: if he were neuer so litle in league with him. *Cæsar* fell grieuously sicke at BRVNDVSIVM: but being recouered againe he entred into ROME, pacified all things, and kept *Lepidus* in his wonted degree. But when he came to bring his souldiers into Colonies, then the storme began to rise: for the owners cryed out that they were tyrannized, being driuen out of their inheritances: the old souldiers they complained that promise was not kept with them. [TLN 787–8] *Fuluia* and some others practised to set them on, to the end to draw a warre into ITALIE, and by this meanes to make *Antonius* come againe besotted by *Cleopatra*. These things proceeded so farre that *Fuluia* tooke armes, for she was then in the campe, her sword by her side, and commanded like a Captaine. *Cæsar* on the other side being angry, sent her daughter home to her, vnto whom he was betrothed, and led his armie against the NVRSINIANS and SENTINATES the allies of *Fuluia*. In the meane space *Lucius Antonius* departed in the night with speed, and entred into ROME by treason: vsed it as a citie taken in warre, and draue out *Lepidus*. *Cæsar* left *Suluidienus* to besiege the SENTINATES, returned to ROME, and draue out *Lucius*, followed him and shortened his iourney as he was going into GAVLE, shut him vp, and besieged him a great time in PEROVSE, and compelled him through famine to yeeld himselfe, and to craue pardon, which he graunted him. PEROVSE was burnt by a strange accident: for one of the chiefest of the citie hauing set his house on fire, after he had wounded himselfe with his dagger, a boisterous wind being risen vpon it, so dispersed the flames abrode, that it burnt all the houses besides. *Cæsar* caused some of his Captaines to be killed that were against him. He condemned the NVRSINIANS in a great summe of money, and because they could not pay it, he draue them out of their citie and territorie. Afterwards he suppressed some troubles raised in NAPLES by *Tiberius Claudius Nero*, father of *Tiberius Cæsar*, and fauourer of *Fuluia*: who seeing her selfe vnder foot, she fled vnto ATHENS. But *Cæsar* to preuent a new conspiracie, sent *Lucius Antonius* far from ROME, to commaund the legions that were in SPAINE: he gaue him also commissioners to looke into him, and to obserue his actions. He finely draue out *Lepidus* also into AFRICK with sixe legions. On the other side *Fuluia* being dead, *Cæsar* and *Antonius* agreed being ready to fight: after that they made peace with *Pompey* that gouerned SICILIA. Immediatly after that he went into GAVLE, to appease some troubles that happened there, and sent *Agrippa* before, who compelled the AQVITANS to submit themselues, and pacified al GAVLE. On the other side *Cneus Caluinus* subdued the CERETANIANS in SPAINE. And because the legions had committed certaine insolencies, whereupon they fell together by the eares, and the enemies had the better hand: after he had sharpely reproued them, he took the tenth man of the two first bands, and belaboured *Iubellius* with a cudgell. In the mean time *Cæsar* sent at times troups of men of armes into DALMATIA, and ILLYRIA, to the end to breath them for other warres that were a hatching, as that of SI-[58]CILIA was the first. For *Menas* the pyrat, *Sextus Pompeius* Lieutenant, hauing for despite brought his fleet vnto *Cæsar*, and taken his part, vnto whom also he deliuered the Iles of SARDINIA and CORSICA, with three legions: *Cæsar* did him great honors, & refused to deliuer him againe vnto *Pompey*, who asked him of him. Besides that *Pompey* complained of *Antonius*, and pretending to haue iust occasions, he tooke armes againe. Wherfore *Cæsar* sent for *Antonius* and *Lepidus* out of GRECE and AFRICKE to come and aide him. *Antonius* came to the hauen of BRVNDVSIVM: but vpon the sudden, not knowne wherfore, he tooke sea againe, & returned from whence he came. *Lepidus* came too late, which made *Cæsar* (seeing all the weight fall on his armes) that he sent his Lieutenants against *Pompey*: who fought with them by sea &

by land, & had the better, and put *Cæsar* to great trouble, who had like to haue bin killed by a slaue also, that wold haue reuēged the death of his maisters father, that was a proscript. After that *Antonius* being come to TARENTVM, with intention to make war against *Cæsar:* *Octauia* sister of the one, and wife of the other, agreed them, so that they did yet prolong with *Lepidus* their *Triumuirate* for fiue yeares more. *Antonius* went against the PARTHIANS, and *Cæsar* prepared to set vpon *Pompey* againe. Hereupon *Menas* being angry for that he was not so well accounted of as he thought he deserued: he returned againe to ioyne with *Pompey* with 7. gallies. *Cæsars* fleet hauing sustained great hurt by tempest, was also beaten by *Menas*. *Lepidus* wan LILYBEE, & tooke certaine neighbor villages. *Cæsar* hauing repaired his ships and army by sea, and made it stronger then before vnder the conduct of *Agrippa*, who sailed vnto LIPARE, he gaue battell by sea vnto *Pompeys* Lieutenants. But they being aided by *Menas* (that was returned the second time) he ouercame and wan thirtie shippes. But the other fleet that *Cæsar* himselfe brought, was wholly ouerthrowne by *Pompey*, neare vnto TAVROMENION, and *Cæsar* brought to that extremitie, that he was readie to kill himselfe. But *Cornificius* ran to the shore who saued him, and brought him to the campe: from whence he retired further off, and very quickly (but with great daunger) vnto MESSALA. After certaine encounters where *Pompey* euer had the better, insomuch as *Lepidus* was suspected to leane on that side, *Cæsar* resolued to commit all to the hazard of a latter battell: and to draw *Pompey* vnto it, he cut him so short of victuals, that he was constrained to come to blowes, and the fight was verie cruell: wherein *Agrippa* bestirred himselfe so valiantly, that he wan the victorie, sunke 28. ships, brake and spoiled the most part of the rest, and tooke two of the chiefest Captaines *Pompey* had: one of the which called *Demochares*, killed himselfe with his owne hands. Now for *Pompey*, who but a litle before had about three hundred and fiftie saile, he fled away with all speed only with seuenteene, and went to MESSINA so discouraged, that leauing all hope and his armie he had by land, he went to the Ile of CEPHALONIE, where being somewhat come to himselfe, he determined to repaire to *Antonius*. But *Tisienus* a Frenchman (his lieutenāt of the armie by land) led all his troupes vnto *Lepidus*: some GREEKE historians report that it was to *Cæsar*. *Plemminius* was within MESSINA with eight legions, and did capitulate with *Lepidus* to render vp the towne to him: wherupon *Agrippa* hapned to come thither: who maintained, that they ought to regard *Cæsar* that was absent then. But that stood him in no stead, for *Lepidus* entred the towne, & gaue the spoile of it as well to *Plemminius* soldiers as to his. Therupon *Cæsar* vndertooke a thing worthie of memory, which was: that being vnarmed he went into *Lepidus* campe, & turning by the blows of the darts that were thrown at him by some, which hit his cloke & pierced it: he took hold of an ensigne of a legion. Then the souldiers all of them armed followed him, and left *Lepidus*: who shortly after lost empire and army: he that with 20. legions promised himself SICILIA and a great deale more, *Cæsar* gaue him his life, and the office of soueraigne Bishop of ROME, whither he sent him. Some say he was banished. Vpō these stirs there rose a sedition in *Cæsars* campe through the insolencie of the souldiers, that ran euen to his iudgement seat, vsing great menaces. But he wisely appeased all, punished the authours of the tumult, and did cassiere all the tenth legion with great shame and ignominie, because the souldiers of the same did outbraue him in words. He dispersed and sent some others to their houses, and gaue vnto them that had vsed themselues gently, two thousand Sesterces for euery souldier: which is thought to amount neare to fiftie crownes. He made them to be mustred, and found that they were fiue and fortie legions, fiue and twentie thousand horsmen, and sixe and thirtie thousand lightly armed. Afterwards he did great honours vnto his Lieutenant *Agrippa* for his notable seruice, and commaunded *Statilius Taurus* to go into AFRICKE to take possession of the Prouinces of *Lepidus*. Whilest *Antonius* made warre with the PARTHIANS, or rather infortunately they made [59] warre with him to his great confusion: [TLN 1743–4] his Lieutenant *Titius* found the meanes to lay hands vpon *Sextus Pompeius* that was fled into the Ile of SAMOS, and then fortie yeares old: whom he put death by *Antonius* commandement: for which fact he was so hated of the people of ROME, that though he had giuen them the pastime of certaine playes at his owne costs and charges, they draue him out of the Theater.

Moreouer, *Cæsar* thinking to haue sailed out of SICILIA into MAVRITANIA, the sea being rough stayed him: which was the cause that he sent his armie into ILLYRIA, and set vpon the IAPVDES, which did him much mischiefe, yet at the last he ouercame them. Then he ranne vpon the PANNONIANS, and the DALMATIANS, whom he made tributaries, being hurt in his thighes, in his armes, and in one of his knees, in this warre against the ILLYRIANS. On the other side, *Messala* his Lieutenant fought against the SALASSIANS, dwelling in a valley enuironed with high mountaines of the Alpes: and after diuerse ouerthrowes, he made them subiect to the Empire. And shortly after *Cæsar* was chosen Consull the second time: but he resigned the office the same day vnto *Autronius Pætus*, being about to make himselfe friends against *Antonius*: who being stayed about *Cleopatra*, gaue his wife occasion to returne from ATHENS to ROME. Now after the fire of enmitie betwixt these two competitours had bene a hatching a certaine time: it stood either of them both vpon to seeke all the meanes to ouerthrow his companion. The straunge proceedings of *Antonius* in fauour of *Cleopatra* hastened the warre, whereupon followed the battel of ACTIVM, the flying of these wicked louers, and the beginning of the Monarchy of *Cæsar*, confirmed by the conquest of ÆGYPT, and the tragicall death of *Antonius* and *Cleopatra*. The which we touch briefly, the whole being largely set downe in the life of *Antonius*.

APPIAN

MACCALLUM (1910, pp. 648–52) first calls attention to evidence that Appian's raising Pompey as a major concern is a likely source for *Ant*. MacCallum stresses particularly Pompey's republicanism (Appian 3.82, 5.1; *Ant*. 1189 ff.), his father's reputation (4.36; *Ant*. 285–9 and 362), Octavius's suspicion that Lepidus favored Pompey (5.3; *Ant*. 1735–6), Pompey's lordship of the sea (5.15, 5.18, 5.67; *Ant*. 283–5), his popularity (5.25; *Ant*. 285–9, 361–6, 468–72—with a similar account in Goulart [1602, p. 56] for a period preceding events shown in *Ant*.—487 and 627), Antony's regret at Fulvia's death (5.59; *Ant*. 219–23), Menas's preferring to continue Pompey's war with the triumvirs (5.70; *Ant*. 1280–1 and 1301–2), and the question of Antony's responsibility for Pompey's death in 5.144, where Appian reports the rumor that Antony's officer L. Munatius Plancus, using Antony's signet and without his knowledge, ordered the execution (cf. *Ant*. 1741–4). He concludes (p. 648), "I do not think there can be any serious doubt about Shakespeare's having consulted the 1578 translation of the *Bella Civilia* for this play, at any rate for the parts dealing with Sextus Pompeius. The most important passage is the one [1743–4] which records Antony's indignation at Pompey's death. Now of that death there is no mention at all in the *Marcus Antonius* of Plutarch; and even in the *Octavius Caesar Augustus* by Simon Goulard . . . it is expressly attributed to Antony [as noted by VOLLMER, 1887, p. 240 n., who also compares Appian]."

Some of MacCallum's evidence—Pompey's enthusiasm for liberty and his lordship of the sea—is questioned with insufficient consideration by SCHANZER (1956,

Shakespeare's Appian, pp. xxiii–vii), who nevertheless adds further parallels on Lucius and Fulvia (especially 5.19 for Fulvia's motive, also explained by Plutarch and Goulart, at *Ant.* 787–8; 5.43 for 734–6, 738–41), as well as on Octavius's unpopularity (5.68 for 631–2), and points out that in *Ant.* (p. xxiii) "the indebtedness to Appian is less extensive than in *Julius Cæsar*. Where in the earlier play it is connected mainly with the character of Antony, in the later play it centres on the figures of Sextus Pompeius and of Lucius Antonius. . . . [*xxv*] Perhaps an even clearer indication of Shakespeare's knowledge of Appian than is provided by the references to Pompey is found in the allusions to the war waged by Antony's brother, Lucius, against Cæsar. All that we learn in Plutarch about this war is contained in one sentence [see p. 416]. . . . Goulard . . . describes the war in greater detail [see p. 464], but makes no mention of the cause for which Lucius fought. That this cause was Republicanism [cf. 738–41], the ending of the Triumvirate and the restoration of the power of the Senate, is repeatedly emphasized in Appian's detailed account of the war [similarly NELSON, 1943, p. 244]. . . . [*xxvi*] According to Appian's narrative Lucius at no time claimed to be fighting in the name of Antony. . . . On the other hand his confederates, Fulvia and Manius, are described by Appian [5.19] as using Antony's supposed grievances as their justification for the struggle, sharing none of Lucius' idealistic motives for the war. This peculiar situation, in which the confederates have different war-aims, is accurately reflected in the play [e.g., 787–8]. . . . [*xxviii*] [Sh.] drew on Appian's *Civil Wars* for his *Julius Cæsar* and *Antony and Cleopatra*, and . . . he read the relevant portions shortly before or during the composition of these plays."

NELSON (1943, pp. 224–58) in a diss. unnoticed by Schanzer finds various parallels in Appian, many remote, some concerning Pompey's career before Philippi (4.83–100: lordship of the sea and early popularity, control of Sicily—also at 4.25—and proscription by the triumvirate [*Ant.* 361], as well as his father's reputation) and his republican pretensions (e.g., 4.138); some facts on the triumvirs' meeting in Rome (*Ant.* 2.2 and Appian 5.63–5: persons present, timing of Antony's commission to Ventidius, division of empire; see also VOLLMER, 1887, pp. 216, 222); the war of Lucius and Fulvia against Octavius (5.19, 5.43); and echoes of Cassius's statements on justice (4.97–8) in *Ant.* 216 ff. He states (p. 229), "The Appianic narrative seems to lie back of Shakespeare's plot and give it validity and direction. The dramatist would perceive the immense value of such a figure as the young Pompey . . . upholding the lost cause of the old free democracy. . . . Sextus Pompey is a curious, vacillating figure in the *History*: half pirate and half Republican, . . . a good leader but not a great captain of men, for he lacked decision. . . . [*230*] He is not quite a tragic figure either in Appian or Shakespeare, but he has some elements of greatness and is a worthy foil, as Lepidus is not, to the great opponents in the tragedy and a not unworthy latter-day inheritor of the Republican tradition." Sh.'s Pompey "is a representative of the dying Republican Rome; he is for a necessary while the barrier between the clashing wills of Octavius and Antony; and in his fall he prefigures the inevitable decline of the last great opponent to Octavius Caesar, Antony. . . . All this is clearly in the play, and is not in Plutarch, not even implicit in his casual and unjointed mention of Sextus; and it is all in Appian."

Nelson (p. 258) and DICKEY (1957, p. 151) note that the moral reflections on "generall peace" in W. B.'s *Continuation* affixed to the tr. of Appian, especially pp. 397–8, may have contributed to suggesting 2581–3, while BARROLL (1958–9, *HLQ*, p. 33 n.) cites Appian's mention of "Scaurus" (5.142) as Sh.'s source for Scarrus and (1969, p. 230, n. 45) "suggestive parallelisms" for 2126 (see n.).

Others who discuss Appian as a source include LANGBAINE (1691, p. 455; see p. 384), THEOBALD (1909, pp. 74–5), CHAMBERS (1930, 1:478), MUIR (1957, pp. 201–6, and 1977, pp. 220–3), BULLOUGH (1964, 5:247–8), WALTER (ed. 1969, p. 297), BARROLL (1970, p. 287, n. 33), and ADELMAN (1973, p. 202, n. 18: a woolly remark that Appian's "sense of incomplete knowledge" is "perfectly" reflected in *Ant.*).

The excerpt given here includes the main sections likely to have influenced *Ant.*

The Romanes Warres (1578)

"APPIANUS Alexandrinus *of the Romaine Civill warres*" was entered on the Stationers' Register to H[enrie] Bynneman and Rafe Newbery on 1 July 1578 (Arber, *Transcript*, 2:148) and published in quarto with the following (abridged) title page: "AN AVNCIENT | Historie and exquisite Chronicle | *of the Romanes warres, both* | Ciuile and Foren. | Written in Greeke by the noble Orator and Histo- | riographer, *Appian of Alexandria. . . .* | IMPRINTED AT LONDON | *by Raufe Newbery, and* | Henrie Bynniman. | Anno. 1578." For a discussion of W. B. (William Barker?), mentioned on the title page of the *Foreign Wars*, as well as on the general title page of two copies in the possession of the Folger Library, as translator of the whole work, see SCHANZER (1956, *Shakespeare's Appian*, pp. xi–xvi).

In the following modified diplomatic reprint, the quarto's black letter is reproduced as roman, incidental italic being preserved; the marginal glosses are reproduced in the quarto's roman with incidental italic. The prose is relined, and the beginning of each page in the quarto indicated by bracketed italic numbers. Book and section numbers (e.g., 5.18), appearing in square brackets, match the system commonly used in scholarly references to Appian since Schweighäuser (1785). Long *s* is printed *s*, and other archaic types have been converted to modern equivalents. Obvious typographical errors have been silently corrected.

Passages corresponding with *Ant.* are preceded by TLNs in square brackets. The following parallels have been found (*Ant.* TLNs are listed, with parenthetical page references to Appian in this edition): 283–5 (469, 472), 285–9 (471), 361–6 (471), 468–72 (471), 487 (471), 627 (471), 631–2 (472), 734–6 (472), 738–41 (471), 787–8 (469), 1280–1 (473), 1301–2 (473), 1741–4 (475).

The text is based on the copy in the Huntington Library (*STC* 713). Excerpts from Appian have been edited by SCHANZER (1956, *Shakespeare's Appian*) and, more briefly, BULLOUGH (1964, 5:338–41).

[The Romanes Warres]

[*314*] [TLN 283–5] The Citie in the meane time, was in great penurie, their prouision of corne beyng stopped by *Pompey*. In *Italie*, tillage beyng almost lefte for the continuaunce of warre, and that that there was, being consumed of the Soldiours: and in the Citie, theeues and murderers by night, were vnpunished, for what soeuer was done, was imputed to the Souldiour. The commons shutte vp theyr shoppes, and were withoute officers, whiche woulde not [*315*] serue where thefte was suffred.

But *Lucius*, beyng well affected to the common wealth, and greeued with the power of the three Princes, continuyng longer than the time appoynted, contended with *Cæsar*: for he onely promised helpe to the olde possessioners, making supplication to all the officers, & they promised their seruice to him. Wherby, bothe *Antonies* Soldiours, and *Cæsar* himself, accused him as an enimy to him, and *Fuluia* also, as stirrers of warre out of time. [TLN 787–8] But a deuise of *Manius* preuayled, which persuaded *Fuluia*, that if *Italie* were in quiet, *Antony* woulde remayne with *Cleopatra* in *Aegipt*, but if warres were styrred, hee woulde come quickly. Then *Fuluia* of a womannishe passion, incensed *Lucius*, & when *Cæsar* wente to place the newe inhabitancies, *Antonies* chyldren and *Lucius* wente with them, that *Cæsar* shoulde not haue the whole thankes, by goyng alone. *Cæsars* horsemenne scoured the coaste towarde *Sicelie*, that *Pompey* shoulde not spoyle it. *Lucius* eyther afrayde in deede, or fayning to bee afrayde, that these horsemen were sente agaynst him and *Antonies* children, wente in haste to the inhabitauncies of *Antonie*, to gette a garde about him, accusing *Cæsar*, as vnfaithfull to *Antony*. But he answered, that he kept faith & friendship with *Antonie*, & that *Lucius* sought to moue warre, for y^t he was offended with the rule of thē three, by the which the newe inhabitants might take full possession, & that the horsemen were yet in the coast, & did their duties. [5.20] Whē *Antonies* Soldiours vnderstoode this, they made a meeting with him at *Theano*, and were reconciled to him with these conditions.

' That he shuld deuide no lāds but to such as serued at *Philippi*.

' That the money of the condemned men, & their landes, should be equally 'diuided among *Antonies* Souldiours.

' That hereafter one alone should not leuy men.

' That two legiōs of *Antonies* should serue *Cæsar* against *Pōpey*.

' That the *Alpes* towarde *Spaine* shoulde be open to them that *Cæsar* sent, 'and not be shutte by *Asinius*.

' That *Lucius* should put away his garde, and exercise his office with 'quietnesse.

These were the couenants, whereof onely the two last were [*316*] kepte. And *Saluidienus* passed the *Alpes* spyte of them that kepte them, the rest were defeated. Wherfore *Lucius* went to *Preneste*, affirmyng he was afrayde of *Cæsar* hauyng a garde aboute him, and he none. *Fuluia* also went to *Lepidus*, saying, she was afrayde of hir children, for she trusted him better than *Cæsar*. And they bothe wrote to *Antonie*, certaine freendes carying their letters, that might certifie him of all thyngs, the copies whereof I haue long sought, and can not finde. Then the chiefe of the armies, agreed to take vp thys matter, and affirmed they woulde compell hym that were vnwillyng. They sente for *Lucius* friendes

[5.19]
Lucius *taketh parte vvith the old hushandemen.*

Manius *counsel.*

Fuluia Antonies *vvife stirreth vvarre.*

Begynnyng of suspition.

Teano, *a citie in* Via Appia. *An other in* Apulia. *Conditions betvvene* Cæsar & Antonies *soldiours.*

Preneste *novve* Pilestrina *a Citie in* Latio.
[5.21]

Fuluia *fleeth to* Lepidus.

to come to them, whiche they denying to doe, *Cæsar* accused them, as well to the chiefe of the armies, as to the officers of the Cities.

Then great resorte was made to *Lucius* out of the Citie, beseechyng him to haue compassion of afflicted *Italie*, and take some man, that eyther with him, or with the Capitaynes might make an ende of the matter. And where as *Lucius* had regarde both of them that spake, and also of the thyngs spoken, *Manius* answeared sharpely. That *Antonie* onely gathered money of strange 'nations, but *Cæsar* did gette mens loue by preuention of the armies and fitte 'places of *Italy*. For by fraude he had gotten *Fraunce*, which was *Antonies* prouince, 'and for xviij. cities, that should be giuen to the Soldiours, he ransacked almoste 'all *Italy*. And also gaue money to foure and thirty legions, not onely to eight 'and twentie that fought in hys quarrell: and that he had spoyled Temples in 'pretence of warre agaynst *Pompey*, whiche was not yet begon, for all the greate 'dearth in the Citie, but in deede to winne the fauour of the Souldiours agaynst '*Antonie*, in so muche as the goodes of the attaynted, are not solde before they 'be giuen to thē: but if he seeketh peace, in good fayth, he must make accompt 'of things he hath done, and hereafter do nothing but by consent of bothe. This was the bolde answeare of *Manius*, that neyther *Cæsar* shoulde doe any thing alone, nor the couenaunts betweene him and *Antonie* remayne firme, that is, that either of them should haue full authoritie in their prouinces, and each confirme others actes.

[*317*] *Cæsar* seeyng that they soughte warre, prepared hymselfe for it, [5.23] but the two legiõs that wer placed about of *Ancona*, and first serued his father, and after *Antony*, for the loue they bare to them both, sente Ambassadors to *Rome*, to pray them to haue respect to peace. And when *Cæsar* aunswered that he swerued not with *Antony*, but *Lucius* wyth hym, the Embassadors conferring with the officers of *Antonyes* Souldyoures, sente a common Embassage to *Lucius*, requiring hym to be contente to committe hys difference wyth *Cæsar*, to arbitrement, affirmyng they woulde take vppon them, excepte he woulde condiscende. Hauing obteyned their request, *Gabij* was appoynted the place of meeting, in the midde way betweene *Rome* and *Preneste*. There was prepared a seate for the Iudges, and two chayres to shewe the cause. *Cæsar* came firste, and sente Horsemen that way that *Lucius* shoulde come, eyther to see what *Lucius* dyd, or whether there were any traynes layde. They lyghted vpon *Antonyes* Horsemen, whyche came as forerunners of *Lucius*, or to see if all were cleere: they fell to fight, and some were kylled. Wherefore *Lucius* wente backe for feare of treason (as he sayde) and beeing called of the chiefe of the army, promising hym to conducte him safe, he refused. [5.24] Thus the pacifyers beeyng deceyued, warre was threatned wyth bitter wordes betweene them. *Lucius* hadde sixe legions, of the leuie whiche he toke when he was created Consull, besyde eleuen of *Antonyes*, vnder Captayne *Caleno*, and all those in *Italy*.

Cæsar hadde foure Legions at *Capua*, and certayne bandes for his person.
Saluidienus broughte other syxe Legions out of *Spayne*.
Lucius had money of the prouinces that *Antony* had pacyfyed.
Cæsar hadde of all them that came vnto hym by lotte, excepte *Sardinia*, whyche was then in warre.
He gote much of Temples, promising to render it with interest, that is,

Great resorte to Lucius.

[5.22]

Manius ansvver sharpe.

Souldioures of Ancona *labour for peace.*

Gabij *a people, destroyed by* Tarquinius Superbus. *Meeting at* Gabij.

A fight by chance.

The daye frustrate. The vvarre breaketh. Lucius *povver.*

Cæsars povver. Antium *vvas a Citie in* Latio, *very good vpon the Sea.* Lannuuium, *novv* Indouina. Nemore, *not farre from* Aritia. Tibure *novve* Tiuoli.

of *Capitolio, Antio, Lanuuio, Nemore, Tibure,* in the whyche Cities be treasures
at this day of holy money.

[TLN 285–9, 361–6, 468–72, 627] Out of *Italy* all things were not quiet,
for *Pompey,* by resorte of condemned Citizens, and auntient possessioners, was
greatly [*318*] increased, both in mighte, and estimation: for they that feared
their life, or were spoyled of their goodes, or lyked not the present state, fledde
all to hym. And this disagreemente of *Lucius,* augmented hys credite: [TLN
487] beside a repayre of yong men, desirous of gayne and seruice, not caring
vnder whome they went, bycause they were all *Romanes,* sought vnto him. And
among other, hys cause seemed most iust. He was waxed riche by booties of
the Sea, and he hadde good store of Shyppes, with their furniture. *Murcus* also
brought him two legions, and fiue hundred archers, much money, and fourescore
Shippes: and he had another army from *Cephalenia.* Wherefore mē thynke, that
if he had then inuaded *Italy,* he might easily haue gotte it, which being afflicted
with famine and discord, loked for him. But *Pompey* of ignorance had rather
defend his owne, than inuade others, till so he was ouercome also. . . .

[*325*] When it was tolde *Cæsar* that *Lucius* was comming to hym, he went
straight to meete him, and they bothe came in sight, accompanied with their
friends, in the habite of a General. Then *Lucius* sending aside all hys friends,
wente on with two Sergeants, signifying what he meant: and *Cæsar* following
that beneuolence, shewed the lyke token of modestie. And when he saw *Lucius*
come within his trenche, that so he might shew himselfe to be in his power,
he firste wente oute of the Trenche, that *Lucius* might be free to saue hymselfe.
Thys they dyd outwardly by tokens of courtesy, [5.42] and when they were
come to the ditche, and had saluted eche other, *Lucius* thus begā.

‘   If I had made this warre with straungers, I would haue bin ashamed (O
‘*Cæsar*) to haue bin ouercome, and more ashamed to yeelde myselfe: from the
‘whiche ignominie, I woulde easilye haue deliuered my life: But bicause I haue
‘dealt with a Citizen of lyke authoritie, and that for my country, I thinke it no
‘[*326*] shame for such a cause to be ouercome of such a manne, which I speake,
‘not that I refuse to suffer any thyng that thou wilt put vpon mee, beyng come
‘to this campe, wythout an Herauld, but to aske pardon for other, iuste and
‘commodious for thyne estate. Whych, that thou mayste vnderstande the more
‘playnly, I wyll separate theyr cause from mine, that after thou shalt vnderstand
‘that I am the onelye cause, thou mayste exercise thine anger vppon me. Thinke
‘not that I will inuey against thee licentiously, which now were oute of tyme,
‘but wyll onelye tell the truth, which I cannot dissemble.

‘   [TLN 738–41] I tooke thys warre agaynste thee, not that I woulde bee a
’Prince, if I ‘hadde dispatched thee: but that I myghte haue broughte the Common
‘wealth to the rule of the Senate, whyche is nowe taken awaye by the power of
‘three, as thou thy selfe canste not denye.

‘   For when you begunne it, confessyng it vnlawfull, you sayde it was nec-
‘essarye for a tyme, *Cassius* and *Brutus* beyng alyue, who coulde not be reconciled
‘vnto you. They being taken awaye, the reste, (if any rest there be) being afraide
‘of you, and takyng armes, not agaynste the Common wealth, and youre tyme
‘beeyng ended, I requyred that the oppressed Senate myghte be restored, not
‘regardyng my brother before my Countrey. For I hoped to haue perswaded him

*Treasure houses
of holy money.*

[5.25]

Pompey
increaseth.

Resort to
Pompey.

Cephalenia, *an
Ilande in the*
Ionian *Sea.*
Pompey   [5.26]
loseth his occasion.
Honor of   [5.41]
Pompey.

Cæsar *meeteth
wwith* Lucius.

Lucius *to*
Cæsar.

471

'at his retourne, and I made haste to doe it in the tyme of myne offyce. If thou
'wouldest haue doone so, thou shouldest haue hadde the glorye alone, but bycause
'I could not perswade thee, I wente to the Cittye, and thought to gette it by
'strength and force, being a Senatoure, and a Consull.

'   [TLN 734–6] These were the onelye causes of this warre, not my brother,
'not *Manius*, not *Fuluia*, nor the landes diuided to the Souldyoures, that wanne
'the fielde at *Philippi*: not the pitie of the olde possessioners cast out of the
'landes: for by myne authoritie, some were appoynted to landes for my brothers
'[327] Legions, the olde owners spoyled. But thys calumniation thou dyddest
'deuise, that thou myghtest putte the faulte of the warre from thy selfe, to me,
'and the newe inhabiters. And by thys arte, wynnyng the heartes of the olde
'Souldyoures, thou hast wonne also the victory: for it was persuaded them, that
'I woulde putte them out by violence. These deuices were to be vsed, when
'thou madest warre agaynste me. Nowe beeyng Conqueroure, if thou bee an
'ennimie of thy Countrey, make mee an enimie also, that coulde not remedie
'it, beeyng lette by famyne. [5.44] And thys I speake freelie, gyuing my selfe
'(as I sayde) into thy handes, shewyng what I thought of thee before, and nowe
'also, beeyng with thee alone. Thus much of my selfe.

'   Now, as concernyng my friendes, and the whole army: if thou wilte beleeue
'me, I wyll gyue thee most profitable councell. Doe not vse them hardly for my
'cause, and matter: and seeyng thou arte a man, and subiect to vnstable fortune,
'make not thy friendes the slower to venture, for thee, if they shall see examples
'gyuen of thee, nothyng to be hoped, but to the Conqueroures. And if thou
'reiect all my councell, as of thyne enimie, I maye not bee ashamed to craue
'pardon of thee, that thou wouldest not exacte punishmente of my friendes for
'my faulte or missefortune, but rather turne all vppon mee, whyche am the
'cause of all these troubles: for I haue lefte them behynde me of purpose, least
'if I shoulde speake these things in theyr hearyng, I shoulde seeme to seeke
'myne owne cause. . . .

[337] [TLN 283–5] In the meane time the cytie was oppressed with famine,
for neyther durst the Merchauntes bring any corne from the East bicause of
Pompeis being in *Sicelie*, nor from the Weast of *Corsica* & *Sardinia*, where *Pompeis*
shippes also lay: nor frō *Africa*, where the nauies of the other conspiratours
kepte their stations. Being in this distresse, they alleaged, that the discorde of
the rulers was the cause, and therefore required that peace might be made with
Pompey, vnto the whiche when *Cæsar* woulde not agree, *Antonie* thought warre
was needefull for necessitie, and bycause mo-[338]ny wāted, a decree was made
by *Antonies* aduise, that euery maister should pay the half of .xxv. drāmes, for
euery slaue y^t he had, which was determined to haue bene done in the war of
Cassius, & that somewhat also shoulde be payde of euery mans heritage. The
people tore the decree with great furie, & obiected the consuming of treasure
publike, the spoylyng of prouinces, the sacking of *Italie*, and all for priuate
displeasure, and yet all woulde not serue, but muste nowe put newe impositions
vpon them that haue nothing left. They assembled and murmured, & cōpelled
thē that would not, and with threatnings to spoyle and burne theyr houses,
[5.68] gathered all the people. [TLN 631–2] Then *Cæsar* with a fewe of his
freends and garde, came to them to excuse themselues, but they threw stones
and droue him away, which when *Antonie* heard, he came to help him. To him

[5.67]

Famine in
Rome.

Cæsar vvyll not
agree to peace
vvith Pompey.

A payment put
vpon the people.

The people resist
the decree of
Cæsar *and*
Antony.

The people resist
Cæsar.

VVho buyeth
friendship to
deere shal smart
as Antony did.

comming the holy way, the people did nothing, bycause he was willing to agree with *Pompey*, but prayde him to departe, which when he would not do, they threw stones at him. Then he brought in his soldiours that were without the walles, & not about him, into the citie, being diuided into market places and streates, wounded & set vpon the multitude & killed thē in the streates as they came. And they could not easily flee for yᵉ multitude, nor breake through by runnyng, so that many were hurte and killed, crying and yellyng from their houses.

So *Antonie* hadde muche ado to escape and *Cæsar* by him was, euidently preserued and got away. Thus did *Antonie* delyuer *Cæsar* from present perill. The bodies of the commons that were killed, were caste into the riuer to auoyde the griefe of the sight, which came not so to passe, for the Souldiours, fished for them as the streame carried them, and tooke from them their apparell, whiche grieued the beholders. Thus this euill ended with enuie of the Princes, and yet no remedie for the lacke of things, whereat the people grutched and suffered. [5.69] *Antonie* wished *Libo* hys freendes, to call him out of *Sicelie*, to congratulate for the alliance made, and he would procure greater matter, and saue him harmelesse. They wrote letters to *Libo*, and *Pompey* was content he should goe. And when he was come to the Ile called *Pithecusa*, and now *Aenaria*, the people assembled again and praied [339] *Cæsar*, to send him letters of safecōduit to come to treat of peace, which he did, although against his wil. The people also cōpelled *Mutia*, mother to *Pompey*, to go vnto him, threatning els to burne hir, & help to make peace. When *Libo* perceyued how the enimies were inclined, he desired to speake with the Captaines, that they might togither agree in the couenants, the which the people cōpelled thē with much a do, & so *Antonie* & *Cæsar* went to *Baia*. [5.70] [TLN 1280–1, 1301–2] All other persuaded *Pompey* earnestly to peace, only *Menodorus* wrote frō *Sardinia* that he should make open warre, or dryue off, whyles the dearth continued, that hee might make peace with the better cōditions, & bad him take heede of *Murcus*, who was a mouer for peace, as one that sought to be in his authoritie. Wherefore *Pompey* put away *Murcus*, and vsed his counsell no more, whome before hee honoured for his worthinesse and wisedome: whereat *Murcus* tooke displeasure and wente to *Siracuse*, and to suche as were sent after him to keepe him, spake openly agaynst *Pompey*, wherewith he beyng angrie killed diuerse of the beste aboute *Murcus*, and sent to kill him, and to say that his slaues had done it, whiche beyng done, he hanged certayne of *Murcus* slaues as though they had done it. The whiche craft was not hid, nor the wickednesse that he did against *Bithynius*, a noble man and a valiant warriour, and constant to him from the beginnyng, & his friende in *Spaine*, from whence he came willingly to serue him in *Sicelie*. [5.71] When he was dead, other men tooke in hand to persuade him to peace, & accused *Menodorus* as desirous of his office by sea, not so much caring for his master, as for his owne power. *Pōpey* folowyng their coūsell, sayled to *Aenaria*, wᵗ many chosen ships, himself being in a gorgious galley with six ores on a seate, & so did passe *Dicearchia* proudly, towarde the euening, the enimies loking vpon him. The next morning stakes were set in the sea, & bridges made, into one of yᵉ which ioyning to the lād, *Cæsar* came with *Antonie*. *Pompey* and *Libo* entred the other bridge, in such distance, yᵗ one could not heare an other, vnlesse they spake alowd. *Pompey* required societie of rule, in

Cæsar *escapeth* by Antonies *meanes.* Dead bodies cast into the ryuer, and after spoyled.

Antonies *coūsel.* The alliance of the mariage betvveene Cæsar and his sister Scribonia. Pythecusa, *vvas named* Aenaria of Aeneas, *and novv* Ischia *of strength, it vvas the inhabitance of the marquesse of* Piscara. Baia *vvas a* Citie not farre *frō* Naples, *vvhere the old* Romanes *had* great delight. Menodorus counsell. Murcus *is put* from Pompey. Siracuse, *novv* Saragosa, a goodly citie of Sicelie. Murcus *and* Bithynius *killed of* Pompey.

Novv Ischia. Dicearchia, *novv* Puzzolo, Puteoli, *an old* ruined citie,

place of *Lepidus*. They onely graūted his return to his countrie, then al was dashed. Till oftē messages wer sēt between, offring diuerse cōditiōs on both sides. [*340*] *Pompey* required that such condemned men as were with him for *Cæsars* death, might be safe in exile, & that the other men of honour & proscribed, might be restored to their countrey and goodes. The dearth continuing, & the people vrgyng peace, it was graunted that they should recouer the fourth part of their goodes, as redeeming it of the new possessioners, and wrote of it to the cōdemned men, thinkyng they would accept it, which tooke the offer, beyng now afrayde of *Pompey*, for his wickednesse committed agaynst *Murcus*, to whom they went & moued him to agree. He tore his cloke, as betrayed of them, whom he had defended, and oft called for *Menodorus*, as one expert in matters of state, and onely constant in faith. [*5.72*] At length, by the exhortatiō of *Murcia* his mother, & *Iulia* his wife, they three met agayne, vpon an old peere of the sea, beyng wel garded, where they cōcluded with these cōditions.

nearer Naples *than* Baia, *beyng three myles asunder by lande, to the* vvhich *Caligula made a bridge by the sea, meeting of* Cæsar, Antony *and* Pompey.

Pompey *in a rage.*

That peace shoulde be, bothe by sea and lande, and the Merchantes haue free course.

The conditions of peace, betvveene Antony, Cæsar & Pompey.

That *Pompey* should take his garrisons out of *Italie*, & receiue no more fugitiues, nor keepe no nauies in *Italie*.

That he should rule in *Cicelie, Corsica* and *Sardinia*, and those other Ilandes that now he had, so long as the rule should be continued to *Antonie* and *Cæsar*.

That he should send to the people of *Rome*, the corne that now was due.

That he should also rule *Pelopenesus*, besides the former Iles.

That he should exercise the office of Consul in his absence by his freende, and be admitted to the colledge of the Bishops.

That the noble mē that were banished, might returne home, except them that were condemned by publique iudgement of *Cæsars* death.

That they that were fled for feare should be restored to their goodes. And they that were cōdemned, only to the fourth parte.

That the slaues that had serued vnder *Pompey*, shoulde be free.

That the free men shoulde haue the same stipendes, that the old Soldiours of *Antonie* and *Cæsar* had.

These were the conditions of peace, whiche beyng written were sent to *Rome*, to be kept of the holy Virgins.

[5.73]

[*341*] Then they desired the one to banquet the other, and the lotte fell first to *Pompey*, who receiued them in his greate gally, ioyned to the peere.

Pompey *banqueteth* Cæsar *and* Antony, *and they him.*

The next day, *Cæsar* and *Antony* feasted hym in their Tentes, pitched on that peere, that euery man might eate on the shore, but peraduenture for their more safetie, for the Shippes were at hand, the gard in order, and the guestes with their weapons vnder their clokes. It is sayd, that *Menodorus* when they banqueted in *Pompeys* Shippe, sente one to *Pompey*, to put him in remembrance, that nowe was the time to reuenge his father and brothers death, for he would see that none should scape the Shippe: and that he aunswered, as became him then for his person and place: *Menodorus* might haue done it without me, it agreeth with *Menodorus* to be periured false, but so may not *Pompey*.

Menedorus *councell.*

Ansvvere of Pompey.

In that supper, *Pompeys* daughter, wife [i.e., niece] to *Libo*, was espoused to *Marcellus, Antonyes* nephew, sonne to *Cæsars* sister.

The next day, the Consuls were appoynted for foure yeares, first *Antony*

Consuls appoynted.

and *Libo*, and that *Antony* mighte make a substitute, next *Cæsar* and *Pompey*, then *Aenobarbus*, and *Sosius*, lastly *Cæsar* and *Antony*, thrice Consuls, and as it was hoped, to restore to the people the gouernement of the common wealth.

These things being concluded, they departed, *Pompey* with his Shippes to *Sicelie*, and they by land to *Rome*.

[5.74]

At the newes of this peace, the Citie and all *Italy* made great ioy, by the which, ciuill warre, continuall musters, insolencie of garrisons, running away of slaues, wasting of Countreys, decay of tillage, and aboue all, most greate famine was taken away: therefore, sacrifices were made by the way to the Princes, as to preseruers of the Countrey. The Citie had receyued them with a goodly triumph, hadde not they entred by nighte, bycause they would not charge the Citizens. Onely they were not partakers of the common ioy, that had the possession of the banished mens goodes, who should returne by the league, and be their heauie enimies. . . .

Reioyce for peace.

[369] Thys was he that now is in bondage [i.e., Pompey].

[5.144]

[TLN 1741–4] *Titius* commaunded hys army to sweare to *Antony*, and put hym to death at *Mileto*, when he hadde lyued to the age of fortye yeares, eyther for that he remembred late displeasure, and forgot olde good turnes, or for that he had such commaundemente of *Antony*.

Titius putteth *Pompey* to death at *Mileto, a Citie in the endes of* Ionia *and* Caria. Plancus.

There bee that saye, that *Plancus* and not *Antony*, dyd commaunde hym to dye, whyche beeyng president of *Syria*, had *Antonyes* signet, and in greate causes wrote letters in hys name. Some thynke it was done wyth *Antonyes* knowledge, he fearyng the name of *Pompey*, or for *Cleopatra*, who fauoured *Pompey* the great.

Some thynke that *Plancus* dyd it of hymselfe for these causes, and also that *Pompey* shoulde gyue no cause of dissention betweene *Cæsar* and *Antony*, or for that *Cleopatra* woulde turne hyr fauour to *Pompey*.

PEMBROKE

Pembroke's *Garnier* is generally scouted in the 19th c. as having had no effect on *Ant.* According to WHITE (ed. 1861, 12:5) on Pembroke and Daniel, Sh. "was in no way indebted to either."

Many 20th-c. scholars stress differences between the two plays and believe Sh. may have read *Antonius* without letting it affect his own conception.

FURNESS (ed. 1907, pp. 510, 513): "Its date renders it possible that it may have been read by Shakespeare. But if Shakespeare ever looked into it, I think he read no further than to the end of the *Argument*, where he found the statement that Garnier had drawn his material from Plutarch,—an ample notice that, in material for his play, the English dramatist could gain nothing from the French. . . .

[513] "Cleopatra's character is not altogether colourless, but is as far removed as possible from any Shakespearian glow. Her love is boundless, her self-reproach endless, her self-abasement abysmal, her knowledge of mythology extensive, and, had we not had some experience with [the *Cléopâtre captive* of] Jodelle, we should consider her achievement in soliloquy phenomenal."

MACCALLUM (1910, p. 61) is also cautious on the question of influence: "The grounds for believing that Shakespeare was influenced by Garnier's *Marc Antoine* are very slight; for believing that he was influenced by Daniel's *Cleopatra* are somewhat stronger; that he was influenced by Garnier's *Cornélie* [in *JC*] are stronger still; but they are even at the best precarious. In all three instances the evidence brought forward rather suggests the obligation as possible than establishes it as certain. But it seems extremely likely that Shakespeare would be acquainted with dramas that were widely read and were written by persons none of whom can have been strange to him; and in that case their stateliness and propriety may have affected him in other ways than we can trace or than he himself knew." He notes (p. 58) that Antony's dying words in *Ant.* 3024–5 are "not unlike" Cleopatra's in Garnier (see Pembroke's ll. 2019–20) and observes a further parallel between Pembroke's 1848–52 and *Ant.* 3261–6; see also nn. 2060–5 and 2884.

FARNHAM (1950, pp. 140, 155): "It may be that Shakespeare . . . knew the Countess of Pembroke's *Antonius*. . . .

[*155*] "If Shakespeare read *Antonius*, he found in it an idealized and sentimentalized pair of lovers that he was not disposed to use for his own dramatic purposes. Moreover, he found no very remarkable poetry. Hence if he did read *Antonius*, the reading produced no telltale effects upon *Antony and Cleopatra*. *Antonius* has a fifth act concerned with the actions of Cleopatra which follow the death of Antony, and at the end of Shakespeare's play the space given to those actions is large. But Shakespeare did not need to learn from *Antonius* that in a tragedy having to do with Cleopatra's ruination of Antony the death of Cleopatra could take over the stage after the death of Antony and yet be something better than an anticlimax. *Antonius* shows a dramatic appreciation of the destiny which brought the great Roman empire under the rule of one man and thereby brought the Pax Romana into a war-torn world—an appreciation not so profound, certainly, as that shown in *Antony and Cleopatra*, but genuine."

DICKEY (1957, p. 163) sees similarities but not influence: "More important, [than the question] whether Shakespeare had read *Antonius* or not, is Garnier's emphasis on certain themes from Plutarch which Shakespeare in turn emphasizes in his play. The interesting thing is that both authors deal not only with the same story but also with the same political and ethical problems and that both by very different methods indeed come to rather similar conclusions." Garnier's play (p. 168) "is more effectively handled than Jodelle's, despite its overemphatic, lengthily explicit moralizing. It moves us one step closer to Shakespeare's conception of the tragedy because, despite passages on fortune, it places the blame for tragedy squarely on the lovers. It attempts to demonstrate politics as well as ethics, showing not only the fatal end of guilty love but the consequences of this love to the Romans and Egyptians. Despite these sophisticated aims, so much of the play is taken up by self-recriminations that our feeling for Antony and Cleopatra is, if sympathetic, no catharsis."

WADDINGTON (1966, p. 217): "Relevant to Shakespeare is the example provided by his predecessors and contemporaries on the stage [for typological pairing of Hercules and Mars]. *The Tragedie of Antonie*, in which Antony is compared to the effeminate Hercules, also presents Antony implicitly associating himself with Mars and Hercules." See also p. 610.

BROWER (1971, pp. 346–7): Sh. "had almost certainly read Daniel's *The Tragedy of Cleopatra*, and perhaps also the Countess of Pembroke's translation of Garnier, *The Tragedy of Antonie*; but he could not have found in these long-winded and relatively simple plays anything like a model for *Antony and Cleopatra*. The titles indicate a major difference from Shakespeare—neither author was capable of embracing the two dramas in a single vision [similarly LEE, ed. 1907, 36:xxi]. Both works are related to the moral narrative tradition of the *Mirror for Magistrates*, though the 'complaints' are given a superficially Senecan look by assigning speakers and interspersing the lamentations and moralizing reflections with messenger speeches and with choruses on mythological parallels, on the 'healthful succour' of Death, on the evils of declining greatness and disorder. Of the two plays, *Antonie* is of the more purely complaining type, with many direct and flat lamentations by the hero on his ruin through passion and ruthless destiny. Terms common in Elizabethan heroic tragedy appear frequently: greatness, glory, passions, prowess, honour, reason. (A similar list could be compiled from Daniel's play.) There are fragmentary glimpses of Shakespeare's major theme, for example, when Antonie grieves over the loss of [*347*] his 'great Empire' [126], [quotes 'scarse . . . nations' (130–1)] or when he confesses with earnest ineptness 'So I me lost' [1169]."

Wilson and Schanzer, in contrast, stress verbal echoes. WILSON (ed. 1950, p. x, n. 2) finds phrases "strikingly similar" to those in *Ant.*; see nn. 822–5, 2060–5, 2085–6, 2173, 3026–30, and 3296–8. SCHANZER (1956, *N&Q*, pp. 152–4) finds more—see nn. 5–10, 822–5, 1354–60, 2060–5, 2887, and 3081–5—and concludes (p. 154) that Sh. "had read the Countess of Pembroke's *Antonius* shortly before or during the composition" of *Ant.* He states (1963, pp. 150–2, 178, 180–1), "In its general presentation of the love-story the Countess of Pembroke's *Antonius* . . . [*151*] is, surprisingly, not at such a far remove from Shakespeare's as one would expect. . . . It differs chiefly from Shakespeare's presentation in its omission of anything that derogates from its eulogistic portrayal of Cleopatra. Though, of course, more simple and less vital, she is basically Shakespeare's Cleopatra of Act V, with no hint of Shakespeare's Cleopatra of Acts I–IV. . . .

"While the picture of this paragon among women thus remains untarnished, Antonius's part in the love-affair is severely con-[*152*]demned by various speakers. . . .

"In *Antonius*, then, as in Shakespeare's play, we find side by side both condemnation and glorification of the love of Antony and Cleopatra. What we do not find in Garnier's play, and what is all-important in Shakespeare's, is a weighing of what Antony loses against what he gains, an alternate calling into question of the values of worldly glory and of the glory of their love." The decisive similarity is this (p. 178): "Antonius shares with Shakespeare's Antony the experience of believing himself betrayed and deserted by the woman who is above all precious to him and for whom he has sacrificed all his worldly fortunes [see Pembroke's ll. 132–43, 889–92; *Ant.* 2780–5, 2840–7]. . . .

[*180*] "Garnier's drama is thus much closer to *Antony and Cleopatra* than Daniel's, both in its concentration on Antonius's tragic [*181*] suffering and in its portrayal of the nature of that suffering." See also p. 527.

Schanzer is the first to show an awareness that Sh.'s sense of Antony's tragic greatness seems to owe more to Pembroke's extended dramatic focus on Antony's inner conflict and soul-searching than to Plutarch. STEPPAT (1987, pp. 255–71) finds that Pembroke's Antony is like Sh.'s in recollecting his onetime soldiership at Philippi (*Ant.* 2060–5, Pembroke's ll. 967–70); the placing of this recollection in Antony's mouth after his defeat, not the historical event as such, links the two plays, as does Antony's talk of Octavius's cowardice (*Ant.* 2178–9, Pembroke 1065–6, 1111–12). Steppat further observes that in both plays Antony desires vengeance on Cleopatra (*Ant.* 2772–3, Pembroke 909–10), resolves to die before receiving her false message (*Ant.* 2848–9, several passages in Pembroke, e.g., 273–4, 1009–10), and perceives the threat of humiliation in Octavius's triumph (*Ant.* 2907–13, Pembroke 28–31). Antony's complaint that Fortune has forsaken him (*Ant.* 2775–6, Pembroke 65, 980–2) is followed in both plays by a statement on the power of Cleopatra's eyes (*Ant.* 2781–2, Pembroke 79, 116–19). There are further echoes of various kinds (including *Ant.* 2340–50, Pembroke 398–405; *Ant.* 2666–9, Pembroke 1344–5; *Ant.* 3534–5, Pembroke 1927–8), Sh.'s practice being, as in his use of Plutarch, creative refashioning rather than slavish copying. Even apart from single echoes, it is conceivable that Sh.'s superior imagination was stimulated by Pembroke's presentation of Antony's tragic experience. Careful reading shows that Antony's death in Cleopatra's arms appears in Pembroke as in Sh. a more worthwhile sacrifice than it does in Plutarch; moreover, Pembroke's strategy of holding in tension two contrasting attitudes to the love relationship may have contributed to Sh.'s complex technique of mutual comment and observation. Thus Pembroke's influence on Sh. is both conceptual and, in places, verbal.

Those who see no direct influence of Pembroke's Garnier on *Ant.* also include COLLIER (ed. 1858, 6:131 n.), HALLIWELL (ed. 1865, 15:195), DYCE (ed. 1866, 7:495), GENÉE (1872; 1878, 1:346), WARD (1875; 1899, 2:186), SYMONS (in IRVING & MARSHALL, ed. 1889, 6:113), HERFORD (ed. 1899, 9:260), ANDERS (1904, p. 89), NEILSON (ed. 1906, p. 1060), WOLFF (1907; 1913, 2:259), NEILSON & HILL (ed. 1942, p. 1244), HUBBELL (1953, p. 138), SIMMONS (1973, *Shakespeare's Pagan World*, p. 127), and WILLIAMSON (1974, p. 133).

Others who think Sh. may have read Pembroke or who recognize degrees of influence include CHAMBERS (1930, 1:478), MUIR (1957, pp. 207–9: notes parallels to *Ant.* 382, 3267, in Pembroke's ll. 768 ff.; 1969, pp. 197, 200; and 1977, p. 225), BULLOUGH (1964, 5:231, 358 ff.: notes parallels, especially for *Ant.* 2884–7 in Pembroke's 546 ff., 3034–44 in 1672; however, he lists the play as an "analogue"), LABRIOLA (1966, p. 174), WALTER (ed. 1969, pp. 8, 297–8: rejects verbal echoes), and LEE (1971, p. 58). *Antonius* is included here for comparison with Plutarch and so that readers may see the context of elements directly echoed in *Ant.*

Antonius (1592)

The play was entered together with *A Discourse of Life and Death* on the Stationers' Register to William Ponsonby on 3 May 1592 (Greg, *Bibliography*, no. 108). A quarto was published with the following title page: "A | Discourse of Life | *and Death.* | Written in French by *Ph.* | *Mornay.* | Antonius, | *A Tragœdie written also in French* | by *Ro.Garnier.* | Both done in English by the | *Countesse of Pembroke.* | [device] | AT LONDON, | Printed for *William Ponsonby.* | 1592." At the end, on O2ᵛ, the play is dated "At Ramsburie. 26. of Nouember. | 1590." The printer was probably John Windet. Another edition of the play appeared in octavo in 1595 (*STC* 11623).

The following is a modified diplomatic reprint of the 1592 quarto. The quarto's italic text with incidental roman is inverted. Except for a few turnovers, the verse lineation is retained, but prose is relined. The beginning of each page in the quarto is indicated by a bracketed signature number in the text or the right margin. Factotums, flowerets, and other typographical ornaments have been removed. Ornamental initials have been replaced by regular capitals, and the capitals that conventionally follow display letters reduced. Long *s* is printed *s*, and other archaic types have been converted to modern equivalents. Obvious typographical errors have been silently corrected.

The beginnings of passages corresponding with *Ant.* are marked by TLNs in square brackets. The following parallels have been found (*Ant.* TLNs are listed, with Pembroke TLNs in parentheses): 5–10 (1963), 77–8 (873), 83 (68), 225 (80), 382 (768), 550 (1219), 728 (889), 822–5 ([Argument] sig. F1ʳ), 1038–42 (1187), 1047–51 (1228), 1316–18 ([Argument] sig. F1ʳ), 1348–50 (522, 672), 1354–60 (768 ff.), 1759–61 (1447), 2060–5 (1071, 1109), 2085–6 (446), 2173 (1069), 2780–5 (132–43, 889–92), 2840–7 (132–43, 889–92), 2848–9 (1009–10), 2884–7 (546 ff.), 2884 (1993), 2887 (1993), 2907–13 (28–31), 3024–5 (2019–20), 3026–30 ([p. 480: Argument] sig. F1ᵛ), 3034–44 (1672), 3081–5 (1901), 3261–6 (1848–52), 3267 (768), 3296–8 (1963).

The text is based on the copy in the Huntington Library (*STC* 18138). Variants in the Huntington Library's copy of the 1595 octavo are recorded at the end of the text. Variants, not recorded, are found in different copies of both editions. The play has been edited by BARNWELL (1865, pp. 1–73), LUCE (1897), and BULLOUGH (1964, 5:358–406).

[Antonius]

The Argument. [F1ʳ]

After the ouerthrowe of *Brutus* and *Cassius*, the libertie of *Rome* being now vtterly oppressed, and the Empire setled in the hands of *Octauius Cæsar* and *Marcus Antonius*, (TLN 822–5, 1316–18) who for knitting a straiter bonde of amitie betweene them, had taken to wife *Octauia* the sister of *Cæsar*) *Antonius* vndertooke a iourney against the Parthians, with intent to regaine on them the honor wonne by them from the Romains, at the discomfiture and slaughter of *Crassus*. But comming in his iourney into Siria, the places renewed in his remembrance the long intermitted loue of *Cleopatra* Queene of Aegipt: who before time had both in Cilicia and at Alexandria, entertained him with all the exquisite delightes and sumptuous pleasures, which a great Prince and voluptuous Louer could to the vttermost desire. Whereupon omitting his enterprice, he made his returne to Alexandria, againe falling to his former loues, without any regard of his vertuous wife *Octauia*, by whom neuertheles he had excellent Children. This occasion *Octauius* tooke of taking armes against him: and preparing a mighty fleet, encountred him at Actium, who also had assembled to that place a great number of Gallies of his own, besides 60. which *Cleopatra* brought with her from Aegipt. But at the very beginning of the battell *Cleopatra* with all her Gallies betooke her to flight, which *Antony* seeing could not but follow; by his departure leauing to *Octauius* the greatest victorye [F1ᵛ] which in any Sea Battell hath beene heard off. Which he not negligent to pursue, followes them the next spring, and besiedgeth them within Alexandria, where *Antony* finding all that he trusted to faile him, beginneth to growe iealouse and to suspect *Cleopatra*. She thereupon enclosed her selfe with two of her women in a monument she had before caused to be built, thence sends him woord she was dead: which he beleeuing for truth, gaue himselfe with his Swoord a deadly wound: but died not vntill a messenger came from *Cleopatra* to haue him brought to her to [TLN 3026–30] the tombe. Which she not daring to open least she should be made a prisoner to the *Romaines*, and carried in *Cæsars* triumph, cast downe a corde from an high window, by the which (her women helping her) she trussed vp *Antonius* halfe dead, and so got him into the monument. The Stage supposed Alexandria: the Chorus, first Egiptians, and after Romane Souldiors. The Historie to be read at large in *Plutarch* in the life of *Antonius*.

The Actors.

Antonius.
Cleopatra.
Eras and ⎫ *Cleopatras* women.
Charmion. ⎭
Philostratus a Philosopher.
Lucilius.
Diomede Secretary to *Cleopatra*.
Octauius Cæsar.
Agrippa.
Euphron, teacher of *Cleopatras* children.
Children of *Cleopatra*.
Dircetus the Messenger.

Act. *1*.

Antonius.

Since cruell Heau'ns against me obstinate,
Since all mishappes of the round engin doo
Conspire my harme: since men, since powers diuine,
Aire, earth, and Sea are all iniurious:
And that my Queene her self, in whome I liu'd,
The Idoll of my hart, doth me pursue;
It's meete I dye. For her haue I forgone
My Country, *Cæsar* vnto warre prouok'd
(For iust reuenge of Sisters wrong my wife,   10
Who mou'de my Queene (ay me!) to iealousie)
For loue of her, in her allurements caught
Abandon'd life, I honor haue despisde,
Disdain'd my freends, and of the statelye Rome
Despoilde the Empire of her best attire,
Contemn'd that power that made me so much fear'd,
A slaue become vnto her feeble face.
    O cruell, traitres, woman most vnkinde,
Thou dost, forsworne, my loue and life betraie:
And giu'st me vp to ragefull enemie,   20
Which soone (ô foole!) will plague thy periurye.
    Yelded *Pelusium* on this Countries shore,   [F2ᵛ]
Yelded thou hast my Shippes and men of warre.
That nought remaines (so destitute am I)
But these same armes which on my back I weare.
Thou should'st haue had them too, and me vnarm'de
Yeelded to *Cæsar* naked of defence.
Which while I beare let *Cæsar* neuer thinke   [TLN 2907–13]
Triumph of me shall his proud chariot grace
Not think with me his glory to adorne,   30
On me aliue to vse his victorie.
    Thou only *Cleopatra* triumph hast,
Thou only hast my freedome seruile made,
Thou only hast me vanquisht: not by force
(For forste I cannot be) but by sweete baites
Of thy eyes graces, which did gaine so fast
Vpon my libertie, that nought remain'd.
None els hencefoorth, but thou my dearest Queene,
Shall glorie in commaunding *Antonie*.
    Haue *Cæsar* fortune and the Gods his freends,   40
To him haue Ioue and fatall sisters giuen
The Scepter of the earth: he neuer shall
Subiect my life to his obedience.
But when that Death, my glad refuge, shall haue
Bounded the course of my vnstedfast life,

And frosen corps vnder a marble colde
Within tombes bosome widdowe of my soule:
Then at his will let him it subiect make:
Then what he will let *Cæsar* doo with me:
Make me limme after limme be rent: make me   50
My buriall take in sides of *Thracian* wolfe.
    Poore *Antonie*! alas what was the day,
The daies of losse that gained thee thy loue!   [
Wretch *Antony*! since then *Mægæra* pale
With Snakie haires enchain'd thy miserie.
The fire thee burnt was neuer *Cupids* fire
(For Cupid beares not such a mortall brand)
It was some furies torch, *Orestes* torche,
Which sometimes burnt his mother-murdering soule
(When wandring madde, rage boiling in his bloud,   60
He fled his fault which folow'd as he fled)
Kindled within his bones by shadow pale
Of mother slaine return'd from Stygian lake.
    Antony, poore *Antony*! since that daie
Thy olde good hap did farre from thee retire.
Thy vertue dead: thy glory made aliue
So ofte by martiall deeds is gone in smoke:
Since then the *Baies* so well thy forehead knewe   [TLN 83]
To Venus mirtles yeelded haue their place:
Trumpets to pipes: field tents to courtly bowers: 70
Launces and Pikes to daunces and to feastes.
Since then, ô wretch! in stead of bloudy warres
Thou shouldst haue made vpon the Parthian Kings
For Romain honor filde by *Crassus* foile,
Thou threw'st thy Curiace off, and fearfull healme,
With coward courage vnto *Ægipts* Queene
In haste to runne, about her necke to hang
Languishing in her armes thy Idoll made:
In summe giuen vp to *Cleopatras* eies.
Thou breakest at length from thence, as one encharm'd   [TLN 225]
Breakes from th'enchaunter that him strongly helde.   81
For thy first reason (spoyling of their force
The poisned cuppes of thy faire Sorceres)
Recur'd thy sprite: and then on euery side   [
Thou mad'st againe the earth with Souldiours swarme.
All Asia hidde: Euphrates bankes do tremble
To see at once so many Romanes there
Breath horror, rage, and with a threatning eye
In mighty squadrons crosse his swelling streames.
Nought seene but horse, and fier sparkling armes: 90

---

54 then] *Om.* 1595

Nought heard but hideous noise of muttring troupes.
The *Parth*, the *Mede*, abandoning their goods
Hide them for feare in hilles of *Hircanie*,
Redoubting thee. Then willing to besiege
The great *Phraate* head of *Media*,
Thou campedst at her walles with vaine assault,
Thy engins fit (mishap!) not thither brought.
   So long thou stai'st, so long thou doost thee rest,
So long thy loue with such things nourished
Reframes, reformes it selfe and stealingly   100
Retakes his force and rebecomes more great.
For of thy Queene the lookes, the grace, the woords,
Sweetenes, alurements, amorous delights,
Entred againe thy soule, and day and night,
In watch, in sleepe, her Image follow'd thee:
Not dreaming but of her, repenting still
That thou for warre hadst such a Goddes left.
   Thou car'st no more for *Parth*, nor *Parthian* bow,
Sallies, assaults, encounters, shocks, alarmes,
For diches, rampiers, wards, entrenched grounds: 110
Thy only care is sight of *Nilus* streames,
Sight of that face whose guilefull semblant doth
(Wandring in thee) infect thy tainted hart.
Her absence thee besottes: each hower, each hower
Of staie, to thee impatient seemes an age.   [F4ʳ]
Enough of conquest, praise thou deem'st enough,
If soone enough the bristled fieldes thou see
Of fruitfull *Ægipt*, and the stranger floud
Thy Queenes faire eyes (another *Pharos*) lights.
   Returned loe, dishonoured, despisde,   120
In wanton loue a woman thee misleades
Sunke in foule sinke: meane while respecting nought
Thy wife *Octauia* and her tender babes,
Of whom the long contempt against thee whets
The sword of *Cæsar* now thy Lord become.
   Lost thy great Empire, all those goodly townes.
Reuerenc'd thy name as rebells now thee leaue:
Rise against thee and to the ensignes flocke
Of conqu'ring *Cæsar*, who enwalles thee round
Cag'd in thy holde, scarse maister of thy selfe,   130
Late maister of so many nations.
   Yet, yet, which is of grief extreamest grief,   [TLN 780–5, 2840–7]
Which is yet of mischiefe highest mischiefe,
It's *Cleopatra* alas! alas, it's she,
It's she augments the torment of thy paine,
Betraies thy loue, thy life alas!) betraies,
Cæsar to please, whose grace she seekes to gaine:
With thought her Crowne to saue, and fortune make

Onely thy foe which common ought haue beene.
  If her I alwaies lou'd, and the first flame   140
Of her heart-killing loue shall burne me last:
Iustly complaine I she disloyall is,
Nor constant is, euen as I constant am,
To comfort my mishap, despising me
No more, then when the heauens fauour'd me.
  But ah! by nature women wau'ring are,   [F⁴
Each moment changing and rechanging mindes.
Vnwise, who blinde in them, thinkes loyaltie
Euer to finde in beauties company.

Chorus.   150

  The boyling tempest still
    Makes not Sea waters fome:
    Nor still the Northern blast
    Disquiets quiet streames:
    Nor who his chest to fill
    Sayles to the morning beames,
    On waues winde tosseth fast
    Still kepes his Ship from home.
  Nor *Ioue* still downe doth cast
    Inflam'd with bloudie ire   160
    On man, on tree, on hill,
    His darts of thundring fire:
    Nor still the heat doth last
    On face of parched plaine:
    Nor wrinkled colde doth still
    On frozen furrowes raigne.
  But still as long as we
    In this low world remaine,
    Mishapps our dayly mates
    Our liues do entertaine: 170
    And woes which beare no dates
    Still pearch vpon our heads,
    None go, but streight will be
    Some greater in their Steads.
  Nature made vs not free   [G
    When first she made vs liue:
    When we began to be,
    To be began our woe:
    Which growing euer more
    As dying life dooth growe,   180
    Do more and more vs greeue,
    And tire vs more and more.
  No stay in fading states,
    For more to height they retch,

484

Their fellow miseries
The more to height do stretch.
They clinge euen to the crowne,
And threatning furious wise
From tirannizing pates
Do often pull it downe.   190
In vaine on waues vntride
To shunne them go we should
To *Scythes* and *Massagetes*
Who neare the Pole reside:
In vaine to boiling sandes
Which *Phœbus* battry beates,
For with vs still they would
Cut seas and compasse landes.
The darknes no more sure
To ioyne with heauy night: 200
The light which guildes the dayes
To follow *Titan* pure:
No more the shadow light
The body to ensue:
Then wretchednes alwaies
Vs wretches to pursue.   [G1^v]
O blest who neuer breath'd,
Or whome with pittie mou'de,
Death from his cradle reau'de,
And swadled in his graue: 210
And blessed also he
(As curse may blessing haue)
Who low and liuing free
No princes charge hath prou'de.
By stealing sacred fire
Prometheus then vnwise,
Prouoking Gods to ire,
The heape of ills did sturre,
And sicknes pale and colde
Our ende which onward spurre,   220
To plague our hands too bolde
To filch the wealth of Skies.
In heauens hate since then
Of ill with ill enchain'd
We race of mortall men
Full fraught our breasts haue borne:
And thousand thousand woes
Our heau'nly soules now thorne,
Which free before from those
No earthly passion pain'd.   230
Warre and warres bitter cheare
Now long time with vs staie,

And feare of hated foe
Still still encreaseth sore:
Our harmes worse dayly growe,
Lesse yesterdaye they were
Then now, and will be more
To morowe then to daye.

[G

Act. 2.

Philostratus.   240

What horrible furie, what cruell rage,
O *Ægipt* so extremely thee torments?
Hast thou the Gods so angred by thy fault?
Hast thou against them some such crime conceiu'd,
That their engrained hand lift vp in threats
They should desire in thy hart bloud to bathe?
And that their burning wrath which nought can quench
Should pittiles on vs still lighten downe?
We are not hew'n out of the monst'rous masse
Of *Giantes* those, which heauens wrack conspir'd: 250
Ixions race, false prater of his loues:
Nor yet of him who fained lightnings found:
Nor cruell *Tantalus*, nor bloudie *Atreus*,
Whose cursed banquet for *Thyestes* plague
Made the beholding Sunne for horrour turne
His backe, and backward from his course returne:
And hastning his wing-footed horses race
Plunge him in sea for shame to hide his face:
While sulleine night vpon the wondring world
For mid-daies light her starrie mantle cast.   260
But what we be, what euer wickednes
By vs is done, Alas! with what more plagues,
More eager torments could the Gods declare
To heauen and earth that vs they hatefull holde?
With Souldiors, strangers, horrible in armes   [G
Our land is hidde, our people drown'd in teares.
But terror here and horror, nought is seene:
And present death prizing our life each hower.
Hard at our ports and at our porches waites
Our conquering foe: harts faile vs, hopes are dead: 270
Our Queene laments: and this great Emperour
Sometime (would now they did) whom worlds did feare,
Abandoned, betraid, now mindes no more
But from his euils by hast'ned death to passe.
Come you poore people tir'de with ceasles plaints
With teares and sighes make mournfull sacrifice

486

On *Isis* altars: not our selues to saue,
But soften *Cæsar* and him piteous make
To vs, his pray: that so his lenitie
May change our death into captiuitie.   280
   Strange are the euils the fates on vs haue brought,
O but alas! how farre more strange the cause!
Loue, loue (alas, who euer would haue thought?)
Hath lost this Realme inflamed with his fire.
Loue, playing loue, which men say kindles not
But in soft harts, hath ashes made our townes.
And his sweet shafts, with whose shot none are kill'd,
Which vlcer not, with deaths our lands haue fill'd.
   Such was the bloudie, murdring, hellish loue
Possest thy hart faire false guest *Priams* Sonne,   290
Fi'ring a brand which after made to burne
The *Troian* towers by *Græcians* ruinate.
By this loue, *Priam, Hector, Troilus*,
Memnon, Deiphobus, Glaucus, thousands mo,
Whome redd *Scamanders* armor clogged streames
Roll'd into Seas, before their dates are dead.   [G3ʳ]
So plaguie he, so many tempests raiseth,
So murdring he, so many Cities raiseth,
When insolent, blinde, lawles, orderles,
With madd delights our sence he entertaines.   300
   All knowing Gods our wracks did vs foretell
By signes in earth, by signes in starry Sphæres:
Which should haue mou'd vs, had not destinie
With too strong hand warped our miserie.
The *Comets* flaming through the scat'red clouds
With fiery beames, most like vnbroaded haires:
The fearefull dragon whistling at the bankes,
And holie *Apis* ceaseles bellowing
(As neuer erst) and shedding endles teares:
Bloud raining downe from heau'n in vnknow'n showers: 310
Our Gods darke faces ouercast with woe,
And dead mens Ghosts appearing in the night.
Yea euen this night while all the Cittie stoode
Opprest with terror, horror, seruile feare,
Deepe silence ouer all: the sounds were heard
Of diuerse songs, and diuers instruments,
Within the voide of aire: and howling noise,
Such as madde *Bacchus* priests in *Bacchus* feasts
On *Nisa* make: and (seem'd) the company,
Our Cittie lost, went to the enemie.   320
   So we forsaken both of Gods and men,

298 raiseth] *i.e.*, raseth

So are we in the mercy of our foes:
And we hencefoorth obedient must become
To lawes of them who haue vs ouercome.

Chorus.

[G.

Lament we our mishaps,
  Drowne we with teares our woe:
  For Lamentable happes
  Lamented easie growe:
    And much lesse torment bring
    Then when they first did spring.
We want that wofull song,
  Wherwith wood-musiques Queene
  Doth ease her woes, among,
  Fresh springtimes bushes greene,
    On pleasant branche alone
    Renewing auntient mone.
We want that monefull sounde,
  That pratling *Progne* makes
  On fieldes of *Thracian* ground,
  Or streames of *Thracian* lakes:
    To empt her brest of paine
    For *Itys* by her slaine.
Though *Halcyons* doo still,
  Bewailing *Ceyx* lot,
  The Seas with plainings fill
  Which his dead limmes haue got,
    Not euer other graue
    Then tombe of waues to haue:
And though the birde in death
  That most *Meander* loues
  So swetely sighes his breath
  When death his fury proues,
    As almost softs his heart,
    And almost blunts his dart:
Yet all the plaints of those,
  Nor all their tearfull larmes,
  Cannot content our woes,
  Nor serue to waile the harmes,
    In soule which we, poore we,
    To feele enforced be.
Nor they of *Phœbus* bredd
  In teares can doo so well,
  They for their brother shedd,
  Who into *Padus* fell,
    Rash guide of chariot cleare
    Surueiour of the yeare.

330

340

350

[G4

360

488

Nor she whom heau'nly powers
  To weping rocke did turne,
    Whose teares distill in showers,   370
    And shew she yet doth mourne,
      Where with his toppe to Skies
      Mount *Sipylus* doth rise.
Nor weping drops which flowe
  From barke of wounded tree,
    That *Myrrhas* shame do showe
    With ours compar'd may be,
      To quench her louing fire
      Who durst embrace her sire.
Nor all the howlings made   380
  On *Cybels* sacred hill
  By Eunukes of her trade,
  Who *Atys, Atys* still
    With doubled cries resound,
    Which *Echo* makes rebound.   [G4ᵛ]
Our plaints no limits stay,
  Nor more then doo our woes:
  Both infinitely straie
  And neither measure knowes.
    In measure let them plaine: 390
    Who measur'd griefes sustaine.

Cleopatra. Eras. Charmion. Diomede.

Cleopatra.

That I haue thee betraid, deare *Antonie*,
My life, my soule, my Sunne? I had such thought?
That I haue thee betraide my Lord, my King?
That I would breake my vowed faith to thee?
Leaue thee? deceiue thee? yeelde thee to the rage
Of mightie foe? I euer had that hart?
Rather sharpe lightning lighten on my head: 400
Rather may I to deepest mischiefe fall:
Rather the opened earth deuower me:
Rather fierce *Tigers* feed them on my flesh:
Rather, ô rather let our *Nilus* send,
To swallow me quicke, some weeping *Crocodile*.
  And didst thou then suppose my royall hart
Had hatcht, thee to ensnare, a faithles loue?
And changing minde, as Fortune changed cheare,
I would weake thee, to winne the stronger, loose?
O wretch! ô caitiue! ô too cruell happe!   410

376 do] doth 1595

And did not I sufficient losse sustaine
Loosing my Realme, loosing my liberty,
My tender of-spring, and the ioyfull light   [H1ʳ
Of beamy Sunne, and yet, yet loosing more
Thee *Antony* my care, if I loose not
What yet remain'd? thy loue alas! thy loue,
More deare then Scepter, children, freedome, light.
    So ready I to row in *Charons* barge,
Shall leese the ioy of dying in thy loue:
So the sole comfort of my miserie   420
To haue one tombe with thee is me bereft.
So I in shady plaines shall plaine alone,
Not (as I hop'd) companion of thy mone,
O height of griefe! *Eras.* Why with continuall cries
Your griefull harmes doo you exasperate?
Torment your selfe with murthering complaints?
Straine your weake breast so oft, so vehemently?
Water with teares this faire alablaster?
With sorrowes sting so many beauties wound?
Come of so many Kings want you the hart   430
Brauely, stoutly, this tempest to resist?
Cl. My eu'lls are wholy vnsupportable,
No humain force can them withstand, but death.
Eras. To him that striues nought is impossible.
Cl. In striuing lyes no hope of my mishapps.
Eras. All things do yeelde to force of louely face.
Cl. My face too louely caus'd my wretched case.
My face hath so entrap'd, so cast vs downe,
That for his conquest *Cæsar* may it thanke,
Causing that *Antony* one army lost   440
The other wholy did to *Cæsar* yeld.
For not induring (so his amorouse sprite
Was with my beautie fir'de) my shamefull flight,
Soone as he saw from ranke wherin he stoode   [H1ᵛ
In hottest fight, my Gallies making saile:
Forgetfull of his charge (as if his soule   [TLN 2085–6]
Vnto his Ladies soule had bene enchain'd)
He left his men, who so couragiouslie
Did leaue their liues to gaine him victorie.
And carelesse both of fame and armies losse   450
My oared Gallies follow'd with his Ships
Companion of my flight, by this base parte
Blasting his former flourishing renowne.
Eras. Are you therefore cause of his ouerthrowe?
Cl. I am sole cause: I did it, only I.
Er. Feare of a woman troubled so his sprite?
Cl. Fire of his loue was by my feare enflam'd.
Er. And should he then to warre haue ledd a Queene?

490

Cl. Alas! this was not his offence, but mine.
Antony (ay me! who else so braue a chiefe!)   460
Would not I should haue taken Seas with him:
But would haue left me fearfull woman farre
From common hazard of the doubtfull warre.
  O that I had beleu'd! now, now of *Rome*
All the great Empire at our beck should bende.
All should obey, the vagabonding *Scythes*,
The feared *Germains*, back-shooting *Parthians*,
Wandring *Numidians, Brittons* farre remoou'd,
And tawny nations scorched with the Sunne.
But I car'd not: so was my soule possest,   470
(To my great harme) with burning iealousie:
Fearing least in my absence *Antony*
Should leauing me retake *Octauia*.
Char. Such was the rigour of your destinie.
Cl. Such was my errour and obstinacie.   [H2^r]
Ch. But since Gods would not, could you doe withall?
Cl. Alwaies from Gods good happs, not harms, do fall.
Ch. And haue they not all power on mens affaires?
Cl. They neuer bow so lowe, as worldly cares.
But leaue to mortall men to be dispos'd   480
Freelie on earth what euer mortall is.
If we therin sometimes some faultes commit,
We may them not to their high maiesties,
But to our selues impute; whose passions
Plunge vs each day in all afflictions.
Wherwith when we our soules do thorned feele,
Flatt'ring our selues we say they dest'nies are:
That Gods would haue it so, and that our care
Could not empeach but that it must be so.
Char. Things here belowe are in the heau'ns begot,   490
Before they be in this our wordle borne:
And neuer can our weaknes turne awry
The stailes course of powerfull destenie.
Nought here force, reason, humaine prouidence,
Holie deuotion, noble bloud preuailes:
And Ioue himselfe whose hand doth heauens rule,
Who both to Gods and men as King commaunds,
Who earth (our firme support) with plenty stores,
Moues aire and sea with twinckling of his eie,
Who all can doe, yet neuer can vndoe   500
What once hath been by their hard lawes decreed.
  When *Troian* walles, great *Neptunes* workmanship,
Enuiron'd were with *Greekes*, and Fortunes whele
Doubtfull ten yeares now to the campe did turne,
And now againe towards the towne return'd:
How many times did force and fury swell   [H2^v]

491

In *Hectors* veines egging him to the spoile
Of conquer'd foes, which at his blowes did flie,
As fearfull shepe at feared wolues approche:
To saue (in vaine: for why? it would not be)   510
Pore walles of *Troie* from aduersaries rage,
Who died them in bloud, and cast to ground
Heap'd them with bloudie burning carcases.

    No, Madame, thinke, that if the ancient crowne
Of your progenitors that *Nilus* rul'd,
Force take from you; the Gods haue will'd it so,
To whome oft times Princes are odiouse.
They haue to euery thing an end ordain'd;
All worldly greatnes by them bounded is;
Some sooner, later some, as they think best: 520
None their decree is able to infringe.
But, which is more, to vs disastred men   [TLN 1348–50]
Which subiect are in all things to their will,
Their will is hidd: nor while we liue, we know
How, or how long we must in life remaine.
Yet must we not for that feede on dispaire,
And make vs wretched ere we wretched bee:
But alwaies hope the best, euen to the last,
That from our selues the mischief may not growe.

    Then, Madame, helpe your selfe, leaue of in time   530
Antonies wracke, lest it your wracke procure:
Retire you frrom him, saue from wrathfull rage
Of angry *Cæsar* both your Realme and you.
You see him lost, so as your amitie
Vnto his euills can yelde no more reliefe.
You see him ruin'd, so as your support
No more hencefourth can him with comfort raise.   [H5(=
With-draw you from the storme: persist not still
To loose your selfe: this royall diademe
Regaine of *Cæsar. Cl.* Soner shining light   540
Shall leaue the daie, and darknes leaue the night:
Sooner moist currents of tempestuous seas
Shall waue in heauen, and the nightlie troopes
Of starres shall shine within the foming waues,
Then I thee, *Antonie,* leaue in depe distres.
I am with thee, be it thy worthy soule   [TLN 2884–7]
Lodge in thy brest, or from that lodging parte
Crossing the ioyles lake to take hir place
In place prepared for men Demy-gods.

    Liue, if thee please, if life be lothsome die: 550
Dead and aliue, *Antonie,* thou shalt see
Thy princesse follow thee, folow, and lament,
Thy wrack, no lesse her owne then was thy weale.
Char. What helps his wrack this euer-lasting loue?

492

Cl. Help, or help not, such must, such ought I proue.
Char. Ill done to loose your selfe, and to no ende.
Cl. How ill thinke you to follow such a frende?
Char. But this your loue nought mitigates his paine.
Cl. Without this loue I should be inhumaine.
Char. Inhumaine he, who his owne death pursues.   560
Cl. Not inhumaine who miseries eschues.
Ch. Liue for your sonnes. *Cl.* Nay for their father die.
Cha. Hardhearted mother! *Cl.* Wife kindhearted I.
Ch. Then will you them depriue of royall right?
Cl. Do I depriue them? no, it's dest'nies might.
Ch. Do you not them not depriue of heritage,
That giue them vp to aduersaries handes,
A man forsaken fearing to forsake,   [H5(=3)ᵛ]
Whome such huge numbers hold enuironned?
T'abandon one gainst whome the frowning world   570
Banded with *Cæsar* makes conspiring warre.
Cl. The lesse ought I to leaue him lest of all.
A frend in most distresse should most assist.
If that when *Antonie* great and glorious
His legions led to drinke *Euphrates* streames,
So many Kings in traine redoubting him;
In triumph rais'd as high as highest heaun;
Lord-like disposing as him pleased best,
The wealth of *Greece*, the wealth of *Asia*:
In that faire fortune had I him exchaung'd   580
For *Cæsar*, then, men would haue counted me
Faithles, vnconstant, light: but now the storme,
And blustring tempest driuing on his face,
Readie to drowne, *Alas*! what would they saie?
What would himselfe in *Plutos* mansion saie?
If I, whome alwaies more then life he lou'de,
If I, who am his heart, who was his hope,
Leaue him, forsake him (and perhaps in vaine)
Weakly to please who him hath ouerthrowne?
Not light, vnconstant, faithlesse should I be,   590
But vile, forsworne, of treachrous crueltie.
Ch. Crueltie to shunne, you selfe-cruell are.
Cl. Selfe-cruell him from crueltie to spare.
Ch. Our first affection to our self is due.
Cl. He is my selfe. *Ch.* Next it extendes vnto
Our children, frends, and to our countrie soile.
And you for some respect of wiuelie loue,
(Albee scarce wiuelie) loose your natiue land,
Your children, frends, and (which is more) your life,   [H4ʳ]

566 them not] them 1595

493

With so strong charmes doth loue bewitch our witts: 600
So fast in vs this fire once kindled flames.
Yet if his harme by yours redresse might haue.
Cl. With mine it may be clos'de in darksome graue.
Ch. And that, as *Alcest* to hir selfe vnkinde,
You might exempt him from the lawes of death.
But he is sure to die: and now his sworde
Alreadie moisted is in his warme bloude,
Helples for any succour you can bring
Against deaths stinge, which he must shortlie feele.
    Then let your loue be like the loue of olde   610
Which *Carian* Queene did nourish in hir heart
Of hir Mausolus: builde for him a tombe
Whose statelinesse a wonder new may make.
Let him, let him haue sumtuouse funeralles:
Let graue thereon the horror of his fights:
Let earth be buri'd with vnburied heaps.
Frame ther *Pharsaly*, and discolour'd stream's
Of depe *Enipeus*: frame the grassie plaine,
Which lodg'd his campe at siege of *Mutina*.
Make all his combats, and couragiouse acts: 620
And yearly plaies to his praise institute:
Honor his memorie: with doubled care
Breed and bring vp the children of you both
In *Cæsars* grace: who as a noble Prince
Will leaue them Lords of this most gloriouse realme.
Cl. What shame were that? ah Gods! what infamie?
With *Antonie* in his good happs to share,
And ouerliue him dead: deeming enough
To shed some teares vpon a widdowe tombe?
The after-liuers iustly might report   630   [H4
That I him onlie for his empire lou'd,
And high state: and that in hard estate
I for another did him lewdlie leaue?
Like to those birds wafted with wandring wings
From foraine lands in spring-time here arriue:
And liue with vs so long as Somers heate,
And their foode lasts, then seke another soile.
And as we see with ceaslesse fluttering
Flocking of seelly flies a brownish cloud
To vintag'd wine yet working in the tonne,   640
Not parting thence while they swete liquor taste:
Afte., as smoke, all vanish in the aire,
And of the swarme not one so much appeare.
Eras. By this sharp death what profit can you winne?

---

632 state] estate 1595

Cl. I neither gaine, nor profit seke therin.

Er. What praise shall you of after-ages gett?

Cl. Nor praise, nor glory in my cares are sett.

Er. What other end ought you respect, then this?

Cl. My only ende my onely dutie is.

Er. Your dutie must vpon some good be founded.   650

Cl. On vertue it, the onlie good, is grounded.

Er. What is that *vertue*? *Cl.* That which vs beseemes.

Er. Outrage our selues? who that beseeming deemes?

Cl. Finish I will my sorowes dieng thus.

Er. Minish you will your glories doing thus.

Cl. Good frends I praie you seeke not to reuoke

My fix'd intent of folowing *Antonie*.

I will die. I will die: must not his life,

His life and death by mine be folowed?

   Meane while, deare sisters, liue: and while you liue,   660

Doe often honor to our loued Tombes.   [11ʳ]

Straw them with flowrs: and sometimes happelie

The tender thought of *Antonie* your Lorde

And me poore soule to teares shall you inuite,

And our true loues your dolefull voice commend.

Ch. And thinke you Madame, we from you will part?

Thinke you alone to feele deaths ougly darte?

Thinke you to leaue vs? and that the same sunne

Shall see at once you dead, and vs aliue?

Weele die with you: and *Clotho* pittilesse   670

Shall vs with you in hellish boate imbarque.

Cl. Ah liue, I praie you: this disastred woe   [TLN 1348–50]

Which racks my heart, alone to me belonges:

My lott longs not to you: seruants to be

No shame, no harme to you, as is to me.

   Liue sisters, liue, and seing his suspect

Hath causlesse me in sea of sorowes drown'd,

And that I can not liue, if so I would,

Nor yet would leaue this life, if so I could,

Without, his loue: procure me, *Diomed*,   680

That gainst poore me he be no more incensd.

Wrest out of his conceit that harmfull doubt,

That since his wracke he hath of me conceiu'd

Though wrong conceiu'd: witnesse you reuerent Gods,

Barking *Anubis, Apis* bellowing.

Tell him, my soule burning, impatient,

Forlorne with loue of him, for certaine seale

Of her true loialtie my corpse hath left,

T'encrease of dead the number numberlesse.

   Go then, and if as yet he me bewaile,   690

If yet for me his heart one sigh fourth breathe

Blest shall I be: and farre with more content   [11ᵛ]

Depart this world, where so I me torment.
Meane season vs let this sadd tombe enclose,
Attending here till death conclude our woes.
Diom. I will obey your will. *Cl.* So the desert
The Gods repay of thy true faithfull heart.

Diomed.

And is't not pittie, Gods, ah Gods of heau'n!
To see from loue such hatefull frutes to spring?   700
And is't not pittie that this firebrand so
Laies waste the trophes of *Philippi* fieldes?
Where are those swete allurements, those swete lookes,
Which Gods themselues right hart-sicke would haue made?
What doth that beautie, rarest guift of heau'n,
Wonder of earth? Alas! what doe those eies?
And that swete voice all *Asia* vnderstoode,
And sunburnt *Afrike* wide in deserts spred?
Is their force dead? haue they no further power?
Can not by them *Octauius* be surpriz'd?   710
Alas! if *Ioue* in middst of all his ire,
With thunderbolt in hand some land to plague,
Had cast his eies on my Queene, out of hande
His plaguing bolte had falne out of his hande:
Fire of his wrathe into vaine smoke should turne,
And other fire within his brest should burne.
Nought liues so faire. Nature by such a worke
Her selfe, should seme, in workmanship hath past.
She is all heau'nlie: neuer any man
But seing hir was rauish'd with her sight.   720   [I
The Allablaster couering of hir face,
The corall coullor hir two lipps engraines,
Her beamie eies, two Sunnes of this our world,
Of hir faire haire the fine and flaming golde,
Her braue streight stature, and hir winning partes
Are nothing else but fiers, fetters, dartes.
Yet this is nothing [to] th'enchaunting skilles
Of her cælestiall Sp'rite, hir training speache,
Her grace, hir Maiestie, and forcing voice,
Whither she it with fingers speach consorte,   730
Or hearing sceptred kings embassadors
Answer to eache in his owne language make.
Yet now at nede she aides hir not at all
With all these beauties, so hir sorowe stings.
Darkned with woe hir only studie is

---

733 she] it 1595

To wepe, to sigh, to seke for lonelines.
Careles of all, hir haire disordred hangs:
Hir charming eies whence murthring looks did flie,
Now riuers grown, whose well spring anguish is,
Do trickling wash the marble of hir face. 740
Hir faire discouer'd brest with sobbing swolne
Selfe cruell she still martireth with blowes.
　　Alas! It's our ill happ, for if hir teares
She would conuert into hir louing charmes,
To make a conquest of the conqueror,
(As well shee might, would she hir force imploie)
She should vs saftie from these ills procure,
Hir crowne to hir, and to hir race assure.
Vnhappy he, in whome selfe-succour lies,
Yet self-forsaken wanting succour dies. 750

Chorus. [I2ᵛ]

O swete fertile land, wherin
　　Phœbus did with breath inspire
　　Man who men did first begin,
　　Formed first of *Nilus* mire.
　　Whence of *Artes* the eldest kindes,
　　Earthes most heauenly ornament,
　　Were as from their fountaine sent,
　　To enlight our mistie mindes.
　　Whose grosse sprite from endles time, 760
　　As in darkned prison pente,
　　Neuer did to knowledg clime.
Wher the *Nile*, our father good,
　　Father-like doth neuer misse
　　Yearely vs to bring such food,
　　As to life required is:
　　Visiting each yeare this plaine,
　　And with fatt slime cou'ring it, [TLN 382, 1354–60, 3267]
　　Which his seauen mouthes do spitt,
　　As the season comes againe. 770
　　Making therby greatest growe
　　Busie reapers ioyfull paine,
　　When his flouds do highest flowe.
Wandring Prince of riuers thou,
　　Honor of the *Æthiops* lande,
　　Of a Lord and master now
　　Thou a slaue in awe must stand.
　　Now of *Tiber* which is spred
　　Lesse in force, and lesse in fame
　　Reuerence thou must the name, 780 [I3ʳ]
　　Whome all other riuers dread,

497

For his children swolne in pride,
  Who by conquest seeke to treade
  Round this earth on euery side.
Now thou must begin to sende
  Tribute of thy watrie store,
  As Sea pathes thy stepps shall bende,
  Yearely presents more and more.
  Thy fatt skumme, our frutefull corne,
  Pill'd from hence with theeuish hands   790
  All vncloth'd shall leaue our lands
  Into foraine Countrie borne.
  Which puft vp with such a pray
  Shall therby the praise adorne
  Of that scepter *Rome* doth sway.
Nought thee helps they hornes to hide
  Farre from hence in vnknowne grounds,
  That thy waters wander wide,
  Yearely breaking bankes, and bounds.
  And that thy Skie-coullor'd brookes   800
  Through a hundred peoples passe,
  Drawing plots for trees and grasse
  With a thousand turn's and crookes.
  Whome all weary of their way
  Thy throats which in widenesse passe
  Powre into their Mother Sea.
Nought so happie haplesse life
  "In this worlde as freedome findes:
  "Nought wherin more sparkes are rife
  "To inflame couragious mindes.   810
  "But if force must vs enforce
  "Nedes a yoke to vndergoe,
  "Vnder foraine yoke to goe
  "Still it proues a bondage worse.
  "And doubled subiection
  "See we shall, and feele, and knowe
  "Subiect to a stranger growne.
From hence forward for a King,
  Whose first being from this place
  Should his brest by nature bring   820
  Care of Countrie to embrace,
  We at surly face must quake
  Of some *Romaine* madly bent:
  Who, our terrour to augment,
  His *Proconsuls* axe will shake.
  Driuing with our Kings from hence
  Our establish'd gouernment,
  Iustice sworde, and Lawes defence.
Nothing worldly of such might

[13ᵛ

But more mightie *Destinie*,   830
By swift *Times* vnbridled flight,
Makes in ende his ende to see.
Euery thing *Time* ouerthrowes,
Nought to ende doth stedfast staie:
His great sithe mowes all away
As the stalke of tender rose.
Onlie Immortalitie
Of the Heau'ns doth it oppose
Gainst his powerfull *Deitie*.
One daie there will come a daie   840
Which shall quaile thy fortunes flower,
And thee ruinde low shall laie   [14ʳ]
In some barbarous Princes power.
When the pittie-wanting fire
Shall, O *Rome*, thy beauties burne,
And to humble ashes turne
Thy proud wealth, and rich attire,
Those guilt roofes which turretwise,
Iustly making Enuie mourne,
Threaten now to pearce Skies.   850
As thy forces fill each land
Haruests making here and there,
Reaping all with rauening hand
They finde growing any where:
From each land so to thy fall
Multitudes repaire shall make,
From the common spoile to take
What to each mans share maie fall.
Fingred all thou shalt beholde:
No iote left for tokens sake   860
That thou wert so great of olde.
Like vnto the auncient *Troie*
Whence deriu'de thy founders be,
Conqu'ring foe shall thee enioie,
And a burning praie in thee.
For within this turning ball
This we see, and see each daie:
All things fixed ends do staie,
Ends to first beginnings fall.
And that nought, how strong or strange,   870
Chaungles doth endure alwaie,
But endureth fatall change.

[Act. 3.]

M. Antonius. Lucilius.   [TLN 77–8]   [I4

M. Ant.

Lucil, sole comfort of my bitter case,
The only trust, the only hope I haue,
In last despaire: Ah! is not this the daie
That death should me of life and loue bereaue?
What waite I for that haue no refuge left,
But am sole remnant of my fortune left?   880
All leaue me, flie me: none, no not of them
Which of my greatnes greatest good receiu'd,
Stands with my fall: they seeme as now asham'de
That heretofore they did me ought regarde:
They draw them back, shewing they folow'd me,
Not to partake my harm's, but coozen me.
Lu. In this our world nothing is stedfast found,
In vaine he hopes, who here his hopes doth groūd.
Ant. Yet nought afflicts me, nothing killes me so,   [TLN 728, 2780–5, 2840–7]
As that I so my *Cleopatra* see   890
Practize with *Cæsar*, and to him transport
My flame, her loue, more deare then life to me.
Lu. Beleeue it not: Too high a heart she beares,
Too Princelie thoughts. *Ant.* Too wise a head she weare[s]
Too much enflam'd with greatnes, euermore
Gaping for our great Empires gouerment.
Lu. So long time you her constant loue haue tri'de.
Ant. But still with me good fortune did abide.
Lu. Her changed loue what token makes you know?
An. Pelusium lost, and *Actian* ouerthrow,   900
Both by her fraud: my well appointed fleet,   [K1
And trustie Souldiors in my quarell arm'd,
Whom she, false she, in stede of my defence,
Came to persuade, to yelde them to my foe:
Such honor *Thyre* done, such welcome giuen,
Their long close talkes I neither knew, nor would,
And treacherouse wrong *Alexas* hath me done,
Witnes too well her periur'd loue to me.
But you O Gods (if any faith regarde)
With sharpe reuenge her faithles change reward.   910
Lu. The dole she made vpon our ouerthrow,
Her Realme giuen vp for refuge to our men,
Her poore attire when she deuoutly kept
The solemne day of her natiuitie,
Againe the cost, and prodigall expence
Shew'd when she did your birth day celebrate,
Do plaine enough her heart vnfained proue,

Equally toucht, you louing, as you loue.
Ant. Well; be her loue to me or false, or true,
Once in my soule a cureles wound I feele. 920
I loue, nay burne in fire of her loue:
Each day, each night her Image haunts my minde,
Her selfe my dreames: and still I tired am,
And still I am with burning pincers nipt.
Extreame my harme: yet sweeter to my sence
Then boiling Torch of iealouse torments fire:
This grief, nay rage, in me such sturre doth kepe,
And thornes me still, both when I wake and slepe.
    Take *Cæsar* conquest, take my goods, take he
Th'onor to be Lord of the earth alone, 930
My Sonnes, my life bent headlong to mishapps:
No force, so not my *Cleopatra* take.
So foolish I, I can not her forget, [K1ᵛ]
Though better were I banisht her my thought.
Like to the sicke, whose throte the feauers fire
Hath vehemently with thirstie drouth enflam'd,
Drinkes still, albee the drinke he still desires
Be nothing else but fewell to his flame:
He can not rule himselfe: his health's respect
Yeldeth to his distempred stomackes heate. 940
Lu. Leaue of this loue, that thus renewes your woe.
Ant. I do my best, but ah! can not do so.
Lu. Thinke how you haue so braue a captaine bene,
And now are by this vaine affection falne.
Ant. The ceasles thought of my felicitie
Plunges me more in this aduersitie.
For nothing so a man in ill torments,
As who to him his good state represents.
This makes my rack, my anguish, and my woe
Equall vnto the hellish passions growe, 950
When I to minde my happie puisance call
Which erst I had by warlike conquest wonne,
And that good fortune which me neuer left,
Which hard disastre now hath me bereft.
    With terror tremble all the world I made
At my sole worde, as Rushes in the streames
At waters will: I conquer'd Italie,
I conquer'd *Rome*, that Nations so redoubt.
I bare (meane while besieging *Mutina*)
Two Consuls armies for my ruine brought, 960
Bath'd in their bloud, by their deaths witnessing
My force and skill in matters Martiall.
    To wreake thy vnkle, vnkinde *Cæsar*, I
With bloud of enemies the bankes embru'd
Of stain'd *Enipeus*, hindering his course [K2ʳ]

Stopped with heapes of piled carcases:
When *Cassius* and *Brutus* ill betide
Marcht against vs, by vs twise put to flight,
But by my sole conduct: for all the time
Cæsar heart-sicke with feare and feauer laie.   970
Who knowes it not? and how by euery one
Fame of the fact was giu'n to me alone.
    There sprang the loue, the neuer changing loue,
Wherin my hart hath since to yours bene bound:
There was it, my *Lucil*, you *Brutus* sau'de,
And for your *Brutus Antonie* you found.
Better my happ in gaining such a frende,
Then in subduing such an enemie.
Now former vertue dead doth me forsake,
Fortune engulfes me in extreame distresse: 980
She turnes from me her smiling countenance,
Casting on me mishapp vpon mishapp,
Left and betraide of thousand thousand frends,
Once of my sute, but you *Lucil* are left,
Remaining to me stedfast as a tower
In holy loue, in spite of fortunes blastes.
But if of any God my voice be heard,
And be not vainely scatt'red in the heau'ns,
Such goodnes shall not glorilesse be loste,
But comming ages still therof shall boste.   990
Lu. Men in their frendship euer should be one,
And neuer ought with fickle Fortune shake,
Which still remoues, nor will, nor knowes the way,
Her rowling bowle in one sure state to staie.
Wherfore we ought as borrow'd things receiue
The goods light she lends vs to pay againe:
Not holde them sure, nor on them builde our hopes   [K:
As one such goods as cannot faile, and fall:
But thinke againe, nothing is dureable,
Vertue except, our neuer failing hoste: 1000
So bearing saile when fauouring windes do blowe,
As frowning Tempests may vs least dismaie
When they on vs do fall: not ouer-glad
With good estate, nor ouer-grieu'd with bad.
Resist mishap. *Ant.* Alas! it is too stronge.
Mishappes oft times are by some comfort borne:
But these, ay me! whose weights oppresse my hart,
Too heauie lie, no hope can them relieue.
There rests no more, but that with cruell blade   [TLN 2848-9]
For lingring death a hastie waie be made.   1010
Lu. Cæsar, as heire vnto his Fathers state:
So will his Fathers goodnes imitate,
To you warde: whome he know's allied in bloud,

Allied in mariage, ruling equallie
Th'Empire with him, and with him making warre
Haue purg'd the earth of *Cæsars* murtherers.
You into portions parted haue the world
Euen like coheir's their heritages parte:
And now with one accord so many yeares
In quiet peace both haue your charges rul'd.   1020
Ant. Bloud and alliance nothing do preuaile
To coole the thirst of hote ambitious breasts:
The sonne his Father hardly can endure,
Brother his brother, in one common Realme.
So feruent this desier to commaund:
Such iealousie it kindleth in our hearts.
Sooner will men permit another should
Loue her they loue, then weare the Crowne they weare.
All lawes it breakes, turns all things vpside downe: [K3ʳ]
Amitie, kindred, nought so holie is   1030
But it defiles. A monarchie to gaine
None cares which way, so he maie it obtaine.
Lu. Suppose he Monarch be and that this world
No more acknowledg sundrie Emperours.
That *Rome* him onelie feare, and that he ioyne
The East with west, and both at once do rule:
Why should he not permitt you peaceablie
Discharg'd of charge and Empires dignitie,
Priuate to liue reading *Philosophie*,
In learned *Greece, Spaine, Asia*, anie lande?   1040
Ant. Neuer will he his Empire thinke assur'de
While in this world *Marke Antonie* shall liue.
Sleeples Suspicion, Pale distrust, colde feare
Alwaies to princes companie do beare
Bred of Reports: reports which night and day
Perpetuall guests from Court go not away.
Lu. He hath not slaine your brother *Lucius*,
Nor shortned hath the age of *Lepidus*,
Albeit both into his hands were falne,
And he with wrath against them both enflam'd.   1050
Yet one, as Lord in quiet rest doth beare
The greatest sway in great *Iberia*:
The other with his gentle Prince retaines
Of highest Priest the sacred dignitie.
Ant. He feares not them, their feeble force he knowes.
Lu. He feares no vanquisht ouerfill'd with woes.
Ant. Fortune may chaunge againe. *L.* A down-cast foe
Can hardlie rise, which once is brought so lowe.
Ant. All that I can, is done: for last assay
(When all means fail'd) I to entreatie fell,   1060
(Ah coward creature!) whence againe repulst   [K3ᵛ]

Of combate I vnto him proffer made:
Though he in prime, and I by feeble age
Mightily weakned both in force and skill.
Yet could not he his coward heart aduaunce
Baselie affraid to trie so praisefull chaunce.
This makes me plaine, makes me my selfe accuse,
Fortune in this hir spitefull force doth vse
'Gainst my gray hayres: in this vnhappie I   [TLN 2173]
Repine at heau'ns in my happes pittiles.   1070
A man, a woman both in might and minde,   [TLN 2060-5]
In *Marses* schole who neuer lesson learn'd,
Should me repulse, chase, ouerthrow, destroie,
Me of such fame, bring to so lowe an ebbe?
Alcides bloud, who from my infancie
With happie prowesse crowned haue my praise.
Witnesse thou *Gaule* vnus'd to seruile yoke,
Thou valiant *Spaine*, you fields of *Thessalie*
With millions of mourning cries bewail'd,
Twise watred now with bloude of *Italie*.   1080
Lu. Witnesse may *Afrique*, and of conquer'd world
All fower quarters witnesses may be.
For in what part of earth inhabited,
Hungrie of praise haue you not ensignes spredd?
An. Thou know'st rich *Ægypt* (*Ægypt* of my deeds
Faire and foule subiect) *Ægypt* ah! thou know'st
How I behau'd me fighting for thy kinge,
When I regainde him his rebellious Realme:
Against his foes in battaile shewing force,
And after fight in victorie remorse.   1090
  Yet if to bring my glorie to the ground,
Fortune had made me ouerthrowne by one
Of greater force, of better skill then I;   [H
One of those Captaines feared so of olde,
Camill, Marcellus, worthy *Scipio*,
This late great *Cæsar*, honor of our state,
Or that great *Pompei* aged growne in armes;
That after haruest of a world of men
Made in a hundred battailes, fights, assaults,
My bodie thorow pearst with push of pike   1100
Had vomited my bloud, in bloud my life,
In midd'st of millions felowes in my fall:
The lesse hir wrong, the lesse should my woe:
Nor she should paine, nor I complaine me so.
  No, no, wheras I should haue died in armes,
And vanquisht oft new armies should haue arm'd,

1072 *Marses*] *Mars his* 1595

New battailes giuen, and rather lost with me
All this whole world submitted vnto me:
A man who neuer saw enlaced pikes
With bristled pointes against his stomake bent,
Who feares the field, and hides him cowardly
Dead at the verie noise the souldiors make.

His vertue, fraude, deceit, malicious guile,
His armes the arts that false *Vlisses* vs'de,
Knowne at Modena, wher the *Consuls* both
Death-wounded were, and wounded by his men
To gett their armie, warre with it to make
Against his faith, against his countrie soile.
Of *Lepidus*, which to his succours came,
To honor whome he was by dutie bounde,
The Empire he vsurpt: corrupting first
With baites and bribes the most part of his men.
Yet me hath ouercome, and made his pray,
And state of *Rome*, with me hath ouercome.
Strange! one disordred act at *Actium*
The earth subdu'de, my glorie hath obscur'd.
For since, as one whome heauens wrath attaints,
With furie caught, and more then furious
Vex'd with my euills, I neuer more had care
My armies lost, or lost name to repaire:
I did no more resist. *Lu.* All warres affaires,
But battailes most, daily haue their successe
Now good, now ill: and though that fortune haue
Great force and power in euery wordlie thing,
Rule all, do all, haue all things fast enchaind
Vnto the circle of hir turning wheele:
Yet seemes it more then any practise else
She doth frequent *Ballonas* bloudie trade:
And that hir fauour, wauering as the wind,
Hir greatest power therin doth oftnest shewe.
Whence growes, we dailie see, who in their youth
Gatt honor ther, do loose it in their age,
Vanquisht by some lesse warlike then themselues:
Whome yet a meaner man shall ouerthrowe.
Hir vse is not to lende vs still her hande,
But sometimes headlong back a gaine to throwe,
When by hir fauor she hath vs extolld
Vnto the topp of highest happines.
Ant. Well ought I curse within my grieued soule,
Lamenting daie and night, this sencelesse loue,
Whereby my faire entising foe entrap'd
My hedelesse *Reason*, could no more escape.
It was not fortunes euer chaunging face,
It was not Dest'nies chaungles violence

[TLN 2060-5]
1110

1120

[K4^v]

1130

1140

1150

505

Forg'd my mishap. Alas! who doth not know
They make, nor marre, nor any thing can doe.
Fortune, which men so feare, adore, detest,   [L 1
Is but a chaunce whose cause vnknow'n doth rest.
Although oft times the cause is well perceiu'd,
But not th'effect the same that was conceiu'd.   1160
Pleasure, nought else, the plague of this our life,
Our life which still a thousand plagues pursue,
Alone hath me this strange disastre spunne,
Falne from a souldior to a Chamberer,
Careles of vertue, careles of all praise.
Nay, as the fatted swine in filthy mire
With glutted heart I wallow'd in delights,
All thoughts of honor troden vnder foote.
So I me lost: for finding this swete cupp
Pleasing my tast, vnwise I drunke my fill,   1170
And through the swetenes of that poisons power
By stepps I draue my former witts astraie.
I made my frends, offended me forsake,
I holpe my foes against my selfe to rise.
I robd my subiects, and for followers
I saw my selfe besett with flatterers.
Mine idle armes faire wrought with spiders worke,
My scattred men without their ensignes strai'd:
Cæsar meane while who neuer would haue dar'de
To cope with me, me sodainlie despis'de,   1180
Tooke hart to fight, and hop'de for victorie
On one so gone, who glorie had forgone.
Lu. Enchaunting pleasure, *Venus* swete delights
Weaken our bodies, ouer-cloud our sprights,
Trouble our reason, from our harts out chase
All holie vertues lodging in their place.
Like as the cunning fisher takes the fishe   [TLN 1038–42]
By traitor baite wherby the hooke is hidde:
So *Pleasure* serues to vice in steede of foode   [L 1
To baite our soules theron too licourishe.   1190
This poison deadlie is alike to all,
But on great kings doth greatest outrage worke,
Taking the Roiall scepters from their hands,
Thenceforward to be by some straunger borne:
While that their people charg'd with heauy loades
Their flatt'rers pill, and suck their mary drie,
Not ru'lde but left to great men as a pray,
While this fonde Prince himselfe in pleasur's drowns:
Who heares nought, sees nought, doth nought of a king,
Seming himselfe against himselfe conspirde.   1200
Then equall Iustice wandreth banished,
And in hir seat sitts greedie Tyrannie.

506

Confus'd disorder troubleth all estates,
Crimes without feare and outrages are done.
Then mutinous *Rebellion* shewes hir face,
Now hid with this, and now with that pretence,
Prouoking enimies, which on each side
Enter at ease, and make them Lords of all.
The hurtfull workes of pleasure here behold.
An. The wolfe is not so hurtfull to the folde,   1210
Frost to the grapes, to ripened fruits the raine:
As pleasure is to Princes full of paine.
Lu. Ther nedes no proofe, but by th' *Assirian* kinge,
On whome that Monster woefull wrack did bring.
An. Ther nedes no proofe, but by vnhappie I,
Who lost my empire, honor, life therby.
Lu. Yet hath this ill so much the greater force,
As scarcelie anie do against it stand:
No, not the Demy-gods the olde world knew,   {TLN 550}
Who all subdu'de, could *Pleasures* power subdue.   1220
   Great *Hercules, Hercules* once that was   [L3(= 2)^r]
Wonder of earth and heau'n, matchles in might,
Who *Anteus, Lycus, Geryon* ouercame,
Who drew from hell the triple-headed dogg,
Who *Hydra* kill'd, vanquishd *Achelous,*
Who heauens weight on his strong shoulders bare:
Did he not vnder *Pleasures* burthen bow?
Did he not Captiue to this passion yelde,   {TLN 1047–51}
When by his Captiue, so he was enflam'de,
As now your selfe in *Cleopatra* burne?   1230
Slept in hir lapp, hir bosome kist and kiste,
With base vnsemelie seruice bought her loue,
Spinning at distaffe, and with sinewy hand
Winding on spindles threde, in maides attire?
His conqu'ring clubbe at rest on wal did hang:
His bow vnstringd he bent not as he vs'de:
Vpon his shafts the weauing spiders spunne:
And his hard cloake the freating mothes did pierce.
The monsters free and fearles all the time
Throughout the world the people did torment,   1240
And more and more encreasing daie by day
Scorn'd his weake heart become a mistresse plaie.
An. In onelie this like *Hercules* am I,
In this I proue me of his lignage right:
In this himselfe, his deedes I shew in this,
In this, nought else, my ancestor he is.
   But goe we: die I must, and with braue ende
Conclusion make of all foregoing harmes:
Die, die I must: I must a noble death,
A glorious death vnto my succor call: 1250

I must deface the shame of time abus'd,
I must adorne the wanton loues I vs'de
With some couragiouse act: that my last daie   [L3(=
By mine owne hand my spotts may wash away.
   Come deare *Lucill*: alas! why wepe you thus!
This mortall lot is common to vs all.
We must all die, each doth in homage owe
Vnto that God that shar'd the Realmes belowe.
Ah sigh no more: alas: appeace your woes,
For by your griefe my griefe more eager growes.   1260

Chorus.

Alas, with what tormenting fire,
Vs martireth this blinde desire
   To staie our life from flieng!
How ceasleslie our minds doth rack,
How heauie lies vpon our back
   This dastard feare of dieng!
Death rather healthfull succor giues,
Death rather all mishapps relieues
   That life vpon vs throweth: 1270
And euer to vs doth vnclose
The doore, wherby from curelesse woes
   Our wearie soule out goeth.
What Goddesse else more milde then shee
To burie all our paine can be,
   What remedie more pleasing?
Our pained hearts when dolor stings,
And nothing rest, or respite brings,
   What help haue we more easing?
Hope which to vs doth comfort giue,   1280
And doth o[u]r fainting hearts reuiue,
   Hath not such force in anguish:
For promising a vaine reliefe
She oft vs failes in midst of griefe,
   And helples letts vs languish.
But Death who call on her at nede
Doth neuer with vaine semblant feed,
   But when them sorow paineth,
So riddes their soules of all distresse
Whose heauie weight did them oppresse,   1290
   That not one griefe remaineth.
Who feareles and with courage bolde
Can *Acherons* black face beholde,
   Which muddie water beareth:
And crossing ouer, in the way

Is not amaz'd at Perruque gray
   Olde rustie *Charon* weareth:
Who voide of dread can looke vpon
The dreadfull shades that rome alone,
   On bankes where sound no voices: 1300
Whom with her fire-brands and her Snakes
No whit afraide *Alecto* makes,
   Nor triple-barking noyses:
Who freely can himselfe dispose
Of that last hower which all must close,
   And leaue this life at pleasure:
This noble freedome more esteemes,
And in his hart more precious deemes,
   Then Crowne and kingly treasure.
The waues which *Boreas* blasts turmoile   1310
And cause with foaming furie boile,
   Make not his heart to tremble:
Nor brutish broile, when with strong head
A rebell people madly ledde   [L3ᵛ]
   Against their Lords assemble:
Nor fearfull face of Tirant wood,
Who breaths but threats, and drinks but bloud,
   No, nor the hand which thunder,
The hand of *Ioue* which thunder beares,
And ribbs of rocks in sunder teares,   1320
   Teares mountains sides in sunder:
Nor bloudie *Marses* butchering bands,
Whose lightnings desert laie the lands
   Whome dustie cloudes do couer:
From of whose armour sun-beames flie,
And vnder them make quaking lie
   The plaines wheron they houer:
Nor yet the cruell murth'ring blade
Warme in the moistie bowells made
   Of people pell mell dieng   1330
In some great Cittie put to sack
By sauage Tirant brought to wrack,
   At his colde mercie lieng.
How abiect him, how base think I,
Who wanting courage can not dye
   When need him therto calleth?
From whom the dagger drawne to kill
The curelesse griefes that vexe him still
   For feare and faintnes falleth?
O *Antonie* with thy deare mate   1340
Both in misfortunes fortunate!
   Whose thoughts to death aspiring

Shall you protect frrom victors rage,
Who on each side doth you encage,
  To triumph much desiring.
That *Cæsar* may you not offend

[L

Nought else but Death can you defend,
  Which his weake force derideth,
And all in this round earth containd,
Pow'rles on them whom once enchaind

1350

  Auernus prison hideth:
Where great *Psammetiques* ghost doth rest,
Not with infernall paine possest,
  But in swete fields detained:
And olde *Amasis* soule likewise,
And all our famous *Ptolemies*
  That whilome on vs raigned.

Act. 4.

Cæsar. Agrippa. Dircetus
the Messenger.

1360

Cæsar.

You euer-liuing Gods which all things holde
Within the power of your celestiall hands,
By whom heate, colde, the thunder, and the winde,
The properties of enterchaunging mon'ths
Their course and being haue; which do set downe
Of Empires by your destinied decree
The force, age, time, and subiect to no chaunge
Chaunge all, reseruing nothing in one state:
You haue aduaunst, as high as thundring heau'n

1370

The *Romains* greatnes by *Bellonas* might:
Mastring the world with fearfull violence,
Making the world widow of libertie.

[L

Yet at this daie this proud exalted *Rome*
Despoil'd, captiu'd, at one mans will doth bende:
Her Empire mine, her life is in my hand,
As Monarch I both world and *Rome* commaund;
Do all, can all; fourth my commaund'ment cast
Like thundring fire from one to other Pole
Equall to Ioue: bestowing by my worde

1380

Happes and mishappes, as Fortunes King and Lord.
  No Towne there is, but vp my Image settes,
But sacrifice to me doth dayly make:
Whither where *Phæbus* ioyne his morning steedes,
Or where the night them weary entertaines,
Or where the heat the *Garamants* doth scorche,

510

Or where the colde from *Boreas* breast is blowne:
All *Cæsar* do both awe and honor beare,
And crowned Kings his verie name do feare.
    Antonie knowes it well, for whom not one   1390
Of all the Princes all this earth do rule,
Armes against me: for all redoubt the power
Which heau'nly powers on earth haue made me beare.
    Antonie, he poore man with fire enflam'de
A womans beauties kindled in his heart,
Rose against me, who longer could not beare
My sisters wrong he did so ill entreat:
Seing her left while that his leud delights
Her husband with his *Cleopatra* tooke
In *Alexandrie*, where both nights and daies   1400
Their time they pass'd in nought but loues and plaies.
    All *Asias* forces into one he drewe,
And forth he sett vpon the azur'd waues
A thousand and a thousand Shipps, which fill'd   [M1^r]
With Souldiors, pikes, with targets, arrowes, darts,
Made *Neptune* quake, and all the watrie troupes
Of *Glauques*, and *Tritons* lodg'd at *Actium*.
But mightie Gods, who still the force withstand
Of him, who causles doth another wrong,
In lesse then moments space redus'd to nought   1410
All that proud power by Sea or land he brought.
Agr. Presumptuouse pride of high and hawtie sprite,
Voluptuouse care of fonde and foolish loue,
Haue iustly wrought his wrack: who thought he helde
(By ouerweening) Fortune in his hand.
Of vs he made no count, but as to play,
So fearles came our forces to assay.
    So sometimes fell to Sonnes of Mother Earth,
Which crawl'd to heau'n warre on the Gods to make,
Olymp on *Pelion, Ossa* on *Olymp*,   1420
Pindus on *Ossa* loading by degrees:
That at hand strokes with mightie clubbes they might
On mossie rocks the Gods make tumble downe:
When mightie *Ioue* with burning anger chaf'd,
Disbraind with him *Gyges* and *Briareus*,
Blunting his darts vpon their brused bones.
For no one thing the Gods can lesse abide
In dedes of men, then Arrogance and Pride.
And still the proud, which too much takes in hand,
Shall fowlest fall, where best he thinks to stand.   1430
Cæs. Right as some Pallace, or some stately tower,

1389 do] doth 1595

511

Which ouer-lookes the neighbour buildings round
In scorning wise, and to the Starres vp growes,
Which in short time his owne weight ouerthrowes.
   What monstrous pride, nay what impietie
Incenst him onward to the Gods disgrace?   [M 1

When his two children, *Cleopatras* bratts,
To *Phœbe* and her brother he compar'd,
Latonas race, causing them to be call'd
The Sunne and Moone? Is not this folie right?   1440
And is not this the Gods to make his foes?
And is not this himself to worke his woes?
Agr. In like proud sort he caus'd his head to leese
The Iewish king *Antigonus*, to haue
His Realme for balme, that *Cleopatra* lou'd,
As though on him he had some treason prou'd.
Cæs. Lydia to her, and *Siria* he gaue,   [TLN 1759–61]
Cyprus of golde, *Arabia* rich of smelles:
And to his children more *Cilicia,*
Parth's, Medes, Armenia, Phœnicia: 1450
The kings of kings proclaiming them to be,
By his owne worde, as by a sound decree.
Agr. What? Robbing his owne countrie of her due
Triumph'd he not in *Alexandria*,
Of *Artabasus* the *Armenian* King,
Who yelded on his periur'd word to him?
Cæs. Nay, neuer *Rome* more iniuries receiu'd,
Since thou, ô *Romulus*, by flight of birds
With happy hand the *Romain* walles did'st build,
Then *Antonies* fond loues to it hath done.   1460
Nor euer warre more holie, nor more iust,
Nor vndertaken with more hard constraint,
Then is this warre: which were it not, our state
Within small time all dignitie should loose:
Though I lament (thou Sunne my witnes art,
And thou great *Ioue*) that it so deadly proues:
That *Romain* bloud should in such plentie flowe,   [M 2
Watring the fields and pastures where we goe.
What *Carthage* in olde hatred obstinate,
What *Gaule* still barking at our rising state,   1470
What rebell *Samnite*, what fierce *Pyrrhus* power,
What cruell *Mithridate*, what *Parth* hath wrought
Such woe to *Rome*? whose common wealth he had,
(Had he bene victor) into *Egipt* brought.
Agr. Surely the Gods, which haue this Cittie built
Stedfast to stand as long as time endures,
Which kepe the Capitoll, of vs take care,
And care will take of those shall after come,
Haue made you victor, that you might redresse

Their honor growne by passed mischieues lesse. 1480
Cæs. The seelie man when all the Greekish Sea
His fleete had hidd, in hope me sure to drowne,
Me battaile gaue: where fortune, in my stede,
Repulsing him his forces disaraied.
Him selfe tooke flight, soone as his loue he saw
All wanne through feare with full sailes flie away.
His men, though lost, whome none did now direct,
With courage fought fast grappled shipp with shipp,
Charging, resisting, as their oares would serue,
With darts, with swords, with Pikes, with fierie flames. 1490
So that the darkned night her starrie vaile
Vpon the bloudie sea had ouer-spred,
Whilst yet they held: and hardlie, hardlie then
They fell to flieng on the wauie plaine.
All full of Souldiors ouerwhelm'd with waues:
The aire throughout with cries and grones did sound:
The Sea did blush with bloud: the neighbor shores
Groned, so they with shipwracks pestred were, [M2ᵛ]
And floting bodies left for pleasing foode
To birds, and beasts, and fishes of the sea. 1500
You know it well *Agrippa. Ag.* Mete it was
The *Romain* Empire so should ruled be,
As heau'n is rul'd: which turning ouer vs,
All vnder things by his example turnes.
Now as of heau'n one onely Lord we know:
One onely Lord should rule this earth below.
When one self pow're is common made to two,
Their duties they nor suffer will, nor doe.
In quarell still, in doubt, in hate, in feare;
Meane while the people all the smart do beare. 1510
Cæs. Then to the ende none, while my daies endure,
Seeking to raise himselfe may succours finde,
We must with bloud marke this our victorie,
For iust example to all memorie.
Murther we must, vntill not one we leaue,
Which may hereafter vs of rest bereaue.
Ag. Marke it with murthers? who of that can like?
Cæ. Murthers must vse, who doth assurance seeke.
Ag. Assurance call you enemies to make?
Cæs. I make no such, but such away I take. 1520
Ag. Nothing so much as rigour doth displease.
Cæs. Nothing so much doth make me liue at ease.
Ag. What ease to him that feared is of all?
Cæ. Feared to be, and see his foes to fall.
Ag. Commonly feare doth brede and nourish hate.
Cæ. Hate without pow'r, comes comonly too late.
Ag. A feared Prince hath oft his death desir'd.

Cæ. A Prince not fear'd hath oft his wrong conspir'de.
Ag. No guard so sure, no forte so strong doth proue,   [M
No such defence, as is the peoples loue.   1530
Cæs. Nought more vnsure more weak, more like the winde,
Then *Peoples* fauor still to chaunge enclinde.
Ag. Good Gods! what loue to gracious Prince men beare!
Cæs. What honor to the Prince that is seuere!
Ag. Nought more diuine then is *Benignitie*.
Cæ. Nought likes the *Gods* as doth *Seueritie*.
Ag. Gods all forgiue. *Cæ.* On faults they paines do laie.
Ag. And giue their goods. *Cæ.* Oft times they take away.
Ag. They wreake them not, ô *Cæsar*, at each time
That by our sinnes they are to wrathe prouok'd.   1540
Neither must you (beleue, I humblie praie)
Your victorie with crueltie defile.
The Gods it gaue, it must not be abus'd,
But to the good of all men mildlie vs'd,
And they be thank'd: that hauing giu'n you grace
To raigne alone, and rule this earthlie masse,
They may hence-forward hold it still in rest,
All scattred power vnited in one brest.
Cæ. But what is he, that breathles comes so fast,
Approching vs, and going in such hast?   1550
Ag. He semes affraid: and vnder his arme I
(But much I erre) a bloudie sworde espie.
Cæs. I long to vnderstand what it may be.
Ag. He hither comes: it's best we stay and see.
Dirce. What good God now my voice will reenforce,
That tell I may to rocks, and hilles, and woods,
To waues of sea, which dash vpon the shore,
To earth, to heau'n, the woefull newes I bring?
Ag. What sodaine chaunce thee towards vs hath brought?
Dir. A lamentable chance. O wrath of heau'ns!   1560
O Gods too pittiles! *Cæs.* What monstrous happ   [M
Wilt thou recount? *Dir.* Alas too hard mishapp!
When I but dreame of what mine eies beheld,
My hart doth freeze, my limmes do quiuering quake,
I senceles stand, my brest with tempest tost
Killes in my throte my wordes, ere fully borne.
Dead, dead he is: be sure of what I say,
This murthering sword hath made the man away.
Cæs. Alas my heart doth cleaue, pittie me rackes,
My breast doth pant to heare this dolefull tale.   1570
Is *Antonie* then dead? To death, alas!
I am the cause despaire him so compelld.
But souldiour of his death the maner showe,
And how he did this liuing light forgoe.
Dir. When *Antonie* no hope remaining saw

514

How warre he might, or how agreement make,
Saw him betraid by all his men of warre
In euery fight as well by sea, as lande;
That not content to yeld them to their foes
They also came against himselfe to fight: 1580
Alone in Court he gan himself torment,
Accuse the Queene, himselfe of hir lament,
Call'd hir vntrue and traytresse, as who sought
To yeld him vp she could no more defend:
That in the harmes which for hir sake he bare,
As in his blisfull state, she might not share.
   But she againe, who much his furie fear'd,
Gatt to the Tombes, darke horrors dwelling place:
Made lock the doores, and pull the hearses downe.
Then fell shee wretched, with hir selfe to fight.   1590
A thousand plaints, a thousand sobbes she cast
From hir weake brest which to the bones was torne.
Of women hir the most vnhappie call'd,   [M4ʳ]
Who by hir loue, hir woefull loue, had lost
Hir realme, hir life, and more, the loue of him,
Who while he was, was all hir woes support.
But that she faultles was she did inuoke
For witnes heau'n, and aire, and earth, and sea.
Then sent him worde, she was no more aliue,
But lay inclosed dead within hir Tombe.   1600
This he beleeu'd; and fell to sigh and grone,
And crost his armes, then thus began to mone.
Cæs. Poore hopeles man! *Dir.* What dost thou more attend
Ah *Antonie*! why dost thou death deferre:
Since *Fortune* thy professed enimie,
Hath made to die, who only made thee liue?
Sone as with sighes he had these words vp clos'd,
His armor he vnlaste, and cast it of,
Then all disarm'd he thus againe did say:
My Queene, my heart, the grief that now I feele,   1610
Is not that I your eies, my Sunne, do loose,
For soone againe one Tombe shal vs conioyne:
I grieue, whom men so valorouse did deeme,
Should now, then you, of lesser valor seeme.
   So said, forthwith he *Eros* to him call'd,
Eros his man; summond him on his faith
To kill him at his nede. He tooke the sworde,
And at that instant stab'd therwith his breast,
And ending life fell dead before his fete.
O *Eros* thankes (quoth *Antonie*) for this   1620
Most noble acte, who pow'rles me to kill,
On thee hast done, what I on mee should doe.
   Of speaking thus he scarce had made an ende,

And taken vp the bloudie sword from ground,
But he his bodie piers'd; and of redd bloud
A gushing fountaine all the chamber fill'd.
He staggred at the blowe, his face grew pale,
And on a couche all feeble downe he fell,
Swounding with anguish: deadly cold him tooke,
As if his soule had then his lodging left.   1630
But he reuiu'd, and marking all our eies
Bathed in teares, and how our breasts we beatt
For pittie, anguish, and for bitter griefe,
To see him plong'd in extreame wretchednes:
He prai'd vs all to haste his lingr'ing death:
But no man willing, each himselfe withdrew.
Then fell he new to crie and vexe himselfe,
Vntill a man from *Cleopatra* came,
Who said from hir he had commaundement
To bring him to hir to the monument.   1640
    The poore soule at these words euen rapt with Ioy
Knowing she liu'd, prai'd vs him to conuey
Vnto his Ladie. Then vpon our armes
We bare him to the Tombe, but entred not.
For she, who feared captiue to be made,
And that she should to *Rome* in triumph goe,
Kept close the gate: but from a window high
Cast downe a corde, wherin he was impackt.
Then by hir womens helpt the corps she rais'd,
And by strong armes into hir windowe drew.   1650
    So pittifull a sight was neuer sene.
Little and little *Antonie* was pull'd,
Now breathing death: his beard was all vnkempt,
His face and brest all bathed in his bloud.
So hideous yet, and dieng as he was,
His eies half-clos'd vppon the Queene he cast:
Held vp his hands, and holpe himself to raise,   [N1ʳ
But still with weakenes back his bodie fell.
The miserable ladie with moist eies,
With haire which careles on hir forhead hong,   1660
With brest which blowes had bloudilie benumb'd,
With stooping head, and bodie down-ward bent,
Enlast hir in the corde, and with all force
This life-dead man couragiously vprais'de.
The bloud with paine into hir face did flowe,
Hir sinewes stiff, her selfe did breathles growe.
    The people which beneath in flocks beheld,
Assisted her with gesture, speech, desire:
Cri'de and incourag'd her, and in their soules

[M4ᵛ]

1649 helpt] help 1595

516

Did sweate, and labor, no white lesse then shee. 1670
Who neuer tir'd in labor, held so long
Helpt by hir women, and hir constant heart, [TLN 3034–44]
That *Antonie* was drawne into the tombe,
And ther (I thinke) of dead augments the summe.
The Cittie all to teares and sighes is turn'd,
To plaints and outcries horrible to heare:
Men, women, children, hoary-headed age
Do all pell mell in house and strete lament,
Scratching their faces, tearing of their haire,
Wringing their hands, and martyring their brests. 1680
Extreame their dole: and greater misery
In sacked townes can hardlie euer be.
Not if the fire had scal'de the highest towers:
That all things were of force and murther full;
That in the streets the bloud in riuers stream'd;
The sonne his sire saw in his bosome slaine,
The sire his sonne: the husband reft of breath
In his wiues armes, who furious runnes to death.
Now my brest wounded with their piteouse plaints [N1ᵛ]
I left their towne, and tooke with me this sworde, 1690
Which I tooke vp at what time *Antonie*
Was from his chamber caried to the tombe:
And brought it you, to make his death more plaine,
And that therby my words may credite gaine.
Cæs. Ah Gods what cruell happ! poore *Antonie*,
Alas hast thou this sword so long time borne
Against thy foe, that in the ende it should
Of thee his Lord the cursed murthr'er be?
O Death how I bewaile thee! we (alas!)
So many warres haue ended, brothers, frends, 1700
Companions, coozens, equalls in estate:
And must it now to kill thee be my fate?
Ag. Why trouble you your selfe with bootles griefe?
For *Antonie* why spend you teares in vaine?
Why darken you with dole your victorie?
Me seemes your self your glorie do enuie.
Enter the towne, giue thankes vnto the Gods.
Cæs. I cannot but his tearefull chaunce lament,
Although not I, but his owne pride the cause,
And vnchaste loue of this *Ægyptian*. 1710
Agr. But best we sought into the tombe to gett,
Lest shee consume in this amazed case
So much rich treasure, with which happelie
Despaire in death may make hir feed the fire:
Suffring the flames hir Iewells to deface,
You to defraud, hir funerall to grace.
Sende then to hir, and let some meane be vs'd

With some deuise so holde hir still aliue,
Some faire large promises: and let them marke
Whither they may by some fine conning slight   1720
Enter the tombes. *Cæsar*. Let *Proculeius* goe,   [N2
And fede with hope hir soule disconsolate.
Assure hir so, that we may wholie gett
Into our hands hir treasure and hir selfe.
For this of all things most I doe desire
To kepe hir safe vntill our going hence:
That by hir presence beautified may be
The glorious triumph *Rome* prepares for me.

Chorus of Romaine
Souldiors.   1730

Shall euer ciuile bate
   Gnaw and deuour our state?
   Shall neuer we this blade,
   Our bloud hath bloudie made,
   Lay downe? these armes downe lay
   As robes we weare alway?
   But as from age to age,
   So passe from rage to rage?
Our hands shall we not rest
   To bath in our owne brest?   1740
   And shall thick in each land
   Our wretched trophees stand,
   To tell posteritie,
   What madd Impietie
   Our stonie stomakes ledd
   Against the place vs bredd?
Then still must heauen view
   The plagues that vs pursue:
   And euery where descrie
   Heaps of vs scattred lie,   1750
   Making the straunger plaines   [N2
   Fatt with our bleeding raines,
   Proud that on them their graue
   So manie legions haue.
And with our fleshes still
   Neptune his fishes fill
   And dronke with bloud from blue
   The sea take blushing hue:
   As iuice of *Tyrian* shell,
   When clarified well   1760
   To wolle of finest fields
   A purple glosse it yelds.

But since the rule of *Rome*,
    To one mans hand is come,
    Who gouernes without mate
    Hir now vnited state,
    Late iointlie rulde by three
    Enuieng mutuallie,
    Whose triple yoke much woe
    On *Latines* necks did throwe: 1770
I hope the cause of iarre,
    And of this bloudie warre,
    And deadlie discord gone
    By what we last haue done:
    Our banks shall cherish now
    The branchie pale-hew'd bow
    Of *Oliue, Pallas* praise,
    In stede of barraine bayes.
And that his temple dore,
    Which bloudie *Mars* before   1780
    Held open, now at last
    Olde *Ianus* shall make fast:
    And rust the sword consume,   [N3^r]
    And spoild of wauing plume,
    The vseles morion shall
    On crooke hang by the wall.
At least if warre returne
    It shall not here soiourne,
    To kill vs with those armes
    Were forg'd for others harmes: 1790
    But haue their pointes addrest,
    Against the *Germains* brest,
    The *Parthians* fayned flight,
    The *Biscaines* martiall might.
Olde Memorie doth there
    Painted on forhead weare
    Our Fathers praise: thence torne
    Our triumphes baies haue worne:
    Therby our matchles *Rome*
    Whilome of Shepeheards come   1800
    Rais'd to this greatnes stands,
    The Queene of forraine lands.
Which now euen seemes to face
    The heau'ns, her glories place:
    Nought resting vnder Skies
    That dares affront her eies.
    So that she needes but feare
    The weapons *Ioue* doth beare,
    Who angrie at one blowe
    May her quite ouerthrowe.   1810

Act. 5.

Cleopatra. Euphron. Children of Cleopatra.
Charmion. Eras.

Cleop.

O cruell Fortune! ô accursed lott!
O plaguy loue! ô most detested brand!
O wretched ioyes! ô beauties miserable!
O deadlie state! ô deadly roialtie!
O hatefull life! ô Queene most lamentable!
O *Antonie* by my fault buriable!   1820
O hellish worke of heau'n! alas! the wrath
Of all the Gods at once on vs is falne.
Vnhappie Queene! ô would I in this world
The wandring light of day had neuer sene?
Alas! of mine the plague and poison I
The crowne haue lost my ancestors me left,
This Realme I haue to straungers subiect made,
And robd my children of their heritage.
    Yet this is nought (alas!) vnto the price
Of you deare husband, whome my snares entrap'd: 1830
Of you, whom I haue plagu'd, whom I haue made
With bloudie hand a guest of mouldie Tombe:
Of you, whome I destroid, of you, deare Lord,
Whome I of Empire, honor, life haue spoil'd.
    O hurtfull woman! and can I yet liue,
Yet longer liue in this Ghost-haunted tombe?
Can I yet breathe! can yet in such annoy,
Yet can my Soule within this bodie dwell?
O Sisters you that spinne the thredes of death!   [N4
O *Styx*! ô *Phlegethon*! you brookes of hell!   1840
O Impes of *Night*! *Euph.* Liue for your childrens sake:
Let not your death of kingdome them depriue.
Alas what shall they do? who will haue care?
Who will preserue this royall race of yours?
Who pittie take? euen now me seemes I see
These little soules to seruile bondage falne,
And borne in triumph. *Cl.* Ah most miserable!
Euph. Their tender armes with cursed corde fast bound   [TLN 3261–6]
At their weake backs. *Cl.* Ah Gods what pittie more!
Eph. Their seelie necks to ground with weaknesse bend.   1850
Cl. Neuer on vs, good Gods, such mischiefe sende.
Euph. And pointed at with fingers as they go.
Cl. Rather a thousand deaths. *Euph.* Lastly his knife
Some cruell caytiue in their bloud embrue.
Cl. Ah my heart breaks. By shadie bankes of hell,
By fieldes wheron the lonely Ghosts do treade,
By my soule, and the soule of *Antonie*

I you beseche, *Euphron*, of them haue care.
Be their good Father, let your wisedome lett
That they fall not into this Tyrants handes.   1860
Rather conduct them where their freezed locks
Black *Æthiopes* to neighbour Sunne do shewe;
On wauie *Ocean* at the waters will;
On barraine cliffes of snowie *Caucasus*;
To Tigers swift, to Lions, and to Beares;
And rather, rather vnto euery coaste,
To eu'rie land and sea: for nought I feare
As rage of him, whose thirst no bloud can quench.
    Adieu deare children, children deare adieu:
Good *Isis* you to place of safetie guide,   1870   [N4ᵛ]
Farre from our foes, where you your liues may leade
In free estate deuoid of seruile dread.
    Remember not, my children, you were borne
Of such a Princelie race: remember not
So manie braue Kings which haue *Egipt* rul'de
In right descent your ancestors haue bene:
That this great *Antonie* your Father was,
Hercules bloud, and more then he in praise.
For your high courage such remembrance will,
Seing your fall with burning rages fill.   1880
    Who knowes if that your hands false *Destinie*
The Scepters promis'd of imperiouse *Rome*,
In stede of them shall crooked shepehookes beare,
Needles or forkes, or guide the carte, or plough?
Ah learne t'endure: your birth and high estate
Forget, my babes, and bend to force of fate.
    Farwell, my babes, farwell, my hart is clos'de
With pitie and paine, my self with death enclos'de,
My breath doth faile. Farwell for euermore,
Your Sire and me you shall see neuer more.   1890
Farwell swete care, farwell. *Chil.* Madame Adieu.
Cl. Ah this voice killes me. Ah good Gods! I swounde.
I can no more, I die. *Eras.* Madame, alas!
And will you yeld to woe? Ah speake to vs.
Eup. Come children. *Chil.* We come. *Eup.* Follow we our chaunce.
The Gods shall guide vs. *Char.* O too cruell lott!
O too hard chaunce! Sister what shall we do,
What shall we do, alas! if murthring darte
Of death arriue while that in slumbring swound
Half dead she lie with anguish ouergone?   1900
Er. Her face is frozen. *Ch.* Madame for Gods loue   [TLN 3081–5] [O1ʳ]
Leaue vs not thus: bidd vs yet first farwell.
Alas! wepe ouer *Antonie*: Let not
His bodie be without due rites entomb'de.
Cl. Ah, ah. *Char.* Madame. *Cle.* Ay me! *Cl.* How fainte she is?

Cl. My Sisters, holde me vp. How wretched I,
How cursed am! and was ther euer one
By Fortunes hate into more dolours throwne?
  Ah, weeping *Niobe*, although thy hart
Beholdes it selfe enwrap'd in causefull woe   1910
For thy dead children, that a sencelesse rocke
With griefe become, on *Sipylus* thou stand'st
In endles teares: yet didst thou neuer feele
The weights of griefe that on my heart do lie.
Thy Children thou, mine I poore soule haue lost,
And lost their Father, more then them I waile,
Lost this faire realme; yet me the heauens wrathe
Into a Stone not yet transformed hath.
  Phaetons sisters, daughters of the Sunne,
Which waile your brother falne into the streames   1920
Of stately *Po*: the Gods vpon the bankes
Your bodies to banke-louing Alders turn'd.
For me, I sigh, I ceasles wepe, and waile,
And heauen pittiles laughes at my woe,
Reuiues, renewes it still: and in the ende
(Oh crueltie!) doth death for comfort lende.
  Die *Cleopatra* then, no longer stay
From *Antonie*, who thee at *Styx* attends:
Goe ioine thy Ghost with his, and sobbe no more
Without his loue within these tombes enclos'd.   1930
Eras. Alas! yet let vs wepe, lest sodaine death
From him our teares, and those last duties take   [O1ᵛ]
Vnto his tombe we owe. *Ch.* Ah let vs wepe
While moisture lasts, then die before his feete.
Cl. Who furnish will mine eies with streaming teares
My boiling anguish worthilie to waile,
Waile thee *Antonie, Antonie* my heart?
Alas, how much I weeping liquor want!
Yet haue mine eies quite drawne their Conduits drie
By long beweeping my disastred harmes.   1940
Now reason is that from my side they sucke
First vitall moisture, then the vitall bloud.
Then let the bloud from my sad eies out flowe,
And smoking yet with thine in mixture growe.
Moist it, and heate it newe, and neuer stopp,
All watring thee, while yet remaines one dropp.
Cha. *Antonie* take our teares: this is the last
Of all the duties we to thee can yelde,
Before we die. *Er.* These sacred obsequies
Take *Antony*, and take them in good parte.   1950
Cl. O Goddesse thou whom *Cyprus* doth adore,
Venus of *Paphos*, bent to worke vs harme
For olde *Iulus* broode, if thou take care

Of *Cæsar*, why of vs tak'st thou no care?
Antonie did descend, as well as he,
From thine owne Sonne by long enchained line:
And might haue rul'd by one and self same fate,
True *Troian* bloud, the statelie *Romain* state.
  Antonie, poore *Antonie*, my deare soule,
Now but a blocke, the bootie of a tombe,   1960
Thy life, thy heate is lost, thy coullor gone,
And hideous palenes on thy face hath seaz'd.
Thy eies, two Sunnes, the lodging place of loue,   [TLN 5–10, 3296–8]   [O2ʳ]
Which yet for tents to warlike *Mars* did serue,
Lock'd vp in lidds (as faire daies cherefull light
Which darknesse flies) do winking hide in night.
  Antonie by our true loues I thee beseche,
And by our hearts swete sparks haue sett on fire,
Our holy mariage, and the tender ruthe
Of our deare babes, knot of our amitie: 1970
My dolefull voice thy eare let entertaine,
And take me with thee to the hellish plaine,
Thy wife, thy frend: heare *Antonie*, ô heare
My sobbing sighes, if here thou be, or there.
  Liued thus long, the winged race of yeares
Ended I haue as *Destinie* decreed,
Flourish'd and raign'd, and taken iust reuenge
Of him who me both hated and despisde.
Happie, alas too happie! if of *Rome*
Only the fleete had hither neuer come.   1980
And now of me an Image great shall goe
Vnder the earth to bury there my woe.
What say I? where am I? ô *Cleopatra*,
Poore *Cleopatra*, griefe thy reason reaues.
No, no, most happie in this happles case,
To die with thee, and dieng thee embrace:
My bodie ioynde with thine, my mouth with thine,
My mouth, whose moisture burning sighes haue dried:
To be in one selfe tombe, and one selfe chest,
And wrapt with thee in one selfe sheete to rest.   1990
  The sharpest torment in my heart I feele
Is that I staie from thee, my heart, this while.
Die will I straight now, now streight will I die,   [TLN 2884, 2887]
And streight with thee a wandring shade will be,
Vnder the *Cypres* trees thou haunt'st alone,   [O2ᵛ]
Where brookes of hell do falling seeme to mone.
But yet I stay, and yet thee ouerliue,
That ere I die due rites I may thee giue.
  A thousand sobbes I from my brest will teare,
With thousand plaints thy funeralles adorne: 2000
My haire shall serue for thy oblations,

My boiling teares for thy effusions,
Mine eies thy fire: for out of them the flame
(Which burnt thy heart on me enamour'd) came.

    Wepe my companions, wepe, and from your eies
Raine downe on him of teares a brinish streame.
Mine can no more, consumed by the coales
Which from my breast, as from a furnace, rise.
Martir your breasts with multiplied blowes,
With violent hands teare of your hanging haire,   2010
Outrage your face: alas! why should we seeke
(Since now we die) our beawties more to kepe?

    I spent in teares, not able more to spende,
But kisse him now, what rests me more to doe?
Then lett me kisse you, you faire eies, my light,
Front seate of honor, face most fierce, most faire!
O neck, ô armes, ô hands, ô breast where death
(Oh mischief) comes to choake vp vitall breath.
A thousand kisses, thousand thousand more   [TLN 3024–5]
Let you my mouth for honors farewell giue: 2020
That in this office weake my limmes may growe,
Fainting on you, and fourth my soule may flowe.

At Ramsburie. 26. of Nouember.

1 5 9 0.

DANIEL

Nineteenth-c. scholars share the view of COLLIER (ed. 1843, 8:3), who speaks of "the 'Cleopatra' of Samuel Daniel, . . . to which Shakespeare was clearly under no obligation. Any slight resemblance between the two is to be accounted for by the fact, that both poets resorted to the same authority for their materials—Plutarch."

    CASE (ed. 1906, pp. ix–x) is the first to note resemblances between *Ant.* and Daniel's play of 1594: "*Cleopatra*, especially as first written and first altered a few years later [1599], is a stately rhymed tragedy after the Senecan model. It takes up the story of Cleopatra after Antony's death. . . . [x] It has, here and there in the earlier version, resemblances more or less slight to passages in *Antony and Cleopatra*. . . .

    "Though . . . Shakespeare had . . . Daniel's . . . work before him, however small his use of it, such resemblances in thought as, for instance, the effective retrospect to *Cydnus* here [Daniel's ll. 1465–8, *Ant.* 3474–5 and, less closely, 3615–16], might easily occur independently to writers of the same age exercising their genius on the same subject." Among further parallels with the 1594 *Cleopatra*, Case notes Daniel's ll. 67–8 for *Ant.* 3032–4 and 3263–4, 52 for 3060; see also nn. 555–6, 3259–60, 3260–7.

FURNESS (ed. 1907, pp. 514–15): "Daniel's poems were deservedly popular, and this *Tragedy* appeared in the successive editions of them. . . . So many successive editions imply a wide circle of readers, and the supposition is not violent that in this circle Shakespeare was included. . . .

"As far as any dramatic aid is concerned, Shakespeare could have found none whatever in Daniel's *Tragedy*. There is no action in it. . . . Whatever influence Daniel had on Shakespeare must be detected not in any action, but in similarity of thought or expression; of this, with two or three possible exceptions [see below], I can find no traces that are indubitable, or even worthy of serious consideration. Naturally there are passages from Plutarch, even following the very words, which are common to both poets, but therein it is Plutarch, not Daniel, whom Shake—[515]speare has followed. . . . That Shakespeare had read Daniel's *Cleopatra* is of course possible; that it is even probable, is not impossible; but that he was indebted to it, or was influenced by it, in the faintest degree, in the delineation of any of his characters, is, I think, chimerical." He notes a parallel to *Ant.* 3201–2 in Daniel's ll. 139–40 and to 3538–9 in 1134; see also nn. 221–3, 550, 3473–5.

ELLEHAUGE (1930–1, p. 207): *Ant.* "gives no definite answer to [the] question: what were Cleopatra's motives of suicide? . . . Shakespeare departs considerably from Plutarch and shapes a Cleopatra more treacherous than Plutarch's and with her motives of death less pure. . . . He may have taken a hint [about motives] from the dramatist Daniel. . . . In his play Cleopatra's fear of personal disgrace is more pronounced than in Plutarch." But he qualifies: "The most probable reason is to be found in Shakespeare's personal observation and experience, especially in his relations with the famous 'dark lady of the sonnets.' "

FARNHAM (1950, pp. 156–7) is the first to present a more comprehensive and cogent case that Daniel "had his effect upon *Antony* [157] *and Cleopatra*, chiefly because he had spontaneous poetry in him, despite his allegiance to cut-and-dried Senecanism, and because Shakespeare was therefore not averse to reading him and not unappreciative of some of his best images and turns of phrase. Daniel had the imaginative power to take a long step beyond Garnier and the Countess of Pembroke in what he did with the character of Cleopatra. He gave his Cleopatra a certain complexity and thus made her more subtly tragic than the heroine of *Antonius*." In particular, as Farnham shows, Daniel's Cleopatra has (p. 164) "royal pride as her dominant motive" more than does Sh.'s, yet the (p. 174) "regal greatness of spirit" Sh. gives her allows him to make use of Daniel's poetry. Farnham states (p. 165), "The signs that Shakespeare knew Daniel's *Cleopatra* in its earlier form are of a kind to indicate that he read it just before writing *Antony and Cleopatra*, retained in his memory certain details, and put them to his own uses casually, perhaps with occasional refreshment of his memory as he wrote. Plutarch was Shakespeare's standby; but Daniel seems to have been helpful." He notes a parallel to *Ant.* 3232 in Daniel's l. 276 (pp. 166–7), to 3247–9 in 317–20 (p. 167), to 3284 in 277 (p. 166), and to 3532 in 1570 (p. 171); see also n. 3540–1. He concludes that some of these correspondences (p. 172) "may of course be accidental. But it is most unlikely that all of them are."

LEAVENWORTH (1953; 1974, pp. 107–8) perceives that Sh.'s "debt to Daniel in *Antony and Cleopatra* has been much larger than anyone has so far seen fit to recognize. . . . [*108*] Several of Shakespeare's most pregnant and gripping moments have been struck from the impact of his dramatic genius upon the metal of Daniel's moral perceptiveness. Daniel may be credited with casting Plutarch's account into a carefully weighed and artistically organized poem with many original and penetrative insights into the human feelings of the historical figures. Daniel brought the historical events into an artistic moral focus and arranged them in a significant order. . . . Shakespeare actively searched through *Cleopatra* and such other writings of Daniel's as were handy [*Letter from Octavia* but also Sonnet 31 from *Delia*, which Leavenworth (p. 95) considers a source for 2197–8] for whatever ideas they might offer [especially (p. 87) 'suggestions of dramatically striking episodes']. While Shakespeare only occasionally attempted to improve upon the thought content of his borrowings from Daniel, he managed to charge all of them with the electrifying immediacy of his own poetic gift." In Sh.'s borrowings, Daniel's reflective abstraction usually becomes (p. 94) "living conflict": see, for example, Daniel's ll. 151–6, dramatically illustrated in *Ant.* 299–311. Moreover, Sh. is (pp. 96–7) "indebted to Daniel for [97] the emphasis placed upon Cleopatra's revulsion from the thought of contributing to Caesar's triumph [see also Furness, p. 515; Farnham, pp. 168–9]." Further echoes include Daniel's l. 1585 for *Ant.* 2711–12 (p. 98), 605 for 3339–40 (p. 89), and 672–82 for 3389–3400 (pp. 89–90).

DICKEY (1957, pp. 169–71): Sh. "had been attracted enough by Daniel's version of the love tragedy to imitate it in some particulars. The verbal parallels are interesting only as proof that Shakespeare knew Daniel. More interesting are Daniel's changes in action and characterization which Shakespeare adopted, for these make even stronger the significance of Cleopatra's influence on her lover. Where the other playwrights, Jodelle and Garnier, had been content to preach about the debilitating folly of Antony's love, Daniel suggests ways of showing on the stage the expense of spirit caused by lust in action.

"The most important connections between Daniel's play and *Antony and Cleopatra* are these: first Daniel's Dolabella like Shakespeare's betrays Caesar's plans to Cleopatra because he loves her. . . .

"Second, although in *Julius Caesar* Shakespeare reminds us of the wildness of Antony's youth, *Antony and Cleopatra*, like Daniel's play, emphasizes Antony's virtues before he goes to Egypt. . . .

[*170*] "Third Daniel's Cleopatra unlike those of Jodelle and Garnier is almost an old woman. . . . Only Daniel and Shakespeare present her as 'wrinkled deep in time' [see n. 555–6].

"Fourth, in the opening soliloquy, Cleopatra mourns the ruin of her Antony, in words which . . . recall Shakespeare's Cleopatra musing on Antony while he is in Rome. . . .

"Fifth only Daniel and Shakespeare heighten Cleopatra's horror of the Roman triumph by picturing her fear of Octavia's mockery. . . .

[*171*] "Finally there are not only verbal parallels between the last scene of

Daniel's play and the end of Shakespeare's [as noted by Farnham], but a similarity in conception. The idea of poetic justice that animates Boccaccio's *De Casibus* reappears in Daniel, whose Cleopatra like Shakespeare's surrenders her amorous limbs to the embrace of death. Only in Daniel and Shakespeare among dramatists does Cleopatra approach death as if death were another lover"—though the idea appears also in *Rom.*

NORMAN (1958, p. 17): "Daniel's conception of Cleopatra as an overwhelming character—one worthy of an entire drama—influenced Shakespeare's picture of his heroine sufficiently to bring about a long act devoted to her personal tragedy." Norman observes (p. 18), "By considering that Act V of *Antony and Cleopatra* was written under the influence of Daniel, we can explain Shakespeare's audacious use of a double climax in the play [with Cleopatra's death more than an anticlimax after Antony's]." He notes (p. 13) a parallel for *Ant.* 3348–51 in Daniel's 113 ff.; see also nn. 3218–21, 3260–7, 3389–3400, 3438–45.

In contrast to Farnham and Dickey, SCHANZER (1963, pp. 153–4, 171) argues that Daniel's play is less close to *Ant.* in some respects than is Pembroke's: Daniel's Cleopatra, "unlike the Cleopatra of [Pembroke's] *Antonius* (and of Shakespeare's play) . . . has only come to love Antony after his death." In Daniel (p. 154), "one's moral bearings are never in doubt. Her liaison with Antony is seen as infamous. . . . For the repentant, regenerate Cleopatra our utmost sympathy and admiration is evoked. . . . But the effect of this is merely to draw us closer to Cleopatra, not to make us question the comparative value of Love and Empire. . . . [*171*] Unlike Garnier, who leaves us wavering between opposed views on fate and human responsibility, Daniel, by reconciling all apparent contradictions and reiterating a coherent and systematic view of human history, allows no room [as Sh. does] for such uncertainty in the minds of his readers." Schanzer does not dispute the verbal echoes.

SIMMONS (1973, *Shakespeare's Pagan World*, pp. 128–30): "Daniel seizes the moral significance of Cleopatra's death that *Antonius* merely touches in Cleopatra's exchange with Charmian." More clearly than in Garnier, Cleopatra's "death becomes the moral palliative for both love and honor; it justifies the lovers to history. . . . Instead of dying merely to share her lover's poor fortune and to join him in death, as in *Antonius*, Daniel's Cleopatra must die to pay a debt to Antony for not having loved him, to prove to him and to the world that now she does love him, and to perform [*129*] a rite that will be a marriage in death, thus consummating her own new 'religious' feelings. . . . [*130*] Shakespeare [as in 3538] takes over the crucial elements in Daniel's dramatic and moral view of Cleopatra's suicide. Both plays dramatize a new Cleopatra rising from Antony's ruin and both invest her suicide with high moral significance that clarifies and illuminates the tragic experience. Her fulfillment in death, through her attaining the means and the resolution, gives genuine dramatic conflict to both versions."

Others who think Sh. may have read Daniel or who recognize degrees of influence include MACCALLUM (1910, pp. 58–61), WILSON (ed. 1950, pp. viii–ix), PEARSON (1954, p. 129), MICHEL & SERONSY (1955, p. 572: they note also [p. 571]—following a suggestion by MacCallum, p. 59—a parallel to *Ant.* 3495 in Daniel's 1. 1501), PHIALAS (ed. 1955, p. 167), MUIR (1957: gives parallels, especially to *Ant.* 3060, 3105–6, in Daniel's 1172, 1439–40, and "resolution" in 1582 [p. 212], to *Ant.* 3245 in 1163 [p. 214], to 3254–5 in 1169, to 3389–3400 in 672 ff. [p. 213], to 3445 in 1085 [p. 214], to 3467–8 in 1164–6; 1969, pp. 197, 200; and 1977, pp. 227, 229), NORMAN (1959, p. 8), BULLOUGH (1964, 5:231–2, 235–6, 406 ff.: cites parallels, especially to *Ant.* 3534–6 in Daniel's 1116 ff.; some others are very remote), STIRLING (1964, p. 303), SAMPSON (1966, pp. 77–8), MAXWELL (1967, p. 139), GÜNTHER (1968, p. 107), RIEMER (1968, p. 12), ALTMANN (1969, pp. 230, 238), BATTENHOUSE (1969, p. 170: argues also for an unconvincing pun on *nil us*-nihilism-liberty in *Ant.* 3495 [p. 167] and Daniel's 1198, 1501, 1701 [p. 423, n. 49]), WALTER (ed. 1969, pp. 8, 298), LEE (1971, p. 58), BARTON (1973, pp. 10–11), KERMODE (in EVANS, ed. 1974, p. 1343), and WILLIAMSON (1974, pp. 238–41). STEEVENS (ed. 1778) notes parallels in Daniel's 1507–10 and 1523–6 for *Ant.* 3563–5, 1664 for *Ant.* 3586; see also n. 3572.

Those who believe Daniel's *Cleopatra* of 1594 did not influence *Ant.* include GERVINUS (1850, tr. 1883, p. 722), WHITE (ed. 1861, 12:5), HALLIWELL (ed. 1865, 15:195), DYCE (ed. 1866, 7:495), GENÉE (1872; 1878, 1:346), WARD (1875; 1899, 2:186), SYMONS (in IRVING & MARSHALL, ed. 1889, 6:113), HERFORD (ed. 1899, 9:260), ANDERS (1904, p. 89), MOORMAN (1904, p. 70), NEILSON (ed. 1906, p. 1060), LEE (ed. 1907, 36:xx), WOLFF (1907; 1913, 2:259), HUBBELL (1953, p. 138), SCHILLING (1953, p. 222), WILSON (1957, p. 171), and BROWER (1971, pp. 346–8; see p. 477).

CASE (ed. 1906, pp. x–xii) suggests the possibility that *Ant.* inspired changes in Daniel's substantially rev. version of 1607. He observes that this version "draws somewhat nearer to the contemporary [i.e., Jacobean] drama by replacing relation and soliloquy to a great extent by dialogue, so that not only is the play more dramatic, but characters familiar to us in *Antony and Cleopatra* now play a greater part, *viz.*, Charmian and Iras; others, Dircetas and Diomedes, are employed for the first time; Gallus becomes an interlocutor where he was but mentioned. It introduces the incident of 'Dircetus' bringing Antony's sword to Cæsar . . . and, by means of his relation [in 1607, 1.2], the story of the events preceding Antony's death, on the [*xi*] lines followed by Shakespeare in [4.12 (latter part), 13, 14, 15], though of course with the comparative brevity of a narration. . . . [*xii*] Daniel re-wrote his play because he had seen another treatment of the theme, namely, Shakespeare's." And FARNHAM (1950, p. 158): "It is possible that the recast *Cleopatra* of 1607 owes something to *Antony and Cleopatra*. Similarities in phrases and ideas that cannot be accounted for by reference to Plutarch have been found between *Antony and Cleopatra* and the matter that is new in the *Cleopatra* of 1607 [see Case], but they are not so close as such similarities between *Antony and Cleopatra* and the earlier *Cleopatra*. The question rests mainly on the fact that Daniel did three things as he recast his play: he frequently brought dialogue into the place of soliloquy or narrative; he introduced new characters, who are in Plutarch, it is true, but who are also in *Antony and Cleopatra*; and, more particularly, he introduced a scene in which Dircetus brings

Antony's sword to Octavius and relates the events preceding Antony's death very nearly as Shakespeare represents them."

SCHÜTZE (1936–7, pp. 63, 65, 71) argues against an influence of *Ant.* on Daniel: "It must not be forgotten that Shakespeare and Daniel used the same source. Shakespeare clings closely to the biographer [Plutarch]—and so does Daniel in his report [1.2 in 1607] as in most of the other scenes. . . . [65] There is no trace of the rich life of Shakespeare's drama in the new version of *Cleopatra*. . . .

[71] "The revision of *Cleopatra* was caused by the poet's wish to see his drama performed." In German.

LEAVENWORTH (1953; 1974, pp. 101–2, 108–9), countering Case (see above), argues tellingly against an influence of *Ant.* on Daniel: "Nothing Daniel wrote followed North more closely than this new scene [1.2 in 1607] in which Dircetus narrates Antony's death. . . . It is more likely that Daniel took the character of Dircetus from the Countess of Pembroke's *Antonie*, who also was simply a 'Nuntius' like Daniel's and who spelled his name the same way. Shakespeare's Dercetas is a full-blooded character who could scarcely have stood as a model to the faceless messenger in *Cleopatra*.

"The character of Diomedes is even farther removed from Shakespeare. The early version of *Cleopatra* has the unnamed Nuntius receive Cleopatra's order to bring her the two asps, and he does so disguised as a rustic. In the new version this Nuntius is given the name Diomedes, and the narration is most simply converted into representation. But the name of Cleopatra's trusted servant is furnished by Plutarch, not by Shakespeare. Gallus scarcely could be called an 'interlocutor' [CASE, ed. 1906, p. x]. He is barely mentioned, true enough, in the early version of the poem; but in the new version he is merely addressed once by Caesar and has [102] not a single word to say. His 'part' in the play was consequently not enlarged [similarly DENNETT, 1951, p. cvii], and this fact in itself supports the conclusion that Shakespeare's dramatization was unknown to Daniel." Leavenworth comments (pp. 108–9) on the "improbable" notion "that Daniel revised his *Cleopatra* because he had seen Shakespeare's popular dramatization": "This theory sees the revision as a popularization of the previous version. But it is hard to see how anyone could be persuaded that the new *Cleopatra* would be more entertaining on the stage than the old. Neither is stageable in a popular sense. And Daniel, having had by 1607 considerable experience in the licensing of plays for the Children of the Queen's Revels, certainly knew the difference between a popular play and the type of dramatic poem which he and Fulke Greville and others at that time chose to write. . . . Had Daniel borrowed from Shakespeare the inspiration for remodeling *Cleopatra*, he surely [109] would have betrayed an acquaintance with Shakespeare's richer and more dynamic characterizations." Leavenworth believes (pp. 102–7) that Daniel's 1607 version influenced *Ant.*, Sh. adding, as before, poetic enrichment to Daniel's thought; yet the evidence is doubtful.

SCHANZER (1957, pp. 379–81), similarly: "Daniel modelled the changes in his play [in 1607] for the most part on the Countess of Pembroke's *Antonius*, and . . . there is nowhere any indication of the influence of *Antony and Cleopatra* upon the choice of new characters, the thoughts they express, or the dramatic situations in which they are placed. What, then, of . . . the verbal parallels between the additions to *Cleopatra* and Shakespeare's play? . . .

[*380*] "Those who maintain that . . . Daniel was the borrower have to explain how any man, much less a poet of Daniel's ability, could see a performance of *Antony and Cleopatra* and then, in revising his play on the same subject, borrow from it only a few paltry expressions. On the other hand, for Shakespeare to have picked up these verbal crumbs would have been quite natural, since there is little in Daniel's play to have fired his imagination. It is, therefore, far more reasonable to assume that Shakespeare, after having read *Cleopatra* in one of the earlier versions, also skimmed through the added material in the revised form of the play."

Those who think the *Cleopatra* of 1607 may have influenced *Ant.* include also DENNETT (1951, p. cvii, briefly) and MUIR (1957, pp. 215–16; not in 1977).

Others who see *Ant.* as a possible source for *Cleopatra* (1607) include ANON. (1893, p. 439: the "motive" of Daniel's alterations in 1607 is the appearance of *Ant.*), CHAMBERS (1923, 3:275, and 1930, 1:477), WITHERSPOON (1924, pp. 108–9), NEILSON & HILL (ed. 1942, p. 1244), WILSON (ed. 1950, pp. viii–ix, as well as ANON., 1950, p. 830), REES (1953, pp. 91–3, and 1958, pp. 294–5), SISSON (ed. 1954, p. 1124), MICHEL & SERONSY (1955, pp. 576–7), PHIALAS (ed. 1955, p. 158), THOMAS (1958, p. 156), NORMAN (1959, p. 8), BULLOUGH (1964, 5:215, 231–2), BARROLL (1965, pp. 138–42), SERONSY (1967, pp. 49–50), RIEMER (1968, p. 12), KERMODE (in EVANS, ed. 1974, p. 1343), MUIR (1977, p. 236), and LAMB (1980, pp. 33, 183–4), while an influence of *Ant.* on Daniel is rejected by MÜLLER (1914, pp. 49, 55), TRAUB (1938, p. 14, n. 7), BEAUCHAMP (1955, pp. 101, 104), REES (1964, pp. 107–10), and SAMPSON (1966, pp. 68–79: scrutinizing Case's and others' evidence, agrees with Schütze and Schanzer).

There are different views also regarding the influence of Daniel's *Letter from Octavia* on *Ant.* FURNESS (ed. 1907, p. 515) remarks that the *Letter* is "unattractive and lacking in earnestness, and with no trace whatsoever of any influence" on Sh.

FARNHAM (1950, pp. 172–3) disagrees: "The *Letter* . . . represents Octavia as writing to Antony after she has tried to take provisions and men to him for his intended war against Parthia and has been stopped at Athens. It shows her as a noble, long-suffering, modest, sweet-tempered, and ever-faithful wife begging Antony to leave Cleopatra and come back to her.

"Two separate passages in *Antony and Cleopatra* indicate that Shakespeare knew the 'Argument' attached to Daniel's *Letter* [i.e., 209–10 (first noted by BALD, 1924, p. 776) and 1005–7]. . . . Thus Shakespeare presents Antony as unable to forget Cleopatra at the time of his marriage to Octavia and as even [*173*] then unfaithful to Octavia in thought. Plutarch does not speak of a breaking of Egyptian fetters when he tells of Antony's being impelled to leave Cleopatra by the disturbing news. . . . Nor does Plutarch make Antony incapable of forgetting Cleopatra at the time of his marriage to Octavia. . . . But the Antony bound by Egyptian fetters is in Daniel's 'Argument', and so is the Antony whose heart is in the East even as he marries Octavia."

And REES (1960, pp. 81–2): "Octavia's intention in the *Letter* is to try to make Antony realize and repent of the sufferings he causes her, but, as she begins to write, the thought strikes her that Antony may receive her letter at some time when he is 'dallying' [l. 12] in Cleopatra's arms and he will blush to have her see him receive letters from his wife. . . . [82] *Antony and Cleopatra* opens [cf. 30–43] with the very scene that Daniel's Octavia imagines [as noted by NORGAARD, 1955, p. 57]. . . .

"The device of the imagined reception of the letter in Daniel's *Letter from Octavia* works well to give some life to Octavia herself and some immediacy to the whole situation. It seems likely that the effectiveness of it struck Shakespeare's imagination, but he adds to the effect by making his Cleopatra taunt Antony with fear of his wife and of Caesar equally. The situation in the *Letter from Octavia* is a personal one between Octavia, Antony and Cleopatra: in *Antony and Cleopatra*, on the other hand, Antony's position and ambition are ever present."

Others who believe Daniel's *Letter* influenced *Ant.* include LEAVENWORTH (1953; 1974, p. 92), DICKEY (1957, p. 172), MUIR (1957: notes a parallel for *Ant.* 957—see n.—in the Argument [p. 210] and a similarity between the account of Cleopatra's wiles in stanza 36 and Sh.'s presentation of her in 1.3, 2.5, and Act 4 [p. 211]; 1977, pp. 227–8), BULLOUGH (1964, 5:237–8), and WALTER (ed. 1969, p. 298). The *Letter* is included here to show the context of parts used by Sh.

The Tragedie of Cleopatra (1594)

"The tragedye of Cleopatra" was entered on the Stationers' Register to Simon Waterson on 19 Oct. 1593 (Greg, *Bibliography*, no. 132). A duodecimo in eights was published in 1594 with the following title page: "DELIA | *and* | ROSAMOND | augmented. | CLEOPATRA | By | *Samuel Daniel* | *Ætas prima ca-* | *nat veneres postre-* | *ma tumul-* | *tus.* | 1594. | Printed at London for *Simon Waterson*, and | are to be sold in Paules Church-yarde at the | signe of the Crowne." The play has the separate title "THE | Tragedie of | *Cleopatra.*" on H4. The printers were James Roberts and Edward Allde, as stated on N8[v] in the colophon to the collection. Before the writing of *Ant.*, further editions of the play appeared in octavo in 1595 (*STC* 6255, new 6243.5); in duodecimo in 1598 (*STC* 6243.6); in quarto in *The Poeticall Essayes*, 1599 (*STC* 6261); in folio in *The Works*, 1601 (*STC* 6236, with a variant edition in 1602, *STC* 6237); and in octavo in *Certaine Small Poems Lately Printed*, 1605 (*STC* 6239).

The following is a modified diplomatic reprint of the 1594 edition, since no convincing correspondences based on variants in the 1599 or any other edition (as recorded in the collation) are to be found in *Ant.*, despite BULLOUGH's (1964, 5:235) preference for 1599. In the Argument and choruses, printed in 1594 in italic with incidental roman, italic and roman are inverted. Except for a few turnunders and turnovers, the verse lineation is retained, but prose is relined. The beginning of each page in the 1594 text is indicated by a bracketed signature number in the text or the right margin. Dedicatory verses on H5–H7 are not reproduced, nor are lace and other ornaments. Ornamental initials and display capitals have been replaced by regular capitals, and the capitals that conventionally follow display letters reduced. Long *s* is printed *s*, and other archaic types have been converted to modern equivalents. Obvious typographical errors have been silently corrected.

The beginnings of passages corresponding with *Ant.* are marked by TLNs. The following parallels have been found (*Ant.* TLNs are listed, with Daniel TLNs in parentheses):

59 (244), 221–3 (542), 299–311 (151–6), 401–20 (940, 1549), 550 (17), 555–6 (157), 2590–6 (1053–62), 2711–12 (1585), 2826–31 (35), 3032–4 (67–8), 3060 (52, 1172, 1439–40), 3105–6 (1172, 1439–40), 3201–2 (139–40), 3218–21 (61), 3232 (276), 3245 (1163), 3247–9 (317–20), 3254–5 (1169), 3259–60 (1143), 3260–7 (61), 3284 (277), 3339–40 (605), 3348–51 (113 ff.), 3368–3406 (669), 3389–3400 (672 ff.), 3438–45 (1079), 3467–8 (1163–6), 3473–5 (1463), 3495 (1198, 1501, 1701), 3532 (1570), 3534–6 (1116 ff.), 3538–9 (1134), 3541 (1590), 3562 (1545), 3563 (1507–10, 1523–6), 3565 (1507–10, 1523–6), 3572–3 (1641), 3586 (1664).

The text is based on the copy in the Houghton Library, Harvard (*STC* 6254, new 6243.4). Variants in the Folger Library's copy of the 1595 octavo, the British Library's imperfect copy of the 1598 duodecimo (the only known extant copy; see also Greg, *Bibliography*, 3:1049–50), the Houghton Library's copy of the 1599 quarto, the British Library's copy of the 1601 folio and the Huntington Library's copy of its 1602 variant, and the British Library's copy of the 1605 octavo are recorded at the end of the text. Variants from the uncorrected 1594 text in the Huntington Library that are retained in later editions are marked (u), and readings from the list of errata on sig. A2ᵛ in 1594 (*errata*). Variants, not recorded, are found in different copies of several editions. The play has been edited by GROSART (1885, 3:1–94), LEDERER (1911), BULLOUGH (1964, 5:406–49), and SAMPSON (1966). DENNETT (1951) has edited the heavily revised 1607 version (*STC* 6240).

[The Tragedie of Cleopatra]

THE ARGVMENT. [H8

After the death of *Antonius, Cleopatra* (liuing still in the Monument shee had caused to be built,) could not by any means be drawne forth, although *Octauius Cæsar* verie earnestly laboured it: & sent *Proculeius* to vse all diligence to bring her vnto him: For that hee though[t] it woulde be a great ornament to his Tryumphes, to get her aliue to Rome. But neuer woulde shee put herselfe into the hands of *Proculeius*, although on a time he found the meanes, (by a window that was at the top of the Monument,) to come downe vnto her: where hee perswaded her (all hee might) to [H8ᵛ] yeeld herselfe to *Cæsars* mercie. Which shee, (to be ridd of him,) cunningly seemed to grant vnto. After that, *Octauius* in person went to visite her, to whom shee excus'd her offence, laying all the

fault vpon the greatnes, and feare shee had of *Antonius*, and withall, seemed
verie tractable, and willing to be disposed of by him.

Where-vpon, *Octauius* (thinking himselfe sure) resolu'd presently to send
her away to Rome. Whereof, *Dolabella* a fauorite of *Cæsars*, (and one that was
grown into some good liking of her,) hauing certified her, shee makes her
humble peticion to *Cæsar*, that he would suffer her to sacrifize to the ghost of
Antonius: which being granted her, shee was brought vnto his Sepulcher, where
after her rites performed, shee returned to the Monument, and there dined,
with great magnificence. And in dinner time, came there one in the habite of
a Countriman, with a basket of figgs vnto her, who (vnsuspected) was suffered
to carry them in. And in that basket (among the figges) were conuaid the
Aspicks wherewith shee did herselfe to death. Dinner beeing [11ʳ] ended, shee
dispatched Letters to *Cæsar*, contayning great lamentations: with an earnest
supplication, that shee might be entomb'd with *Antonius*. Wherevpon, *Cæsar*
knowing what shee intended, sent presently with all speed, messengers to haue
preuented her death, which notwithstanding, before they came was dispatched.

Cesario her sonne, which shee had by *Iulius Cæsar*, (conuaied before vnto
India, out of the danger of the warrs,) was about the same time of her death,
murthered at Rhodes: trained thether by the falshood of his Tutor, corrupted
by *Cæsar*. And so heereby, came the race of the *Ptolomies* to be wholy extinct,
& the florishing ritch Kingdome of Egipt vtterly ouer-throwne and subdued.

The Scæne supposed
Alexandria.

THE ACTORS.

CLEOPATRA.   OCTAVIVS CÆSAR.
PROCVLEIVS.   DOLABELLA.
TITIVS, Seruaunt to DOLABELLA.
ARIVS.————— } two Philosophers.
PHILOSTRATVS. }
SELEVCVS. Secretary to CLEOPATRA.
RODON. Tutor to CÆSARIO.
NVNTIVS.

The CHORVS. all Egiptians.

ACTVS PRIMVS.

[12ʳ]

CLEOPATRA.

Yet doe I liue, and yet doth breath possesse
This hatefull prison of a loathsome soule:

Can no calamitie, nor no distresse
Breake hart and all, and end a life so foule?
Can *Cleopatra* liue, and with these eyes
Behold the deerest of her life bereft her?
Ah, can shee entertaine the least surmise
Of any hope, that hath but horror left her?   10
Why should I linger longer griefes to try?
These eyes that sawe what honor earth could giue mee,
Doe now behold the worst of misery:
The greatest wrack wherto Fortune could driue mee.
Hee on whose shoulders all my rest relyde,
On whom the burthen of my ambition lay:
The *Atlas* and the Champion of my pride,   [TLN 550] [I.
That did the world of my whole fortune sway;
Lyes falne, confounded, dead in shame and dolors,
Following th'vnlucky party of my loue.   20
Th'Ensigne of mine eyes, th'vnhappy collours,
That him to mischiefe, mee to ruine droue.
And now the modell made of misery,
Scorne to the world, borne but for Fortunes foile,
My lusts haue fram'd a Tombe for mee to lie,
Euen in the ashes of my Countries spoyle.
Ah, who would think that I were shee who late,
Clad with the glory of the worlds chiefe ritches,
Admir'd of all the earth, and wondred at,

---

3 possesse] extend 1599+
4–14 My life beyond my life, nor can my graue
    Shut vp my griefes, to make my end my end?
    Will yet confusion haue more then I haue?
    Is th'honor, wonder, glory, pompe and all
    Of *Cleopatra* dead, and she not dead?
    Haue I out-liu'd my selfe, and seene the fall
    Of all vpon me, and not ruined?
    Can yet these eyes endure the gastly looke
    Of desolations darke and ougly face,
    Wont but on fortunes fairest side to looke,
    Where nought was but applause, but smiles, and grace? 1599+ (*om.* eyes 1601, 1602)
15 Hee on whose] Whiles on his 1599+
17 The . . . Champion] My Atlas, and supporter 1599+
18 my whole fortune] all my glory 1599+
19 Who now thrown down, disgrac'd, confoūded lies
    Crusht with the weight of shame and infamie, 1599+
20 my loue] my eies 1599; mine eies 1601, 1602, 1605
21–6 The traines of lust and imbecilitie,
    Whereby my dissolution is become
    The graue of *Ægypt* and the wracke of all;
    My vnforeseeing weakenesse must intoome
    My Countries fame and glory with my fall. 1599+
27 Ah] Now 1599+
28–9 With all the ornaments on earth inrich'd,
    Enuiron'd with delights, compast with state, 1599+

Glittring in pompe that hart and eye bewitches: 30
Should thus distress'd, cast down from of that heigth,
Leuell'd with low disgrac'd calamitie,
Vnder the waight of such affliction sigh,
Reduc'd vnto th'extreamest misery.
Am I the woman, whose inuentiue pride,   [TLN 2826–31]
(Adorn'd like *Isis*,) scornd mortalitie?
Ist I that left my sence so without guide,
That flattery would not let him know twas I?
Ah, now I see, they scarce tell truth, that praise vs,
Crownes are beguild, prosperity betraies vs.   40
VVhat is become of all that statelie traine,   [I3ʳ]
Those troopes that wont attend prosperitie?
See what is left, what number doth remaine,
A tombe, two maydes, and miserable I.
And I t'adorne their tryumphes, am reseru'd
A captiue kept to beautifie their spoyles:
VVhom *Cæsar* labours, so to haue preseru'd,
And seekes to entertaine my life with wiles.
No *Cæsar* no, it is not thou canst doe it.
Promise, flatter, threaten extreamitie,   50
Imploy thy wits, and all thy force vnto it,
I haue both hands, and will, and I can die.   [TLN 3060]
Though thou of Country, kingdom, & my Crowne,
Though thou of all my glory dost bereaue me,
Though thou hast all my Egipt as thine owne,
Yet hast thou left me that which will deceiue thee.
That courage with my blood and birth innated,

---

30 hart . . . bewitches] harts and eies bewitch'd 1599 +
37 that . . . guide] would haue my frailty so belide 1599 +
38 would . . . twas] could perswade *I* was not 1599 +
39 Ah . . . scarce tell truth] Well . . . but delude 1599 +
  now] then 1605
40 Crownes are beguild] Greatnesse is mockt 1599 +
41–3 And we are but our selues, although this clowd
    Of interposed smokes make vs seeme more:
    These spreading parts of pompe wherof w'are prou'd,
    Are not our parts, but parts of others store:
    Witnesse these gallant fortune-following traines,
    These Summer Swallowes of felicitie
    Gone with the heate, of all see what remaines, 1599 + (smoake makes 1605)
44 A tombe . . . miserable] This monument . . . wretched 1599 +
46 beautifie their] honor others 1599 +
49 But *Cæsar*, it is more then thou canst do, 1599 +
51 vnto it] thereto 1599 +
53 Country, kingdom] both my country 1599 +
54 Though . . . dost] Of powre, of means & al doost quite 1599 +
55 all . . . as] wholy *Egypt* made 1599 +
  my] mine 1598

Admir'd of all the earth, as thou art now:
Cannot by threates be vulgarly abated,
To be thy slaue, that rul'd as good as thou.   60
Consider *Cæsar* that I am a Queene,   [TLN 3218–21, 3260–7]
And scorne the basenes of a seruile thought:
The world and thou, dost know what I haue beene,
And neuer thinke I can be so low brought,
That Rome should see my scepter-bearing hands,
Behinde mee bounde, and glory in my teares.   [
That I should passe, whereas *Octauia* stands   [TLN 3032–4]
To view my misery, that purchast hers.
No, I disdaine that head that wore a Crowne,
Should stoope to take vp that which others giue: 70
I must not be, vnlesse I be mine owne.
Tis sweet to die when we are forst to liue.
Nor had I troubled now the world thus long,
And beene indebted for this little breath,
But that I feare, *Cæsar* would offer wrong
To my distressed seede after my death.
Tis that which dooth my deerest blood controule.
Tis that (alas) detaines mee from my Tombe,
Whilst Nature brings to contradict my soule,
The argument of mine vnhappy wombe.   80
O lucklesse issue of a wofull Mother,
Th'vngodly pledges of a wanton bed;
You Kings design'd, must now be slaues to other,
Or els not bee (I feare) when I am dead.
It is for you I temporise with *Cæsar*,
And liue this while for to procure your safetie.

---

59 Cannot . . . vulgarly] Can neuer be so abiectly 1599 +
61 Consider . . . am] Thinke *Cæsar* I that liu'd and raign'd 1599 +
62–4 Doe skorne to buy my life at such a rate,
     That I should vnder neath my selfe be seene,
     Basely induring to suruiue my state: 1599 +
69 that wore] which wore 1599 +
73 troubled . . . long] staide behind my selfe this space 1599 +
74–5 Nor paid such intrest for this borrow'd breath,
     But that hereby I seeke to purchase grace 1599 +
76 To] For 1599 +
77 Tis] It's 1599 +
78 Tis that] That's it 1599 +
79 Whilst] VVhiles 1599 +
81 O] You 1599 +
   a] an 1601 +
82 Th'vngodly] The wretched 1599 +
83 now be slaues] subiects liue 1599 +
84 not . . . feare)] I feare, scarse liue, 1599 +
86 liue . . . for to procure] staie . . . to mediate 1599 +

For you I fayne content, and soothe his pleasure,
Calamitie heerein hath made me crafty.
But tis not long, Ile see what may be done,   [14ʳ]
And come what will, this stands, I must die free.   90
Ile be my selfe, my thoughts doe rest thereon,
Blood, chyldren, nature, all must pardon mee.
My soule yeelds honour vp the victory,
And I must bee a Queene, forget a mother:
Yet mother would I be, were I not I,
And Queene would I not now be, were I other.
   But what know I, if th'heauens haue decreed,
And that the sinnes of Egipt haue deseru'd,
The *Ptolomeyes* should faile, and none succeed,
And that my weakenes was thereto reseru'd.   100
That I should bring confusion to my state,
And fill the measure of iniquitie:
Licentiousnes in mee should end her date,
Begunne in ill-dispensed libertie.
If so it be, and that my heedles waies,
Haue this so great a dissolation rais'd,
Yet let a glorious end conclude my dayes,
Though life were bad, my death may yet be prais'd,
That I may write in letters of my blood,
A fit memoriall for the times to come: 110
To be example to such Princes good
That please themselues, and care not what become.
   And *Anthony*, because the world doth know,   [TLN 3348–51]   [14ᵛ]
That my mis-fortune hath procured thine,
And my improuidence brought thee so low,

---

89 tis . . . see] this is but to trie 1599 +
90 And] For 1599 +
91 And die my selfe vncaptiu'd, and vnwon. 1599 +
95 Yet] Though 1599 +
96 I not . . . I] not be now, could I be 1599 +
103 Licentiousnes . . . end her date] Luxuriousnesse . . . raise the rate 1599 +
104 Begunne in] Of loose and 1599 +
105–8 If it be so, then what neede these delaies?
     Since I was made the meanes of miserie:
     Why shuld I striue but to make death my praise,
     That had my life but for my infamie? 1599 +
109 That I may] And let me 1599 +
112 That] As 1599 +
113 because] although 1605
    doth know] takes note 1599 +
114 mis-fortune . . . thine] defects haue only ruin'd thee 1599 +
115 improuidence . . . low] ambitious practises are thought 1599 +

To lose thy glory, and to ruine mine:
By grapling in the Ocean of our pride,
To sinke each others greatnes both together,
Both equall shipwrack of our states t'abide,
And like destruction to procure to eyther: 120
If I should now (our common faulte) suruiue,
Then all the world must hate mee if I doe it,
Sith both our errors did occasion giue,
And both our faults haue brought vs both vnto it.
I beeing first inamour'd with thy greatnes,
Thou with my vanity bewitched wholy:
And both betrayd with th'outward pleasant sweetnes,
The one ambition spoyld, th'other folly.
For which, thou hast already duly paid,
The statute of thy errors dearest forfeit: 130
VVhereby thy gotten credite was decayd,
Procur'd thee by thy wanton deadly surfeit.
And next is my turne, now to sacrifize

---

116 *Replaced by insertion:*
   The motiue and the cause of all to be:
   Though God thou know'st, how iust this staine is laid
   Vpon my soule, whom ill successe makes ill:
   Yet since condemn'd misfortune hath no ayd
   Against proud luck that argues what it will,
   I haue no meanes to vndeceiue their mindes,
   But to bring in the witnesse of my bloud,
   To testifie the faith and loue that bindes
   My equall shame, to fall with whom I stood.
   Defects I grant I had, but this was worst,
   That being the first to fall I dy'd not first.
      Though I perhaps could lighten mine own side
   With some excuse of my constrained case
   Drawn down with powre: but that were to deuide
   My shame: to stand alone in my disgrace.
   To cleere me so, would shew m'affections naught,
   And make th'excuse more hainous then the fault.
   Since if I should our errours disunite,
   I should confound afflictions onely rest,
   That from stearn death euen steales a sad delight
   To die with friends or with the like distrest;
   And since we tooke of either such firme hold
   In th'ouerwhelming seas of fortune cast,
   What powre should be of powre to reunfold
   The armes of our affections lockt so fast, 1599 + (Yet God thou know'st, this staine is wrongly
      . . . And my condemn'd 1605)
117 By] For 1599 +
118 To sinke] We sunke 1599 +
119 And both made shipwracke of our fame beside, 1599 +
120 And . . . procure to] Both wrought a like destruction vnto 1599 +
121–32 *Om.* 1599 +
133 next . . . now] therefore I am bound 1599 +

To Death, and thee, the life that doth reproue mee,
Our like distresse I feele doth sympathize,
And euen affliction makes me truly loue thee.
VVhich *Anthony*, (I must confesse my fault,)   [15ʳ]
I neuer did sincerely vntill now;
Now I protest I doe, now am I taught,   [TLN 3201-2]
In death to loue, in life that knew not how.   140
For whilst my glory in that greatnes stood,
And that I saw my state, and knew my beauty,
Saw how the world admir'd mee, how they woode,
I then thought all men, must loue me of dutie,
And I loue none: for my lasciuious Courte,
(Fertile in euer-fresh and new-choyce pleasure,)
Affoorded me so bountiful disport,
That I to thinke on loue had neuer leysure.
    My vagabond desires no limits found,
      For lust is endlesse, pleasure hath no bound.   150
Thou, comming from the strictnes of thy Citty,   [TLN 299-311]
The wanton pompe of Courts yet neuer learnedst:
Inur'd to warrs, in womans wiles vnwittie,
Whilst others fayn'd, thou fell'st to loue in earnest.
    Not knowing women like them best that houer,
      And make least reckning of a doting Louer.
And yet thou cam'st but in my beauties waine,   [TLN 555-6]
When new-appearing wrinkles of declining,
Wrought with the hand of yeeres, seem'd to detaine
My graces light, as now but dimly shining.   160
Euen in the confines of mine age, when I   [15ᵛ]
Fayling of what I was, and was but thus:
VVhen such as wee, doe deeme in iealosie
That men loue for them-selues, and not for vs.
Then, and but thus, thou didst loue most sincerely,
(O *Anthony*,) that best deseru'dst it better.
Thys Autumne of my beauty bought so deerely,
For which (in more then death) I stand thy debter.
VVhich I will pay thee with most faithfull zeale,

---

141 that] her 1599+
148 thinke] stay 1599+
152 And neuer this loose pomp of monarchs learnest, 1599-1602; And this loose pomp of monarchs
    neuer learnest, 1605
153 womans] womens 1599+
155 women] how we 1599+
166 that] who 1605
    deseru'dst] deseru'st 1599+
169 most . . . zeale] so true a mind 1599+

And that ere long, no *Cæsar* shall detaine me;   170
My death, my loue and courage shall reueale,
The which is all the world hath left t'vnstaine me.
    And to the end I may deceiue best, *Cæsar*,
Who dooth so eagerly my life importune,
I must preuaile mee of this little leisure,
Seeming to sute my minde vnto my fortune.
Whereby I may the better mee prouide,
Of what my death and honor best shall fit:
A seeming base content, must warie hide
My last disseigne, till I accomplish it.   180
    That heereby yet the world shall see that I,
    Although vnwise to liue, had wit to die.
                                Exit.

CHORVS.   [

Behold what Furies still
Torment their tortur'd brest.
Who by their doing ill,
Haue wrought the worlds vnrest.
Which when being most distrest,
Yet more to vexe their sp'rit,   190
The hidious face of sinne,
(In formes they most detest)
Stands euer in their sight.
Their Conscience still within,
Th'eternall larum is,
That euer-barking dog that calls vppon theyr miss.

No meanes at all to hide
Man from himselfe can finde:
No way to start aside
Out from the hell of mind.   200
But in himselfe confin'd,

170–2 (Casting vp all these deepe accoumpts of mine)
       That both our soules, and all the world shall find
       All recknings cleer'd, betwixt my loue and thine. 1599+
173 And . . . deceiue best,] But . . . preuent proud 1599+
177 Whereby . . . mee] Thereby with more conuenience to 1599+
178 Of] For 1599+
179 A seeming] An yeelding 1599+
192 most] must 1599+

Hee still sees sinne before:
And winged-footed paine,
That swiftly comes behind,   [16ᵛ]
The which is euer more,
The sure and certaine gaine
Impietie doth get.
And wanton loose respect, that dooth it selfe forget.

And CLEOPATRA now,
Well sees the dangerous way   210
Shee tooke, and car'd not how,
Which led her to decay.
   And likewise makes vs pay
For her disordred lust,
Th'int'rest of our blood:
Or liue a seruile pray,
Vnder a hand vniust,
As others shall thinke good.
This hath her riot wonne,
And thus shee hath her state, her selfe and vs vndunne.   220

Now euery mouth can tell,
What close was muttered:
How that shee did not well,
To take the course shee did.
   For now is nothing hid,
Of what feare did restraine.   [17ʳ]
No secrete closely done,
But now is vttered.
The text is made most plaine
That flattry glos'd vpon,   230
The bed of sinne reueal'd,
And all the luxurie that shame would haue conceal'd.

The scene is broken downe,
And all vncou'red lyes,
The purple Actors knowne
Scarce men, whom men despise.
   The complots of the wise,
Proue imperfections smoake:
And all what wonder gaue
To pleasure-gazing eyes,   240
Lyes scattered, dasht, all broke.
Thus much beguiled haue

---

239 what] that 1598

Poore vnconsiderat wights,
These momentary pleasures, fugitiue delights.   [TLN 59]

ACTVS SECVNDVS.   [

Cæsar. Procvleivs.

Kingdoms I see we winne, we conquere Climates,
Yet cannot vanquish harts, nor force obedience,
Affections kept in close-concealed limits,
Stand farre without the reach of sword or violence.   250
Who forc'd doe pay vs duety, pay not loue:
Free is the hart, the temple of the minde,
The Sanctuarie sacred from aboue,
Where nature keepes the keyes that loose and bind.
No mortall hand force open can that doore,
So close shut vp, and lockt to all mankind:
I see mens bodies onely ours, no more,
The rest, anothers right, that rules the minde.
   Behold, my forces vanquisht haue this Land,
Subdu'de that strong Competitor of mine: 260
All Egipt yeelds to my all-conquering hand,
And all theyr treasure and themselues resigne.
Onely this Queene, that hath lost all this all,
To whom is nothing left except a minde:
Cannot into a thought of yeelding fall,
To be dispos'd as chaunce hath her assign'd.   [
   But *Proculei*, what hope doth shee now giue,
   Will shee be brought to condiscend to liue?
Proc. My Lord, what time being sent from you to try,
To win her foorth aliue, (if that I might)   270
From out the Monument, where wofully
Shee liues inclos'd in most afflicted plight;
No way I found, no meanes how to surprize her,
But through a Grate at th'entry of the place,
Standing to treate, I labour'd to aduise her,
To come to *Cæsar*, and to sue for grace.   [TLN 3232]
Shee saide, shee crau'd not life, but leaue to die,   [TLN 3284]
Yet for her children, prayd they might inherite,
That *Cæsar* would vouchsafe (in clemency,)
To pitty them, though shee deseru'd no merite.   280

---

261 yeelds] *Om.* 1598

So leauing her for then; and since of late,
With *Gallus* sent to try another time,
The whilst hee entertaines her at the grate,
I found the meanes vp to the Tombe to climbe.
Where in discending in the closest wise,
And silent manner as I could contriue:
Her woman mee descri'd, and out shee cryes,
Poore *Cleopatra*, thou art tane aliue.
With that the Queene raught frō her side her knife,
And euen in acte to stab her martred brest,   290   [18ᵛ]
I stept with speed, and held, and sau'd her life,
And forth her trembling hand the blade did wrest.
Ah *Cleopatra*, why should'st thou (said I,)
Both iniurie thy selfe and *Cæsar* so?
Barre him the honour of his victory,
VVho euer deales most mildly with his foe?
Liue and relye on him, whose mercy will
To thy submission alwaies ready be.
   With that (as all amaz'd) shee held her still,
Twixt maiestie confus'd and miserie.   300
Her proud grieu'd eyes, held sorrow and disdaine,
State and distresse warring within her soule:
Dying ambition dispossest her raigne,
So base affliction seemed to controule.
Like as a burning Lampe, whose liquor spent
With intermitted flames, when dead you deeme it,
Sendes foorth a dying flash, as discontent,
That so the matter failes that should redeeme it.
So shee (in spight) to see her low-brought state,
(When all her hopes were now consum'd to nought,)   310
Scornes yet to make an abiect league with Fate,
Or once discend into a seruile thought.
Th'imperious tongue vnused to beseech,
Authority confounds with prayers, so   [K1ʳ]
Words of commaund conioyn'd with humble speech,
Shew'd shee would liue, yet scorn'd to pray her foe.
   Ah, what hath *Cæsar* heere to doe, said shee,   [TLN 3247-9]
In confines of the dead in darknes liuing?
Will hee not graunt our Sepulchers be free,
But violate the priuiledge of dying?   320
What, must hee stretch forth his ambitious hand
Into the right of Death, and force vs heere?
Hath misery no couert where to stand
Free from the storme of pryde, ist safe no where?

---

315 Words of commaund] That words of powre 1605
318 liuing] lying 1599+

Cannot my land, my gold, my Crowne suffise,
And all what I held deere, to him made common,
But that he must in this sort tirannize,
Th'afflicted body of an wofull woman?
Tell him, my frailty, and the Gods haue giuen,
Sufficient glory, if hee could content him: 330
And let him now with his desires make euen,
And leaue mee to this horror, to lamenting.
Now hee hath taken all away from mee,
What must hee take mee from my selfe by force?
Ah, let him yet (in mercie) leaue mee free
The kingdom of this poore distressed corse.
No other crowne I seeke, no other good.
Yet wish that *Cæsar* would vouchsafe this grace,   [K]
To fauour the poore of-spring of my blood.
Confused issue, yet of Roman race.   340
If blood and name be linkes of loue in Princes,
Not spurres of hate; my poore *Cæsario* may
Finde fauour notwithstanding mine offences,
And *Cæsars* blood, may *Cæsars* raging stay.
But if that with the torrent of my fall,
All must bee rapt with furious violence,
And no respect, nor no regard at all,
Can ought with nature or with blood dispence:
Then be it so, if needes it must be so.
There stayes and shrinkes in horror of her state.   350
VVhen I began to mitigate her woe,
And thy great mercies vnto her relate;
Wishing her not dispaire, but rather come
And sue for grace, and shake off all vaine feares:
No doubt shee should obtaine as gentle doome
As shee desir'd, both for herselfe and hers.
And so with much a-doe, (well pacifide
Seeming to bee,) shee shew'd content to lyue,
Saying shee was resolu'd thy doome t'abide,
And to accept what fauour thou would'st giue.   360
And heere-withall, crau'd also that shee might
Performe her last rites to her lost belou'd.   [K]
To sacrifize to him that wrought her plight:
And that shee might not bee by force remou'd.
   I graunting from thy part this her request,
   Left her for then, seeming in better rest.

326 what] that 1598
330 if . . . him] could he be content 1601+
332 lamenting] lament 1601+
354 all vaine] idle 1605

Cæs. But doost thou thinke she will remaine so still?
Pro. I thinke, and doe assure my selfe shee will.
Cæs. Ah, priuate men sound not the harts of Princes,
  VVhose actions oft beare contrarie pretences.   370
Pro. Why, tis her safety for to yeeld to thee.
Cæs. But tis more honour for her to die free.
Pro. Shee may thereby procure her childrens good.
Cæs. Princes respect theyr honour more then blood.
Pro. Can Princes powre dispence with nature than?
Cæs. To be a Prince, is more then be a man.
Pro. There's none but haue in time perswaded beene.
Cæs. And so might shee too, were shee not a Queene.
Pro. Diuers respects will force her be reclam'd.
Cæs. Princes (like Lyons) neuer will be tam'd.   380
  A priuate man may yeeld, and care not how,
  But greater harts will breake before they bow.
  And sure I thinke sh'will neuer condiscend,
  To lyue to grace our spoyles with her disgrace:
  But yet let still a warie watch attend,
  To guard her person, and to watch the place.   [K2ᵛ]
    And looke that none with her come to confer:
    Shortly my selfe will goe to visite her.

CHORVS.

OPINION, howe doost thou molest   390
  Th'affected minde of restles man?
  Who following thee, neuer can,
  Nor euer shall attaine to rest.
For getting what thou saist is best,
  Yet loe, that best hee findes farre wide
  Of what thou promisedst before:
  For in the same hee lookt for more,
  Which proues but small when once tis tride.
Then something els thou find'st beside,
  To draw him still from thought to thought: 400
  When in the end all proues but nought.

370 actions oft] purposes 1605
371 for to] to come 1601+
374 respect . . . then] are not ally'd vnto their 1605
385 watch] troupe 1601+
394 For getting] Forgetting 1598

Farther from rest hee findes him than,
Then at the first when he began.

O malcontent seducing guest,
    Contriuer of our greatest woes:
    Which borne of winde, and fed with showes,   [K3ʳ]
    Doost nurse thy selfe in thine vnrest.
Iudging vngotten things the best,
    Or what thou in conceite design'st.
    And all things in the world doost deeme,   410
    Not as they are, but as they seeme:
    Which shewes, their state thou ill defin'st:
And liu'st to come, in present pin'st.
    For what thou hast, thou still doost lacke:
    O mindes tormentor, bodies wracke,
    Vaine promiser of that sweet rest,
    Which neuer any yet possest.

If wee vnto ambition tende,
    Then doost thou draw our weakenes on,
    With vaine imagination   420
    Of that which neuer hath an end.
Or if that lust we apprehend,
    How doth that pleasant plague infest?
    O what strange formes of luxurie,
    Thou straight doost cast t'intice vs by?
    And tell'st vs that is euer best,
Which wee haue neuer yet possest.
    And that more pleasure rests beside,
    In something that we haue not tride.   [K3ᵛ]
    And when the same likewise is had,   430
    Then all is one, and all is bad.

This *Anthony* can say is true,
    And *Cleopatra* knowes tis so,
    By th'experience of their woe.
    Shee can say, shee neuer knew
But that lust found pleasures new,
    And was neuer satis-fide:
    Hee can say by proofe of toyle,
    Ambition is a Vulture vile,
    That feedes vpon the hart of pride: 440
And findes no rest when all is tride.
    For worlds cannot confine the one,
    Th'other, listes and bounds hath none.
    And both subuert the minde, the state,
    Procure destruction, enuie, hate.

And now when all this is prou'd vaine,
   Yet *Opinion* leaues not heere,
   But sticks to *Cleopatra* neere.
   Perswading now, how she shall gaine
Honour by death, and fame attaine.   450
   And what a shame it were to liue,   [K4^r]
   Her kingdome lost, her Louer dead:
   And so with this perswasion led,
   Dispayre doth such a courage giue,
That naught els can her minde relieue.
   Nor yet diuert her from that thought:
   To this conclusion all is brought.
   This is that rest this vaine world lends,
   To end in death that all thing ends.

ACTVS TERTIVS.   460

PHILOSTRATVS. ARIVS.

How deepely *Arius* am I bounde to thee,
That sau'dst frō death this wretched life of mine:
Obtayning *Cæsars* gentle grace for mee,
When I of all helps els dispayr'd but thine?
Although I see in such a wofull state,
Life is not that which should be much desir'd:
Sith all our glories come to end theyr date,
Our Countries honour and our owne expir'd.
Now that the hand of wrath hath ouer-gone vs,   470
Liuing (as 'twere) in th'armes of our dead mother,
With blood vnder our feete ruine vpon vs,   [K4^v]
And in a Land most wretched of all other,
When yet we reckon life our deerest good.
And so we liue, we care not how we liue:
So deepe we feele impressed in our blood,
That touch which nature with our breath did giue.
And yet what blasts of words hath learning found,
To blow against the feare of death and dying?
What comforts vnsicke Eloquence can sound,   480
And yet all fayles vs in the poynt of trying.

---

459 thing] things 1598 +
463 sau'dst] sau'st 1598
471 Liuing (as 'twere)] We liue but as 1605

For whilst we reason with the breath of safety,
VVithout the compasse of destruction liuing:
VVhat precepts shew wee then, what courage lofty
In taxing others feares in counsell giuing?
VVhen all thys ayre of sweet-contriued words,
Prooues but weake armour to defend the hart.
For when this lyfe, pale feare and terror boords,
Where are our precepts then, where is our arte?
O who is he that from himselfe can turne,   490
That beares about the body of a man?
Who doth not toyle and labour to adiorne
The day of death, by any meanes he can?
All this I speake to th'end my selfe t'excuse,
For my base begging of a seruile breath,
Wherein I graunt my selfe much t'abuse,   [K
So shamefully to seeke t'auoyd my death.
Arius. Philostratus, that selfe same care to liue,
Possesseth all alike, and grieue not then
Nature dooth vs no more then others giue: 500
Though we speak more then men, we are but men.
And yet (in truth) these miseries to see,
VVherein we stand in most extreame distresse:
Might to our selues sufficient motiues be
To loathe this life, and weigh our death the lesse.
For neuer any age hath better taught,
VVhat feeble footing pride and greatnes hath.
How 'improuident prosperity is caught,
And cleane confounded in the day of wrath.
See how dismaid Confusion keepes those streetes,   510
That nought but mirth & Musique late resounded,
How nothing with our eye but horror meetes,
Our state, our wealth, our pride & all confounded.
Yet what weake sight did not discerne from far
This black-arysing tempest, all confounding?
Who did not see we should be what we are,
When pride and ryot grew to such abounding.
When dissolute impiety possest,
Th'vnrespectiue mindes of such a people:
VVhen insolent Security found rest   520   [K
In wanton thoughts, with lust and ease made feeble.
Then when vnwary peace with fat-fed pleasure,
New-fresh inuented ryots still detected,

484 lofty] loftly 1595, 1598
496 much t'abuse] I much abuse 1598
519 such a] prince, and 1599+
521 with] which 1605

Purchac'd with all the *Ptolomies* ritch treasure,
Our lawes, our Gods, our misteries neglected.
Who saw not how this confluence of vice,
This innondation of disorders, must
At length of force pay back the bloody price
Of sad destruction, (a reward for lust.)
O thou and I haue heard, and read, and knowne   530
Of lyke proude states, as wofully incombred,
And fram'd by them, examples for our owne:
Which now among examples must be numbred.
For this decree a law from high is giuen,
An auncient Canon, of eternall date,
In Consistorie of the starres of heauen,
Entred the booke of vnauoyded Fate;
That no state can in heigth of happines,
In th'exaltation of theyr glory stand:
But thither once ariu'd, declyning lesse,   540
Ruine themselues, or fall by others hand.
Thus doth the euer-changing course of things,   [TLN 221-3]
Runne a perpetuall circle, euer turning:
And that same day that highest glory brings,   [K6^r]
Brings vs vnto the poynt of back-returning.
For senceles sensualitie, doth euer
Accompany felicity and greatnes.
A fatall witch, whose charmes do leaue vs neuer,
Till we leaue all in sorrow for our sweetnes;
When yet our selues must be the cause we fall,   550
Although the same be first decreed on hie:
Our errors still must beare the blame of all,
This must it be, earth aske not heauen why.
   Yet mighty men with wary iealous hand,
Striue to cut off all obstacles of feare:
All whatsoeuer seemes but to withstand
Theyr least conceite of quiet, held so deere;
And so intrench themselues with blood, w^t crymes,
With all iniustice as theyr feares dispose:
Yet for all thys wee see, how oftentimes   560
The meanes they worke to keep, are means to lose.
And sure I cannot see, how this can stand
With great *Augustus* safety and his honor,
To cut off all succession from our land,
For her offence that puld the warrs vpon her.
Phi. Why must her issue pay the price of that?

---

538 heigth] heigh 1605
563 safety] glory 1605
564 To . . . from] T'extinguish the succession of 1605
566 *Phi.* Must all her yssue be confounded now? 1605

Ari. The price is life that they are rated at.
Phi. Cæsario to, issued of *Cæsars* blood?   [K6
Ari. Pluralitie of *Cæsars* are not good.
Phi. Alas what hurt procures his feeble arme?   570
Ari. Not for it dooth, but that it may doe harme.
Phi. Then when it offers hurt, represse the same.
Ari. Tis best to quench a sparke before it flame.
Phi. Tis inhumane, an innocent to kill.
Ari. Such innocents, sildome remaine so still.
  And sure his death may best procure our peace,
  Competitors the subiect deerely buies:
  And so that our affliction may surcease,
  Let great men be the peoples sacrifice.
    But see where *Cæsar* comes himselfe, to try   580
  And worke the mind of our distressed Queene,
  To apprehend some falsed hope: whereby
  Shee might be drawne to haue her fortune seene.
    But yet I thinke, Rome will not see that face
    (That quel her chāpions,) blush in base disgrace.

SCENA. SECVNDA.   [K7

CÆSAR, CLEOPATRA, SELEVCVS,
DOLABELLA.

Cæs. What *Cleopatra*, doost thou doubt so much
  Of *Cæsars* mercy, that thou hid'st thy face?   590
  Or doost thou think, thy'offences can be such,
  That they surmount the measure of our grace?
Cleo. O *Cæsar*, not for that I flye thy sight
  My soule this sad retyre of sorrow chose:
  But that my'oppressed thoughts abhorring light,
  Like best in darknes, my disgrace t'inclose.
  And heere to these close limmits of dispaire,
  This solitary horror where I bide:
  Cæsar, I thought no Roman should repaire,
  More after him, who heere oppressed dyde.   600
  Yet now, heere at thy conquering feete I lye,

567 *Ari.* Yea all that from the roots of kings did grow, 1605
568 *Cæsario* to, issued] And sweet *Cæsario* sprong 1605
582 To . . . falsed] With some deluding 1605
584 thinke] trust 1605
585 quel] queld 1599+

Poore captiue soule, that neuer thought to bow:
VVhose happy foote of rule and maiestie,
Stoode late on y^t same ground thou standest now.

Cæs. Rise Queene, none but thy selfe is cause of all. [TLN 3339–40] [K7^v]
And yet, would all were but thyne owne alone:
That others ruine had not with thy fall
Brought Rome her sorowes, to my tryumphs mone.
For breaking off the league of loue and blood,
Thou mak'st my winning ioy a gaine vnpleasing: 610
Sith th'eye of griefe must looke into our good,
Thorow the horror of our owne blood-shedding.
And all, we must attribute vnto thee.

Cleo. To mee? *Cæsar* what should a woman doe
Opprest with greatnes? What was it for mee
To contradict my Lord, beeing bent thereto?
I was by loue, by feare, by weakenes, made
An instrument to such disseignes as these.
For when the Lord of all the Orient bade,
Who but obeyd? who was not glad to please? 620
And how could I with-draw my succouring hand,
From him that had my hart, or what was mine?
Th'intrest of my faith in straightest band,
My loue to his most firmely did combine.

Cæs. Loue? alas no, it was th'innated hatred
That thou and thine hast euer borne our people:
That made thee seeke al meanes to haue vs scattred,
To disvnite our strength, and make vs feeble.
And therefore did that brest nurse our dissention, [K8^r]
VVith hope t'exalt thy selfe, t'augment thy state: 630
To pray vpon the wrack of our contention,
And (with the rest our foes,) to ioy thereat.

Cleo. O *Cæsar*, see how easie tis t'accuse
Whom fortune hath made faultie by their fall,
The wretched conquered may not refuse
The titles of reproch he's charg'd withall.
    The conquering cause hath right, wherein y^u art,
    The vanquisht, still is iudg'd the worser part.
Which part is mine, because I lost my part.
No lesser then the portion of a Crowne. 640
Enough for mee, alas what needed arte

---

604 y^t] ye 1599–1602
610 a gaine] againe 1605
611 griefe must looke] griefs looke not 1605
612 Thorow] But thor'w 1605
622 or] and 1599 +
625 alas] ah no 1605
641 what] was 1605

To gaine by others, but to keepe mine owne?
But heere let weaker powers note what it is,
To neighbour great Competitors too neere,
If we take part, we oft doe perrish thus,
If neutrall bide, both parties we must feare.
    Alas, what shall the forst partakers doe,
    When following none, yet must they perrish to?
But Cæsar, sith thy right and cause is such,
Bee not a heauie weight vpon calamitie: 650
Depresse not the afflicted ouer-much,
The chiefest glory is the Victors lenitie.
Th'inheritaunce of mercy from him take,   [K8
Of whom thou hast thy fortune and thy name:
Great *Cæsar* mee a Queene at first did make,
And let not *Cæsar* now confound the same.
Reade heere these lines which still I keep with me,
The witnes of his loue and fauours euer:
And God forbid this should be said of thee,
That *Cæsar* wrong'd the fauoured of *Cæsar*.   660
For looke what I haue beene to *Anthony*,
Thinke thou the same I might haue been to thee.
And heere I doe present thee with the note,
Of all the treasure, all the Iewels rare
That Egipt hath in many ages got;
And looke what *Cleopatra* hath, is there.
Seleu. Nay there's not all set down within that roule,
I know some things shee hath reseru'd a part.
Cle. What vile vnggrateful wretch, dar'st thou cõtroule   [TLN 3368–3406]
Thy Queene & soueraine? caitiue as thou art.   670
Cæs. Hold, holde, a poore reuenge can worke so feeble hands.
Cle. Ah *Cæsar*, what a great indignitie   [TLN 3389–3400]
Is this, that heere my vassale subiect stands,
T'accuse mee to my Lord of trechery?
If I reseru'd some certaine womens toyes,
Alas it was not for my selfe (God knowes,)
Poore miserable soule, that little ioyes   [L1
In trifling ornaments, in outward showes.
But what I kept, I kept to make my way
Vnto thy *Liuia*, and *Octauias* grace.   680
That thereby in compassion mooued, they
Might mediat thy fauour in my case.
Cæs. Well *Cleopatra*, feare not, thou shalt finde
What fauour thou desir'st, or canst expect:
For *Cæsar* neuer yet was found but kinde
To such as yeeld, and can themselues subiect.

---

680 *Octauias*] *Octauius* 1605

And therefore giue thou comfort to thy minde;
Relieue thy soule thus ouer-charg'd with care,
How well I will intreate thee thou shalt find,
So soone as some affayres dispatched are.   690
Til whē farewel. *Cl.* Thanks thrise renowned *Cæsar*,
Poore *Cleopatra* rests thine owne for euer.
Dol. No meruaile *Cæsar* though our greatest sp'rits,
  Haue to the powre of such a charming beautie,
  Beene brought to yeeld the honour of their merits:
  Forgetting all respect of other dutie.
  Then whilst the glory of her youth remain'd
  The wondring obiect to each wanton eye:
  Before her full of sweet (with sorrow wain'd,)
  Came to the period of this misery.   700
  If still, euen in the midst of death and horror,   [L1ᵛ]
  Such beauty shines, thorow clowds of age & sorow,
  If euen those sweet decayes seeme to plead for her,
  Which from affliction, mouing graces borrow;
    If in calamity shee could thus moue,
    What could she do adorn'd with youth & loue?
  VVhat could she do then, when as spreading wide
  The pompe of beauty, in her glory dight?
  When arm'd with wonder, shee could vse beside,
  Th'engines of her loue, Hope and Delight?   710
    Beauty daughter of Meruaile, ô see how
  Thou canst disgracing sorrowes sweetly grace?
  VVhat power thou shew'st in a distressed brow,
  That mak'st affliction faire, giu'st teares their grace.
  VVhat can vntressed locks, can torne rent haire,
  A weeping eye, a wailing face be faire?
    I see then, artlesse feature can content,
    And that true beauty needes no ornament.
Cæs. What in a passion *Dolabella?* what? take heede:
  Let others fresh examples be thy warning;   720
  What mischiefes these, so idle humors breed,
  VVhilst error keepes vs from a true discerning.
  Indeed, I saw shee labour'd to impart
  Her sweetest graces in her saddest cheere:
  Presuming on the face that knew the arte   [L2ʳ]
  To moue with what aspect so eu'r it were.
  But all in vaine, shee takes her ayme amisse,
  The ground and marke, her leuel much deceiues;
  Time now hath altred all, for neither is
  Shee as shee was, nor wee as shee conceiues.   730

---

696 respect] respects 1598
711 Beauty . . . Meruaile] Daughter of Meruaile beauty 1605

And therefore now, twere best she left such badnes,
Folly in youth is sinne, in age, tis madnes.
   And for my part, I seeke but t'entertaine
In her some feeding hope to draw her forth;
The greatest Trophey that my trauailes gaine,
Is to bring home a prizall of such worth.
And now, sith that shee seemes so well content
To be dispos'd by vs, without more stay
Shee with her chyldren shall to Rome be sent,
Whilst I by *Syria* thither take my way.   740

CHORVS.

O Fearefull frowning NEMESIS,
   Daughter of *IVSTICE*, most seuere,
   That art the worlds great Arbitresse,
   And Queene of causes raigning heere.
Whose swift-sure hand is euer neere   [L2ᵛ
   Eternall iustice, righting wrong:
   Who neuer yet deferrest long
   The proudes decay, the weakes redresse.
But through thy powre euery where,   750
   Doost raze the great, and raise the lesse.
   The lesse made great, doost ruine to,
   To shew the earth what heauen can doe.

Thou from dark-clos'd eternitie,
   From thy black clowdy hidden seate,
   The worlds disorders doost discry:
   Which when they swell so proudly great,
Reuersing th'order nature set,
   Thou giu'st thy all-confounding doome,
   Which none can know before it come.   760
   Th'ineuitable destinie,
Which neyther wit nor strength can let,
   Fast chayn'd vnto necessitie,
   In mortall things doth order so,
   Th'alternate course of weale or wo.

---

731 twere . . . badnes] leaue her vnto her sadnesse 1605

O how the powres of heauen do play
  With trauailed mortalitie:
  And doth their weakenes still betray,   [L3ʳ]
  In theyr best prosperitie.
When beeing lifted vp so hie,   770
  They looke beyond themselues so farre,
  That to themselues they take no care:
  Whilst swift confusion downe doth lay,
Theyr late proude mounting vanitie:
  Bringing theyr glory to decay.
  And with the ruine of theyr fall,
  Extinguish people, state and all.

But is it iustice that all wee
  Th'innocent poore multitude,
  For great mens faults should punisht be,   780
  And to destruction thus pursude.
O why should th'heauens vs include,
  Within the compasse of theyr fall,
  Who of themselues procured all?
  Or doe the Gods (in close) decree,
Occasion take how to extrude
  Man from the earth with crueltie?
  Ah no, the Gods are euer iust,
  Our faults excuse theyr rigor must.

This is the period Fate set downe   790   [L3ᵛ]
  To Egipts fat prosperity:
  Which now vnto her greatest growne,
  Must perrish thus, by course must die.
And some must be the causers why
  This reuolution must be wrought:
  As borne to bring theyr state to nought.
  To change the people and the crowne,
And purge the worlds iniquitie:
  Which vice so farre hath ouer-growne.
  As wee, so they that treate vs thus,   800
  Must one day perrish like to vs.

---

769 In] Euen in 1598
778 is it] it is 1595

ACTVS QVARTVS.

SELEVCVS. RODON.

Sel. Neuer friend *Rodon* in a better howre,
    Could I haue met thee then eu'en now I do
    Hauing affliction in the greatest powre
    Vpon my soule, and none to tell it to.
    For tis some ease our sorrowes to reueale,
    If they to whom wee shall impart our woes
    Seeme but to feele a part of what wee feele,   810   [I
    And meete vs with a sigh but at a cloze.
Rod. And neuer (friend *Seleucus*) found'st thou one
    That better could beare such a part with thee:
    Who by his owne, knowes others cares to mone,
    And can in like accord of griefe agree.
    And therefore tell th'oppression of thy hart,
    Tell to an eare prepar'd and tun'd to care:
    And I will likewise vnto thee impart
    As sad a tale as what thou shalt declare.
        So shal we both our mournful plaints combine,   820
        Ile waile thy state, and thou shalt pitty mine.
Sel. Well then, thou know'st how I haue liu'd in grace
    With *Cleopatra*, and esteem'd in Court
    As one of Counsell, and of chiefest place,
    And euer held my credite in that sort.
    Tyll now in this confusion of our state,
    When thinking to haue vs'd a meane to climbe,
    And fled the wretched, flowne vnto the great,
    (Follow'ing the fortune of the present time,)
    Am come to be cast downe and ruin'd cleene.   830
    And in the course of mine owne plot vndonne.
    For hauing all the secretes of the Queene
    Reueal'd to *Cæsar*, to haue fauour wonne:
    My trechery is quited with disgrace,   [I
    My falshood loath'd, and not without great reason
    Though good for him, yet Princes in this case
    Doe hate ye Traytor, though they loue the treason.
    For how could hee imagine I would be
    Faithfull to him, being false vnto mine owne?
    And false to such a bountious Queene as shee,   840
    That had me rais'd, and made mine honor known.
    Hee saw twas not for zeale to him I bare,
    But for base feare, or mine owne state to settle.

804 Neuer friend *Rodon*] Friend *Rodon* neuer 1605

Weakenes is false, and faith in Cowards rare,
Feare findes out shyfts, timiditie is subtle.
And therefore scornd of him, scornd of mine own.
Hatefull to all that looke into my state:
Despis'd *Seleucus* now is onely growne
The marke of infamy, that's pointed at.
Rod. Tis much thou saist, and ô too much to feele,   850
  And I doe grieue and doe lament thy fall:
  But yet all this which thou doost heere reueale,
  Cōpar'd with mine, wil make thine seem but smal.
  Although my fault be in the selfe-same kind,
  Yet in degree far greater, far more hatefull;
  Mine sprong of myschiefe, thine from feeble mind,
  I staind with blood, thou onely but vngratefull.
  For vnto mee did *Cleopatra* gyue   [L5ʳ]
  The best and deerest treasure of her blood,
  Louely *Cæsario*, whom shee would should liue   860
  Free from the dangers wherein Egipt stood.
  And vnto mee with him this charge she gaue,
  Heere *Rodon*, take, conuay from out thys Coast,
  This precious Gem, the chiefest that I haue,
  The iewell of my soule I value most.
  Guide hym to INDIA, leade him farre from hence,
  Safeguard him where secure he may remaine,
  Till better fortune call him back from thence,
  And Egipts peace be reconcil'd againe.
  For this is hee that may our hopes bring back,   870
  (The rysing Sunne of our declyning state:)
  These be the hands that may restore our wrack,
  And rayse the broken ruines made of late.
  Hee may gyue limmits to the boundles pryde
  Of fierce *Octauius*, and abate his might:
  Great Iulius of-spring, hee may come to guide
  The Empire of the world, as his by right.
    O how hee seemes the modell of his Syre?
  O how I gaze my *Cæsar* in his face?
  Such was his gate, so dyd his lookes aspyre;   880
  Such was his threatning brow, such was his grace.
  High shouldred, and his forehead euen as hie.   [L5ᵛ]
  And ô, (if hee had not beene borne so late,)
  He might haue rul'd the worlds great Monarchy,
  And nowe haue beene the Champion of our state.
    Then vnto him, ô my deere Sonne, (she sayes,)
  Sonne of my youth, flye hence, ô flye, be gone:
  Reserue thy selfe, ordain'd for better dayes,
  For much thou hast to ground thy hopes vppon.

860 should] haue 1605

Leaue mee (thy wofull Mother) to endure,   890
The fury of thys tempest heere alone:
Who cares not for herselfe, so thou be sure,
Thou mayst reuenge, when others can but mone.
Rodon will see thee safe, *Rodon* will guide
Thee and thy waies, thou shalt not need to feare.
Rodon (my faithfull seruaunt) will prouide
What shall be best for thee, take thou no care.
And ô good *Rodon*, looke well to his youth,
The wayes are long, and daungers eu'ry where.
I vrge it not that I doe doubt thy truth,   900
Mothers will cast the worst, and alwaies feare.
    The absent daunger greater still appeares,
    Lesse feares he, who is neere the thing he feares.
And ô, I know not what presaging thought
My sp'rit suggests of luckles bad euent:
But yet it may be tis but loue doth dote,
Or idle shadowes which my feares present.
But yet the memory of myne owne fate,
Makes mee feare his. And yet why should I feare?
His fortune may recouer better state,   910
And hee may come in pompe to gouerne heere.
But yet I doubt the *Genius* of our Race
By some malignant spirit comes ouer-throwne:
Our blood must be extinct, in my disgrace,
Egypt must haue no more Kings of theyr owne.
Then let him stay, and let vs fall together,
Sith it is fore-decreed that we must fal.
Yet who knowes what may come? let him go thither,
What Merchaunt in one Vessell venters all?
Let vs deuide our starrs. Goe, goe my Sonne,   920
Let not the fate of Egypt find thee heere:
Try if so be thy destiny can shunne
The common wracke of vs, by beeing there.
But who is hee found euer yet defence
Against the heauens, or hyd him any where?
Then what neede I to send thee so far hence
To seeke thy death that mayst as well die heere?
And heere die with thy mother, die in rest,
Not trauayling to what will come to thee.
Why should wee leaue our blood vnto the East,   930
VVhen Egipt may a Tombe sufficient be?
    O my deuided soule, what shall I doe?
    VVhereon shall now my resolution rest?

907 which] with 1599+
917 fal] all 1605

What were I best resolue to yeeld vnto
When both are bad, how shall I know the best?
Stay; I may hap so worke with *Cæsar* now,
That hee may yeeld him to restore thy right.
Goe; *Cæsar* neuer will consent that thou
So neere in blood, shalt bee so great in might.
Then take him *Rodon*, goe my sonne fare-well.   [TLN 401–20]
But stay; ther's something els that I would say: 941
Yet nothing now, but ô God speed thee well,
Least saying more, that more may make thee stay.
Yet let mee speake: It may be tis the last
That euer I shall speake to thee my Sonne.
Doe Mothers vse to parte in such post-hast?
VVhat, must I ende when I haue scarce begun?
Ah no (deere hart,) tis no such slender twine
VVhere-with the knot is tyde twixt thee and mee.
That blood within thy vaines came out of mine,   950
Parting from thee, I part from part of mee:
And therefore I must speake. Yet what? O sonne.
 Here more she wold, whē more she could not say.
Sorrow rebounding backe whence it begun,   [L7ʳ]
Fild vp the passage, and quite stopt the way:
VVhen sweet *Cæsario* with a princely sp'rite,
(Though comfortlesse himselfe) did comfort giue;
VVith mildest words, perswading her to beare it.
And as for him, shee should not neede to grieue.
And I (with protestations of my part,)   960
Swore by that faith, (which sworne I did deceaue)
That I would vse all care, all wit and arte
To see hym safe; And so we tooke our leaue.
Scarce had wee trauail'd to our iourneyes end,
VVhen *Cæsar* hauing knowledge of our way,
His Agents after vs with speed doth send
To labour mee, *Cæsario* to betray.
VVho with rewards, and promises so large,
Assaild mee then, that I grew soone content;
And backe to *Rhodes* dyd reconuay my charge,   970
Pretending that *Octauius* for him sent,
To make hym King of Egipt presently.
 And thither come, seeing himselfe betrayd,
And in the hands of death through trecherie,
VVayling his state, thus to himselfe he sayd.
 Loe heere brought back by subtile traine to death,
Betrayde by Tutors fayth, or Traytors rather:

959 neede] yeeld 1598
962 and] all 1595, 1598

My faulte my blood, and mine offence my birth,   [L⁷
For beeing sonne of such a mightie Father.
　　From INDIA, (whither sent by Mothers care,   980
To be reseru'd from Egypts common wracke,)
To *Rhodes*, (so long the armes of Tyrants are,)
I am by *Cæsars* subtile reach brought back.
Heere to be made th'oblation for his feares,
Who doubts the poore reuenge these handes may doe him:
Respecting neyther blood, nor youth, nor yeeres,
Or how small safety can my death be to him.
　　And is this all the good of beeing borne great?
Then wretched greatnes, proud ritch misery,
Pompous distresse, glittering calamity.   990
Is it for this th'ambitious Fathers sweat,
To purchase blood and death for them and theirs?
Is this the issue that theyr glories get,
To leaue a sure destruction to theyr heyres?
O how farre better had it beene for mee,
From low discent, deriu'd of humble birth,
To'haue eate the sweet-sowre bread of pouerty,
And drunke of *Nilus* streame in *Nilus* earth:
Vnder the cou'ring of some quiet Cottage,
Free from the wrath of heauen, secure in minde,   1000
Vntoucht when sad euents of Princes dotage,
Confounds what euer mighty it dooth find.   [L⁸
And not t'haue stoode in theyr way, whose condition,
Is to haue all made cleere, and all thing plaine,
Betweene them and the marke of theyr ambition,
That nothing let the full sight of theyr raigne.
Where nothing stands, that stands not in submission;
Where greatnes must all in it selfe containe.
Kings will be alone, Competitors must downe,
Neere death he stands, that stands too neer a Crowne.   1010
　　Such is my case, for *Cæsar* will haue all:
My blood must seale th'assurance of his state:
Yet ah weake state that blood assure him shall,
Whose wrongfull shedding, Gods and men do hate.
Iniustice neuer scapes vnpunisht still,
Though men reuenge not, yet the heauens will.
　　And thou *Augustus* that with bloody hand,
Cutt'st off succession from anothers race,
Maist find the heauens thy vowes so to withstand,

---

994 To] So 1605
995 farre] much 1599+
998 streame] streams 1599+
1003 And . . . way] Out of the way of greatnesse 1605

That others may depriue thine in like case.   1020
When thou maist see thy proude contentious bed
Yeelding thee none of thine that may inherite:
Subuert thy blood, place others in theyr sted,
To pay this thy iniustice her due merite.
    If it be true, (as who can that deny
VVhich sacred Priests of *Memphis* doe fore-say,)   [L8ᵛ]
Some of the of-spring yet of *Anthony*,
Shall all the rule of this whole Empire sway.
And then *Augustus*, what is it thou gainest
By poore *Antillus* blood, or this of mine?   1030
Nothing but thys thy victory thou stainest,
And pull'st the wrath of heauen on thee and thine.
    In vaine doth man contende against the starrs,
    For what hee seekes to make, his wisdom marrs.
        Yet in the mean-time we whom Fates reserue,
The bloody sacrifices of ambition,
VVe feele the smart what euer they deserue,
And wee indure the present times condition.
    The iustice of the heauens reuenging thus,
    Doth onely sacrifice it selfe, not vs.   1040
        Yet tis a pleasing comfort that dooth ease
Affliction in so great extreamitie,
To thinke theyr like destruction shall appease
Our ghostes, who did procure our misery.
But dead we are, vncertaine what shall bee,
And lyuing, wee are sure to feele the wrong:
Our certaine ruine wee our selues doe see.
They ioy the while, and wee know not how long.
    But yet *Cæsario*, thou must die content,
    For men will mone, & God reuenge th'innocent.   1050   [M1ʳ]
        Thus he cōplain'd, & thus thou hear'st my shame.
Sel. But how hath *Cæsar* now rewarded thee?
Rod. As hee hath thee. And I expect the same   [TLN 2590–6]
    As fell to *Theodor* to fall to mee:
    For he (one of my coate) hauing betrayd
    The young *Antillus*, sonne of *Anthony*,
    And at his death from of his necke conuayd
    A iewell: which being askt, he did deny:
    Cæsar occasion tooke to hang him straight.
    Such instruments with Princes liue not long.   1060
    Although they neede such actors of deceit,

1034 what] that 1599+
1040 sacrifice] satisfie 1594 (*errata*), 1595+
1044 who] which 1595, 1598
1061 such] vs, 1594(u), 1595, 1598

Yet still our sight seemes to vpbrayd their wrong;
And therefore we must needes this danger runne,
And in the net of our owne guile be caught:
Wee must not liue to brag what we haue done,
For what is done, must not appeare theyr fault.
    But heere comes *Cleopatra*, wofull Queene,
    And our shame will not that we should be seene.
                   Exeunt.

CLEOPATRA.   1070   [M

What, hath my face yet powre to win a Louer?
Can this torne remnant serue to grace me so,
That it can *Cæsars* secrete plots discouer
What he intends with mee and mine to do?
VVhy then poore Beautie thou hast doone thy last,
And best good seruice thou could'st doe vnto mee.
For now the time of death reueal'd thou hast,
Which in my life didst serue but to vndoe mee.
    Heere *Dolabella* far forsooth in loue,   [TLN 3438–45]
Writes, how that *Cæsar* meanes forthwith, to send   1080
Both mee and mine, th'ayre of Rome to proue:
There his Tryumphant Chariot to attend.
I thanke the man, both for his loue and letter;
Th'one comes fit to warne mee thus before,
But for th'other, I must die his debter,
For *Cleopatra* now can loue no more.
    But hauing leaue, I must goe take my leaue
And last farewell of my dead *Anthony*:
Whose deerely honour'd Tombe must heere receaue
This sacrifice, the last before I dye.   1090
    O sacred euer-memorable Stone,   [M
That hast without my teares, within my flame,
Receiue th'oblation of the wofull'st mone
That euer yet from sad affliction came.
And you deere reliques of my Lord and Loue,
(The sweetest parcells of the faithfull'st liuer,)
O let no impious hand dare to remoue
You out from hence, but rest you heere for euer.
Let Egypt now giue peace vnto you dead,

1065 brag] bray 1594(u), 1595, 1598
1078 didst] did 1598

That lyuing, gaue you trouble and turmoyle: 1100
Sleepe quiet in this euer-lasting bed,
In forraine land preferr'd before your soyle.
And ô, if that the sp'rits of men remaine
After their bodies, and doe neuer die,
Then heare thy Ghost thy captiue Spouse complaine,
And be attentiue to her misery.
But if that laborsome mortalitie,
Found this sweet error, onely to confine
The curious search of idle vanity,
That would the deapth of darknes vndermine: 1110
Or rather, to giue rest vnto the thought
Of wretched man, with th'after-comming ioy
Of those conceiued fieldes whereon we dote,
To pacifie the present worlds anoy.
If it be so, why speake I then to th'ayre?   [M2ᵛ]
But tis not so, my *Anthony* doth heare: [TLN 3534–6]
His euer-liuing ghost attends my prayer,
And I doe know his houering sp'rite is neere.
And I will speake, and pray, and mourne to thee,
O pure immortall loue that daign'st to heare: 1120
I feele thou aunswer'st my credulitie
VVith touch of comfort, finding none elswhere.
Thou know'st these hands entomb'd thee heer of late,
Free and vnforst, which now must seruile be,
Reseru'd for bands to grace proude *Cæsars* state,
Who seekes in mee to tryumph ouer thee.
O if in life we could not seuerd be,
Shall Death deuide our bodies now a sunder?
Must thine in Egypt, mine in Italie,
Be kept the Monuments of Fortunes wonder?   1130
If any powres be there where as thou art,
(Sith our owne Country Gods betray our case,)
O worke they may theyr gracious helpe impart,
To saue thy wofull wife from such disgrace.   [TLN 3538–9]
Doe not permit shee should in tryumph shew
The blush of her reproch, ioyn'd with thy shame:
But (rather) let that hatefull Tyrant know,
That thou and I had powre t'auoyde the same.
But what doe I spend breath and idle winde,   [M3ʳ]
In vaine invoking a conceiued ayde?   1140
Why doe I not my selfe occasion find
To breake the bounds wherein my selfe am stayd?

1115 If . . . then] Then do I speake but onely 1605
1130 the] in 1598
1132 owne] *Om.* 1601, 1602

VVords are for them that can complaine and lyue,   [TLN 3259–60]
VVhose melting harts compos'd of baser frame,
Can to theyr sorrowes time and leysure gyue,
But *Cleopatra* may not doe the same.
No *Anthony*, thy loue requireth more:
A lingring death, with thee deserues no merit,
I must my selfe force open wide a dore
To let out life, and so vnhouse my spirit.   1150
These hands must breake the prison of my soule
To come to thee, there to enioy like state,
As doth the long-pent solitary Foule,
That hath escapt her cage, and found her mate.
This Sacrifice to sacrifize my life,
Is that true incense that doth best beseeme:
These rites may serue a life-desiring wife,
Who dooing them, t'haue done enough doth deeme.
My hart blood should the purple flowers haue beene,
Which heere vpon thy Tombe to thee are offred,   1160
No smoake but dying breath should heere been seene,
And this it had beene to, had I beene suffred.
But what haue I saue these bare hands to doe it?   [TLN 3245, 3467–8]   [M3
And these weake fingers are not yron-poynted:
They cannot peirce the flesh be'ing put vnto it,
And I of all meanes els am disapoynted.
But yet I must a way and meanes seeke, how
To come vnto thee, what so ere I doo.
O Death, art thou so hard to come by now,   [TLN 3254–5]
That wee must pray, intreate, and seeke thee too?   1170
But I will finde thee where so ere thou lye,
For who can stay a minde resolu'd to die?   [TLN 3060, 3105–6]
    And now I goe to worke th'effect in deede,
Ile neuer send more words or sighes to thee:
Ile bring my soule my selfe, and that with speed,
My selfe will bring my soule to *Anthony*.
Come goe my Maydes, my fortunes sole attenders,
That minister to misery and sorrow:
Your Mistres you vnto your freedom renders,
And quits you from all charge yet ere to morrow.   1180
    And now by this, I thinke the man I sent,
Is neere return'd that brings mee my dispatch.
God graunt his cunning sort to good euent,

1163 hands . . . it] silly hands 1605
1165 the . . . it] with them which stands 1605
1167 a way] away 1598
     a . . . seeke] some way endeuour 1605
1174 sighes] sights 1605
1180 quits . . . all] will discharge your 1599 +

And that his skill may well beguile my watch.
So shall I shun disgrace, leaue to be sorie,
Fly to my loue, scape my foe, free my soule;
So shall I act the last of life with glory,   [M4ʳ]
Dye like a Queene, and rest without controule.
                              Exit.

                    CHORVS.   1190

Misterious Egipt, wonder breeder,
   strict religions strange obseruer,
State-ordrer Zeale, the best rule-keeper,
   fostring still in temprate feruor:
O how cam'st thou to lose so wholy
   all religion, law and order?
And thus become the most vnholy
   of all Lands that *Nylus* border?   [TLN 3495]
How could confus'd Disorder enter
   where sterne Law sate so seuerely?   1200
How durst weake lust and ryot venter
   th'eye of Iustice looking neerely?
Could not those means that made thee great,
Be still the meanes to keepe thy state?

Ah no, the course of things requireth
   change and alteration euer:
That same continuaunce man desireth,
   th'vnconstant world yeeldeth neuer.   [M4ᵛ]
Wee in our counsels must be blinded,
   and not see what dooth import vs: 1210
And often-times the thing least minded,
   is the thing that most must hurt vs.
Yet they that haue the stearne in guiding,
   tis their fault that should preuent it,
For oft they seeing their Country slyding,
   take their ease, as though contented.
Wee imitate the greater powres,
The Princes manners fashion ours.

1187 of life with] act of my 1594(u)
1192 religions] religious 1595, 1598
1207 same] stayd 1605
1215 For . . . seeing] Who when they see 1605
1216 take . . . though] for their priuate are 1605

Th'example of their light regarding,
    vulgar loosenes much incences: 1220
Vice vncontrould, growes wide inlarging,
    Kings small faults, be great offences.
And this hath set the window open
    vnto lycence, lust and ryot:
This way Confusion first found broken,
    whereby entred our disquiet.
Those lawes that olde *Sesostris* founded,
    and the *Ptolomies* obserued,
Heereby first came to be confounded,
    which our state so long preserued.   1230
The wanton luxurie of Court,   [M
Dyd forme the people of like sort.

For all (respecting priuate pleasure,)
    vniuersally consenting
To abuse theyr time, theyr treasure,
    in theyr owne delights contenting:
And future dangers nought respecting,
    whereby, (O howe easie matter
Made this so generall neglecting,
    Confus'd weakenes to discater?)   1240
Cæsar found th'effect true tryed,
    in his easie entrance making:
Who at the sight of armes, discryed
    all our people, all forsaking.
For ryot (worse then warre,) so sore
Had wasted all our strength before.

And thus is Egipt seruile rendred,
    to the insolent destroyer:
And all their sumptuous treasure tendred,
    all her wealth that did betray her.   1250
Which poyson (O if heauens be rightfull,)
    may so far infect their sences,
That Egipts pleasures so delightfull,   [M
    may breed them the like offences.
And Romans learne our way of weaknes,
    be instructed in our vices:
That our spoyles may spoyle your greatnes,
    ouercome with our deuises.

1227 olde *Sesostris*] *Zoroaster* 1594(u), 1595, 1598
1236 delights] delight 1595, 1598
1251 heauens] heauen 1599 +

Fill full your hands, and carry home
Inough from vs to ruine Rome.   1260

ACTVS QVINTVS.

DOLABELLA, TITIVS.

Dol. Come tell mee *Titius* eu'ry circumstaunce
  How *Cleopatra* did receiue my newes:
  Tell eu'ry looke, each gesture, countenaunce,
  That shee did in my Letters reading vse.
Tit. I shall my Lord so farre as I could note,
  Or my conceite obserue in any wise.
    It was the time when as shee hauing got
  Leaue to her Deerest dead to sacrifize;   1270
  And now was issuing out the Monument,
  With Odors, Incense, Garlands in her hand,   [M6ʳ]
  When I approcht (as one from *Cæsar* sent,)
  And did her close thy message t'vnderstand.
    Shee turnes her backe, and with her takes mee in,
  Reades in thy lynes thy strange vnlookt for tale:
  And reades, and smyles, and stayes, and doth begin
  Againe to reade, then blusht, and then was pale.
  And hauing ended with a sigh, refoldes
  Thy Letter vp: and with a fixed eye,   1280
  (Which stedfast her imagination holds)
  Shee mus'd a while, standing confusedly.
  At length. Ah friend, (saith shee,) tell thy good Lord,
  How deere I hold his pittying of my case:
  That out of his sweet nature can afford,
  A miserable woman so much grace.
  Tell him how much my heauy soule doth grieue
  Mercilesse *Cæsar* should so deale with mee:
  Pray him that he would all the counsell giue,
  That might diuert him from such crueltie.   1290
  As for my loue, say *Anthony* hath all,
  Say that my hart is gone into the graue
  With him, in whom it rests and euer shall:
  I haue it not my selfe, nor cannot haue.
  Yet tell him, he shall more commaund of mee

1283 saith] said 1598

Then any, whosoeuer lyuing, can.   [M
Hee that so friendly shewes himselfe to be
A right kind Roman, and a Gentleman.
Although his Nation (fatall vnto mee,)
Haue had mine age a spoyle, my youth a pray,   1300
Yet his affection must accepted be,
That fauours one distrest in such decay.
    Ah, hee was worthy then to haue been lou'd,
Of *Cleopatra* whiles her glory lasted;
Before shee had declyning fortune prou'd,
Or seene her honor wrackt, her flower blasted.
Now there is nothing left her but disgrace,
Nothing but her affliction that can moue:
Tell *Dolabella*, one that's in her case,
(Poore soule,) needes rather pitty now then loue.   1310
But shortly shall thy Lord heare more of mee.
And ending so her speech, no longer stayd,
But hasted to the Tombe of *Anthony*.
And this was all shee did, and all shee said.
Dol. Ah sweet distressed Lady. What hard hart
Could chuse but pitty thee, and loue thee too?
Thy worthines, the state wherein thou art
Requireth both, and both I vow to doo.
Although ambition lets not *Cæsar* see
The wrong hee doth thy Maiestie and sweetnes,   1320   [M
VVhich makes him now exact so much of thee,
To add vnto his pride, to grace his greatnes.
Hee knowes thou canst no hurt procure vs now,
Sith all thy strength is seaz'd into our hands:
Nor feares hee that, but rather labours how
Hee might shew Rome so great a Queene in bands.
That our great Ladies (enuying thee so much
That stain'd thē all, & hell'd them in such wonder,)
Might ioy to see thee, and thy fortune such,
Thereby extolling him that brought thee vnder.   1330
But I will seeke to stay it what I may;
I am but one, yet one that *Cæsar* loues,
And ô if now I could doe more then pray,
Then should'st yᵘ know how far affection moues.
But what my powre and prayer may preuaile,
Ile ioyne them both, to hinder thy disgrace:
And euen this present day I will not fayle
To doe my best with *Cæsar* in this case.

1302 such] her 1605
1306 flower] flowre thus 1605
1322 his pride] himselfe 1605

Tit. And Sir, euen now her selfe hath Letters sent,
    I met her messenger as I came hither,   1340
    With a dispatch as hee to *Cæsar* went,
    But knowe not what imports her sending thither.
    Yet this hee told, how *Cleopatra* late
    Was come from sacrifice. How ritchly clad   [M7^v]
    VVas seru'd to dinner in most sumptuous state,
    VVith all the brauest ornaments shee had.
    How hauing dyn'd, shee writes, and sends away
    Him straight to *Cæsar*, and commaunded than
    All should depart the Tombe, and none to stay
    But her two maides, and one poore Countryman.   1350
Dol. Why then I know, she sends t'haue audience now,
    And meanes t'experience what her state can doe:
    To see if Maiestie will make him bow
    To what affliction could not moue him to.
    And ô, if now shee could but bring a view
    Of that fresh beauty shee in youth possest,
    (The argument where-with shee ouer-threw
    The wit of *Iulius Cæsar*, and the rest,)
    Then happily *Augustus* might relent,
    Whilst powrefull Loue, (far stronger thē ambition)   1360
    Might worke in him, a mind to be content
    To graunt her asking, in the best condition.
    But beeing as shee is, yet doth she merite
    To be respected, for what shee hath been:
    The wonder of her kinde, of rarest spirit,
    A glorious Lady, and a mighty Queene.
    And now, but by a little weakenes falling
    To doe that which perhaps sh'was forst to doe: [M8^r]
    Alas, an error past, is past recalling,
    Take away weakenes, and take wemen too.   1370
       But now I goe to be thy Aduocate,
    Sweet *Cleopatra*, now Ile vse mine arte.
    Thy presence will mee greatly animate,
    Thy face will teach my tongue, thy loue my hart.

1342 knowe] knowes 1594(u), 1595, 1598
1362 To condescend vnto her small petition 1605
1364 what shee hath] her hauing 1605
1365 rarest] so rare 1605

SCENA SECVNDA.

NVNTIVS.

Am I ordaind the carefull Messenger,
And sad newes-bringer of the strangest death,
VVhich selfe hand did vpon it selfe infer,
To free a captiue soule from seruile breath?   1380
Must I the lamentable wonder shew,
VVhich all the world must grieue and meruaile at?
The rarest forme of death in earth below,
That euer pitty, glory, wonder gat.
Chor. What newes bring'st y^u, can Egipt yet yeeld more
Of sorrow then it hath? what can it add
To th'already ouer-flowing store
Of sad affliction, matter yet more sad?
Haue wee not seene the worst of our calamitie?   [M
Is there behind yet something of distresse   1390
Vnseene, vnknowne? Tell if that greater misery
There be, that we waile not that which is lesse.
Tell vs what so it be, and tell at fyrst,
For sorrow euer longs to heare her worst.
Nun. VVell then, the strangest thing relate I will,
That euer eye of mortall man hath seene.
    I (as you know) euen from my youth, haue stil
Attended on the person of the Queene.
And euer in all fortunes good or ill,
With her as one of chiefest trust haue beene.   1400
And now in these so great extreamities,
That euer could to Maiestie befall,
I did my best in what I could deuise,
And left her not, till now shee left vs all.
Chor. VVhat is shee gone. Hath *Cæsar* forst her so?
Nun. Yea, shee is gone, and hath deceiu'd him to.
Chor. What, fled to INDIA, to goe find her sonne?
Nun. No, not to INDIA, but to find her Sunne.
Chor. Why thē there's hope she may her state recouer.

1382 must] may 1605
1383 in] on 1605
1385 bring'st] brings 1598
1387 To] Vnto 1605
1389 the . . . our] our worst 1605
1391 Vnseene . . . that] Vnknowne? if there be 1605
1392 There . . . is] Relate it, that we do not waile the 1605

Nun. Her state? nay rather honor, and her Louer.   1410
Chor. Her Louer? him shee cannot haue againe.
Nun. VVell, him shee hath, w^t him she doth remaine.
Cho. Why thē she's dead. Ist so? why speak'st not thou?   [N1^r]
Nun. You gesse aright, and I will tell you how.
    Whē she perceiu'd al hope was cleane bereft her,
  That *Cæsar* meant to send her straight away,
  And saw no meanes of reconcilement left her,
  VVork what she could, she could not work to stay.
  Shee calls mee to her, and she thus began.
  O thou whose trust hath euer beene the same   1420
  And one in all my fortunes, faithfull man,
  Alone content t'attend disgrace and shame.
  Thou, whom the fearefull ruine of my fall,
  Neuer deterrd to leaue calamitie:
  As did those other smooth state-pleasers all,
  VVho followed but my fortune, and not me.
  Tis thou must doe a seruice for thy Queene,
  VVherein thy faith and skill must doe their best:
  Thy honest care and duty shall be seene
  Performing this, more then in all the rest.   1430
  For all what thou hast done, may die with thee,
  Although tis pitty that such faith should die.
  But this shall euer-more remembred be,
  A rare example to posterity.
  And looke how long as *Cleopatra* shall
  In after ages liue in memory,
  So long shall thy cleere fame endure withall,   [N1^v]
  And therefore thou must not my sute deny;
  Nor contradict my will. For what I will   [TLN 3060, 3105–6]
  I am resolu'd: and this tis thou must doe mee: 1440
  Goe finde mee out with all thy arte and skill
  Two Aspicqs, and conuay them close vnto mee.
  I haue a worke to doe with them in hand,
  Enquire not what, for thou shalt soone see what,
  If the heauens doe not my disseignes withstand,
  But doe thy charge, and let mee shyft with that.
    Beeing thus coniur'd, by her t'whom I had vow'd
  My true perpetuall seruice, forth I went,
  Deuising how my close attempt to shrowde,
  So that there might no arte my arte preuent.   1450
  And so disguis'd in habite as you see,

1415, 1417 her] *Om.* 1601+
1425 other] others 1599+
1440 tis . . . mee] now must it be 1601+
1442 vnto] to 1601+
1445 heauens] heauen 1598

Hauing found out the thing for which I went,
I soone return'd againe, and brought with mee
The Aspicqs, in a basket closely pent.
Which I had fill'd with figges, and leaues vpon.
And comming to the Guarde that kept the dore,
What hast thou there? said they, and lookt thereon.
Seeing the figgs, they deem'd of nothing more,
But sayd, they were the fairest they had seene.
Taste some, said I, for they are good and pleasant.   1460
No, no, sayd they, goe beare them to thy Queene.   [N
Thinking mee some poore man y^t brought a Present.
Well, in I went, where brighter then the Sunne,   [TLN 3473–5]
Glittering in all her pompous ritch aray,
Great *Cleopatra* sate, as if she'had wonne
Cæsar and all the world beside this day.
Euen as shee was when on thy cristall streames,
O CYDNOS shee did shew what earth could shew.
VVhen Asia all amaz'd in wonder, deemes
VENVS from heauen was come on earth below.   1470
Euen as shee went at first to meete her Loue,
So goes shee now at last againe to finde him.
But that first, did her greatnes onely proue,
This last her loue, that could not liue behind him.
Yet as shee sate, the doubt of my good speed,
Detracts much from the sweetnes of her looke:
Cheere-marrer Care, did then such passions breed,
That made her eye bewray the care shee tooke.
But shee no sooner sees mee in the place,
But straight her sorrow-clowded brow shee cleeres,   1480
Lightning a smile from out a stormy face,
Which all her tempest-beaten sences cheeres.
    Looke how a stray'd perplexed trauailer,
When chas'd by thieues, and euen at poynt of taking,
Discrying suddainly some towne not far,   [N
Or some vnlookt-for ayde to him-ward making;
Cheeres vp his tired sp'rits, thrusts forth his strength
To meete that good, that comes in so good houre:
Such was her ioy, perceiuing now at length,
Her honor was t'escape so proude a powre.   1490
Foorth from her seate shee hastes to meet the present,
And as one ouer-ioyd, shee caught it straight.
And with a smyling cheere in action pleasant,
Looking among the figges, findes the deceite.

___

1468 O] Cleere 1601+
1478 care] griefe 1601+

And seeing there the vgly venemous beast,
Nothing dismayde, shee stayes and viewes it well.
At length, th'extreamest of her passion ceast,
VVhen shee began with words her ioy to tell.
   O rarest Beast (sayth shee) that Affrick breedes,
How deerely welcome art thou vnto mee?   1500
The fayrest creature that faire *Nylus* feedes   [TLN 3495]
Mee thinks I see, in now beholding thee.
VVhat though the euer-erring world doth deeme
That angred Nature fram'd thee but in spight?
Little they know what they so light esteeme,
That neuer learn'd the wonder of thy might.
Better then Death, Deathes office thou dischargest,   [TLN 3563, 3565]
That with one gentle touch canst free our breath:
And in a pleasing sleepe our soule inlargest,   [N3ʳ]
Making our selues not priuie to our death.   1510
If Nature err'd, ô then how happy error,
Thinking to make thee worst, shee made thee best:
Sith thou best freest vs from our liues worst terror,
In sweetly bringing soules to quiet rest.
VVhen that inexorable Monster Death
That followes Fortune, flyes the poore distressed,
Tortures our bodies ere hee takes our breath,
And loades with paines th'already weake oppressed.
How oft haue I begg'd, prayd, intreated him
To take my life, and yet could neuer get him?   1520
And when he comes, he comes so vgly grim,
That who is he (if he could chuse) would let him?
Therefore come thou, of wonders wonder chiefe,   [TLN 3563, 3565]
That open canst with such an easie key
The dore of life, come gentle cunning thiefe,
That from our selues so steal'st our selues away.
VVell did our Priests discerne something diuine
Shadow'd in thee, and therefore first they did
Offrings and worshyps due to thee assigne,
In whom they found such misteries were hid.   1530
Comparing thy swift motion to the Sunne,
That mou'st without the instruments that moue:
And neuer waxing old, but alwaies one,   [N3ᵛ]

1496 stayes] sayes 1605
    viewes] viewe 1595
1505 so] of 1605
1508 canst] can 1599
1520 and . . . him] which he would neuer do 1601+
1522 Attended on with hideous torments to. 1601+
1531 swift] sweet 1594(u), 1595, 1598 (*illegible*)

573

Doost sure thy strange diuinitie approue.
And therefore to, the rather vnto thee
In zeale I make the offring of my blood,
Calamitie confirming now in mee
A sure beliefe that pietie makes good.
Which happy men neglect, or hold ambiguous,
And onely the afflicted are religious.   1540
    And heere I sacrifize these armes to Death,
That Lust late dedicated to Delights:
Offring vp for my last, this last of breath,
The complement of my loues deerest rites.
With that shee bares her arme, and offer makes   [TLN 3562]
To touch her death, yet at the touch with-drawes,
And seeming more to speake, occasion takes,
Willing to die, and willing too to pause.
    Looke how a Mother at her sonnes departing   [TLN 401–20]
For some far voyage, bent to get him fame,   1550
Doth intertaine him with an idle parling,
And still doth speake, and still speakes but the same;
Now bids farewell, and now recalls him back,
Tells what was told, and bids againe fare-well,
And yet againe recalls; for still doth lack
Something that loue would faine and cannot tell.
Pleas'd hee should goe, yet cannot let him goe.   [N
So shee, although shee knew there was no way
But this, yet this shee could not handle so
But shee must shew that life desir'd delay.   1560
Faine would shee entertaine the time as now,
And now would faine yᵗ Death would seaze vpõ her.
Whilst I might see presented in her brow,
The doubtfull combat tryde twixt Life and Honor.
Life bringing Legions of fresh hopes with her,
Arm'd with the proofe of Time, which yeelds we say
Comfort and Help, to such as doe refer
All vnto him, and can admit delay.
But Honor scorning Life, loe forth leades he
Bright Immortalitie in shyning armour: [TLN 3532]
Thorow the rayes of whose cleere glory, shee   1571
Might see Lifes basenes, how much it might harm her.
Besides, shee saw whole Armies of Reproches,
And base Disgraces, Furies fearefull sad,

1534 sure thy strange] therein a 1605
1542 late] hath 1595
1570 Cleere Immorralitie arm'd all in flames: 1605
1571 the . . . cleere] whose bright shining rayes of 1605
1572 Lifes . . . her] how base was life that her defames 1605

Marching with Life, and Shame that still incroches
Vppon her face, in bloody collours clad.
Which representments seeing worse then death
Shee deem'd to yeeld to Life, and therfore chose
To render all to Honour, hart and breath;
And that with speede, least that her inward foes   1580
False flesh and blood, ioyning with lyfe and hope,   [N4^v]
Should mutinie against her resolution.
And to the end shee would not giue them scope,
Shee presently proceeds to th'execution.
And sharply blaming of her rebell powres,   [TLN 2711–12]
False flesh, (sayth shee,) and what dost thou cōspire
With *Cæsar* to, as thou wert none of ours,
To worke my shame, and hinder my desire?
Wilt thou retaine in closure of thy vaines,
That enemy Base life, to let my good?   [TLN 3541]
No, know there is a greater powre constraines   1591
Then can be countercheckt with fearefull blood.
For to the minde that's great, nothing seemes great.
And seeing death to be the last of woes,
And life lasting disgrace, which I shall get,
What doe I lose, that haue but life to lose?
   This hauing said, strengthned in her owne hart,
And vnion of her selfe sences in one
Charging together, shee performes that part
That hath so great a part of glory wonne.   1600
And so receiues the deadly poysning touch.
That touch that tryde the gold of her loue pure,
And hath confirm'd her honor to be such,
As must a wonder to all worlds endure.
Now not an yeelding shrinke or touch of feare,   [N5^r]
Consented to bewray least sence of paine:
But still in one same sweete vnaltred cheere,
Her honor did her dying thoughts retaine.
   Well, now this work is done (saith she,) here ends
This act of life, that part the Fates assign'd mee: 1610
What glory or disgrace heere this world lends,
Both haue I had, and both I leaue behinde mee.
And now ô Earth, the Theater where I
Haue acted this, witnes I dye vnforst.

1575 with Life] therewith 1605
1576 bloody] blushing 1605
1577 worse] farre worse 1605
1610 the] of 1594(u), 1595, 1598
1610, 1612 mee] *Om.* 1599 +
1611 or disgrace heere] of disgraces 1605

575

Witnes my soule parts free to *Anthony*,
And now proude Tyrant *Cæsar* doe thy worst.
   This sayd, shee stayes, and makes a suddaine pause,
As twere to feele whither the poyson wrought:
Or rather els the working might be cause
That made her stay, as likewise may be thought.   1620
For in that instant I might well perceiue,
The drowsie humor in her falling brow:
And how each powre, each part opprest did leaue
Theyr former office, and did sencelesse grow.
Looke how a new-pluckt branch against the Sunne,
Declynes his fading leaues in feeble sort,
So her disioyned ioyntures as vndonne,
Let fall her weake dissolued limmes support.
Yet loe that face the wonder of her life,   [N⁹
Retaines in death, a grace that graceth death,   1630
Couller so liuely, cheere so louely rife,
That none wold think such beauty could want breath.
And in that cheere, th'impression of a smile
Did seeme to shew shee scorned Death and *Cæsar*,
As glorying that shee could them both beguile,
And telling death how much her death did please her.
VVonder it was to see how soone shee went,
Shee went with such a will, and did so haste it,
That sure I thinke shee did her paine preuent,
Fore-going paine, or staying not to taste it.   1640
And sencelesse, in her sinking downe shee wryes   [TLN 3572–3]
The Diadem which on her head shee wore,
Which *Charmion* (poore weake feeble mayd) espyes,
And hastes to right it as it was before.
For *Eras* now was dead, and *Charmion* too
Euen at the poynt, for both would imitate
Theyr Mistres glory, striuing like to doo.
But *Charmion* would in this exceede her mate,
For shee would haue this honour to be last,
That should adorne that head that must be seene   1650
To weare a Crowne in death, that life held fast,
That all the world might know shee dyde a Queene.
And as shee stood setting it fitly on,   [N
Lo in rush *Cæsars* Messengers in haste,
Thinking to haue preuented what was doone,
But yet they came too late, for all was past.

1618 twere] if 1605
1620 as . . . be] and intertain'd her 1599+
1641 sinking] shrinking 1598
1651 a . . . that] that . . . which 1605
1652 might] may 1601, 1602

For there they found stretch'd on a bed of gold,
Dead *Cleopatra*, and that proudly dead,
In all the riche attyre procure shee could,
And dying *Charmion* trymming of her head.   1660
And *Eras* at her feete, dead in like case.
Charmion, is this well doone? said one of them.
Yea, well sayd shee, and her that from the race
Of so great Kings discends, doth best become.   [TLN 3586]
And with that word, yeelds too her faithful breath,
To passe th'assurance of her loue with death.
Chor. But how knew *Cæsar* of her close intent?
Nun. By letters which before to him shee sent.
For when shee had procur'd this meanes to die,
Shee writes, and earnestly intreates, shee might   1670
Be buried in one Tombe with *Anthony*.
Whereby then *Cæsar* gess'd all went not right.
And forth-with sends, yet ere the message came
Shee was dispatcht, he crost in his intent,
Her prouidence had ordred so the same
That shee was sure none should her plot preuent.

CHORVS.   [N6ᵛ]

Then thus we haue beheld
Th'accomplishment of woes,
The full of ruine, and   1680
The worst of worst of ills.
And seene all hope expeld,
That euer sweet repose
Shall re-possess: the Land
That Desolations fills,
And where Ambition spills
With vncontrouled hand,
All th'issue of all those,
That so long rule haue hell'd:
To make vs no more vs,   1690
But cleane confound vs thus.

And canst O *Nylus* thou,
Father of floods indure,
That yellow *Tyber* should

1685 Desolations] Desolation 1595 +

With sandy streames rule thee?
Wilt thou be pleas'd to bow
To him those feete so pure,
Whose vnknowne head we hold   [N7
A powre diuine to bee?
Thou that didst euer see   1700
Thy free banks vncontroul'd   [TLN 3495]
Liue vnder thine owne care:
Ah wilt thou beare it now?
And now wilt yeeld thy streams
A pray to other Reames?

Draw backe thy waters floe
To thy concealed head:
Rockes strangle vp thy waues,
Stop *Cataractes* thy fall.
And turne thy courses so,   1710
That sandy Dezarts dead,
(The world of dust that craues
To swallow thee vp all,)
May drinke so much as shall
Reuiue from vastie graues
A lyuing greene, which spredd
Far florishing, may gro
On that wide face of Death.
Where nothing now drawes breath.

Fatten some people there,   1720   [N7
Euen as thou vs hast doone,
With plenties wanton store,
And feeble luxurie:
And them as vs prepare
Fit for the day of mone
Respected not before.
Leaue leuell'd Egipt dry,
A barraine pray to lye,
Wasted for euer-more.
Of plenties yeelding none   1730
To recompence the care
Of Victors greedy lust,
And bring forth nought but dust.

And so O leaue to bee,
Sith thou art what thou art:

1702 care] cure 1594 (*errata*), 1595
1724 vs] we 1595

Let not our race possess
Th'inheritance of shame,
The fee of sin, that wee
Haue left them for theyr part:
The yoke of whose distress   1740
Must still vpbraid our blame,
Telling from whom it came.
Our weight of wantonnes,   [N8^r]
Lyes heauy on their hart,
Who neuer-more shall see
The glory of that worth
They left who brought vs forth.

O thou all seeing light,
High President of heauen,
You Magistrates the starres   1750
Of that eternall court
Of *Prouidence* and *Right*,
Are these the bounds y'haue giuen
Th'vntranspassable barres,
That limit pride so short,
Is greatnes of this sort,
That greatnes greatnes marres,
And wracks it selfe, selfe driuen
On Rocks of her owne might?
Doth Order order so   1760
Disorders ouer-thro?
                    FINIS.

A Letter from Octavia to Marcus Antonius (1599)

"*A letter sent from* OCTAVIA *to her husband* MARCUS ANTHONIUS *into Egipt*" was entered on the Stationers' Register to Simon Waterson on 9 Jan. 1599 (Arber, *Transcript*, 3:134). The work is included in *The Poeticall Essayes* with the following title page on A1: "A | LETTER | FROM OCTA- | VIA TO MARCVS | ANTONIVS. | SAMVEL DANIEL. | [device] | AT LONDON | Printed by P. Short for Simon | Waterson. 1599."

In this modified diplomatic reprint of the 1599 quarto, the Argument's italic with incidental roman is inverted. The verse lineation is retained, but prose is relined. The beginning of each page in the quarto is indicated by a bracketed signature number in the text or the right margin. The dedication to the Countess of Cumberland on A2 is not reproduced, nor are lace and other ornaments and factotums. Display capitals have been replaced by regular capitals, and the capitals that conventionally follow display letters reduced. Long *s* is printed *s*. Obvious typographical errors have been silently corrected.

The beginnings of passages corresponding with *Ant.* are marked by TLNs. The following parallels have been found (*Ant.* TLNs are listed, with parenthetical page references to Daniel in this edition): 30–43 (581), 209–10 (580), 957 (580), 1005–7 (580).

The text is based on the copy in the Houghton Library, Harvard (*STC* 6261).

The Argument. [B

Vpon the second agreement (the first being broken through iealousie of a disproportion of eminencie) betweene the *Triumuiri Octauius Cæsar, Marcus Antonius*, and *Lepidus: Octauia* the sister of *Octauius Cæsar*, was married to *Antonius*, as a linke to combine that which neuer yet, the greatest strength of nature, or anie power of nearest respect could long holde togither, who made but the instrument of others ends, and deliuered vp as an Ostage to serue the oportunitie of aduantages, met not with that integritie she brought: but as highlie preferred to affliction encountered with all the greeuances that beate vppon the miserie of greatnes, exposed to stand betwixt the diuers tending humours of vnquiet parties. [TLN 209–10, 1005–7] For *Antonie* hauing yet vpon him the fetters of AEgypt, layde on by the power of a most incomparable beautie, could admit no new lawes into the state of his affection, or dispose of himself being not himselfe, but as hauing his heart turned Eastwarde whither the point of his desires were directed, touchte with the strongest allurements that ambition, and a licencious soueraintie could draw a man vnto: could not trulie descend to the priuate loue of a ciuill nurtred Matrone, [TLN 957] whose entertainment bounded with modestie and the nature of her [B1ᵛ] education, knew not to cloth her affections in any other colours then the plain habit of truth: wherein she euer suted al her actions, and vsed all her best ornaments of honestie, to win the good liking of him that helde her but as a Curtaine drawne betweene him and *Octauius* to shadow his other purposes withall; which the sharpe sight of an equallie iealous ambition could soone pierce into, and as easily looke thorow and ouer bloud and nature as he to abuse it: And therefore to preuent his aspiring, he armes his forces either to reduce *Antonie* to the ranke of his estate, or else to disranke him out of state and al. When *Octauia* by the imploiment of *Antonie* (as being not yet ready to put his fortune to her triall) throwes her selfe, great with child, and as big with sorrowe, into the trauaile of a most laboursome reconciliation: taking her iourney from the farthest part of *Greece* to find *Octauius*, with whom her care and teares were so good agents that they effected their Commission beyond all expectation: and for that time quite disarmed their wrath, which yet long could not hold so. For *Antonius* falling into the relaps of his former disease, watching his oportunity got ouer againe into *Egypt*, where he so forgot himselfe, that he quite put off his own nature, and wholly became a prey to his pleasures, as if hee had wound himselfe out of the respect of Country, bloud and alliance, which gaue to *Octauia* the cause of much affliction, and to me the Argument of this Letter.

A Letter sent from *Octauia* to her   [B2ʳ]
husband *Marcus Antonius*
into Egypt.

1

To thee (yet deere) though most disloiall Lord,
Whom impious loue keepes in a barbarous land,
Thy wronged wife *Octauia* sendeth word
Of th'vnkind wounds receiued by thy hand,
Grant *Antony*, ô let thine eyes afford
But to permit thy heart to vnderstand
The hurt thou dost, and do but read her teares
That still is thine though thou wilt not be hers.

2   10

Although perhaps, these my complaints may come   [TLN 30–43]
Whilst thou in th'armes of that incestious Queene
The staine of *Aegypt*, and the shame of *Rome*
Shalt dallying sit, and blush to haue them seene:
Whilst proud disdainfull she, gessing from whome
The message came, and what the cause hath beene,
Wil skorning saie, faith, this comes from your Deere,
Now sir you must be shent for staying heere.

3   [B2ᵛ]

From her indeed it comes, delitious dame,   20
(Thou royal Concubine, and Queene of lust)
Whose Armes yet pure, whose brests are voide of blame,
And whose most lawfull flame proues thine vniust:
Tis shee that sendes the message of thy shame,
And his vntruth that hath betraid her trust:
Pardon, deare Lord, from her these sorrowes are
Whose bed bringes neither infamie nor warre.

4

And therefore heare her wordes, that too too much
Hath heard the wronges committed by thy shame;   30
Although at first my trust in thee was such
As it held out against the strongest fame;
My heart would neuer let in once a touch
Of least beliefe, till all confirmd the same:
That I was almost last that would belieue
Because I knew mee first that most must grieue.

5

How oft haue poore abused I tooke parte
With falshood onely for to make thee true?
How oft haue I argued against my heart   40
Not suffring it to know that which it knew?
And for I would not haue thee what thou arte

581

I made my selfe, vnto my selfe vntrue:
So much my loue labourd against thy Sinne
To shut out feare which yet kept feare within.

6

   For I could neuer thinke th'aspiring mind
Of worthie and victorious *Antonie*,
Could be by such a *Syren* so declind,
As to be traynd a pray to Luxury: 50
I could not thinke my Lord would be s'vnkind
As to despise his Children, *Rome* and me:
But ô how soone are they deceiud that trust
And more their shame, that wilbe so vniust.

7

   But now that certaine fame hath open layd
Thy new relaps, and straunge reuolt from mee,
Truth hath quite beaten all my hopes awaie
And made the passage of my sorrowes free:
For now poore hart, there's nothing in the waie 60
Remaines to stand betwixt despaire and thee;
All is throwne downe, there comes no succors newe
It is most true, my Lord is most vntrue.

8

   And now *I* may with shame inough pull in
The colours I aduaunced in his grace
For that subduing powre, that him did win
Hath lost me too, the honour of my face:
Yet why should I bearing no part of sinne
Beare such a mightie part of his disgrace? 70
Yes though it be not mine, it is of mine;
And his renowne being clips'd, mine cannot shine.

9

   Which makes me as I do, hide from the eie
Of the misiudging vulgar that will deeme,
That sure there was in me some reason why
Which made thee thus, my bed to disesteeme:
So that alas poore vndeseruing I
A cause of thy vncleane deserts shall seeme,
Though lust takes neuer ioy in what is due, 80
But still leaues known delights to seeke out new.

10

   And yet my brother *Cæsar* laboured
To haue me leaue thy house, and liue more free,
But God forbid, *Octauia* should be led
To leaue to liue in thine, though left by thee,
The pledges here of thy forsaken bed,

582

Are still the obiects that remember me
What *Antony* was once, although false now,
And is my Lord, though he neglect his vow.   90

11

These walles that here do keepe me out of sight
Shall keepe me all vnspotted vnto thee,
And testifie that I will do thee right,
Ile neuer staine thy house, though thou shame me:
The now sad Chamber of my once delight
Shall be the temple of my pietie
Sacred vnto the faith I reuerence,
Where I will paie my teares for thy offence.   100   [B4ʳ]

12

Although my youth, thy absence, and this wrong
Might draw my bloud to forfeit vnto shame,
Nor need I frustrate my delights so long
That haue such meanes to carrie so the same,
Since that the face of greatnesse is so strong
As it dissolues suspect, and beares out blame,
Hauing all secret helps that long thereto
That seldome wants there ought but will to do:

13

Which yet to do, ere lust this heart shall frame   110
Earth swallow me aliue, hel rap me hence:
Shall I because despisd contemne my shame,
And ad disgrace to others impudence?
What can my powre but giue more powre to fame?
Greatnesse must make it great incontinence;
Chambers are false, the bed and all wil tell,
No doore keepes in their shame that do not well.

14

Hath greatnesse ought peculiar else alone
But to stand faire and bright aboue the base?   120
What doth deuide the cottage from the throne,
If vice shall laie both leuell with disgrace?
For if vncleannesse make them but all one
What priuiledge hath honor by his place?
What though our sinnes go braue and better clad,
They are as those in rags as base as bad.

15   [B4ᵛ]

I know not how, but wrongfullie I know
Hath vndiscerning custome plac'd our kind
Vnder desart, and set vs farre below   130
The reputation to our sexe assign'd;
Charging our wrong reputed weakenes, how

VVe are vnconstant, fickle, false, vnkinde:
And thogh our life with thousand proofs shewes no
Yet since strength saies it, weaknes must be so.

16

Vnequall partage to b'allow'd no share
Of power to do of lifes best benefite;
But stand as if we interdicted were
Of vertue, action, libertie and might: 140
Must yoYet oft our narrowed thoughts look more u haue all,
and not vouchsafe to direct
spare
Our weaknes any intrest of delight?
Is there no portion left for vs at all,
But sufferance, sorrow, ignorance and thrall?

17

Thrice happie you in whom it is no fault,
To know, to speake, to do, and to be wise:
VVhose words haue credit, and whose deeds though naught
Must yet be made to seeme far otherwise:
You can be onely heard whilst we are taught   150
To hold our peace, and not to exercise
The powers of our best parts, because your parts
Haue with our fredome robb'd vs of our hearts.

18   [C1ʳ]

We in this prison of our selues confin'd
Must here shut vp with our own passions liue
Turn'd in vpon vs, and denied to find
The vent of outward means that might relieue:
That they alone must take vp all our mind;
And no roome left vs, but to thinke and grieue,   160
Yet oft our narrowed thoughts look more direct
Then your loose wisdoms borne with wild neglect.

19

For should we to (as God forbid we should)
Carrie no better hand on our desires
Then your strength doth; what int'rest could
Our wronged patience paie you for your hires?
What mixture of strange generations would
Succeed the fortunes of vncertaine Sires?
What foule confusion in your blood and race   170
To your immortall shame, and our disgrace?

20

What? are there bars for vs, no bounds for you?
Must leuitie stand sure, though firmnes fall?
And are you priuiledg'd to be vntrue,
And we no grant to be dispens'd withall?

584

Must we inuiolable keepe your due,
Both to your loue, and to your falshood thrall?
Whilst you haue stretch'd your lust vnto your will
As if your strength were licenc'd to do ill.   180

21 [C1ᵛ]

O if you be more strong then be more iust,
Cleere this suspition, make not the world to doubt
Whether in strong, or weake be better trust,
If frailtie, or else valour be more stout:
And if we haue shut in our harts from lust
Let not your bad example let them out,
Thinke that there is like feeling in our blood,
If you will haue vs good, be you then good.

22 190

Is it that loue doth take no true delight
In what it hath, but still in what it would,
Which drawes you on to do vs this vnright,
Whilst feare in vs of loosing what we hold
Keepes vs in still to you, that set vs light,
So that what you vnties, doth vs infold?
The loue tis thou that dost confound vs so
To make our truth the occasion of our wo.

23

Distressed woman kind that either must   200
For louing loose your loues, or get neglect;
Whilst wantons are more car'd for, then the iust
And falshood cheerisht, faith without respect:
Better she fares in whom is lesser trust,
And more is lou'd that is in more suspect.
VVhich (pardon me) shewes no great strength of mind
To be most theirs, that vse you most vnkind.

24 [C2ʳ]

Yet wel it fits for that sinne euer must
Be tortur'd with the racke of his own frame,   210
For he that holds no faith shall find no trust,
But sowing wrong is sure to reape the same:
How can he looke to haue his measure iust
That fils deceipt, and reckons not of shame,
And being not pleas'd with what he hath in lot
Shall euer pine for that which he hath not?

25

Yet if thou couldst not loue, thou mightst haue seem'd,
Though to haue seem'd had likewise beene vniust:
Yet so much are leane shewes of vs esteem'd   220
That oft they feed, though not suffice our trust:
Because our nature grieueth to be deem'd

585

To be so wrong'd, although we be and must.
And it's some ease yet to be kindly vs'd
In outward shew, though secretly abus'd.

26

But wo to her, that both in shew despis'd,
And in effect disgrac'd, and left forlorne,
For whom no comforts are to be deuis'd,
Nor no new hopes can euermore be borne: 230
O *Antony*, could it not haue suffiz'd
That I was thine, but must be made her skorne
That enuies all our bloud, and doth deuide
Thee from thy selfe, onely to serue her pride?

27

[C2ᵛ]

What fault haue I committed that should make
So great dislike of me and of my loue?
Or doth thy fault but an occasion take
For to dislike what most doth it reproue?
Because the conscience gladlie would mistake   240
Her own misdeedes which she would faine remoue,
And they that are vnwilling to amend
Will take offence because they will offend.

28

Or hauing run beyond all pardon quite
They flie and ioine with sin as wholy his,
Making it now their side, their part, their right,
And to turne backe would shew t'haue done amisse:
For now they thinke not to be opposite
To what obraides their fault, were wickednesse: 250
So much doth follie thrust them into blame
That euen to leaue of shame, they count it shame.

29

Which do not thou, deere Lord, for *I* do not
Pursue thy fault, but sue for thy returne
Backe to thy selfe; whom thou hast both forgot
With me, poore me, that doth not spight but mourne:
And if thou couldst as well amend thy blot
As I forgiue, these plaints had beene forborne:
And thou shouldst be the same vnto my hart   260
VVhich once thou were, not that which nowe thou art.

30

[C3ʳ]

Though deepe doth sit the hard recouering smart
Of that last wound (which God grant be the last)
And more doth touch that tender feeling part
Of my sad soule, then all th'vnkindnes past:
And *Antony* I appeale to thine own hart,

586

(If th'hart which once was thine thou yet still hast)
To iudge if euer woman that did liue
Had iuster cause, then wretched I, to grieue.   270

31

For comming vnto *Athens* as I did,
Wearie and weake with toile, and all distrest,
After I had with sorrow compassed
A hard consent, to grant me that request:
And how my trauaile was considered
And all my care, and cost, thy selfe knowes best:
That wouldst not moue one foot from lust for me
That had left all was deere to come to thee:

32   280

For first what great ado had I to win
My'offended brother *Cæsars* backward will?
And praid, and wept, and cride to staie the sinne
Of ciuill rancor rising twixt you still:
For in what case shall wretched I be in,
Set betwixt both to share with both your ill?
My bloud said I with either of you goes,
Who euer win, I shall be sure to lose.

33   [C3ᵛ]

For what shame should such mighty persons get   290
For two weake womens cause to disagree?
Nay what shall I that shall be deem'd to set
Th'inkindled fire, seeming inflam'd for mee?
O if I be the motiue of this heate
Let these vnguiltie hands the quenchers bee,
And let me trudge to mediate an accord
The Agent twixt my brother and my Lord.

34

With praiers, vowes and tears, with vrging hard
I wrung from him a slender grant at last,   300
And with the rich prouisions I prepard
For thy (intended *Parthian* war) made haste
Weighing not how my poore weake body far'd,
But all the tedious difficulties past:
And came to *Athens*; whence I *Niger* sent
To shew thee of my comming and intent.

35

Whereof when he had made relation:
I was commanded to approch no neare;
Then sent I backe to know what should be done   310
With th'horse, and men, and monie I had there:
Whereat perhaps when some remorse begun

To touch thy soule, to thinke yet what we were,
Th'Inchantres straight steps twixt thy hart & thee
And intercepts all thoughts that came of mee.

36

She armes her teares, the ingins of deceit
And all her batterie, to oppose my loue:
And bring thy comming grace to a retraite
The powre of all her subtiltie to proue: 320
Now pale and faint she languishes, and straight
Seemes in a sound, vnable more to moue:
Whilst her instructed followers plie thine eares
With forged passions, mixt with fained teares.

37

Hard-harted lord, say they, how canst thou see
This mightie Queene a creature so diuine,
Lie thus distrest, and languishing for thee
And onely wretched but for beeing thine?
Whilst base *Octauia* must intitled bee   330
Thy wife, and she esteem'd thy concubine:
Aduance thy heart, raise it vnto his right
And let a scepter baser passions quit.

38

Thus they assaile thy natures weakest side
And worke vpon th'aduantage of thy mind,
Knowing where iudgment stood least fortified
And how t'incounter follie in her kinde:
But yet the while O what dost thou abide,
Who in thy selfe such wrastling thoughts dost finde?   340
In what confused case is thy soule in
Rackt betwixt pitie, sorrow, shame and sin?

39

I cannot tell but sure I dare beleeue
My trauails needs must some cōpassion moue:
For no such locke to bloud could nature giue
To shut out pitie, though it shut out loue:
Conscience must leaue a little way to grieue
To let in horror comming to reproue,
The guilt of thy offence that caus'd the same,   350
For deepest woūds the hand, of our owne shame.

40

Neuer haue vniust pleasures beene compleet
In ioyes intire, but still feare kept the dore
And held back something from that ful of sweet
To intersowre vnsure delights the more:
For neuer did all circumstances meete

588

With those desires which were cõceiu'd before,
Something must still be left to check our sinne,
And giue a touch of what should not haue bin.   360

41

Wretched mankinde, wherefore hath nature made
The lawfull vndelightfull, th'vniust shame?
As if our pleasure onelie were forbade,
But to giue fire to lust, t'ad greater flame;
Or else but as ordained more to lade
Our heart with passions to confound the same,
Which though it be, yet ad not worse to ill,
Do, as the best men do, bound thine owne will.

42   370   [D1ʳ]

Redeeme thy selfe, and now at length make peace
With thy deuided hart opprest with toile:
Breake vp this war, this brest dissention cease,
Thy passions to thy passions reconcile;
I do not only seeke my good t'increase,
But thine owne ease, and liberty the while:
Thee in the circuite of thy selfe confine,
And be thine owne, and then thou wilt be mine.

43

I know my pitied loue, doth aggrauate   380
Enuy and wrath for these wrongs offered:
And that my suffrings adde with my estate
Coales in thy bosome, hatred on thy head:
Yet is not that, my fault, but my hard fate,
Who rather wish to haue beene vnpitied
Of all but thee, then that my loue should be
Hurtfull to him that is so deere to me.

44

Cannot the busie world let me alone
To beare alone the burthen of my griefe,   390
But they must intermeddle with my mone
And seeke t'offend me with vnsought reliefe?
Whilst my afflictions labour'd to moue none
But only thee; must pitie play the thiefe,
To steale so many harts to hurt my hart,
And moue apart against my deerest part?

45   [D1ᵛ]

Yet all this shall not preiudice my Lord
If yet he will but make returne at last,
His sight shall raze out of the sad record   400
Of my inrowled griefe all that is past;
And I will not so much as once affoord

589

Place for a thought to thinke I was disgrac'st:
And pity shall bring backe againe with me
Th'offended harts that haue forsaken thee.

46

   And therfore come deer lord, least longer stay
Do arme against thee all the powers of spight,
And thou be made at last the wofull pray
Of full inkindled wrath, and ruin'd quite: 410
But what presaging thought of bloud doth stay
My trembling hand, and doth my soule affright?
What horror do I see, prepar'd t'attend
Th'euent of this? what end vnlesse thou end?

47

   With what strange formes and shadowes ominous
Did my last sleepe, my grieu'd soule intertaine?
I dreamt, yet ô, dreames are but friuolous,
And yet Ile tell it, and God grant it vaine.
Me thought a mighty *Hippopotamus*   *a sea Horse.*   420
From *Nilus* floting, thrusts into the maine,
Vpon whose backe a wanton Mermaide sate,
As if she ruld his course and steerd his fate.

48   [D2ʳ]

   With whom t'incounter, forth another makes,
Alike in kind, of strength and powre as good:
At whose ingrappling *Neptunes* mantle takes
A purple colour dyde with streames of bloud,
Whereat, this looker on, amaz'd forsakes
Her Champion there, who yet the better stood;   430
But se'ing her gone straight after her he hies
As if his hart and strength laie in her eyes.

49

   On followes wrath vpon disgrace and feare,
Whereof th'euent forsooke me with the night,
But my wak'd cares, gaue me, these shadowes were
Drawne but from darknes to instruct the light,
These secret figures, natures message beare
Of cōming woes, were they desciphered right;
But if as clouds of sleepe thou shalt them take,   440
Yet credit wrath and spight that are awake.

50

   Preuent great spirit the tempests that begin,
If lust and thy ambition haue left waie
But to looke out, and haue not shut all in,
To stop thy iudgement from a true suruay
Of thy estate; and let thy hart within

590

Consider in what danger thou doost lay
Thy life and mine, to leaue the good thou hast,
To follow hopes with shadowes ouercast.   450

51

Come, come away from wrong, from craft, frō toile,
Possesse thine owne with right, with truth, with peace;
Breake from these snares, thy iudgement vnbeguile,
Free thine owne torment, and my griefe release.
But whither am I caried all this while
Beyond my scope, and know not when to cease?
Words still with my increasing sorrowes grow;
I know t'haue said too much, but not ynow.
    Wherefore no more but only I commend   460
    To thee the hart that's thine, and so I end.

FINIS.

Other Sources, Influences, and Analogues
DRAMATIC VERSIONS

The search for influences on *Ant.* from versions other than the Countess of Pembroke's and Daniel's—especially those by Cinthio, Jodelle, Sachs, and Brandon, and the anon. *Caesar's Revenge*—begins with the earliest of these plays, Giraldi Cinthio's *Cleopatra tragedia* (c. 1542, pub. 1583). KLEIN's (1867, 5:352) belief that it was known to Sh.—based on such parallels as the appearance of Maecenas, Agrippa, Proculeius, Octavius, and the eunuch; Antony's moods and his curses against Cleopatra after the lost battle; and his commanding his shield bearer to kill him—is rebutted by MOELLER (1888, p. 23), FURNESS (ed. 1907, pp. 514–15), and MACCALLUM (1910, p. 310 n.), who point out common origins in Plutarch.

Picking up a cautious hint from MACCALLUM (1910, p. 435, n. 1; see n. 3398), MUIR (1969, pp. 197–206; also 1977, pp. 230–3) argues for Sh.'s acquaintance with Etienne Jodelle's *Cléopâtre captive* (performed 1552–3, pub. 1574): Jodelle (ed. F. Gohin, Paris, 1925, pp. 75–7) resembles Sh. in (p. 202) "the theatrical violence of his heroine's behavior" in the scene with Seleucus (3368–3406), though Muir also notes that the similar motives for her suicide (*Ant.* 3450–64 and Jodelle, p. 86) could have been developed independently by both dramatists from Plutarch.

MOELLER (1888, p. 23) sees a resemblance between Act 3 of Hans Sachs's play *Die Königin Cleopatra aus Egipten mit Antonio, dem Römer* (1560)—where two of Antony's soldiers discuss Cleopatra's pernicious influence on their master—and *Ant.* 1.1, but he points to Plutarch (Ch. 58; see p. 436) as probable common source. WILLIAMSON (1974, p. 181) sees Sachs as a "harbinger" of Sh.: "Both write for the popular stage; both use the whole story of Antony and Cleopatra, preserving (with some modifications in Shakespeare) the chronicle structure of Plutarch's narrative; both present a wanton Cleopatra (though Shakespeare's is more than that too); both see treachery of the principals reflected in that of their followers; and both divide

591

the action in two movements: for Sachs the signal is the shift of place to Rome, and for Shakespeare the scene on Pompey's barge [2.7]."

Several scholars have found parallels to *Ant.* in the anon. *Tragedy of Caesar's Revenge* (1595, pub. 1607), despite the late publication date. BARROLL (1958, *JEGP*, p. 715, n. 13) refers to it in passing as sharing with *Ant.* the thematic principle of sloth in Mark Antony. COUCHMAN (1961, p. 423, n. 22) points out that Antony's *bonus genius* in *Caesar's Revenge* 1312–23 (ed. F. S. Boas, Malone Society Rpts., 1911) "talks surprisingly like" Octavius in *Ant.* 491–507. JORGEN-SEN (1965, p. 172) sees *Caesar's Revenge* as "a structural model" for *Ant.* since it has "a compelling woman, an internal struggle, the poignancy of recollected soldiership, and a scene constructed so as to highlight the strain in Antony's breaking away from Egypt." WADDINGTON (1966, p. 217), quoting ll. 879–88 of *Caesar's Revenge* (ed. Boas), notes the linking of "mythological incidents [Mars-Venus, Hercules-Deianira] which Shakespeare uses as structural archetype." WEIS (1983, *SJH*, pp. 178–86) believes that (p. 178) "in its choice of metaphor and simile relating to Cleopatra and her lovers, *CR* curiously anticipates *Ant.*, and a detailed parallel study of the language of the two plays at key points strongly argues in favour of a close link between them." He provides a close textual comparison and finds a verbal echo of the play's l. 154 (ed. Boas) in *Ant.* 612–13 (p. 184)—a parallel first noted by BLISSETT (1956, pp. 568–9), who thought *Ant.* was the source—of 707 ff. in *Ant.* 1797 ff. (p. 185), of Pompey's lament about his fall (689 ff.) in *Ant.* 2091–5, of the iterative metaphor "triumph-heart-ride" (3.3.1303–5) in *Ant.* 2663–6 (p. 182), of the Dido-Aeneas analogy (3.3.1357–9) in *Ant.* 2884–7—(p. 184) "the most striking (and unique) parallel between the two plays," Weis claims, though Pembroke's ll. 1952–8 also allude to the analogy—as well as a less likely echo of the image of ships (3.3.1343–4) in *Ant.* 2893–4 (p. 183). Weis concludes (pp. 185–6), "*Caesar's Revenge* acted primarily as a stimulus, both stylistically and the-matic-[*186*]ally. It could hardly be maintained that the play is original in its conception of Cleopatra and her lovers. Even so, the metaphoric density of its language, coupled with an initially ambiguous view of Cleopatra, as well as its sheer scope, may go some way to accounting for Shakespeare's considered use of it in a play about Roman history and Antony and Cleopatra in particular." RONAN (1987, pp. 174–9) discerns an echo of *Caesar's Revenge* 922–38, 943 (ed. Boas) in *Ant.* 163–4 and, less convincingly, of 757–63 in *Ant.* 1290–4 and of 820–4 in *Ant.* 3141–60.

Samuel Brandon's Senecan *Tragicomoedi of the Vertuous Octavia* (1598) may be echoed in *Ant.* or have acted as an influence. CASE (ed. 1906, pp. xxii–iii), not having seen the play, cites W. J. CRAIG's privately communicated conclusion that Sh. "had cast an eye" over it; Case finds an echo of ll. 341–58 (ed. R. B. McKerrow, Malone Society Rpts., 1909) in Octavius's welcome to his sister (*Ant.* 1796–1809). CHAMBERS (1930, 1:478) says merely that Brandon's play may be a source. ADELMAN (1973, p. 186), without arguing for Brandon as a direct source, refers to his idea that Cleopatra's skin was dark (ed. McKerrow, ll. 1341–2; see also *Ant.* 555–6) as exemplifying Elizabethan opinion; she cites a similar description in Robert Greene's *Ciceronis amor* (1589; *Complete Works*, ed. A. B. Grosart, 1881–6, 7:142; first cited by KITTREDGE, ed. 1941), as well as George Gascoigne's poem "In praise of a gentlewoman who though she were not verye fayre, yet was she as harde fauoured as might be" (*Complete Poems*, ed. W. C. Hazlitt, 1869, 1:487). See also n. 10. More directly, WILLIAMSON (1974, pp. 238–44) argues that Octavia's interview with a messenger in Brandon's Act 2 inspired two passages in *Ant.*—181–6 (resembling Brandon's 562–3, ed. McKerrow) and 1068–80 (531–64)—noting (p. 244) "similarities of subject-matter, of character-role, of details of the scene, and of dramatic purpose." The influence of Brandon on *Ant.* is rather summarily rejected, with insufficient consideration of evidence, by ANDERS (1904, p. 148), CREIZENACH (1916, 5:438), NELSON (1943, p. 223), MUIR (1957, p. 216, n. 2), and BULLOUGH (1964, 5:238), who believes Sh. "drew nothing from this dull pedagogy unless it were a determination to make his virtuous Octavia as reticent as Brandon's is loquacious."

For surveys of dramatic accounts of Antony and Cleopatra, see especially JAMESON (1832; 1879, pp. 277–85), WARD (1875; 1899, 2:186–7), KOCH (ed. 1882, 9:244, 247–9), MOELLER (1888 and 1907), BRADFORD (1898; 1936, pp. 189–206), LEE (1898; 1925, p. 410 n., and ed. 1907, 36:xvi–xix, 1–iii), EVERETT (1905, pp. 252–63), FURNESS (ed. 1907, pp. 507–83), HILLEBRAND (ed. 1926, pp. xiii–xviii), TRAUB (1938), ABOUL-ENEIN (1954), BEAUCHAMP (1955), DICKEY (1957, pp. 173–5), BULLOUGH (1964, 5:222–38), MORRISON (1974, pp. 113–25), WILLIAMSON (1974), PATRICK (1975, pp. 64–76), ARDINGER (1976), and HUGHES (1983, pp. 85–92). A survey of late medieval and early Renaissance nondramatic accounts of Antony and Cleopatra is given by WILLIAMSON (1972, pp. 145–51).

CLASSICAL WORKS

Many Shn. borrowings, especially from Virgil, Ovid, Horace, Apuleius, and a few other authors, have been traced.

Virgil's *Aeneid* is often seen as having influenced *Ant.*'s themes and, occasionally, style. Brief remarks by FOARD (1893, p. 356), KNIGHT (1931; 1965, pp. 286, 297), SCHANZER (1963, p. 159), and ERSKINE-HILL (1970, p. 32) comparing or contrasting the lovers' story in *Ant.* to that of Dido and Aeneas are extended in BROWER's (1971, p. 351) reflection on *Ant.* as "an imaginative sequel to the *Aeneid*: what might have happened had Aeneas stayed in Carthage and not fulfilled his fate. Like Aeneas, Antony cannot altogether put behind him the 'Roman thought' [164] of the role that historical destiny (*fata Romana*) and the heroic code require him to play." Sh. thus adapted to Cleopatra "Dido's role of temptress and heroic queen": "Cleopatra is not only like Dido a woman capable of jealous fury; she also equals her lover in nobility, as Dido equalled Aeneas. Both women are conscious of their responsibilities as 'president' [1878] of a kingdom. Both belong to the company of 'the greatest' [3407], and both have a high regard for reputation, for *fama*." HAMILTON (1973, p. 248) locates parallel concepts: "In the first act of the play the similarities between the two stories are played on, but with the stress falling on the need to leave off love-making and return to duties. The forceful reminder of his proper role [in 1.2] moves Antony to act quickly." Thus "exactly paralleling Aeneas's action in Book Four of the *Aeneid*, Antony [at 276–9] orders his men to prepare the ships while he goes to notify the queen of his departure."

Other scholars stress differences. SCHANZER (1963, p. 150) observes that while Virgil approves of Aeneas's deserting Dido, Sh. does not condemn Antony's choice of love. ADELMAN (1973, pp. 70–8) refers to the various sources available to the Elizabethans of the story of Dido and Aeneas—Virgil, Chaucer, Marlowe—to show the significance of the composite story for *Ant.* In the *Aeneid* 8.675 ff. (ed. H. R. Fairclough, Loeb, rev. ed., vol. 2, 1956)—and here Adelman expands DICKEY, 1957, p. 147—"that Antony's defeat is seen as the farthest extension of Aeneas's victory over Turnus is not merely political propaganda for Caesar Augustus: Antony and Cleopatra are shown to represent the human frailty that Rome was founded to overcome. . . . [71] For Cleopatra is a new Dido, and Antony's passion for her a new threat to Roman civilization; the victory of Octavius over Antony's foreign passion reenacts Aeneas's heroic founding of Rome." Thus "Aeneas sees Antony's defeat at Actium as preparation for his own battle with Turnus; Antony recalls Aeneas immediately after his defeat at Actium [hardly; no sooner than at 2886]. The cross-reference is striking. Indeed, almost all the central elements in *Antony and Cleopatra* are to be found in the *Aeneid*: the opposing values of Rome and a foreign passion; the political necessity of a passionless [72] Roman marriage; the concept of an afterlife in which the passionate lovers meet. . . . [73] But in the play, a new set of values is posited as an alternative to, though not necessarily a substitute for, the Virgilian values. . . . In the *Aeneid*, the values which must prevail are supremely temporal and spatial: the poem concerns the establishment of a civilization in a particular place and the historical continuity of that civilization. But in *Antony and Cleopatra*, the values of the foreign passion are posited, and these values are supremely nontemporal and nonspatial. . . . [74] As the Aeneas whom Antony recalls after Actium is revised, so the whole of *Antony and Cleopatra* may be seen as a revision of the scene on Vulcan's shield [Bk. 8], in some sense as a revision of the *Aeneid* itself." See n. 3306–8.

MIOLA (1983, pp. 124–7) observes that Antony's leave-taking in 1.3 follows *Aeneid* 4.297 ff., and he discusses (pp. 154–5) the evocation of the Dido-Aeneas myth in Cleopatra's death scene. COLIE (1974, p. 179, n. 18) considers the *Aeneid* a general source for Antony's elevated style of speech. FISCH (1970, p. 65), like WALTER (ed. 1969), believes the movement of the play's world toward "vniuersall peace" (2581, see n.) recalls Virgil's vision of the ages of the world in the fourth eclogue.

Parallels in Ovid involve less Shn. reevaluation. ZIELINSKI (1905, pp. 17–18) observes, "Psychologically Shakspeare's Cleopatra [especially in 299–427] is developed from the Ovidian [in *Heroides* 7], not the Virgilian Dido; her nervousness [18] comes from thence, even if the fatal admixture of an instinctive, fox-like cunning, lacking in the Ovidian puella, belongs only to the English poet—or rather Plutarch" (in German; BALDWIN, 1944, 2:424–5, and HIGHET, 1949, pp. 205–6 and 621, n. 47, agree; MACCALLUM, 1910, pp. 653–6, objects, thinking the parallel—see also n. 325–6—fortuitous). HAMILTON (1973), who believes Sh. employs (p. 249) "brush-stroke suggestions" of the literary tradition of noble lovers, sees Cleopatra as like Ovid's Dido in the *Heroides*, noting both (p. 248) "verbal echoes" and "correspondence between incidents." Thus Cleopatra's behavior in 1.2 is "reminiscent of the fluctuating moods of Dido and her counterparts in the *Heroides*." W. B. C. WATKINS (1950, pp. 24–31) sees *Ant.* as resembling Ovid's *Amores* in characters and situations but Sh. as transcending Ovid by (p. 31) "spiritualizing sensuality." ADELMAN (1973, p. 84) cites as underlying traditions for *Ant.* Ovid's *Metamorphoses* 4 and *Ars amatoria* 2 on the Mars-Venus affair, where Ovid's playful lightheartedness contrasts with Lucretius's seriousness; see also p. 598. Others see a parallel in the story of Hercules, who in *Heroides* 9 and *Fasti* 2.317 ff. is "reduced to a position of ignominious servitude by Omphale, as Samson was by Delilah" (WARNER, 1957, p. 139, quoting the Loeb tr. of *Heroides* by G. Showerman, 1914, p. 113; similarly WILSON, ed. 1950: see n. 1050–1; SCHANZER, 1963, p. 159; and WADDINGTON, 1966, p. 212). ROSE (1969, p. 387) calls attention to the "dilemma of choice" between reason and the emotions in politics as a theme in *Ant.*, well expressed in Ovid's "non bene conveniunt nec in una sede morantur | maiestas et amor" ("Majesty and love do not go well together, nor tarry long in the same dwelling-place," *Metamorphoses* 2.846–7, tr. F. J. Miller, 2 vols., Loeb, 1958–60, 1:119). BROWER (1971, p. 124) and HILL (1984, p. 227) note that Antony's suicide evokes that of the mad Ajax as described in *Metamorphoses* 13. Parallels with single passages are noted especially by ANDERS (1904, pp. 29–30; see n. 1354–60), FRIPP (1930, pp. 98–128; see nn. 381–2, 544, 3306–8), THOMSON (1952, pp. 148–50; see nn. 381–2, 544), WILKINSON (1955, esp. p. 413: Antony's "alleging" in 329 recalls Ovid's Aeneas in *Heroides* 7), and HUNTER (1969, pp. 236–9: the story of Io in *Metamorphoses* 1.107–943 and Virgil's *Georgics* 3.146–56 reflected in 1993–4); see also nn. 22, 62, 2682–3, 2804, 2811, 2871, 3016–20.

Horace is claimed to have inspired some of the conceptual polarities embodied in Cleopatra. In a seminal essay WESTBROOK (1947, pp. 392–8), anticipated in a general remark by KOCH (ed. 1882, 9:245; see also brief references in VOLLMER, 1887, pp. 219, 244 n., 269 n.), suggests that Sh. drew Cleopatra's tragic heroism from Horace's Cleopatra Ode (*Carmina* 1.37), making it (p. 393) "royal pride that brings her to self-destruction" rather than "the frenzy of a desperate mind" as in Plutarch, and that Sh. used *Epode* 9 for his picture of the hostile Roman attitude to her (pp. 396–8). LABRIOLA (1966, p. 180), however, rightly objects that Plutarch "furnishes material for the same ideas." MUIR (1957, pp. 205–6, and 1977, pp. 224–5) believes Sh. may have been acquainted with the ode but points out that his presentation of Cleopatra's suicide may be independently developed from Plutarch. COMMAGER (1958, pp. 54–5) notes that in *Ant.* "private lives play against [55] public issues, and the counterpoint recalls Horace's" in the ode. However, Commager is aware of the differences: "On Shakespeare's boards the conflict is played out principally in terms of Antony, in whom love vies with honour, East with West. Horace could hardly share the Englishman's distanced perspective, and even had he felt free to treat the subject in the same way, it is unlikely that he would have anticipated Shakespeare's tacit, and Dryden's explicit, verdict that the world was well lost. Horace's treatment of Cleopatra represents not so much a divided allegiance as a fondness for seeing every situation in a double aspect. The tendency is habitual, and the Cleopatra Ode, in its technique, stands as a kind of manifesto of the Horatian imagination." PEARCE (1961–2, pp. 249–50) gamely and improbably freights Horace's two-word description of Cleopatra after Actium, *vultu sereno* (in the ode, l. 26), with the whole of Act 5: "Her countenance is 'clear' because her mind is made up, 'cleared' of doubts or fears; 'bright' and 'shining' (with satisfaction) because she has outwitted Octavian and evaded capture. . . . [*250*] The Cleopatra we find in Act Five of *Antony and Cleopatra* is clearly a development, by way of Plutarch, of Horace's initial image." More plausibly, JONES (ed. 1977, on 5.2), who thinks the last three stanzas of the ode may have influenced Sh.'s concept of Cleopatra's "inner transformation," sees (pp. 45–6) Horace's poetry as a stylistic model for *Ant.* See also nn. 22, 220–1, 807, 883, 3459.

Apuleius's account of Isis, ancestress of Venus, in *The Golden Ass* has emerged as a probable source for Cleopatra's aspirations to the Egyptian goddess's role. STARNES (1945, pp. 1021–50), the first to trace in depth Sh.'s debt to Apuleius, finds his concept of Cleopatra (p. 1038) "colored throughout by his recollection of Apuleius' portrait of Venus," with parallels particularly between the jealous Venus of Bk. 5 and Cleopatra's conduct in *Ant.* 2.5, as well as Venus's technique in winning Paris (10.32 ff., tr. W. Adlington, 1566; rev. S. Gaselee, Loeb, 1915) and the Cydnus description in *Ant.* 902–31. Starnes believes Sh.'s Apuleius may have been the Latin version (e.g., Venice, 1521). LLOYD (1959, *ShS*, pp. 90–1, 93) in a strained argument notes that in Apuleius (tr. Adlington; Chiltern Library, 1946, pp. 221–3) "the procreative principle is given the name of Ceres or Venus, according to whether its maternal [which Lloyd thinks illustrated in 2346–7] or amorous quality is stressed. The goddess is also invoked as queen of the dead. . . . [*91*] Venus, Bellona, Juno [the last in 2053, 3041]: the names of Isis might be Cleopatra's, and if one cared with her Roman detractors to stress the element of witchcraft, one could add the name of Hecate." The implication is that "for a critic who sees Cleopatra as exercising a creative more than a destructive influence on Antony, the function of Isis in the novel is not unlike Cleopatra's." Thus Lloyd believes that at 2886–7 Cleopatra, in retaining sovereignty in death, resembles Apuleius's Isis. Apuleius supplies precedent for Cleopatra's usurping of male domination: he (p. 93) "puts it in martial terms by making Isis Bellona." Lloyd qualifies, however: "There is clearer indication of Plutarch [i.e., *Moralia*; see p. 394] in Shakespeare's play than of Apuleius. That is perhaps because the two sources are different in kind. One [Plutarch] is a full and circumstantial account of a cult, the other is a poetic evocation. Isis is the same figure in both, with a common emphasis on that wifely and maternal devotion in which Cleopatra [doubtfully] resembles her." See n. 3562. WADDINGTON (1966, p. 216) states that Apuleius's Isis "is Venus in her local habitat; Shakespeare retains the Isis analogy because it is literally appropriate to the Egyptian Queen and thus integrates perfectly with the extensive symbolic nexus that he develops from the Egyptian scene and character." Cleopatra's renunciation of the moon as her planet (3490) signals "the casting off of the false and the assumption of the true mythic identity. When Cleopatra disclaims the fleeting moon of Isis, it is replaced in her personal cosmos by the eastern star of Venus [3560]." While FISCH's (1970, p. 61) account of Apuleius's Isis is brief and general, WHITAKER (1972, pp. 156–8; see n. 902–31), ADELMAN (1973, pp. 66–7), and ADLARD (1975, p. 327; see n. 552) supply more detail from Apuleius to show how the goddess becomes a mythic prototype for Cleopatra. TOBIN (1979, pp. 225–8, and 1984, pp. 130–5) finds (1984, p. 130) "three passages in *The Golden Asse* [tr. Adlington; Tudor Translations, ed. W. E. Henley, 1893, 4:99, 128, 236] which shed light on Antony's irascible and concupiscible weaknesses" and believes Sh. (p. 133) "has deliberately limited his attractiveness while enhancing that of Cleopatra"; a fourth passage from Apuleius, though (4:129), in which Jupiter makes Psyche immortal, "supports the ultimate stress upon their immortal unity and equality." See nn. 449, 2334, 3562. For Tobin (p. 135), "there is much that is brave and noble, done in the high Roman fashion [3102] in *Antony and Cleopatra*, but in its sources the tragedy is at times not so much Roman as Milesian."

Various conceptual parallels or analogues with other classical works have been noted. In a general way, ADAMS (1967, pp. 44–52) quotes Heliodorus's *Aethiopica* and *Clitophon and Leucippe* to prove that "the love which surmounts massive obstacles of birth and politics and defies [45] death is the concept which vitalizes the Greek romance; this concept soars to an apogee" in *Rom.* and *Ant.* There is no evidence that Sh. was familiar with these romances. BROWER (1971, p. 350) believes that the tragic attitude toward the pity and glory of heroic agon as dramatized in *Ant.* "would be familiar to a reader of the *Iliad*," of which Sh. "had some knowledge." BELL (1973, pp. 256–7) quotes the (p. 256) "heroic idiom" of *Iliad* 2.64 (*Chapman's Homer*, ed. A. Nicoll, Princeton, 1967, 1:528) as a literary and heroic convention recalled in *Ant.* 44, but he qualifies (p. 257): "The convention at this point is only suggested, for Antony here is not wholly the Homeric hero. The 'nobleness of life' [47] for him remains romantic love, not manly battle. Yet in employing the convention of the Homeric hero, Shakespeare limits our expectation temporarily to tales of men involved in the physical struggles of time, while at the same time they are attracted by the timeless realm of reputation among men and honor from Jove. He defines an area of human experience that straddles the worlds of time and timelessness." For Homer, see also nn. 902–3 and 2871. Bell (p. 258) also traces to Seneca Stoic conventions reflected in Antony's conduct, noting the praise of the "man of meane estate" in *Agamemnon* 102–7 (John Studley's tr. in *Seneca: His Tenne Tragedies*, ed. Thomas Newton, 1581; Tudor Translations, ed. C. Whibley, 1927, 2:105) as background for Antony's "well diuided disposition" (584) and the "advice" of Epistle 70 (*Senecae epistulae*, ed. L. D. Reynolds, OUP, 1965, 1:203–5) for 2848–9. Expanding on THOMSON (1952, p. 149), WAITH (1962, pp. 118–19) notes that, in his longing for revenge and death (see n. 2772–3), Antony resembles Hercules in Seneca's *Hercules Oetaeus*; JONES (ed. 1977, p. 37), that Seneca's description of Antony's liberality in *De beneficiis* 6.3 resembles Sh.'s. See also n. 2804. THEOBALD (ed. 1733) sees in 622–5 (see n.) an imitation of Juvenal's tenth satire.

HILL (1984, p. 219) believes it is "tempting" to equate Antony's choice of the *vita voluptuosa* with Paris's choice of Venus as discussed by Fulgentius (*Fulgentius the Mythographer*, tr. L. G. Whitbread, Columbus, 1971, pp. 64 ff.).

Before the 20th c. there are hardly any attempts to trace parallels to philosophical concepts underlying or suggested in *Ant.*, and such concepts are usually viewed as analogues or illustrative parallels rather than sources. Thus MACCALLUM (1910, pp. 445–53) believes *Ant.* reflects both Aristophanes's and Diotima's ideas of love in Plato's *Symposium*, as well as the love of beauty described in *Phaedrus.* ERSKINE-HILL (1970, p. 46, and 1983, p. 159) invokes Plato's chariot of the soul in *Phaedrus* 246ff. (*Dialogues*, tr. B. Jowett, OUP, 1892, 1:452–3, 460–1) as interpretive background to Antony's concupiscence (coming to Sh. through Plutarch; see p. 420), commenting that "unrestrained appetite only brings the chariot to grief." The "horse of the mind" image is associated with 578 (see n.) by ADELMAN (1973, pp. 59–60), with 1989 by MIOLA (1983, p. 139, n. 27), and with various further instances of horse imagery in *Ant.* by ROSS (1980, pp. 386–7). RACKIN (1972, p. 202) cites Plato's theories of the rational principle of the soul, the unreliability of sense appearance, and the necessity of measuring and numbering (in *Republic* 10) to explain the Roman moralistic view in the play. WHITAKER (1972, p. 111), speculating on "cosmological contexts," finds *Timaeus* helpful in distinguishing between the realms of time and eternity in *Ant.*, time being viewed in the dialogue as "motion that reflects the perfection and stasis of eternal, unchanging forms. Therefore, existence in a world of time is always becoming, changing, perishing, and never having real being," while *Ant.* enacts a "movement out of the sublunary world [of change] into the eternal perfection of the superlunary cosmos." ADELMAN (1973, pp. 67, 207, n. 51) briefly cites *Phaedrus* 274 (ed. H. N. Fowler, Loeb, 1914, pp. 561–3), on Egypt as birthplace of the arts, as part of the traditions underlying the play's Egyptian associations.

KROOK (1967; 1969, pp. 201–7) names Aristotle's *megalopsuchia* (greatness of soul, nobility) as *Ant.*'s (p. 201) "prevailing ethos": Mark Antony in particular (p. 203) "reads like an inspired dramatization of the Magnificent Man and the Magnanimous Man of the *Nicomachean Ethics* [4.3; ed. H. Rackham, Loeb, 1934] rolled into one."

WILLIAMSON (1968, p. 428) employs Boethius's thoughts on evil Fortune in *The Consolation of Philosophy* 2.8 (ed. J. J. Buchanan, New York, 1957) to explain Sh.'s representation of Cleopatra's resolution for suicide: she "connects her change with Fortune [in 3201–8] and announces that, like Boethius' sufferer in adversity, she sees the mundane gifts of Fortune for what they are and is a free person who can willingly embrace the only remedy Fortune really fears on earth—death." This is the Fortune tradition used by Sh., not Plutarch's *fortuna publica* (in *Moralia*).

ADELMAN (1973, pp. 84–8) observes that Lucretius's "high seriousness" regarding Venus and her relation to Mars in *De rerum natura* (probably chiefly 4.1058 ff.; ed. W. H. D. Rouse, Loeb, rev. ed. 1937), contrasting with Ovid's playfulness (see p. 595), was very likely known to Sh.—since Lucretian ideas (p. 210, n. 74) "were becoming current"—and may have influenced the lovers' mythic elevation in the play. For Lucretius, see also n. 2826–31.

COLIE (1974, p. 194) sees a "theoretical precedent" in Longinus, *On the Sublime*, for Antony's speech style, marked by "generosity, magnitude, magnanimity."

Many commentators have turned to writings on mythical, natural, or political history as sources or analogues. Thus FOARD (1893, p. 356), anticipating scholars who focus more precisely on Ovid, places the lovers of the play in the tradition of mythical history, mentioning in general terms Hercules and Omphale, Mars and Venus, Dido and Aeneas, and other celebrated lovers.

The elder Pliny's *Natural History*, especially 5.9 (noted by GREY, 1754, 2:204; see n. 1354–60), along with John Pory's tr. of Leo's *History of Africa* (1600; mentioned by MALONE in STEEVENS, ed. 1793), is recognized as a source for Egyptian local color by a number of scholars, including ANDERS (1904, pp. 37, 235–6), who adds De Jode's *Speculum orbis terrae* (1593) without claiming it as a source (see n. 1361–4), MACCALLUM (1910, p. 333), DRAPER (1933, p. 235), SCHANZER (1956, *N&Q*, p. 154), MUNRO (ed. 1957, 6:1212), ADELMAN (1973, pp. 187, 206–7, n. 45), and, briefly, KURIYAMA (1977, p. 336). See also n. 2826–31.

NELSON (1943, pp. 259–69) unlocks the question of Sh.'s debt to Dio Cassius, believing much of Sh.'s Pompey material could have come thence: Sh. (p. 261) "merely reviewed his Appian at the time of the composition of the play and then turned to Dio [particularly 48.17–19; *Roman History*, tr. E. Cary, Loeb, vol. 5, 1917] for further light on the affair. It may be, too, that the loss of Appian's story of the final conflict prompted him to the reading of Dio's interesting, if anti-Antonian, version of the triumph of Octavius." However, the parallels from Dio are not clearly closer to *Ant.* than is Appian's account. Nelson (pp. 262–3) spots a "free adaptation" of Dio 49.4 in Ventidius's speeches on sensible policy for a lieutenant in *Ant.* 3.1. Other possibly Dionic scenes in the play are 2.7 (Antony's Bacchic dancing denounced by Octavius, in Dio 50.27; see also 48.38, noted by VOLLMER, 1887, p. 231 n.), 3.5 (Octavius's treatment of Lepidus and Antony's anger at Pompey's death, in Dio 49.11 f. [noted also by Vollmer, p. 217], 49.18, 50.20, 54.15), and 3.13 (Cleopatra's interview with Thidias, in Dio 51.6–8; noted by Vollmer, p. 218). Nelson concludes that (p. 268) "the histories of Appian and Dio added background of character and setting [to *Ant.*], especially in the Pompey episodes." WILLIAMSON (1971, pp. 180–90), who does not mention Nelson, also finds borrowings in 3.1 (see n. 1494–1537), where Sh. (p. 185) "diverges briefly from his general conception of Antony's character as he adapts it from the tolerant biographer [Plutarch] and draws it instead from the more cynical picture of Antony Dio gives [49.21, 23; see also Vollmer, pp. 217, 232 n., 233 n.]." She comments (p. 187), "The Ventidius scene has seemed tangential from the main action of *Antony and Cleopatra*. If Shakespeare is echoing Dio here, the sense of disjunction about the episode may be explained." A further likely Dionic loan—as noted also by Vollmer (pp. 218, 259 n.)—is Enobarbus's desertion of Antony (p. 190): "A minor event in Plutarch; it is of exemplary importance in Dio [50.13, tr. Cary]; and in Shakespeare it is the culmination of a series of such desertions that form a definite pattern in the tragic action."

Possible though remote echoes from several further classical historians (Eutropius, Florus, Suetonius, Velleius) are also suggested by NELSON (1943, pp. 259–69). For Suetonius, see also nn. 1691 and 2391; for a possible source in Florus, n. 1066–7.

Antony's intemperance in revelry is graphically scathed in Cicero's *Oratio philippica secunda* 1.63, cited by DICKEY (1957, p. 146) and ERSKINE-HILL (1970, p. 33, and 1983, p. 147) as among Plutarch's sources and hence indirectly part of the influences on Sh.'s characterization.

DICKEY (1957, pp. 146–55), followed by BULLOUGH (1964, 5:218–22), surveys classical and medieval accounts of Antony and Cleopatra, most of them condemning the lovers as voluptuaries, to show what an Elizabethan or Jacobean audience, and perhaps Sh., might have learned from such sources. Dickey's list for antiquity includes Cicero, Horace, Virgil, Velleius, Lucan (in Arthur Gorges's tr. of 1614), Josephus, Suetonius, Plutarch, Florus, Dio, Athenaeus, and Sidonius; for the Middle Ages, Boccaccio, Chaucer—the only one to praise Cleopatra as a martyr of love—and Lydgate.

GILDON (1710, pp. 415–16, 468) cites classical parallels for 2187–90 in Virgil, Horace, Ovid, Seneca, and others. For further classical borrowings and parallels, see DELIUS (1883, pp. 93–4, 101–2: mythology), VOLLMER (1887, pp. 215–70: especially historians but also Horace), ROOT (1903, passim: mythology), BALDWIN (1944, passim: parallels, mostly derivative, in Homer, Ovid, Virgil, Horace, Juvenal, Quintilian, Pliny, Florus), and THOMSON (1952, pp. 148–50: Ovid, Virgil, Seneca). As curiosities one may add THEOBALD (1909, passim), who collects an array of mostly unconvincing classical analogues to prove Sh.'s (or rather Bacon's) learning, and JAGGARD (1933, pp. 17, 27), who gives vague parallels from Lucan and Thucydides in an attempt to prove Sh.'s acquaintance with rare books and hence with the book trade.

MEDIEVAL WORKS AND THE BIBLE

Sources and analogues from the medieval period often refer to single passages. Thus ANDERS (1904, p. 152) claims that the Herod of the miracle plays, particularly in Coventry where Sh. might have seen them, is alluded to at 1625–6 (see also n. 107–8); JAGGARD (1933, p. 8), that Sh. was thinking of Albertus Magnus's *Boke of Secretes* (anon. tr. 1525), especially the title, in 88–9.

Several scholars discover parallels or echoes in Chaucer. SCHANZER (1960, "*Ant.* and *The Legend of Good Women*," pp. 335–6; see n. 435) suggests Sh. may have drawn on the "Legend of Cleopatra" (*The Legend of Good Women*) for his references to Cleopatra's early husbands, the Ptolemy brothers, whom both Chaucer and Sh. run together. In more general terms, BATTENHOUSE (1969), claiming that (p. 169) "Chaucer was certainly being ironic in his *Legend of Good Women*," believes both Chaucer and Sh. (p. 170) "understood Cleopatra as belonging entirely and topmost among Cupid's saints, yet as tragic because that kind of sainthood is blind and self-defeating." Antony's posture of courtly romance against the "calumniating" demands of time, as in the opening scene, reminds BELL (1973, p. 256) of *Troilus and Criseyde* 1.432–4 (*Works*, ed. F. N. Robinson, Boston, 1957). As background for the art-nature relationship mentioned in Cleopatra's dream (3317–20) and in Enobarbus's description of her (909–13), MACK (1973, p. 105) quotes *The Physician's Tale* 7–18. MUIR (1977, p. 224) grants Sh.'s acquaintance with Chaucer's treatment of Cleopatra but rightly points out that he could have developed his version independently from Plutarch.

Expanding FOARD (1893, p. 356) and DORAN (1965, p. 32), HAMILTON (1973, pp. 246–7, 251) places Antony and Cleopatra in the tradition of noble lovers and points to bk. 8 of John Gower's *Confessio amantis* (ed. R. Pauli, 1857, 3:361–2)—where they rank with Tristram and Iseult, Jason and Medea, Paris and Helen, Theseus and Ariadne, Pyramus and Thisbe—as well as to John Lydgate's *Temple of Glas* (ed. J. Schick, 1891, p. 33) and *The Complaint of the Black Knight* (*Minor Poems*, ed. H. MacCracken, 1934, 2:397–8, ll. 365–71), works which rate the lovers' suffering with that of Achilles and Polyxena, Arcite, and Palamoun, their fame also with that of Ceyx and Alcyone, Hero and Leander. For further illustration Hamilton mentions Lydgate's *Minor Poems*, 2:410–18 and 438–42; the anon. *Assembly of Ladies* (*Complete Works of Geoffrey Chaucer*, ed. W. W. Skeat, OUP, 1894–7, 7:395, ll. 456–62, an analogue borrowed from Doran); Lydgate's *The Court of Love* (Skeat's *Chaucer*, 7:432, l. 873); and George Pettie, *A Petite Pallace of Pettie his Pleasure* (ed. H. Hartman, New York, 1938, pp. 146, 174–5). ALVIS (1978, pp. 194–6) concentrates on Tristram and Iseult to show that, like them (p. 195), "Antony and Cleopatra find their completion [i.e., self-exaltation] in a death which they deliberately embrace."

Biblical parallels are numerous and often speculative. DRAPER (1933, p. 236) attributes the Egyptian local color and allusions to Palestine in *Ant.* to Sh.'s knowledge of Ps. 22, 68, 78, and 105; Job 39:13; Lam. 4:3; the gospels for Holy Innocents and Epiphany. FRIPP (1938, 2:678–83) cites additional scriptural parallels: Exod. 1–12, 16:3, 18:8–10, and 20:2; Deut. 7:15 and 28:60; Ezek. 16:26, 23:2–3, 19, and 32:12; Ezra 9:1 and Heb. 11:24–6 for *Ant.* 209–10 and 225–7; Ezek. 29:3–4 (Bishops' Bible) as recalled at 1037–41; 2 Kings 18:21 as alluded to at 1345–7 and 2233–5; Prov. 2:16–18, 5:3–5, and 7:6–27 as drawn on for 1361 ff. and 2101–2; Prov. 7:27 (Geneva) for 2781; and—first noticed by CARTER (1905, p. 454)—Exod. 22:18 for 2806. ADELMAN (1973, pp. 66–7) acknowledges the biblical picture of Egypt as being among the traditions underlying the play. SEATON (1946, pp. 219–24), followed by LINDSAY (1947, p. 66), MUIR (1957, pp. 217–19), BATTENHOUSE (1969, pp. 176–81), WALTER (ed. 1969, pp. 34–5), SLATER (ed. 1971, p. 33), WHITAKER (1972, pp. 181–95), SHAW (1974, pp. 229–31), and SCHAMP (ed. 1978, pp. 137–8), argues for cosmic and apocalyptic echoes from Rev.—(p. 221) "the great visions of *Revelation* exalted the conceptions and fired the poetry of the later part" of *Ant.*—holding that (p. 224) "this most worldly pair, children of luxury and riot, must indeed be viewed *sub specie æternitatis*, as if children of light. The lovers themselves undergo a purification of their passion; and it may well have been brought about by their creator's self-submission to the poetry and the mystery" of Rev. She notes echoes at 24–5 (Rev. 21:1; see n.), 552 (17:1–2, 18:7; see n.), 1825 ("like a refrain" in Rev.; see n.), 2325–7 (6:13, 9:1–2), 2340–50 (16:20–1), 2881–2 (7:3–8, suggested by LEA in Seaton, p. 223), 2941–3 (21:1–2), 2951–5 (8:10, 8:13, 9:6, 10:6; see n. 2951–2), 3011–13 (8:12), 3264–9 (11:8–10), 3296–3306 (10:1–6), 3473–5 (21:2; see n.), and 3560 (2:28), most of which—as MUIR (1977, p. 237) thinks—were probably unconscious. Further questionable parallels: Salome's demanding John the Baptist's head for 1627–8 (CARTER, 1905, p. 453; WALTER, ed. 1969), the Last Supper for 4.2 (MURRY, 1936, p. 362: esp. 2424–7, see n.; CUTTS, 1966–7, p. 149: 2445, 2451; BATTEN-HOUSE, 1969, p. 173), the Judas story for 4.9 (MURRY, 1936, pp. 366–7), the Samson story of Judg. 13–16 for Antony's temptation by a woman (BRYANT, 1961, p. 181), the eve of Christ's passion for 2833 (ANON. in WALTER, ed. 1969), and the Annunciation for 3233–7 (BENOIT, 1976, p. 4, who also finds "Christian terminology" at 3225–32). Parallels to single passages or episodes, mostly far-fetched or fortuitous, are given by GREY (1754, 2:207–8), Isa. 36:6 for 2233–5; BLUMHOF (ed. 1870), Ps. 2:4 for 3537–8, where HUNTER (ed. 1870) thinks the idea "founded" rather on Luke 16:25; MURRY (1936, pp. 365–6), Matt. 10:22 for 2201–4; HANKINS (1953, p. 231), Job 30:15 and Isa. 60:8 for 2826 ff.; PIPER (1967, no. 10), Mark 14:25 for 3532–3; BATTENHOUSE (1969, p. 174), John 19:5 and 19:27 for 2675; WALTER (ed. 1969), Matt. 2:15 for 105–8, Isa. 2:4 for 942–3, 2 Cor. 6:10 for 1407–8, Matt. 10:16 for 3517, and (1969, p. 138) Exod. 7:14–12:33 for 2341–50 (see also n.); FISCH (1970, p. 64), Isa. 66 and Mark 9:44 f. for 3495–3500; BARROLL (1984, p. 247), Matt. 25 for 3527–8. There are further collected parallels in WORDSWORTH (1864; 1892, passim), BURGESS (1903, pp. 36–7, 46), CARTER (1905, pp. 451–6), NOBLE (1935, pp. 238–40), and SHAHEEN (1987, pp. 175–86). See also nn. 264, 622–5, 2287–91, 2304–6. Albrecht Dürer's woodcuts in his *Apocalypse* (1498 and 1511) suggest echoes in *Ant.* to MORRIS (1968, pp. 252–62, followed by SHAW, 1974, pp. 229–31): (p. 259) 2173–4 may reflect Dürer's *Die babylonische Buhlerin*, which shows a "Lady in Venetian Dress" (of 1495) holding up an "elaborately-wrought 'cup of golde' towards 'the kynges of the earth,' " while (p. 254) 2325–7 suggests *Der Sternenfall*; (p. 256) 2881–2 recalls *Die vier Engel, die Winde aufhaltend, und die Besiegelung der Auserwählten*; and (p. 254) 2951–2 evokes *Die sieben Engel mit den Posaunen*. The images of 3296–3306 (p. 259) are "clarified" by *Die Verteilung der weissen Gewänder und der Sternenfall*, as well as by Dürer's angel in *Johannes das Buch verschlingend* and the angel in the corresponding picture in the 1568 Bishops' Bible, and (p. 260) 3304–6 echoes *Das Tier aus dem Meere und das Tier aus dem Festlande*. Morris offers no evidence that the similarities are more than fortuitous.

RENAISSANCE WORKS

Spenser and Marlowe are likely near-contemporary influences. Most Spenserian debts and parallels concern *The Faerie Queene*. Expanding on DICKEY (1957, p. 40) and

BARROLL (1958, *TxSE*, p. 71, n. 20), SCHANZER (1963, pp. 158–9) points to the coupling of Antony and Hercules as love's victims in *F.Q.* 5.8.2 (in Variorum ed. of *Works*, ed. E. Greenlaw et al., Baltimore, 1936), while Dickey (p. 40), WADDINGTON (1966, p. 213), BLISSETT (1967, p. 158), and ADELMAN (1973, p. 81) link the figurative unmanning of Artegall in *F.Q.* 5.5 with that of Hercules to give resonance to what one interpretation sees as Cleopatra's similar treatment of Antony. ERSKINE-HILL (1970, pp. 27–30, 37, and 1983, pp. 141–3, 150, acknowledging suggestions by POTTS, 1958, pp. 202, 204), like Barroll (1958, *TxSE*, p. 76; see n. 902–31), regards the Bower of Bliss (*F.Q.* 2.12, ed. Greenlaw et al., 1933) as an influence on Enobarbus's description of Cleopatra (909–26): the corresponding passage in Plutarch "reminded" Sh. of the Bower, for (p. 142) "prominent in Spenser's handling . . . is the theme of art and nature sinisterly mingling as they strive to outvie one another"; Sh. "deliberately retained and added to the qualities of a Spenserian poetic set-piece which the passage in North already suggested." Antony's "this great Faiery" (2662) recalls Spenser's title (noted also by STEEVENS, ed. 1793, who instances *F.Q.* for the merging of beauty and power in "fairy"; see also n. 2662): (p. 150) "It may be" that Sh. "wishes to remind us of Spenser here," for Sh. "has turned the allegory of Guyon and Acrasia upside down." Adelman (1973) notes various parallels, especially (pp. 61–7) the numerous references to serpents, crocodiles, and the Nile; (pp. 83, 88–90) Mars and Venus in Bk. 1 proem and Bk. 2; (pp. 123–4) temperance, whose "exemplar" in *Ant.* is Octavius, in Bk. 2; and (pp. 211–12, n. 82) the power of love in 5.8. See also n. 552. The notion of grace as bounty, favor, and liberality throughout *Ant.* reminds McALINDON (1973, p. 202) of E. K.'s gloss on the Three Graces as "Goddesses of al bountie" in the April eclogue of *The Shepheardes Calender* (*Poetical Works*, ed. J. C. Smith and E. de Selincourt, OUP, 1912, p. 434). MACK (1973, pp. 97, 103) notes that love's fetters as felt by Antony (e.g., 209) are allegorized in Spenser's House of Busyrane, *F.Q.* 3.12. ZEEVELD (1974, pp. 127–8, 137) sees *Ruines of Rome* and the Bower of Bliss in *F.Q.* 2.12 as parallels for the theme of idleness causing decay of empire. Cleopatra's protean fickleness recalls to FARMER (1977, p. 114) the verdict of Nature in the *Mutabilitie Cantoes*: "Cleopatra's inconstancy in deserting Antony in the very element of inconstancy, the sea, ultimately serves the cause of love's constancy." See also n. 381–2.

Most comments concerning Marlowe are on Sh.'s debt to *Dido, Queen of Carthage*. Acknowledging ELLIS-FERMOR's (1927, p. 21) tracing of echoes from *Dido* in the barge speech (909–26) and her general feeling that (p. 19) "the play of *Dido* constantly reminds us of the like balance of forces" in *Ant.*, as well as POIRIER's (1951, pp. 84–5) "When she [Dido] has just fallen a prey to overwhelming passion, she behaves with the same coquetry as Shakespeare's Cleopatra. She sends for Aeneas, but when he appears in her presence she denies having summoned him. The Queen of Carthage also resembles the Queen of Egypt when, alone with her confidante, she compares Aeneas' excellencies to [85] those of her former lovers," HARRISON (1956, p. 60) ventures, "As without struggle Antony accepts his doom, so the analogy with Marlowe's Aeneas is made more immediate in Marlowe's neglect of

Virgil's epic theme of Rome in favor of the human theme of man and woman. Shakespeare's Antony wavers briefly between the claims of love and duty, Marlowe's Aeneas parleys briefly between love and the Spenserian ideal of the active life, finally escaping Carthage only on receiving the divine mandate from Hermes" (cf. STILLING, 1976, p. 278: while Marlowe's Aeneas finally chooses empire, Antony remains under Cleopatra's influence). Finding (p. 61) "similarities of situation, sequence of mood, and language," Harrison cites an array of parallels (from C. F. Tucker Brooke's ed., 1930): (pp. 61–3) *Dido* 3.4.56–7 for *Ant.* 44–5, where the heroes' protestations of loyalty (p. 61) "prelude their defection"; 4.4.122 for 345; 3.4.28–9 for 408–10; 4.4.133 for 425–6; 3.1.112–18 and 4.4.48–9 for 902–31, particularly the water imagery and the Cupids; and, less strikingly, 4.3.55 for 209–10; 4.4.4 for 305 with similar errands for Anna and Alexas; 4.4.13 for 315; 4.4.17 for 329, 333, 340, where the heroes similarly attempt to gain a hearing; 4.4.16, 26–7, for 330–1; 5.1.169 for 341–2; 5.1.156, misreading "a goddess," for 402–3; 3.4.37 for 418; 5.1.188–91, 259–60, for 586–9, where (p. 62) "each heroine pictures similarly the mixed emotions of her absent lover"; and 3.1.62–6 for 597–607, where Charmian's (p. 63) "intimacies with her mistress" suggest those of Marlowe's Anna. He concludes that *Dido* anticipates *Ant.* "in the famous Cydnus passage [where LABRIOLA, 1966, p. 180, sweepingly objects that Sh. is closer to Plutarch than to Marlowe] and in the management of nonclassical situations involving the protagonists." SCHANZER (1963, pp. 159–60) agrees, while STEANE (1964, pp. 29–30, 38, 59–61), finding atmospheric and stylistic links, comments: (p. 30) "As in Shakespeare's play there is a sense of the immensity of creation and of human beings proportionate to it, so in Marlowe's, poetry makes the universe the lovers' stage, and the lovers actors great enough to fill it." There is (p. 59) "a similar 'feel' in the substance of the poetry. Marlowe's imagery here is very like" Sh.'s. There are local echoes—when crowds swarm to gaze on Aeneas (*Dido* 3.1.71, ed. Tucker Brooke) as on Cleopatra (926–31) and when both women deify their men (*Dido* 4.4.45, *Ant.* 3317); for the cosmic note beginning both plays see n. 24–5—as well as the structural parallel of (p. 38) "two worlds, inimical to each other." BROWER (1971, p. 352; see also his pp. 99–103) thinks *Dido* "offered the most likely example for the Shakespearian blend in *Antony and Cleopatra* of the Virgilian heroic and the Ovidian erotic." ADELMAN (1973, pp. 177–83) in a searching app. notes similarities in the heroes' effeminacy (434–6, 1943, and esp. 1985–6 recalling *Dido* 4.3.31–6, in *Complete Plays*, ed. I. Ribner, New York, 1963), the notion of immortality (3047 and 3531–2 suggested by *Dido* 4.4.123), the queens' willingness to sacrifice kingdom to passion (1124 recalling *Dido* 5.1.146–7), and, more generally and remotely, the image of eyes resting on the beloved as an alternative to empire as well as the (p. 179) "emphasis on speaking in a way worthy of oneself"; Sh. uses Marlowe's (p. 180) "image of the lovers dying to meet one another in the afterlife [2883 and 3538 echoing *Dido* 5.1.318, 328] and the process by which they echo one another as they die." She notes, however, that (p. 180) "the process by which both playwrights test the assertive power of language" is more significant than the verbal echoes. Yet in both plays, this power "ultimately fails to conquer mundane reality; in fact, both playwrights seem deliberately to emphasize the discrepancy between words [*182*] and action." See also nn. 225 and 3047. DONNO (1956, p. 231) thinks *Ant.* 3090–7 recalls *2 Tamburlaine* 3025–33 and 3070–6 (ed. Tucker Brooke, OUP, 1910), where the hero's anguish at Zenocrate's death turns similarly to defiance of the gods. Following WILSON (ed. 1950), Adelman (1973, p. 98) and MACK (1973, p. 106, n. 8) see debt to *1 Tamburlaine* 467 ff., Menaphon's description of Tamburlaine's cosmic dimension, in such hyperbole as *Ant.* 3296–8. ROSE (1969, p. 387) cites *Dr. Faustus* to show that the description of *Edward II* in the Prologue establishes as theme—analogous to *Ant.*—the conflict of love and empire; Brower (1971, p. 353) finds that Cleopatra blends "Ovid's sophisticated woman of Rome with the 'immortal' Helen of Marlowe's *Faustus*"; HUME (1973, p. 285) alludes to the similar conception in *Faustus* and in *Ant.* of the "tragic fall, though with a persuasive and sensitive presentation of the temptation."

ADELMAN (1973, pp. 68–101) devotes part of a chapter, "Tradition as Source," to the treatment of the Dido-Aeneas and Mars-Venus legends in classical, medieval, and Renaissance literature and art, finding—as reflected in *Ant.*—a cosmic significance in the relationships of lovers.

Various other literary sources and analogues have been proposed. Thus BRAD-BROOK (1954, p. 470) finds that in Cleopatra's "dream" of Antony (especially 3296–3306) Sh. echoes a passage in Thomas Nashe's *Christ's Teares over Ierusalem* (1593; see *Works*, ed. R. B. McKerrow, 1910, 2:170–1).

JORGENSEN (1965, p. 169) declares that John Lyly's *Campaspe* (c. 1581), with its struggle between lover and conqueror in Alexander, "offered" Sh. "suggestions for the grouping of characters into patterns of conflict" in *Ant.*, the rough soldier Hephaestion resembling to some extent Enobarbus (similarly JONES, 1971, p. 239). Jorgensen also finds (p. 174) in Barnaby Rich's *Allarme to England* (1578) and *A Right Exelent and Pleasaunt Dialogue, Betwene Mercury and an English Souldier* (1574, sigs. M1ᵛ-M3) as well as Robert Wilson's *The Coblers Prophesie* (1594, sigs. A3, D3-E4ᵛ) "the conqueror shamefully tarrying in dotage"—Mars in Venus's lap—which "became for Tudor soldier-alarmists a favorite symbol of the deterioration of England as a warlike state and of the folly of soldiers dallying in love."

NEVO (1967, pp. 116–18) agrees with WHITER (1794; 1967, pp. 160–6) that Cleopatra's dream in 3289 ff. reflects popular pageants, court masques, and royal processions, particularly Ben Jonson's *Masque of Hymen* and *Masque of Blackness* (both 1605; for the latter, see also BRADBROOK, 1969, p. 118, and ADELMAN, 1973, pp. 186–7, who considers it among analogues for the swarthiness of [p. 187] the "proverbial Elizabethan Ethiopian," like whom Cleopatra describes herself at 555–6; see also n. 10); they also think Jonson's *Hymenaei*, produced in cooperation with Inigo Jones, may have suggested the cloud imagery at 2826 ff. (see n. 2833). MIOLA (1983, p. 157) surmises an influence of *Hymenaei* on the guards' entering Cleopatra's monument at 3241 and 3334. FUJITA (1968–9, pp. 27–8) points up resemblances to Cleopatra's sumptuously royal death in the dumb show preceding the first act of George Gascoigne's *Jocasta* (1566), a tr. of Lodovico Dolce's *Giocasta*.

MORGAN (1968, pp. 131, 136) suggests that the perspective picture as described in 1170–1 parallels George Puttenham's likening of imagination to a perspective glass (*The Arte of English Poesie*, 1589, pp. 14–15), while the satyr-play element in 2.7 recalls Puttenham's account (on p. 21) of ancient pantomime.

ERSKINE-HILL (1970, pp. 29–30, and 1983, pp. 143–4), acknowledging advice from A. J. Smith, considers the moralistic allusions to the lovers in Ludovico Ariosto's *Orlando furioso* 7.19 (tr. John Harington, 1591, p. 50) and in Torquato Tasso's *Gerusalemme liberata* 16.4–7 (tr. Edward Fairfax as *Godfrey of Bulloigne*, 1600, p. 281) as background to Sh.'s stress on temperance in *Ant*. ADELMAN (1973, p. 65) notes Tasso's association of the enchantress Armida with Cleopatra, esp. at 16.3–7 and 20.118 (ed. John C. Nelson, New York, 1963), as among the traditions for the queen's dubious supernatural charms; see n. 642. For Ariosto, see also n. 2380–1; for Tasso, nn. 902–3 and 2826–31.

ERSKINE-HILL (1983, p. 155; similarly 1970, p. 43) regards Ben Jonson's *The Poetaster* (1601), esp. 4.5–4.6 (ed. C. H. Herford and P. Simpson, OUP, 1932, 4:279–82), along with Goulart (see p. 459), as an influence on the characterization of Octavius, who resembles Jonson's "dignified and authoritative guarantor of human order, decorum and literary values." For Jonson, see also n. 570.

WHITAKER (1972, pp. 144–5) sees parallels to the macrocosmic imagery of Cleopatra's "dream" (3289 ff.) in the astronomical comparisons used in various sonnets of Sidney's *Astrophil and Stella* (c. 1581–3) as well as John Davies's *Nosce teipsum* (1599). SIMMONS (1973, *Shakespeare's Pagan World*, pp. 118–19) considers *Ant.*'s conflict of love and reason in the light of *Astrophil*, where *amor vulgaris* weakens the poet's reason without being rejected, and of John Donne's "The Canonization," where the lovers (p. 119) "are poetically exalted to sainthood." ZEEVELD (1974, pp. 136–7, n. 73) believes the (p. 136) "sophistical mischievous sensuality" in the Cydnus description, 901 ff., to be "strongly reminiscent" of the "extravagant sensuality in the bathing of the princesses in the River Ladon," in Sidney's *Arcadia* (ed. A. Feuillerat, 1912, 1:215–18), but the similarities are vague. See also n. 424.

Donne's notion of love's bondage as the highest freedom in "Elegie XIX: To His Mistris Going to Bed" is cited by MACK (1973, p. 104) as an example of literary formulas reworked by Sh. and implicit in 2664, 2668–9, 3616—by contrast, one might add 209–10. TANNER (1985–6, pp. 417–30) discusses similarities between Donne's *Songs and Sonnets* and *Ant*.

Numerous further influences and analogues of various kinds, some from works not strictly literary (in the same sense as the above), have been noticed.

GREEN (1870, p. 541) surveys reflections of emblems and devices in *Ant*.

Though ROBERTSON (1897; 1909, pp. 111–12) sees no influence of Montaigne, TAYLOR (1925, pp. 24–5, less convincingly pp. 56–7) finds a number of verbal echoes, especially *Ant*. 199–200 (John Florio's Montaigne of 1603, Tudor Translations, ed. W. E. Henley, 3 vols., 1892–3, 1:39), 319–20 (3:369), 497–8 (1:338), 1422–3 (2:68, 3:21), 2382 (2:192), 3062–6 (2:196), 3102 (2:65), and 3204–8 (2:23). REYHER (1947, p. 543) believes Sh. drew the idea expressed in 3143–5 from the *essai* "Comment nous pleurons et rions d'une mesme chose," 1.37; further parallels given by GRUDIN (1979, pp. 173–4) include paradoxical statements on morality and truth in Florio's Montaigne of 1603 (ed. J. I. M. Stewart, New York, 1933, p. 990) echoed in 440–3, Montaigne's p. 975 in 802–9, and pp. 972–4 in 952 (see n.).

JORGENSEN (1951, pp. 387–92) claims that Sh.'s presentation of Enobarbus's death was influenced by Sir Lewis Lewkenor's *The Estate of English Fugitives under the King of Spaine* (1595). See n. 2700–20.

RIBNER's (1952, pp. 244–6) belief, anticipated in a parallel noted by CASE (ed. 1906; see n. 3562), that George Peele's *Famous Chronicle of King Edward the First* (1593) gave Sh. the idea of applying asps to Cleopatra's breast rather than to her arm is exploded by REEVES (1952, pp. 441–2) and NORGAARD (1952, pp. 442–3). Norgaard points instead to more likely sources in Thomas Cooper's *Thesaurus linguae romanae & britannicae* (1584, sig. 7E1^r) and Galen's *De theriaca ad Pisonem* (Ch. 8)—the latter noted by HALLIWELL (ed. 1865, on l. 3567, quoting from Thomas Browne, *Vulgar and Common Errors* 5.12) and CASE (ed. 1906). Norgaard also cites Paul of Aegina's 7th-c. medical epitome, 5.19 (which, together with Cooper and Galen, is mentioned likewise by WATSON, 1978, pp. 411–14), Michael Glycas's 12th-c. work, and Domitius Calderinus's *Commentarii in M. Valerium Martialem* (Venice, 1474, sig. H5^v), the last noted previously by THEOBALD (ed. 1733, on 3566). These works—with paintings and cameos—were all accessible to Sh. THOMAS (1963, p. 176, n. 9) summarizes the sources on the "two asps-two breasts version." Besides Cooper, she mentions especially Richard Reynoldes, *A Chronicle of All the Noble Emperours of the Romaines* (1571, fol. 17), and William Fulbecke, *An Historicall Collection of the Continuall Factions, Tumults, and Massacres of the Romans and Italians* (1601, pp. 196–7), both quoted by FARNHAM (1950, pp. 195–6); Thomas Nashe's *Christ's Teares over Ierusalem* (*Works*, ed. R. B. McKerrow, 1910, 2:140), noted by CASE (ed. 1906); Holbein's woodcut *The Death of Cleopatra*, used by Froben as the title page for works by Erasmus (Arthur B. Chamberlain, *Hans Holbein the Younger*, New York, 1913, 1:198); and Boccaccio's *De casibus*. Thomas adds general references to Hugh of St. Victor, St. Bernard, Bonaventura, and the Franciscan tradition on the paradoxical union of *concupiscentia* and *caritas* as an idea relevant in Cleopatra's death (p. 182, n. 12). MIOLA (1983, p. 156) discusses the transformation of Cesare Ripa's symbolism of serpents in *Iconologia* (rpt. in *The Renaissance and the Gods* 21, New York, 1976, pp. 125–6, 407–9) in Cleopatra's death scene.

Marcellus Palingenius in *Zodiacus vitae*, tr. Barnabe Googe as *The Zodiake of Life* (1565), may have provided some of *Ant.*'s image strands (recorded by HANKINS, 1953, pp. 47, 81, 121, 151, 163, 191, 203, 230–1). Hankins (p. 121) also sees echoes from Roger Ascham's *The Scholemaster* (1570; ed. E. Arber, English Rpts., 1870, p. 75) in Sh.'s use of Lethe, citing 647 and 1458.

STARNES & TALBERT (1955, pp. 132–3) believe Sh. derived the concept of "dotage" in Antony from Cooper's *Thesaurus* (s.v. *Cleopâtra*), where it is the key to the character and may have been (p. 133) "the cue" for Sh.'s interpretation of Antony and his emphasis on Octavius's restraint.

MORRIS (1968–9, pp. 271–8) specifies various sources for descriptions of Queen

Elizabeth's personality as mirrored in Cleopatra, naming—apart from Sh.'s experience and hearsay—records of royal passage and progresses, accounts by foreign visitors, and state papers and letters, most of the last group probably unknown to Sh. See nn. 902–31 and 1877–9. While MUIR (1969, pp. 199–200) does not believe Sh. echoes Elizabeth, RINEHART (1972, pp. 81–6) finds possible parallels, noting reflections of Elizabeth's court in 77–155 and 603 (see nn.) and both queens' awareness of their public character (see n. 3407–10).

KALMEY (1978, pp. 280–7) perceives that the widely held contempt of certain Renaissance historians for Octavius's pre-Augustan demagogy may have influenced Sh., citing Richard Reynoldes (*A Chronicle of All the Noble Emperours of the Romaines*, 1571), William Fulbecke (*An Historicall Collection of the Continuall Factions . . . of the Romans and Italians*, 1601, pp. 17–18, 171–2), and Pedro Mexia (*The Historie of all the Romane Emperors*, tr. W. T., 1604, pp. 27 ff.), as well as Plutarch (ed. W. W. Skeat, 1904, frequent references), Suetonius (*History of Twelve Caesars*, tr. P. Holland, 1606, Tudor Translations, ed. W. E. Henley, 1899, 1:86 ff., 101 ff.), Appian (*Auncient Historie*, tr. W. B., 1578, frequent references), and Eutropius (*A Briefe Chronicle*, tr. N. Haward, 1564, fol. 69ᵛ); MIOLA (1983, p. 162, n. 56) adds Seneca, *De clementia* 1.11.1–3.

SHAPIRO (1982, pp. 1–15) believes *Ant.*'s disjunctive structure was influenced by plays written for and performed by children's troupes.

For various influences on Enobarbus's description of Cleopatra on the Cydnus, see nn. 902–31, 902–3, 906–9. Among less likely ones are a picture of Venus mentioned in *The Voyage of Captain John Saris to Japan* (1613; ed. E. M. Satow, 1900, p. 83), to which SHAW-SMITH (1973, p. 93) sees an allusion in 912–13, and Joseph of Exeter's *De bello troiano* 3.169–75, which DRONKE (1980, pp. 172–4) thinks Sh. used for the opening lines of the speech, 902–9, as well as for the picture of Venus at 912–13 and the conceit at 929–31 (see *Joseph Iscanus, Werke und Briefe*, ed. L. Gompf, Leiden and Köln, 1970, p. 126). HALLIWELL (ed. 1865, 15:275) cites an analogous description of a ship in *Richard Cœur de Lion* (ed. K. Brunner, Wien and Leipzig, 1913, ll. 61–76; a possible echo of 67 in the "Silken Tackle" of *Ant.* 922). For comparisons of the speech with Plutarch, see pp. 393–4.

For influences on or parallels to Antony's speech at 2826–31, see n.

FRIEDMAN (1969, pp. 481–4) notes various analogues in Michael Drayton's *Mortimeriados* (1596), especially a similarity between Edward III at 2715–16 (*Works*, ed. J. W. Hebel et al., vol. 1, Oxford, 1931) and Octavius in *Ant.* 2395; Mortimer's farewell epistle at 2717–18 (in rev. of 1603, *The Barons Warres*, 6.681–8; see *Works*, vol. 2, 1932) and *Ant.* 3062–6; (p. 483) "the boundlessness, the disavowal of limits, the free use of hyperbole" in 2612–18 (6.561–8) and *Ant.* 3296–3301; Mortimer's being likened to Hercules at 689, 2594, 2652, 2870, and *Ant.* 402, 2491–2, 2803. See also n. 902–31. These parallels show the two poets' independent (p. 481) "interest in similar historical situations and in characters who command admiration despite the ambiguity of their moral natures."

Scholars have noted a number of further analogues from Renaissance works for interpretive concepts or myths.

Renaissance authors quoted by PHILLIPS (1940, pp. 188–205) for qualities essential to a successful governor are chiefly Sir Thomas Elyot, *The Gouernour* (1531, passim); Desiderius Erasmus, *Institutio principis christiani* (1516; tr. L. K. Born as *The Education of a Christian Prince*, New York, 1936, p. 189); Baldassare Castiglione's *The Courtier*, tr. Thomas Hoby (1561; Everyman's Library, 1928, p. 276); Tigurinus Chelidonius's *A Most Excellent Hystorie, Of the Institution and Firste Beginning of Christian Princes*, tr. James Chillester (1571, ch. 4, as well as pp. 60 ff.); and George Buchanan, *De iure regni apud Scotos* (1579, tr. Philalethes, 1689, p. 28), to prove that Antony and Lepidus (p. 189) "are eliminated because they do not possess, as Octavius clearly does, the special qualities [continence, self-control, prudence, concern with welfare of the state, wisdom, etc.] which, according to Renaissance thinking, mark a man for the vocation of government." For Elyot, see also n. 3176–9.

FARNHAM (1950, pp. 179–80, 194–6) and DICKEY (1957, pp. 156–60) cite Elizabethan moralists from the 1560s on as background to *Ant.*, to show the prevailing disparagement of the lovers; Dickey argues that Sh.'s view is similar.

BARROLL (1958, *JEGP*, pp. 708–20) mentions various authorities for the thematic link he sees among lechery, gluttony, and sloth in *Ant.*, though he does not distinguish influences from analogues. Mentioned are *The Life and Death of Mary Magdalene* (1565), Marlowe's *Dr. Faustus*, Francis Thynne's *Emblemes and Epigrames* (1600), Thomas Lodge's *Wits Miserie* (1596), Lawrence Humfrey's *The Nobles* (1563), Ariosto's *Orlando furioso* (tr. John Harington, 1591), William Langland's *Piers the Plowman* (c. 1387), Guillaume de Deguileville's *Pilgrimage of the Life of Man* (tr. John Lydgate, 1426–30), Ben Jonson's *Volpone* (1606), Joseph Hall's *Mundus alter et idem* (1605), Francis Meres's *Palladis tamia* (1598), and Jeremias Bastingius's *Exposition . . . upon the Catechisme* (1589).

SCHANZER (1963, pp. 155–9) points to Xenophon's *Memorabilia* 2.1.21 ff. (tr. E. C. Marchant, Loeb, 1923, p. 95), Cicero's *De officiis* 1.32, Whitney's *Choice of Emblemes* (1586, p. 40), and Tasso's *Gerusalemme liberata* 16.3–7 (tr. Edward Fairfax as *Godfrey of Bulloigne*, 1600), as sources for the "choice of Hercules" theme, which he—anticipated by HERFORD (ed. 1899, 9:261) and BARROLL (1958, *TxSE*, pp. 72–3)—regards as an analogue to Antony's choice between two opposed ways of life. COATES (1978, pp. 45–52), expanding on this topic, refers to Xenophon as well as to the *Punica* of Caius Silius Italicus (tr. J. D. Duff, Loeb, 1934, 2:327–33), where Virtue and Vice appear in a dream to the elder Scipio, as origins of a Neoplatonic allegory of the (p. 45) "attainment of human wholeness" in the blending of pleasure and virtue—the (p. 52) "statement" also of *Ant.* Coates considers particularly the description of Hercules in Vincenzo Cartari's *Imagines deorum* (Lyons, 1581, pp. 190, 227–8, 234)—especially his moral rather than physical courage, his role as god of eloquence, and his descent into Hades, linked by Cartari with human beings' descent into their own nature to bridle its impulses—a description that, together with Natale Conti's remarks in *Mythologiae* (Lyons, 1605, p. 697) on Hercules's education by Chiron in both arms and law, suggests to Coates Hercules's role as complete man, a model for Sh.'s Herculean Antony.

Among Renaissance authorities named by WADDINGTON (1966, pp. 210–24) to illustrate various aspects of the Mars-Venus myth—especially the concept of *concordia discors*, a theme in *Ant.*—are Pico della Mirandola, George Chapman, and Leone Ebreo (i.e., Judah Abravanel), as well as the iconographic tradition. See also pp. 394–5 and n. 1050–1. For the rival myth of Hercules and Omphale, with its emphasis on the hero's effeminacy, Waddington mentions numerous other authorities—Abraham Fraunce, George Chapman, Angelo Poliziano, Sir Philip Sidney, John Weever, Richard Linche, Andreas Alciati, George Puttenham, Thomas Wilson—as background rather than as sources. For further Hercules-Omphale parallels and analogues, see BARROLL (1958, *TxSE*, pp. 71–2). For Chapman, see also nn. 1029 and 2826–31.

WILLIAMSON (1968, p. 428) refers to Machiavelli's concept of Fortune in *Il principe* (1513–14), ch. 25 (tr. L. Ricci, rev. E. R. P. Vincent, New York, 1940, p. 91), to show that in *Ant.* Sh. "seems, like Machiavelli, to interpret human affairs as partially the product of character and partially ruled by Fortune."

WALTER (ed. 1969, p. 31) cites the *Homily against Gluttony and Drunkenness* to illustrate how, as in Lepidus's case, drunkenness may lead to cruelty and arbitrary use of authority.

Several scholars dwell on Neoplatonic analogues. TRACI (1970, pp. 96–135) outlines aspects of the philosophy of love that he finds embodied in *Ant.* from Plato's *Symposium*, Ovid's poems on love, Andreas Capellanus's *Art of Courtly Love*, Marsilio Ficino's *Commentary on Plato's 'Symposium'*, and Leone Ebreo's *Dialoghi d'amore*, but without claiming that Sh. (p. 135) "is indebted to any of them as sources." BIRKINSHAW (1972, pp. 37–44) refers generally to Ficino, Pico della Mirandola, Baldassare Castiglione's *The Courtier* (tr. Thomas Hoby, 1561), which Sh. (p. 39) "had almost certainly read," Giordano Bruno's *De gli eroici furori* (1585), as well as Spenser's *Fowre Hymnes* (1596) and the July eclogue of *The Shepheardes Calender* (1579) to support his claim that, as in 560–1 (where he thinks Cleopatra alludes to the [p. 43] "little death of sex," seen by Ficino to touch the divine) or in 590 and 2668 (where as in Ficino and Pico virtue between two extremes becomes infinite), *Ant.* shows "neo-erotic Platonism" at work. To illustrate the resemblance between Cleopatra's transcendent love and that described by the Neoplatonists, LABRIOLA (1975, pp. 20–36) cites Plotinus, Ebreo, Castiglione, Bruno, Agrippa, Copernicus, and Betussi. HILL (1984, pp. 232–5) discusses the motif of the kiss of death, symbolizing the soul's liberation through love—described in Lorenzo de' Medici's preface to his sonnets and in Pico's *Commento*—as analogue to such statements as 3023–5, 3046–8, or 3542–4.

ADELMAN (1973, pp. 80, 93–4) refers to Vincenzo Cartari's (*Imagines deorum*, French tr. by Antoine du Verdier as *Les images des dieux des anciens*, Lyons, 1581, pp. 484, 498, 513–14, 621) account of Bacchus's dual role of conqueror and drunkard, as well as his occasional hermaphroditism, to explain that god's resemblance to Antony.

ZEEVELD (1974, pp. 124–6), who sees *Ant.* as (p. 124) "a tragedy of empire," cites Statutes of the Realm, the Act of Appeals of 1533, and other historical documents to illustrate the Tudor notion of empire.

HALLETT (1976, p. 82) thinks Pompey's career exemplifies the doctrine of Fortune's wheel as expounded in Thomas Sackville's Induction in the *Mirror for Magistrates* (1563; ed. J. Haslewood, 1815, 2:312).

Criticism

For surveys of criticism on *Ant.*, see NAKAMURA (1960, pp. 1–70), SCHANZER (1963, pp. 146–50), LABRIOLA (1966), BROWN (1968, pp. 11–21), TRACI (1970, pp. 11–22), GURA (1974, pp. 110–19), CRAWFORD (1978, pp. 82–121), and STEPPAT (1980).

General Assessments

Because it flouts conventions, *Ant.* tends to reflect changes of critical fashion. Before the Restoration, the theatrical presentation of the story of Antony and Cleopatra is mentioned to make satirical (ANTON, 1616; see p. 687) or educative (BRATHWAIT, 1631; see p. 631) points touching social life. After the Restoration and particularly in the 18th c., when critical responses reflect a common concern with order and with normative standards for judging dramatic art, critics who admire *Ant.* have to come to terms with its unclassically expansive and loose-limbed structure. Thus ROWE (ed. 1709, 1:[x]xviii) speaks of Sh.'s "Carelessness" in scattering locale so widely, though he praises *"The Manners of his Characters,"* in which Sh. "may be generally justify'd" since manners are (p. xxx) "proper to the Persons represented." ANON. (1747, p. 42), however, defends the violation of the unities: *"Dryden's Play [All for Love]* is most correctly poetical with the Unities; *Shakespear's* is most pathetically Natural without 'em. The first is the finish'd Performance of a great Poet, the last the hasty Production of a true Dramatick Genius." *Ant.'s* irregularity in structure as well as characterization may explain the preference given to *All for Love* in the 18th-c. theater. No critic of the period places *Ant.* among Sh.'s greatest works. WARBURTON (ed. 1747, 1:e1) assigns it to the second of four classes of literary merit, along with a motley group comprising *Jn., H5, R3, H8, Tim.,* and *Cym.* JOHNSON (ed. 1765), for whom *Ant.* exemplifies Sh.'s natural inventiveness, admires the play's entertaining variety (7:254)—"This Play keeps curiosity always busy, and the passions always interested"—rather than Sh.'s artistic control of structure and characterizations, of which he approves less.

Romantic critics, with a new imaginative apprehension of individual consciousness as against the bounds of social convention, are fascinated by the unique power of Cleopatra's individuality and—in keeping with their stress on the intensity of creative imagination—discover that the beauty and strength of her passion outshine any moral flaw (see also p. 641). This fascination leads to the praise expressed by HAZLITT (1817; 1930, 4:228)—"This is a very noble play. Though not in the first class of Shakespear's productions, it stands next to them, and is, we think, the finest of his historical plays"—and especially COLERIDGE (1818; 1960, 1:77), who believes *Ant.* may be, "in all exhibitions of a giant power in its strength and vigor of maturity, a formidable rival of the *Macbeth, Lear, Othello*, and *Hamlet*. . . . Of all perhaps of Shakespeare's plays the most wonderful" is *Ant.*

The romantic sense of organic unity brought to bear on this drama withers in the course of the 19th c. Coleridge's high ranking of *Ant.* is sometimes endorsed by critics (e.g., HERAUD, 1865, pp. 374, 376; HUDSON, 1872, 2:365–7) who, going even further in raising the lovers above moral censure, exemplify a 19th-c. tendency for moral judgment and romantic fascination to drift apart and verge, each in its own way, on the sentimental: thus while HUGO (ed. 1860; 1868, 7:7–23) celebrates (p. 23) "l'amour infini" as the play's (p. 21) "vérité morale," DOWDEN (1875; 1877, pp. 306–17), though alive to the way the lovers' Dionysian passion and pleasure (p. 311) "toil after the infinite," believes that Sh., with a severity as unflinching as Milton's, finally exposes the sensuous splendor as (p. 313) "a deceit, a snare." Whereas SWINBURNE (1879; 1902, p. 191), for whom Cleopatra is "the perfect and the everlasting woman," calls *Ant.* (1909, p. 76) "the greatest love-poem of all time," SHAW (1900; 1931, 31:xxvii) declares that it "must needs be as intolerable to the true Puritan as it is vaguely distressing to the ordinary healthy citizen," owing to its depiction of debauchery and wantonness. ULRICI (1839; 1868–9, tr. 1876, 2:201–8), for whom Sh. is the poet of world history, and GERVINUS (1850, tr. 1883, pp. 722–45), who considers him as an ethical teacher, find the play's idea in the vengeance following the yielding of public honor to private pleasure; Dowden, like Gervinus, inquires into Sh.'s personality and assigns *Ant.* to his gloomy third period, "Out of the depths." Some German critics fault the play's lack of elevating idealism (e.g., Gervinus, pp. 723–5; KREYßIG, 1858; 1877, 1:462–3). A group of rationalist critics emerging originally from the Hegelian "right" (e.g., Ulrici; SNIDER, 1876; 1877, 2:260–84; MOULTON, 1903; 1907, pp. 128–40) focuses on the play's political and moral conflicts and vindicates the structure as suited to represent such conflicts. Disapproval of the structure lingers, however, particularly in Germany (e.g., FREYTAG, 1863; 1890, tr. 1894, pp. 71–2, 386–7; GENÉE, 1872; 1878, 1:345–6; BENEDIX, 1873, pp. 358–9), because of classicist doctrine as well as efforts on the part of dramatists and scholars to unshackle national drama from Sh.'s overpowering influence.

In the 20th c., *Ant.*'s literary excellence is rarely questioned. A brief survey of major critical attitudes and concerns will illuminate reasons for what has become an explosion of interest in this play. BRADLEY (1906; 1909, pp. 279–308) transmits to the 20th c. the romantics' grasp of *Ant.*'s ambivalent complexity. Though displeased with the structure (in the wake of Freytag, 1863), Bradley sets *Ant.* in a class by itself, sensing, though not fully accounting for, the play's paradoxical vision (pp. 282, 305): "Although *Antony and Cleopatra* may be for us as wonderful an achievement as the greatest of Shakespeare's plays, it has not an equal value. . . .

[*305*] "A comparison of Shakespearean tragedies seems to prove that the tragic

emotions are stirred in the fullest possible measure only when such beauty or nobility of character is displayed as commands unreserved admiration or love; or when, in default of this, the forces which move the agents, and the conflict which results from these forces, attain a terrifying and overwhelming power. . . . It [*Ant.*] does not attempt to satisfy these conditions, and then fail in the attempt. It attempts something different, and succeeds as triumphantly as *Othello* itself. In doing so it gives us what no other tragedy can give, and it leaves us, no less than any other, lost in astonishment at the powers which created it." Bradley observes (p. 292) that the "peculiar effect" of *Ant.* depends on the "absence of decidedly tragic scenes and events" in the first half, as well as on a strongly emphasized "element of reconciliation" in the "final tragic impression" (see also 1904; 1905, p. 84).

Among comments on *Ant.*'s value early in the century, before fresh critical methods gain ground, are ELIOT's (1920; 1950, p. 99) ranking of *Ant.* with *Cor.* as Sh.'s "most assured artistic success"—contrasting with *Ham.*, (p. 98) "most certainly an artistic failure"—and, less erratically despite some crabbed notebook rambling, BRECHT's (1920, tr. 1979, p. 15) highlighting of the dramatic action: *Ant.* is "a splendid drama which really gripped me. The more central the place apparently taken by the plot, the richer and more powerful are the developments open to its exponents. They haven't got faces, they only have voices. . . . I love this play and the people in it." Against a long-standing (and still thriving) tradition of disparaging female sexuality, one that has shaped much critical response to Cleopatra, defenses of her conduct and moral status are mounted by GRINDON (1909, passim), SIMPSON (1928; 1950, pp. 27–37), and latterly FITZ (1977, pp. 297–316). Reacting against criticism solely of character, SCHÜCKING (1919, tr. 1922, p. 112) takes *Ant.* as a prime example of Sh.'s "supreme interest in the single scene." The result, he claims, is an inconsistent Cleopatra: a harlot in the first acts, as required by the action, she suddenly becomes a noble queen in the last two, psychological plausibility being sacrificed to (p. 114) "episodic intensification." For answers to Schücking, see pp. 694–5.

From the 1930s on, critics achieve fresh insights concerning structure, image patterns, mythical analogues, archetypes, Antony's heroic nobility, *Ant.*'s relation to the other Roman plays, and the play's paradoxes. Sh.'s use of Elizabethan stage conventions is reexamined by GRANVILLE-BARKER (1930; 1946, 1:367–458), who calls attention to the unlocalized scene to defend *Ant.*'s structure, with its (p. 367) "large field of action" expressed in the symbolic contrast between Rome and Egypt. He stresses the sense of dimension: "Here is the most spacious of the plays. It may lack the spiritual intimacy of *Hamlet*, the mysterious power of *Macbeth*, the nobilities of *Othello*, may reach neither to the heights nor depths of *King Lear*; but it has a magnificence and a magic all its own, and Shakespeare's eyes swept no wider horizon." KNIGHT (1931; 1965, especially pp. 199–350) concentrates on *Ant.*'s "spatial" structure (see also *The Wheel of Fire*, 1930, pp. 3–4): (p. 19) "In no play is the imperial theme of government more magnificently presented; in none is it more vividly silhouetted as transitory against the infinite brilliance and imperial theme of love. . . . [25] In the *Hamlet*-world there is ever an emphasis on death and disease, in *Antony and Cleopatra* on forces of life and health." *Ant.* is (p. 31) "the Everest of Shakespearian drama." And again (p. 199): "Here finite and infinite are to be blended. Throughout we have a new vital complexity surpassing other plays; a wider horizon, a richer content. It is probably the subtlest and greatest play in Shakespeare, or, at least, paragoned only by *The Tempest.* The action compasses the Mediterranean and its citied shores; the Roman empire is revivified at its climacteric of grandeur and shown as something of so boundless and rich a magnificence that the princes who sway its destiny appear comparable only to heroes of myth, or divine beings." Stretching the thematic approach a little, GRIFFITHS (1945, p. 39; partly anticipated by GUNDOLF, 1926, pp. 7–35), who considers Cleopatra a Dionysian impulse (see also KNIGHT, 1931; 1965, pp. 25, 304), believes "the play exists much more than any other of Shakespeare's in its ecstatic moments, its pure sensations, its gusts of sheer passion: pride, jealousy, remorse, anger, above all love, absolute sole lord of Life and Death, presented with rapturous lyrical energy."

Not enchanted by the love theme, critics who regard the play as a study of statecraft or kingship reach quite different conclusions, disparaging the subversion of reason by passion. Thus PHILLIPS (1940, pp. 188–205) considers especially Antony's and Octavius's behavior against the background of Renaissance views on the personal conduct of rulers, a method applied by STEMPEL (1956, pp. 59–72; countered by TRACI, 1970, pp. 18–19) also to Cleopatra; DICKEY (1957, pp. 144–202) and BARROLL (e.g., 1958, *MLR*, pp. 327–43; *JEGP*, pp. 708–20) find classical, medieval, and Renaissance attitudes toward the lovers mostly unfavorable, a view, they assert, Sh. shares.

A few remain distant from the play or consider it a failure. WHITAKER (1965, pp. 276–310; similarly 1974, pp. 143–6), echoing Freytag (1863), criticizes it for not presenting a tragic choice and declares that, since it (p. 282) "lacks a true dramatic climax and becomes merely a series of events," it is (p. 296) "far inferior" to *Lr.* and *Mac.* MASON (1966; 1970, pp. 229–76) claims Sh. fails to write a successful love tragedy because Antony's fall is not dramatically motivated (he is answered by ENRIGHT, 1970, pp. 69–118, and BAYLEY, 1976, pp. 238–44). FITCH (1968, pp. 3–17), like Gervinus (1850), misses the sublime and ideal (p. 16): "The entire atmosphere of the play militates against any feeling of intimate involvement on the part of the spectator"; instead it establishes (p. 17) "a psychic distance where indifference and awe are curiously commingled."

More positive, and less reminiscent of 19th-c. attitudes, is WIMSATT's (1948; 1954, pp. 95–100) Thomistic argument that, since the lovers choose evil passion not as such but as a lesser good before a greater, Sh. is able to create sympathy for a (p. 97) "richly human state of sin." And yet (p. 100), "the greatest poems for the Christian will never be that kind, the great though immoral, which it has been our labor to describe [p. 95: 'a poem which embodies a clear approval of an evil choice and its evil emotion']. *Antony and Cleopatra* will not be so great as *King Lear.* The testimony of the critical tradition would seem to confirm this. The greatest poetry will be morally right, even though perhaps obscurely so, in groping confusions of will and knowledge."

WARNER (1957, p. 139) views *Ant.* as a dramatization of "a theme that is deeply rooted in myth and legend, the ruin of the strong man by his sexual weakness," the clearest analogue being the myth of Hercules and Omphale (first pointed out by SCHLEGEL, 1811, tr. 1846, p. 416). WAITH (1962, pp. 113–21), who also analyzes Antony as Herculean hero, notes Cleopatra's admiration of his heroic dimension and holds that their mutual dedication ennobles them. And BROWER (1971, p. 353): "The 'wonderful', the quality that Renaissance critics admired in heroic poetry, is salient in our total impression of *Antony and Cleopatra*, most variously heroic of all Shakespearian tragedies. The ease with which Shakespeare moves in this play from heroic tragedy to divine comedy, both high and low, shows that he had recovered for modern literature the freedom of Homer."

A different critical issue is the twofold catastrophe, with the lovers' deaths occurring in separate acts (e.g., GRANVILLE-BARKER, 1930; 1946, 1:399–400; WILSON, 1957, pp. 179–80; MILLS, 1960, p. 161, and 1964, p. 59; see also pp. 668–9).

SCOTT (1983) discusses production aspects of the dramatic text; BARROLL (1984) examines *Ant.* more substantially to show Sh.'s approach to the problem of tragic heroism.

Among recent critics who devote extended discussions to the Roman plays as a group, SIMMONS (1973, *Shakespeare's Pagan World*, pp. 109–63) argues that Sh. shows protagonists as heroically aspiring to realize a vision of perfection in an imperfect world; tragedy results when they fail. Moreover, behind both Antony's empire (of love) and that of Octavius there looms Augustinian irony in that the *Pax Romana* is doomed to be replaced—as Sh. is aware—by the *civitas Dei*. CANTOR (1976, pp. 127–208) holds that the "liberation of Eros" is closely bound up with the "politics of Empire," since the lovers' mutual attraction rests on their lofty political status and their passion aspires to (p. 187) "a new kind of public eminence." See also pp. 625 ff.

In a materialistic analysis of ideological concepts, DOLLIMORE (1983, pp. 204–17) asserts that *Ant.* and *Cor.* call into question the notion of martial *virtus* at a time of decline for the Jacobean aristocracy.

A growing number of critics in the 20th c., picking up where Bradley (1906) left off, believe *Ant.* represents an interplay of condemnation of passionate folly (see Dowden, 1875) and celebration of love (Hugo, 1860; Knight, 1931). Exploring this interplay has become a major critical concern. As an effort to reconcile opposing views, with a stress on ambiguity, paradox, and tension, this concern reflects the outlook of New Criticism but not always its methods. TRAVERSI (1938; 1969, 2:208–32; again 1963, pp. 79–203), the first major spokesman for what is almost a via media between opposing values in the play, argues that the conflicting attitudes toward the lovers—mainly Roman contempt and Egyptian apotheosis—are not resolved one-sidedly, since each is qualified by the other. His extended analysis shows that the lovers' flawed nobility is indicated by pervasive interaction of images of fertility and corruption. For others who discuss the play's paradoxes and ambiguities, see pp. 647 ff. SCHANZER (1963, p. 183) considers it "by far the greatest, as well as the most quintessential, of Shakespeare's Problem Plays," a category including also *JC* and *MM*, (p. 6) "in which we find a concern with a moral problem which is central to it, presented in such a manner that we are unsure of our moral bearings, so that uncertain and divided responses to it in the minds of the audience are possible or even probable." And RABKIN (1967, p. 188): "As a play about Rome and love, as the vehicle of some of Shakespeare's most memorable poetry, and as one of the last of his tragedies, *Antony and Cleopatra* is unique. It is not, however, an aberration from his other work; rather, as a simultaneously exultant and despairing dramatization of the unresolvable dialectic between opposed values that claim us equally and of the necessary tragedy of choice, it is a paradigm of Shakespeare's art." KROOK (1967; 1969, pp. 199–201), who perceives that Sh.'s view of love as both ennobling and destructive reflects a Christian consciousness, groups *Ant.* with *Cor.* as heroic drama based on Aristotelian *megalopsuchia* (greatness [of soul] or nobility), a species that (p. 199) "at this level of artistic accomplishment probably occurs nowhere else in European literature."

The ambivalent relationship of opposites in *Ant.* continues to engage critics. MARKELS (1968) examines the conflict between public and private values as a theme running through the canon and culminating in *Ant.*, where these values emerge as mutually conditioning. In this view Antony, by refusing to choose between Rome and Egypt, endorses and transcends both, Cleopatra following his initiative.

ADELMAN (1973), in a brilliant critical study incorporating discussions of the mythological and legendary traditions relevant to *Ant.*, especially Mars and Venus as well as Dido and Aeneas, substantiates the view of those who find Roman emphasis on logic and empirical evidence set against the play's poetry, which by means of paradox and hyperbole affirms the superiority of the imaginative dimension over the rational. Yet Adelman also shows that Roman logic, though transcended, is never denied its significance in the play.

To SIEMON (1973, p. 317), *Ant.* is the culmination of Sh.'s tragic vision: "Through its brilliant fusion of the wide point of view of medieval drama, with its marked emphasis upon a social and political world, and the intensity of feeling developed through the paradoxical view of human nature which distinguishes the tragedies from *Hamlet* to *Lear, Antony and Cleopatra* gives dramatic form to a tragic conception at once old and new. . . . It is only in *Antony and Cleopatra* that we find a fully developed vision of a world irremediably flawed, and yet one whose like we shall never see again. In its complete embodiment of such a world view the play represents a new accomplishment for Elizabethan tragedy."

MACK, who (ed. 1960, p. 15) considers *Inferno, Purgatorio*, and *Paradiso* guides to tone for *Mac., Lr.*, and *Ant.*, gives this account of the play's complexity (1973, pp. 79–81, 83–4): *Ant.* "is the delight of audiences and the despair of critics. Its delight for audiences springs, in part at least, from its being inexhaustible to contemplation. . . . No doubt its delight for today's audiences owes something also to its being the most accessible of the major Shakespearean tragedies to twentieth-century sensibilities, especially those not much experienced in drama apart from that of the realistic stage. There are no witches, . . . no ghosts, no antic madmen, no personages who are paragons of good or evil, nor even any passions (such, for example, as Coriolanus's contempt for the Roman commoners) which require of today's spectator an act of imaginative adjustment. . . . [80] If the play is inexhaustible to contemplation, it is at the same time remarkably inaccessible to interpretation, or at any rate to a consensus of interpretation, as the critical record shows. There seems to be a delicacy combined with intricacy in the play's interior balance that no criticism can lay hold of for long without oversimplifying or oversetting. . . . [81] We are never brought close to them [the protagonists] by a secret shared, a motive, conscious or unconscious, suddenly divulged. We watch them always from a distance, uncertain how far to accept their actions—and which actions—at face value, how far to believe the commentary of the observers in which Shakespeare again and again frames them, and even how to reconcile one action with the next. . . . [83] A great deal of the play's language seems calculated to question or explode our habitual safe norms and logical expectations; for it bristles with startling oxymorons, contradictions, and abrupt reversals. . . . What these effects convey is the [84] same intricate balance of opposing impulses and conflicting attitudes that characterize the play throughout. Somewhere behind them we may sense not only the playwright's effort to achieve a style that will accommodate the story he has to tell in its extremes of grandeur and folly, dignity and humiliation, but, just possibly, the mood of serious play . . . that seems to shine out in all Renaissance works that draw heavily on the vein of paradox [e.g., Erasmus's *Praise of Folly* or Donne's defense of "inconstancy in women" in several works]. Not impossibly, Shakespeare was himself conscious of his propinquity in this instance to that honorable tradition."

FICHTER (1980, pp. 99–111), arguing that the ambivalence of love and empire is meant to be understood in the light of Christian revelation, perceives (p. 100), "In the pre-Christian world of Shakespeare's play the transcendence to which the lovers aspire is tragically impossible"; *Ant.* (p. 103) "stands chronologically and metaphysically between the quest traditions of Roman epic and Christianity" (see also pp. 654–5).

Recent psychoanalytic criticism (e.g., SCHWARTZ, 1977; 1980, p. 30) examines the "interpenetration of opposites, self and other, male and female" and finds Antony struggling "between masculine hardness and feminine fluidity, finally choosing both and neither, a new synthesis." Other critics who discuss problems of gender identity and status (or related matters), largely from psychoanalytic or feminist perspectives, include DUSINBERRE (1975, p. 290: Antony with his excess of feeling is the play's "fullest man"), NOVY (1977; 1980, pp. 262–4, and 1984, pp. 91–2: the lovers are both actor and audience to each other; 1984, pp. 122–4: the lovers' relationship is marked by stability and equality; 1984, pp. 196–7: neither lover has a narrow conception of gender), BERGGREN (1980, p. 25: Cleopatra enters a maternal phase at the end), GOHLKE (1980, pp. 159–61: Antony's view of himself as womanish destroys his sense of identity), DASH (1981, pp. 209–47: Cleopatra unites sexual and political roles, as well as love and marriage; see also RICHMOND, 1978, pp. 338–9), FRENCH (1981, p. 252: *Ant.* provides a vision of constancy integrated with sexuality as a feminine principle), WHEELER (1981, pp. 208–11: there is mutual interchange of masculine and feminine qualities in both lovers), BAMBER (1982, pp. 45–70: unlike Cleopatra, Antony is unsure of his identity), KASTAN (1982, pp. 124–5: lovers' deaths are a triumph of mutual commitment), ERICKSON (1985, pp. 123–47: Antony shows a [p. 133] "capacity for cross-gender identification"; he participates in [p. 145] "maternal bounty"), FABER (1985, pp. 71–104: lovers' empire is the need for an integrated self), NEELY (1985, pp. 138–9: Antony experiences conflict between roles as soldier and lover, Cleopatra none between those of queen and lover; gender roles in the play are polarized, not reversed), KROHN (1986, pp. 89–96: unconscious fantasy of emasculation threatens Antony's relation to Cleopatra), and GREENE (1987, pp. 24–40: lovers attempt to transform themselves into androgynous beings).

Critics who consider *Ant.* a superlative achievement include, besides those quoted, ANON. (1824, p. 49: because of Cleopatra), HUDSON (ed. 1855; 1872, 2:365–7: *Ant.* leaves the most profound impression of Sh.'s greatness), HERAUD (1865, pp. 374, 376: because of idealism of love), HALL (1869; 1871, p. 253: language, structure, character), KOCH (ed. 1882, 9:245: Cleopatra), WHITE (ed. 1883, 3:787: poetry), VOLLMER (1887, p. 219: characterizations), CORSON (1889, p. 252: moral spirit), SYMONS (1889; 1919, p. 1: Cleopatra), FOARD (1893, p. 355: love), LEE (ed. 1907, 36:xxx: Cleopatra), HARRIS (1909; 1911, p. 304: supreme expression of Sh.'s passion for Mary Fitton; with *Ham.*, Sh.'s "supremest work"), MATHEW (1922, p. 280: love), MURRY (1924, p. 38: loyalty redeeming tragic waste, *Ant.* and *Lr.* as Sh.'s "greatest triumph as an artist"), RIDLEY (ed. 1935, p. viii, and ed. 1954, p. l: Sh.'s "high-water mark" for technical brilliance), MENON (1938, p. 152: Sh. almost overconfident in his masterly historical sense), CECIL (1944; 1949, p. 7: a uniquely virtuosic political play), STAUFFER (1949, pp. 232–3: characterization, moral values, poetry; *Ant.* and *Lr.* are supreme in Sh.), GODDARD (1951, 2:184: *Ant.* best represents all aspects of Sh.'s genius), HARRISON (1951, p. 203: verse, characterization, structure; p. 226: *Ant.* is not deep tragedy but "a thing of beauty incomparable"), HALLIDAY (1954, p. 166: poetry), PEARSON (1954, p. 125: like W. H. AUDEN, he thinks *Ant.* is "the culmination of verse drama in the Elizabethan age"), SPEAIGHT (1955, p. 149: triumph of transcendent humanism; the "most dazzling" even if not most profound of Sh.'s visions), RUPPEL (1957, p. 188: most powerful historical tragedy in world literature; perfect image of late Hellenism, as stated also by GUNDOLF, 1926, p. 13, and 1928; 1949, 2:429), WILSON (1957, p. 177: love), FERGUSSON (1961; 1970, p. 249: love), DAICHES (1962; 1968, p. 70: poetry), ALEXANDER (1964, p. 238: virtuosity), ARTHOS (1964, pp. 62, 64, 66: love), FOAKES (1964, *DUJ*, p. 66: most brilliant of Sh.'s later tragedies, mainly [p. 76] because of Antony's Rubens-like vitality), HAUSER (1964, tr. 1965, 1:343–5: Sh.'s most mannerist creation, poetic climax of his work), NOWOTTNY (1964, p. 75: records her and the classicist H. E. BUTLER's opinion that *Ant.* is the world's greatest play), HAINES (1968, p. 121: color, atmosphere, poetry), BRODWIN (1971, pp. 223, 253–4: greatest tragedy of "Worldly Love" ever written), EVANS (1973, 5:26: reconciliation of language and character), KERMODE (in EVANS, ed. 1974, p. 1343: interplay of theme and poetry), CHAMPION (1976, pp. 240–1, 264–5: Sh.'s most powerful delineation of secular values between which human beings struggle to choose), DORIUS (1978, p. 302: richest relationship between the sexes in Sh.), FUZIER (1978, p. 73: Sh.'s most successful version of the tragedy of a couple), TOLMIE (1978, p. 113: Sh.'s most coherent work of art), and JEFFORD (1982, 1:270, 276: love; musicality of Cleopatra's last speeches).

Others who emphasize strengths in *Ant.* include BRÄKER (1780, tr. 1979, p. 84: entertaining masterpiece), DAVIES (1783, 2:334, 367: action, character, manners), SEYMOUR (1805, 2:83: written in Sh.'s best manner), HAZLITT (1813; 1930, 5:191: "one of the best" of Sh.'s historical plays), KEATS (a letter of 1820 states that *Ant.* is his favorite play; see L. M. JONES, 1977, pp. 43–4), HETTNER (1852, pp. 33–4: characterization), GRIFFIN (1870, p. 76: irregular grandeur), BODENSTEDT (1874; 1887, p. 354: characterization and poetry), DOWDEN (1875; 1877, p. 307: compelling characters "seen through a golden haze of sensuous splendour"), FRIESEN (1876, 3:224–5, 259: great psychological tragedy, though not as great as Coleridge claims), SNIDER (1876; 1877, 2:265: language, thought, and characterization), BASEDOW (1893, 1:112 n.: gripping), WENDELL (1894, p. 314: masterpiece of historical fiction), LOUNSBURY (1901, p. 96: characterization), GARNETT & GOSSE (1903, 2:243–4: variety), STRINDBERG (1909, tr. 1966, p. 278: a heavy play but not tiresome as the comedies are), SAINTSBURY (1910; 1934, p. 75: variety), KOSTER (1915; 1916, pp. 105–6: agrees with Coleridge), WINCHESTER (1922, pp. 66–7: *Ant.* powerful in its immediate impact, a spell broken when passion is recognized as transient), GILLET (1930, pp. 242, 263–4: one of Sh.'s most marvelous works, hymn to love and nirvana), LEAVIS (1936, pp. 167–8: supports Bradley), MISSENHARTER (1938–9, p. 422: love), WOLFF (1944; 1945, p. 106: the heroic essence of antiquity), RÜEGG (1951, p. 250: pathos supreme in Sh., yet too much historical chronicle to be equal to the major tragedies), SCHILLING (1953, pp. 222–3: acute perception of Hellenism; similarly RUPPEL, 1957, p. 188), CLAUDEL (whose opinion that *Ant.* contains superb poetry but is not very good as a play is recorded by SPEAIGHT, 1955, p. 122), WRIGHT (1958, p. 37: "pity for the weakness of man and admiration for his heroism"), IMAM (1959, pp. 51–61: characterization, poetry), SHARPE (1959, p. 74: intense passion, vast scope), HARBAGE (1963, p. 436: "both glamorous and astringent," of a different order from the major tragedies), HOWARTH (1964, p. 84: uniquely elusive), ENRIGHT (1970, pp. 69–71, 118: admirable as tragedy), BIRKINSHAW (1972, p. 44: Sh.'s "most prophetic" play in exploring the frontiers of passion to their inevitable limit), HAWKES (1973, p. 178: complex probing of the value of love), AOKI (1978, pp. 1–45: vacillation of characters and their humanistic generosity unique in this play), and PLANCHON (1979, p. 62: first theatrical dream of a magic Orient by an Occidental).

Those who stress faults and weaknesses in *Ant.* include AYRENHOFF (1783; 1813, pp. 13–16: structure), STENDHAL (1821; 1972, 5:175: "assez froid," presumably because of rhetorical poetry), DUPORT (1828, 2:57–8: tragic dignity), BENEDIX (1873, pp. 358–60: structure), and FRENZEL (1877, 1:258–9: structure).

For descriptions of responses to this play among students, see ROSENBLATT (1938, pp. 273–6), ENRIGHT (1970, pp. 69–70), and HENN (1972, p. 117).

Ant. has often been compared, contrasted, or discussed in conjunction with various works by Sh. and by others. Significant contributions include comparisons with *Tro.* by GERVINUS (1850, tr. 1883, pp. 725–6), FURNIVALL (ed. 1877, 1:lxxxii–iii), NICOLL (1952, p. 150), DICKEY (1957), and NOCHIMSON (1977, pp. 99–127); with *R2* by BURTON (1968; 1970, pp. 34–9, and 1973, passim); with *H4* and *H5* by MORLEY & GRIFFIN (1895, 11:93–4), SCHANZER (1963, pp. 162–7), JONES (1971, pp. 231–9), and SIMMONS (1973, *Shakespeare's Pagan World*, pp. 153–5); with *Rom.* by COLERIDGE (1818; 1960, 1:77, 2:256), HUGO (ed. 1860; 1868, 7:22–3), KOCH (ed. 1882, 9:246), DICKEY (1957), and ROZETT (1985, pp. 152–64); with *JC* by GERSTENBERG (1766; 1890, p. 162), GENÉE (1872; 1878, 1:347), WINCHELL (1881, pp. 205–9), PHILLIPS (1940, pp. 188–9), CHARNEY (1959, pp. 355–67), and SPENCER (1967, pp. 20–9); with *Ham.* by KNIGHT (1931; 1965, pp. 23–5), MENDEL (1960, pp. 223–36), and VINCENT (1978, pp. 90–120); with *Oth.* by OSBORN (1966, pp. 272–4), BRODWIN (1971, pp. 226, 252), and RICHMOND (1971, pp. 158–76); with *Lr.* by BRANDES (1895, tr. 1935, pp. 470, 476), WILSON (1957, pp. 159–209), HAWKES (1973, pp. 178–93), SNYDER (1979, pp. 164–5), CLAYTON (1983, pp. 131–4), and MATCHETT (1984, pp. 327–37); with *Mac.* by GAWALEWICZ (1888, pp. 163–280), BRANDL (1922, pp. 397–8), KNIGHT (1931; 1965, pp. 327–42), MASON (1966; 1970, pp. 257–60), WILLSON (1969, p. 7), BROWNE (1976, passim), LONG (1976, pp. 220–59), and VERMA (1986, pp. 838–52); with *Cor.* by DOWDEN (1875; 1877, p. 280), ELIOT (1920; 1950, p. 99), KNIGHTS (1959, pp. 143–50), RIBNER (1960, pp. 168–201), WHITAKER (1965, pp. 276–96), KROOK (1967; 1969, p. 199), ERSKINE-HILL (1970, pp. 38–43, and 1983, pp. 152–5), MURAKAMI (1970–1, pp. 28–55), SIMMONS (1973, *ShS*, pp. 95–101), and VINCENT (1978, pp. 90–120); with *Tmp.* by VERPLANCK (ed. 1846, *Ant.*, p. 6) and MARKELS (1968, pp. 171–6); with *Ven.* by BONJOUR (1962, pp. 73–80) and LEVER (1962, pp. 81–8); with *PhT* by KNIGHT (1931; 1965, pp. 349–50); and with *Son.* by GERVINUS (1850, tr. 1883, p. 731), CARTWRIGHT (1859, pp. 21–31), MASSEY (1866; 1872, pp. 481–2), COURTHOPE (1903, 4:47), HARRIS (1909; 1911, pp. 324–8), ACHESON (1913, pp. 198–200), BROWN (1949, pp. 216–32, and 1957, pp. 160–252), HOLLOWAY (1961, pp. 99–100), NANDY (1964, p. 194), SJÖBERG (1975–6, pp. 11–12), FERRARA (1977, pp. 34–49), ALVIS (1978, p. 197), ESTRIN (1982, pp. 177–88), and COOK (1986, pp. 72–88).

As for non-Shn. works, there are comparisons with Aeschylus's *Oresteia* by CLAY (1844, pp. 12–13) and WHALLON (1980, pp. 127–32); with Euripides's *Bacchae* by VATKE (1869, pp. 82–3) and JEPSEN (1953, pp. 95–101); with Plato's *Symposium* by MacCALLUM (1910, pp. 445–53); with Dante by QUINONES (1968, pp. 275–6); with *The Castle of Perseverance* by STROUP (1964, p. 296); with Grimald's *Archipropheta* by BLACKBURN (1971, p. 98); with Drayton's *Mortimeriados* by FRIEDMAN (1969, pp. 481–4); with Chapman's *Bussy D'Ambois* by IDE (1980, pp. 128–31); with Ford's *The Broken Heart* by HAPGOOD (1971, pp. 5–6); with Webster's *The Duchess of Malfi* by BRODWIN (1971, p. 252); with Scève's *Délie* by MOURGUES (1976, pp. 73–9); with Racine's *Bérénice* by WHATLEY (1974–5, pp. 96–114);

with Milton's *Paradise Lost* by L. D. (1900, pp. 377–81) and SCHANZER (1963, pp. 149–50) and with *Samson Agonistes* by DOWDEN (1875; 1877, p. 315), FRYE (1968, pp. 139–46), and CAMÉ (1977, pp. 69–70, responding to BLONDEL, 1977, p. 162); with Dryden's *All for Love* by ANON. (1747, pp. 41–2), HILL (1759, pp. 35–6), SCOTT (1808; 1883, 5:307–15), DELIUS (1869, pp. 22–3), HANNMANN (1903, passim), DOBRÉE (1928, pp. 717–18), LEAVIS (1936, pp. 158–69), WALLERSTEIN (1943, pp. 170–1), KLEINSCHMIT VON LENGEFELD (1951, pp. 88–106), MCCUTCHION (1961, pp. 46–64), QUENNELL (1963, pp. 290–2), HOPE (1965, pp. 144–65), PALMER (1965, pp. 8–9), SCHARF (1970, pp. 53–96), NELSON (1972, pp. 42–7), NOVAK (1978, pp. 375–87), and SHIMIZU (1982, pp. 59–74); with Pope's *The Rape of the Lock* by BARKER (1975, p. 39); with Goethe's *The Singer's Book* and Keats's "Fame" by KNIGHT (1931; 1965, pp. 346–8); with Brontë's *Wuthering Heights* and Joyce's *Ulysses* by GRIFFITHS (1945, pp. 40–3); with Dostoyevski's *The Brothers Karamazov* by LANDAUER (1920; 1962, pp. 311–12); with James's *The Ambassadors* by COURSEN (1961, pp. 382–4) and KNOEPFLMACHER (1965, pp. 333–44); with Tennyson's "A Dream of Fair Women" by MADDEN (1968, pp. 416–17); with Ibsen's *Rosmersholm* by DURBACH (1986, pp. 1–16); with Shaw's *Caesar and Cleopatra* by SHAW himself (1900; 1931, 31:xxvii–xxxvi) and REHBACH (1916, pp. 117–34); with Claudel's *Le soulier de satin* by ERWIN (1974, pp. 65–77); with D'Annunzio's *Francesca da Rimini* by BLANCO (1952, pp. 414–44); with Shawqi's *The Death of Cleopatra* by YAGHMOUR (1986, pp. 7–24); with Natsume Soseki's *Gubijinso* by MORIYA (1959, pp. 1–12); with Anouilh's *The Lark* and Wilder's *Our Town* by MCMANAWAY (1962, pp. 1–5); with Lawrence's *Lady Chatterley's Lover* by MENDEL (1968, pp. 52–60); and with Plath's "Edge" by ACHARYA (1979, pp. 54–7).

Genre

TRAGEDY

Critics disagree as to whether *Ant.* is a tragedy (F1's designation) or a history and —if it is a tragedy—where its tragic quality lies. HAZLITT (1817; 1930, 4:306), commenting on *Jn.*, asserts that "the actual truth of the particular events, in proportion as we are conscious of it, is a drawback on the pleasure as well as the dignity of tragedy." JAMESON (1832; 1879, p. 253) responds that historical reality heightens the "moral effect" of tragedy: that "the arts of Cleopatra" had a "real existence" makes them suited to be "a subject of contemplation and a lesson of conduct." CORSON (1889, p. 252), however, distinguishes moral from historical considerations: *Ant.* "is, to all intents and purposes, a tragedy, the moral interest predominating over the historical or political. The latter is, indeed, entirely subservient to the former—constituting a background against which individualities are exhibited." FARNHAM (1950, p. 205): "As Shakespeare proceeds with the creation of his last tragic world, he comes logically to that view of the tragic scheme of things which we find in *Antony and Cleopatra*. Seeing tragedy more and more as a product of flaw in character, he sees less and less of mystery in its causation. Then suddenly the mysteries of evil and injustice cease to challenge him." Aware of the lovers' nobility, HOPE (1965, p. 151) highlights the tragedy of choice: *Ant.* "is a play based on a genuinely tragic opposition of values to be decided by a choice having the seriousness of a public action of the utmost moment. This opposition of values arises from the claims of two different views of life, two worlds [i.e., public and private virtues] whose values are absolute, undeniable, and in the circumstances irreconcilable. To grasp the nature of the claims and the implications of the choice demands characters of superior intelligence and real greatness of spirit; to make the choice demands an heroic act of will only to be found in persons with the rare quality of magnanimity; for magnanimity requires not only personal capacity for it, but the position in which the public and the private virtues can be exercised to the full. It is this that makes *Antony and Cleopatra* tragic. The two principals have the nobleness of nature to match the choice demanded of them." And to BROWER (1971, p. 318), Antony's heroic nobility is tragic: "In Antony nobility is seen in its most complete form, at times glorified by love, at times debased by it, or defeated by a failure of the self. In Cleopatra love rises to nobility, and though Antony's failure is not brushed over, her vision and death renew our certainty of his greatness, and beyond that our certainty that greatness, though inherently tragic, is attainable. Shakespeare achieves this twofold purpose of displaying the tragedy of the heroic and the heroism of love while picturing love in its sensuous fullness and gaiety, and the heroic in its pomp and self-aggrandizement, even to the point of burlesque." Sh. brings "these all but contradictory aims to controlled and harmonious expression." It is (p. 330) "Antony's consciousness of self-betrayal, fitful at first and then flat and final, that makes him a tragic hero of the purest kind." Cleopatra's career, like his, is invested with (p. 353) "the tragic sense of the destructiveness inherent in greatness," yet since unlike him she never undergoes Dido's "passionate inner experience of lost 'reputation,'" it is "Antony alone who is a truly tragic figure in the tradition of ancient and Renaissance heroic tragedy."

CAMPBELL (1904, p. 189) comments on the tragic end: "The countryman who brings the asp to Cleopatra [3492 ff.] bears those traces of rusticity of which Shakespeare's audience were so fond, yet the tragic burden of his basket of figs may well check the rising merriment that would else have marred the pathos of the close. . . . But for this half page, the drama from Act III. sc. ix. to the end has a purely tragic effect that is unequalled except in Shakespeare." So does BARTON (1973, pp. 18–19), discussing the redemption of both lovers' moral flaws in Cleopatra's death: "Cleopatra dies perfectly, as a tragedy queen. In doing so, she not only redeems the bungled and clumsy nature of Antony's death in Act IV by catching it up and transforming it within her own, flawless farewell; she crystallises and stills all the earlier and more ambiguous tableaux of the play—Cydnus, her appearance throned in gold as the goddess Isis, even the dubious spectacle presented to the Roman messenger in the opening scene. This is a divided catastrophe of a very special kind. Not only does it alter the way we feel about the previous development of the tragedy, hushing our doubts about Cleopatra's faith, it makes us understand something about historical process. After all, there does seem to have been something about Cleopatra's death as the story [19] was perpetuated in time that made it impossible for Cinthio and Jodelle, Garnier and Daniel, not to mention Chaucer and Spenser, to condemn her, whatever the overall moral pattern of the poem or play in which she appeared. There are no satirical comedies about Antony's infatuation with an Egyptian whore."

For SIEMON's (1973, p. 317) view of *Ant.*'s merging of personal and political tragedy, see p. 616. Those who consider *Ant.* a love tragedy include BODENSTEDT (1874; 1887, p. 341), OECHELHÄUSER (ed. 1877; 1895, p. 89), MACCALLUM (1910, p. 341), RIDLEY (ed. 1935, pp. vii–viii, and ed. 1954, p. xlix), TRAUB (1938, p. 35), VIERTEL (1953; 1970, p. 29), and GÜNTHER (1965; 1967, 2:69); similar terms are used by RAPP (1862, p. 211: psychology of despairing love); by EMERSON (1890, p. 126), ETTY (1903–4, pp. 302, 307–8), BRANDL (1922, pp. 405–6), and MATHEW (1922, p. 274), who speak of "passion" tragedy; by BINDER (1939, p. 163) and THOMPSON (1971, pp. 143–5), who call it "romantic" tragedy; and by those who discuss *Ant.* in connection with other love tragedies, especially DICKEY (1957), MARSH (1960 and 1976), MASON (1966; 1970), and BRODWIN (1971). Others who discuss it as tragedy emphasize various thematic and structural considerations: BAKER (1907, p. 283: completeness of Cleopatra's control over Antony), ELLIS-FERMOR (1936; 1953, p. 267: assurance of transcendent nobility), LYMAN (1940, p. 104: noble lovers' loss of material happiness), WILSON (1957, pp. 176–7: ennoblement and purification through suffering), STEIN (1959, pp. 603, 606: Cleopatra's grandeur of imagination as opposed to sordid necessity), BRYANT (1961, pp. 174, 191: lovers' selflessness), WHITNEY (1963, p. 66: man's separation from mother goddess; psychoanalytical), KUCKHOFF (1964, pp. 417, 432: tragic conflict of Antony), UÉNO (1967–8, pp. 1–36: audience identification with hero), FROST (1968, p. 136: moral tragedy), IWAMOTO (1968, pp. 99–129: tragedy lacking pity and fear), ENRIGHT (1970, p. 118: sense of triumph and pleasure at end), BARTON (1971, 3:251–2: transfiguring triumph at end), LEE (1971, pp. 56–7: terror and pity arise at end), SIMMONS (1973, *ShS*, pp. 95, 99: heroic tragedy), CHAMPION (1976, pp. 240, 264–5: social tragedy, struggle between secular values), FUZIER (1978, pp. 69–70: separate tragedies of Antony and Cleopatra explain structural pattern), and BULMAN (1985, pp. 212–13: heroic tragedy).

HISTORICAL PLAY

Critics who group *Ant.* with the histories (not necessarily the Roman plays) usually do so to explain the loose structure. ROWE (ed. 1709, 1:[x]xviii) speaks of *Ant.* as a history play in an attempt to account for its violation of the unities: "Almost all his [Sh.'s] Historical Plays comprehend a great length of Time, and very different and distinct Places: And in his *Antony* and *Cleopatra*, the Scene travels over the greatest Part of the *Roman* Empire." Similarly DAVIES (1783, 2:367–8): "The simplicity of the fable is necessarily destroyed, by exhibiting such a croud of events, happening in distant periods of time, a fault common to histo-[368]rical plays."

WHITE (ed. 1883, 3:787) denies *Ant.* the artistic standing of tragedy: "This drama is properly a history rather than a tragedy. In form and motive it is much more like an historical play than, for example, *Coriolanus* and *Julius Cæsar* are. In its design there is no art. Whatever it has of moral significance or of ethical value and interest pertains merely to the actual characters of its personages, and the historical incidents in which they figured, and not at all to any special manipulation of these, or to any informing of the drama by the individual spirit of the writer. . . . Indeed, this play is, in its structure, little more than a very bald dialoguing of North's version of Plutarch's life of Marcus Antonius." ADAMS (1923, pp. 398–9), more favorably: "The play, though ranked among the tragedies, belongs in technique to . . . the chronicle. It is not designed so much to produce in us the emotions of pity and fear, as to excite our wonder. . . . It is in truth a splendid historical pag-[399]eant, full of moving armies, of battles on land and sea, of varied action rapidly shifting from Italy to Greece and to Egypt." Others who treat *Ant.* as a history play include GERSTENBERG (1766; 1890, p. 163), SCHLEGEL (1811, tr. 1846, p. 416), HAZLITT (1813; 1930, 5:191, briefly, and 1817; 1930, 4:228), KEMBLE (ed. 1813, p. ii), CAMPBELL (ed. 1838, p. lxi), CLARKE (1863, p. 217), RÜMELIN (1865; 1866, pp. 113–14), ROBERTSON (1930, p. 125), HARRISON (ed. 1934, 5:358–9, and 1951, p. 226), and RÜEGG (1951, p. 266).

A few see historical and tragic elements as fused. ULRICI (1839; 1868–9, tr. 1876, 2:205) notes that "the tragic end of Roman history" rises "to the general historical view of the whole." WENDELL (1894, p. 326): "If we once accept the conventions of chronicle-history, this play reveals an artist, objective in temper and consummate master of his art, who has told a historic story with supreme artistic truth; and the story, impregnated at once with the sense of irony which we have learned to know and with a more profound sense than ever of the evil which woman may wreak, is a story which supremely, dispassionately expresses the tragedy of world-decadence." BRADLEY (1904; 1905, p. 3) groups *R3, R2, JC, Ant.*, and *Cor.* as "tragic histories or historical tragedies, in which Shakespeare acknowledged in practice a certain obligation to follow his authority, even when that authority offered him an undramatic material. Probably he himself would have met some criticisms to which these plays are open by appealing to their historical character, and by denying that such works are to be judged by the standard of pure tragedy." For ALDEN (1922, p. 280), Antony's tragedy is acted out within a chronicle framework: Sh. "composed a drama which is at the same time chronicle-history and personal tragedy. In structure it reverts, in an extraordinary degree, to the old loose chronicle method. . . . Nor can it be said that the interest in this larger drama of the decaying empire is slight or mean. But in the midst of it we are led to concentrate on the tragedy of Antony." STROUP (1964, p. 290) believes *Ant.* "belongs to Polonius' 'tragical-historical' kind," taking its shape from the late morality play: it is (p. 295) "out of Antony's character-struggle, his psychomachia, that the tragedy develops. . . . The soul-warfare of the morality play is indicated." Others who discuss *Ant.* as both history play and tragedy include KOCH (ed. 1882, 9:245–6), SECCOMBE & ALLEN (1903; 1904, 2:98–9), QUILLER-COUCH (1922, pp. 183–4), HILLEBRAND (ed. 1926, p. xxvi), HORNE (1945, pp. 145, 151–2), HOUGHTON (ed. 1962, p. 8), and MUIR (1972, p. 156).

ROMAN PLAY

The series of Roman plays is usually taken to comprise *JC, Cor.*, and *Ant.*, rarely *Tit.* Comment is mostly directed to issues of political life, morality, classical learning, the Roman tragic hero, and the pagan setting, recent critics devoting as much attention to the heroic individual as to political considerations. Critics who group *Ant.* with the Roman plays do not necessarily call it a history play as distinct from tragedy.

SCHLEGEL (1811, tr. 1846, p. 414), the first to treat these plays as a group, admires Sh.'s art in transforming Roman history into effective stage drama: "In the three Roman pieces . . . the moderation with which Shakspeare excludes foreign appendages and arbitrary suppositions, and yet fully satisfies the wants of the stage, is particularly deserving of admiration. . . . Under the apparent artlessness of adhering closely to history as he found it, an uncommon degree of art is concealed. . . . The public life of ancient Rome is called up from its grave, and exhibited before our eyes with the utmost grandeur and freedom of the dramatic form, and the heroes of Plutarch are ennobled by the most eloquent poetry."

GOETHE (1813–16, tr. 1921, pp. 177–8), who finds a central idea in each play, disagrees about the characters' Roman qualities: "It is said that he [Sh.] has delineated the Romans with wonderful skill. I cannot see it. They are Englishmen to the bone; but they are human, thoroughly human, and thus the Roman toga presumably fits them. . . . [*178*] It would be hard to find a poet each of whose works was more thoroughly pervaded by a definite and effective idea than his.

"Thus *Coriolanus* is permeated by the idea of anger at the refusal of the lower classes to recognize the superiority of their betters. In *Julius Cæsar* everything hinges on the idea that the upper classes are not willing to see the highest place in the State occupied, since they wrongly imagine that they are able to act together. *Antony and Cleopatra* expresses with a thousand tongues the idea that pleasure and action are ever incompatible."

ULRICI (1839; 1868–9, tr. 1876, 2:183, 201–3, 205) considers the Roman plays as illuminating constitutional history: Sh. has "divided his historical dramas into two great cycles [Roman and English], and dramatically carried ancient and modern history through the principal stages of their development. The first cycle of Roman plays brings before us the political life and the history of the progress of the Roman people (the basis of modern political life) in all its essential moments; *Coriolanus* gives us the contests between the plebeians and patricians and the progressive development of the republic; *Julius Cæsar*, the last, fruitless struggles of the dying republic with the rise of the new monarchical form of government; *Antony and Cleopatra*, the downfall of the oligarchy and the nature of the empire; *Titus Andronicus*, the inevitable decay of the ancient spirit and position of the Roman empire, in face of the Germanic nations, and the new principle of life which the latter introduced into the political history of Europe. . . . [*201*] *Antony and Cleopatra* must obviously be regarded as a continuation of *Julius Cæsar*; in the former we have the old times at war with the new, in the latter, these elements are exhibited in their separation, and become themselves engaged in conflict with one another. The oligarchy is restored, the Roman world is divided, and Antony, Octavius and Lepidus govern the empire. . . . *Several* individuals at the head of the state is an ever insolvable contradiction. An oligarchy, therefore, can only represent a point of transition, it collapses as soon as it has accomplished its purpose. The history of this decay, in the form of given concrete relations and facts, constitutes the historical substance of the drama; the necessity of the transition from the oligarchy to monarchy is its historical truth. . . . [*202*] History did not as yet desire the overthrow of the Roman empire, and therefore made Octavius its ruler. But even under other circumstances the first demands of history—which is [*203*] itself essentially action—are moderation, prudence and self-control. He who does not possess these qualities . . . is not destined to take an independent part in the great piece of machinery; it thrusts him off into perdition. . . . [*205*] The great Cæsar had to fall in order to make way for the little Augustus; this is the tragic end of Roman history, and contains the terrible truth which is proclaimed in every line of the piece." LLOYD (1856; 1858, sig. 14^r) is the first English critic who similarly describes *Ant.* as showing the transition to autocracy.

MÉZIÈRES (1860; 1886, p. 460, in French) comments, Sh. "does not neglect the moral viewpoint which he usually brings to bear on his conceptions. His three Roman plays resemble each other in the moral character which he bestows on them. He brings into conflict passion and duty, but in order to show that one of them is punished if it does not subordinate itself to the other." In a study dealing largely with characters, as well as with the play's relation to Plutarch, MACCALLUM (1910, p. 344) echoes Ulrici on the political conflicts uniting the series. DRAPER (1933, pp. 225, 241–2), examining realistic features of Roman life added to Plutarch, finds a measure of classical learning in details of local color but notes that *Ant.*'s dramatic structure is unclassical. Especially in *Ant.* and *Cor.*, Sh. presents (p. 225) "no significantly Elizabethan characters or situations," since he follows Plutarch closely. Draper observes (p. 241) that *Ant.* "with its carefulness of detail, would seem to be the best criterion of Shakespeare's classical learning; but, even here, it is broad rather than deep, and scattered rather than full or systematic; and apparently he made no effort to supplement such knowledge as he had. Indeed, a greater knowledge would have helped him little; for the use of it would merely have been a stumbling block to many of his audiences; and classical [*242*] dramatic structure, running counter to the strongly intrenched conventions of Elizabethan stagecraft, had already met its nemesis in the plays of Jonson."

PHILLIPS (1940, pp. 188–9, 204–5) views *JC* and *Ant.* as forming a "monarchic cycle" in harmony with Elizabethan political thought: "In dwelling upon the love affair the dramatist only [*189*] magnified one link in the chain of political events which runs, consistent and unbroken, through ten acts. For it seems evident that the political thinking of the later play, like the historical narrative, is taken up where *Julius Caesar* ended. . . .

[204] "With the accession of Octavius as Augustus at the end of *Antony and Cleopatra* the cycle which began with *Caesar* is complete. . . . The political action of the two plays, following this pattern, is not only continuous in development, but consistent in philosophy and conformable to the principles of political thinking about the nature and structure of states generally accepted in Shakespeare's day. . . . Out of the welter of divided and conflicting authorities emerges the one man who, according to the political standards of the Renaissance, is qualified to be the natural head of the Roman body politic. With nothing to indicate that the promise [205] of civil peace and order will not be fulfilled, the political action of *Antony and Cleopatra*, unlike that of the earlier play, can end conclusively and happily, for the normal state-structure has been re-established." However, Phillips is aware that the political action is (p. 203) "subordinate" in this "drama of splendid passion." BARROLL (1958, *MLR*, pp. 327–43), drawing on the medieval theory inherited by the Elizabethans of Octavius as the ideal ruler and of Rome as the providentially ordained last empire to rise before Christ's eternal kingdom, shares many of Phillips's conclusions.

CHARNEY (1961, pp. 11, 28), without ignoring dramatic context, examines the poetic style and image patterns marking each Roman play as distinct; see pp. 674–5.

TRAVERSI (1963, pp. 10, 14, 17–18) sees the choice facing the tragic hero as a link between *Ant.* and *Cor.*: "In both *Antony and Cleopatra* and *Coriolanus—Julius Caesar*, written so much earlier, stands a little apart in this respect from the two greater masterpieces—we are conscious of the smooth progress of a single narrative current, unimpeded from the beginning of the action to its logical conclusion. . . . [14] Already, in the series of plays on English history, political processes are shown, as the dramatist must show them, in terms of individual motives and personal idiosyncrasies. The same feature, extended and developed, can be found in the Roman plays. At the centre of the public scene there is placed in each case the figure of a hero who is faced, in his related greatness and weakness, with a *choice* the consequences of which are of decisive importance, not only for himself, but for the world around him. . . . [17] The political and the personal elements, which Shakespeare had elsewhere treated with varying degrees of emphasis but which seem always to have been associated in his maturing thought, are now brought together in a new and distinctively Roman vision for which Plutarch provided the foundation. The *whole* has become again, much as it had been in the English historical plays but on a vaster and more universal scale, an ordered society, at the head of which stands the individual hero, at once indispensable [18] to its functioning and needing its support, confirming by the quality of his public choices its unity and purpose. He finds himself obliged to choose between reason and passion, between the elements in his personality which make for harmony and fulfilment and those which lead to his isolation and final undoing, by forcing him to follow unilaterally a self-centred impulse. . . . The tragedy proceeds in each case from flaws in the hero's character, which reflect themselves in his failure to discharge the public duty which his situation imposes upon him; but, it has to be added, the failure itself is one which, by its very nature, vindicates the forces of unity and integration which his choice has spurned and, in one play at least, in *Antony and Cleopatra*, the partial passion which leads the protagonists inexorably to ruin is itself shown as possessing true nobility and a measure of transforming greatness."

SIMMONS (1973, *Shakespeare's Pagan World*, pp. 3, 8, 10, 13–14) is aware that the Roman plays operate in a pagan world seen in a Christian light: *JC, Ant.*, and *Cor.* "are indeed essentially different from Bradley's Great Four [*Ham., Oth., Lr., Mac.*] and . . . the most important factor in their integral relationship is the historically pagan environment out of which each tragedy arises. In all three of these dramas, a kind of problem play stands between the critic and the tragedy because the conflict of opposing sides does not, as in Bradley's Four, involve the struggle between characters associated with the clarifying absolutes of good and evil. There are no villains—no Macbeth, Claudius, Iago, Goneril, Regan, or Edmund. . . . [8] Shakespeare accurately represents Rome as a pagan world in which the characters must perforce operate with no reference beyond the Earthly City. All attempts at idealistic vision by the tragic heroes, all attempts to rise above the restrictions of man and his imperfect society, are tragically affected by the absence of revelation and the real hope of glory. Implying this historical distinction, Shakespeare views his Roman world with the cosmic irony of what that world could not know.

"The Roman heroes do not have access to St. Augustine's Heavenly City. . . .

[*10*] "In his Roman tragedies Shakespeare is at one and the same time recreating the historical reality of the glory that was Rome and perceiving that reality in a Christian perspective. . . .

[*13*] "As treated by Shakespeare, the aspirations of the Roman [*14*] heroes have the potentiality for absolute sanction when the proper relationship is revealed between the temporal and the divine. Without this proper relationship and the means of atonement, the Roman hero's vision is necessarily flawed. But the substance of that vision is never dramatically rejected even though in the tragic blindness of the human condition the virtue can only be paradoxical. To discard the vision would be to discard the aspiration in man that traditionally proved his essential alienation from the imperfections of the world and his distinction among the creatures: [quotes 'Kingdomes . . . Man', 46–7]." See also SIMMONS (1985, 2:480–3).

CANTOR (1976, pp. 128, 132, 208) compares the armed city state of *Cor.* to *Ant.*'s rootless world of non-political desires: "To understand why Antony apparently prefers a life of love rather than politics, one must consider how the terms of his choice have changed since the time of the Republic. In the Empire, the rewards of public life begin to look hollow, whereas private life [i.e., eros] seems to offer new sources of satisfaction. . . . The Imperial regime works to discourage spiritedness and encourage eros, or, more accurately expressed, by removing the premium the Republic places on spiritedness, the Empire sets eros free with a new power. . . . [*132*] As long as the city lives under the constant threat of war, the common good is evident, at least in its most rudimentary form: the Romans realize they need each other if only to protect themselves. But once the threat of war is removed, private interests and appetites have the chance to assert themselves, unhindered by the need to unite the community against common enemies. One might in fact trace the absence of any references to the common good of Rome in *Antony and Cleopatra* to the absence of any common enemies for Romans [i.e., as a whole]. . . . [*208*] It is above all the cosmopolitan setting of *Antony and Cleopatra* that is responsible for the impression of universality the play makes, and this expansiveness is but the reverse side of *Coriolanus'* restriction to the narrow horizons of a single polis. Both plays revolve around the same issue, namely, what is meant by being bounded by the city and what is meant by being free of it, or, alternatively phrased, what is meant by being rooted in the city and what is meant by being uprooted from it. . . . The plays thus approach from different angles the one problem of the relationship of the city and man."

And ALVIS (1977, pp. 69–70, 72–3), opposing CHARNEY's (1961, p. 207) view that the Roman plays differ in tone, style, theme, purpose, and handling of subject, compares them to the major tragedies and finds within the Roman group strong intrinsic similarities: "The Roman protagonists are not speculative men (not even Brutus), nor do they often have opportunity to engage in prolonged exercises of private introspection. Their life is lived out in a public arena where hortatory rather than deliberative rhetoric prevails. This emphasis on public display is especially characteristic of *Julius Caesar* and *Coriolanus*, but we find it also in *Antony and Cleopatra*. Although the action presents lovers contending against their fate, neither Cleopatra nor Antony dwell upon questions concerning the nature of love itself. Unlike the protagonists of the major tragedies who universalize their particular dilemmas, Shakespeare's Roman heroes remain closely tied to their particular circumstances. The philosophical comments given by the plays are made, so to speak, at one remove since there are no adequate spokesmen among the dramatis personae. And Shakespeare's moral judgments are rendered at the expense of the central [*70*] characters. Being but little aware of the meaning of their own activities the protagonists must be viewed with considerable irony. If the heroes of the major tragedies lack full understanding of their world, as I suppose they do, the Roman characters suffer a more damaging disability in that they steadfastly refuse even the attempt to see themselves clearly. They display unreflective minds, temperamentally indisposed to self-assessment in terms of principle. . . . In *Hamlet, Macbeth, Othello* and *Lear* all the calamities suffered in the course of the play do in fact arise from some act of obvious moral wrong-doing; but in the Roman plays ignorance and intellectual misconceptions, rather than conscious malice, cause the ills that befall society and individuals.

"Limitations of intellect are less disturbing to the contemplating observer than displays of bad will. Perhaps for this reason the mood of the Roman plays seems relatively detached, even studiously distant, compared to the anguish of the dramas by which Shakespeare is principally known. . . .

[*72*] "The Roman plays also explore the consequences of self-regard, but theirs

is a different kind of scrutiny resembling Marlowe's and Chapman's depiction of Titanic figures who seek to assert their nobility against an ignoble, or at least unglamorous, society. Like Chapman's Bussy, Shakespeare's Roman heroes die in this effort, attesting by their deaths to a grandeur and purity of purpose which cannot be matched by their opponents. They are extraordinary beings, in spiritual amplitude superior to their society. Yet they are all tragically limited, and the fact that they are all limited in the same way indicates the precise direction of Shakespeare's interpretation of antique heroism. . . . The three Roman plays make similar statements upon the consequences of living for self-glory. . . .

[73] "The Roman protagonists exemplify a common failure of perception which significantly limits their achievement. . . . Brutus' statesmanship, Coriolanus' magnanimity, Cleopatra's and Antony's love are fundamentally misconceived. . . . [The lovers] achieve glory over a paltry, unbeglamored Caesar, [but] they lose the good attained by the less self-conscious lovers of the comedies. . . . Rome appears to stand for a radically defective view of human virtue, an aberrant *paideia*. The plays which Shakespeare made from Plutarchian history proclaim his purpose of testing the eligibility of the secular humanist premises underlying Renaissance enthusiasm for Rome." See also ALVIS (1979, pp. 115–34).

DOLLIMORE (1983, pp. 204–17) argues that *Ant.* and *Cor.*, staged in a period when the aristocracy's power declined, (p. 204) "effect a sceptical interrogation" of notions of honor and *virtus* as martial ideals; in *Ant.* the lovers' (p. 217) "sexual infatuation" transfers the desire for power (p. 216) "from the battlefield to the bed" (similarly CANTOR, 1976, pp. 187, 192–203).

GOLDBERG (1983, p. 165) believes the Roman plays reflect James I's "sense of himself as royal actor" and sees Antony as a hero in whom "the absolutism that James espoused in his own self-division is tragically revealed."

Others who comment on *Ant.* as a Roman play include RUSKIN (1865; 1905, 18:112, and 1883–6; 1908, 33:215), STAPFER (1879, tr. 1880, especially p. 424), KOCH (ed. 1882, 9:4), BRINCKER (1884, pp. 159–60), EMERSON (1890, pp. 72–7), MOULTON (1903; 1907, pp. 111–13), WOLFF (1907; 1913, 2:255–6), MEINCK (1910, pp. 10–16, 31–6, 46–7, 52–3), HIRZEL (1912, pp. 140–3), LANGE (1920), LEVI (1925, pp. 291–4), GILLET (1930, p. 241), HEUER (1938, pp. 75–84), GLUNZ (1940, pp. 61–2), CHAMBRUN (1947, p. 387), TACHIBANA (1947; 1948, passim), GODDARD (1951, 2:207–8), SEWELL (1951, p. 125), WALKER (1951, pp. 287–93), EVANS (1952; 1964, pp. 185–200), SCHILLING (1953, pp. 222–3), SISSON (1960, pp. 133–9), HANEA (1961, pp. 429–50), AHERN (1963), SPENCER (1963, pp. 28–38), BULLOUGH (1964, "Shakespeare's Roman Plays," pp. 1–8), NOEL (1965, pp. 186–9), BIANCHI (1970, passim), ALVIS (1973, pp. 247–353), MUIR (1974, pp. 45–63), PAYNE (1974, p. 56), ZEEVELD (1974, pp. 138–9), POWELL (1975, pp. 166–224), PLATT (1976, pp. 246–61), KRANZ (1977, passim, and 1982, pp. 371–80), SPEAIGHT (1977, pp. 308–21), GREEN (1979, pp. 243–57), MIOLA (1983, pp. 116–63), and SIEGEL (1986, pp. 117–20, 129–32).

TRAGEDY AND COMEDY

Noted early, the mingling of tragic and comic in *Ant.* becomes an important concern of critics only in the 20th c. BRATHWAIT (1631, pp. 196–7), the first to comment, issues a warning to gentlewomen: "Be your actions neuer so darkely shrouded, nor your amorous encounters cunningly carried; there will be euer some priuate Pencill to portray them, some quicke-sighted eye to display them. Loues en-[*197*]teruiew betwixt *Cleopatra* and *Marke Anthony*, promised to it selfe as much secure freedome as fading fancy could tender; yet the last Scene clozed all those Comicke passages with a Tragicke conclusion." BETTINELLI (1788; 1799, 5:309, in Italian), a Voltairean, frowns at comic buffoonery in *Ant.*: "I find the English taste brutal. . . . The great tragedian Shakespeare . . . has, in *Cleopatra*, Augustus, Antony, Lepidus, Pompey, Agrippa, and Maecenas drink together, singing songs in chorus, intoxicated as they are." TIECK (1794; 1920, p. 159) too disapproves of the comic episodes.

KNIGHT (1931; 1965, p. 254) is the first who is sensitive to the comic element: "Antony and Cleopatra are both essentially sportive. There is, indeed, sometimes a delicate, sometimes a boisterous humour running throughout. The spirit of the romantic comedies is here blended with tragedy. . . . We touch that peculiar quality, whereby the elements of this drama are transformed by a clear yet altering medium, a vision which sees its subject all levelled under a strange optimism, in which Antony's sensuousness is pure as a boy's pranks, the tragic agony of Cleopatra cleansed by girlish merriment." MACK (ed. 1960, p. 15), asserting that in tone *Ant.* may be compared to the *Paradiso*, calls the play "bright" as against *Mac.* and *Lr.*: "The humor of *Macbeth* and *King Lear* is either grim or pitiful: a drunken porter at the gate of hell, a court jester shivering on a stormy heath. The humor of *Antony and Cleopatra* is neither grim nor pitiful, although sometimes acrid enough. . . . We are encouraged by Shakespeare in this play to disengage ourselves from the protagonists, to feel superior to them, even to laugh at them, as we rarely are with his earlier tragic persons." EVERETT (ed. 1964, pp. xxiii–iv): *Ant.* "is tragic . . . in the expression of an irremediable loss, incurred consciously and borne responsibly. . . . And yet it is also comic, not only in the sense of containing the satirical or the farcical (for [*xxiv*] Shakespeare's tragedies also do that) but also in the expression of an ineffaceable lightheartedness."

For J. O. SMITH (1964, pp. 37–8), the comic elements shatter illusion without undermining the lovers' tragic nobility: "If there is any single great theme of literature this is it: the destruction of the *faux-semblant* and attendant illusions by the intervention, bitter or glorious, of reality. Tragedy works with this theme and is inseparable from it, and the problem of *Antony and Cleopatra* is that the lovers either do not have illusions or, if they do, never substitute for them other visions of their predicament. . . . In *Antony and Cleopatra* all exorcism fails. . . . Exorcism works to dispel illusion, but the poetry of *Antony and Cleopatra* works to create illusion. . . .

[*38*] "Comedy too traditionally penetrates illusions; it is the incongruity of

what is supposed and what is that produces laughter. But *Antony and Cleopatra* relates most immediately and most helpfully to comedy, since its tragic dimensions are attained (in Acts IV and V) by an excess and a concentration of emotion not anticipated in the earlier acts." Sh. (p. 48) "balances hyperbole with comic suggestion—the Antony as Colossus and the Antony as ruffian, the Cleopatra equal to all visions of herself and the Cleopatra raging at the servant who has betrayed her. But the counterpoint does not work here . . . to qualify the grandeur of these people and to cheat them of their incredible dignity. It works rather to suggest, by contrast, the range of behavior this dignity allows itself and the heights to which it succeeds."

ADELMAN (1973, pp. 49, 52), however, believes the comic elements do tell against the lovers' tragic stature: "The insistence upon scope, upon the infinite variety of the world, militates against the tragic experience. We simply are not permitted the luxury of the tragic vision: our attempt to see the universe solely in terms of the protagonists is continually thwarted. . . . The dramatic contrasts and the varied repetitions insist that we move among several versions of experience, among the comic and satiric as well as the tragic. . . . [52] The play is essentially a tragic experience embedded in a comic structure. In that sense it is as treacherous and painful as life itself."

SIMMONS (1973, *Shakespeare's Pagan World*, pp. 152–3, 156) suggests the necessity of comic elements for love's triumph: "The pure holiday spirit of Egypt encourages the radically comic, sometimes bordering on farce. . . . [153] The comedy of love is the basis of the protagonists' tragedy.

"Nowhere more than in the aspiration of love [for perfect realization of the emotional life] does the comic spirit emerge. . . . [Yet] there is potential for comedy as well as for tragedy in the discrepancy between the real and the ideal. . . . [156] She [Cleopatra] steps forward like the queen of comedy, arranging the happy ending of marriage and thereby winning the admiration and approval of the Roman world's highest moral sense. The comic purging and reconciliation take place to our delight while we are moved by the tragedy of its requiring the lovers' death." Their graves are narrow, but they win the height of fame.

PAYNE (1974, p. 80), however, thinks the play does not end on a comic note: "The lovers' apotheosis is for them a comic resolution. . . . But we are left with Caesar in a world of boundaries, a tragic world where ecstasy is temporary, occasional, and suspect." To LONG (1976, pp. 252–3), "the comedy of Dionysos dominates the play. . . . [253] The ribald comedy of disbelief in Rome is as much a part of Dionysiac life as is the lyricism of Egyptian passion. . . . The exuberance of laughter is . . . an intrinsic part of the exuberance of sexuality." Others who discuss the mixture of tragic with comic in *Ant.* include ANON. (1789, p. 20), SYMONS (1889; 1919, p. 5), SHAW (1900; 1931, 31:xxix, and 1921; 1932, 25:261), WEEKES (1928, p. 188), O'CONNOR (1948; 1960, pp. 170–1), MALEKIN (1957, p. 104), QUAYLE (1958, pp. 130–66), PROSER (1965, pp. 189–90), SIEGEL (1965, pp. 152–221), MORGAN (1968, pp. 128–39), RIEMER (1968, pp. 50, 57–8), SIMMONS (1969, p. 496), TRACI (1970, pp. 73–8), KELLY (1972, pp. 84–141), EVANS

(1973, pp. 34–5), PAYNE (1973, p. 279), CANTOR (1976, p. 183), DAWSON (
pp. 138–46), TOLMIE (1978, p. 131), VINCENT (1978, pp. 7–8, and 1982, p
53–86), and MANLOVE (1981, pp. 91–5).

OTHER CATEGORIES

Ant. is sometimes described as a mixture of numerous genres. Thus MACCALLUM
(1910, p. 343): "These three aspects of this strange play, as a chronicle history, as
a personal tragedy and as a love poem, merge and pass into each other." And GARBER
(1974, p. 126): *Ant.* "partakes at once of tragedy, chronicle, 'Roman play', 'problem
play', and even, to a certain extent, comedy. This mixture of modes is in fact exactly
what we should expect" of Sh. at the top of his powers. For a similar view, see
RICHMOND (1971, p. 166), DORIUS (1975, p. 89, and 1978, p. 296), and NEELY
(1985, p. 162), who is perceptive on the interplay of genre and gender.

Some suggest that the play transcends tragedy. MACKAIL (1930, pp. 88–9):
"It is a tragedy, but it is more than that. . . . [89] We might apply to it with
justice the term, often carelessly flung about or thoughtlessly misused, of a super-
tragedy or super-drama." And RIEMER (1968, p. 110): In *Ant.* Sh. "has liberated
from the overpowering, and in one sense constricting, world of tragedy a story
which contained ample material for tragic treatment. He has banished from this
play all those metaphysical and even moral considerations which tragedies (and other
versions of this story) possess, and he has, instead, made these tragic possibilities
parts of the play's dialectic. The result is a unique work of dramatic literature which
is able to deal with one of the greatest and most celebrated love-stories dispassionately, without ever becoming arid or unimaginative, and one which can contemplate
great historical and public themes from a purely human point of view."

Others would classify *Ant.* not as tragedy but as romance—or a combination
of the two. Thus STAUFFER (1949, p. 247): "In the sense that its protagonists finally
create their own glowing worlds, the play is not the next-to-the-last of the tragedies,
but the first and greatest of the dramatic romances." And UPHAUS (1978, pp.
310–11, 318): *Ant.* "has it both ways—tragedy and [*311*] tentative romance. . . .
[*318*] The fall of Antony and Cleopatra is only tragic to the extent that we share
Caesar's assumptions about time, the value of individual life, and the worth of
worldly possessions. If we do not share Caesar's view, as Antony and Cleopatra
finally do not, then we are left in the peculiar position, as Caesar is, of applying a
tragic view to two seemingly tragic characters who, in fact, disclaim every attribute
of tragedy, including death. In which case the Roman guard is absolutely right:
all's not well because Caesar, like tragedy, has been 'beguiled' [*358*] by an Alexandrian romance." Similar views include those of MARKELS (1968, p. 151),
ROHRMOSER (1971, p. 93), BRADBROOK (1976, p. 176), TOMOKIYO (1977, pp.
50–75), DORIUS (1978, p. 306), and GHOSH (1985–6, pp. 1–20).

STEMPEL (1956, p. 72) regards *Ant.* as tragical satire that treats infatuation
ironically: "Oscar J. Campbell has advanced the theory that *Timon of Athens* and
Coriolanus represent a mixed genre, tragical satire, which was modeled on Jonson's

atire (New York, 1943), pp. 198–217]. . . . Almost every
applies to *Coriolanus* is met by *Antony and Cleopatra*. In both
one is set in the first scene by uncomplimentary references to
h Antony and Coriolanus (not to speak of Cleopatra) are slaves
passion, which is revealed again and again by their actions; their
external. Both vacillate between 'unnatural extremes of emo-
y a divided loyalty. The deaths of the protagonists are not tragic:
Corio.... g automatically to deliberate provocation, is trapped into arousing
the mob which destroys him; Antony kills himself because of a false report of
Cleopatra's death which she herself has concocted to test his reaction; Cleopatra . . .
meets an ironically just demise [p. 71: 'What more fitting end for the serpent who
has fed Antony with delicious poison than to die by her own weapon?']." STIRLING's
(1956, pp. 182, 184, 191) discussion of *Ant.* as satirical tragedy is similar, as is
NOCHIMSON's (1977, pp. 99–127) view that Sh., as in *Tro.*, ironically deflates the
lovers' pretension to tragic status.

SCHANZER (1963, p. 183) considers *Ant.* a problem play (see also pp. 615–16):
"Though not a pioneer in any field, *Antony and Cleopatra* develops and brings to perfection methods and techniques used with less consummate skill before. It is by far
the greatest, as well as the most quintessential, of Shakespeare's Problem Plays."

And for KROOK (1967; 1969, pp. 199–200), *Ant.* belongs to a type of play
manifesting a heroic view of life characterized by Aristotelian *megalopsuchia* (*Nicomachean Ethics* 4.3), or magnanimity, a quality including pride, passion for honor, and
courage: "It is a different species of drama, remarkably interesting in itself, which
is represented in Shakespeare's work only by this play and *Coriolanus*, and at this
level of artistic accomplishment probably occurs nowhere else in European literature.
I propose to call it *heroic drama*, using the term 'heroic' in a sense patently different
from that in which it is commonly applied to Restoration tragedy or [200] French
neoclassic tragedy, and in a way which clearly distinguishes the heroic from the
tragic yet shows them to be closely connected."

Themes and Significance

ILLICIT PASSION

Critics since the 18th c. have often focused their attention on ruinous consequences
of the lovers' passion. GENTLEMAN (ed. 1774, 6:261), regarding Antony's fall: "A
double moral may be inferred, namely, That indolence and dissipation may undo
the greatest of men; and that beauty, under the direction of vanity, will not only
ruin the possessor, but admirer also." COLERIDGE (1818; 1960, 1:77): "This play
should be perused in mental contrast with Romeo and Juliet;—as the love of passion
and appetite opposed to the love of affection and instinct." SKOTTOWE (1824, 2:240):
Sh. "read the inmost thoughts of Antony; he has given them an everlasting record;
and the pages on which they are impressed, will long be referred to as instructive
lessons against the indulgence of the passions, and the sacrifice of the judgment to

the will." GERVINUS (1850, tr. 1883, pp. 477–8) sees passion as seducing Antony from duty: "In Antony [478] there is represented as the catastrophe in the hero's fate the faithless rupture of old and new formed ties of policy, of friendship, and of marriage, in order to keep faith with an unworthy paramour." And DOWDEN (1875; 1877, p. 307) describes *Ant.* as "a divinisation of pleasure, followed by the remorseless Nemesis of eternal law."

CROCE (1920, tr. 1920, pp. 241–2) sees *Ant.* as a tragedy of passion's over-powering the will: "The tragedy of the good and evil will, is sometimes followed, sometimes preceded by another tragedy, that of the will itself. Here the will, instead of holding the passions in control—making its footstool of them—allows itself to be dominated by them in their onrush; or it seeks the good, but remains uncertain, dissatisfied as to the path chosen; or finally, when it fails to find its own way, a way of some sort, and does not know what to think of itself or of the world, it preys upon itself in this empty tension.

"A typical form of this first condition of the will is voluptuousness, which overspreads a [242] soul and makes itself mistress there, inebriating, sending to sleep, destroying and liquefying the will. When we think of that enchanting sweetness and perdition, the image of death arises at the same instant, because it truly is death, if not physical, yet always internal and moral death, death of the spirit, without which man is already a corpse in process of decomposition. The tragedy of *Antony and Cleopatra* is composed of the violent sense of pleasure, in its power to bind and to dominate, coupled with a shudder at its abject effects of dissolution and of death."

For SHAW (1900; 1931, 31:xxvii–ix), who takes offense at what he regards as Sh.'s glorification of destructive passion, see p. 643.

Many see Antony as ruined by passion, including ULRICI (1839; 1868–9, tr. 1876, 2:201–2), HÜLSMANN (1856, pp. 225–6), MÉZIÈRES (1860; 1886, p. 460), CLARKE (1863, p. 220), RÜMELIN (1865; 1866, p. 114), VISCHER (1869–87; 1905, 6:158–9), GENÉE (1872; 1878, 1:347–9), KÖNIG (1875, pp. 248–9), STAPFER (1879, tr. 1880, pp. 390–1), BULTHAUPT (1883; 1911, 2:227), CORSON (1889, pp. 252–4, 260–1, 303), SYMONS (1889; 1919, pp. 5–6), EMERSON (1890, p. 126), FOARD (1893, p. 357), MOORE (1895, pp. 613–19), SHARP (1902, pp. 141–3), STEPHEN (1902, 4:35), MOULTON (1903; 1907, pp. 128–30), JUSSERAND (1904, tr. 1909, 2:263–4), CASE (ed. 1906, p. xiv), CHAMBERS (ed. 1907; 1925, p. 249), MacCRACKEN, PIERCE, & DURHAM (1910, p. 190), MASEFIELD (1911; 1954, pp. 137–8), SMEATON (1911, p. 445), KELLER (ed. 1912, 5:187–8), ALDEN (1922, p. 281), BRANDL (1922, p. 398), WINCHESTER (1922, pp. 66–8), PHILLIPS (1940, pp. 196–8), HORNE (1945, p. 146), CAMPBELL (ed. 1949, pp. 980, 983), REEG (1950, p. 96), CUNNINGHAM (1955, p. 10), BARROLL (1958, *JEGP*, pp. 708–20: discusses Antony's vices), WRIGHT & LaMAR (ed. 1961, pp. ix–x), MILLS (1964, pp. 35, 59), DRAPER (1965, *EA*, p. 232), UHLIG (1967, pp. 86–7), and ERSKINE-HILL (1970, p. 41); others who describe the lovers' passion as ruinous or morally corrupt include JAMESON (1832; 1879, pp. 271–3), VEHSE (1851, 1:274, 2:72), RAPP (1862, pp. 211–12), HALL (1869; 1871, pp. 252–3), TALBOT (1887,

p. 227), SHERMAN (1901, pp. 316–18), MATTHEWS (1913, pp. 267–9), DICKEY (1957, p. 177), KNIGHTS (1959, pp. 143–4), FROST (1964, pp. 40–1), BATTEN-HOUSE (1969, pp. 162, 182), and FITCH (1969, p. 229).

GOETHE (1813–16, tr. 1921, p. 178) introduces a polarity as the play's "idea": "pleasure and action are ever incompatible." SKOTTOWE (1824, 2:239) observes that, though Antony is powerless against Cleopatra's charm, his intellectual ability impresses on his mind the "deepest sense of his folly" (similarly SCHLEGEL, 1811, tr. 1846, p. 416). Many of the critics cited above expand these perceptions into an emphasis on the struggle within Antony between will and judgment, passion and reason (e.g., CORSON, 1889, p. 303: "The disastrous consequences of his insane persistence to fight at sea . . . cause Antony to rise to a deep and mortifying sense of his infatuation and enslavement. It is in representing the moral struggle which ensues that he is kept within the pale of our sympathy").

Some among those who see Antony as choosing passion add further insights. WIMSATT (1948; 1954, pp. 94–7): "There are two main ways in which a poem may approach vileness—that is, in which it may be ethically defective: (1) by asserting an unacceptable philosophy; (2) by approving, commending, or inviting an immoral choice or passion. . . .

[95] "A harder case is the second . . . that of a poem which embodies a clear approval of an evil choice and its evil emotion. An answer to the question how we are to find poetic value in such a poem may be suggested in the statement that on the assumption of a Socratic ethic we might have more difficulty in doing so. On the Christian grounds of an ethic of will, we may find the distinction easier. The fact indeed that it seems to us possible to distinguish this class, the simply immoral, from the other, the philosophically wrong, marks the great difference between an ethic where the virtuous man is he who resists temptation and that where the virtuous man is he who is never tempted. But once admit temptation, and much is open to us—a wide realm of motives which may be profoundly moving and sympathetic though falling short of the morally acceptable. We have a question of how much good can be the cause of sin. Here I would be strictly Thomistic. . . . The human sinner, so we are instructed in the classic explanation, does not choose evil *qua* evil—a contradiction, since *bonum* is defined as *terminus appetitus*. He chooses a lower good or one inappropriate to the moment—*quod non est vel nunc vel hoc modo bonum* [not good now, or in this way]. But of lower and inappropriate goods there are many levels, lower and higher, and in the gamut of human goods which in some situations the virtuous man foregoes, there is room for an indefinite range of complexity, richness, and sympathy.

"As a ground on which to explore this principle I choose the *Antony and Cleopatra* of Shakespeare. . . .

[96] "What is celebrated in *Antony and Cleopatra* is the passionate surrender of an illicit love, the victory of this love over practical, political, and moral concerns, and the final superiority of the suicide lovers over circumstance. . . . [97] There is no escaping the fact that the poetic splendor of this play, and in particular of its concluding scenes, is something which exists in closest juncture with the acts of

suicide and with the whole glorified story of passion. . . . Even though, or rather because, the play pleads for certain evil choices, it presents these choices in all their mature interest and capacity to arouse human sympathy. The motives are wrong, but they are not base, silly, or degenerate. . . . If one will employ the classic concept of 'imitation', the play imitates or presents the reasons for sin, a mature and richly human state of sin."

Like SCHANZER (1963, p. 163), who finds a morality structure (though not a morality ethos) in Antony's inner struggle, STROUP (1964, pp. 295–6) considers *Ant.* in the light of the psychomachia tradition: "At the very center . . . is the microcosm, the soul of a man. It is really out of Antony's character-struggle, his psychomachia, that the tragedy develops. . . . The emphasis is not so much upon *hamartia* here as upon the equally divided qualities of soul: [quotes 3146]. Certainly the soul-warfare of the morality play is indicated. . . .

[296] "Kept to the fore, his psychomachia helps to shape the drama. At the opening he is found deep in sin; like Mankind in the *Castle of Perseverance* he repents and reforms; like Mankind through his uncontrolled will he slides back, and recognizing his failures and his Queen's deceit, he despairs; but unlike Mankind, being deceived by the Queen, he tries suicide, then welcomes his punishment, and concludes his life by asking that his nobility and magnanimity be remembered. . . . Though his salvation may be left to the gods, their pattern of testing him is clear enough."

ALVIS (1978, pp. 185–6) asserts that Antony's and Cleopatra's conduct is to be judged by an "ideal of love evident from the sonnets and comedies" rather than by their standards or by Roman values. The lovers' artificial (p. 186) "erotic exaltation" causes Antony's ruin: "Contrary to Plutarch, Shakespeare appears to suggest that given the debased status of politics under the empire Antony may act nobly in preferring a life of love to the degenerate power struggle taking place in Rome. However, approval of the choice does not entail . . . an approval of the *manner* of the love; and it is the tragedy of waste caused by ignorance of love's proper end which constitutes the real subject of the play."

Some hold that the play, though celebrating passion, as a whole shows its hollowness, not its triumph. DOWDEN (1875; 1877, pp. 308, 311, 313–16) thinks Sh. demonstrates the "fact" of human limitations against all self-glorification: "The spirit of the play, though superficially it appear voluptuous, is essentially severe. That is to say, Shakspere is faithful to the fact. . . .

[311] "Measure things only by the sensuous imagination, and everything in the world of oriental voluptuousness, in which Antony lies bewitched, is great. The passion and the pleasure of the Egyptian queen, and of her paramour, toil after the infinite. . . . [313] This sensuous infinite is but a dream, a deceit, a snare. . . . Shakspere, in his high impartiality to fact, denies none of the glory of the lust of the eye and the pride of life. He compels us to acknowledge these to the utmost. But he adds that there is another demonstrable fact of the world, which tests the visible pomp of the earth, and the splendour of sensuous passion, and finds them wanting. . . .

[*314*] "If we would know how an artist devoted to high moral ideals would treat such a character as that of [*315*] the fleshly enchantress we have but to turn to the Samson Agonistes. . . . The severity of Shakspere, in his own dramatic fashion, is as absolute as that of Milton. . . . [*316*] Let her [Cleopatra] possess all her grandeur, and her charm. Shakspere can show us more excellent things which will make us proof against the fascination of these."

SYMONS (1889; 1919, pp. 5–6) finds in the scenes in which Cleopatra does not figure "a running comment of moral interpretation" and "a sane and weighty [6] criticism" of "absolute abandonment of everything to the claims of love."

Building on DANBY's (1949; 1952, p. 148) rejection of "love romanticism" in *Ant.*, KNIGHTS (1949, pp. 318–19, 322) sees Sh. as "placing" the lovers' self-exaltation: "Those who most glorify the passion of the lovers draw largely on the great speeches of Cleopatra just before her death. And although it may be argued that these great utterances represent a culmination or transcendence of what has gone before, the impression I always receive is that the part has been taken for the whole, and the total meaning thereby obscured. If we are to understand these last scenes fully, and with them the nature and meaning of the whole tragedy, we must read them with a present consciousness of *all* that has preceded them. . . . [*319*] In the great central scenes—with a deliberate avoidance of glamour—the dramatist seems insistently to demand that we question ourselves about the nature and conditions of the energy which the lovers release in each other. . . .

[*322*] "It is, of course, one of the signs of a great writer that he can *afford* to evoke sympathy or even admiration for what, in his final judgment, is discarded or condemned. In *Antony and Cleopatra* the sense of potentiality in life's untutored energies is pushed to its limit, and Shakespeare gives the maximum weight to an experience that is finally 'placed'. If we do not feel both the vitality and the sham vitality, both the variety and the monotony, both the impulse towards life and the impulse towards death, we are missing the full experience of the play. It is perhaps this that makes the tragedy so sombre in its realism, so little comforting to the romantic imagination." This view is questioned by SCHANZER (1963, pp. 149–50) and MEHL (1983; 1986, pp. 174–5).

DICKEY (1957, pp. 176, 179, 201–2) claims that Sh.'s treatment accords with the ancient literary tradition condemning the lovers as lustful, for all their "golden world": "We find very little in Shakespeare's *Antony and Cleopatra* on the insecurity of high estate or the inevitable decline of empire [as in the Senecans], but we find a great deal on the dire consequences of indecorum on the part of princes and on the terrible end of excessive passion. . . . [*179*] Traditionally Antony and Cleopatra are examples of rulers who threw away a kingdom for lust, and this is how, despite the pity and terror which Shakespeare makes us feel, they appear in his play. . . . [*201*] There is nothing niggardly about the world that Shakespeare has built for his peerless amorists to win and lose. There is nothing overtly ascetic, nor do we find any of that smug moral snobbishness that mars other plays about the lovers. Yet this golden world is tarnished; Shakespeare is always shifting his viewpoint so that each magnificent wayward gesture is countered either by a glimpse of its futility or

by a sober estimate of its cost both to the lovers and to
feeling as the Senecans wanted us to feel but did not suc
that the most magnificent love affair the world [*202*] has ev
fire in the night and like a great fire left sad ashes in the mc
and luxury of the play, its scale and size, shock us by a pai
mundi which other playwrights preach in vain follows upon our
the most glittering world conceivable lying in ruins." BARROLL
341–3) takes a similar view.

FROST (1964, p. 40) thinks a Jacobean audience would not   ... the
lovers' self-ennoblement: Sh. "through the mouths of the lovers, al...iost makes us
see the action temporarily from their view-point; but their view-point is never
constant, and their emotion leads to cloying sensuality, waste and death. . . .
Cleopatra's final speech must be seen as a miracle of self deception [ALVIS, 1978,
p. 197 calls it 'a recourse to the grotesque, which she mistakes for the sublime'].
True, she declares 'husband, I come' [3538]; but the Jacobean audience must have
seen the play in a different moral and eschatological context to our own. They must
at least have found it more difficult to accept death as a consummation of adulterous
love, or to believe that even the Elysian fields were open to a courtesan. The word
'husband' must remind them that Antony was anything but her husband; the wife
who truly served her husband's interests was Octavia; Cleopatra destroys him."

HALLETT (1976, pp. 88–9), seeing *Ant.* as a study of the effects of reliance
on mundane values, believes that Sh. demonstrates the vanity of erotic life: "That
Shakespeare should turn his attention abruptly from the problem of evil in a mul-
tileveled world [of heaven, earth, hell] to a study of man's relationship to the
mundane world at almost the very moment Donne and others were complaining
that all coherence was gone should not be surprising. . . .

"To a man used to thinking in historic as well as dramatic terms, the Rome
of Antony and Cleopatra must have seemed, metaphorically, just such a [mundane]
world—Rome, the paradigmatic physical world, and the lovers, the embodiments
of masculinity and femininity. . . . Shakespeare has observed and recorded—without distortion—the futile lives of these demigods stripped of their wings. As always,
he was able to pierce through to the fundamental issue—whether, spiritual love
gone, eros can support the weight of the world. . . . [89] In *Antony and Cleopatra*,
Shakespeare has given us an almost clinical analysis of eros, its power and glory,
but also its ultimate inability to sustain itself and those who venture all in its cause."
This view is questioned by VINCENT (1982, pp. 75–6).

To show how Sh. keeps the audience from accepting the principals' false claims
to nobility and dignity, STIRLING (1956) examines the subversive use of irony and
satire (pp. 159, 182, 184, 190–1): Sh. "did not 'see life truly and think about it
romantically' [SHAW, 1900; 1931, 31:xxviii], and . . . there is no meretricious
sublimity cast even over the ending of *Antony and Cleopatra*. Instead, it is engagingly
satirical throughout. . . . [*182*] When the protagonists self-consciously assume a
flawed stature [i.e., one whose flaw they do not recognize], the role is ironically
denied them; when they are simply themselves they achieve a subdued dignity. The

however, is qualified by satire which constantly keeps the tragedy within
...ds of moral realism. . . . *[184]* [*Ant.* is] a tragedy in which satire and seriousness are in continual suspension. The satire, moreover, is directed constantly at
claims of tragic stature which the protagonists assert for themselves. . . . [*190*] In
Antony and Cleopatra he [Sh.] offered protagonists who combine impressive qualities
with an artless and self-conscious claim to the 'nobleness of life' [47], which is
satirized almost to the end. . . . [*191*] The audience . . . perceives events not in
the manner of Antony or Cleopatra but of Shakespeare," who undercuts their pretensions. Similar statements on ironic deflation are made by STEMPEL (1956, p.
72), BRYANT (1961, p. 191), BATTENHOUSE (1969, pp. 162, 182), and BENOIT
(1976, pp. 3–4); see also ALVIS (1978, p. 197), as well as NOCHIMSON's (1977,
pp. 99–127) discussion of "deflation of tragic possibility."

Sh.'s relentless exposure both of the lovers' erotic appetite and of Octavius's
lust for power drives FITCH (1968, pp. 16–17)—even more than GERVINUS (1850,
tr. 1883, p. 725), who finds "degradation" pervading *Ant.*—away from the play:
"Unfortunately we have no deep sense of identification with either of the protagonists.
Our sympathies are not profoundly moved. . . .

"Moreover, the entire atmosphere of the play militates against any feeling of
intimate involvement on the part of the spectator. The conflict between Pleasure
and Power; the staging on a World which is coldly geopolitical and presided over
by a capricious Fortune rather than warmed by the im-[*17*]pulses of Nature or made
significant by the visitations of the Gods; the portrayal of a love that is doting, or
devious, that is without courage or honor or faith, that may exalt in death but only
degrades in life, that forever verges upon gluttony and lust even though at last it
may reach toward the sublime; the power of a perspective which thrusts out to a
scene larger than can be contained in any theater; the precedence of the poet over
the playwright; and the resolution of temporal urgencies into the bliss of an eternal
ecstasy: all these actions and values drive us to a psychic distance where indifference
and awe are curiously commingled."

With ULRICI (1839; 1868–9, tr. 1876, 2:201–5; see pp. 625–6), some claim
that *Ant.* shows private passion as public calamity. STEMPEL (1956, p. 72) summarizes: "The degradation of a strong man enslaved by lust to a woman who is the
embodiment of physical desire in its most attractive form is traced to its disastrous
conclusion. The point of the play, however, is that Antony is one of the contenders
for the rule of an empire, and that the morbid disease which has destroyed him
must be removed completely as a source of danger to the state." Others who discuss
this topic include MÉZIÈRES (1860; 1886, p. 460), BLUMHOF (ed. 1870, pp. 12–
13), PHILLIPS (1940, pp. 194–8), and BARROLL (1958, *MLR*, pp. 339–43). BRANDL
(1894, p. 185, in German) calls *Ant.* "a mirror of manners, not of course for ancient
Egypt but for the city on the Thames and at the time when the House of Stuart
felt itself pressed by its extravagance toward absolutism." And KÜHNE (1902, p.
12) sees austere Rome as corrupted by contact with Eastern immorality.

Among those who take note of corrupt political life and corrupt erotic passion,
GERVINUS (1850, tr. 1883, p. 725) finds the play depressing: "The poet had to

represent a debased period in Antony and Cleopatra; he did this in
historical truth; but this ought not to have prevented him from casting
a better state of human nature, which might comfort and elevate us amiα
degradation." Others who remark on the debased period include ULRICI
1868–9, tr. 1876, 2:204–5), HÜLSMANN (1856, p. 225), KREYβIG (1858;
1:463), BLUMHOF (ed. 1870, pp. 12–13), and GREGOR (1935; 1948, p. 399).

TRANSCENDENT LOVE

The romantics are the first to discover that the intensity and imaginative force of
love have an esthetic appeal that transcends ruinous lust and sensuality. SCHLEGEL's
(1811, tr. 1846, pp. 416–17) attraction to the lovers is strong enough to outweigh
his disapproval of their moral flaws (as well as of the play's diffuse structure): "The
principal personages . . . are most emphatically distinguished by lineament and
colouring, and powerfully arrest the imagination. . . . Although the mutual passion
of herself [Cleopatra] and Antony is without moral dignity, it still excites our
sympathy as an insurmountable fascination:—they seem formed [417] for each
other." HAZLITT (1817; 1930, 4:230) feels that the "grandeur" ("beauty" in 1817,
p. 99) of Cleopatra's death and the "strength of her affections" almost redeem her
faults, COLERIDGE (1818; 1960, 1:77) that the "depth and energy" of her passion
lessen his "sense of criminality"; see pp. 688, 690, for both. HUGO (ed. 1860;
1868, 7:21–2, in French) goes further "In the eyes of posterity as in Shakespeare's
the wife of Antony is no longer Octavia, it is Cleopatra." Hence "the intensity of
the passion is its legitimacy: such is the moral truth that emerges manifestly from
the work. . . . [22] They love each other; and such is the grandeur of their love
that we forget their crimes."

HILLEBRAND (ed. 1926, pp. xxii–iii) explains how poetic imagination idealizes
the lovers: "There *is* a glamor about the loves of Antony and Cleopatra, just as there
is a glamor about every supreme manifestation of man's nature. . . . [*xxiii*] The
world quickly forgets men of middling virtues and vices, but it is stirred by greatness,
whether in saints or sinners. It admires great haters, great robbers, great lovers, all
persons in whom the vitality of human nature is powerfully affirmed. This is not a
matter of moral approbation, but of imaginative excitation. . . . And of course in
every great love story, however illicit the passion may be, it is surrounded by
attendant qualities which everyone must reckon to be good,—loyalty, trust, self-
sacrifice, courage. Out of such materials the world has made the unforgettable tales
of Dido and Æneas, Tristan and Iseult, Lancelot and Guinevere, and has cherished
the historic loves of Abelard and Héloïse and of Antony and Cleopatra."

KNIGHT (1931; 1965, pp. 200, 225, 227) holds that the spiritual quality of
love in *Ant.* transcends the grossly sensual: "Our view is directed not to the material
alone, nor to the earth alone, but rather to the universal elements of earth, water,
air, fire, and music, and beyond these to the all-transcending visionary humanism
which endows man with a supernatural glory. . . . [*225*] The sensuously beautiful
is never developed for its own sake: it is a necessary accompaniment to a spiritual

love—but that love itself, at its finest moments, so far transcends the sensuous that all sensuous suggestion melts, like morning mist, to nothingness in its sun. . . . [227] This play is not merely a story of a soldier's fall, but rather a spelled land of romance achieved and victorious: a paradisal vision expressed in terms of humanity's quest of love." WILSON (1957, p. 177) too rises to hyperbole: "There is an enno-blement and a purification through suffering: an ennoblement for the tragic pro-tagonists; a purification for us the spectators who share in their suffering vicariously and in their triumphant reconciliation. Both Antony and Cleopatra are mortal and fallible, exceedingly liable to acts of passion, of human folly, and to the sufferings which they entail. They are also great human beings, true to the grandeur of their aims. These aims surpass the human measure and the protagonists suffer tragic eclipse; but they have lived greatly; they are not pitiable in defeat; rather, they achieve the utmost human grandeur in their tragic eclipse and in their deaths affirm for us the supreme value—in this world—of human love. Though they show us the tragic frailty of mankind, even at its worthiest, yet this spectacle is inspiring, uplifting, an affirmation, at the same time, of human dignity, of the dignity of the love of man and woman. It is not too much, perhaps, to say that the play contains the greatest affirmation of this value in the world's literature." BROWER (1971, p. 318) sees *Ant.* as portraying heroic love in the Virgilian tradition, ennobling both lovers: "In Antony nobility is seen in its most complete form, at times glorified by love, at times debased by it, or defeated by a failure of the self. In Cleopatra love rises to nobility, and though Antony's failure is not brushed over, her vision and death renew our certainty of his greatness, and beyond that our certainty that greatness, though inherently tragic, is attainable." Others who see them as ennobled or justified by love include RÖTSCHER (1846, Pt. 2, pp. 311–12), HERAUD (1865, p. 375), HEYSE (in BODENSTEDT, ed. 1867; 1873, vol. 7, *Ant.*, pp. vi–viii), VATKE (1868, pp. 334, 340), HUDSON (1872, 2:367–9), BODENSTEDT (1874; 1887, pp. 341, 352–3), KOCH (ed. 1882, 9:245–6), PEART (1892, p. 217), WINTER (1892, pp. 221, 223), MABIE (1900; 1912, pp. 271–2), FURNESS (ed. 1907, pp. xi–xv), WOLFF (1907; 1913, 2:266–7, 271–2), HANFORD (1912, p. 388), QUILLER-COUCH (1922, pp. 184–5, 205–6), DYBOSKI (1923, p. 24), BAB (1925, pp. 280–1), TOLMAN (1925, p. 161), RIDLEY (ed. 1935, pp. vii–viii; 1937, pp. 190–1; and ed. 1954, pp. lii–iv), WILCOX (1936, pp. 542–4), ALEXANDER (1939, pp. 176, 178), MEIßNER (1940; 1954, pp. 73–4), WOLFF (1944; 1945, pp. 106–7), CHAMBRUN (1947, p. 394), REYHER (1947, pp. 540–1), CRAIG (1948, pp. 280–1), POGSON (1950, pp. 107–8), RÜEGG (1951, p. 263), DAICHES (1956, pp. 5–6), MUNRO (ed. 1957, 6:1214), BEHRENS (1959, p. 37), FERGUSSON (1961; 1970, pp. 249, 257), HYMAN (1961, pp. 40, 50), McCUTCHION (1961, p. 55), MUIR (1961, *KN*, p. 262), HOUGHTON (ed. 1962, pp. 8–10), SCHANZER (1963, p. 148), BULLOUGH (1964, *Narrative and Dramatic Sources of Shakespeare*, 5:252–3, and "The Uses of History," pp. 112, 114), FOAKES (1964, *DUJ*, p. 74), SCHWARTZ (1965, p. 46), FUJII (1967, pp. 35–6), RIEHLE (1968, p. 145), MOORE (1969, p. 655), NICOL (1969, pp. 100–1), WALTER (ed. 1969, pp. 17–19), COLMAN (1971, p. 23), DUNBAR (1971, pp. 232, 242), BOSE (1972, p. 61), HAMILTON (1973, p.

251), Colie (1974, pp. 204–5), Grene (1974, pp. 34–5), Maxwell-Mahon (1975, p. 44), Yokomori (1978, pp. 83–98), and Weiß (1979, p. 169); Holloway's (1961, pp. 100–1, 104–5) argument that the lovers' search for nobility transcends lust is similar. Discussing Sh.'s use of Marlowe's "heroic idiom," Logan (1987, p. 15) finds that the lovers "achieve a heroic majesty in love as they die."

Those who, like Knight (1931) and Wilson (1957), see *Ant.* as affirming the glory of humanity include Wilson (ed. 1950, p. xxxvi), Nowottny (1964, p. 77), Hope (1965, p. 159), Mendilow & Shalvi (1967, pp. 242–3), Simmons (1969, pp. 509–10, and 1973, *Shakespeare's Pagan World*, pp. 162–3), Colman (1971, p. 23), Grene (1974, pp. 34–5), and Stansfield (1975, pp. 395–7).

Some believe *Ant.* celebrates love as higher than reason. Swinburne (1879; 1902, pp. 190–1), opposing moral utilitarianism, identifies Sh. with Antony as lover: "Even as that Roman [Antony's] grasp relaxed and let fall the world, so has Shakespeare's self let go for awhile his greater world of imagination, with all its all but infinite variety of life and thought and action, for love of that more infinite variety which custom could not stale. Himself a second and a yet more fortunate Antony, he has once more laid a world, and a world more wonderful than ever, at her feet. He has put aside for her sake all other forms and figures of womanhood. . . . [*191*] Shakespeare has elsewhere given us in ideal incarnation the perfect mother, the perfect wife, the perfect daughter, the perfect mistress, or the perfect maiden: here only once for all he has given us the perfect and the everlasting woman." Against her (p. 189), "all the glory of the world with all its empires . . . [*190*] are less than straws in the balance." Shaw (1900; 1931, 31:xxvii–ix), countering, sniffs at Sh.'s folly in glorifying love: *Ant.* "must needs be as intolerable to the true Puritan as it is vaguely distressing to the ordinary healthy citizen, because, after giving a faithful picture of the soldier broken down by debauchery, and the [*xxviii*] typical wanton in whose arms such men perish, Shakespear finally strains all his huge command of rhetoric and stage pathos to give a theatrical sublimity to the wretched end of the business, and to persuade foolish spectators that the world was well lost by the twain. . . . [*xxix*] Let realism have its demonstration, comedy its criticism, or even bawdry its horse-laugh at the expense of sexual infatuation, if it must; but to ask us to subject our souls to its ruinous glamor, to worship it, deify it, and imply that it alone makes our life worth living, is nothing but folly gone mad erotically."

Others acknowledge the splendor of Sh.'s celebration of love. Thus Stauffer (1949, pp. 233–4): Sh. "takes the classical tragic theme—the conflict between love and duty—and treats it romantically. The classic solution is the triumph of duty over love." Yet he "is no rational or mechanical moralist. . . . [*234*] He wagers all for love. Shakespeare is at one with Aristotle in holding that in the truly moral nature instinct and intelligence are in harmony, as in Cleopatra. But in this play he is a romantic rather than an Aristotelian in believing that if they cannot be harmonized, then instinct must be chosen." And Traci (1970, pp. 134–5): "Whatever the nature of love, the play asserts, whether sublime, holy, degrading, or merely comic—or all of these—there is something unreasonable, inexplicable, even magical in its essence. . . . Love's mystery or magic is all that can explain the inexplicable. It is, after all, a divine madness. . . . [135] However magical and mysterious the nature of love, the movement and tone of the play would argue (like Plato's Diotima) that 'the mystery of man and woman' is 'a divine thing, for conception and generation are a principle of immortality in the mortal creature' [*Symposium*, 206c]." Others who believe *Ant.* celebrates or glorifies love include REHBACH (1916, p. 124), RICHTER (1930, p. 145), POGSON (1950, p. 107), DIETRICH (1965, p. 200), MOORE (1969, p. 669), BRODWIN (1971, pp. 253–4), BIRKINSHAW (1972, pp. 38, 43), and NAUMANN (1978, pp. 428–9). To explain the celebration, critics sometimes describe the lovers as linked in mental or spiritual partnership: thus PEART (1892, p. 220) believes Antony is attracted to Cleopatra by mental "comradeship," into which "mere sexuality" hardly enters; MACCALLUM (1910, p. 446), by "elective affinity": (p. 447) "They are alike in their emotionalism, their impressibility, their quick wits, their love of splendour, their genial power, their intellectual scope, their zest for everything." CADOUX's (1938, pp. 89–90) view is similar.

The transcendent value of love is often thought proved by the lovers' deaths. SCHLEGEL (1811, tr. 1846, p. 417) suggests *Liebestod*: "As they die for each other, we forgive them for having lived for each other." MURRY (1922, *Countries of the Mind*, p. 26) similarly feels that "at the last the mutual devotion is complete," HOUGHTON (ed. 1962, p. 8) that "Antony and Cleopatra are genuine lovers, and in their death they are not divided. . . . Nothing in their lives became them like the leaving of it." Others who believe they die for each other, not for base motives, include HUGO (ed. 1860; 1868, 7:21–3), MACCALLUM (1910, pp. 451–3), SPENCER (ed. 1948, p. ix), WEILGART (1952, p. 63), HYMAN (1961, p. 50), MATTHEWS (1962, p. 177), NOVAK (1969, p. 23), FISCH (1970, p. 62), HAMILTON (1973, p. 251), MCALINDON (1973, p. 200), ROTHSCHILD (1976, pp. 423–5), and STILLING (1976, pp. 288–9).

Their deaths are seen by many as a triumph over mortality. HUGO (ed. 1860; 1868, 7:23, in French) suggests "the two lovers in dying have exchanged the kiss of an eternal betrothal. Between her and him, there is no more separation to be feared, no divorce possible." KNIGHT (1931; 1965, p. 262) goes further: "Cleopatra and Antony find not death but life. This is the high metaphysic of love which melts life and death into a final oneness; which reality is indeed no pulseless abstraction, but rather blends its single design and petalled excellence from all life and all death, all imperial splendour and sensuous delight, all strange and ethereal forms, all elements and heavenly stars; all that is natural, human, and divine; all brilliance and all glory." BETHELL (1944, p. 129) speaks theologically: "The strong sinner may enter heaven before the prudential legislator. In *Antony and Cleopatra* the strong sinners meet their purgatory here. They do not desire or seek it; it is forced upon them from without—grace which visits them in the guise of defeat. Changes of character inexplicable by psychological determinism are readily explained if we perceive that Shakespeare is applying theological categories. Earthly defeat is the providential instrument of eternal triumph." STAUFFER (1949, p. 248): "The asp brings Cleopatra 'liberty' [3487]. Death is not negation, but a liberation that finds new heaven, new earth, and an assurance of a reunion which alone gratifies immortal longings." And SCHWARTZ (1961–2, p. 557): "In loving each other as persons, in the full development of their mortal nature, the lovers have in a sense transcended their mortality. . . . Just as there is a shackling of accidents in love, so there is a bolting up of change in death. What we happen to believe about such matters outside the play really does not matter. In the dreamy context of these last scenes, we believe for the moment in the lover's intimation that there is forever and forever in love. It is as though the dream, now 'past the size of dreaming' [3317], has suddenly become real, and the actual world is itself but a dream." Others who see the lovers' deaths as triumphant consummation or fulfillment beyond mortality include WILSON (1929, pp. 63–4), GILLET (1930, p. 263), MUIR & O'LOUGHLIN (1937, p. 209), BUCK (1938, pp. 120–2), SPENCER (1943; 1961, p. 173), CHAMBRUN (1947, p. 394), FLUCHÈRE (1948, tr. 1953, pp. 258, 263–4), GODDARD (1951, 2:206), VIERTEL (1953; 1970, p. 28), PEARSON (1954, pp. 138, 145), SISSON (ed. 1954, p. 1124), SPEAIGHT (1955, p. 149, and 1977, p. 321), MC-FARLAND (1958–9, pp. 219–22, 224–5, 228), LERNER (1961, p. 28, and 1964, pp. 131–5), LEVER (1962, p. 87), MATTHEWS (1962, p. 178), ARTHOS (1964, p. 61), DYSON (1964, p. 637), HOROWITZ (1965, pp. 65, 67–70), ORNSTEIN (1966, pp. 45–6), FUJII (1967, pp. 35–6), MENDILOW & SHALVI (1967, pp. 242–3), BURCKHARDT (1968, pp. 279–82), QUINONES (1968, pp. 275–6), MOORE (1969, p. 655), MUIR (1969, p. 206), MATSUMOTO (1971, pp. 1–17), HENN (1972, p. 136), MORRIS (1972, p. 45), NEVO (1972, pp. 354–5), RACKIN (1972, pp. 210–11), LONG (1976, p. 257), MÜLLER-SCHWEFE (1978, p. 172), and MARCHANT (1984, p. 175). For a similar view, see GOLDMAN (1985, p. 132).

A few critics discuss whether the triumphant poetry in Cleopatra's death scene (5.2) is consonant with earlier parts of the play, where love seems more like dotage. KNIGHT (1931; 1965, p. 24) asserts, "Cleopatra's final speech is the outstanding effect in the whole play: dramatically and poetically. If we must be guilty of bias, it would be safer to start with such poetic splendours and remain true to them at the risk of lesser infidelities. Yet there is no need for that. We can find our legitimate pieces of 'ethic' and fit them into our whole picture quite easily—but only if we allot them a secondary, not a primary, attention; if we remember to read the parts with reference to the whole, not the whole with reference to one, arbitrarily chosen, part. In the language of imaginative interpretation Cleopatra is wholly 'good': that is she, and her play, are aureoled in completeness, assertion, brightness, all things positive and happy." KNIGHTS (1949, pp. 318–19, 321–2) argues conversely that the poetry of triumph is "placed" by the central scenes, where the value of the love affair is questioned; see p. 638. SCHWARTZ (1961–2, pp. 556–7), however, claims that Act 5 gives point to all that has gone before: "If we take seriously the 'moralistic' view of the play, we ought to find the [557] whole of Act V superfluous. The lust-ridden Antony has already died his fool's death—what sort of climax can occur after that? Actually, the last act impresses us with its extraordinary 'rightness'. We expect to see Cleopatra join Antony in death, of course. But more than this, we expect the manifold themes of the play to be brought into precise focus and given final statement." This final vision, epitomized by Cleopatra, leaves the play's world at the end (p. 558) "fully realized." And Harris (1977, p. 231) thinks the poetry of Cleopatra's death affirms "the value of the lovers' lives and deaths" even though their actions through most of the play deny it (pp. 220–1): "Putting poetry and action in conflict, pitting word against word, deed against deed, is the dominant dramaturgical pattern in the play. Within that overall pattern is a more specific and more artful design. While the actions of the lovers consistently support the condemning Roman judgments of them, the poetic claims for the magnitude and importance of the lovers' passion only gradually gain the credit which action on the stage can give. The poetry of praise makes us want to believe the lovers' claims; yet, throughout most of the play, we actually witness [*221*] only snatches and suggestions of the magnificence promised by the poetry. When the very carefully arranged presentation of Cleopatra's death visually confirms the values so forcefully expressed in the poetry, as I believe it does, we sense an appropriate and coherent closure." Grene (1978; 1988, pp. 13–35) holds that the poetry affirms the lovers' nobleness.

In the play as a whole the Egyptian world of love, vitality, and spirit is felt to transcend the dour discipline and imperial rationality of Rome. Knight (1931; 1965, pp. 269, 324): "The values of War or Empire and Love are ever twin supremities in Shakespeare; more crudely, we can name them 'efficiency' and 'sentiment'; more nobly, the great spiritual heritages of West and East. . . . [*324*] Our love-theme, which ranges equally through all the natural imagery, is shown as a force not to be denied, more potent than kings, controlling their actions by its own passivity. We watch the dualism of East and West, spirit and action, death and life: and all are finally blended in love. And it must be remembered that Eastern splendour is closely associated in Shakespeare with love's ideal, which ideal is often imaged as set beyond a sea: hence the consummate symbolic accuracy of Cleopatra, Love's Queen, at Egypt, contrasted with Caesar, empire-symbol, at Rome. Between these two Antony wavers. His final surrender to love and death completes the pattern of his story. . . . The final effect is a blending, a melting, with a victory for the finer, over the cruder, ideal." Bethell (1944, pp. 128–9), also believing "the choice which Antony has to make between Rome and Egypt is . . . heavily weighted by Shakespeare on the Egyptian side," affirms, "Antony chose Egypt, intuition, the life of the spontaneous affections, with its moral and aesthetic corollaries; of all which Cleopatra is the focus and symbol. . . . [*129*] The Egyptian values are affirmative; the Roman, negative or restrictive: the good life may be built upon the Egyptian, but not upon the Roman." Lings (1966, p. 85): "In the light of what the East stands for, Roman 'virtues' are no more than human limitations. . . . Conversely, the 'vices' of Egypt amount to a breaking down of the barriers of human limitations. In Shakespeare's other representations of 'the pearl of great price', the Divine Qualities of the Spirit are symbolized by outstanding human virtues. But in this play the stress is on the Spirit's incomparability, the lack of any common measure between this world and the next; and as a symbol of the celestial, it is the function of Egypt to convey to us something of the next world's elusive mysteriousness that passes human comprehension." ESKIN (1967, p. 62) speaks of "an almost mystical culmination at the end," owing to Sh.'s expanding Egyptian values "into a romantic commitment." And LONG (1976, pp. 228–9, 251–2): "Everything in *Antony and Cleopatra* [depends] on a romantic apprehension of the Dionysiac. . . . [229] I shall call the vitality of Egypt Dionysiac, and thus try to do justice to its fructifying chaos of fertility. . . . [251] Egypt's ability to generate such powers [of poetic and playful extravagance], with their attendant human qualities of sexual vitality and laughter, not only mocks the absurd pretension and juvenile insolence of Roman imperialism. It mocks all moralistics too, having in itself as it does the very essence of the Dionysiac which is seen by Shakespeare, here as in festive comedy, as a *sine qua non* of full psychic life. . . . [252] If we do not feel both the festal laughter of Egyptian lyricism [cf. KNIGHT, 1931; 1965, p. 254: sportive spirit as part of the lovers' view of life] and the ribald laughter directed at Rome we shall read the play more solemnly than it requires and miss the very essence of the vision of the Dionysiac which it has to impart." Others who describe Egyptian values as superior to Roman include NAKAMURA (1961, p. 136), HERBERT (1965, pp. 64–6), and KERNAN (1975, 3:440).

MORAL AMBIGUITY, DIALECTICAL TENSION, PARADOX

A growing number of critics, reflecting New Critical methodology, are aware that ambiguity and dialectical tension affect the interpretation of themes, characters, and structure. Early origins of such a perception are already to be found in the romantic period. SCHLEGEL (1811, tr. 1846, p. 416) is the first to remark on both lovers' ambiguous complexity: "In Antony we observe a mixture of great qualities, weaknesses, and vices. . . . The seductive arts of Cleopatra are in no respect veiled over; she is an ambiguous being made up of royal pride, female vanity, luxury, inconstancy, and true attachment." Many echo Schlegel but resolve the ambiguity by either extolling or condemning the lovers. BRADLEY (1906; 1909, p. 304), however, declining simple solutions, insists that both attitudes are evoked almost equally: "With all our admiration and sympathy for the lovers we do not wish them to gain the world." TRAVERSI (1938; 1969, 2:219), who believes "it is the play's achievement to leave room for *both* estimates of the personal tragedy, the realistic as well as the lyrical," traces the ambivalent presentation of the lovers throughout the play (pp. 208–32; at greater length, 1963, pp. 79–203). DANBY (1949; 1952, p. 130) perceives that "if it is wrong to see the 'mutual pair' [48] as a strumpet and her fool, it is also wrong to see them as a Phoenix and a Turtle," and FARNHAM (1950, p. 177) regards flawed nobility as Sh.'s concern: "The love of Antony and Cleopatra, like themselves, never ceases to be deeply flawed, however much it becomes capable of arousing admiration. It is like them in having a paradoxical nobility." Farnham does not believe (p. 180) "that the final effect of Shakespeare's play is a romantic washing out of the faults of his hero and heroine. Certainly the spirit in which he deals with their faults is not that of the preaching moralist; but neither is it that of the preaching romanticist who, because of sympathy for Antony and Cleopatra, would free them from the judgment of the moralist. . . . [*205*] Shakespeare's growing interest in the paradox he has discovered in deeply flawed yet noble character becomes very distinctly his sustaining interest in the writing of tragedy." CAPUTI (1965, p. 190) tries to explain why Sh. "both exalts and exposes the lovers": "It is in the lovers and their minions that we meet the tendency to embrace diversity, to fuse disparates, to take hold of experience in such a way as to feel all possibilities at once, to make every moment expressive of the fullness of all moments. . . . They [the lovers] are, in fact, their best selves even as they are their worst selves. Their approach to the data of the world is inclusive, where the Roman approach is exclusive; they find beauty in experience not by distinguishing one thing from another, but by unifying and harmonizing its multiplicity, diversity, and discord. The commitment contains tragedy, pain, and ruin, but accepting the world as it does, pleasurable with painful, lesser selves with greater, and grounded as it is in the assumption that such acceptance makes for grandeur of experience, experience with magnitude, it has no terror." Among others who stress that the lovers are both noble and flawed are W. B. C. WATKINS (1950, pp. 24–6), HAWKES (1963, p. 11), QUINN (1963, pp. 13, 17), YAMADA (1965, pp. 28–39), AOYAMA (1969, pp. 12–13, 23–4), SLATER (ed. 1971, pp. 10–11), and MILWARD (1973, p. 239).

Some see Cleopatra's death as counterpointing the triumph of love. BOAS (1896, p. 483) and BRADFORD (1898; 1936, p. 203) find her reasons for suicide ambiguous and, with JAMESON (1832; 1879, p. 254), her character enigmatic, but they do not consider the effect of her death on the love theme and on the play's end. BRADLEY (1906; 1909, p. 304), who does, believes that, since Cleopatra's glorious death is out of tune with her earlier conduct, triumph sours into disillusion: "Why is it that, although we close the book in a triumph which is more than reconciliation, this is mingled, as we look back on the story, with a sadness so peculiar, almost the sadness of disenchantment? Is it that, when the glow has faded, Cleopatra's ecstasy comes to appear, I would not say factitious, but an effort strained and prodigious as well as glorious, not, like Othello's last speech, the final expression of character, of thoughts and emotions which have dominated a whole life? Perhaps this is so, but there is something more, something that sounds paradoxical: we are saddened by the very fact that the catastrophe saddens us so little; it pains us that we should feel so much triumph and pleasure." KURIYAMA (1977, pp. 327–8, 349–50) explains the mingling of sadness and elation as felt by Bradley by noting that *Liebestod*, not necessarily a world-well-lost fantasy, derives pleasure from fulfillment of desire but also pain from the necessary incompleteness of fulfillment; as *Ant.* shows, one (p. 350) "can only attain partial happiness." TRAVERSI (1938; 1969, 2:228) stresses that Cleopatra's baby "will, in due course, turn out to be the aspic," that (p. 229) "the sleep, though associated with images of peace and fulfillment, will be that of death." NANDY (1964, pp. 193–4) also does not see Cleopatra's death as fulfilling desire: "The triumphant assertion of love at its [*Ant.*'s] close does not blunt the perception of what is negative and unrealized about it and makes it

potentially vulnerable to the charge of romanticism in the pejorative sense. . . .
Unlike the *Liebestod* [194] of romantic love, Cleopatra's death involves a wonderfully
realistic assessment of the objective features of the world around her. Shakespeare,
unlike Wagner [in *Tristan and Isolde*], is not enshrining Death for Love as valuable
in itself." For a similar discussion of Cleopatra's death, see BULMAN (1985, pp.
208–12). RIEMER (1968, pp. 75–6) believes Sh. "cannot allow his heroine to achieve
that fixity and permanence for which she yearns after the death of her lover: to a
considerable degree she has been able to achieve purity of spirit, to have distilled
the fire and air within her, but Shakespeare is still intent in reminding us that this
achievement is not absolute and perhaps not as desirable as it seems. Here [76] is
the play's structural paradox: the work has been tending almost relentlessly towards
this achievement in Cleopatra, but once its attainment is in sight, Shakespeare
withdraws from giving it the full endorsement it seems to have required." For others
who discuss ambiguity or paradox in Cleopatra, see pp. 692–3.

The dialectical tension of Antony's tragic dilemma is sometimes analyzed as
basic to the play's meaning. Though the ambiguity of his character is a commonplace
(TATE, 1680, sig. A4^v, being the first to speak of "all the Defects and Excellencies
of his Mind"), it is hardly considered unresolvable before HERFORD (1916; 1921,
pp. 41–2): "Antony is held by his serpent of old Nile in the grip of a passion which
insolently tramples on moral and institutional bonds, private and public alike; which
brings the lovers to ruin and to death; and which yet invests their fall with a
splendour beside which the triumph of their conqueror appears cold and mean.
There is no conflict, no weighing of love and empire, as great alternatives, against
each other . . . nor does Shakespeare take sides with either; he neither reprobates
Antony, like Plutarch, for sacrificing duty to love, nor glorifies him, like the author
of the Restoration drama, *All for Love, or the World Well Lost*; still less does he seek
to strike a balance between these views. He is no ethical theorist trying exactly to
measure right or wrong, but a great poet whose comprehensive soul had room,
together, for many kinds of excellence incompatible in the experience of ordinary
men. That Antony's passion for Cleopatra not only ruins his colossal power in the
state but saps his mental and moral strength is made as mercilessly clear in Shakespeare as in Plutarch. . . . But it is [42] equally clear that this passion enlarges
and enriches his emotional life." TRAVERSI (1938; 1969) stresses Antony's self-
deception and folly (e.g., 2:218) but also his (p. 221) "poetic 'redemption' " by
means of the "rottenness" in the world around him: "The over-ripeness of that world
is variously related to the personal tragic theme; if it is a fitting background to the
story of mature passion, which indeed springs from and reflects it, it also lends
point to Antony's assertion of the supremacy of his personal feeling. Antony undoubtedly gambled away his dignity as 'a triple pillar of the world' [19], but the
corruption and treachery of that world in part redeems his folly and justifies the
contempt which at certain moments he expresses for it." LYMAN (1940, p. 88)
regards *Ant.* as the story of "a Janus-soul in his perplexity and tragic downfall," a
"grandeur-delusion that founders a noble soul": "Like Hamlet, Antony cannot resolutely choose one difficult alternative and resign the other." For DANBY (1949;

1952, p. 151), both choices are sordid, *Ant.* showing "the 'man of men' [605] soldiering for a cynical Rome or whoring on furlough in a reckless Egypt. It is the tragedy of the destruction of man, the creative spirit, in perverse war and insensate love—the two complementary and opposed halves of a discreating society." And to MACK (1973, p. 112), Antony is both devoted lover and strumpet's fool: "Antony, ever attracted by the sweeping magnanimity of his nature to an imagined literary world of perfect devotion between man and woman . . . is set down in the slippery Roman world he has himself helped create, suffers deeply—but always too, like Quixote, a little comically—from the incongruities between the code he is attracted to and that world's demands, yet refuses equally to be discomfited (either by Cleopatra's treasons or his own), and in the end wagers with his life that there is a valency in the code's perspective, though again it can never cancel out the world's perspective, since both are true." DOWNER (1975, p. 253) believes Antony as tragic hero is faced with unclear alternatives: "The world of government is ambivalent, the world of love is ambivalent; and yet he must choose. And in either choice lies destruction" (contrast MARKELS, 1968, p. 9, who argues that Antony refuses to choose and thus transcends both). For others who comment on unresolvable complexity in Antony, see pp. 680–1.

Many feel that the conflict of values in *Ant.* is not resolved, at least not one-sidedly. PHILIPS (1887, 1:25) briefly states that almighty love, the play's major concern, is morally dubious and yet majestic; MORGAN & VINES (ed. 1893–8, p. xx) and HERFORD (1916; 1921, p. 41) go further, declaring that Sh. sides with neither the lovers nor their foes. For TRAVERSI (1938; 1969, 2:208–9), love's triumph and the exposure of folly interact: "Is *Antony and Cleopatra* . . . a tragedy of lyrical inspiration, justifying love by presenting it as triumphant over death, or is it rather a remorseless exposure of human frailties, a presentation of [209] spiritual possibilities dissipated through a senseless surrender to passion? Both interpretations . . . can be defended; but to give each its due, to see them less as contradictory than as complementary aspects of a unified artistic creation, is as difficult as it proves, in the long run, to be necessary for a proper understanding of the play." DANBY's (1949; 1952, pp. 130, 148) attitude is similar. SPENCER (1958, pp. 377–8) perceives that the paradox of values ironically subverts any one-sided interpretation: "A one-dimensional reading of the tragedy would seem scarcely convincing. Certainly a narrow didacticism, whether moralistic or political, gradually dissolves in the cumulative ironies and contradictions of character, plot, and catastrophe. . . . What we have in the tragedy . . . is the mirror held up to the disturbance of values when two large and incompatible cultures come into conflict. . . . [378] What Shakespeare precisely intended we can never know. But who is to say that an age which nurtured the art of John Donne would not have found itself even more at home than we with the cumulative paradox that lies at the very heart" of *Ant.?* Contrast the view of STIRLING (1956; see pp. 639–40).

SHAPIRO (1966) argues that the audience desires reversals of intense feelings as a means of lessening psychic tensions; Sh. satisfies that need by (p. 20) "sustaining a controlled ambivalence," that is, by (p. 30) "continually intruding satire, pain, and the world of fact into lyric scenes, thus restoring balance to the audience." Hence the play oscillates between the opposing values of (p. 25) "world" and "pleasure." BLISSETT (1967, pp. 151–66) discusses dramatic irony in *Ant.* as a device that emphasizes constantly shifting values by counterpointing them against one another. MARSH (1976, pp. 199–200; similarly 1960, p. 27) inches slightly closer to affirming love's triumph without ignoring its limits: "I cannot see this as an anti-romantic play, which denies any real value to the lovers' passion. I cannot see it as a simple romance either, which sees the world well lost for love, for the love that has been shown can only exist in the world. . . . [*200*] This play . . . concentrates on the worth of a love that is allowed both intensity and scope. Its tragic end is the tragedy of all close human relationships, for no matter how strong the love, or what obstacles it has overcome or over what suffering it has triumphed, it cannot survive death. But to love at all, this play seems to say, it is necessary to be fully alive, and since all are doomed to die, it is better to love and die than to be like Caesar, who will die without having lived." And ADELMAN (1973, pp. 169–70) is aware that no one "meaning" can account for the complex mystery of *Ant.*: "Literary criticism frequently assumes that the knot can be untied: that every work will have a single explicable meaning. But this assumption may be counter to the process of Shakespeare's art, which usually functions to suggest that our experiences are larger than the intellectual formulations in which we attempt to embody them. . . . [*170*] Comedy, tragedy, and romance are here distinct versions of life: limited and human attempts to understand the nature of an action which remains essentially baffling." Others who think Sh. leaves the conflict of values and motives unresolved include BAILEY (1929, pp. 188–9), DELIUS (1947, p. 76), GOLDBERG (1961, pp. 44, 60, 62–3), SCHANZER (1963, pp. 145–6), GRACE (1964, p. 122), NANDY (1964, pp. 173–4), SMITH (1966, pp. 190–1), NEVO (1967, p. 125), UÉNO (1967–8, pp. 30–2), EDWARDS (1968, p. 121), RIEMER (1968, p. 77), GIANAKARIS (ed. 1969, p. xv), LEE (1969, pp. 14–16), NICOL (1969, pp. 87, 94–5), BARTON (1971, pp. 249–50), INGLEDEW (ed. 1971, p. xviii), LEE (1971, pp. 31–2, 57), TAYLOR (1971, pp. 149–50), FRENCH (1972, p. 233), CRAIG & BEVINGTON (ed. 1973, p. 1071), MUIR (1973, p. 170), KERMODE (in EVANS, ed. 1974, pp. 1345–6), FELPERIN (1977, pp. 107–12), BEVINGTON (ed. 1980, p. 1284), ERICKSON (1985, pp. 145–7), MACDONALD (1985, p. 80), and HALL (1989, pp. 140, 155).

A similar view is that Sh. carefully balances opposites. TRAVERSI (1938; 1969, 2:211) considers the balance achieved in the opening scene characteristic of the whole: "The scene, in fact, by relating the political action to emotion poetically expressed, calls in the characteristic Shakespearean way for a balance in judgment which will have to be maintained throughout the play. On the one hand, Antony's readiness to turn away from outside events is given a certain weight by his first opulent gesture of triumphant love; on the other, that gesture is itself finally subjected to criticism, seen in its double nature as splendid and yet mean, a product of personal degradation. To bear *both* judgments in mind, refusing to neglect one in order to exalt the other, is to respond truly to the intention of the play." ROSEN

(1960, p. 147) sees *Ant.* as "a tangled skein" intermingling good and evil: "What people do is not always what they know they should do, and there is neither the illusion that the traditional currency of virtue will find conventional reward nor the delusion that evil will of necessity meet with retributive punishment. Opposing values and beliefs are very often held in tenuous balance because they are presented as having equally compelling merit." Hence Sh.'s "play world is not unlike the real world" (similarly CECIL, 1944; 1949, pp. 23–4; HAWKES, 1963, pp. 8, 11; BURKE, 1964, pp. 26–7; SHANKER, 1975, p. 211; and JONES, ed. 1977, pp. 12–13, 31). Others who comment on balance of opposites include MACK (ed. 1960, pp. 19, 21, 23), GOLDBERG (1961, p. 63), EAGLETON (1967, p. 123), RABKIN (1967, pp. 185, 188), LEE (1971, p. 57), BARTON (1973, pp. 6, 17), DORIUS (1978, p. 296), and GREGSON (1983, p. 220).

ROSEN's (1960, p. 147) view that in *Ant.* "good grows up together with evil almost inseparably" is echoed by FOAKES (1964, "Shakespeare's Later Tragedies," p. 109) and SHANKER (1975, p. 210: "It all boils down to a Manichean view that evil is essential to define good, that the energy of the one creates the other"). SHAPIRO (1975, p. 36) similarly sees the play's paradox in that "the destruction which comes about through excess necessarily precedes and is an integral part of the process of creation."

DANBY (1949; 1952, p. 132) stresses the ambiguity of both Egyptian and Roman values: "It is the logic of a peculiarly Shakespearian dialectic. Opposites are juxtaposed, mingled, married; then from the very union which seems to promise strength dissolution flows." The opposites are (p. 140) "Rome [p. 143: politics and policy] and Egypt, the World and the Flesh. . . . [*146*] Egypt is a force as universal as Rome—as hot as the other is cold, as inevitably self-renewing as the other is inescapably deadly. . . . Neither of these is final, because between them they have brought down Antony" (cf. BAMBER, 1982, pp. 46–55). Thus *Ant.* is (p. 149) "an account of things in terms of . . . the two great contraries that maintain and destroy each other, considered apart from any third sphere which might stand over against them." SPENCER (1958, pp. 377–8) similarly thinks Sh. "is neither Roman nor Egyptian in his dramatic stance. . . . There is no clear resolution in behalf of any of the characters, as there tends to be in the other major tragedies. The virtue whose feature the dramatic mirror shows here [in *Ant.*] is an as yet undefined synthesis lying [*378*] beyond both Rome and Egypt but partaking of the values of both." For CHARNEY (1961, p. 114; not unlike TRAVERSI, 1938; 1969, 2:208–9), Egypt and Rome form a "tragic unity": "Taken alone, the Roman point of view simplifies the tragedy into a morality play, and the Egyptian one transforms the tragedy into a paean of transcendental love. If the tragic choices in this play are between different kinds of rightness, then we need both of these views to understand the meaning of the action." And MARKELS (1968, p. 9) argues that instead of choosing between the Rome of public duty and the Egypt of private appetite, Antony "resolves the conflict by striving equally toward both values and rhythmically making each one a measure and condition of the other. . . . Antony grows larger in manhood until he can encompass both Rome and Egypt [contrast HOY, 1973, p. 62], affirming the values that both have taught him until both are fulfilled." The Rome-Egypt ambiguity is also noted by W. B. C. WATKINS (1950, p. 34), ALTMANN (1969, pp. 58–9), WERTIME (1969, pp. 1–12), HOMAN (1970, p. 468), and KITTREDGE & RIBNER (ed. 1971, p. 1325).

A few critics remark on the confrontation of flawed reality and poetic imagination. STEIN (1959, p. 605) thinks that, despite the lovers' folly and the play's tragic conclusion, the lyric tone of love's nobleness survives in that "the defeated possess their dream." S. M. SMITH (1964, p. 176) comments on the contrast of the lovers' imperfections and the poetic picturing of death as fulfillment. PROSER (1965, p. 234), who sees art as surpassing nature in *Ant.*, declares that Cleopatra's apotheosis "is a direct appeal to the imaginative sensibilities in spite of, indeed, because of, what we realistically know of both the queen and her lover. It is a question of art's perfecting nature before our eyes. Or to put the matter another way, it is a question of our 'realizing' Antony's and Cleopatra's failings in a new light, a light which reveals in Cleopatra's endless subterfuges and betrayals the transcendent variety and contradiction of nature herself, and in Antony's self-deluded loyalty to her, that impassioned devotion to life in its mystery which can make a man a hero." SHAPIRO (1966, p. 30) finds the audience led imaginatively into the lovers' dreamworld but also continually guided back to the world of fact. Expanding TRAVERSI's (1938; 1969, 2:224) discovery of "balance between decay and fruitfulness" in *Ant.*, LYONS (1968; 1971, p. 186) observes that the play "celebrates the infinity of love within the lovers' fantasy and confronts the inevitability of the decomposition of life into death. . . . Decay is accommodated and creativity celebrated." MORGAN (1968) thinks *Ant.* operates as (p. 128) "a conflict between imagination and reason," (p. 134) "a persistent struggle of the subjective imagination to impose its own fantasy on the actual." ADELMAN (1973, passim) discusses the way the play's poetry affirms the superiority of the imaginative dimension over the rational and the reality of action (echoed by COOKE, 1979, pp. 85–9). WILLIAMSON (1974, p. 215) and SCHULMAN (1976, pp. 155, 174) note that the lovers' imagination, though triumphant in poetry, cannot overcome or shape external reality. WEIS (1983, *English*, pp. 1–11) discusses the tension between rational perception and imagination, BULMAN (1985, pp. 191, 197) that between heroic hyperbole and diminished reality, and MACDONALD (1985, pp. 78–99) that between active command of language or imagination and reality. MULRYNE (1982, pp. 155–67) examines the paradoxical relation between solemn ritual and crudely inefficient stage presentation in the final scenes.

Others caution that the poetic imagination may be self-flattering fiction. Responding to KNIGHTS's (1959, p. 149) insight that the Antony of Cleopatra's dream (3292 ff.) "may not be fancy—the poetry invests it with a substantial reality; but it is not the Antony that the play has given us," GOLDBERG (1961, p. 61) asks, "How substantial *is* the 'substantial reality'?" and comments (p. 63), "If . . . the art embodies the light by which the action, the world of the play, may be evaluated . . . the action also casts its shadow back on the art. For the imagination (natural, or human, or both) that created Antony is given no absolute guarantee. Clearly, the reality may be said to be Dolabella's Antony as readily as Cleopatra's; and by the same token, the 'high order' [3636] of the art may be no more real or significant than the ever-dissolving flux in which it seeks that order, its images no more than pleasing fictions to flatter our immortal longings, our immortal longings no more than the insatiable itch of desire." HOMAN (1970, pp. 464–5) sees Cleopatra's fifth-act transformation from whore to spouse "by the sheer force of her imagination" as illusion: "Souls less given to the theater are perfectly right in calling an asp an asp. . . . The illusion itself is [465] a paradox since Cleopatra offers us not an empire, nothing as solid as Rome, but merely words, words, words. . . . If Shake-speare [in *Ant.* and *Son.*] views love impartially, both celebrating and condemning it, perhaps he may be equally impartial in viewing that imagination and the actor's skill which distinguish Cleopatra no less than her patent sexuality" (contrast BROCK-BANK, 1963, p. 34, and particularly ORNSTEIN, 1966, p. 46, who speaks of a "triumph of love and art" at the end of the play).

The play's paradoxes are sometimes considered from a Christian perspective. RIBNER (1960, pp. 168–9, 172) remarks on the lovers' sinfulness: "In these final Roman plays Shakespeare probed the paradox of a road to damnation which might be heroic and awe-inspiring. . . . [169] The destructive power of evil and the magnificence of evil are simultaneously displayed. . . . [172] Whatever triumph Antony and Cleopatra may achieve is in defiance of the Christian moral order, and that we should emotionally share in this sense of triumph while we perceive that it is rooted in sin is a reflection of the paradox which this play in its totality embodies." For KROOK (1967; 1969, pp. 216–18), Sh.'s view of love as both ennobling and destructive reflects a Christian consciousness: "It is distinctly no part of the pagan-heroic view of life to take sexual love as seriously as it is taken here. Plato repudiates it; Aristotle ignores it; Stoicism endures it; and all the pagan moralists treat it as appetite plain and simple. . . . The conception of sexual love as a marriage of true minds, as admitting of a dimension other than the purely carnal, comes to Shakespeare not from any pagan source but from the Romance tradition of medieval and Renaissance Europe." Besides the high seriousness and the Romance tradition, however, there is also (p. 217) "the more specifically 're-naissance' element" of "uninhibited sensuality," the " 'renaissance' of the body and the senses."

Yet the glory of love in mind and body is offset (p. 218): "The obverse side is the sense of loss [quotes 2784–5] which the contemplated spectacle induces in the developed Christian mind. Remembering Plutarch, one sees how much simpler it all was for the pagan consciousness, which contrived to keep the two sides perfectly separate and distinct, contenting itself with a matter-of-fact recital of the events, laced with some straight and simple moralizing about the pity of it. For the Christian sensibility, the matter is altogether more complex: its awareness of the beauty and splendor of sexual passion is persistently interfused with the knowledge of its de-structive power; and it is this double consciousness, operating simultaneously, of which the true pagan has no experience, that is the primary symptom of the radical ambiguity of the play." And FICHTER (1980, pp. 99–100, 103, 110) argues that the ambivalent presentation of both love and empire is meant to be understood from a Christian perspective that remains oblique in the play: "As Antony [*100*] and Cleopatra paradoxically assert for themselves a love transcending death and a triumph emerging from defeat we are meant to recognize an impulse that is completed in Christian miracle; but we are also meant to realize that in the pre-Christian world of Shakespeare's play the transcendence to which the lovers aspire is tragically impossible. . . . The *Pax Romana* [adumbrating the *Pax Christiana*] is the result of the manipulations of [Octavius,] one of Shakespeare's most self-serving and irre-ducibly political characters. . . . [*103*] On one hand the play looks to Augustan empire as the culmination of historical processes, and on the other hand it conveys the feeling that the energies of its principals are misdirected, that their goals are insufficient to their needs. . . . The play describes yearnings for which it envisions no moral or aesthetic gratification [see also PLATT (1976, p. 261): *Ant.* makes one long for a better world]. . . . [Ll. 2880–2 provide] a comment on the aimlessness of a universe lacking moral focus from the perspective of one that has achieved coherence through divine revelation. . . . [*110*] Antony and Cleopatra remain con-strained by a dialectic of equally delimiting choices—empire and romantic love, world and flesh, Roman morality and Alexandrian amorality; but by confounding their alternatives, by insisting on both love *and* empire, death *and* immortality, they approach Christian paradox as closely as is possible without divine intercession."

On the whole, critical outlooks that stress ambiguities, dialectical tensions, and plurality of significance—though difficult to summarize—have achieved pen-etrating insights into this play. The growth of such critical attitudes, with their awareness that no single "meaning" can account for the play's complexity, in the 20th c., and especially since the 1960s, is connected to some extent with a growing tendency toward pluralism in society and culture, conditions that have made possible a fresh appreciation of Sh.'s affinity to the tradition of paradox.

MYTH AND ARCHETYPE

Ant. has been interpreted in the light of the mythic analogues of Hercules, Isis-Osiris, Dionysus versus Apollo, Mars-Venus, Dido-Aeneas, and others. Expanding on WARBURTON (ed. 1747; see n. 1050–1), SCHLEGEL (1811, tr. 1846, p. 416) describes *Ant.* as showing "Hercules in the chains of Omphale, drawn from the fabulous heroic ages into history, and invested with the Roman costume." The Hercules-Omphale parallel is also recognized by HÜLSMANN (1856, p. 227), HEYSE (in BODENSTEDT, ed. 1867; 1873, vol. 7, *Ant.*, p. v), FOARD (1893, p. 356), GUNDOLF (1926, p. 26, and 1928; 1949, 2:446), WAITH (1962, p. 113), BLISSETT (1967, pp. 157–9), and those who note sources: WILSON (ed. 1950; see n. 1050–1), WARNER (1957, p. 139), BARROLL (1958, *TxSE*, pp. 70–1), SCHANZER (1960, "Three Notes on *Ant.*," p. 21, and 1963, pp. 158–9), KERMODE (1961; 1971, p. 98, n. 20), WADDINGTON (1966, pp. 211–12), ADELMAN (1973, pp. 81, 209, n. 69), and MACK (1973, p. 96); see also p. 595.

The idea of Antony's effeminacy is rejected, however, by BUCK (1938, pp.

106–7), who claims what Cleopatra loves is his masculine independence, and qualified by WARNER (1957, p. 143), who finds Antony's loss of masculine honor transformed to a triumph of love by poetic imagination.

WAITH (1962) describes Antony as a type of Hercules (p. 115): "Some of the most striking identifications with Hercules are made shortly before Antony's death. They emphasize certain characteristics which he continues to share with his former protector. Notable among these is Antony's violent rage, the more conspicuous for being allied with an extravagant generosity, shown on occasion to those who have merited rage. Bounty and rage, mingling and interacting, account for a large share of Antony's heroic nature." Rage, his (p. 116) "most Herculean trait," is applauded by Cleopatra in 3.13: "The spectacle of Antony *furens* is one which she admires rather than fears. From this time she never wavers in her commitment (p. 117)." After Antony's final defeat (4.12), his suspicion of betrayal again issues in rage (pp. 119–20): "Both Hercules and Antony want more than anything to recover some part of their lost honour in order to make themselves worthy of a hero's death. Both of them wish that revenge upon a perfidious woman [Deianira, Cleopatra] might atone for their [*120*] guilt towards an innocent woman [Megara, Octavia], as well as punishing an infamous betrayal." Yet "Antony's rage at Cleopatra is brought to an abrupt end by the news that she has killed herself for his love [4.14], just as Hercules' rage at Deianira ends when Hyllus reveals her innocent intentions, her horror at the outcome, and her suicide. But the difference between Antony and Hercules is brought out by Antony's response to the news. To Hercules the full import of this news is that an old prophecy has been fulfilled, and that he is meeting the heroic death promised him. He is able to reassert his old self and muster the fortitude necessary to face the flames of his funeral pyre because it is clear that Deianira was merely instrumental in his undoing, and of no real importance. He then dismisses her from his thoughts. The news brought by Mardian means to Antony that Cleopatra, instead of betraying him, has given him a model of heroic death, and that life without so wonderful a woman is not worth living. There is Herculean fortitude in his suicide; there is also the final assertion of love. The meaning of Antony's tragedy does not lie entirely in the Herculean pattern."

SCHANZER (1963, p. 156) refers to Hercules's choice between Pleasure and Virtue: "Consciously or not, it may have played its part in shaping his [Sh.'s] presentation of the Antony and Cleopatra story in terms of the hero's choice between two opposed ways of life, seen at least from the Roman point of view as the opposition between the path of *virtus* and of *voluptas*, as well as the hero's position between two women embodying these values." See p. 609 for classical sources. BLISSETT (1967) notes that the choice of pleasure and the resulting enslavement by Omphale combine with the analogue of Cleopatra as (p. 158) "Circe-like enchantress binding the hero with erotic magic" to lead to (p. 159) "the spectacle of the destruction of the hero by a harlot sorceress" as one, though not the dominant, impression of the play. COATES (1978, pp. 51–2) sees Sh. as reconciling the alternatives facing Hercules: "What seems to strengthen the connection of Antony with the Renaissance

Hercules and his choice, is Cleopatra's description of him after his death [3292 ff.]. There are too many points of similarity to the Hercules who blends pleasure with virtue to be dismissed as coincidence. . . . In the continuing controversy concerning the play . . . the 'Choice of Hercules' [a popular allegory based on his hesitation between Vice and Virtue] is a suggestive piece of evidence. It tends to make against the view that Shakespeare's intentions are mainly ironical, that he is debunking the lovers. The linking of the 'Choice of Hercules' with *Antony and Cleopatra* gives a fuller value to Enobarbus's death [since he is overwhelmed by Antony's heroic curbing of avarice], strengthens the case for accepting [52] Antony's courage at the end as genuine, and above all, allows us to accept the poetry of acts IV and V as what it surely is, the real expression of something real: nothing so callow as 'the world well lost' but a statement of Pleasure reconciled to Virtue." Others who comment on Herculean parallels include WARBURTON (ed. 1747; see n. 2804), HEATH (1765, pp. 463–4; see n. 2806), JAMESON (1832; 1879, p. 273), HERFORD (ed. 1899, 9:261), KNIGHT (1931; 1965, p. 247), SOELLNER (1958, *CL*, p. 321), FOAKES (1964, *DUJ*, pp. 75–6), ADELMAN (1973, pp. 81, 135; see also n. 2803), COSTA DE BEAUREGARD (1974, pp. 107–11), BONO (1984, pp. 151–67), HILL (1984, pp. 225–7), ROBERTSON (1984, pp. 65–75), MOSELEY (1986, pp. 123–6), and HILLMAN (1987, pp. 442–51).

GÜNTHER (1934, pp. 576–9, in German) identifies Cleopatra with Isis as representing a (p. 578) "tellurian [earthly] marshland empire" and Antony with Osiris as spouse of Isis; he sees in Octavius an "embodiment of masculine force as uranian [heavenly] power of spirit." LLOYD (1959, *ShS*, p. 94) also discusses Cleopatra as Isis: Sh. "was acquainted with the cult of Isis from Plutarch's essay [in *Moralia*], and from Apuleius. They [the classical authors] are echoed in his portrait of Cleopatra and her values, but denied to Antony [who is not identified with Osiris]. If we see Antony's tragedy as the centrepiece of the play, its structure is faulty. The fifth act falls, on the contrary, into place as the necessary final stage in the evolution of the play's values, if we see as its subject the statement of the divine humanity which is common to Isis and Cleopatra." ADLARD (1975, pp. 324–8) believes Cleopatra, like Isis who (p. 328) "includes all goddesses," is "at once a woman of intelligence and royal spirit and a sensual plaything"; the four elements "coexist in her (though at her death she renounces all but air and fire) in a Blakean interplay of contraries, as Egyptian mud coexists with and complements Egyptian wisdom." Thus Cleopatra unites pleasure and wisdom: "She can play like a child and rule like a queen, as may be expected from one who is not only Venus but Ceres, Diana, Athena, Bellona, and many others." Comments on Isis-Osiris analogues include those by GUNDOLF (1926, p. 17, and 1928; 1949, 2:435), FISCH (1970, p. 65), KURIYAMA (1977, pp. 335–7), and BONO (1984, pp. 191–213); for sources, see also pp. 596–7.

A Dionysus-Apollo analogue is occasionally suggested. GUNDOLF (1928; 1949, 2:431, in German; similarly 1926, p. 15) summarizes: Cleopatra is "the goddess of living and dying, as Antony is the god of Bacchic intoxication and the Herculean fall—both full of mythic fire. . . . Opposed to these two forces of life is Octavian

Caesar, the firm master spirit, earth-reason, level-headed knowledge of proportion, limit, and weight of things," analogous to the Roman god Terminus or to Apollo. Gundolf sees a development in the play (p. 451) "from Dionysian heroic joy to Dionysian agony and night." RUPPEL (1957, p. 188, in German): "As in Cleopatra the ancient wanton goddesses of the East celebrate once more their last triumph, glowing with intoxication and the melancholy of their end ere they sink into dust . . . before the new Roman gods of state, so in Antony Dionysus returns home for the last time to the East, whence he came, and there finds his grave." LONGO (1974, p. 34) sees Antony as "meeting ground" of the "Dionysian and Apollonian states," finally sacrificing Apollo for Dionysus. LYMAN & SCOTT (1975, pp. 56, 95) agree: "Rome and its personification in Octavius Caesar stand for the Apollonian principle [p. 55: the 'tendency to impose form and order upon the world']; Egypt and its personification in Cleopatra for the Dionysian [p. 55: 'life unfettered by forms or boundaries']. Antony is desperately, helplessly, and ultimately, fatally, caught between the two. The drama explores the many facets and forms of conflict that arise when these two principles meet. . . . In the end, Rome and Apollonianism triumph over Egypt and Dionysianism. . . . [95] Both Antony and Cleopatra follow the Dionysian principle of equating love and death with nobility." Eros alone can provide resistance against the Apollonian victory (p. 98).

DANBY'S (1949; 1952, p. 150) brief "The play is Shakespeare's study of Mars and Venus—the presiding deities of Baroque society" is given force by WADDING-TON (1966, pp. 210, 221): *Ant.* "is a romance which is designed to evoke primarily the mythical and cosmological affair of Mars and Venus, rather than the unrelated characters of Hercules and Isis—though the latter are subsumed typologically by Mars and Venus. . . .

[221] "When Antony and Cleopatra are perceived as types of Mars and Venus rather than Hercules and Omphale, the consequences for an interpretation of the play are far-reaching because the necessity of a moral response to the action becomes less relevant and it is possible to concur with the lovers' own estimate of their situation. While it is true that a minor strand of allegorical tradition demanded a moral response to this apparently adulterous relationship of pagan gods, the dominant Renaissance interpretation regarded the legend of Mars and Venus as embodying the profoundly significant concept of *concordia discors*." But ADELMAN (1973, pp. 100–1) cautions, "We should not expect the fable of Mars and Venus to define the meaning of *Antony and Cleopatra*. Indeed, iconography and mythography can never serve as a definition of meaning, for only the play can define itself. But iconography and mythography can provide a context for the play; they can serve to identify those images which the original audience might have felt to be particularly significant and to suggest the range of signification. The analogy with Mars and Venus operates precisely to define the range of meaning in *Antony [101] and Cleopatra*. For in the play it is suggested that the lovers are larger than human, that their union is somehow cosmic like that of their great prototypes, the union of male and female, war and love, strife and friendship. And at the same time, of course, they are the merely human adulterous lovers whom strict morality must condemn. The play

takes on the quality of a myth that offers its contrary perspectives of interpretation and value within itself: and, like the mythographers, the play insists that we see all the perspectives at once. If it is the fault of the lovers that they do not see from the moral perspective, it is the fault of the Romans that they, rather like some critics, see only from that perspective." Mars-Venus analogues are also discussed by BONO (1984, pp. 167–90) and HILL (1984, pp. 214–19). For Mars-Venus sources, see also pp. 394–5, 610.

For Dido-Aeneas analogues and sources, mainly Virgil, Ovid, and Marlowe, see pp. 593–5, 603–4.

Various other mythic or archetypal interpretations have been proposed. GOD-DARD (1951, 2:195): "It is with the semi-mythological Cleopatra, the ancestral image of Woman she evokes within him [Antony], the gypsy, Egypt, the Serpent of old Nile, that he is in love. The fascination is mutual, and she in turn endows him with superhuman attributes. He is anything to her from the demi-Atlas of the Earth to Mars."

HOLLAND (1964, pp. 268–9), referring to Freudian theory, finds in Cleopatra the fruitful mother and loving charmer, Venus and Isis; in Octavia the virginal Diana; and in furious Fulvia the revenging death goddess Persephone—the three constituting the famous triple goddess. The idea, he acknowledges, is perhaps fanciful.

FRYE (1967, pp. 70–2): *Ant.* "is the definitive tragedy of passion, and in it the ironic and heroic themes, the day world of history and the night world of passion, expand into natural forces of cosmological proportions. . . . [71] The Egypt of the play includes the Biblical Egypt, the land of bondage, and the Egypt of legend in which serpents and crocodiles are spawned from the mud of the Nile. Cleopatra, the serpent of the Nile, is a Venus rising from it in Enobarbus' speech [901 ff.]; she wears the regalia of Isis; she is a *stella maris*, a goddess of the moon and the sea. She has affinities with the kind of goddess figure that both Hebraic and Classical religions kept trying to subdue by [72] abuse: . . . she has many characteristics of her sister whore of Babylon. This last gives a curiously apocalyptic tone to the play. . . .

"But *Antony and Cleopatra* is not a morality play, and Egypt is not hell: it is rather the night side of nature, passionate, cruel, superstitious, barbaric, dissolute, what you will, but not to be identified with its vices, any more than Rome can be identified with its virtues." FRYE (1986, p. 133) considers Antony in his last days "a force of nature."

And FISCH (1970, pp. 59, 65–7): Sh. "is dealing *directly* in this play with a pair of characters who lay claim to mythological status and who at every turn adopt the posture of figures in a fertility ritual. . . . [65] The world moves on, as it must, towards the 'time of universal peace' of which Octavius speaks in Act IV, vi [2581], recalling to us Vergil's vision of the ages of the world in the fourth *Eclogue*. The drama of universal history sets up its rhythm in the play, and the ritual enactments of Isis and Osiris in their temporary incarnations as Cleopatra and Antony are accordingly diminished in size and significance. Their own tragedy observes the mythic unity of place; it is confined to one corner of Egypt: but the play as a whole, as is notorious, bursts the last fetters of classical restraint. . . . The closed myth-world of tragedy is exploded, for the theme of world history has taken its place. . . . [66] As Cleopatra takes the centre of the stage for her final exit she is not only herself rehabilitated in a characteristically Shakespearian fashion, but the world of mythology is rehabilitated too. . . . [67] The final speeches of Cleopatra suggest not the meeting of Mars and Venus nor of Isis and Osiris, but rather of Cupid and Psyche. . . . And at this point where the soul is born and its grace is discovered, Paganism transcends itself and glimpses those permanent and fundamental relations of love which give meaning not only to all human marriages but to the vast and seemingly impersonal march of history itself."

Among further discussions are those by STOESSL (1935, 3:275: the lovers are autumn figures, falling like ripe fruit to prepare for a new year), GRIFFITHS (1945, p. 39: *Ant.* exists in its "pure sensations" and passions, from pride and jealousy to love as "absolute sole lord of Life and Death"), NOSWORTHY (1956, p. 4: Cleopatra resembles the phoenix), RUPPEL (1957, pp. 190–1: Eros closely linked to Thanatos; suggested by GUNDOLF, 1926, p. 25, and 1928; 1949, 2:445), WARNER (1957, p. 139: *Ant.* thematizes a strong man's ruin by his sexual weakness, as in Adam and Eve, Tammuz and Ishtar, Samson and Delilah), ARMSTRONG (1969, pp. 45, 48: Cleopatra's domain is the outermost margin of formed order, represented by the snake), ROHRMOSER (1971, pp. 86–7: defeat of mythical world of Eros by historical world of rationality), ASAHARA (1978, pp. 1–26: the lovers are grandly mythological figures toward the end, though of lesser stature earlier in the play), and DAVIDSON (1980, pp. 35–51: Cleopatra as Circe, Venus, Eve, and the Whore of Babylon).

DRAME À CLEF

Linking biographical and psychological interests, a few critics since the mid-19th c. have speculated on Elizabethan "models" for Sh.'s characters.

CARTWRIGHT (1859, pp. 22–3, 26–7, 31), with riotous ingenuity, finds *Ant.* tallying with *Son.* and both with real life: "The two ladies readily answer for themselves—Cleopatra being, of course, the lady with the raven black eyes; and Octavia, Mrs. W. Shakspere.

"Enobarbus also . . . is easily recognized as Lord Southampton, who was in after-life 'a great captain in the Spanish wars, and in the Low Countries'. . . .

[23] "Cæsar is the good Shakspere, who thus beautifully portrays the contest and ultimate ascendancy of his moral feelings over his evil inclinations: [quotes 981–8]. . . . [26] Pompey is William Herbert. . . . [27] Menas, the pirate, is Thomas Thorpe, the piratical publisher. . . . [31] Antony is evidently not the Mark Antony of history, but the fully developed Shakspere of 1593—an archangel ruined; . . . the character of Marlowe is drawn with extraordinary accuracy [in Lepidus]."

For others who see the Dark Lady as a model for Cleopatra or who stress similarities between them, see p. 698.

To MASSEY (1866; 1872, p. 482), Cleopatra is Penelope Rich: "The model from which Shakspeare drew his Cleopatra was, like his statue of Hermione, a very real woman all a-thrill with life. . . .

"There was a woman in the North, whom Shakspeare had known, quite ready to become his life-figure, for this siren of the east; her name was Lady Rich." WALTER (ed. 1969, pp. 305−6) surmises an influence of Penelope Rich on the characterization of Cleopatra and of her lover Charles Blount ('Lord' Mountjoy, Earl of Devonshire) on that of Antony.

HARRIS (1911, pp. 196−7, 204), anticipated by COURTNEY (13 Nov. 1906), names Mary Fitton as an influence: "We may assume before proof that Shakespeare will identify himself with the lover, Antony; but a little doubt of the perfectness of the portraiture must remain in us; for Antony was a great captain and fighter. . . . [197] Hamlet-Shakespeare is here in a *rôle* only partially suited to him and consequently Antony is not one of Shakespeare's best character pictures. . . . [204] His superb mistress, Mary Fitton, finds at length in Cleopatra a part that suits her to perfection." See also HARRIS (1909; 1911, pp. 304−5).

BROWN (1949, p. 229) disagrees with the Fitton theory: "We shall never know, it seems, who the Dark Lady was. The Pembroke-Fitton theory of man right fair and woman colour'd ill has been discredited. . . . She may, in her final and most glorious embodiment as Cleopatra, have been more of a remembered fancy than a woman of fact." He enlarges on Cleopatra as Dark Lady (p. 216): *Ant.* "is essentially a hymn of forgiveness. By the time that Shakespeare had finished with the Dark Lady in this tremendous tragedy, she had declared her immortal longings and made Death proud to take her." See also BROWN (1957, pp. 308−9).

Some critics object to hunting for biographical allegories. WENDELL (1894, p. 326): "The unanswerable question . . .—as to whether Beatrice and Cleopatra be different portraits of the same living woman who inspired the *Sonnets*,—is impertinent. The Shakspere with whom we may legitimately deal is not the man, who has left no record of his actual life, but the artist, who has left the fullest record of his emotional experience. To search for the actual man is at once unbecoming and futile." DEMPEWOLF (1914, p. 59, in German) also concludes that it is "quite pointless" to hunt for biographical models.

HARMAN (1925, pp. 123−4), a Baconian, arranges his identifications to suit his theory: "The plays which, in my belief, were produced under the influence of the writer's recollections of Essex, are *Macbeth, Antony and Cleopatra* and *Coriolanus*. . . . [124] When he drew the character of Octavius, my belief is that he saw the analogy of Cecil; of Antony that of Essex; of Cleopatra that of Queen Elizabeth, and of Enobarbus . . . that of himself." So do the Oxfordians OGBURN & OGBURN (1952, p. 1166): "This play, in which he [the Earl of Oxford] was Antony—as he was Antonio in others—was intended as a symbolic though authoritative account of his relationship with the Queen." For another Oxfordian, see CLARK (1931; 1974, pp. 349−57).

OTHER THEMES

Various further themes have been suggested. HAZLITT (1817; 1930, 4:228) sets the tone for many later critics when he speaks of a Rome-Egypt clash: *Ant.* "presents a fine picture of Roman pride and Eastern magnificence: and in the struggle between the two, the empire of the world seems suspended." BRANDES (1895, tr. 1935, p. 461) sees Sh. as immersed in "a world-catastrophe! He has no mind now to write of anything else. What is sounding in his ears, what is filling his thoughts, is the crash of a world falling to ruin." GRINDON (1909, p. 21) points to a character contrast: "This is one of the plays wherein Shakespere gives us failure in a high nature [Antony's] on the one hand and the success of a low nature [Octavius's] on the other. And he leaves us with hope and expectation that the failure will not be eternal, while the low success will never rise beyond itself." HEUER (1938, p. 75, in German) believes the play deals with "the problem of fate" as an "essential theme," man being "given opportunity for resistance." To BOWLING (1956–7, p. 251, similarly 1964, p. 239), *Ant.* shows various characters divided against themselves, with "duality and disaster" ensuing.

KOTT (1961, tr. 1964, pp. 128, 130) thinks of the heroes as encaged by the play's world: *Ant.* "is a tragedy about the smallness of the world. . . . [*130*] The theme of *Antony and Cleopatra* could be taken from Racine: dignity and love cannot be reconciled with the struggle for power which forms the matter of history. But neither the world nor the struggle for power is shown in the abstract. The heroes are restless, like big animals in a cage. The cage gets smaller and smaller, and they writhe more and more violently." But TROY (in SISSON, ed. 1961, pp. 26–7): *Ant.* "may . . . be taken as Shakespeare's tragedy of the soul in space, of the soul struggling [*27*] in a universe of illimitable space of which it is only a limited and self-limiting fragment."

DAICHES (1962; 1968, pp. 71, 87, 95) believes *Ant.* "is—to summarise it crudely—about the different roles that man can play on the various stages which human activity provides for him, and about the relation of these roles to the player's true identity. . . . [*87*] The play is in fact both triumph and tragedy; Antony, and more especially Cleopatra, achieve in death what they have been unable to achieve in life: the triumph lies in the achievement, the tragedy in that the price of the achievement is death. . . . [*95*] Is the play about human frailty or human glory? We are left with the feeling that one depends on the other, an insight too subtly generous for any known morality." WAIN (1964, p. 129) sees *Ant.* as Sh.'s "last full-scale treatment" of the "theme of lovers held asunder by the world." WHITAKER (1965, pp. 284, 294, similarly 1974, pp. 143–4) alone claims Sh.'s interest to be narrative rather than interpretive: Sh. "gives us no hint of any thesis or any purpose that has ordered his telling of the story. He neither calls them [the lovers] dead lechers nor implies that for their love the world was well lost. Their story is its own justification and its own reward. . . . [*294*] He wrote . . . what might aptly have been called 'The lamentable dotage and death of Mark Antony, with the tragical fall of amorous Cleopatra.' " WILLIAMSON (1968, p. 426) notes that Sh. "uses the concept of Fortune to interpret his source story," adding: "Fortune seems an appropriate figure to preside over *Antony and Cleopatra*, not only because the play involves love and war, two of her special provinces, but also because both of the principals have many qualities in common with her." To HARDING (1969, p. 251), *Ant.* exemplifies female attempts at manly heroism: "When he came to *Antony and Cleopatra* Shakespeare was still interested to explore the theme of the woman's usurpation of the man's role. . . . The crucial disaster is made to occur only because Cleopatra interferes in the military campaign." GODSHALK (1973, p. 150) observes that "the pattern of instability and insecurity is basic, and encompasses all elements of the play. The action is based on this instability and on the struggle to attain some kind of permanence in a world which seems to deny its very existence." WEITZ (1975, pp. 35–6), finding "a form of generation and corruption that destroys itself in its perfection," asks: "Is . . . one theme in the play that there is in Antony's love for Cleopatra a coming into being (the intensity of fire) of a love (the rarefaction of air) that destroys in its very perfection? It seems to me that it is. . . . [36] *Antony and Cleopatra* is not Dryden's 'All for Love or the World Well Lost' or Enobarbus' 'Don't lose your head when you lose your heart'. Rather, there is something unique: that there is in the world . . . a kind of perfume which in its loveliness suffocates. Without the suffocation, no loveliness: that is the full choice. The alternative is the gap of boredom."

Partly building on ULRICI (1839; see pp. 625–6), some believe *Ant.* deals with political problems. Thus CECIL (1944; 1949, pp. 5, 8–9, 15–16, 20–1) emphasizes the contest for world leadership: "If *Antony and Cleopatra* is meant to be a typical Shakesperean tragic drama, with love as its theme, it is a failure. But we enjoy it: and one does not enjoy failures. Perhaps these neat categories of tragedy and love story do not apply to it. . . . [8] With him [Sh.] the love-story is seen always in its relation to the rivalry between Octavius and Antony. A large part of the play is concerned with this only, and not with the love-story at all. We see Antony with Octavius and Pompey and his soldiers quite as [9] much as we see him with Cleopatra. We also see Pompey, Octavius and the soldiers by themselves, without Antony. Shakespeare conceives his play as a piece of history; its interest is largely political. . . .

[*15*] "Destiny, so Shakespeare suggests, a supernatural destiny is working behind the visible scene to promote its secret purpose. These great persons, apparently so [*16*] powerful, and with the world at their feet, are in reality no more than puppets in the fingers of a mysterious and irresistible fate [similarly EVERETT, 1905, p. 254]. The personal drama is seen as part of a huge impersonal historical process. . . . [*20*] The incoherent heterogeneous material which is his subject-matter is all made to relate to a single presiding theme. This theme is not love; it is success. This fact is the master-key to the riddle of the play. Shakespeare looks at the chaotic spectacle of the great world convulsed in the struggle for power and happiness; and, he asks 'What sort of man is successful in it?' . . .

[*21*] "But Shakespeare does not stop here. To so profound a mind as his, the achievement of worldly power cannot be a final test of success. He goes on to ask, 'Is worldly success really worth having?' "

STEMPEL's (1956, pp. 62–3) argument that Sh.'s concern is the safety of the state is strained: "The spread of chaos on the level of political organization, in particular, was feared by men of the Renaissance. Shakespeare's classical plays reflect this fear; it is the ultimate source of the conflict of values in all of them, including *Antony and Cleopatra*. . . .

"Is this far-reaching disturbance of order merely a background for the portrayal of a great love or is it the dominant theme of the play? . . . Even Phillips [1940, p. 188], who has carefully analyzed the political significance of the play, feels that this aspect is subordinate to the love story. . . . [*63*] If this is true, why does Shakespeare prolong the action beyond the death of Antony by adding scenes depicting Cleopatra's dealings with Octavius and her final suicide? The splendid infatuation, for all practical purposes, ends with the death of Antony. . . . If, however, the major theme is the safety of the state, then the death of Antony does not remove the chief danger to political stability—Cleopatra. She has ensnared Julius Caesar, Pompey, and Antony—how will Octavius fare? The last act shows us that Octavius is proof against the temptress, and the play ends, as it should, with the defeat and death of the rebel against order." Stempel's view is rebutted by TRACI (1970, pp. 18–19).

G. R. SMITH (1974, p. 15) sees *Ant.* as showing a decline in standards of political conduct: "Had Shakespeare wanted to write a tragedy of middle-aged, classical and heroical figures in love, there was always the tale of Dido and Aeneas, which has all kinds of possibilities in King Cambyses' or any later vein. The choice of Antony and Cleopatra as a subject, with its very heavy emphasis upon political chicanery and deceit, is a deliberate Shakespearean choice. It continues his studies of politics at the highest levels of government, and once more what we have been shown is not at all flattering to heads of state."

Those who discuss political order and its disturbance include also RÖTSCHER (1846, Pt. 2, pp. 305–7), LLOYD (1856; 1858, sig. 14^r), KREYßIG (1858; 1877, 1:437–8), BLUMHOF (ed. 1870, pp. 12–13), SNIDER (1876; 1877, 2:261–3), FRENZEL (1877, 1:257), SYMONS (1889; 1919, p. 5), GILLET (1930, pp. 241–2), PHILLIPS (1940, pp. 188–9, 204–5; see pp. 626–7), WALKER (1951, p. 290), MERI (1958, pp. 252, 255), NELSON (1966, pp. 199, 203), ROSE (1969, pp. 379, 388), WILLIAMSON (1970, pp. 241, 251), and ZEEVELD (1974, pp. 124, 138–9).

By contrast, some put more stress on the lovers' personal relationship, as do VATKE (1868, p. 308, in German: Sh. "in this tragedy puts political and historical elements far behind the purely personal") and CORSON (1889, p. 252). This priority, implicit in most discussions of the lovers, is given special turns by DUTHIE (1951, pp. 152–3: brief contrast with *H5*, where external action is important in itself), ROTHE (1961, p. 326, in German: *Ant.* focuses on private relations, like a "chamber drama"), HAPGOOD (1971, p. 5: the three protagonists struggle for personal supremacy, not for rule of the world), and particularly BECKERMAN (1977, p. 112), who highlights the lovers' efforts to perfect their devotion: "The spectacle of Antony's and Cleopatra's defeat as kings interests us but little. Their painful struggle to touch each other truly is what finally holds our attention"; for a similar discussion, see CHRISTOPHER (1976, pp. 59–73) on "private war and peace" in *Ant*.

Others who discuss themes include BIRCH (1848, p. 478: no certainty of immortality for pagans), NICLAS (1917, p. 71: war and love), CONSTANTIN-WEYER (1929, p. 60: enchantment), KOLBE (1930, p. 138: gamble for world power; cf. KNIGHT, 1931; 1965, p. 253), LÜTHI (1957; 1966, p. 121: loss of world in frenzied licentiousness), BONJOUR (1964, p. 91: clash of love and action), BÖSE (1966, p. 70: love verging on insanity), BURGE (1966, pp. 123–45: problems of identity), IZAGUIRRE (1966, p. 2a: death and immortality), SAKURAI (1969, pp. 37–55: truth and falsehood), BREASTED (1970, Pt. 3: theatrical uses of self), DIAS (1972, p. 465: love's conflict with powers of the world), KINDRED (1972, pp. 178–9: futility of mediation between love and empire; based on GOETHE, 1813–16, tr. 1921, p. 178), WHITAKER (1972, pp. 7, 109, 194: time and eternity), OTSUKI (1975: psychoanalytic concepts), SIRCAR (1975, pp. 579–675: identity and fulfillment), SJÖBERG (1975–6, pp. 13–14: master-servant relations), FERRARA (1977, pp. 27–8: sex and power), BRENNAN (1978, pp. 313–29: identity and role-playing), TOLMIE (1978, p. 113, and HOSOKAWA, 1979, pp. 23–32: absoluteness and relativity), DEGENHART (1980, pp. 29–39: conflict of psychic elements), PAULIN (1980, pp. 161–7: pastoral elements), BAYLEY (1981, p. 137: sense of predestination), JAMES (1981, pp. 127, 130, 140: ruin of nobility), RAEBURN (1982, 1:263: "the fragility of human beings when they place themselves totally at risk"), TRAVERSI (1982, pp. 197–226: imagination and reality), JOSE (1983, pp. 487–504: truth of heart beneath surface), KRANZ (1984, pp. 90–8: speed and rational certainty), TUCKER (1984, pp. 176–81: differences in personality types), GOLDMAN (1985, pp. 112–13: greatness and its way of acting on the world), and HOOKS (1987, pp. 37–49: power and submission).

Technique

STRUCTURE

ROWE (ed. 1709, 1:[x]xviii, also xxxi) justifies Sh.'s "carelessness" in violating the unities of time and place (cf. GILDON, 1710, p. 413: "The Play is full of Scenes strangely broken: many of which exceed not ten Lines") by taking *Ant*. as a history play not subject to the rules of tragedy, a classification supported by JOHNSON (ed. 1765; 1968, 7:68), DAVIES (1783, 2:367–8), and ULRICI (1839; 1868–9, tr. 1876, 2:208). A different defense is adopted by ANON. (1747, p. 42), who contrasts *Ant*. with Dryden's *All for Love* as "most pathetically Natural" since it lacks the unities.

Using *Ant*. as a leading case, JOHNSON (ed. 1765; 1968, 7:76–7) mounts a sustained attack on the unities, asserting that an audience does not follow the play's movement from place to place: "The objection arising from the impossibility of passing the first hour at Alexandria, and the next at Rome, supposes, that when the play opens the spectator really imagines himself at Alexandria, and believes that his walk to the theatre has been a voyage to Egypt, and that he lives in the days of Antony and [77] Cleopatra. Surely he that imagines this may imagine more. He that can take the stage at one time for the palace of the Ptolemies, may take it in half an hour for the promontory of Actium. . . .

"The truth is, that the spectators are always in their senses, and know, from the first act to the last, that the stage is only a stage, and that the players are only players. They come to hear a certain number of lines recited with just gesture and elegant modulation. The lines relate to some action, and an action must be in some place; but the different actions that compleat a story may be in places very remote from each other; and where is the absurdity of allowing that space to represent first Athens, and then Sicily, which was always known to be neither Sicily nor Athens, but a modern theatre." Then again he holds the play's delightful variety against what he calls its lack of structural art (ed. 1765, 7:254): "The continual hurry of the action, the variety of incidents, and the quick succession of one personage to another, call the mind forward without intermission from the first Act to the last. But the power of delighting is derived principally from the frequent changes of the scene. . . .

"The events, of which the principal are described according to history, are produced without any art of connection or care of disposition." His delight in variety is shared by KEMBLE (ed. 1813, pp. ii–iii), DRAKE (1817, 2:492–3), GUIZOT (ed. 1821, 3:1), and HÜLSMANN (1856, p. 225).

Some 18th-c. critics defend *Ant.*'s dramatic unity, especially GERSTENBERG (1766; 1890, p. 163, in German), who notes "unity of purpose and composition" or coherence in the play, and ESCHENBURG (ed. 1778, 6:385–6, in German; echoed by LE TOURNEUR, ed. 1779, 6:287, in French): "One finds more connection of scenes in some other of our poet's plays than in this; yet his great art of making everything work toward one common end, to direct the reader's and spectator's eye on one principal object—this true *unity*, overlooked and misunderstood by many critics and [386] imitators of Shakespeare—will not be found missing here." AYRENHOFF (1783; 1813, pp. 14–15), however, castigates Sh.'s neglect of the unities in *Ant.*

Uncertainty over the play's structure continues in the 19th c. SCHLEGEL (1811, tr. 1846, p. 416) is irritated by the unfocused background yet fascinated by the lovers' characters, the play's main interest: "The fulness and variety of political and warlike events, to which the union of the three divisions of the Roman world under one master necessarily gave rise, were perhaps too great to admit of being clearly exhibited in one dramatic picture. . . . Many things, which are transacted in the background, are here merely alluded to, in a manner which supposes an intimate acquaintance with the history; but a work of art should contain, within itself, every thing necessary for its being fully understood. Many persons of historical importance are merely introduced in passing; the preparatory and concurring circumstances are not sufficiently collected into masses to avoid distracting our attention. The principal personages, however, are most emphatically distinguished by lineament and colouring, and powerfully arrest the imagination." HAZLITT (1817; 1930, 4:228, 230–1) defends more vigorously Sh.'s harmonizing of opposites, such as the struggle between "Roman pride" and "Eastern magnificence" and his contrast between the oriental life of luxury and Antony's military hardships reported in 1.4: "The jealous attention which has been [*231*] paid to the unities both of time and place has taken away the principle of perspective in the drama, and all the interest which objects derive from distance, from contrast, from privation, from change of fortune, from long-cherished passion; and contracts our view of life from a strange and romantic dream, long, obscure, and infinite, into a smartly contested, three hours' inaugural disputation on its merits by the different candidates for theatrical applause." LLOYD (1856; 1858, sig. K0^r) observes that loose structure is proper to Sh.'s concern with reckless dissoluteness. An attempt to find a coherent pattern in *Ant.*'s political conflicts is offered by the Neo-Hegelian SNIDER (1876; 1877, 2:265–6): "There are manifestly two main movements, though other divisions are possible, according to the stand-point of the critic. The first division exhibits the various conflicting elements of the Roman World, and ends in their apparent reconciliation. It has three distinct threads or groups of characters, each of which has a locality of its own. The central figures of these groups are, respectively, Antony and Cleopatra, Octavius, Pompey. The second movement shows the disruption of the truce and the struggle of the hostile principles and individuals, till their final and complete subordination to one man—Octavius. Here there are essentially two threads—that [*266*] of Antony and Cleopatra on the one hand, and that of Octavius on the other."

Still, the sprawling structure more often irritates critics. GERVINUS (1850, tr. 1883, p. 724) attributes his dissatisfaction to the lack of fusion of the psychological and historical strands: "By the too numerous and discordant interruptions, that psychical continuity is destroyed which is necessary to the development of such a remarkable connection of the innermost affections as that between Antony and Cleopatra. Let the reader think over the purport of the various historical plays of our poet; he will nowhere find the external actual material of history impregnated with a sensible or sensual connection of so much importance. Let him look over the purely psychological dramas, and nowhere will he find a connection of the affections so incessantly crossed by external public affairs of such an opposite nature." VATKE (1868, pp. 322–3, 338–9), though not wholly reconciled to *Ant.*'s structure, is readier than Gervinus to see coherence in the way the lovers' story pushes historical elements into the background (similarly SCHIRMER, in SCHÜCKING, ed. 1962, pp. 192–5). Continuing the debate begun by Gervinus, DELIUS (1875–6, p. 345) limits the psychological interest to Acts 4 and 5, a narrowing rejected by CORSON (1889, p. 256).

FREYTAG (1863; 1890, tr. 1894, pp. 71–2, 387), from a doctrinaire Neo-Aristotelian viewpoint, believes Sh. sacrificed a true structural climax to the extended tragic elevation of Cleopatra at the close: In Act 3 "Antony has withdrawn from Cleopatra, has been reconciled with Octavianus, and has re-established his authority. But the spectator has long [*72*] had a presentiment that he will return to Cleopatra. The inner necessity of this relapse is amply motived from the first act. Notwithstanding this, one demands rightly to see this momentous relapse. . . . And yet, it is presented in only brief sections. . . . [*387*] The exaltation of this character [Cleopatra] in a desperate situation, under the fear of death, was a fascinating subject for him [Sh.], and to a certain extent rightly so; for herein was an opportunity for a most peculiar, gradual intensification. Shakespeare, then, sacrificed to these scenes a part of the action."

Discontent with the structure pervades the 19th c. and continues into the 20th: see especially SCOTT (1808; 1883, 5:307), ANON. (1819, pp. 167–8), GRABBE (1827; 1977, 2:440), HALLAM (1839; 1854, 3:88), COLERIDGE (1851, 2:183), MONTÉGUT (ed. 1868; 1878, 8:3, 5, 7), VISCHER (1869–87; 1905, 6:157–8), GENÉE (1872; 1878, 1:346–7, and 1905, pp. 325–7), BENEDIX (1873, pp. 358–9), KÖNIG (1875, p. 249), FRENZEL (1877, 1:259), OECHELHÄUSER (ed. 1877; 1895, p. 89), STAPFER (1879, tr. 1880, pp. 424–5), BULTHAUPT (1883; 1911, 2:43–4), BOAS (1896, pp. 473–4), SECCOMBE & ALLEN (1903; 1904, 2:98), ETTY (1903–4, p. 308), BRADLEY (1904; 1905, pp. 71, 260), CASE (ed. 1906, pp. xiv–xv), WOLFF (1907; 1913, 2:260), MATTHEWS (1913, pp. 264–5), PELLISSIER (1914, pp. 6–8), and CAMPBELL (ed. 1949, p. 980). Nevertheless, general assertions of the play's unity and coherence come from HORN (1827, 4:77), VEHSE (1851, 1:275–6), HUDSON (1872, 2:360, 387), PHILIPS (1887, 1:25), EMERSON (1890, pp. 71–2), MORGAN & VINES (ed. 1893–8, pp. xviii–xix), EVERETT (1905, p. 254), STRINDBERG (1909, tr. 1966, pp. 276–7), SWINBURNE (1909, p. 76), ZANCO (ed. 1931, pp. xvii–xx), SQUIRE (1935, p. 71), and OPPEL (1949, p. 87).

In the 20th c. fresh defenses of structure evolve. MOULTON (1903; 1907, p. 131) makes Antony, torn between Octavius as representing "life rising to public duty" and Cleopatra as "life falling to private passion," the structural focus. Many share or develop this idea (e.g., BETHELL, 1944, p. 124; DANBY, 1949; 1952, p. 146; WILSON, 1957, p. 178; KUCKHOFF, 1964, p. 417; VINCENT, 1978, pp. 21–8); see also STROUP's (1964, pp. 289–98) view of *Ant.* as a psychomachia harking back to the morality tradition. MARKELS (1968, passim) discusses the public and private worlds in *Ant.* in detail, concluding that Antony refuses to choose and straddles both (similarly JOHNSON, 1979, passim).

A further topic of 20th-c. discussion is the play's dual catastrophe, noted by SHERMAN (1901, p. 316): "There are really two tragedies fused into one. The tragedy of Antony culminates in Act IV; the tragedy of Cleopatra [essentially that she (p. 318) 'comes to death when she has but begun to live'] is developed in Act V." WILSON (1957, pp. 179–80) believes the placing of the two deaths affirms love's triumph: "The crisis of Actium leads us immediately to the catastrophe of Antony in Act IV, upon which the catastrophe of Cleopatra logically follows in Act V. . . . [*180*] With splendid craftsmanship, Shakespeare apportions the deaths of Antony and Cleopatra to separate acts, so that the one becomes preparatory for the other and the transition from one to the other cumulative, a unified movement in which the devotion, the courage, and dignity of both the lovers is interacting and mutually ennobling; the death of Cleopatra gives final unity to the whole movement figuring as a reunion with Antony, the crowning symbol of their love triumphant."

But, as MILLS (1964, p. 59; also in 1960, p. 161) argues, "To have Cleopatra glorified and transfigured is to forgive her treatment of Antony, to imply that it was well worth the destruction of the great Roman to bring about her regeneration. If the tragedy of Antony and the tragedy of Cleopatra are to interact to intensify each other, as they do, it is necessary *not* to have a transfiguration of Cleopatra; the poignancy of Antony's tragedy is intensified by Cleopatra's unregeneracy, and it increases the pathos and tragedy of Cleopatra that she is never penitent, not even conscious of the debacle she has wrought. That she does change somewhat, that she does attain some realization of what Antony was, is to be recognized. That she did not realize it earlier, and to a much greater degree, is her tragedy: the too little and the too late. Thus the tragedy of Cleopatra is different in kind from that of Antony; the play contains the tragedy of Antony and then the tragedy of Cleopatra." BARTON (1973, p. 18), however, discussing the twofold catastrophe, thinks Cleopatra's death as tragedy queen "redeems" Antony's suicide by "transforming it within her own, flawless farewell." Other comments on the dual catastrophe include those by BRADLEY (1906; 1909, p. 299), GRANVILLE-BARKER (1930; 1946, 1:399–400), KNIGHT (1931; 1965, pp. 311, 318), MURRY (1936, pp. 372, 377), ALEXANDER (1939, p. 178), BINDER (1939, pp. 79–84), CRAIG (1948, pp. 268, 280), WILSON (ed. 1950, p. xxxii), STEMPEL (1956, p. 63), LLOYD (1959, *ShS*, p. 94), RIBNER (1960, pp. 171–2), MCMANAWAY (1962, pp. 1–5), MILLS (1964, pp. 5–6), FITCH (1968, p. 6), MARKELS (1968, p. 140), RIEMER (1968, pp. 61, 63), MIYAUCHI (1970, pp. 1–13, and 1978, pp. 224–5, 330), RACKIN (1972, pp. 207–8), FOREMAN (1978, p. 160), FUZIER (1978, pp. 69–74), BOWERS (1982, pp. 31–3), and LEVIN (1987, pp. 147–62).

Elizabethan dramatic conventions are studied from opposite perspectives by Schücking and Granville-Barker. SCHÜCKING (1919, tr. 1922, pp. 119–46) claims *Ant.* is composed of a succession of episodic scenes, character consistency being subordinated to requirements of action in each scene. Thus Cleopatra (here Schücking is anticipated by ANON., 1849, pp. 280–3), an (p. 126) "essentially vulgar, and profoundly immoral creature" in the first three acts, is suddenly transformed into an ideally noble queen in the last two. Against Schücking's unsubtle view of Cleopatra, STOLL (1928; 1930, pp. 12–19), KIRSCHBAUM (1944; 1962, pp. 99–110), CRAIG (1948, pp. 268–75), and STEWART (1949, pp. 64–78) affirm the consistency of her characterization.

Ant.'s coherence, on the other hand, is partly a product of Sh.'s mastery of stagecraft, according to GRANVILLE-BARKER (1930; 1946, 1:367–458). The fast-changing scenes of Acts 3 and 4 show Sh.'s best artistry (p. 11): "His drama is attached solely to its actors and their acting. . . . They carry place and time with them as they move." Granville-Barker also calls attention to the technique of un-localized scenes that provide continuous action (p. 379): "Each scene has an effective relation to the next, which a pause between them will weaken or destroy." If a pause at a "turn of the action" is required, it would be convenient somewhere between 3.3 and 3.6 (where BRADLEY, 1906; 1909, p. 286, places the "downward turn" of the action), or, better, between 3.6 and 3.7 (p. 380; similarly BOWERS,

1964, p. 50, and JONES, 1971, p. 227). The whole play should stress the Rome-Egypt conflict (already suggested by Hazlitt, 1817, and picked up by MABIE, 1900; 1912, p. 271) as a structural polarity (p. 371): "For a broad picturesque contrast, Roman and Egyptian are set against each other; and this opposition braces the whole body of the play, even as conflict between character and character will sustain each scene." Among other discussions of the Rome-Egypt contrast, often a commonplace, are those by KNIGHT (1931; 1965, p. 269), BETHELL (1944, pp. 120–9), DANBY (1949; 1952, pp. 130, 132, 140, 146), PEARSON (1954, pp. 134–5), SPENCER (1958, pp. 377–8), CHARNEY (1961, pp. 93–112), HERBERT (1965, pp. 55–9), HOROWITZ (1965, pp. 41–4), SEN GUPTA (1972; 1977, pp. 32–60), KERNAN (1977–8, pp. 48–56: within discussion of place and plot in Sh.), DAWSON (1978, pp. 141–2), CHAUDHURI (1981, pp. 188–9), FRENCH (1981, pp. 255–6), WOLF (1982, pp. 328–32), PEARSON (1984, pp. 173–5), BARBER (1985, pp. 92–8), JORGENSEN (1985, pp. 114–15, 119–20), FRYE (1986, p. 136), and LEGGATT (1988, pp. 174–6). Vindication of Sh.'s short-scene technique is also offered by KNIGHT (1931; 1965, pp. 322–3: scenes convey impression of vast space), WEBSTER (1942; 1957, pp. 257–8: scenes carefully interlocked), BRUNNER (1957, pp. 162–3: effect of wide-ranging political events on chief characters), OPPEL (1963, pp. 265–6: contrasting sequence of scenes in Act 4), COGHILL (1964, pp. 72–6) and ADELMAN (1973, pp. 41–2): juxtaposition and contrast of scenes, CLEMEN (1968, pp. 4–5: rhythmic contrasts of mood and place), CHARNEY (1970, p. 29: short scenes create sense of urgency), GEORGE (1980, pp. 136–9: changing scenes represent poles of conflict), and FRICKER (1983, 2:321–2: simple plot and tension in lovers' relations unify action). Critics who call the technique of fast-changing scenes cinematic include DANBY (1949; 1952, p. 128), STYAN (1960; 1963, p. 215, and 1967; 1975, p. 122), HAUSER (1964, tr. 1965, 1:344), CHARNEY (1970, pp. 28–9), and FLESCH (1987, pp. 289–92). Discussions of the structural use of contrast, antithesis, and parallelism are also offered by LÜDEMANN (1913, pp. 123–33), WALZEL (1916, pp. 17–18), FRICKER (1951, pp. 197–213), BEAUCHAMP (1955, pp. 162–5), SCHANZER (1963, pp. 133, 138), SMITH (1966, pp. 192, 202–3), RIEMER (1968, p. 35), KINDRED (1972, pp. 176–7), KOPPENFELS (1972; 1978, pp. 581–2), PAYNE (1973, p. 265), RAMM (1974, p. 119), and BRITO (1978, pp. 32–46).

ADELMAN (1973, pp. 41–9) argues that the structural use of multiple contrast permits, perhaps even requires, competing interpretations of the action to exist simultaneously without resolution, just as (pp. 30–9) the recurrent device of framing, with characters commenting on one another, involves the audience in uncertainties of judgment. This assessment is echoed by CULLUM (1981, pp. 197–8). Adelman's study is partly anticipated by BINDER's (1939, passim) thoughtful analysis of the way *Ant.*'s undulating rhythm of scene shifts actually imposes order on the complex relations between such polarities as love and duty, Egypt and Rome.

Devoid of reference to multiple contrasts is TRACI's (1970, p. 153 et passim) strained view of *Ant.*'s imitating the love act: "The progress of the play . . . follows the marriage of the lovers even to the birth of the baby Cleopatra sees at her breast

[3562] and to her creation of another Antony [3615], the Emperor Antony, who is reborn in the dream told to Dolabella. The entire movement of the play seems to imitate that of the love-act itself." Cf. KNIGHT (1931; 1965, pp. 229–36) on imagery of mating.

ELLIS-FERMOR (1960; 1961, p. 85) discusses the graded prominence of characters: "In the plays of Shakespeare's maturity, we perceive a third dimension, akin to the depth given by perspective to a painting; in dimensions and tone alike the characters [messengers, soldiers, guards, and especially Taurus] retreat successively from the foreground towards a background where they reach a virtual vanishing point. . . . [87] The dramatic function of perspective in *Antony and Cleopatra* is to evoke . . . the sense at once of vastness, of coherence, and of significance." This extension of the action in space creates the impression of a (p. 86) "limitlessly extended" universe, conveyed by (p. 88) "continuous regression in the spatial grouping of the minor figures." For a similar view, see STROUP (1964, pp. 292–4).

Some try to divide the action into a sequence of parts or phases, including RICE (1968, pp. 347–75), RIEMER (1968, pp. 37–77), ALTMANN (1969, pp. 13–15), HARTSOCK (1970, p. 59), COLMAN (1971, p. 10), JONES (1971, p. 230), RAMM (1974, pp. 119–27), DOWNER (1975, pp. 251–2), STANSFIELD (1975, p. 386), CHRISTOPHER (1976, p. 59), BECKERMAN (1977, p. 100), BAMBER (1982, pp. 49–54), and LYONS (1983, pp. 63–77). Among specific structural techniques, the use of narration as against dramatic action is discussed by DELIUS (1875–6, p. 343), RALEIGH (1907, p. 125), SCHLÜTER (1958, pp. 43–4, 136–7, 140–1), and GREYERZ (1965, pp. 58–61: esp. ll. 901 ff.). Comments on the structural use of time progression include those by CLARKE (1879, p. 220), SEN GUPTA (1961, pp. 132–46), KAULA (1964, pp. 211–23), BELL (1973, pp. 253–64), FOY (1974, pp. 218–64), and WALLER (1976, pp. 116–20); on the rapid changes of place and time, HAINES (1927, p. 58, as well as ALTMANN, 1969, pp. 13, 204: particularly place), BALESTRI (1970, pp. 294–346), LEE (1971, p. 20), and MAGUIN (1978, pp. 61–7). Concerning the sequence of events shown in the play, DANIEL (1879, pp. 239–40) suggests there are "twelve days represented on the stage; with intervals." In his scheme, the first day corresponds to 1.1–1.4, with an interval of perhaps 40 days following; the second to 1.5–2.3; the third to 2.4 (interval follows); the fourth to 2.5–2.7 as well as 3.3 (possibly interval follows); the fifth to 3.1–3.2 (interval follows); the sixth to 3.4–3.5 (interval follows); the seventh to 3.6 (interval follows); the eighth to 3.7; the ninth to 3.8–3.10 (interval follows); the tenth to 3.11–4.3; the eleventh to 4.4–4.9; and the twelfth to 4.10–5.2. KITTREDGE (ed. 1941) substantially agrees, except for day 3 ("or next day but one") and days 8 and 9, which he sees as one day; his total is thus 11 days.

EVANS (1979, pp. 223–80) examines gaps between the characters' and the audience's views of dramatic situations, as well as conflicts of such awareness among the principal characters. GRUBER (1985, pp. 31–46) focuses on the opening scenes to show how characterization is complicated by the visible interplay of character and actor, and WORTHEN (1986, pp. 295–308) discusses the dialectic between character and the actor's presentation.

Discussions of other structural techniques include those by ENGELEN (1927, pp. 123–8), PRICE (1948, p. 110), SPENCER (ed. 1948, pp. iv–vi), CLEMEN (1952, passim, and 1972, pp. 121–2), BARNET (1957, pp. 331–4), SEHRT (1960, pp. 188–90), UNGERER (1964, pp. 99–100), PERRET (1966, pp. 67–72), BLISSETT (1967, p. 152), FUJITA (1967, pp. 1–16), SCHANZER (1969, pp. 109–10), DOWNER (1975, pp. 240–54), HEFFNER (1976, pp. 154–62), LEVITH (1978, pp. 59–61), and HIRSH (1981, pp. 142–7).

LANGUAGE AND STYLE

DRYDEN (1678; 1962, 1:231), in his Preface to *All for Love*, professes to "imitate" the style of "the divine" Sh. Otherwise 17th-c. critics do not comment on the style of *Ant.*, which is discussed more substantially in the course of the 18th c.'s debate on Sh.'s classical sophistication, with pros and cons. Whereas LA PLACE (ed. 1746, 3:xxii) amuses himself at the "ton Bourgeois" and "air un peu *Bourguemestre*" of *Ant.*'s principals, as forming a "peinture naïve" of ancient manners, UPTON (1746; 1748, p. 89; followed by DODD, 1752, 1:151, n. 1) hails the learning evident in Sh.'s adopting from Plutarch Antony's "Asiatic manner of speaking," which accords with Antony's temper in being "very rodomontade." JOHNSON's (ed. 1765, 7:254) reply to Upton seems to suggest that Antony can sound as pompous as Octavius: "I think his [Antony's] diction not distinguishable from that of others: the most tumid speech in the Play is that which *Caesar* makes to *Octavia* [probably 1796–1809]." More perceptive on the relation of speech to character, SEWARD (1750, 1:lxvi) credits Sh. with giving *Ant.*'s principals "Rapidity and Boldness of Metaphors" proper to their natures. Response to Sh.'s rhetorical art is divided, however: HURD (1757; 1811, 1:77) praises his "artful management" in handling compound epithets (e.g., 578), but KAMES (1762; 1785, 2:249–50) dislikes the descriptive personifications (e.g., 902 ff.). A fruitful topic first broached in this period is imagery. DUFF (1770, p. 148) notes the sympathy aroused for Cleopatra by means of the "baby" image at 3562, and both WARTON (1778; 1871, 3:291, on 2826 ff.) and WHITER (1794; 1967, pp. 160–6, on 3289 ff.) recognize images of pageantry, while DOUCE (1807, 2:293) disapproves of anachronistic card imagery.

HAZLITT (1817; 1930, 4:231; similarly KNIGHT, ed. 1841; 1849, p. 423) appreciates the splendor of 2826 ff., "without doubt, one of the finest pieces of poetry" in Sh. And COLERIDGE (1818; 1960, 1:77) describes *Ant.*'s style with a Horatian phrase: "*Feliciter audax* is the motto for its style comparatively with his other works, even as it is the general motto of all his works compared with those of other poets."

On verse, the 19th c. notes Sh.'s abundant use of hypermeters (SEYMOUR, 1805, 2:84; VERPLANCK, ed. 1846, *Ant.*, pp. 6–7; also CASE, ed. 1906, pp. xiii–iv) signaling the "autumnal richness" of late Sh. (Verplanck, p. 7; similarly LLOYD, 1856; 1858, sig. K4^r; BOAS, 1896, p. 473; HERFORD, ed. 1899, 9:259–60; MABIE, 1900; 1912, p. 271; later BAB, 1925, pp. 276–7). BATHURST (1857, pp. 130–5) speaks of a free handling of verse except in the (p. 132) "political parts" and faults an overall lack of (p. 130) "dignity" (but WENDELL, 1894, pp. 320–1: *Ant.*'s "phrasing throughout is far above [*321*] the indignity of actual life"). SAMPSON (1889, pp. 227, 236), who gives the first extended treatment of *Ant.*'s meter, concludes, "The many irregularities do not grate upon us. . . . The deviations from strict metre are intentional; even more, warrantable; in many cases adding to the strength of the verse. . . . [*236*] The irregularities render the verse rugged, but thereby make it . . . more suited to the subject." (In the 20th c., HALLIDAY, 1954, p. 164, also notes that the use of enjambment, "breaking down the last barrier of the verse form," yields a "source of impetus and energy.")

Other 19th-c. comments are by HERAUD (1865, pp. 381–2: economy and compression of style), DELIUS (1870, pp. 267–8: prose), JANSSEN (1897, 1:62–4: prose), FRIESEN (1876, 3:248: Octavius's speech dispassionate, the lovers' passionate), WHITE (ed. 1883, 3:787: general praise), BRINCKER (1884, pp. 159–60: no bombast; similarly LEE, 1898; 1925, p. 412: "In their moments of supreme exaltation, both Antony and Cleopatra employ direct language which is innocent of rhetorical involution"; also LEE, ed. 1907, 36:xiii), SYMONS (1889; 1919, p. 3: coolly restrained style, no heady passion), as well as ADLER (1895, pp. 305–17) and WYNDHAM (1895, 1:xciv–vi), who compare North's Plutarch. SHAW (1932, 24:76–7) perceives that in *Ant.* Sh. "is so much the word-musician that mere practical intelligence, no matter how well prompted by dramatic instinct, cannot enable anybody to understand his works or arrive at a right execution of them without the guidance of a fine ear. At the great emotional climaxes we find passages which are Rossinian in their reliance on symmetry of melody and impressiveness of march to redeem poverty of meaning. . . . [77] The right way to declaim Shakespear is the sing-song way."

The 20th c. to about 1930 does not expand much on earlier discussions. After general praise of the play's style by LUCE (1907, p. 327), VOIGT (1908, pp. 3–5) surveys metaphors in *Ant.*, the successful use of which is shown by ANON. (1926, pp. 681–2). NEWBOLT (1916, pp. 183–5, and 1926, pp. 272–7) finds bombast and inconsistencies of tone, mostly in Acts 1–4. BAYFIELD (1920, passim) rearranges lineation according to a strained theory of Sh.'s common use of tri- and quadrisyllabic metrical feet. MURRY (1922, *The Problem of Style*, pp. 36–9) lauds the style of 5.2 as completely adequate to the emotion while Cleopatra passes (p. 38) "from the dignity of a queen to the perfect intimacy of the lover." KLEIN (1930, pp. 20–2, 35–6) examines prose-verse transitions. In the most substantial contribution since Sampson (1889), GRANVILLE-BARKER (1930; 1946, 1:410–23) shows how verse is fitted to mood.

The 1930s are a renaissance for studies of style and particularly imagery, with contributions by Spurgeon, Knight, and Clemen. Discussing imagery apart from dramatic context, SPURGEON (1935, pp. 350, 352; similarly 1930, pp. 40–5) emphasizes the effect created by the domination of imagery of the universe in *Ant.*: "The group of images in *Antony and Cleopatra* . . . peculiar to this play, consists of images of the world, the firmament, the ocean and vastness generally. That is the dominating note in the play, magnificence and grandeur, expressed in many ways. . . .

[*352*] "This vastness of scale is kept constantly before us by the use of the word 'world', which occurs forty-two times, nearly double, or more than double, as often as in most other plays, and it is continually employed in a way which increases the sense of grandeur, power and space, and which fills the imagination with the conception of beings so great that physical size is annihilated and the whole habitable globe shrinks in comparison with them." BETHELL (1944, pp. 117–19), restating Spurgeon on image patterns, speaks of *Ant.*'s (p. 117) "Brobdingnagian imagery."

KNIGHT (1931; 1965, pp. 200 ff.) analyzes four major themes illuminated by image patterns: (p. 205) "imperial magnificence" by imagery of world, sea, and empire; (p. 206) "physical and sensuous love-themes" by images of feasting; "mating of elements" or harmony in nature, by images of blending; and the "spiritual" elements of love, by imagery of fire and light. *Ant.*'s poetry transcends sensuality (pp. 200–1, 203–4, 236): "This poetry is both metaphysical and emotional: but the emotion is ever thrice-distilled . . . so finely wrought in delicate yet vividly dynamic phrase or word that we find a maximum of power within a minimum of sense-appeal, either visual or aural. There are sense-effects, and they are powerful: but they are always so refined, visually and aurally, that we must recognize them to possess only a secondary delight. . . .

[*201*] "There is a pre-eminence of thin or feminine vowel-sounds, 'e' and 'i' [examples given include 381–2, 565–6, 590, 952, 2836]; and a certain lightness and under-emphasis of passion, which yet robs it of no intrinsic power; a refusal of the resonant and reverberating stress, an absence of any direct or prolonged sensuous pleasure in phrase, word, or syllable. . . . [*203*] Throughout there is a certain tenuousness and ethereality in the phraseology and rhythms of which these 'i'-sounds are single instances. . . . [*204*] The style of *Othello* is like a large glowing coal; that of *Macbeth* like the sparks from an anvil; *Lear*, like a rocket; *Timon*, like phosphorus churned to flame in a tropic ocean. That of *Antony and Cleopatra* is like a thin, blazing, electric filament, steadily instinct with keenest fire. . . . [*236*] Everywhere we should observe especially the idea of 'melting', 'dissolving'—it is a crucial theme in the play. For the blending of elements is similar to that blending of the sexes in love which is our main story: and from that we pass, even farther, to a blending of life and death." Thus in 3201–8 death appears as (p. 312) "dear nurse to life, eternity calling back the child of time to its bosom." BROCKBANK (1963, p. 33) endorses Knight's recognition of the "tragic equation between death and nourishment."

CLEMEN (1936; 1977, pp. 159–67), more attentive than Spurgeon and Knight to dramatic context, discusses examples of image patterns that illuminate scene, atmosphere, and details of characterization. TRAVERSI (1938; 1969, 2:219–25; also 1963, p. 146) shows how the (p. 224) "balance between decay and fruitfulness," especially in Cleopatra's imagery, evolves (p. 225) "a certain tragic greatness for Cleopatra's passion . . . out of the impermanence of the flesh and the corrupt world with which it is organically connected."

CHARNEY (1957, pp. 149–61, and 1961, pp. 7, 79–141), like Spurgeon, finds in the world imagery the play's (1961, p. 93) "most general pattern" but, alive to dramatic context as well as to (p. 7) "presentational imagery" conveyed in the theater rather than the text, demonstrates how world imagery follows the dramatic action: (p. 80) "There are at least three distinct movements in this imagery. Before Actium the world is the material domain of the Roman Empire, in which Antony is a 'triple pillar' [19]; after his defeat there is only the memory of the world lost; and his death marks [81] a devaluation of the world, as if his departure removed its source of value." Within the world imagery a (p. 93) "strong symbolic contrast" between sensual Egypt and temperate Rome organizes the play (similarly GRANVILLE-BARKER, 1930; 1946, 1:371, discussing structure), Egypt being characterized by imagery of (p. 95) "eating and drinking, hotness, and indolence," Rome by "temperance, coldness, and business" (see also HERBERT, 1965, pp. 55–9; HOROWITZ, 1965, pp. 41–4; and SEN GUPTA, 1972; 1977, pp. 32–60). Charney analyzes image patterns that mark Antony's decline, particularly those created by allusions to sword and armor, dissolution, and vertical dimension. He finds *Ant.* with its hyperbolical style (p. 28) "one of the richest [plays] in imagery and stylistic effects and *Julius Caesar* one of the most sparse. The two plays offer an illustrative contrast between a carefully limited and controlled 'Roman' style and a hyperbolical and evocative 'Egyptian' style" (similarly 1959, p. 367).

Further discussions of imagery, a favorite approach to the play, include those by SITWELL (1948, pp. 136–43), KYD (1951, pp. 325–33, satirically), NICOLL (1952, pp. 151–2), NOSWORTHY (1956, p. 4), MUIR (1961, *KN*, pp. 249–64, and 1973, pp. 158–70), DAICHES (1962; 1968, pp. 70–95), HOUGHTON (ed. 1962, pp. 11–15), SCHIRMER (in SCHÜCKING, ed. 1962, pp. 198–9), TOMLINSON (1962, p. 118), ISHIDA (1963, pp. 1–9), NEVO (1967, pp. 111–27), LYONS (1968; 1971, pp. 160–86), TRACI (1970, pp. 62–95), LEE (1971, pp. 33–6), SLATER (ed. 1971, pp. 20–6), HENN (1972, pp. 128–35), ADELMAN (1973, pp. 121–57), HOOVER (1973, pp. 80–113), and MATTHEWS (1977–8, passim; 1981, pp. 3–23: image and gesture). On water imagery see LOMBARDO (1959; 1971, pp. 42–67), VENET (1977, passim), and ANSARI (1983, pp. 79–93); on imagery of Fortune LLOYD (1962, pp. 548–54; on Fortune see also WILLIAMSON, 1968, pp. 423–9; HALLETT, 1976, pp. 75–89, and KIEFER, 1983, pp. 319–29); on theater imagery LYONS (1962, pp. 266–72), WALL (1971, 3:257–60), and FARMER (1977, pp. 107–20), and also TROY (in SISSON, ed. 1961, pp. 28–30, briefly) and BRENNAN (1978, pp. 313–29) on the lovers' strategies of self-dramatization; on religious imagery MATTHEWS (1962, pp. 205–7); on death imagery MACMULLAN (1963, pp. 399–410) and HOLLAND (1964, pp. 273, 282); on oaths and imprecations COPPEDGE (1967, pp. 316–39); on body-politic imagery JEWETT (1972, pp. 148–90); on imagery of unity and disintegration KINDRED (1972, pp. 149–72) and SMITH (1977, pp. 15–28); on moon imagery COSTA (1978, pp. 47–64); on farewells M. S. A. SMITH (1978, pp. 65–77); on revelry and carousing VAN WOENSEL (1978, pp. 78–100); on imagery of fixity and motion SNYDER (1980, *ShS*, pp. 114–21); on vertical-stage imagery GOLDMAN (1985, pp. 128–32, 136). Critics who discuss metaphors include SPENCER (1958, pp. 373–8: metaphors of paradox),

RIGHTER (1962, pp. 187–9: theater metaphors), and HOMAN (1971, pp. 407–8: theater as metaphor in 5.2).

To show how style supports the universalizing of individual action, MARKELS (1968, p. 156) argues that abstract diction and indirect syntax enhance a sense of cosmic forces' using human characters for their ends: "By the use of metonymy, inversion, infinitive phrases, and passive constructions, the style keeps subordinating the persons to their actions, which are then universalized by the abstractness of the diction. The characters turn up syntactically only as the objects of verbs and prepositions, and as the subjects of the subordinate clauses; they are made to seem the impersonal media through which cosmic forces work on the world."

HUME (1973, pp. 281, 283–5) examines the relation of speech to character: "The characters are sharply differentiated by their language. . . . [283] The characteristic Egyptian language of Cleopatra [e.g., 345–7] is utterly different from the speech of Caesar [e.g., 458–63]; there is no significant overlap whatever. . . . [284] Antony and Cleopatra exhibit a striking duality in their imagery. The grand is set against the degraded. There is a soaring, often astronomical terminology which they use again and again: heaven, moon, sun, earth, stars, space, kingdom, wide arch of ranged empire, world, ocean, fire, air, tree imagery, great sphere, eternity, orb, thunder. Set against this imagery of transcendental grandeur are terms of degradation, poison, treachery, and decay: snakes, slime, poison, serpents, cistern, discandying, gnats, flies, sty, dung, mud, breeding serpent's poison, ooze, creeps, dungy earth. This combination of the high and low accurately mirrors the ambiguous nature of the protagonists, and it can be seen again in the terms used to describe them.

"Caesar's language is nothing like this. What is startling about it is its almost total lack of vivid terms or striking characteristics. . . . [285] His abstract and dispassionate speech [similarly FRIESEN, 1876, 3:248] gives the impression that he is a man of little feeling or imagination." See also EHRL (1957, pp. 172–4: Antony's language marked by war imagery, Cleopatra's by fickleness, self-confidence, impatience, and voluptuousness; her metaphors blend her person with the elements).

COLIE (1974, pp. 201–2, 206) comments on hyperbole: "At the beginning, Antony speaks hyperbolically, bombastically. . . . It is Cleopatra who checks his overstatement, questions the sincerity of his hyperbole. . . . By the third act, something has begun to happen which demonstrates the identity of the lovers: the hyperbolical style with which Antony began the play now issues from Cleopatra's mouth [quotes 2341–50]. . . . [202] Early in the play, Antony and Cleopatra are separately hyperbolical; as their unity grows, they adapt to each other's modes of speech. These lovers are in many ways temperamentally alike, and they become more so as their meaning for each other becomes more conscious and more motivating in their lives. . . . They are true to one aspect of the Attic (or 'Senecan') prescription, after all, in that they express 'themselves' truly in their language—this is to say, then, that their style *must* in honesty be bombastic, which according to Attic prescription should mean that their style matches the variability and shoddiness of their characters. . . . [206] What at first sounds like bombast in Antony's speech

is naturalized in the course of the play, until his way of speaking beco
against which other men are judged. . . . During the course of the pl
Antony and Cleopatra grow into their rhetorical measure. At the play's start,
had called a spade a spade, or even a shovel: in contrast, Antony and Cleopatra
spoke in love's arrogant, idealized overstatements. By the end of the play, Philo's
linguistic practice is blocked out by Antony's hyperbole coming true, until we too
believe that 'the nobleness of life' [47] is for such lovers to embrace." See also DORAN
(1965, pp. 26–51) and ADELMAN (1973, pp. 102–57) on hyperbole.

Critics who discuss baroque or mannerist style in *Ant.* include LINDHEIM (1954,
pp. 247–9), HAUSER (1964, tr. 1965, 1:342–6), ROERECKE (1965, pp. 182–95),
and HOY (1973, pp. 62–4). For versification, see also BINDER (1939, pp. 141–
57), GRIFFITH (1947, pp. 163–5), SEDLAK (1970, pp. 154–209), and DUNBAR
(1971, pp. 231–45); for prose CRANE (1951, pp. 177–81) and VICKERS (1968,
pp. 380–8); for Antony's language especially DRAPER (1946, pp. 430–2) and
CHARNEY (1957, pp. 149–61); for bawdy PARTRIDGE (1947; 1968, passim), TRACI
(1970, pp. 136–60), COLMAN (1974, passim), and BRAND (1976, pp. 98–107:
sex imagery); for comparisons of language with North's Plutarch, see pp. 393–4;
for grammar, see studies by BURTON (1967–8, pp. 148–54; 1970, 1st pub. 1968,
pp. 34–9; and 1973, pp. 266–72 et passim) and HOUSTON (1988, pp. 179–97:
syntactical tone). Other discussions include those by BOAS (ed. 1935, pp. xx–ii:
general appraisal), RIDLEY (ed. 1935, pp. ix–x, and ed. 1954, pp. liv–vi: praise
of dramatic poetry), VAN DOREN (1939, pp. 232–8: little dramatic action, but
verbal intensity), MIRIAM JOSEPH (1947, passim: rhetorical devices), ELIOT (1950,
pp. 205–6, and 1955–6, n. pag.: verse and prose), EVANS (1952; 1964, pp.
191–7: variety of language), BEAUCHAMP (1955, pp. 166–78: style compared to
other dramatic versions of the story), MAHOOD (1957; 1965, passim: wordplay),
BONJOUR (1959, pp. 136–46: dramatic irony in opening scenes), LLOYD (1959,
SQ, pp. 461–8: Roman style), MILNER (1966, pp. 153–8: colloquial style at
climactic moments), WALTER (ed. 1969, pp. 34–42: image patterns, hyperbole,
puns; pp. 42–6: verse and prose), HAPGOOD (1971, pp. 1–12: verbal sound effects;
tone of private not political struggles), PARTRIDGE (1971, pp. 210–20: on ll.
379–427), BOSE (1972, pp. 60–1: word music), EVANS (1973, 5:31–2: quality of
regal ritual in the language), JONES (ed. 1977, pp. 43–7: lyrical style modeled on
Horace's *Odes*), WECKERMANN (1978, pp. 261–7: communication problems), BE-
REK (1981, pp. 295–304: language of action), and JACKSON (1984, pp. 128–48:
descriptions and metaphors of triumph).

Special comments on Enobarbus's "barge" speech (901–31) include those by
LE BLANC (1745, tr. 1747, 2:167–8), MARMONTEL (1746, 1:124), SCOTT (1808;
1883, 5:312–13), JEFFREY (1817, p. 474), BRADFORD (1898; 1936, pp. 204–5),
DOUGLAS (1909, pp. 583–9), HALLIDAY (1954, pp. 161–2), BARROLL (1958,
TxSE, pp. 61–78), TRAVERSI (1963, pp. 115–17), GREYERZ (1965, pp. 58–61),
PROSER (1965, pp. 197–200), BOSE (1966, pp. 81–97), GÜNTHER (1968, pp.
98–100), MORGAN (1968, pp. 131–3), ALTMANN (1969, pp. 60–102), ERSKINE-
HILL (1970, pp. 26–8), RACKIN (1972, pp. 204–6), DOWNER (1975, pp. 242–

1978, pp. 105–6); see also CIONI (1986, pp. 73–

n German) remarks on Agrippa and Maecenas: "Their intel-
listinguished, but it is just enough to restore peace and sleep
to a.   orld and teach it that for the time being there is to be an end to
all distinc.   . . I cannot help seeing them in silk garments as they were worn
by sixteenth-century diplomats." As GRANVILLE-BARKER (1930; 1946, 1:456–7)
sees them, they "hover after Cæsar to the end, putting in the tactful word—which
ripens to flattery . . . the minute [457] he is secure in power. Such men, of such
a measure, are always forthcoming." Others who discuss Agrippa include OECHEL-
HÄUSER (ed. 1877; 1895, p. 95: his role to be merged with Dolabella's in productions), TRAVERSI (1963, pp. 112–13: his flattery and insinuation in 2.2), and
WERTIME (1969, pp. 48–52: in 2.2 he flatters Antony's sense of personal honor).

ANTONY

Among the earliest characteristics noted is his complex fusion of nobility and corruption. Thus TATE (1680, sig. A4ᵛ): "You find his [Sh.'s] *Anthony* in all the Defects
and Excellencies of his Mind, a Souldier, a Reveller, Amorous, sometimes Rash,
sometimes Considerate, with all the various Emotions of his Mind." DAVIES (1783,
2:367) speaks of Antony's "boundless generosity, as well as unexampled dotage."
And SCHLEGEL (1811, tr. 1846, pp. 416–17): "In Antony we observe a mixture
of great qualities, weaknesses, and vices; violent ambition and ebullitions of magnanimity; we see him now sinking into luxurious enjoyment and then nobly ashamed
of his own aberrations,—manning himself to resolutions not unworthy of himself,
which are always shipwrecked against the seductions of an artful woman. . . . [417]
The open and lavish character of Antony is admirably contrasted with the heartless
littleness of Octavius."

Nineteenth-century critics sometimes stress either the lover or the ruler. KNIGHT
(ed. 1841; 1849, pp. 420–2), giving a companion sketch of Antony to JAMESON's
(1832) of Cleopatra, sees him as poetical lover: "The *Antony* of this play is of course
the Antony of *Julius Cæsar*;—not merely the historical Antony, but the dramatic
Antony drawn by the same hand. . . . We cannot think meanly of him. He is one
great either for good or for evil. . . . [421] The reckless short-sighted voluptuary
was never drawn more truly. His entire policy is shaped by his passion. . . . [422]
Antony was of the poetical temperament—a man of high genius—an orator, who
could move the passions dramatically—a lover, that knew no limits to his devotion,
because he loved imaginatively. When sorrow falls upon him, the poetical parts of
his character are more and more developed; we forget the sensualist." Others who

comment on his poetic nature include KREYβIG (1858; 1877, 1:454), BRANDES (1895, tr. 1935, pp. 465–6), and ORNSTEIN (1966, pp. 39–42).

ULRICI (1839; 1868–9, tr. 1876, 2:201–3), however, stresses that he is unfit as a ruler: he combines a "straightforward, frank disposition" with the vices of his times, notably (p. 202) "love of dominion, ambition, inconstancy, arrogance, and excessive voluptuousness." His "old heroism" is "extinguished, stifled by the atmosphere of excessive love of pleasure," Cleopatra finally making him "a moral renegade." Antony is beaten by Octavius because "the history of his day preeminently called for prudence and consistency": (p. 203) "He who does not possess these qualities—he who, like Antony, cannot control himself . . .—is not destined to take an independent part in the great piece of [historical] machinery." And GERVINUS (1850, tr. 1883, pp. 730, 741), similarly severe on Antony's political defects, dwells on his inward emptiness: "We see him everywhere needing a prop, a supporter, never able to stand alone. . . . His imitation of Hercules or Bacchus refers to this trait; he leans against a tutelar god, who, according to Shakespeare and to Plutarch, turns from him when he is to perish. With a nature thus ever needing support, he encounters this paragon of female weakness, Cleopatra, like ivy leaning on ivy. . . . [741] By nothing more striking than this poetical image [2826 ff.] could the poet . . . comprise his judgment respecting the whole life of this man, who astonished and deceived the world with his splendid nothingness, with his seeming greatness and seeming nobleness, in a thousand changing forms."

Several comment on Antony's inner struggle, suggested by Schlegel (1811). Thus SKOTTOWE (1824, 2:238–40): "He is fully alive to, and bitterly laments [239] the folly and degradation of his conduct; but his firmest resolves are feebly opposed against the potent spell of his [quotes 'graue . . . end' (2781–3)]. . . . History has alike recorded Antony's intellectual ability and his corporeal frailty: a victim to the latter, enough of the former doubtless survived to impress on his memory the deepest sense of his folly, the weakness and the unworthiness of his infatu-[240]ation. Shakspeare read the inmost thoughts of Antony." SNIDER (1876; 1877, 2:281–2): in Act 4 "he fights, not to save an empire, but to preserve his relation to the Egyptian Queen. . . . The deepest principle of his nature [p. 271: 'gratification of the senses'] is assailed; he might dally away the world, but he cannot surrender the tie to Cleopatra. . . . The internal conflict now [in 4.12] arises more fiercely than ever; she to whom he has sacrificed a world has betrayed him. What agony could be more intense? . . . [282] His career is made up of a series of external conflicts on account of his passion, and internal conflicts with his passion." CORSON (1889, p. 303): "The disastrous consequences of his insane persistence to fight at sea [in 3.7] . . . cause Antony to rise to a deep and mortifying sense of his infatuation and enslavement. It is in representing the moral struggle which ensues that he is kept within the pale of our sympathy. He is not wholly despicable." And MOULTON (1903; 1907, pp. 130–1): "The rivalry of the state and the individual is . . . to be seen within the personality of Antony himself: it is [131] the conflict, for Antony, between his public and his private life. . . . For this competing public and private life of Antony there is an external measure in the movement of the play: Antony conjoining himself with Cæsar is the life rising to public duty; Antony inclining to Cleopatra is the life falling to private passion."

In the 20th c. Antony attracts further comment as lover. BRADLEY's (1906; 1909, pp. 294, 296–8) statements on Antony as lover (and on his nobility), though more lyrical, partly recall Knight's (1841): "We do not feel the hero of the tragedy to be a man of the noblest type, like Brutus, Hamlet, or Othello. . . . Yet, for all this, we sympathise warmly with Antony, are greatly drawn to him, and are inclined to regard him as a noble nature half spoiled by his time. . . . His nature tends to splendid action and lusty enjoyment. But he is neither a mere soldier nor a mere sensualist. He has imagination, the temper of an artist who revels in abundant and rejoicing appetites, feasts his senses on the glow and richness of life, flings himself into its mirth and revelry, yet feels the poetry in all this. . . . [296] When he meets Cleopatra he finds his Absolute. She satisfies, nay glorifies, his whole being. . . . [297] To love her is what he was born for. What have the gods in heaven to say against it? To imagine heaven is to imagine her; to die is to rejoin her. To deny that this is love is the madness of morality. He gives her every atom of his heart. . . . [298] He is more than love's pilgrim; he is love's martyr." And KNIGHT (1931; 1965, p. 258 n., expanded in 1958, pp. 193–4) picks up F1's spelling "Anthony"—see n. 3305—suggestive of his flowery nature, as denoting the lover (see also 1931; 1965, p. 288 et passim). IDE (1980, pp. 114–21) and SUMMERS (1984, pp. 115–36) discuss Antony as heroic lover.

MURRY (1936, pp. 367–8, 377) points to his followers' loyalty: "The royalty that draws loyalty to it, that compels loyalty indeed, but by an internal, not an external compulsion, whereby the servant is at once the lover and the friend, and knows that he becomes his own true self only in serving his lord—this royalty is, in the lord himself, superhuman. . . . [368] Shakespeare's prodigious art consists first and foremost in convincing us of Antony's royalty. . . . [377] We have watched Antony ennoble the sacrifice of his friends, and be the more ennobled by that sacrifice; and we have watched him die royally."

A number of 20th-c. critics expand the idea of his unresolved complexity (see also pp. 684–5). LYMAN (1940, pp. 93–4, 98), for example, sees Antony as Janus-faced: "He has two soul-sides. . . . The Roman is the one the world sees: a great captain, the triple pillar of the world, but with his best days behind him; yet an old lion, one who with his sword had quartered the world. . . . [94] This Antony looks back into the past for his own identity, and scarcely finds it in the present. Over against him, shrined in the present, towers the Alexandrian god. Says Cleopatra: [3292 ff.]. Antony's stature in Cleopatra's eyes is more than human; his magnanimity and might outreach humanity. . . .

"Transfer this conception of him from Cleopatra's mind to Antony's and you have the material of delusions of grandeur. . . . Indeed, throughout the play Antony proclaims himself in grandiose vaunts which ring as if he thought himself omnipotent. . . . [98] One face is that of a man, a great Roman captain; the other, that of a god, Jove-like rather than Egyptian, although his Olympus is Alexandria."

And FARNHAM (1950, p. 139) speaks of both lovers' "paradoxical nobility," with Antony for all his flaws capable of rising at his end to (p. 182) "an unselfish consideration of Cleopatra's future that shows deepened love for her" (ROSEN, 1960, pp. 122, 158, however, argues that, although Antony repeatedly and unsuccessfully tries to renounce Cleopatra, his death does not glorify his love: what matters most to him is his [p. 158] "honorable reputation").

Others find him less complex. Thus PHILLIPS (1940, pp. 193–8), like Ulrici (1839), discusses Antony's incontinency, and his vices are further stressed by STEM-PEL (1956, p. 69), DICKEY (1957, pp. 179, 183), and BARROLL (1958, *JEGP*, pp. 708–20).

For DRAPER (1965, *Psychiatric Quarterly*, pp. 451–2; similarly 1945, pp. 40–2), he is a sybarite: "Not melancholy debility but phlegmatic lust makes him desert the battle and steer his ship after the fleeing Cleopatra, and then forgive her for the unforgivable. He has changed from the choleric Roman of Act I, who left her at political behest, into a phlegmatic voluptuary, who has no thought of consequences, in fact, no thought at all; and Enobarbus notes with soldierly disgust a 'diminution' in his general's intellect [2385]. . . . Plutarch has obligated the playwright to [452] set aside accepted medical theory, and depict advancing years as turning the soldier into the sybarite; and such a change implies a protracted tension in which native ideals and obvious good sense give way by degrees to overwhelming passion.

"The younger Antony of *Julius Caesar*, sharp politician and successful general, properly looked forward to becoming a power in the state; but the older Antony, having achieved great power and a time of life that ought to have brought wisdom, looks forward more and more only to Cleopatra; and, as the tragedy unfolds, the inner conflict of this strange transition becomes close to psychosis, a conflict between past and present, between intellect and emotion, that reduces the sufferer to bad judgment at Actium and later in Egypt to instability and utter folly."

More favorably, a number of critics stress his magnanimity. STAUFFER (1949, pp. 238, 240–1): "If Antony is to fail tragically, it must be because he is false to his own conception of himself rather than false to his social obligations, for Shake-speare has intentionally portrayed a political world that 'is not worth leave-taking' [3549].

"And if Antony is to fail tragically, he must be built up to towering stature. His own integrity as a soldier must outweigh the world's opinion, and his love for Cleopatra must outweigh his integrity. He is larger than the world, and his love is larger than himself. . . .

[240] "Perhaps Antony is the most comprehensive character that Shakespeare set his hand to. . . . [241] Even his enemies acknowledge that his greatness can be destroyed only by himself: ['He . . . heart' (3132–7)]. Basically, Shakespeare makes confidence into a moral quality in Antony. He has no lack-luster doubts or palterings. No matter how rapidly his moods shift, no matter how recklessly he remains a 'child o' th' time' [1450], at every moment he is master of himself and others. This headlong certainty of purpose is here interpreted as but another manifestation of generosity, magnanimity."

STEIN (1959, pp. 586, 588–90): "What is the process . . . which finally permits Antony, against great odds, to project an authentic tragic self which is the image that emerges triumphantly from all the others? . . .

[588] "Antony may be considered Shakespeare's manliest man. . . . The manliest man will be most admired by other men, not only for his virtues but for his faults. . . .

[589] "Antony savors moments, can put himself wholly into a moment; and this would appear to be a major source of both strength and weakness. But a source of this ability, to push matters a little further back, must be located in the man's heroic self-confidence. It is a rich and complex confidence. At the worst it may seem to approach petulance at one extreme and megalomania at another. . . . But it is a real and unquestionable base of strength, from which he can freely admit real weakness, which is always complicated in effect; and though he can also extravagantly display the shallow forms of weakness to which strength and confidence are conventionally subject, no superficial extravagance on his part quite counters the steady presence of an essential confidence. Gesture after gesture reaffirms the rich resource he draws upon, and proves—whether or not in the main assertion at least moment by moment—a 'nobleness of life' [47]. The old term, which does not [590] simplify the problem in its context, is 'magnanimity'—that authentic generosity of imagination that shapes with spontaneous grace the superior response to ordinary and immediate concerns." And KROOK (1967; 1969, p. 203) sees Antony in Aristotelian terms as "the Magnificent Man and the Magnanimous Man of the *Nicomachean Ethics* [4.3] rolled into one." Others who remark on his generosity or magnanimity include KREYβIG (1858; 1877, 1:454–9), PEART (1892, pp. 218–19), WOLFF (1907; 1913, 2:269), WINCHESTER (1922, pp. 69–70), RICHTER (1930, p. 142), CRAIG (1948, pp. 275–80), WAITH (1950, pp. 272–3, and 1971, pp. 108–10), SCHILLING (1953, pp. 224–5, 228–32), JENKINS (1958–60, p. 34), HUNTER (1966, pp. 21–5), MARKELS (1968, pp. 130–40), MOORE (1969, p. 673), WALTER (ed. 1969, pp. 25–9), ERSKINE-HILL (1970, pp. 34–8), ADELMAN (1973, pp. 128–30), FISKIN (1975, pp. 98–9), and MARCHANT (1984, pp. 164–5). See also STAPFER (1879, tr. 1880, pp. 380–1), who believes Antony desires others' happiness as an element of his own well-being.

WAITH (1962, pp. 114–16, 121) stresses Antony's dedication to Cleopatra's image of his heroism: "Out of the fragments of the Roman image of Antony grows the great image presented in Cleopatra's speeches in the fifth act—an image which owes as [115] much to the ideals of romance as to the older heroic ideal. The hero is re-created and yet . . . not entirely made anew, for the process in which Cleopatra has so important a part is a reassertion of qualities Antony already possesses, a shift of emphasis, a rediscovery of self.

"The Antony who commits suicide at the end of the play is no longer a world-conqueror in the obvious sense of the term, yet neither is he the defeated man we have seen after Actium. In his own way he has conquered the world and himself. . . . [116] He would end his life not only to recover a soldier's honour but to be worthy of Cleopatra. . . . Where the pursuit of the beloved led to shameful self-betrayal at Actium, here it is the affirmation of an ideal exalted in romances and in Renaissance love-poetry generally: the lover finds only in the beloved the completing of himself. . . . [*121*] Antony's suicide is in one sense a recognition of the impossibility of achieving Cleopatra's ideal in the world. It is a noble Roman's death, but more than that, it is a dedication of himself to Cleopatra, the final custodian of his heroic image." For Waith's (1962) analysis of Antony as Herculean hero, see p. 656.

Antony's understanding of himself divides critics. CHARNEY (1957, p. 149) analyzes his tragedy as one not of self-knowledge but of will: Sh.'s "Antony resembles Hamlet in this respect: both have an acute awareness of their moral situation, but they are without the power to change it. Their tragedy does not come from a blindness or error of judgment, but from a deep-seated paralysis of will. Hamlet, however, is catapulted into a tragedy to which he remains alien and unreconciled, whereas Antony seems to choose his fate deliberately and knowingly." Heilman and Nochimson, though, believe Antony does not recognize his flaws. HEILMAN (1964, pp. 19–20, 27): "Macbeth has to suppress the knowledge of what he is up to in order to be up to it, whereas in doing what he does Antony drifts away from knowledge of it. In Macbeth we see the quelling of conscience by action; in Antony, the decay of conscience in passion. . . . [*20*] Shakespeare sensed Antony as a man in whom the clear knowing of self and of moral options has been all but deadened by the [erotic] impulses that determine his direction. . . . This is Shakespeare's new version of the tragic hero in relation to the problem of self-knowledge. . . . [*27*] Antony poses a question raised by none of the other heroes: can the man of charm look within? *Dare* he? What substance might he find by which to estimate the thing done, the life lived? . . . The flow of his psychic energy is all outward. . . . Shakespeare is here imagining, as he does in no other tragedy, a world where all vital powers conspire against self-knowledge." And NOCHIMSON (1977, p. 103): "Antony's lack of perceptiveness in studying himself is clearly a source of many of the problems that develop for him. This could evoke a tragic response in us if, sooner or later but too late to save himself, he arrived at a realisation of error. . . . This is very much not the case. In fact, throughout the play, Antony's insistence upon his greatness, in the face of mounting contradictory evidence, is a dominant motif." Nochimson also observes (p. 113), "We can feel tragically about Antony only if before his end that crowns all he creates for us a sense of stature that makes us feel his loss as significant. . . . [*120*] The death of the Antony that Shakespeare has depicted for us could not cause the crown of the earth to melt, and, as though to make sure that no one will miss this point, Shakespeare repeats it in Act V. The Antony of Cleopatra's dreams is a magnificent figure indeed. But we have not seen such a figure in Shakespeare's play."

The conflict between Egyptian passion and Roman reason in Antony is a further topic of discussion. DANBY (1949; 1952, p. 146): "His human stature is greater than either Cleopatra's or Caesar's. Yet there is no sphere in which he can express himself except either Rome or Egypt, and to bestride both like a Colossus and keep his balance is impossible. The opposites play through Antony and play with him, and finally destroy him." STROUP (1964, pp. 289–98) sees Antony's psychomachia as resembling mankind's in the morality plays; MARKELS (1968, p. 9) argues that, in refusing to choose between Roman public duty and Egyptian private appetite, Antony finally encompasses both (similarly STILLING, 1976, p. 280). A different estimate is that of HOY (1973, p. 62), who thinks Antony remains lost in dotage throughout and never veers from passion to public duty.

Voicing an opinion often implied by others, PURDOM (1963, pp. 166–9) argues that Antony is the play's sole protagonist, Cleopatra being far less important.

Others who praise or defend Antony include GRIFFITH (1775, p. 473), BRÄKER (1780, tr. 1979, pp. 83–4), HÜLSMANN (1856, pp. 226–9), LLOYD (1856; 1858, sig. K3ᵛ), KREYβIG (1858; 1877, 1:454–9), MÉZIÈRES (1860; 1886, pp. 452–5), VISCHER (1869–87; 1905, 6:158–61, 170, 173), BLUMHOF (ed. 1870, pp. 19–22), MINTO (1874; 1885, p. 285), FRIESEN (1876, 3:244, 254–5), OECHELHÄUSER (ed. 1877; 1895, p. 92), TALBOT (1887, p. 228), MORLEY & GRIFFIN (1895, 11:93, 95), WEEKES (1928, p. 189), GRANVILLE-BARKER (1930; 1946, 1:423–35), RICHTER (1930, p. 142), BOAS (ed. 1935, pp. viii–xi), NEILSON & HILL (ed. 1942, p. 1245), CRAIG (1948, pp. 275–80), WILSON (ed. 1950, pp. xxiv–xxxii), OLIVIER (ed. 1952, pp. 4–6), PARKER (1955, pp. 147–8), WRIGHT (1958, pp. 42–5), McFARLAND (1958–9, pp. 221–4), RIBNER (1960, pp. 172–6, 180–2), ALEXANDER (1964, p. 240), JONES (1967, pp. 73–85), HAINES (1968, pp. 121–4), WERTIME (1969, pp. 13–123), ERSKINE-HILL (1970, pp. 34–8), BROWER (1971, pp. 320–37), INGLEDEW (ed. 1971, pp. xxv–ix), McALINDON (1973, pp. 195–200), LYMAN & SCOTT (1975, pp. 73–91, 97), CHAMPION (1976, pp. 246–7), and CLAYTON (1981, p. 96). See also LEWIS (1927, p. 154), who claims that Sh., being attached in "romantic devotion" to his "warlike demigods," is "in love with Antony."

Others who dislike or attack him include DUPORT (1828, 2:57), TIECK (ed. 1831, 5:378), THÜMMEL (1881; 1887, 2:29, 32–3), WINCHELL (1881, pp. 207–9), and BERKELEY (1953, pp. 1–13; 1955–6, pp. 96–9; 1956–7, pp. 286–7; and 1964, pp. 138–42).

Those who discuss the complexity of his character include DRAKE (1817, 2:493), GUIZOT (ed. 1821, 3:2), DE QUINCEY (1832; 1890, 6:272–3), TYRRELL (ed. 1851–3, 3:367), HUDSON (ed. 1855; 1872, 2:383–5), STAPFER (1879, tr. 1880, pp. 379–93), SHARP (1902, pp. 141–3), HERFORD (1916; 1921, pp. 41–2), LANDAUER (1920; 1962, pp. 308–9), ANDERSON (1927; 1966, p. 160), PERGER (1936, p. 113), WILCOX (1936, pp. 533–7), SCHMIDT (1938, pp. 349–50), TRAVERSI (1938; 1969, 2:208–32; and 1963, pp. 79–203), URBAN (1939, passim), DANBY (1949; 1952, pp. 146–7, 151), GODDARD (1951, 2:193–4), BROWN (1953, pp. 294–6), DRAPER (1960, p. 219), GOLDBERG (1961, pp. 50–6), BOWLING (1964, pp. 239–46), KUCKHOFF (1964, p. 417), MENDL (1964, p. 176), HAPONSKI (1967), GARDNER (1968, pp. 19–29), STAMPFER (1968, pp. 253–6), SERIO (1970, p. 16), MURAKAMI (1970–1, pp. 29–40), LYMAN & SCOTT (1975, pp. 73–91, 97), CANTOR (1976, pp. 155–6), FERRARA (1977, pp. 63–80), JONES (ed. 1977, pp. 37–40), DORIUS (1978, pp. 315–17), NAUMANN (1978, pp. 420–1), and

VINCENT (1978, pp. 32–172). BARROLL (1969, pp. 159–235, and 1984, pp. 83–125) also discusses Antony's complexity.

The following are among those who comment on his problems of identity: KNIGHT (1931; 1965, p. 276), WILCOX (1936, pp. 533–7), URBAN (1939, passim), POGSON (1950, p. 114), KAULA (1964, pp. 217–20), NANDY (1964, p. 183), HUNTER (1966, pp. 21–5), GARDNER (1968, pp. 19–29), BARROLL (1969, pp. 179–80), SERIO (1970, pp. 16–17), TRACI (1970, pp. 119–21, 148), WHITAKER (1972, pp. 54–99), SIMMONS (1973, *Shakespeare's Pagan World*, pp. 133–6), GARBER (1974, pp. 131–3), CANTOR (1976, pp. 189–90), SCHWARTZ (1977; 1980, pp. 29–30), BRENNAN (1978, pp. 313–29), VAN LAAN (1978, pp. 215–22), VINCENT (1978, pp. 32–172), WILDERS (1978, pp. 100, 116, and 1988, pp. 226, 229), GOHLKE (1980, pp. 159–60), SNYDER (1980, *SEL*, p. 207), WHEELER (1981, pp. 208–10), BAMBER (1982, pp. 45–70), BLISS (1983, p. 86), DOLLIMORE (1983, pp. 210–11), ERICKSON (1985, pp. 123–47), and STOCKHOLDER (1987, pp. 148–62).

Those who consider the reasons for his fall include HORN (1827, 4:43–67), KREYβIG (1858; 1877, 1:451), CLARKE (1863, p. 218), THÜMMEL (1881; 1887, 2:29, 32–3), EMERSON (1890, pp. 517–21), JUSSERAND (1904, tr. 1909, 2:262–4), MACCALLUM (1910, pp. 391–412), WAITH (1950, p. 271), SPALDING (1953, p. 158), MACLURE (1954–5, pp. 119–20), LÜTHI (1957; 1966, pp. 121–3), MILLS (1964, pp. 7–35), BRANDÃO (1978, pp. 101–14), and SUJAKU (1978, pp. 231–42).

Critics who discuss his chivalric heroism include FRIESEN (1876, 3:244), ECKHOFF (1954, pp. 60–2), and WILLIAMSON (1974, pp. 200–6); his heroism is regarded as soldierly by EMERSON (1890, pp. 517–21), BORINSKI (1955, pp. 104–6), and NANDY (1964, p. 181). For his language, see also DRAPER (1946, pp. 426–32), SEN GUPTA (1972; 1977, pp. 44–8), HUME (1973, pp. 280–300), COLIE (1974, p. 175), MIYAUCHI (1978, passim), and SMITH (1983, pp. 57, 71–8). MOMMSEN (in WILDENBRUCH, 1914, p. 3) affirms that Sh.'s Antony is an accurate portrait of the historical figure.

CHARMIAN AND IRAS

ELLIOTT (1885, pp. 337–8, 340, 342–4) discusses their fidelity: "They are the confidential handmaids of a voluptuous and capricious queen, and attendants in the innermost circle of a dissolute court.

"We need not therefore expect to find in them any very high qualities of mind or morals. Like most around them they are quick-witted and ready-spoken, much given to [338] laughter and merry jesting, and by no means particular as to the matter or manner of their jokes. . . .

[340] "Charmian is a thorough teaze. She delights in playing counter to her companion's mood. . . .

"But at other times when the Majesty of Egypt wants soothing . . . Charmian can be as acquiescent as any one, and eeks most faithfully all her mistress' wishes. . . .

[342] "But Charmian is no mere girl, no butterfly sunning herself in the splendour of the court. . . . Iras and she, whilst they basked in Cleopatra's glorious summer of pomp and luxury, remain true to her in disaster, and do not forsake her in death. As they partook of her prosperity they share her disaster. . . . [343] Of the three, Iras is the first to die. But there is no hysterical passion about her end. . . . Charmian is left to triumph for a moment over Cæsar's disappointment and to sing her sovereign's requiem. Her firmness never fails her. . . .

[344] "All Shakspeare's women are faithful and attached to those they serve, but in Charmian and Iras alone do we see this faithfulness follow them to the grave. Judging them by their first appearance we see little to warrant such devotion of character and such firmness of purpose. They seem giddy and heartless. In fact, Charmian welcomes the prediction that she shall survive her mistress, but when the hour comes that Cleopatra determines to atone for her cowardice by her death, and share Antony's fate as she brought about his downfall, there is no clinging to life as would seem natural in so young and careless a girl, but a stoical calmness that embraces death as a boon and enables her to die with the light of triumph in her eyes and a smile of scorn upon her lips."

GRANVILLE-BARKER (1930; 1946, 1:457–8) also sees both as rising to dignity: "Iras is the more fragile, the more placid; Charmian, the 'wild bedfellow' [128], will be the quicker of her tongue, when a word may be slipped in. It is an impudent tongue too; she has no awe of her betters. Worthless little trulls, no doubt! But when disaster comes, and Antony's men, all save one, make their peace with the conqueror, for these two there is no question. They also see what lies behind Cæsar's courtesy; and the timid, silent Iras suddenly breaks silence with [3428–9]—revealing herself in a dignity of spirit of her own. Another moment and she is trembling again; one would think she could hardly carry her share of the heavy robe and crown. Her service consummated by her mistress' kiss, she dies, as the people of the [458] East can, so they say, by pure denial of life. Charmian . . . is of fiercer breed. Quick, desperate, agonized, sticking to her task to the end—when all is over she is at it still, fighting her Queen's battles still, mocking the enemy. She laughs in triumph as she too dies."

Morgan and Wertime discuss Charmian as foil to Cleopatra. MORGAN (1968, p. 138): "Charmian is, in a sense, Cleopatra's double, or under-study, as the dramatically more prominent and complex Enobarbus has been Antony's. . . . When the Queen is 'marble-constant' [3490], pure symbol, the queenliness in the waiting-woman shines out. . . . Charmian throughout, though lightly sketched, is more like the North-Plutarch Cleopatra than her mistress is. Steadily good-humoured, devoted and affectionate, in all her scenes Charmian is the guardian of a clear-sighted but sympathetic estimate of human value: the value of the imperfect, mortal being." And WERTIME (1969, pp. 142–3): "Cleopatra's first encounter with the messenger [in 2.5] is also pivotal in Charmian's career as a choric commentator. To this point . . . Charmian's relationship to the queen has paralleled Enobarbus's relationship to Antony: both begin in a state of detached amusement toward the love affair, skeptical of its stability and power to endure; both move toward a more positive

attitude regarding it—Enobarbus in 1
reminiscences—as they are drawn out o
flow of action; both, even, find their o1
their masters. But here they part ways. A1
in Act II, scene ii is the beginning of th
Charmian's tactful reticence toward Cleop̣
the former's total acceptance of her mistre
that eventually unites them in death."

Others who discuss Charmian and Ira,
2:386: they show moral and social qualities
CLARKE (1863, p. 240: their devotion and obe
moving devotion), OECHELHÄUSER (ed. 1877;
patra is), MORGAN & VINES (ed. 1893–8, p. x
ADLER (1895, p. 304: good character despite ligh
speak Cleopatra's language in a minor key), MA   ₋₁924, p. 404: reflectors
of Cleopatra), GUNDOLF (1926, pp. 17–18, and 1928; 1949, 2:435: reflect Cleopatra's combination of queen and harlot), KNIGHT (1931; 1965, pp. 320–1: "sta-
bilize and solidify the marbled theme [321] of Love above the flux of change"),
ARTHOS (1964, p. 63: choose to die for love), RICE (1968, pp. 372–3: at Cleopatra's
death Charmian sustains tragic mood), MUIR (1972, p. 168: Charmian's love and
loyalty), CHAMPION (1976, p. 263: they reveal Cleopatra's deceptiveness), SHINTRI
(1977, p. 248: they are worthy of Cleopatra's affection), BRENNAN (1978, pp.
328–9: they are shills; they prompt the audience), TOLMIE (1978, p. 130: between
1.3 and 4.13 Charmian learns much about Antony's relationship to Cleopatra), and
VINCENT (1978, pp. 53–4: Charmian in 1.2 mocks idea of Fortune but is caught
up in a tragic plot).

CLEOPATRA

The satirist ANTON (1616; 1617, p. 46) includes Cleopatra, though not clearly
Sh.'s, in his attack on the theaters: "Why are *women* rather growne so mad, | That
their *immodest feete* like *planets* gad | With such *irregular motion* to base *Playes*, | Where
all the *deadly sinnes* keepe *hollidaies*. | There shall they see the *vices* of the *times*, |
Orestes incest, *Cleopatres* crimes." After the Restoration, in an age more concerned
with Sh.'s truth to nature, CAVENDISH (1664, p. 245) praises his capacity for
portraying women, including Cleopatra, "to the Life": (p. 246) "One would think
that he had been Metamorphosed from a Man to a Woman, for who could Describe
Cleopatra Better than he hath done." WESLEY's (1685, p. 3) lines probably allude
to 3538 and 3566: "I come she cryed, I com' dear *Hony!* | And then kickt up with
Tony! Tony." The 18th c. rarely finds much to admire in her. JOHNSON (ed. 1765,
7:254), whose classical taste is offended by her lack of decorum, deplores "the
feminine arts, some of which are too low, which distinguish *Cleopatra*." Few in this
period comment on her death or her reasons for suicide. GILDON (1710, p. 413),
the most explicit, flatly asserts that she kills herself "to avoid being carry'd in

DAVIES (1783, 2:367) speaks of her "generous reso-
submit to embrace life upon ignoble terms." Later critics
patra's motive is fear of humiliation include HORN (1827,
ON (1832; 1879, p. 275), ANON. (1849, p. 282), GERVINUS
3, p. 739), LLOYD (1856; 1858, sig. K3ʳ), SYMONS (1889; 1919,
), LEWES (1893, tr. 1894, p. 257), BRANDL (1894, p. 189), BRANDES
, tr. 1935, p. 475), BRADLEY (1906; 1909, pp. 301–2), DANBY (1949; 1952,
p. 144–5), RÜEGG (1951, p. 265), ROSEN (1960, p. 156), FOAKES (1964, *DUJ*,
p. 72), and WILLIAMSON (1970, pp. 250–1). FRYE (1986, p. 128) thinks her
suicide motivated "by her total refusal to be a part of someone else's scene."

DAVIES (1783, 2:365–6) is the first to recognize an ennobling value in her
death: "Cleopatra's preparation for death is animated to a degree of sublimity which
greatly raises the character of the Egyptian princess, and makes us lament her in
death whom living we could not praise, [366] though it was impossible not to
admire her."

The romantics find Cleopatra's ambivalence fascinating. Thus SCHLEGEL (1811,
tr. 1846, pp. 416–17): "The seductive arts of Cleopatra are in no respect veiled
over; she is an ambiguous being made up of royal pride, female vanity, luxury,
inconstancy, and true attachment. Although the mutual passion of herself and
Antony is without moral dignity, it still excites our sympathy as an insurmountable
fascination:—they seem formed [417] for each other, and Cleopatra is as remarkable
for her seductive charms as Antony for the splendour of his deeds. As they die for
each other, we forgive them for having lived for each other." Others who believe
she dies for love include HUGO (ed. 1860; 1868, 7:22–3: death is the lovers' hymen,
or marriage, as in *Rom.*), FURNESS (ed. 1907, pp. xii–xiv), KNIGHT (1931; 1965,
p. 313), GODDARD (1951, 2:198–203), PEARSON (1954, pp. 144–6), WAIN (1964,
p. 138), NEVO (1972, pp. 341–2), HYMEL (1979, pp. 2–4), and MARCHANT
(1984, pp. 166, 175).

Cleopatra's ennoblement in death, suggested by Davies (1783) and Schlegel
(1811), is partly granted by HAZLITT (1817; 1930, 4:228–30), who lavishes praise
on the characterization: "The character of Cleopatra is a master-piece. . . . She is
voluptuous, ostentatious, conscious, boastful of her charms, haughty, tyrannical,
fickle. The luxurious pomp and gorgeous extravagance of the Egyptian queen are
displayed in all their force and lustre. . . .

[229] "Cleopatra's whole character is the triumph of the voluptuous, of the
love of pleasure and the power of giving it, over every other consideration. . . .

[230] "She had great and unpardonable faults, but the grandeur of her death
almost redeems them. She learns from the depths of despair the strength of her
affections. She keeps her queen-like state in the last disgrace, and her sense of the
pleasurable in the last moments of her life. She tastes a luxury in death."

Many later critics likewise see Cleopatra as ennobled in her death scene. Among
these is BRADLEY (1906; 1909, pp. 299–300, 303): "Cleopatra stands in a group
with Hamlet and Falstaff. . . . They are inexhaustible. . . . [300] What raises

Cleopatra at last into pure tragedy is, in part, that which some critics have denied her, her love for Antony. . . .

[*303*] "That which makes her wonderful and sovereign laughs at definition. . . . The spirit of fire and air within her refuses to be trammelled or extinguished; burns its way through the obstacles of fortune and even through the resistance of her love and grief; and would lead her undaunted to fresh life and the conquest of new worlds. It is this which makes her 'strong toil of grace' [*3616*] unbreakable; speaks in her brows' bent and every tone and movement; glorifies the arts and the rages which in another would merely disgust or amuse us; and, in the final scenes of her life, flames into such brilliance that we watch her entranced as she struggles for freedom, and thrilled with triumph as, conquered, she puts her conqueror to scorn and goes to meet her lover in the splendour that crowned and robed her long ago, when her barge burnt on the water like a burnished throne, and she floated to Cydnus on the enamoured stream to take him captive for ever."

RIBNER (1960, p. 182) believes she is regenerated in the final act when she rejects lust and accepts "a love which is all giving and self-sacrifice" (suggested also by BETHELL, 1944, p. 131).

HARRIER (1962, pp. 64–5) too stresses her growing commitment to Antony: "When we first see her in the fifth act she is contemplating the nobility of suicide. Her words are Roman words about bolting up change with one act, but she parleys with Proculeius until she is caught. . . . She has indeed planned on suicide only if her terms are not met, with her commitment to Antony only partially felt and acknowledged. What happens is that Cleopatra is again surprised by the power of Antony. As Julius Caesar returned to claim his revenge, Antony returns to claim his love. . . .

"Not until line [*3328*] does Cleopatra ask Dolabella what Caesar means to do with her, and not until line [*3332*] does she know. The intervening lines are the [*65*] most important in Cleopatra's dramatic life. They establish the spirit in which she goes to her death, and that spirit comes to this: although she has indulged her will to live to its last ounce, she now realizes that life without Antony is meaningless. The loss—not of herself and her kingdom—but of Antony—strikes her fully for the first time. . . .

"The rhetoric of her suicide develops her conviction, just found, that to regain Antony more than balances all losses. She is humble not before the gods and fortune but before Antony. Her baser elements of earth and water she submits to Antony's fire and air, for she is a kind of Caliban to his Ariel."

And MCALINDON (1973, pp. 208–10) sees her as finally conquering passion: "One must not lose sight of the art with which Cleopatra seeks to ensure that her fortune and Antony's mingle entirely and that his name will be buried in hers. Her constancy is studied and involves a determination to acquire Antony's Roman and masculine virtues. . . . [*209*] The very strength of Cleopatra's grief—her perception of just how weighty her loss has been—helps her to become a queen over her passion. Her desolation begins to make a better life in the sense that it teaches her the paltriness of that luck or good fortune which is now embodied in [*210*] Caesar. . . . Her final change, effected by courage, is from levity to gravity, from weakness into unchanging nobility, from bondage to liberty, from concubine to wife, from becoming into being."

Other comments on grandeur or nobility in her death scene include those by GUIZOT (ed. 1821, 3:4), SINGER (ed. 1826, 8:379), RÖTSCHER (1846, Pt. 2, p. 322), VATKE (1868, p. 334), GRIFFIN (1870, p. 81), FRIESEN (1876, 3:256–9), OECHELHÄUSER (ed. 1877; 1895, pp. 96–9), THÜMMEL (1881; 1887, 1:85–7), EMERSON (1890, pp. 190–1), SHERMAN (1901, pp. 317–18), ETTY (1903–4, pp. 307–9), WOLFF (1907; 1913, 2:266–7), GLEICHEN-RUSSWURM (1909, pp. 58–72), EISINGER (1925, pp. 105–7), BUCK (1938, pp. 101–22), FRIPP (1938, 2:676–85), SCHNEIDER (1947; 1953, pp. 153–4), WILSON (ed. 1950, pp. xxxii–vi), ECKHOFF (1954, pp. 62–5), WILSON (1957, pp. 173–7), WRIGHT (1958, p. 47), BAKER (1959–60, p. 9), BRYANT (1961, pp. 183–8), LERNER (1961, pp. 35–7), NAKAMURA (1961, pp. 122–7), TORBARINA (1962, p. 5), THOMAS (1963, pp. 174–83), BOWERS (1965; 1967, pp. 60–2), GREEN (1966, pp. 17–20), MENDILOW & SHALVI (1967, pp. 236–42), FUJITA (1968–9, pp. 21–31), ALTMANN (1969, pp. 265–7), AOYAMA (1969, pp. 13, 21–2), MOORE (1969, pp. 668–70), WALTER (ed. 1969, pp. 19–24), WEIDHORN (1969, pp. 304–6), BROOKS (1972, pp. 21–2), SIMMONS (1973, *Shakespeare's Pagan World*, pp. 156–63), CHAMPION (1976, pp. 261–5), FERRARA (1977, pp. 49–63), HARRIS (1977, pp. 219–31), DORIUS (1978, pp. 339–49), STAMM (1978, pp. 72–80), PITT (1981, pp. 43–5), and BOORMAN (1987, pp. 246, 250). A similar assessment is that of GOLDMAN (1985, p. 132).

COLERIDGE (1818; 1960, 1:77), though he does not comment on her death beyond admiring the "momentary flashes of nature counteracting the historic abstraction," affirms with Hazlitt (1817) the power of Cleopatra's passion to redeem moral flaws: "The art displayed in the character of Cleopatra is profound in this, especially, that the sense of criminality in her passion is lessened by our insight into its depth and energy, at the very moment that we cannot but perceive that the passion itself springs out of the habitual craving of a licentious nature, and that it is supported and reinforced by voluntary stimulus and sought-for associations, instead of blossoming out of spontaneous emotion."

Inchbald and, in more detail, Jameson adopt a psychological approach to Cleopatra as woman rather than queen. As INCHBALD (ed. 1808, vol. 4, *Ant.*, pp. 3–5) notes, the reader is "introduced to the queen of Egypt, in her undress, as well as in her royal robes; he will be, as it were, admitted to her toilet, where, in converse with her waiting-woman, she will suffer [*4*] him to arrive at her most secret thoughts and designs: and he will quickly perceive, that the arts of a queen with her lover, are just the same as those practised by any other beauty." Noting "those minute touches of nature, by which Shakspeare proves the queen to be a woman," Inchbald maintains that Sh. (p. 5) "gives those royal personages more endearments, far, than splendour can bestow, in exposing them as part of the human species; and claiming, from that tender tie, more lenity to their faults—more reverence to their virtues."

JAMESON (1832; 1879, pp. 254, 256, 262, 271, 276, 278): "Cleopatra is a brilliant antithesis, a compound of contradictions, of all that we most hate with what we most admire. . . . What is most astonishing in the character of Cleopatra is its antithetical construction—its *consistent inconsistency*. . . . [*256*] She dazzles our faculties, perplexes our judgment, bewilders and bewitches our fancy; from the beginning to the end of the drama we are conscious of a kind of fascination against which our moral sense rebels, but from which there is no escape. . . . [*262*] With all her violence, perverseness, egotism, and caprice, Cleopatra mingled a capability for warm affections and kindly feeling, or, rather, what we should call in these days a constitutional *good-nature*; and was lavishly generous to her favourites and dependants. . . . [*271*] In Cleopatra the passion is of a mixt nature, made up of real attachment, combined with the love of pleasure, the love of power, and the love of self. . . . In the midst of all her caprices, follies, and even vices, womanly feeling is still predominant in Cleopatra, and the change which takes place in her deportment towards Antony, when their evil fortune darkens round them, is as beautiful and interesting in itself as it is striking and natural. Instead of the airy caprice and provoking petulance she displays in the first scenes, we have a mixture of tenderness, and artifice, and fear, and submissive blandishment. . . . [*276*] Coquette to the last, she must make Death proud to take her. . . . The idea of this frail [an adjective rejected by SIMPSON, 1928; 1950, p. 32], timid, wayward woman dying with heroism, from the mere force of passion and will, takes us by surprise. . . . [*278*] He [Sh.] alone has dared to exhibit the Egyptian queen with all her greatness and all her littleness—all her frailties of temper—all her paltry arts and dissolute passions, yet preserved the dramatic propriety and poetical colouring of the character, and awakened our pity for fallen grandeur without once beguiling us into sympathy with guilt and error."

Others who consider her more as woman than queen include WARD (1875; 1899, 2:187), STAPFER (1879, tr. 1880, pp. 393–408), TIMON (1889, p. 465), GRINDON (1909, pp. 8, 11, 57, et passim), HARRIS (1909; 1911, pp. 310–28, and 1911, pp. 196–216), WINCHESTER (1922, pp. 79–90), HILLEBRAND (ed. 1926, pp. xxxii–iv), SIMPSON (1928; 1950, pp. 28, 30), GERWIG (1929, pp. 153–70), OLIVIER (ed. 1952, pp. 6–9), HUBBELL (1953, pp. 132–45), J. O. SMITH (1964, p. 48), TAYLOR (1964, pp. 63–6), BROWNE (1976, pp. 150–77), and OKI (1978, pp. 10–24, and 1979, pp. 23–64).

Later in the 19th c. Cleopatra is sometimes seen as Woman, especially by SWINBURNE (1879; 1902, p. 191: "the perfect and the [Blakean] everlasting woman"; rebutted by CORSON, 1889, p. 274, as "crazy") and BRANDES (1895, tr. 1935, p. 462: "the woman of women, quintessentiated Eve, or rather Eve and the serpent in one"; echoed by STOLL, 1928; 1930, p. 13, and KNIGHT, 1931; 1965, p. 297 and particularly p. 304).

Cleopatra's mingling of virtues and vices, first noted by Schlegel (1811), leads some to think that both fear of humiliation and loyalty to Antony move her to suicide. Thus BOAS (1896, p. 483): "She will not linger behind her hero among the petty figures that now make up the world. And her resolve to die is quickened by her aesthetic horror of being exhibited in Caesar's triumph." BRADFORD (1898; 1936, p. 203), however, cannot decide: "It is more than doubtful whether she kills herself for love of him [Antony] or in sheer desperation to avoid the scorn and vengeance of Octavius. . . . If she had been confident of Octavius' favor, confident of reigning in Rome as she had reigned in Alexandria, Antony's poor dust might have tossed forgotten in the burning winds of Egypt. And yet, I do not know."

CASE (ed. 1906, pp. xvii–xx) believes Sh. suggests both motives, and FARNHAM (1950, pp. 196–200) is perceptive on their interplay: Sh. "pays his compliments in two directions with marked evenhandedness, now to the tradition [represented by Daniel] that Cleopatra was really moved to end her life by concern for herself and her honor, and now to the tradition [represented by Garnier] that she was really moved to do so by love for Antony. . . . [197] As Shakespeare's Cleopatra builds up a conviction that she must kill herself, she is swayed alternately by the thought of Caesar's triumph and the thought of Antony. The thought of the triumph is the first to take hold upon her. While Antony is still alive she comes to a decision that if she can avoid being led in triumph only by dying, then she will die. . . . But after Antony has been lifted into the monument and has died in her arms, the thought of him seems to drive away the thought of the triumph. Immediately after his death, she makes up her mind that she cannot abide in a dull world from which he is absent. . . .

"When next we see Cleopatra, just before her interview with Proculeius, her mind has reverted to the triumph and to the escape from Caesar's power that suicide will provide. . . . [198] But as Proculeius leaves and she begins to talk with Dolabella, her mind turns again to the incomparable Antony whom she has lost. . . . [199] The assurance given by Dolabella that Caesar will lead her in triumph remains fixed in Cleopatra's mind while Caesar 'words' her [3425], and as Caesar departs it becomes the cause of her first effective step toward suicide. . . .

[200] "Now [3461 ff.] Antony comes back into her mind. He remains there and is dominant during the few moments of life that are left to her. She will not see her own greatness belittled on the Roman stage, and neither will she see Antony's." Finally, Farnham does grant her nobility (p. 202): "If we are to understand that the love of Cleopatra for Antony, like her character, continues to be deeply flawed to the end of her life, we are nevertheless to understand that, like her character, it has its measure of nobility. If Cleopatra never comes to have a love for Antony to match his love for her, she at least comes to have magnificent visions of what it would be like to achieve such a love, and her climactic vision leads her to call him husband as she dies." ROTH (1951–2, pp. 58–9) challenges Farnham's analysis, claiming that Sh. resolves ambiguity (p. 59) "on the side of full tragic pity." Others who consider her motives mixed include MACCALLUM (1910, pp. 426–8, 436), RIDLEY (ed. 1954, pp. xlv–ix), MILLS (1960, p. 159, and 1964, pp. 55–6: cannot decide), WAITH (1962, p. 214, n. 6), and SUJAKU (1977, pp. 205–32).

Cleopatra's ambivalence is given fresh emphasis in the 20th c., notably in TRAVERSI's (1938; 1969, 2:223–4) analysis of her blend of corruption and tragic greatness: "Cleopatra, like Antony, is to be judged not only through her own words

692

but through the reaction of those who surround her. Even Enobarbus' famous account of her meeting with Mark Antony at Cydnus (II. ii) is at least as much an exposure as a glorification. The beauty unquestionably conveyed by his description is, like so much else in this play, deliberately over-ripe, artificially opulent in its effect. . . .

"The presence of these two contrasted elements in the description corresponds to the essential diversity of the character. Cleopatra, though [*224*] the creature of the world which surrounds her, can at times emerge from it, impose upon her surroundings a vitality which is not the less astonishing for retaining to the last its connection with the environment it transcends. This combination of 'nature' with artifice, vitality with corruption, in a single, infinitely complex creation, is at once the essence of her personality and the key to the conflicting estimates which her relations to Antony inspire in the course of the tragedy." The complexities of the characterization (p. 225) "have one principal aim—to evolve a certain tragic greatness for Cleopatra's passion out of its very stressed imperfections, out of the impermanence of the flesh and the corrupt world with which it is organically connected."

DANBY (1949; 1952, p. 145) thinks she incarnates "the Flesh, deciduous, opulent, and endlessly renewable," Sh. giving her everything (p. 146) "except his final and absolute approval." And to FARNHAM (1950, p. 139), Cleopatra, like Antony, is a study in flawed nobility. Others who, expanding upon Schlegel, consider her ambiguous or paradoxical include ULRICI (1839; 1868–9, tr. 1876, 2:203–4), HÜLSMANN (1856, pp. 227–9), FURNIVALL (ed. 1877, 1:lxxxii–iii, lxxxvi), DOUG-LAS (1909, pp. 588–9), HERFORD (1912, p. 78), GUNDOLF (1926, pp. 22–4, and 1928; 1949, 2:441–4), JEPSEN (1953, pp. 95–6, 101), SPENCER (1958, p. 375), ROSEN (1960, pp. 152–5), KAULA (1964, pp. 220–3), UNGERER (1964, pp. 95–9), SHAPIRO (1966, p. 30), UÉNO (1967–8, pp. 19–25), MORGAN (1968, p. 137), RICE (1968, pp. 370–1), RIEMER (1968, p. 61), HOMAN (1970, pp. 464–5), LEE (1971, pp. 51–7), HUME (1973, pp. 280–300), LONGO (1974, pp. 32–4), HON-IGMANN (1976, p. 169), SANDERS & JACOBSON (1978, pp. 133–5), and DAVIDSON (1980, pp. 35–51).

To explain Cleopatra's transcending mere sexuality, PEART (1892, pp. 219–20) considers her as companion to Antony: her "secret charm . . . [*220*] denotes alliance, association, comradeship, a permanent condition, into which mere sexuality does not necessarily enter. The women who are real companions to men are not shocked by conventionality or dread of echoes. The high-minded Octavia could not have lowered herself to midnight brawls, to hunting sports, or gaming revels. . . . For Cleopatra it was but the indulgence of a natural taste inherited from a race of voluptuaries. She gave herself up to the delights of this companionship, which was as entrancing to her as to Antony. . . . With a woman's quick tact she knew when to change the intoxications of pleasure for higher thought. . . . She was a comrade in high places as well as low." Others who discuss her love or try to explain her attraction for Antony, though on the whole hardly bettering JAMESON (1832; 1879, e.g., pp. 257–60, 271–3), include HEINE (1838, tr. 1891, 1:302–10), HUDSON (ed. 1855; 1872, 2:377–8), BAHNSEN (1877–8; 1905, pp. 230–1, 234, 237), SYMONS (1889; 1919, pp. 11–12), MORGAN & VINES (ed. 1893–8, pp. xxvii–

ix), THISELTON (1899, pp. 25–6), CONRAD (1900, pp. 257–60), MACCALLUM (1910, pp. 446–7), GILLET (1930, pp. 251–4), BOAS (ed. 1935, pp. xi–xv), WILCOX (1936, pp. 537–9), CADOUX (1938, pp. 89–90), ELLIS (1947, pp. 147–57), DEMIZU (1967, ch. on Cleopatra's love), JOSEPHS (1967, p. 18), STAMPFER (1968, pp. 242–8), KINDRED (1972, pp. 146–8), COLIE (1974, pp. 188–94), PAYNE (1974, pp. 66–9), DUSINBERRE (1975, pp. 67–9), LABRIOLA (1975, pp. 20–36), TANIFUJI (1977, pp. 1–34), NAUMANN (1978, pp. 420, 424–5), and SANDERS & JACOBSON (1978, pp. 130–3).

Reacting against character analysis inherited from the 19th c., SCHÜCKING (1919, tr. 1922, pp. 121, 123, 127–8, 130, 132) asserts Sh. sacrifices consistency of character to episodic structure: "If we now regard the Cleopatra of Shakespeare's drama we are astonished to find how inferior she is to the original. . . . Plutarch gives us no clearly outlined picture of her character, but she certainly is not the great courtesan whom Shakespeare shows us in the first acts of his play. The first thing we miss is her culture. . . . As a matter of fact, we never see her acting as queen at all. . . .

[*123*] "The essential vulgarity of her character is also shown by the pride which, like every courtesan, she takes in having had so many distinguished lovers. . . .

[*127*] "The contradiction between this picture of Cleopatra and the character Shakespeare gives her in the last two acts, after the position of Antony has become hopeless, is astonishing. The consistent development of the character . . . would require that she should endeavour to extricate herself from the fate that threatens Antony. . . .

"We may be quite certain, however, that Cleopatra is not faithless to Antony. In this case there is no suspicion [*128*] of treachery even in the original. If in the beginning of the play Shakespeare appears to have deprived her of some of the good qualities she possesses in Plutarch, he makes up for this by raising her at this stage of the action actually above Plutarch's estimate. . . . [*130*] Now [at 3088–3106] for the first time, when she feels her loss so deeply that it makes her as poor as any peasant girl, does she really look like a queen, and a queen she remains during the negotiations of the last act. There is something truly sublime in her attitude, which resembles that of a Thusnelda in chains. . . .

[*132*] "It cannot well be doubted that this woman, who now is inwardly as well as outwardly a queen, has but little in common with the harlot of the first part."

STOLL (1928; 1930, pp. 12–17, 19), however, disputes any inconsistency in the characterization: "On the stage, as in life, a character has a right to change— in Cleopatra's case, to cease from changing—under stress of love and in the presence of death. . . . She is no Doll Tearsheet or Doll Common in the early scenes, nor a sublime queen . . . in the later ones. She is vain and voluptuous, cunning and intriguing, wrangling and voluble, humorous and vindictive, to the end. . . . [*13*] In her inconsistency she is consistent [as found by JAMESON, 1832; 1879, p. 254]. But the chief means by which the dramatist makes her so is the identity, through all her changes, of her tone and manner. She changes as a vivacious, amorous, designing woman changes, not so as to lose her identity, like Proteus. . . .

[*14*] "And in the same audacious, sensuous key, for all her exaltation, she expresses herself on her deathbed. She is tenderer with her women, and stronger and more constant, than she has ever been; but her thoughts of Antony, though now an inviolable shade, are not celestial or Platonic. They are steeped in amorousness, and she is waiting, coiled on her couch. She loves him more than at [*15*] the beginning; but neither now nor at his death is she, as Professor Schücking declares, 'all tenderness, all passionate devotion and unselfish love' [p. 129]. . . . What is it that nerves her up to make haste and apply the asp? Pride, fear to be made a show of at Rome, and—something deeper. 'Love is enough', but not enough for her. [*16*] [Quotes 'If . . . haue' (3553–5).] Without kissing what would heaven be—nay, without jealousy? . . . [*17*] Few women who have had more lovers than one can easily forget the circumstance; and Cleopatra is not so much boasting as (out of her extensive experience) making comparisons, and declaring that Antony overtops them all and their mutual love is greater than any other she has shared. . . .

[*19*] "But the preëminently felicitous touch, I think, which links her most unmistakably with all her earlier self, and thus effectually contradicts any impression of sublimity, is in her sense of humor."

Others who answer Schücking by demonstrating Cleopatra's consistency include HERFORD (1923, p. 50), CRAIG (1948, pp. 268–75), and STEWART (1949, pp. 64–78). Further discussions of unity and consistency in the character include those by RÖTSCHER (1846, Pt. 2, pp. 308–11, 319, 322), MONTÉGUT (ed. 1868; 1878, 8:8–9), GRANVILLE-BARKER (1930; 1946, 1:435–48), URBAN (1939, pp. 42–9), DRAPER (1945, pp. 92–3, and 1965, *Psychiatric Quarterly*, pp. 454–5), HILLEMANN (1945, pp. 54–5), CRAIG (ed. 1951; 1961, pp. 1071–2), STIRLING (1956, pp. 176–7), McGINN (1960, pp. 57–80), WATSON (1960, pp. 322–3), MUIR (1961, *KN*, pp. 249–51), PROSER (1965, pp. 225–35), WILLIAMSON (1969, pp. 129–38), ENRIGHT (1970, pp. 87–8), INGLEDEW (ed. 1971, pp. xxxix–xlii), BURTON (1973, pp. 266–72), DAVIDSON (1973, p. 31), FISKIN (1975, pp. 100–5), SHAPIRO (1975, pp. 40–1), SCHULMAN (1976, pp. 154–74), DASH (1981, p. 243), MEHL (1983; 1986, pp. 172–3), and EDWARDS (1986, p. 150). A related assessment is that of FARMER (1977, pp. 113–15), who discusses her mutability and imagistic connection to Proteus.

SIMPSON (1928; 1950, pp. 27–8, 30, 32, 35) claims the play is Cleopatra's tragedy even more than Antony's: "Cleopatra is not only the greatest of his [Sh.'s] heroines but the culmination of feminine characterisation in all literature. . . . [*28*] Cleopatra is the only heroine [in Sh.] treated individually, that is, apart from the man's character with whom her life is conjoined. . . . The play, in fact, might have been called Cleopatra [contrast CECIL, 1944; 1949, p. 16, and JAMES, 1981, p. 140] as appropriately as that of Hamlet is called *Hamlet*, of Othello *Othello*. This is not in any way to depreciate Antony, for only by estimating him aright can the greatness of Cleopatra be gauged and understood. . . .

[*30*] "The portrayal of a woman of temperament remains something of a challenge to all creative writers of fiction as well as drama. As no other, before him or since, Shakespeare succeeded here. . . . [*32*] We prefer to think the poet's chief concern was with Cleopatra. . . .

[*35*] "From beginning to end there is abundant evidence Cleopatra has greatness of character and courage as well as charm." (GRINDON, 1909, passim, too stresses charm and greatness of character, but also womanly fears—e.g., p. 15; see also JAMESON, 1832; 1879, pp. 271–6.) Simpson's spirited defense of Cleopatra is remarkable despite its rather vague terms.

GRIFFITHS's (1945, p. 45) argument is partly similar to Simpson's: "The conventional view of the play's structure is . . . that it is Antony's tragedy. If my contention is right, Cleopatra is even more important structurally and spiritually. Cleopatra, as Lady Macbeth does not, transcends the hero. . . . Cleopatra is incomparably the more interesting, complex, and in her own sphere, love, more gifted." Griffiths also views her as embodying the Dionysian impulse (pp. 41–4). Other critics for whom she is the chief protagonist are FITZ (1977, p. 314) and BOWERS (1982, p. 33).

For KNIGHT (1931; 1965, pp. 297, 302, 309, 313), as for Swinburne (1879), she is eternal woman and divine lover: "Cleopatra and her girls at Alexandria are as the Eternal Femininity waiting for Man. A certain eternity broods over this still, languorous Alexandria. . . . [*302*] Death, the feminine, calls back the adventurer, Life, to her bosom. So Cleopatra awaits Antony; and so Antony finally dies into the arms of Cleopatra's love. . . . [*309*] She, more than any other, is the play. Hence the femininity in the vowel-sounds and the style generally . . . and its shifting, dazzling, opalescent interplay of imagery. . . . Cleopatra is the divinity of this play in the sense that Desdemona is the divinity of *Othello*. . . . Cleopatra is divine by nature of her divine variety and profusion. . . .

[*313*] "Out of her varying moods, passions, experiences, one fact emerges: her serene love of Antony. This, among all else fleeting, is, ultimately, changeless and still, the centre and circumference of her personality, of the play." Knight also sees in her Eve's and Lady Macbeth's (p. 316) "vein of pure evil; necessary in so rich a feminine creation," and speaks of (p. 317) "the twin potentialities of woman: the divine and the satanic—. . . qualities which . . . blend in Cleopatra."

KIRSCHBAUM (1944; 1962, pp. 102–3, 107, 109) takes issue with both Schücking (1919) and Knight, asserting she remains a courtesan to the end: Sh. "has subtly— but effectively—employed a device of speech decorum which does adumbrate a unified psychology in Cleopatra. . . . The [*103*] obvious harlot and the queenly lover both draw their metaphors from the same storehouse—or bagnio [e.g., 535– 6, 1025–6, 3546–7, 3553–5]. . . . [*107*] In her suicide, imagery, statement, attitude show still the same basic psychology. She is still, however transformed [cf. 3488–91], the same courtesan—avid of love, impatient, jealous of rivals, quick-tempered, voluptuous, feline, thinking in sheerly female terms. . . .

[*109*] "What Schücking and Knight do not note enough is that Shakespeare never for a moment ceases to picture Antony and Cleopatra as voluptuaries."

Stressing political order as Sh.'s main concern, STEMPEL (1956, p. 63) finds

Cleopatra the "chief danger to political stability" and "the rebel against order," a "symbol of Antony's slavery to desire," the "tempter and the temptation" destroying the balance of Antony's nature. More attentive to character, MILLS (1964, p. 56) thinks "it was not accidental that the first word she speaks in the play is 'If' [21]. The appropriate symbol for her is a big interrogation point." He analyzes her tragedy as distinct from Antony's (p. 59) and finds her unregenerate ("never penitent, not even conscious of the debacle she has wrought"), neither transfigured nor glorified at the end. See also MILLS (1960, pp. 159, 161).

Among those more sympathetic to her is LLOYD (1959, *SQ*, p. 466), who sees Cleopatra as exposing "the guileful surface of Rome": "She, whose nature has always been abused and exploited by Rome, not only exposes the Roman intention and method to us, but sees it foiled by her own steadfastness." A similar view is that of MCFARLAND (1958–9, pp. 214–15).

KURIYAMA (1977, pp. 328–31) uses recherché psychoanalysis to demonstrate that she is both male and female symbol and incestuously loved earth mother. To FARMER (1977, p. 117), too, Cleopatra "in her sexual completeness approaches androgyny." Less arcane than these, FITZ (1977, p. 314) strengthens Simpson's (1928) argument for Cleopatra, not Antony, as primary character: "Any attempt to reach a canonical decision on the identity of a single hero in a play of such generic unorthodoxy as *Antony and Cleopatra* is probably foolhardy and possibly distorting in itself. Nevertheless, . . . there are good reasons for considering Cleopatra to be the play's protagonist. . . . Not only does the play culminate in Cleopatra's death scene, but she has . . . more speeches than Antony; indeed, the most in the play. . . . But most important, she learns and grows as Antony does not." Fitz finds Cleopatra struggling against "her own artificial theatricality"—as when she actually dies mentioning Antony's name after her pretense at 2819—and "her own inconstancy"—as in 3488–91.

Fitz's views are challenged by BAMBER (1982, pp. 55, 66–7), who argues that Cleopatra with her preexistent and fixed identity does not struggle, as does Antony, for self-knowledge but merely plays shifting roles. Recent feminist critics who, dependent more on a modern than a Renaissance framework of ideas, discuss Cleopatra's femininity include BERGGREN (1980, p. 25) and DASH (1981, pp. 209–47).

Besides those quoted, critics who praise the characterization of Cleopatra include GRIFFITH (1775, p. 475), DRAKE (1817, 2:493), VILLEMAIN (1827, 3:174), MAGINN (1837; 1860, p. 162), CAMPBELL (ed. 1838, p. lxi), HALLAM (1839; 1854, 3:88), COURTENAY (1840, 2:268, 274), DE QUINCEY (1842, 20:186), CLAY (1844, pp. 12–13), CLARKE (1863, p. 219), TAINE (1863, tr. 1874, 1:329), HEYSE (in BODENSTEDT, ed. 1867; 1873, vol. 7, *Ant.*, pp. vi–vii), GILES (1868, pp. 143–4), MONTÉGUT (ed. 1868; 1878, 8:8–9), BLUMHOF (ed. 1870, pp. 22–4), BODENSTEDT (1874; 1887, pp. 351–3), WILKES (1876; 1882, p. 367), KOCH (ed. 1882, 9:245–7), DOWDEN (1885; 1896, p. 374), GOWING (1888, pp. 82–3), SYMONS (1889; 1919, pp. 1–2), BASEDOW (1893, 1:111–12), BRINK (1893, tr. 1895, pp. 90–1), LEE (1898; 1925, pp. 411–12), EVERETT (1905, p. 255), SCHELLING (1908; 1935, 1:574), LEVI (1925, p. 294), CLARK (1936, p. 41), SORENSEN (1936, pp. 21–4), PARROTT (ed. 1938, p. 861), ROSENBLATT (1938, pp. 273–6), SPENCER (1940, pp. 344–6),

CHAMBRUN (1947, pp. 393–4), KOIKE (1960, pp. 32–45), HERBERT (1965, pp. 64–5), BOSE (1966, pp. 81–95), KERMODE (in EVANS, ed. 1974, p. 1346), PÜSCHEL (1977, pp. 20–2), SHINTRI (1977, p. 95), DORIUS (1978, pp. 317–20), TOLMIE (1978, p. 131), and SUZMAN (in COOK, 1980, p. 137).

Others who disapprove of the characterization include AYRENHOFF (1783; 1813, p. 9), TIECK (1794; 1920, p. 298), SKOTTOWE (1824, 2:239–40), DUPORT (1828, 2:57), ANON. (1849, pp. 277–91), SAINT-MARC GIRARDIN (1860; 1870, 4:402–3), and CANNING (1884, pp. 14–19).

Those who praise or defend her character include BRÄKER (1780, tr. 1979, pp. 83–4), ANON. (1824, p. 49), VATKE (1868, p. 331), ANON. (1871, pp. 344–59), KELLER (ed. 1912, 5:192–4), CADOUX (1938, pp. 85–8), BEHRENS (1959, p. 37), SEN GUPTA (1972; 1977, pp. 51–5), and CLAYTON (1981, p. 96).

Others who disapprove of her character include HOPKINSON (ed. 1795, 1:vii), BENDA (ed. 1825, 9:441–2), TALBOT (1887, p. 229), WILSON (1887, pp. 64–5), WETZ (1890, 1:470–2), SHAW (1900; 1931, 31:xxvii), ETTY (1903–4, pp. 303–4, 307–9), BAILEY (1929, p. 189), ZANCO (ed. 1931, pp. xxv–xxxii), DAVID (1935, pp. 145–9), CAMPBELL (ed. 1949, pp. 982–3), BARROLL (1958, *TxSE*, pp. 61–78), BANDEL (1959–60, p. 10), FROST (1964, p. 40), KUCKHOFF (1964, pp. 418–21), FITCH (1968, pp. 11–12, 16), and MURAKAMI (1970–1, pp. 28–40).

She is compared with Falstaff by BOAS (1896, p. 475), LUCE (1907, pp. 325–6), MACKENZIE (1924, pp. 402–4), WILSON (1957, pp. 172–3), FITCH (1968, pp. 11–12), and CALDERWOOD (1987, p. 186), and with the Dark Lady of *Son.* by GERVINUS (1850, tr. 1883, p. 731), CARTWRIGHT (1859, p. 22), RAPP (1862, p. 212), HEYSE (in BODENSTEDT, ed. 1867; 1873, vol. 7, *Ant.*, p. vi), FURNIVALL (ed. 1877, 1:lxxxii), KOCH (ed. 1882, 9:247), SYMONS (1889; 1919, p. 2), BRANDES (1895, tr. 1935, pp. 462–3, 470–2), COURTHOPE (1903, 4:45, 47, 178), COURTNEY (13 Nov. 1906), WOLFF (1907; 1913, 2:267–8), HARRIS (1909; 1911, pp. 324–8), ACHESON (1913, pp. 198–200), CREIZENACH (1916, 5:437), LANDAUER (1920; 1962, pp. 314–15), IMELMANN (ed. 1923, pp. 194–5), MACKENZIE (1924, pp. 367–8), CHAMBRUN (1938, pp. 154–5, and 1947, pp. 392–3), BROWN (1949, pp. 216–32, and 1957, pp. 160–252), VIERTEL (1953; 1970, pp. 28–9), BREWER (1966, pp. 100–6), SCHMID (1972, pp. 54–7), SCHAMP (ed. 1978, pp. 126–8), and ERICKSON (1985, pp. 125–7). For comparisons of Sh.'s play with others about Cleopatra, see especially MOELLER (1888, pp. 17–24), EVERETT (1905, pp. 254–5), TRAUB (1938, pp. 21–37), ELLIS (1947, pp. 146–58), PATRICK (1975, p. 70), ARDINGER (1976, pp. 85–117), and KENNEDY (1981, 1:99–116). A vain attempt to Christianize her (CUNNINGHAM, 1955, pp. 9–17) is refuted by DONNO (1956, pp. 227–33). She is considered as an Egyptian by JONES (1965, pp. 82–5) and ADELMAN (1973, pp. 184–8). The relation between her and the goddess Isis is examined by LLOYD (1959, *ShS*, pp. 88–94) and ADLARD (1975, pp. 324–8). Rather like GUNDOLF (1926, p. 17, and 1928; 1949, 2:435), EAGLETON (1986, p. 88) calls her an "image of Nature." Cleopatra is compared to Clytemnestra in Aeschylus's *Oresteia* by WHALLON (1980, pp. 127–32), to Cathy Earnshaw in Brontë's *Wuthering Heights* by GRIFFITHS (1945, pp. 40–2), and to Elizabeth I by GREY (1754, 2:201), STAPFER (1879, tr. 1880, pp.

403–4), MORRIS (1968–9, *HLQ*, pp. 271–8), MUIR (1969, pp. 197–206, and 1977, pp. 236–7), RINEHART (1972, pp. 81–6), BRAND (1976, pp. 101–2), and JANKOWSKI (1987, p. 22); see also nn. 77–155, 603, 902–31, 1165–8, 1620–83, 1877–9, 3088–90, 3407–10. Critics who discuss the importance of the boy actor in the characterization include GRANVILLE-BARKER (1930; 1946, 1:435–48), BOAS (1937, pp. 74–6), SPEAIGHT (1955, p. 135, and 1977, p. 311), WRIGHT & LAMAR (ed. 1961, p. xiii), JAMIESON (1964, pp. 32–4), RACKIN (1972, pp. 201–11), OZAKI (1977, pp. 289–318), BRENNAN (1978, p. 327), and GRUBER (1985, pp. 39–46). DAN-OBEITIA FERNANDEZ (1986, pp. 55–73) discusses Cleopatra's role taking, and BARROLL (1984, pp. 130–84) offers a substantial analysis of Cleopatra as tragic character.

CLOWN

KREYßIG (1858; 1877, 1:453) holds that the Clown's humor underscores Cleopatra's tragic isolation in suffering. CLARKE (1863, p. 240) remarks on the contrast between the Clown and Cleopatra: "The most powerful, or rather the most genuine piece of individual portraiture among the insignificant actors in this drama, is that of the country clown who brings Cleopatra the serpent—the asp. The utter indifference and boorish obtuseness dawning into an expression of humour, thrown into this character, is excessively happy. There is no human animal more stupidly regardless of death and its consequences than your genuine country lout. . . . It was, indeed, a consummately artistic and altogether picturesque idea to place that primitive lump of humanity in juxtaposition with the gorgeous Eastern magnificence, the rich fancy."

Boas and Wright are among those who discuss his comic function. BOAS (ed. 1935, p. xix): "The Clown who brings Cleopatra the asps, like the condemned convict in *Measure for Measure*, is one of those little miracles of realistic vitality which Shakespeare throws as largesse on his already crowded canvas, and, like the Porter in *Macbeth*, he introduces a few moments of unexpected comedy. . . . He knew how a brief relaxation such as the Porter and the Clown supply heightens and does not lessen an audience's power of reaction to tragic tension. Yet the Clown, as is the way with Shakespeare's fools, is very far from speaking folly, and might as fittingly have been entitled Soothsayer." And WRIGHT (1958, p. 49): "One of a long series of Shakespearean clowns, he is one of the least voluble: . . .—scarce 250 words. . . . It is perhaps just as well that there is no opportunity for him to utter more than a few of those malapropisms that the Elizabethans thought so hilarious but that quickly grow tiresome to us except on the lips of a master like Bottom or Dogberry. This clown, like all the others, fancies himself as a wit, and has the true masculine relish for a snide comment on the ladies." TRAVERSI (1963, p. 199) observes that besides comic relief the Clown "speaks with the voice of a necessary realism against Cleopatra's entranced contemplation of self-justifying poetic illusion"; similarly, FROST (1964, p. 38) believes he warns Cleopatra against indulging in sensual love: he "begs Cleopatra to give the worm nothing [3520], not to feed sensuality, for it is not worth it." SIMMONS (1973, *Shakespeare's Pagan World*, pp. 161–2), however, seeing the Clown as an instrument to affirm the value of love, asserts that "his comic [*162*] confusion of sexuality with death, death with life, and life with immortality laugh the complexities of the play into affirmation."

Among other discussions of the Clown are those by GRIFFITH (1775, p. 475: one of Sh.'s "inspired" clowns), DOUCE (1807, 2:97: country fellow with due portion of wit and satire), HORN (1827, 4:70: terrifying humor), OECHELHÄUSER (ed. 1877; 1895, p. 96: stupid, garrulous, elderly), MASELLI (1920, pp. 411–15: comic contrast with Cleopatra's gravity), SISSON (1922, p. 142: his tragic irony shows Sh.'s attitude), KNIGHT (1931; 1965, pp. 316–17: "acts as the embassy of the heavenly spheres," warning Cleopatra of the [p. 317] "twin potentialities of woman: the divine and the satanic"), CECIL (1944; 1949, p. 19: shows how little the misfortunes of the great mean to the humble), SCHÖNE (1960, p. 229: a secret philosopher), CHARNEY (1961, p. 100: vulgar, well-meaning; comic relief; his speech full of overtones of Eve and the serpent), STROUP (1964, p. 298: carries out soothsayer's prophecies), CANTOR (1976, pp. 180–2: his skepticism moderates any exultation at Cleopatra's death), and BOWERS (1983, pp. 285–8: embodies person-ified Death, to be seen in traditional funerary imagery).

DECRETAS

Comments on Decretas include those by TRAVERSI (1963, pp. 177, 187: cynical at first, Decretas later speaks with dignity of his dead master) and WILLIAMSON (1970, pp. 247–8: his yielding to Octavius only after his master's death contrasts with the desertions of the living Antony by others).

DOLABELLA

This character has tricked (cf. 3290) commentators into speculation. TOLMAN (1925, pp. 166–7) considers him as lover: "Cleopatra is eloquent [at 3289 ff.] both because she is praising her beloved Antony, and because she is captivating Dolabella. Her rapturous words are about Antony, but they are also directed at her new admirer. The young man is deeply moved, so moved that his allegiance to Cæsar breaks down. He serves the queen, and not his master. ['I . . . know't.' (3324–33)]

[*167*] "Then Octavius enters and tries to reassure Cleopatra. But her eyes have been opened, and she perceives the insincerity of his words. Cæsar departs. Dolabella immediately returns to declare his love, to give the queen the fullest possible information, and to take a last farewell. [3438–48]" Tolman speaks of an "embryonic love-affair, acting itself out before us on the very brink of the grave."

MURRY (1936, pp. 355–6), more restrained (like most critics), finds that Dolabella senses but does not fully understand Cleopatra's grief: "The contrast between the ecstasy of Cleopatra's imaginative dream [3292 ff.], and the tenderness of Dolabella's human sympathy [3321 ff.], . . . springs from and is rooted in the world of actuality. . . . Dolabella stands by the [*356*] Queen—gentle with a man's gentleness, wondering, anxious, eager to comfort and reassure. But she, in her ecstasy, is beyond his ken. He admits it in so many words. He, too, has loved

Antony; he grieves for him and he grieves for her. But the region where her mind and heart are wandering is strange to him. At the nature of her grief he must conjecture; yet the vibration of it strikes him to the heart. [3321–6] It is the incommensurability of Cleopatra's loss, the incommensurability of her suffering, which Dolabella thus registers. It is, in respect of the world which he inhabits and represents—the real world—superhuman. Shakespeare finds a word for it—. . . a symbol of the magnificence he communicates to us. It is the word 'royal' [3572]."

Smith and Rice try to build interpretations on etymology of the name. SMITH (1966, p. 208): "Wordplay on Dolabella's name serves to contrast Antony's bounty with Caesar's. For all that his name means 'fine trick', Dolabella does not 'laugh when boys or women tell their dreams' [3289], though Cleopatra asks him if that is not his *trick*. He is sympathetic, straightforward, and honest with her, scorning to deceive her by false pretences as to Caesar's bounty." RICE (1970, pp. 403–5; similarly 1968, pp. 240–4) derives the name from *dolor*, not δόλος: Sh. "makes him into an incarnation of his name, which may mean 'beautiful grief'. His compassion and depth of feeling sharply differentiate him from Octavius Caesar, the general to whom Dolabella is the chief aide-de-camp, and he seems to represent a principle of susceptibility to feeling or the passion of compassion, which Shakespeare may be defending against the Stoical rationality of Octavius. . . . In his reaction to Cleopatra's speech Dolabella's words convey no other motive for his subsequent betrayal of Caesar than an empathetic 'grief' which suggests the significance of his name, [3321–6]. [404] Dolabella's telling Cleopatra of Octavius' intention is an act of pity, [3329–33]. . . . Shakespeare gives Dolabella no motivation for his betrayal of his master, Caesar. . . . All of Caesar's other officers, including Proculeius whom Antony told Cleopatra to trust, carry out his order faithfully, although Dolabella appears in the play's last line to be Caesar's right hand man, [3635–6]. . . . [405] As a foil to Caesar, whose only motivation is to 'o'ertake pursued success' Dolabella resembles some of the other minor characters, who act feelingly rather than logically."

WERTIME (1969, pp. 196–7, 199–200) believes Dolabella is gradually taught by Cleopatra to recognize his limitations: "Dolabella is filled with the Roman sense of urgency, an urgency, moreover, typical of a young man who finds himself displaced from his usual sphere of knowledge and scrambles to recover his poise. . . . [197] What he replies, 'Gentle madam, no' [3314], can be interpreted as widely as the play itself, as either dryly satiric or drenched with sympathy, depending on one's attachment to or antipathy for Rome. The context, and Dolabella's character, make it likely that both gentle satire and sympathy are involved. . . .

[199] "Dolabella's expected refusal to acknowledge her imagined Antony gives Cleopatra the opportunity to push beyond or beneath, the role of poet to the role of poet-as-rhetorician. . . . While it is one of her theatrical tactics to plunge Dolabella ever deeper into incomprehension, he, in fact, [200] *is* becoming illuminated by her total performance. What essentially he is learning is the nature of Cleopatra herself, and his response at the end of the lesson partakes of a heightened self-awareness as well as heartfelt sympathy."

701

GODSHALK (1977, pp. 69–74), at the other extreme from Tolman (1925), unconvincingly argues that Dolabella is Octavius's secret agent, manipulating Cleopatra's death at his master's command and thus cementing her defeat (p. 73): "Unlike Enobarbus, Dolabella does not betray his lord."

BOOTH (1979, pp. 115–17) attempts to show that the roles of Dolabella and Proculeius were doubled.

Others who comment on Dolabella include STIRLING (1956, pp. 179–81: functions to limit Cleopatra's illusions), GOLDBERG (1961, p. 59: his deepest emotions are linked with worldly success), WAIN (1964, pp. 139–40: hard Roman common sense, grave and sensible), PROSER (1965, pp. 180–2: audience realize his limits but recognize that he is right in his realism; p. 220: betrays his master's confidence), BLISSETT (1967, pp. 163–4: Cleopatra changes him; first *eiron*, he later obeys her will), RIEMER (1968, pp. 68–9: articulates the play's resistance to Cleopatra's vision of Antony), ALTMANN (1969, pp. 256–7: unlike Seleucus he acts out of admiration, love, and pity), BARROLL (1969, pp. 220–1, and 1984, pp. 124–5: his ideals come close to Antony's when he puts a woman above political duty), MOORE (1969, pp. 670–1: prose of self-assurance, but he rises to meet Cleopatra's grief), WILLIAMSON (1970, p. 248: audience sympathizes with his contribution to a defeat for his master), ADELMAN (1973, p. 46: temporarily deserts Octavius for love of Cleopatra), BELL (1973, p. 263: his confusion at Cleopatra's vision of Antony is ours), and HEFFNER (1976, p. 155: becomes Cleopatra's messenger rather than Octavius's).

ENOBARBUS

Admiring the characterization, WARBURTON (ed. 1747, 7:142) refers to Enobarbus as "frank and rough"; DAVIES (1783, 2:367), as "the rough old warrior, shrewd in his remarks and humorous in his plain-dealing." STEEVENS (ed. 1793; see n. 2210–13) calls him "the buffoon of the play." GRIFFITH (1775, p. 474) speaks of his remorse after deserting Antony: if Sh. "had not given us a representation of this character, I should hardly have been brought to imagine that a breast capable of harbouring such treachery and vileness, could ever, at the same time, have contained a spirit of so much honour, and so strong a sense of shame." HAZLITT (1817; 1930, 4:232) finds his repentance "the most affecting part of the play."

MORGANN (1777; 1972, p. 174 n.) perceives he is "in effect the Chorus of the Play; as Menenius Agrippa is of Coriolanus." Enobarbus's choric function attracts frequent comment. HUDSON (1872, 2:370–1, 373) considers him both a character and an ironical commentator, a link between author and audience: "Through him the Poet keeps up a secret understanding with us. . . . Enobarbus is himself far from understanding the deep wisdom and sagacity of what he utters [illustrated by, e.g., 239 ff.]. . . .

"Nevertheless Enobarbus is to all intents and purposes one of the persons of the drama, and not in any sort a mere [371] personified emanation of the author. . . . So that we have in him at once a character and a commentary. . . . [373] Aside

702

from his function as chorus, he is perhaps, after Octavia, the noblest character in the drama. His blunt, prompt, outspoken frankness smacks delightfully of the hardy Roman soldier brought face to face with the orgies of a most un-Roman levity; while the splitting of his big heart with grief and shame for having deserted the ship of his master, which he knew to be sinking, shows him altogether a noble vessel of manhood. That Antony's generosity kills him, approves, as nothing else could, how generous he is himself."

WILSON (1948, pp. 406–7): "He is the absorption of the external chorus of Renaissance drama into the characterization and action of the tragedy. . . . His words always have strong dramatic power because spoken by a very human character, himself caught in the tragic action around him. . . . [407] His shrewdly judging others, then ironically falling into tragic error in judging himself, makes him finally one of us—ties him intimately into the tragic web of the play. For him, as for Antony and the rest of us, character is fate; he is rightly the close companion of the erring hero of a great poetic tragedy.

"This full humanity of Enobarbus makes possible his technical success as a semi-chorus. It separates him from the impersonal pseudo-Senecan choruses in numerous Renaissance neo-classical plays, many of them about Antony and Cleopatra, with their stiff reporting of off-stage events and their staid moralizing upon the vicissitudes of fortune and the wages of sin. It gives him kinship, rather, with the humanized choruses of Aeschylus and Sophocles."

GRIFFITHS (1945, p. 41) speaks of his choric function in archetypal terms: Sh. "clearly intends him as an example of the truth-seer who perishes, the blinded prophet. Shakespeare no doubt regards Enobarbus's reason as a revealer of truth divorced from charity and the affective will, the lightning-flash into the nature of things—the human heart only excepted—the wisdom of Silenus. His vision has the aloofness of the Lucretian gods. . . . But Enobarbus is also a human being, and by passing judgement on Antony in his own person and acting against him by going over to Octavius he attempts to live, to be, to incarnate the vision of reason, and thereby delivers himself into the tragic process." NOCHIMSON (1977, pp. 112–13), more plausibly, doubts his choric accuracy, at least regarding Antony: "Enobarbus is wrong many times in the play. He is wrong when he regards Antony as being primarily a soldier [cf. 684–5]. He is wrong again, at least in his timing, when he decides that Antony's cause is hopeless and that, recovery being impossible, he may as well leave. He is wrong finally in thinking that Antony's last, generous gesture to him makes him 'alone the villain of the earth' [2611]. . . . [*113*] Enobarbus is more likely to be right when he is seeing flaws in the fabric of Antony's character than when he is praising him. . . . Enobarbus's characteristic loyalty to his master is such that we should trust his judgement more when he is critical of Antony than when he persists in presenting an image of a figure who never was. So it is probable that the most important use that Shakespeare is making of Enobarbus in this play is to emphasise the weaknesses that always dominated Antony's character." Others who comment on Enobarbus as chorus as well as character include HUDSON (ed. 1855, 8:463), STAPFER (1879, tr. 1880, pp. 417–24), SYMONS (1889;

1919, p. 6), Morgan & Vines (ed. 1893–8, pp. xxix–xxx), Lee (ed. 1907, 36:xlviii–l), Lucas (1927, pp. 67–9), Sprague (1935, pp. 217–23), Lyman (1940, pp. 97–8), Pogson (1950, p. 112), Jepsen (1953, p. 97), Spencer (1964; 1968, pp. 15–16), Dietrich (1965, pp. 198–200), Blissett (1967, pp. 160–2), Uéno (1967–8, pp. 11–13), Traci (1970, pp. 46–8), Williamson (1970, pp. 246–7), Shanker (1975, pp. 198–200), and Erskine-Hill (1983, p. 140).

Clarke (1863, p. 234) discusses the consistency of the characterization: "Enobarbus stands in the record of those who deserted a kind master in the winter of his fortunes; but he also numbers with the few who have expiated to the uttermost the baseness of their ingratitude. . . . He [Sh.] knew that it would be offering an undue violence to humanity to introduce . . . a moral anomaly, a fellow-being with a Janus-nature, bluntly and sincerely honest up to a certain stage in his career; and then, with the suddenness of a pantomime trick, convert him into a remorseless, callous self-seeker." Enobarbus oscillates "between inconstancy and steadiness, with the gradual and stronger leaning to inconstancy." Clarke goes on to trace in detail Enobarbus's conflict between self-interest and fidelity (pp. 234–9).

MacCallum (1910, pp. 349, 351, 353–9) devotes a lengthy discussion, much of it (as far as p. 356) similarly stated by others, to Enobarbus's soldierly nature, his loyalty, and his inner conflict: "He is the only one of the more prominent personages who is practically a new creation in the drama, the only one in whose delineation Shakespeare has gone quite beyond the limits supplied by Plutarch. . . . [351] Practical intelligence, outspoken honesty, real capacity for feeling, are still the fundamental traits, and we have evidence of them all from the outset. But, in the first place, they have received a peculiar turn from the habits of the camp. . . . Indeed he is a soldier, if not only, at any rate chiefly and essentially; and a soldier of the adventurer type. . . . [353] Yet he is by no means indifferent to real charm, to the spell of refinement, grace and beauty. Like many who profess cynicism, and even in a way are really cynical, yet he is all the more susceptible to what in any kind will stand his exacting tests, especially if in contrast with his own rough jostling life of the barracks and of the field. . . . [354] And this responsiveness to what is gracious, has its complement in his responsiveness to what is magnificent. He has an ardent admiration for his 'Emperor'. . . . [355] But with all his enthusiasm for Antony, he is from the first critical of what he considers his weaknesses and mistakes, just as with all his enthusiasm for Cleopatra he has a keen eye for her affectations and interferences. . . . [356] He is raised above the common run of the legionaries by his devotion to his master. . . . The tragedy of Enobarbus' position lies in this: that in that evil time his reason can furnish him with no motive for his loyalty except self-interest and confidence in his leader's capacity; or, failing these, the unsubstantial recompense of fame. . . . His instincts pull him one way, his reason another, and in such an one instincts unjustified by reason lose half their strength. . . . [357] Enobarbus' heart is right, but in the long run it has no chance against the convincing arguments of the situation." Enobarbus, in fact, as MacCallum observes, remains a rationalist to the end (pp. 357–9): "Even his revulsion of feeling is brought about by the appeal to his worldly wisdom. . . . Enobarbus' penitence, though sudden, is all rationally explained. . . . He is made to realise that he has taken wrong measures in [*358*] his own interest, by Octavius' treatment of the other deserters. [Quotes 2590–8.] Then the transmission to him of his treasure with increase, makes him feel that after all loyalty might have been a more profitable investment: ['Oh *Anthony* . . . Gold' (2612–15)]. . . . [*359*] He succumbs less through his own fault than through the fault of the age; and this is his grand failure."

JORGENSEN (1951, pp. 387–92) finds that Enobarbus's death is modeled after doctrine explained in Sir Lewis Lewkenor's *The Estate of English Fugitives under the King of Spaine* (1595). LOMBARDO (1960; 1971, pp. 11–41) perceives a prismatic quality in Enobarbus, saying Sh. uses him to reveal other characters and situations.

JONES (1971, pp. 239–41) shows the significance of the Vice tradition and comments on the changes in Enobarbus: "As Antony's bluff soldierly counsellor, Enobarbus probably owes something in general conception to Lyly's Hephaestion in *Campaspe* [similarly JORGENSEN, 1965, p. 169]. His role is to oppose his commander's love-in-idleness by exalting the military life over amorous entanglements. But in the way Enobarbus is presented, and especially in the relationship he early establishes with the audience, Shakespeare was probably drawing on the earlier Tudor tradition of the Vice. Not, of course, that there is anything seductively vicious about Enobarbus' point of view: quite the reverse. But he can be said to represent a structural principle of opposition to the dominant values of Egypt, just as the Vice habitually called in question the dominant values of the play in which he appeared. . . .

[*240*] "The Bastard Faulconbridge in *King John* is the character who seems to have served as Shakespeare's chief model for Enobarbus; and he shows even more clearly the strength of the Vice tradition. . . . [*241*] In the first part [of the play] Enobarbus is largely the sardonic, often amusing commentator, but in the second his tone is changed. He is now no longer detached, but tragically involved in Antony's fall, and in this development he follows the Bastard." And SIMMONS (1973, *Shakespeare's Pagan World*, p. 138) remarks on the moral significance of Enobarbus's position: "In a comedy Enobarbus, with his charitable skepticism, would be confirmed at the close. In *Antony and Cleopatra*, where a comic reconciliation is thwarted, the comic 'plain man' himself has a distinctive tragic fall. Nevertheless, Enobarbus comes close to being the moral center of vision. He is a part of the Roman world, but rises above its absurd pretensions in his awareness that there is little to distinguish his world from the world of pirates and thieves. . . . He holds a superior moral position in the play not only because he sees the limitations of Rome but because he sees a proper place for Egypt in the soldier's life. He becomes, in fact, the greatest support for Antony's desire to maintain both worlds." To SANDERS & JACOBSON (1978, pp. 105–6) Enobarbus is the ironist in the play, notably in the barge speech (902–56), where he admires Cleopatra but also tempers his admiration by showing awareness of the lovers' romantic folly.

Those who discuss the changes in Enobarbus during the play include GERVINUS (1850, tr. 1883, pp. 743–4), HERAUD (1865, pp. 381–2), STAPFER (1879, tr. 1880, pp. 417–24), GRINDON (1909, pp. 30–5), GRANVILLE-BARKER (1930;

1946, 1:451–3), KNIGHT (1931; 1965, pp. 269–74), HODGSON (1936, pp. 88–99), DONNO (1956, pp. 228–30), JONES (1967, pp. 78–80), PANDURANGAN (1968, pp. 227–30), RICE (1968, pp. 229–35), AOYAMA (1969, pp. 17–18), WERTIME (1969, pp. 148–83), TANIFUJI (1970, pp. 51–72), INGLEDEW (ed. 1971, pp. xlviii–liii), LEE (1971, pp. 39–41), SLATER (ed. 1971, pp. 34–5), WHITAKER (1972, pp. 68–78), CANTOR (1976, pp. 146–8), FERRARA (1977, pp. 34–49), HARRIS (1977, pp. 223–6), NUNES (1978, pp. 10–31), and NEELY (1985, pp. 151–6).

Among those who discuss his tragic inner conflict or his death are SNIDER (1876; 1877, 2:283), GRINDON (1909, pp. 31–5), SCHALL (1915), WINCHESTER (1922, pp. 78–9), GUNDOLF (1926, p. 17, and 1928; 1949, 2:434), HILLEBRAND (ed. 1926, p. xxxviii), MURRY (1936, pp. 365–7), STAUFFER (1949, pp. 236–7), SPEAIGHT (1955, pp. 144–5, and 1977, p. 316), BOWLING (1956–7, pp. 254–5), MACK (1960, p. 17), RIBNER (1960, pp. 176–7), DRAPER (1961, pp. 138–9), KAULA (1964, p. 216), ORNSTEIN (1966, p. 42), SMITH (1966, pp. 192–3, 201, 206–7), MARKELS (1968, pp. 127–8), RICE (1968, pp. 232–5), SIMMONS (1969, pp. 499–502), WALTER (ed. 1969, pp. 32–4), ENRIGHT (1970, pp. 105–7), TANIFUJI (1970, pp. 51–72), INGLEDEW (ed. 1971, pp. xlviii–liii), NEVO (1972, p. 332), ADELMAN (1973, p. 131), SHAPIRO (1975, p. 39), STILLING (1976, pp. 286–8), HARRIS (1977, pp. 223–6), NAUMANN (1978, pp. 419, 421–2), SANDERS & JACOBSON (1978, pp. 121–2), VINCENT (1978, pp. 248–53, and 1982, pp. 78–9), BARROLL (1984, pp. 232–7), MARCHANT (1984, p. 167), PEARSON (1984, p. 176), and BOORMAN (1987, pp. 243–4).

Comments on his soldierly nature are offered by KREYβIG (1858; 1877, 1:443–4), DOUGLAS (1909, pp. 588–9), MACKENZIE (1924, p. 371), BOAS (ed. 1935, pp. xvii–xviii), CHAMBRUN (1947, p. 390), and MCMANAWAY (1973, p. 142); on his loyalty KREYβIG (1858; 1877, 1:444), BLUMHOF (ed. 1870, pp. 24–5), THÜMMEL (1881; 1887, 2:182–4), MURRY (1936, pp. 365–7), WILCOX (1936, p. 542), HEUER (1938, pp. 77–9), NEILSON & HILL (ed. 1942, p. 1245), CAMPBELL (ed. 1949, pp. 981–2), ARTHOS (1964, pp. 62–3), J. O. SMITH (1964, p. 45), and WEINSTOCK (1971, pp. 464–5); his sense of humor VATKE (1868, pp. 328–9), CREIZENACH (1916, 5:443–4), WINCHESTER (1922, pp. 77–8), RICHTER (1930, p. 145), WILSON (1948, pp. 407–8), ALTMANN (1969, p. 155), and SEN GUPTA (1972; 1977, pp. 48–9); his language Sen Gupta (pp. 48–51) and HUME (1973, pp. 286, 297); and his misogyny WOODBRIDGE (1984, pp. 294–7). Miscellanea include SHAW's (1897, *SatR*; 1932, 24:147) brief and cryptic remark on the "bogus characterization" of Enobarbus and SUZUKI's (1979, pp. 11–18) comments on Enobarbus as supporting Antony's greatness and the progress of action.

EROS

SWINBURNE (1879; 1902, p. 192) calls Eros "the freedman transfigured by a death more fair than freedom through the glory of the greatness of his faith."

GRINDON (1909, pp. 35–7), who traces his development in detail, finds merit in his fidelity and sympathy: "Eros is another of the pathetic figures whom everybody loves, and knowing the end of him invests everything he does through the play with an interest all its own. What a burden this man's heart has borne under this pledged oath to kill his master with his own hand should fortunes fall to the lowest. After Actium, what poignancy will there be in his rushing off to fetch Cleopatra to try to bring comfort to his master! . . . Eros sees his own dreaded hour facing him. 'Thou art sworn, Eros . . . do't; the time has come' [2897, 2902]. . . . When he [Antony] is putting on the armour for the last victory there is evidently something wrong with Eros, for his master says: ['Thou . . . Dispatch.' (2521–2)]. [36] [Is it] the extra heartache of the desertion of Enobarbus which some one has to tell the master? . . . It is to Eros that Antony utters the wondrous story of 'black vesper's pageants' [2833], and Eros knows what it all means. . . . When he is next wanted by Antony he shrinks from it. He has to be called no fewer than four times. . . . Eros knows there is no more delay. He ventures in with, 'What would my lord?' [2889] He listens scared and trembling. . . . The sword is drawn—but it enters the heart of Eros himself, and the faithful soul with his last gasp says: 'Thus do I escape the sorrow of Antony's death' [2936]. And if the two do [37] meet where the souls couch on flowers, Eros will resume his old service to the master 'wherein the worship of the whole world lies' [2924]."

MacCallum (1910, pp. 366–7) comments on his loyalty: "Often for the slave . . . the sole chance of escape from a condition of spiritual as well as physical servitude would lie in personal enthusiasm for the master, in willing self-absorption in him. . . . [367] So it is the quondam slave, Eros the freedman, bred in the cult of it, who bears away the palm. . . . Eros by breaking his oath and slaying himself, does his master a better service. He cheers him in his dark hour by this proof of measureless attachment." To Hodgson (1936, p. 90), Eros is the young "body-servant" who, "like Seyton [in *Mac.*] . . . has become his master's friend as well" (see also Willson, 1969, p. 7). And Battenhouse (1969, p. 176) somewhat fancifully sees Eros symbolizing throughout "paganism's dark analogue of agape, its passion parody of Saving Passion." Thus when in 4.12 Cleopatra enters to Antony's call for Eros, "the whole situation figuratively seems to epitomize Antony's plight: he would call in Eros to solace him, yet Cleopatra herself stands for *eros.*"

Others who comment on Eros include Horn (1827, 4:58–9, 70–1: love for Antony), Kreyβig (1858; 1877, 1:445: heroic virtue, surpassing that of the great leaders), Blumhof (ed. 1870, p. 26: gains our admiration and love), Oechel-häuser (ed. 1877; 1895, p. 95: Antony's faithful companion), Gundolf (1926, p. 17, and 1928; 1949, 2:434: becomes Antony's friend in death), Urban (1939, pp. 53–4: his devotion enhances Antony's nobility), Knight (1958, p. 193: symbolic name, Love), Coghill (1964, pp. 72–6: gesture of love in killing himself; symbolic significance of name), Frost (1964, pp. 41–2: name suggests sensual passion, deceiving Antony to death), Smith (1966, p. 193: must choose between obedience and devotion), and McAlindon (1973, pp. 195–6: symbolically unites bondage and freedom, love and war).

LEPIDUS

Commenting on his political role, CLARKE (1863, p. 225) calls him "the pottering peace-maker between his coadjutors, Octavius and Antony," adding, "Lepidus was a peace-botcher from timidity; moreover, he was stupid, sensual, and swinish." EMERSON (1890, p. 75) notes his usefulness: "Lepidus is permitted a voice in the councils only that he may bear the blame. But he is, temporarily, a very necessary man, since Antony or Cæsar with him can foil the other. Notwithstanding both see the weakness of the master-of-horse, each finds some good when the other dispraises him. A strong man in his place would have held the balance of power in the Roman world." MACCALLUM (1910, pp. 369, 371) finds his efforts as trimmer contemptible: "It is mere indolence and flaccidity of temper that makes him ready to play the peace-maker, and his efforts are proof of incompetence rather than of nobility. . . . [*371*] His deposition, which must come in the natural course of things, is mentioned only casually and contemptuously: [1732–7]. Accused of letters written to Pompey! So he had been at his old work, buttering his bread on both sides." KINDRED (1972, pp. 81–4) regards him as weak, though—like Pompey— a potential unifier between Antony and Octavius: "As the action opens he is occupying what seems like a firm position as an equal member of the partnership that rules the world. . . . However, a realistic assessment of the power distribution in the Roman world as portrayed in *Antony and Cleopatra* would have to conclude that Lepidus is decidedly a weak third. . . . [*82*] That he is allowed to remain as long as he does in a position of titular equality must be attributed on the one hand to Caesar's need for the loyalty he commands among certain Italian factions in his war against Pompey, and on the other to Antony's desire to use him as a buffer between himself and Caesar. . . . [*83*] Although he has great potential as an effective link, he is not even allowed the dignity of suggesting the match between Octavia and Antony which temporarily resolves the differences between the two giants. . . . [*84*] The disaster of Lepidus, almost a foregone conclusion from the beginning of the play, is finally accomplished beyond any doubt verbally in Act III, Scene ii, in a conversation between Agrippa and Enobarbus: [1545–52]." From this angle Lepidus's (p. 85) "sole function" is "to dramatize the enmity between Caesar and Antony."

Some sense his comic quality. Thus HUDSON (ed. 1855; 1872, 2:373): "The Lepidus of the play . . . bears a strong likeness to the veritable pack-horse of the Triumvirate, trying to strut and swell himself up to the dimensions of his place, and thereby of course only betraying his emptiness the more. . . . Vain, sycophantic, unprincipled, boobyish, he serves as a capital butt to his great associates, while his very elevation only renders him a more provoking target for their wit." STAPFER (1879, tr. 1880, p. 412): "Lepidus is at all events amusing; he is such an unequivocal nonentity that he becomes positively comic." BOWLING (1956–7, p. 252) finds his reluctance to make choices amusing yet fatal: "In Lepidus, the idea of duality is developed with comic effect. . . . Lepidus [in 3.2] gets himself into the awkward and ridiculous situation of trying to praise *both men equally* by asserting that *neither has an equal*. As we know, Lepidus' comical attempt to pursue an intermediate course between Antony and Caesar ended in tragic failure. If he had firmly chosen either side, he might have saved himself." To VINCENT (1978, p. 130), he is out of place because he strives to make the play's world comic: "Lepidus, though he is universally regarded by Romans as a weakling and a non-entity, is not by all standards a despicable character. He is the mild-natured triumvir, who believes the three men should subordinate their differences to the business of running the empire. He is a much-strained embodiment of the spirit of civilized toleration and compromise, a spirit which is broken in the passionate masculine rivalry of Antony and Caesar. Lepidus is in a technically comic position, in which he attempts to be a reconciler of opposites. But what is rich and valuable in a comic world is promiscuous pandaring in a tragic world."

Other contributions include GRANVILLE-BARKER's (1930; 1946, 1:455), who admires the characterization: "It is a sketch of a mere sketch of a man; but done with what skill and economy, and how effectively placed as relief among the positive forces of the action! Shakespeare (as dramatist) had some slight affection for the creature too. For a last speech, when Octavia is tearfully taking leave as she sets forth with her Antony, he gives him the charming 'Let all the number of the stars give light | To thy fair way' [1616–17]." And HUME's (1973, pp. 282–3), who examines his language: "He says almost nothing, usually contenting himself with such interjections as 'here's more news' [465]. What is remarkable is the concentration in so few lines of so many phrases like 'beseech', 'entreat', 'let me', and 'pray you' [680, 693, 707]; he is always begging in a bleating voice to which the sound of 'beseech' and 'entreat' seems very appropriate. He is obsequious even to Enobarbus: [283] [Quotes 679–81]. . . . *Quiet* is another of his motifs (none of Antony's 'thunder' for him [cf. 2256])."

Others who comment on Lepidus include ULRICI (1839; 1868–9, tr. 1876, 2:202: good but weak, lacking spirit and energy), KREYβIG (1858; 1877, 1:445, 459–60: instinctive love of peace makes him mediator), BLUMHOF (ed. 1870, p. 26: good-natured but weak), OECHELHÄUSER (ed. 1877; 1895, p. 94, and 1881, p. 34: good-natured and insignificant bonhomme; comic quality), THÜMMEL (1881; 1887, 2:179–80: professional and weak-minded apostle of peace), CORSON (1889, p. 279: a mere cipher), ADLER (1895, p. 304: good-natured, limited), LEE (ed. 1907, 36:xlviii: cast in mold of Polonius), GUNDOLF (1926, pp. 20–1, and 1928; 1949, pp. 438–9: his foolishness enhances Antony's and Octavius's greatness), HILLEBRAND (ed. 1926, pp. xxxvi–vii: his tragedy is to hold balance of power and be unable to use it), PHILLIPS (1940, pp. 190–2: born to obey not to rule), CHAMBRUN (1947, p. 390: pretentious character, language banal), RÜEGG (1951, pp. 269–70: the great need him as buffer), SMITH (1966, pp. 197–8: trimmer, representing middle way), BLISSETT (1967, p. 154: helpless inconsistency of his images in 1.4), STAMPFER (1968, pp. 217–18: his remarks on Antony in 1.4 indulgent but ambiguous), INGLEDEW (ed. 1971, p. liii: semicomic), G. R. SMITH (1974, pp. 1–2: his incompetence becomes clear in 1.4), and BARROLL (1984, p. 226: "unctuous and humble-mannered hypochondriac").

MENAS

OECHELHÄUSER (ed. 1877; 1895, p. 96, in German) describes Menas in 2.7 as "an insidious, evil character; he displays the open manners of a sailor, but more roughly drawn than his master," and CORSON (1889, p. 292) cryptically asserts, "Menas is a grand old representative servant of a time that has passed away." KNIGHT (1958, p. 192) thinks the Greek Menas (cf. μηνύω, betray; μηνίω, be wroth), like Menecrates, has a "minatory" sound (rebutted by LEVIN, 1976, p. 54 as "considering too curiously"; see n. 483): "Menas is clearly a rough, and even dishonourable— as a Roman would not be—adventurer." To ROSE (1969, p. 386), more plausibly, his ethic is that of the Romans: "Menas' idea of nobility, like that of Caesar and his lieutenants, is basically that what is expedient is also noble." ALTMANN (1969, p. 155) compares him to Enobarbus: "Menas seems altogether more likable than Agrippa and Maecenas, because like Enobarbus he is honest in his speech and shrewd in estimating the consequences of the Roman leaders' actions. Furthermore, like Enobarbus, he has a sense of humor—something none of the other Romans demonstrates, not even the Egyptian Roman Antony." So does WILLIAMSON (1970, p. 245): "Menas' resolve to desert Pompey begins an important pattern of action in the play: the desertion of the unfortunate Antony by his followers. This pattern culminates in Enobarbus' leaving Antony, an almost entirely Shakespearian development of his source. Menas' similarities to Enobarbus should not escape us—both are plain, blunt soldiers who speak their minds. Both seek to persuade their leaders of what seems to them the best course to follow; and when they fail, both leave their leaders. Indeed, Menas' lack of scruple in tempting Pompey to dishonorable means to power only serves to heighten by contrast the good advice that Antony gets about his affairs from Enobarbus and other followers, whose desertion seems sadly justified by Antony's flight at Actium. . . . We cannot escape the impression that desertion is rife in the world of the play."

Others who comment on Menas include CAPELL (1779 [1774], 1:31: Pompey's "fast friend"), CARTWRIGHT (1859, p. 27: allusion to Thomas Thorpe, the London bookseller—an unlikely idea), GRANVILLE-BARKER (1930; 1946, 1:456: pragmatic), CANTOR (1976, pp. 138–9: has no guidance from Pompey but must try to read his mind), and SWANDER (1985, pp. 165–87: in F1 [p. 165] "mysteriously, obstinately, fascinatingly silent" owing to his mute appearances at 614 and 3108).

MENECRATES

CAPELL (1779 [1774], 1:31) contrasts him with Menas: "Menecrates is also his [Pompey's] friend; but not in favour, like Menas, from being discontented, and disapproving his patron's conduct." GRANVILLE-BARKER (1930; 1946, 1:456) remarks on his speech: "Menecrates is needed to offer a sententious check to Pompey's soaring confidence. [Quotes 622–5.] A philosophic pirate, indeed; and we may see, if we will, the more pragmatic Menas, chafing, but scornfully silent in the background." For comments on Menecrates, see also KNIGHT (1958, p. 192: minatory name) and CANTOR (1976, pp. 139–41: in 2.1 he asserts that the gods [p. 141] "know better than men themselves what is in the interest of mankind").

OCTAVIA

JAMESON (1832; 1879, pp. 286–7) rejects Hazlitt's criticism of Octavia: "I do not understand the observation of a late critic, that in this play 'Octavia is only a dull foil to Cleopatra' [HAZLITT, 1817; 1930, 4:229]. Cleopatra requires no foil, and Octavia is not dull. . . . The subject of the drama being the love of Antony and Cleopatra, Octavia is very properly kept in the background, and far from any competition with her rival: the interest would otherwise have been unpleasantly divided, or rather, Cleopatra herself must have served but as a foil to the tender, virtuous, dignified, and generous Octavia, the very *beau idéal* of a noble Roman lady. . . .

[287] "The character of Octavia is merely indicated in a few touches, but every stroke tells. We see her with 'downcast eyes sedate and sweet, and looks demure',—with her modest tenderness and dignified submission—the very antipodes of her rival! Nor should we forget that she has furnished one of the most graceful similes in the whole compass of poetry, where her soft equanimity in the midst of grief is compared to 'The swan's down feather | That stands upon the swell at flood of tide, | And neither way inclines' [1594–6]."

Many others, especially in the 19th c., praise her character. Thus HUDSON (ed. 1855; 1872, 2:375–6): "Octavia has furnishings enough for the heroine of a great [376] tragedy. . . . The Poet has hardly done justice to her sweet and solid qualities; and indeed, from the nature of the case, the more justice she had received, the more she would have suffered from the perilous brilliancy of her rival. Yet he shows that he fully knew and felt her beauty and elevation of character, by the impression that others take of her." FOAKES (1964, *DUJ*, pp. 67–8), similarly noting that to all characters she is "chastely [68] beautiful," agrees that she possesses "qualities that link her with the heroines of the 'great' tragedies, with Ophelia, Desdemona, Cordelia." SNIDER (1876; 1877, 2:278–9): "She is the true Roman wife, who is by no means devoid of deep emotion, but it is the quiet, pure emotion of the Family; her feeling is confined to the bounds of an ethical relation, and herein she is the direct contrast to Cleopatra, whose passion is hampered by no limitations. She tried to perform her duty to both [279] husband and brother; but that husband had as his deepest impulse sensual, instead of conjugal, love, and that brother had as his strongest principle political supremacy, instead of fraternal affection, even if he possessed the latter also. . . . Thus the Family sank before the thirst of passion and before the thirst for power." And LEWES (1893, tr. 1894, pp. 257–8): "She is sincerely fond of Antony; she knows how to prize his gifts and qualities; she hopes, as is the way with good women, to cure him, through her influence, of the sins and weaknesses which have stained his life. . . . But [258] she is far from loving him with passion; she knows nothing of passion. It is plain, from the beginning, that so unequal a marriage can never fulfil the hopes based upon it. Antony is not in a position to appreciate Octavia's good and noble qualities."

KREYβIG (1858; 1877, 1:462), however, thinks her a mediocrity, and DEV-RIENT (1869, p. 120) calls her unamiable and sanctimonious ("unliebenswürdige Betschwester"). MACCALLUM (1910, pp. 364–6), like Lewes, believes she does not really love Antony: "Without affection to bring it out, there will be no answering affection in a woman like Octavia. She will be true to all her obligations, so long as they are obligations, but no love will be roused to make her do more than is in her bond. And of love there is in the play as little trace on her part as on Antony's. It is brother and sister, not husband and wife, that exchange the most endearing terms. . . . [365] This diplomatic alliance interferes . . . little with Octavia's sisterly devotion to Octavius. . . . And much is gained by this for the play. In the first place the hero no longer, as in the biography, offends us by fickleness in his grand idolatry and infidelity to a second [366] attachment, on the one hand, or by ingratitude to a long-suffering and loving wife on the other. But just for that reason Octavia does not really enter into his life, and claims no full delineation. . . . She is sister first and essentially, and wife only in the second place because her sisterly feeling is so strong."

MACKENZIE (1924, p. 404) too discusses Octavia's limitations: "Cleopatra's power over Antony is that she can ride level with him wherever the wind of the spirit blows—outride him if she will. . . .

"It is for lack of that life that Octavia fails. She is clean and generous and noble, of a marble beauty like the Cnidian Demeter. But she cannot spend herself. She does not give the impression of a woman merely cold. She can feel, and deeply; she can give her strength *for* Antony, as Fulvia does. But she cannot give it *to* him. That is not in her, for she cannot accept his."

Although she has a small part, GRANVILLE-BARKER (1930; 1946, 1:448) admires the poetry given her (e.g., 966–7, 1697–9, 1716–17): "She is meant to be a negative character, set in contrast to Cleopatra; but if only as an instance of what Shakespeare can do by significant 'placing' [cf. 957–9], by help of a descriptive phrase or so, and above all by individualizing her in the music of her verse, she ranks among the play's achievements."

She is sometimes considered a focus for contrary forces in *Ant.* Thus DANBY (1949; 1952, p. 142): "Her importance is apt to be overlooked unless her careful positioning is noted. . . . She is woman made the submissive tool of Roman policy where Cleopatra always strives to make the political subservient to her. . . . Where Caesar and Cleopatra are simple and opposite, Octavia—like Antony—is a focal point for the contraries. There is nothing in her as a 'character-study' to account for the effect her presence has." And BOWLING (1956–7, pp. 252–4), who maintains that divided loyalties lead to her failure: "Like Lepidus, Octavia also tries to maintain a middle position between Antony and Caesar. Although her love, unlike Lepidus', is sincere and unselfish, still she makes a serious error in attempting to love them both equally. . . . [253] [At 963] the folio stage direction . . . describes Octavia as entering 'between' Antony and Caesar. . . . [*254*] Even after Caesar tells her that Antony has returned to Cleopatra [in 3.6], Octavia still refuses to make a choice. Instead, she now makes to Caesar a statement closely paralleling and almost exactly repeating her previous remarks to Antony: [1834–6]. Here she does not make so much distinction between them as to call one 'husband' and the other 'brother'. Instead, she refers to them both identically as 'two friends'. This is Octavia's last speech in the play, and it reveals that she remains to the end, not a completely devoted wife but a woman whose loyalty is equally and tragically divided between her husband and her brother."

LONGO (1974) regards her as (p. 31) "the image of Apollonian civility" representing a dead Roman world (p. 32) "symbolized by Mars, cold, and land."

Others who comment on Octavia include BRÄKER (1780, tr. 1979, p. 84: charming, but only a shadow to Cleopatra), GUIZOT (ed. 1821, 3:3: pure and virtuous), HORN (1827, 4:53–4: prosaic virtue; marries Antony for her brother's sake), CAMPBELL (ed. 1838, p. lxi: devoted and dignified), HÜLSMANN (1856, pp. 229–30: her virtue and beauty), CARTWRIGHT (1859, p. 22: allusion to Sh.'s wife—a doubtful idea), CLARKE (1863, p. 239: sweet, womanly, dignified), BLUM-HOF (ed. 1870, p. 26: admirable morality), GRIFFIN (1870, p. 78: dull and still), OECHELHÄUSER (ed. 1877; 1895, p. 100: dutiful and virtuous, Juno to Cleopatra's Venus; her love for Antony is like her love for Octavius), CANNING (1884, p. 17: virtuous; Sh. should have brought her to the fore), CORSON (1889, p. 299: beauty of her womanhood), MORGAN & VINES (ed. 1893–8, pp. xxx–i: sluggish, bewildered, feeble), BRANDL (1894, p. 187: dry, cold, loves Octavius more than Antony), ADLER (1895, pp. 302–3: noble and dutiful), DOCCIOLI (1907, p. 593: loves Antony but is poor in spirit), GLEICHEN-RUSSWURM (1909, pp. 54–8: tragedy of family relations), GRINDON (1909, pp. 48, 56: errs in leaving Antony after 3.4), KELLER (ed. 1912, 5:195: cold, passionless, cannot hold Antony), WINCHESTER (1922, p. 75: moral dignity of character), ZANCO (ed. 1931, pp. xxv–vii: her morality obscured by Cleopatra's brilliance), BOAS (ed. 1935, p. xvii: dutiful devotion), SCHANZER (1954, pp. 379–80: resembles Blanche in *Jn.*; similarly DUSINBERRE, 1975, pp. 294–6, and see also n. 1700–5), SPEAIGHT (1955, p. 136: her exquisite poetry), RIBNER (1960, pp. 177–8: ideal of womanhood against which Cleopatra's abandonment to passion may be measured), CHARNEY (1961, pp. 108, 120–1: exemplar of coldness), GOLDBERG (1961, pp. 42–3: virtue subject to irreconcilable conflicts of desire), MARKELS (1968, p. 34: legalistic Roman impersonality), INGLEDEW (ed. 1971, p. liii: virtuous, passive, pathetic), LEE (1971, pp. 32–3: attempts to unite husband and brother when their division is clear), KINDRED (1972, pp. 90–3: no credible link between husband and brother), PAYNE (1974, pp. 74–5: caught between husband's rage and brother's policy), SHINTRI (1977, p. 203: noble womanhood), VINCENT (1978, pp. 131–3: cannot comprehend the rift between Antony and Octavius within her own character, conflict remains external to her), DASH (1981, p. 226: "perhaps" an "incestuous bond" between her and Octavius), and BARROLL (1984, pp. 224–6: has no moral energy).

OCTAVIUS

WARBURTON (ed. 1747, 7:186), admiring Sh.'s portrait, dislikes the character: "It is observable with what judgment *Shakespear* draws the character of *Octavius*. *Antony* was his Hero; so the other was not to shine: yet being an historical character, there was a necessity to draw him *like*. But the ancient historians his flatterers, had delivered him down so fair, that he seems ready cut and dried for a Hero. Amidst these difficulties *Shakespear* has extricated himself with great address. He has admitted all those great strokes of his character as he found them, and yet has made him a very unamiable character, deceitful, mean-spirited, narrow-minded, proud and revengeful." So does SCHLEGEL (1811, tr. 1846, p. 417): "The open and lavish character of Antony is admirably contrasted with the heartless littleness of Octavius, whom Shakspeare seems to have completely seen through, without allowing himself to be led astray by the fortune and the fame of Augustus." STAPFER (1879, tr. 1880, pp. 409–11) finds him revolting, yet denies that he has any personality: "In the whole range of historical figures it would be difficult to find one more disagreeable, more ugly, and more repulsive than Cæsar's nephew, Octavius. . . . [*410*] If ever in history there was a man predestined to win, it was Octavius, and all his skill, which was of a negative rather than of a positive order, simply consisted in offering no obstacle to his good fortune, but in letting things work for him, and in floating on the stream of events which carried him on of itself. . . . [*411*] A passive instrument in the hands of fortune, tame and colourless, without one ray of poetry in his nature, Octavius both in history and in Shakespeare is an absolutely vapid and insipid personage. . . . At most, he only fills in the tragedy the place of the principal agent in Antony's predestined downfall."

ULRICI (1839; 1868–9, tr. 1876, 2:204) takes a more balanced view, granting Octavius's "moderation," the "chief of political virtues," and his "inward moral right," but noting that it becomes "a mere mask to his love of dominion." EMERSON (1890, pp. 520–1) stresses his political talents, which Antony lacks: "It is the civic character of Octavius that is most important in *Antony and Cleopatra*. He belongs to the underplot, and personal motives have less place. Everywhere he acts as the personator of imperialism. It is in this civic character also that Octavius is most true to history, and for this he was most admired by the Romans. . . . [*521*] While always seeking the advancement of self, he sought it through the advancement of the empire. This he sought not to enlarge by war, but to unify in peace, establishing the empire because in sympathy with the minutiæ of governmental administration. . . . This moderation, self-restraint, is the one virtue in which he pre-eminently surpassed Antony. He was Antony's superior as a ruler, and the empire was safer in his hands." BRADLEY (1906; 1909, p. 290), like Stapfer, highlights his function as agent rather than his individuality: "His figure is invested with a certain tragic dignity, because he is felt to be the Man of Destiny, the agent of forces against which the intentions of an individual would avail nothing." Seeing Octavius as (p. 289) "laying a trap" in marrying his sister to Antony, Bradley calls him (p. 290) "neither attractive nor wholly clear" and regards him with (p. 288) "respect, fear, and dislike."

FURNESS (ed. 1907, pp. x–xi), however, partly anticipated by VATKE (1868, pp. 322, 334, 336–7), defends Octavius's nobility: Sh. "intends us to accept Cæsar's love for Anthony as perfectly sincere and very deep-seated. . . .

[*xi*] "Moreover, does it not injure the tragedy as a work of art that the Power, representing Justice, which is to crush Anthony should be of a character no more elevated than Anthony's own? . . . A man who is pure craft and selfishness ought not to be entrusted with the sword of Heaven."

And PHILLIPS (1940, pp. 199–203) regards Octavius's political virtues as the personal qualities that satisfy Renaissance requirements for an ideal monarch: "He and his role in history came to symbolize the inevitability and justice of the monarchic form of the state. . . .

"The very characteristic which deprives him of dramatic appeal is [*200*] one of his chief virtues as a governor. Unlike his great rival, he allows his political reason to be swayed by no form of excess or passion. . . .

"There is a certain magnanimity and nobility of character which further qualifies Octavius for the exalted position which destiny holds for him. The virtue is particularly manifested in his attitude toward Cleopatra in the closing scenes of the play. . . . [*201*] Her frustration of his schemes does not alter his admiration or prevent the funeral honors which he pays her in the end. . . .

[*202*] "But that which chiefly marks Octavius for 'the specialty of rule' is his ability to act consistently with reference to a just and legitimate political cause, the welfare of the state which the restoration of the monarchy will accomplish. . . . [*203*] Relentlessly he fulfills his own destiny and Rome's, so that in the end Thyreus can truly say that he 'performs The bidding of the fullest man, and worthiest to have command obey'd' [2257–9]."

To most, however, he is less than ideal. Thus BARROLL (1970, pp. 280–1), commenting on the narrowness of his ambition: "Caesar has trodden a well-worn, if subtle course, from simple acquisition to dreams of glory, but in his preoccupations, he has failed to grasp a truism which must be considered if one is to 'possess' the time [*1451*]. To seek dominance over men [*281*] by controlling solely the material objects of their desires is ultimately to ignore the range of human personality. For there is the ever-present danger of losing this control if what some men desire cannot be measured in purely material terms. A goal such as Caesar's is constantly vulnerable to those whose desires may roam beyond his horizon." See also BARROLL (1984, pp. 195–224).

And ERSKINE-HILL (1970, pp. 43–5, and 1983, pp. 156–7), discussing Sh.'s depiction of a ruler traditionally temperate and beneficial as a character (1983, p. 155) "not wholly admirable": Sh. (p. 156) "accepts the traits attributed to Augustus by Jonson [in *Poetaster*, 1601] and Goulart [in *Life of Octavius Caesar Augustus*, 1602] but, in a relatively rounded and naturalistic portrayal, gives them a human basis which at once modifies and fills out the picture. Youth, vulnerability, defensiveness and determination are the foundations of Caesar's character in the play. . . .

[*157*] "In effect Shakespeare has given us in Caesar our embodiment of Temperance, but with a psychological subtlety of portrayal which reduces the attrac-

tiveness of the quality, though not its evident effectiveness in the world of affairs. Caesar's condemnation of Antony's excess, and certainly his capacity to act from a grasp of the total political and human situation, both take their origin from his deeply felt resentful and competitive attitude to the older man."

SIMMONS (1973, *Shakespeare's Pagan World*, p. 123) finds that "the moral ambiguity of Octavius lies in his ability to use his honor to justify and support his rise. Unlike Pompey and Antony, Octavius never permits his sense of honor to conflict with opportunity and political exigencies. By adroitly turning the weaknesses of others against themselves, he can create with 'perfect honour' [396] the very opportunities he seizes, not unlike the equally ambivalent and enigmatic Bolingbroke in *Richard II*. . . . Perhaps the final scenes best clarify Octavius's conception of honor as a public virtue: while he is culpable in trying to dupe Cleopatra with appeals to his honorable nature, that private dishonor would serve the public honor of his triumphant return to Rome. The virtue of Octavius is therefore completely relative; its failure as an absolute criterion is that it leaves the man a moral question mark, if not a cipher." And LYMAN & SCOTT (1975, p. 73) point to the bleak world he heralds: "Octavius, the bureaucrat, not only ushers in the Augustan age; he also introduces the Roman norm that will soon sweep through the Occident—man will be divorced from his purposes; action will be self-defeating; existence will depend on a deadening rationalism; being will become nothingness."

Critics who express dislike of Octavius or his role include GRIFFITH (1775, p. 473), GUIZOT (ed. 1821, 3:2), BENDA (ed. 1825, 9:442), HÜLSMANN (1856, p. 229), CLARKE (1863, pp. 220–1), OECHELHÄUSER (ed. 1877; 1895, pp. 93–4), SWINBURNE (1879; 1902, p. 192), THÜMMEL (1881; 1887, 2:179), GRINDON (1909, pp. 37–41), MACCALLUM (1910, pp. 378–90), BOAS (ed. 1935, pp. xv–xvii), PEARSON (1954, pp. 133–6), MCFARLAND (1958–9, pp. 208–11), MATTHEWS (1962, pp. 66–7), KUCKHOFF (1964, pp. 422–5), RICE (1968, pp. 253–80), WERTIME (1969, pp. 186–91), LEE (1971, pp. 38–9), GODSHALK (1973, pp. 162–3), G. R. SMITH (1974, pp. 15–16), NOCHIMSON (1977, p. 126), KALMEY (1978, pp. 275–87), M. H. SMITH (1978, pp. 117–26), and FRENCH (1981, p. 257).

Others who are sympathetic to him or his role include CANNING (1884, pp. 17, 21, 28), ADLER (1895, pp. 301–2), LEE (ed. 1907, 36:xlv–vi), BRANDL (1922, p. 407), GUNDOLF (1926, pp. 26–8, and 1928; 1949, 2:446–9), GRANVILLE-BARKER (1930; 1946, 1:449–51), URBAN (1939, pp. 54–60), BRYANT (1961, pp. 188–9), SPENCER (1963; 1966, p. 31), FOAKES (1964, *DUJ*, pp. 74–5), STAMPFER (1968, pp. 260–1), WALTER (ed. 1969, pp. 29–32), WILLIAMSON (1970, p. 244), MARTIN (1975, p. 296), CANTOR (1976, pp. 199–200), and MIYAUCHI (1978, pp. 266–91).

Those who discover both good and ill in him include HORN (1827, 4:73–4), RÖTSCHER (1846, Pt. 2, p. 306), GERVINUS (1850, tr. 1883, pp. 742–3), HUDSON (ed. 1855; 1872, 2:375), LLOYD (1856; 1858, sig. I4ᵛ), KREYßIG (1858; 1877, 1:460–1), MÉZIÈRES (1860; 1886, pp. 456–7, 459), VISCHER (1869–87; 1905, 6:160, 176), BLUMHOF (ed. 1870, pp. 25–6), FRIESEN (1876, 3:251–2), SNIDER

(1876; 1877, 2:270, 284), MORGAN & VINES (ed. 1893–8, pp. xxv–vii), HIL-LEBRAND (ed. 1926, pp. xxxiv–vi), ZANCO (ed. 1931, pp. xxxiii–v), RIDLEY (1937, pp. 191–2, and ed. 1954, p. liv), DANBY (1949; 1952, pp. 143–4), MACLURE (1954–5, p. 119), WILSON (1957, pp. 160–1), RIBNER (1960, pp. 177–8), GOLD-BERG (1961, pp. 48–9), NAKAMURA (1961, pp. 119–22), TRAVERSI (1963, pp. 99–102), BULLOUGH (1964, *Narrative and Dramatic Sources of Shakespeare*, 5:249), KAULA (1964, pp. 216–17), HUNTER (1966, pp. 22, 24), NELSON (1966, pp. 200–1), ORNSTEIN (1966, pp. 38–9), SMITH (1966, pp. 192, 196), RIEMER (1968, pp. 38–9), MOORE (1969, pp. 671–4), ROSE (1969, p. 381), INGLEDEW (ed. 1971, pp. xliv–viii), SLATER (ed. 1971, pp. 15–17), KERMODE (in EVANS, ed. 1974, p. 1345), DORIUS (1978, pp. 320–4), SANDERS & JACOBSON (1978, pp. 103–4), and TOLMIE (1978, p. 122).

For comments on his language, see particularly SEN GUPTA (1972; 1977, pp. 38–44) and HUME (1973, pp. 280–300). SHAW (1897, *SatR*; 1932, 24:147) briefly asserts that Octavius "is deeper than the usual Shakespearean stage king."

PHILO AND DEMETRIUS

HORN (1827, 4:43, in German) resents Philo's disrespect as "impudent servant": "convinced of the hero's total decay," Philo "has the vile courage to mock the hero behind his back and ridicule him with base jesting." OECHELHÄUSER (ed. 1877; 1895, p. 95, in German) rates him socially higher, as not only "half servant" but also "half friend" of Antony. GRANVILLE-BARKER (1930; 1946, 1:456) remarks on both characters: "soldiers ingrain, [they] move for a moment in contrast, make their indignant protest against epicene Egypt and Antony in its toils; they have served their purpose, and we see them no more."

SMITH (1966, p. 207) ventures etymologies: "As the play opens, Philo is describing Antony's excesses to Demetrius. 'Philo', of course, is judicious devotion as opposed to 'Eros', passion. The name Demetrius is derived from 'Demeter', the goddess of natural fertility and harvest bounty, and her name suggests 'beyond measure'. Shakespeare begins to play with these concepts in Philo's opening words. . . . Philo talks too much like Caesar to be needed after the latter has stated his case in Act I, scene iv. Neither does Demetrius appear again, but the train of thought set in motion by his name continues through repeated references to Antony's bounty."

But RIEMER (1968, pp. 26, 28) points out that they are chorus rather than characters: "The First Folio . . . conveniently identified these speakers as Philo and Demetrius; but in fact they are not named in the play, they are given no individuality at all, and they are soon swept away by the impetus of the action. Neither has anything to do for the rest of the play (indeed, Demetrius' total role is about five lines of verse at the end of this scene), and neither he nor even the more voluble Philo is in any sense a 'character': their function is choric, and the opening speech is the product of a voice, of an undifferentiated Roman figure expressing an opinion. The contrast with Shakespeare's normal manner of tragic exposition is revealing. . . .

[28] "Philo's speech thus presents a definite and impassioned view of Antony

offered in such forceful terms that it is not likely to be glossed over or forgotten quickly. . . . Philo's attitude is that of the Renaissance moralists and those writers who attempted to cast this material into the form of an orthodox, didactic tragedy."

To ENRIGHT (1970, pp. 72–3), they are male chauvinists: "Antony is seen as serving Cleopatra's lust: and what Philo and his colleagues object to is the idea of a woman using a man, and not (which is the natural order of things) a man making use of a woman. . . . [73] For these soldiers, women are essentially camp followers, and the camp doesn't follow *them*; they are there to be used and disposed of."

PAYNE (1974, pp. 57–8) comments on Philo's Roman narrowness: "We are introduced to the Roman point of view through Philo's estimate of Antony's fall from greatness resulting from his association with Cleopatra: [4–14]. This is an example of dualistic perception par excellence: on the one hand we have Philo's past impression of Antony as Mars, who once devoted his 'office and devotion' entirely to 'the [58] scuffles of great fights', but on the other hand we have Antony as Philo sees him now, a man who has sacrificed his former greatness to become in effect Cleopatra's slave who fans her to cool her lust. Like Pompey and Caesar—and to a lesser extent Enobarbus and Agrippa—Philo would have Antony carefully measure out his experience according to an absolute set of Roman standards based on the absolutes of time and space. . . .

"The magnificent entrance of Antony and Cleopatra with their exotic retinue dramatizes the Roman fear of excess, but at the same time it demonstrates the inadequacy of Philo's perspective and of the Roman ethic."

MIYAUCHI (1978, p. 77) speculates that, because cautious of speech, Philo like Demetrius may be "entrusted by Octavius Caesar to have a good look at Antony's behaviour at Cleopatra's court." And SANDERS & JACOBSON (1978, p. 95) see Philo determined to impress his companion: "What is it that Demetrius says to Philo which, as the play begins, we are just too late to hear? . . . We might guess that Demetrius has resisted the flow of Philo's witty disapproval with some show of easy tolerance. Philo's judgement has been questioned, and Philo is a man proud of his perceptions. . . . At any rate he has a stake in the performance; he is the moral impresario of the show."

Others who comment on Philo and Demetrius include KNIGHT (1931; 1965, p. 211: Philo praises Antony's prowess), HONIGMANN (1959, p. 27: Demetrius's name perhaps unconsciously suggested to Sh. by Plutarch's *Comparison of Demetrius with Antonius*), CHARNEY (1961, pp. 83, 107: Philo from his personal and Roman viewpoint right about Antony, but has not reckoned with the world of love), STROUP (1964, p. 297: they are chorus presenting Roman view), STAMPFER (1968, p. 224: Philo master of ceremonies), WERTIME (1969, pp. 16–19: Philo concerned with Antony's occupation not his individuality), BROWER (1971, pp. 319–20, 322: Philo's impersonal and remote tone with its [p. 319] "epic generality" suggests Antony's heroic greatness), WHITAKER (1972, pp. 25–30: Philo's speech suggests Antony's actual greatness), PAYNE (1973, pp. 266–7: Roman perspective, contrasting Antony's past and present), ROTHSCHILD (1976, pp. 416–17: their consciousness is Plutarch's, not Sh.'s), JONES (ed. 1977, pp. 8–10: Philo uses metaphors he does not fully understand), NAUMANN (1978, pp. 405–6: speak as Romans would), VINCENT (1978, pp. 33–8: Philo has no idea of Antony's inner life), HIBBARD (1980, p. 104: Philo the ideal Roman soldier, voice of destiny), and PEARSON (1984, p. 172: not choric figures).

POMPEY

CAPELL (1779 [1774], 1:31) speaks of Pompey's virtues and weaknesses: "The character of Pompey is mark'd by—a high sense of honour; and by a natural honesty, join'd with irresolution and a backwardness to engage in great actions." GERVINUS (1850, tr. 1883, p. 744), however, like most critics, sees little virtue in his motives: "The young Pompey, a frank but thoughtless soul, the image of political levity opposed to the moderate Octavius, fights for the cause of freedom in company with pirates, foolishly brave, without friends. He cannot wait for the consequences of the discord between Octavius and Antony; he knows that his insurrection even re-unites them; but wantonly and vainly he thinks all the better of himself because he is able to force Antony out of Egypt. This confidence rests on the predictions of hope, on the command of the sea, on the love of the people, on all the most deceitful things in the world. . . . As Pompey understands the cause of freedom, he is satisfied, not that one man should be as good as another, but that he himself should be equal to the mightiest. . . . He shows what an adept he is in the revels and debaucheries that are bringing Rome to ruin." SANDERS & JACOBSON (1978, p. 100) agree that Sh. has created "a Pompey more interested in cupping it with the best of them than in running the world single-handed. . . . If this play were about the world well lost for pleasure, Pompey must be its hero, for it is he who is offered a chance Antony never has, and he it is who, for pleasure's sake, spurns it with never a regret."

Many others also comment on his failure. For SNIDER (1876; 1877, 2:274–5), Pompey represents a failure of republican principle: "Pompey, from the first, exhibits no great strength of purpose, no firm reliance on his principle. He stands as the representation of the old republican constitution of Rome, in opposition to the tendency to imperialism. . . . But he is clearly not the man to be at the head of a great political movement. He has, moreover, a [275] scrupulosity which makes him sacrifice his cause to a moral punctilio. Such a man ought never to begin a rebellion whose success is not his highest principle. . . . He really joins the Triumvirate in the division of the world, and thus utterly abandons the principle which he represented. Logically, he is now absorbed in the new idea by his own action and he disappears as a factor of the drama."

Pompey and Antony are (p. 276) "alike in surrendering their grand opportunity" (similarly LLOYD, 1856; 1858, sig. K2^v). According to a "moral test," Snider rather wetly asserts, Pompey is "the hero of this play, as Brutus is, by the same criterion, the hero of *Julius Cæsar*," but this "test" has no validity against the "world-historical" force of Octavius. WERTIME (1969), likewise noting Pompey's general similarity to Antony (p. 63: "Pompey's fortunes are a miniature of Antony's.

The two men are similar in character, and are instinctively more friendly toward each other than any of the other world-sharers"), observes particular characteristics (pp. 64–6): "Imagery of the sea informs Pompey's role in the play from first to last. . . . He uses a moon image [628] which, if carried to its logical conclusion, is ominous, the moon's inevitable rising and setting being the same motion essentially as the turn of Fortune's wheel. . . . [65] His principle of action is a democratic one which denies the essential dynamic of political power, the elevation of an individual to a status of superman. But Pompey ignores, apparently, the root of his own rise to power, and, having [in 2.6] proclaimed his noble reason for making war, abruptly does an about-face [66] and settles for a political compromise that undercuts his lofty motives." BOWLING (1956–7, pp. 251–2) discusses Pompey's inner division: "Pompey's duality, although not developed at great length, is very significant. Whereas Antony's distinguishing characteristic is honor and Caesar's is political ambition, Pompey is equally divided between these two interests. Pompey is strongly ambitious to be Emperor of the Roman Empire, but he is so honorable that he will not seize the most practical means of achieving his ambition. . . . What Pompey wishes [in 2.7] is that Fortune (in the form of Menas) had thrust duality upon him without his having to make a choice. Then he would have both ambition and honor at the same time, without having to give up one in order to get the other. . . . [252] In the present instance, although Pompey seems to think that he makes a decision in favor of honor, he does not really do so. He merely leaves things as they are, regretting that they are not otherwise. This moment's hesitation is the cause of his ultimate downfall, for Caesar . . . later makes new wars on Pompey and finally strips him of both his honor and his profit."

McFARLAND (1958–9, pp. 211–12) examines how Pompey's Machiavellianism fails him: "The opening of Act Two affords us an opportunity to observe in detail the requirements for success in the world. The scene is Pompey's headquarters at Messina, and we see Pompey as the Machiavel *manqué*. He projects himself grandly into the future, weaving plans and policy in a manner worthy of Octavius; he reviews for himself the worldly deficiencies of both Antony and Octavius, and concludes by saying: ['*Lepidus* . . . him.' (632–4)]. Pompey's careless use of the word 'love' in describing the people's view of him, and in describing the possibilities of the relationship of Lepidus to the other members of the triumvirate, indicates that for him, as for Octavius, the reality of love does not exist. . . .

[212] "To this extent Pompey seems the ideal Machiavel; confidence in the reality of the world, willingness to live in the future, inability to love—all these seem his credentials. But still another element obtrudes in Pompey, a fatal tendency to govern his attitudes by rigid formulas removed from the flux of experience—in this instance, the notion of justice: [quotes 616–17]. The successful Machiavel can scarcely build his policy on the merely hypothetical justice of the merely hypothetical gods. And Pompey allows himself to take seriously the so-called love of the populace. And he thinks of Antony's relation to the world in terms of honor, wishing that the Epicurean cooks may sharpen Antony's appetite so that 'sleep and feeding may prorogue his honour' [646]. Completely involved in the struggle for power, he

nonetheless permits himself the luxury of hiding his [own] aims, not from his enemies but from himself—he adopts, with pompous words, the persona of the avenger of his father, of the heir to the idealism of Brutus: ['What . . . Father.' (1193–1202)]. Constricted by dead formulations, his motivations obscured from himself, Pompey cannot survive in the power struggle." Pompey has to learn that (p. 213) "the moralistic trimmer has no place" in the play's scale of values.

KINDRED (1972), seeing him as a (p. 87) "potential linking force" between Antony and Octavius, observes that, like Lepidus, he serves (p. 89) "the purpose of reinforcing the theme of disorder and disruption by at first promising to effect reconciliation and then, not merely failing to achieve [90] it, but instead contributing to further disorder and dissension." To G. R. SMITH (1974, p. 4), his miscalculations doom him from the first: "Pompey begins by saying that if the great gods be just, they shall assist just men—like himself, presumably [616–17]. The subjunctive is ominous in that context, and we know from many previous Shakespearean portraits of self-announced righteousness that Pompey's self-righteousness may also be a bad sign. Pompey soon shows himself confident (as Brutus had been) that Antony is a poor thing, that he sits at dinner in Egypt, that Caesar is losing public support, and that Lepidus is estranged from both. Of these four assertions the first three are quite wrong and the fourth is not yet true. . . . A man who makes such errors and in such bouquets is sure to be a loser. The audience has already seen enough to know how wrong Pompey is." VINCENT (1978, pp. 136–7), like SCHANZER (1963, p. 165), compares him to Hotspur, going on to discuss his career in terms of "Fortune and Nature": "At first they seem united; Pompey's waxing fortunes seem a result of the participation of natural forces, like the sea and the high-spirited Roman youth, in his cause: ['I . . . full.' (626–9)]. Yet as Pompey's fortune is coming to the full, it ebbs in a natural fellow-feeling with Antony and the others [in 2.7]." Pompey is a semicomic character: "Menas renders the failure of Pompey's martial ambitions in language suggestive of a comic event: 'Pompey doth this day laugh away his fortune' [1302]. Pompey succumbs to the flattering comic illusion that he is being admitted to the club, to a share in the triumvirate's power. . . . We might feel that Pompey's relenting in his war is not such an ignominious failure; that it springs perhaps from a humane and civilized impulse. But such natural, comic [137] impulses prove insidious and destructive in the tragic world of Rome, a world in which comic actions are negative ones. . . . By the end of Pompey's cause, Fortune and Nature have become entirely antithetical; at the feast on Pompey's galley, Pompey can only recoup his fortunes by the unnatural act of murdering his dinner guests."

In a different vein, BOAS (ed. 1935, pp. xviii–xix; similarly BOAS, 1896, p. 480) discusses Pompey as Sh.'s contemporary: "In Pompey Shakespeare succeeds less in making much of the Pompey of history than of reproducing in Roman guise a sea-dog of the Elizabethan age. . . . [xix] Shakespeare puts his heart less into the signing of the treaty or into suggesting Pompey's naval genius than into depicting the hearty carousal on the galley, wherein in fine Tudor style the treaty is celebrated in wine and song."

Others who comment on Pompey include ANON. (1614, sig. B3^r: his conduct [in 2.7] a pattern to all Christians; a likely allusion to *Ant.* rather than Plutarch or other dramatic versions, as argued by SANER, 1969, pp. 117–20), GRIFFITH (1775, p. 468: no difference between receiver and thief), GUIZOT (ed. 1821, 3:3: forgets his sacred mission to avenge his father), BENDA (ed. 1825, 9:442: noble sense of honor), ULRICI (1839; 1868–9, tr. 1876, 2:202: hasty, energetic, thoughtless, and inexperienced), KREYβIG (1858; 1877, 1:460: shabby sense of decency), CART-WRIGHT (1859, pp. 25–6: allusion to William Herbert—an unlikely idea), CLARKE (1863, pp. 228–9: frank and generous, soldier of fortune), BLUMHOF (ed. 1870, p. 26: represents decline of Roman virtues), OECHELHÄUSER (ed. 1877; 1895, p. 94: reckless sailor, but not evil), THÜMMEL (1881; 1887, 2:180–2: cupidity cancels honor), CORSON (1889, p. 281: feeble representative of the old constitution), EMER-SON (1890, pp. 75–6: by accepting his enemies' proposals, he loses all claim to leadership), ADLER (1895, p. 304: bold naval hero with some wit), BRANDL (1922, p. 407: misses opportunity, like Antony), GUNDOLF (1926, p. 21, and 1928; 1949, 2:439–40: his initial strength and subsequent failure enhance the triumvirs' gran-deur), GRANVILLE-BARKER (1930; 1946, 1:455–6: facile optimism, suspect, [p. 456] "carries too much sail for his keel"), PHILLIPS (1940, pp. 192–3: ruins his advantages), CHAMBRUN (1947, p. 390: young, audacious, loyal), HARRISON (1951, p. 212: a lesser Macbeth), WILSON (1957, p. 164: a comically diminished Antony, missing opportunity), CHARNEY (1961, pp. 84–6: incapable of world rule), TRA-VERSI (1963, pp. 124–6: confused; has lost the will to see situation clearly), HUNTER (1966, p. 22: becomes a man of the past when he fails to grasp his opportunity), SMITH (1966, pp. 192, 197: must choose between personal integrity and ambition; an exemplar of the mean between conflicting forces, hence doomed), BLISSETT (1967, pp. 154–5: a certain loser from the start), ALTMANN (1969, pp. 151–4: reasons for defying triumvirate are confused), ADELMAN (1973, pp. 27–9: in 2.1 his judg-ment of Antony tells as much about him as about the accused), BELL (1973, p. 259: enlightened Renaissance nobility, for an Elizabethan audience), HUME (1973, pp. 283, 289–91: honor and justice his key concepts), SHANKER (1975, pp. 197–8, 201: honest man in world of power politics), CHAMPION (1976, pp. 257–8: mor-alistic trimmer), PLATT (1976, p. 246: his desire for power is weak), TOLMIE (1978, pp. 124–5: does not follow his verbal absolutes [e.g., 675–6] through), and BAR-ROLL (1984, pp. 227–32: his problem is self-knowledge).

PROCULEIUS

McGINN (1960, pp. 68–9) speculates: "Named by Antony as the only one of [69] Caesar's men whom Cleopatra should trust [3059], Proculeius may have been a sycophant of Antony's before Actium just as he now is of the conquering Caesar. Doubtless extremely personable, he has been selected, whether he knows it or not, as a decoy to distract the attention of the Queen while Gallus overpowers her guards."

BARROLL (1969, pp. 217–18) argues that on the whole the audience remains sympathetic to him: "Proculeius pursues . . . a Thidias-like function of plying

Cleopatra with flattery, but unlike Thidias who forfeited audience-sympathy through the patronizing tone he adopted both toward Enobarbus and Anthony, Proculeius is never portrayed as a 'jack' [2265]. Even if he does come near forfeiting the audience's favor as he continues to reassure the captured queen about his master's 'bounty' [3250], he does indicate other sensitivities in his reply to Dolabella. [Quotes 3276–83.]

"This latter may, of course, be mere blandishment, but the injunction to gentleness suggests some perception of the human misery in front of him. More importantly, we cannot take his injunction as hypocritical, as a way of hinting to Dolabella about the tone to be adopted, for then Dolabella's own subsequent sympathy [*218*] would be suspect and his betrayal of Caesar unmotivated. . . . He [Proculeius] is some sort of professional soldier with the social status of an Eros, or of an Enobarbus. . . . With a talent for smooth talk, but with limited authority, with an ability to improvise on orders which he has not the faintest idea of disobeying, he is capable not only of a professional contempt for Cleopatra's concept of the security of her fortified position, but also of an impulse of sympathy for a beautiful and unhappy queen." See also BARROLL (1984, pp. 123–4).

BOOTH (1979, pp. 115–17) tries to show that Proculeius's and Dolabella's roles were doubled.

Others who comment on Proculeius include MACCALLUM (1910, p. 450: eager to preserve Cleopatra's life), BERKELEY (1950, p. 534; 1953, p. 8; 1956–7, p. 286; and 1964, p. 140: Octavius's tool), TRAVERSI (1963, pp. 191–3: covers Octavius's intrigue with a gesture of generosity), ROSE (1969, p. 386: for him Octavius represents political ideal of kingship), WILLIAMSON (1970, p. 248: his loyalty to his master is unappealing), and HEFFNER (1976, p. 155: true ambassador in his loyalty to his master).

SCARUS

CLARKE (1863, p. 233) comments on his loyalty: "Scarus alone, of his [Antony's] principal officers, remains attached to him"; Sh. "has made Scarus the most energetic and the most cheerful of them all."

MACCALLUM (1910, pp. 359–60) expands: "First of these [honest characters] is Scarus, the simple and valiant fightingman, who resents the infatuation of Antony and the ruinous influence of Cleopatra as deeply as Enobarbus, but whose unsophisticated soldier-nature keeps him to his colours with a troth that the less naïf Enobarbus could admire but could not observe. It is from his mouth that the most opprobrious epithets are hurled on the absconding pair, the [*360*] 'ribaudred nag of Egypt, whom leprosy o'ertake' [1989–90]. . . . But as soon as he hears they have fled toward Peloponnesus, he cries: ''Tis easy to't; and there will I attend | What further comes' [2015–16]. He attends to good purpose, and is the hero of the last skirmish; when Antony's prowess rouses him to applause, from which he is too honest to exclude reproach: [2628–30]. Then halting, bleeding, with a wound that from a T has been made an H, he still follows the chase. It is a little touch of irony, apt to be overlooked, that he, who has cursed Cleopatra's magic and raged because kingdoms were kissed away, should now as grand reward have his merits commended to 'this great fairy' [2662], and as highest honour have leave to raise her hand—the hand that cost Thyreus so dear—to his own lips. Doubtless, despite his late outbreak, he appreciates these favours as much as the golden armour that Cleopatra adds. Says Antony, 'He has deserved it, were it carbuncled | Like holy Phoebus car' [2682–3]. He has: for he is of other temper than his nameless and featureless original in Plutarch, who is merely a subaltern who had fought well in the sally. . . . Not so Scarus. He is still at his master's side on the disastrous morrow and takes from him the last orders that Antony as commander ever gave."

BARROLL (1958–9, *HLQ*, p. 39), assuming the Soldier at 1931 and Scarus to be one, finds him to be "the typical loyal soldier, praising, cursing, encouraging, and fighting hard for his emperor, remaining until the last possibility for action. His exit here [2773] is a departure which suggests a larger finality."

Others who comment on Scarus include OECHELHÄUSER (ed. 1877; 1895, p. 95: tough old soldier), BATTENHOUSE (1969, pp. 173–4, doubtfully: parody of Christ's beloved disciple John), and VINCENT (1978, pp. 238–9: his spirit of broad comedy in 4.7).

SOOTHSAYER

SNIDER (1876; 1877), claiming (2:273) "Enobarbus manifestly thinks [cf. 950, 1322] that his master ought to go back at once to Egypt," regards the Soothsayer's utterances as reinforcement through the "medium" of "the prophetic emotion." He (p. 274) "urges very strongly the return to Egypt—the reason whereof he says he has not in his tongue, but in his feeling, in his instinctive perception of the future. . . . The Soothsayer thus utters in his peculiar form that which has already been told; the principle of Antony is subordinate to the principle of Octavius—the higher end must vindicate its superior power. This is not only known, but is now felt."

To CECIL (1944; 1949, p. 15), this "strange figure" is the voice of fate: "Ostensibly he is only a tame fortune-teller hanging about the Court for the entertainment of idle people. Nobody seems to take his predictions very seriously. They are wrong. When Cleopatra's ladies ask him about their future, in occult terms the soothsayer foretells their dreadful end. And when Antony casually asks him whether he or Octavius is likely to get the better of the other, he replies: ['stay . . . Noble.' (983–96)].

"Destiny . . . is working behind the visible scene to promote its secret purpose. These great persons, apparently so [16] powerful, and with the world at their feet, are in reality no more than puppets in the fingers of a mysterious and irresistible fate."

STROUP (1964, pp. 295, 298) balances him against the Clown (enlarging on BOAS, ed. 1935, p. xix): "The Soothsayer, perhaps the Clown even who fetches immortality for three, represents these affairs [of the stars, as against the personal and private]; and though the spiritual forces are not so clearly operative as in the moralities or in Marlowe or in Shakespeare elsewhere (as in *Hamlet* or *Lear* or *Macbeth*), they are always present to the minds of the principals. . . . [*298*] The episode of the Soothsayer (I.ii) and that of Cleopatra's actual death [3472 ff.] involve some of the same witty characters, and the Soothsayer in the one balances the Clown in the other. More to the point, the Clown is the very means for carrying out the Soothsayer's prophecies. The same wit, especially the same ironic *double entendre*, prevails in the words of the two."

And GARBER (1974, pp. 128–9) sees him voicing Antony's inner awareness: "The soothsayer appears at a pivotal moment in Antony's thought. We have met him before [in 1.2] at Cleopatra's palace . . . forecasting in riddle the course of the drama, predicting to Cleopatra's attendants that they will outlive their mistress. . . . In this first encounter the soothsayer is thus parallel to the soothsayer of *Julius Caesar* or to the earlier monitory dreams. . . . We have by now accepted the official place of soothsayers and augurers in the Egyptian court as a major distinguishing factor between the worlds of Egypt and Rome. When the soothsayer appears again, however, he is in Rome; and this subtly but completely alters the comfortable climate of belief. Antony has just accepted the hand of Octavia in a political marriage calculated [*129*] to bring peace between him and Caesar. With her good-night to him the soothsayer enters and is catechized by Antony on the prospects of the future [975–88]. Plainly, this is in part an internal monologue of the sort we examined in *Macbeth*. . . . The voice of warning we hear through him is Antony's own voice, projecting a brooding internal premonition of disaster. The soothsayer, like the witches, is here simultaneously an internal and an external character."

Others who comment on the Soothsayer include OECHELHÄUSER (ed. 1877; 1895, p. 96: elevated pathos of his speeches), MACK (1960, p. 27: his entry in 2.3 a visual surrogate for Antony's own personal intuition), NEVO (1972, pp. 321–2: reveals Antony's real inclination), SIMMONS (1973, *Shakespeare's Pagan World*, pp. 142–3: knows only Fortune, not concerned with humanity's responsibility for its fate), JONES (ed. 1977, p. 13: in 1.2 reminds audience of the women's fate, of which they are ignorant), and VINCENT (1978, p. 53: in 1.2 introduces idea of Fortune's connection with tragedy).

THIDIAS

OECHELHÄUSER (ed. 1877; 1895, pp. 95–6, in German) imagines the kind of actor needed: "Caesar wants to entice Cleopatra to turn away from Antony, perhaps even to kill him. To this end he chooses Thyreus [Thidias], who by Caesar's own witness is skilled in oratory and artful, a man who knows how to flatter a coquette's vanity. His appearance must be suited to the task. Young, handsome, versatile, with a flexible and ingratiating voice, he progresses rapidly in Cleopatra's favor until Antony returns and furiously interrupts the scene of the hand kiss. Thyreus at first tries to defy Antony, with a parvenu's pride and in the vain hope of having already gained a foothold with Cleopatra; when Antony however tears him away from her, his [96] part is played out; he endures his ignominious fortune silently in suppressed rage and cowardly fear." Others who comment on Thidias include KNIGHT (1958, p. 193: etymology of "Thyreus"), TRAVERSI (1963, pp. 146–9: his speech covers deep contempt for Cleopatra), BARROLL (1969, pp. 192–4: in him Octavius extends himself to saucy familiarity with Cleopatra; see also Barroll, 1984, pp. 104–6), and SEN GUPTA (1972; 1977, pp. 32–3: speaks falsehood, but eloquently).

VENTIDIUS

LLOYD (1856; 1858, sig. I5^v) sees Ventidius as reflecting the times: "The self-imposing sophistry with which Ventidius persuades himself that in prudentially foregoing a military success to save or curry favour with Antony, he is still true to the principle of soldierly ambition, only proves how entirely the ancient warlike spirit is debased and lost." HUNTER (1966, p. 22), similarly: "Ventidius, who knows how to avoid seeming to be a hero, is the real man of the time." WERTIME (1969, pp. 76–7) comments on how he reflects the consequences of Antony's weakness, which calls for his practical attitude: "Ventidius, a realist like Enobarbus, accepts the conditions of political power as his guide to achievement. But his lesson is more than an exposure of great men; he recognizes that, in the military hierarchy, the leader sets the upper limit of soldierly virtue no matter how good or bad he is. [77] The question is not one merely of how much glory a captain gains through his lieutenant, but also one of the consequences of the captain's moral failures. Antony's shirking his duty as a triumvir has forced Ventidius to stop short of total victory over the Parthians; this has tainted not only Ventidius's achievement, but has worked to Antony's detriment as well." SHAPIRO (1975, pp. 39–40) remarks on his lack of emotion: "The true antithesis of Antony is his lieutenant, Ventidius, who has that discretion which grants distinction between a soldier and his sword; that is, who is not excessively emotional even in matters of valor and ambition. . . . Nonetheless, unlike Antony, Ventidius is not a great hero, nor will he ever be. This, then, lends support to [40] the paradoxical hypothesis upon which the play revolves: that only excess can create, although it must destroy to do so."

NOCHIMSON (1977, pp. 109–11) notes how he punctures Antony's heroic nobility: "Nothing [110] that happens during Ventidius's three appearances on stage gives us any reason to question his loyalty to Antony; quite to the contrary, he seems able to admire his leader even while noting in him a significant flaw—jealousy of the accomplishments of his subordinates. . . .

"The question is why Shakespeare included Ventidius. . . . [111] The way in which Shakespeare prepares carefully for Ventidius's one real speech by having him appear silently on two prior occasions suggests the importance that he is attaching to this character. . . . Shakespeare wants not only to qualify our understanding of Antony's prowess as a general but also to underscore his pettiness and weakness of character."

And TOLMIE (1978, p. 116) thinks he is judicious because he "wisely refuses to do his utmost. . . . He is placed at the centre of the play, monitored by 'ambition, the soldier's virtue' [1519–20], to have Antony's experience for him and to speak important truths about all Roman experience. An absolute performance in defeating the Parthians, in doing Antony 'good' [1522], would in the immediate sequel 'offend' the Antony who sent him to defeat them [1523]. . . . Ventidius himself would perish because his 'good' to Antony would be seen to constitute an 'outcaptaining' offence. The Roman soldier Ventidius here knows the Roman oscillation, instability, alteration and reversal so well that he makes choices of the lower performance rather than the absolute performance, the full 'gain' which would actually 'darken' him in this peculiarly unstable Roman world [1521]." Others who comment on Ventidius include CLARKE (1863, pp. 229–30: his worldly prudence and wisdom), SMITH (1966, p. 193: must choose between honor for Rome and prudence for himself), and CANTOR (1976, p. 138: must try to read his general's mind, has no clear guidance).

Antony and Cleopatra *on the Stage*

The Text

The efforts by stage directors to translate Sh.'s text into theatrical experience always alter the original play: *Ant.* on stage is never identical with the play Sh. wrote. Audiences in the theater often are unaware of the many changes arising from the director's taste, interpretations, and idiosyncracies or from adjustments to the thoughts and feelings of the time. The alterations are made mainly by cutting, transposing, adding, and rewriting.

THE VERSIONS

The following essay analyzes the reshaping of *Ant.* as it occurs in various printed acting versions, printed eds. marked for use as promptbooks, and MSS and typescripts used for production. The texts discussed are drawn from SHATTUCK's (1965, pp. 33–42) list of 47 unpublished promptbooks plus a few later productions. Omitted are incomplete or duplicate promptbooks and partbooks (Shattuck's nos. 8, 9, 12, 15, 16, 19, 20–26, 29–31, 33, 35), and some others. An attempt has been made to give a representative cross section of English and American versions, of conservative texts and freer adaptations, and of varying renditions of a single text.

Concentration is on the texts rather than the performances. Collations of stage versions beyond the ones discussed here are provided by HALSTEAD (1979, vol. 12), who, however, is not always reliable. The versions discussed are, in chronological order:

1. Capell (for Garrick): Antony and Cleopatra; an historical Play, written by William Shakespeare: fitted for the Stage by abridging only; and now acted, at the

Theatre-Royal in Drury-Lane, by his Majesty's Servants. London: Printed for J. and R. Tonson in the Strand, 1758.

Edward Capell does not make drastic changes apart from shortening the play. His version is among the most faithful to F1—especially in retaining Enobarbus's death scene and Seleucus. But he dispenses with some of the nonrealistic or non-historical material, for instance, Antony's desertion by Hercules. The harsh criticism that calls this version for Garrick a "murderous work" (see Calvert [no. 12], p. xii, quoting a letter to the *Morning Post*, 6 Nov. 1866) does not seem justified.

2. Garrick: David Garrick's promptbook (prepared in collaboration with Capell) used for production at Drury Lane (3 Jan. 1759). [Shattuck, no. 1; Folger Library: Ant, 3]

About Garrick's promptbook "marked [in ink] by Edward Capell in preparation for the acting edition," PEDICORD (1981, 4:398, n. 14) remarks that "there are only minor and unimportant differences between the marked copy and the printed version." Shattuck seems to imply that the "further cuts in pencil" are not Capell's. Whoever made them, the additional cuts indicated in ink or pencil render the version more like 19th-c. distortions of the play, especially those concentrating on love and neglecting history.

3. Bell's Sh.: Antony and Cleopatra, A Tragedy, by Shakespeare. An Introduction, and Notes Critical and Illustrative, are added, by the Authors of the Dramatic Censor [Francis Gentleman]. London: Printed for John Bell, 1774. (Cornmarket Press Facsimile, 1969.)

Bell's is a complete text marked for possible deletions and with footnotes arguing in favor of certain cuts and sometimes praising or criticizing the original play.

4. Colman (Kemble?): Shakspeare's Tragedy of Antony and Cleopatra; with alterations, and with additions from Dryden; as now perform'd at the Theatre-Royal, Covent-Garden. London: Printed and Publish'd by J. Barker, 1813. (Cornmarket Press Facsimile, 1970.)

Colman's version, in addition to cutting and transposing, merges Sh.'s play with Dryden's *All for Love* (as the title of the adaptation indicates). Also the few scenes and passages that correspond generally with F1 are full of verbal changes. Colman's deviation from the original in giving the gist of the description of Cleopatra in the barge to Antony instead of to Enobarbus is approved by Francis Gentleman in Bell (no. 3; p. 30): "We think him [Dryden] inferior to *Shakespeare*, though he has disposed the description better, by putting it in *Antony's* mouth."

Because it was produced at Kemble's theater, the Colman version has been attributed to Kemble—and still is even though "Kemble's name does not appear

on the title-page; and the work is not included in his collection of plays in 1815"
(ODELL, 1920, 2:66). But see no. 5.

5. Kemble: John Philip Kemble's promptbook used for production at Covent
Garden (15 Nov. 1813). [Shattuck, no. 2; Nuffield Library, Stratford-upon-Avon:
50.02 (1813)]

Kemble's promptbook, marked in his hand, seems to support the view that
the ed. of 1813 is indeed by him and not by Colman. It contains mainly added
directions in ink for stage business, but hardly any substantive alterations in the
text.

6. Kemble MS: The so-called second stage version made by John Philip Kemble
is a MS copy of the whole play in Kemble's hand (n.d.; sold 1821). [Shattuck, no.
3; Folger Library: S.a.125]

Kemble's manuscript version was purchased by George Lamb at the Kemble
sale in 1821 but is not otherwise dated. The quality of the adapter's work, however,
suggests a date after 1813 because it improves many of Colman's (no. 4) numerous
deficiencies. The main principle of revision, says FURNESS (ed. 1907, p. 590), is
"omission; there are not many transpositions, and no additions of moment," and
he concludes that with the omission of "fifteen characters" almost automatically "the
play is shortened by many hundred lines." Actually, some of the characters' parts
do not altogether disappear but are taken over by others. As ODELL (1920, 2:56)
points out, Kemble had a "predilection . . . for giving definite names" to anonymous
characters, as in the case of Cleopatra's Messenger. Other changes in Kemble's
version (including his 10 short transitions between scenes) are not particularly
conspicuous.

7. Macready: William Charles Macready's handwritten version (13 July 1833).
[Shattuck, no. 4; Folger Library: S.a.130]

Macready is held by some to be the arranger of the Cumberland version by
D. G. (no. 8), but despite some similarities in detail the two versions represent
different approaches. Macready's text is "much cut and adulterated with Dryden,"
according to LAMB (1980, p. 61), and this adulteration distinguishes the manuscript
from Cumberland's published text by D. G. One possible reason for a confusion of
the two versions is Macready's participation as Antony in Alfred Bunn's production
at Drury Lane (21 Nov. 1833)—for which his adaptation was used (see ODELL,
1920, 2:177, and ALLEN, 1971, p. 219)—and his assumed brief involvement as
Antony in Kemble's production (no. 5) at Covent Garden in 1813 (see Lamb, p.
60). In addition, both "Theatres Royal," Drury Lane and Covent Garden, were
under Bunn's management from 1833–5, and Covent Garden was taken over by
Macready in 1837 (see Odell, 1920, 2:119–23). It seems that the connection of

Macready and Bunn in one way or other with the two theaters and two productions has led to the later publication of an edited amalgam of productions at the "Theatres [plur.] Royal" but not of one identifiable production. As Lamb (p. 61) points out, of the two versions (Macready's and D. G.'s) "the manuscript copy seems closer to the stage production: for example, the purported acting edition [Cumberland's] omits the scene at Misenum [2.6], but reviewers were warm in their praise of Stanfield's painted Promontory of Misenum." On the whole, however, Cumberland's version corresponds with F1 more closely than does the MS, not only in ignoring Dryden but also in the order of lines and scenes.

8. Cumberland: Antony and Cleopatra: A Historical Play, In Five Acts, By William Shakespeare. Printed from the Acting Copy, with Remarks, Biographical and Critical, by D. G. [George Daniel]. . . . As performed at the Theatres Royal, London. London: Davidson, [1833?], (Cumberland's British Th. 355.)

9. Phelps: Samuel Phelps's promptbook used at Sadler's Wells (22 Oct. 1849). [Shattuck, no. 5; Folger Library: Ant, 8]

Though the Folger Library copy (SHATTUCK, no. 5) is based on an "unidentified full text" (HALSTEAD, 1979, 12: SS 910d, S AC5) and that of the Nuffield Library in Stratford-upon-Avon is made in the text of STEEVENS (ed. 1793), the stage directions show that both extant copies of Phelps's promptbook derive from Steevens's ed. Despite heavy cuts, Phelps's version is "restored" (Shattuck) or "Shakespeare undiluted" (ODELL, 1920, 2:275) in lacking the borrowings from Dryden found in Colman (no. 4) and Macready (no. 7).

10. Glyn: Isabella Glyn's copy of the text used for readings (1855?). [Shattuck, no. 6; Folger Library: Ant, 2]

Isabella Glyn was Phelps's Cleopatra in 1848, and this version shows strong resemblances to Phelps's promptbook (no. 9) but more severely excises indecent words and passages. SHATTUCK (1965, p. 34) considers it a reading copy ca. 1855, HALSTEAD (1979, 12: SS 910d) a promptbook of 1852. The text is pp. 343–480 from vol. 7 of an unidentified *Works*.

11. Calvert: Charles Calvert's text (no. 12) marked perhaps for his production at the Prince's at Manchester (10 Sept. 1866) or for Jean Davenport Lander's production (see no. 15) in Brooklyn (1874). [Shattuck, no. 7; New York Public Library, Lincoln Center, Theatre Collection: *NCP.164539]

This preparation copy (early stage of a promptbook) was owned by George Becks (an actor in Lander's company) and bequeathed to the New York Public Library in Jan. 1905. Becks's reconstruction of Lander's performances (no. 15) may have been influenced by his knowledge of Calvert's version; SHATTUCK (1965, p. 34) thinks that this copy was "perhaps used for Mrs. Lander's production."

12. Calvert: Shakspeare's Tragedy of Antony and Cleopatra, Arranged for Representation in Four Acts. By Charles Calvert, Prince's Theatre, Manchester. Edinburgh: Printed by Schenck and M'Farlane, [1867?].

The main features of the play that need excision, according to Calvert, are the historical "diffuseness" (p. v) and the "large number of comparatively insignificant characters. . . . Their absence makes the remaining parts more prominent and acceptable to trained performers" (pp. vi–vii). Calvert asserts that he has "not presumed to add a syllable" (p. vii).

13. Lacy: Antony and Cleopatra. A Tragedy, in Five Acts. By William Shakespeare. Thomas Hailes Lacy, Theatrical Publisher. [London, 1867?] (Lacy's Acting Ed. 75.)

Lacy's publication claims (p. 3) to be a rendition of a production by Charles Calvert at the Prince's Th. in Manchester 1866 and again at the Prince of Wales Th. in Liverpool in 1867. The performance is criticized (p. 6) as having "more scenery and less Shakespeare." Because, cuts apart, Calvert's contemporaneous version (no. 12) is faithful to F1, it is hard to believe this one can also be his. In cutting complete scenes, Lacy condenses the action and at the same time reduces the number of scene changes—to such an extent, however, as to render some of the goings-on unintelligible. According to ODELL (1920, 2:303), the version is "a poor thing."

14. Halliday: Shakspeare's Tragedy of Antony and Cleopatra. Arranged and Adapted for Representation by Andrew Halliday. *First performed at the Theatre Royal Drury Lane (under the Management of* Mr. F. B. Chatterton*) on the 20th of September*, 1873. London: Tinsley Brothers, 1873.

Halliday's text tries to be "agreeable to modern audiences." Halliday "struck out the episode of Pompey (which has little to do with the main story), and removed many shifting scenes which tend to interrupt the action and confuse the spectator" (p. vi), in order to concentrate on "the 'Passion of the Single Pair.' " Assuming that Sh. "would have introduced better 'sensations' than 'noises heard off', hand-to-hand combats, and alarums," he "attempted an improvement" (p. vii), the addition of spectacular visual presentations at the end of each act. ODELL (1920, 2:305) quotes a reviewer: "No line is spoken that is not Shakespeare's, but then the lines of Shakespeare that are not spoken are very many indeed," and calls (2:259) this version "a curtailed Antony and Cleopatra . . . gorgeously mounted with spectacle, dance and song."

15. Lander: Jean Davenport Lander's promptbook used at Brooklyn Th. (2 and 3 Sept. 1874), and George Becks's memorial reconstruction of it. [Shattuck, nos. 13 and 14; New York Public Library, Lincoln Center, Theatre Collection: *NCP.342925, and Folger Library: Ant, 1]

The two extant texts connected with Lander's production are a promptbook made up by George Becks, using an unidentified ed. (Shattuck, no. 13), and his memorial reconstruction (Shattuck, no. 14). The main promptbook (Shattuck, no. 11), which, according to Shattuck, was based on Halliday (no. 14), is lost from the Theatre Collection of the New York Public Library, Lincoln Center (*NCP.342921); it was used last in 1982. George Becks's memorial reconstruction (Shattuck, no. 14) reflects a theatergoer's (or an actor's) experience of the production in giving fuller descriptions than the promptbook does of stage business and gestures.

Like Halliday (no. 14), Lander neither integrates her own poetry into the play nor alternates between Sh.'s and some other author's wording. The similarities between Lander and Calvert (nos. 11 and 12) are undeniable. Interestingly, a review of Calvert's production at the Prince's Th., pasted into the back of Becks's memorial reconstruction, mentions details from the performance connected with nos. 11 and 12.

16. Langtry: Shakespeare's Play of Antony & Cleopatra, as performed for the first time under Mrs. Langtry's Management, at the Royal Princess's Theatre, London, on Tuesday, 18th November, 1890. London: The Leadenhall Press, [1890].

Lillie Langtry's version is almost as short as Halliday's (no. 14). The author of the preface, Arthur Symons, praises her (p. viii) for "having done more for this incomparable drama than anyone has ever done for it before." ODELL (1920, 2:387) describes the production as "sumptuous," but, in contrast with Symons, as one in which Langtry was a "most inadequate Egyptian queen." Furthermore, he stresses (2:443) that "she knew only too well that it [the strength of her revival] could not be in her acting, and therefore she lavished money on the scenery."

17. Louis Calvert: Messrs. Louis Calvert & Richard Flanagan's Second Annual Shakespearian Season, Queen's Theatre, Manchester, February 16th, 1897. Antony and Cleopatra: Arranged for Representation in Four Acts, and Produced by Louis Calvert. Illustrated by James Magnus. Manchester: Jesse Broad & Co. Ltd, [1897?].

Louis Calvert's text bears strong resemblances to that of his father, Charles Calvert (no. 12), prepared 30 years earlier, although the 1897 ed. has fewer cuts and sticks more closely to F1. Still, much of the text, especially the death scenes and the ending of the play, are modeled on Charles Calvert's version.

18. Hanford: Charles Hanford's promptbook used for a touring production in America (1900?). [Shattuck, no. 18; Folger Library: Ant, 6]

The most striking characteristic of this version is the return to a division of the play into five acts, with choruses and tableaux between each. It may be for practical reasons only that Eros doubles with Lepidus, Agrippa with Demetrius in Acts 2, 3, and 4 and with Proculeius in Act 5, Mardian with Scarus, the Soothsayer with Decretas in Act 5 and with Thyreus in Act 4, and Maecenas with Canidius

—but it is certainly not just by chance (though it may be convenient) that Enobarbus is made to double with the Clown.

Hanford takes pains to curtail politics, but the cuts in his version are less conspicuous than the additions. He tends to overstate what is implicit in the poetry. The first act, for example, closes at 427 with an additional "Farewell Cleopatra" spoken by Antony, and a repeated "Farewell! Farewell!" concludes his speech. Hanford makes lavish use of spectacle, music, lighting, and choruses.

19. Beerbohm Tree: Two of Herbert Beerbohm Tree's promptbooks (chosen from a list of 11 in Shattuck) used in connection with production at His Majesty's (27 Dec. 1906). [Shattuck, nos. 27 and 28; Bristol, Drama Department, Theatre Collection: HBT 193/27, case 193; HBT 193/28, case 193A]

20. Beerbohm Tree: Shakespeare's Antony and Cleopatra, as arranged for the stage by Herbert Beerbohm Tree. With Illustrations from Photographs by F. W. Burford. London: Warrington & Co., 1907.

Herbert Beerbohm Tree considers the topic of the play "a world-passion redeemed by love" (p. [5]) and by his scenic arrangement almost forces attention from Rome to Egypt and the love theme. Though he omits Enobarbus's death and Antony's victory over Caesar (concentrating instead on the defeats), he does more justice to the play than do, for instance, Halliday (no. 14) or Langtry (no. 16). BERRY (1983, p. 97) finds Beerbohm Tree's "arrangement of scenes . . . excellent." Contemporary critics contradict one another about the length and number of scenes. *The Standard* (28 Nov. 1906) announces before the opening: "At His Majesty's it [the play] will be given in four acts and 18 scenes." Elsewhere (*The Daily Express*, 28 Nov. 1906) Tree also "let it be known that his version would have four acts and 18 scenes, which is several scenes more than was actually played" (Berry, p. 89). COURTNEY (1906) counts—one night before the opening—"in Mr. Tree's version, who has done his best to reduce the story within manageable dimensions . . . as many as seventeen scenes," which, of course, could mean 18. Berry (p. 89), however, counts 12, LAMB (1980, p. 91) finds 14, and *The Daily Express* (31 Oct. 1906) announces that "the five acts, as is usual with Mr. Tree's Shakespearian representations, will be given in three, but nothing of dramatic value in the play will be omitted. . . . The story gains in cohesion and simplicity by this reduction in the number of the intervals." The three versions by Beerbohm Tree discussed have 4 acts and 13 scenes.

Beerbohm Tree's two full promptbooks (Shattuck's nos. 27 and 28) are based on proof sheets of his acting ed. (1907). Changes marked in ink and colored pencils in Shattuck's no. 27 are carried out in the interleaved no. 28, the final promptbook made by Edward Broadley, Beerbohm Tree's stage manager. The complicated rearrangement of scenes is identical in all three texts, and the differences affect mainly single lines or words or details of the staging. One gets the impression that the ed. may have been published for nonprofessional readers rather than for use in performance. This assumption finds support in some other differences between ed. 1907 and Shattuck's no. 27. The retaining of passages that may be hard to follow in a swift performance suggests that a profounder understanding is expected from readers of ed. 1907; the scene in which Antony is deserted by Hercules (2467 ff.), for example, is marked for omission in Shattuck's no. 27 but retained in ed. 1907.

21. Ames: The typewritten text prepared by Winthrop Ames for production at the New Th., New York (8 Nov. 1909). [Shattuck, no. 36; New York Public Library, Lincoln Center, Theatre Collection: *NCP+.51624B]

22. Ames: [Proof sheets of] William Shakespeare's Antony and Cleopatra as arranged for presentation at the New Th. [by Winthrop Ames. New York, 1909]. (Shattuck, no. 37; New York Public Library, Lincoln Center, Theatre Collection: *NCP.38 × 1111)

23. Sothern/Marlowe: Two copies of the promptbook (chosen from a list of 4 in Shattuck) used by E. H. Sothern and Julia Marlowe in Winthrop Ames's production. [Shattuck, nos. 32 and 34; New York Public Library, Lincoln Center, Theatre Collection: *NCP, and Museum of the City of New York: 43.430.621]

Nos. 21–23 are versions of Winthrop Ames's American production, which, according to an unidentified review (Nov. 1909, Theatre Collection), "differs from any other which has ever been prepared." Only two years after Beerbohm Tree's publication of his *Ant.*, Winthrop Ames's text was prepared for publication (no. 22). In referring to the production, Shattuck (pp. 39–40) also lists a typescript of the director's (no. 21) as well as four promptbook versions used by his leading actors, Edward H. Sothern and Julia Marlowe.

The director's typescript probably represents the version actually performed. But the three renditions discussed here, as well as a preparation copy in the Museum of the City of New York (Shattuck, no. 34), had some bearing on the production at the New Th. Reviews of the performances seem to refer sometimes to what is documented in Ames's texts, sometimes rather to the Sothern/Marlowe versions. All versions arrange the play in five acts. Ames asserts (p. 5) that "the present version adheres more nearly to Shakespeare's play than any other acting version now extant." Like Beerbohm Tree, he has cut scenes of "intrinsic historical interest" and all "political" scenes except that on Pompey's galley, "for the sake of brevity and concentration upon the main tragic theme" (p. 6). Another unidentified review praises the "thoughtful" elimination of "the episodic element."

The difference between Sothern/Marlowe and Ames consists mainly in the rearrangement and designation of scenes, less in the cutting of passages.

24. Bridges-Adams: Text with cuts used for production at Stratford-upon-Avon (29 June 1931). [Shattuck, no. 39; Nuffield Library: 71.21/1931A (2179)]

W. Bridges-Adams's 1931 production of *Ant.* was not his first. His "Stratford tenure" was highlighted by "four seasons of *Antony and Cleopatra*, from 1921 to

1931," with what is described as "nonstop" productions (LAMB, 1980, p. 101). He confines his intervention in the text to cutting and refrains from transpositions and additions.

25. Bankhead: The text used by Tallulah Bankhead (William Strunk's acting version) for production at the Mansfield Th., New York (10 Nov. 1937) under the direction of Reginald Bach. [Shattuck, no. 41; New York Public Library, Lincoln Center, Theatre Collection: *NCP.49 × 168]

Reginald Bach's production with Tallulah Bankhead as Cleopatra "left out the politics and proceeded in old-fashioned 'static tableaux' " (LAMB, 1980, p. 218, n. 110). It resumes the style of Halliday (no. 14) or Hanford (no. 18). In other respects the text is like Langtry's (no. 16) in the neglect of characterization, causal relations, and above all language and poetry for the sake of theatrical effects. The prose text of Tallulah Bankhead's version assembles only the highlights of the play to form an almost incoherent puzzle of fragments; ATKINSON (*New York Times*, 11 Nov. 1937, 30:2) speaks of "gayly scattered scenes . . . badly edited." There are relatively few transpositions, however.

26. Atkins: Robert Atkins's promptbook used at Stratford-upon-Avon (23 Apr. 1945). [Shattuck, no. 42; Nuffield Library: 71.21/1945A (5366)]

According to SHATTUCK (1965, p. 41) Robert Atkins's promptbook was "originally used in B. Iden Payne's production in 1935 [and] . . . erased and reused." (The surviving text of Ben Iden Payne's production [Shattuck, no. 40] turns out to be an "unused copy.") The achievement of Atkins's version is the absence of any distorting intervention such as additions or transpositions. If there are shortcomings, they may be the reduction of poetry and the deletion of passages conveying emotions in Caesar.

27. Nunn: Trevor Nunn's promptbook used at Stratford-upon-Avon (15 Aug. 1972). [Not in Shattuck; Nuffield Library: 71.21/1972 ANT (S. 1293)]

Nunn's promptbook neglects anything in the text beyond what is necessary to keep the action going: his text is strongly simplified.

One year after the Stratford production, Nunn revived *Ant.* at the Aldwych in London (1973). The text of the London production is even more severely cut than the 1972 version, the most noticeable change being the placing (perhaps another step back to the 19th c.) of 1.5 (the mandragora scene) after 2.2 (the barge scene).

28. Brook: Peter Brook's promptbook used for production at Stratford-upon-Avon (4 Oct. 1978). [Not in Shattuck; Nuffield Library: 72.902 at 71.21 (S. 2658)]

Brook's production was repeated a year later at the Aldwych in London. His promptbook is the least cut stage text.

RESHAPING THE PLAY

The following pairs are considered substantially the same, and the second in each case is mentioned only when it differs in occasional details: Capell (no. 1) and Garrick (no. 2); Colman (no. 4) and Kemble (no. 5); Charles Calvert (nos. 12 and 11), as well as Charles Calvert (no. 12) and Louis Calvert (no. 17); Tree (nos. 20 and 19); Ames (nos. 22 and 21). Similarly, references to Lander (no. 15) and Sothern/Marlowe (no. 23) apply substantially to all their versions discussed here, unless otherwise specified.

The play in standard reading editions consists of 5 acts and 42 scenes. This organization varies in acting versions. Charles Calvert, Halliday, Lander, Louis Calvert, and Beerbohm Tree have only 4 acts, and Bankhead has 15 scenes without act division.

Regardless of the act-scene arrangement, all stage versions make cuts and sometimes other adjustments. Some versions proceed by cutting only (Capell, Bell, Cumberland, Phelps, Glyn, Bridges-Adams, Atkins, Nunn, Brook), others mainly by transposing (Charles Calvert, Lacy, Halliday, Lander, Langtry, Louis Calvert, Beerbohm Tree, Ames, Sothern/Marlowe, Bankhead), and still others mainly by adding and rewriting (Colman, Kemble, Macready, Hanford). With certain differences Nunn also belongs to the last category: he does not add to the text, but he paraphrases difficult passages (e.g., 2741–6), summarizes them (e.g., 1832–3), or substitutes glosses from the Signet ed. (1964) for "hard" words in F1 (e.g., 2148). Certain scenes in particular are affected by a mixture of cutting, transposing, rewriting—Cleopatra's encounters with the Messenger, the battle scenes, Antony's desertion by Hercules, the circumstances of Enobarbus's desertion and death, and the other death scenes.

Cutting

To shorten a long play, directors normally delete material unnecessary for understanding the action that can be cut without transitions or substitutions. A few scenes are retained in all texts, though they may be cut to some extent: these are (with labels modeled on the ones used by Brook in no. 28) 1.1 (the lovers); 1.2 (the Soothsayer, news from Rome); 1.3 (Antony's departure); 1.5 (mandragora); 2.2 (Caesar and Antony meeting); 3.11 (Antony's retreat); 3.13 (Thidias); 4.12 ("All is lost"); 4.14 (death of Eros); 5.2 (the Monument). The last two—4.14 and 5.2 —are severely changed and cut.

The opening scene (1.1) is practically uncut, and there are no serious deletions in 1.3. 1.2 is considerably shortened in a number of stage versions. The first half of the scene—the banter between Cleopatra's women and the Soothsayer—is condensed in all but Lander and Beerbohm Tree. The extent of the cuts varies from the deleting of single lines or short paragraphs (begun by Capell) to the dropping of the bawdy passage at 80–169 (first marked for omission by Bell's ed. and later deleted by most published texts and Bankhead), and to the cutting of everything up to 156 and so beginning the scene with Cleopatra's entrance (first done by

Kemble MS and followed on the whole by Macready, Cumberland, and Phelps). Brook is alone in almost fully preserving this section. In other versions short cuts of 1.2 affect mainly indecent material or sententious sayings.

Some episodes or portions of scenes are particularly susceptible to alteration, even though the results are not identical. Ames cuts 1.4 entirely, and Hanford almost entirely (deleting 446–508 and 514–22). The complete deletion of Caesar's first scene certainly indicates a lack of interest in the play's political issues; cuts are similarly motivated in a group of texts (e.g., Macready and Atkins) that shorten or omit some of Caesar's speeches in this scene. Another group of texts attempts to shorten by cutting speeches by Lepidus or the Messenger as well (e.g., Kemble MS and Halliday). Furthermore, many eliminate some of Caesar's description of Antony's debaucheries (ca. 435–63) and also the gross portions (especially the reference at 497–9 to the "stale of Horses") in Caesar's praise of Antony's former soldierly qualities (ca. 491–507). Whether such cuts are made out of respect for Caesar's prestige or out of prudishness is hard to say, because the representatives of both attitudes are not among those who cut: Capell and Bell do not cut at all, and Glyn and Phelps delete only some four to six lines from the scene.

The Egyptian equivalent of the Roman 1.4, the mandragora scene (1.5), is retained in all texts, but references especially to the eunuch and to sexual activities, including Cleopatra's reminiscences of her past with Julius Caesar, along with her bursts of temper, are often cut (ca. 533–48, 597–610). While Capell and Brook are the exceptions in shortening practically not at all, Beerbohm Tree exceeds the others in deleting Alexas's appearance altogether (556–613).

The cutting of the entire first Pompey scene (2.1) shows some disregard for the political theme of the play, but, no doubt because of Pompey's relatively slight significance, Capell, Colman, Kemble MS, Cumberland, Glyn, Calvert, Lacy, Halliday, Lander, Hanford, Ames, Sothern/Marlowe, and Bankhead eliminate it. The others make some attempts at shortening the scene by the deletion of single lines, most of which contain figurative language (e.g., 641, 644–7) or cruxes (e.g., 624–5) or the parts of minor characters. This local shortening is done with some variation by Langtry, Beerbohm Tree, Atkins, and Nunn. Macready cuts more extensively, with the obvious intention of concentrating fully on the news of Antony's approaching, thus preparing for the first meeting of Caesar and Antony in the following scene.

The stage versions usually retain Antony's and Caesar's speeches in 2.2 but omit the material spoken by minor characters. The dialogue of Enobarbus, Agrippa, and Maecenas (containing the "barge speech") is, however, retained in all, though condensed out of recognition by Colman and purged of references to Cleopatra's bawdy past (e.g., 941–56) by most. Praise of Octavia's beauty (825–8) is sometimes excised, as are details of Pompey's power (862–6). These cuts indicate that Cleopatra is without a serious rival and that Pompey has no real share in the struggle for world supremacy.

The relative insignificance of Octavia is demonstrated by the handling of 2.3. The first part of the scene (963–73) consists of the parting of the newly betrothed couple and Caesar, the second of Antony's encounter with the Soothsayer (974–98), and the third of Antony's decision to return to Egypt (999–1010). Capell, Colman, Cumberland, Lacy, Lander, and Bankhead cut the entire scene, as if to wipe out any conflict in Antony between pleasure and his marriage for peace, as well as to remove Octavia's function as peacemaker. Another group of texts—represented by Kemble MS and Halliday—omit the betrothal and parting (963–73; Kemble MS in addition shortens the ensuing dialogue with the Soothsayer), whereas a further group—led by Bell and followed by Macready—suppresses Antony's dialogue with the Soothsayer and most of Antony's ensuing soliloquy (ca. 975–1007) as if to cancel Antony's fear of Caesar. With a sense of climactic scene endings, Kemble MS concludes with Antony's "I'th'East my pleasure lies" (1007); this ending is followed by Sothern/Marlowe and Nunn. All attempt to focus on Antony only.

There is little disagreement about the relative insignificance of 2.4 (1011–23), the short meeting of Lepidus with Maecenas and Agrippa that takes up the triumvirs' decision of 2.2 to meet Pompey at Mount Misenum. It is deleted in all but Bell and Kemble MS, and it is one of the only two cuts of entire scenes in Brook's text.

Cleopatra's first encounter with the Messenger (2.5) is less interesting for its cutting than its transposition (see pp. 749–50). But 2.6 (1175–1332), Pompey's first direct meeting with his political opponents, is comparable with 2.3. The entire scene is omitted by Colman, Cumberland, Halliday, Langtry, and Hanford; Kemble MS omits Pompey's meeting with the triumvirs and retains only Enobarbus and Menas (as Mecænas), while Bell deletes even the latter section (1280–1332). The 20th-c. versions cut this scene less drastically, omitting only single lines. Bell alone pays due attention to the political ramifications, and in canceling the remainder of the scene this version focuses on Pompey's invitation (1279) to the feast on his galley (2.7). Of those who remove 2.6 entirely—including Kemble MS, which cuts all of Pompey in 2.6—all but Langtry are consistent in cutting 2.1 as well, to concentrate on the political confrontation of Antony and Caesar rather than admit further complications by introducing a third party, Pompey. Of these, Kemble MS, Cumberland, and Halliday also cut the reconciliation of the triumvirs on Pompey's galley (2.7) and thereby get rid of Pompey altogether. Of the others who also eliminate 2.7—Bell, Langtry, and Lander—Francis Gentleman in Bell is driven by a sense of propriety to dispense with this scene and to preserve the other two Pompey scenes: he calls 2.7 (p. 301) an "incoherent scene of revelry" with "very little concern with, or influence upon, the plot." Lander cuts 2.1 and 2.7 but retains 2.6, a scene with more plot details and dramatic force than the other two. When 2.7 is not entirely cut, it is often trimmed of the servants' discussion of Lepidus at the beginning (1335–50). None of the stage texts leaves that dialogue untouched; some (Capell, Colman, Calvert, Nunn, and Brook) retain only a minimum. The scene-ending in F1 (1493) is also changed: Macready omits 1432–93; Hanford stops at 1388; Lacy and Sothern/Marlowe (Shattuck, no. 32) end with the song at 1471; Shattuck's no. 34 adds some 10 lines after it. Certainly the song concluding Act 2, as in no. 32, makes a more spectacular ending. Beerbohm Tree's last line is 1485, and Nunn inserts 1493 into 1490 to end the scene with "sound out."

In all stage versions but Bell, Phelps, and Brook, 3.1 (with Ventidius in Parthia *"as it were in triumph"*) is cut. Like many short scenes in *Ant.*, 3.1 has fewer than 50 lines (1494–1537) and only minor characters and is therefore easily deleted.

In 3.2 the dialogue of Enobarbus and Agrippa (1538–63) is cut (Kemble MS, Phelps, Glyn, Atkins, Nunn, and Brook retain it), with Kemble MS deleting only 1546–61 and Nunn only 1548–9, 1552–3, 1555–61. Also deleted is the parting of Caesar, Antony, and Octavia (1564–1619), first cut by Capell, who is followed by most published versions (except Bell, Calvert, and Langtry) as well as by Kemble MS and Bankhead among the unpublished promptbooks. The first section is obviously cut to save time; the second probably because Antony's and Caesar's manliness is violated by the references to their tears and because the section shows—unfavorably in the view of the love-theme enthusiasts—Antony's concern for a woman who is not Cleopatra. In addition, the cutting of 3.2 avoids the portrayal of a somewhat too close relationship between brother and sister, and it further minimizes Octavia's role in the play so as to give more prominence to Cleopatra.

Probably for the same reason, some versions cut 3.4 and 3.6, the remaining two of four Octavia scenes in the play. Scene 3.4 is the only intimate encounter of Antony and Octavia, and those who omit it (Capell, Macready, Cumberland, Calvert, Lacy, Halliday, Lander, Langtry, Hanford, Ames, Sothern/Marlowe) avoid showing a personal meeting of Antony and his wife. Kemble MS leads those retaining it. The four Octavia scenes (2.3, 3.2, 3.4, 3.6) are handled with a certain arbitrariness: Capell, Cumberland, Lacy, and Lander cut the first three but retain 3.6; Bankhead deletes 2.3 and 3.2; Sothern/Marlowe omit 3.2 and 3.4; Colman and Kemble MS dispense only with 2.3; Macready, Calvert, Halliday, Langtry, and Ames cut 3.4; Sothern/Marlowe (Shattuck, no. 34) are alone in cutting 3.6. Those who cut 3.4 reduce Octavia by robbing her of the little emotional display she has in the original. At the same time omitting this dialogue of the newly married couple extenuates Antony's reckless determination to let her go. Since in 3.6 Octavia is a symbol of dissension in contrast to 2.3, where she symbolizes reconciliation, it is inconsistent to cut only one of them. A distortion also occurs on stage when in the cutting of the Octavia sections in 3.2 (1564–1619) and in 3.6 (1792–1857) Octavia is reduced to a mute presence in the former and to nonexistence in the latter: her arrival in Rome in 3.6 is completely cut by Halliday and Hanford, while all others shorten throughout the scene, but especially in the Octavia section. By retaining 3.6 (with or without Octavia) the others make this scene a catalyst for the political and military actions that follow. The first part, consisting of Caesar's (with Agrippa's and Maecenas's) reacting to Antony's "Contemning Rome" (1751–91), is deleted altogether by Lander and to a great extent by Halliday. All others shorten throughout mainly for the sake of simplification—an additional indication of which is the usual omission of the list of Antony's allies (1825–33) in the second part of the scene.

Scene 3.3, which follows up on 2.5—both showing a spiteful and irrational Cleopatra with the Messenger—is, like 2.5, not only shortened but often otherwise transformed (see pp. 749–50). Though the two scenes are interdependent, 3.3 is not retained by Macready and Cumberland.

In the short 3.5 (1726–50) Eros and Enobarbus discuss political changes—Lepidus's decline and Pompey's death. Because of the scene's brevity and because it anticipates information discussed from Caesar's point of view in 3.6, many adapters feel justified in cutting it. It is, for example, the second of only two scenes cut entirely in Brook. Other eds., however, recognize the impact of the political evaluation provided by Antony's friends and retain it (Kemble MS, Macready, Phelps, Glyn, and Beerbohm Tree, who transposes it to follow 1485).

All sections of 3.7 (Cleopatra and Enobarbus on her presence in the battle [1858–80], discussions of Antony's wish to fight by sea [1881–1930], comments on Antony's decision [1931–59]), are deemed superfluous only by Langtry—presumably because her interest is more with the emotional drama and with Cleopatra specifically than with the struggle between passion and reason in Antony. In other versions, smaller adjustments are made: the speeches after the exit of Antony and Cleopatra at 1939, i.e., comments on the situation made by a Soldier, a Messenger, and Canidius, are ignored by Bell, Halliday, and Beerbohm Tree (who adds "We'll fight by sea!" to Antony's speech after 1939). With the same apparent intention of ending the scene impressively, Colman and Bankhead cut at 1930 with Antony's "Away my *Thetis*"; Macready, Calvert, Lander, Hanford, Ames, Sothern/Marlowe, and Atkins close with Canidius's statement that they are "Womens men" (1943); and Nunn's last line praises Caesar's speed (1948–9).

Glimpses of the sea battle are presented in the short scenes 3.8 and 3.9, and they are cut seemingly for practical reasons: 3.8 is deleted first by Colman (but not by Kemble MS, Glyn, Nunn, and Brook); 3.9 is retained only in Capell, Bell, Colman, Macready, Glyn, Calvert, Nunn, and Brook. The simplification of the battle, however, eliminates much of the play's oscillation between politics and love, Rome and Egypt, the two sides of the fight. If 3.8 is cut and 3.9 retained, the balance is lost; it is preserved by the retention of both scenes (Capell, Bell, Glyn, Nunn, Brook) or in the deletion of both (Phelps, Lander, Hanford, Ames, Sothern/Marlowe, Bankhead). The same applies to 4.1 and 4.2, where similarly the alternation between Caesar's and Antony's sides is destroyed in some texts by the removal of one scene of the pair.

The scene describing Antony's shameful flight from various perspectives (3.10) is completely cut only by Cumberland but is considerably shortened by some others to omit difficult or indecent passages, to dispense with a minor character (Scarus), or to reduce Enobarbus's significance. Bell and Lander keep only Enobarbus's opening speech (1977–80) and continue with his and Canidius's talk about desertion, of which Lander cuts Enobarbus's final lines (2020–2); Kemble MS and Langtry omit this last section (ca. 2006–19); Hanford cuts everything after Canidius's evaluation of Antony's behavior (2006–11); Nunn shortens single lines in order to avoid figurative language (e.g., 2007–8), as he does elsewhere.

Antony's appearance afterward (3.11) is sometimes shortened between 2068 and 2099 (in Colman, followed by Kemble MS and most others except Macready, Cumberland, Halliday, Langtry, Bankhead, and Brook) so that Cleopatra asks for Antony's forgiveness and receives it at once. The more regular practice is to condense

Antony's speech of self-reproach and shame (2031–48) or even delete it (Colman, Macready, Phelps, Lander, Langtry, Hanford, Beerbohm Tree, Ames, Sothern/ Marlowe, Atkins, Nunn).

The deletion of 3.12, the scene in which Antony's Ambassador talks to Caesar, in almost half of the versions (Macready, Lacy, Halliday, Lander, Hanford, Beerbohm Tree, Ames, Sothern/Marlowe, Bankhead) primarily avoids a change of locale and has 3.13 as an uninterrupted continuation of 3.11 in Egypt. It also suggests some lack of interest in Caesar (as a character and as a triumvir) in ignoring his treatment of Antony's Ambassador and his orders for Thidias. As earlier, the play's balance is further weakened in the deletion of this scene and in the retention of its counterpart, 3.13. Directors intend to emphasize Antony and Cleopatra, it seems, and therefore they are satisfied with having Caesar's answer to Antony's request come indirectly from Thidias and the Ambassador in 3.13.

One of the longest scenes of the play, 3.13 (2152–2388), consists of several sections: (1) Cleopatra and Enobarbus (2152–66); (2) Antony with his Ambassador (2167–93); (3) servant and Enobarbus (2194–2204); (4) Cleopatra and Thidias (2205–54); (5) Antony and Enobarbus, joining them (2255–65); (6) Antony and Thidias (2266–2332); (7) Antony and Cleopatra: fury and reconciliation (2333–81); (8) Enobarbus (2382–8). All stage versions cut down all these sections in some way, but it is striking how severely Enobarbus's comments are reduced: his speech on judgment (2187–93) is deleted in practically all versions, as is his concluding speech about Antony's diminished reason and Enobarbus's plan to leave him (2382–8) in Lacy, Hanford, Beerbohm Tree, Ames, Sothern/Marlowe, and Bankhead. Only Halliday and Colman shorten in another area (2152–93) to keep the Thidias episode. Directors' ideas about famous speeches are divided: Nunn cuts the whole of Antony's furious outbursts (2269–75), Kemble MS their continuation (2286–99), others, like Macready, Lander, and Atkins, omit his moment of fresh courage ("I will be trebble-sinewed" [ca. 2362–6]) or the wish to have a feast (ca. 2367–9).

Scenes 4.1 ("He calles me Boy") and 4.2 ("He will not fight with me, *Domitian?*") portray Caesar and Antony in turns as personal rivals, no longer as politicians competing for power. Stage versions ignore the relationship of these two scenes; the cuts affect Caesar as well as Antony, and no reason for the lack of balance is apparent. Only Caesar's scene (4.1) is cut in Bell, Kemble MS, Ames, and Sothern/Marlowe, whereas only Antony's scene (4.2) is deleted by Phelps, Glyn, Lacy, Beerbohm Tree, Atkins, and Nunn. This practice is hard to justify, especially because the two scenes are strongly linked by the reaction of both competitors to the topic of single combat. Both scenes are retained only by Macready and Brook; both are cut by Capell, Colman, Cumberland, Calvert, Halliday, Lander, Langtry, Hanford, and Bankhead.

The scene with Antony's soldiers on guard, 4.3 (2467–2501), is enacted exclusively by minor and anonymous characters and therefore susceptible to cutting. In addition, stage versions tend to delete material not absolutely necessary for understanding the action. Accordingly, Antony's desertion by Hercules—as the soldiers interpret the supernatural music—is cut by many and retained (though sometimes shortened, transposed, or otherwise changed) by Calvert, Hanford, Beerbohm Tree, Sothern/Marlowe (Shattuck, no. 32), Nunn, and Brook. Calvert is typical: he omits 2467–82 (the relief of the sentry) but preserves 2483–2501 (the music and its origin).

An interest in heroism perhaps prevented directors from cutting 4.3, though they may delete 4.4 (2502–51), Antony's arming, the first part of which also provides atmosphere rather than action (2502–25). As Bell's note points out, these scenes (p. 333) "add to a superfluity of business, and explain nothing new." All of 4.4 is kept by Capell, Glyn, Lacy, Hanford, Sothern/Marlowe, Bankhead, and Brook, and nearly all by Phelps. Halliday retains the lovers' moments of tenderness (2502–33) but deletes the military business. Conversely, Kemble MS, with the progress of the action in mind, preserves the military lines (2527–33) but cuts the romantic. Many delete the core of the scene (ca. 2527–34, 2536–7, 2545–6); Nunn's cuts ignore the meter (at 2540 he eliminates "well-sed," at 2542–4 "rebukeable . . . Complement").

A major concern in Act 4 is Antony's decline, from which the part of Enobarbus cannot be detached. Changes made in the Enobarbus scenes 4.5 (his desertion, 2552–74), 4.6 (his two speeches of repentance, 2575–2620), and 4.9 (his death, 2694–2735) sometimes grossly distort the original. The excision of the desertion scene (in Bell, Colman, Calvert, Lacy, Langtry, Ames, Sothern/Marlowe, and Bankhead) not only suppresses the result of Enobarbus's gradual alienation from his general but also the exhibition of Antony's generosity when he sends Enobarbus's treasure after him.

Enobarbus's repentance automatically disappears with the omission of the whole scene in Hanford, Ames, Sothern/Marlowe, and Bankhead, but his two speeches (2590–8, 2611–20) specifically are cut by Colman, whereas Nunn crosses out merely 2616–17. Only Halliday and Langtry cut the first part of 4.6 (2575–89), deleting Caesar's instructions for the battle and beginning with Enobarbus's speech of repentance (2590). Colman retains Caesar but omits Enobarbus.

It is not quite clear why 4.9 (2694–2735) of all scenes is banned from the text without some kind of substitution—whether Enobarbus is simply forgotten or is not recognized as significant enough to have a death scene of his own, or whether the manner of his death is deemed too mysterious, like the desertion of Hercules (4.3). His death is neither presented nor reported in Colman, Macready, Cumberland, Langtry, Hanford, Beerbohm Tree, Ames, Sothern/Marlowe, and Bankhead; in Ames's text 4.5–4.11 are cut and Enobarbus simply stops existing. In Cumberland's 4.3 and Beerbohm's 4.1, Enobarbus receives the treasure sent after him by Antony and disappears from the play after deciding to die (2620).

Not all of those who retain 4.9 (Capell, Bell, Kemble MS, Phelps, Glyn, Calvert, Lacy, Halliday, Lander, Atkins, Nunn, Brook) leave the scene untouched. Only Capell and Bell do not cut at all; Glyn and Atkins cut the soldiers' dialogue before Enobarbus's speech to the moon; Lacy cuts most of the soldiers' lines after the speech to the moon but retains 2730, the record of Enobarbus's death; so does Nunn, who makes sure to cut 2735 as if to exclude the possibility that Enobarbus "may recouer yet." Nunn and Brook, in addition, delete—for whatever reason—2716 ("Nobler then my reuolt is Infamous"). In Kemble MS and Halliday, Enobarbus exits and dies offstage.

Antony's rising fortunes in battle are described in 4.7, 4.8, and 4.10, but to simplify the action directors cut extensively. Antony's perspective rather than Caesar's is presented. 4.7 is omitted by Bell, Colman, Cumberland, Calvert, Lacy, Phelps, Halliday, Lander, Langtry, Beerbohm Tree, Ames, Sothern/Marlowe (Shattuck, no. 34), and Bridges-Adams. The remaining versions show a great deal of editorial intervention: because of some lack of understanding of the dialogue or doubts about the audience's sensibility, Antony's talk with Scarus about the *H*-shaped wound is cut in Kemble MS (2621–46), Macready (2631–3), and Sothern/Marlowe (2631–6), whereas Nunn crosses out only Scarus's first speech (2628–30). Agrippa, who opens the scene in F1 (2621–5), does not appear in Kemble MS, Hanford, Sothern/Marlowe, Atkins, Nunn, and Brook. The scene's ending is changed: in Kemble MS and Hanford Scarus's encouraging remark that he has "Roome for six scotches more" (2636) is the last line; in Sothern/Marlowe and Nunn, the optimistic ending is Eros's line assuring a "faire victory" (2639); in Atkins, Scarus ends the scene aggressively with his "sport to maul a Runner" (2642); and in Brook, who retains the pun on Scarus's wound, the scene ends on this line (2633). Only Capell and Bankhead do not cut anything from this scene at all.

Calvert, Halliday, Beerbohm Tree, Ames, and Sothern/Marlowe (Shattuck, no. 34) cut 4.8 entirely, and others shorten it. Brook's interference is unintelligible: in Antony's "We haue beate him to his Campe" speech (2649 ff.), this first sentence, as well as 2650–2 ("to morrow . . . escap'd") and 2656–9, is cut. Even Nunn does not go so far here (he cuts only 2653–5), and Atkins, who cuts almost the whole speech, preserves the famous opening sentence (with some of 2650), moving it to precede 2628.

The deletion of 4.10 ("Their preparation is to day by Sea") further simplifies the battle and diverts attention from Caesar's activities, which are being watched and discussed by Scarus and Antony. The scene is not in Bell, Cumberland, Calvert, Lacy, Halliday, Lander, Langtry, Beerbohm Tree, Ames, Sothern/Marlowe, and Atkins. For similar reasons 4.11 (2747–51), a quick glance into Caesar's camp, is deleted by all except Capell, Glyn, and Brook.

Both Antony's defeat and his despair in 4.12 (2752–2808) are considered indispensable by all stage texts: none cuts this scene entirely. However, some versions—Bell, Cumberland, Calvert, Lacy, Halliday, Lander, Langtry, Hanford, Ames—omit Scarus's and Antony's comments on the battle and begin with Antony's "All is lost" speech (2765); others begin with Scarus's speech at 2757 (Phelps, Sothern/Marlowe, Atkins); Nunn cuts the images of Fortune (2761–3). Most of the versions under discussion omit the crux at 2776–80 (see nn. 2776–8, 2780) and shorten Antony's "Vanish" speech (2790–2806) in one way or other. The intention seems to be to diminish or to soften Antony's outbursts addressed directly to Cleopatra.

In the original, 4.13 (2809–22) shows Cleopatra's immediate reaction to Antony's verbal attacks of 4.12, the retreat to her Monument. Because most versions want to avoid a change of locale, this scene is cut by all except Bell and Colman. (The latter keeps the first three lines, however, and substitutes for the rest lines not in F1.) Among the strong reasons for keeping 4.13 are its transitional function and, more important, its vital information that Cleopatra will feign her death. Gentleman's reason for a possible cutting is (p. 343) that "the purport of it is afterwards sufficiently explained." If this argument were taken seriously it would mean that the audience, like Antony, does not know that Cleopatra is alive, a situation similar to that in *WT* when both characters and audience learn that Hermione has not died. Moreover, in keeping the audience as ignorant as Antony, the ed. indirectly applies his interpretation (p. 345) of Antony's following actions to the audience as well: "Here the portrait of a man, over powered with amorous credulity, is most faithfully described." Perhaps, as ODELL (1920, 2:19) explains, Gentleman marks "lines that he thinks might be omitted in representation . . . [but] does not pretend that these [his texts] are acting-versions."

The death of Eros and suicide of Antony in 4.14 (2823–2995) and Antony's death in 4.15 (2996–3106) are shortened and also otherwise drastically changed (see pp. 752–3). Though no one cuts 4.14 entirely, some suppress Eros's death. Even more incomprehensibly, 4.15 is deleted altogether in Langtry's version. In this Langtry is preceded only by Bell's text, which marks 4.15 for deletion (p. 93): "Though this scene is enriched with some great sentiments as to poetical fancy, and is in favour of *Cleopatra*, yet we are doubtful how it would answer in representation," presumably because it is awkward to have the entire scene on the upper stage (see pp. 753–6, 781–5).

Not all texts have a scene ending after 3107; some omit 5.1, some insert Enobarbus's repentance and death scenes (4.6 and 4.9) before or after 4.15 (see pp. 751–2). Scene 5.1 may be retained or cut: Capell, Bell, Kemble MS, Macready, Cumberland, Phelps, Glyn, Calvert, Atkins, Nunn, and Brook keep it; Colman cuts first and others follow. Those omitting 5.1 (or even 5.1 and 4.15) or shortening it obviously want to have the protagonists' deaths close together, and some of them hasten the action preceding Cleopatra's death by having her captured by Proculeius almost immediately after Antony dies. This is done by Colman and Macready (who rewrite and add a couple of lines in 5.1), by Calvert, Lander, and Langtry. Hanford and Beerbohm Tree arrange at this point for the later discovery of Antony's body: the former has, while Caesar is announced, "Cleo. and her women draw the curtains on arch quickly to hide Antony and stand in front of arch," the latter *"They place Antony's body on a couch. Silence."*

Bell, the only version reproducing F1's 5.1 more or less faithfully, praises (p. 353) Caesar's speech on the dead Antony—*"Octavius's* panegyric on his deceased friend, and late foe is generous, sensible, and manly"—while admitting that Caesar's instructions to Proculeius and his arrangements for the handling of Cleopatra show (p. 354) "double-dealing, ambition, and much more of the politician than the honest man." His behavior is even called (p. 356) "equivocal" and "treacherous." This unflattering portrayal of Caesar (as well as a diversion from the love theme) is avoided by Colman, Lacy, Halliday, Lander, Langtry, Hanford, Beerbohm Tree, Ames, Sothern/Marlowe, and Bankhead, who cut the whole scene (3108–99). Only the gist of it is preserved in Kemble MS, Macready, Calvert, Atkins, and Nunn, all of whom dispense with or shorten considerably the very speech ("Oh Anthony . . ." [3152–68]) praised in Bell's footnote. Similarly, Caesar's first reaction to the news of Antony's death—"The breaking of so great a thing" (3126–31)—is completely cut in Kemble MS and Macready, and only the two last lines ("The . . . world") are retained by Atkins and Nunn; it is moved by Calvert to follow 3601. The main reason for the deletion is probably the textual difficulty at 3127–9 ("The . . . dennes"); Nunn typically strives for a down-to-earth text.

Cleopatra's part in the last scene (5.2 up to 3587) is subjected to numerous short omissions but mainly to the excision of whole sections or severe cuts in the following areas: Cleopatra's defying Fortune and conversation with Proculeius until she is captured (at 3241) are entirely cut by Beerbohm Tree and Macready; they are considerably shortened in Kemble MS, Lander, Hanford, and Sothern/Marlowe, and somewhat less severely in Phelps, Glyn, Atkins, and Nunn. Interestingly, Cleopatra's "desolation" speech (3201–8) and her dream (3292–4, 3296–8, 3300–10) are strongly affected by cutting, probably not only because they hinder the speedy consummation of Cleopatra's reunion in death with Antony but also because of the amount of figurative language used, perhaps considered too difficult for an audience. Her opening monologue (3201–8) is crossed out by Colman and Hanford and shortened by Halliday (omitting 3206–8) and Atkins (omitting 3206–8). Of Cleopatra's dream, the dolphin image (3306–10) is canceled in Kemble MS and Lander; the comparison of nature and fancy (3317–20) is banned by Kemble MS, Lander, Sothern/Marlowe, and Atkins and shortened by Ames (omitting "Nature . . . quite" [3317–20]). These lines disappear with the excision of all or a large portion of the dialogue of Cleopatra and Dolabella (3275–3333) in Colman (who cuts all but 3300–4), Cumberland (who cuts 3296–3311), Calvert (who cuts 3272–3320), Langtry (who cuts 3285–3320), Hanford (who cuts 3272–3327), Beerbohm Tree (who cuts 3295–3327), and Bankhead (who cuts 3285–3320). Capell, Bell, Lacy, Ames, and Brook alone do not shorten this section of 5.2.

Speeding the action is probably also one reason for the frequent omission of the Seleucus episode (3366–3423). Another reason for cutting or shortening it is, of course, that it may be too difficult for an audience unfamiliar with the play to grasp who is deceiving whom. Its deletion also helps to get rid of a minor character, Seleucus. The episode is cut altogether in Colman, Macready, Calvert, Halliday, Lander, Beerbohm Tree, Ames, and Sothern/Marlowe; deleted almost entirely in Bankhead (she cuts 3364–3406); and shortened by all others (though Capell and Bell do so sparingly).

Between Caesar's exit and the arrival of the Clown (3424–80) Cleopatra talks a second time with Dolabella (3435–47) and prepares for her suicide. In this section she displays a wide range of emotions, among them fear of humiliation in Rome. It is not clear whether the long deletions in this area serve to keep Cleopatra heroic or whether they are meant to dispense with the rude and gross descriptions of that procession and her reception; certainly the excision of references to the procession emphasizes her motivation for suicide as love for Antony, not fear of Caesar. The dialogue with Dolabella is cut (in Hanford, Sothern/Marlowe, and Bankhead) or shortened (in Macready, Lander, and Nunn). The dialogue of Cleopatra and her women after Dolabella's exit is condensed in Kemble MS, Macready, Lander, Hanford, Sothern/Marlowe, and Nunn.

The deletion in some versions of the Clown who brings the asps helps shorten the scene as well as dispense with a bawdy minor character. It also removes a comic character from a tragic scene. The necessity of having somebody else get the basket with the "worm" is taken care of by the substitution of Charmian, who brings the asps in Colman, Kemble MS, Macready, and Bankhead. Only Capell, Bell, Cumberland, and Glyn do not shorten the Clown's passages at all, and Ames and Brook cross out only three lines each. Before the Clown's arrival Cleopatra philosophizes about the deed she is about to perform and the means of doing it (3486–91): this speech is completely cut in Calvert, Beerbohm Tree, and Atkins and is deprived of its philosophy and imagery by Lander, Langtry, and Hanford, who eliminate 3486–91. The other deletions in these and the other versions involve mainly difficult sentences and bawdy. All this shortening serves not only to simplify but also to keep focus on the lovers' reunion and to dissociate Cleopatra's suicide from any heroic or superhuman aspirations.

There is a great variety of endings. Minor differences apart, the ending corresponds with F1 in Capell, Bell, and Colman, the latter merely adding a "Grand Funeral Procession." Music and spectacle conclude Macready ("Dead march. The curtain falls"), Lacy ("Dead March, Tableau, and Curtain"), and Halliday ("Soldiers lower their weapons. Mournful music").

Caesar's last appearance in F1 (3595–3636) provokes innumerable changes. He is transformed in two ways: some cut him down to a figure without distinctive characteristics, possibly in order to make the protagonists more memorable; others try to cover up anything negative associated with him as if to balance the lovers' emotional greatness by Caesar's unimpaired political grandeur. After finding Cleopatra dead, he often delivers only one speech (consisting of 3600, 3628–35), which dispenses with all of F1's speculation about Cleopatra's death and Caesar's personal response to it. In Cumberland, Phelps, and Atkins his sole function is to arrange the funeral and take control. Some adapters go further and do not even let Caesar give orders for the funeral and the return to Rome: Glyn, Lacy, and Halliday end the play at 3630 ("famous"); so does Beerbohm Tree (followed basically by Nunn), who also reverses 3635–6, so that the last word is *Rome*, thus emphasizing politics rather than "Solemnity." Ames and Sothern/Marlowe likewise reverse the last two lines. Kemble MS concedes to Caesar a little more emotion by retaining such personal remarks as "but . . . Grace" (3614–16) and leaving Caesar's last speech (3623–36) almost untouched. Kemble is followed in this by Brook.

Some stage versions eliminate the political conclusion in favor of a *Liebestod*. Calvert is the first to arrange his cuts so that Antony will be found dead with Cleopatra. During Cleopatra's preparations for her death, Antony's body is on stage covered with a mantle. Arriving immediately after Cleopatra's suicide, Caesar delivers the "Brauest . . . way" lines (3599–3601). These lines as well as Proculeius's *"Raising the mantle from the body of* ANTONY," the confirmation by Agrippa that Antony is dead, and a concise statement of sadness by Caesar as he orders preparations for the funeral and return to Rome (3125–32, 3140–2, 3628–35) present the lovers as if their deaths were simultaneous.

Lacy considers another possibility (p. 79): "If the piece ends at Cleopatra's death, slow and mournful Music from the application of the second *asp. Curtain descending slowly.*" This tentative suggestion is put into practice by Lander, who has Cleopatra die after "O *Anthony*" (3566). Langtry's and Hanford's versions also emphasize that love and not fear of a triumphal procession is Cleopatra's motivation. Bankhead's ending is eccentric: Caesar has a short appearance (3337–64, 3407–23) though without Seleucus. But after Cleopatra's death (incidentally, her words after her exclamation of "O *Anthony!*" are not cut), Charmian—"(As though too dazed to realize fully what has happened)"—comments: "It is well done and fitting for a princess descended of so many royal kinds [sic]" (3585–6). This ending is not only unusual but also un-Shn. in that a minor character speaks the final eulogy and concludes the play.

Transposing, Adding, and Rewriting

Adapters do not content themselves with shortening the play. Whether to create longer continuous scenes rather than to retain several short ones without transitions, to avoid constantly changing locales (and scenery) or to intensify emotions, to convey an idea corresponding with the tastes of a particular time, or to serve practical and theatrical purposes such as covering cuts, quite a few stage versions of *Ant.* abound in transpositions of scenes and passages. Three versions in particular—Colman, Macready, and Hanford—and sometimes Kemble MS contain numerous passages not in F1. ODELL (1931, 7:111–12) remarks on the last performance in the old Broadway Th. on 7 Mar. 1859, "I am sorry to say that the text used contained a large admixture of Dryden; not that I do not love Dryden's All for Love, but that I prefer Dryden and Shakespeare each by himself."

The Beginning of the Play

F1's order in 1.1, consisting of Philo's introductory speech about Antony's changed identity (4–14), the protagonists' appearance, and the comments by Demetrius (70, 74–6) and Philo (71–3), is retained by Bell, Phelps, Glyn, Calvert, Lacy, Halliday, Lander, Hanford, Ames, Atkins, Nunn, and Brook, though some editions change the speakers, probably to dispense with the two choric figures who never appear again. The other stage versions present the beginning of *Ant.* in basically four different ways:

1. Capell inserts 51 lines from 2.2 (895–954) at 68 before the scene continues with 74–6. The result of this rearrangement is a double comment on the protagonists: Enobarbus's lines are given to Thyreus, but the description of the barge and

praise of Cleopatra's charms still serve to explain Antony's unsoldierly behavior and to make less severe Demetrius's and Philo's concluding criticism. Capell thereby also significantly changes Enobarbus's role. PEDICORD, Garrick's ed., points out (1981, 4:399), "The idea behind the shift of the most famous scene of the play to the first act, surely Garrick's brainchild, was to establish at the outset Cleopatra as a gloriously wonderful woman." Still, the magic of the description is reduced by the subsequent physical presence of the "strumpet" and her "fool." LAMB (1980, p. 47) thinks the "passage carries much more dramatic weight in its original placement in Act II." Capell's rearrangement is followed nevertheless by Cumberland and Colman, though the latter has not the full barge speech but only the portions not given to Antony, conflated with lines from 1.2 and spoken by Canidius. In Garrick's promptbook (no. 2) the barge scene (895–954, 74–6)—though the speakers still are Dolabella and Thyreus—is restored to its original position at the end of 2.2.

2. Kemble MS gives Philo's opening speech to Enobarbus and Enobarbus's barge description to Thyreus. The text interrupts F1's 1.1 after 14 (i.e., before the protagonists' entrance), inserts a portion from Enobarbus's conversation with Agrippa and Maecenas (897–8, 901–48), and then resumes F1's Act 1. It is indeed a drastic deviation from Sh.'s play to have Enobarbus disapprove of Antony so early, but to do so is consistent with taking away from Enobarbus the positive description of Cleopatra. Likewise Kemble gives 70 to Thyreus and 71–3 to Enobarbus. Thus Antony's infatuation is contrasted with Enobarbus's critical distance. Macready follows Kemble's arrangement with Eros, Philo, and Thyreus as speakers (adding some material from Dryden and from Caesar's and Lepidus's speeches in 1.4 between 14 and 881 ff.), as do Sothern/Marlowe, but without the change in speakers.

3. Langtry opens the play with the first Caesar scene (1.4), a strange beginning if—as Arthur Symons writes in the preface (p. viii) to Langtry's version—"the centre . . . is the fatal love which is the glory and the shame of Antony and Cleopatra." But as if trying to make up for the political beginning, she has Cleopatra's and Antony's first appearance in the next scene (consisting of F1's 1.1 and 1.2) enacted aboard Cleopatra's barge. However, even a beginning centered on Caesar's and Lepidus's talk about the former and the present Antony seems more reasonable than giving Philo's speech to Enobarbus: at least Lepidus and Caesar comment critically on Antony's transformation elsewhere in the play. Beerbohm Tree also begins with Caesar's and Lepidus's dialogue of 1.4; his 1.2 consists of 1.1, 1.2, and 1.3, and he has Philo's opening speech (given as in Kemble MS to Enobarbus) follow Antony's and Cleopatra's first appearance, appending Demetrius's line 70 and Philo's and Demetrius's 71–6 as one speech given to Enobarbus. This heavy criticism at the beginning of the play by Antony's opponents as well as by his friends and followers is sustained by Beerbohm Tree (Shattuck, no. 28) in 1.2: Cleopatra begins with 21–69; 1–14 are spoken by Enobarbus; and Antony himself renders 231 and 19–20, thus connecting his decision to leave Egypt with an awareness of his transformation. Then follow 70–96 (spoken by Demetrius and Enobarbus). BERRY (1983, p. 95) concludes from the existence of various versions by

Beerbohm Tree that "Tree's arrangements were in a continuous development until the best solution was reached."

4. Bankhead has the most exotic beginning of all. Scene 1 consists of the barge speech from 2.2 (881–940), spoken by Thyreus and Lepidus, and 1.4; it postpones, as do the versions of Langtry and Beerbohm Tree, the entrance of Antony and Cleopatra to the second scene. Her text thus begins with a positive comment on Cleopatra and a negative one on Antony, prolonging suspense by delaying the protagonists' appearance. Bankhead must have been convinced of her physical attractiveness and persuasiveness as an actress, because in this arrangement a Cleopatra who does not live up to her advance description would ruin the effect.

Kemble's practice of having Enobarbus speak Philo's part is continued by Lander, Ames, and Calvert's promptbook. Others introduce Enobarbus in 1.1 in similarly critical functions: Macready has Philo and Enobarbus share a speech resembling Philo's original lines 17–20; Enobarbus is substituted for Demetrius in Phelps, Glyn, Lacy, and Calvert's promptbook, but, unlike Kemble MS, they do not take the barge speech away from him. Other substitutions for Philo are Eros (in Phelps, Lacy, and Halliday), Scarus (in Calvert, Langtry, and Ames), Ventidius (in Atkins and Nunn), and Canidius (in Calvert's promptbook); substitutions for Demetrius are Thyreus (in Calvert, Langtry, and Ames) and Diomedes (in Halliday).

The Messenger Scenes and Octavia

The most conspicuous instances of transposition and cutting involve the encounters of Cleopatra and the Messenger who reports Antony's and Octavia's marriage in 2.5 (1024–1174, esp. 1052–1174) and who gives Cleopatra more details about Octavia in 3.3 (1620–83). Because he seems less anonymous than others of his kind who report news and then disappear, perhaps also to reduce the cast, numerous stage versions make him one of Cleopatra's attendants: Seleucus in Kemble MS; Mardian in Macready, Cumberland, Phelps, Glyn, Lacy, Halliday, Lander, and Hanford; Diomedes in Calvert and Ames. The two scenes are separated—as in F1—in half the stage texts (Capell, Bell, Colman, Kemble MS, Phelps, Glyn, Lacy, Atkins, Nunn, and Brook). But some of these are altered in other ways: Colman, for instance, has 3.4 (the parting of Antony and Octavia) immediately follow 2.5 (Cleopatra's first learning of the marriage); since the audience knows that Antony is sending Octavia away, the effect of Cleopatra's jealous reaction to the description of her rival is much diminished. Langtry's version, however, agrees with Colman's.

The other versions (except Cumberland and Macready) merge 2.5 and 3.3, some incorporating additional scenes and others ordering various scenes in ways that achieve particular effects. "Octavia" scenes (2.3, 3.2) precede these merged "Messenger" scenes in Calvert and Langtry, and 3.6 (Octavia being informed of Antony's desertion) follows in Calvert, the arrangement emphasizing the clash between duty (Antony's Roman marriage) and passion (his return to Cleopatra). Hanford, Beerbohm Tree, Ames, Sothern/Marlowe (Shattuck, no. 34), and Bankhead incorporate 1.5 (Cleopatra assuaging her longing for Antony with mandragora, music, and bawdy) with the other two, showing the audience what awaits Antony outside Rome. In Beerbohm Tree the scene is placed immediately after Antony's "And though I make this marriage for my peace, I'th'East my pleasure lies" (1006–7). Hanford's version is even more manipulated: his third act (containing 1.5, the main part of 2.5 [1029–1173], and 3.3 [1620–83]) concludes with additional lines for Cleopatra (composed by Hanford), as well as a "vision in her [Cleopatra's] mind's eye." Cleopatra imagines the "Marriage of Antony and Octavia," hears a "Wedding Chorus," and finally "Falls in Center in faint." Octavia's arrival in Rome (3.6) follows directly, presumably to illustrate the confrontation of Roman sobriety and Egyptian pleasure. The arrangement of 3.3 immediately followed by 3.6, omitting 3.2 and 3.4, makes it hard to understand Octavia's return to Rome, since the audience does not know that she has ever left. ODELL's (1920, 2:303) response to such texts—"I do not know how a careless auditor could have known what it was all about"—is typical of a theatergoer's confusion. Halliday incorporates 1.5 and 3.7 (Cleopatra's coaxing Antony into fighting by sea), Lander 3.6, 3.7, and 3.13 (aftermath of the defeat at Actium): these two versions emphasize Antony's subjection to Cleopatra.

Cumberland and Macready cut 3.3 entirely and have only one short meeting between Cleopatra and the Messenger.

Other versions delete passages from the Messenger scenes deemed indecent or vulgar; the general effect is to eliminate references unfavorable to Cleopatra. But Bell's ed. marks possible cuts in 2.5 (1075–80, 1097–8, 1101–11, 1118–32) expressly to improve Cleopatra's image: "The vulgar and virago spirit of *Cleopatra*, shames every idea of her character; she is in this scene a perfect *Covent-Garden* amazon, wherefore, to soften her as much as possible, we curtail" (p. 36). Attempting to moderate verbal exchanges and actions, most versions omit the mention of Antony being bound to Octavia "For the best turne i'th'bed" (1097–8); the various references to *Eunuch* (1028–36) are shortened to remove the word or punning exchanges on it. Passages showing Cleopatra striking the Messenger or threatening to do so are often altered, shortened, or deleted: Colman substitutes "spurn" for "strike" at 1076; Bell suggests eliminating 1118–32, Calvert 1123–37.

The Fourth Act

Transpositions and alterations in Act 4 are frequent, and the main effect of the shifting of scenes and episodes is a simplification of the action. In the attempt to diminish the alternating focus on the opposing sides, adapters part with anything not directly related to the war. Most of them, in addition, concentrate on Antony's side of the battle and neglect Caesar's. Halliday notes at the bottom of his list of dramatis personae that *"The Second Act takes place in Rome. The rest of the Play in Egypt,"* and this structure seems to have created a precedent. Macready is an exception because of his avid interest in visual effects: the battle scenes, which in F1 are mainly described by means of sounds, reports, and soldiers passing over the stage, are replaced with tableaux (e.g., Macready's 3.2 following 1948–9). His techniques are imitated elsewhere (though not in battle scenes) by Halliday and Hanford.

The Battles, Hercules, and Enobarbus

Rearrangements made to facilitate the staging of the battle scenes automatically affect scenes not directly connected with the war.

Only Hanford, Nunn, and Brook retain 4.3 (2467–2501), Antony's desertion by Hercules, in its original position. What little remains of it in Hanford (he labels it 5.1 and has it in a room of Cleopatra's Monument) is changed almost beyond recognition. The speakers are not Antony's guard but Charmian, Iras, and the Soothsayer, and the scene opens with a long SD conveying an image of luxury, leisure, and pleasure: Antony is presented without armor—a lover, not a soldier. And while Charmian is singing a song of praise, "Low Thunder rolls" and the Soothsayer announces that the thunder indicates "the God Hercules, Whom Antony loved Now leaves him." This stirs Antony to call for his armor at 2503 and to proceed from a moment of tenderness with Cleopatra to war.

Beerbohm Tree has F1's 4.3 at the beginning of his 4.2, which is a combination of 4.3, 4.10, 4.12, 4.14, 4.15, and presents—exceptional among stage versions—Antony's desertion by Hercules without cuts. The position of Hercules' desertion in Sothern/Marlowe is similar to that in Beerbohm Tree: their Act 5 is a condensed version of the last two acts. The first scene, staged "Under the walls of Alexandria," is a combination of fragments of the original 4.7 and of 4.8. Again, Antony's nobility is stressed, while references to details of war (such as the wordplay on Scarus's wounds) are left out. Their second scene is patched together from F1's 4.3 (2467–2501), parts of 4.12 (2757–2808), 4.13 and 4.14 (2809–2960), 4.15 (2996–3106), 5.2 (3201–3333, 3448, 3427–33, 3449–3601, 3628–35).

As the cuts (see pp. 742–3) suggest, Enobarbus's part is strongly affected—mainly reduced—but even more so by other changes made in Act 4. Halliday alone adds to the significance given to Enobarbus's desertion (4.5) in F1. In transposing its report (2554–74) to follow immediately Antony's utterances of shame and self-reproach after the naval battle (2023–47), he makes it the ultimate reason for the rejection of Cleopatra by Antony, who declines her attempts at reconciliation and pleas for forgiveness (2050, 2076–99, 2765–2808), and the reason for her subsequent flight to the Monument. At the same time this combination of events changes Antony's character, making him an agent of uncontrolled rage.

Kemble MS is the first to combine the scenes of Enobarbus's repentance and preparation for death, 4.6 and 4.9 (it has 2590–2616 ["*Enob. Alexas* . . . thought"] followed by 2715–20 ["O Emperor"—for "Oh *Anthony* . . . *Anthony!*"]), and to move Enobarbus's death offstage (see pp. 742–3). Halliday combines speeches as in Kemble MS but moves the scene to follow Antony's death (between 3107 and 3201), thus having Enobarbus's exit to his offstage death intensify the sense of doom. Halliday's scene continues with Cleopatra's lamentation and preparations for death. Unfortunately Halliday's grouping of the three death scenes is imitated by Calvert (in the published version as well as in no. 11). Keeping 4.6 and 4.9 separate, he combines the latter with 4.3 and puts Hercules's desertion (2483–2501) immediately after, inserting the whole (as his 4.4) between 4.14 and 4.15 as a response to Antony's suicide and an anticipation of his death. Calvert cuts some of the soldiers' lines in 4.9 but retains the remark that "the hand of death hath raught him" (2730). The music of hautbois in 4.3 and the drums sounding at the moment of Enobarbus's death are the links between the two scenes and perhaps are meant to signify the deaths of a giant and a plain soldier in the use of two instruments, one associated with the supernatural and the other with war.

Antony's Suicide

The suicide and death scenes of Antony (4.14, 4.15) often depart from F1 in motivation, in timing, and in theatrical presentation. In particular, Antony's attempt to kill himself, which is in the original linked with Eros and involves the necessity of transporting the wounded Antony to Cleopatra's Monument, suffers changes. It is striking how many attempts are made to cancel, reduce, or ignore the significance of Eros's example for Antony. Francis Gentleman in Bell (p. 346), disapproving of Antony's suicide, tries to ameliorate the act by lessening Eros's influence in order to make Antony more independently responsible: "If there can be an argument for a man's desiring, or contributing to his own death, *Marc Antony* certainly here advances it, and with dignity of feeling: desiring assistance in this point from a friend, or a dependant, was common amongst the *Romans*, but we think not justifiable to ask or be complied with." Accordingly, he suggests the cutting of 2915–22, i.e., Antony's repeated plea for Eros's help. The same lines are deleted by Kemble MS, Beerbohm Tree, Ames, Bankhead, and Brook. Nunn extends the omission (he crosses out 2921–5, 2927–33 ["*Ant.* . . . Chiefe"]) and sacrifices some of Antony's repeated pleading for assistance, as well as Eros's emotional expressions of loyalty.

Hanford indirectly dehumanizes Sh.'s Antony and makes him to a certain extent more noble: Antony's request that Eros kill him and Eros's suicide are crossed out (2888–2945), and Antony's decision to be "Conqueror" of himself (2897) is followed immediately by his "Falling" and the desperate question "How, not dead? Not dead?" (2945). Neither Colman nor Macready retains Eros's death, and a reluctance to accept Antony's dependence on Eros finds similar expression in the deletion of "Thy Master dies thy Scholler" (2944) in Kemble MS (cutting 2943–5 ["and . . . thee"]) and Nunn. Other versions prefer the omission of the credit for a "Noblenesse in Record" given by Antony to both Eros and Cleopatra, and they cut 2939–41 (Beerbohm Tree, Ames). A third group is unhappy with Antony's description of himself as a "Bride-groome" who goes into his grave "As to a Louers bed" (2939–43 are eliminated by Macready, Calvert, and Langtry).

The simplification (if not falsification) of Antony's motivation is most apparent in Kemble MS, Colman, and Macready. In 4.7 of Kemble MS Antony learns from the report by Seleucus that Cleopatra has died and then by Eros that Enobarbus too is dead. In order to bring these two pieces of information together, Kemble writes a transition in which Eros says (after 2889): "I come, my Lord.—Here's one brings word of Enobarbus's death.—" To which Antony answers, "I have forgiven him." This way of handling the two deaths results in an intensification of the sense of downfall, but it also emphasizes love as the leading motive in this phase of the play. It is Enobarbus whom Antony has forgiven, but it is Cleopatra for whom he mourns. The opposite is intended in Colman and Macready. Both stress the noble Roman rather than the lover in Antony: when Antony learns of Cleopatra's "death" (F1's 4.13), a dialogue with Eros (invented by Macready) restores Antony's personal dignity. He is reacting to Cleopatra's death with lines 2870–1, 2874–80, 2882–9, when Eros announces that Caesar is at the gate. This piece of news does not frighten Antony, because he has already decided to die: "*Anton*: Why let him enter: He's welcome now. *Eros*: Would you be taken? *Anton*: Yes: I would be taken;— But as a Roman ought, good Eros. *Eros*: What means my lord?" Then follow 2890–2.

The evaluation of Antony's attempted suicide as either nobleness or weakness also affects an ambiguous detail of stage business. In F1, at 2851 Antony says to Mardian: "Oh thy vilde Lady, she has rob'd me of my Sword," and at 2916 he urges Eros: "Draw that thy honest Sword." The question arises whether Antony kills himself with his sword or with that of Eros. CAPELL (1779 [1774], 1:47) believes the latter (see nn. 2851, 2944–5) and adds in his stage text at 2943 the direction "(*taking Eros' sword*)." He is followed in this by Bell and Cumberland. SPRAGUE (1944, p. 332) disagrees, particularly since if Antony kills himself with Eros's sword "it is this sword, accordingly, which Dercetas now carries away to show Octavius!" Others take it for granted that Antony uses his own sword (Calvert, Lacy, Halliday, Lander, Langtry, Beerbohm Tree, Bankhead, Atkins, and Nunn) and have the direction at 2944 or 2945 "*Falling on his sword*" (Nunn has it at 2943 after "Louers bed"). Of these, Lacy, Halliday, and Lander strive for visual effects and have an elaborate SD for Eros at 2935: "(stabs himself with the sword—*then throws it convulsively at the feet of* Antony *as he staggers back and falls*, up, L[eft])." This direction makes Antony's use of his sword a refusal of Eros's and promotes him from a "Scholler" to a master again.

Antony's Death

In F1, Antony is borne to Cleopatra at the end of 4.14, and a new scene begins with Cleopatra in her Monument, "*aloft.*" This arrangement is retained in Capell, Bell, Beerbohm Tree, and Brook. A slightly varied rendition of it is realized either in having a discovery of Cleopatra and her women on the main stage or in using a staircase or raised platform (instead of the balcony) to represent the Monument. Beerbohm Tree follows F1 in having (at 3011, his postponed beginning of this scene) Cleopatra and the women "*seen at the window of the monument.*" To avoid a long section played on the balcony, he introduces a new scene at 3037: "*Within the*

Monument." The idea of discovering the actors on the main stage is introduced by Colman (*"The Interior of a Monument.* Cleopatra, Charmion, *and* Iras, discover'd") and picked up by Cumberland (who is the first to explicitly mention "a couch"), Lacy (*"a grated door . . . opening in flat over a wide staircase"*), Lander, Langtry, Ames, and Nunn.

Transportation of Antony to Cleopatra varies in those texts retaining Antony's command to bear him "where *Cleopatra* bides" (2985). Kemble MS has an extra scene (4.8) that is practical and spectacular at the same time: it stages a procession for bearing the dying Antony to Cleopatra: *"A Street. Mournful Music. Titius & Guards,* pass towards the Monument, bearing *Antony* on his Litter." The next scene stages Antony's arrival at the Monument. The passage of time is indicated by *"Mournful Music."* George Becks's reconstruction of Lander's versions also recalls "Music—slow & solemn March" after 2995.

Though all references to Antony's weight are cut in Kemble MS, the drawing up of Antony with cords and ropes is described in full detail as first done by Capell and Bell. (See also pp. 785–7.) Cumberland and Lacy follow Kemble, but instead of Antony's being drawn up to the battlements of the Monument, he is *"borne by the Four Officers. . . . They place him on the couch . . . and exeunt."* In Atkins, Antony is "brought in on a bier" and then Cleopatra kneels near him. Obviously Atkins builds on B. Iden Payne's (Stratford-upon-Avon, 15 Apr. 1935) simplified staging (Shattuck, no. 40; Nuffield Library: 71.21/1935A [7925]): at the beginning of 4.15 Antony is brought in on a bier by four soldiers, and the directions demand, "Get Ant. into 'Monument.' " This was possible because the new stage of the Shakespeare Memorial Th. at Stratford was furnished with "permanent steps that divided the two levels" of the stage (LAMB, 1980, p. 126). In 5.2, the same architecture also makes possible the capture of Cleopatra in full view (not with Proculeius suddenly seizing her from behind). For further remarks on the effects of this stage in Payne's production (especially the stage's size and the separation of audience and actors), see Lamb (pp. 126–7).

A continuous staging of Antony's suicide and his death in Cleopatra's arms is achieved by Macready: he has Cleopatra rush on stage announcing her approach from "without" and calling, "Where is my lord? Where is he?" The practice of having Cleopatra come to Antony instead of having him borne to her is picked up by Halliday (*"Enter* Cleopatra *agitated . . ."* at 2996), by Sothern/Marlowe (*"Enter Cleopatra . . ."*), and by Bankhead (at 3013). Also in Hanford, Antony's suicide and the final reunion with Cleopatra are staged continuously—in the same room in Cleopatra's Monument in which the desertion by Hercules took place. The room has an "Arch with Curtains to draw up R[ight] in flat" with a "Couch covered" inside; the arch is "backed by Egyptian Tapistry-wings." But Hanford's version is exceptional in having Eros (who survives) and Scarus "rush to Antony and raise him up gently" at 2950. "They take Antony up to couch in Arch" and "They rise him up," probably to a sitting position, when Cleopatra and her women enter so that when Cleopatra "Rushes to Antony" as she begins to speak (at 3006–7) she can embrace him. Hanford expands, so it seems, on Edmund Tearle's staging of the

Monument scene (in England in the 1890s: Shattuck, no. 17; Nuffield Library: 72.902 TEA [9010]). At the beginning of Tearle's Act 5 (F1's 4.15) Antony is "Discovered . . . on couch apparently dead." In Tearle's version it is not a question of bringing Antony up to Cleopatra but of getting him closer to her so that he can utter his last words. Cleopatra's comment on his heaviness ("Heere's sport . . . come" [3038–44]) and the SD *"They heaue . . . Cleopatra"* are replaced by "They raise his head."

Antony's death on a couch certainly conveys a sense of Victorian refinement. In Macready and Beerbohm Tree Antony's body is somewhat more realistically placed *"on bed"* (Macready) or "on a couch" after his death. Bankhead, trying to keep up a sense of royalty, is not satisfied with a bier or a couch; instead "They lift Antony up to the throne" at 3039 and he dies an emperor, just as Cleopatra will be all queen in her death. Colman's rendition of Antony's death surpasses all other attempts at ennobling his suicide as well as his manner of dying: not only does his Antony not die as Eros's (alias Ventidius's) scholar, but the scene ends with *"Exit* Mark Anthony, *supported by his Guard—other Soldiers join their shields, on which they place the corse of* Ventidius, *and bear it away."* The passage of time before Antony's reappearance in the Monument is suggested by an intervening Caesar scene. Cleopatra and her women are discovered in the *"Interior of a Monument,"* and the dying Antony enters (the SD at ca. 3011 says *"Enter* Antony, *supported by the Guard"*) announcing, "I'm dying, Cleopatra, dying!" Apparently this noble Roman dies while standing upright (perhaps leaning on Cleopatra, who embraces him at 3044). Sothern/Marlowe's staging is similar: Antony's attempt at suicide ends with his guards' refusal to strike him dead (2957) and is followed immediately by the scene of Cleopatra and her women in the Monument (2996 ff.). Antony's death speeches are made more prominent and intimate by being accumulated and transposed to follow the "heaving aloft"; both "I am dying" speeches are retained, so that the order of lines is 2996–3015, then the drawing him up (3038–48), and then his last conversation with Cleopatra (3016–25, 3049–3106). The practical purpose is, of course, to avoid having the dying Antony shout to Cleopatra above that he is dying.

In Bell's text Francis Gentleman accounts for the possibility of omitting Antony's stage death altogether: after Antony is borne off (still alive), Caesar enters to F1's 5.1; the audience and Caesar thus learn of Antony's death when Decretas brings Antony's sword. In Langtry's version, since it cuts 4.15 and 5.1 completely, it is Cleopatra's task to convey that Antony has died: Antony and his guard have an *Exeunt* at 2995 and the scene continues with Cleopatra's "My desolation. . . ."

Cleopatra "swoons" or "faints" in most texts somewhere between 3080 and 3083 and is seen recovering at about 3087. The exceptions are Kemble MS, Phelps, Glyn, Calvert, Ames, Bankhead, and Brook, who do not insert any SDs. Macready has Cleopatra faint at 3070 ("I can no more"), and Lacy, Halliday, Lander, Hanford, Sothern/Marlowe, and Atkins feel that a little more show is needed. Lacy, the first to insert at 3080 *"(she falls in a burst of grief on Antony),"* is followed by Halliday, Lander, Hanford, and Sothern/Marlowe. Atkins's SDs are ambiguous; possibly he stresses an extraneously occidental if not Christian implication: Cleopatra at 3080 "faints over his body" and then after "Our Lampe is spent" (3100) puts a religious metaphor into gesture: "Folds Anthony's hands on his breast." But it is equally possible that in imitation of representations of Tutankhamen he is making Antony an Egyptian.

Despite cuts and transpositions, some texts follow the standard practice of ending the scene and act with the bearing off of Antony's body (3107). Capell, Bell, Kemble MS, Sothern/Marlowe, and Brook correspond with F1. Some others introduce modern devices beyond or instead of the *Exeunt* to indicate an end of scene: Bankhead has a curtain at 3100 and resumes the action at 3200 with Cleopatra's "My desolation" speech, followed by her capture by Proculeius; Atkins replaces F1's SD at 3107 by "Fade"; and Nunn adds "Door closing." Others expand and embellish F1's modest *"Exeunt, bearing of [f] Anthonies body"*: *"She faints on Antony's body, as the Act Drop falls"* (Cumberland); Cleopatra *"(Kneeling, C[enter], and with her arms extended aloft as invoking the protection of the gods—*Iras *and* Charmian *in great despondency—Tableau)"* (Lacy).

The Deaths of Cleopatra and Her Women

The manner of Cleopatra's death is practically alike in most versions: she applies one asp to her breast, the other one to her arm. Capell first inserted these directions (at 3555 and 3566; see nn.), inferring them from F1; he also notes that Cleopatra kisses her women at 3543 and that Iras *"falls."* Charmian, according to Capell's notation, applies an asp to herself at 3578 and dies at 3587 as in F1. Capell is followed in all this business verbatim by Bell, and also by Cumberland. F1 is retained—without Capell's inferential expansions—by Phelps, Glyn, Nunn, and Brook. Cleopatra applies only the first asp to her breast in Colman, Kemble MS, Halliday, Lander (Shattuck, no. 14), Langtry, Beerbohm Tree, Ames, Sothern/Marlowe, and Atkins. The application of the asps is not mentioned at all in Calvert and Lander (Shattuck, no. 13), though both retain the Clown and the delivery of the asps (Calvert cuts 3544–55, Lander 3552–63). Those who have the play end with Cleopatra's "O *Anthony*" (3566) naturally omit the second asp.

The deaths of Charmian and Iras are treated quite inconsistently. Iras's death (see also n. 3544), for which there is no SD in F1, is noted at 3543 (as in Capell) by Kemble MS, Lacy, Halliday, Langtry, and Lander. Charles and Louis Calvert are criticized by SHAW (1932, 24:82) who complains: "I do not see why Cleopatra should ungratefully take Iras's miraculous death as a matter of course by omitting the lines beginning 'Have I the aspic in my lips', nor why Charmian should be robbed of her fine reply to the Roman's 'Charmian, is this well done?' 'It is well done, and fitted for a princess descended of so many royal kings'. No doubt the Cleopatras of the palmy days objected to anyone but themselves dying effectively." Nunn, however, whose text does not add a SD for Iras's death, adds an interesting piece of business in performance. DAVID (1978, p. 163) points out that "Iras, instead of dying of grief when Cleopatra kisses her, had surreptitiously applied an asp before the embrace. To Cleopatra's question, 'Have I the aspic in my lips?' one was tempted to reply 'No, she took one when you weren't looking.' " Macready alone does not describe Iras's death. Neither of the two women is recorded as dying by Colman, Calvert, Hanford, and Bankhead: Colman simply does not mention Charmian anymore; Calvert has her retire (at 3494, after bringing forward the Clown) and Iras reenter instead with Mardian (at 3531) to bring the robe and crown. In Hanford and Bankhead it is also Iras who brings the robe, but neither her death nor Charmian's is recorded. All the others (Bell, Cumberland, Macready, Beerbohm Tree, Ames, Sothern/Marlowe, Atkins, Nunn, and Brook) follow Capell in the notation of Charmian's applying the asp (taking it from Cleopatra) and follow F1 in the moment of her death. The treatment of the women recalls the handling of Eros. The indefinite ends of the three may arise from neglect, but the purpose may have been to avoid competition in death between the protagonists and their subordinates.

Attitudes toward Cleopatra's death are reflected in her position on stage. Opinions are balanced as to an ascent or a fall. Capell's version has a detailed description of how and where Cleopatra is supposed to die: at 3538 she *"Goes to a bed, or sofa, which she ascends; her women compose her on it. Iras sets the basket, which she has been holding upon her own arm, by her."* Cleopatra's raised position corresponds with her regal dress and the noble act. Capell is followed verbatim by Bell, substantially by Colman, and is expanded in Kemble MS, which has Cleopatra ascend not just to a couch but to her throne.

Cumberland and Macready also emphasize Cleopatra's greatness visually. They go further than the others in integrating Iras and Charmian as a decorative frame rather than as Cleopatra's rivals: Cleopatra *"ascends the steps to the couch"* in Macready (at 3538), and at 3543 (usually the moment where others record Iras's death) *"They embrace her and kneel beside her, as she sits on the bed."* Her women die after her so as to keep the lovers' union in death uninterrupted. Before Iras brings the aspics, *"Cleopatra draws away the curtain before the bed*: We're now alone in secrecy and silence; And is not this like lovers? I may kiss Those pale cold lips: Octavia does not see me!" These lines, interpolated from Dryden, help make Cleopatra's death a genuine *Liebestod*. Her last words are expanded. As she dies with Antony's name on her lips, she describes (again as in Dryden): "Already, death, I feel thee in my veins!—A heavy numbness creeps through every limb." Cumberland's device of raising Cleopatra in her death is to put the women in a lower position: both are required to fall (Iras at 3543 and Charmian at 3587).

Death and Cleopatra's falling are connected by Lacy, Halliday, Bankhead, and Lander. Her death is obviously associated with a visual giving up of all worldly possessions and functions; Cleopatra is no longer a queen but a woman. Thus Lacy makes her rise before her death to emphasize the fall: she *"(rises from couch—advances to front of stage*, c[enter])" at 3531 and *"falls on a bed and dies"* at 3567. Bankhead illustrates this idea even more directly: at 3567 Cleopatra "(*falls from the throne and dies)"*—though it is unclear when she ascends the throne (probably at 3531 when she is being dressed in her robe and crown). SPRAGUE (1944, pp. xv–xvi) classifies this staging as "business out of keeping with the plain meaning of what Shakespeare wrote" and quotes as "an awful example . . . Miss Bankhead's standing, as Cleopatra, while she applied the asps, then plunging forward to a sprawling, unlovely death!" The renunciation of royalty is seen as a sacrifice in Halliday and Lander. Halliday's last scene is set in a Temple of Isis, and when Cleopatra dies she *"Falls on altar"* (3567). Lander follows him in this but picks up Macready's interpretation when Cleopatra, before she dies, takes "the mantle off Antony's face" (3539). The stage versions' division over whether Cleopatra rises like a princess descended of so many royal kings or falls like a lass, even though one unparalleled, simply underscores the paradox that is central to her character.

Performances

FIRST ATTEMPTS

No documents or records have survived about a performance of Sh.'s *Ant.* before the closing of the theaters in 1642. There is, however, some indirect evidence that the play may have been performed. NICOLL (1923, pp. 315–16) prints the document dated ca. 12 Jan. 1669 giving performance rights to Thomas Killigrew, in which *Ant.* is included in "A Catalogue of part of His Ma^{tes} Servants Playes as they were formerly acted at the Blackfryers." Also, not only do Samuel Daniel's alterations in his 1607 ed. of *Cleopatra* suggest familiarity with Sh.'s *Ant.* (see pp. 528–30), but allusions in the plays of other dramatists before 1623 have been used—though without consensus—to support the possibility that *Ant.* was staged before its publication in F1. One of these bits of evidence (see also p. 381) is the appearance of two asps called *"Cleopatraes* birds" in Barnabe Barnes's *Divils Charter* (1607). CHAMBERS (1930, 1:478) and others accept this passage as support for the theory of a performance before 1607; KITTREDGE (ed. 1936, p. 1285) does not. BALDWIN's (1927, pp. 198–9, n. 2) argument that the casting of *The False One* (ca. 1620) was influenced by that of *Ant.* is too speculative to bear much weight.

Theories have also been advanced about the theater in which the earliest performance may have taken place. REES (1953, pp. 91–3) tentatively suggested that the account of Cleopatra's and her maids' hauling Antony aloft in rolls of taffeta may reflect Daniel's memory of an actual performance of Sh.'s play, presumably either at the Globe or at court (see p. 787). LAMB (1980, pp. 182–3) incautiously specifies that Daniel's vague terms *pulley* and *frame* (which may only mean "hoisting device" and "contrivance") refer to a pulley block (through which taffeta could not be threaded) and implies "winch-and-gallery" staging at the Globe. BARROLL (1965, pp. 153–4) bases his conviction that the first performance of *Ant.* took place at court on the assumption that after the accession of James I in 1603, most likely court "or other private performances were, for long periods of time, the only legitimate outlets for plays in or about London" (p. 154), because they were "exempt . . . from city plague restrictions" between 1603 and 1611. (See also pp. 383–4.) Unfortunately, however, no record confirms the assumption. *Ant.* is mentioned neither in the surviving Revels Accounts for 1604–5 and 1611–12 nor in the Chamber Accounts (from which names of plays are generally omitted).

The stage history of *Ant.* is marked by irregularities and also some mysteries. With its frequent changes of locale, battle scenes, and scenes difficult to stage (4.14 and 5.2), the play has obviously intimidated many directors. Not surprisingly, the stage career of *Ant.* is primarily one of stage sets and spectacle and only secondarily one of the principal actors. Most of the following information about performances is based on FURNESS (ed. 1907), ODELL (1920 and 1927–49), KINDERMANN (1957–74), VAN LENNEP et al. (1960–8, and SCHNEIDER, 1979), TREWIN (1964), LAMB (1980), MULLIN (1980), LEITER (1986), and SHATTUCK (1965 and 1987). Shattuck provides most of the dates of first performances.

In the early English stage history of *Ant.* not Sh.'s play but its most important adaptation, John Dryden's *All for Love* (1678), was performed either by itself or amalgamated with parts of Sh.'s *Ant.* FURNESS (ed. 1907, pp. 473–7) gives a detailed discussion of Dryden's tragedy, which in the words of HALL (1880, p. 56) is "not an alteration of Shakspere, but merely an imitation of his style based upon the incidents of Antony and the Egyptian Queen." NICOLL (1921, p. 21) calls it "far more a suggested than an adapted play" and "the finest of the Restoration . . . tragedies." VAN LENNEP et al. (1960–8), indexed by SCHNEIDER (1979, p. 253), record some 140 performances from 1677 to 1790. In the United States the first Shn. *Ant.* (George Vandenhoff's in 1846) was likewise preceded by a performance of Dryden's adaptation in New York in 1767–8 (DUNN, 1939, p. 79).

The adaptation by Sir Charles Sedley also had a history of performances when Sh.'s play had none, though according to WILSON (ed. 1950, p. xxxvii) Sedley's is "an exceedingly poor version of the story in rhyming verse"; NICOLL (1923, p. 110) finds it inferior to Dryden's. VAN LENNEP et al. (1960–8, 1:254–5) list performances on 12 and 14 Feb. 1677 and think one on 13 Feb. probable. Sedley's play was published as *Beauty the Conqueror* or *The Death of Marc Antony* in 1702. Another adaptation, Henry Brooke's, was published in 1778 though not performed (ODELL, 1920, 1:367). GENEST (1832, 6:63) notes that it contains only "one third, or perhaps one half" of Sh.'s play.

According to NICOLL (1923, p. 167), changing tastes and stage conditions caused Restoration adaptations to be preferred to Sh.'s plays: "pseudo-classic criticism" fostered "the tendency to make more unified and more symmetrical the romantically irregular plots of Shakespeare," and "Shakespeare's works, written for the platform of the Globe, were being adapted for performance in the picture-frame of the Duke's and the Theatre Royal." For an extensive treatment of Sh. adaptations, see BRANAM (1956) and SPENCER (1927).

The series of quasi-Shn. performances was interrupted only once before the 19th c. by a production of Sh.'s play—Capell's version for Garrick (3 Jan. 1759 at Drury Lane), with David Garrick and Mary Ann Yates in the title parts. The production was not very popular—ODELL (1920, 1:424) calls it "one of the failures of his [Garrick's] career"—and there were only six performances (Odell, 1:367). Odell (1:425) speculates that "perhaps the scene shifted too often for conservative followers of the unities!" DAVIES (1783, 2:369) blames the inexperience and youth of Mrs. Yates and (2:368) Garrick's lack of a "person . . . sufficiently important and commanding." Despite his magnificent stage presence, Garrick's short stature evidently told against him.

It was 54 years before the original play—or something bearing Sh.'s name—was produced again in London. On 15 Nov. 1813 John Philip Kemble directed a revival at Covent Garden, one of his "so-called versions of Shakespeare" (ODELL, 1920, 2:70), with Charles Mayne Young and Harriet Faucit as the principal actors. LAMB (1980, p. 59) thinks that the actors were "swamped by the spectacle," the high points of which were the on-stage battle at Actium and the funeral procession at the end of the play. Neither scene, of course, is in Sh.

Attempts at producing Sh.'s *Ant.* outside England and the United States began in the 19th c. (although adaptations of *Ant.* in foreign languages came into European theaters before Sh.'s play in translation did; see pp. 775–7). A Finnish version was produced by Kaarlo Bergbom in 1897 (KINDERMANN, 1957–74, 9:670–1). An Australian performance was given on 26 Dec. 1912 at the Theatre Royal in Melbourne; Oscar Ashe was actor-director with Lily Brayton as his partner. A Czechoslovakian *Ant.* was prepared during World War I by Karl Hugo Hilar (Kindermann, 1957–74, 10:185–6); the production was strongly influenced by Max Reinhardt's expressionistic style. The Comédie Française mounted a production in 1918 under Firmin Gémier, and another right after World War II in 1945. A Russian production was done in 1923 in Leningrad, and Per Lindberg did a Swedish production, in cubist style (Kindermann, 1957–74, 9:647), in 1926–7 in Stockholm.

The first performance of a German tr. of Sh.'s play seems to have been given at the German theater in Pest (May 1857) by the Hungarian National Th. (BINAL, 1972, p. 243). In Vienna, the first Cleopatra in a German tr. was Adele Sandrock (with Friedrich Mitterwurzer as Antony) in 1895 or 1896 (KINDERMANN, 1957–74, 8:150), succeeded by Lotte Medelsky, who played opposite Raoul Aslan at the Burg Th. in 1923 under Max Burckhard. Between these two, there were guest performances by Eleonora Duse in 1899 in Berlin, Breslau, and Munich. Duse's earlier appearances as Cleopatra were in Milan in 1888 in Arrigo Boito's tr. and in St. Petersburg and Moscow in 1891 (STAHL, 1947, p. 520). Herbert Beerbohm Tree also gave a guest performance in Germany (1906 in Berlin). See STAHL (1907, pp. 365–7).

STAGE, SETTING, TEXT

Un-Shakespearean Spectacle

Kemble's directions for the stage setting at the opening of *Ant.*, quoted by FURNESS (ed. 1907, p. 589) from Kemble's undated MS, are as follows: "The Palace in Alexandria should be of the most magnificent orders of the purest Grecian architecture; yet the decorations and furniture of every apartment should remind one that the scene lies in Egypt. *Portico of the Palace:* Stage open as far back as possible. View of the sea, ships, etc., The Pharos, Pompey's Pillar, Cleopatra's Obelisk, Statues of Hercules, Alexander, Anubis." For approximately 100 years after Kemble's production of 1813, most revivals of *Ant.* were marked by such lavishness of setting (and costume and properties) and by the introduction of much un-Shn. spectacle and of material from plays other than Sh.'s. Increasing use of huge, three-dimensional scenery made quick changes of the set impossible and led to long waiting periods between scenes (LAMB, 1980, pp. 73–4). As a consequence, productions also followed Kemble's example of presenting abbreviated versions with fewer changes of scene.

Alfred Bunn's production of "that hopelessly impossible thing [Sh.'s *Ant.*] for the picture-stage" (ODELL, 1920, 2:176) at Drury Lane (21 Nov. 1833), with William Charles Macready and Louisa Anne Phillips as the principals, certainly expanded on Kemble's techniques (see also pp. 729–30). So did George Vandenhoff's production of the play in New York City (Park Th., 27 Apr. 1846), with himself as Antony and Harriet Bland as Cleopatra. One reviewer (see ODELL, 1931, 5:182) thought the production worth seeing, if only for Vandenhoff's opening, which gave a "view of the ancient city of Alexandria," and for the "panoramic view of the naval fight of Actium." Although the two principal actors were well received, there were only six performances.

Samuel Phelps's lavish production at Sadler's Wells (22 Oct. 1849), with himself as Antony and Isabella Glyn as Cleopatra, shared with the earlier revivals the emphasis on spectacle and display, but it was also the first recorded performance after Garrick's that "gave Shakespeare undiluted" (ODELL, 1920, 2:275) though somewhat shortened (see p. 730). Some scenes of Phelps's *Ant.* were especially spectacular: the protagonists' first appearance in the play (1.1) surrounded by dancers; the banquet on Pompey's galley (2.7); and the lovers' meeting in Alexandria after Antony's victory over Caesar (4.8), where each appears with a long train of followers. The production was a great success and ran for 22 nights (LAMB, 1980, p. 65).

On 7 Mar. 1859 the old Broadway Th., New York, presented a production with Edward Eddy as Antony and Elizabeth Ponisi as Cleopatra. ODELL (1931, 7:112) reports that, like the spectators of earlier English productions, the audience was "in exceeding raptures over some of the very beautiful scenes," and the production ran for "three solid weeks." That "the text used contained a large admixture of Dryden" (Odell, 7:111) indicates a similarity to the versions of Kemble and Macready (see pp. 729–30). Kyrle Bellew revived the play at Palmer's Th. in New York on 8 Jan. 1889 in similar style. The elaborate scenery, as usual, required compression of the play: SHATTUCK (1987, 2:122) calls this version a "tidy package of fourteen scenes divided into six acts." Bellew cut considerably, especially in Act 3, and also transposed scenes, beginning with the first Caesar scene (1.4), as in some English versions.

In George James Vining's production at the Princess's in London (15 May 1867), with Henry Loraine and Isabella Glyn, "the main attraction after Miss Glyn" was—according to LAMB (1980, p. 75), and unfortunately for Loraine—the scenery, an original creation by Thomas Grieve and Frederick Lloyds for Charles Calvert's *Ant.* at the Prince's in Manchester, 10 Sept. 1866 (ODELL, 1920, 2:362; Lamb, p. 77). Vining's production showed "the great advance in *vraisemblance* of Egyptian effect over the production of Phelps" (Odell, 2:362). Even more highly praised was

761

that of Frederick Chatterton (Drury Lane, 20 Sept. 1873). As Odell (2:363) puts it, Chatterton's opulent style of production provided "a scenic holiday for London playgoers," and "the director, scene-painter, and choreographer were applauded more vigorously than the principals" (Lamb, pp. 80–1). More exotically, the rich production at the Broadway Th., New York (26 Nov. 1877), with Rose Eytinge as Cleopatra and F. B. Warde as Antony, integrated a ballet into the performance. Despite this attraction it had only "a respectable run and no more" (ODELL, 1938, 10:403) and "moved out on December 15th."

If comparison is possible, Lewis Wingfield's London revival with Lillie Langtry on 18 Nov. 1890 outdid Chatterton's of 1873. The *Illustrated London News* (29 Nov. 1890, p. 679) and other magazines featured pictures of Cleopatra's barge and the "elaborate two-story set for the last scene" (LAMB, 1980, p. 81). One reviewer warned those "who are inclined to be disappointed with the play after the First Act is over . . . 'Wait for the end', and don't leave until the Curtain has descended on that gracious figure of the Queen of Egypt, attired in her regal robes, crowned with her diadem, holding her sceptre, but dead in her chair of state" (*Punch*, 6 Dec. 1890, p. 268).

Thirty years after the first Manchester revival by Charles Calvert (1866), his son Louis Calvert directed the play at the Queen's in Manchester (16 Feb. 1897), with himself as Antony and Janet Achurch as Cleopatra. The production as a whole was praised as much more interesting and much less expensive than Mrs. Langtry's (LAMB, 1980, p. 84) and was probably the only modest one during the period. The same production and cast, however, went to the Olympic in London (24 May 1897) with added "scenic embellishments" and incidental music (Lamb).

Frank Benson directed *Ant.* for the Stratford Festival on 14 Apr. 1898 with himself and his wife, Constance, as the principals. DAY & TREWIN (1932, p. 81) report that it was "the costliest production ever seen in Stratford. . . . Herr [Michael] Balling composed special music, and the settings recreated some of the magnificence of Roman Egypt. Cleopatra . . . died in a monument of ebony and silver." TREWIN (1960, p. 95) calls Benson's "adjustments," in comparison with the drastic textual interferences customary at that time, "fairly mild" in getting "the thirty-eight scenes into fourteen." The production was not breathtaking, but "Stratford cheered the massive Egyptian halls and far sea horizons" (Trewin, 1960, p. 95), and probably for the first time since Garrick, Antony was "hoisted . . . aloft upon the butt-ends of [the guards'] halberds for the waiting Cleopatra, Iras, and Charmian to draw him in to safety" (Trewin), in a Monument "painted with hieroglyphics and Egyptian gods" (LAMB, 1980, p. 88). Benson and his wife were again the principal actors in his second revival at The Lyceum in London (29 Mar. 1900).

Before Benson's third *Ant.* at the Stratford Festival on 23 Apr. 1912, one English and two American revivals were staged: Charles Hanford's touring production in America (ca. 1900; see pp. 732–3), Herbert Beerbohm Tree's revival at His Majesty's in London (27 Dec. 1906), and Winthrop Ames's at the New Th. in New York (8 Nov. 1909). Beerbohm Tree's "love of the panorama" (FITZGERALD, 1908, p. 79), his interest in visual rather than dramatic elements, his liking for tableaux

762

with almost cinematic devices, resulted in a stage sensation that thrilled the first-night audience. Tree's four-act version is discussed above (pp. 733–4). His trans-positions of scenes had a practical reason, as LAMB (1980, p. 91) points out: they "allowed the heavy three-dimensional pieces of more elaborate sets—such as Cleo-patra's palace, Pompey's barge, and the monument interior—to be put into place while the action of the 'short scene' was in progress." Responses to Tree's tableaux were divided. Fitzgerald (p. 81) thinks that in *Ant.* "any attempts at stage sensation, realistic treatment, should be taboo," whereas SPEAIGHT (1973, p. 126) sees that "Tree, alert as ever to seize an opportunity which Shakespeare had missed, picked on a single reference to Cleopatra's appearance as the goddess Isis" to present her mysterious power. The visual frame of the performance was a sphinx projected on a drop screen at the opening of the play and again after the final tableau of "Cleopatra upright at stage left, Antony supine at right, and Iras and Charmian stretched in graceful attitudes on the floor" (see Lamb, p. 96; *Times* [London], 28 Dec. 1906, p. 3; *Punch*, 2 Jan. 1907, p. 2).

Ames's production—which opened the 1909 season on 8 Nov. at the New Th., New York, with Julia Marlowe and E. H. Sothern in the title parts—was a failure, partly because the principals disagreed severely with the original stage manager, Louis Calvert (who finally left), partly because of "acoustical problems" (the actors spoke badly and their lines were often "drowned out by noise from the ventilating system" [SHATTUCK, 1987, 2:281]). Not even the setting, with "huge Egyptian pillars framing a vista of the Nile and its farther shore, a backdrop adapted from one of [Jules] Guérin's paintings" (Shattuck), saved the event. Moreover, "scene shifting took so long that after the initial performance two entire scenes, including that aboard Pompey's galley, had to be dropped in order to end the play before midnight" (Shattuck, 2:280).

Two more productions, though dating from the twenties and thirties, seem to continue the traditions of staging established in the early 19th c. In 1923, at the State Th. in Leningrad, the artist Pavel A. Schillingowsky provided what SPEAIGHT (1973, p. 220) calls a "handsome, if conventional, décor of steps and pillars" in which "Beerbohm Tree would have been at home," and at the Stratford Festival in 1931 W. Bridges-Adams "used tableau curtains at four different stage depths . . . in much the same scheme as Phelps's wing-and-groove arrangement eighty years earlier" (LAMB, 1980, p. 124).

Later Ways

Later ways of producing the play were influenced to a great extent by new technical facilities, such as revolving stages or permanent step constructions, which enabled directors to put new conceptions into practice. Modern productions also tended to avoid tableaux, processions, and spectacular scenery and to use instead stylized sets or even an almost bare, Elizabethan kind of stage.

Firmin Gémier staged the French adaptation by Lucien Népoty at the Comédie Française on 27 Feb. 1918, with himself as Antony and Ida Rubinstein as Cleopatra.

Despite the simple staging—two flights of stairs sloping into the audience—Gémier used considerable scenery and added what JACQUOT (1964, p. 50) calls "un morceau de bravoure," an orgy at Cleopatra's concluding his Act 2, which Gémier defended as being in Plutarch (Jacquot). According to BLANCHE (in GRIVELET, 1960, p. 271), music from the three orchestras was "more than enough to drown such poetry as the translation had managed to preserve" (in French; tr. SPEAIGHT, 1973, p. 184, and also quoted by Jacquot, p. 50). André Gide's free prose version of sixteen scenes in six acts, written for and used by Rubinstein at the Théâtre National de l'Opéra in June 1920, was also the basis of Jean-Louis Barrault's Shn. production at the Comédie Française (27 Apr. 1945), with Marie Bell as Cleopatra (see Jacquot, pp. 95, 96). In Speaight's opinion (p. 233), 23 changes of scene, "even with Jean Hugo's ravishing [Italianate] décors, instead of painting a decipherable map of the Mediterranean world, left it in unrelated fragments."

A mixture of traditional spectacle and attempts at stylizing the setting was likewise evident in Rollo Peters's production at the Lyceum Th. in New York on 19 Feb. 1924, with Jane Cowl and himself in the main parts. A reviewer (CORBIN, *New York Times*, 20 Feb. 1924, 22:1, and 24 Feb. 1924, 7:1:1) lamented the long waiting periods for the scenery to be shifted and the cutting of many scenes to make up for the loss of time, the perennial problem of earlier English productions. On the other hand, he was disappointed with the modest stylized Monument for which "Miss Cowl's stage director merely hangs two little tapestries on a scene used for the interior of her palace and lets it go at that" (2 Mar. 1924, 8:1:1).

Bridges-Adams's first Stratford Festival of 1921 was a pioneering and greatly influential revival of *Ant.* It was the first "nonstop" production, with only one interval and an "almost uncut" text (LAMB, 1980, p. 101; see also pp. 734–5). Dorothy Green and Edmund Willard were the principals. The fact that Bridges-Adams did the play for three more Stratford Festivals (15 July 1924; 11 July 1927; 29 June 1931) suggests that it was a challenge for him. His second *Ant.* (Stratford, 1924) was believed to be "the finest of the Stratford season" (Lamb, p. 112). To guarantee smooth changes of location in the 1921 production, the director "installed a cyclorama [curved background screen] at Stratford and made extensive use of traverse curtains" (Lamb, p. 109).

The following year saw the second "nonstop" production at the Old Vic (4 Dec. 1922) under Robert Atkins. His protagonists were Wilfrid Walter and Esther Whitehouse. Like Bridges-Adams, Atkins used traverse curtains. He refrained altogether from spectacular scenic effects and produced the play on an "almost bare stage" with a "semipermanent Elizabethan setting [achieved] by putting up a false proscenium (covered in black velour) with a couple of doors on each side, and a small apron stage" (LAMB, 1980, pp. 101, 106–7). Robert Atkins's second *Ant.*, produced for the Stratford Festival in 1945 (23 Apr.) with Claire Luce and Anthony Eustrel, likewise presented an almost full text (see also p. 735) and continuous action. Lamb (pp. 101–2) sums up the achievements of Atkins and Bridges-Adams: "The first revolutionary productions . . . broke with the tradition of pictorial realism, but they did not give up all the conventions of the nineteenth-century stage.

They did not, for example, give up the curtain." The full text and continuous action, however, were attempted by most following directors. An example is Guthrie McClintic's production at the Martin Beck Th. in New York (1947) with Katharine Cornell and Godfrey Tearle, in which the text was treated (BROWN, 1986, pp. 22–3) "in a respectful fashion . . . the cutting and transposing [being limited to] one scene."

Andrew Leigh, Atkins's successor at the Old Vic, revived *Ant.* during his first season in 1925, with Edith Evans as Cleopatra and Baliol Holloway as Antony. Harcourt Williams's revival at the same theater (24 Nov. 1930) resorted to the "traverse curtains customarily used at the financially hard-pressed Old Vic" (LAMB, 1980, p. 118) but "skillfully combined [them with] semi-permanent settings." To save time, Williams worked with "discoveries" rather than entrances of characters in certain scenes—a practice criticized as an impediment by Granville-Barker (WILLIAMS, 1935, p. 96); Williams later agreed that "discovering" diminished the impetus of the play.

B. Iden Payne presented *Ant.* for the Stratford Festival at the Sh. Memorial Th. on 15 Apr. 1935. The Stratford production was described as "surprisingly pictorial" (TREWIN, 1964, p. 168) in using, for example, "giant Egyptian columns with friezes" (LAMB, 1980, p. 126). The advantage of the new Stratford stage, which was divided into two levels by permanent steps, was at the same time a problem: "The separation of stage from auditorium was much too marked, as was the division between the two stage levels" (Lamb).

The last London *Ant.* before World War II was produced by Theodore Komisarjevsky at the New Th. (14 Oct. 1936), with Eugenie Leontovich and Donald Wolfit. TREWIN (1964, p. 155) ridicules the balletic, "extravagantly fantasticated" costumes. CROSSE (1953, p. 98) criticizes Komisarjevsky's "liberties with the text," which were "not needed to save scene-shifting, so it is to be supposed that he thought his arrangements better than Shakespeare's." As an example he cites Caesar's "*Anthony*, Leaue thy lasciuious Vassailes . . ." (491 ff.), for which Komisarjevsky "actually brought Antony on to the stage so that Octavius was made to deliver the lines straight at him." But Komisarjevsky's was also the first really experimental production: he used a single fixed set (consisting mainly of steps with a platform and a backdrop), which changed its function by means of varied lighting. Favorable reviews point out that the décor as well as the "concept of costume . . . may have been ten years ahead of its time" (see LAMB, 1980, p. 127). More critical responses complain that despite the possible advantages of such a setting, in this particular theater it did not work. "In the monument scene none of the players was visible from the side boxes" (Lamb, p. 127; *Times* [London], 15 Oct. 1936, p. 12).

A quasi-Elizabethan stage was created for Glen Byam Shaw's first English postwar revival of *Ant.* at the Piccadilly Th. in London (20 Dec. 1946), with Edith Evans and Godfrey Tearle. The costumes were a "free treatment of the Renaissance style," according to ST. CLARE BYRNE (1948, p. 31), though "with some suggestions of Roman and Egyptian." Shaw's set was similar to Komisarjevsky's: a two-story structure, used as a permanent setting, "supplied Elizabethan stage features without imitating Elizabethan style" (LAMB, 1980, p. 134). TREWIN (1964, p. 203) regrets that "unhappily, owing to the problems of this particular theatre, the structure had to be set too far downstage; in consequence it seemed cramped and heavy."

For Glen Byam Shaw's Stratford production on 28 Apr. 1953 the stage had been remodeled in order to reduce the distance between actors and spectators. The revival, with Peggy Ashcroft and Michael Redgrave, was later presented at the Prince's in London and also taken on a Continental tour. The stage in Shaw's production was bare apart from a "sort of false inner-proscenium frame" and temporary stairs, but "lighting and color scheme quickly established the visual contrast between East and West" (LAMB, 1980, pp. 145, 146). A single set was used also in Robert Helpmann's production at the Old Vic (5 Mar. 1957), with Keith Michell and Margaret Whiting. Like Bridges-Adams's and Atkins's, Helpmann's was a "nonstop" revival with an almost complete text. The simple permanent set (with some Egyptian obelisks) was varied by lighting devices: "When . . . the upstage area was blacked out, the four plinths farther downstage became Roman pillars. Egyptian emblems and Cleopatra's chaise set Alexandria at one side of the stage, while the imperial eagle established Rome at the other" (Lamb, p. 156). The plinths were also used as the Monument to which Antony was lifted, and for the final scene different lighting created the inside of the Monument. Memorable and new in Helpmann's production were the "overlapping entrances and exits" through which he "established the spaciousness of his setting" (Lamb, p. 158).

For the Festival of Britain in 1951 Michael Benthall, with Vivien Leigh and Laurence Olivier in the title parts, directed *Ant.* at the St. James Th. in London (11 May) and later at the Ziegfeld Th. in New York (20 Dec.). In this enthusiastically received revival, Benthall went beyond Bridges-Adams's idea of the cyclorama (1921) by using a revolving stage for the first time; this device permitted a "continuous action . . . from Egypt to Rome and back again" (VENEZKY, 1951, p. 336). Benthall was also the first to stage *Ant.* on alternate nights with Shaw's *Caesar and Cleopatra* as a "prologue to Shakespeare's romantic tragedy" (ATKINSON, *New York Times*, 21 Dec. 1951, 22:2). In addition to allowing smooth change of locale in Sh.'s play, the revolving stage helped create a connection between it and Shaw's: "An aloof sphinx . . . begins 'Caesar and Cleopatra' and concludes 'Antony and Cleopatra'— thus defining the full circle of the theme" (Atkinson, 30 Dec. 1951, 11:1:1). LAMB (1980, p. 140) outlines the staging of the Monument scenes for which "a rather substantial and naturalistic monument topped by a sphinx was brought onstage. . . . Antony was lifted up to the top of the platform, which was only about six feet high. For the last scene, the turntable moved to show the other side of the monument." Bernard Hepton's production at the Birmingham Repertory Th. in Feb. 1961, with Elizabeth Sprigg and Tony Steedman, likewise used a revolving stage (TREWIN, 1963, pp. 177–9).

In two ways the first *Ant.* done by the RSC seems to elaborate on Benthall's achievements: Trevor Nunn prepared the play for the Stratford Festival (15 Aug. 1972) as part of a sequence called "The Romans" (including *Cor., JC, Ant.*, and *Tit.*). The principal actors were Richard Johnson and Janet Suzman. Like other directors, Nunn used "lighting, costumes, props, and changes of level" to stress the contrast between Rome and Egypt (LAMB, 1980, p. 165) and the newly installed hydraulic machinery of the Stratford theater to "instantly supply a new locale with a different typography" (Lamb). Michael Kahn tried something similar to "The Romans" in producing *Ant*. "in tandem" with *JC* at the American Sh. Festival Th., Stratford, Conn., in 1972. Salome Jens was his Cleopatra. Both triumvirates were played by the same actors, with Paul Hecht as Antony (BROWN, 1986, p. 18).

Although there were a few revivals, including one at Stratford, Conn., in 1960, according to BROWN (1986, p. 18), "the only important productions" of the sixties were those of Michael Langham at Stratford, Ont., in 1967, and of Peter Dews at Chichester, Eng., in 1969. Langham's production (31 July 1967) is deemed by LAMB (1980, p. 160) "in some ways . . . the most significant English *Antony and Cleopatra* of the decade," mainly because the director did not try to smooth out the play's sudden switching from one time and place to another. What other directors had tried in order "to correct Shakespeare's bluntness by filling in . . . transitions" (KERR, *New York Times*, 17 Sept. 1967, 2:1:1) was not attempted by Langham, whose production was "all speed and abruptness . . . bumping tableaux into one another" (Kerr), thus emphasizing Sh.'s employment of what we know today as "cinematic jump-cuts." This kind of staging "carried [Robert] Helpmann's 1957 overlapping technique somewhat farther" (Lamb, p. 161). SPRAGUE & TREWIN (1971, p. 112): Today "more and more, scenes, in their rapid progress, are juxtaposed or imaginatively overlapped. Frank Hauser did this excitingly in his Oxford Playhouse [*Ant*.] (1965) when, for example, the often-cut Syrian scene (III.i) . . . was set immediately against the revellers on Pompey's galley (II.vii)."

Four more productions in the 1970s (all described by LAMB [1980, pp. 172–3] as "variations on Robert Atkins's historic production of 1922") had in common the use of an almost bare stage: Robin Phillips's rendition for the Stratford, Ont., Festival (19 May 1976), with Keith Baxter and Maggie Smith; Frank Dunlop's revival at the Young Vic, London (Oct. 1976), with Michael Graham Cox and Delphine Seyrig; Toby Robertson's production at the Prospect Th. at the Old Vic, London (Aug. 1977), with Alec McCowen and Dorothy Tutin; and Peter Brook's version at the Stratford Festival (4 Oct. 1978), with Alan Howard and Glenda Jackson, which moved to the Aldwych in London (12 June 1979). TREWIN (1980, p. 157), WARREN (1980, pp. 177–8), and NEUFELD (1986, pp. 34–5) praise Brook's version; LONEY (1980, p. 92) and Lamb (pp. 174–8) are less enthusiastic.

A bare platform was also used by Alf Sjöberg in his last Sh. revival at the Royal Dramatic Th. in Stockholm (22 Nov. 1975). The naked stage was "furnished only with the most essential scenic elements" (MARKER, 1986, p. 32). In this "antiheroic view of the play, Antony [Anders Ek] became a kind of suffering Strindbergian pilgrim on a painful journey of self-discovery. . . . Ulla Sjöblom's Cleopatra shared both Antony's existential soul-sickness and his alienation from 'the new, cold, and realistic age' represented by Caesar" (Marker, pp. 32–3).

Two unconventional productions of *Ant*. were directed by Joseph Papp in 1959 and 1963, preceded, however, by a less successful reading version presented by Papp at the Heckscher Th., New York, in 1958: "George Scott's Antony, modeled after General MacArthur, didn't work, and under the circumstances Colleen Dewhurst failed to flourish as Cleopatra" (*Best Plays*, 1958–9, p. 52). Papp's "free" *Ant.* with the same actors for the 1959 New York Sh. Festival, a concert version with music by David Amram, is called by GELB (*New York Times*, 14 Jan. 1959, 28:1) "the best bargain in town." And FUNKE (*New York Times*, 21 June 1963, 33:1) says about its revival for the New York Sh. Festival's ninth season in 1963 at the open-air Delacorte Th. in Central Park (this time with Michael Higgins as Antony): "Mr. Papp has a tendency toward surplus foolery" sometimes verging "on burlesque." However, "if he has not mastered the play, he has succeeded in making it blunt, straight, serviceable and interesting."

Tony Richardson's modern-dress production at the Bankside Globe in London (9 Aug. 1973) with Julian Glover and Vanessa Redgrave, is called by some the "play's first important experimental postwar rendition" (BROWN, 1986, p. 19). Two provocative productions of *Ant.* were staged in 1979: Estelle Parsons did the play at the Interart Th., New York (19 Apr.–13 May), with Kathleen Gaffney and Francisco Prado. Brown (p. 20) praises the production: "The bilingual modern dress interpretation mingled Spanish and English in the dialogue, had a gorgeous Cleopatra . . . in the mold of a 1940s Hollywood movie queen . . . and a super-macho Antony." The Romans were played by Hispanic Americans, the Egyptians by blonde Anglo-Saxons, and "ethnic differences" were successfully exploited for the "clash between . . . cultures" (HOLMBERG, 1980, p. 196). Robert Colonna's Rhode Island Sh. Th. production at the Swanhurst Th., Newport (2–12 Aug.), was placed "in a *Cabaret*-like world of between-the-wars Berlin" (Brown, p. 19). Many dances were appropriately integrated into the performance. Enobarbus even danced in his death scene (NEUSE, 1980, p. 186).

All in all, activities in England have come full circle after a little more than 200 years since Garrick. Adrian Noble's production at The Other Place, Stratford (6 Oct. 1982), with Helen Mirren (Michael Croft's Cleopatra by the National Youth Th. in 1965) and Michael Gambon, seems to have returned to what the play itself offers. BROWN (1986, p. 19) describes the revival as "reducing scenic investiture in order to concentrate on dramatic values," and SHRIMPTON (1984, p. 173) stresses the intimacy and simplicity of the entire presentation: "The remarkable achievement of this sparse but striking production argues . . . that hard living and high thinking must not yet be allowed to perish utterly from the English theatre." On the other hand, Peter Hall's production at the Olivier Th., London (1987), with Judi Dench and Anthony Hopkins, was a Renaissance *Ant.*, using "rust-red for Egypt, dimming to brownish grey-blue for Rome" (EVERETT, 1987, p. 439), but despite excellent acting it did not achieve "exceptionality."

THE ACTORS

Reports about the principal actors concentrate on Cleopatra more often than on Antony, though sometimes commenting on their suitability as partners.

Propriety if not prudishness in the 19th c. accounts for some miscast Cleopatras—often with inadequate Antonys—because some good actresses refused to play a morally dubious character; for example, Sarah Siddons, Kemble's sister, declined to be cast in Kemble's production at Covent Garden (15 Nov. 1813). ODELL (1920, 2:70) finds that with only nine performances, the revival got "exactly the success it deserved. Of course [Charles Mayne] Young and Mrs. [Harriet] Faucit were rather prosaic actors to select for Antony and the Nile-serpent." William Charles Macready and Louisa Anne Phillips were considered miscast for different reasons in Alfred Bunn's production at Drury Lane (21 Nov. 1833)—Miss Phillips for her "pointed features" and inadequate acting (LAMB, 1980, p. 65), and Macready, who had not wanted to take the role, for being convincing only in "portraying suffering and fortitude" (p. 64).

Some noted 19th-c. productions suggest that the conception of Cleopatra was not at all stable. The varying ages and reputations of the Cleopatras—from virginal to more experienced—often contrasted with the more consistently advanced ages of the roué Antonys. LAMB (1980, p. 72) points out that Frederick Chatterton in 1873 at Drury Lane and Lewis Wingfield in 1890 at the Princess's "had as their Cleopatras a seventeen-year-old novice [Ellin Wallis] and a celebrated beauty who was a mistress of the Prince of Wales [Lillie Langtry]"; the discrepancy in the actors' ages (James Anderson was 54 when he played Antony with Ellin Wallis) seemed to pass unnoticed.

The performances of one Victorian Cleopatra, Isabella Glyn, resulted in three epoch-making productions. Samuel Phelps's pioneering revival at Sadler's Wells (22 Oct. 1849), which ODELL (1920, 2:321) calls one of his "four most notable productions," was done in a mixture of styles, with tunic and buskins for Antony and Victorian costumes for the women (LAMB, 1980, p. 68). The *Illustrated London News* (27 Oct. 1849, p. 285) praised Phelps's realistic makeup as well as the acting and thought that "Miss Glyn's performance of *Cleopatra* is the most superb thing ever witnessed on the modern stage." See also SALGĀDO (1975, p. 314). Glyn developed a more erotic Cleopatra in two later revivals of the play: in the production at The Standard (Mar. 1855) under John Douglass, with Henry Marston as Antony, and with Henry Loraine in George James Vining's production at the Princess's (15 May 1867), using Lacy's acting ed. (see p. 731). Lamb (p. 75) summarizes the tension: "The forty-four-year-old actress whose performance . . . expressed such ripe sexuality was properly got up in a Mid-Victorian crinoline-style costume." Odell (2:303), however, criticizes Glyn's Cleopatra as "too ladylike to give [the Messenger] the beating that Shakespeare's Cleopatra thought he so richly deserved."

Lillie Langtry's performance in the 1890 production was less remarkable than her physical appearance. She was found impressive in only two scenes: when she struck the Messenger with the jewels that she had intended as a reward (a piece of stage business from Lacy's acting ed.) and in her death scene (see LAMB, 1980, p. 83). Her partner, Charles Coghlan, hardly received comment except that he "supported" Langtry's "most inadequate Egyptian queen" (ODELL, 1920, 2:387). Elizabeth Ponisi had a different problem in the 1859 production at the old Broadway

Th. in New York (7 Mar.). Whereas Edward Eddy's performance as Antony was praised, Ponisi was (ODELL, 1931, 7:112) "too stout to be any kind of serpent; and [she] never had a profile." Eddy repeated his success with Julia Dean Hayne on 25 Apr. 1859 and at the New Bowery with Alice Grey (or Gray) on 17 Sept. 1860. WINTER (1916, p. 459) praises Rose Eytinge's Cleopatra, in particular her physiognomy and temperament and "her knowledge of all the arts of female coquetry," as the best he had ever seen in his sixty or seventy years of playgoing. Eytinge's Antony was F. B. Warde in the production at the Broadway Th. (26 Nov. 1877).

In Kyrle Bellew's production at Palmer's Th. (New York, 8 Jan. 1889), according to ODELL (1945, 14:20), Bellew as Antony and Cora Brown Potter (Urquhart) as Cleopatra made "a combination that could hardly be surpassed for lack of suitability to the superhuman lovers of Shakespeare's massive poetic tragedy." Brown Potter's persuasiveness depended on the "see-through effect of her skirts" (SHATTUCK, 1987, 2:122), which shocked the audience, and on her bare breasts in Antony's (Bellew's) and her death scenes (Shattuck, 2:123). A similar approach, however, was taken in the Comédie Française production (27 Feb. 1918) under Firmin Gémier. Parents—and critics, all quoting, citing, or translating BLANCHE's account (originally in *Mercure de France*, 1918; quoted by GRIVELET, 1960, p. 271) of Cleopatra's orgy—were outraged to have their children watch the "beautiful naked thighs kicking in the air under the embrace of rough boxers" (in French; tr. SPEAIGHT, 1973, p. 185; see also JACQUOT, 1964, pp. 48, 50).

Two examples illustrate that neither youth nor revealing costume nor an air of indecency was necessary to do Cleopatra right. The first American revival outside New York was at the Baldwin Th. in San Francisco (21 Sept. 1898) with Helena Modjeska at the age of 58 as Cleopatra. SHATTUCK (1987, 2:135) comments, "That would seem indeed 'wrinkled deep in time'. But not so with Modjeska. She was never more girlish." Constance Collier, Beerbohm Tree's Cleopatra in the production at His Majesty's (London, 27 Dec. 1906), had, according to TREWIN (1964, p. 40), "a natural majesty of bearing and tone," whereas "Tree, concerned with the look of the thing, seemed to have only half his mind on Antony." Critics noted that Collier's "oriental sensuality" as an "imperious young Cleopatra" (LAMB, 1980, pp. 92–3) was unequalled by Beerbohm Tree's stature as a lover, though Tree was "effective as the Roman soldier and, toward the end, the picture of ruin" (Lamb, p. 92). The highest praise was given to Lyn Harding, whose "gruff Enobarbus ruled the night" (Trewin, p. 41).

Youthfulness was considered a fault, however, in Julia Marlowe's impersonation of Cleopatra as "more girl than woman" at the New Th. in New York (8 Nov. 1909) under Winthrop Ames. She was also criticized for making "Cleopatra as nearly like herself as possible" (SHATTUCK, 1987, 2:282); like Sarah Siddons, she had "long since declared she wished to play only 'good women' " (Shattuck, 2:279), and she had accepted the "honor of inaugurating America's 'national' theatre" only reluctantly. E. H. Sothern as Antony "got some credit for his explosion of rage" (Shattuck, 2:282) in the Thidias scene.

Age seemed insignificant in Robert Helpmann's production at the Old Vic (5 Mar. 1957). Keith Michell was 30 when he played Antony and Margaret Whiting 23 as Cleopatra, both younger "than their parts required" (SPEAIGHT, 1973, p. 271). Nevertheless, Margaret Whiting—especially in her death scene—was found convincing. When in Peter Dews's production of *Ant.* for the Chichester Festival (23 July 1969) the principals were played by older actors, Margaret Leighton and John Clements, "their performances had to depend . . . more on other qualities than those of great lovers" (LEITER, 1986, p. 30). Accordingly, they were "praised for beautifully spoken, intelligently detailed, rather small-scale performances," and they "projected disillusion, wryness, and a sense of long domesticity" (LAMB, 1980, p. 163).

If Brown Potter's "weakest point" was her voice—"it was harsh, metallic, monotonous" (SHATTUCK, 1987, 2:122)—Janet Achurch (in Louis Calvert's production at the Queen's in Manchester, 16 Feb. 1897) was accused of arbitrary intonation, hysterical laughter, and inarticulate sounds (LAMB, 1980, p. 86). In addition, SHAW (1932, 24:79) found that Achurch's "beauty is not the beauty of Cleopatra. . . . She is not even the English . . . Cleopatra, the serpent of old Thames," while (p. 81) "Calvert looks as if he not only had the boars put on the spit, but ate them. He is inexcusably fat." An unconvincing serpent of old Nile was also a problem in Frank Benson's productions at Stratford (14 Apr. 1898) and at The Lyceum in London (29 Mar. 1900), with himself as Antony and his wife, Constance, as Cleopatra. Both times Mrs. Benson was thought miscast (Lamb, p. 88). TREWIN (1960, p. 95) recalls that in the "first performance, [Constance Benson] could only indicate Cleopatra"; at The Lyceum her "Cleopatra was 'hysterical, but only after the manner of the pampered parlour boarder' " (Trewin, p. 115, quoting *The Morning Post*, 30 Mar. 1900, p. 3). In Benson's third revival, at the Stratford Festival in 1912 (23 Apr.), Dorothy Green became his partner. Critics consider this Benson's best production of the play because he "had apparently grown in the role" (Lamb, p. 88) and especially because of Dorothy Green: she was 25 years old and "a promising Cleopatra . . . a role she would make more and more her own in later revivals at Stratford and the Old Vic" (Lamb, p. 90). DAY & TREWIN (1932, p. 119) praise hers as "a magnificent impersonation of a capricious, vain, innately human woman," and in W. Bridges-Adams's Stratford Festival of 1921, for example, she was called the "best living Cleopatra, febrile and seductive [who] had splendid assistance from the Antony of Edmund Willard" (Day & Trewin, p. 168).

Cleopatra's gypsy qualities were stressed in Jane Cowl's presentation at the Lyceum Th. in New York (19 Feb. 1924). A reviewer (CORBIN, *New York Times*, 20 Feb. 1924, 22:1, and 24 Feb. 1924, 7:1:1) praised Cleopatra's "transferring midnight revels to the streets of Alexandria, changing clothes with drink-dulled Antony [played by Rollo Peters] to make his awakening ridiculous."

SPEAIGHT (1973, p. 217) declares the performance of Lotte Medelsky at the Burg Th., Vienna, in 1923 "probably the finest Cleopatra of the century on any European stage"—a testimony to her versatile talent, since she usually played more homely parts such as Gretchen in Goethe's *Faust* (KINDERMANN, 1939, pp. 139, 145). Medelsky's Antony, Raoul Aslan, however, was "too neurotic for a part that should be played on anything but the nerves" (Speaight, p. 217).

English productions in the twenties showed a certain continuity in their choice of the principal actors. Dorothy Green was Bridges-Adams's Cleopatra also in the Stratford Festivals of 1924 and 1927 and in Harcourt Williams's revival at the Old Vic (24 Nov. 1930); Baliol Holloway was Bridges-Adams's Antony (with Dorothy Green) in 1924 and Andrew Leigh's in 1925 (with Edith Evans); Edith Evans had played Dryden's Cleopatra before, and Baliol Holloway had been in four of Benson's *Ant.* productions, once as Antony (SPEAIGHT, 1973, p. 149; LAMB, 1980, pp. 113–14). In the 1925 production Edith Evans was particularly convincing in her "projection and diction [which] were so marvelous that Old Vic audiences lost not a line of her Cleopatra" (Lamb, p. 116). Some critics thought her "venturesome" because she approached the part with "mind and technique over matter" and a "certain coldness," especially in the earlier phases of the play (Lamb, p. 115). Some found Holloway more moving than Evans. In Bridges-Adams's 1927 production (11 July) in the Cinema at Stratford (temporarily used as the Festival Th.), Dorothy Green, with Wilfrid Walter as Antony, elaborated on other actresses' earlier frivolous presentations; her "scantily clad Cleopatra—the conventional picture of the naughty seductress—" showed that "heroine and harlot are not contradictory interpretations . . . but merely different facets" of Cleopatra (Lamb, p. 113).

Instead of exposing the physical attractions of their Cleopatras, other directors returned to Elizabethan dress. Harcourt Williams used Renaissance costumes in his 1930 revival at the Old Vic, with "touches of ancient Egypt as well as Rome" (LAMB, 1980, pp. 118–19), as did Bridges-Adams in his 1931 production, still at the Stratford Cinema. In Williams's performance the Renaissance costumes helped John Gielgud (who thought himself miscast as Antony because he did not look physically strong enough) "to build up a young frail body to a more heroic stature" (WILLIAMS, 1935, p. 94); in Bridges-Adams's revival "Stratford audiences could not get used to the new Cleopatra . . . in a pink farthingale" (Lamb, p. 124), but the director explained: "It is the only way of saving a line like 'Cut my lace, Charmian' from absurdity" (DAY & TREWIN, 1932, p. 216). According to TREWIN (1964, p. 136), the protagonists under Bridges-Adams, as played by Dorothy Massingham and Gyles Isham, remained "below the crest as the lovers." Under Williams, however, John Gielgud was found convincing, and so was Dorothy Green—"verging on middle age . . . and . . . experienced" (Lamb, p. 122).

Because of the weak principals, very few positive comments were made about the productions of *Ant.* under the new directors at both Stratford and the Old Vic. (Harcourt Williams was replaced at the Old Vic in 1933 by Henry Cass; Bridges-Adams's successor at Stratford in 1934 was B. Iden Payne.) Wilfrid Lawson and Mary Newcombe were Henry Cass's Antony and Cleopatra at the Old Vic in 1934 (17 Sept.). TREWIN (1964, p. 162) describes Lawson as a "sore failure," and LAMB (1980, p. 126) concedes that "Mary Newcombe's blonde Cleopatra had variety and poetic force but seemed overly Western." The star of the production was Maurice

Evans as Octavius Caesar. Payne's Cleopatra in 1935 (15 Apr.), Catherine Lacey, was a "beautiful miniature" (Trewin, p. 168), while his Antony, Roy Emerton, "did not have sufficient vitality or detailed invention to carry out his concept of the character" (Lamb, p. 127, citing *Times* [London], 16 Apr. 1935).

Rather than their acting, the actors' delivery was often faulted. Unanimously, critics made fun of Eugenie Leontovich's "heroic misadventure with the English language" (LAMB, 1980, p. 127) in Komisarjevsky's production at the New Th., London (14 Oct. 1936), and they felt sorry for "young Donald Wolfit" as Antony (Lamb, p. 129). More successful was George Hayes's Clown's speaking (SPRAGUE & TREWIN, 1971, p. 69) "in a sustained eerie whisper." Regarding Robert Atkins's second *Ant.*, produced for the Stratford Festival in 1945 (23 Apr.), TREWIN (1964, p. 197) sums up: "Had the sound of Claire Luce's speech matched her subtlety, she would have been Cleopatra indeed; the Antony [Anthony Eustrel] was less plausible." Tallulah Bankhead and Conway Tearle, the principals in Reginald Bach's revival at the Mansfield Th. in New York (10 Nov. 1937), were similarly censured. ATKINSON (*New York Times*, 11 Nov. 1937, 30:2) harshly calls the production a "cacophony of noisy heartiness signifying nothing but incompetence on a high occasion," but he praises John Emery (Bankhead's husband) as Caesar and Fania Marinoff as Charmian. SPRAGUE (1953, p. 214, n. 20) labels this production one of his "*worst* Shakespearian memories."

Critics were also divided about the principal actors under Glen Byam Shaw's direction at the Piccadilly Th., London (20 Dec. 1946). TREWIN (1964, p. 204) regretted that Edith Evans (who at 57 was playing her second Cleopatra after her 1925 Old Vic appearance) "was not a Cleopatra for fire and air: the tragedy did not exalt" and that Godfrey Tearle was "too unambitious to achieve all he might have done." CROSSE (1953, p. 151), however, praised this production as almost the best *Ant.* he had seen, especially Edith Evans in 4.8, "when she stood with arms uplifted on the upper stage, while Antony and his victorious soldiers cheered her from below."

Godfrey Tearle's achievements as Antony were more convincing in Guthrie McClintic's 1947 revival at the Martin Beck Th. in New York. SPEAIGHT (1973, p. 241): "Tearle's Antony flickered with a greatness going suicidally to seed." Equally strong was Katharine Cornell: "There was no Cleopatra within sight on the British stage in whom the paradox of the character could have been stated so triumphantly."

Two more Cleopatras and Antonys were applauded by audiences as well as by critics. In Michael Benthall's production in 1951 at the St. James Th. in London and at the Ziegfeld Th. in New York, ATKINSON (*New York Times*, 21 Dec. 1951, 22:2) found Vivien Leigh and Laurence Olivier "perfectly matched in a production that conveys the richness, fire and majesty of Shakespeare. . . . Miss Leigh's Cleopatra is superb. . . . Mr. Olivier's Antony is worthy of her mettle." Of Glen Byam Shaw's production at Stratford (28 Apr. 1953), SPEAIGHT (1973, p. 250) says: "There was Peggy Ashcroft to remind us that where Dryden had written the part for a woman, Shakespeare had written it for a boy. . . . Redgrave and Dame Peggy . . . never allowed the play to become bogged down in a cloying sensuality." Their performances were nonetheless erotic. LAMB (1980, p. 151) approves of the actress's playing Cleopatra as a cunning, passionate Greek because this interpretation was more "compatible with her own stage appearance. . . . This Cleopatra was pale-faced and red-haired, a ragingly selfish but irresistible nymphomaniac." Michael Redgrave's "physical appearance and poetical delivery stressed the heroic Antony" in conflict with "dissoluteness, vanity and overworked charm" (*Times* [London], 29 Apr. 1953, p. 8; Lamb, p. 149, citing R. Findlater, *Michael Redgrave*, 1956, p. 128).

The "star draw" (BROWN, 1986, p. 27) was not enough in Jack Landau's revival of *Ant.* at the Festival Th., Stratford, Conn. (31 July 1960), and the Expo 67 World Festival, Montreal: Katharine Hepburn and particularly Robert Ryan "lacked . . . stage experience and had particular difficulty in the rendering of the verse." Similarly, Christopher Plummer and Zoe Caldwell, the principals in Michael Langham's production at Stratford, Ont. (31 July 1967), though they brought "vitality, variety, and humor" to the performance (LAMB, 1980, p. 162), were accused of lacking "regality" (Lamb) and of "assassinat[ing] the play" (BARNES, *New York Times*, 29 Oct. 1967, 83:4).

Recent actors have found some surprising nuances in their parts. In Peter Dews's revival for the Chichester Festival (23 July 1969) Keith Baxter managed to alter the conception of Octavius: "Baxter's Caesar was first a boy, awkward, tugging at his toga, worshiping Antony. . . . With Octavia's rejection, Caesar became a man and an avenger" (LAMB, 1980, p. 164, quoting Bryden in *The Obs.*, 27 July 1969). And whereas in Trevor Nunn's first RSC revival of the play, as part of the cycle "The Romans" (15 Aug. 1972), Richard Johnson presented a traditional Antony, "physically and emotionally large, deep in sexual thralldom, and wild with moral regret" (Lamb, p. 169), Janet Suzman, unlike other Cleopatras, was "a cunning political animal who schemes for the world and loses it through being too clever by half" (Lamb, p. 167, quoting Margaret Tierney in *Plays and Players*, Oct. 1972, p. 43). Even more startling was Tony Richardson's modern-dress *Ant.* at the Bankside Globe in London (9 Aug. 1973), which was intended to be a "comment on international power politics" (Lamb, p. 170). Cleopatra (Vanessa Redgrave) appeared as a "rasping Vamp leering through out-sized orange sunspecs, her slacks held up by red suspenders, and green plastic combs in her hair" (*Time*, 20 Aug. 1973, p. 43), and Antony (Julian Glover) was "a dandyish, cigar-smoking subaltern in khakis" (Lamb, p. 170).

In various ways, four productions in the seventies refrained from stressing the sexual elements in Cleopatra. In Robin Phillips's rendition for the Stratford, Ont., Festival (19 May 1976) with Maggie Smith and Keith Baxter, Smith "made a sophisticated yet vulnerable Cleopatra" (LAMB, 1980, p. 173). In Frank Dunlop's revival at the Young Vic, London (Oct. 1976), with Delphine Seyrig and Michael Graham Cox, Seyrig "was judged intelligent but perhaps lacking in intensity" (Lamb). In Toby Robertson's Elizabethan-costumed production at the Prospect Th. at the Old Vic, London (Aug. 1977) with Dorothy Tutin and Alec McCowen, Tutin made "a politically wise Cleopatra, and a sharp observer of her own mercurial changes in mood" (Lamb). In Peter Brook's version at the Stratford Festival (4 Oct. 1978), with Glenda Jackson and Alan Howard, Jackson "portrayed a Cleopatra of considerable wit and authority" in a "severe short hairdo" (Lamb, p. 176).

Recently, in Adrian Noble's production at The Other Place (Stratford, 1982), Helen Mirren as a "marvellous Cleopatra" was praised more than her partner, Michael Gambon (SHRIMPTON, 1984, p. 173). Though Gambon was convincing as "an ageing man from a passionate race," she was the "heart of the play" and "most impressive when she was most intimate." In Peter Hall's revival at the Olivier Th., London (1987), Judi Dench's achievements, rather than Anthony Hopkins's (despite his "grizzled charm"), made the play successful: "Her Cleopatra is admirably attentive to the nuances and contours of the role . . . and never for an instant fails to interest" (EVERETT, 1987, p. 439).

LATER ADAPTATIONS

The free adaptations found in the early stage history of *Ant.* have had their counterparts in foreign languages and later especially in film and opera. The first French rendition of *Ant.* was by Mme Émile de Girardin in 1847; better known today is André Gide's prose version (pub. 1921; see p. 764). Adaptations in German are more numerous. STAHL (1947, passim) and others record an amateur version in Biberach, 1759–60; duodramas (i.e., arrangements for two performers with music) by J. C. Kaffka in Berlin, 1779, and by Leopold Naumann, with music by Franz Danzi, in Mannheim, 1780 (see KÜHN, 1908, p. 9); a probably unperformed version by Christian Adam Horn, 1796 (see LEDERER, 1907, pp. 220–6). They also note better-known versions by Julius Pabst, performed in Dresden, 1852, with Marie Bayer-Bürck and Emil Devrient; by Heinrich Laube, Burg Th., Vienna, 1854, with Bayer-Bürck and Josef Wagner; by Karl Gutzkow, 1852, first performed in Munich, 1908; by F. A. Leo, in Berlin and Weimar, 1870, with Louise Hettstedt and Ludwig Barnay; by Gisbert von Vincke, in Riga, 1876, and in Freiburg, 1880; by Feodor Wehl, in Stuttgart, 1877; by Franz Dingelstedt, Burg Th., Vienna, 1878–9; and by Robert Buchholz, in Hamburg, 1881. Of these adaptations, only Dingelstedt's continued to hold the stage, although FURNESS (ed. 1907, p. 580) thinks it can be only "leniently termed a version" and should be called "a perversion." It was first performed on 30 Oct. 1878 at the Vienna Burg Th. by Dingelstedt with Charlotte Wolter and Adolf (von) Sonnenthal (Stahl, 1947, p. 409; KINDERMANN, 1957–74, 7:185, and 1964, p. 20) as the principals.

In the 20th c., Sh.'s *Ant.* has sometimes been reduced to the story of Cleopatra and Antony or of Cleopatra and Caesar. Bernard Miles's and Ron Pember's production entitled "Shakespeare's Rome" at the Mermaid Th., London, on 13 Oct. 1981, was a conflation by Miles and Julius Gellner of *JC* and *Ant.* WARDLE (*Times* [London], 14 Oct. 1981, p. 14) liked Carmen Du Sautoy's Cleopatra better than Timothy Dalton's Antony, "a fiery opportunist in the first play [*JC*], then an unshaven voluptuary who goes through the entire second play in a dressing gown."

Several film adaptations were produced before World War I: two American versions in 1908 (directed by William V. Ranous and by J. Stuart Blackton) and one in 1912 called *Cleopatra* (directed by Charles L. Gaskill, who also wrote the script), with Helen Gardner as Cleopatra, Robert Gaillard, and Harley Knoles; an Italian adaptation, *Marcantonio e Cleopatra* (directed by Enrico Guazzoni, who also wrote the script) in 1913 with Amleto Novelli as Antony and Gianna Terribili Gonzales as Cleopatra; and at least three (possibly four) movies about the Cleopatra story produced by Charles Pathé. LIPPMANN (1964, p. 113) describes Guazzoni's story as impressions of Sh., a term also applicable to Adrian Johnson's script for *Cleopatra*, a movie directed by J. Gordon Edwards in 1917 with Theda Bara as Cleopatra and Fritz Leiber as Julius Caesar. Guazzoni's *Ant.* is praised by reviewers for "the historicity, the imaginative creation of atmosphere, the lavish settings, the battle and crowd scenes, the moonlight effects" (BALL, 1968, p. 166)—that is, for the same characteristics found in popular 19th-c. stage productions.

Charles L. Gaskill's movie of 1912 is probably the first "mammoth, or perhaps colossal," film of the play (BALL, 1968, p. 147), with "only Shakespearean bits" (Ball, p. 339). Although DAISNE (1975, 2:129) classifies it as an adaptation of Plutarch, J. Gordon Edwards's 1917 film is a similar concoction of "Plutarch, [Victorien] Sardou, Shakespeare, and a lot of Adrian Johnson" (Ball, p. 253). Cecil B. deMille's movie *Cleopatra* (1934), with Claudette Colbert as Cleopatra, Henry Wilcoxon as Antony, and Warren William as Julius Caesar, apparently owes little to Sh.

The connection between Charles Pathé's earliest (1903) hand-colored *Cleopatra* and Sh. is doubtful; his 1910 version is classified by DAISNE (1975, 2:208) as Sh.'s, whereas BALL (1968, p. 112) says it is a "mixture of Shakespeare, Plutarch, [Victorien] Sardou, and invention." The director of the latter film was either Henri Andréani or Albert Capellani; Cleopatra was played by Madaline Roche (or Madeleine Roch). Pathé's 1913 movie was called *Cleopatra* in England but *Antony and Cleopatra* in the United States. Ball (p. 165) thinks it is a "padded remake or reissue of its 1910 film," and though the *Film Index* (New York, 1941, 1:433) classifies it as not based on Sh., Ball (p. 345) finds Sh.'s influence undeniable. As early as 1918 a burlesque called *Cleopatsy* was produced by Charles Pathé with Dora Rogers as Cleopatra; another, subtitled in the tradition of Polonius a "histerical history" (Ball, p. 265), was done in 1924. In 1951 a 33-minute version of Sh.'s play for students was released by Parthian Productions in England (LIPPMANN, 1964, p. 117).

Two mammoth television productions were based on Sh., but on the Roman plays rather than on *Ant.* alone. In 1963, a nine-hour serialized version called "The Spread of the Eagle" (consisting of *Cor., JC, Ant.*) was broadcast by BBC television in Britain (MANVELL, 1971, p. 131, n. 2), and a Spanish-English coproduction appeared in 1972 with such stars as Charlton Heston (Antony), Eric Porter (Enobarbus), John Castle (Octavius), Hildegard Neil (Cleopatra), and Jane Lapotaire (Charmian). See DAISNE (1975, 2:209).

Jane Lapotaire became Colin Blakely's Cleopatra in Jonathan Miller's production for the BBC and Time-Life television series in 1981. PEARCE (*CahiersE* 20, 1981, p. 109) praises the "minute attention to authentic detail" as a "satisfying experience" and the "rich costumes" as a "visual treat." Though this lavishness calls to mind

19th-c. un-Shn. spectacle, the intention, as Miller explained it, was to present "Egypt and Rome as the Elizabethans would have conceived them" (Pearce, p. 108). Another reviewer (ROTHWELL, *SQ* 32, 1981, p. 399) laments: "The possibility of using the camera to move back and forth between Rome and Egypt never gets thoroughly exploited"; that is, "conventional cutaways" were used. Miller shortened the play and "deliberately play[ed] down the political in favor of the private lives of the principals" (Rothwell). This Victorian approach did not result, however, in making the lovers greater or more heroic. Although Jane Lapotaire's performance was praised as so strong that it will "serve as models for actresses in the future" (Rothwell), she did not look right as Cleopatra. And Colin Blakely was, even without comparison with someone like Charlton Heston, "of Lilliputian stature" and seemed "cruelly miscast" (Rothwell). Pearce (p. 109) nevertheless found Blakely's performance moving in his "long drawn-out suicide." Emrys James as Enobarbus was most convincing. It seems that this production duplicated lapses of earlier stage renditions and did not even utilize the technical potential of film.

As for musical versions, DEAN (1964, p. 96) concedes that because the scripts have not survived, the connection with Sh. of an opera, oratorio, or cantata may be "tenuous or even imaginary." In some instances a composer's interest in Sh. is known, but the results are not. Verdi, for instance, "considered an 'Antony and Cleopatra', with libretto by [Arrigo] Boito" (Dean, p. 90) but apparently did not write it; Berlioz wrote a cantata on *Ant.*, but it was based on a French play and not on Sh.'s, though he "headed [it] with a Shakespearean quotation" (CUDWORTH, 1964, p. 77).

The earliest known opera based on Sh.'s *Ant.* was written in 1816 by Henry Rowley Bishop. Though CUDWORTH (1964, p. 75) calls Bishop the "most fearsome despoiler" of Sh., he concedes that, as a "general deranger of other men's work," Bishop only continues "the tradition begun with Davenant and Dryden." SQUIRE (1916, p. 76) thinks that the musical version by Count E. F. von Sayn-Wittgenstein (1883) and the ballet of Rodolphe Kreutzer, *Les amours d'Antoine et de Cléopâtre* (1808), "seem possibly, from their titles, to be founded on Shakespeare." Another operatic version was composed by Gian Francesco Malipiero in Florence (1938). DEAN (1964, p. 156) describes it as having a shortened libretto that cut "all the scenes outside Egypt except that on Pompey's galley (with Enobarbus's description of Cleopatra inserted) and a brief battle-piece for Actium." Samuel Barber composed the most recent opera of *Ant.*, his opus 40. The libretto (New York: G. Schirmer, 1966; rev. Franco Zeffirelli, 1975) says that it is Sh.'s text in a three-act version commissioned by the Metropolitan Opera Association at Lincoln Center, New York. The first performance inaugurated the new Met on 16 Sept. 1966.

Staging the Monument Scenes at the Globe

Early eds. and commentators spend little time discussing how Antony's death (4.15) and Cleopatra's capture (5.2) were originally staged. Scholars devote a certain amount of attention to 5.2 because SDs must be supplied to clarify the dialogue between

Proculeius and Cleopatra, but they do not examine the Monument scenes closely until they start trying to discover the structure and resources of the Globe playhouse. They then study 4.15 with particular care because its SDs call for the use of a platform other than the main stage and suggest the presence of flying machinery. Many of the attempts to determine how the Monument scenes were staged therefore appear in scholarship on Elizabethan-Jacobean playhouses rather than in eds.

Naturally, the proposed reconstructions of the Monument scenes' staging differ according to critics' opinions about the physical resources and form of the Globe. The reconstructions also depend on an assumption, often merely implicit, about the F1 text. If F1 allows us to discern how Sh. wanted the Monument scenes to be performed, then he must have written these scenes with a specific staging in mind. If F1 indicates how the Monument scenes were actually staged, then it must have been printed from a MS used at the Globe or include recollections of or notes from a performance; neither possibility is at all likely. Readers should bear in mind that many of the proposed stagings can be accepted only if one also accepts the underlying opinions about the kind of evidence provided by F1 and about the Globe's stage.

Both scenes contain textual problems relevant to the staging. Some argue that 4.15 was revised for performance. In 5.2, the SP *"Pro."* is repeated at 3238 and 3241, and there are no SDs for Cleopatra's capture. Critics must answer two questions to reconstruct the staging of Antony's death. First, how was the Monument represented, and where did the actors stand? Second, how was Antony raised aloft to Cleopatra? To reconstruct the staging of 5.2, critics must explain where the actors stood so that Cleopatra appeared safe in her Monument, and how the Romans entered to seize her.

ANTONY'S DEATH (4.15)

Staging and the Text of 4.15

Before the 20th c., eds. assume that Cleopatra and her attendant women stand in some elevated location—the *"aloft"* of 2996—to which they raise the dying Antony. SDs are added to indicate this position, and eds. evidently assume a two-level staging when they alter the dialogue to clarify Cleopatra's "I dare not" (3026) answer to Antony's request for a kiss. (Eds. add—see textual notes—"descend," "come down," "open," or "ope the gates" to either of the lovers' lines.) No one suggests that 4.15 presents *textual* difficulties related to staging until researchers working on the Elizabethan stage or on the staging of 4.15 advance this view. Only then do eds. and textual scholars begin to entertain the idea.

R. RHODES (1922, pp. 51–4) argues that "the death of Antony was not originally played in the balcony" but was performed there in a later production. He believes that F1 reflects "alterations for a revival—maybe when the Globe . . . was rebuilt" (p. 54). Rhodes asserts that, in the scenes before 4.15, lines containing the word *Monument* are hypermetrical, "which plainly shows that the words have been altered, as if they were added during a rapid revision" (p. 53). (In fact, only

2821 and 2973 are clearly hypermetrical.) Rhodes cites the repeated SP for Proculeius (3241) as further evidence that "some alteration or abridgement has taken place" (p. 53).

When JENKIN (1945) attempts to reconstruct 4.15's staging, he also discovers textual problems in F1. These problems are "the repetitions, inconsistencies, and contradictions in the earlier part of the scene" (p. 1). Jenkin believes that Diomedes's "Looke out o'th other side your Monument, His Guard haue brought him thither" (3008–9) does not make sense unless Antony enters some distance away ("thither") and on some "other side" of the Monument. (Jenkin claims [p. 12] that no one else has commented on this problem. In fact, LAWRENCE [1927, p. 120] observes that "the Guard, bearing Antony, come on below. . . . [So,] if Diomed entered from the back of the upper stage, Cleopatra would face him as he spoke, a position which would explain his reference to the other side." WILLIAMS [1954, pp. 70–1] and BECKERMAN [1962, p. 230] also advocate this blocking as a way to make sense of 3008. F1, however, gives no indication that Diomedes should enter aloft.) The repetitions that trouble Jenkin are Cleopatra's call to "draw" Antony up (3014–15, 3035–6) and Antony's "I am dying, Egypt, dying" (3022, 3050). Jenkin finds Cleopatra's speeches "I dare not" (3026–36) and "Heere's sport indeede" (3038–44) inappropriate and indecorous, and he remarks that "there is no 'exeunt' for Diomed and the Guard" (p. 2). These peculiarities, he concludes, appear because "there were two versions of the beginning of this scene, and . . . both versions (or parts of both) have got into the First Folio in a confused form" (p. 2). Jenkin's reconstruction of the two versions is based entirely on his efforts to imagine how Sh. planned to stage 4.15. He leaves it up to "textual experts" (p. 14) to explain how the versions were combined in F1.

According to Jenkin, most of the text to line 3037 ("*Ant.* Oh quicke, or I am gone.") was included in the first version, which was to be staged in close imitation of the action described in Plutarch (see p. 450). Cleopatra enters on the inner stage (a recess in the tiring-house facade, beneath the balcony) and speaks to Antony from behind some property gates. After refusing to admit him through these gates, she goes to the tiring-house balcony to hoist him up. Reconstructing the text of this first version, Jenkin deletes "*aloft*" from 2996, omits 3008, changes the "thither" of 3009 to "hither," and omits 3011–15 except for "O *Antony, Antony, Antony*" (3013). The first version otherwise follows F1, but it ends at 3037. Jenkin speculates that Sh., having written up to 3037, saw that hoisting Antony in front of the audience would cause delay and distraction and therefore rewrote the scene.

In the second version, Jenkin claims, Sh. followed North less literally. Cleopatra enters on the tiring-house balcony and speaks with Diomedes, who enters on the main stage. The "other side" of the Monument is represented by a property wall behind Cleopatra; she turns and looks over it as if to see Antony. The SD for Antony's entrance (3010) is omitted. At "let's draw him hither" (3015), Cleopatra and her attendants begin pulling on ropes that pass over the property wall. Lines 3016–37 are not spoken here. Cleopatra delivers the "Heere's sport indeede" speech (3038–43), and at 3043 Antony is lifted over the property wall. Cleopatra speaks

3044, and the women carry Antony to the inner stage below, descending a staircase within the tiring-house. Once below, Antony is placed on a bed, and the lovers speak the exchange of 3016–25. They continue with 3046 and follow F1 for the rest of the scene, except that Antony's second "dying" line (3050) is dropped. In this second version, Jenkin entirely omits Cleopatra's "I dare not" speech (3026–36) and Antony's "Oh quicke" line (3037), and he does not mention the SD at 3045. This reconstruction of 4.15 accounts for those aspects of the scene that Jenkin finds problematic, but it calls for extensive emendation and an elaborate staging. F1 includes no SDs that point to such a staging, and the scheme requires a more spacious balcony than there is reason to believe existed.

WILSON (ed. 1950, p. 128, n. 1) credits Jenkin for having "first brought to light" the repetition of the "draw" lines (3014–15, 3035–6) and the "dying" lines (3022, 3050) and suggests that "we are here confronted with notes for a proposed cut of some seventeen lines" (by Wilson's lineation); "Peace" (3016) through "Assist good Friends" (3036) were marked for deletion. Wilson also argues that "Cleopatra's speech once ended 'O *Antony, Antony, Antony*' " and that Cleopatra's first "draw" lines (3014–15) were written by the cutter, to replace those at 3035–6. The cutter's instructions also indicated how 3022 could be inserted in the text remaining, as 3050, in order to emphasize "Antony's dying condition." Wilson believes that F1 was printed from Sh.'s "draft" and that either the author or the bookholder made indications for a time-saving cut in this MS, "with a view to making a cut in the prompt-book later" (pp. 129–30).

RIDLEY (ed. 1954, pp. 195–6) agrees with Wilson that a cut may have been indicated by someone other than Sh., but he explains it differently. All the text, including 3014–15, was originally present, so by moving 3022 to 3050 the cutter could eliminate 3016–36 without having to rewrite 3035–6 as 3014–15. Ridley speculates that Sh.'s MS could have contained the redundancy of 3014–15 and 3035–6 if the playwright, having written up to 3015, had suddenly decided not to heave Antony aloft immediately but to insert 3016–36. Having done so, "either he forgot to delete the now worse than unwanted *Help, Charmian . . . hither*, or his indications of deletion were neglected."

GREG (1955, p. 403) also notes the repetitions but dislikes Wilson's explanation. (He does not refer to Ridley's account.) Greg argues that "there are other possible explanations, which do not involve the book-keeper and seem intrinsically more probable." He favors the conjecture that Sh., arriving at 3034, "became dissatisfied with what he had written" and struck out the dialogue from "O *Antony*" (3013) through "Demuring vpon me" (3034), knitting together what remained of 3013 and 3034 and relocating 3022.

THOMAS (1958, pp. 156–7) rejects Jenkin's staging plan and argues against a cut because it allows no time for raising Antony. She suggests that Cleopatra's two calls to draw Antony up indicate the beginning and end of "the prolonged process." Thomas admits that 4.15 could have included the repetitions when it was first written, but she thinks the scene was originally composed without 3015–36;

the passage was inserted later, to gain time for hoisting Antony up to the Monument. Thomas thus agrees that 4.15 was revised.

GALLOWAY (1958, pp. 330–5) argues that the difficulties in F1 have been exaggerated and do not warrant the conclusion that 4.15 was altered. Apart from the repetitions, "Jenkin's other objections to the scene are flimsy" (p. 332). Galloway offers interpretations to clarify the passages that trouble Jenkin and attempts to explain the two repetitions without speculating about the text. He concludes that "the Folio is the sole authority for *Antony and Cleopatra* and the case for its corruption in the First Monument Scene rests not on bibliographical evidence or critical acumen but on two 'repetitions' merely because they are repetitions" (p. 334).

Staging Antony's Death

The SDs *"aloft"* (2996) and *"They heaue Anthony aloft to Cleopatra"* (3045) indicate that Cleopatra stands in some elevated location, and that Antony is raised to this location. Critics examining how 4.15 was staged at the Globe concentrate on two problems that correspond to these SDs: They try to specify where Cleopatra and Antony enter and to explain exactly how Antony was raised.

Representing the Monument—Tiring-House or "Tent"?

Although critics agree that, when Cleopatra enters *"aloft"* (2996), she is on a level higher than that on which Antony enters, they disagree about where she actually stands. In other words, they disagree about how the Monument was represented. Two proposals are most widely accepted. In both Antony enters on the main, lower stage, but in one Cleopatra enters on the upper level of the tiring-house (at a window or on a balcony) and in the other she stands on a specially erected platform or scaffold (often identified with a "tent" structure). Only one other possibility has been proposed. SAUNDERS (1954, p. 74, and 1960, p. 412) suggests that *"aloft"* could have been the main stage level, "and the lower level could have been represented—why not?—by the yard." According to Saunders's proposal, Diomedes, Antony, and the Guard all enter in the "yard alley," an area surrounding the stage. When *"They heaue Anthony aloft to Cleopatra"* (3045), the dying general is lifted over the railing at the stage's edge. This plan has several advantages over performing 4.15 on the tiring-house balcony or a Monument property. Antony can be raised safely and simply, and there is ample space for performance. The scene is also clearly visible, as it might not be if played upstairs in the tiring-house, especially behind a railing. Moreover, since the main stage has distinct sides, Antony's entrance can be performed so that Diomedes' "Looke out o'th other side your Monument" (3008) makes perfect sense. Finally, there is no need to erect a large, sturdy Monument property. GARDNER (ed. 1963, p. 224) advocates Saunders's plan, but other commentators hardly mention it. STYAN (1967, p. 25, n. 1), defending the balcony staging against Saunders's view that the scene should be acted on the main stage, notes that, although "space on the balcony is cramped, the scene of Antony's death is one which calls for a minimum of movement, and its ritualistic importance would be pointed by placing it prominently on the upper level." The decisive questions about Saunders's proposal are whether players at the Globe really entered the yard for certain scenes and whether "aloft" can indicate the main stage when an entrance into the yard has no special SD. KING's research (1971, pp. 35–6) indicates that "aloft" always designates a location above the main stage.

Most critics favor a staging in which Cleopatra stands in a window or balcony on the tiring-house facade. To justify this placement, commentators must show that the location existed at the Globe (it is now doubted that there were windows in the facade [KING, 1971, p. 31]), that it provided enough room to play Antony's death, that the action would be visible from it, and that Antony could be raised to it. CAPELL (ed. 1768, similarly in the 1758 version with Garrick) is the first to specify Cleopatra's location, giving the SD, *"Enter, at a Window, above."* In a later note on 4.15, Capell explains "this upper stage" on which Cleopatra enters (1779 [1774], 1:51): "The platform was double, the hinder or back part of it rising some little matter above that in the front; and this serv'd them . . . for Cleopatra . . . to draw up Antony dying." SDs in subsequent eds. follow Capell's lead, but there are no other notes on the blocking of the first Monument scene before COLLIER (ed. 1843): "We are to suppose Cleopatra in her tomb, and elevated [Collier does not say how] at the back of the stage." DELIUS (ed. 1856) also describes the Monument as a structure elevated at the rear of the stage, adding that it has an opening at which Cleopatra and her women appear. BLUMHOF (ed. 1870) has Cleopatra enter on the rear stage (similarly BINDER, 1939, p. 77) or on a projecting structure provided with side entrances, apparently a balcony on the facade of the tiring-house. R. RHODES (1922, pp. 51–4) advocates a staging in the balcony, as do CHAMBERS (1923, 3:115–16), LAWRENCE (1927, pp. 119–20), and HARRISON (1951, pp. 221–2). Only Lawrence refers to the way the scene should be managed, noting the difficulty of Diomedes' "other side" line (3008) and making some suggestions about Antony's hoisting (see pp. 785–7).

GRANVILLE-BARKER (1930; 1946, 1:403–5) is the first to examine closely how the scene must be performed if the balcony represents the Monument. He identifies several problems that must be overcome if the scene is played there: assuming that ropes were used to raise Antony, he fears that the balustrade along the front of the balcony would have made it difficult to draw the general onto the upper station. He is also concerned about (p. 405) "the effect of the rest of the scene, of Antony's death and Cleopatra's lament over him, played behind the balustrade as behind bars." He concludes, "The balustrade must, one presumes, have been removed for the occasion or made to swing open." Such an arrangement would have been convenient, but Granville-Barker offers no reason to think it actually existed. (See p. 785.)

ADAMS (1942, pp. 346–9) gives a more detailed explanation of how 4.15 could be staged in the upper story of the tiring-house. The tiring-house's facade was concave, he claims, and its second story held a balcony flanked by large bay windows (for whose existence there is no documentary evidence). Cleopatra first appears at one window, speaks with Diomedes when he comes on below, and crosses the balcony to the other window in response to his "other side" line (3008). (Most proponents of a balcony staging consider such a minor movement, or even a simple turning of the head, sufficient to make sense of 3008, unlike advocates of a tent staging, who think the Monument's sides must be more clearly defined.) If Antony's death were played in a window, it would be even less visible than behind a balustrade, but Adams solves this problem by not lowering Antony to the floor of the upper-story stage. Raised lying flat on his shield, the general is balanced on the windowsill for the rest of the scene. (See p. 785.)

WILSON (ed. 1950, p. 230) introduces the first "tent" plan into the debate. He asserts that the proposals of Granville-Barker, Jenkin, and Adams all require an inner stage behind the balcony's main platform in order to have room for the action. (This is true of Jenkin, uncertain with Granville-Barker, and clearly not the case in Adams's solution, though Adams elsewhere argues that many scenes were played on recessed inner stages at the main level and in the second story of the tiring-house.) Wilson complains that the use of an inner stage in 4.15 "ignores the *textual* fact . . . that dead bodies have to be carried away [to comply with 3107] . . . a thing unnecessary upon the inner stages with their curtains." For this reason alone, Wilson suggests a radically new way to stage both Monument scenes: "Sh.'s Monument was a square painted wooden structure, with a barred gate in front . . . and a flat roof, erected by servitors at the end of 4.14 on the outer stage over the central trap (through which Cleo. etc. [sic] could enter and thence climb to the roof by a concealed stair), and immediately underneath the 'heavens', above which was the winch for 'heaving Ant. aloft', while his body was, I assume, borne off down the stair at the end of 4.15. If so, it would remain in position during the brief interval scene (5.1), be inexpensive to make, and quick to erect." Wilson gives no evidence to support these claims. RIDLEY (ed. 1954), in a separate appendix on the staging of the Monument scenes, opposes Wilson's suggestion and explains the disadvantages of a property Monument: "It might at first seem to help" with the "other side" line (3008), since Cleopatra can actually go to the opposite side of the structure to see Antony enter at the second door, but "this is more than counterbalanced by the fact that the entry of the guard with Antony [from one of the stage doors] would be obscured [by the Monument] from some of the audience. And there is no real difficulty in staging the episode with the existing stage" (p. 248). Ridley also notes that Wilson's reason for using a property Monument "rests on [the] unwarranted assumption" that dead bodies were absolutely never carried off the inner stage but only shielded by closing the curtains. His general objections to the tent solution are even more telling. They identify the main problems that advocates of the "tent" staging must resolve: the structure, if sturdy, could not be set up quickly; it would occupy a large portion of the stage during 5.1, a fairly long scene; and it would not help much in staging Cleopatra's capture.

Such a detailed comparison of the tent and balcony proposals is rare in the commentary on these scenes; most critics adopt one or the other theory with little justification of their preference. Several variations on the tent staging are advanced in the 1950s, but no critic tries to answer Ridley's objections. W. SMITH (1951, pp. 27–9; 1975, pp. 44–7) thinks that 4.15 was performed using a low scaffold that had no balustrade and was reached by four or five steps at the side; the scaffold sometimes served as a dais in other plays. Antony could easily be slid onto the top of this structure, and it would provide a clearly visible location for his death. Only BECKERMAN (1962, p. 230) refers to this suggestion, objecting that "wherever scaffolds are otherwise used . . . the term 'aloft' or 'above' is never introduced."

HODGES (1953, pp. 58–9) advocates a tent staging of the sort Wilson proposes. He describes an "impermanent special structure" (p. 58) erected against the facade of the tiring-house, between the two doors. This "small temporary structure" (p. 60) has a solid roof on which several persons can stand, and its front and sides may be hung with curtains. Its roof is slightly lower than the floor of the balcony, and actors can step down to it when the central balustrade is removed. Whether Hodges believes this structure remained on stage during the entire performance or was set up between 4.14 and 4.15 is not clear. He points out the advantages such a structure offers (visibility, clarification of 3008, easy raising of Antony), notes that it could be used for actions that other critics assign to the inner stage, and suggests that it may have existed at the Globe as a vestige of street theaters' "booths."

NAGLER (1958, pp. 61–2) endorses Hodges's proposal, describing the tent as a permanent structure projecting from the tiring-house facade. He also notes that Ludwig Tieck proposes a similar arrangement in his account of Sh.'s stage in *Der junge Tischlermeister* (1836). WICKHAM (1963, 2:39, and 1969, pp. 142–3) also advocates staging the Monument scenes with a tent, although he is unspecific about the structure's form. In 1954 WILLIAMS (pp. 70–4) offers a balcony plan and does not even mention the tent, but in 1968 (pp. 73–5) he describes a staging very similar to what Hodges suggests. GURR (1970, p. 98) endorses a tent plan, assumes that the structure was low enough so that Antony could be raised by hand, and indicates that it could have been either separate from or attached to the tiring-house. THOMSON (1983, p. 52) is the only critic besides Wilson who clearly opts for a tent structure that stands separate from the tiring-house and also considers how the actors are supposed to get on top of it. Cleopatra and her women would have reached its top by a sort of external staircase ("upstairs treads concealed from most of the audience").

HOTSON (1959, pp. 201–4) proposes a tent plan based on his singular theory about the Globe's structure. According to Hotson's reconstruction of the playhouse, the tiring-house is used only for seating. The actors enter and exit the stage from two "houses" of scaffolding, erected on opposite sides of the stage. The sides of these houses can be curtained to represent closed rooms or buildings, and the actors perform some scenes in them. Hotson declares that the Monument scenes take place on the upper story of one of the houses, to which Antony is lifted by hand. WEINER (1961, pp. 15–34) advances an equally ingenious proposal, describing a tent structure that would be sturdy, yet quick to erect and disassemble. The rear edge of the tent's solid roof is attached with hinges to the edge of the balcony, so it can be folded down against the tiring-house wall when not in use. The tent's two legs fold up behind it. The structure is set up in the same way one raises a table's drop leaf. Weiner's device may seem too ingenious to be believed, and there is no evidence that it actually existed at the Globe, but Sabbattini recommends a similar construction for large trap doors, as RONAYNE (1981, pp. 219–21) reports.

E. RHODES (1971, pp. 41–6) describes how the Monument scenes could have been staged on the balcony of the "Theatrum Orbi" depicted in Robert Fludd's *Ars memoriae* (1619). Rhodes will not identify Fludd's illustration as the Globe or the Blackfriars, but he claims that the practicability of staging the Monument scenes in the Theatrum shows that they were supposed to be performed using a balcony. Since Rhodes avoids saying that the Globe looked like Fludd's illustration, it is hard to see what this argument has to do with a performance at the Globe.

After RIDLEY (ed. 1954) presents the main objections to a property Monument, advocates of a staging in the balcony spend little time arguing that the balcony is the best location for 4.15. Instead they concentrate on the two main difficulties of this location: making Antony's death visible and raising him to the balcony.

GRANVILLE-BARKER's (1930; 1946, 1:403–5) idea of a removable balustrade is not very popular with later critics. I. SMITH (1956, p. 128) believes that this convenience would be desirable, allowing adaptation of balcony scenes as they call for more or less visibility, but he does not attempt to prove that the balustrade at the Globe really could be removed. BECKERMAN (1962, p. 231) thinks such an arrangement could have existed, but he provides no evidence that it actually did. Most critics who argue for staging 4.15 in the balcony try to make Antony's death visible despite the obstruction. JENKIN (1945, p. 8) brings Antony down to the main stage to die (see pp. 779–80), and ADAMS (1942, p. 347, n. 18) refuses to lower him to the upper-level floor, balancing him (on his shield) in a windowsill. HOSLEY (1964, p. 64) makes Antony visible over the balustrade by seating him in a chair, in which he is also raised to the balcony. I. SMITH (1956, p. 151) has Antony placed on a couch, after he has been hoisted up.

Raising Antony to the Balcony

The great advantage of a staging that uses a property Monument is that Antony can be lifted to its top by the Guard, for such a structure is usually thought to be relatively low. Only WILSON (ed. 1950, p. 230) advocates using ropes or flying machinery in conjunction with a property Monument. In contrast, all the proponents of a balcony staging assume that some mechanical aid must be used to raise Antony. The exceptions are CHARNEY (1957, p. 156) and THOMSON (1988, pp. 87–9). In an article on imagery, Charney digresses to assert that Antony could be lifted by hand, "even if the Elizabethan balcony were eight to twelve feet above the main stage," but does not explain how such a feat could be accomplished. Thomson also argues that Antony could be raised to balcony level by his men, suggesting that Sh. wanted the action to be awkward: (p. 87) "Antony is lifted up to Cleopatra in the gallery but not on to it, and . . . is lowered again to the main stage after he dies"; Cleopatra (p. 88) "in a window or behind a balustrade," leans out to embrace

Antony as his men hold him up to her from 3046 to 3074. Thomson believes (p. 88) "the distance to be covered would be reduced to a manageable ten feet or so," but it is hard to see how even that distance could be negotiated. Because Antony's men cannot be expected to raise him a full ten feet in the air, Cleopatra must bend down to reach him. But since she is doing so over a balustrade or windowsill, she can hardly reach any lower than the level of her feet. Even if we assume the balcony floor to be only eight feet higher than the main stage, this plan makes for a most precarious, strained embrace.

In the early reconstructions of the Globe, scholars usually assume that there was machinery for flying effects in the part of the tiring-house that projected over the stage. LAWRENCE (1927, pp. 119–20) has no doubt that a winch in the huts, used for descents of the gods, was employed to hoist Antony up. He also introduces the example most often cited to clarify the hoisting, a scene from Haughton's *Englishmen for My Money* (1598) in which the line coming down from the winch must pass close to the edge of the balcony, so that someone standing there can reach out to the person being raised.

GRANVILLE-BARKER (1930; 1946, 1:404) worries that "the hoisting of a full-grown man ten or twelve feet in the air asks some strength. However, this could be provided ostensibly by 'her Maides', actually by stagehands helping from behind the curtains." He seems to think that the women in the balcony haul Antony up with a line that passes from their hands directly down to the stage, rather than one that rises to a winch or passes through a pulley above the balcony. ADAMS (1942, p. 349) believes flying machinery was used, but he also observes the weakness of the boy actors and suggests that Cleopatra and her maids pull on dummy ropes, while the line actually bearing Antony is taken up by a winch in the huts. HOSLEY (1964, p. 63) and I. SMITH (1956, p. 151) accept this proposal. Smith points out another reason why Antony cannot be raised without a winch or pulley: "If the ropes originated at a point no higher than window-sill or balcony rail, the last two or three feet would be an undignified scramble to get the dying man over the edge and safely in."

Recent studies of Elizabethan and Jacobean playhouses have questioned whether flying machinery was available in the public theaters. BECKERMAN (1962, p. 106) argues that no such equipment was available at the Globe, and although KING (1971, p. 148) cautions that "there is no proof" for Beckerman's positive banning of the gear, he concedes that "such machinery was not *required* in the vast majority of plays, which suggests that it was also not available in the vast majority of playhouses." THOMSON (1983, pp. 41–2), however, says that flying effects were not unusual. Those critics who doubt the presence of flying machinery at the Globe have not examined how this limitation affects the staging of 4.15. King says nothing, and Beckerman concludes only (p. 231) that "Antony was raised in a manner which, we must assume, was not ludicrous."

Whether the ropes go up to a winch, through a pulley, or directly from the stage to the hands of the women in the balcony, one must resolve a second problem—how Antony is attached to the lifting line and what he is suspended in.

ADAMS (1942, p. 349) suggests that Antony could have been carried in and hoisted up while lying "on his great shield." WILSON (ed. 1950) adopts this idea in his SDs. I. SMITH (1956, p. 151, n. 3) though usually loyal to Adams's proposals, objects to the idea that, once Antony is hoisted to Cleopatra's level, he remains lying on his shield, balanced in a window. HOSLEY (1964, pp. 63–5) proposes that a chair be used to carry Antony onstage and hold him while he is winched up to the balcony. A chair can be suspended easily and safely, so that Antony will not tumble out, and the audience can see him over the balustrade because he remains sitting in the chair once he reaches the balcony. Hosley notes that SDs in other plays by Sh. direct that ill or wounded characters be borne in on chairs.

REES (1953, pp. 91–3) suggests that a description of Antony's hoisting in the 1607 ed. of Samuel Daniel's *Tragedie of Cleopatra* reflects the way Antony was raised at the Globe. The passage is not included in the 1594 ed., and Rees argues that certain elements of the description are too technical to have been invented by Daniel and are not indicated in Plutarch. She therefore suggests that Daniel saw a production of *Ant.* and based his description on the staging of 4.15. In this description (sig. O[=G] 8ᵛ), Cleopatra "drawes [Antony] vp in rowles of taffatie," which Rees understands "to mean that lengths of taffeta (presumably thrown from Cleopatra's window) were wrapped round Antony and that he was actually drawn up by means of them" (p. 92). Further on, the passage relates how Charmion and Eras "Tugd at the pulley." There were two pauses in the lifting ("The frame stood still, the body at a stay," and "then againe It comes to stay"), and Antony hung, "showring out his blood On th'under lookers." Rees argues that "the dramatic pauses and the picture of the suspended body . . . might be a reminiscence of the way the . . . scene was actually managed . . . or perhaps when he saw it such hitches occurred rather by accident than design but impressed Daniel as life-like and effective" (p. 93). R. WALKER (1953, p. 349) supports the suggestion that Antony was lifted in cloths thrown out from above, arguing that a similar staging in 1898 may reflect a traditional way of handling the scene. Though cautious in accepting Rees's proposal that Daniel saw *Ant.*, THOMAS (1958, pp. 153–7) remarks that in Daniel's description "the gradualness of the procedure is especially emphasized" (p. 157). Thomas believes this supports her claim that the hoisting began at 3015 and lasted until about 3045. LAMB (1980) uses the passage in Daniel's play to reconstruct the staging of 4.15. She agrees that Daniel may have seen *Ant.* and asserts that "the passage seems to be a naive reproduction of winch-and-gallery staging" (p. 183). Lamb does not discuss the mechanical details but suggests that "the two pauses in the hoist operation . . . were deliberate," misleadingly implying that Rees does not mention this possibility. Lamb argues that (p. 184) "If . . . the Folio repetitions are intentional, the stops in the hoisting are cued to particular lines in Shakespeare's text," and she concludes (p. 185) that Antony hung in midair during 3028–34 and 3038–43.

CLEOPATRA'S CAPTURE (5.2)

Most critics since THEOBALD (ed. 1733) assume that Sh. intended to stage Cleopatra's capture as it is described by Plutarch, since the dialogue in 5.2 is modeled after the conversations reported in the *Life of Antony* (see pp. 451–2). Many critics also propose stagings in which the Monument is represented by the same location as in 4.15, even though 5.2 has no SD "aloft" or "above." Proculeius's exclamation at 3246–8 is obviously spoken as he disarms the queen, and the staging of the rest of the scene is clear. The problematic section runs from Cleopatra's entrance to 3246, and the crucial moment is at 3241, where the SP "*Pro.*" is repeated and the dialogue indicates that the Romans have entered the Monument.

The Repeated SP at 3241

Most explanations for the repetition of "*Pro.*" have some bearing on the staging of 5.2.

A few critics do not believe the repetition originated during the printing of F1. GRANVILLE-BARKER (1930; 1946, 1:406, n. 32) observes that "the unnatural hiatus between Proculeius' two speeches, if they are both his . . . *may* point to some change in staging, or in the stage itself, or to the shifting of the play from one theater to another of different resources." GREG (1955, p. 400) notes that "If Shakespeare had not made up his mind respecting the mechanics of the action, or if he thought it best to leave them to the actors to work out on stage, he would naturally leave a blank for the direction and repeat the speaker's name." Similarly, JONES (ed. 1977, p. 275) proposes that Sh. "may have left [the stage business] deliberately vague so as to make it adaptable to different stage conditions."

Most eds. and critics reassign 3241–2 (see textual notes). MALONE (ed. 1790) states that the attribution of these lines to Proculeius "was an error of the compositor." RIDLEY (ed. 1954, pp. 254–5) suggests that "The erroneous speech-heading was not just a matter of careless substitution, but rather of the transference of a proper name from text to speech-heading." Line 3241, which Ridley thinks was Gallus's, began, "*Proculeius*, you see how easily . . ." and the proper name was mistaken for a speech prefix. Ridley does not explain why the SP for Gallus was ignored.

A few critics assign both 3240 and 3241–2 to Proculeius (see textual notes) and argue that an intervening passage was omitted. JENKIN (1945, p. 9) asserts that "something must have been spoken by Gallus (or by someone else) to account for the second *Pro.* A mere stage direction would not justify the second prefix." HINMAN (1963, 2:509, n. 1) and HOSLEY (1964, pp. 69–70) agree that 3241–2 is correctly assigned to Proculeius, but they believe only a SD is missing. They explain that a SP may indeed be repeated after nothing more than a SD, and Hosley provides examples of this practice from the Folio and other contemporary plays. Hinman attributes the omission of the SD to an error in casting off, noting that (2:508) "we are concerned with a decidedly 'tight' page . . . a page that could hardly accommodate the stage direction so obviously wanting."

THISELTON (1899, p. 26) mentions another possible reason for the repetition. The new SP at 3241 may indicate "the commencement of a new scene, the interval being taken up with the movements of Proculeius."

Staging the Capture

If Plutarch is followed, Cleopatra must seem safe in her Monument while she speaks to the Romans outside it, and some of them must enter unnoticed so as to surprise and capture her.

From F2 (1632) through ROWE (ed. 1714), 3241–2 are given to Charmian, and no SD for the capture is inserted. POPE (ed. 1725) assigns 3241 to Charmian and 3242 to Proculeius but makes no other change. THEOBALD (ed. 1733) opens the discussion of 5.2's staging by adding SDs and a note. Cleopatra enters "above," apparently on a balcony. After 3240, "Gallus, *and guard, ascend the Monument by a Ladder, and enter at a back-Window.*" Gallus speaks 3241, Proculeius 3242. Cleopatra draws a dagger, and "*The Monument is open'd*; Proculeius *rushes, in and disarms the Queen.*" These SDs correspond to Plutarch's account, as Theobald points out, but it is not entirely clear how the actions he indicates should be performed on stage.

HANMER's (ed. 1744) SDs are similar to Theobald's, but he omits the reference to "*a back-Window*" by which Gallus and the guard enter. JOHNSON (ed. 1765) retains it. He gives both 3240 and 3241–2 to Proculeius but places the SD to ascend the Monument after 3241, not 3240. 3241 thus becomes an instruction to Gallus rather than an exclamation on success. Johnson also suggests that 3241 has been "misplaced" and would better follow 3232, allowing Gallus more time to enter the Monument.

CAPELL (ed. 1768 and the 1758 version with Garrick) assigns 3241–2 to Proculeius but marks them as commands to Gallus, who waits while Proculeius sneaks into the Monument. Capell also seems to abandon the two-level staging he assumed at 2996. He does not add "above" or "below" to the entrances, and his SDs do not indicate that the Romans ascend the Monument. The scene is located in "*A Room in the Monument.*" The Romans enter "*to the Door of the Monument, without,*" and while "Gallus *maintains converse with* Cleopatra," Proculeius and the Guard exit and "*Re-enter, into the Monument, from behind.*" A later note of Capell's (1779 [1774], 1:52–3), however, suggests that he may have considered a two-level staging of 5.2, for he describes the general function of the "upper stage" and remarks on its utility in "the monument scenes in this act." Yet Capell's SDs seem designed for a staging in which both the Romans and Cleopatra stand on the main platform, negotiating through a door until the queen is captured.

MALONE (ed. 1790) adopts some of Capell's SDs. The Romans enter "*to the gates of the Monument*" instead of its "*Door,*" and Cleopatra's speech at 3201–8 is preceded by the SD "*within.*" Malone explains that "Cleopatra and her attendants speak all their speeches till the queen is seized, within the monument," but he does not explicitly say how the Monument is represented. Apparently Cleopatra stands behind some property gates erected at the rear of the stage, which the soldiers approach after entering through a stage door. Commanded by Gallus, who delivers 3241–2, Proculeius climbs up a ladder to the balcony and, *"having descended, came behind* CLEOPATRA. *Some of the guard unbar and open the gates."* Most subsequent eds. follow Malone's staging, but COLLIER (ed. 1843) places Cleopatra upstairs. His SDs do not indicate that Cleopatra descends to the main stage after her capture. DELIUS (ed. 1856) and BLUMHOF (ed. 1870) add SDs similar to Collier's, but Blumhof argues against using a ladder to scale the Monument. He proposes that Proculeius exit the stage below, ascend by the stairs within the tiring-house, and enter on the upper stage to surprise Cleopatra.

Several 20th-c. commentators and eds. examine 5.2's staging, but their remarks are usually less detailed than their comments on 4.15. The stagings proposed differ on three points: whether Cleopatra stands on the balcony or on the main stage, whether some sort of barrier separates her from the Romans, and whether the Romans climb the Monument in view of the audience.

If Cleopatra enters on the balcony, the first part of 5.2 is easily visible and audible, and yet the queen seems safe from the Romans. But if she is captured on the balcony, Cleopatra must either be brought down to the main stage or her interview with Caesar and the climactic suicide must be performed upstairs. GRAN-VILLE-BARKER (1930) first notes this problem: having stated (1946, 1:405) that "obviously she is not still upon . . . an upper stage," he argues against having the Guard scale the Monument so as to descend and enter behind her, adding (p. 406, n. 31), "If Cleopatra had to be *brought* down to the lower stage, it would be ten times worse." RIDLEY (ed. 1954, p. 252) and I. SMITH (1956, *SQ*, p. 169) explain the obvious disadvantages of bringing Cleopatra to the main stage. Yet several 20th-c. scholars still accept a blocking in which Cleopatra is captured above. R. RHODES (1922, p. 51) believes that part of 5.2 takes place on the balcony, and CHAMBERS (1923, 3:115–16) and HARRISON (1951, p. 223) casually remark that the scene is played there. Some later critics link the balcony location with an onstage ascent of the Monument. BINDER (1939, p. 81) states that the soldiers climb to the upper stage, and ADAMS (1942, pp. 349–50, n. 19), who believes that bay windows flanked the balcony, imagines that "the Roman soldiers who slipped into the well-secured Monument while Cleopatra, in one bay-window, was held in conversation by Proculeius on the outer stage (V.ii), clambered up by way of the rope inadvertently left dangling (in IV.xv) from the other bay-window." E. RHODES (1971, pp. 46–8) also advocates a staging in the gallery, basing his plan on the "Theatrum Orbi" depicted in Fludd's *Ars memoriae*. He expects the latter part of 5.2 to be played on the main stage, but he does not believe a SD is missing; the dialogue alone, he thinks, makes the descent to the main stage clear.

Some critics believe a tent structure should represent the Monument in 5.2 as well as in 4.15. In WILSON's (ed. 1950) SDs, Cleopatra stands inside a property Monument and speaks through a gate on its front. To capture her the guards climb ladders to the structure's roof and descend through a trap door. Cleopatra thus begins 5.2 on the main stage, and after the Monument is opened the actors can use the entire platform for the rest of the scene. HOTSON (1959, p. 201) also uses a property Monument but claims that "from the opening of 4.13 . . . the upper room of the monument is the scene of all the action involving Cleopatra." She does not even descend for her suicide. WILLIAMS (1968, p. 78) places Cleopatra on a property Monument like that of Hodges, to be captured "by a sudden movement and entry," but adds that "It is in her capture, and in being passed from hand to hand, that she is brought down to the main stage level."

Wilson's staging resembles Malone's in that Cleopatra enters and speaks from behind property gates and is captured by guards who scale the Monument and descend to enter behind her. I. SMITH (1956, *SQ*, p. 169) also believes gates were used, but he places them so as to close off the inner stage, thus following Malone's directions even more closely than does Wilson. JENKIN (1945, p. 10) too installs gates on the lower level, but he does not have the guards climb up to the Monument's top. A property wall is erected at the rear of the balcony and Gallus and the Guard climb over it as if they have scaled the Monument from the side invisible to the audience. They capture Cleopatra on the lower stage, after descending by the tiring-house staircase. This elaborate scheme requires a very spacious balcony. In SISSON's (ed. 1954) SDs, Cleopatra enters on the balcony, but after Proculeius asks to negotiate she descends to parley from behind gates. Property gates do make the Monument seem secure, and they correspond to the description in Plutarch; RIDLEY (ed. 1954, p. 251), however, explains their drawbacks: "Where, for the first thirty-five lines of the scene, are Cleopatra and her attendants supposed to be? Malone assumed that they were on the inner stage, with a barred gate across the opening. That is all very well for the dialogue with Proculeius, and it is according to North. But it is very far from well for Cleopatra's opening speech. . . . Nor does it make effective the entry of the guard, who would be even less visible [than Cleopatra]."

In SAUNDERS's (1954, pp. 72–4) reconstruction of 5.2, the entire lower stage represents the Monument's interior. Cleopatra stands on the main stage and parleys with Proculeius, who stands in the yard alley on one side of the stage. Gallus and the guards climb onto the main stage from the other side to surprise and capture the queen. GARDNER (ed. 1963, p. 224) endorses this proposal, and JONES (ed. 1977) seems sympathetic to it.

FURNESS (ed. 1907, p. 338) records none of the staging proposals for 5.2: "I see no need of any stage-direction at all. It is, at least for me, quite sufficient to see that the Romans rush in and seize the Queen. In these thrilling moments, how they got in, I neither know nor care." HARRISON's (ed. 1937) SDs indicate that he agrees, and although HODGES (1953, p. 60) proposes using a Monument property in 4.15, he says of 5.2 that "most of it, if not all, took place on the main stage, the monument being understood." RIDLEY (ed. 1954, pp. 253–4) defends and elaborates this approach. The main stage represents the Monument's interior. Cleopatra and her maids enter "through the curtains of the inner stage, to mark that they come from another room in the monument," and Proculeius is admitted as "a single emissary." At 3241, "the guards break in from behind, either through the curtains or through the ordinary doors." PHIALAS's (ed. 1955) SDs correspond to this plan, and HOSLEY (1964, pp. 67–8) and BARROLL (1969, p. 216) also endorse it.

CONCLUSION

The reconstructed stagings of the Monument scenes often tell us more about scholars' efforts to determine the physical conditions of Elizabethan-Jacobean playhouses than about how 4.15 and 5.2 were originally performed. By excluding those stagings that seem least likely, however, we may determine how these scenes were probably presented.

If the tentlike Monument that some critics describe was a permanent feature of Sh.'s stage, it would surely have been used in 4.15. The presence of such a structure at the Globe, however, seems questionable. The advantages of a temporary Monument property are outweighed by its drawbacks. Such a structure clarifies the "other side" line, but 3008 can be made sensible in a balcony staging if Proculeius enters at one door and indicates Antony coming in the other. And although a property Monument allows us to raise Antony without ropes, it would be easier to arrange gear for hoisting Antony than to erect a special platform for the sole purpose of raising him without such gear. If, then, 4.15 was indeed staged aloft, the tiring-house balcony most probably represented Cleopatra's Monument.

The difficulties of a balcony staging are not insuperable. Although we may reject the assumption of an inner stage behind the main part of the balcony, there will still be enough room for several persons. As for the balustrade's obscuring Antony's death, Hosley's suggestion that Antony sit in a chair is an easy solution that can be adopted even if the chair is not used for raising him. The most serious problem in a balcony staging is getting Antony up. Even if the balcony floor were only eight feet above the main stage and several people were helping, lifting Antony that high and then getting him over the balustrade would not be easy or decorous. The problem is not Antony's weight, but the height to which he must be raised. Though the dialogue indicates that the action should appear difficult, it should not be so hard to execute that there is a chance of failure, or so clumsy that it arouses laughter.

If flying machinery existed at the Globe, it would surely have been used in 4.15. If a winch was not available, a simple pulley, a hook, or perhaps even tackle could be installed above the balcony so that Cleopatra and her maids could pull down on the line, using their own weight to raise Antony. Such an arrangement seems much more likely than a line passing directly down to the stage from the hands of the people in the balcony, for that solution would oblige the boy actors to lean over the balustrade and pull Antony up hand over hand. If the balcony were particularly spacious, they might back up to pull on a line going over the balustrade, but for the last few feet they would still have to lean precariously over the balcony's edge. We must also consider that, with a rope passing directly from balcony to stage, Antony risks being dragged up the face of the tiring-house or catching on the underside of a projecting balcony. As for the container in which Antony is raised, Hosley's chair seems the most practical choice if flying machinery is assumed, but a lighter, flexible container, perhaps a cloth sling recalling the taffeta described by Daniel, might have been used if Antony was drawn up using a pulley or a line passing directly from the actors in the balcony down to the stage.

It is inconceivable—if only because of the number of characters in the scene —that all of 5.2 was performed on the balcony or a property Monument's roof; if we cannot bring Cleopatra down from such a location, she should not be captured aloft. Since bringing her down takes time and requires us to change Cleopatra's entrance SD and add other SDs after her capture, we cannot admit such a reconstruction. Cleopatra must enter on the main stage. Can she do so behind property gates massive enough to make her seem safe from the Romans? Hardly. We would lose most of her speeches until the gates were opened, and if the Guard entered behind the same gates the audience would not understand what was happening at 3241. If the Romans actually climbed up to the balcony in view of the audience, as Malone proposes, the audience would realize that Cleopatra was about to be captured, but this arrangement requires adding a SD based only on the description in Plutarch. Performing the scene as Furness suggests, on the main stage and without gates, seems the most practical, effective staging for 5.2. The earlier speeches are easily seen and heard, and the only SD to be added is the entrance of the Romans between 3240 and 3241.

BIBLIOGRAPHY

The place of publication is London unless otherwise indicated. For editions of *Antony and Cleopatra*, see pp. xiv ff.; for abbreviations, see pp. xxv ff.

Abbott, E[dwin] A. *A Shakespearian Grammar.* 3rd ed., rev. & enl. 1870. (Rpt. New York: Dover, 1966. 1st ed. 1866.)

Aboul-Enein, A. M. "Cleopatra in French and English Drama from Jodelle to Shakespeare." Trinity Coll., Dublin, diss., 1954.

Abraham, Lyndall. "Alchemical Reference in *Antony and Cleopatra.*" *Sydney Studies in English* 8 (1982–3), 100–4.

Absens. "[*Ant.* 921.]" 9 *N&Q* 9 (3 May 1902), 342.

Acharya, Shanta. "An Analysis of Sylvia Plath's 'Edge.' " *Literary Criterion* 14, No. 3 (1979), 52–7.

Acheson, Arthur. *Mistress Davenant: The Dark Lady of Shakespeare's Sonnets.* London, New York, & Chicago, 1913.

Adams, F. " 'Antony and Cleopatra', [578]." 8 *N&Q* 2 (8 Oct. 1892), 283.

———. "Arm-gaunt." 8 *N&Q* 2 (26 Nov. 1892), 426.

Adams, John Cranford. *The Globe Playhouse: Its Design and Equipment.* 2nd ed. New York, 1961. (Rpt. New York: Barnes & Noble, 1973. 1st ed. 1942.)

Adams, Joseph Quincy. *A Life of William Shakespeare.* Boston, 1923.

Adams, Martha L. "The Greek Romance and William Shakespeare." *Studies in English* (Mississippi) 9 (1967), 43–52.

Adams, Robert M. *Proteus, His Lies, His Truth: Discussions of Literary Translation.* New York, 1973.

Addis, John, Jr. " 'Embosed' and 'Imbost.' " 4 *N&Q* 1 (16 May 1868), 454–5.

Adee, A. A. "Cleopatra's 'Billiards.' " *The Literary World* 14 (21 Apr. 1883), 131.

Adelman, Janet. *The Common Liar: An Essay on* Antony and Cleopatra. Yale Stud. in Eng. 181. New Haven, 1973.

Adlard, John. "Cleopatra as Isis." *Archiv* 212 (1975), 324–8.

Adler, Fritz. "Das Verhältniß von Shakespeare's 'Antony and Cleopatra' zu Plutarch's Biographie des Antonius." *SJ* 31 (1895), 263–317.

Ahern, Matthew J., Jr. "The Roman History Play, 1585–1640: A Study Indicating How Plays Dealing with Roman History Reflect Changing Political and Social Attitudes in England During this Period." Tulane Univ. diss., 1963. (*DA* 24 [1963], 3319A.)

Albright, Evelyn May. *Dramatic Publication in England, 1580–1640.* MLA Monograph Ser. 2. New York, 1927.

Alden, Raymond M. *Shakespeare.* Master Spirits of Lit. New York, 1922.

Aldus, Paul J. "Analogical Probability in Shakespeare's Plays." *SQ* 6 (1955), 397–414.

————. Letter. *SQ* 7 (1956), 133–4.

Alexander, Peter. *Shakespeare.* Home Univ. Libr. 252. 1964.

————. *Shakespeare's Life and Art.* 1939. (Repub. New York, 1961. Rpt. Westport, Conn.: Greenwood, 1979.)

Allen, Charles. *Notes on the Bacon-Shakespeare Question.* Boston, 1900.

Allen, Shirley S. *Samuel Phelps and Sadler's Wells Theatre.* Middletown, Conn., 1971.

Altmann, Ruth. "Shakespeare's Craftsmanship: A Study of His Use of Plutarch in *Antony and Cleopatra.*" Univ. of Washington diss., 1969. (*DA* 30 [1969], 2474A.)

Alvis, John [E.]. "The Coherence of Shakespeare's Roman Plays." *MLQ* 40 (1979), 114–34.

————. "The Religion of Eros: A Re-Interpretation of *Antony and Cleopatra.*" *Renascence* 30 (1978), 185–98.

————. "Shakespeare's Roman Tragedies: Self-Glorification and the Incomplete Polity." Univ. of Dallas diss., 1973. (*DA* 35 [1974], 1034A.)

————. "Unity of Subject in Shakespeare's Roman Plays." *Pubs. of the Arkansas Philological Assn.* 3, No. 3 (1977), 68–75.

Amner, Richard (1736–1803). Contributor to v1793. (Presumably Steevens himself.)

Anders, H[enry] R. D. *Shakespeare's Books: A Dissertation on Shakespeare's Reading and the Immediate Sources of his Works.* Schriften der Deutschen Shakespeare-Gesellschaft 1. Berlin, 1904.

Anderson, Donald K., Jr. "A New Gloss for the 'Three-nook'd world' of *Antony and Cleopatra.*" *ELN* 17 (1979), 103–6.

Anderson, Ruth L. *Elizabethan Psychology and Shakespeare's Plays.* 2nd ed. New York, 1966. (1st ed. Iowa City, 1927. Rpt. New York: Haskell House, 1944.)

Anonymous. Contributor to ARD2.

————. Contributor to CAM1.

————. Contributor to CAM2.

————. Contributor to *St. James's Chr.*

————. Contributor to v1773.

————. *An Examen of the New Comedy, Call'd The Suspicious Husband. With Some Observations upon Our Dramatick Poetry and Authors; To which is added, A Word of Advice to Mr. G—rr—ck; and a Piece of Secret History.* 1747.

————. *A Horrible Cruel and bloudy Murther, Committed at Putney in Surrey on the 21. of Aprill last 1614.* 1614.

————. "Metaphors." *TLS,* 14 Oct. 1926, pp. 681–2.

————. MS Notes *apud* Halliwell 1868.

————. MS Notes in Furness's Copy of F2 *apud* v1907.

————. "On the Character of Cleopatra." *Cornhill Magazine* 12 (1871), 344–59.

————. "*Original Observations and Conjectures on* Shakespear." *Gent. Mag.* 60 (1790), 125–8.

————. [Review of *Antonio e Cleopatra,* by Antonio Marescalchi.] *Nuovo Giornale Letterario d'Italia* 20 (1789), 20.

————. [Review of *Sulla poesia,* by Giovanni Torti, & *Idee elementari sulla poesia romantica,* by Ermes Visconti.] *Biblioteca Italiana* 13 (Feb. 1819), 147–69.

————. [Review of Wilson ed.] *TLS,* 29 Dec. 1950, p. 830.

————. "Samuel Daniel." *Macmillan's Magazine* 68 (1893), 433–40.

————. "Shakspeare's Character of Cleopatra." *Fraser's Magazine* 40 (1849), 277–91.

————. "Shakspeare's Females." 5 *Port Folio* 17 (1824), 47–52.

Ansari, A. A. "Antony and Cleopatra: An Image of Liquifaction." *Aligarh Journal of English Studies* 8 (1983), 79–93.

Anton, Robert. *The Philosophers Satyrs*. New ed. as *Vices anotimie*. 1617. (1st ed. 1616.)

Aoki, Kazuo. "An Essay on *Antony and Cleopatra*." *Ippan Kenkyu Kokoku* (Seikei Univ.) 14 (1978), 1–45.

Aoyama, Seiko. "Magnificence and Folly: A Study of Value in *Antony and Cleopatra*." *Collected Essays by the Members of the Faculty* (Kyoritsu Women's Junior Coll.) 13 (1969), 12–25.

Arber, Edward, ed. *A Transcript of the Registers of the Company of Stationers of London*. 5 vols. London & Birmingham, 1875–94. (Rpt. New York: Peter Smith, 1950.)

Ardinger, Barbara R. "Cleopatra on Stage: An Examination of the *Persona* of the Queen in English Drama, 1592–1898." Southern Illinois Univ. diss., 1976. (*DA* 37 [1976], 3634A.)

Armstrong, John. *The Paradise Myth*. OUP, 1969.

Arthos, John. *The Art of Shakespeare*. 1964.

Asahara, Sanae. "Myth-Ritual Patterns in *Antony and Cleopatra*." *Edgewood Review* 5 (1978), 1–26.

Auden, Wystan H. (1907–73). Contributor to Pearson 1954.

[Ayrenhoff, Cornelius Hermann von.] *Kleopatra und Antonius: Ein Trauerspiel in vier Aufzügen*. . . . New ed. Wien, 1813. (1st ed. 1783.)

B., C. "Shakspeare's 'Antony and Cleopatra.' " 1 *N&Q* 3 (8 Mar. 1851), 190–1.

B., C. C. " 'Antony and Cleopatra', [920–1]." 7 *N&Q* 12 (25 July 1891), 63.

B., C. F. "A Word with 'Shakespeare's Scholar.' " *Putnam's Monthly Magazine* 9 (1857), 286–7.

Bab, Julius. *Shakespeare: Wesen und Werke*. Stuttgart, 1925.

Babb, Lawrence. *The Elizabethan Malady: A Study of Melancholia in English Literature from 1580 to 1642*. East Lansing, Mich., 1951.

Badham, Charles (1813–84). Contributor to CAM2.

Bahnsen, Julius. "Charakterzüge aus Shakespeares Frauenwelt." *Wie Ich Wurde Was Ich Ward*. Ed. Rudolf Louis. München, 1905. Pp. 184–240. (Written 1877–8.)

Bailey, John. *Shakespeare*. 1929.

Bailey, N[athan]. *Dictionarium Britannicum*. 1730. (Rpt. Anglistica & Americana 50. Hildesheim & New York: Olms, 1969.)

———. *An Universal Etymological English Dictionary*. 1721. (Rpt. Anglistica & Americana 52. Hildesheim & New York: Olms, 1969.)

Bailey, Samuel. *On the Received Text of Shakespeare's Dramatic Writings and its Improvement*. 2 vols. 1862–6.

Baker, Donald C. "The Purging of Cleopatra." *ShN* 9, No. 6; 10, No. 1 (1959–60), 9.

Baker, George Pierce. *The Development of Shakespeare as a Dramatist*. New York, 1907. (Rpt. New York: AMS, 1965.)

Bald, R. C. "Shakespeare and Daniel." *TLS*, 20 Nov. 1924, p. 776.

Baldwin, Thomas W. *The Organization and Personnel of the Shakespearean Company*. Princeton, 1927.

———. *William Shakspere's Small Latine & Lesse Greeke*. 2 vols. Urbana, 1944.

Balestri, Charles A. "English Neoclassicism and Shakespeare: A Study in Conflicting Ideas of Dramatic Form." Yale Univ. diss., 1970. (*DA* 31 [1970], 6537A.)

Ball, Robert H. *Shakespeare on Silent Film: A Strange Eventful History*. 1968.

Bamber, Linda. *Comic Women, Tragic Men: A Study of Gender and Genre in Shakespeare*. Stanford, 1982.

Bandel, Betty. "Cleopatra's Creator." *ShN* 9, No. 6; 10, No. 1 (1959–60), 10.

Barber, Charles. *Early Modern English*. 1976.

————. *The Theme of Honour's Tongue: A Study of Social Attitudes in the English Drama from Shakespeare to Dryden.* Gothenburg Studies in English 58. Göteborg, 1985.

Baret, John. *An Alvearie or Triple Dictionarie, in Englishe, Latin, and French.* [1573.]

Barker, Rosalind. "A Note on Belinda's 'sev'nfold Fence.' " *W&L* 3, No. 1 (1975), 39.

Barnet, Sylvan. "Recognition and Reversal in *Antony and Cleopatra.*" *SQ* 8 (1957), 331–4.

Barnwell, Robert G., ed. *The Works of Mary Sidney, Countess of Pembroke.* 1865.

Barroll, J[ohn] Leeds. "Antony and Pleasure." *JEGP* 57 (1958), 708–20.

————. "The Characterization of Octavius." *ShakS* 6 (1970), 231–88.

————. "The Chronology of Shakespeare's Jacobean Plays and the Dating of *Antony and Cleopatra.*" *Essays on Shakespeare.* Ed. Gordon R. Smith. University Park, 1965. Pp. 115–62.

————. "Enobarbus' Description of Cleopatra." *TxSE* 37 (1958), 61–78.

————. "Scarrus and the Scarred Soldier." *HLQ* 22 (1958–9), 31–9.

————. "Shakespeare and Roman History." *MLR* 53 (1958), 327–43.

————. "Shakespeare and the Art of Character: A Study of Anthony." *ShakS* 5 (1969), 159–235.

————. *Shakespearean Tragedy: Genre, Tradition, and Change in* Antony and Cleopatra. Washington, D.C., 1984.

Barry, Henry, Rev. (b. 1781 or 1782). Contributor to COL1.

[Bartholomaeus Anglicus.] *Batman vppon Bartholome, his Booke* De Proprietatibus Rerum. 1582. (Rpt. Anglistica & Americana 161. Introd. Jürgen Schäfer. Hildesheim & New York: Olms, 1976.)

Barton, Anne. *"Nature's piece 'gainst fancy": The Divided Catastrophe in* Antony and Cleopatra. An Inaugural Lecture. 1973.

————. "Shakespeare: His Tragedies." *English Drama to 1710.* Ed. Christopher Ricks. History of Lit. in the Eng. Lang. 3. 1971. Pp. 215–52.

————. *See* Righter, Anne.

Basedow, Hans von. *Shakespearesche Charaktere.* Vol. 1 of *Charaktere und Temperamente: Dramaturgische Studien.* Berlin, 1893.

[Bathurst, Charles.] *Remarks on the Differences in Shakespeare's Versification in Different Periods of his Life.* 1857.

Battenhouse, Roy W. *Shakespearean Tragedy: Its Art and Its Christian Premises.* Bloomington & London, 1969.

Bayfield, M[atthew] A. *A Study of Shakespeare's Versification.* Cambridge, 1920.

Bayley, John. *Shakespeare and Tragedy.* London & Boston, 1981.

————. *The Uses of Division: Unity and Disharmony in Literature.* London & New York, 1976.

Beauchamp, Virginia W. "Dramatic Treatment of Antony and Cleopatra in the Sixteenth and Seventeenth Centuries: Variations of Dramatic Form upon a Single Theme." Univ. of Chicago diss., 1955.

Beckerman, Bernard. "Past the Size of Dreaming." *Twentieth Century Interpretations of* Antony and Cleopatra. Ed. Mark Rose. Englewood Cliffs, N.J., 1977. Pp. 99–112.

————. *Shakespeare at the Globe, 1599–1609.* New York, 1962.

[Becket, Andrew.] *A Concordance to Shakespeare: Suited to all the Editions.* 1787.

————. *Shakspeare's Himself Again.* 2 vols. 1815.

Behrens, Ralph. "Cleopatra Exonerated." *ShN* 9, No. 5 (1959), 37.

Bell, Arthur H. "Time and Convention in *Antony and Cleopatra.*" *SQ* 24 (1973), 253–64.

Benedix, Roderich. *Die Shakespearomanie: Zur Abwehr.* Stuttgart, 1873.

Benoit, Raymond. "The Prophecy in the Play: *Antony and Cleopatra.*" *Greyfriar: Siena Studies in Literature* 17 (1976), 3–7.

Berek, Peter. "Doing and Undoing: The Value of Action in *Antony and Cleopatra.*" *SQ* 32 (1981), 295–304.

Berggren, Paula S. "The Woman's Part: Female Sexuality as Power in Shakespeare's Plays." *The Woman's Part: Feminist Criticism of Shakespeare.* Ed. Carolyn R. S. Lenz, Gayle Greene, & Carol T. Neely. Urbana, 1980. Pp. 17–34.

Berkeley, David S. "Antony, Cleopatra, and Proculeius." *N&Q* 195 (1950), 534–5.

————. "The Crux of *Antony and Cleopatra.*" *Bulletin of the State Univ. of Oklahoma Agricultural & Mechanical College: Arts & Sciences Studies, Humanistic Ser. No. 4,* 50, No. 2 (1953), 1–13.

————. Letter. *CE* 18 (1956–7), 286–7.

————. "On Desentimentalizing Antony." *N&Q* 209 (1964), 138–42.

————. "On Oversimplifying Antony." *CE* 17 (1955–6), 96–9.

Berkowitz, Steven. Private Contributor.

Berry, J. Wilkes. "Two Hoops in Shakespeare's *Antony and Cleopatra.*" *CEA* 35, No. 3 (1973), 29–30.

Berry, Ralph. "Beerbohm Tree as Director: Three Shakespearean Productions." *Essays in Theatre* 1 (1983), 81–100.

Bertram, Paul. *White Spaces in Shakespeare: The Development of the Modern Text.* Cleveland, 1981.

The Best Plays of 1958–59. Ed. Louis Kronenberger. The Burns Mantle Yearbook. New York & Toronto, 1959.

Bethell, S[amuel] L. *Shakespeare and the Popular Dramatic Tradition.* 1944.

Bettinelli, Saverio. "Dialogo [d'amore] XIV. *Balli.* Amore e Melpomene." *Opere edite o inedite in prosa ed in versi.* 2nd ed. Vol. 5. Venezia, 1799. Pp. 289–314. (1st ed. 1788.)

Bianchi, Adriano. *Le tragedie romane: Giulio Cesare, Antonio e Cleopatra, Coriolano.* Università degli studi, Perugia, Facoltà di magistero. Roma, 1970.

Binal, Wolfgang. *Deutschsprachiges Theater in Budapest. Von den Anfängen bis zum Brand des Theaters in der Wollgasse (1889).* Wien, 1972. (Vol. 10, No. 1 of *Theatergeschichte Österreichs.* Ed. Österreichische Akademie der Wissenschaften.)

Binder, Rudolf. *Der dramatische Rhythmus in Shakespeares "Antonius und Cleopatra."* Würzburg-Aumühle, 1939.

Birch, William J. *An Inquiry into the Philosophy and Religion of Shakspere.* 1848. (Rpt. New York: Haskell House, 1972.)

Birkinshaw, Philip. "Heroic Frenzies: Neo-erotic Platonism in *Antony and Cleopatra.*" *UCTSE* 3 (1972), 37–44.

Blackburn, Ruth H. *Biblical Drama Under the Tudors.* The Hague & Paris, 1971.

Blackstone, William (1723–80). Contributor to v1785.

Blair, Alexander, M. D. (1834–96). Contributor to CAM2.

Blake, N[orman] F. *Shakespeare's Language: An Introduction.* 1983.

Blakiston, J. M. G. "The Three Nook'd World." *TLS,* 17 Sept. 1964, p. 868.

Blanche, Jacques-Emile. Contributor to Grivelet 1960.

Blanco, Julio Enrique. "Las pruebas del alter ego en D'Annunzio y en Shakespeare (Francesca da Rimini y Antony and Cleopatra)." *Ideas y Valores* 6 (1952), 414–44.

Blayney, Peter W. M. *The Texts of King Lear and their Origins.* Vol. 1: *Nicholas Okes and the First Quarto.* Cambridge, 1982.

Bliss, Lee. *The World's Perspective: John Webster and Jacobean Drama.* New Brunswick, N.J., 1983.

Blissett, William. "Dramatic Irony in *Antony and Cleopatra.*" *SQ* 18 (1967), 151–66. (Paper presented Apr. 1962.)

———. "Lucan's Caesar and the Elizabethan Villain." *SP* 53 (1956), 553–75.

Blondel, Jacques. "La tentation dans *Samson Agonistes.*" *EA* 30 (1977), 158–68.

B[lount], T[homas]. *Glossographia.* 1656. (Rpt. Anglistica & Americana 32. Hildesheim & New York: Olms, 1972.)

Boaden, James (1762–1839). Contributor to SING1.

Boas, Frederick S. *Shakspere and His Predecessors.* 1896.

Boas, Guy. "The Influence of the Boy-actor on Shakespeare's Plays." *ContempR* 152 (1937), 69–77.

Bodenstedt, Friedrich. *Shakespeare's Frauencharaktere.* Vierte vermehrte Auflage. Berlin, 1887. (1st ed. 1874.)

Böse, Petra. *"Wahnsinn" in Shakespeares Dramen: Eine Untersuchung zu Bedeutungsgeschichte und Wortgebrauch.* Studien zur Englischen Philologie, n. F. Band 10. Tübingen, 1966.

Bonjour, Adrien. "L'anticipation tragique dans les scènes initiales d'*Antoine et Cléopâtre.*" 2 *EdL* 2 (1959), 136–46.

———. "From Shakespeare's Venus to Cleopatra's Cupids." *ShS* 15 (1962), 73–80.

———. "Shakespeare and the Toil of Grace." *Shakespeare 1564–1964: A Collection of Modern Essays by Various Hands.* Ed. Edward A. Bloom. Providence, R.I., 1964. Pp. 88–94.

Bono, Barbara J. *Literary Transvaluation: From Vergilian Epic to Shakespearean Tragicomedy.* Berkeley & London, 1984.

Boorman, S[tanley] C. *Human Conflict in Shakespeare.* London & New York, 1987.

Booth, Stephen. "Speculations on Doubling in Shakespeare's Plays." *Shakespeare: The Theatrical Dimension.* Ed. Philip C. McGuire & David A. Samuelson. New York, 1979. Pp. 103–31.

Borinski, Ludwig. " 'Soldat' und 'Politiker' bei Shakespeare und seinen Zeitgenossen." *SJ* 91 (1955), 87–120.

Bose, Amalendu. "The barge she sat in." *Calcutta Essays on Shakespeare.* Ed. Amalendu Bose. Calcutta, 1966. Pp. 81–97.

———. "Shakespeare's Word-music." *Studies in Elizabethan Literature: Festschrift to Professor G. C. Bannerjee.* Ed. P[othukuchi] S. Sastri. New Delhi, 1972. Pp. 57–63.

Boswell, James. Contributor to v1821.

Bowers, Fredson. "The Concept of Single or Dual Protagonists in Shakespeare's Tragedies." *RenP*, 1982, pp. 27–33.

———. "Death in Victory: Shakespeare's Tragic Reconciliations." *Studies in Honor of DeWitt T. Starnes.* Ed. Thomas P. Harrison et al. Austin, 1967. Pp. 53–75. (Delivered 1964; first pub. *SoAB* 30 [1965], 1–7.)

———. "Establishing Shakespeare's Text: Notes on Short Lines and the Problem of Verse Division." *SB* 33 (1980), 74–130.

———. *On Editing Shakespeare.* Rpt., with additions, Charlottesville, 1966. (First pub. as *On Editing Shakespeare and the Elizabethan Dramatists* [OUP, 1955].)

———. "Shakespeare's Art: The Point of View." *Literary Views: Critical and Historical Essays.* Ed. Carroll Camden. Chicago, 1964. Pp. 45–58.

Bowers, John M. " 'I am Marble-Constant': Cleopatra's Monumental End." *HLQ* 46 (1983), 283–97.

Bowling, Lawrence E. "Antony's Internal Disunity." *SEL* 4 (1964), 239–46.

———. "Duality in the Minor Characters in *Antony and Cleopatra.*" *CE* 18 (1956–7), 251–5.

Bradbrook, Frank W. "Thomas Nashe and Shakespeare." *N&Q* 199 (1954), 470.

Bradbrook, M[uriel] C. *The Living Monument: Shakespeare and the Theatre of His Time.* Cambridge, 1976.
―――――. *Shakespeare the Craftsman.* The Clark Lectures 1968. 1969.
Bradford, Gamaliel, Jr. "The Serpent of Old Nile: A Study of the Cleopatra of Tragedy." *Elizabethan Women.* Ed. Harold Ogden White. Boston, 1936. Pp. 189–206. (First pub. *Poet Lore* 10 [1898], 514–32.)
Bradley, A[ndrew] C. *Shakespearean Tragedy: Lectures on* Hamlet, Othello, King Lear, Macbeth. 2nd ed. 1905. (1st ed. 1904.)
―――――. "Shakespeare's *Antony and Cleopatra.*" *Oxford Lectures on Poetry.* 2nd ed. 1909. Pp. 279–308. (Rpt. 1970 [Papermacs]; 1st ed. 1909; first pub. *The Quarterly Review* 204 [1906], 329–51.)
B[rae], A. E. "Shakspeare's Use of 'Captious' and 'Intenible.' Shakspeare's 'Small Latin.' " 1 *N&Q* 3 (21 June 1851), 497–9.
Bräker, Ulrich. *A Few Words About William Shakespeare's Plays.* . . . Tr. Derek Bowman. London & New York, 1979. (Written in Ger. c. 1780.)
Branam, George C. *Eighteenth-Century Adaptations of Shakespearean Tragedy.* Berkeley & Los Angeles, 1956. (Rpt. Norwood, Pa.: Norwood Eds., 1976.)
Brand, Alice G. "Antony and Cleopatra and the Nature of Their Sexuality." *The Bard* 1 (1976), 98–107.
Brandão, Nielson das Neves. "Defeat in *Antony and Cleopatra.*" *Signal* 1, No. 1 (1978), 101–16.
Brandes, Georg. *William Shakespeare: A Critical Study.* Tr. William Archer, Mary Morison, & Diana White. 2 vols. 1898. (Reissued 1 vol., New York, 1935. 1st Danish ed. 1895–6.)
Brandl, Alois. *Shakespeare: Leben—Umwelt—Kunst.* Neue Ausgabe. Berlin, 1922. (1st ed. 1894.)
Brathwait, Richard. *The English Gentlewoman, drawne out to the full Body.* . . . 1631.
Breasted, Barbara. "I. Comus and the Castlehaven Scandal. II. Public Standards in Fiction: A Discussion of Three Nineteenth-Century Novels—George Eliot's *Middlemarch* and Jane Austen's *Pride and Prejudice* and *Emma.* III. *Antony and Cleopatra*: Theatrical Uses of the Self." Rutgers Univ. diss., 1970. (*DA* 31 [1970], 4112A.)
Brecht, Bertolt. *Diaries 1920–1922.* Ed. Herta Ramthun. Tr. John Willett. New York, 1979. (Remarks on *Ant.* dated 17 Aug. 1920.)
Brennan, Anthony S. "Excellent Dissembling: Antony and Cleopatra Playing at Love." *Midwest Quarterly* 19 (1978), 313–29.
Brewer, D. S. "The Ideal of Feminine Beauty in Medieval Literature, Especially 'Harley Lyrics', Chaucer, and Some Elizabethans." *MLR* 50 (1955), 257–69.
Brewer, Leighton. *Shakespeare and the Dark Lady.* Boston, 1966.
Brincker, Friedrich. *Poetik Shakespeare's in den Römerdramen* Coriolanus, Julius Caesar *und* Antony and Cleopatra. Münster, 1884. (Münster diss.)
Brink, Bernhard ten. *Five Lectures on Shakespeare.* Tr. Julia Franklin. 1895. (1st Ger. ed. 1893.)
Brito, João Batista B. de. "Duality in *Antony and Cleopatra.*" *Signal* 1, No. 1 (1978), 32–46.
Brockbank, J. P. "Shakespeare and the Fashion of These Times." *ShS* 16 (1963), 30–41.
Brodwin, Leonora L. *Elizabethan Love Tragedy 1587–1625.* London & New York, 1971.
Bronson, B. H. "Arme-gaunt." *TLS*, 8 Oct. 1938, p. 644.
Brook, G[eorge] L. *The Language of Shakespeare.* 1976.
Brooke, C[harles] F. Tucker, ed. *Shakespeare's Plutarch.* 2 vols. 1909.

Brooks, Harold F. Contributor to ARD2.

————. "Lady Macbeth; Cleopatra; Volumnia." *Shakespeare's Jacobean Tragedies: Report of the Fifteenth International Shakespeare Conference 1972.* Stratford-upon-Avon, 1972. Pp. 21–2.

Broussard, Mercedes. "Mother and Child: Cleopatra and the Asp." *CEA* 37, No. 1 (1974), 25–6.

Brower, Reuben A. *Hero & Saint: Shakespeare and the Graeco-Roman Heroic Tradition.* OUP, 1971.

Brown, Huntington. "Enter the Shakespearean Tragic Hero." *EIC* 3 (1953), 285–302.

Brown, Ivor. *Dark Ladies.* 1957.

————. *Shakespeare.* 1949.

Brown, John Russell. *Shakespeare's Plays in Performance.* 1966.

————, ed. *Shakespeare*, Antony and Cleopatra: *A Casebook.* 1968.

Brown, Langdon. Contributor to Leiter 1986.

Browne, Marlene C. "Shakespeare's Lady Macbeth and Cleopatra: Women in a Political Context." Brown Univ. diss., 1976. (*DA* 38 [1977], 274A.)

Browne, William S., Rev. (b. 1829). Contributor to Wright, William Aldis, MS Notes (–1892). Letter (24 July 1885) to Wright in Trinity Coll., Cambridge: Add. MS. b. 59 (292).

Brunner, Karl. *William Shakespeare.* Tübingen, 1957.

Bryant, J[oseph] A., Jr. *Hippolyta's View: Some Christian Aspects of Shakespeare's Plays.* Lexington, Ky., 1961.

Buck, Eva. "Cleopatra, eine Charakterdeutung. Zur Interpretation von Shakespeares 'Antony and Cleopatra.' " *SJ* 74 (1938), 101–22.

Bucknill, John C. *The Medical Knowledge of Shakespeare.* 1860.

B[ulloch], J[ohn]. *"New Readings in Shakespeare*, No. XVII." *Aberdeen Herald*, 26 Aug. 1865, p. 2.

————. *Studies on the Text of Shakespeare.* 1878.

B[ullokar], I[ohn]. *An English Expositor: Teaching the Interpretation of the hardest words vsed in our Language.* 1616. (Rpt. Anglistica & Americana 71. Hildesheim & New York: Olms, 1971.)

Bullough, Geoffrey. "Shakespeare's Roman Plays." *Bulletin of the Department of English: A Shakespeare Number* (Univ. of Calcutta) 6, Nos. 1–2 (Serial Nos. 19–20) (1964), 1–8.

————. "The Uses of History." *Shakespeare's World.* Ed. James Sutherland & Joel Hurstfield. 1964. Pp. 96–115.

————, ed. *Narrative and Dramatic Sources of Shakespeare.* Vol. 5: *The Roman Plays*: Julius Cæsar, Antony and Cleopatra, Coriolanus. London & New York, 1964.

Bulman, James C. *The Heroic Idiom of Shakespearean Tragedy.* Newark, N.J., London, & Toronto, 1985.

Bulthaupt, Heinrich. *Shakespeare.* Vol. 2 of *Dramaturgie des Schauspiels.* 10th ed. Oldenburg & Leipzig, 1911. (1st ed. 1883.)

Burckhardt, Sigurd. *Shakespearean Meanings.* Princeton, 1968.

Burge, Barbara J. " 'Nature Erring From Itself', Identity in Shakespeare's Tragedies: A Study of the Use of 'I am not what I am' and Its Related Variations in the Delineation of Character." Univ. of Pittsburgh diss., 1966. (*DA* 27 [1967], 4216–17A.)

Burgess, W[illiam]. *The Bible in Shakespeare.* 1903. (Rpt. New York: Haskell House, 1968.)

Burke, Kenneth. "Shakespearean Persuasion." *AR* 24 (1964), 19–36.

Burton, Dolores M. "Aspects of Word Order in Two Plays of Shakespeare." *Computer Studies in the Humanities and Verbal Behavior* 3 (1970), 34–9. (First pub. as "Toward a Theoretical Description of Deviant Sequence," *Proceedings of the 23rd National Conference of the Assn. for Computing Machinery* [Princeton, 1968], 801–5.)

————. *Shakespeare's Grammatical Style: A Computer-Assisted Analysis of* Richard II *and* Antony and Cleopatra. Austin & London, 1973.

————. "Some Uses of a Grammatical Concordance." *CHum* 2 (1967–8), 145–54.

Butler, Harold Edgeworth (1878–1951). Contributor to Nowottny 1964.

Cadoux, Arthur T. *Shakespearean Selves: An Essay in Ethics.* 1938.

Cairncross, Andrew S. " 'Antony and Cleopatra', [1989]." *N&Q* 220 (1975), 173.

Calderwood, James L. *Shakespeare & the Denial of Death.* Amherst, 1987.

The Cambridge Ancient History. Vol. 10: *The Augustan Empire 44 B.C.–A.D. 70.* Ed. S[tanley] A. Cook, F[rank] E. Adcock, & M[artin] P. Charlesworth. Cambridge, 1952.

Camden, Carroll. "Elizabethan Chiromancy." *MLN* 62 (1947), 1–7.

[Camden, William.] *Remaines of a Greater Worke, Concerning Britaine.* 1605.

Camé, J.-F. "A Note on Shakespeare's *Cleopatra* and Milton's *Dalila.*" *CahiersE* 12 (1977), 69–70.

Campbell, John. *Shakespeare's Legal Acquirements Considered.* 1859.

Campbell, Lewis (1830–1908). Contributor to CAM2.

————. Contributor to Wright, William Aldis, MS Notes in a copy of CAM1 in Trinity Coll., Cambridge: MS. Adv. C. 18. 57. (References to letters of 12 Feb. 1879 and 24 June 1879.)

————. *Tragic Drama in Aeschylus, Sophocles, and Shakespeare.* 1904. (Rpt. New York: Russell & Russell, 1965.)

Canning, Albert S. G. *Thoughts on Shakespeare's Historical Plays.* 1884.

Cantor, Paul A. *Shakespeare's Rome: Republic and Empire.* Ithaca & London, 1976.

Caputi, Anthony. "Shakespeare's *Antony and Cleopatra*: Tragedy Without Terror." *SQ* 16 (1965), 183–91.

Carr, R[alph] H., ed. *Plutarch's Lives of Coriolanus, Caesar, Brutus, and Antonius in North's Translation.* OUP, 1906.

Carter, Thomas. *Shakespeare and Holy Scripture, with the Version he Used.* 1905.

Cartwright, Robert. *The Footsteps of Shakspere.* 1862.

————. *New Readings in Shakspere.* 1866.

[?————.] *The Sonnets of William Shakspere, Rearranged and Divided into Four Parts. With an Introduction and Explanatory Notes.* 1859.

[Cavendish, Margaret.] *CCXI Sociable Letters, Written by the Twice Noble, Illustrious, and Excellent Princess, the Lady Marchioness of Newcastle.* 1664. (Rpt. Menston: Scolar, 1969.)

[Cawdrey, Robert.] *A Table Alphabeticall, conteyning and teaching the true writing, and vnderstanding of hard vsuall English wordes.* 1604. (Rpt., introd. Robert A. Peters; Gainesville, Fla.: Scholars' Facsimiles & Rpts., 1966.)

Cecil, David. " 'Antony and Cleopatra.' " *Poets and Story-Tellers.* 1949. Pp. 3–24. (Delivered 1943; first pub. Glasgow, 1944.)

Cercignani, Fausto. *Shakespeare's Works and Elizabethan Pronunciation.* OUP, 1981.

Chambers, E[dmund] K. *The Elizabethan Stage.* 4 vols. OUP, 1923.

————. *Shakespeare: A Survey.* 1925. (First pub. in Red Letter Sh., 1904–8; *Ant.* 1907.)

————. *William Shakespeare: A Study of Facts and Problems.* 2 vols. OUP, 1930.

Chambrun, Clara Longworth de. *Shakespeare Rediscovered.* New York & London, 1938.

————. *Shakespeare retrouvé: Sa vie. Son œuvre.* Paris, 1947.

Champion, Larry S. *Shakespeare's Tragic Perspective*. Athens, Ga., 1976.

Charney, Maurice. "Shakespeare's Antony: A Study of Image Themes." *SP* 54 (1957), 149–61.

―――. *Shakespeare's Roman Plays: The Function of Imagery in the Drama*. Cambridge, Mass., 1961.

―――. "Shakespeare's Style in *Julius Caesar* and *Antony and Cleopatra*." *ELH* 26 (1959), 355–67.

―――. " 'This Mist, My Friend, Is Mystical': Place and Time in Elizabethan Plays." *The Rarer Action: Essays in Honor of Francis Fergusson*. Ed. Alan Cheuse & Richard Koffler. New Brunswick, N.J., 1970. Pp. 24–35.

Chaudhuri, Sukanta. *Infirm Glory: Shakespeare and the Renaissance Image of Man*. OUP, 1981.

Chedworth, John. *Notes upon Some of the Obscure Passages in Shakespeare's Plays*. 1805.

Christopher, Georgia B. "The Private War and Peace in *Antony and Cleopatra*." *A Festschrift for Professor Marguerite Roberts, on the Occasion of Her Retirement from Westhampton College, University of Richmond, Virginia*. Ed. Frieda E. Penninger. Richmond, Va., 1976. Pp. 59–73.

Cioni, Fernando. " 'The fancy outwork nature': Enobarbo e la sua descrizione di Cleopatra." *Analysis: Quaderni di Anglistica* 4 (1986), 73–93.

Clark, Cumberland. *Shakespeare and Psychology*. 1936. (Rpt. Folcroft, Pa.: Folcroft Libr. Eds., 1976.)

Clark, Eva T. *Hidden Allusions in Shakespeare's Plays*. 3rd rev. ed. Ed. Ruth L. Miller. Port Washington, 1974. (1st ed. 1931.)

Clarke, Charles Cowden. *Shakespeare-Characters; Chiefly Those Subordinate*. 1863.

―――, & Mary Cowden Clarke. *The Shakespeare Key: A Comprehensive Guide to All Features of Shakespeare's Style, Dramatic Construction, and Expression*. 1879. (Rpt. New York: Ungar, n.d.)

Claudel, Paul (1868–1955). Contributor to Speaight 1955.

Clay, Charles J. *A Comparison Between the Female Characters of the Greek Tragedians and Those of Shakspeare*. Second Prize, St. Paul's School. Prolusiones Literariae. 1844.

Clayton, Thomas. " 'Is this the promis'd end?': Revision in the Role of the King." *The Division of the Kingdoms: Shakespeare's Two Versions of King Lear*. Ed. Gary Taylor & Michael Warren. Oxford Sh. Stud. OUP, 1983. Pp. 121–41.

―――. " 'Mysterious by This Love': The Unregenerate Resurrection of 'Antony and Cleopatra.' " *Jadavpur Univ. Essays and Studies III, Special Issue: A Festschrift in Honour of S. C. Sen Gupta*. Ed. Jagannath Chakravorty. Calcutta, 1981. Pp. 95–116.

Clemen, Wolfgang. *The Development of Shakespeare's Imagery*. 2nd ed. 1977. (1st ed. 1951. 1st Ger. ed. Bonn, 1936.)

―――. "Der dramatische Rhythmus in 'Antonius und Cleopatra.' " *Programm des Schauspielhauses Zürich, 28 Nov. 1968*. Pp. 4–5.

―――. *Shakespeare's Dramatic Art*. 1972.

―――. *Wandlung des Botenberichts bei Shakespeare*. Sitzungsberichte der Bayerischen Akademie der Wissenschaften, philosophisch-historische Klasse, Jahrgang 1952, Heft 4. München, 1952.

Coates, John. " 'The Choice of Hercules' in 'Antony and Cleopatra.' " *ShS* 31 (1978), 45–52.

Cobden-Sanderson, T. J. "*Antony and Cleopatra*." *TLS*, 16 May 1912, p. 206.

C[ockeram], H[enry]. *The English Dictionarie: or, an Interpreter of hard English Words*. 1623. (Rpt. Menston: Scolar, 1968.)

Coghill, Nevill. *Shakespeare's Professional Skills.* Cambridge, 1964.

Coleridge, Hartley. *Essays and Marginalia.* Ed. Derwent Coleridge. 2 vols. 1851.

Coleridge, Samuel Taylor. *Coleridge's Shakespearean Criticism.* Ed. Thomas Middleton Raysor. 2 vols. Rev. ed. London & New York, 1960. (1st ed. Cambridge, Mass., 1930. Notes for lecture on *Ant.*, probably 1818.)

Coles, E[lisha]. *An English Dictionary.* 1676. (Rpt. Anglistica & Americana 76. Hildesheim & New York: Olms, 1973.)

Colie, Rosalie L. *Shakespeare's Living Art.* Princeton, 1974.

Collier, J[ohn] Payne. *Notes and Emendations to the Text of Shakespeare's Plays, from Early Manuscript Corrections in a Copy of the Folio, 1632.* 2nd ed., rev. & enl. 1853. (1st ed., 1852.)

Colman, E[rnest] A. M. *The Dramatic Use of Bawdy in Shakespeare.* 1974.

————. *The Structure of Shakespeare's* Antony and Cleopatra. Sydney, 1971.

Commager, Steele. "Horace, *Carmina* 1.37." *The Phoenix: The Journal of the Classical Assn. of Canada* 12 (1958), 47–57.

Conrad, Hermann. "Shakspere und die Frauen." *Preußische Jahrbücher* 101 (1900), 243–70.

Constantin-Weyer, M[aurice]. *Shakespeare.* Maîtres des Littératures 1. Paris, 1929.

Cook, Albert. "Shakespeare's *Antony and Cleopatra,* [3538–41]." *Expl* 6 (1947), no. 9.

Cook, Elizabeth. *Seeing Through Words: The Scope of Late Renaissance Poetry.* New Haven & London, 1986.

Cook, Judith. *Women in Shakespeare.* 1980.

Cooke, Michael G. *Acts of Inclusion: Studies Bearing on an Elementary Theory of Romanticism.* New Haven & London, 1979.

Cooper, Thomas. *Thesavrvs Lingvae Romanæ & Britannicæ.* 1565. (Rpt. Menston: Scolar, 1969.)

Coppedge, Walter R. "Shakespeare's Oaths and Imprecations." Indiana Univ. diss., 1967. (*DA* 28 [1968], 2643A.)

Corson, Hiram. *An Introduction to the Study of Shakespeare.* Boston, 1889.

————. "Note on a Passage in Shakespeare [*Ant.* 3304–6]." *The Nation* 426 (28 Aug. 1873), 144–5. (Rpt. 5 *N&Q* 1 [18 Apr. 1874], 303.)

Costa, Maria Gláucia de V. "The Moon and Cleopatra: A Case of Parallelism in *Antony and Cleopatra.*" *Signal* 1, No. 1 (1978), 47–64.

Costa de Beauregard, Raphaelle. "*Antony and Cleopatra*: A Play to Suit the New Jacobean Taste." *Caliban* 10 (1974), 105–11.

Cotgrave, John. *The English Treasury of Wit and Language.* 1655.

Cotgrave, Randle. *A Dictionarie of the French and English Tongves.* 1611. (Rpt. Menston: Scolar, 1968.)

Couchman, Gordon W. "*Antony and Cleopatra* and the Subjective Convention." *PMLA* 76 (1961), 420–5.

Coursen, Herbert R., Jr. "The Mirror of Allusion: *The Ambassadors.*" *NEQ* 34 (1961), 382–4.

Courtenay, Thomas P. *Commentaries on the Historical Plays of Shakspeare.* 2 vols. 1840.

Courthope, W[illiam] J. *A History of English Poetry.* 6 vols. 1895–1910. Vol. 4. 1903.

Courtney, W. L. "Shakespeare's 'Antony and Cleopatra': The Dark Lady." [Periodical Unidentified], 13 Nov. 1906.

Cowling, G[eorge] H. *Music on the Shakespearian Stage.* Cambridge, 1913. (Rpt. New York: AMS, 1976.)

Craig, Hardin. *An Interpretation of Shakespeare.* New York, 1948.

Craig, W[illiam] J. (1843–1906). Contributor to ARD1.

Crane, Milton. *Shakespeare's Prose.* Chicago, 1951.

Crawford, John. *Romantic Criticism of Shakespearian Drama.* Romantic Reassessment 79. Salzburg, 1978.

Creizenach, Wilhelm. *Geschichte des neueren Dramas.* 5 vols. Halle a. S., 1893–1916. Vol. 5. 1916.

Croce, Benedetto. *Ariosto, Shakespeare and Corneille.* Tr. Douglas Ainslie. London & New York, 1920. (Rpt. New York: Russell & Russell, 1966. 1st It. ed. 1920.)

Croft, John. *Annotations on Plays of Shakespear.* York, 1810.

Crosby, Joseph (1822–91). Contributor to HUD2.

———. "The Banquet Scene in 'Antony and Cleopatra.' " *Shakespeariana* 1 (1883–4), 122–3.

———. Letters to various people [1870–84]. Folger MS Y.c.1372 (1–260). (Pub. in *One Touch of Shakespeare: Letters of Joseph Crosby to Joseph Parker Norris, 1875–1878.* Ed. John W. Velz and Francis N. Teague. Washington, London, & Toronto, 1986.)

———. "Notes on 'Antony and Cleopatra.' " *Shakespeariana* 1 (1883–4), 45–8.

———. "On a Passage in 'Antony and Cleopatra.' " 5 *N&Q* 7 (16 June 1877), 464–5.

Crosse, Gordon. *Shakespearean Playgoing 1890–1952.* 1953.

Cruickshank, C[harles] G. *Elizabeth's Army.* 2nd ed. OUP, 1966. (1st ed. 1946.)

Cudworth, Charles. "Song and Part-Song Settings of Shakespeare's Lyrics, 1660–1960." *Shakespeare in Music.* Ed. Phyllis Hartnoll. 1964. Pp. 51–89.

Cullum, Graham. " 'Condemning Shadows Quite': *Antony and Cleopatra.*" *Philosophy and Literature* 5 (1981), 186–203.

Cunningham, Dolora G. "The Characterization of Shakespeare's Cleopatra." *SQ* 6 (1955), 9–17.

Cutts, John P. "Charmian's 'Excellent Fortune!' " *AN&Q* 5 (1966–7), 148–9.

D., J. " 'Take In.' " 6 *N&Q* 2 (16 Oct. 1880), 304–5.

D., L. *"Antony and Cleopatra."* New Ireland Review 12 (1900), 377–81.

Daiches, David. "Guilt and Justice in Shakespeare." *Literary Essays.* Edinburgh & London, 1956. Pp. 1–25. (Delivered Aug. 1954.)

———. "Imagery and Meaning in *Antony and Cleopatra.*" *More Literary Essays.* Edinburgh, 1968. Pp. 70–95. (First pub. *ES* 43 [1962], 343–58.)

Daisne, Johan, ed. *Dictionnaire filmographique de la littérature mondiale.* 2 vols. Ghent, 1971–5.

Danby, John F. "*Antony and Cleopatra*: A Shakespearian Adjustment." *Poets on Fortune's Hill: Studies in Sidney, Shakespeare, Beaumont & Fletcher.* 1952. Pp. 128–51. (First pub. as "The Shakespearean Dialectic: An Aspect of 'Antony and Cleopatra,' " *Scrutiny* 16 [1949], 196–213.)

Daniel, Peter A. Contributor to CAM1.

———. *Notes and Conjectural Emendations of Certain Doubtful Passages in Shakespeare's Plays.* 1870. (Rpt. New York: AMS, 1972.)

———. "Time-Analysis of the Plots of Shakspere's Plays." *New Shakspere Society's Transactions 1877–9.* [1879.] Pp. 117–346.

Dañobeitia Fernández, María Luisa. "Cleopatra's Role Taking: A Study of *Antony and Cleopatra.*" *Revista Canaria de Estudios Ingleses* 12 (Apr. 1986), 55–73.

Daphinoff, Dimiter. "Zur Behandlung der Quellenfrage in der englisch-deutschen Studienausgabe der dramatischen Werke Shakespeares." *SJH,* 1975, pp. 179–93.

Dash, Irene G. *Wooing, Wedding, and Power: Women in Shakespeare's Plays.* New York, 1981.

David, Richard. *The Janus of Poets.* Cambridge, 1935.

———. *Shakespeare in the Theatre.* Cambridge, 1978.

Davidson, Clifford. "*Antony and Cleopatra*: Circe, Venus, and the Whore of Babylon." *Shakespeare: Contemporary Critical Approaches*. Ed. Harry R. Garvin. Lewisburg, Pa., 1980. Pp. 31–55.

———. "Shakespeare's Cleopatra: Circe, Venus, and the Whore of Babylon." *ShN* 23 (1973), 31. (Delivered Oct. 1972.)

Davies, H. Neville. "Jacobean *Antony and Cleopatra*." *ShakS* 17 (1985), 123–58.

Davies, Thomas. *Dramatic Miscellanies: Consisting of Critical Observations on Several Plays of Shakspeare*. 3 vols. 1783–4. Vol. 2. 1783.

Dawson, Anthony B. *Indirections: Shakespeare and the Art of Illusion*. Toronto, 1978.

Dawson, Giles E. Private Contributor.

Dawson, R. MacG. "But Why Enobarbus?" *N&Q* 232 (1987), 216–17.

Day, M[uriel] C., and J[ohn] C. Trewin. *The Shakespeare Memorial Theatre*. London & Toronto, 1932.

Dean, Winton. "Shakespeare and Opera." *Shakespeare in Music*. Ed. Phyllis Hartnoll. 1964. Pp. 89–145.

Degenhart, Karen. "*Antony and Cleopatra*: Psychic Elements in Conflict." *Lapis* 6 (1980), 29–39.

D[eighton], K[enneth]. " '*Antony and Cleopatra*', [1340–2]." 10 *N&Q* 8 (19 Oct. 1907), 303.

———. "Conjectural Emendations in Shakespeare." *Gent. Mag.* 302 (1907), 85–7.

———. *The Old Dramatists: Conjectural Readings*. Calcutta, 1898.

Delamaine, Charles J. "A Curious Crux in '*Antony and Cleopatra*.' " *The Herald* (Boston), 24 Dec. 1916, p. 8.

Delius, N[icolaus]. "Die Bühnenweisungen in den alten Shakespeare-Ausgaben." *SJ* 8 (1873), 171–201.

———. "Dryden und Shakespeare." *SJ* 4 (1869), 6–40. (Article dated 1868.)

———. "Klassische Reminiscenzen in Shakespeare's Dramen." *SJ* 18 (1883), 81–103.

———. "On Shakspere's Use of Narration in His Dramas. Part II." *New Shakspere Society's Transactions*, 1st Ser., Nos. 3–4 (1875–6), 332–45.

———. "Die Prosa in Shakespeare's Dramen." *SJ* 5 (1870), 227–73.

Delius, Rudolf von. *Shakespeare: Eine Neudeutung seines Geistes*. Reinbek, 1947.

Demizu, Shunzo. *Shakespeare's Tragedy*. Kyoto, 1967.

Dempewolf, Walter. *Shakespeares Modelle*. Jena, 1914. (Jena diss.)

Dennett, Drayton N. "Samuel Daniel's Tragedy of Cleopatra: A Critical Edition." Cornell Univ. diss., 1951.

Dent, R[obert] W. *Shakespeare's Proverbial Language: An Index*. Berkeley & London, 1981.

De Quincey, Thomas. "The Cæsars: Augustus Cæsar." *The Collected Writings*. New ed. by David Masson. Vol. 6. Edinburgh, 1890. Pp. 268–81. (First pub. *Blackwood's* 32 [1832], 949–55.)

———. "Shakspeare." *Encyclopædia Britannica*. 7th ed. Vol. 20. Edinburgh, 1842. Pp. 169–88. (Written 1838.)

Devrient, Otto. *Zwei Shakespeare-Vorträge*. Karlsruhe, 1869.

Dey, E. Merton. " '*Antony and Cleopatra*.' " 10 *N&Q* 12 (11 Dec. 1909), 464–5.

———. " '*Antony and Cleopatra*', [48–9, 2124, 3304–6]." 10 *N&Q* 10 (28 Nov. 1908), 424–5.

———. " '*Antony and Cleopatra*', [306–13]." 10 *N&Q* 10 (29 Aug. 1908), 165.

———. " '*Antony and Cleopatra*', [2345]." 10 *N&Q* 11 (30 Jan. 1909), 85.

Dias, Walter. *Shakespeare: His Tragic World. Psychological Explorations*. New Delhi, 1972.

Dickey, Franklin M. *Not Wisely But Too Well: Shakespeare's Love Tragedies.* San Marino, Calif., 1957.

Dietrich, Rainer. "Shakespeares Gesinnung: Thesen und Bedenken." *SJH*, 1965, pp. 184–204.

Dillon, Janette. " 'Solitariness': Shakespeare and Plutarch." *JEGP* 78 (1979), 325–44.

[Dobrée, Bonamy.] "Cleopatra and 'That Criticall War.' " *TLS*, 11 Oct. 1928, pp. 717–18.

Dobson, E[ric] J. *Phonology.* Vol. 2 of *English Pronunciation 1500–1700.* 2nd ed. OUP, 1968. (1st ed. 1957.)

Doccioli, Matilde. "La donna nei drammi dello Shakespeare." *Rassegna nazionale* 156 (1907), 584–94.

Dodd, William. *The Beauties of Shakespear.* 2 vols. 1752. (Rpt. London: Cass, 1971.)

Dollimore, Jonathan. *Radical Tragedy: Religion, Ideology and Power in the Drama of Shakespeare and his Contemporaries.* Chicago & London, 1983.

Donno, Elizabeth Story. "Cleopatra Again." *SQ* 7 (1956), 227–33.

Doran, Madeleine. " 'High Events as These': The Language of Hyperbole in *Antony and Cleopatra.*" *QQ* 72 (1965), 26–51.

Dorius, R. J. *"Antony and Cleopatra." How to Read Shakespearean Tragedy.* Ed. Edward Quinn. New York, 1978. Pp. 293–354.

———. "Shakespeare's dramatic Modes and *Antony and Cleopatra.*" *Literatur als Kritik des Lebens: Festschrift zum 65. Geburtstag von Ludwig Borinski.* Ed. Rudolf Haas, Heinz-Joachim Müllenbrock, & Claus Uhlig. Heidelberg, 1975. Pp. 83–96.

Douce, Francis. *Illustrations of Shakspeare, and of Ancient Manners.* 2 vols. 1807.

Douglas, James. " 'Antony and Cleopatra.' " *Harper's Monthly Magazine* 119 (1909), 583–9.

Dowden, Edward. *Shakspere: A Critical Study of his Mind and Art.* 3rd ed. 1877. (1st ed. 1875.)

———. "Shakspere's Portraiture of Women." *Transcripts and Studies.* 2nd ed. 1896. Pp. 338–77. (First pub. *ContempR* 47 [1885], 517–35.)

Downer, Alan S. "Heavenly Mingle: *Antony and Cleopatra* as a Dramatic Experience." *The Triple Bond: Plays, Mainly Shakespearean, in Performance.* Ed. Joseph G. Price. University Park & London, 1975. Pp. 240–54.

Drake, Nathan. *Shakspeare and his Times.* 2 vols. 1817.

Draper, John W. *The Humors & Shakespeare's Characters.* Durham, 1945.

———. " 'Hybris' in Shakespeare's Tragic Heroes." *EA* 18 (1965), 228–34.

———. "Minor Plots in Shakespearean Tragedy." *RLMC* 14 (1961), 133–40.

———. "The Realism of Shakespeare's Roman Plays." *SP* 30 (1933), 225–42.

———. "Shattered Personality in Shakespeare's Antony." *Psychiatric Quarterly* 39 (1965), 448–56.

———. "Speech-Tempo and Humor in Shakespeare's Antony." *Bulletin of the Institute for the History of Medicine* 20 (1946), 426–32.

———. "Subjective Conflict in Shakespearean Tragedy." *NM* 61 (1960), 214–21.

Dronke, Peter. "Shakespeare and Joseph of Exeter." *N&Q* 225 (1980), 172–4.

Dryden, John. "Preface to *All for Love: or The World Well Lost* (1678)." *Of Dramatic Poesy and Other Critical Essays.* Ed. George Watson. Vol. 1. London & New York, 1962. Pp. 221–31.

Duff, William. *Critical Observations on the Writings of the Most Celebrated Original Geniuses in Poetry.* 1770. (Rpt., introd. William Bruce Johnson; Delmar, N.Y.: Scholars' Facsimiles & Rpts., 1973.)

Duhring, L[ouis] A. (1845–1913). Contributor to v1907.

Dunbar, Georgia. "The Verse Rhythms of Antony and Cleopatra." *Style* 5 (1971), 231–45.

Dunn, Esther Cloudman. *Shakespeare in America.* 1939. (Rpt. New York: Blom, 1968.)

Duport, Paul. *Essais littéraires sur Shakspeare.* 2 vols. Paris, 1828.

Durbach, Errol. "*Antony and Cleopatra* and *Rosmersholm*: 'Third Empire' Love Tragedies." *CompD* 20 (1986), 1–16.

Dusinberre, Juliet. *Shakespeare and the Nature of Women.* 1975.

Duthie, George Ian. *Shakespeare.* 1951.

Dyboski, Roman. *Rise and Fall in Shakespeare's Dramatic Art.* Shakespeare Assn. Papers 9. 1923.

Dyce, Alexander. *Strictures on Mr. Collier's New Edition of Shakespeare, 1858.* 1859.

Dyche, Thomas, & William Pardon. *A New General English Dictionary.* 1740. (Rpt. Anglistica & Americana 81. Hildesheim & New York: Olms, 1972.)

Dyson, H. V. D. "This Mortal Coil—II: Shakespeare and Life in Death." *The Listener*, 16 Apr. 1964, pp. 637, 639.

Eagleson, Robert D. "Propertied As All The Tuned Spheres: Aspects of Shakespeare's Language." *The Teaching of English* 20 (1971), 4–15.

Eagleton, Terence. *Shakespeare and Society: Critical Studies in Shakespearean Drama.* London & New York, 1967.

———. *William Shakespeare.* Oxford, 1986.

Eckhoff, Lorentz. *Shakespeare: Spokesman of the Third Estate.* Tr. R. I. Christophersen. Oslo Stud. in Eng. 3. Oslo & OUP, 1954.

Edwards, Philip. *Shakespeare: A Writer's Progress.* OUP, 1986.

———. *Shakespeare and the Confines of Art.* 1968.

Edwards, Thomas (1699–1757). MS Notes *apud* v1778.

———. *A Supplement to Mr. Warburton's Edition of Shakespear. Being the Canons of Criticism, and Glossary.* 1748. (2nd ed. 1748. 7th ed.: *The Canons of Criticism, and Glossary.* By Thomas Edwards, Esq. 1765. Rpt. London: Cass, 1970.)

Edwards, W[illiam] A. *Plagiarism.* Cambridge, 1933.

Ehrl, Charlotte. *Sprachstil und Charakter bei Shakespeare.* Schriftenreihe der Deutschen Shakespeare-Gesellschaft, n. F. Band 6. Heidelberg, 1957.

Eisinger, Fritz. *Das Problem des Selbstmordes in der Literatur der englischen Renaissance.* Überlingen, 1925. (Freiburg diss.)

Eliot, T[homas] S[tearns]. "Hamlet and His Problems." *The Sacred Wood: Essays on Poetry and Criticism.* 7th ed. 1950. Pp. 95–103. (1st ed. 1920.)

———. "Shakespeares Verskunst." *Blätter des Deutschen Theaters in Göttingen* 89 (1955–6). (First pub. *Der Monat* 2 [No. 20, 1950], 198–207. Donald Gallup, *T. S. Eliot: A Bibliography*, 1969, p. 290, no. D238: "An unpublished lecture given on T. S. Eliot's German tour, based upon earlier unpublished lectures on Shakespeare delivered in Edinburgh in 1937. Translated anonymously by Gerhard Hensel.")

Ellehauge, Martin. "The Use of His Sources Made by Shakespeare in *Julius Cæsar* and *Antony and Cleopatra*." *Englische Studien* 65 (1930–1), 197–210.

[Elliott, M(adeleine) Leigh-Noel.] *Shakspeare's Garden of Girls.* 1885.

Ellis, Oliver C. de C. *Cleopatra in the Tide of Time.* The Poetry Lovers' Fellowship Pub. 1947.

Ellis-Fermor, U[na] M. *Christopher Marlowe.* 1927.

———. *The Jacobean Drama: An Interpretation.* 3rd ed. 1953. (1st ed. 1936.)

———. "The Nature of Plot in Drama." *Shakespeare the Dramatist and Other Papers.* Ed.

Kenneth Muir. London & New York, 1961. Pp. 78–101. (First pub. *E&S* NS 13 [1960], 65–81.)

Elton, Charles I. *William Shakespeare: His Family and Friends.* Ed. A. Hamilton Thompson. 1904.

Elze, K[arl]. "Notes and Conjectural Emendations on *Antony and Cleopatra* and *Pericles.*" *Englische Studien* 9 (1886), 267–90.

——. *Notes on Elizabethan Dramatists with Conjectural Emendations of the Text.* New ed. in one vol. Halle a. S., 1889. (Formerly pub. in 3 ser., 1880, 1884, 1886.)

Emerson, Oliver F. "*Antony and Cleopatra.*" *Poet Lore* 2 (1890), 71–7, 125–9, 188–92, 516–23.

The Encyclopædia Britannica. 11th ed. 29 vols. 1910–11.

Engelen, Julia. "Die Schauspieler-Ökonomie in Shakespeares Dramen." *SJ* 63 (1927), 75–158.

Enright, D[ennis] J. *Shakespeare and the Students.* London & Toronto, 1970.

Erickson, Peter. *Patriarchal Structures in Shakespeare's Drama.* Berkeley, 1985.

Erskine-Hill, Howard. "Antony and Octavius: The Theme of Temperance in Shakespeare's 'Antony and Cleopatra.'" *RMS* 14 (1970), 26–47.

——. *The Augustan Idea in English Literature.* 1983.

Erwin, John W. "Hero as Audience: *Antony and Cleopatra* and *Le Soulier de Satin.*" *MLS* 4, No. 2 (1974), 65–77.

Eskin, Stanley G. "Politics in Shakespeare's Plays." *BuR* 15, No. 3 (1967), 47–64.

Estrin, Barbara L. " 'Behind a dream': Cleopatra and Sonnet 129." *Women's Studies* 9 (1982), 177–88.

Etty, J. L. "Studies in Shakespeare's History. VII.—Antony and Cleopatra." *Macmillan's Magazine* 89 (1903–4), 302–9.

Evans, B[enjamin] Ifor. *The Language of Shakespeare's Plays.* 3rd ed. 1964. (1st ed. 1952.)

Evans, Bertrand. *Shakespeare's Tragic Practice.* OUP, 1979.

Evans, Gareth Lloyd. *Shakespeare.* Pt. 5: 1606–16. Writers and Critics [72]. Edinburgh, 1973.

Everett, Barbara. "On a Sumptuous Scale." (Rev. of *Ant.* at the Olivier Th.) *TLS*, 24 Apr. 1987, p. 439.

Everett, William. "Six Cleopatras." *The Atlantic Monthly* 95 (1905), 252–63.

Faber, M. D. "*Antony and Cleopatra*: The Empire of the Self." *Psychoanalytic Review* 72 (1985), 71–104.

Fairholt, F[rederick] W. *Costume in England: A History of Dress from the Earliest Period till the Close of the Eighteenth Century.* 1846.

Farmer, Harold. " 'I'll give thee leave to play': Theatre Symbolism in Antony and Cleopatra." *ESA* 20 (1977), 107–20.

Farmer, Richard. *An Essay on the Learning of Shakespeare.* 2nd, enl. ed. Cambridge, 1767. (1st ed. 1767.)

Farnham, Willard. *Shakespeare's Tragic Frontier: The World of His Final Tragedies.* Berkeley, 1950; Oxford, 1973.

Felperin, Howard. *Shakespearean Representation: Mimesis and Modernity in Elizabethan Tragedy.* Princeton, 1977.

Fergusson, Francis. "*Antony and Cleopatra.*" *Shakespeare: The Pattern in His Carpet.* New York, 1970. Pp. 249–57. (First pub. in Sisson ed. 1961, Laurel Sh., pp. 7–17.)

——. "Poetry and Drama." *Symbolism and Modern Literature: Studies in Honor of Wallace Fowlie.* Ed. Marcel Tetel. Durham, 1978. Pp. 13–25.

Ferrara, Fernando. "Sesso e potere. Le truffe di Cleopatra." *Annali-Anglistica* 22 (1977), 27–80.

Fichter, Andrew. " 'Antony and Cleopatra': 'The Time of Universal Peace.' " *ShS* 33 (1980), 99–111.

Fisch, Harold. " 'Antony and Cleopatra': The Limits of Mythology." *ShS* 23 (1970), 59–67.

Fiskin, A. M. I. "Antony and Cleopatra: Tangled Skeins of Love and Power." *UDQ* 10, No. 2 (1975), 93–105.

Fitch, Robert E. "No Greater Crack?" *SQ* 19 (1968), 3–17.

––––––. *Shakespeare: The Perspective of Value.* Philadelphia, 1969.

Fitz, L. T. "Egyptian Queens and Male Reviewers: Sexist Attitudes in *Antony and Cleopatra* Criticism." *SQ* 28 (1977), 297–316.

––––––. *See* Woodbridge, Linda.

Fitzgerald, Percy. *Shakespearean Representation: Its Laws and Limits.* 1908.

Fleay, F. G. "On Metrical Tests Applied to Shakespeare." In C[lement] M. Ingleby. *Occasional Papers on Shakespeare: Being the Second Part of Shakespeare the Man and the Book.* 1881. Pp. 50–141.

Flesch, William. "Proximity and Power: Shakespearean and Cinematic Space." *Educational Theatre Journal* 39 (1987), 277–93.

Florio, John. *A Worlde of Wordes.* 1598. (Rpt. Anglistica & Americana 114. Hildesheim & New York: Olms, 1972.)

Fluchère, Henri. *Shakespeare.* Tr. Guy Hamilton. 1953. (1st Fr. ed. 1948.)

Foakes, R[eginald] A. "Shakespeare's Later Tragedies." *Shakespeare 1564–1964: A Collection of Modern Essays by Various Hands.* Ed. Edward A. Bloom. Providence, R.I., 1964. Pp. 95–109.

––––––. "Vision and Reality in *Antony and Cleopatra.*" *DUJ* 25 (1964), 66–76.

Foard, James T. "Shakespeare's Classical Plays." *Manchester Quarterly* 12 (1893), 333–71.

Foreman, Walter C., Jr. *The Music of the Close: The Final Scenes of Shakespeare's Tragedies.* Lexington, Ky., 1978.

Fortescue, J. W. "The Army: Military Service and Equipment. (§1 The Soldier)." *Shakespeare's England: An Account of the Life & Manners of his Age.* 2 vols. OUP, 1916. 1:112–26.

Foy, Ted C. "Shakespeare's Use of Time: A Study of Four Plays." Univ. of Delaware diss., 1974. (*DA* 35 [1974], 2220–1A.)

Franciscus. "Shakspeare's Designation of Cleopatra." 1 *N&Q* 3 (7 June 1851), 465.

Franz, Wilhelm. *Die Sprache Shakespeares in Vers und Prosa. Shakespeare-Grammatik* in 4. Auflage überarbeitet und wesentlich erweitert. Halle a. S., 1939. (First pub. as *Shakespeare-Grammatik* in 1898–9. 2nd ed., 1909; 3rd ed., 1924; 4th ed. incl. all material from *Orthographie, Lautgebung und Wortbildung in den Werken Shakespeares mit Ausspracheproben,* Heidelberg, 1905, and *Shakespeares Blankvers,* 2. Auflage, Tübingen, 1935.)

French, A[ntony] L. *Shakespeare and the Critics.* Cambridge, 1972.

French, Marilyn. *Shakespeare's Division of Experience.* New York, 1981.

Frenzel, Karl. *Berliner Dramaturgie.* Vol. 1. Hannover, 1877. (Pp. 256–64: review of a performance May 1871.)

Freytag, Gustav. *Technique of the Drama.* Tr. from 6th Ger. ed. (1890) by Elias J. MacEwan. 2nd ed. Chicago, 1894. (Rpt. St. Clair Shores, Mich.: Scholarly Press, n.d. 1st Ger. ed. 1863.)

Fricker, Robert. *Das ältere englische Schauspiel.* 3 vols. Bern & München, 1975–87. Vol. 2. 1983.

––––––. *Kontrast und Polarität in den Charakterbildern Shakespeares.* Schweizerische Anglistische Arbeiten 22. Bern, 1951.

Friedman, Stanley. "*Antony and Cleopatra* and Drayton's *Mortimeriados.*" *SQ* 20 (1969), 481–4.

Friesen, Herm[ann] Freih[err] von. *Will[iam] Shakspere's Dramen: Von 1601 bis zum Schlusse seiner Laufbahn*. Vol. 3 of *Shakspere-Studien*. Wien, 1876.

Fripp, Edgar I. *Shakespeare, Man and Artist*. 2 vols. OUP, 1938.

———. "Shakespeare's Use of Ovid's *Metamorphoses*." *Shakespeare Studies: Biographical and Literary*. OUP, 1930. Pp. 98–128.

Frost, David L. "*Antony and Cleopatra*—All for Love; or the World Ill-Lost?" *Topic* 4 (No. 7) (1964), 33–44.

———. *The School of Shakespeare: The Influence of Shakespeare on English Drama, 1600–1642*. New York, 1968.

Frye, Northrop. *Fools of Time: Studies in Shakespearean Tragedy*. Toronto, 1967.

———. *Northrop Frye on Shakespeare*. Ed. Robert Sandler. New Haven & London, 1986.

Frye, Roland M. *Shakespeare: The Art of the Dramatist*. Boston, 1970.

———. "Theological and Non-theological Structures in Tragedy." *ShakS* 4 (1968), 132–48. (Delivered Sept. 1966.)

Fujii, Takeo. "A New Heaven in *Antony and Cleopatra*." *Kansai Gaikokugo University Kenkyu Ronshu* 12 (1967), 17–36.

Fujita, Makoto. "The Stage of *Antony and Cleopatra*." *Eigo Eibungaku Ronso* 17 (1967), 1–16.

Fujita, Minoru. "The Concept of the Royal in Shakespeare." *ShStud* 7 (1968–9), 1–32.

Furness, Horace Howard, ed. *The Tempest*. A New Variorum Ed. of Sh. Philadelphia, 1892.

Furnivall, F. J. " 'Embossed.' " 4 *N&Q* 11 (21 June 1873), 507.

Fuzier, Jean. "*Antony and Cleopatra*'s Three-Stage Tragic Structure: A Study in Development." *CahiersE* 13 (1978), 69–74.

Galloway, David. " 'I am dying, Egypt, dying': Folio Repetitions and the Editors." *N&Q* 203 (1958), 330–5.

Gantillon, P. J. F. "Arm-gaunt." 5 *N&Q* 12 (27 Sept. 1879), 244.

Garber, Marjorie B. *Dream in Shakespeare: From Metaphor to Metamorphosis*. New Haven, 1974.

Gardner, C. O. "Themes of Manhood in Five Shakespeare Tragedies: Some Notes on *Othello, King Lear, Macbeth, Antony and Cleopatra* and *Coriolanus*." *Theoria* 30 (1968), 19–43.

Garnett, Richard, & Edmund Gosse. *English Literature: An Illustrated Record*. 4 vols. London & New York, 1903.

Gawalewicz, Marian. *Sylwetki i Szkice Literackie*. Cracow, 1888.

Genée, Rudolph. *Shakespeare's Leben und Werke*. New ed. Vol. 1 of *Shakespeare's dramatische Werke*, tr. Franz Dingelstedt et al. Leipzig, 1878. (1st ed. 1872.)

———. *William Shakespeare in seinem Werden und Wesen*. Berlin, 1905.

[Genest, John.] *Some Account of the English Stage, from the Restoration in 1660 to 1830*. 10 vols. Bath, 1832.

George, Kathleen. *Rhythm in Drama*. Pittsburgh, 1980.

Gerarde, John. *The Herball or generall Historie of Plantes*. 1597.

[Gerstenberg, Heinrich Wilhelm von.] "Achtzehnter Brief ('Beschluß')." *Briefe über Merkwürdigkeiten der Litteratur*. Stuttgart, 1890. Pp. 159–66. (Written 1766.)

Gervinus, G[eorg] G. *Shakespeare Commentaries*. Tr. F. E. Bunnètt. Rev. ed. 1883. (1st Ger. ed. Leipzig, 1849–50; 1st ed. of tr., 2 vols., 1863.)

Gerwig, George W. *Shakespeare's Ideals of Womanhood*. East Aurora, N.Y., 1929.

Ghosh, Gauri P. "*Antony and Cleopatra*: The First Recoil from the Tragic Impasse." *Journal of the Dept. of English, Univ. of Calcutta* 20, No. 2 (1985–6), 1–20.

[Gildon, Charles.] *The Lives and Characters of the English Dramatick Poets. . . . By Gerard Langbaine, [rev. Charles Gildon]. [1699.]* (Rpt. New York & London: Garland, 1973.)

[————.] "Remarks on the Plays of Shakespear." In supplementary vol. 7 (1710) added to Nicholas Rowe, ed., *The Works of Shakespear*, 6 vols., 1709. Pp. 257–444. (Rpt. New York: AMS, 1967.)

Giles, Henry. *Human Life in Shakespeare*. Boston, 1868.

Gillet, Louis. *Shakespeare*. Paris, [1930].

Gleichen-Russwurm, Alexander Freiherr von. *Shakespeares Frauengestalten*. Nürnberg, [1909].

Glunz, Hans H. *Shakespeares Staat*. Frankfurt a. M., 1940.

Goddard, Harold C. *The Meaning of Shakespeare*. 2 vols. Chicago, 1951.

Godshalk, W[illiam] L. "Dolabella as Agent Provocateur." *RenP*, 1977, pp. 69–74.

————. *Patterning in Shakespearean Drama: Essays in Criticism*. De proprietatibus litterarum. Series practica 69. The Hague, 1973.

Goethe, Johann Wolfgang von. *Goethe's Literary Essays: A Selection in English arranged by J. E. Spingarn*. New York, 1921. (Incl. tr. of "Shakespeare und kein Ende," written 1813–16.)

Gohlke, Madelon. " 'I wooed thee with my sword': Shakespeare's Tragic Paradigms." *The Woman's Part: Feminist Criticism of Shakespeare*. Ed. Carolyn R. S. Lenz, Gayle Greene, & Carol T. Neely. Urbana, 1980. Pp. 150–70.

Goldberg, Jonathan. *James I and the Politics of Literature*. Baltimore & London, 1983.

Goldberg, S. L. "The Tragedy of the Imagination: A Reading of *Antony and Cleopatra*." *CR* 4 (1961), 41–64.

Goldman, Michael. *Acting and Action in Shakespearean Tragedy*. Princeton, 1985.

Gould, George. *Corrigenda and Explanations of the Text of Shakspere*. A new issue [enl. ed.]. 1884. A second continuation. 1887. (1st ed. 1881.)

Gourlay, Patricia S. "Shakespeare's Use of North's Plutarch in the Roman Plays, with Special Reference to *Julius Caesar*." Columbia Univ. diss., 1969. (*DA* 31 [1970], 1757A.)

Gowing, Aylmer. "The Graphic Gallery of Shakespeare's Heroines. Olivia—Cleopatra—Miranda." *The Theatre* NS 12 (1888), 80–4.

Grabbe, Christian Dietrich. "Über die Shakspearo-Manie." *Werke*. Ed. Roy C. Cowen. Vol. 2. München, 1977. Pp. 417–45. (First pub. *Dramatische Dichtungen*, vol. 2 [Frankfurt a. M., 1827], pp. 329–84.)

Grace, William J. *Approaching Shakespeare*. New York & London, 1964.

Grant, Michael. *Cleopatra*. 1972.

Granville-Barker, Harley. *Prefaces to Shakespeare*. 2 vols. Princeton, 1946–7. Vol. 1. 1946. (1st ed. 1930.)

Gray, Henry D. "Antony's Amazing 'I Will To Egypt.' " *MP* 15 (1917–18), 43–52.

————. "Chronology of Shakespeare's Plays." *MLN* 46 (1931), 147–50.

Green, David C. *Plutarch Revisited: A Study of Shakespeare's Last Roman Tragedies and Their Source*. Jacobean Drama Stud. 78. Salzburg, 1979.

Green, Henry. *Shakespeare and the Emblem Writers*. 1870.

Green, J. T. "Shakespearean Women Contrasts: Cleopatra, Cordelia and Isabella." *FHP* 3, No. 5 (1966), 17–23.

Greene, James J. "*Antony and Cleopatra*: The Birth and Death of Androgyny." *Hartford Studies in Literature* 19, Nos. 2–3 (1987), 24–44.

Greg, W[alter] W. *Bibliography of the English Printed Drama to the Restoration*. 4 vols. 1939–59.

————. *The Editorial Problem in Shakespeare: A Survey of the Foundations of the Text*. 3rd ed. OUP, 1954. (1st ed. 1942.)

————. *The Shakespeare First Folio: Its Bibliographical and Textual History*. OUP, 1955.

————, ed. *Pericles*. Sh. Quartos in Collotype Facsimile 5. OUP, 1940.

Gregor, Joseph. *Shakespeare: Der Aufbau eines Zeitalters.* 3rd ed. München, 1948. (1st ed. 1935.)

Gregson, J. M. *Public and Private Man in Shakespeare.* London & Canberra, 1983.

Grene, David. *The Actor in History: A Study in Shakespearean Stage Poetry.* University Park & London, 1988. (Rev. from lectures given in 1978.)

Grene, W. D. "Antony and Cleopatra." *Hermathena* 118 (1974), 33–47.

Grey, Zachary. *Critical, Historical, and Explanatory Notes on Shakespeare.* 2 vols. 1754. (Rpt. New York: AMS, 1973.)

[————.] *Remarks upon a Late Edition* [by Bishop Warburton] *of Shakespear; with a Long String of Emendations borrowed . . . from the Oxford Edition.* [1755.]

Greyerz, Georg von. *The Reported Scenes in Shakespeare's Plays.* Bern, 1965.

Griffin, Alice. *The Sources of Ten Shakespeare Plays.* New York, 1966.

Griffin, G[ilderoy] W. "Antony and Cleopatra." *Studies In Literature.* Baltimore, 1870. Pp. 76–82.

Griffith, [Elizabeth]. *The Morality of Shakespeare's Drama Illustrated.* 1775. (Rpt. Eighteenth Century Sh. 14. London: Cass, 1971.)

Griffith, Hubert. "Antony, Cleopatra, and Others." *The New English Review* 14 (1947), 162–7.

Griffiths, G. S. "*Antony and Cleopatra.*" *E&S* 31 (1945), 34–67.

Grill, Cynthia. "Antony, Cleopatra, and Proculeius." *N&Q* 205 (1960), 191.

Grimes. Contributor to CAM1.

Grindon, [Rosa] Leo. *A Woman's Study of* Antony and Cleopatra. Manchester, 1909.

Grivelet, Michel. "La critique dramatique française devant Shakespeare." *EA* 13 (1960), 264–82.

Grosart, Alexander B., ed. *The Complete Works in Verse and Prose of Samuel Daniel.* 5 vols. 1885–96. (Rpt. New York: Russell & Russell, 1963.)

Gruber, William E. "The Actor in the Script: Affective Strategies in Shakespeare's *Antony and Cleopatra.*" *CompD* 19 (1985), 30–48.

Grudin, Robert. *Mighty Opposites: Shakespeare and Renaissance Contrariety.* Berkeley, 1979.

Günther, Albrecht E. "Antonius und Kleopatra: Ein Schauspiel auf mythischer Grundlage." *Deutsches Volkstum* 16 (1934), 573–9.

Günther, Alfred. *William Shakespeare.* Vol. 2. Friedrichs Dramatiker des Welttheaters. 2nd ed. Velber, 1967. (1st ed. 1965.)

Günther, Peter. "Shakespeares *Antony and Cleopatra*: Wandel und Gestaltung eines Stoffes." *SJH,* 1968, pp. 94–108.

Gundolf, Friedrich. *Shakespeare, sein Wesen und Werk.* 2 vols. Zweite Auflage. Berlin, 1949. (1st ed. 1928.)

————. "Shakespeares Antonius und Cleopatra. Festvortrag." *SJ* 62 (1926), 7–35.

Gura, Timothy J. "The Function of the Hero in Shakespeare's Last Tragedies." Northwestern Univ. diss., 1974. (*DA* 35 [1974], 3681A.)

Gurr, Andrew. *The Shakespearean Stage 1574–1642.* Cambridge, 1970.

H., L. Contributor to mTHEO2.

H., M. "*Original Elucidations of* Shakespear." *Gent. Mag.* 60 (1790), 306–7.

Haines, Charles. *William Shakespeare and His Plays.* London & New York, 1968.

Haines, C[harles] M. "The Development of Shakespeare's Stagecraft." *A Series of Papers on Shakespeare and the Theatre . . . by Members of the Shakespeare Assn.* OUP, 1927. Pp. 35–61.

Hall, A. "[*Ant.* 578.]" 8 *N&Q* 2 (8 Oct. 1892), 283.

Hall, Henry T. (1813–79). Contributor to HUD2.

———. *Shaksperean Fly-Leaves and Jottings.* New & enl. ed. 1871. (Rpt. New York: AMS, 1970. 1st ed. 1869.)

———. *Shakspere's Plays: the Separate Editions of, with the Alterations Done By Various Hands.* 2nd ed. Cambridge, 1880. (1st ed. 1873.)

Hall, Michael. *The Structure of Love: Representational Patterns and Shakespeare's Love Tragedies.* Charlottesville, 1989.

Hallam, Henry. *Introduction to the Literature of Europe, in the Fifteenth, Sixteenth, and Seventeenth Centuries.* 4th ed. 3 vols. 1854. (1st ed. 1839.)

Hallett, Charles A. "Change, Fortune, and Time: Aspects of the Sublunar World in *Antony and Cleopatra.*" *JEGP* 75 (1976), 75–89.

Halliday, F[rank] E. *The Poetry of Shakespeare's Plays.* London & New York, 1954.

Halliwell[-Phillipps], J[ames] O. *Selected Notes upon Shakespeare's Tragedy of* Antony and Cleopatra. 1868.

———. *Some Account of the Popular Belief in Animated Horse-Hairs, Alluded to by Shakespeare in the Play of Antony and Cleopatra.* N.p., 1866.

Halstead, William P. *Shakespeare as Spoken: A Collation of 5000 Acting Editions and Promptbooks of Shakespeare.* 12 vols. Ann Arbor, Mich., 1972. Vol. 12.

Hamilton, Donna B. "*Antony and Cleopatra* and the Tradition of Noble Lovers." *SQ* 24 (1973), 245–51.

Hanea, V. "Concepţiile antifeudale ale lui Shakespeare în 'Tragediile Romane.' " *Analele Universităţii Bucureşti* (Seria Ştiinţe Sociale, Filologie) 10 (1961), 429–50.

Hanford, James H. "Suicide in the Plays of Shakespeare." *PMLA* 27 (1912), 380–97.

Hankins, John E. *Backgrounds of Shakespeare's Thought.* Hassocks, Sussex, 1978.

———. *Shakespeare's Derived Imagery.* Lawrence, Kans., 1953.

Hannmann, Friedrich. *Dryden's tragödie "All for Love or the World well Lost" und ihr verhältnis zu Shakespeare's "Antony and Cleopatra."* Rostock, 1903. (Rostock diss.)

Hapgood, Robert. "Hearing Shakespeare: Sound and Meaning in 'Antony and Cleopatra.' " *ShS* 24 (1971), 1–12.

Haponski, William Charles. "Shakespeare's Ambiguous Heroes." Cornell Univ. diss., 1967. (*DA* 28 [1968], 3670A.)

Harbage, Alfred. *See* Kyd, Thomas.

———. *William Shakespeare: A Reader's Guide.* New York & Toronto, 1963.

Harding, D. W. "Women's Fantasy of Manhood." *SQ* 20 (1969), 245–53.

Harman, Edward G. *The "Impersonality" of Shakespeare.* 1925. (Written 1919.)

Harrier, Richard C. "Cleopatra's End." *SQ* 13 (1962), 63–5.

Harris, Duncan C. " 'Again for Cydnus': The Dramaturgical Resolution of *Antony and Cleopatra.*" *SEL* 17 (1977), 219–31.

Harris, Frank. *The Man Shakespeare and his Tragic Life Story.* 2nd rev. ed. 1911. (1st ed. 1909.)

———. *The Women of Shakespeare.* [1911].

Harrison, G[eorge] B. "A Note on *Coriolanus.*" *Joseph Quincy Adams Memorial Studies.* Ed. James G. McManaway, Giles E. Dawson, & Edwin E. Willoughby. Washington, D.C., 1948. Pp. 239–52.

———. *Shakespeare's Tragedies.* 1951.

Harrison, Thomas P. "Shakespeare and Marlowe's *Dido, Queen of Carthage.*" *TxSE* 35 (1956), 57–63.

Harting, James E. *The Ornithology of Shakespeare*. Old Woking, 1864. (Rpt. Unwin Brothers, 1978.)

Hartsock, Mildred E. "Major Scenes in Minor Key." *SQ* 21 (1970), 55–62.

Hauser, Arnold. *Mannerism*. Tr. Eric Mosbacher. 2 vols. New York, 1965. (Ger. ed. 1964.)

Hawkes, Terence. *Shakespeare's Talking Animals: Language and Drama in Society*. 1973.

———, & Michael Quinn. "Two Points of View on Antony and Cleopatra." *AWR* 13 (Winter 1963), 7–18.

Hawkins, Sir John (1719–89). Contributor to v1778.

Hazlitt, William. *Complete Works*. Ed. P. P. Howe. 21 vols. 1930–4. ("Characters of Shakespear's Plays: *Antony and Cleopatra*," vol. 4 [1930], pp. 228–32, first pub. 1817; "A View of the English Stage or A Series of Dramatic Criticisms: *Antony and Cleopatra* [16 Nov. 1813]," vol. 5 [1930], pp. 190–2.)

Heath, Benjamin (1704–66). Contributor to v1773.

[———.] *A Revisal of Shakespear's Text*. 1765.

Heffner, Ray L., Jr. "The Messengers in Shakespeare's *Antony and Cleopatra*." *ELH* 43 (1976), 154–62.

Heilman, Robert B. "From Mine Own Knowledge: A Theme in the Late Tragedies." *CentR* 8 (1964), 17–38.

Heine, Heinrich. "Shakespeare's Maidens and Women: Cleopatra." *The Works*. Tr. Charles G. Leland. Vol. 1. 1891. Pp. 302–10. (1st Ger. ed. 1838.)

Heninger, S[imeon] K., Jr. *A Handbook of Renaissance Meteorology*. Durham, 1960.

Henley, Samuel (1740–1815). Contributor to v1785.

Henn, T[homas] R. *The Living Image: Shakespearean Essays*. 1972.

Heraud, John A. *Shakspere: His Inner Life as Intimated in his Works*. 1865.

Herbert, T. Walter. "A Study of Meaning in *Antony & Cleopatra*." . . . *All These To Teach: Essays in Honor of C. A. Robertson*. Ed. Robert A. Bryan et al. Gainesville, Fla., 1965. Pp. 47–66.

Herford, C[harles] H. *Shakespeare*. The People's Books 6. London & Edinburgh, [1912].

———. "Shakespeare's Treatment of Love and Marriage." *Shakespeare's Treatment of Love & Marriage and Other Essays*. 1921. Pp. 1–43. (First pub. *Edda* 3 [1916], 92–111.)

———. *A Sketch of Recent Shakesperean Investigation 1893–1923*. [1923].

Hettner, Hermann. *Das moderne Drama: Aesthetische Untersuchungen*. Braunschweig, 1852.

Heuer, Hermann. "Lebensgefühl und Wertwelt in Shakespeares Römerdramen." *Zeitschrift für neusprachlichen Unterricht* 37 (1938), 65–90.

Hibbard, G. R. "Feliciter audax: Antony and Cleopatra, [2–35]." *Shakespeare's Styles: Essays in honour of Kenneth Muir*. Ed. Philip Edwards, Inga-Stina Ewbank, & G[eorge] K. Hunter. Cambridge, 1980. Pp. 95–109.

Highet, Gilbert. *The Classical Tradition: Greek and Roman Influences on Western Literature*. OUP, 1949.

Hill, James L. "The Marriage of True Bodies: Myth and Metamorphosis in *Antony and Cleopatra*." *REAL—The Yearbook of Research in English and American Literature* 2 (1984), 211–37.

[Hill, John.] *A Letter to the Hon. Author of the New Farce, Called the Rout. To which is subjoined, An Epistle to Mr. G——k, upon That, and other Theatrical Subjects. With an Appendix; containing Some Remarks upon the new-revived Play of Antony and Cleopatra*. 1759.

Hillemann, Felix. *Shakespeares Kleopatra: Ein Entwurf ihrer Problemeinheit*. Marburg, 1945. (Marburg diss.)

Hillman, Richard. "Antony, Hercules, and Cleopatra: 'the bidding of the gods' and 'the subtlest maze of all.' " *SQ* 38 (1987), 442–51.

Hinman, Charlton. *The Printing and Proof-reading of the First Folio of Shakespeare.* 2 vols. OUP, 1963.

Hirsh, James E. *The Structure of Shakespearean Scenes.* New Haven & London, 1981.

Hirzel, Rudolf. *Plutarch.* Das Erbe der Alten 4. Leipzig, 1912.

Hodges, C[yril] Walter. *The Globe Restored: A Study of the Elizabethan Theatre.* 2nd ed. OUP, 1968. (1st ed. 1953.)

Hodgson, Geraldine. "Enobarbus—The Enigma." *The Church Quarterly Review* 122 (1936), 88–99.

Hoeniger, F[rederick] D., ed. *Pericles.* The [New] Arden Sh. 1963.

Holaday, Allan. "Antonio and the Allegory of Salvation." *ShakS* 4 (1968), 109–18.

Holland, Norman N. *The Shakespearean Imagination.* New York, 1964.

Holloway, John. *The Story of the Night: Studies in Shakespeare's Major Tragedies.* 1961.

Holmberg, Arthur. "Estelle Parson's *Antony and Cleopatra.*" *SQ* 31 (1980), 195–7.

Homan, Sidney R. "Divided Response and the Imagination in *Antony and Cleopatra.*" *PQ* 49 (1970), 460–8.

———. "When the Theater Turns to Itself." *NLH* 2 (1971), 407–17.

Honda, Akira. "Antonius to Antony." *Hosei Daigaku Bungakubu Kiyo* (Hosei Univ. Stud. in Eng. and Am. Lit.) 3 (1958), 1–15.

Honigmann, E[rnst] A. J. *Shakespeare, Seven Tragedies: The Dramatist's Manipulation of Response.* London & New York, 1976.

———. "Shakespeare's Plutarch." *SQ* 10 (1959), 25–33.

Hook, Frank S. Letter. *CE* 17 (1955–6), 365–6.

Hooks, Roberta. "Shakespeare's *Antony and Cleopatra*: Power and Submission." *American Imago* 44 (1987), 37–49.

Hoover, Sr. Mary Frederic. "A Study of Imagery in Shakespeare's Sonnets, 'Troilus and Cressida', 'Macbeth', 'Antony and Cleopatra', and 'The Winter's Tale.' " Case Western Reserve Univ. diss., 1973. (*DA* 34 [1974], 5103A–4A.)

Hope, A[lec] D. "All for Love, or Comedy as Tragedy." *The Cave and the Spring: Essays on Poetry.* Adelaide, 1965. Pp. 144–65.

Horn, Franz. *Shakspeare's Schauspiele, erläutert.* 5 vols. Leipzig, 1823–31. Vol. 4. 1827.

Horne, Herman H. *Shakespeare's Philosophy of Love.* Raleigh, N.C., 1945.

Horowitz, David. *Shakespeare: An Existential View.* New York, 1965.

Hosley, Richard. "The Staging of the Monument Scenes in *Antony and Cleopatra.*" *LC* 30 (1964), 62–71.

Hosokawa, Makoto. "Absoluteness and Relativity in *Antony and Cleopatra.*" *Kenkyu Hokoku* 14A (1979), 23–32.

Hotson, Leslie. *Shakespeare's Sonnets Dated and Other Essays.* 1949.

———. *Shakespeare's Wooden O.* 1959.

Houston, John P. *Shakespearean Sentences: A Study in Style and Syntax.* Baton Rouge & London, 1988.

Howard-Hill, T[revor] H. *Compositors B and E in the Shakespeare First Folio and Some Recent Studies.* Columbia, S.C., 1976.

———. "New Light on Compositor E of the Shakespeare First Folio." 6 *Library* 2 (1980), 156–78.

———. *A Reassessment of Compositors B and E in the First Folio Tragedies.* Columbia, S.C., 1977.

————. "Spelling and the Bibliographer." 5 *Library* 18 (1963), 1–28.

Howarth, Robert G. *A Pot of Gillyflowers: Studies and Notes.* Cape Town, 1964.

Hoy, Cyrus. "Jacobean Tragedy and the Mannerist Style." *ShS* 26 (1973), 49–67.

Hubbell, Lindley W. *Lectures on Shakespeare.* Tokyo, [1953]. (Rpt. New York: AMS, 1972.)

Hudson, H[enry] N. *Shakespeare: His Life, Art, and Characters.* 2 vols. Boston, 1872. (Rpt. New York: AMS, 1973. Rev. from ed. 1855.)

Hülsmann, Eduard. *Shakespeare: Sein Geist und seine Werke.* Leipzig, 1856.

Hughes, Derek. "Art and Life in *All for Love.*" *SP* 80 (1983), 84–107.

Hulme, Hilda M. *Explorations in Shakespeare's Language: Some Problems of Lexical Meaning in the Dramatic Text.* 1962.

————. "The Spoken Language and the Dramatic Text: Some Notes on the Interpretation of Shakespeare's Language." *SQ* 9 (1958), 379–86.

Huloet, Richard. *Abcedarivm anglicolatinvm.* 1552. (Rpt. Menston: Scolar, 1970.)

[————.] *Hvloets Dictionarie, newelye corrected . . . by John Higgins.* 1572.

Hume, Robert D. "Individuation and Development of Character Through Language in *Antony and Cleopatra.*" *SQ* 24 (1973), 280–300.

Hunter, G. K. "The Last Tragic Heroes." *Later Shakespeare.* Stratford-upon-Avon Stud. 8. Gen. Eds. John Russell Brown & Bernard Harris. 1966. Pp. 11–28.

Hunter, Joseph. *New Illustrations of the Life, Studies, and Writings of Shakespeare.* 2 vols. 1845. (Rpt. New York: AMS, 1976.)

Hunter, Robert G. "Cleopatra and the '*Oestre Junonicque*.' " *ShakS* 5 (1969), 236–9.

Hurd, Richard. "Notes on the Art of Poetry." *The Works.* 1811. 1:63–277. (Rpt. Anglistica & Americana 44. Hildesheim & New York: Olms, 1969. First pub. 1757.)

Hyman, Stanley Edgar. "English Neo-Classicism." *Poetry and Criticism: Four Revolutions in Literary Taste.* New York, 1961. Pp. 39–55.

Hymel, Cynthia D. "Shakespeare's *Antony and Cleopatra* [3495–3530]." *Expl* 37, No. 4 (1979), 2–4.

Ide, Richard S. *Possessed with Greatness: The Heroic Tragedies of Chapman and Shakespeare.* Chapel Hill, 1980.

Imam, Syed Mehdi. "Studies of Shakespeare's Plays: II. *Antony and Cleopatra.*" *Mother India* 11 (1959), 51–61.

Ingleby, C[lement] M. "Misprinted Articles and Pronouns in Shakspeare." 6 *N&Q* 6 (9 Sept. 1882), 205–6.

————. *Occasional Papers on Shakespeare: Being the Second Part of Shakespeare the Man and the Book.* 1881.

————. *Shakespeare Hermeneutics, or The Still Lion, Being an Essay towards the Restoration of Shakespeare's Text.* 1875. (Rpt. New York: Haskell House, 1971.)

————. *Shakespeare, the Man and the Book.* 2 vols. 1877–81. *Part the First.* 1877.

Ingleby, Holcombe. " 'Anthony and Cleopatra', II.ii. [920–1]." 7 *N&Q* 11 (7 Mar. 1891), 182.

————. " 'Antony and Cleopatra', [641, 743]." 7 *N&Q* 12 (4 July 1891), 3.

Ingram, John K. "On the 'Weak Endings' of Shakspere, with Some Account of the History of the Verse-Tests in General." *New Shakspere Society's Transactions,* 1st Ser., Nos. 1–2 (1874), 442–64. (Rpt. Vaduz: Kraus, 1965.)

Ishida, Higashi. "Concerning Antony and Cleopatra." *Osaka Literary Review* 2 (1963), 1–9.

Iwamoto, Fujio. "*Antony and Cleopatra*: The World of Cleopatra." *Miyagi Kyoiku Univ. Bulletin* 2 (1968), 99–129.

Izaguirre, Ester de. "El tema de la muerte en cinco tragedias de Shakespeare." *La Prensa* (Buenos Aires), 11 Sept. 1966.

Jackson, Russell. "The Triumphs of *Antony and Cleopatra*." *SJH*, 1984, pp. 128–48.

Jackson, Zachariah. *A Few Concise Examples of Seven Hundred Errors in Shakspeare's Plays*. 1818. (2nd ed., enl., 1818.)

————. *Shakspeare's Genius Justified: Being Restorations and Illustrations of Seven Hundred Passages in Shakspeare's Plays*. 1819.

Jacobson, Howard. "*Antony and Cleopatra*: Gentle Madam, No." *Shakespeare's Magnanimity: Four Tragic Heroes, Their Friends and Families*. By Wilbur Sanders & Howard Jacobson. London & Toronto, 1978. Pp. 95–135.

Jacquot, Jean. *Shakespeare en France: Mises en scène d'hier et d'aujourd'hui*. Paris, 1964.

Jaggard, William. *Shakespeare Once a Printer and Bookman*. Stratford on Avon, 1933.

James, Max H. " 'The Noble Ruin': *Antony and Cleopatra*." *CollL* 8 (1981), 127–43.

Jameson, [Anna B.]. *Shakspeare's Heroines: Characteristics of Women, Moral, Poetical, and Historical*. 2nd ed. 1879. (Rpt. New York: AMS, 1967. First pub. as *Characteristics of Women, Moral, Poetical, and Historical*, 2 vols., 1832; 2nd ed. first pub. 1833.)

Jamieson, Michael S. "Shakespeare's Celibate Stage: The Problem of Accommodation to the Boy-Actress in *As You Like It, Antony and Cleopatra* and *The Winter's Tale*." *Papers Mainly Shakespearian*. Coll. G[eorge] I. Duthie. Aberdeen Univ. Stud. 147. Edinburgh & London, [1964]. Pp. 21–39.

Jankowski, Theodora A. " 'On a tribunal silver'd': Cleopatra, Elizabeth I, and the Female Body Politic." *ShN* 37 (1987), 22.

Janssen, Vincent F. *Die Prosa in Shaksperes Dramen. Erster Teil: Anwendung*. Pt. 1 of *Shakspere-Studien*. Strassburg, 1897.

Jefford, Barbara. "*Antony and Cleopatra*." *Shakespeare in Perspective*. Ed. Roger Sales. Vol. 1. 1982. Pp. 270–6.

[Jeffrey, Francis.] Review of *Characters of Shakespeare's Plays*, by William Hazlitt. *Edinburgh Review* 28 (1817), 472–88.

Jenkin, Bernard. "*Antony and Cleopatra*: Some Suggestions on the Monument Scenes." *RES* 21 (1945), 1–14.

Jenkins, Harold, ed. *Hamlet*. The [New] Arden Sh. 1981.

Jenkins, Raymond. "The Tragic Hero of Aristotle and Shakespeare." *RenP*, 1958–60, pp. 29–35.

Jepsen, Laura. *Ethical Aspects of Tragedy: A Comparison of Certain Tragedies by Æschylus, Sophocles, Euripides, Seneca and Shakespeare*. Gainesville, Fla., 1953.

Jervis, Swynfen. *Proposed Emendations of the Text of Shakspeare's Plays*. 1860.

Jewett, Mike. "Shakespeare's Body Politic Imagery." Univ. of Missouri diss., 1972. (*DA* 33 [1973], 5180A–1A.)

Johnson, Anthony L. *Readings of* Antony and Cleopatra *and* King Lear. Pisa: ETS Disenciclopedia 2, 1979.

Johnson, Samuel (1709–84). "Contributor" to CAM1.

————. *A Dictionary of the English Language*. 2 vols. 1755. (4th, rev. ed., 2 vols., 1773.)

————. "Preface to Shakespeare, 1765." *Johnson on Shakespeare*. Ed. Arthur Sherbo. Vol. 1. Vol. 7 of *The Yale Edition of the Works*. New Haven & London, 1968. Pp. 59–113. (Also "General Observation" on *Ant*. Vol. 2, vol. 8 of *Works*, p. 873.)

Joicey, G. " 'Antony and Cleopatra', II.ii." 7 *N&Q* 12 (25 July 1891), 62; (3 Oct. 1891), 262–3.

————. " 'Antony and Cleopatra', [578], [1155–6], [1712–13], [3259], [1864–5]." 7 *N&Q* 12 (31 Oct. 1891), 342–3.

————. " 'Antony and Cleopatra', [578]." 8 *N&Q* 1 (11 June 1892), 470.

Jones, Eldred. *Othello's Countrymen: The African in English Renaissance Drama.* OUP, 1965.

Jones, Emrys. *The Origins of Shakespeare.* OUP, 1977.

————. *Scenic Form in Shakespeare.* OUP, 1971.

Jones, Leonidas M. "Keats's Favorite Play." *ELN* 15 (1977), 43–4.

Jones, Tom. " 'Antony and Cleopatra', [306–13]." 10 *N&Q* 10 (31 Oct. 1908), 345.

Jones, William M. "Protestant Zeal in the Personality of Shakespeare's Mark Antony." *McNR* 18 (1967), 73–85.

Jorgensen, Paul A. "Antony and the Protesting Soldiers: A Renaissance Tradition for the Structure of *Antony and Cleopatra.*" *Essays on Shakespeare.* Ed. Gordon R. Smith. University Park, 1965. Pp. 163–81.

————. "Enobarbus' Broken Heart and *The Estate of English Fugitives.*" *PQ* 30 (1951), 387–92.

————. *William Shakespeare: The Tragedies.* TEAS 415. Boston, 1985.

Jose, Nicholas. "*Antony and Cleopatra*: Face and Heart." *PQ* 62 (1983), 487–505.

Josephs, Lois. "Shakespeare and a Coleridgean Synthesis." *SQ* 18 (1967), 17–21.

Jusserand, J[ean] J. *A Literary History of The English People: From the Renaissance To the Civil War.* [Vol. 2, pt. 2, of the *History.*] 1909. (1st Fr. ed. 1904.)

Kable, William S. "Compositor B, The Pavier Quartos, and Copy Spellings." *SB* 21 (1968), 131–61.

Kalmey, Robert P. "Shakespeare's Octavius and Elizabethan Roman History." *SEL* 18 (1978), 275–87.

Kames, Henry Home, Lord. *Elements of Criticism.* 6th ed. 2 vols. Edinburgh, 1785. (Rpt. New York: Garland, 1971–2. 1st ed. 1762.)

Kastan, David S. "Shakespeare and 'The Way of Womenkind.' " *Daedalus* 111, No. 3 (1982), 115–30.

Kaula, David. "The Time Sense of *Antony and Cleopatra.*" *SQ* 15, No. 3 (1964), 211–23.

Keightley, Thomas. *The Shakespeare-Expositor: An Aid to the Perfect Understanding of Shakespeare's Plays.* 1867. (Rpt. New York: AMS, 1973.)

Kellner, Leon. *Restoring Shakespeare: A Critical Analysis of the Misreadings in Shakespeare's Works.* Leipzig & London, 1925. (Rpt. New York: Biblo, 1969.)

Kelly, William J. "The Comic Perspective in Shakespeare's *Henry V, Hamlet,* and *Antony and Cleopatra.*" Univ. of Oregon diss., 1972. (*DA* 33 [1973], 6874A.)

Kennedy, William J. "Audiences and Rhetorical Strategies in Jodelle, Shakespeare, and Lohenstein." *Assays: Critical Approaches to Medieval and Renaissance Texts.* Vol. 1. Ed. Peggy A. Knapp & Michael A. Stugrin. Pittsburgh, 1981. Pp. 99–116.

Kermode, Frank. "Antony and Cleopatra." *The Riverside Shakespeare.* Textual ed. G. Blakemore Evans. Boston, 1974. Pp. 1343–6.

————. "The Banquet of Sense." *Renaissance Essays: Shakespeare, Spenser, Donne.* 1971. Pp. 84–115. (First pub. *Bulletin of the John Rylands Univ. Libr.* 44 [1961], 68–99.)

Kernan, Alvin. " 'The full stream of the world' (ii): *Antony and Cleopatra.*" *The Revels History of Drama in English.* Vol. 3. Ed. J[ohn] Leeds Barroll et al. 1975. Pp. 436–45.

————. "Place and Plot in Shakespeare." *YR* 67 (1977–8), 48–56.

K[ersey], J[ohn]. *A New English Dictionary: Or, a Compleat Collection Of the Most Proper and Significant Words.* 1702. (Rpt. Anglistica & Americana 120. Hildesheim & New York: Olms, 1974.)

Kiefer, Frederick. *Fortune and Elizabethan Tragedy.* San Marino, Calif., 1983.

Kimura, Teruhira. "Observations upon Some Textual and Annotatory Problems in *Antony and Cleopatra.*" *ShStud* 20 (1981–2), 91–107.

Kindermann, Heinz. *Das Burgtheater: Erbe und Sendung eines Nationaltheaters.* Wien & Leipzig, 1939.

————. *Theatergeschichte Europas.* 10 vols. Salzburg, 1957–74.

Kindred, Jerome C. "Unity and Disunity in *Antony and Cleopatra.*" Univ. of Texas diss., 1972. (*DA* 33 [1973], 3588A–9A.)

King, T[homas] J. *Shakespearean Staging, 1599–1642.* Cambridge, Mass., 1971.

Kinnear, Benjamin G. *Cruces Shakespearianæ: Difficult Passages in the Works of Shakespeare.* 1883.

Kirschbaum, Leo. "Shakespeare's Cleopatra." *Character and Characterization in Shakespeare.* Detroit, 1962. Pp. 99–110. (First pub. *ShAB* 19 [1944], 161–71.)

Klein, J[ulius] L. *Geschichte des Drama's.* 13 vols. Leipzig, 1865–76. Vol. 5. 1867.

Klein, Magdalene. *Shakespeares dramatisches Formgesetz.* Untersuchungen zur Sprach- und Literaturgeschichte, n. F. Heft 4. München, 1930.

Kleinschmit von Lengefeld, Wilhelm Freiherr. "Ist Shakespeares Stil barock? Bemerkungen zur Sprache Shakespeares und Drydens." *Shakespeare-Studien: Festschrift für Heinrich Mutschmann.* Ed. Walther Fischer & Karl Wentersdorf. Marburg, 1951. Pp. 88–106.

Knight, Charles. *Studies of Shakspere.* 1849. (First pub. in ed. 1841. Rpt. New York: AMS, 1972.)

Knight, G[eorge] Wilson. *The Imperial Theme: Further Interpretations of Shakespeare's Tragedies Including the Roman Plays.* 3rd ed. 1951. (Rev. ed. 1965; 1st ed. 1931.)

————. *The Sovereign Flower or Shakespeare as the Poet of Royalism Together with Related Essays.* 1958.

Knights, L[ionel] C. "On the Tragedy of Antony and Cleopatra." *Scrutiny* 16 (1949), 318–23.

————. *Some Shakespearean Themes.* 1959.

Knoepflmacher, U. C. " 'O rare for Strether!' *Antony and Cleopatra* and *The Ambassadors.*" *NCF* 19 (1965), 333–44.

Knowles, Richard. Private Contributor.

————, ed. *As You Like It.* With a Survey of Criticism by Evelyn Joseph Mattern. A New Variorum Ed. of Sh. New York, 1977.

Kökeritz, Helge. *Shakespeare's Pronunciation.* New Haven, 1953.

König, Wilhelm. "Eine Emendation zu *Antonius und Cleopatra.*" *SJ* 10 (1875), 381–2.

————. "Ueber den Gang von Shakespeare's dichterischer Entwickelung und die Reihenfolge seiner Dramen nach demselben." *SJ* 10 (1875), 193–258.

Koike, Noriko. "Kureopatora no Seikaku Bunseki—Sheikusupia no Butai Giko o Chushin to shite." *Eibungaku* 16 (1960), 32–45.

Kolbe, F[rederick] C. *Shakespeare's Way. A Psychological Study.* 1930.

Koppenfels, Werner von. "*Antony and Cleopatra.*" *Shakespeare-Handbuch: Die Zeit—Der Mensch—Das Werk—Die Nachwelt.* Ed. Ina Schabert. 2nd ed. Stuttgart, 1978. Pp. 527–35. (1st ed. 1972.)

Koster, Edward B. *William Shakespeare Gedenkboek 1616–1916.* 2nd ed. Den Haag, 1916. (1st ed. 1915.)

Kott, Jan. *Shakespeare Our Contemporary.* Tr. Boleslaw Taborski. New York, 1964. (1st Polish ed. 1961.)

Kozikowski, Stanley J. "Shakespeare's *Antony and Cleopatra* [3558–9]." *Expl* 35, No. 4 (1977), 7–8.

Kranz, David L. "Shakespeare's New Idea of Rome." *Rome in the Renaissance: The City and the Myth.* Ed. Paul Ramsey. Medieval and Renaissance Texts & Stud. 8. Binghamton, N.Y., 1982. Pp. 371–80.

————. "Shakespeare's Roman Vision." Univ. of California diss., 1977. (*DA* 38 [1977], 4846–7A.)

————. " 'Too Slow a Messenger': The Certainty of Speed in *Antony and Cleopatra*." *CEA* 47, Nos. 1–2 (1984), 90–8.

Krebs, H. "The Pronunciation of 'Anthony.' " 6 *N&Q* 1 (7 Feb. 1880), 123.

Kreyßig, Fr[iedrich A.]. *Vorlesungen über Shakespeare, seine Zeit und seine Werke.* 2 vols. 3rd ed. Berlin, 1877. (1st ed. 1858–60.)

Krohn, Janis. "The Dangers of Love in *Antony and Cleopatra*." *International Review of Psychoanalysis* 13 (1986), 89–96.

Krook, Dorothea. "Tragic and Heroic: Shakespeare's *Antony and Cleopatra*." *Elements of Tragedy.* New Haven, 1969. Pp. 184–229. (First pub. *Scripta Hierosolymitana* 19 [1967], 231–61.)

Kuckhoff, Armin-Gerd. *Das Drama William Shakespeares.* Schriften zur Theaterwissenschaft 3, No. 1. Berlin, 1964.

Kühn, Walter. "Shakespeare's Tragödien auf dem deutschen Theater im 18. Jahrhundert. Theaterbearbeitungen und Kritiken." Diss. München, 1908.

Kühne, W[aldemar]. *Venus, Amor und Bacchus in Shakespeare's Dramen: Eine medicinisch-poetische Studie.* Braunschweig, 1902.

Kuriyama, Constance B. "The Mother of the World: A Psychoanalytic Interpretation of Shakespeare's *Antony and Cleopatra*." *ELR* 7 (1977), 324–51.

Kyd, Thomas [Alfred Harbage]. "Cosmic Card Game." *ASch* 20 (1951), 325–33.

Kynaston, John (1728–83). Contributor to *St. James's Chr.*

Labriola, Albert C. "An Organization and Analysis of the Post-Variorum Criticism of *Antony and Cleopatra*." Univ. of Virginia diss., 1966. (*DA* 27 [1967], 3430A.)

————. "Renaissance Neoplatonism and Shakespeare's Characterization of Cleopatra." *HUSL* 3 (1975), 20–36.

Lamb, Margaret. Antony and Cleopatra *on the English Stage.* Rutherford, N.J., London, & Toronto, 1980.

Landauer, Gustav. *Shakespeare.* Ed. Martin Buber. Hamburg, 1962. (Written 1917–18; first pub. 1920.)

Langbaine, Gerard. *An Account of the English Dramatick Poets.* 1691. (Rpt. Menston: Scolar, 1971; New York: Garland, 1973.)

Lange, Alfred. *Die Einführung der Personen in Shakespeare's Römerdramen.* Leipzig, 1920. (Leipzig diss.)

Law, Robert Adger. "On the Dating of Shakspere's Plays." *ShAB* 11 (1936), 46–51.

————. "The Text of 'Shakespeare's Plutarch.' " *HLQ* 6 (1942–3), 197–203.

Lawrence, William J. *The Physical Conditions of the Elizabethan Public Playhouse.* Cambridge, Mass., 1927.

Lea, Kathleen M. Contributor to Seaton 1946.

Leavenworth, Russell E. *Daniel's "Cleopatra": A Critical Study.* Salzburg Stud. in Eng. Lit.: Elizabethan and Renaissance Stud. 3. Salzburg, 1974. (Univ. of Colorado diss., 1953.)

Leavis, F. R. " 'Antony and Cleopatra' and 'All for Love': A Critical Exercise." *Scrutiny* 5 (1936), 158–69.

[Le Blanc, Jean B.] *Letters on the English and French Nations.* 2 vols. 1747. (Written 1737–44; 1st Fr. ed. 1745.)

Lederer, Max, ed. *Daniel's "The Tragedie of Cleopatra" nach dem Drucke von 1611.* Materialien zur Kunde des älteren Englischen Dramas 31. Louvain, 1911.

————. "Zu *Antonius und Cleopatra* in Deutschland." *SJ* 43 (1907), 220–6.

Lee, Robin. " 'Antony and Cleopatra'. Theme: Structure: Image." *Crux* 3 (1969), 11–16.

————. *Shakespeare: Antony and Cleopatra.* Stud. in Eng. Lit. 44. 1971.

Bibliography

L[ee, Sidney?]. (1859–1926). Contributor to EV1.

———. *A Life of William Shakespeare*. 4th ed. of rev. version. 1925. (1st ed. 1898.)

Leggatt, Alexander. *Shakespeare's Political Drama: The History Plays and the Roman Plays*. London & New York, 1988.

Leiter, Samuel L., ed. *Shakespeare Around the Globe: A Guide to Notable Postwar Revivals*. Westport, Conn., 1986.

L[eo], F[riedrich] A. *Beiträge und Verbesserungen zu Shakespeare's Dramen nach handschriftlichen Aenderungen in einem von J. Payne Collier Esq. aufgefundenen Exemplare der Folio-Ausgabe von 1632*. Berlin, 1853.

———. "Robert Sprenger's Bemerkungen zu Dramen Shakespeare's." *SJ* 27 (1892), 217–24.

———. *Shakespeare-Notes*. 1885.

———. "Shakespeare's 'Antony and Cleopatra', Act II. Sc. 2. [807]." 4 *N&Q* 3 (27 Feb. 1869), 191.

———, ed. *Four Chapters of North's Plutarch*. London & Strassburg, 1878.

Lerner, Laurence. "Love and Gossip: or, How Moral is Literature?" *EIC* 14 (1964), 126–47.

———. "Tragedy: Religious and Humanist." *Review of English Literature* 2, No. 4 (1961), 28–37.

Lettsom, William Nanson. Contributor to W. S. Walker, *A Critical Examination of the Text of Shakespeare*, 1860.

[———.] "New Readings in Shakespeare." *Blackwood's* 74 (1853), 451–74.

———. "Shakspeare Correspondence." 1 *N&Q* 7 (16 Apr. 1853), 377–8.

Lever, J. W. "Venus and the Second Chance." *ShS* 15 (1962), 81–8.

Levi, Cesare. "I drammi romani di Shakespeare." *I libri del giorno*, June 1925, pp. 291–4.

Levin, Harry. *Shakespeare and the Revolution of the Times: Perspectives and Commentaries*. New York: OUP, 1976.

———. "Two Monumental Death-Scenes: *Antony and Cleopatra*, 4.15; 5.2." *Shakespeare—Text, Language, Criticism: Essays in Honour of Marvin Spevack*. Ed. Bernhard Fabian & Kurt Tetzeli von Rosador. Hildesheim, Zürich, & New York, 1987. Pp. 147–63.

Levith, Murray J. *What's in Shakespeare's Names*. London & Sydney, 1978.

Lewes, Louis. *The Women of Shakespeare*. Tr. Helen Zimmern. 1894. (1st Ger. ed. 1893.)

Lewis, Wyndham. *The Lion and the Fox: The Rôle of the Hero in the Plays of Shakespeare*. 1927.

Lindheim, Bogislav von. "Syntaktische Funktionsverschiebung als Mittel des barocken Stils bei Shakespeare." *SJ* 90 (1954), 229–51.

Lindsay, Jack. Letter. *RES* 23 (1947), 66.

Lings, Martin. *Shakespeare in the Light of Sacred Art*. 1966.

Linthicum, M[arie] Channing. *Costume in the Drama of Shakespeare and his Contemporaries*. OUP, 1936. (Reissued New York: Russell & Russell, 1963.)

Lippmann, Max. *Shakespeare im Film*. Wiesbaden, 1964.

Lloyd, Julius (1830–92). Contributor to CAM1.

Lloyd, Michael. "Antony and the Game of Chance." *JEGP* 61 (1962), 548–54.

———. "Cleopatra as Isis." *ShS* 12 (1959), 88–94.

———. "Plutarch's Daemons in Shakespeare." *N&Q* 205 (1960), 324–7.

———. "The Roman Tongue." *SQ* 10 (1959), 461–8.

Lloyd, W[illiam] Watkiss. " 'Antony and Cleopatra', [920–1]." 7 *N&Q* 12 (4 July 1891), 4.

———. " 'Antony and Cleopatra', [1335]." 7 *N&Q* 11 (31 Jan. 1891), 82.

———. *Essays on the Life and Plays of Shakespeare. . . . Contributed to the Edition of the Poet by S. W. Singer, 1856.* 1858.

822

————. " 'Pyramid.' " 7 *N&Q* 11 (11 Apr. 1891), 283.

Logan, Robert A. "The Sexual Attitudes of Marlowe and Shakespeare." *Hartford Stud. in Lit.* 19, Nos. 2–3 (1987), 1–23.

Lombardo, Agostino. *Ritratto di Enobarbo: Saggi sulla letteratura inglese.* Pisa, 1971. ("Le immagini dell'acqua in *Antony and Cleopatra*," pp. 42–67, first pub. *EM* 10 [1959], 107–33; "Ritratto di Enobarbo," pp. 11–41, first pub. *EM* 11 [1960], 33–58.)

Loney, Glenn M. "Europe in the Seventies." *Theatre Crafts* 14, No. 1 (1980), 23, 86–97.

Long, John H. "*Antony and Cleopatra*: A Double Critical Reversal." *RenP*, 1964, pp. 28–34.

Long, Michael. *The Unnatural Scene: A Study in Shakespearean Tragedy.* 1976.

Longo, Joseph A. "Cleopatra and Octavia: Archetypal Imagery in *Antony and Cleopatra*." *UDR* 10, No. 3 (1974), 29–37.

Lounsbury, Thomas R. *Shakespeare as a Dramatic Artist: With an Account of His Reputation at Various Periods.* New York, 1901.

————. *The Text of Shakespeare.* New York, 1906.

Lucas, F[rank] L. *Tragedy: Serious Drama in Relation to Aristotle's Poetics.* 1927.

Luce, Alice, ed. *The Countess of Pembroke's "Antonie."* Litterarhistorische Forschungen 3. Weimar, 1897.

Luce, Morton. *A Handbook to the Works of William Shakespeare.* 1907. (Rpt. New York: AMS, 1972.)

Lüdemann, Ernst August. *Shakespeares Verwendung von gleichartigem und gegensätzlichem Parallelismus bei Figuren, Situationen, Motiven und Handlungen.* Bonner Studien zur Englischen Philologie 7. Bonn, 1913.

Lüthi, Max. *Shakespeares Dramen.* 2nd ed. Berlin, 1966. (1st ed. 1957.)

Lyman, Dean B. "Janus in Alexandria: A Discussion of 'Antony and Cleopatra.' " *SR* 48 (1940), 86–104.

Lyman, Stanford M., & Marvin B. Scott. *The Drama of Social Reality.* New York: OUP, 1975.

Lyons, Charles R. "*Antony and Cleopatra*: The Reality of 'Nilus' Slime' and the Dream of an Eternal Marriage." *Shakespeare and the Ambiguity of Love's Triumph.* Stud. in Eng. Lit. 68. The Hague & Paris, 1971. Pp. 160–86. (First pub. as "The Serpent, The Sun and 'Nilus Slime': A Focal Point for the Ambiguity of Shakespeare's 'Antony and Cleopatra,' " *RLMC* 21 [1968], 13–34.)

Lyons, Clifford. "The Dramatic Structure of Shakespeare's *Antony and Cleopatra*." *RenP*, 1983, pp. 63–77.

————. "Stage Imagery in Shakespeare's Plays." *Essays on Shakespeare and Elizabethan Drama in Honor of Hardin Craig.* Ed. Richard Hosley. Columbia, Mo., 1962. Pp. 261–74.

Mabie, Hamilton W. *William Shakespeare: Poet, Dramatist, and Man.* New ed. New York, 1912. (1st ed. 1900.)

McAlindon, T[homas]. *Shakespeare and Decorum.* 1973.

MacCallum, M[ungo] W. *Shakespeare's Roman Plays and Their Background.* With a Foreword by T. J. B. Spencer. 1967. (First pub. 1910.)

MacCracken, H[enry] N., F[rederick] E. Pierce, & W[illard] H. Durham. *An Introduction to Shakespeare.* New York, 1910.

McCutchion, David. "Creation and Contrivance: Dryden's Adaptation of *Antony and Cleopatra* Set Against the Background of His Age." *JJCL* 1 (1961), 46–64.

Macdonald, Ronald R. "Playing Till Doomsday: Interpreting *Antony and Cleopatra*." *ELR* 15 (1985), 78–99.

McFarland, Thomas. "Antony and Octavius." *YR* 48 (1958–9), 204–28.

McGinn, Donald J. "Cleopatra's Immolation Scene." *Essays in Literary History Presented to J. Milton French*. Ed. Rudolf Kirk & C[harles] F. Main. New Brunswick, N.J., 1960. Pp. 57–80.

Mack, Maynard. "*Antony and Cleopatra*: The Stillness and the Dance." *Shakespeare's Art: Seven Essays*. The Tupper Lectures on Sh. Ed. Milton Crane. Chicago, 1973. Pp. 79–113.

———. "The Jacobean Shakespeare: Some Observations on the Construction of the Tragedies." *Jacobean Theatre*. Stratford-upon-Avon Stud. 1. Gen. Eds. John Russell Brown & Bernard Harris. 1960. Pp. 10–41.

Mackail, J[ohn] W. *The Approach to Shakespeare*. OUP, 1930.

Mackay, Charles. *New Light on Some Obscure Words and Phrases in the Works of Shakspeare and his Contemporaries*. 1884.

Mackenzie, Agnes Mure. *The Women in Shakespeare's Plays*. 1924.

McKenzie, D. F. "Compositor B's Role in *The Merchant of Venice* Q2 (1619)." *SB* 12 (1959), 75–90.

McKerrow, Ronald B. *An Introduction to Bibliography for Literary Students*. OUP, 1927.

———. *Prolegomena for the Oxford Shakespeare: A Study in Editorial Method*. OUP, 1939.

MacLure, Millar. "Shakespeare and the Lonely Dragon." *UTQ* 24 (1954–5), 109–20.

McManaway, James G. "All's Well with Lafew." *Shakespeare's Art: Seven Essays*. Ed. Milton Crane. Chicago, 1973. Pp. 137–50.

———. "Notes on Act V of *Antony and Cleopatra*." *ShStud* 1 (1962), 1–5.

———. "Recent Studies in Shakespeare's Chronology." *ShS* 3 (1950), 22–33.

MacMullan, Katherine V. "Death Imagery in *Antony and Cleopatra*." *SQ* 14 (1963), 399–410.

Madden, J. L. "Peacock, Tennyson and Cleopatra." *N&Q* 213 (1968), 416–17.

Maginn, William. "Dr. Farmer's Essay on the Learning of Shakspeare Considered." *Fraser's Magazine* 20 (1839), 254–73. (Rpt. in *Miscellaneous Writings*, vol. 3: *The Shakespeare Papers*, New York, 1856, pp. 229–71.)

———. "Shakspeare Papers.—No. V. His Ladies.—I. Lady Macbeth." *The Shakespeare Papers*. New ed. 1860. Pp. 142–87. (First pub. *Bentley's Miscellany* 2 [1837], 550–67.)

Maguin, J. M. "A Note on Shakespeare's Handling of Time and Space Data in *Antony and Cleopatra*." *CahiersE* 13 (1978), 61–7.

Mahood, M[olly] M. *Shakespeare's Wordplay*. 1965. (1st ed. 1957.)

Malekin, Peter. "Tragedy and Comedy—A Western View." *The Aryan Path* 28 (1957), 100–4.

Malone, Edmond (1741–1812). Contributor to v1778, v1785, v1793, v1821.

———. *A Second Appendix to Mr. Malone's Supplement to the Last Edition of the Plays of Shakspeare*. 1783.

———. *Supplement to the Edition of Shakspeare's Plays Published in 1778*. 2 vols. 1780.

Manlove, Colin N. *The Gap in Shakespeare: The Motif of Division from* Richard II *to* The Tempest. 1981.

Manvell, Roger. *Shakespeare and the Film*. 1971.

Manwayring, Henry. *The Seaman's Dictionary*. 1644. (Rpt. Menston: Scolar, 1972.)

Marchant, Robert. *A Picture of Shakespeare's Tragedies*. Retford (Eng.), 1984.

Markels, Julian. *The Pillar of the World*: Antony and Cleopatra *in Shakespeare's Development*. Columbus, Ohio, 1968.

Marker, Frederick J. Contributor to Leiter 1986.

[Marmontel, Jean F., & Jean G. Bauvin.] *L'Observateur littéraire*. Vol. 1. Paris, 1746.

Marsh, D[erick] R. C. "The Conflict of Love and Responsibility in *Antony and Cleopatra.*" *Theoria* 15 (1960), 1–27.

————. *Passion Lends Them Power: A Study of Shakespeare's Love Tragedies.* Sydney, Manchester, & New York, 1976.

Marshall, Julian. " 'Antony and Cleopatra', [919–24]." 9 *N&Q* 9 (3 May 1902), 342.

Martin, Leslie H. " 'All for Love' and the Millenarian Tradition." *CL* 27 (1975), 289–306.

Masefield, John. *William Shakespeare.* Home Univ. Libr. Rev. ed. 1954. (1st ed. [1911].)

Maselli, Antonio. "Un *contadino.*" *Gli umili nella tragedia greca e shakespeariana.* Alatri, 1920. Pp. 411–15.

Mason, H[arold] A. *Shakespeare's Tragedies of Love: An Examination of the Possibility of Common Readings of* Romeo and Juliet, Othello, King Lear *&* Anthony and Cleopatra. 1970. ("Angelic Strength—Organic Weakness?", pp. 229–53, first pub. *Cambridge Quarterly* 1 [1966], 209–36; "Telling *versus* Shewing," pp. 254–76, first pub. *Cambridge Quarterly* 1 [1966], 330–54.)

Mason, John Monck. (1726–1809). Contributor to MAL, v1793, v1803.

————. *Comments on the Last Edition of Shakespeare's Plays.* 1785.

Massey, Gerald. *The Secret Drama of Shakspeare's Sonnets Unfolded, with the Characters Identified.* 2nd ed. 1872. (Rpt. New York: AMS, 1973. First pub. as *Shakspeare's Sonnets Never Before Interpreted,* 1866.)

Matchett, William H. "Reversing the Field: *Antony and Cleopatra* in the Wake of *King Lear.*" *MLQ* 45 (1984), 327–37.

Mathew, Frank. *An Image of Shakespeare.* 1922. (Dated 1915–20. Rpt. New York: Haskell House, 1972.)

Matsumoto, Hiroshi. "Defeat and Victory of Antony: An Essay on *Antony and Cleopatra.*" *English Quarterly* 9 (1971), 1–17.

Matthews, Honor. *Character & Symbol in Shakespeare's Plays.* Cambridge, 1962.

Matthews, [James] Brander. *Shakspere as a Playwright.* New York, 1913.

Matthews, Roger. "*Antony and Cleopatra*: Enter the Imagest: A Work in Progress." *Studies in English Literature* (Tokyo), Eng. No. (1981), 3–23.

————. "The Shakespeare Line: A Study of 'Antony and Cleopatra.' " Trinity Coll., Dublin, diss., 1977–8. (*DA* 39 [1979], 4694C.)

Maxwell, J. C. " 'Rebel Powers': Shakespeare and Daniel." *N&Q* 212 (1967), 139.

————. "Shakespeare's Manuscript of 'Antony and Cleopatra.' " *N&Q* 196 (1951), 337.

Maxwell-Mahon, W. D. "Character and Conflict in 'Antony and Cleopatra.' " *Crux* 9, No. 3 (1975), 39–44.

Mayhew, Anthony L. "The Pronunciation of 'Anthony.' " 6 *N&Q* 1 (27 Mar. 1880), 264.

Mehl, Dieter. *Shakespeare's Tragedies.* Cambridge, 1986. (1st Ger. ed. Berlin, 1983.)

Meinck, Carl. *Über das örtliche und zeitliche Kolorit in Shakespeares Römerdramen und Ben Jonsons "Catiline."* Studien zur Englischen Philologie 38. Halle a. S., 1910.

Meißner, Paul. *Shakespeare.* Zweite Auflage bearbeitet von Martin Lehnert. Berlin, 1954. (1st ed. 1940.)

Mendel, Sydney. "Hamletian Man." *Ar Q* 16 (1960), 223–36.

————. "Shakespeare and D. H. Lawrence: Two Portraits of the Hero." *WascanaR* 3, No. 2 (1968), 49–60.

Mendilow, A[dam] A., & Alice Shalvi. *The World and Art of Shakespeare.* Jerusalem, 1967.

Mendl, R[obert] W. S. *Revelation in Shakespeare.* 1964.

Menon, C. Narayana. *Shakespeare Criticism: An Essay in Synthesis.* OUP, 1938.

Meredith, Peter. " 'That pannelled me at heeles': *Antony and Cleopatra* [2777]." *ES* 55 (1974), 118–26.

Meri, G. "Antoniy i Kleopatra." *Šekspirovski Sbornik* 2 (1958), 245–55.

Mézières, A[lfred]. *Shakespeare: Ses œuvres et ses critiques.* 4th ed. Paris, 1886. (First pub. 1860.)

Michel, Laurence, & Cecil C. Seronsy. "Shakespeare's History Plays and Daniel: An Assessment." *SP* 52 (1955), 549–77.

Mills, L[aurens] J. "Cleopatra's Tragedy." *SQ* 11 (1960), 147–62.

———. Letter. *SQ* 7 (1956), 133.

———. *The Tragedies of Shakespeare's Antony and Cleopatra.* Bloomington, Ind., 1964.

Milner, Ian. "Shakespeare's Climactic Style." *Charles University on Shakespeare.* Ed. Zdeněk Stříbrný. Praha, 1966. Pp. 151–8. (Paper read Apr. 1964.)

Milward, Peter. *Shakespeare's Religious Background.* 1973.

Minsheu, John. *Ductor in Linguas, the gvide into tongves.* 1617. (Rpt., introd. Jürgen Schäfer; Delmar, N.Y.: Scholars' Facsimiles & Rpts., 1978.)

Minto, William. *Characteristics of English Poets: From Chaucer to Shirley.* 2nd ed. Edinburgh & London, 1885. (1st ed. 1874.)

Miola, Robert S. *Shakespeare's Rome.* Cambridge & New York, 1983.

Miriam Joseph, Sr. *Shakespeare's Use of the Arts of Language.* Columbia Univ. Stud. in Eng. & Comp. Lit. 165. New York, 1947.

Missenharter, Hermann. "Antonius und Kleopatra." *Die Literatur* 41 (1938–9), 422.

[Mitford, John.] "Conjectural Emendations on the Text of Shakspere, with Observations on the Notes of the Commentators." *Gent. Mag.* NS 22 (1844), 115–36, 451–72.

Miyauchi, Bunshichi. *Immortal Longings: The Structure of Shakespeare's* Antony and Cleopatra. Tokyo, 1978.

———. "Preliminary Remarks on *Antony and Cleopatra*, Act V." *SELL* 1 (1970), 1–13.

Moeller, Georg Hermann. *Die Auffassung der Kleopatra in der Tragödienliteratur der romanischen und germanischen Nationen.* Ulm, 1888.

———. "Beiträge zur Dramatischen Cleopatra-Literatur." *Schulprogramm.* Schweinfurt, 1907.

Mommsen, Theodor (1817–1903). Contributor to Wildenbruch 1914.

Moore, Ella A. "Moral Proportion and Fatalism in 'Antony and Cleopatra.' " *Poet Lore* 7 (1895), 613–19.

Moore, John R. "The Enemies of Love: The Example of Antony and Cleopatra." *Kenyon Review* 31 (1969), 646–74.

Moorman, F. W. "Shakespeare's History Plays and Daniel's 'Civile Wars.' " *SJ* 40 (1904), 69–83.

Morgan, Margery M. " 'Your Crown's Awry': *Antony and Cleopatra* in the Comic Tradition." *Komos* 1 (1968), 128–39.

Morgann, Maurice. "An Essay on the Dramatic Character of Sir John Falstaff." *Shakespearian Criticism.* Ed. Donald A. Fineman. OUP, 1972. Pp. 141–215. (First pub. 1777.)

Moriya, Sasaburo. *"Gubijinso* to *Hamuretto* to *Antoni* to *Kureopatora."* *Journal of Literature and Linguistics* 9 (1959), 1–12.

Morley, Henry, & W[illiam] H. Griffin. *English Writers: An Attempt Towards A History of English Literature.* 11 vols. 1887–95. Vol. 11. 1895.

Morris, Helen. "Queen Elizabeth I 'Shadowed' in Cleopatra." *HLQ* 32 (1968–9), 271–8.

———. "Shakespeare and Dürer's Apocalypse." *ShakS* 4 (1968), 252–62.

Morris, Ivor. *Shakespeare's God: The Role of Religion in the Tragedies.* 1972.

Bibliography

Morrison, Mary. "Some Aspects of the Treatment of the Theme of Antony and Cleopatra in Tragedies of the Sixteenth Century." *Journal of European Studies* 4 (1974), 113–25.

Moseley, C. W. R. D. "Cleopatra's Prudence: Three Notes on the Use of Emblems in *Antony and Cleopatra*." *SJH*, 1986, pp. 119–37.

Moulton, Richard G. *Shakespeare as a Dramatic Thinker*. 1907. (Rpt. Norwood, Pa.: Norwood Eds., 1977. 1st pub. as *The Moral System of Shakespeare*, 1903.)

Mourgues, Odette de. "Deux triomphes de l'hyperbole." *De Shakespeare à T. S. Eliot: Mélanges offerts à Henri Fluchère*. Ed. Marie-Jeanne Durry, Robert Ellrodt, & Marie-Thérèse Jones-Davies. Collection "Etudes Anglaises" 63. Paris, 1976. Pp. 73–9.

Müller, Amandus. *Studien zu Samuel Daniels Tragödie Cleopatra: Quellenfrage und literarischer Charakter*. Leipzig, 1914. (Leipzig diss.)

Müller-Schwefe, Gerhard. *William Shakespeare: Welt—Werk—Wirkung*. Berlin & New York, 1978.

Muir, Kenneth. " 'Antony and Cleopatra', [2240–5]." *N&Q* 206 (1961), 142.

———. "Elizabeth I, Jodelle, and Cleopatra." *Renaissance Drama* NS 2 (1969), 197–206.

———. "The Imagery of 'Antony and Cleopatra.' " *KN* 8 (1961), 249–64.

———. *Shakespeare the Professional and Related Studies*. 1973.

———. "Shakespeare's Roman World." *LHY* 15, No. 2 (1974), 45–63.

———. *Shakespeare's Sources. I: Comedies and Tragedies*. 1957.

———. *Shakespeare's Tragic Sequence*. 1972.

———. *The Sources of Shakespeare's Plays*. 1977.

———, ed. *Macbeth*. The [New] Arden Sh. 9th ed. 1962; paperback rpt. 1983. (1st ed. 1951; 1st paperback ed. 1964.)

———, & Sean O'Loughlin. *The Voyage to Illyria: A New Study of Shakespeare*. 1937.

Mullin, Michael. *Theatre at Stratford-upon-Avon: A Catalogue-Index to Productions of the Shakespeare Memorial/Royal Shakespeare Theatre 1879–1978*. 2 vols. Westport, Conn., 1980.

Mulryne, J. R. "The Paradox on the Stage: *Antony and Cleopatra*." *Le Paradoxe au temps de la Renaissance*. Ed. Marie-Thérèse Jones-Davies. Paris, 1982. Pp. 155–68.

Murakami, Toshio. "Cleopatra and Volumnia." *ShStud* 9 (1970–1), 28–55.

Murry, John Middleton. "Metaphor." *Countries of the Mind, 2nd Series*. OUP, 1931. Pp. 1–16. (Rpt. Freeport, N.Y.: Books for Libraries, 1968.)

———. "The Nature of Poetry." *Discoveries: Essays in Literary Criticism*. 1924. Pp. 11–44. (Delivered Sept. 1922.)

———. "North's Plutarch." *Countries of the Mind, 2nd Series*. OUP, 1931. Pp. 78–96. (Rpt. Freeport, N.Y.: Books for Libraries, 1968. First pub. *TLS*, 12 Sept. 1929, pp. 689–90.)

———. *The Problem of Style*. OUP, 1922. (Delivered 1921.)

———. *Shakespeare*. 1936.

———. "Shakespeare and Love." *Countries of the Mind*. 1922. Pp. 9–28.

Nagler, A[lois] M. *Shakespeare's Stage*. Tr. Ralph Manheim. New Haven, 1958.

Nakamura, Mutsuo. "An Appreciation of 'Antony and Cleopatra' Mainly from the Standpoint of Its Three Principal Themes." *Journal of the Faculty of Textile Science and Technology* (Shinsu Univ.), Ser. D, Arts No. 4, 28 (1961), 117–37.

———. "A Historical Study on the Criticism of Shakespeare's Antony and Cleopatra." *Journal of the Faculty of Textile and Sericulture* (Shinsu Univ.), Ser. D, Arts & Sciences No. 3, 25 (1960), 1–70.

Nandy, Dipak. "The Realism of Antony and Cleopatra." *Shakespeare in a Changing World*. Ed. Arnold Kettle. 1964. Pp. 172–94.

Nares, Robert. *A Glossary.* New rev. and enl. ed. by James O. Halliwell & Thomas Wright. 2 vols. 1876. (Earlier eds. in 1822, 1825, 1859, 1867, 1872.)

Naumann, Walter. *Die Dramen Shakespeares.* Darmstadt, 1978.

Naylor, Edward W. *Shakespeare and Music.* Rev. ed. 1931. (Rpt. New York: Da Capo & Blom, 1965. 1st ed. 1896.)

Neely, Carol T. *Broken Nuptials in Shakespeare's Plays.* New Haven & London, 1985.

Nelson, C. E. "*Antony and Cleopatra* and the Triumph of Rome." *University Review—Kansas City* 32 (1966), 199–203.

Nelson, Lawrence G. "Classical History in Shakespeare." Univ. of Virginia diss., 1943.

Nelson, Raymond S. "Eros Lost." *Iowa English Bulletin: Yearbook* 22 (1972), 42–7.

Neufeld, Mary D. Contributor to Leiter 1986.

Neuse, Richard. "A Cabaret Version of *Antony and Cleopatra.*" *SQ* 31 (1980), 186–7.

Nevo, Ruth. "The Masque of Greatness." *ShakS* 3 (1967), 111–28.

———. *Tragic Form in Shakespeare.* Princeton, 1972.

The New English Dictionary. See *Oxford English Dictionary.*

The New Grove Dictionary of Music and Musicians. Ed. Stanley Sadie. 20 vols. 1980.

The New York Times Theater Reviews 1870–1919 (6 vols., New York, 1975); *1920–1970* (10 vols., New York, 1971–2); *1971–82* (6 vols., New York, 1973–84).

Newbolt, Henry. "A Note on Antony and Cleopatra." *A Book of Homage to Shakespeare.* Ed. Israel Gollancz. OUP, 1916. Pp. 183–5.

———. *Studies Green and Gray.* 1926.

———. *The Tide of Time in English Poetry.* 1925.

Nichols, James. " 'Antony and Cleopatra', Act IV. Sc. 9. [2732]." 3 *N&Q* 8 (30 Sept. 1865), 264.

———. *Notes on Shakespeare.* 2 pts. 1861–2. (2nd ed. 1862.)

Nichols, John. *See* Theobald, Lewis.

Nicholson, Brinsley M. (1824–92). Contributor to CAM1 and CAM2.

———. Contributor to Wright, William Aldis, MS Notes (–1892) in Trinity Coll., Cambridge: Add. MS. b. 58 (158).

———. "*Antony and Cleopatra.*" 3 *N&Q* 7 (20 May 1865), 395.

———. "[*Ant.*]" 8 *N&Q* 1 (5 Mar. 1892), 182–3.

———. "Dr. Mackay's Thirteen Celtic Derivations: Part I." *The Antiquarian Magazine & Bibliographer* 3 (1883), 177–82.

———. "Three Explanations and Two 'Probable Opinions.' " 4 *N&Q* 8 (15 July 1871), 41–2.

Niclas, Lisbeth. *Der Charakterkontrast in Shakespeares Tragödien.* Halle a. S., 1917. (Halle diss.)

Nicol, Bernard de Bear, ed. *Varieties of Dramatic Experience: Discussions on Dramatic Forms and Themes Between Stanley Evernden, Roger Hubank, Thora Burnley Jones and Bernard de Bear Nicol.* 1969.

Nicoll, Allardyce. *Dryden as an Adapter of Shakespeare.* Pub. for the Sh. Assn. [1921].

———. *A History of Restoration Drama 1660–1700.* Cambridge, 1923.

———. " 'Passing Over the Stage.' " *ShS* 12 (1959), 47–55.

———. *Shakespeare.* 1952.

Noble, Richmond. *Shakespeare's Biblical Knowledge and Use of the Book of Common Prayer.* 1935.

———. *Shakespeare's Use of Song With the Text of the Principal Songs.* OUP, 1923.

Nochimson, Richard. "The End Crowns All: Shakespeare's Deflation of Tragic Possibility in *Antony and Cleopatra.*" *English* 26 (1977), 99–132.

Noel, J. "Shakespeare's Roman Plays." *RLV* 31 (1965), 186–9.

Norgaard, Holger. [Follow-up of Reeves's "A Supposed Indebtedness of Shakespeare to Peele."] *N&Q* 197 (1952), 442–3.

———. "Shakespeare and Daniel's 'Letter from Octavia.' " *N&Q* 200 (1955), 56–7.

Norman, Arthur M. Z. "Daniel's *The Tragedy of Cleopatra* and *Antony and Cleopatra.*" *SQ* 9 (1958), 11–18.

———. "Source Material in 'Antony and Cleopatra.' " *N&Q* 201 (1956), 59–61.

———. " 'The Tragedie of Cleopatra' and the Date of 'Antony and Cleopatra.' " *MLR* 54 (1959), 1–9.

Nosworthy, J. M. "Symbol and Character in 'Antony and Cleopatra.' " *ShN* 6 (1956), 4.

Novak, Maximillian E. "Criticism, Adaptation, Politics, and the Shakespearean Model of Dryden's *All for Love.*" *Studies in Eighteenth-Century Culture* 7. Madison, 1978. Pp. 375–87.

Novak, Rudolf. "Die Geschichte ist das Drama: Anmerkungen zu Shakespeares 'Antonius und Cleopatra.' " *Neue Wege* 25 (1969), 23–4.

Novy, Marianne. *Love's Argument: Gender Relations in Shakespeare.* Chapel Hill, 1984.

———. "Shakespeare's Female Characters as Actors and Audience." *The Woman's Part: Feminist Criticism of Shakespeare.* Ed. Carolyn R. S. Lenz, Gayle Greene, & Carol T. Neely. Urbana, 1980. Pp. 256–70. (First pub. in *Shakespearean Metadrama*, ed. John W. Blanpied [Rochester, 1977], pp. 17–40.)

Nowottny, Winifred. "Shakespeare's Tragedies." *Shakespeare's World.* Ed. James Sutherland & Joel Hurstfield. 1964. Pp. 48–78.

Nunes, Herta Maria F. de Queiroz. "Enobarbus: 'He is of Note.' " *Signal* 1, No. 1 (1978), 10–31.

Oakeshott, Walter. "Shakespeare and Plutarch." *Talking of Shakespeare.* Ed. John Garrett. 1954. Pp. 111–25.

Obertello, Alfredo. "La morte di Cleopatra in Shakespeare: Nota interpretativa." *VeP* 38 (1955), 696–9.

O'Connor, Frank [O'Donovan, Michael]. *Shakespeare's Progress.* Cleveland, 1960. (Rev. ed. of *The Road to Stratford*, 1948.)

Odell, George C. D. *Annals of the New York Stage.* 15 vols. New York, 1927–49.

———. *Shakespeare: From Betterton to Irving.* 2 vols. 1920. (Rpt., introd. Robert H. Ball; New York: Dover, 1966.)

Oechelhäuser, Wilhelm. *Einführungen in Shakespeare's Bühnen-Dramen und Charakteristik sämmtlicher Rollen.* 3rd, rev. ed. Minden, 1895. (First pub. in ed. 1877.)

———. "Die Zechbrüder und Trunkenen in Shakespeare's Dramen." *SJ* 16 (1881), 25–38.

Ogburn, Dorothy & Charlton. *This Star of England: "William Shake-speare," Man of the Renaissance.* New York, 1952.

Oki, Hiroko. "A Study of *Antony and Cleopatra*—With Special Reference to Cleopatra." *Eigo Eibeibungaku Ronso* 12 (1979), 23–64.

———. "A Woman in Shakespeare—Cleopatra." *Eigo Eibeibungaku Ronso* 11 (1978), 10–24.

Onions, C[harles] T. *A Shakespeare Glossary.* Enl. and rev. throughout by Robert D. Eagleson. OUP, 1986. (1st ed. 1911.)

Oppel, Horst. *Das Shakespeare-Bild Goethes.* Mainz, 1949.

———. *Shakespeare: Studien zum Werk und zur Welt des Dichters.* Heidelberg, 1963.

Orger, John G. *Critical Notes on Shakspere's Histories and Tragedies.* 1890.

Ornstein, Robert. "The Ethic of the Imagination: Love and Art in 'Antony and Cleopatra.' " *Later Shakespeare.* Stratford-upon-Avon Stud. 8. Gen. Eds. John Russell Brown & Bernard Harris. 1966. Pp. 31–46.

Bibliography

Orson, S. W. *Shakespeare Emendations*. MS. 1891. (In Furness Sh. Libr.)

Osborn, Neal J. "Kenneth Burke's Desdemona: A Courtship of Clio?" *HudR* 19 (1966), 267–75.

Otsuki, Kenji. *Psychoanalytic Insight of the Poet Shakespeare: Analytic Appreciation of his Five Great Tragedies*. Tokyo, 1975.

The Oxford Classical Dictionary. Ed. N[icholas] G. L. Hammond & H[oward] H. Scullard. 2nd ed. OUP, 1970. (1st ed. 1949.)

The Oxford English Dictionary. Ed. James A. H. Murray et al. 12 vols. & suppl. OUP, 1933. (Orig. pub. as *A New English Dictionary on Historical Principles*, 10 vols., 1888–1928.)

Ozaki, Yoshiharu. "Shakespeare no Boy Cleopatra." *Shakespeare no Engekiteki Fudo*. Ed. Nihon Shakespeare Kyokai. Tokyo, 1977. Pp. 289–318.

Palmer, Roderick. "Treatments of Antony and Cleopatra." *CEA* 27, No. 4 (1965), 8–9.

Pandurangan, Prema. "Shakespeare's Enobarbus." *The Aryan Path* 39 (1968), 227–30.

Parker, M[arion] D. H. *The Slave of Life: A Study of Shakespeare and the Idea of Justice*. 1955.

Partridge, A[stley] C. *The Language of Renaissance Poetry: Spenser, Shakespeare, Donne, Milton*. 1971.

————. *Orthography in Shakespeare and Elizabethan Drama: A Study of Colloquial Contractions, Elision, Prosody and Punctuation*. 1964.

Partridge, Eric. *Shakespeare's Bawdy: A Literary & Psychological Essay and a Comprehensive Glossary*. New ed. 1968. (1st ed. 1947; rev. ed. 1955.)

Patrick, J. Max. "The Cleopatra Theme in World Literature up to 1700." *The Undoing of Babel: Watson Kirkconnell, The Man and His Work*. Ed. J[ames] R. C. Perkin. Toronto, 1975. Pp. 64–76.

Paulin, Bernard. "L'Elément pastoral dans *Antoine et Cléopâtre* de Shakespeare." *Le genre pastoral en Europe du XVe au XVIIe siècle*. Ed. Claude Longeon. Saint-Etienne, 1980. Pp. 161–7.

Paulys Real-Encyclopädie der classischen Altertumswissenschaft. Neue Bearbeitung. Ed. Georg Wissowa et al. 24 vols. Stuttgart, 1894–1963. Zweite Reihe, vols. 1A–10A, 1920–72. Supplement vols. 1–15, München, 1903–78.

Payne, Michael. "Erotic Irony and Polarity in *Antony and Cleopatra*." *SQ* 24 (1973), 265–79.

————. *Irony in Shakespeare's Roman Plays*. Salzburg Stud. in Eng. Lit., Elizabethan Stud. 19. Salzburg, 1974.

Pearce, Donald. "Horace and Cleopatra: Thoughts on the Entanglements of Art and History." *YR* 51 (1961–2), 236–53.

Pearce, T. M. "Shakespeare's *Antony and Cleopatra*, [3497–3631]." *Expl* 12 (1953–4), no. 17.

Pearson, Jacqueline. "Romans and Barbarians: The Structure of Irony in Shakespeare's Roman Tragedies." *Shakespearian Tragedy*. Ed. Malcolm Bradbury & David Palmer. New York, 1984. Pp. 158–82.

Pearson, Norman Holmes. "Antony and Cleopatra." *Shakespeare: Of an Age and For All Time*. The Yale Festival Lectures. Ed. Charles Tyler Prouty. [Hamden, Conn.], 1954. Pp. 125–47.

Peart, S. E. "The Comradeship of Antony and Cleopatra." *Poet Lore* 4 (1892), 217–21.

Peck, Francis. *New Memoirs of the Life and Poetical Works of Mr. John Milton*. 1740.

Pedicord, Harry W., & Fredrick L. Bergmann. *The Plays of David Garrick*. Vol. 4: *Garrick's Adaptations of Shakespeare, 1759–1773*. Carbondale & Edwardsville, 1981.

Pelling, C. R. B., ed. *Plutarch: Life of Antony*. Cambridge Greek and Latin Classics. Cambridge, 1988.

Pellissier, Georges. *Shakespeare et la superstition shakespearienne*. Paris, 1914.

Percy, Thomas, Bish. (1729–1811). Contributor to MAL.

Perger, Arnulf. *Die Wandlung der dramatischen Auffassung.* Berlin, 1936.

Perret, Marion. "Shakespeare's Use of Messengers in *Antony and Cleopatra.*" *Drama Survey* 5 (1966), 67–72.

[Perring, Philip.] " 'Antony and Cleopatra', [1989]: 'Ribaudred Nagge.' " 10 *N&Q* 7 (20 Apr. 1907), 301.

————. *Hard Knots in Shakespeare.* 2nd ed., enl. 1886. (1st ed. 1885.)

Philips, Carl. *Lokalfärbung in Shakespeares Dramen. Erster Teil.* Höhere Bürgerschule der Stadt Köln: Jahres-Bericht (No. 5) über die Zeit von Ostern 1886 bis Ostern 1887, erstattet von dem Rektor Professor Dr. Otto Thomé. Köln, 1887.

Phillips, James E., Jr. *The State in Shakespeare's Greek and Roman Plays.* New York, 1940. (Rpt. New York: Octagon, 1972.)

Piper, H. W. "Shakespeare's *Antony and Cleopatra*, [3531–3]." *Expl* 26 (1967), no. 10.

Pitt, Angela. *Shakespeare's Women.* Newton Abbott & Totowa, N.J., 1981.

Planchon, Roger. "Trembler devant Shakespeare." *CahiersE* 16 (1979), 59–68.

Platt, Michael. *Rome and Romans According to Shakespeare.* Jacobean Drama Stud. 51. Salzburg, 1976.

Pogson, Beryl. *In the East My Pleasure Lies: An Esoteric Interpretation of Some Plays of Shakespeare.* 1950. (Rpt. New York: Haskell House, 1974.)

Poirier, Michel. *Christopher Marlowe.* 1951. (Rpt. [Hamden, Conn.:] Archon, 1968.)

Pollard, Alfred W. *Shakespeare Folios and Quartos: A Study in the Bibliography of Shakespeare's Plays 1594–1685.* 1909. (Rpt. New York: Cooper Square, 1970.)

————. *Shakespeare's Fight with the Pirates and the Problems of the Transmission of his Text.* 2nd ed., rev. Cambridge, 1920. (1st ed. 1917.)

————, et al. *Shakespeare's Hand in the Play of 'Sir Thomas More.'* Cambridge, 1923.

Potts, Abbie F. *Shakespeare and The Faerie Queene.* Ithaca, N.Y., 1958.

Powell, Henry W. "Shakespeare's Rome: Major Themes in the Late Political Plays." Univ. of North Carolina diss., 1975. (*DA* 37 [1976], 1568–9A.)

Prenter, N. Hancock. " 'Antony and Cleopatra', [919–24]." 9 *N&Q* 9 (22 Mar. 1902), 222–3.

Price, Hereward T. "Mirror-scenes in Shakespeare." *Joseph Quincy Adams Memorial Studies.* Ed. James G. McManaway, Giles E. Dawson, & Edwin E. Willoughby. Washington, D.C., 1948. Pp. 101–13.

Prideaux, W. F. "[*Ant.* 920–1.]" 7 *N&Q* 12 (12 Sept. 1891), 203.

Proser, Matthew N. *The Heroic Image in Five Shakespearean Tragedies.* Princeton, 1965.

Püschel, Ursula. "Lebensanspruch und Menschenwürde: Shakespeares Frauengestalten." *SJW* 113 (1977), 7–29.

Purdom, C[harles] B. *What Happens in Shakespeare: A New Interpretation.* 1963.

Pye, Henry James. *Comments on the Commentators on Shakespear.* 1807.

Q. Contributor to *St. James's Chr.*

Quayle, Calvin K. "Humor in Tragedy." Univ. of Minnesota diss., 1958. (*DA* 19 [1959], 2687A.)

Quennell, Peter. *Shakespeare, the Poet and his Background.* 1963. (Pub. in New York as *Shakespeare, a Biography.*)

Quiller-Couch, Arthur. "Antony and Cleopatra." *Studies In Literature, Second Series.* Cambridge, 1922. Pp. 169–206.

[Quincy, Josiah P.] *Manuscript Corrections from a Copy of the Fourth Folio of Shakspeare's Plays.* Boston, 1854.

Quinn, Michael. *See* Hawkes, Terence.

Quinones, Ricardo J. "Time in Dante and Shakespeare." *Symposium* 22 (1968), 261–84.

Quirk, Randolph, et al. *A Grammar of Contemporary English.* 1972. (7th impr., corrected, 1978.)

Rabkin, Norman. *Shakespeare and the Common Understanding.* New York, 1967.

Rackin, Phyllis. "Shakespeare's Boy Cleopatra, the Decorum of Nature, and the Golden World of Poetry." *PMLA* 87 (1972), 201–12.

Raeburn, Anna. "*Antony and Cleopatra*." *Shakespeare in Perspective.* Ed. Roger Sales. Vol. 1. 1982. Pp. 263–9.

Raleigh, Walter. *Shakespeare.* Eng. Men of Letters. 1907.

Ramm, Dieter. *Die Phasenstruktur der Shakespeareschen Tragödien.* Studienreihe Humanitas: Studien zur Anglistik. Frankfurt a. M., 1974.

Ransom, John Crowe. "On Shakespeare's Language." *SR* 55 (1947), 181–98.

Rapp, Moriz. *Studien über das englische Theater.* Tübingen, 1862.

Rawlinson, Sir W. Contributor to v1773.

Ray, Robert H. "The 'Ribaudred Nagge' of *Antony and Cleopatra*, [1989]: A Suggested Emendation." *ELN* 14 (1976–7), 21–5.

Reeg, Ludwig. *Shakespeare und die Weltordnung.* Stuttgart, 1950.

Rees, Joan. "An Elizabethan Eyewitness of *Antony and Cleopatra?*" *ShS* 6 (1953), 91–3.

———. Letter. *RES* NS 9 (1958), 294–5.

———. *Samuel Daniel.* Liverpool, 1964.

———. "Samuel Daniel's 'Cleopatra' and Two French Plays." *MLR* 47 (1952), 1–10.

———. "Shakespeare's Use of Daniel." *MLR* 55 (1960), 79–82.

Reeves, John D., & Holger Norgaard. "A Supposed Indebtedness of Shakespeare to Peele." *N&Q* 197 (1952), 441–3.

Rehbach, Wilhelm. "Shaw's 'Besser als Shakespeare.' " *SJ* 52 (1916), 84–140.

Reid, S. W. "Some Spellings of Compositor B in the Shakespeare First Folio." *SB* 29 (1976), 102–38.

Reinhold, Heinz. "Die metrische Verzahnung als Kriterium für Fragen der Chronologie und Authentizität im Drama Shakespeares und einiger seiner Zeitgenossen und Nachfolger." *Archiv* 181 (1942), 83–96.

Reyher, Paul. *Essai sur les idées dans l'œuvre de Shakespeare.* Paris, 1947.

Rhodes, Ernest L. "Cleopatra's 'Monument' and the Gallery in Fludd's *Theatrum Orbi*." *RenP*, 1971, pp. 41–8.

Rhodes, R[aymond] Crompton. *The Stagery of Shakespeare.* Birmingham, 1922.

Ribner, Irving. *Patterns in Shakespearian Tragedy.* 1960.

———. "Shakespeare and Peele: The Death of Cleopatra." *N&Q* 197 (1952), 244–6.

Rice, Julian C. "The Allegorical Dolabella." *CLAJ* 3 (1970), 402–7.

———. "Renaissance Perspectives on Antony and Cleopatra: A Study of Themes, Sources, and Elizabethan Skepticism." Univ. of California diss., 1968. (*DA* 29 [1968], 1877A–8A.)

Richmond, Hugh M. *Shakespeare's Sexual Comedy: A Mirror for Lovers.* Indianapolis, 1971.

Richmond, Velma B. "Shakespeare's Women." *Midwest Quarterly* 19 (1978), 330–42.

Richter, Helene. *Shakespeares Gestalten.* NS, Beiheft 18. Marburg, 1930.

Rider, John. *Bibliotheca scholastica.* 1589. (Rpt. Menston: Scolar, 1970.)

Ridley, M[aurice] R. *Shakespeare's Plays: A Commentary.* 1937.

Riehle, Wolfgang. "Antonius und Kleopatra (*Antony and Cleopatra*)." *Shakespeare-Kommentar zu den Dramen, Sonetten, Epen und kleineren Dichtungen.* By Werner Habicht, Dieter Mehl, et al. Introd. Wolfgang Clemen. München, 1968. Pp. 143–6.

————. *Das Beiseitesprechen bei Shakespeare: Ein Beitrag zur Dramaturgie des elisabethanischen Dramas.* München, 1964. (München diss.)

Riemer, A[ndrew] P. *A Reading of Shakespeare's* Antony and Cleopatra. Sydney Stud. in Lit. Sydney, 1968.

Righter, Anne. *See* Barton, Anne.

————. *Shakespeare and the Idea of the Play.* 1962.

Rinehart, Keith. "Shakespeare's Cleopatra and England's Elizabeth." *SQ* 23 (1972), 81–6.

Ritson, Joseph (1752–1803). Contributor to v1793.

————. *Cursory Criticisms on the Edition of Shakespeare Published by Edmond Malone.* 1792. (Rpt. Eighteenth Century Sh. 20. London: Cass, 1970. Together with *Malone's Letter to the Rev. Richard Farmer.*)

————. *Remarks, Critical and Illustrative, on the Text and Notes of the Last Edition of Shakspeare.* 1783.

Roberts, G. J. "Shakespeare and 'Scratching.' " *N&Q* 228 (1983), 111–14.

Robertson, J[ohn] M. *The Genuine in Shakespeare.* 1930.

————. *Montaigne and Shakspere.* 1897. (2nd, rev. ed. 1909. Rpt. New York: Haskell House, 1968.)

Robertson, Patricia R. " 'This Herculean Roman': Shakespeare's Antony and the Hercules Myth." *Pubs. of the Arkansas Philological Assn.* 10, No. 2 (1984), 65–75.

Roerecke, Edith M. "Baroque Aspects of *Antony and Cleopatra.*" *Essays on Shakespeare.* Ed. Gordon R. Smith. University Park, 1965. Pp. 182–95.

Rötscher, Heinrich Th. *Cyclus dramatischer Charaktere.* Pt. 2. Berlin, 1846.

Rohrmoser, Günter. *Shakespeare: Erfahrung der Geschichte.* Das Wissenschaftliche Taschenbuch, Abt. Geisteswissenschaften, 2. München, 1971.

Ronan, Clifford J. *"Caesar's Revenge* and the Roman Thoughts in *Antony and Cleopatra.*" *ShakS* 19 (1987), 171–82.

Ronayne, John. "Decorative and Mechanical Effects Relevant to the Theatre of Shakespeare." *The Third Globe.* Ed. C[yril] Walter Hodges, S[amuel] Schoenbaum, & Leonard Leone. Detroit, 1981. Pp. 190–221.

Root, Robert K. *Classical Mythology in Shakespeare.* Yale Stud. in Eng. 19. New York, 1903. (Rpt. New York: Gordian, 1965.)

Rose, Paul Lawrence. "The Politics of *Antony and Cleopatra.*" *SQ* 20 (1969), 379–89.

Rosen, William. *Shakespeare and the Craft of Tragedy.* Cambridge, Mass., 1960.

Rosenblatt, Louise M. *Literature As Exploration.* New York, 1938.

Ross, Gordon N. "Enobarbus on Horses: *Antony and Cleopatra,* [1866–8]." *SQ* 31 (1980), 386–7.

Roth, Robert. "Another World of Shakespeare." *MP* 49 (1951–2), 42–61.

Rothe, Hans. *Shakespeare als Provokation.* München, 1961.

Rothschild, Herbert B., Jr. "The Oblique Encounter: Shakespeare's Confrontation of Plutarch with Special Reference to *Antony and Cleopatra.*" *ELR* 6 (1976), 404–29.

Rouse, W[illiam] H. D., ed. *Plutarch's Lives. Englished by Sir Thomas North.* 10 vols. 1898.

Rozett, Martha Tuck. "The Comic Structures of Tragic Endings: The Suicide Scenes in *Romeo and Juliet* and *Antony and Cleopatra.*" *SQ* 36 (1985), 152–64.

Rüegg, August. *Shakespeare: Eine Einführung in seine Dramen.* Sammlung Dalp 79. Bern, 1951.

Rümelin, Gustav. *Shakespearestudien.* Stuttgart, 1866. (First pub. in *Morgenblatt für gebildete Leser* in 1865 as "Shakespearestudien eines Realisten.")

Ruppel, K. H. *"Antonius und Cleopatra*: Werkgestalt und Bühnenerscheinung." *SJ* 93 (1957), 186–95.

Ruricola. Letter. *Gent. Mag.* 17 (1747), 179.

Rushton, W[illiam] L. "Present Pleasure." 4 *N&Q* 10 (26 Oct. 1872), 330–1.

————. *Shakespeare Illustrated By the Lex Scripta.* The First Part. 1870.

Ruskin, John. *The Works.* Libr. Ed. by E. T. Cook & Alexander Wedderburn. 39 vols. London & New York, 1902–12. (*Sesame and Lilies*, vol. 18 [1905], pp. 1–187, delivered 1864, first pub. 1865; *Valle Crucis*, vol. 33 [1908], pp. 205–54, written c. 1883–6.)

Russell, D[onald] A. *Plutarch.* 1973.

St. Clare Byrne, M. "Fifty Years of Shakespearian Production: 1898–1948." *ShS* 2 (1949), 1–20.

————. Introd. to *A History of Shakespearean Production.* Arr. by the Arts Council of Great Britain and The Society for Cultural Relations with the U.S.S.R. 1948. (1st ed. 1947.)

Saint James's Chronicle; or, The British Evening-Post. Ed. Henry Baldwin. 1765.

Saint-Marc Girardin, [François A.]. *Cours de littérature dramatique.* 10th ed. 5 vols. Paris, 1868–70. Vol. 4. 1870. (1st ed. 1860.)

Saintsbury, George. *Shakespeare.* Cambridge & New York, 1934. (Rpt. from *Cambridge History of English Literature*, vol. 5, 1910, pp. 186–249.)

Sakurai, Shoichiro. "Truth and Falsehood: A Study of *Antony and Cleopatra*." *English Literature Quarterly* 7 (1969), 37–55.

Salgādo, Gāmini. *Eyewitnesses of Shakespeare. First Hand Accounts of Performances 1590–1890.* London & New York, 1975.

Sampson, John. "An Arme-gaunt Steede." *TLS*, 30 Apr. 1920, p. 272.

Sampson, Martin W. "An Examination of the Metre of 'Antony and Cleopatra.' " *Shakespeariana* 6 (1889), 227–36.

Sampson, Sr. Helen Lucy. "A Critical Edition of Samuel Daniel's *The Tragedie of Cleopatra*." Univ. of St. Louis diss., 1966. (*DA* 27 [1967], 3017A.)

Sanders, Wilbur, & Howard Jacobson. *Shakespeare's Magnanimity: Four Tragic Heroes, Their Friends and Families.* London & Toronto, 1978.

Saner, Reginald. "*Antony and Cleopatra*: How Pompey's Honor Struck a Contemporary." *SQ* 20 (1969), 117–20.

Satin, Joseph, ed. *Shakespeare and His Sources.* Boston, 1966.

Saunders, J. W. "Staging at the Globe, 1599–1613." *SQ* 11 (1960), 402–25. (Rpt. in *The Seventeenth-Century Stage*, ed. G[erald] E. Bentley [Chicago, 1968], pp. 235–66.)

————. "Vaulting the Rails." *ShS* 7 (1954), 69–81.

Schäfer, Jürgen. *Shakespeares Stil: Germanisches und romanisches Vokabular.* Frankfurt a. M., 1973.

Schall, M. "Schuld und Sühne des Enobarbus in Shakespeares *Antonius und Cleopatra*." *Der Reichsbote: Sonntagsblatt* (Berlin) No. 46 (1915).

Schanzer, Ernest. " 'Antony and Cleopatra' and the Countess of Pembroke's 'Antonius.' " *N&Q* 201 (1956), 152–4.

————. " 'Antony and Cleopatra' and 'The Legend of Good Women.' " *N&Q* 205 (1960), 335–6.

————. "Daniel's Revision of His *Cleopatra*." *RES* NS 8 (1957), 375–81.

————. "A Plot-Chain in 'Antony and Cleopatra.' " *N&Q* 199 (1954), 379–80.

————. "Plot-Echoes in Shakespeare's Plays." *SJH*, 1969, pp. 103–21.

————. *The Problem Plays of Shakespeare: A Study of* Julius Caesar, Measure for Measure, Antony and Cleopatra. 1963.

————. "Three Notes on 'Antony and Cleopatra.' " *N&Q* 205 (1960), 20–2.

————, ed. *Shakespeare's Appian: A Selection from the Tudor Translation of Appian's "Civil Wars."* Eng. Rpts. Ser. 13. Liverpool, 1956.

Scharf, Gerhard. *Charaktergestaltung und psychologischer Gehalt in Drydens Shakespeare-Bearbeitungen.* Hamburger Philologische Studien 14. Hamburg, 1970.

Schelling, Felix E. *Elizabethan Drama, 1558–1642.* 2 vols. New York, 1935. (First pub. 1908.)

Schilling, Kurt. *Shakespeare: Die Idee des Menschseins in seinen Werken.* München & Basel, 1953.

Schirmer, Walter F. "Zum Verständnis des Werkes." *Antonius und Cleopatra.* Tr. A. W. von Schlegel & L. Tieck. Ed. L[evin] L. Schücking. Reinbek, 1962. Pp. 185–201.

Schlegel, August W. von. *A Course of Lectures on Dramatic Art and Literature.* Tr. John Black, rev. A. J. W. Morrison. 1846. (Delivered 1808; 1st Ger. ed., 2 vols., 1809–11; tr. John Black, 2 vols., 1815; rpt. of 1846 ed. New York: AMS, 1965.)

Schlüter, Kurt. *Shakespeares dramatische Erzählkunst.* Schriftenreihe der Deutschen Shakespeare-Gesellschaft, n. F. Band 7. Heidelberg, 1958.

Schmid, Eduard Eugen. *Shakespeare und die Schwarze Dame.* München, 1972.

Schmidt, Alexander. *Sacherklärende Anmerkungen zu Shakespeare's Dramen.* Leipzig, 1842.

————. *Shakespeare-Lexicon.* 2 vols. Berlin, 1874–5. (2nd ed. 1886; 3rd ed., enl. by Gregor Sarrazin, 1902; rpt. Berlin & New York: de Gruyter, 1971; New York: Blom.)

Schmidt, Wolfgang. "Shakespeares Leben und der Sinn der Tragödien: Einige Leitgedanken." *NS* 46 (1938), 339–53.

Schneider, Reinhold. "Tod und Unsterblichkeit in Shakespeares Drama." *Über Dichter und Dichtung.* Köln & Olten, 1953. Pp. 142–56. (Essay dated 1947.)

Schöne, Annemarie. "Shakespeares weise Narren und ihre Vorfahren." *Jahrbuch für Ästhetik und Allgemeine Kunstwissenschaft* 5 (1960), 202–45.

Schücking, Levin L. *Character Problems in Shakespeare's Plays.* 1922. (Rpt. Gloucester, Mass.: Smith, 1959. 1st Ger. ed. 1919.)

Schütze, Johannes. "Daniel's 'Cleopatra' und Shakespeare." *Englische Studien* 71 (1936–7), 58–72.

Schulman, Norma M. "A 'Motive for Metaphor': Shakespeare's *Antony and Cleopatra.*" *HUSL* 4 (1976), 154–74.

Schwalb, Harry M. "Shakespeare's *Antony and Cleopatra*, [80–4]." *Expl* 8 (1949–50), no. 53.

Schwartz, Elias. "The Idea of the Person and Shakespearian Tragedy." *SQ* 16 (1965), 39–47.

————. "The Shackling of Accidents: *Antony and Cleopatra.*" *CE* 23 (1961–2), 550–8.

Schwartz, Murray M. "Shakespeare through Contemporary Psychoanalysis." *Representing Shakespeare: New Psychoanalytic Essays.* Ed. Murray M. Schwartz & Coppélia Kahn. Baltimore & London, 1980. Pp. 21–32. (First pub. *HUSL* 5 [1977], 182–98.)

Scott, Michael. *Antony and Cleopatra: Text and Performance.* London & Atlantic Highlands, N.J., 1983.

Scott, Walter. Introd. to *All For Love.* In *The Works of John Dryden.* Illustrated with Notes . . . by Sir Walter Scott, rev. and corrected by George Saintsbury. Vol. 5. Edinburgh, 1883. Pp. 305–15. (1st ed. 1808.)

Scullard, H[oward] H. *From the Gracchi to Nero: A History of Rome from 133 B.C. to A.D. 68.* 4th ed. 1976. (1st ed. 1959.)

Seaton, Ethel. "*Antony and Cleopatra* and the *Book of Revelation.*" *RES* 22 (1946), 219–24.

Seccombe, Thomas, & J[ohn] W. Allen. *The Age of Shakespeare (1579–1631).* 2nd ed. 2 vols. 1904. (1st ed. 1903.)

Sedlak, Werner. *Blankversveränderungen in Shakespeares späteren Tragödien. Eine Interpretation von Othello, King Lear, Macbeth und Antony and Cleopatra. Mit einem Ausblick auf J. Websters Duchess of Malfi und Th. Middletons Women Beware Women sowie einem Anhang zu Hamlet.* München, 1970. (München diss.)

Sehrt, Ernst Th. *Der dramatische Auftakt in der elisabethanischen Tragödie: Interpretationen zum englischen Drama der Shakespearezeit.* Abhandlungen der Akademie der Wissenschaften in Göttingen, philologisch-historische Klasse, 3. Folge, 46. Göttingen, 1960.

Sen Gupta, S[ubodh] C. *Aspects of Shakespearian Tragedy.* 2nd ed. Calcutta: OUP, 1977. (1st ed. 1972.)

———. *The Whirligig of Time: The Problem of Duration in Shakespeare's Plays.* Bombay, 1961.

Seng, Peter J. "Shakespearean Hymn-Parody?" *Renaissance News* 18 (1965), 4–6.

Serio, John. "The Tragedy of Antony." *The Cresset* 33, No. 8 (1970), 16–17.

Seronsy, Cecil [C.]. *Samuel Daniel.* TEAS 49. New York, 1967.

Seward, Thomas (1708–90). Contributor to *The Works of Mr. Francis Beaumont, and Mr. John Fletcher. . . . Ed. by the late Mr. Theobald, Mr. Seward of Eyam in Derbyshire, and Mr. Sympson of Gainsborough.* 10 vols. 1750.

Sewell, Arthur. *Character and Society in Shakespeare.* OUP, 1951.

Seymour, E. H. *Remarks, Critical, Conjectural, and Explanatory, upon the Plays of Shakspeare.* 2 vols. 1805.

Shaheen, Naseeb. *Biblical References in Shakespeare's Tragedies.* Newark, Del., 1987.

Shanker, Sidney. *Shakespeare and the Uses of Ideology.* Stud. in Eng. Lit. 105. The Hague & Paris, 1975.

Shapiro, Michael. "Boying her Greatness: Shakespeare's Use of Coterie Drama in 'Antony and Cleopatra.' " *MLR* 77 (1982), 1–15.

Shapiro, Stephen A. "The Varying Shore of the World: Ambivalence in *Antony and Cleopatra.*" *MLQ* 27 (1966), 18–32.

Shapiro, Susan C. "To 'O'erflow the Measure': The Paradox of the Nile in *Antony and Cleopatra.*" *Studies in the Humanities* 4, No. 2 (1975), 36–42.

Sharp, Frank C. *Shakespeare's Portrayal of The Moral Life.* New York, 1902.

Sharpe, Robert B. *Irony in the Drama: An Essay on Impersonation, Shock, and Catharsis.* Chapel Hill, 1959.

Shattuck, Charles H. *Shakespeare on the American Stage.* Vol. 2: *From Booth and Barrett to Sothern and Marlowe.* Washington, D.C., 1987.

———. *Shakespeare on the American Stage.* Vol. 1: *From the Hallams to Edwin Booth.* Washington, D.C., 1976.

———. *Shakespeare's Promptbooks: A Descriptive Catalogue.* Urbana, 1965.

Shaw, [George] Bernard. *Works.* Standard Ed. 34 vols. 1931–51. ("Better than Shakespear?", vol. 31 [1931], pp. xxvii–xxxvi, first pub. in *Three Plays for Puritans*, 1900; review of *Oth.* and *Ant.* [in *SatR* 83 (1897), 603–5], vol. 24 [1932], pp. 144–51; "Shakespear in Manchester [*Ant.* produced by Louis Calvert at Queen's Th., 1897]," vol. 24 [1932], pp. 76–83; "Tolstoy: Tragedian or Comedian?", vol. 25 [1932], pp. 260–6, first pub. in *Pen Portraits and Reviews*, 1921.)

Shaw, John. " 'In Every Corner of the Stage': *Antony and Cleopatra*, IV.iii." *ShakS* 7 (1974), 227–32.

Shaw-Smith, R. "*Antony and Cleopatra*, [912]." *SQ* 24 (1973), 92–3.

Sherman, L[ucius] A. *What is Shakespeare? An Introduction to the Great Plays.* New York, 1901.

Shimizu, Masako. "A Stylistic Study of Shakespeare's *Antony and Cleopatra* in Comparison with Dryden's *All for Love.*" *Igakukai-shi Ippankyoyo-hen* 8 (1982), 59–74.

Shintri, Sarojini. *Woman in Shakespeare.* Research Pub. Ser. 32. Dharwad, 1977.

Shirley, Frances A. *Shakespeare's Use of Off-Stage Sounds.* Lincoln, Nebr., 1963.

Shrimpton, Nicholas. "Shakespeare Performances in Stratford-upon-Avon and London, 1982–3." *ShS* 37 (1984), 163–73.

Siegel, Aaron H. "The Dramatic Function of Comic Elements in Three Shakespearean Love Tragedies." Univ. of Southern California diss., 1965. (*DA* 26 [1965], 2193A.)

Siegel, Paul N. "Foreshadowings of Cleopatra's Death." *N&Q* 203 (1958), 386–7.

———. *Shakespeare's English and Roman History Plays: A Marxist Approach.* Rutherford, N.J., London, & Toronto, 1986.

Siemon, James E. " 'The Strong Necessity of Time': Dilemma in *Antony and Cleopatra.*" *ES* 54 (1973), 316–25.

Sigurdson, Paul A. "To Weet Or Not To Weet." *ShN* 36 (1986), 52.

Simard, Rodney. "Source and *Antony and Cleopatra*: Shakespeare's Adaptation of Plutarch's Octavia." *SJW* 122 (1986), 65–74.

Simmons, J[oseph] L. " 'Antony and Cleopatra' and 'Coriolanus', Shakespeare's Heroic Tragedies: A Jacobean Adjustment." *ShS* 26 (1973), 95–101.

———. "The Comic Pattern and Vision in *Antony and Cleopatra.*" *ELH* 36 (1969), 493–510.

———. *Shakespeare's Pagan World: The Roman Tragedies.* Charlottesville, 1973.

———. "Shakespeare's Treatment of Roman History." *William Shakespeare: His World, His Work, His Influence.* Ed. John F. Andrews. 3 vols. New York, 1985. 2:473–88.

Simpson, Lucie. "Shakespeare's Cleopatra." *The Secondary Heroes of Shakespeare and Other Essays.* 1950. Pp. 27–37. (First pub. *Fortnightly Review* NS 129 [1928], 332–42.)

Simpson, Percy. *Proof-reading in the Sixteenth, Seventeenth and Eighteenth Centuries.* OUP, 1935.

———. *Shakespearian Punctuation.* OUP, 1911.

Singer, S[amuel] W. "Could Shakspeare Have Designated Cleopatra 'Yond Ribald-Rid Nag of Egypt'?" 1 *N&Q* 3 (12 Apr. 1851), 273–4.

———. *The Text of Shakespeare Vindicated from the Interpolations and Corruptions Advocated by John Payne Collier Esq. in His Notes and Emendations.* 1853.

Sipe, Dorothy L. *Shakespeare's Metrics.* New Haven, 1968.

Sircar, Bibhuti B. *An Appreciation of William Shakespeare: Ten Plays with Critical Estimates.* Calcutta, 1975.

Sisson, Charles J. *Le goût public et le théâtre élisabéthain jusqu'à la mort de Shakespeare.* Dijon, [1922].

———. *New Readings in Shakespeare.* Sh. Problems 8. 2 vols. Cambridge, 1956.

———. "The Roman Plays." *The Living Shakespeare.* Ed. Robert Gittings. 1960. Pp. 127–39.

Sitwell, Edith. *A Notebook on William Shakespeare.* 1948.

Sjöberg, Alf. "Sekundärrollen: Herre och tjänare-visionen i *Antonius och Kleopatra.*" *Dramaten* 6 (1975–6), 9–15, 47.

Skeat, Walter W. " 'Antony and Cleopatra', [50]." 7 *N&Q* 2 (13 Nov. 1886), 385.

———. *A Glossary of Tudor and Stuart Words Especially from the Dramatists.* Ed. with Additions by A. L. Mayhew. OUP, 1914. (Rpt. Anglistica & Americana 4. Hildesheim & New York: Olms, 1968.)

———, ed. *Shakespeare's Plutarch.* New ed. 1880. (1st ed. 1875.)

Skinner, Stephen. *Etymologicon Linguae Anglicanae.* 1671. (Rpt. Anglistica & Americana 58. Hildesheim & New York: Olms, 1970.)

Skottowe, Augustine. *The Life of Shakespeare.* 2 vols. 1824.

Smeaton, Oliphant. *Shakespeare, His Life and Work.* Everyman's Libr. London & New York, [1911].

Smith, A[lbert] J. *Literary Love: The Role of Passion in English Poems and Plays of the Seventeenth Century.* 1983.

Smith, Constance I. "A Further Note on A. and C. [54]." *N&Q* 203 (1958), 371.

Smith, Gerald A. " 'Good Brother' in *King Lear* and *Antony and Cleopatra.*" *SQ* 25 (1974), 284.

Smith, Gordon R. "The Melting of Authority in *Antony and Cleopatra.*" *CollL* 1 (1974), 1–18.

Smith, Irwin. " 'Gates' on Shakespeare's Stage." *SQ* 7 (1956), 159–76.

―――. *Shakespeare's Globe Playhouse.* New York, 1956.

―――. "Their Exits and Reentrances." *SQ* 18 (1967), 7–16.

Smith, J. E. " 'Antony and Cleopatra', II.ii. [920–1.]" 7 *N&Q* 10 (22 Nov. 1890), 402–3.

Smith, J. Oates. "The Alchemy of *Antony and Cleopatra.*" *BuR* 12, No. 1 (1964), 37–50.

Smith, Maria S. A. "Last Farewells in *Antony and Cleopatra.*" *Signal* 1, No. 1 (1978), 65–77.

Smith, Marion B. *Dualities in Shakespeare.* Toronto, 1966.

Smith, Michael H. "Men of Ice: The Dehumanizing Effects of Ambition in Shakespeare's *Antony and Cleopatra.*" *Signal* 1, No. 1 (1978), 117–26.

Smith, Sheila M. " 'This Great Solemnity': A Study of the Presentation of Death in *Antony and Cleopatra.*" *ES* 45 (1964), 163–76.

Smith, Stella T. "Imagery of Union, Division, and Disintegration in *Antony and Cleopatra.*" *Claflin College Review* 1, No. 2 (1977), 15–28.

Smith, Warren. "Evidence of Scaffolding on Shakespeare's Stage." *RES* NS 2 (1951), 22–9.

―――. *Shakespeare's Playhouse Practice: A Handbook.* Hanover, N.H., 1975.

Smithers, G. V. "Guide-lines for Interpreting the Uses of the Suffix '-ed' in Shakespeare's English." *ShS* 23 (1970), 27–37.

Snider, Denton J. *"Antony and Cleopatra." System of Shakespeare's Dramas.* Vol. 2. St. Louis, 1877. Pp. 260–84. (First pub. *Journal of Speculative Philosophy* 10 [1876], 52–69.)

Snyder, Susan. *The Comic Matrix of Shakespeare's Tragedies*: Romeo and Juliet, Hamlet, Othello, *and* King Lear. Princeton, 1979.

―――. "Ourselves Alone: The Challenge to Single Combat in Shakespeare." *SEL* 20 (1980), 201–16.

―――. "Patterns of Motion in 'Antony and Cleopatra.' " *ShS* 33 (1980), 113–22.

Soellner, Rolf. "The Four Primary Passions: A Renaissance Theory Reflected in the Works of Shakespeare." *SP* 55 (1958), 549–67.

―――. "The Madness of Hercules and the Elizabethans." *CL* 10 (1958), 309–24.

Sorensen, Catherine. "Whom Everything Becomes." *The Silver Falcon* (Hunter Coll., N.Y.), 1936, pp. 21–4.

Sorgenfrey, Clemens. Private Contributor.

Spalding, K[enneth] J. *The Philosophy of Shakespeare.* Oxford, 1953.

Speaight, Robert. *Nature in Shakespearian Tragedy.* 1955.

―――. *Shakespeare: The Man and his Achievement.* 1977.

―――. *Shakespeare on the Stage: An Illustrated History of Shakespearian Performance.* 1973.

Spedding, James. "Note on a Passage in Shakspeare." 5 *N&Q* 1 (18 Apr. 1874), 303–4.

Spence, R. M. " 'Antony and Cleopatra', Act I. Sc. 5.—'Arm-gaunt' [578]." 5 *N&Q* 10 (28 Sept. 1878), 244.

―――. " 'Antony and Cleopatra', [28]." 9 *N&Q* 5 (27 Jan. 1900), 62.

Spencer, Benjamin T. *"Antony and Cleopatra* and the Paradoxical Metaphor." *SQ* 9 (1958), 373–8.

Spencer, Hazelton. *The Art and Life of William Shakespeare.* New York, 1940.

————. *Shakespeare Improved. The Restoration Versions in Quarto and on the Stage.* New York, 1927. (Rpt. New York: Ungar, 1963.)

Spencer, Lois. "The Antony Perspective." *London Review* 2 (1967), 20–9.

Spencer, T[erence] J. B. *William Shakespeare: The Roman Plays—Titus Andronicus, Julius Caesar, Antony and Cleopatra, Coriolanus.* Bibliographical Ser. of Supplements to "British Book News" on Writers and Their Work 157. Gen. Ed. Geoffrey Bullough. 1963. (Rpt. with additions 1966.)

————, ed. *Shakespeare's Plutarch.* Harmondsworth, 1964. (Reissued Penguin Sh. Libr., 1968.)

Spencer, Theodore. *Shakespeare and the Nature of Man.* The Lowell Lectures 1942. 2nd ed. New York, 1961. (1st ed. 1943.)

Spevack, Marvin. "The Editor as Philologist." *TEXT* 3 (1987), 91–106.

————. "Shakespeare's Language." *William Shakespeare: His World, His Work, His Influence.* Ed. John F. Andrews. 3 vols. New York, 1985. 2:343–61.

Sprague, Arthur Colby. *Shakespeare and the Actors: The Stage Business in His Plays (1660–1905).* Cambridge, Mass., 1944. (Rpt. New York: Russell & Russell, 1963.)

————. *Shakespeare and the Audience: A Study in the Technique of Exposition.* Cambridge, Mass., 1935.

————. *Shakespearian Players and Performances.* 1954. (First pub. 1953.)

————, & J. C. Trewin. *Shakespeare's Plays Today.* Columbia, S.C., 1971.

Sprenger, Robert. *Bemerkungen zu Dramen Shakespeares.* Programm des Realprogymnasiums zu Northeim. Northeim, 1891.

Spurgeon, Caroline F. E. *Shakespeare's Imagery and What It Tells Us.* Cambridge, 1935.

Squire, John. *Shakespeare As A Dramatist.* 1935. (Rpt. New York: Haskell House, 1971.)

Squire, W. Barclay. "Shakespearian Operas." *A Book of Homage to Shakespeare.* Ed. Israel Gollancz. OUP, 1916. Pp. 75–83.

Stahl, Ernst Leopold. "Die englischen Shakespeare-Aufführungen 1906–7." *SJ* 43 (1907), 362–73.

————. *Shakespeare und das deutsche Theater.* Stuttgart, 1947.

Stahr, Adolf. *Cleopatra.* Berlin, 1864.

Stamm, Rudolf. *"Antony and Cleopatra:* Cleopatra als Objekt der Kritik und der Teilnahme des Publikums." *Sympathielenkung in den Dramen Shakespeares: Studien zur publikumsbezogenen Dramaturgie.* Ed. Werner Habicht & Ina Schabert. Texte und Untersuchungen zur Englischen Philologie 9. München, 1978. Pp. 72–81.

————. "The Transmutation of Source Material." *The Shaping Powers at Work.* Heidelberg, 1967. Pp. 74–84. (First pub. as "Elizabethan Stage-Practice and the Transmutation of Source Material by the Dramatists," *ShS* 12 [1959], 64–70.)

Stampfer, Judah. *The Tragic Engagement: A Study of Shakespeare's Classical Tragedies.* New York, 1968.

Stansfield, Dale B. "Montaigne and Shakespeare, Renaissance or Baroque?" Univ. of Wisconsin diss., 1975. (*DA* 36 [1976], 6057A.)

Stapfer, Paul. *Shakespeare and Classical Antiquity.* Tr. Emily J. Carey. 1880. (Rpt. New York: Franklin, 1970. 1st Fr. ed. 1879.)

Starnes, D[e Witt] T. "Shakespeare and Apuleius." *PMLA* 60 (1945), 1021–50.

————, & Ernest W. Talbert. *Classical Myth and Legend in Renaissance Dictionaries*. Chapel Hill, 1955.

Stauffer, Donald A. *Shakespeare's World of Images: The Development of His Moral Ideas*. New York, 1949.

Staunton, H. "Unsuspected Corruptions of Shakspeare's Text." *Athenæum* No. 2372 (12 Apr. 1873), 473–4; No. 2374 (26 Apr. 1873), 534–5.

Steane, J[ohn] B. *Marlowe: A Critical Study*. Cambridge, 1964.

Steevens, George (1736–1800). Contributor to v1803.

Stein, Arnold. "The Image of Antony: Lyric and Tragic Imagination." *KR* 21 (1959), 586–606.

Stempel, Daniel. "The Transmigration of the Crocodile." *SQ* 7 (1956), 59–72.

Stendhal. *Mélanges*. Vol. 5: *Littérature*. Vol. 49 of *Œuvres complètes*. Ed. Victor Del Litto. New ed. Genève, 1972. (Remark on *Ant.* dated 8 Jan. 1821.)

Stephen, Leslie. *Studies of a Biographer*. 4 vols. 1898–1902. Vol. 4. 1902.

Steppat, Michael. *The Critical Reception of Shakespeare's* Antony and Cleopatra *from 1607 to 1905*. Bochum Stud. in Eng. 9. Amsterdam & Atlantic Highlands, N.J., 1980.

————. "Shakespeare's Response to Dramatic Tradition in *Antony and Cleopatra*." *Shakespeare—Text, Language, Criticism: Essays in Honour of Marvin Spevack*. Ed. Bernhard Fabian & Kurt Tetzeli von Rosador. Hildesheim, Zürich, & New York, 1987. Pp. 254–79.

Sternfeld, F[rederick] W. *Music in Shakespearean Tragedy*. London & New York, 1963.

Stewart, J[ohn] I. M. *Character and Motive in Shakespeare: Some Recent Appraisals Examined*. London & New York, 1949.

Stilling, Roger. *Love and Death in Renaissance Tragedy*. Baton Rouge, 1976.

Stirling, Brents. "Cleopatra's Scene with Seleucus: Plutarch, Daniel, and Shakespeare." *SQ* 15, No. 2 (1964), 299–311.

————. *Unity in Shakespearian Tragedy: The Interplay of Theme and Character*. New York, 1956.

Stockholder, Kay. *Dream World: Lovers and Families in Shakespeare's Plays*. Toronto, 1987.

Stoessl, Otto. *Geist und Gestalt*. Vol. 3 of *Gesammelte Werke*. Wien, 1935.

Stoll, Elmer Edgar. "Cleopatra." *Poets and Playwrights*. Minneapolis, 1930. Pp. 1–30. (First pub. *MLR* 23 [1928], 145–63.)

Strachan, L. R. M. "The Spelling 'Anthony.'" *N&Q* 167 (1934), 85–6.

Strindberg, August. *Open Letters to the Intimate Theater*. Tr. Walter Johnson. Seattle & London, [1966]. (1st Swedish ed. 1909.)

Stroup, Thomas B. "The Structure of *Antony and Cleopatra*." *SQ* 15, No. 2 (1964), 289–98.

Stull, Joseph S. "Cleopatra's Magnanimity: The Dismissal of the Messenger." *SQ* 7 (1956), 73–8.

Styan, J[ohn] L. *The Elements of Drama*. Cambridge, 1960. (Paperback ed. with new Preface 1963.)

————. *Shakespeare's Stagecraft*. Cambridge, 1967. (Rpt. 1975 with new Preface dated 1970.)

Sujaku, Shigeko. "Fall and Fortune of Antony." *Eibei Bungaku Kenkyu* (Baiko Women's Coll.) 14 (1978), 231–42.

————. "Love and Honor for Cleopatra." *Eibei Bungaku Kenkyu* (Baiko Women's Coll.) 13 (1977), 205–32.

Summers, Joseph H. *Dreams of Love and Power: On Shakespeare's Plays*. OUP, 1984.

Suzman, Janet. Contributor to Cook 1980.

Suzuki, Hisako. "Enobarbus as an Excellent Supporting Actor in *Antony and Cleopatra*." *Eibungaku Kenkyukai Kaishi* (Ferris Women's Coll.) 12 (1979), 11–18.

Swander, Homer. "Menas and the Editors: A Folio Script Unscripted." *SQ* 36 (1985), 165–87.

Swinburne, Algernon Charles. *Shakespeare.* OUP, 1909. (Written 1905.)

———. *A Study of Shakespeare.* 4th ed. 1902. (1st ed. 1879.)

Symons, Arthur. "Antony and Cleopatra." *Studies In The Elizabethan Drama.* 1919. Pp. 1–20. (Rpt. New York: AMS, 1972; first pub. in Irving & Marshall ed., vol. 6 [1889]: 119–24.)

Tachibana, Tadae. *A Survey of Shakespeare: His Roman Plays.* [In Japanese.] 2nd ed. Tokyo, 1948. (1st ed. 1947.)

Taine, H[ippolyte A.]. *History of English Literature.* Tr. H. van Laun. 5th ed. 2 vols. Edinburgh, 1874. (Tr. first pub. 1871; 1st Fr. ed. 1863–4.)

Talbot, Bertram. "Shakespeare's View of Women's Relations with and Influence on Men of Mark." *Winchester College Shakspere Society, Noctes Shaksperianae: A Series of Papers by Late and Present Members.* Ed. Charles Halford Hawkins. Winchester & London, 1887. Pp. 223–52.

Tanifuji, Isamu. "Aspects of Love in *Antony and Cleopatra.*" *Kiyo* 7–8 (1977), 1–34.

———. "Enobarbus' Minor Tragedy in *Antony and Cleopatra.*" *ESELL* 57 (1970), 51–72.

Tanner, John S. " 'Here is my Space': The Private Mode in Donne's Poetry and Shakespeare's *Antony and Cleopatra.*" *Iowa State Journal of Research* 60 (1985–6), 417–30.

Tate, N[ahum]. *The Loyal General: A Tragedy. Acted at the Duke's Theatre.* 1680.

Taylor, Anthony B. "The Non-existent Carbuncles: Shakespeare, Golding, and Raphael Regius." *N&Q* 230 (1985), 54–5.

Taylor, Archer. " 'He that will not when he may; when he will shall have nay.' " *Studies in Old English Literature in Honor of Arthur G. Brodeur.* Ed. Stanley B. Greenfield. Waldo Hall, Corvallis, Ore., 1963. Pp. 155–61.

Taylor, George Coffin. *Shakspere's Debt to Montaigne.* Cambridge, Mass., 1925.

Taylor, Marion A. "Not Know Me Yet?" *Ball State Teachers College Forum* (now *BSUF*) 5 (Autumn 1964), 63–6.

Taylor, Michael. "The Conflict in Hamlet." *SQ* 22 (1971), 147–61.

Theobald, Lewis. Letters to William Warburton; originals in Folger Library. Phillipps MS 8565. Pub. in *Illustrations of the Literary History of the Eighteenth Century.* By John Nichols. 8 vols. 1817–58. 2:204–655. (Rpt. New York: Kraus & AMS, 1966.)

———. *Shakespeare Restored.* 1726. (Rpt. London: Cass, 1971.)

Theobald, William. *The Classical Element in the Shakespeare Plays.* 1909.

Thiselton, Alfred E. " 'Antony and Cleopatra', [28]." 9 *N&Q* 4 (2 Dec. 1899), 453.

———. *Some Textual Notes on the Tragedie of Anthony and Cleopatra: With Other Shakespeare Memoranda.* 1899.

Thomas, Helen S. " 'Breeze' and 'Bees', 'Sailes' and 'Tailes': *A&C* [1989–94]." *CEA* 37, No. 1 (1974), 23–4.

Thomas, Mary O. "Cleopatra and the 'Mortal Wretch.' " *SJ* 99 (1963), 174–83.

———. "The Opening Scenes of *Antony and Cleopatra.*" *SAQ* 71 (1972), 565–72.

———. "Plutarch in *Antony and Cleopatra.*" Duke Univ. diss., 1956.

———. "The Repetitions in Antony's Death Scene." *SQ* 9 (1958), 153–7.

Thompson, Karl F. *Modesty and Cunning: Shakespeare's Use of Literary Tradition.* Ann Arbor, 1971.

Thomson, J[ames] A. K. *Shakespeare and the Classics.* 1952.

Thomson, Leslie. "*Antony and Cleopatra,* Act 4 Scene 16: 'A Heavy Sight.' " *ShS* 41 (1988), 77–90.

Thomson, Peter. *Shakespeare's Theatre.* 1983.

Thümmel, Julius. *Shakespeare-Charaktere.* 2 vols. 2nd ed. Halle a. S., 1887. (1st ed. 1881.)

Tieck, Ludwig. *Das Buch über Shakespeare: Handschriftliche Aufzeichnungen* [c. 1794]. Aus seinem Nachlaß herausgegeben von Henry Lüdeke. Neudrucke deutscher Literaturwerke des 18. und 19. Jahrhunderts Nr. 1. Halle a. S., 1920.

Tiessen, Ed[uard]. "Beiträge zur Feststellung und Erklärung des Shakspearetextes." *Englische Studien* 2 (1879), 185–204, 440–75.

Tilley, Morris P. *A Dictionary of the Proverbs in England in the Sixteenth and Seventeenth Centuries: A Collection of the Proverbs Found in English Literature and the Dictionaries of the Period.* Ann Arbor, 1950.

Timon, Dr. [M. P. de Haan]. *Shakespeare's Drama in seiner natürlichen Entwicklung dargestellt.* Leyden, 1889.

Tobin, J. J. M. "Apuleius and *Antony and Cleopatra*, Once More." *SN* 51 (1979), 225–8.

———. *Shakespeare's Favorite Novel: A Study of* The Golden Asse *As Prime Source.* Lanham, New York & London, 1984.

Tollet, George (1725–79). Contributor to v1778.

Tolman, Albert H. "The Fifth Act of 'Antony and Cleopatra.' " *Falstaff and Other Shakespearean Topics.* New York, 1925. Pp. 161–8.

Tolmie, L. W. " 'Least cause' / 'All cause': Roman Infinite Variety: An Essay on *Antony and Cleopatra*." *Southern Review* 11 (1978), 113–31.

Tomlinson, T. B. "Shakespeare as Idealist—Recent Trends in Criticism." *CR* 5 (1962), 108–18.

Tomokiyo, Yoko. "The Dramatic World of *Antony and Cleopatra*." *Chofu Gakuen Woman's Junior College Kiyo* 10 (1977), 50–75.

Torbarina, Josip. "The 'Nakedness' of the Shakespearian Tragic Hero." *SRAZ* 12 (1962), 3–7.

Traci, Philip J. *The Love Play of Antony and Cleopatra: A Critical Study of Shakespeare's Play.* Stud. in Eng. Lit. 64. The Hague & Paris, 1970.

Traub, Walther. *Auffassung und Gestaltung der Cleopatra in der englischen Literatur.* Würzburg, 1938.

Traversi, Derek. *An Approach to Shakespeare.* 3rd ed. 2 vols. 1968–9. (1st ed. 1938.)

———. *The Literary Imagination: Studies in Dante, Chaucer, and Shakespeare.* Newark, N.J., London, & Toronto, 1982.

———. *Shakespeare: The Roman Plays.* 1963.

Trench, Richard C. *Plutarch—His Life, His Parallel Lives, and His Morals: Five Lectures.* 2nd ed. 1874. (1st ed. 1872.)

Trewin, J[ohn] C. *Benson and the Bensonians.* With a Foreword by Dorothy Green. 1960.

———. *The Birmingham Repertory Theatre 1913–1963.* 1963.

———. "Shakespeare in Britain." *SQ* 31 (1980), 153–61.

———. *Shakespeare on the English Stage 1900–1964: A Survey of Productions.* 1964.

Troy, William. " 'Antony and Cleopatra': The Poetic Vision." In Sisson ed. 1961. Laurel Sh. Pp. 21–31.

Tucker, Kenneth. "Psychetypes and Shakespeare's *Antony and Cleopatra*." *Journal of Evolutionary Psychology* 5 (1984), 176–81.

Turner, Paul, ed. *Selected Lives from the Lives of the Noble Grecians and Romans.* 2 vols. 1963.

Turner, Robert Kean. Private Contributor.

Tyrwhitt, Thomas (1730–86). Contributor to v1778.

[———.] *Observations and Conjectures upon Some Passages of Shakespeare.* Oxford, 1766. (Rpt. London: Cass, 1969.)

Uéno, Yoshiko Y. "*Antony and Cleopatra*: The Last Phase of Shakespearean Tragedy." *ShStud* 6 (1967–8), 1–36.

Uhlig, Claus. *Traditionelle Denkformen in Shakespeares tragischer Kunst.* Britannica et Americana 15. Hamburg, 1967.

Ulrici, Hermann. *Shakespeare's Dramatic Art.* Tr. from 3rd Ger. ed. by L. Dora Schmitz. 2 vols. 1876. (1st Ger. ed. 1839; 2nd ed. 1847; 3rd ed. 1868–9.)

Ungerer, Friedrich. *Dramatische Spannung in Shakespeares Tragödien.* München, 1964. (München diss.)

Uphaus, Robert W. "Shakespearean Tragedy and the Intimations of Romance." *CentR* 22 (1978), 299–318.

Upton, John. *Critical Observations on Shakespeare.* 2nd ed. 1748. (Rpt. New York: AMS, 1973. 1st ed. 1746.)

Urban, Wilhelm. *Die dämonische Persönlichkeit des Antonius in Shakespeares "Antony and Cleopatra."* Marburg, 1939. (Marburg diss.)

Urkowitz, Steven. "Interrupted Exits in *King Lear.*" *Educational Theatre Journal* 30 (1978), 203–10.

V., F. J. "Conjectural Notes on Shakspeare and Other Writers." 4 *N&Q* 11 (15 Mar. 1873), 210–11.

Van Doren, Mark. *Shakespeare.* New York, 1939.

Van Laan, Thomas F. *Role-playing in Shakespeare.* Toronto, 1978.

Van Lennep, William, et al. *The London Stage 1660–1800.* 5 pts. in 11 vols. Carbondale, Ill., 1960–8. *Index.* Ed. Ben R. Schneider, Jr. 1979.

Van Woensel, Maurice J. F. "Revelry and Carousing in Shakespeare's *Antony and Cleopatra.*" *Signal* 1, No. 1 (1978), 78–100.

Vatke, Theodor. "Shakespeare und Euripides: Eine Parallele." *SJ* 4 (1869), 62–93.

———. "Shakespeare's Antonius und Kleopatra und Plutarch's Biographie des Antonius." *SJ* 3 (1868), 301–40.

Vehse, Eduard. *Shakespeare als Protestant, Politiker, Psycholog und Dichter.* 2 vols. Hamburg, 1851.

Venet, Gisèle. "Images et structures dans *Antoine et Cléopâtre.*" *EA* 30 (1977), 281–302.

Venezky, Alice. "Current Shakespearian Productions in England and France." *SQ* 2 (1951), 335–42.

Verma, Rajiva. "Winners and Losers: A Study of *Macbeth* and *Antony and Cleopatra.*" *MLR* 81 (1986), 838–52.

V[erplanck], G[ulian C.]. "III. Zu Antonius und Cleopatra." *SJ* 12 (1877), 320–1.

Vickers, Brian. *The Artistry of Shakespeare's Prose.* 1968.

Viertel, Berthold. "Antonius und Kleopatra." *Schriften zum Theater.* Ed. Gert Heidenreich. München, 1970. Pp. 28–31. (First pub. *Programmheft des Burgtheaters Wien, 28 Feb. 1953.*)

Villemain, [Abel F]. "Essai littéraire sur Shakspeare." *Mélanges historiques et littéraires.* Vol. 3. Paris, 1827. Pp. 141–87.

Vincent, Barbara C. "The Anatomy of Antony: A Study of the Literary Worlds in Shakespeare's *Antony and Cleopatra.*" Rutgers Univ. diss., 1978. (*DA* 39 [1978], 904A–5A.)

———. "Shakespeare's *Antony and Cleopatra* and the Rise of Comedy." *ELR* 12 (1982), 53–86.

Vischer, Friedrich Th. *Shakespeare-Vorträge.* Ed. Robert Vischer. 6 vols. Stuttgart & Berlin, 1899–1905. Vol. 6. 1905. (Delivered 1869–87.)

Voigt, Hermann. *Gleichnisse und Metaphern in Shakespeare's Dramen und in seinen Quellenschriften.* Strassburg, 1908. (Strassburg diss.)

Vollmer, Adolf. "Shakespeare und Plutarch." *Archiv* 78 (1887), 215–70.

W., J. S. "Shakspeare's 'Small Latin'.—His Use of 'Triple.' " 1 *N&Q* 4 (12 July 1851), 26–7.

Waddington, Raymond B. "Antony and Cleopatra: 'What Venus did with Mars.' " *ShakS* 2 (1966), 210–27.

Wain, John. *The Living World of Shakespeare: A Playgoer's Guide.* 1964.

Waith, Eugene M. *The Herculean Hero in Marlowe, Chapman, Shakespeare and Dryden.* New York & London, 1962.

———. "Manhood and Valor in Two Shakespearean Tragedies." *ELH* 17 (1950), 262–73.

Walker, Alice. "Principles of Annotation: Some Suggestions for Editors of Shakespeare." *SB* 9 (1957), 95–105.

———. *Textual Problems of the First Folio:* Richard III, King Lear, Troilus & Cressida, 2 Henry IV, Hamlet, Othello. Vol. 7 of *Shakespeare Problems,* ed. J. Dover Wilson. Cambridge, 1953.

Walker, Roy. "Antony and Cleopatra." *TLS,* 29 May 1953, p. 349.

———. "The Northern Star: An Essay on the Roman Plays." *SQ* 2 (1951), 287–93.

Walker, William S. *A Critical Examination of the Text of Shakespeare.* [Ed. W. Nanson Lettsom.] 3 vols. 1860.

———. *Shakespeare's Versification.* 1854.

Wall, Stephen. "Shakespeare: His Later Plays." *English Drama to 1710.* Ed. Christopher Ricks. Hist. of Lit. in the Eng. Lang. 3. 1971. Pp. 253–77.

Waller, G[ary] F. *The Strong Necessity of Time: The Philosophy of Time in Shakespeare and Elizabethan Literature.* The Hague & Paris, 1976.

Wallerstein, Ruth. "Dryden and the Analysis of Shakespeare's Techniques." *RES* 19 (1943), 165–85.

Walter, J. H. "Four Notes on 'Antony and Cleopatra.' " *N&Q* 214 (1969), 137–9.

Walzel, O. "Shakespeares dramatische Baukunst." *SJ* 52 (1916), 3–35.

Warburton, William (1698–1779). Contributor to THEO1, HAN2.

———. "Contributor" to Lounsbury 1906.

———. Correspondent of Lewis Theobald in mTHEO2, mTHEO3.

Ward, Adolphus W. *A History of English Dramatic Literature to the Death of Queen Anne.* Rev. ed. 3 vols. 1899. (1st ed. 2 vols., 1875.)

Warner, Alan. "A Note on *Antony and Cleopatra.*" *English* 11 (1957), 139–44.

Warren, Roger. "Shakespeare at Stratford and the National Theatre, 1979." *ShS* 33 (1980), 169–80.

Warton, Thomas (1728–90). Contributor to Malone 1780.

———. *History of English Poetry from the Twelfth to the Close of the Sixteenth Century.* Ed. W. Carew Hazlitt. 4 vols. 1871. (Rpt. Anglistica & Americana 18. Hildesheim & New York: Olms, 1968. First pub. 1774–81. Vol. 3. 1778.)

Waterhouse, Ruth. "Shakespeare's *Antony and Cleopatra,* [442–3, 478–81]." *Expl* 33 (1974), no. 17.

Watkins, Ronald. *On Producing Shakespeare.* 1950.

Watkins, W[alter] B. C. *Shakespeare and Spenser.* Princeton, 1950.

Watson, Curtis B. *Shakespeare and the Renaissance Concept of Honor.* Princeton, 1960.

Watson, Gilbert. "The Death of Cleopatra." *N&Q* 223 (1978), 409–14; 224 (1979), 133–7.

Webster, Margaret. *Shakespeare Today.* 1957. (First pub. as *Shakespeare without Tears,* New York, 1942.)

Weckermann, Hans-Jürgen. *Verständigungsprobleme in Shakespeares Dramen.* Bochum Stud. in Eng. 7. Amsterdam, 1978.

Weekes, A. R. "Shakespeare: Antony and Cleopatra." *The University Correspondent*, 1 Dec. 1928, pp. 188–9.

Weidhorn, Manfred. "The Relation of Title and Name to Identity in Shakespearean Tragedy." *SEL* 9 (1969), 303–19.

Weilgart, Wolfgang J. *Shakespeare Psychognostic: Character Evolution and Transformation.* Tokyo, 1952. (Rpt. New York: AMS, 1972.)

Weiner, Albert B. "Elizabethan Interior and Aloft Scenes: A Speculative Essay." *Theatre Survey* 2 (1961), 15–34.

Weinstock, Horst. "Loyal Service in Shakespeare's Mature Plays." *SN* 43 (1971), 446–73.

Weis, René J. A. " 'Antony and Cleopatra': The Challenge of Fiction." *English* 32 (1983), 1–14.

————. "*Caesar's Revenge*: A Neglected Elizabethan Source of *Antony and Cleopatra*." *SJH*, 1983, pp. 178–86.

Weiβ, Wolfgang. *Das Drama der Shakespeare-Zeit.* Sprache und Literatur 100. Stuttgart, Berlin, Köln, & Mainz, 1979.

Weitz, Morris. "Literature Without Philosophy: 'Antony and Cleopatra.' " *ShS* 28 (1975), 29–36.

Wells, Stanley. *Re-Editing Shakespeare for the Modern Reader.* Oxford Sh. Stud. OUP, 1984.

————, & Gary Taylor. *William Shakespeare: A Textual Companion.* OUP, 1987.

Wendell, Barrett. *William Shakspere: A Study in Elizabethan Literature.* New York, 1894. (Rpt. New York: Haskell House, 1971.)

Wentersdorf, Karl. "Shakespearean Chronology and the Metrical Tests." *Shakespeare-Studien: Festschrift für Heinrich Mutschmann.* Ed. Walther Fischer & Karl Wentersdorf. Marburg, 1951. Pp. 161–93.

Werstine, Paul. "Compositor B of the Shakespeare First Folio." *Analytical & Enumerative Bibliography* 2 (1978), 241–63.

————. "Compositors and Cases in the Folio *Othello*." Sh. Assn. of America seminar paper.

————. "Folio Editors, Folio Compositors, and the Folio Text of *King Lear*." *The Division of the Kingdoms: Shakespeare's Two Versions of* King Lear. Ed. Gary Taylor & Michael Warren. Oxford Sh. Stud. OUP, 1983. Pp. 247–312.

————. "Line Division in Shakespeare's Dramatic Verse: An Editorial Problem." *Analytical & Enumerative Bibliography* 8 (1984), 73–125.

Wertime, Richard A. "Excellent Falsehood: Theme and Characterization in *Antony and Cleopatra*." Univ. of Pennsylvania diss., 1969. (*DA* 30 [1969], 2983A.)

[Wesley, Samuel.] *Maggots: Or, Poems on Several Subjects, Never before Handled.* 1685.

Westbrook, Perry D. "Horace's Influence on Shakespeare's *Antony and Cleopatra*." *PMLA* 62 (1947), 392–8.

Wetz, W[ilhelm]. *Shakespeare vom Standpunkte der vergleichenden Litteraturgeschichte.* Vol. 1: *Die Menschen in Shakespeares Dramen.* Worms, 1890.

Whaley, John (1710–45). Correspondent of Styan Thirlby.

Whallon, William. *Problem and Spectacle: Studies in the Oresteia.* Heidelberg, 1980.

Whatley, Janet. "L'orient désert: *Bérénice* and *Antony and Cleopatra*." *UTQ* 44 (1974–5), 96–114.

Wheeler, Richard P. *Shakespeare's Development and the Problem Comedies.* Berkeley, 1981.

Whitaker, Juanita J. "*Antony and Cleopatra*: Cosmological Contexts and the Dramatic Achievement." Univ. of Wisconsin diss., 1972. (*DA* 33 [1972], 736A.)

Whitaker, Virgil K. *The Mirror up to Nature: The Technique of Shakespeare's Tragedies.* San Marino, Calif., 1965.

———. "Shakespeare the Elizabethan." *RUS* 60, No. 2 (1974), 141–51.

White, Richard G. *Shakespeare's Scholar. Being Historical and Critical Studies of his Text, Characters, and Commentators, with an Examination of Mr. Collier's Folio of 1632.* New York, 1854.

White, Thomas Holt (1763–1841). Contributor to v1793.

———. "*Further Remarks on* Shakespeare's *Plays.*" *Gent. Mag.* 57 (1787), 478–80.

———. "*New Observations on* Shakspeare." *Gent. Mag.* 53 (1783), 933–5.

Whiter, Walter. *A Specimen of a Commentary on Shakspeare: Being the Text of the First (1794) Edition Revised by the Author and Never Previously Published.* 2nd, rev. ed. Ed. Alan Over & Mary Bell. 1967.

Whiting, Bartlett J. & Helen W. *Proverbs, Sentences, and Proverbial Phrases From English Writings Mainly Before 1500.* Cambridge, Mass., 1968.

Whitney, Cynthia L. K. "The War in 'Antony and Cleopatra.' " *L&P* 13 (1963), 63–6.

Wickham, Glynne. *Early English Stages, 1300–1660.* Vol. 2, pt. 1. 1963.

———. *Shakespeare's Dramatic Heritage.* 1969.

Wigginton, Waller B. " 'One way like a Gorgon': An Explication of *Antony and Cleopatra*, 2.5.116–17." *PLL* 16 (1980), 366–75.

Wilcox, John. "Love in *Antony and Cleopatra.*" *Papers of the Michigan Academy of Science, Arts and Letters* 21 (1936), 531–44.

Wildenbruch, Ernst von. "Einleitende Worte zu einer Vorlesung von 'Antonius und Cleopatra.' " *SJ* 50 (1914), 1–3.

Wilders, John. *The Lost Garden: A View of Shakespeare's English and Roman History Plays.* 1978.

———. *New Prefaces to Shakespeare.* Oxford, 1988.

Wilkes, George. *Shakespeare, from an American Point of View; Including an Inquiry as to his Religious Faith, and his Knowledge of Law.* 3rd, rev. ed. New York, 1882. (1st ed. London, 1876.)

Wilkinson, L[ancelot] P. *Ovid Recalled.* Cambridge, 1955.

Williams, George W. Private Contributor.

———. "Shakespeare's *Antony and Cleopatra*, [2182]." *Expl* 20 (1962), no. 79.

Williams, Harcourt. *Four Years at the Old Vic 1929–1933.* 1935.

Williams, Raymond. *Drama In Performance.* New [rev.] ed. 1968. (1st ed. 1954.)

W[illiams], W. "Notes on *Antony and Cleopatra.*" *Parthenon* 1 (17 May 1862), 89.

Williamson, Marilyn L. "Antony and Cleopatra in the Late Middle Ages and Early Renaissance." *MichA* 5 (1972), 145–51.

———. "Did Shakespeare Use Dio's Roman History?" *SJH*, 1971, pp. 180–90.

———. "Fortune in *Antony and Cleopatra.*" *JEGP* 67 (1968), 423–9.

———. *Infinite Variety: Antony and Cleopatra in Renaissance Drama and Earlier Tradition.* Mystic, Conn., 1974.

———. "Patterns of Development in *Antony and Cleopatra.*" *TSL* 14 (1969), 129–39.

———. "The Political Context in *Antony and Cleopatra.*" *SQ* 21 (1970), 241–51.

Willoughby, Edwin E. *The Printing of the First Folio of Shakespeare.* OUP, 1932.

Willson, Robert F., Jr. "A Note on Symbolic Names in *Macbeth* and *Antony and Cleopatra.*" *CEA* 31, No. 8 (1969), 7.

Wilson, Elkin C. "Shakespeare's Enobarbus." *Joseph Quincy Adams Memorial Studies*. Ed. James G. McManaway, Giles E. Dawson, & Edwin E. Willoughby. Washington, D.C., 1948. Pp. 391–408.

Wilson, Harold S. *On the Design of Shakespearian Tragedy*. Toronto, 1957.

Wilson, H[arold] Schütz. "Shakspeare's Two Characters of Antony and Cleopatra." *The Theatre* NS 9 (1887), 59–68, 127–39.

Wilson, J[ohn] Dover. *Six Tragedies of Shakespeare: An Introduction for the Plain Man*. 1929.

Wimsatt, W[illiam] K., Jr. "Poetry and Morals: A Relation Reargued." *The Verbal Icon*. Lexington, Ky., 1954. Pp. 85–100. (First pub. *Thought* 23 [1948], 281–99.)

Winchell, Walter B. "Shakspere's Two Delineations of Mark Antony." *The Hamilton Literary Monthly* 15 (1881), 205–9.

Winchester, C[aleb] T. *An Old Castle and Other Essays*. 1922. (Rpt. Freeport, N.Y.: Books for Libraries Press, Essay Index Rpt. Ser. 1971. Written before 1920.)

Winter, William. *Old Shrines and Ivy*. New York, 1892.

————. *Shakespeare on the Stage*. 3rd Ser. New York, 1916. (Rpt. New York: Blom, 1968–9.)

Witherspoon, Alexander M. *The Influence of Robert Garnier on Elizabethan Drama*. Yale Stud. in Eng. 65. New Haven, 1924. (Rpt. [Hamden, Conn.:] Archon, 1968.)

Wolf, William D. " 'New Heaven, New Earth': The Escape from Mutability in *Antony and Cleopatra*." *SQ* 33 (1982), 328–35.

Wolff, Emil. "Shakespeare und die Antike." *Antike und Abendland* 1 (1945), 78–107. (First pub. *Die Antike* 20 [1944], 134–74.)

Wolff, Max J. *Shakespeare: Der Dichter und sein Werk*. 2 vols. 3rd ed. München, 1913. (1st ed. 1907.)

Woodbridge, Linda. *Women and the English Renaissance*. Urbana & Chicago, 1984.

————. *See* Fitz, L. T.

Woolrych, H. F. "The Pronunciation of 'Anthony.' " 6 *N&Q* 2 (4 Dec. 1880), 453–4.

Wordsworth, Charles. *On Shakspeare's Knowledge and Use of the Bible*. 4th, rev. ed. 1892. (1st ed. 1864; 2nd, enl. ed. 1864; 3rd, rev. enl. ed. 1880. Rpt. of 1880 ed. New York: AMS, 1973.)

Worthen, W. B. "The Weight of Antony: Staging 'Character' in *Antony and Cleopatra*." *SEL* 26 (1986), 295–308.

Wray, George Octavius, Rev. (1822–93). Contributor to Wright, William Aldis, MS Notes (–1892) in Trinity Coll., Cambridge: Add. MS. b. 61 (100).

Wright, Austin. "*Antony and Cleopatra*." *Shakespeare: Lectures on Five Plays*. Carnegie Ser. in Eng. 4. Ed. A[lbert] Fred Sochatoff et al. Pittsburgh, 1958. Pp. 37–51.

Wright, Joseph. *The English Dialect Dictionary*. 6 vols. 1898–1905.

Wright, William Aldis. MS Notes in copy of CAM 1, Trinity Coll., Cambridge: MS Adv. C. 18. 57.

————. "Shakespeariana." MS Notes (–1892) in Trinity Coll., Cambridge: Add. MS. b. 58; Add. MS. b. 59; Add. MS. b. 61.

Wyndham, George, introd. *Plutarch's Lives of the Noble Grecians and Romans, Englished by Sir Thomas North, Anno 1579*. 6 vols. Tudor Translations 7–12. 1895–6. Vol. 1. 1895.

Yaghmour, Fakhry H. "Cleopatra in the Tragedies of Shakespeare and Shawqi." *Dirāsāt* 13, No. 12 (1986), 7–24.

Yamada, Yutaka. "*Antony and Cleopatra*—Paradoxical Value of Nobleness." *Prelude* 8 (1965), 28–39.

Yates, D. E. "Arme-Gaunt." *TLS*, 22 Oct. 1938, p. 678.

Yokomori, Masahiko. "An Essay on *Antony and Cleopatra.*" *Kenkyu Kiyo* 12 (1978), 83–98.

Yonge. Contributor to Mayhew 1880.

Z., X. "Shakspeare's 'Antony and Cleopatra.' " 1 *N&Q* 3 (22 Feb. 1851), 139–40.

Zeeveld, W[illiam] Gordon. *The Temper of Shakespeare's Thought.* New Haven & London, 1974.

Zielinski, Th[addäus]. "Marginalien." *Philologus* 64 (1905), 17–19.

INDEX

Compiled by Sabine U. Bückmann-de Villegas

EDITIONS COLLATED

The following chronological lists of sigla represent the lists (pp. xiv ff.) of editions and related works whose readings are recorded in the textual notes. The form and scope of the notes are explained on pp. xxi ff.

F1	1623		COL2	1853
F2	1632		HUD1	1855
F3	1663–4		SING2	1856
F4	1685		DYCE1	1857
ROWE1	1709		COL3	1858
ROWE2	1709		STAU	1859
ROWE3	1714		WH1	1861
POPE1	1723		GLO	1864
POPE2	1728		KTLY	1864
THEO1	1733		HAL	1865
THEO2	1740		DYCE2	1866
HAN1	1744		CAM1	1866
WARB	1747		COL4	1877
THEO4	1757		HUD2	1881
JOHN1	1765		WH2	1883
CAP	1768		OXF1	[1891]
v1773			NLSN	1906
v1778			ARD1	1906
MAL	1790		RIDa	1935
RANN	1791–		KIT1	1936
v1793			CAM3a	1950
v1803			ALEX	1951
v1821			RIDb	1954
SING1	1826		SIS	1954
KNT1	1841		ARD2	1954
COL1	1843		CAM3b	1964
			EVNS	1974

Unusual readings and corrections are occasionally given from the following:

mF2J	−1700		GAR	1758		HALD	1873
mF4Q	1685–		mF2FL20	−1765		WORD1	1883
mF4FL33	−1723		JOHN2	1765		IRV	1889
mPOPE	−1723		JOHN3	1768		CAM2	1892
mTHEO1	1723–33		HAN3	1771		RLF1	1895
mTBY2	1723–33		CAPN	1779–83 [1774]		EV1	1899
mTHEO2	1729–34		v1785			v1907	
mTHEO3	1729–36		mTYR	−1786		BAYF	1920
mLONG	−1733?		mSTV2	1791–1802		BOAS	1935
mTBY3	1733–47		mF2TCC	−1800		EV2	1935
HAN2	1745		MAUN	1839		PEN1	1937
HAN47	1747		mCOL1	−1853		N&H	1942
mTBY4	1747–53		COLNE	1853		YAL2	1955
mWARB	1747–79		DEL2	1856		SISNR	1956
mCAP2	1751		BLUM	1870		MUN	1957
THEO3	1752		HTR	1870		CLN2	1962
mF2FL21	1754–65		DEL4	1872		PEL2	1969